THE
SCIENCE OF SOCIETY

PUBLISHED UNDER THE AUSPICES OF THE SUMNER CLUB
ON THE FOUNDATION ESTABLISHED
IN MEMORY OF
PHILIP HAMILTON McMILLAN OF THE CLASS OF 1894
YALE COLLEGE

THE
SCIENCE OF SOCIETY

BY

WILLIAM GRAHAM SUMNER

*Late Professor of Political and Social Science
in Yale University*

AND

ALBERT GALLOWAY KELLER

*Professor of the Science of Society
in Yale University*

VOLUME II

NEW HAVEN
YALE UNIVERSITY PRESS
LONDON: HUMPHREY MILFORD; OXFORD UNIVERSITY PRESS
1928

CONTENTS

VOLUME II

PART IV

SELF-MAINTENANCE: RELIGION

* An asterisk after a section-number indicates that there is in the *Case-Book* a section corresponding to that number.

EXPLANATORY NOTE

Inasmuch as the authors aim always at a display of the inter-connection of society's institutions—to that end employing a re-iteration of cross-reference—it seems proper to equip each volume not alone with its own table of contents but also with those of pre-ceding and succeeding volumes. For this reason the following Tables of Contents of Volumes I, III, and IV are here inserted.

CONTENTS

VOLUME I

* An asterisk after a section-number indicates that there is in the *Case-Book* a section corresponding to that number.

PART II

SELF-MAINTENANCE: INDUSTRIAL ORGANIZATION

Part III

Self-Maintenance: Regulative Organization

VOLUME III

PART V

SELF-PERPETUATION

VOLUME IV

PART IV

SELF-MAINTENANCE: RELIGION

CHAPTER XXI

THE ALEATORY ELEMENT

§194. **Chance.** The presence of nature and fellow-men—the natural and social environments[1]—constitutes a pair of basic and objective life-conditions for society. Adjustments to their presence evolve into the industrial organization and property and into the military and regulative systems that have now been sketched, just as adjustment to the life-condition of bi-sexuality results in the institutions of marriage and the family. In the process of adjustment to all these there emerges yet another life-condition, basic and elemental as they and equally suited, as involving a dominant interest, to form the nucleus of an accretion of mores, the core of a comprehensive institution. This added life-condition is the element of chance or luck.[2] The momentousness of chance in the affairs of societal life is tacitly accepted by everyone, though it is seldom discerningly recognized. Just because perception is here somewhat dulled by familiarity it becomes necessary to recall rather fully the nature and the bearings of the fortuitous element in life.

In the course of earthly existence efforts and results are found not to be strictly in proportion, though experience shows a correlation between them upon which the race, in actual living, has had to depend. The same energy put forth upon successive occasions in hunting has resulted now in plenty, easily obtained, and again merely in fruitless fatigue. In all ages and stages variation from the expected is always taking place. The liner drives upon a derelict, drifting awash; the tire picks up a nail; the billiard-balls collide just as a hard shot and an excellent position are about to be won; the grounder hits an uneven spot and jumps over the fielder's head. Then disappointed men groan over bad luck and "jinxes." The liner shaves the derelict; the nail merely scratches the surface of the tire; a kiss results in making a shot and attain-

[1] Ch. III, above.
[2] The immediately following paragraphs are taken with little alteration from Keller, "The Luck Element," in *Sci. Mo.*, IV, 145 ff.

ing a position uncontemplated; a safe hit is deflected into a fielder's hands. Then fortune's favorites exult over good luck and talk of rabbits'-feet and horse-shoes. Luck may play a trivial part in human life; it may also make or ruin. Whether any particular exhibition of it is of much or little consequence depends upon circumstances; a slight push is nothing to a man who is standing in the middle of a flat field where it may mean a good deal if he is rope-walking. Upon the primitive stage mischance is the more significant because men live, so to speak, on the edge of existence where it does not take much to shove them over.

That the efforts of man in the struggle for existence are thwarted by forces which he does not understand is true at all stages. When men set out to collect subsistence, to kill beasts, to breed domestic animals, to till the soil, they adapt their efforts to what they know or think they know about the right way in which to get what they want. Drought, inundation, hail, lightning, cattle-disease, insects, heat, and cold traverse their efforts and defeat their purposes. Though the intervention of these incidents is as much a part of nature as the reproductiveness of plants and animals, to man they seem exceptional, hostile, capricious, malignant because they are not favorable to what he wants and because he has not learned devices by which he can ward off their intervention. Sometimes they fall in with his interest and do him a service upon which he had not calculated, as when a swarm of locusts that eat up a crop are themselves better food, according to local taste, than the crop would have been. This element enters into the struggle for existence as good or ill luck; that struggle, indeed, seems to turn into a calculus of luck. As knowledge extends, the element of hazard may be dealt with by devices or met with resignation. Man takes what is favorable or satisfactory to himself, that is, good luck, as in the order of things and spends little reflection upon it unless it is exceptional and sensational. Ill luck comes to thwart him as if sent by some superior, malignant, unreachable power.

Among civilized men the play of the luck element is felt in connection with changes in values, whereas uncivilized men regard prices as fixed and resent the alterations made by white men. Fluctuations in value are known under the name of the conjuncture, that is, the relation of the two sides of the market, supply and demand, when regarded in their effect upon the interests of the parties. The conjuncture is now subject to world-causes. Convulsions in nature,

political disputes or treaties, inventions, fashions, migrations, wars, diseases
of plants or animals, may produce great changes in the conjuncture. Heavy
demand is thrown on some things; nearly all demand is withdrawn from others.
To the individual property-holder or investor these changes come as good or
bad luck. The investment-market may record all the fluctuations due to fact
and to anticipation; still the element of hazard can never be eliminated. It is
most important and necessary to look forward, to exercise prudence, and to
prepare for what is coming, if it can be foreseen. If no attempt were made to
foresee, the fluctuations would be far greater and much more abrupt. Risk,
however, is always present. In some respects it rises into highest intensity in
civilized society. The stock-exchange becomes for civilized men the temple of
luck; it surpasses by far all the methods and institutions of hazard and of
forecasting which it has superseded.

Though the experience of men seems to have been that chance
brought loss rather than profit; though in any case men's minds
have dwelt more upon their ill than upon their good fortune;
nevertheless there has always lurked in those minds the lure of the
possible something-for-nothing. A good part of the race's life on
earth has been spent in toying with the element of chance, often
for itself alone but oftener under the hope of material gain. Tylor[3]
thinks that games of chance are a survival from divination and
magic. There has been a never-ending fascination in the fall of the
cards, the turn of the wheel, the fortuitous in general; one even
hears of the gaming or gambling "instinct."[4] Gambling is almost
universal on the primitive stage, where no game without a stake
is much valued. The passion for gaming has had its molding effect
upon the mores, especially in the case of a frontier-society such as
California used to be, and, among the mores, even upon the language of a nation. Witness the terms current in our own society
and used by many a godly person who would be horrified if he knew
their origin; for they are derived from the so-called "national
game."

What wonder, in view of these various considerations, that the
luck element in life has occupied men's thoughts through the ages?
They have loved it and feared it; they have played with it as with
no other interest. "Interest" is the word for their attitude toward
it. The passion for getting something for nothing and the fear of
getting nothing for something have always fascinated the human
mind.

[3] *Prim. Cult.*, I, 70 ff.   [4] §436, below.

§195. What Luck Is. It would be entirely irregular if the presence of this luck element among the life-conditions had not evoked, in the course of evolution, an important set of societal adaptations. What institutions then correspond to its presence in the field? This question must be approached by way of a preliminary understanding as to the nature of luck. Science, of course, recognizes no such thing as chance in the sense of a result without a sufficient cause; it cannot believe that anything ever "just happened," or was a "mere coincidence" or "causeless spontaneity." Tossing a coin or drawing lots "is committing the decision of a question to a mechanical process, itself in no way unnatural or even extraordinary, but merely so difficult to follow that no one can say beforehand what will come of it."[5] The most fortuitous event can be explained if there is knowledge enough. The liner had reached a certain point of latitude and longitude, at a certain instant, as the result of numerous contributing causes—steam-pressure, head-winds, gales, strikes, temperament of captain, and so on—the action of any one of which could have been predicted if knowledge had been sufficient. Similarly with the derelict into which it crashes. The collision was therefore as much in the natural order of things as is the burning of a finger thrust into living flame. There was no miracle or magic about it. The nail lay in such a position that it was bound to make a puncture or merely to scratch the tire. The billiard-balls were sure to meet at the exact spot where they did, being driven as they were. The inequality in the ground being such as it was and the baseball coming as it did, the result could be indefinitely repeated if the conditions could be duplicated. It is all a question of knowing and foreseeing. To omniscience there could be no luck; to advancing knowledge there is less luck; and as one set of phenomena after another is included within the range of rational explanation the conviction has grown that throughout the universe regularity reigns to the total exclusion of chance.

Luck then is a name for that which is inexplicable on a given stage of knowledge or in view of men's unwillingness to take the trouble to get or to apply that knowledge. It is variation from the expected. "Chance is the emergence of a situation not rendered

5 Tylor, *Prim. Cult.*, I, 70.

necessary by what was previously known."[6] It is what men are too ignorant or too unenterprising to figure out. Omitting the latter consideration as representing the entrance of the personal equation, the importance assigned to luck varies inversely with the amount of knowledge or directly with the amount of the inexplicable. This means, however, since the knowable is immeasurably vast, that the luck element will always be an immense factor in human destiny. It is most difficult to eliminate, as is shown by the ill success of all attempts to rid any game of the "breaks." Perhaps it is superfluous to point out that recognition of this relation of chance and knowledge is current. If a man "takes no chance" it means that he is informing himself to the utmost; indeed, he may even be fully informed and "betting on a sure thing." After a poor man with a little money has exhausted his knowledge, say about investment-conditions, he is prone to "take a chance" on the rest. After listening awhile to a person whining over his bad luck, is one not exasperated sometimes into a partial personal investigation of the case, with the result that, when he knows, he refuses to accede to the appeal to the inexplicable and finds "not so much bad luck as bad management"? When the small boy lays his finger upon the hot stove, his elders comfort him and say, "Hard luck, son!" It is just that, and not folly or bad judgment, in the case of one who knows no better. In our condolence we put ourselves in his place; whereas if a grown man should do the same thing and howl over his experience, the answer might be: "Serves you right! You knew better than to do that. Anyhow you ought to have known better." Now the savage is like the child: his knowledge, beyond the restricted sphere of immediate experience, is small; manifestly, he is "taking a chance" on almost everything he does. The explicable, to him, is an exceedingly limited range; and the amplitude of the inexplicable, the unreckonable, is correspondingly wide. Add to this the fact that ill luck, even a little of it, is a vastly more serious matter to him than to civilized man, and the significance to his destiny of the luck element—the "aleatory element,"[7] as we shall henceforth call it—is indefinitely enhanced. It

[6] Cantor, *Zufall*, 4.

[7] From Latin *alea*, meaning a die. Lea (*Inquisition*, II, 442) says of the Inquisition that its gains were "aleatory," that is, at risk, doubtful, dependent on luck.

forms for him, as the facts show, one of the major conditions of life on earth; and his adaptation to it, as he sees it, works out into an important set of societal structures.

The aleatory element plays in the inexplicable and varies in importance with the amount that is unaccountable; that is, it varies inversely with the amount of knowledge, theoretically ranging from zero with infinite knowledge to infinity with zero knowledge.

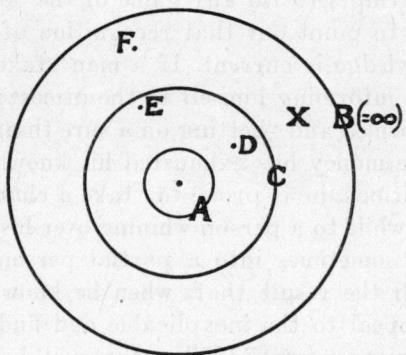

In the figure, let circle A represent the positive knowledge of primitive man, while circle B represents universal knowledge (a condition designated by the sign of infinity). The band between A and B represents the domain of chance as the primitive man sees it. Suppose that for civilized man the range of knowledge has been extended to circle C. Then much that was for the primitive man a part of the aleatory element (say D, an eclipse; or E, a comet) is seen to occur in accordance with law and can even be predicted with precision or probability; whims of spirits do not come in any longer to account for it. The realm of the aleatory element has been encroached upon from within and reduced to the band X. But since the area enclosed by B is infinite while that enclosed by C (or A) is definite, the band X is also infinite and the domain of chance has been no whit lessened. The savage has no comprehension of the scope of the unknown; the realization of life's enveloping mystery comes only to the most enlightened, scientifically informed minds. However, upon the most enlightened stage of modern science, X is no longer taken to represent a realm of chance (lawless caprice); but the universality of law is inferred from successive experiences of finding it prevailing within the erstwhile range of chance (say, between A and C) now invaded and reduced by knowledge. This view is characteristic of emancipated minds alone. F, the origin of life, let us say, is as yet unknown. It may be unknowable, but whether it is or is not, it must lie within the realm of law, not of caprice. Being as yet inexplicable, it remains in X. It will be noted that, to the men in A, what is outside of A seems less than does X to the more emancipated in C. The unknown and unknowable are most impressive to those who know the most. However, the ways of men are such that those who are somewhat more advanced have regularly ridiculed, censured, and contemned the less advanced, calling them "superstitious," because the latter have continued to regard what is outside their circle of knowledge (say outside of A) in precisely the same way as most of the former have regarded what is outside their circle (say outside of C). To this figure we shall presently return for further illustration.[8]

§196. Good and Bad Luck. It may be objected that there is just as much good luck as ill luck, and the optimist will doubtless seize the occasion to vociferate that all is for the best in this best of worlds. Irrespective of general theory, however, a fact of observation is that the tendency of human nature is to take good luck to be normal and as the matter of course and to confine attention pretty largely to the ill fortune.

"Very characteristic of the Milano [of Sarawak] is their intense belief in a world of spirits, which makes them refer all the events of their lives to the agency of these spirits. For all the ills of mankind malevolent spirits are directly responsible, though, on the other hand, they do not usually consider good fortune to be the gift of the gods, as if the good things of life were man's normal lot."[9]

Perfect health is not normal, yet people go on the theory that it is and grumble at illness as a misfortune. Age brings on a series of discomforts; they are perfectly normal; still we refuse to consider the good days as good fortune and we go on complaining about the bad ones. That man was a great philosopher who kept a diary which he consulted at times of discomfort, being always able to find some occasion when he was worse off; so was Odysseus, who adjured himself: "Bear up, heart! ere this thou hast endured more grievous ill!"[10]

One does not take much pleasure in past joys when he is being plagued; he subscribes rather to the sentiment about sorrow's crown of sorrows being the remembrance of happier things. It is not to be denied that discontent, however unpleasant as a personal habitude, may yet be a good racial quality; for it leads to new variations and adjustments, while content may mean lack of motion and change; it is therefore, in a sense, expedient that the

8 §208, below.
9 Lawrence and Hewitt, in JAI, XXXVIII, 388.
10 Homer, *Odyssey*, XX, 18.

race forgets good fortune and grunts, squirms, and strives under ill. The final word of Goethe's ripe wisdom is that the inveterate striver may be saved.[11]

Engrossment in the present is the rule among peoples whose representative faculties are relatively weak; to them ill luck is more important than good luck because, while the latter may be highly desirable, the former is supremely undesirable. It may mean present death; or a disablement, such as a broken and ill-set limb, permanent and in the highest degree disadvantageous on a low stage of civilization; or some hideous disease. The experience of good luck never relieves people on that stage of the present fear of ill; indeed, a run of good fortune frightens them to the last degree, for it is a sure harbinger of calamity. Polycrates is full of anxiety over his long stretch of good luck; he tries to sacrifice the thing he prizes most; it is thrown back to him by the gods; and he prepares for his doom.

Luck-beliefs run out into a sort of fatalism; as Achilles says to Priam, it is useless to mourn "for there is no recourse for cruel sorrow. The gods have apportioned it to miserable mortals to live in woe, while they themselves are without care. There are on Zeus's threshold two jars of gifts such as he gives, one of woes and the other of benefits. To whomsoever Zeus, wielder of the thunderbolts, gives them mixed, he encounters now the evil and again the good; but to whomsoever he gives of the woeful gifts alone, him he makes an object of contempt. Ravenous hunger goads him over the divine earth and he wanders about esteemed neither by gods nor by men."[12] The later Greeks reiterated that no man may be called happy till he is dead.[13] They adhered to a rude calculation of the average distribution of good and ill luck and were so assured that no one mortal could ever depart far from the average that they made a deity of the force which appeared to rule the variations. If a man has wife and children he has given "pledges unto fortune" —that is, he has opened so many more avenues by which adverse fate may reach him.

It is necessary to step very softly when things go well, with an eye always aslant toward the perennial menace of ill. If one recalls

---

[11] *Faust*, II, act V, 878-879.   [12] Homer, *Iliad*, XXIV, 49; 523 ff.
[13] Sophocles, *Œd. Tyr.*, 1524 ff.

the manifold dangers surrounding human life before the barrier of civilization was built up to afford it some protection, he will not be surprised at the prevalence of interest in avoiding ill as over against interest in attaining good. It is necessary to set ourselves in the situation of primitive man to realize this; anyone can help himself to do that if he will realize that the savage was really involved in a struggle for existence, whereas none of us are. We struggle for a standard of living; if we lose out utterly, still existence is assured to us by the society in which we live. Our far-away ancestors, on the contrary, and their present-day representatives, the nature-peoples, lived and live in a direct relation to physical environment that is full of perils of a vital order. They were and are victims of a vivid fear of calamity; the "free and noble savage" is a philosopher's phantasm.

"It is not too much to say that the horrible dread of unknown evil hangs like a thick cloud over savage life and embitters every pleasure."[14] This is something of an exaggeration, but is much nearer the truth than statements of the opposite tenor. "The *curriculum vitæ* of the heathen Bawenda is a long succession of fear, superstition, suppression and misery. From birth to death they are haunted by their gods, by the ghosts of their ancestors, by all sorts of hobgoblins, and tremble with fear of their witch-doctors and chiefs."[15] Says Sieroshevski[16] of the Yakuts: "Their dependence on luck is tragic"; the great mass of them is just above misery. If prices rise a little, or one is cheated by his neighbor or by the merchant, or loses calves, such blows easily upset the household budget. They sell what they have, go hungry, run in rags, cannot work; their cattle run down, the milk fails. They fall into a condition from which only a stroke of good luck can free them. It is said of the Dyaks that their struggle has to be carried on in the midst of dangers that are not understood and for which guidance is necessary.[17] "On the spiritual side, the Cheyenne's life was hedged about by a multitude of barriers of ritual and custom. . . . Yet he lived in constant fear of doing some forbidden thing which would bring him bad luck. The list of the proscribed acts is a long one. They had to do with the most ordinary operations of

14 Lubbock, *Preh. Times*, 571.　　15 Gottschling, in JAI, XXXV, 371.
16 *Yakuts* (Russ.), 67, 426.　　17 Roth, *Sarawak*, 191.

life: with his eating, drinking, and sleeping, with the members of his family, his life in the lodge, his hunting, and his war journey. In all that he did at home and abroad he was closely bound by custom which had become law."[18]

The contrast between bad and good luck is so great—nothing for something *versus* something for nothing—that it has rivetted the attention of men in all ages. Why work, when bad luck may defeat you? Why exert yourself, when good luck may do for you in a moment more than effort could do in a lifetime? The author of the book of Ecclesiastes[19] had observed this: "I returned, and saw under the sun that the race is not to the swift, nor the battle to the strong, neither yet bread to the wise, nor yet riches to men of understanding, nor yet favour to men of skill; but time and chance happeneth to them all." "What the ant, Reason, painfully gathers together, that the wind, chance, heaps up in a trice."[20] Man's experience is as if he were dealing with a superior power which sometimes favors him but oftener withholds what he wants and frustrates his best efforts. It takes some sophistication to arrive at the common sense of the peasant in the *Electra*,[21] who says: "No idle man, even if he has the names of the gods upon his lips, can earn his living without hard work."

That it is "human nature" to be engrossed in the avoidance of ill luck, and that omens and portents are more likely to presage calamity than to warn of the coming of prosperity, have been brought out over and over again by shrewd observers. Says the negro Jim, after asserting that good-luck signs are few and of no use anyway: "What you want to know when good luck's a-comin' for? want to keep it off?"[22]

§197. Adjustment to the Aleatory Element. The aleatory element, especially in its negative phase of ill fortune, fills the perspective of the race's childhood with an enduring and real menace. The unreckonable enters into a situation that is vital. Comfort and even life itself depend upon some expedient in adjustment. Inasmuch as this element formed one of the major condi-

18 Grinnell, *Cheyenne*, II, 193.   19 IX, 11.
20 Schiller, *Fiesco*, act II, scene 4.   21 Euripides, *Electra*, 80.
22 Clemens, *Huckleberry Finn*, ch. VIII, near end.

tions of his life, primitive man was not slow to sense the discomfort that enforces adaptation. His attitude could not be one of indifference nor could his mind develop or harbor the refined faith of the civilized man; no more could he evolve the philosophy of the stoic or the more enlightened resignation of the agnostic. Yet he must forthwith do something to avoid ill, and for that he must have some explanation of the inexplicable. He was not at all the victim of intellectual curiosity; if this matter had not touched compellingly upon his most vital interests he would never have sensed the need of explanation; there had to be something accounting for the aleatory element, precisely in order to deal practically with it. He was not after any intellectual gratification. The question was simply what to do; how to insure against ill that always threatened and was not to be accounted for upon any basis of actual experience. Some effort to solve the issue "will continue to flourish so long as man confronts the unknown, and is puzzled and alarmed by it—that is, so long as the unknown menaces his everyday comfort. It is not ignorance *per se* that shakes him, but ignorance that is practical, pressing and personal."[23]

Such was the issue that lay before the primitive folk in the face of this peculiar and inevitable life-condition. If anybody imagines that they attacked and solved it by a conscious, rational, "heuristic" procedure, he has yet a great deal to learn about the early stages of society's evolution. Primitive people could not even have formulated the issue; much less could they have applied enlightened methods of investigation to it. They felt it in a dull sort of way, and squirmed and fumbled about to dodge the pain of it or to secure some alleviation. How, automatically and un-rationally, to get hold of some explanation of the inexplicable—that was a heavy problem for childlike minds with but slight and unreliable equipment of matter and method. The mental operations of the race were largely phantasy until science arose.

In default of a more exact term, we have used the word "rational" to indicate procedure in the light of knowledge, as opposed to a mental process which, though it may be quite reasonable so far as working out the logical sequences from its premises is concerned, issues in what we know to be wrong conclusions. Indeed, the savage is reasonable enough, in most cases, in arriving at his premises; under his circumstances, nobody could do any better. His

23 Mencken, in *Amer. Mercury*, November, 1925, 383.

main difficulty is ignorance. It is no wonder that he ascribes his ills to spiritual sources; nevertheless we shall often describe such a proceeding as irrational— and shall be conforming to usage in so doing—although we shall hope not to be charged with denying that he is using his reason as well as he can, or can be expected to do. If there were a word that meant "inability to arrive at correct conclusions because of inevitable error due to ignorance," that would be the term for which we have faithfully searched. Not having been able to discover it, we shall use instead "irrationality," with the proviso just made. We fully realize that future generations will have the same right to apply the term to us that we have to employ it in respect to primitive men.

It is not alone the savage man who gropes and fumbles in the face of the aleatory element. He has no science to use; but many who have do not use it. Where they do not flee incontinently to primitive devices of a magical or semi-magical nature, such as prophecies, omens, and revelations, they take recourse to imaginary constructions of scarcely greater reliability. The dreams of some imaginative soul are hailed as the solution of the ills of life, and with as little critical examination or verification on facts as ever the savage displayed in regard to the pronouncements of his medicine-men. Modern people have the same old capacity for believing what they would like to believe, and that in the face of repeated demonstrations of the futility and peril of that procedure. They know, as the savage did not, that vision after vision has proved illusory; that men have been disillusioned and disenchanted over and over again; they laugh at the simplicity of the credulous native; and yet they ignore facts and plunge ahead along the same old path.24 The "philosophic" solution is the attractive one; it can never be refuted except by experience; and experience can be ignored or interpreted.

Socialism is one of these philosophic attempts to deal with the ills of life. To miss this point is to miss the significance of the system. It too wishes to deal with the aleatory element; it is a revolt against the inequality which results both from effort and from luck, as well as from the abuse of political power in the state. Effort can always be renewed and the relation between effort and product is rational; political abuses admit of direct treatment and reform. There remains the element of contingency which determines the fate of the multitudes, especially when there are included in it the factors of heredity and social conditions of birth which for the individual constitute his initial "chance" in life. We are still far from that point at which those adults who procreate the multitude will refuse to beget children whose initial chances they are not able to make favorable. Socialism has proposed to let them alone and even set them free from any anxiety on this point while it aims to act upon the consequences by using the machinery of the state. It is sometimes spoken of as a system of insurance by which the gainers by the aleatory element shall share with the losers by it, the fallacy of this notion being in the fact that some would insure others, that is, would pay their premiums for them. Its greatest error is the same as that which was in the ghost-fear policy; its methods would destroy capital. Capital, however, is the great rational means of dealing with the aleatory element, after science has reduced it to rationality. Whatever lessens the care, prudence, and knowledge of the exposed person or puts his ill fortune on somebody else increases the total risk for society.

24 Ward (*Thobbing*) illustrates this tendency in many fields.

Nowadays civilized man has at hand a practical adaptation to the aleatory element which is the fine fruit of some of primitive man's primæval gropings toward safety and surety in the face of mischance, namely, insurance. It is necessary here to form a conception of insurance as of a major expedient in encountering the ills of life. Of all things desired by man, security against mischance in its innumerable forms is supremely precious. To be safe in a world of insecurities is impossible; nevertheless approximation to that state is much. The general principles of insurance, whether developed in connection with corporate life or religion or government,[25] are always the same; insurance is a generic conception covering the methods of attaining security, of which the modern devices are but specific, highly elaborated, and scientifically tested examples. Insurance, in itself, does not lessen the losses involved; what it does is to distribute them so they can more easily be borne. It reduces a variable of shattering loss to a constant of endurable loss. It is always loss, be it noted—bearable loss incurred in order to avoid utter calamity. In insurance-operations recourse is had to the laws of chance and actuaries figure out about what amount of mischance must be reckoned on; then this is distributed in the form of premiums paid on policies.

Insurance is a grand device and is now a highly technical process; but its roots go farther back than one would think, offhand. Man on earth, having always had an eye to the avoidance of ill luck, has tried in all ages somehow to insure himself—to take out a "policy" of some sort on which he has paid regular premiums in some form of self-denial or sacrifice. His methods of so doing, rude as they were and mistaken, were susceptible of replacement and rectification. Only by some such device was existence possible in the presence of the menacing inexplicable. The aleatory element is incalculable at any particular stage because it always contains elements which are beyond human knowledge at that stage; when these elements have been reduced to rationality by science and art in respect to one point after another, they straightway recur a little farther on. The arts are thus ever surmounting the unidentifiable obstructive or destructive forces and conditions; in the form of civilization a system of defenses is built up within which

[25] §§8, 52, 128, 160, above, and 287, 335, below.

human life is passed;[26] then "accidents" happen again on this stage, especially in the use of the apparatus of defense and achievement against nature—railroads, explosives, machinery. The investments of the civilized man on which his life depends are the sport of a new set of contingencies—of a different order from those which affect the food-quest of the savage but no less destructive. At every stage there are inexpugnable obstacles; by acquiring knowledge they are rendered imperfectly expugnable and sometimes, later on, are removed altogether. It is in the earlier stages of this process that the aleatory element holds men most irremediably helpless. When their minds were fixed on luck as the secret to the problem of life, they did not see the place of labor or capital in that problem; they wasted capital by their devices to win luck. What was the use of working if, after all, success or failure waited on chance?

The attitude of primitive man toward this element is characteristically human. In the struggle for existence, animals as well as men are not successful strictly in proportion to effort or intent. The animal, having made an effort and lost, goes on tranquilly and with no worry about the insufficiency of its understanding, to other experiences. At most he looks foolish or runs away in passing fright if the unexpected experience is painful; he does not notice the situation and reflect upon it. Whitman, in his "Song of Myself," expresses his admiration of this enviable imperturbability:

I think I could turn and live with animals, they are so placid and self-contained,
I stand and look at them long and long.
They do not sweat and whine about their condition,
They do not lie awake in the dark and weep for their sins,
They do not make me sick discussing their duty to God,
Not one is dissatisfied, not one is demented with the mania of owning things,
Not one kneels to another, nor to his kind that lived thousands of years ago,
Not one is respectable or unhappy over the whole earth.

With man, as these sentiments intimate, the case is different. He is concerned before a painful exhibition of the aleatory element and worries over it. Of the Melanesian it is said: "Anxiety in the face of real or imaginary ill is the keynote to which he is attuned.

26 Keller, *Soc. Evol.*, 177 ff.

Mistrust is the immediate consequence."[27] The ills of life caused reflection, however rudimentary. Pain is a signal of maladjustment, physical or other; it is, in many of its aspects, most salutary; all the way up through the organic scale it has been pain and death which have forced a superior adaptation. When that adaptation has been attained the tendency is to settle down upon it and remain quiescent. But the condition of well-being, comfort, and self-satisfaction has never promoted evolution; it generally means stagnation except perhaps for highly self-conscious beings who are imaginative enough to contrast present comfort with past pain, and rational enough and sufficiently endowed with foresight to struggle after an even safer insurance, in the form of wealth of various sorts, against calamity. Exceptions of this sort are not primitive; man was for long ages so feeble in the matter of foresight as to live on the very edge of things rather than endure an increment of present discomfort in order to secure the future. This was found true even in relation to the food-supply. When the Fuegians were heard howling and lamenting at every sunrise, the interpreter, being questioned, said: "People very sad, cry very much."[28] Apparently they hated to see the new day and to feel the spur to renewed struggle; yet after expressing their sentiments they went perforce and doggedly forward with their routine.

It was the painfully unusual rather than the pleasurably so that forced men to reflect and theorize. On the evidence it appears, further, that primitive life was more familiar with the distressful fortuity than the happy one. It was misery, loss, pain, disease—in short, the ills of life—that enforced attention. They have made it imperative for man to ask who is tormenting him and to hit upon some theory of escape and mode of reconciliation as a policy of welfare. The ills of life spare nobody and they afflict the same victim over and over again. What shall we do, in our common and recurring misery, in order not to bear all this again? The most brutal of men at last suffers enough to make him join with the rest of his fellows in asking this question. And for its answering man has always been, and still is, but poorly fitted; his case on the primitive stage may be summed up in a phrase: he is at the

27 Von Pfeil, *Südsee*, 133.
28 Fitzroy, *Adventure and Beagle*, II, 179.

sport of vicissitude and chance. He cannot, we repeat, either remain indifferent or take the stoical or agnostic attitude; he must have some explanation or, better, some expedient for preventing or dodging recurrences. What he feels is fear[29]—fear of the mysterious and menacing Unknown. This is no natural excitant like hunger and love, which drive at once to natural action; it is not so elemental and underived as these. It is far older and deeper, however, than other excitants, such as wonder and curiosity, to a higher mental activity and to the consequent accumulation of a mental outfit of notions and theories.

§198. Mental Outfit. The aleatory element represents a great and crucial question-mark in human living. The issue is presented as one of adjustment to be secured, if at all, through men's characteristic mode of mental and societal adaptation.[30] It is necessary at this point—for the task of explaining the inexplicable is certainly the heaviest that was ever assigned to men—to be resolved somewhat more clearly as to what sort of mental resources they had to go on in those remote periods of cultural evolution. Comparison of the mental differences between civilized and uncivilized man reveal the fact that they do not inhere so much in the original constitution of the mind as in its contents. There are doubtless some differences due to the action of natural selection, but the likenesses are the commanding features. The mind is there; and it is not different in kind upon the various stages of civilization. Peculiarities of the primitive mind are referable to what is in it or, still better, to what is not in it. When a suggestion comes to one who has a small stock of ideas, he connects it with one of them, in all likelihood wholly erroneously, whereas he who has many ideas may make a more nearly correct connection. Education gives a choice of many categories to which to refer suggestions.

A single illustration may bring out the fact that the savage can understand a situation if it is brought home to him in terms of concrete experience. Certain Africans were complaining that they could get calico at 4d a yard at Blantyre, ten days' march distant, while the local trader was charging them 5d. "To have said, 'All right, you go down to Blantyre and buy your calico'

29 §14, above.
30 §§18-20, above; Keller, Soc. Evol., ch. I.

would not have convinced the native at all that it was not an exorbitant charge. He would think nothing of going down ten days to expend 8*d* on two yards of calico. Time is not money to the African." An old trader, being consulted, advised as follows: "There are always ways and means of explaining to the natives. I say all right you go and hunk me up a load of calico from Blantyre for nothing, and I will then sell you as many yards as you like for 4*d*." This argument carried instantaneous conviction.[31]

Working upon what outfit of experience it has, the primitive mind arrives at logical conclusions; and the chief reason for the difference between its conclusions and ours is that it has had comparatively little to work on. The mental outfit or content does not come from being human; it derives from life in society. The mind cannot be filled to any great extent except with what it gets from others; some reflection is required for a civilized man to realize that his mental outfit springs out of the experience of millions of the living and the dead. Men are now so used to the diffusion of ideas over space and through time that they take it for granted; it requires some effort to set themselves in the condition of primitive man in this regard. Also by habitually working upon a relatively copious outfit of mental materials, they have got into certain critical and self-corrective attitudes toward phenomena that the savage could not have developed any more than can a child. Said a Spanish priest of his charges: "In many things they are big children who must be treated like little ones."[32] Civilized men know that things are not always what they seem; they have traditional, re-verified tests of reality; they have learned to stand off from phenomena and to scrutinize and compare. In short, they have a fuller mental outfit and tested ways of dealing with it. They are less unsophisticated.

In particular, men now know, though they often forget or ignore it under pressure of emotion, that there is no necessary relation whatever between purposes and results.

To take an extreme case, the purpose of the woman who gets up at night to give her child medicine is praiseworthy; but if she lays hand upon the wrong bottle and gives him poison, the quality of her intention will not alter the result. That a boy does not know that the gun he points at another is loaded is no element in the situation, once the trigger is pulled and the spark shot into the powder.

[31] Stigand, *Elephant,* 280, 281.
[32] Worcester, *Philippine Isl.,* 482.

The necessary relation is not between intentions and consequences but between acts and consequences; that is sure and constant. The order is: purpose—act—consequence. The relation between purposes and acts would be equally sure and constant with that between acts and consequences if knowledge were complete; whereas in the absence of knowledge the realization of purposes through acts must be, except perhaps for a relatively few instinctive actions, purely accidental. The sureness of the realization of purposes by acts, that is, the transmutation of purposes into desired consequences, varies directly with the amount of knowledge available.[33] The winning order is: purpose—knowledge—act—consequence. The very reason for the existence of knowledge is that the act may be suited to the intent so as to realize the desired result. This is man's characteristic process of adjustment and he practises it ever more successfully and consciously as he goes on through his course; but where knowledge is feeble there can be no sure and steady advance from purposes to results.

Men's ways of dealing with material things and with ideas have come out to some extent in preceding connections and will be illustrated throughout this book. Though there is no reason to undertake here a survey of the qualities of the primitive mind,[34] certain of its most general traits should be before us. First, then, intellectual curiosity is undeveloped; in fact, none but the most highly civilized have risen to the height of disinterested inquiry into causes and of understanding of causality. Savages have insight which, though it is often an acute summing-up of experience, rests solely upon the direct demonstration of practice. Proverbs, apothegms, maxims, fables, myths, legends, and riddles—little pellets of practical wisdom or folk-experience—reveal the natural mode of the unlettered. "It is astonishing to mark what a number of questions relating to the prudent conduct of life are canvassed in Proverbs: occupation, profit, business in general, intercourse with superiors and inferiors and with different classes of men generally, one's attitude to rulers, and numberless others."[35] The unusual excites uneasiness for a time, but if it produces no experience

[33] §195, above.
[34] Spencer, *Prin. Soc.*, I, chs. VI, VII; Boas, *Mind of Prim. Man,* offers a criticism of older views.
[35] Kautzsch, in *Hastings's Dict. Bible,* 728.

it is soon disregarded. Men of a lower culture are also wont to apply the idea of agency rather than of cause; it is easier, more obvious, more anthropomorphic. "We think with less strain if we think in terms of persons. In fact, the race has always personalized the less tangible and more abstract things, for by such means it has been possible to tie up floating and evasive conceptions so that they can be found again and dealt with. The vast impersonalities that control our destiny—Nature, Chance, God—are rendered into terms that men are more used to handle."[36]

Again, it has been maintained that primitive man is not behind cultured man in the logic of his mental operations; that his manifest errors are due to wrong premises rather than inherent in the progress of his mental operations. He acts from primary motives only: interest, as he understands it, and desire; yet, once set upon a train of deduction, he lunges on through to the bitterest end with a simple inexorability of logic astonishing to his more civilized brothers. He is doubtless "alogical" in getting his premises: "My experience in the field," says an excellent observer,[37] "has persuaded me of the complete futility of the theories which attribute to the savage a different type of mind and different logical faculties. The native is not 'prelogical' in his beliefs, he is alogical, for belief or dogmatic thinking does not obey the law of logic among savages any more than among ourselves." When, however, he sets out to develop his dogmas, he reasons forward on astonishingly straight lines, like a child, not being led astray by stray flights of fancy. Miss Kingsley[38] thinks that the longer you know and study the West African and his institutions the more convinced you are that his chief mental trait is to be narrowly logical. He is no dreamer, no doubter; for him "everything is real, very real, horribly real." He is not critical and failure does not convert him. He knows there is a future life, and just what it is; he knows there is another world and how to get there. He does not have to weigh and reflect; he becomes for some reason disgruntled with this existence and acts on his premises at once; he commits suicide in as matter-of-fact a way as one would purchase a ticket to go to New York. His mental processes are simple and unperturbed; his

36 Keller, *War to Peace*, 14.   37 Malinowski, in JAI, XLVI, 418, note.
38 *W. Afr. Stud.*, 124; Lippert, *Kgchte.*, II, 332.

"native hue of resolution" is not clouded by reflections and bal-
ancings. His observations, outside a limited range, are seldom correct and his inferences are faulty but his mind advances without
misgiving and accepts consequences without flinching. His chief
errors are referable to a lack of criticism which would require
analysis, comparison, and true generalization—operations impossible in the absence of an accumulation of experiences which the
savage, like the child, could not possibly have in available form.
Hence his mental processes remain uncorrected. Perhaps the highest mental operation of the savage, one common enough with men
on higher grades of civilization, is "reasoning from analogy" and
from association. Association continued through time produces an
impression of actual connection in fact and logic; and analogy,
which is a "partial identity,"[39] extends this relation to other
things that are in any way parallel. The tendency in reasoning to
assign weight to analogy, to jump at conclusions under the hypnotic influence of suggestive parallels, has been a pest in the developing science of society.

It is evident that these logical difficulties, if one choose to call
them logical, are the results of lack of knowledge rather than of
defects of mental constitution; they reside in the character of the
mental outfit rather than in that of the mind. How is it that men
have learned to refer effects to causes rather than to agents? It
is not by an alteration of the nature of their minds; rather is it by
a comparison of accumulated cases. This involves the presence of
records or collections which the savage cannot have.

"The Dyak feels the need of guidance from the powers around and above him
in his going out and coming in, in his precarious farming, in his occupations
in the sombre depths of the jungle, in his boating over the dangerous rapids,
or the treacherous tides of the swift rivers. He is aware that death and destruction may suddenly confront him in many a hidden danger, and he longs
for something to hint to him when to advance and when to recede. He is a
'questioning humanity'; and he has devised for himself an 'answering nature.' "[40]

In some of the museums for archæology may be seen collections
of stone objects which have been produced solely by natural forces,
though they look so much like ancient artifacts that only a trained
eye can detect the difference. The object of these collections is to

[39] Barth, *Phil.*, ch. IV; §453, below.   [40] Roth, *Sarawak*, I, 191.

educate observation so as to avoid error in the ascription of human agency. This case, on the border-line between causation and agency, may show that the question as to the presence of the one or the other is the question as to where that line of distinction falls; it is always drawn at the limit of experience, illuminated by knowledge. Having now an accumulation of recorded experiences, men have learned not to attribute disease to an agent-man or agent-spirit; not to put a supernatural being behind the wind, the growing tree, the cracking ice, or the crackling fire. It is the experience of life, corrected and re-corrected and stored up in tradition, that teaches the art of adjustment to things as they are rather than as they seem. The savage knows that art well, so far as he goes. He is well aware of the habits of animals or the quality of different kinds of wood or stone. Beyond his little range of positive knowledge he falls into phantasy and fallacy, as we all do. Some of us believe in maternal impressions, or talismans, or the infallibility of a political formula or party, or in some fantastic religious dogma; yet from the vantage-ground of modern science we are always smiling patronizingly at the follies and superstitions of the recent past and inferring that we ourselves are emancipated from them—whereas the only correct inference is that future generations will look back patronizingly upon us as we have done upon our forebears.

Is the type of intellect represented in the following passage utterly without parallel at the present day? "The Ten'a have a wonderful faculty for believing or disbelieving what they choose. Their intellect seems to be altogether at their will's command, ready to give or refuse its assent according to the direction which it receives from the will. They never judge of the credibility of a report or statement on the merits of the case. Their criterion is neither the intrinsic credibility of the fact, nor the extrinsic evidence of testimony that may accompany it—although they are generally inclined to believe whatever is being said. The ultimate reason, which can be detected in almost every instance as the one that really determines their belief, is: what benefit shall accrue to me from such a belief? If they see in it their own advantage, nothing more is required. To illustrate this statement, I may be allowed to quote from personal experience. Many a time have Ten'a people offered to me to believe all my teachings and profess themselves Christians, for the consideration of a sack of flour, or a pound of tea, or a head of tobacco. . . . Requesting that the Mission would contribute a gift to the rejoicings of the people, . . . they added, 'if you do so, we shall all believe your teachings, without exception.' This disposition is the cause of the phenomenal credulity with which they accept all the absurd sayings of the medicine-men, because they fear woeful

consequences if they refuse to believe. . . . This frame of mind is partly bred
in them, but mostly acquired through the constant and sedulous exertions of
their parents, relatives and friends. . . . Since . . . their power of belief is
very great, the intensity as well as the extent of their devil-belief is beyond
our conceptions."[41] The fact is, the Ten'a have the "will to believe." The abyss
is not so deep or wide between such laughable primitive credulity, such chame-
leon-mindedness, and the mentality of those who urge one to believe because
it is for his temporal and eternal welfare to do so, or those who refuse to
credit a conclusion of science because it is distasteful to them. Yet no other
persons would pour such withering scorn upon the misguided savage, or ridicule him more contemptuously, or perhaps pity him more condescendingly,
than modern representatives of his way of thinking. When George Eliot[42]
writes: "Experience has . . . long shown that the human brain is a congenial
nidus for inconsistent beliefs," she is not thinking about the savages.

It is contended, not that the process of selection has not elevated the quality of the human mind, but that the difference between the primitive and the sophisticated intelligence is one much
more of content than of quality, of degree rather than of kind;
and that human mental machinery in its more complicated workings goes back to the same simple elements which were present
when the apparatus was still rudimentary. This is what makes the
study of the simple elements worth while.

§199*. **Primitive Accuracies and Fallacies.** The primitive
peoples are accurate enough, and often amazingly unerring, in
dealing with the practical matters of life as they live it.

The Australians, according to experienced observers, are "all there" when
it has to do with the hunt. They are marvellous trackers, for example, like the
American Indian. "Their mental powers are simply developed along the lines
which are of service to them in their daily life."[43] In a country where "to
perish" means to lose one's way and die of thirst, the natives do not get lost.
Footprints are "to the natives an open book." This is what is to be expected of
evolution. Indifference to the new is common. However, "it must always be
remembered that the peculiar intelligence of the blackfellow deprives him of
the capacity of estimating anything complicated, and also prevents initiative
in throwing. He throws a weapon as his father taught him, and is afraid to
initiate an improvement for fear that he may be deemed *kootchi* (uncanny).
He will develop wonderful skill in the use of things that were used by his
father and his father's father but never attempts to get out of the groove. If
they get white men's tools they use them as nearly as possible in the same
way as they used their stone tools. And this applies to the use of weapons."[44]

[41] Jetté, in JAI, XXXVII, 158-159.   [42] Essay on *Evangelical Teaching.*
[43] Spencer and Gillen, *Nat. Tr. Cent. Aust.,* 26; and *North. Tr. Cent. Aust.,*
30; Semon, *Aust. Bush,* 217.
[44] Horne and Aiston, *Cent. Aust.,* 25, 26, 82-83.

Of the Tasmanians it is said: "After having seen something of the natives of Van Diemen's Land, the conviction was forced upon my mind, that they exceeded Europeans in skill, in those things to which their attention had been directed from childhood."[45] Certain Melanesians "are keenly observant of all natural phenomena, and there are few birds or fish or plants whose names even a small boy does not know. This closeness of observation is especially noticeable in all that pertains to fishing and to the gardens, and has led to the creation of an extensive vocabulary connected with these pursuits; the varieties of yams and shell-fish for example appear to the foreigner numberless. . . . No one, however, can be more stupid than an uninterested native. Many things which appeal to us have no interest whatever for him."[46] Similarly of the Kaffirs: "Their wonderful facility for passing judgment in matters of rights has escaped no attentive observer who has stayed for some time among the A-Bantu; and from that alone it can easily be recognized what school of life these natives have gone through, and how necessity has forced them to develop this side of their intellect. . . . But if one wanted to conclude that other intellectual activities which do not so immediately subserve material advantage are to be brought with ease to the same grade of perfection, he would go far astray. Concerning everything that does not fall within the narrow circle of his few needs and leanings, the Kaffir hates to take care; for the thing he likes best is to surrender himself to thoughtless good spirits and to enjoy today, letting tomorrow take care of itself."[47] "Facts are cited showing that the negro is, in certain circumstances, the superior of the white man, and that the development of the faculties stands in direct relation to the environment. Of course it is not meant to imply that the negro is, on the average, the intellectual equal of the European; the point which it is attempted to emphasize is that each is admirably adapted to his surroundings, and therefore it is unfair to compare their respective faculties by simply transferring, as it were, one to the environment of the other; it is merely the first half of the story of the fox and the crane without the compensating sequel. And this has a direct bearing upon the question of the civilisation of the negro; it is ridiculous to clothe a primitive people in a civilisation made to the measure of someone else and expect the result to be a good fit. . . . Take, for instance, a subject which is of little importance for the average modern European, but of the greatest moment for the native, the subject of hunting. Travellers have often commented on the intimate knowledge of natural history possessed by natives, but few have realised that practically *every* individual has a knowledge of the local fauna and flora which in Europe can only be paralleled by that of the specialist. . . . They know every bird, not only by sight, but by its cry, or by its nest. Plants are carefully distinguished, and it is only in speaking to Europeans that general terms . . . are used. The precise food of each animal is known, and every insect has its special name. . . . If they have once been in a place they know every tree and every bush. . . . This superiority in what may be called general observation is particularly striking in cases where the faculty of hearing is concerned."[48]

Of course the native may seem as stupid when he is badgered about some-

---

[45] Roth, *Tasmania*, 31.
[46] Jenness and Ballentyne, *D'Entrecasteaux*, 52.
[47] Fritsch, *Eingeb. S.-Afr.*, 55.
[48] Torday and Joyce, in JAI, XXXVI, 274-277.

thing in which he has no interest, or which he is not up to, as any modern
called upon to plow through metaphysical whimsies. "It must be also remembered that it is difficult to find a Sakai who will, or can, fix his attention on
any one subject for more than a very few minutes at a time; hence it is necessary, after talking about anything for a little while, to let the matter drop
and return to it later. To question an aboriginal, especially a member of one
of the wilder tribes, minutely and elaborately, usually only results in the
visible distress and confusion of the savage."[49] Borneo natives concern themselves solely with what touches their immediate interests: "The same limitation of their knowledge revealed itself in [their indifference to] the names of
animals and plants which they did not use as food or for some other purpose
in their domestic economy." One of the travellers shot a number of small
birds which they had never seen before, and for which they had no name.[50]
Cowan[51] has a chapter on nature-lore and forest-craft which shows the Maori
a master-observer of his local environment. The need of the Shingu natives to
find out the nature of a new thing was exhausted by the question whether the
traveller had made it and what it was called. The excellent observer[52] who
reports this maintains repeatedly out of his wide experience of savages that
the necessary and useful preceded the reflective and sentimental.

Oliveira Martins[53] concludes, apropos of the well-known limitation of interest and curiosity on the part of primitive races that
"from foresight comes curiosity and the first shrine of reason,
for from surprise comes reflection and along with meditation ideas
are at length defined." But the awakening is only partial at first,
and the "explanation" is but another way of admitting ignorance.

Of certain Africans it is said: "Nothing that seems to them inexplicable, supernatural, can impress them; they say to themselves, 'Oh, it is always that way,'
and think no more of it, or why it is 'so.' "[54] But when for some reason the
inexplicable is forced upon attention, generally by fear, the first explanation—
reference to magic—appears. The Australian perceives that the throwing-stick
"gives the spear a surprising impetus, and not being able to explain its mechanical action, he considers that it is magical. This is a good instance of the
manner in which the aboriginal mind works."[55] Among savage Australian
tribes in general there is an "undercurrent of anxious feeling which, though
it may be stilled and forgotten for a time, is yet always present. In his natural
state the native is often thinking that some enemy is attempting to harm him
by means of evil magic, and, on the other hand, he never knows when a medicine man in some distant group may not point him out as guilty of killing
some one else by magic."[56] The Australian is scared by violent whirlwinds,
regarding them as malignant spirits.[57]

[49] Evans, in JAI, XLVIII, 197.   [50] Schwaner, *Borneo*, II, 118-119.
[51] *Maoris*, ch. XV.
[52] Von den Steinen, *Zent. Bras.*, 76, 221.
[53] *Raças*, II, 20.   [54] Von Götzen, *Durch Afr.*, 210.
[55] Howitt, in JAI, XVI, 28, note.
[56] Spencer and Gillen, *Nat. Tr. Cent. Aust.*, 53, 54.
[57] Horne and Aiston, *Cent. Aust.*, 9.

As regards the Congo native, "the stars in their courses make for him no song around the eternal throne, but the smoke ascending from his great bush fires forming a halo round the sun will make him quake with fear because it is an omen of evil. The movements of the sun and the moon awaken no admiration in him, but exhibit some poor conjuring trick, or a shilling mechanical toy, and his eyes and mouth are not big enough to express his wonder."[58] "A frequent statement I have heard made by [Bantu] natives is that lions are more numerous in the rains. Lions have forced themselves on his attention more at that time, so he says there are more. It never occurs to him to think where all the extra lions come from or go to. Anyhow, with the miraculous always at his disposal, he never has to follow an argument farther than one step, and there it can end in a supernatural phenomenon. However, he does not even trouble to assign such an occurrence to a miracle. If asked where they have come from, he says, 'How should I know?' and dismisses the matter from his mind."[59] "A puppet," says Junker,[60] "almost a meter high, cut out of cardboard and gaily painted, which I had hung up in my hut, was frequently the cause of the liveliest scenes. If when the women visited me I suddenly and without being noticed pulled at the thin threads that hung far down from the phantom, the women rushed shrieking and plunging out of my hut and were by reason of their apprehension only with difficulty to be brought back again." "Forked lightning . . . marks the fall of a celt and the wrath of heaven on the stricken object. . . . The Kukis in the event of an earthquake call out 'We are alive; we are alive,' so that the god under the earth, who is conceived of as shaking it to find out if men still inhabit it, shall know they are there and desist. They also attribute earthquakes to the presence of a great snake that coils round the world. When it succeeds in biting its own tail the earth is shaken."[61] The same idea of a god shaking the earth is found in the Malay Archipelago; the natives call out "Idup! Idup!" ("Still alive!") and beat the earth with sticks to make the god keep still.[62]

Preoccupied observers have often reported upon the primitive mind in a manner which is evidence only of their own lack of objectivity. They have started out by imputing to it both likenesses and unlikenesses as compared with their own mental processes and have been surprised and shocked, both ways; in the main, they have confused what is in the savage mind with what it actually is, in the matter of quality, as an instrument. Boas[63] has with some impatience rectified certain impressions thus obtained. In particular, observers without training, and intent only upon some enterprise of their own, have seemed not to accredit the savage with the normal human propensity to become bored at insistent pryings and intrusions or amused at what cannot help but appear to him as imbecilities and futilities in the white man's ideas and behavior. Again, they have not realized that he may esteem politeness above truth, though they themselves are always, among themselves, witnessing to the same preference. Tylor[64] tells of natives who, bored with the persistency of an investigator intent upon proving to them that they could count higher than they said they could, finally decided that the issue was not worth the trouble and furnished a series of terms for higher numbers which, upon expert exami-

[58] Weeks, in JAI, XXXIX, 134.
[60] Afrika, II, 61, 225.
[62] Wilken, in VG, III, 274 ff.
[64] Prim. Cult., I, 241.

[59] Stigand, Elephant, 289.
[61] Hutton, Sema Nagas, 252.
[63] Mind of Prim. Man, passim.

nation, turned out to be "partly nonsense-words and partly indelicate expressions, so that the supposed series of high numerals forms at once a little vocabulary of Tongan indecency, and a warning, as to the probable results of taking down unchecked answers from question-worried savages."

Two authorities on Africa furnish a pair of representative instances. Says one of them:[65] "My experience is that an intelligent native, when asked for information by his master, will, in his anxiety to please, prefer inventing a story to giving none at all, so I accept information of this sort with caution." The other writer[66] corroborates: "One may arrive at conclusions diametrically opposed to the truth by direct interrogation. To a phrase thus expressed: 'That tiger is red, that road is long, is it not?'—the black will without fail answer, nine times in ten: 'Surely.' And a moment later, ask him: 'That tiger is blue, or that road is short?'—the answer will be the same: 'Surely.' All the reports of military men and explorers mention this fact, concluding that the black is an 'arrant' liar. For us, yes, but for him, certainly no, for he simply thinks that the white man wants an affirmative answer and he provides him that satisfaction, which is just as easy for himself. But according to his idea he has made no reply that he thinks true, so far as he himself is concerned, and does not imagine that there is required from him the truth as he sees it."

We have no intention of trying to analyze the savage mind to any degree approaching exhaustiveness and shall concentrate upon certain traits which have special bearing upon the topic before us. Of commanding importance is the fact that a naïve intelligence, whether among savages or civilized people, is prone to take a sequence in time for a sequence in causation. Men have gradually and painfully and partially learned that while causes are antecedents, not every antecedent is a cause. To make with precision this distinction—or that between concomitance and causality[67]—is science. So far as the savage man has any notion of causation, it is all exhausted in the reasoning that if one event follows another it is caused by it. Primitive mental operations show characteristic cases; imitative magic[68] is the grand instance of the *post-propter*.

The Australian believes many a thing that seems ridiculous to us, yet it cannot be said that there is anything but sincerity in his views. "For instance, bone-pointing is regarded as absolute nonsense, and to our superior knowledge it certainly looks so. Now the black argues thus: I point a bone at a man, that man dies. Nothing could be clearer than the cause and effect. The flaw in the argument is the omission from the premises of the fact that the victim knows or thinks that the bone has been so pointed. Take, again, the example of rain-

[65] Moggridge, in JAI, XXXII, 472; Worcester, *Philippine Isl.*, 476-478.
[66] Trilles, *Fân*, 261.
[67] D'Alviella, *Concep. of God*, 295-296.
[68] §302, below.

making, which more often than not comes wrong. An excuse is always ready at hand. In the koonki's last effort, I hear since that the alleged reason of failure now is the presence of the cinematograph, 'All time turn 'em handle too much wind, *pudney* rain,' was the remark."[69] Lichtenstein[70] tells of a stick ornamented with buttons which was given, as a symbol of authority, to a Bushman. Dying, he gave it to his son. The son soon died. Then the stick was returned to the donor; it was thought that all would die if it were kept. Another case reported by the same traveller relates to a ship's anchor, which lay at the mouth of a river; when the king of the Amachosa had a piece of it broken off, the man who did it died. The anchor was thereafter considered a god angry at the injury, was given a name, and was hailed by passers-by. "In Molembo where a pest broke out, soon after the death of a Portuguese in the locality, and was referred to that event, the people tried in every way as long as the memory was fresh to prevent any European from dying within the boundaries of its territory." In Loango there was a taboo against the export of gum-copal because to it they ascribed their many throne-changes.[71] On one of the Nicobar Islands several of the natives began to make earthen pots; "but when they chanced to die soon after, their deaths were ascribed to this dangerous enterprise, and pottery-making was given up. The art has since been lost in that place."[72] Among the Yakuts, in a case where exogamy was the rule, there was on one occasion a union within the sib, "but all condemned that marriage, and when the new-made wife, after the wedding, became blind, they ascribed this calamity to the breach of the ancient custom."[73] Batak legends relate that once when a man married the daughter of his father's sister calamities followed and the custom had to be given up.[74] Again, where images of fabulous animals were put in the chiefs' coffins the notion developed that these images caused the deaths of chiefs. Then it became a crime, not civil but religious, to make one of these images.[75] It is quite possible that many an expedient variation in the mores perished in this manner. "At St. Michael," says Nelson,[76] "a man told me of three hunters who went out one winter during a famine, and after hunting for a long time could find no game. Finally one of them went back to their sledge and took from it the ham of a dog which he had brought with him. After eating some of this he started off again, carrying the bone with him. He had gone only a short distance when he encountered a seal and killed it. This, it was said, was due to the dog's ham-bone which he had with him, and thereafter he carried this bone and adopted a mark to represent it in place of his totem sign, as did his son after him."

These instances serve not only to illustrate the application of the *post-propter* argument to particular instances but also to throw considerable light upon the general efficacy of this sort of reasoning in the creation of fetishes and other details of that

[69] Horne and Aiston, *Cent. Aust.,* 121.
[70] *Reisen,* I, 412; *Travels in S. Afr.,* II, 61.
[71] Bastian, *Afr. Reisen,* 104-105; Bastian, *Deut. Exped.,* I, 193.
[72] Ratzel, *Anthropogeog.,* II, 699-700.
[73] Sieroshevski-Sumner, in JAI, XXXI, 87.
[74] Meerwaldt, in *Bijd.,* XLI, 203.   [75] Nieuwenhuis, *Borneo,* 80.
[76] In BAE, XVIII, pt. I, 325-326.

structure of pseudo-knowledge which constitutes so dominating a part of the mental outfit.

Though apparently worn threadbare early in time, the *post-propter* argument has remained indestructible. "Constantinople was conquered by the Turks on May 19, 1453. On the twelfth of May of the following year occurred a total eclipse of the moon. Again two years later, in 1456, a comet appeared which was visible far and wide in the heavens. No one doubted the causal connection of these recurrences. Public prayers were offered that God might hold off the comet and the Turks."[77] It should be realized also that the well-worn fallacy still flourishes in our midst. Every election affords a chance to bring it out and exercise it. We were told that the election of Cleveland brought on the crisis of 1893, as well as the deficit in the Treasury. Every two years prosperity or adversity is attributed or charged to the administration that has been in power. A pair of instances of a scarcely more extreme type may be cited. A writer is in opposition to the provision for daylight-saving. "Now I should think that two years of daylight saving followed by the influenza is proof enough that nature cannot be changed without ruining the health of the working people as has been shown twice in the past."[78] With this instance may be aligned the conviction of the Serbian peasant that the establishment of a flying-field near the capital was responsible for the drought of 1923. "It is more than probable that if the flight of airplanes over their country were stopped the rain would come again before very long, and then will they have the best of rights to say 'We told you so!' to such doubters of their meteorological theories as there now may be."[79]

The intellect of the savage operates with clearness and accuracy within the range of his knowledge; he knows and exists by utilizing his information when, for instance, it comes to playing upon the instincts and habits of animals. His mind "goes wrong" when he is involved in his "superstitions." The word superstition is deservedly a derogatory term and as such ought not to be applied to primitive tenets. To the Romans it meant an excessive fear of the gods or an unreasonable religious belief. A superstition is essentially a survival; and it is no tribute to anyone to call him a survival or his actions survivalistic. "In the sense of culture-history," Lippert[80] writes, "only that can with good reason be called superstition which reaches up in survivalistic fashion out of a lower stage of development into a higher, and lives on in inner contradiction with it." It is superstition for a modern man to believe in witchcraft; it is not superstition for a savage to do so. Anyone would, in his place. Men are wont to label views resting

77 Cantor, *Zufall*, 5.
78 Letter to the New Haven *Journal Courier*, Jan. 31, 1920.
79 N. Y. *Times*, Oct. 13, 1923.   80 *Kgchte.*, I, 95.

on a stock of knowledge which they think "lower" than their own as superstitious. What is encountered in the savage is plain ignorance—not superstition; he, like the child, knows no better and has had no opportunities to improve by way of learning better. This is no place for a moral judgment or even for a word carrying unconsciously a moral judgment. What vitiates the primitive major premises is ignorance, which puts a wrong construction upon perfectly true facts and sets up a false end incapable of realization. "There is nothing like acute deductive reasoning for keeping a man in the dark; it might be called the technique of the intellect, and the concentration of the mind upon it corresponds to that predominance of technical skill in art which ends in degradation of the artist's function, unless new inspiration and invention come to guide it."[81] The development of astrology and alchemy illustrate the process of getting the major premise wrong and then working on "logically" through ages toward an unrealizable goal, until accumulating experience forces a reëxamination resulting in the rejection of the basic assumption. This case should cause one to notice, in anticipation of later pages, that "superstition" is the forerunner of science; and that without the anxious, fear-inspired observations and labors due to the former there could have been no body of recorded fact capable of destroying the illusory major premise and then of being worked over in later times under more enlightened hypotheses.

§200. Illusion. Perhaps the lair of illusion can best be identified by considering first the range which it finds least congenial. Mores that represent direct reactions upon the natural environment have in them a minimum of reflection, theorizing, and "notions." The relation here between life-conditions and men's responses to them is immediate; the mores-adjustments are all the time and inevitably being carried back to the concrete conditions of life, re-fitted to them in their changing phases, or more expediently harmonized with their durable features. Adjustments and re-adjustments are not the product of study and premeditation; they are matter-of-fact, adopted in the face of specific cases, automatic. Unconscious adaptation by way of automatic selection is

[81] George Eliot, Essay on *The Influence of Rationalism*.

at a maximum.[82] Selection, too, is prompt. If a course of action, a variation in the mores, in connection with the food-quest is inexpedient, the fact is likely to be speedily sensed and the variation given up or modified; for the maintenance-mores are always on trial and, since they are subject to conclusive test, they are promptly subjected to selection before they become so hardened in custom, complicated with theory, and involved in a train of consequences, corollaries, and vested interests not easily recognizable as such, as to persist in the face of disaster. Justification or correction is not much delayed. Hence there are likely to be no very great or persisting illusions in the mores and institutions of elementary self-maintenance. They are readily referred to contact with tangible, material conditions. Hunger is not theorized over by the famished group of savages any more than by animals; there is an effort, which is almost a reflex, to stop it at once; and everyone knows what will stop it. In the matter of self-maintenance societies are still near enough to the tangible and verifiable not to get their feet far off the ground of actuality or to allow their heads to swim about in the clouds of theory and dogma.

Of course, this automatic process produces a "logical" result; it is out of the process that men got the idea of logic in the first place. We believe that much which bears the face and presentment of logic in primitive life and is assigned to the primitive mind, is simply the "logic of events."[83]

Nowhere is there less of illusion than in the range of material self-maintenance. However there are cases even within this range which show unmistakable maladjustment due to its presence; there are customs the effect of which has been to drive whole generations into usages harmful to them, such as the renunciation for no good reason, but for "mere superstition," of useful foods, materials, and activities.[84] The Yakuts, for instance, seeing a camel for the first time just as smallpox was breaking out among them, ever after regarded the useful beast as a malevolent god.[85] In all such cases there has been mental reaction based upon certain conceptions in the mind that had no counterpart in the actual facts of the physi-

82 Keller, Soc. Evol., ch. III, and 132 ff.
83 Keller, Soc. Evol., 93 ff. 84 Sumner, Folkways, §29.
85 Wilken, Vkde., 546.

cal and human environment, that is, upon illusions. This situation
is not paralleled in the animal world; it is with the entrance of the
human mind, with its outfit of illusions—about ghosts, magic, the
evil eye, the supernatural in general—into the field that "the
errorless course of nature" is replaced by one in which errors
multiply on errors. Illusion is imported, even into the mainte-
nance-operations, from a range of speculation about mysterious
agencies in which it seems almost innate; and the farther men get
away from the possibility of concrete verification, the more are
they exposed to illusion. Fortunately for the race, men's illusions
and superstitions are checked up in the long run, though often
very tardily and indirectly, on the hard facts of life. It is the
object of the present section of this book to deal with mankind's
mental outfit of illusions and beliefs and with its evolution and
correction: with the notions, for they really deserve the name,
derived from illusory premises and with the modification and refinement of these toward harmony with actuality. If the word
"phrenology" had not been appropriated to baser uses, this section might well bear that term as a title.

It cannot but have appeared that the grand illusion under which
mankind has labored throughout the ages is that of the existence
of a world of ghosts and spirits. That world has constituted a
third environment, along with the natural and the social, adjustment to which has been believed to be fully as essential to well-
being as adaptation to the more tangible surroundings of nature
and fellow-men. This is the supernatural environment, and cases
of utter unmindfulness of it are not to be found. It is simply another life-condition along with the rest for man to meet in the
struggle for existence. Because it is apprehended by primitive man
in terms not so obvious and familiar to the modern mind, it needs
portrayal before methods of adjustment to it are much considered; for it is a thing of the mind, an unverifiable mental outfit
of views and beliefs, and does not, like the world of things and of
men, exist as from the givings of the waking senses. It is an article
of faith. In treating of it much less may be taken for granted than
has been the case when the institutions under review were more
matter-of-fact than matter-of-fancy.

The conception of the supernatural environment might have

been a mere outlying curiosity in societal evolution had it not been thought to impinge with power upon human living. Its mode of impact is through nothing less than the aleatory element. If primitive tribes over the earth agree on anything, it is that supernatural powers are in control of the luck-element. This fact will be illustrated over and over again in the following chapters; it is, in a sense, the burden of them all. Here is where that tremendous, crucial luck-factor in existence, intangible, rationally irreducible by primitive powers to a form admitting of adjustment to it, is visualized and identified, albeit under illusion, so that an attempt can be made to handle it in the interest of human destiny.

For all men, in every human society that has ever existed, the luck element has formed one of the few dominant life-conditions. It has had to be dealt with in some manner. "It is hardly necessary to prove that every kind of speculation or philosophical dogma was, as a rule of action, foreign to primitive men. They stood face to face with the fact of existence, and the only inference from this fact was anxiety to maintain existence."[86] It was to this end that they strove to deal with the aleatory element. They had a way of accounting for it furnished them from a source that had really no connection with it; they used one mystery to explain another. A sense of exposure to mischance has always been provocative of religious sentiment. The gatherers of edible birds'-nests in Java— an occupation attended with many mishaps—are exceptionally fervid in their service of the spirits, for the latter are conceived to protect men against these hazards.[87] Sins are abjured in calamity. This does not mean that men in peril excogitate dogmas and pass them down to succeeding generations. "Prescriptions about religious commissions and omissions—not teachings about the inner continuity of the world of phenomena, but practical means for protection, whether in life or after death, from injury and misfortune—form, to a greater or less degree, the original stock in all religions of antiquity. . . . It is the religious usages and customs, not the notions out of which these developed, that have constituted the prime subject-matter of tradition."[88]

It is not correct to say that men gratuitously frightened them-

86 Lippert, *Kgchte.*, I, 7; II, 504.   87 Wilken, in VG, III, 272.
88 Pietschmann, *Phön.*, 154.

selves by the imaginings of their own minds. What was behind their supernatural structures—that which these structures accounted for—was what filled them with terror. They feared their ghosts and gods for what they could do in causing calamity— because they personified the aleatory element. It is a shrewd saying that "men are tormented by the ideas they have of things, and not by the things themselves,"[89] but anyone who conceives that there was a mere void behind all man's religious concern has missed one of the great facts of life. There was no thin vacuum; there was the element of chance. No wonder that men were ready to seize upon an explanation of luck which was, as it were, made to order. It is necessary to anticipate broadly by stating that the institution developed in adjustment to the element of the inexplicable and fortuitous—the element of chance or luck, the aleatory element—is religion.

It would be tragic—were it true that the origin of an institution had any bearing upon its developed character—that men were thrown back upon illusion as the only available means of dealing with what is always a momentous and may at any time become the gravest of life-conditions. Naturally, however, that aspect of the matter does not inspire concern in the scientist; seen in proper perspective, it need not disquiet anybody, even the most visionary idealist.

It is evident enough, since there is in the minds of men a conviction—how implicit and unshaken a conviction will presently appear—of the existence of this third environment of ghosts and spirits, that religion, as a response to it, is a mode of self-maintenance belonging with industry, war, and regulation. To most primitive men religion ranks all the other forms of self-preservation in importance; and so long as it is thought to be superlatively indispensable to existence, the question whether it is actual or illusory must remain, so far as the play of cause and consequence is concerned, a matter of irrelevance. As a matter of fact, religion has worked; it has been powerful in securing societal self-maintenance, though not along the lines of efficiency which primitive men have thought they perceived. In truth, the aleatory element, though unanalyzed, was felt and feared vividly enough, and when

[89] Epictetus, *Manual, 5,* quoted in Montaigne, *Essais,* in *Œuvres,* I, 99.

it was once identified with supernatural inmixture into the affairs of men, there was unleashed a powerful force, comparable in its compulsions to hunger and love, namely, a fear of the supernatural or, to use a brief and distinctive term, ghost-fear.[90] Now could the fearsome inexplicable be fearsomely explained. There was set afloat a tremendous major premise gravid with dread deductions none of which over long ages were verifiable or even subject to critical examination by an awe-stricken and worshipful humanity. Only the impersonal evolutionary forces remained unawed, and proceeded imperturbably to curb this new fellow-force into the service of society.

[90] §14, above.

CHAPTER XXII

THE SPIRIT-ENVIRONMENT

§201. Ghost-Fear. What was needed, in the face of the aleatory element, was an explanation of the inexplicable. Nothing in the line of "realities" would do. Perhaps "explanation" is too pretentious a word for what the savage had to have. He was terrified by the aleatory element and under the necessity of somehow dealing with it. He had to have some sort of theory to go on in order to develop methods of procedure. By a sort of marvellous coincidence the theory was there, right at hand; and it was one competent to cover any and all cases, however mysterious and astonishing. The theory was that of the spirit-environment. It is not asserted that the recognition, conscious or unconscious, of the element of chance in life summoned into being the idea of that environment. That conception arose from other sources altogether. Nevertheless it was there, and it explained the otherwise inexplicable. The two conceptions dovetailed together, and out of this situation came that important cluster of institutions which we know as primitive religion. The two conceptions still cling together; inexplicable or unforeseeable calamities are still generalized as "acts of God" or "acts of Providence." What men can understand and provide against they do not so designate. If there had been no aleatory element, there might have been a very different sort of religion or none at all. As it actually has been, the former was a major condition of living to which men automatically adjusted themselves by recourse to the development of religious institutions. The need was very real and the evoked adjustments have been in the highest degree actual—as much so as property, marriage, and the rest. It might appear upon superficial observation that ghost-fear was entirely independent of the struggle for existence; it would then be a purely gratuitous weakness or folly into which men fell though it was inexpedient for their interests. No evolutionist could think that. Ghost-fear is directly and vitally coupled with the struggle for existence through the aleatory element. Savages have a direct and simple notion of the correlation

between their earthly fate and their religion. They build inferences of the most materialistic character on it. Their religion has
no sense except to ward off ill and get good. The worship of the
Christian god seems to them to lack such sense.[1]

On the one side are the inexplicable ills of life; on the other the
inexplicable good fortune. The latter befalls man often enough to
cast a gleam of unearthly light upon human experience: to inflame
the imagination and to stimulate idealization, and so to produce
a world-philosophy altogether opposed to the philosophy of the
struggle for existence. These two phases, bad and good luck, may
be called respectively the negative and the positive side of the
aleatory element. Though at different stages of civilization the
element lies upon different planes and has to do with different
things, its nature and its relation to human life do not change.
The sentiment of man in regard to it is modified a little, but not
much, by education.

Naturally it is at the crises of life that the effect of the aleatory
element is seen in strongest relief. Smith[2] says of the Semite that
everything connected with the propagation of the species on the
one hand, and disease and death on the other, seems to him to
involve the action of superhuman agencies of a dangerous kind.
But here are involved the two elemental issues of all life, self-preservation and self-perpetuation. The inexplicable may be ignored
when the occasion is trivial; it is the entrance of the unreckonable
into a situation vital for the individual or the society that enforces
attention.[3]

§202. The Shock of Death. Reactions on experience are thus
the origin of the mental outfit. The Omahas, being in peril from
strong neighbors, not only esteemed warriors but cultivated religious observances to get supernatural help.[4] The customs produced in response to the need of adjustment, the doctrines which
coördinate the customs, the traditions and rules which have been
deduced from the doctrines, constitute a stock of knowledge or
pseudo-knowledge, or a world-philosophy, which is handed down
from generation to generation, is applied to whatever is unusual

[1] Von Martius, *Beiträge*, I, 463. [2] *Relig. Sem.*, 447.
[3] Lippert, *Kgchte.*, I, 95. [4] Fletcher, in JAI, XXVII, 437.

and painful, and is growing and being corrected all the time. This is the mental outfit of the race. The actual process of correcting and purifying it has followed upon a realization that, being full of error, it did not verify. It has too often been changed by putting a new error in place of an old. Only gradually have some parts of it been made true, that is, verifiable on the ordinary tests of reality. We know that this is so; nevertheless the traditions are sacred, the corrections anything but obvious, and the task of living from day to day absorbs our strength and thought. This makes the whole process automatic. The savages fear the irregular, not the regular; "the things of every day have never yet stimulated their thinking."[5] All men live for the most part unconsciously in the mores. "The great mass of the folkways give us discipline and the support of routine and habit. If we had to form judgments as to all these cases before we could act in them, and were forced always to act rationally, the burden would be unendurable. Beneficent use and wont save us this trouble."[6] It is only with some grand upheaval in our experience that we are shaken out of our routine and inertia. How much the more so with savage man.

Such a shock in the experience of life was death. There is a sentimental notion, the product of carrying back present-day ideas into the interpretation of primitive life, that man was first stirred to reflection by the wonder and mystery of birth.[7] These may well fill with awe the mind of the thoughtful and cultured parent or of the biologist; as for the savage, he was familiar enough with the superficial aspects of reproduction, animal and human, and was not in the way of being impressed by the mysteries of cell-behavior. The "new soul" that had come to earth was not imposing to him; it was a puny spirit in a feeble body and inspired neither respect nor fear; the disposal of the bodies of dead children was careless[8] because there was nothing to be uneasy about. What impresses the savage is power; it was when the great chief or medicine-man died that the mortuary ceremonies were scrupulously, anxiously, and lengthily attended to. If there was no shock in the slipping into the world of a new and weak soul

[5] Lippert, *Kgchte.*, I, 5.   [6] Sumner, *Folkways*, §68.
[7] Lippert, *Kgchte.*, I, 105-106, where this idea is curtly disposed of.
[8] §§226-232, below.

there was a severe one when the powerful, domineering, hard-hitting warrior met his end. Here was something that demanded explanation. Also dissolution might come to one's self, and that prospect stirred the instinct of self-preservation. Apparently the first and most powerful of the excitants to reflection was that event which has represented to many generations of shrinking mortals the supreme and decisive, if not the ultimate ill of earthly existence—death. This reaction must not be confused with any idea of the "sanctity of human life," a conception not harbored by the savage mind. Death was extraordinary and inexplicable, due to some agency without whose intervention it need not be. Death by violence was, among early men as among animals, a common form of life-ending; disease came upon them as something without any antecedent at all; so that people were accustomed to the visible operation of agency and the conception of cause was not thrust upon them. In short, death being inexplicable in the exclusion of agency, it came under the widely extended range of the aleatory element, as perhaps the extreme case of it.

Instances of indifference to life are scattered throughout this book. Take the Papuan who ran to a tree, climbed it, cast himself down from its top, and broke his neck, in a rage because his wife had surreptitiously smoked up his cigarette.[9] Of the Malays of Borneo we read: "Death, to their ignorant and unenlightened minds, displays no terror; and though they shun it with that instinctive fear which is common to both animals and men, they have by no means the dread of the King of Terror common to more enlightened nations."[10] "Suicide is of frequent occurrence among the females, but is rarely resorted to by the males. The women . . . are so keenly sensitive to disgrace that many prefer, if anything untoward happen, to perish by their own act. They cannot bear to be found fault with by those whom they love, and if reproached by their parents or their husbands in at all bitter terms for any irregularity in their conduct they take poison."[11] "Male suicide often takes place [among some tribes in Celebes] when they catch their wives in adultery."[12] Among the Eskimo, "suicide is not of rare occurrence, since, according to the religious ideas of the Eskimo, the souls of those who die by violence go to . . . the happy land. Hence it is considered lawful for a man to kill his aged parents."[13] American Indians commit suicide oftener than is suspected, even boys taking their lives. They do this when ill and sometimes for more trivial reasons. "A Dakota boy . . . shot himself rather than face his companions after his mother had whipped him, and a Pai-Ute boy . . . tried to poison himself with the wild parsnip because he was not well and strong

9 Hagen, *Papua's*, 254.
10 Roth, *Sarawak*, I, 137.
11 Roth, *Sarawak*, I, 117.
12 Riedel, in *Bijd.*, XXXV, 79.
13 Boas, in BAE, VI, 615.

like the other boys."[14] In a number of primitive cases suicide was committed in order to place blood-guilt upon an enemy.[15] Death was often chosen as the lesser of two evils. "On the islands the Indians at the time of the conquest, to avoid being persecuted with fire and sword by the Spaniards, were said to have committed suicide on a wholesale scale by means of cassava juice."[16] Suicide for vengeance may be recalled by a single instance: in a certain East African district, "a young man one day had a violent quarrel with his own mother while cultivating, and eventually beat her with a stick. She ran crying to a village near by, and one of the elders came out and gave the young fellow a thrashing; to every one's astonishment the young man hanged himself that afternoon, and the people of the vicinity told my agent, who went to enquire into it, that he had committed suicide so that his blood relations might lay his death at the door of the elder, and thus start a blood feud against him."[17] The Japanese customs of *harakiri* and *jigai*, which sometimes amount to the commission of suicide on what looks to a Westerner to be very slight cause, will occur to any reader.[18]

§203*. Death Not Inevitable. To us the marvellous thing is life. We think of it as maintained against opposing and disintegrating forces which are sure to win in the end. We know that we die in part each hour and moment; that waste and dead cells are being all the time cast off from the body; and that presently life will fail through the gain of the processes of disintegration over those of restoration. That "all men are mortal" is to us a truism —an axiom that we put into our textbooks on logic as the most undeniable of major premises. Yet we must realize that this modern view, as stated, rests upon scientific discovery and, back of that, upon an accumulation of experience that the savage did not have. "Who amongst us has any consciousness in himself, when in the bloom of life, of the necessity of his own death except as he derives it as a generalization from the imperfect experience outside of himself?"[19] We know that all must die, because we are told so. History always records, at the end, the death of its characters; the kings and captains depart and negative evidence is pretty strong that they are not here. Primitive men see no such universal destiny of death; they take life as the fact and cannot understand that it must end—or begin.[20] Of natural cause they have no idea

[14] Mallery, in BAE, IV, 131.
[15] Lasch, "Rache als Selbstmordmotiv," in *Globus*, LXIV, 39; §177, above.
[16] Roth, in BAE, XXXVIII, 560.   [17] Hobley, in JAI, XXXIII, 358.
[18] Hearn, *Japan*, 314–316, 318.   [19] Lippert, *Kgchte.*, I, 104.
[20] §211, below.

at all. They are familiar with a fact which naturalists emphasize, that most wild animals meet death by violence; and they see many human beings slain. If no slayer actually appears, his existence is assumed. The conviction prevails widely, at any rate, among backward aborigines that death is not according to nature and that it cannot occur in the undisturbed course of events; it is very generally referred to magic.[21] They have, further, no criteria for distinguishing living from non-living things.[22]

Of course when it comes to acquiring a realization of what death means—of the state of non-existence—we are about as helpless as the race has ever been. The belief in the inevitability of death is based upon some observation and much hearsay; and not all even of the hearsay supports it. The induction is not conclusive unless the observation and hearsay are extensive and corroborative and unless alleged exceptions are dismissed on one ground or another; it was necessarily very imperfect for those who lived in small and isolated groups and who had no history. They might easily imagine that some men somewhere did not die.

The Bible says that Enoch and Elijah did not die, and other peoples beside the Hebrews have traditions of translation. Menelaus was not to die but was to be sent to the Elysian fields because he was the husband of the daughter of Zeus; and his case does not stand alone in Homer.[23] When Ponce de León set out, in the sixteenth century, to find the fountain of immortal youth, the induction that all men must die must have been very imperfect in his mind; and similarly with others who believed the same sort of thing.[24] The like is true of men who thought that there could be an "elixir of life."[25] The Miltonic view assumes the original absence of death, before sin "brought death into the world and all our woe."[26]

Evidently death belongs to the aleatory element and is one of its most startling manifestations. Hence it has been an object of anxious and sustained attention, with the result that views about it have filled and moved the minds of men. These views show, together with a variety of detail, an essential parallelism over the earth in regarding death as incidental and also temporary.

[21] §§304, 306, 308, below. [22] Spencer, *Prin. Soc.*, I, ch. IX.
[23] *Odyssey*, IV, 561-569. Heracles, Castor and Polydeuces, *Odyssey*, XI, 300-304, 601-603; Keller, *Hom. Soc.*, 106.
[24] Herodotus, *Hist.*, III, 23; Hopkins, "The Fountain of Youth," in *Jour. Am. Orient. Soc.*, XXVI.
[25] Levick, "Elixir of Life," in N. Y. *Times*, Sept. 9, 1923.
[26] *Paradise Lost*, I, 3.

"It is not difficult to see how, amongst savages having no real knowledge of the causes of disease, which is the common lot of humanity, the very suspicion of such a thing as death from natural causes should be unknown. Death by accident they can imagine, although the results of what we should call accident they mostly attribute to the effects of some evil magic. They are well acquainted with death by violence, but even in this they [for instance, certain Australians] believe . . . that a warrior who happens to be speared in one of the ceremonial fights has lost his skill in warding off or evading a spear, through the evil magic of someone belonging to his own tribe. But I doubt if, anywhere in Australia, the aborigines, in their pristine condition, conceived the possibility of death merely from disease."[27] "Among Central Australian natives there is no such thing as belief in natural death; however old and decrepit a man or woman may be when it takes place, it is at once supposed that it has been brought about by the magic influence of some enemy, and in the normal condition of the tribe the death of one individual is followed by the murder of some one else who is supposed to be guilty of having caused the death. . . . The identity of the guilty man is always revealed by the medicine man."[28] The Papuans of Loyalty Island lay death to witchcraft, misdeeds, or infraction of the taboo.[29] "New Guinea natives in their primitive condition will hardly admit that a death can occur apart from some human agency. Perhaps at some former time deaths from the violence of an enemy were so common that they performed an act of hasty generalization and inferred that the exceptions are only apparent, and that in such case some hidden means were employed. However such an idea arose, it certainly exists in New Guinea very widely. . . . Accepting that the native ascribes sickness and death to a hostile magician, the next matter to settle is as to who the magician is. . . . In some cases, I quite believe that the magician does actually cause sickness and death indirectly, by causing so much fear that ill-health and susceptibility to illness may follow."[30] "There are many reasons given why a child must not be allowed to live if its birth cost its mother her life; the chief is, that every life given has to be avenged; an eye for an eye is an immutable law with the savages. . . . The deceased mother is not supposed to have died of natural causes, or of senile decay; in some way the child took her life and that is said to be ample reason why the child should be buried alive in the grave of its dead mother. A more important consideration is the fact that the mother being dead, there is no one that can be relied on to nourish the child satisfactorily that it may become an useful unit of the tribe."[31] In the Trobriand Islands, "there seems to be some possibility of death by old age, especially in the case of very insignificant old men and women. Several times, when I was asking of what a man had died, I received the answer, 'He was very old and weak and he just died.' But when I asked about M'tabalu, a very old and decrepit man, the chief of Kasana'i, whether he was going to die soon, I was told that, if no *silami* (evil spell) were thrown on him, there was no reason why he should not go on living. Again, it must be remembered that a *silami* is a private thing, not to be talked about except with intimate friends. It must be emphasized

[27] Howitt, *S.E. Aust.*, 357.
[28] Spencer and Gillen, *Nat. Tr. Cent. Aust.*, 476-477.
[29] Ella, in AAAS, 1892, 642.   [30] Strong, in JAI, XLIX, 294.
[31] Holmes, in JAI, XXXII, 423.

that the 'ignorance of natural death' is the general typical attitude expressed in custom and reflected in such legal and moral institutions as exist, rather than some kind of absolute apodictic statement, excluding any contradictions or uncertainties." In this ignorance of natural death "there ought to be distinguished: (1) the ignorance of the necessity of death, of the life coming to an end; (2) ignorance of the natural causes of sickness as we conceive it. Only the second ignorance seems quite prevalent, the action of evil sorcerers being always assumed, except, perhaps, in the above-mentioned cases of very old and insignificant folk."[32]

"The Africans in common with many other primitive peoples believe that there is no such thing as a natural death but that it is caused by magic. It is the most important office of the tribal magician to trace out the criminal."[33] The Bechuana, regarding death as an unnatural effect of magic, expect souls to return and have a notion of life beyond death.[34] The idea is wide-spread that one may die and later come to life again. Holub[35] cites a chief's long speech of welcome, which closed as follows: "Look you, . . . here speaks a mouth that knows more than all those of my people who sit about me; for this mouth was erstwhile once shut, but has opened again. I was several times dead and I have again become a living man!" Holub thinks this "death" to have been "probably unconsciousness due to hyperæmia of the brain." In the French Congo there are two ways, in addition to witchcraft, by which a man may be brought to death; his "bush-soul" may be killed, or he may be a reincarnated soul bringing into its latter life the disease he had in its former one. Such reincarnation is a current doctrine in West Africa.[36] In East Africa, "the vast majority of natives believe that death from natural causes is the work of supernatural and evil magic. . . . Nor is this always mere magic, for the native does not distinguish between the absurdest concoctions and the most deadly poisons, wherefore innumerable cases of so-called witchcraft are undoubtedly simply cases of poisoning. Other harm is done to individuals and communities through dread of supposed injury done to them, as, for instance, when on one occasion a wizard placed some perfectly harmless medicine beside a water-hole, and so deprived a whole community of their water supply for several days. Imagine, then, the futility of impressing on the native the argument that there is no such thing as witchcraft, and his amazement when a person proved to be a wizard by all the tests ever devised is permitted by the European to go unpunished and at large. . . . Among tribes such as the Akikuyu, Akamba, and Wachagga, when a person dies, it is always suspected that the cause was witchcraft or the effects of some injury received, however long ago; in fact a natural death is hardly recognized. So the relatives will harp back to any blow or wound inflicted since birth, and attempt to fix responsibility for the death upon somebody or other. . . . In this connection it may be mentioned that if a person dies elsewhere than in his or her own home, the responsibility falls on anyone who was the cause of his or her absence, as, for instance, if a wife or child were to be enticed away or abducted, or if a man were kidnapped, enslaved or otherwise made away with."[37] In

[32] Malinowski, in JAI, XLVI, 360, note, 402-403.
[33] Starcke, Prim. Fam., 67.   [34] Ratzel, Vkde., I, 299.
[35] Capstadt, II, 180.   [36] Kingsley, Travels W. Afr., 460.
[37] Dundas, C., in JAI, LI, 233, 240-241; Barrett, in JAI, XLI, 23.

Baghirmi people who die of anything else than the weaknesses of old age are supposed to have been the victims of enemy magic, and the medicine-men proceed at once by magical means to detect the ill-doer.[38] In Samoa the belief was that a coco-nut tree stood by the gate of the spirit-world. If a departing soul collided with this, it returned to the body; and those who fell into syncope were supposed to have had this experience.[39] The American Indians "frequently speak of persons who have been very ill and have recovered as dying and returning to life again, and have a gesture sign to express the idea."[40] A high priest of the Pawnee tribe believes that he was once dead. He says that just as he died he entered an Indian village and went to the lodge of his relations. He knew them, but, not being offered a seat, thought he was not welcome. He left the village and then came back to life. In the morning he died and in the afternoon returned to life.[41] Among the Pima Indians, "death is always due to magic, to animals, or to neglect of the ceremonies or tabus."[42] "Many stories have come to the Sia by those who have died only for a time; the heart becomes still and the lips cold and the spirit passes to the entrance of the other world and looks in, but it does not enter, and yet sees it all, and in a short time returns to inhabit its earthly body. Great alarm is felt when one returns in this way to life, but much faith is put in the stories afterwards told by the one who has passed over the road of death."[43] The Shingu Indians find the cause of death always in the malice of another person. If there were only good men, there would be neither disease nor death. They know nothing of a natural termination of the process of life any more than the man who describes them did as a boy.[44]

The Chinese are far from regarding death as an absolute reality and think there is an elixir of immortality,[45] and the ancients did not believe it to be natural and inevitable. Why should not life continue until it was cut off? Hence death always had a positive cause.[46] It was an assassination by man, beast, falling tree, or other display of agency. By the use of a magic plant an old man might become young again.[47] The conception of death as a demon was common; consider the figure of Thanatos in the *Alcestis* of Euripides. In backward parts of the modern world there are legends of people who have been "screamed back" into life.[48] Says Krauss[49] of the South Slavs: "The idea of a natural force working according to laws, whose end-result we call death, passes the power of conception and comprehension of the nature-man. He suspects and believes that the spirit in the body has been overcome by another more powerful spirit and so separated from the body." This easily passes over into the Christian doctrine, but retains a primitive stamp where the Christians are primitive. The Imeritians of the Caucasus consider death a consequence of sin.[50] "Sickness was the greatest stranger in early Kentucky. Death from natural causes was so remarkable, that 'on one occasion when a young man was

[38] Nachtigal, *Sahara,* II, 686.

[39] Ella, in AAAS, 1892, 643.

[40] Mallery, in BAE, X, 306.

[41] Grinnell, *Folk-Tales,* 356.

[42] Russell, in BAE, XXVI, 193.

[43] Stevenson, in BAE, XI, 144.

[44] Von den Steinen, *Zent. Bras.,* 348, 492.

[45] DeGroot, *Relig. Syst.,* I, 241; Harvey, *Chinese Animism,* ch. IV.

[46] Maspero, *Hist. Anc.,* I, 111, 117-124.

[47] Schrader, *Keilinschr.,* 524, 526.

[48] Carstens, in *Am Urquell,* I, 10.

[49] *Südslaven,* 134.

[50] Hahn, in *Globus,* LXXX, 304.

taken sick and died, after the usual manner of nature, the women in the fort sat up all night, gazing at him as an object of beauty.' "[51]

§204. Inferences from Illusion. It is plain from these cases, typical of many more, that there was no clear idea of the nature of death and that it could readily be confused with death-like states. It is difficult yet for the non-expert to discriminate between absence of life and suspended animation. The traditional method of holding a feather or a mirror before the mouth in order to detect the presence or absence of the breath is a device that would have fallen in with the savage theory; for what primitive observation had fastened upon as the most obvious sign of life was the breath. When a man was alive he had it; when he was dead he had it not. Evidently it was the breath that effected the animation. Though observation extended, as will be seen, to other agencies or seats of life, the plain inference from the evidence is that the presence of "the breath of life" was the primordial proof of the animate state and its absence the accepted indication of death. Here is yet another case of the *post-propter* type of conclusion. But what, to the savage intelligence, was this breath? He knew nothing about the aëration of the circulation or about the formation of a vacuum through the action of the diaphragm and other muscles. The physical and chemical processes involved quite eluded him. He thought of the breath as a thing that went out and in. He had to figure it to his mind in some way without having seen it except, in some cases, as vapor. He did figure it—in human form. This, we should say, was an illusion. Whence came the illusion? What was in the savage mind that did not correspond to "realities"?

There are states of illusion in human experience in which the brain gets impressions due to its own condition and not to exciting forces acting on the periphery of the body. These states are called, broadly, hallucinations. They are regarded by us as unreal and as illusory because their sights and sounds do not verify upon the regular tests of reality—practical tests, developed as the result of millennia of experience, traditional and recorded—which, all through these millennia, we have lived by. Such states form, as

[51] From Ex-Gov. Morehead's Boonesborough Address, of May 25, 1840, quoted in Collins, *Hist. of Kentucky*, II, 509.

it were, a set of means between life and death, being often confused with the latter—in fact, hallucination not seldom immediately precedes death—and they are both pathological and natural. In the former category are reckoned fever, delirium, swoon, disorders of the brain-circulation, apoplexy, epilepsy, migraine, hysteria, ecstasy, and trance; forms of "absence of mind" running all the way from reverie to the hysterical and hypnotic state.[52]

A competent writer[53] distinguishes hallucinations as either due to agencies, chiefly toxins, that operate upon the brain or nerves, or as of purely mental origin, where no physical agency is known. The latter type includes suggestion, hypnotism, crystal-gazing, clairvoyance, hysteria, somnambulism, multiple personality, dreams, and so-called telepathy. A narrow escape from drowning is often accompanied by hallucination.

These states productive of illusion are, however, except for one, incidental and sporadic; there is but a single normal and universal type, namely, sleep with dreams. Dreams, coming in a state that is poetically termed the "brother of death," are the only universal experiences in which there is an exit from the world of reality into another world where happenings are not limited as in waking life by material conditions and by identity, coherence, and continuity. It is also possible to observe sleep and dreams in others and to note that reported experiences do not square with actuality; for example, that a sleeper has not moved in the body although he wakes to recount remote excursions and exciting adventures. Such phenomena can be observed over and over again— an indispensable feature for the teaching of anything to the savage. States of suspended animation and unconsciousness, after which life seems to be renewed, have regularly been aligned with sleep.

Passing over, for the present, other aspects of sleep and dreams which will become relevant at later stages of the presentation, we seek first to develop the connections between dreams and death. This comes in dreams about the dead. If there were no such visions it would be very difficult to fix upon an obvious origin of the conception of the soul.

[52] Lehmann, *Overtro*, IV, 254 ff.; Brinton, *Relig. Sent.*, 72-73.
[53] Steen, in *Brit. Med. Jr.*, summarized in N. Y. *Times*, Aug. 16, 1917.

§205. Dreams about the Dead. It is difficult for an educated person to realize the impression made upon an uncritical mind by the dream.[54] The primitive man, whose mind is of that order, has no reason to doubt the actuality of the visions that come in sleep. He knows not "seems"; in his very language "be" and "seem" are not distinguished; even in Latin "to seem" is "to be seen." He has no idea that things are not what they are seen to be, nor can he know that there are states where the brain gets impressions due to its own internal condition. He cannot be criticized and ought not to be ridiculed for believing what looks to be the direct evidence of his senses. Indeed the vivid dream not seldom leaves behind it visible physical results such as sweating and trembling, which might well be taken by the uncritical mind as proof positive of the reality of dream-experience. It is not at all unlikely that the dream was a more common occurrence with the savage than with us; the nature of his food-supply, his periods of hunger and fasting, his abiding sense of jeopardy and anticipation of ill, and the other uncomfortable and irregular experiences of his life might well have made of his sleep a more fitful and less reposeful affair than that of the well-fed and secure. However that may be, the savage has dreams and they mean much to him; that they have been taken very seriously by people no longer barbarous is amply established by the evidence of legend, tradition, myth, and history. Even peoples who have become sophisticated enough to distinguish pretty readily between appearance and reality and who no longer consider dreams real in the strict sense are far from dismissing them as utterly unreal and trivial.

It is precisely the dreams about the dead that enable the savage to form some conception of what it is that passes out of a man when he dies. Let us assume a case which, while it may never have happened just as stated, yet carries the essential truth of the matter; it can be checked up easily enough by the reader of ethnography. Assume the sudden death of some powerful leader whose strength and ferocity have long furnished both a protection and an object of dread. The event startles the minds of his survivors as the thing which is unusual and at the same time affects interest

[54] Puckett, *Folk Beliefs of the Southern Negro*, index, *sub* "Dreams."

alone can. The body may have suffered partial dissolution, may
even have been eaten by the enemy. The leader may have been
dead for some time before his fate was known. In any case, the
breath has gone out of the body and with it the strong and menacing personality has vanished. There is only one usual way of coming into contact with the latter again, as in life, and that is
through the dream. Someone, dreaming in a fitful sleep, actually
sees and hears the dead man, perhaps agonizingly feels the weight
of his heavy and ready hand and rouses up with a yell of fear and
pain. Very likely more than one report the same sort of experience. There is no laughing at one's self over such matters, as we
do over persisting dream-impressions; it is a serious experience.
Taking these dreams as actuality, as they do, it is clear enough to
the members of the group that the chief still lives. His body is
gone, or is stiff and stark. What is it that lives? Evidently that
which left the body at death. What else but the breath?

Further, the chief has been seen just as he was in life; he could
not be recognized under any other guise. He lives on as the same
man, with the same scars, expression, temper, ornaments, weapons,
and so on. How then will that which leaves the body at death be
figured? Evidently not otherwise than as a replica of the living
man, only not visible to the waking eye. This double is, however,
still an object to be feared; in the dream he can inflict pain and
cause a nameless anxiety and dread; he cannot be wounded or
frightened off. The only way to escape him is to awaken; yet even
then, though no longer seen, he is still there. He is a factor to be
reckoned with in all the future so long as memory of him holds
out. What is true of him is true in their own degrees of other dead
persons; and presently there is inevitably constructed by the savage upon the unimpeachable evidences of his senses an unseen
world of beings to whom death has meant no more than a change
of potentiality for good or ill—chiefly, in his mind, for the latter,
inasmuch as the prospect of ill chance is what his apprehensions
dwell upon.

In deriving the soul-idea from the dream rather than from confusion of
personality, or "mana," or any other of the origins for which some writers[55]
contend, we are moved in good part by the consideration that a virtually uni-

[55] Lévy-Bruhl, *Fonc. Ment.*, is a type; see §§258, 303, below.

versal belief must have a virtually universal phenomenon as its source. Dreams are the only illusory states that are universal. It will be recalled[56] that the primitive mind must receive repeated and simple impressions if it is to function in any particular way; sporadic, to say nothing of metaphysical, phenomena will not do.

§206. Projectivism. The man who dies becomes a superior existence, endowed with supernatural powers, and the theories about him form an important part of the mental outfit. Pneumatology, to use a comprehensive term, begins at this point; it covers the conception of superior existences in all its ramifications and deductions. Why the dead man is regarded as a superior existence will appear more clearly as we go on; but it must be noted that such superiority implies no qualitative differences in the man after death from what he was before. Dreams give back the experience, which is derived also from the observation of growth and age, of identity in variation; there is some variation of the dream-figure from the living one, it is true; but the differences are negligible as compared with the likenesses. In the dream the dead man was seen as he appeared in life because that was the only impression of him that the dreamer's brain had to work on. The inevitable conclusion was that the person and personality, disposition and character, of the deceased kept right on into this next existence of his;[57] he remained not only anthropomorphic, but "automorphic." He was with all the rest who had gone through the same experience, and they lived, all together, another life beyond this incident or interruption of death. Their surroundings in this next life were like the ones they had in this life; were not their spirit-figures seen in a setting of natural and fabricated objects, wearing such clothing and ornament as in life? This direct, positive, and continuing apprehension of the dead and of the state of things after death in terms of earthly life has been called "otherworldliness." The term is awkward and experience shows that it is likely to be misunderstood. Since the idea of another life and world is merely a projection of this life and world, we have adopted the term "projectivism"[58] to cover the conception of the next existence in terms of this one.

56 §88, above.   57 Lippert, Kgchte., I, 108.
58 Suggested by Dr. Nathan Miller.

Kenyon Cox[59] utilizes the inevitable tendency of man to construct the imaginary solely upon the basis of actual experience as follows: "As men imagine things unseen always in the terms of things seen, their wildest fancies being but the shifting and the recombination of the elements of known objects, the beings imagined by men are as much within the purview of imitative art as are the beings of the actual world."

The actuality of the next life is a matter of serene and unshaken belief; that life is as real as the next street is to us, and far more so than an unvisited foreign country can be to most men. This being the case, it can be understood that death is robbed of much of the terror it may previously have inspired under the unchecked animal instinct of self-preservation. The fear of death for one's self, as a mere step across the boundary, may be nil and people may commit suicide from a great desire for the life beyond.[60] There was no fear of hell, for the idea did not exist; perhaps the decline of the belief in a place of punishment puts modern men more nearly on a par with the savage and allows of an increase of suicide. A vivid and objective conception of the next life lay in the minds of the Scandinavian warriors when they thought of Valhalla and in those of the Moslems who contemplated Paradise and finally laid their plans to go there, through the expedient of a dose of hashish, a razor-sharp cleaver, and a promiscuous hacking of Christians.[61]

The Cambodians regard assassination with little feeling and go to execution with indifference.[62] Asiatics say that fear of death is a European disease. In June, 1924 a Japanese committed suicide by *harakiri*, or disembowelling, as a protest against the American exclusion-law. The Japanese may not have the same idea that inspires some other Asiatics to suicide—to get revenge upon an importunate creditor,[63] for example, but this traditional custom of *harakiri*, which is an expression of relative contempt for life, certainly roots deep in primitive conceptions. In the case cited, "the newspapers are strongly taking up the suggestion that the suicide should have a national funeral, since, as one publicist declares, 'he has truly expressed the feelings of the Japanese people.' The chief of the Tokio Police Bureau is quoted by the newspapers as saying: 'I was never more profoundly impressed by a suicide, although I have dealt with hundreds of them. There is no indication of insanity, and the fact that the suicide did not disclose his name shows that he was not seeking notoriety. He met his death like an ancient warrior. The police have been ordered to take

[59] *Concerning Painting*, 22.
[60] Steinmetz, "Suicide among Prim. Peoples," in AA, VII, 55.
[61] Worcester, *Philippine Isl.*, 188.   [62] Leclère, in PSM, XLIV, 780.
[63] §§105, 177, above.

the greatest care of the remains. He will probably be shown the honors due to a soldier who died on the battlefield.' "[64]

It should be noted, however, that even such an attitude toward one's own decease does not mean that the fear of death and of the dead is nullified. For now the reader is in a position to see that the real object of fear is the disembodied spirit rather than the mere happening as a result of which that spirit is freed. Here appears the paradox that because there was no understanding of death the predominant interest was death.

§207. The Imaginary Environment. The ensemble of the foregoing views, sketched within broad outlines and later to be filled in more fully, leads to the conception of a world of ghosts and spirits which, since it does not verify according to our tests of reality, cannot now be regarded as other than imaginary. This is the supernatural or imaginary environment; and it forms for primitive man that great illusory major premise[65] from which he deduces, with entire logic, most of the "superstition" for which he is pitied, condemned, or ridiculed. It is demonstrated to him by evidence which he cannot but accept and becomes a matter of faith to which he clings with tenacity. It thoroughly permeates every range of society's life except the most simple and material reactions on physical environment and not infrequently is found even there, in the form, for instance, of taboos on foods, labor, improved implements, and other necessities and desirables of life. Hence it is to be reckoned with as a factor of immense reach, scope, and power in the life of human society. No such conception occurs in the case of the animals. It is a commonplace of logic that everything can be drawn out into the conclusion which has previously been packed into the major premise; hence there is no limit to the train of consequences in human reflection and upon human life that may be deduced from the stupendous premise of the imaginary environment. With the development of that idea an altogether new and virgin tract is opened for the operations of

[64] N. Y. *Times*, June 1, 2 (quoted), 3, 5, 1924; Hearn, *Japan*, 313-315, 508, note.

[65] §200, above.

the human mind; and because the whole conception has remained unverifiable and since the limits of that which is explicable under natural law are so restricted, it is clear that the sweeping hypothesis was sure not only to expand in itself but also to be carried back to account for much with which, in its origin, it had nothing at all to do. The accountability of the unseen world, in the thought of the more primitive peoples—and that means of all peoples in their earlier times, to say nothing of the superstitions of more enlightened ages—is comparable with that of natural law in the minds of the educated of the modern day. To develop the evolution and results of this comprehensive and, as one must call it, fallacious major premise is the object of the present section of this book.

§208. The Explanation of Luck. We have seen that man had the aleatory element, and especially its adverse side, to account for and that his concern admitted of no attitude of indifference. The phenomenon of death was to him a disquieting and impressive one and his observation of death and death-like states, together with his dreams and hallucinations, led him to the conception of another world peopled with superior existences of a thoroughgoing anthropomorphic nature. The idea of a "double" was developed and to this double the term "breath" was widely applied. We may anticipate by stating that these "spirits" were thought to be of a power entirely above the human and wholly capable of bringing to pass the otherwise inexplicable. The otherwise inexplicable is the aleatory element. We left that element ominous but unexplained; we have now found, elsewhere in human experience, that which amply accounts for it. Here, then, we sight the connection which the convergence of our argument begins to show: that the aleatory element is accounted for by the spirits and is, as it were, personified in them.

Of course this position is very naïve and in the case of people who ought to know better—not the savage—represents a survival of primitive thought. "To infer that because you cannot tell how an effect is produced, it is due to spirits, is about as logical as the inference of the man who found the harness on the rack and the horse gone, and concluded that the hostler had eaten the horse. As a fact many persons believe in the reality of spirits for no other reason than that they cannot account for how such effects [as those asserted by spiritualists] are obtained."[66]

It is worth while to recur to the diagram in the preceding chapter.[67] The range of the aleatory element in that diagram may now be taken to be the range of supernatural accountability, or of "higher causes." It includes, in general, whatever lies outside the range of positive knowledge (the band between circles A and B for the primitive; between circles C and B for the more advanced). It is evident that the supernatural explanation was once necessary for D (eclipse) and E (comet) but is so no longer. Knowledge has encroached, since primitive times, to the extent of the band between circles A and C. The emancipated mind concludes that eventually the spirit-explanation will not be needed for what falls between circles C and B (for natural law must prevail in that band also) any more than it is now needed within the band between circles A and C. To such a mind, a universal mystery underlies known and unknown, one as the other, alike. The circle B (full knowledge) is infinity, in any case, and no subtraction from it can lessen it.

The accountability of the spirits for the aleatory element affords a simple, comprehensive basis for the assignment of agency where agency cannot be established according to the direct evidence of the senses. Here is a sweeping premise that cannot be disproved, at any rate not to primitive man. It is the germ of a developing mental outfit of deductions which are turned back with power upon societal life. The spirit-world, with its accountability, forms an entirely actual condition of life to which men are fain to adjust as they do to the natural and social conditions; it is a prodigious and unique addition to the circumstances of earthly life. No science of society can pretend to any degree of adequacy which does not take it into account as a fundamental consideration. The imaginary environment may not be as elemental and primordial as the environment of things and fellow-men, but the reactions to it permeate societal life quite as fully and generally more obviously than do those evoked by nature or men. Persuasions as to spirit-agency are always producing variations that invite selection and also acting selectively upon variations of other provenance. The realm of pneumatology is the range of a reflection and a theorizing the result of which is a mental life quite different from any that could have been developed apart from the illusions out of which that reflection and theorizing grew up. Let

[66] Jastrow, "Sir Oliver's Mystic Teachings Assailed," in N. Y. *Times*, Feb. 8, 1920.

[67] §195, above.

one try to imagine what human life in society might have been without the conception of the world of spirits; a moment's reflection upon the consequences of what never happened is not always so sterile. The adjustment of mankind to the spirit-environment constitutes an uniquely human section of societal life. The evolution of society is as little to be understood without a study of its religious institutions as without taking into account its industrial or regulative organization.

That the aleatory element forms the link between religion and the struggle for existence has been stated above and will be illustrated many times in what is to come. Primitive men built their world-philosophy on the aleatory interest. The blows of ill fortune fell upon them, compelled them to squirm about to evade the pain, and at last forced them to think, however naïvely. They asked: "Who inflicts these blows, and why?" The answer which they gave themselves was that spirits of dead ancestors, somehow dissatisfied with them, inflicted ill.

"When," says Tylor,[68] "people like the American Indians or the African negroes believe that the air around them is swarming with invisible spirits, this is not nonsense. They mean that life is full of accidents which do not happen of themselves; and when in their rude philosophy they say the spirits make them happen, this is finding the most distinct causes which their minds can understand." In Nyassaland they have a hazy idea of some supreme being, "to account for unexplained phenomena, such as thunder, lightning, and small-pox."[69]

Ghost-fear was therefore directly connected with welfare, prosperity, and success in all the immediate interests of life. It fathered the first stock of ideas and theories, the first mental outfit in that sense, of mankind. It is astonishing to find how universally and how without demonstrable contact one with another, primitive races have reached this common solution of the problems of life. Here is perhaps the grandest case of parallelism that societal evolution has to offer. Ghost-fear became the fountain of ever new streams of thought-life. Its immediate consequence was an art of living based upon a life-policy, that is, a prosperity-policy. If the spirits in anger send ill and in pleasure good fortune, what angers, what pleases them? The one will be wrong conduct and the other

[68] *Anth.*, 353.   [69] Stigand, in JAI, XXXVII, 130.

right, that is, conduct respectively unfitted or fitted to the case, inexpedient or expedient for the result that is wanted.

The minds of primitive men all over the globe travelled one course in putting and answering the question about the origin of luck. Primitive religion therefore sprang from the struggle for existence under its aleatory aspect. This philosophy intensified ills; for, inasmuch as misery was due to the wrath of the ghosts, those in misery sacrificed to the offended spirits some part of the little they had. Ghost-fear and fear of the other world have in this respect reacted in all ages unfavorably upon the struggle for existence: they have proved to be not alone the most formidable obstacle to that real knowledge which alone can enable men to deal with the ills of life, but also a source of waste of labor and capital on unproductive structures and enterprises such as tombs, temples, endowments of priests, and pious foundations. The dead have often been the worst enemies of the economic welfare of the living.

Though religious and ecclesiastical remedies for ill luck and hardship have gone to some extent out of fashion, the problem of misfortune and misery occupies as large a part of human interest now as it ever did. The devices for meeting it which are at present proposed and credulously embraced are in part social but above all political. Ill is attributed to the wrong "organization of society" and it is conceived that there is some contrivable alternative system by which ill might be eliminated. It is safe to say that this latter-day phantasy is as profound in the minds of many who harbor it as was the ghost-fear of savages. The only recourse which ever enables men to deal with the ills of life or "accident" is scientific knowledge. If men know the facts and laws of nature they can see before them a rational problem and can plan devices to get what they want and to evade or set aside what they do not want.

CHAPTER XXIII

ANIMISM

§209. Nature of the Soul. The vital element which is supposed to survive death and bodily dissolution is variously termed the ghost, spirit, shade, soul, wraith, specter, apparition, phantom, vision, "haunt." Several of these terms, for example, "spirit" or "shade," come down from primitive conceptions. The word "soul," the etymology of which is uncertain, is perhaps the most inclusive of them all. Using it as such, we now turn to the body of beliefs about souls, their nature, powers, and attributes. This set of doctrines is summed up under the term "animism," derived from the Latin *anima* and established through the writings of Tylor.[1]

The conception of superior existences, or pneumatology, and of the other world did not involve for the savage any such rarefied and metaphysical interpretations as the civilized man is led to weave about it. The former had in mind the actual embodied or disembodied souls and their characteristic, concrete activities. Any such soul must of necessity be anthropomorphic; when it was disembodied it was man raised to a higher power. Souls exhibit, it is true, certain differences in the essence and behavior that go with the incorporeal state; nevertheless there is nothing here that is referable to introspection or self-analysis. The disembodied soul was like the dead man in all respects except where the consensus of the senses did not corroborate the evidence of one or two of them—where, for instance, the soul was regarded as having no substance although that fact was not betrayed to eye or ear but only to touch. The Bible, for example, gives a partial definition of a spirit: "Handle me and see, for a spirit hath not flesh and bones, as ye see me having."[2] The soul was like the double in the dream, always built upon the likeness of the living; like to the living where the dream-double was like, different where, and as, the

---

[1] *Prim. Cult.*, chs. XI ff.; Tylor, *Anth.*, ch. XIV. For an encyclopædic treatment of the nature of the soul, see Frazer, *Golden Bough*, I; Wilken, "Animisme," in VG, III; Wilken, *Vkde.*, 550 ff.; Kruijt, *Animisme.*

[2] Luke, XXIV, 39.

dream-double was different. Both soul and dream-figure have their vague, shadowy, specter-like attributes. This is excellent evidence for the dream-derivation of the soul-idea as developed in the preceding chapter. The extra-human qualities assigned to the double from the experiences of illusion were tenuosity of structure, speed of movement, sudden appearance and disappearance, power of protean transformation, and other equally disquieting characteristics, some of which could scarcely have an origin outside of nightmare.

These are the qualities that come out in the disembodied soul or ghost; it must be understood, however, that the soul, before it becomes a ghost, is conceived to abide in the living person. That is why the person is alive and not dead, "animate" and not "inanimate"; to die he has to "give up the ghost," breathe it out when he "breathes his last," or "expires." Doubtless the invisibility and warmth of the breath, its thinness and evanescence as vapor, were taken into the conception of the soul; certainly no other bodily emission has so many obvious points of harmony with the dream-figment. There were dreams also about the living that were as convincing, though not so terrifying and thought-provoking, as those about the dead; the soul of the living man obviously left him and prowled about upon adventure bent. The embodied as well as the disembodied soul is, in any case, matter for the development of soul-doctrines or animism. Later on it becomes useful in exposition to distinguish the disembodied soul from one which is incorporated in its original receptacle, and to restrict animism to the doctrines about souls in the latter state. But to know the nature of the soul in a living being it is necessary to know also how it is conceived to be when separated from the body. The prime object at present is to acquire a comprehensive impression of the nature of the soul, whether embodied or disembodied.

Absence of animistic beliefs is almost if not quite non-existent.[3] Alleged cases deserve notice by reason of their rarity. We have seen none that seem to us convincing. It is true that some peoples do not pursue the question of the soul and its destiny very far. The African Wapagoro do not believe in ghosts, and so pay little attention to the gods. "If anybody dies, he decays in the ground and with him decays his soul. If one asks 'Does not the soul go

3 §322, below.

to God?' he receives the answer, 'The soul decays in the ground, in what way shall it then go to God?' "[4] The Todas think it not easy to be born, and that when people have once started on the journey of life, they must go on. On being further questioned, they reply: "This makes our heads swim! Better to think of nothing and be at peace. Enough of this!"[5] Such instances are in sharp contrast with the elaborate doctrines developed by other primitive peoples; but the difference is one of degree only.

§210*. Animistic Beliefs. Having brought the argument to this point with the minimum of illustrative material, in order that the interrelations of the aleatory element, the ills of life, the imaginary environment, and animistic beliefs might be as clear as we could make them, we now turn to a selection from the many cases upon which our position rests. And first we must recur to the beliefs about sleep and dreams. "It is a well-established ethnographical fact that savage and semi-civilized men as a rule explain sleep, swoon, and unconsciousness as due to an absence of the sentient entity from the body. The invisible duplicate thus wandering away may be made to return to the body by shouts and by calling the name. Sometimes, as in ordinary sleep, it comes back immediately. In other instances, as when the body is in a state of lethargy or trance, the return of the other-self is postponed for hours, at times for several days."[6] The dream is what happens to the soul while temporarily out of the body. "What a savage experiences during a dream is just as real to him as what he sees when he is awake."[7]

The Australians "universally believe that their deceased ancestors and kindred visit them during sleep, and counsel or warn them against dangers, or communicate to them song-charms against magic."[8] The authors previously quoted tell how the medicine-men get their ideas in dreams, and Howitt thinks that great social changes, for instance the system of classes and totems, could have been brought about, at least in part, by way of these revelations through dreams. The Papuans never awake a sleeper "in an abrupt manner but carefully and gradually, so that the soul shall get time to return to its dwelling."[9] Miss Kingsley[10] says that the Africans are great at dreams and have them

[4] Fabry, in *Globus*, XCI, 223.　　　[5] Reclus, *Prim. Folk*, 215.

[6] DeGroot, *Relig. Syst.*, I, 243.

[7] Spencer and Gillen, *North. Tr. Cent. Aust.*, 450.

[8] Howitt, *S.E. Aust.*, 89.

[9] Krieger, *Neu-Guinea*, 306; Jenness and Ballentyne, *D'Entrecasteaux*, 109; Wilken, in VG, III, 17.

[10] *Travels W. Afr.*, 504, 435.

very noisily but do not seem to attach much importance to them—not so much as do the Indians. Among the Yoruba "the theory of the soul satisfactorily accounts for what the uncivilized man believes to be the incontestable evidence of his dreams."[11] "All their dreams are construed into visits from the spirits of their deceased friends. The cautions, hints, and warnings which come to them through this source are received with the most serious and deferential attention, and are always acted upon in their waking hours."[12] The soul is supposed to live through everything seen in a dream and the dead people who appear in it are believed to be really present.[13] The Galla and Danakil "render a very great respect to dreams—perhaps in reality dream more than other peoples."[14] "The Kayan feels ill—he has bad dreams or adversity and if he does not succeed in getting back his soul its material envelope dies. In the case of distressing dreams, the soul in its flight sees what is dreamed."[15] "If a Dyak dreams of falling into water, he thinks that this accident has really befallen his spirit and sends for a *manang* [medicine-man], who fishes for it and recovers it." It is the shadow-spirit that falls into the water. "No doubt Dyaks often concoct dreams out of their waking thoughts to suit their interest, yet they are implicit believers in the reality of dreams, and will not spare expense to atone by ceremony or sacrifice for a bad one."[16] "When any one dreams of a distant land, as we exiles often do, the Dyaks think that our souls have annihilated space, and paid a flying visit to Europe during the night."[17] The Maoris believe that "the soul leaves the body in dreams and trance. In illness the soul journeys away and is sometimes on the brink of crossing to Hades, but returns—only a few return."[18] In China is retailed the "well-known dream of Chuang-tsze, in which he saw himself in the form of a butterfly. Awakened, he asked himself: 'Am I a man who dreamed he was a butterfly, or a butterfly that dreams he is a man?' "[19] The same beliefs about sleep and dreams are to be found throughout America. Cranz,[20] in his early work on Greenland, states that the Eskimo believe in two souls, the breath and the shadow; that the soul during sleep goes hunting or on other adventure; and he affirms that dreams led to this notion. Instances throughout the Jesuit Relations show that dreams were regarded as real occurrences in the mystery- or spirit-world and therefore were of greater importance than any ordinary daily occurrence.[21] "The importance of dreams in the religion of the Mohave is unusually great, and probably finds no parallel in any other region of the continent. "In short, whatever is dreamed of will come to pass. 'Good luck' is expressed by 'good dreaming.' . . . Sickness is caused by dreaming that one is sick."[22] The Chaco Indians tell amazing yarns concerning their asserted experiences; hence they are held to be liars. But they are narrating their dreams, which are real to them.[23] The Shingu explain the headache after too short sleep

[11] Ellis, *Yoruba*, 131.　　　　　　　[12] Nassau, *Fetichism*, 161.
[13] Gutmann, in *Globus*, XCII, 166.　　　[14] Paulitschke, *Nordost-Afr.*, II, 8.
[15] Nieuwenhuis, *Borneo*, I, 148; many East Indian cases in Wilken, VG, III, 17 ff.
[16] Roth, in JAI, XXI, 112, 135.　　　[17] Roth, *Sarawak*, I, 231.
[18] Tregear, in JAI, XIX, 118.
[19] Grube, in *Veröffent. aus dem K. Museum f. Völkerkunde*, VII, 6.
[20] *Grönland*, I, 241.　　　　　　　[21] McGuire, in AA, III, 266.
[22] Kroeber, in AA, IV, 280.　　　　　[23] Frič, in *Globus*, LXXXIX, 233.

by saying that the shadow has not been able to get back. Other South American Indians considered it harmful to draw a picture of a sleeping person, and wanted to wake him. They believe firmly in all that occurs in dreams; the soul goes forth in the form of a bird, and has greater power.[24] In Homer, a dream was called by the same name as the soul of a dead man; it was "mindless," incorporeal, and dim, like the soul; and the home of dreams was located near the entrance of the spirit world.[25] Familiarity with the Hebrew scriptures and knowledge of the ancients in general[26] reveal many cases bearing upon the topic under review, and mediæval records contain others.

The conception of the nature and attributes of the soul comes out with especial fulness and clarity in the case of a people which has learned to express itself and does so with the candor of unpremeditation but without yet having arrived at the stage of extensive rationalization. Such a people were the Homeric Greeks. A review of the Homeric conception of the soul[27] will cover most of the essential features of other peoples' conceptions as well.

The prevalent terms for soul were words, like the later *pneuma*, signifying "breath" or "wind." The *psyche* was regarded as the energizing principle of the body; yet the body it was with which the personality was identified. The body was the *autos*, or self; the only other Homeric term for the living body is a circumlocution. "Hence it seems that the soul was a separate being for the continued possession of which a man would strive. The soul and the man were a sort of dual personality; when the hero in distress poetically 'addressed his noble soul,' it is a survival of this dualism. Thus there was a close bond between a man and his soul; a strong man had a strong soul, and a weak coward a contemptible one. The soul had various ways of leaving the body: in fainting it was breathed out, to return apparently by the same way when recovery occurred; in death, it departed regularly by way of the mouth, sometimes in a flow of blood, or it followed the spear withdrawn from a wound. In all cases, it 'flies' in haste through the air, departing with mourning. 'And from his limbs his soul was gone in flight to the home of Hades, mourning its fate, leaving behind both manliness and youth.' When the soul had once 'passed the bulwark of the teeth,' it returned no more to vivify the body. It became an *eidōlon*, like in all respects to the dead man, a being which, if the dead body were treated carelessly, might return to earth." Existence in the beyond was conceived of in terms of existence during life (projectivism[28]), for the dead were supposed to retain the feelings of living men: desire for property, love and pride, jealousy and pain; they even bore their old wounds and by appearance and action indicated their station in their former life. Kings and judges

[24] Von den Steinen, *Zent. Bras.*, 340, 510, 511; Koch, in Suppl. to *Intern. Archiv f. Ethnol.*, XIII.

[25] Keller, *Hom. Soc.*, 101, 150, 152; Seymour, *Hom. Age*, 524-525.

[26] Lehmann, *Overtro*, I, 37 ff.

[27] From Keller, *Hom. Soc.*, 101-105, where full references to the text are given.

[28] §206, above.

ruled and judged as before. When the soul of Patroclus appeared to Achilles in a dream, he was like to the dead man even in the matter of clothing; and that the dead retained human desires appears from the cry of Achilles to Patroclus, after the body of Hector had been ransomed: "Continue not thy anger, O Patroclus, if thou, in the home of Hades, dost know that I have loosed Hector. I received much ransom and thou shalt have thy share."[29] Yet the Homeric shades, like as they were to men, were unsubstantial. As "mere *eidōla*" they flew about "beneath the earth" with thin cries, huddling and clinging together like bats dislodged from the roof of a cave, disappearing like smoke, "like a shadow or a dream," "without mind," and forgetful of all unless temporarily resuscitated by a draught of blood. When Achilles in the dream tried to embrace the shade of his comrade, "he did not take him; but the soul fled with a shriek beneath the earth, like smoke, and Achilles roused up in alarm."[30] The disembodied soul, finally freed by having received its "share of the fire," departed to the realm of the Unseen (Aïdēs), never to return; as an *eidōlon* it preserved there much the same qualities which the visitation of Patroclus revealed to Achilles. Odysseus, making the journey to the spirit-world, completes the picture by his description of various shades. Here it is that one encounters the thin twittering of the spirit-voice, as of a bat. This conception of the voice of the dead as a twittering, chirping, or whistling sound is rather wide-spread; Tylor[31] shows its prevalence among Algonquins, Maoris and other Polynesians, Zulus, Romans, and Hebrews.

From this Greek case a tolerably complete idea of the soul, its relation to the dream, and its several qualities may be gained. To it as a preliminary case might be added, by way of a more highly sophisticated conception, the striking apostrophe of the educated Roman to his soul:[32]

> Animula, blandula, vagula,
> Hospes, comesque corporis,
> Quae nunc abibis in loca?
> Pallidula, rigida, nudula.

That the soul comes readily to be identified with the breath has appeared in the foregoing. Tylor[33] has collected a number of cases in which the term for breath is that for soul. Let the reader reflect upon the combinations in English into which the Greek and Latin roots of the terms *psyche*, *anima*, and *spiritus* appear. Evidence, etymological as well as ethnographical, supports this identifica-

---

[29] Homer, *Iliad*, XXIV, 592-595.   [30] Homer, *Iliad*, XXIII, 97-101.
[31] *Prim. Cult.*, I, 408-409; Ellis, *Yoruba*, 103; Codrington, *Melanesians*, 256.
[32] "Hadrian to his Soul," quoted in Pater, *Marius the Epicurean*, 127.
[33] *Prim. Cult.*, I, 388 ff.; see Clodd, *Animism*, for a survey of the meaning of "soul."

tion very strongly and cannot be explained away. A few additions
and variants may be added to Tylor's classic collection.

In the Congo region "there was a curious saying after one had sneezed, viz.,
'It is not I, but someone else,' and this was accompanied by a clapping of the
hands expressive of astonishment." It meant: "I am surprised that you want to
call away my spirit (the spirit is supposed to escape from the nostrils), I am
not the person you think I am."[34] The cessation of visible breathing is with the
Dyak the cessation of life. He has no way of distinguishing a prolonged state
of coma from death, and it is not impossible that sometimes bodies have been
buried before they became corpses.[35] Wilken[36] cites many cases illustrative of
this belief. In Nias the oldest son assimilates the soul of his father by taking
his last breath; if he fails to do so and another does, he must share his inherited position with him. When a chief is dying, not only his sons but also
others, even strangers, crowd about him, hoping to get his last breath. "There
are cases where, while the dying man lies with his face down, someone makes
a hole in the floor in order to get his breath through a bamboo-tube." "The
Tongans figure the soul of man to themselves as an aëriform substance spread
through the whole body and reproducing its entire form, which escapes at the
moment of death like the perfume which emanates from all parts of a
flower."[37] With the Tusayan Indians the soul is the "breath-body" and its
symbol is the downy breast-feather of the eagle.[38] The Sioux believe in the
transfer of qualities by the breath. Previous to the naming of an infant comes
the ceremony of the transfer of character. If the child is a boy, a brave and
good-tempered man, chosen beforehand, takes the infant in his arms and
breathes into his mouth, thereby communicating his own disposition to the
child who will grow up to be a brave and good-natured man. It is thought that
such babies will not cry as much as others. If the child is a girl, it is put into
the arms of a good woman who breathes into its mouth.[39] The function of the
breath in procreation is a matter of belief in some parts of the earth.[40] The
sect of Orphians believed that "the soul is brought by the winds out of the
All, and enters the body with the drawing in of the breath."[41] The "breath of
life" is a common expression among those educated according to Biblical conceptions;[42] the Jews of a later age, in the story of the death of Moses, show
this identification clearly. The Devil (as in Goethe's *Faust*) lurks about and
tries in vain to get hold of the soul of Moses; "then God himself comes down
accompanied by three angels and takes the soul of Moses with the kiss of his
mouth."[43]

Through the common mental modes of association and analogy
there can be gained other and supplementary ideas about what the
soul is conceived to be. To the primitive mind, unaware of later

[34] Weeks, in JAI, XL, 416.   [35] Roth, *Sarawak,* I, 202-203.
[36] In VG, III, 7.   [37] De Quatrefages, *Histoire,* 259.
[38] Emerson, in AA, VII, 237.   [39] Dorsey, in BAE, XI, 482.
[40] §334, below.   [41] Wobbermin, *Mysterienwesen,* 99.
[42] Kautzsch, "Relig. Israel," in *Hastings's Bible Dict.,* 665-666.
[43] Duhm, *Geister,* 54.

commonplaces of knowledge, the shadow was inexplicable. It clung to the person or the thing, changed shape, and was in general tenuous and elusive much as was the dream-figure. Souls are even by us referred to as "shades."

Shadow and breath are interchangeable conceptions of the soul among the Shingu Indians, as among the Eskimo.[44] The Tasmanians' fundamental religious doctrine identified the shadow with the soul. Shades of their ancestors were their guardian deities. An echo, to them, was a "talking shadow."[45] In the Australian shaman's hut "are often secreted shadow spirits stolen from their owners, who are by their loss dying a lingering death, for no man can live without Mulloowil, his shadow. Every one has a shadow spirit which he is very careful not to parade before his enemies, as any injury to it affects himself." If the sorcerer gradually shrinks a shadow's size, the owner sickens and dies. "May your shadow never grow less!"[46] In West Africa, the "animating soul, whether it be only one, or whether it appear in two, three, or even four forms, is practically the same, that talks, hears, and feels, that sometimes goes out of the body in a dream, and that exists as a spirit after the death of the body." Among several tribes, "the same word 'nsisim' means not only soul but also shadow. The shadow of a tree or any other inanimate object and of the human body as cast by the sun is 'nsisim.'"[47] "There are diseases that arise from injury to the shadow-soul. It strikes one as strange at first to see men who have been walking, say, through forest or grass land on a blazing hot morning quite happily, on arrival at a piece of clear ground or a village square, most carefully go round it, not across, and you will soon notice that they only do this at noontime, and learn that they fear losing their shadow." The authoress[48] once asked certain negroes "why they were not anxious about losing their shadows when night came down and they disappeared in the surrounding darkness, and was told that that was all right, because at night all shadows lay down in the shadow of the Great God and so got stronger. . . . Murders are sometimes committed by secretly driving a nail or knife into a man's shadow . . . but if the murderer be caught red-handed at it, he or she would be forthwith killed, for all diseases arising from the shadow-soul are incurable." "This shadow of the man, as visible in the sunlight, is that which actually experiences all that is seen in the dream."[49] "All human beings have souls or shadows . . . which leave their bodies during sleep. They seem to be connected also with the breath, but how they could leave the bodies of sleeping—and still breathing—persons my informants were unable to explain. The Kagoro are doubtful about animals. Some say that since the shadow disappears at death (or rather since they cannot see one) there can be no spirit, others point out that they can appear in dreams. . . . The soul always has

[44] Von den Steinen, *Zent. Bras.*, 364; Tylor, *Anth.*, 345; Clodd, *Magic*, 27-33.
[45] Tylor, reported in JAI, XXII, 138.
[46] Parker, *Euahlayi*, 29.   [47] Nassau, *Fetichism*, 64.
[48] Kingsley, *W. Afr. Studies*, 207-208.
[49] Gutmann, in *Globus*, XCII, 166.

the form and voice of the body it occupies, and an individual has only one."[50] Again, people must not cross over each other's shadows or step over a sleeper; if the latter is ill, or the stepper is, he will pass on the illness.[51]

Among the Cheyenne Indians, "a man's spirit or living principle is called his shade or shadow, . . . that is, the soul, mind, or spiritual part; not the body, the immortal part. Tasoom is also the shadow of any animate thing, as a man, horse, bird, or dog. It is not the shadow of a tree, a rock, or a building. Of a dying person who has lost consciousness and merely breathes, they may say, 'His tasoom has been gone a long time; he is only just breathing.' Those who die become shadows, or spirits. If a man sees his shade, it is a sign that he will soon die. A sick man may send for a friend to come to him, and say: 'Well, my friend, I have sent for you that I may see you once more, for I am about to die. I have seen my shadow.' Women saw their shadows more often than men, and with them the vision was not certainly followed by death. If an old woman had been badly frightened, she might say, 'I was so badly frightened that I saw my shadow.' The idea seems to be that her life was literally frightened out of her body, and for a moment stood before her. The shadow is a mere shape, seen for an instant, and then gone. It is like a shadow in having no detail; no clothing, no features—a silhouette. Years ago Indians commonly refused to be photographed, because they believed that when the picture was taken away the life of the subject was taken away too, and the actual man would die. They regarded the photographic print as the man's shadow. In the same way, in early days when little trade mirrors were first received, many people refused to look into them, because they would see their shadows, and bad luck would follow."[52] This idea about a likeness anticipates a following topic.

Frazer's *Golden Bough*[53] contains a collection of beliefs about the shadow. It should be added that "men, when raised from the dead, shall have no shadow any longer. In India, gods have no shadows; in Persia, Rashiddadin was recognized to be a god from his producing no shadow. . . . The plant of eternal life, Haoma, has no shadow."[54] Dante[55] represents the spirits as without weight and casting no shadow.

The soul is likewise identified with other immaterial and shadowy things, such as the reflection in water or in a mirror. If the reader can set himself in the place of the savage who knows nothing of the existence or behavior of light-rays he can readily understand how the Andamanese, for instance, when they first saw a mirror thought the reflection in it was the soul, that hitherto unseen self.[56]

[50] Tremearne, in JAI, XLII, 158.   [51] Barrett, in JAI, XLI, 36.
[52] Grinnell, *Cheyenne*, II, 93-94.   [53] I, 142 ff.
[54] Müller, *Sacred Books of the East*, IV, xliii, note; *Zendavesta*, pt. I.
[55] *Inferno*, VIII, 27; *Purgatorio*, III, 16 ff.
[56] Man, in JAI, XII, 162.

Frazer[57] gives a number of instances in illustration. He mentions the wide-spread custom of covering mirrors or turning them to the wall after a death in the house. It is feared "that the soul, projected out of the person in the shape of the reflection in the mirror, may be carried off by the ghost of the departed, which is commonly supposed to linger about the home till the burial." In one of Zangwill's stories about modern Jewish life,[58] not only is the mirror turned to the wall but the water-pitcher is emptied out of the window. The latter procedure may be exorcistic.[59]

Connected closely with the reflection is the likeness in the form of portrait or photograph.[60] "Tell me," asked an African woman whose photograph had been taken, "when I am dead, will my face disappear from that?" "No." "But if I move away from water, my image disappears."[61] Many primitive peoples refuse to allow the making of likenesses, whether the subject is man or beast, because they fear that magic may be practised by way of this abstracted item of personality.[62]

Frazer[63] cites instances of these ideas about likenesses, and Andree[64] devotes a chapter to the notion that the portrait carries away the soul. Says Fritsch[65] of his Hottentot types: "The appended collection of portraits would not be so poor in individuals of the tribe in question, had not the superstition that the preparation of such a picture would take away a portion of their life-force caused me over and over again to lose the hoped-for results." A Togo woman "ascribed the death of her child to the photographic fetish of the white man."[66] We have a curious description of the behavior of a Veddah at sight of his own portrait. In order to see what impression it might make, Rütimeyer[67] showed an old tribesman his own picture, reproduced in Schmidt's book on Ceylon. "Here his behavior became very remarkable: first his face took on an expression of dumbfounded amazement, as he and the rest closely observed the picture. But gradually he became restless and ejaculated violent, almost barking sounds; his excitement grew fast, he wanted to thrust the picture with his arrow, and suddenly he drew back about a stride and a half in order to string his bow and lay on an arrow, which he evidently intended to shoot at the picture. His expression was so wild as he did this that I found it advisable to throw away the picture, which I was holding before my body, as hastily as possible, as I had no wish to serve as a target for the enraged Veddah. As soon as the picture was removed he became quiet again." Great difficulty was experienced in photographing the Sikkimese; they exhibited a

[57] Golden Bough, I, 142 ff.; Clodd, Magic, 33-36; Puckett, Folk Beliefs of So. Negro, 81 ff., 139.

[58] Ghetto, 259.

[59] §§227, 276, below.

[60] Clodd, Magic, 23-26.

[61] Vannutelli e Citerni, L'Omo, 118-119.

[62] §301, below.

[63] Golden Bough, I, 148-149.

[64] Eth. Parallelen, 18-20.

[65] Eingeb. S.-Afr., 336.

[66] Klose, Togo, 475.

[67] In Globus, LXXXIII, 207.

lively horror and hid whenever the lens, or the "evil eye of the box," as they
called it, was pointed at them. For they believed that it worked some dark
magic on them and took away their souls with their pictures, thus putting them
into the power of the possessor thereof, to cast spells over them. Similarly
they thought a photograph of the scenery blighted the landscape.[68] This latter
notion is significant of the belief that all things have souls. In Borneo the
natives feared the escape of their souls not only through photography but
through the taking of anthropometric measurements; but "if their souls were
cajoled with a present the danger was less."[69] Most detailed is the reproduction by Jacobs[70] of the Sumatran ideas regarding likenesses. "Through the
making of a likeness, whether photographed, drawn, painted, modelled, cast,
or made in any other way, the maker steals the soul of the person or animal
represented by the likeness. For if one takes the picture of anyone, he takes
along with it a piece of his shadow, that is, of his soul, something which, after
the death of the giver, will bring both the one and the other into serious trouble. After his death, the portrayed party will first notice that there is something lacking in his soul whereby he cannot effect his entrance into the next
world. Then he will make it hot for the possessor of the lacking portion,
whether still alive or already dead, in order to get it back again; but he himself must all this time wander about in unrest, which naturally, as is easily
conceived, must be in the highest degree unpleasant for both parties. So they
do not like to have their portraits made, that is, to have their shadow or soul
stolen."

George Catlin,[71] who succeeded in some way in assembling an unrivalled
collection of Indian portraits, recounts a number of curious and dangerous
experiences in connection with his painting. It is reported that a Mandan
medicine-man had his picture painted and called the process being "made
alive."[72] For many years no Yankton-Dakota would consent to have his likeness taken lest, after his death, one of his "apparitions" should remain in the
picture instead of going to the spirit land.[73] Certain Indians would not pose
for Dellenbaugh,[74] regarding it as "very bad medicine." In ancient countries
of higher culture the connection of soul and likeness appears in derived forms.
Although every Egyptian tried to found liturgies for himself in perpetuity,
the old ones were abandoned in favor of later ones, after three or four generations, in spite of the imprecations. This is why the pictures were made inside
the tomb. The picture of food would suffice for a ghost; a picture of hunting,
of slaves working, of his household in operation, kept up forever for the ghost
the pleasure he had had in these things in life. Statues of the deceased were
also set up in the tomb, or little ones in great number were stored away in the
tomb. To all these the soul of the departed was attached or indwelling. To
avoid his curse, one who violated the tomb must break these statues. Hence
the great number of them hidden away in the tomb by himself or his friends;
also the care with which the access to the tomb was hidden, sometimes nearly
a hundred feet down. In making statues of the dead the Egyptians aimed at

---

[68] Waddell, *Himalayas*, 85 ff.   [69] Nieuwenhuis, *Borneo*, I, 143.
[70] *Groot-Atjeh*, I, 275-276.   [71] *Indians*, 147 ff.
[72] Donaldson, in *Smithson. Rep.*, 1885, II, 81.
[73] Dorsey, in BAE, XI, 484.   [74] *North Amer.*, 144.

portraits, not at ideal beauty, because otherwise the double would not fit the statue after death.[75]

And, finally, even where a people has become used to photography there lurks a suspicion which is readily fanned to flame. The Papuans, says Pratt,[76] "were very keen to see our photographs, and had no difficulty in understanding a picture: therein they differed greatly from the debased Australian aborigines who could never grasp the graphic symbol, and in the famous instance, when shown a picture of Queen Victoria, said it was a ship. They picked out their friends' photographs at once, and recognized them with exclamations of delight. For one of our men, however, our stereoscope proved too much, as the relief of the figures had probably been too realistic; and on being invited to look at a group of our retainers, he no sooner put his eye to the glass than he howled and nearly dropped the instrument. He ran away, saying, 'Mookau meego' ('Man lives there'), and could not be persuaded to look again."

Ideas about the soul, embodied and disembodied, while variant in detail, show a generic relationship carrying back to basic derivations. It is impossible, in a book of this sort, to review them all; we refer again to the special collections of Frazer.[77] There remain certain miscellaneous aspects of animistic belief which ought to be noticed because they are contributory to the understanding of subsequent topics.

"If a Sema away from home build a temporary shelter, he will always burn it when he leaves it, for fear it should take the errant fancy of his soul, which might linger behind or leave him in his sleep to return to his temporary habitation. It is the same conception of the soul which prompts the Sema when migrating to make a hole in the roof of his house just above his bed in order that his *aghongu* may find its way out and accompany him to his new village. In the same way a Sema who is sick goes to the fields to call his soul, whose desertion of the body may be the cause of the illness. The sick man takes a chicken or a dog, kills it, and sets aside a share for his *aghongu*. He calls loudly on his own name. He then returns very slowly home. His soul follows, but may easily be frightened away again. . . . A case once came up before me for adjudication in which an old man named Nikiye, who had been ill for some time, went to the fields to call his soul. It came, and he was climbing slowly back to the village occasionally calling 'Nikiye, Nikiye!' over his shoulder to make sure that the truant soul was following. Unfortunately a personal enemy had observed him, and lay in wait in the bush by the path with a thick stick. As the old man tottered by he sprang from his ambush with a yell, and brought down his stick with a thud on the path immediately behind Nikiye's heels. The frightened soul fled incontinently, and the old fellow himself died of the loss of it two days later."[78] Wilken[79] devotes considerable space to the practice of soul-catching in illness. "Not alone at death, but also at swoon or

[75] Maspero, *Hist. Anc.*, I, 255 ff.   [76] *New Guinea Cannibals*, 318.
[77] *Golden Bough*, especially I, 122 ff.; 216 ff.; 297 ff.
[78] Hutton, *Sema Nagas*, 200; Hutton, in JAI, L, 48.
[79] In VG, III, 12-16, 13, 24-25.

fright does the soul leave the body; with the sick too this is the case. Thus
it is the custom, for example with the Macassars and Buginese, to retain the
soul of a sick child by waving to it with a cloth and calling it back." There is
a Buginese song, sung on occasion of smallpox, which is supposed to call a
sick child's soul back. The Batak, returning from a perilous undertaking, puts
some rice-kernels on his head; this is to assure the soul, to keep it from being
scared off by evil spirits, to keep it at home. There is such a thing as getting
a new soul when the original is lost; the Eskimo *angekok* (sorcerer) can provide one or can exchange a sick soul for a well one which he can get out of an
animal or a child. Also fragments of the soul may go astray and the *angekok*
can collect them and piece them together again.[80] A comrade's soul may follow
and afflict a man: "he will rise in the morning weak and languid, or if he had
been unwell before he would be worse. Although this is not done by witchcraft
a man is held responsible for what his *uga* does, and is made to pay money to
the injured man, and by an act of his will to take off the malignant influence."[81] To be noted here is the fact that, entirely apart from magic or witchcraft, even a friend's soul is dangerous to the living.

Cases are plentiful which illustrate the belief that the soul is
stronger, more beautiful, or otherwise superior to the living man.
It may be endowed with weird or terrifying qualities; it is in any
case a being calculated to inspire awe and fear. The Kootenay Indians believed that souls could go anywhere, "through glass, wood,
or any substance, as through air. The touch of them causes death
and disease. At the death of Indians their spirits may enter into
fishes, bears, trees, etc.; in fact, into anything animate or inanimate."[82] This superiority comes out most clearly when the soul,
disembodied, has become a ghost or higher spirit. It is noteworthy,
in connection with the aspect of the soul, that "most black tribes
think that the gods and spirits of ancestors are white."[83]

The Australians, for instance, believe that the dead turn white and come
back as white men—"jump up white fellow." They have thought that they
recognized in certain whites their deceased countrymen.[84] They could account
for their arrival in no other way, as they knew nothing of any other country
beyond the sea;[85] here is a clear case of the spirit-explanation of the inexplicable. It is not surprising to find, says Curr,[86] that in some aboriginal languages, "white man" and "ghost" are expressed by the same term, as the reader
will notice in the vocabularies. "Some tribes had a vague idea of the white men
being spirits or reappearances of dead persons, and were restrained by awe
alone from attacking them. . . . In the southeastern portion of Australia, the

[80] Nansen, *Esk. Life*, 225.
[81] Codrington, *Melanesians*, 222-223.
[82] Anon., "Northwestern Indians," in PSM, XLIII, 825.
[83] Taylor, *Te Ika*, 579.   [84] Ratzel, *Vkde.*, II, 93.
[85] Bland, in JAI, XVI, 342.   [86] *Aust. Race*, I, 51.

old men used to say that the forms or spirits of the dead went to the west-ward, towards the setting sun; and the natives of Western Australia had the same belief. When, therefore, they saw white men coming over the sea from that quarter, they at once took them to be their deceased relatives re-incarnated, and called them Djenga, or ghosts, as distinguished from Yung-ar, or per-sons."[87] The Melanesians "were sure the voyagers were not men; if they were they would be black. What were they then? They were ghosts, and being ghosts, of necessity those of men who had lived in the world."[88] "Wherever the white has not yet appeared, where he is known only by reputation, when he arrives in a village where his color is extraordinary, as was many times our experience, they take him immediately for a revenant, *khun:* he is the soul of a dead man, a reincarnated spirit."[89] Of the California Digger Indians it is said that "when these Indians first saw the pale faces, as they called the white men, they thought them some of their dead returned to them in a new guise, and one that they by no means liked."[90] The fact that they were greeted as spirits and took instant advantage of the lucky misapprehension assisted some of the Spanish conquistadores in their dealings with the American natives.[91]

That the soul may assume an insect or animal form is the belief of many peoples; and it is involved with and supports a whole series of doctrines covering the relations of men and animals. It has been suggested that since the soul as pulse, breath, shadow, has about it something saltant, light, mobile, fleeting, hovering, the savage, possessing no such adjectives as these, described it in the concrete forms which he knew and which embodied such quali-ties. Thus he saw it as a bird, an insect, a snake, a lizard, a mouse, weasel, or cat; likewise as a mist, ignis fatuus, cloud; and finally as a miniature man, or homunculus. It is a curiosity that the Macassars and Buginese call the soul with the same words with which they allure their fowls when they throw out rice for them.[92]

The butterfly plays here a considerable rôle. The Greek word "psyche" means both soul and butterfly, the latter signification being explained, of course, as symbolic or emblematic.[93] The Burmese and Shans have a great objection to arousing anyone suddenly from sleep, "for fear," as they say, "that his butterfly may not return in time." On the return of a family from a burial, old men tie up the wrists of each member to prevent the escape of his butterfly; the strings remain till they wear away and fall off.[94] The butterfly

---

[87] Smyth, *Vict.,* II, Appendix A, 224.
[88] Codrington, *Melanesians,* 11.   [89] Trilles, *Fân,* 3.
[90] Miller, in PSM, L, 212.
[91] Zimmermann, *Europ. Kol.,* I, 249.
[92] Wilken, in VG, III, 18-19, 23-24. (He quotes Schultze, *Entstehungsge-schichte der Vorstellung Seele,* 334, 335.)
[93] §456, below.
[94] Woodthorpe, in JAI, XXVI, 23, 24.

has remained the "symbol of immortality" and is still to be seen adorning cemetery buildings. The case of the bee-soul has been cited previously. The West African "bush-soul" may be almost any sort of an animal, as a leopard, or a fish or tortoise. It is usually the same, in a family, for a man and his sons and for a woman and her daughters. "There is another peculiarity about the bush-soul; i.e., on its account old people are held in such esteem among the Calabars. However bad these old people's personal record may have been, the fact of their longevity demonstrates the possession of powerful and astute bush-souls."[95] The bird-form of the soul is common;[96] it may have been derived, or strengthened, by the "flying-dream."[97] Maspero[98] shows a picture of an Egyptian mummy holding his own soul in his arms, the soul being represented as a bird with a human head. The Egyptians "believed that the two most important parts of a man did not remain in the tomb, namely the *ba* and the *khu;* these they always represented in the form of waders. . . . The *ba*-crane busied itself in carrying food and drink to the mummy; the *khu*-ibis provided itself with mystical information and protective formulæ for its long and perilous journey to the abode of the gods."[99] The dove-soul has been so commonly believed in as to have become a religious symbol.

From the conception of the soul wandering about in animal form it is not far to the belief in were-wolves and kindred illusions. These hardly come under the heading of transmigration or reincarnation, which immediately follows; for lycanthropy and similar states are supposed to represent the independence of the soul, or, perhaps, some section of the multiple soul, of a living man from his body, not a return of that soul after his death into another body. The two conceptions naturally merge and we shall not strive desperately to keep them apart; but the distinction should be kept in mind. There is an immense literature touching upon the passing of men's souls into animals and upon soul-affinity between men and beasts or even inanimate things; we can no more than indicate its character.

"On one occasion the elders of a large Ao village . . . came to me for permission to tie up a certain man in the village while they hunted a leopard which had been giving a great deal of trouble. The man in question, who was . . . a Christian convert, also appeared to protest against the action of the village elders. He said that he was very sorry that he was a were-leopard, he didn't want to be one, and it was not his fault, but seeing that he was one he supposed that his leopard body must kill to eat, and if it did not both the leopard and himself would die. He said that if he were tied up the leopard would certainly be killed and he would die. To tie him up and hunt the leopard

[95] Kingsley, *Travels W. Afr.*, 460.
[96] Negelein, "Seele als Vögel," in *Globus*, LXXIX.
[97] Lehmann, *Overtro*, IV, 150-151, 153, 155-156, 168-173.
[98] *Hist. Anc.*, I, 182.   [99] March, in JAI, XXVII, 211-213.

was, he said, sheer murder. In the end I gave leave to the elders to tie the man up and hunt the leopard, but told them that if the man died as a result of killing the leopard, whoever had speared the leopard would of course be tried and no doubt hanged for murder, and the elders committed for abetment of the same. On this the elders unanimously refused to take advantage of my permission to tie up the man. I was sorry for this, though I had foreseen it, as it would have been an interesting experiment." Evidently the natives had no interest in verifying the theory and were still less capable of appreciating the humor of the situation. On another occasion, a Sakhuto "died on July 19, 1916, as a result of the leopard which was occupied by his *aghongu* [soul] having been shot by Sakhalu of Sakhalu on June 30 of that year. It was reported to the writer on July 4 that Sakhalu had shot a were-leopard, but it was then believed to be identical with Khozhumo of Kukishe, and it was expected that he would die when the news reached him, as the death of the man concerned does not actually take place till he hears that his leopard body has been killed. The son of Yemithi of Lizotomi, whose leopard-cat body was killed at Sagami, heard the news as he was returning to his village and expired on the spot for no other reason. A curious example of the power of the Sema mind over the Sema body."[100]

Wilken[101] cites as a symptom of transformation into a wolf or other transformation the lack of the little depression in the upper lip; he says that there is a sort of mental illness in some people which leads them to belief in their own were-wolf quality; that this must be distinguished from the popular belief; but that one is connected somewhat with the other. Magic formulas are used to secure transformation, which results in persecution of old people. This author has an extended monograph on "The relation between human, animal, and plant life according to popular belief," which enters very fully into the discussion of transformations. In particular, he cites all sorts of stories about a man's life being bound up with some animal or thing. The Macassars and others give the doctor an iron utensil to keep while a wife is pregnant; he takes care of it and returns it afterwards for a fee. Her soul goes into the iron. A child's fortune is united with that of a bird, animal, or even a piece of half-burned wood, as in the Meleager tale; if the counterpart is faint, the child is; if it dies, so does the child.

"The 'Phalto Bag,' or spiritual tiger, of the Khond country is a curious conception. A person is supposed to be able to change himself or herself into a spiritual tiger. One of the Meriah Agency officers had some trouble in settling a dispute in a village in the Khond country. A man was said to have made himself into a 'Phalto Bag' and eaten up the spirit of a sick man, whose spirit had been wandering, and who therefore could not get well."[102] In a story called *The Tomb of His Ancestors,* Kipling develops a somewhat similar situation.

§211*. Transmigration and Reincarnation. An idea readily derivable from views of this kind is that of transmigration, which leads directly to beliefs connected with fetishism in its various

---

[100] Hutton, *Sema Nagas,* 203, note, 205-206; and in JAI, L, 46.
[101] In VG, III, 25 ff., 291 ff.   [102] Fawcett, in JASB, I, 260.

forms. And the soul is likewise conceived to be born again into human shape. It is difficult for a modern to realize the outlook on life that accompanies an unshaken belief in such now discarded doctrines. Accepted as axiomatic, they invade the existence of individual and society. The organic and even the inorganic world are pervaded by human personalities and must be adjusted to, not by the methods of investigation and discovery of laws but by the use of expedients calculated to avoid, control, or propitiate powerful human beings. The old, dying, do not carry their conservatism with them to the grave; they come back and, even in reincarnation, bring it along with them. Neither nature nor society can be treated with a free hand. Countries like India, where beliefs in transmigration and reincarnation are rife, have had a history shaped in good part by their presence. A few illustrations of such beliefs may stand as representative of many.

Among the Australians it is believed that the spirit-part of a child killed as an infant goes back at once to the particular spot whence it came, and can be born again at some subsequent time, even of the same woman.[103] "Belief in the transmigration of souls, which is general among all the Australian tribes, as far as known, extends to Torres Strait. Those holding this belief imagine that immediately after death, they are changed into white people or Europeans, and as such pass the second and final period of their existence."[104] The Papuans believe that there is a second death, after which follows a change into an insect, for instance a white ant.[105] In the Solomon Islands, "after death a great many ghosts become incarnate in animals. It may be wondered in what way natives determine the particular animal into which the *ataro* of a dead relative has entered. It depends partly on where the man is buried. It is a common practice to bury in the sea both chiefs and common people, and their *ataro* naturally become incarnate in fish, especially in sharks. But even if a man is buried on shore his *ataro* may enter a shark. After his death his skull and other relics may be put into a wooden figure of a shark, which is then securely sealed with canoe gum, and allowed to float in the sea. Watch is kept, and the first thing seen to approach it is the future incarnation of the *ataro*. Usually a shark, it may also be an octopus, a skate, a turtle, or a crocodile. But all *ataro* have not a sea incarnation. When a man or woman grows old, natives watch to see whether any animal persistently associates itself with them. This is often a bird. The bird comes to the house and perches on the old man's shoulder. It must be a young bird. It is fed and treated respectfully as the future home of the man's soul. When he dies his soul is known to be in the bird. His children will not eat any bird of that sort. This taboo seems only to last for a generation. . . . Or again, the *ataro* may go into a stone or a tree.

[103] Spencer and Gillen, *Nat. Tr. Cent. Aust.*, 51-52.
[104] Haddon, in JAI, XIX, 436.   [105] Krieger, *Neu-Guinea*, 182.

This is known by dreams after a man's death. If in the dream the *ataro* of the man is seen at a stone, or by a tree, that is known to be its incarnation. . . . A man will say, I cannot eat such and such a fish or bird, because it is my father or my mother. . . . Obviously totems might originate in this manner. The natives have other opinions as to the origin of totems and clans among them."[106] On the west coast of Africa belief in transmigration is common. If a fetish-doctor or a good trader has died, the natives want to get back his valuable soul, and each baby that arrives is closely watched. "Assortments of articles belonging to deceased members of the house are presented to it, and then, according to the one it picks out, it is decided who that baby really is— See, Uncle So-and-so knows his own pipe, etc.—and I have often heard a mother reproaching a child for some fault say, 'Oh, we made a big mistake when we thought you were so-and-so.' " "The idea of reincarnation . . . exists apparently throughout all Africa, but usually only in scattered cases." Some souls may get a rise in status with their next incarnation. "You often hear a woman saying she will be a man next time, a slave, he will be a freeman." A man's wealth determines the sort of baby in which he is to be reincarnated. "The souls of the dead are sometimes reborn in animals, and occasionally, though but rarely, in plants. In the ideas of the natives, animals, though they differ in shape from a man, possess passions and moral qualities identical with those of the human being. Animals also possess souls which, like the souls of men, go to Deadland. Hence, as men and animals have so many characteristics in common, it does not require any great stretch of the imagination for the native to fancy that the soul may be re-born in an animal. When a plant is concerned, the difference is greater." "As the births at least equal in number the deaths, and the process of being re-born is supposed to have gone on 'from the beginning,' logically there ought to be few, if any, departed souls in Deadland; but the natives do not critically examine such questions as this, and they imagine Deadland to be thickly populated, and at the same time every new-born child, or almost every one, to be a re-born ghost."[107] It might be added that reincarnation is, to West Africans, an especial destiny of royalty.[108] In Borneo one of the souls is conceived to go over into certain fetish-animals, not eaten by the natives, such as gray apes or snakes.[109] The Dyak soul, after a sojourn in the spirit-world of seven times seven times the period passed on earth, returns to enter the bast, blossom, leaf, or fruit of a tree. If any such part of the tree is eaten by any creature, that creature is in a position to collaborate in the propagation of the human race. An animal, say, eats of the tree into which a soul has passed. Then the soul goes over into the body of the animal, and, after the next pairing, is born an animal. If now the animal is eaten by a human being, the soul passes on into him or her, and sex-union brings it into the human state again. But if the blossom, leaf, or other part of the tree dies before being eaten by animal or man, or if the animal that eats it is not used by man, the soul is annihilated.[110] In Tibet, at dawn of the day after cremation, a man whose function it is searches among the ashes

[106] Fox and Drew, in JAI, XLV, 161-162.
[107] Kingsley, *W. Afr. Studies,* 144-145; and in *Travels W. Afr.,* 461, 492, 493; Ellis, *Yoruba,* 129, 133-134.
[108] Bastian, *Deut. Exped.,* I, 196, note; and in *Afr. Reisen,* 258.
[109] Nieuwenhuis, *Borneo,* I, 148.   [110] Perelaer, *Dajaks,* 17.

for the footprints of animals, and according to the footprints found, so, it is believed, will be the rebirth of the soul.[111] One of the two souls, according to the Hurons, becomes at length a turtle-dove or goes to the village of souls, while the other is attached to the body and remains in the grave, never to leave it, "unless some woman bears it again." Proof of reincarnation exists to them in the perfect resemblance which some persons bear to others who are deceased.[112] The wicked, among the Haida Indians, are allowed to enter the bodies of fish and animals;[113] while among the Tarahumari the medicine-man has a hard time rescuing a particularly bad man from the animal kingdom—if his people cannot pay the functionary, the ghost may wander indefinitely as an animal.[114] "The Tlascaltecs supposed that the common people were after death transformed into beetles and disgusting objects, while the nobler became stars and beautiful birds."[115] Even when a man is alive, the Oregon Indians hold that his spirit may exist in the form of a tomtit, a bear, or a flower; and spirits of the dead come, at the call of the medicine-man, as birds or in other forms.[116] Gods are represented on Assyrian monuments as different from men by reason of their wings; angels, cherubs, and seraphs are winged. Feathers are a sign of magical beings, and witches and nymphs are naked if robbed of their feather dress. The departed soul is sometimes clad in feathers, and the unborn soul, as well, is so represented.[117]

Rose[118] in his article on celestial and terrestrial orientation of the dead, expresses the belief that the rites he treats obviously point to a conviction of reincarnation. He notes that in classical times one who was falsely reported dead "had to go through an elaborate pretence of being a new-born child, being swaddled, bathed, and suckled by the women, i.e. having made him over to the dead, his people gave him the same treatment as any other dead man, and welcomed him back as a baby. . . . Very early, it would seem, the idea springs up that there is some sort of a ghostly clearing-house through which all normal spirits, or all those of a particular class, must pass on their way to re-birth. . . . The nearest approach to perfect consistency is perhaps the fairly widespread custom of burying a young child in the house even when adults are buried elsewhere. The baby has died so young that he needs hardly any preparation to become once more a baby-spirit." The dead are pointed toward the original home, except that undesirable ghosts are directed in the wrong way; good ghosts go home to be re-born.

The idea of transmigration and reincarnation is herewith illustrated sufficiently for our purpose, for we are interested in these animistic beliefs less for themselves than for their effects as fac-

---

[111] Bishop, *Tibetans*, 107.
[112] From *Relations des Jésuites*, 1636, quoted by Thomas, in BAE, V, 114.
[113] Harrison, in JAI, XXI, 20.
[114] Lumholtz, in *Scribner's Mag.*, XVI, 444.
[115] Bancroft, *Nat. Races*, III, 512.
[116] Anon., "Northwestern Indians," in PSM, XLIII, 825.
[117] Negelein, in *Globus*, LXXIX, 357-360.
[118] In JAI, LII, 127 ff.

tors in society's evolution.[119] "This belief has formed in many places on earth independently and without transference from place to place;"[120] that is, it is not a product of acculturation but is one of those parallelisms whose presence is to the scientist so significant of the underlying process of societal evolution.

§212*. The Name. To the primitive mind, if a human being has no name, he is not placed, he cannot be designated—in short, he has no real existence. When his name is forgotten by survivors, there comes to him the "second death." Thus a man's name becomes peculiarly identified with himself and is an integral part of him. Anyone who knows and uses it may affect his destiny as much and more than he could if he got hold of his hand or head. Hence a savage would have two names, a real one which was never used and another for common appellation; or he would change his name several times during life for reasons presently to appear. Men have always acquired epithets, titles, and nicknames from personal traits, accidents of association, acts, achievements, sufferings, official positions, or anything else that marked them out from others or identified them. These supersede all others, so that the latter are forgotten. The initiate, who was supposed to be reborn, received a new name. No one's name, least of all a god's, might be taken "in vain," that is, lightly, as if the trivial utterance of it upon the air could have no significance to him. The name plays an important part in magic.[121]

This name-notion is by no means destitute of truth. There is much of personality in a name. In narrower and wider circles amongst ourselves the names of men of influence have prestige and authority through habits of respect, deference, and obedience. The name of Washington, Wellington, or Bismarck illustrates this on the larger scale; that of the ward boss on the smaller. Moses, Confucius, Cæsar, Napoleon, Aristotle, Shakespeare, are names to which their bearers gave a kind of independent existence as disembodied powers in human society. The names are quasi-supernatu-

119 For further evidence see especially Tylor's *Prim. Cult.*, ch. XII, and Frazer's *Golden Bough*.
120 Rohde, *Psyche*, II, 134.
121 §§163, above, and 243, 299-301, below; Clodd, *Magic in Names*, 83-88, 135.

ral beings by themselves; things to conjure with. A book is dedicated "To the Great Name of Charles Darwin." Savage men
conceived of all names as entities connected intimately with personality. Every man was, therefore, as he lived, creating an hypos-
tasis, a hypothetical substance, projection, or essence of himself
—the Napoleonic legend, for instance. The hero was no more than
the grand case, for all men's names, according to their degrees of
importance, were hypostases.

We do not know of a more appropriate connection in which to
introduce this idea than here, under the general topic of animism.
The name, if it is not strictly an aspect of the soul but perhaps a
species of emanation or aura of personality, is closer, we think,
to the conception of that immaterial thing, persistent beyond
death, than to any other item which we distinguish in the mental
outfit.[122]

There are, it is true, occasional cases where the name is lacking; the Bushman of South Africa has no name peculiar to himself,[123] and the same is true
of the Veddahs. "When a Veddah was asked his name he said, 'I am called a
man: when young, I was called the little man: and when old, I shall be called
the old man.' "[124]

In view of the reticence often exhibited on the score of the name, such cases
may not signify much; in general, the name stands for a great deal among
most peoples, and even among the very backward. "You can implore a native
to tell you his name, and even offer him coin to pay him for that information,
but it has no effect. He will tell you some name, if you press him hard enough,
but it won't be his, as you will discover if you try to find him again." Mr.
Hardy, on one occasion, wished to buy a canoe and asked a native who was
standing by if the canoe was his. "The native smiled blandly and shook his
head. 'Don't you know whose it is?' asked Mr. Hardy. 'Don't know; man over
there, p'r'aps,' said the native. 'What's his name?' Mr. Hardy pursued. 'No
name.' The native shook his bushy head. 'Well, show me which is the hut he
lives in.' At this question the man began to fidget, and then, glancing carelessly
at the row of huts, all as like each other as peas, he swept his hand past the
whole lot and said: 'That one.' And that was all the information concerning
the name and possessor of the canoe that Mr. Hardy obtained. Subsequently
he learned that the owner of it was the very man he had been questioning."[125]
Says Hagen[126] of other Papuans: "A native is not so vain or proud of any-

[122] Clodd, *Magic*, 36 ff., especially 106, 224 ff. The author considers personal
names, exchange of names, names of relatives, those acquired at birth, baptism,
and initiation, names of kings and priests, of the dead, and of the gods.
[123] Lichtenstein, *S. Afr.*, II, 49.
[124] Davy, *Account of the Interior of Ceylon*, 117.
[125] Hardy and Elkington, *So. Seas*, 26-27.
[126] *Papua's*, 231.

thing else, save of his external bodily appearance, as he is of his name. He, who stalks about enveloped in nothing but his bark girdle and an endless self-consciousness, desires and assumes that everyone knows his renowned name." It is bad manners to ask a Papuan his name; everyone is supposed to know it instantly. Similar cases could be gathered from many lands; the mind recalls at once the speeches of Homeric heroes.[127] This is human enough; it is always flattering to feel that one has impressed other people so strikingly that his name is readily recalled, and the politician in all ages is triply armed if he can fit the name to the face. These two cases of concealment of the name and pride in it should not, by their contrast and inconsistency,[128] produce any confusion. The savage mind feels none. In any case the name of renown may not be the real one: a Teda, for example, is accustomed to take a new name after the killing of a personal enemy in open conflict.[129] Any dashing or distinguished deed may result in the ostentation of a laudatory name or title.[130]

It is not these aspects of the name as a vaunt which are of moment at this point, though they all bear upon the conception of the name as something more than a label, useful in distinguishing person from person. Our cases aim to bring out the more mystic aspects of the name;[131] if it is not substance of the soul it is a sort of attachment to it.

To certain tribes of India, "as to most people of the lower culture, a name is an integral part of its owner and consequently offers a suitable handle to the sorcerer for his magical operations. This supposed intimate connection of a name with its owner" explains the reason why these tribes avoid naming certain persons and certain places at certain hours. They, after nightfall, "will not use the words 'serpent' or 'tiger,' but describe a 'serpent' as a 'cord' . . . and a 'tiger' as 'the long-tailed thing.' Should the actual names be used, their owners—the serpent and the tiger—would, it is believed, be attracted to the place. . . . The chance of ill-luck may, however, be avoided if he utters . . . magic words . . . before he pronounces those inauspicious names. It is probably to prevent magicians from easily finding out the real name of a person, that the . . . parents give two names to each child."[132] The following anecdote is from the Nicobar Islands: "At noon to-day four young women came from Malacca . . . on some affair of their own, and came to my hut and asked me, 'Where is Solo?' ('Solo' being my name to the Nicobarese). I replied in Nicobarese fashion, 'I don't know.' 'Then who are you?' they asked. I said, 'I am a man.' 'What is your name?' they asked. I said, 'I have no name.' All this is in tone with the Nicobarese manners. I then said, 'Tell me your name and I will tell you mine.' They complied, and then I revealed the fact that I was Solo."[133] The Polynesian custom of choosing friends, when visitors arrive, is accompanied by an exchange of names. Apparently it is like putting one's

127 Keller, *Hom. Soc.*, 113, 167 and references.
128 §215, below.   129 Nachtigal, *Sahara,* I, 350.
130 §449, below.
131 See Clodd, *Magic in Names,* 106, 224 ff.
132 Roy, in JAI, XLIV, 339.   133 Solomon, in JAI, XXXII, 217.

soul in another's keeping to give him one's name. One of the kings of a Samoan district "gave his name to Williams, who thereupon became entitled to the respect due to him, was greeted under his name, and was addressed in the language used in speaking to chiefs of the highest rank." The case of a white man is cited, "who had exchanged names with a Tongan chief, and was therefore regarded as the son of that chief's mother. . . . I am inclined to think that this practice of exchanging names was not a mere formality, but may have involved, or had its origin in, a Polynesian conception under which a man's name was identified with the man himself, and that therefore the person to whom he gave it was, in a sense, the man himself. . . . If, say a pig, had been stolen, and the owner guessed who was the thief, he would give to the pigs or trees of the suspected person his own or another man's name, whereby, according to native ideas, those articles became possessed, or bewitched; for they believed that the spirit of a dead or living man was in the things, and sometimes this belief was sufficient to impel the thief to abandon his property, and settle down elsewhere."[134]

In East Greenland the name is the second soul; that is, the child being named after the last person deceased in the group, the ghost of this person enters into and so becomes the soul, or one of the souls, of the child. "The 'name' . . . is as big as the man and enters the child when, after birth, it is wet around the mouth with water while the dead man's 'name' is uttered. . . . One must take care not to hurt or offend the 'name'; for then it may leave the person and he becomes ill. . . . When the man dies the 'name' remains lying in the corpse in the water or earth where it is deposited until a child is called after him. It then goes into the child and there carries forth its existence. . . . The 'name,' in the period between its presence in two human beings, wanders through a number of animals."[135] The name of the dead remains with the body or migrates through different animals until a child is called by it. Then the dead person has peace; but if the matter is not attended to, evil consequences may follow for the child who should have had the name. In Greenland, and generally, a spiritual affinity is supposed to exist between two people of the same name and the characteristics of the dead are transmitted to those who are called after them. Many races forbid marriage between two of the same name, as if there were a spiritual affinity which was as much a bar to union as is blood-affinity. The name, we have just seen, is regarded in East Greenland as one of the components of an individual. Nansen,[136] who reports this of the Eskimo, adds that there is a similar notion in Norway that the dead seek after names; that if, before her child is born, a woman dreams of a deceased relative she must name her child for him or the child will suffer. This the Lapps too believe.

The feeling for the name was very strong among the North Americans and can be illustrated copiously from them. "The Indian regards his name, not as a mere label, but as a distinct part of his personality, just as much as are his eyes or his teeth, and believes that injury will result as surely from the malicious handling of his name as from a wound inflicted on any part of his physical organism. This belief was found among the various tribes from the Atlantic to the Pacific, and has occasioned a number of curious regulations in regard

---

[134] Williamson, *Cent. Polyn.*, III, 156-160.
[135] Holm, *Eth. Skizze*, 70-71.   [136] *Esk. Life*, 228, 230.

to the concealment and change of names. It may be on this account that both Powhatan and Pocahontas are known in history under assumed appellations, their true names having been concealed from the whites until the pseudonyms were too firmly established to be supplanted."[137] These "curious regulations" respecting names will find an explanation under other headings.[138] A name is like a soul or spirit also in the fact that it can be taken from a slain enemy:[139] "Names and all the privileges connected with them may be obtained, also, by killing the owner of the name, either in war or by murder. . . . In this manner names and customs have often spread from tribe to tribe. A man may even hypothecate his soul in the form of his name: a Kwakiutl Indian, if his credit is poor, may pawn his name for a year, during which time he may not use it. He has to pay about twenty-five per cent for a three months' loan to redeem his name.[140] A new name will often be found, especially in connection with crises in the individual's life, such as his initiation,[141] to denote a new station —really a new man with a new spirit. For example, the captives whom the Iroquois forced to run the gantlet, and who got through, were adopted under a new name.[142]

Elsewhere than among the Americans, who have furnished the bulk of our cases, the name is held in the same esteem. The Borneo head-hunters believe that "without a name there would be no existence—how could a nameless thing be admitted to 'Apo Legan,' or Heaven? The receiving of a name is really the starting-point of life; the bestowal of a name by the parents is probably the most serious of parental duties and is to be performed with ceremonies proportioned to their rank. So essential is the ceremony of naming that in the enumeration of a family an unnamed child is not counted; and should a child die before the ceremony of naming, a Kayan or Kenyah mother would mourn for it no more deeply than had it been stillborn. This is true even when an unnamed child lives to be nearly a year old."[143] Among the Maori, "the priest repeated a long list of names, and when the child sneezed, that which was then being uttered was the one selected, those repeated being the names of ancestors."[144] Of the importance of the name in ancient times, especially in southwestern Asia, more will be seen under the topic of the name-fetish. In Chaldæa the view was that a thing had no existence till it was named.[145] The Bible is full of evidence as to the spiritual quality of the name: "The name of the God of Jacob defend thee"; "The name of the Lord is a strong tower; the righteous man runneth into it and is safe."[146] A modern case is where the departing soul was loosed through manipulation of the name: on the island of Hiddensee, in the Baltic, "as in the north of Brandenburg and elsewhere, they cut the name out of the shirt of the dying, that he may be able to die more easily."[147]

[137] Mooney, in BAE, VII, 343.

[138] §§223, 252, 266, 273, 276, 277, 301, below.

[139] §§229, 249, 252, below.

[140] Boas, in USNM, 1895, 335 (quoted), 341.

[141] §163, above.   [142] Morgan, *League of Iroq.*, 342.

[143] Furness, *Head-Hunters*, 18, corroborated in matter of detail by Nieuwenhuis, *Borneo*, I, 65.

[144] Taylor, *Te Ika*, 184.   [145] Maspero, *Hist. Anc.*, I, 537.

[146] Psalm XX, 1; Proverbs, XVIII, 10.

[147] Heilborn, in *Globus*, LXXVIII, 385.

§213*. Location of the Soul. Theories as to the location of the animating principle in the body serve to fill out the conception of the soul. It resides in any bodily part or attribute the loss of which means death, swoon, or great weakness, as the breath, blood, bodily warmth; or in those members, disturbance of which is attended by death or deathlike states, as the head, heart, pit of the stomach, kidney-fat;[148] or elsewhere for various other reasons, known or unknown. Such words as "courageous," "splenetic," and "atrabiliar" are survivals of the belief that certain emotions, at least, had their seats in specific organs. The cases to be cited tell the story and also throw light both forward and backward over our exposition.

One case of the breath-soul will recall that conception of location. "Among the Seminoles of Florida, when a woman died in child-birth, the infant was held over her face to receive her parting spirit, and thus acquire strength and knowledge for its future use. These Indians could have well understood why at the death-bed of an ancient Roman, the nearest kinsman leant over to inhale the last breath of the departing (et excipies hanc animam ore pio)."[149] The reader may note the possible spread of infection attendant upon such practice. As to the location of the soul in the blood,[150] we are told that "the life in Africa means a spirit, hence the liberated blood is the liberated spirit, and liberated spirits are always whipping into people who do not want them." In the French Congo, "the villagers eat the meat of the sacrifice, that having nothing to do with the sacrifice to the spirits, which is the blood, for the blood is the life."[151] In Tibet, the senior lama or priest lifts the lock at the back of the corpse's head in order to liberate the soul if it is still clinging to the body. The people believe that a drop of blood on the head marks the spot where the soul has made its exit.[152] In Homer,[153] the hero's soul may depart through a wound, in the flow of blood. The ancient notion was that men and beasts were animated by the breath which flowed with the blood in the veins, and was gaseous or fluid. By drinking blood or eating flesh one absorbed this soul.[154] In such case the heart must be closely connected with the blood and soul. In Nyassaland, "the Angoni eat lion and leopard's hearts to make them brave." Among the Yorubas the hearts of human victims were dried, reduced to powder, mixed with rum, and sold to persons who wished to be endowed with great courage. The heart was believed to be the seat of courage, as the ety-

[148] Smyth, *Vict.*, I, 102, 107, 246, 469; II, 289, 313; merely in the fat: I, xxxv, 237; II, 315, 393. One reference in Homer: *Iliad*, XXI, 204.

[149] Tylor, *Prim. Cult.*, I, 391.   [150] Clodd, *Magic*, 12-13.

[151] Kingsley, *Travels W. Afr.*, 447, 451.

[152] Bishop, *Tibetans*, 106.

[153] *Iliad*, IX, 408-409, XX, 403, XIV, 518-519, XVI, 504-505; Keller, *Hom. Soc.*, 103.

[154] Maspero, *Hist. Anc.*, II, 164.

mology of that term in some modern languages would indicate, and the object in devouring it was to assimilate its tenant.[155]

Wilken[156] goes into this matter of the seat of the soul quite fully; especially is it found, in the East Indies, to inhabit the head, and still more particularly the hair. Head-hunting is based largely upon the conviction that thereby the soul of a person, residing in his head, becomes serviceable to his slayer. When the soul leaves the body, it looks to vulgar eyes like a bunch of hair, but to learned men like a man in miniature, a homunculus. The author's lengthy paper on hair-sacrifice supports at every turn the location of the soul in head and hair. He cites the case of gypsies who go to great trouble to cut the hair and beard of the dead, shaving him even in the coffin. Some regard the stomach as the seat of the soul; the modern Greeks call a stomach-plaster an *antipsycho*. To say "my stomach aches" means "my soul aches." The soul is found also to be connected with the breath, heart, shadow, and blood. The idea of the strength residing in the hair is familiar from the Samson story; but that account seems only an isolated feat of fancy until it is aligned with analogous cases.[157] "If a Mu-Kamba cuts his hair or nails, he throws the cuttings into a thicket, for it is believed that if anyone picked any of them up, and burned them, the owner would fall ill. This is a very widespread belief and is traceable to the idea that hair, etc., contains part of the spiritual essence of the owner and that the owner is capable of feeling an injury done to any part of himself, even after it is separated from him. . . . Truly the life of a savage native is a complex matter, and he is hedged round by all sorts of rules and prohibitions, the infringement of which will probably cause his death, if only by the intense belief he has in the rules which guide his life."[158] A scalped warrior was supposed by the Indians to be annihilated;[159] hence scalping really deprived the victim of the future life. The following quotation on the significance of the scalp-lock[160] will carry the case of the soul-location in the hair. Among the Omahas, "the hair was believed to have a vital connection with the life of the body, so that anyone becoming possessed of a portion of it, might work his will upon the man from whom it came. In ceremonial expressions of grief, the throwing of tufts of hair upon the dead, and the laceration of the body [shedding the blood] were equal expressions of the vital loss sustained." The hair, but especially the scalp-lock, represented life; it was used to carry one's ornaments, to consecrate one's self, to triumph over one's enemy. The sign of consecration to the thunder-god "seems to have been a small lock on the crown, parted in a circle from the rest of a man's hair and kept constantly braided. Upon this lock the talisman and the war honours were worn by the warrior, and it was this lock which was cut from the head of a slain enemy, and formed the central object in the triumph ceremonies, for the reason that it pre-eminently represented the life of the man

155 Stigand, in JAI, XXXVII, 123; Ellis, *Yoruba*, 69.

156 In VG, III, 21, 22; "Haaropfer," in VG, III, especially 476, 477; "Schedelvereering," in VG, IV.

157 Clodd, *Magic*, 13-17.   158 Hobley, *A-Kamba*, 101.

159 Mason, *Invention*, 395.

160 Fletcher, in JAI, XXVII, 443; Bancroft, *Nat. Races*, I, 569, II, 605, 606, note.

who had been killed in battle." The reader will recall the Tibetan lock which was lifted to release the soul.

An interesting location for the soul is the pupil of the eye.[161] "The Macusi Indians of Guiana show that at death the small human figure disappears from the pupil of a man's eye, and that the spirit has gone out of him. This is sufficient reason to the Indian for believing in the distinctness of body and spirit, as the two parts separate at death."[162] This case of localization, whether the soul is identified with the spot of light in the pupil, or whether, as seems more likely, with the reflected miniature image looking out through "the windows of the soul," is a significant one. The savage could not recognize the figure he saw in another's eye, distorted as in a convex mirror, as himself; yet it was plainly the image of a human face. Some Papuan tribes locate the soul in the eye;[163] and it was doubtless some such notion that led the Maori chieftain to seek to incorporate the virtues of a brave enemy by swallowing his eye-balls.[164] Natives of the Solomon Islands say they can tell whether a man is genuinely possessed by the appearance of his eye—"out of which a strange soul looks, not the soul of the man possessed."[165] Perhaps the strange Homeric epithet, "base eyeball," that is, "base coward,"[166] is explicable with this idea as a clue. Other localizations of the soul seem more capricious; they may be listed briefly: the great toe;[167] the larynx and left side;[168] the back;[169] the thigh;[170] the saliva;[171] the tongue. The latter organ has been used by most American peoples as an index to life or death in the object symbolized. "The tongue firmly held forth indicates life or vigor or spirit; the tongue dangling helplessly from one corner of the half-open mouth signifies death or captivity doomed to end in death." This organ was supposed to play no small part in procreation.[172]

In later times, as the functions of the different organs have come to be better known, the assignment of the soul to any one part of the body has come to be survivalistic; nevertheless the tendency to seek the seat of the soul in organs whose functions were not well known persisted in some instances until recently; thus the pineal gland came in for a brief season of honor. The

---

[161] Tylor, *Prim. Cult.*, I, 389; Monseur, "L'âme pupilline," in *Rev. de l'Hist. d. Relig.*, LI, 1-23; §292, below. Eye-balls are used as love-charms in the South. Puckett, *Folk Beliefs of the Southern Negro*, 261.

[162] Im Thurn, in JAI, XI, 363.   [163] Krieger, *Neu-Guinea*, 401.

[164] Taylor, *Te Ika*, 352.

[165] Fox and Drew, in JAI, XLV, 169.

[166] Homer, *Iliad*, VIII, 164. *Autenreith's Hom. Dict.* refers to the miniature in the eye; Euripides (*Electra*, 1221; *Orestes*, 389, 469, 1261, 1267) often uses the word *korē*, "maiden," for "eye," because, it is explained, of the small image in the pupil.

[167] Ellis, *Yoruba*, 126.   [168] Nansen, *Esk. Life*, 225.

[169] Altai Tribes. Michailovski, *Shamanism*. (Russ.), 65.

[170] Hebrews: Gen., XXXII, 33; Smith, *Relig. Sem.*, 380.

[171] Clodd, *Magic*, 17-23.   [172] Dall, in BAE, III, 113.

unknown was spiritualized. The habitat of the soul, like the range of the aleatory element, was gradually encroached upon until in the case of the former, and by the educated, the idea of a bodily "seat" has been given up.

Although the soul is supposed to inhere in a special way in various parts of the body, that it is present to some degree in all parts of it is indicated by the necessity, in burial ceremonies—which have to do with the "laying" of the soul—of having at least some shred of the body over which to perform rites. In fact, even a man's property, as a projection of his personality, may be used at a pinch to represent him.[173]

Among the Yoruba, "when a man dies abroad his family make the greatest exertions to obtain something belonging to him, over which the usual rites may be held. Hair or nail-parings are most sought for this purpose, but, if these cannot be obtained, a portion of the clothing worn by the deceased suffices. . . . Through a confusion between objective and subjective connection," the author[174] elucidates, rationalizing on the basis of his own stage of culture, "these relics, which bring the deceased to mind, are supposed to bring the soul to the place where the funeral ceremonies are held." Among the Saoras, "a youth's father had been murdered, and when asked if funeral rites had been performed, he said: 'No; how could we when the Government made way with his body?' " It had been buried after a post-mortem. They said that if they had even one bone or piece of his body, they would go through all the funeral-rites and put up the stone but without some piece of him they could do nothing.[175] In Samoa there was a way around such difficulties. If anyone was killed in battle or died at sea so that his body was not recovered, his soul was supposed to wander in distress. To lay his ghost a mat was spread and the first living thing which came upon it was caught up in it and buried. It was supposed to be his soul.[176] In China body and soul were supposed to go together. Hence bodies were brought home to be buried in order to get the soul there; the contracts of Chinese laborers in France, in 1917, provided for the return of the bodies of the dead, and for funeral-provisions and ceremonies.[177] If the body were lost, still the soul was evoked and buried in Chinese soil.[178] In Homer, since a cenotaph and gifts to the unburied dead would "do him no good," the soul was evidently conceived of as present with the body and absent in its default. "Lack of funeral ceremonies was a terrible misfortune; thus death by drowning was a pitiful and inglorious one, as was death far away from friends, for, in either case, the soul entered the next life without possessions of any kind. It would have been better for Odysseus to have died at Troy, for there he would have been magnificently buried. There was also the idea that the soul which had not gained 'a share of the fire' could not pass the

173 §108, above.   174 Ellis, *Yoruba*, 163.
175 Fawcett, in JASB, I, 257.   176 Ella, in AAAS, 1892, 641.
177 N. Y. *Times*, Feb. 25, 1917.   178 DeGroot, *Relig. Syst.*, III, 847.

river and associate with the shades of those gone before." These considerations explain the stubborn combats over the dead bodies of warriors.[179]

To ideas of this sort about the soul and its location in the body
go back many of the phenomena of sacrifice, head-hunting, and
other religious and magical practices of primitive folk.

In view also of the variety of objects with which the soul is
identified, it is not strange to find a common belief in a plurality
of souls.

Some Australians distinguish three or four: a "soul equivalent," a dream-
spirit, a shadow-spirit, and perhaps an animal-spirit.[180] The Calabar negroes
distinguish four: one that survives death, the shadow, the dream-soul, and the
bush-soul, the latter in the form of a wild animal.[181] The Chukchi distinguish
five or six, of which the owner may lose one or two, but not more, without
endangering his health; the medicine-man cures by replacing losses in souls.[182]
The Yakuts believe a man has three souls and three shadows: the first belonging to every object, the first and second to living things only, the third solely
to human beings, horned cattle, and horses. If a man loses one of these he
suffers discomfort; if two, he is ill; if all three, he dies.[183] It is not needful to
rehearse many cases in full, for all are a good deal alike. The Dyaks run the
number of souls up to seven.[184] One of the souls, according to the Eskimo, is
the life-giving warmth of the body; it is without sense and at death takes
flight into the air.[185] Dorsey[186] has heard an Indian believer in four souls
"quietly discussing this doctrine with an Assinneboine, who believed in only one
soul to each body." The fourth soul, according to the former, "always lingers
with the small bundle of the hair of the deceased, kept by the relatives until
they have a chance to throw it into the enemy's country, when it becomes a
roving spirit, bringing death and disease to the enemy in whose country it
remains. From this belief arose the practice of wearing four scalp feathers
for each enemy slain in battle, one for each spirit. . . . Some Sioux claim a
fifth scalp feather, averring that there is a fifth spirit." The Kootenays of
Oregon believed that a great or strong man had many spirits.[187] The echo of
beliefs in plurality of soul persisted in such views as those of Plato who assigned three souls to man: the vegetative in his digestive organs, the animal in
his breast, and the intelligence in his head.[188]

[179] Keller, *Hom. Soc.*, 117-122, where references to text are given. Consider
the plot of the *Antigone* of Sophocles.
[180] Parker, *Euahlayi*, 35.
[181] Kingsley, *Travels W. Afr.*, 459, and *W. Afr. Studies*, 200.
[182] Bogoras, in AA, III, 98.
[183] Sieroshevski-Sumner, in JAI, XXXI, 108.
[184] Roth, *Sarawak*, I, 269.
[185] Nelson, in BAE, XVIII, pt. I, 422.
[186] In BAE, XI, 484, 517.
[187] Anon., "Northwestern Indians," in PSM, XLIII, 825.
[188] Lippert, *Kgchte.*, II, 268.

§214. All Things Have Souls. Hitherto the idea of the soul has been developed as of a something characteristic of man alone. Incidental detail of the cases cited has perhaps betrayed the fact that he is not unique in this respect. Perhaps the notion of a soul in things was due in part to such qualities as elasticity or freshness or the capacity to throw out a spark; but there is a more comprehensive cause. If one goes back to the dream or hallucination he will readily see that it was not man alone who appeared as a dream-double; doubles of clothing, weapons, and ornaments were also in evidence, as were those of trees, animals, and other features of the dream-background. The conclusion that all things have souls was as natural as that men had them; and this is a belief current among primitive peoples. "Lower psychology" draws no definite line between the souls of men and of beasts.[189] This might have been inferred from preceding cases; the attribution of a soul is not limited to the animal or even to the organic being.

In West Africa there is regularly a pattern that runs around pots to "keep their souls in," that is, to prevent their breaking up on their own account. Any sort of pattern answers, and it need not be carefully done. "Other things besides gods and human spirits have the habit of becoming incarnate. . . . Once I had to sit waiting a long time at an apparently clear bush path, because in front of us a spear's ghost used to fly across the path about that time in the afternoon, and if anyone was struck by it they died. . . . A certain spring I know of is haunted by the ghost of a pitcher."[190] Pots and pitchers are classed with animals, plants, and men as having a spiritual principle. The American negro conceives of a ghostly attack by a whole house.[191] "Every man, woman, and the smallest children, every dog, every pig, every crocodile, has a soul or spirit which does not die."[192] The foundation of all Melanesian and Polynesian religion is pantheism, in the sense of everything having a soul, or being capable of having one, including dead things or utensils.[193] In New Guinea the natives believe that everything having life can speak, and they are always expecting trees, fish, and plants to talk in their particular language.[194] To the Melanesians a pig has a soul or *tarunga:* "when a man sells a pig he takes back from it its *tarunga* in a dracæna leaf, which he hangs up in his house; thus he does not lose more than the fleshly accidents of the pig, the *tarunga* remains waiting to animate some pig that will be born. A pig is an animal of distinction and has a *tarunga;* yams and such things have none; they do not live with any kind of intelligence." There is a word used in parts of Melanesia, never applied

189 Gomme, *Ethnol. in Folklore*, 163.
190 Kingsley, *Travels W. Afr.*, 66, 522.
191 Puckett, *Folk Beliefs of the Southern Negro*, 115.
192 Bastian, *Ideale Welten*, 81.   193 Ratzel, *Vkde.*, II, 289.
194 Cayley-Webster, *New Guinea*, 28.

to the soul of a man but very significant of native belief, namely *nunuai*. "It is the abiding or recurrent impression on the senses that is called a *nunuai;* a man who has heard some startling scream in the course of the day has it ringing in his ears; the scream is over and the sound is gone, but the *nunuai* remains; a man fishing for flying-fish paddles all day alone in his canoe with a long light line fastened round his neck; he lies down tired at night and feels the line pulling as if a fish were caught, though the line is no longer on his neck; this is the *nunuai* of the line. To the native it is not a mere fancy, it is real, but it has no form or substance."[195] It would be difficult to imagine a more striking case than this of the spiritual explanation of the otherwise inexplicable.

Ellis[196] says that man is inclined to assign an indwelling spirit to animals, plants, and even inanimate nature, "partly because he does not perceive any strict line of demarcation between them and partly because he as frequently sees the phantom of such things in his dreams as he does the phantoms of living men. He would be led to extend the indwelling-spirit theory to all nature, because it would account for many things that would otherwise be incomprehensible." In Togo, the negroes believe that the soul of an animal, like that of a man, lives on in the next world; "therefore the ghosts of slain animals are feared and through rites closely analogous to those at the burial of a relative, are to some extent conjured not to do ill to the hunter."[197] A hunter prays to the life-spirit of a female hippopotamus not to bear him ill-will for having killed it and thus cut it off from future maternity;[198] the bones of a slain elephant are heaped up and covered, to propitiate its soul, lest it oppose the hunter's future activities.[199] In Africa, as elsewhere, it is believed that in mining, "a part of the ore must be left, that it may be able to grow again."[200] In India and among the Bataks occurs a festival of the worship of tools or implements, which implies the presence in these of a soul or spirit.[201] The Yakuts believe that the metallic attachments of the wizard's dress do not rust, and so have souls; the tools of a smith also have souls and can give out sounds of themselves.[202] "It is not only every human being nor merely all that we call living beings, but, in fact, all things either created by God or made by the hand of man, and even such immaterial things as the spoken word, an expressed wish, a passing thought or emotion, a magic formula, certain proper names and class-names, an odd number or an even number, that possess each its individual soul or its special spiritual energy. Indeed, soul, spirit, energy, and power are generally convertible terms in the primitive vocabulary. . . . The spirit-substance or soul-stuff, whether residing in aerial or in human bodies, is believed to resemble the human shadow in its form, and to influence man or cattle for good or for evil by 'overshadowing' them. . . . And the absorbing care of the aboriginal . . . is how best to defend himself and his family, his cattle and his crops, his house and his other belongings, against the subtle influence of such baneful energies and the poison-

[195] Codrington, *Melanesians,* 249, 251, 252, 269.

[196] *Yoruba,* 276.   [197] Klose, *Togo,* 261.

[198] Nassau, *Fetichism,* 204.   [199] Stuhlmann, *Mit Emin,* 87.

[200] Bastian, *Afr. Reisen,* 215-216.

[201] Thurston, *S. India,* 360-361; Wilken, in VG, III, 39.

[202] Sieroshevski-Sumner, in JAI, XXXI, 104.

ous malice inhering in most human and non-human souls and spirits." The author[203] says that certain persons with particularly strong individuality or soul-power are called men of "heavy shadow." It seems to us that this writer has assigned a soul to things which are really possessed by an outside spirit and are fetishes;[204] but, if so, it merely indicates the tendency of all categories in an evolutionary sequence to run into one another. In the East Indies everything has a soul: steam, for example, is the soul of boiling water. Things like iron have souls: before working iron, an offering is made to the souls of the iron, hammer, and anvil, during which they are all called by fine names.[205] According to the Dyaks, "gold has a soul, so long as it remains in the lap of the earth. . . . When the metal comes into man's possession the soul escapes, but tries then to take vengeance upon the gold-seeker, by causing him severe fever and other sickness."[206] Perhaps this is their *auri sacra fames*. The Kayans believe that all living things have souls and feelings like their own: "herewith they fill for themselves the cleft which, in the opinion of more developed peoples, separates them from animals and plants." Hence the difficulty in bringing them to burn or destroy anything. To them rice has a soul, and it must be got into a good frame of mind before harvesting. There is an extensive ceremony to this end, in fact, "every new manipulation of the rice is thus accompanied."[207] From a Malay point of view, tin ore is endowed with vitality and the power of growth. Its spirit can assume the form of a buffalo and move underground from place to place. Certain words that would offend the spirit are tabooed, and, as noise is offensive to it, all eating-vessels should be of coconut shell or wood. No animal may be killed in a mine. The miner must wear trousers; yet it is forbidden to wear shoes or to carry an umbrella or to wear a sarong, or Malay skirt, in a mine.[208]

Wilken[209] goes into this matter quite fully for the Malay Archipelago, beginning with Tylor's[210] statement that "among the lower races of mankind there have been observed to hold most explicitly and distinctly the doctrine of object-souls," namely, among the Algonquins, the Karens of Burma, and the Fijians. To these Wilken adds the Dyaks of Borneo and the Bataks of Sumatra. Souls of plants and of inanimate objects as well may leave their habitations and appear in dreams to men; they have a human form except that those of trees are frightful. They are good and bad, and to the latter sacrifices are made, especially when a man has fallen ill after felling a tree. The good spirits, among others those of swords, have a yearly offering. Especially honored is the soul of rice, among the Bataks. With the rest of the islanders the notion of souls in things is less pronounced, although indications of its former universality appear. Rice is endowed with human attributes, and its sexual passion must be roused in order to get a harvest; this is done by sexual performances in the fields at the time of blossoming. There is supposed

[203] Roy, in JAI, XLIV, 324-325.   [204] Ch. XXVIII, below.

[205] Wilken, *Vkde.*, 550-554.

[206] Perelaer, *Dajaks*, 6, 215; Bock, *Borneo*, 95.

[207] Nieuwenhuis, *Borneo*, I, 106, 145, 146.

[208] Skeat, *Malay Magic*, 250 ff.

[209] In VG, III, 37-39, 40-41, 43, 101 (from Mariner, *Tonga Islands*, II, 129; Williams, *Fiji and the Fijians*, I, 242).

[210] *Prim. Cult.*, I, 479.

to be a rice-couple, bride and groom. Further the rice-soul may become angry and has to be handled with care; all sorts of taboos are listed by the author concerning conduct in the fields. Other plants are treated as pregnant women, and people refrain from what might frighten them and cause them to drop their fruit untimely. There must be no uproar near them, nor any fire or light in their neighborhood at night; people must approach them with head uncovered. Various ceremonies also occur in connection with producing palm-wine. Wilken cites Mariner on the Tonga Islands to the effect that "if an animal or a plant die, its soul immediately goes to Bolotoo [the land of souls]; if a stone or any other substance is broken, immortality is equally its reward; nay, artificial bodies have equal good luck with men, and hogs, and yams. If an axe or a chisel is worn out or broken up, away flies its soul for the service of the gods. If a house is taken down or any way destroyed, its immortal part will find a situation on the plains of Bolotoo."

The Bering Strait Eskimo have an elaborate "bladder-festival" to propitiate the souls of slain animals;[211] and the Central Eskimo, when they dig out potstone, put ivory earrings, beads, food, or the like in the hole, as exchange-gifts to the rock.[212] Thus too the Cherokee medicine-man, after pulling up a medicine-plant by the roots, puts a bead in the hole, probably "as compensation to the earth for the plant."[213] Each of the copper plates, so highly esteemed by the Indians of the Northwest, has a house to itself and is regularly fed. No women are allowed in the house.[214] It is suggested that the ring in the plates indicates the presence of a spirit.[215] Among the Kootenay Indians "even little stones, bits of rug, shavings of wood, have their spirits."[216] "As the steam arose when they made a fire on a stone, the Dakotas concluded that stones had life, the steam being their breath, and that it was impossible to kill them."[217] The Hopi call the soul the breath-body. "This breath-body man shares with organic and inorganic nature, and it likewise forms an essential part of objects of human manufacture. The figures which are so constant and prominent in altars have breath-bodies, and it is this essence, not the idol, which is worshipped."[218] The Indians of Ecuador have something the same idea as the Malays about the sexual nature of plants. "The fact that only the women have to brew the manioc beer—which is the rule among all Indians—is due to the same reason as makes the cultivation of the manioc fields a business solely incumbent on the female sex. According to the animistic ideas of the Jibaros, all plants are animated by human spirits, . . . some of male sex, some of female. The manioc, like most other domestic plants, has a woman's soul. Hence—according to the principle 'like is best known by like'—the women have to cultivate this plant just as, in regard to the preparation of the manioc beer, they are believed to have a special power of promoting that mysterious and, to the Indian mind, unintelligible process of nature which is called fermentation."[219]

Not only human but also animal life was thought by the Hebrews to depend

[211] Nelson, in BAE, XVIII, pt. I, 392-393.

[212] Boas, in BAE, VI, 596.   [213] Mooney, in BAE, VII, 339.

[214] Dellenbaugh, *North Amer.*, 375.   [215] Niblack, in USNM, 1888, 336.

[216] Anon., "Northwestern Indians," in PSM, XLIII, 825.

[217] Dorsey, in BAE, XI, 538.   [218] Fewkes, in AA, IX, 161.

[219] Karsten, "Jibaro," in BAE, Bull. LXXIX, 60.

upon the divine breath; Jahweh is a "God of the living spirits of all flesh."[220] The women of Bagdad would not give dolls to their daughters because they conceived of a ghost in every doll which might awake to activity and hurt the children.[221] Krauss[222] thinks that "from the belief that the plant has a soul grew the view that it is the temporary body of a human soul."

The transition from views of this sort to fetishism[223] is not an abrupt one. In fact, there is here a zone of uncertainty as to whether the soul in a thing is one "native" to it or whether it is an alien spirit in "possession" of it. This is why writers limit the genuine belief in the souls of things to so few tribes. Though the above cases have been chosen to illustrate the former alternative, they naturally verge somewhat toward the latter. However, the fact that the soul was not regarded as an exclusive possession of man is now before us; it is one of wide bearing and high significance.

§215. Inconsistencies. In all these notions there is a common element, namely, the attempted explanation of that which is, for the time and place, inexplicable and which belongs, therefore, under the aleatory element. All these ideas are based upon the fundamental illusion or major premise of the double, which forms so apt a means for explaining what would be, apart from this illusion, unaccountable. An underlying principle of such scope should not have been lost to view by reason of immersion in detail. Further, it will have been noted that the ideas of the soul, even those held by the same group or individual, are not seldom contradictory. Students have often raised the question as to how the savage can believe in the insubstantiality of the soul and yet in its ability to inflict blows and even to suffer under them. An instinct for consistency is assumed. It is not to be assumed. In this section on adjustment to the inexplicable, where the impossibility of verification is encountered at every turn, inconsistencies are multiplied; and we might as well have done at once with a natural perplexity at their occurrence.

220 Kautzsch, "Relig. Israel," in *Hastings's Bib. Dict.*, 666; Psalm CIV, 29 ff.; Job, XXXIV, 14 ff.; Num., XVI, 22, XXVII, 16.
221 Andree, *Eth. Parallelen*, 91.   222 *Südslaven*, 36.
223 Chs. XXVIII, XXIX, below.

Says Weeks[224] of the African: "Before the unknown and mysterious he is timid, fearful and very superstitious. He will regard you as a *god,* and yet try to fight you: he will superstitiously believe that you have wonderful occult powers that can stop the rain, cause pestilence, and plagues, and yet he will not attempt to conciliate you, but he will savagely tell you to clear out of his town, and take your witchcraft elsewhere. When fighting with a gun he is timid, nervous, and apparently very cowardly, because he does not understand the mysteries of gunpowder, but give him a shield and a spear and his bravery is evidenced by his boldness in a fight and his utter indifference to wounds and death. The mysterious overawes, paralyses him, but superstitious fears will often arouse the demon of cruelty and vindictiveness, and incite to boldness and recklessness." "The more one looks into these matters the more one becomes clear that in the unorganised and uneducated human mind, be it 'civilised' or be it primitive, there is a horizontal stratification of the most contradictory ideas, which lie absolutely undisturbed in the ordinary course of life."[225]

One must realize that in studying primitive men he is dealing with untrained and unstocked minds to which inconsistency does not appear as a vice. Because it does not perceive relations of things and ideas in any perspective, the primitive mind, where it is not checked up by actual experience, is not aware of inconsistency. Whereas in the grosser and more material life the process of verification on experience is enforced and regular, elsewhere the mode is that of logical deduction from a major premise. The whole spirit-environment, like the dream, is in any case teeming with inconsistencies and contradictions; and when once the accountability of the imaginary environment for the aleatory element is accepted, inconsistency is in the order of events. Logical deductions from this gravid major premise take now one road, now another; and minds seem to entertain alternatives and contradictories and to pass from one to another without a jar, being artlessly hospitable to any number of propositions which appear to a trained intellect to be partly or wholly irreconcilable. That any reconciliation is incumbent seems not to have entered the head of the savage any more than it occurs to a child. These very divergences, however, are a necessary part of the thought-evolution of any age and demand no reconciliation. The main line of development is clearly enough marked; inconsistencies often serve to complete the picture in its details.[226] The same phenomenon of inconsistency does

224 In JAI, XXXIX, 134.
225 Panikkar, in JAI, XLVIII, 285.   226 Keller, *Hom. Soc.,* 102.

not fail to put in its appearance in our own time; it inheres in the unconscious action of us all and does not emerge till we "bethink" ourselves. The savage does not bethink himself even as much as we do, and so he lives on in serene unconsciousness of the "hobgoblin of little minds."[227]

227 Emerson, *Essays*, I, 52.

CHAPTER XXIV

EIDOLISM

§216. Beliefs about Ghosts. The soul is conceived of, then, as persisting after death; and the concourse of disembodied souls of various degrees of power forms the imaginary environment. The existence of the latter, to the primitive man quite as actual and verifiable as that of the natural environment, forms for him a set of conditions within which he must live. It is envisaged by him as an assemblage of agencies, for the conception of cause is too abstract for him. The question now arises as to the character of this environment in its relation to human life. Is it hostile or friendly? Does it weigh down upon or lighten the burdens of men? Recall once more the nature of the aleatory element of whose manifestations the spirits may be said to be the personified multiple agency: that good luck, even if it is merely the absence of bad luck, is accepted as a matter of course, while bad luck engenders uneasiness and care. The former may flow on indefinitely and produce no reflection. A man does not realize that he has a body while he is in perfect health; he thinks, "This is the way a man ought to feel." But the pain of a day occupies his attention more than the health of years. Bad luck seems to preponderate over good to such an extent that men have generally regarded the superior powers as malevolent and malignant, sporting with men, enjoying their misery, revelling in their own superiority and immunity from retaliation. The Greeks of the classical period argued that the gods did not act fairly and were not as honorable and just as men. Prosperity seemed more unstable than adversity; "there is nothing more serviceable to mankind than prudent distrust."[1] The injunction found in the *Trojan Women* of Euripides[2] and in the stately epilogue of that great tragedy of the fortuitous, the *Œdipus Tyrannus*, warns men to count no mortal happy till he is dead; they are bidden to contemplate the fate of a high-minded hero who solved the enigma of the Sphinx and became a powerful king,

---

[1] Euripides, *Helen,* 1617-1618. [2] 509-510.

devoted to the interests of his people, and to see how, though wholly innocent of blameworthy intent, he has now entered a very harbor of ill fortune.

These examples from a developed stage of culture may serve to bring out more clearly the vague convictions which underlie the point of view of primitive peoples. To anticipate slightly,[3] a significant conviction exists among savages that good spirits need no attention; they will go on doing good without it; it is the bad spirits that require bribery and worship. The Greenlanders never think of the spirits while all goes well but when trouble comes the medicine-man must go to the spirit-world and bring back information and advice.[4] The Loango negroes, though believing in a supreme thunder-god, are far more concerned about ghosts and spirits; whereas the former is good and not dangerous, the latter are malevolent and to be feared,[5] for they represent the reverse side of the aleatory element against which men need insurance.

Again, "the supreme deity is Lugaba, who dwells in the sky; he created man and beast; the world belongs to him, his smile is life, and the result of his displeasure sickness and death. This supreme being is not worshipped, nor are offerings made to him; he has no sacred place. Although they talk freely about him, and acknowledge him to be their great benefactor, they accept all his gifts as a matter of course, and make him no offering in return." This is another African illustration of how men have their eyes on bad luck rather than good; and of the fact that the thank-offering is extremely rare. "One must not, therefore, conclude that the Bahima are an irreligious people; like most of the Bantu tribes their religion consists chiefly in dealing with ghosts of departed relatives, and in standing well with them; from the king to the humblest peasant the ghosts call for daily consideration and constant offerings, whilst the deities are only sought in case of great trials or national calamities. . . . Ghosts of people more recently dead receive more attention than those of people who have died long since, though, should a priest attribute illness or other calamity to the negligence of the relations in not taking care of the grave, or making offerings to the ghost of some one long since departed, the hut is restored, and suitable offerings placed in it. Various illnesses are attributed to the influence of ghosts, and offerings are made to propitiate them, according to the advice given by the medicine-man, who is able to discover which ghost has caused illness, and its reason for doing so. Some of the ghosts become very wealthy in cattle and slaves from constant offerings made to them; the cattle are sacred and are watched over by the relations of the deceased person to whose ghost they belong."[6] Seligmann[7] cites a number of

---

[3] §§241, 278, below. [4] Fries, *Grönland*, 144.
[5] Brunache, *Cent. Afr.*, 15.
[6] Roscoe, in JAI, XXXVII, 108-109. [7] In JAI, XLIII, 660-662.

instances of "the belief in the otiose high gods, associated with an active cult of the dead." The former concern themselves but slightly with men, the regulation of human affairs being dependent upon men's efforts seconded by the spirits of the dead. Such beliefs are widespread among the tribes of the Anglo-Egyptian Sudan and their neighbors.

Among the reindeer nomads of the upper Yenesei, the big far-away gods get little attention, and the house-gods more; the latter are never neglected, receiving food and drink at every meal. They play a far greater part in the native life. Some of them are good, but must be kept friendly; most of them are ready to do men ill. Every unrecognized animal-noise at night is referred to them. "The Soyot's life is an enduring worry over these invisible enemies and a steady fight against them."[8]

Wilken[9] gives illustrations from the East Indies. All the events of life are referred to spiritual influences. "In the animistic cult fear reigns over any other mood, such as gratitude, trust, devotion. The spirits from which most is to be dreaded are the ones most eagerly appealed to, the bad therefore more than the good, the lower rather than the higher, those at hand rather than the ones farther removed, the special rather than the general. 'The thoughts of men seldom climb higher than to the top of the aspen-trees.'" The highest spirit is almost neglected; at best he is invoked when the spirits of the dead and other minor spirits have been solicited in vain. "Practically, therefore, the belief in a supreme being has only small significance."

In short, the reason for paying heed to the souls of the dead was that one might escape ill. Built as souls were upon the human plan, practically all their points of difference due to the disembodied status made for their overwhelming predominance over the living; and it is characteristic of the ghosts, as has appeared incidentally in the foregoing, that they are regarded as malevolent or at least as jealously insistent upon their rights and suspicious of intent to withhold their due. The idea of the recently dead as hovering in solicitude over the bereaved living is a distinctly modern and poetically idealized conception. Even if the dead are well disposed to the living their presence or touch is fraught with ill. When the savage pays heed to the ghosts it is regularly because he fears ill from their hand; his very mourning, as will appear, is largely a prophylactic device. The relation between man and ghost resolves itself, in sum, into a relation of rights and duties, with all the rights on one side and all the duties on the other.

The ghosts are conceived of as living in their second existence a life like that of men (projectivism) and so as subjected to a

[8] Olsen, *Primitivt Folk*, 138, 141.
[9] In VG, III, 233-234, 242-260, *passim*.

need of food, clothing, and all the rest of the things that men want. What they eat and wear, however, is not self-procured; it consists of the ghosts or doubles of food or clothing gathered or made by living men. In some cases, it is true, the ghosts in the spirit-world hunt for themselves, at least after a time, and cease to burden the living; the soul of Heracles hunted the shades of the animals he had slain in life.[10] In the great majority of cases, though, the sustenance of the dead, if they are to live on, must come from the earth and must be provided by survivors. The struggle for existence is thus prolonged, as it were, beyond the grave, and is carried on for those who have passed beyond by the doubly burdened living. This is the case in particular for the period immediately succeeding death, before the "laying" of the spirit.

The outcome of this situation is that the ghosts have a right to be supported by survivors and that it is the duty of the latter to afford support. This relation of rights and duties rests upon the basic relation of strength and weakness; the might of the spirits makes their right and the men's fear inspires them to their "sense" of duty. They develop "conscience" under the stress of dread. If the ghosts are believed to incur the obligation to use their power in behalf of the survivors, that is on condition that the latter propitiate them. There is no way by which the men can, of their own power, compel them to live up to obligation; coercitive measures that could force them are of a spiritual nature.[11] Hence the relation of rights and duties is essentially a one-sided affair. When a term is needed to express the attitude of men toward the disembodied souls[12] it is "ghost-fear" that is found most appropriate. "The domain of belief in souls or ghosts is the domain of what is irrational and inexplicable. Hence the domain is that of the dreadful and uncertain. None of the concepts in it are firm."[13] Man has always found a law in human affairs. The first and for a long time only law was that good luck and prosperity go with ghost-fear and faithful fulfilment of duties to ghosts. Very likely this law would be better expressed in the negative. About ghost-fear as a motive are woven all the beliefs and theories about the nature and

10 Homer, *Odyssey*, XI, 601 ff.   11 §277, below.
12 §201, above.   13 Rohde, *Psyche*, I, 43.

ways of ghosts: their powers, prerogatives, and rights, the duties of survivors, the sanctions which they employ if men fail of their duties. These beliefs and theories about ghosts we call "eidolism."

In employing this term, we seek to isolate in some degree beliefs about the recently disembodied soul as an agency of good or ill. "Animism," as we use it, means the doctrine about souls in their original bodies; this narrows the term as used by Tylor[14] to cover the "deep-lying doctrine of Spiritual Beings." By "eidolism" we mean the doctrine about ghosts; while under "daimonism" we shall include the doctrines about spirits of a higher potency and not obviously identifiable as the souls of the recently dead. That it is useful to distinguish this intermediate stage in the series of soul, ghost, and daimon or god, will appear, we hope, in what is to follow. "Ghostism" is the precise term, perhaps, but it is grotesque and also awkward in the matter of its adjectival form. An *eidōlon*,[15] in the Greek, is often plainly a ghost, though it may also be a soul long disembodied and living in the spirit-world. "Eidolism," like other terms in science that are of Greek derivation, is susceptible of receiving a definite connotation. It lends itself also to the formation of adjectival and other forms and is not uncouth; and adherence to the exact spelling of the Greek distinguishes it from commoner English derivatives of the same stem, such as "idol" and "idolatry." This distinction corresponds to one which appears in the usage of savage peoples. Certain Salish Indians, for instance, have three distinct terms which they employ on speaking of those who have passed away: spirit-people, to distinguish between persons in this world and those in the next; the departed, which "seems to express the condition of the departed between the time of leaving their bodies and arriving in the 'spirit-world' "; corpse or ghost, meaning an apparition of the dead.[16]

Belief that life does not end with death is so general among men that actual or alleged cases of disbelief in a future state are extraordinarily significant. All of them merit examination, for right here lies the crux of the question as to whether any people whatsoever has lacked religion altogether.[17] If there are found in a prehistoric grave articles useful for the prosecution of living, it is fair to conclude that they represent provision for a continued existence and that the man in question had the rudiments, at least, of religious belief. We have encountered but few cases of utter disbelief in the survival of the soul after death, and several of these seem to us spurious. "Animism characterizes tribes very low in the scale of humanity, and thence ascends deeply modified in its

[14] *Prim. Cult.*, I, 384.

[15] §210, above. Consider the poetic use of the term: "For I see that those of us who live are nothing else than eidola or insubstantial shadow." Sophocles, *Aias*, 125-126.

[16] Hill-Tout, in JAI, XXXIV, 321.   [17] §322, below.

transmission, but from first to last preserving an unbroken continuity, into the midst of high modern culture. Where doctrines adverse to it are held by individuals or schools, they are usually to be accounted for as due not to early lowness of civilization, but to later changes in the intellectual course, to divergence from, or rejection of, ancestral faiths, and such newer developments do not affect the present inquiry as to a fundamental religious condition of mankind."[18] More commonly, where observers assert there is no religion, it will be found upon closer examination that there is some idea of existence after death and that some attention is paid to the ghost. And it must be realized that savages, who are often extremely reticent, especially to strangers, about their cherished beliefs, are quite likely to deny the existence among them of that upon which they do not want to be questioned.

The Alur of Africa know nothing of life beyond the grave, although they think ghosts return, especially in dreams.[19] Upon questioning the heathen of Baghirmi, Nachtigal[20] found that "all seem to be convinced that with earthly death the life of man totally ceases, yet the manner in which they bury their dead, especially the chiefs, speaks for the unconscious acceptation of a continued existence." The thought of what is to become of them after death worries the Bechuana very little, but there exists, according to their ideas, a class of supramundane beings . . . which fall into connection with the shades of the dead."[21] Some Siberians are reported as believing that death ends all.[22] The Samoyeds have only a vague notion about life beyond the grave, believing that all ends with death; Castren[23] implies that there was earlier a more definite notion of the future life which the shamans obscured in order to increase their own power. Now the people think that shamans only have continued existence. Of the Hill Arrians of India it is said that "of what happens to the soul after death they have no certain belief. The doctrine of transmigration is unknown among them." Yet "in times of drought, ravages of wild beasts and sickness, vows are made and prayers such as 'Oh ancestor, be not angry with us!' are offered."[24] The Kubus of Sumatra seem to have no idea of a state after death; they say, "When we are dead, we are dead."[25] The Miwok Indians of California believe in the annihilation of the soul after death; though even here all do not entertain such a conviction.[26] The Toba Indians of Paraguay have no clear idea but only a very vague conception of the soul and its destiny in the beyond. "I believe," writes Koch,[27] "that the conception of a

[18] Tylor, *Prim. Cult.*, I, 385.
[19] Stuhlmann, *Mit Emin*, 529.
[20] *Sahara*, II, 686.
[21] Fritsch, *Eingeb. Süd-Afr.*, 167.
[22] Patursson, *Siberien*, 154.
[23] *Finn. Mythol.*, 264 (quoted in Michailovski, *Shamanism* (Russ.), 7).
[24] Painter, in JASB, II, 152.
[25] Forbes, in JAI, XIV, 125.
[26] Powers, in *Contrib. N. Amer. Ethnol.*, III, 348-349.
[27] In *Globus*, LXXXI, 108.

'higher being,' a 'god,' was first introduced by the missionaries . . . and that the Indians understand by it all that is unknown and frightful to them, above all the ghosts of the dead."

Cases of this order cited in disproof of a universal belief in the continuance of life after death, seem to us highly inconclusive; at any rate the weight of evidence is overwhelmingly in the other direction. Men believe universally, or all but universally, in the persistence of the soul, at least as far as the ghost-form.

§217*. The Ghost-Status. The souls of the dead are not ordinarily thought of as proceeding at once to the spirit-world or as always remaining there, once arrived, never again to visit their haunts in life. It is a general theory that the soul remains in the neighborhood of the dead body for a varying period; and many peoples believe that it may return temporarily from the spirit-world. Under these conditions it is a ghost or eidolon. If it were not for these ideas there would be no point in setting eidolism off from animism in general, or from daimonism; eidolism has to do with the soul after it is disembodied and before it becomes a daimon, that is, with the transition-period in the life of the soul. Transition-stages are traditionally instructive; the period of the "keeping" of fire[28] is such a stage. Eidolism has to do with the mortuary ceremonies and the "laying" of the ghost rather than with the developed cult typical of more advanced stages in the evolution of religion.

When it comes to illustration of eidolistic beliefs, the only difficulty is one of renunciation of material. The ghost-belief of the Melanesians "goes out from the belief that the ghosts are the souls of the dead."[29] "Europeans it is true speak of the spirits of the sea or of the storm or of the forest; but the native idea which they represent is that ghosts haunt the sea and the forest, having power to raise storms and to strike a traveller with disease, or that supernatural beings never men do the same."[30] Among the Trobriand Islanders, "there appears to be no one definite, dogmatic answer" about the actual abode of the departed. They "are invisible, and so is everything that belongs to them, and that is the reason why their villages can be there without being in anybody's way."[31] The Bangala call the embodied spirit *elimo* and the disembodied *mongoli*. Immediately after death the *mongoli* visits the nether regions, later to come above ground, and to make its haunts in the bush or on

28 §90, above.   29 Von Pfeil, *Südsee*, 143.
30 Codrington, *Melanesians*, 123.   31 Malinowski, in JAI, XLVI, 369.

the river-banks according as its people lived in one or the other location. They make a noise called *bie-bie,* and "are supposed to speak sometimes through the members of their own family, not always in the language of the present day, but in the archaic language known only to the old people." This last point is very significant of their ancestral quality. The land and water are full of them, so that "the timorous folk are afraid to travel at night."[32] The negroes of West Africa carry on conversation with dead relatives and friends, "and I have often seen a man, sitting at a bush fire or in a village palaver house, turn round and say, 'You remember that, mother?' to the ghost that to him was there."[33] On the occasion of Junker's[34] arrival at a certain African village, a bundle of spears was laid at his feet, the local chief explaining that "this was a greeting from his dead father's *kipa,* and that his own presents would follow later." "On the whole the evil spirits are preferably out at night, and therefore the Soyot very reluctantly departs from the nearest environs of the yurt after dark"; the same was true of the ancient Lapps.[35] The Hyperboreans believe that the dead go about on earth as invisible beings, living the earthly life over again.[36] The Hurons bury the dead child by a path that its soul may enter the body of some passing woman and be born again.[37] Succeeding chapters will contain many cases which directly or by implication sustain the ghost-theory. It has persisted or recurred among the sophisticated. "In Greece in earlier time the view, reaching even beyond Homer, was expressed that nothing at all outlasted death; even Attic orators could speak to their public with an expression of doubt about the hope of lasting consciousness. But such doubts related to the theoretic view about the persistence of the life of the soul. Even an unbeliever, if he were otherwise a true son of his city and rooted in her old customs, could in his last testament earnestly attend to the lasting cultus of his soul and of the souls of those who belonged to him. This is what Epicurus did, to the wonderment of later generations. Even the unbeliever held closely to the cult, as to the rest of the traditional, and the cult generated yet again and again, in the case of many, the belief which alone justified it."[38]

The interval of sojourn during which the ghost is thought to remain near the corpse ranges from a common minimum of three or four days to a year or more. Indeed, since the grave becomes a fetish,[39] the idea is at least implicit that the soul remains near the body, at least in some vague way, for a long time. Such an inconsistency should not perplex anyone.[40] The matter of concern in the present instance is the period of sojourn between death and departure for the spirit-world. There is generally some ceremony to mark the end of this interval, a "second funeral" which may take

---

[32] Weeks, in JAI, XL, 368, 369.
[33] Kingsley, *W. Afr. Studies,* 63.
[34] *Afrika,* III, 23.
[35] Olsen, *Primitivt Folk,* 139.
[36] Patursson, *Siberien,* 154.
[37] *Relations des Jésuites,* 1636, 128-139, quoted in Thomas, in BAE, V, iii.
[38] Rohde, *Psyche,* I, 257-258.
[39] §§250, 251, below.
[40] §215, above.

place after the exposure of the body and the removal or wasting
of the flesh or, again, some funeral-feast or other rite whose object
is the "laying" of the ghost.[41] The length of the interval of sojourn determines roughly the extent of the mortuary ceremonies.

The varying periods may be set down in semi-tabular form: a few hours to
a few days;[42] breath-soul leaves within twenty-four hours, material one later;[43]
three days;[44] four days;[45] seven days;[46] nine days;[47] ten to twelve days;[48]
thirteen days;[49] fourteen days.[50] In Homer the time was eleven days in the
case of Hector and over seventeen in that of Achilles.[51] Among the Amur
peoples the period is "several months";[52] among some Indians, one month.[53]
For the Ibo of Africa, it is thirty-two days for everyone except infants.[54]
Forty,[55] forty-nine,[56] and a hundred days[57] are other estimates. In Korea the
period for a poor man is three days, for a middle-class man nine, for a noble-
man or high official three months, and for royalty nine months.[58] Several peoples reckon the period as a year.[59] Among the Iroquois the journey to the
spirit-world took a year, during which there was mourning; mourning was
later reduced to ten days, the journey, on a revised schedule, taking but three
days.[60] The Hudson Bay Eskimo allow a four years' sojourn.[61] Certain West
Africans, finally, show a curious variation: they "hold that there is a definite
earthly existence belonging to each soul of a human kind. Suppose a soul has
a thirty years' bodily existence belonging to it. If that soul's body is killed at
twenty-five, the remaining five years must be spent, if it is left alone, in knock-

[41] Thomas, in JAI, XLVII, 209.   [42] Johnston, *Uganda*, II, 693-694.
[43] Perelaer, *Dajaks*, 219.
[44] Central Eskimo: Boas, in PSM, LVII, 629; Siberian tribes: Michailovski,
Shamanism (Russ.), 13; East Iranians: Geiger, *Ostiran. Kultur*, 263.
[45] Australians: Dawson, *Aust. Aborig.*, 51; Tibetans: Bishop, *Tibetans*, 108;
Bering Str. Eskimo: Nelson, in BAE, XVIII, pt. I, 314-315.
[46] Dyaks: Perelaer, *Dajaks*, 220; South China: Rehatsek, in JASB, I, 328.
[47] Coast of West Africa: Ratzel, *Vkde.*, I, 175, 610; White Russians: *Russian Ethnog.* (Russ.), I, 112.
[48] Paraguay Indians: Koch, in *Globus*, LXXXI, 46.
[49] India in the time of Manu: Bühler, *Laws of Manu*, III, 247, note.
[50] Tonga Islands: "Anthrop. Miscell.," in JAI, X, 460; Nicaragua: Sapper,
in *Globus*, LXXVIII, 273-274.
[51] Keller, *Hom. Soc.*, 120, where references to the text are given.
[52] Schimkjewitch, in *Globus*, LXXIV, 272.
[53] Allison, in JAI, XXI, 313.   [54] Thomas, in JAI, XLVII, 179.
[55] *Russian Ethnog.* (Russ.), II, 126, and in the New Testament.
[56] Tibetans: Waddell, *Buddhism*, 488-489; some Malays: Ratzel, *Vkde.*, II,
461.
[57] Solomon Islands: Somerville, in JAI, XXVI, 403.
[58] Bishop, *Korea*, 287.
[59] Tasmanians: Roth, *Tasmania*, 132; Ges of Brazil: Von Martius, *Beiträge*,
I, 291; Tarahumari of Mexico: Lumholtz, *Inter. Cong. Anthrop.*, Chicago, 1893,
112; Kaffirs: Kropf, *Kaffir-English Dict.*, 240.
[60] Morgan, *League of Iroq.*, 174.   [61] Turner, in BAE, XI, 193.

ing about its old haunts, homes, and wives. In this state it is called a Sisa and is a nuisance." The difficulty is that not having reached its full term of life it has not learned the way down to the spirit-world—a knowledge that "grows gradually on a man's immortal soul (the other three souls are not immortal), and naturally, not having been allowed to complete his life, his knowledge is imperfect."[62]

§218*. Mortuary Practices. During the interval of sojourn the doings of the ghosts are diverse in detail but alike in the large. For a time the soul remains in close connection with the corpse; in fact, as certain Siberian tribes believe, it cannot at once understand that it has left the body and learns this only after three days, when it observes that its feet no longer leave impressions in the ashes.[63] A state of nervousness and bewilderment seems often to characterize the new ghost. Its presence in or near the body is very actual to the believer.

The Dyaks, for instance, strew rice upon the corpse either for the use of the soul, saying, "That is for you"; or for the soul to take to some destination, the giver enjoining: "That I send to my forefathers," or "That is for so-and-so."[64] Among the Bulgars the body is addressed as if alive and messages and requests are given it for the dead whom the soul will meet in the place whither it will soon go.[65] If a pregnant woman dies, the South Russian Jews proceed to remove the child before the burial, the husband or friend whispering in the ear of the corpse, "I pray you, give the child."[66] Said a Palermo peasant: "My husband's soul has not left the room yet. It often takes three days for the soul to settle, and sometimes we have to call upon it from the street." "Is it still in the body?" she was asked. "Oh, no, it left the body at once, it always does, but the soul does not leave the house immediately, you know."[67]

The continued presence of the soul near the grave, even after the decay of the body, is a common tenet of uncivilized people which has lasted far down into civilization.

"The Kubu think that the souls of their relatives hover as ghosts over the place where their bones lie."[68] After fourteen days the Nicaragua medicine-man captures the errant soul and brings it, enclosed in a bottle, to the grave, "where it returns again into the heart of its quondam possessor."[69] Chinese literature copiously illustrates the belief that the grave is inhabited by the soul

[62] Kingsley, *Travels W. Afr.,* 517.

[63] Michailovski, *Shamanism* (Russ.), 13.

[64] Perelaer, *Dajaks,* 221.   [65] Krauss, *Bulgaren,* 427.

[66] Weissenberg, in *Globus,* XCI, 361.   [67] Alec-Tweedie, *Sunny Sicily,* 14.

[68] Anon., "Orang Kubus," in *Globus,* XXVI, 46.

[69] Sapper, in *Globus,* LXXVIII, 273-274.

of the man who lies therein[70] and the notion has furnished material for many a European poem, serious or jocose; consider the "In Questa Tomba Oscura" which Beethoven set to music.[71]

That there is, at one and the same time, "an adhesion of the freed soul to the remains of the body which it once inhabited"[72] and a passage of the soul to the spirit-world, seldom or never to return, is one of those inconsistencies which do not at all disconcert the primitive mind. However, the commonest version of ghost and body connection is, perhaps, that it persists between the first and second funerals. The body is first buried or exposed to the weather or fire until the flesh is removed, and then comes the expediting of the soul to the spirit-world. Between these two "funerals" the ghost is thought to be near at hand and is avoided or conciliated accordingly by ceremonies which are the simplest forms of the soul-cult.

The Papuans set up a post into which the ghost goes between the first and second funerals.[73] During a hundred days "the property of the dead man is sacred; his coconuts, his canoe, his house—no one may touch them any more than if he were alive—and his dog is allowed to go and starve in the bush; no one will care for it." Meanwhile the man's body has been buried for five days, in a sitting posture, with the head exposed to the ravages of ants. Thereafter the head is "scrubbed clean with sand and salt water, and bleached in the sun until it is white." For the rest of the period the skull is perched on a post and supplied with pipes, tobacco, and food, and at the end of the period it is stored with those of former chiefs or household lords. When the flesh is completely gone from the bones they are cleaned and buried "either in the ground, or sometimes in a cairn of stones, like an altar, about which various old 'properties' are placed."[74] The West African soul which has not completed its allotted period of existence in the body "will cause sickness and throw stones. It will fall off roofs and play the mischief with its wives' subsequent husbands. . . . A man's soul, however, can be taught the way [to the spirit-world] in the funeral 'custom' made by his relatives and the priests."[75] Among the Kaffirs the chief was buried in the cattle-kraal. Persons were appointed to watch the grave, and cattle were given them to milk. The village was abandoned except for three people. At the end of a year or longer, the watching was given up and the grave-watchers received some of the cattle as their wages.[76] Up to the time when the soul is to be expedited to the spirit-world, the Golds of Siberia think it resides in a *fanga,* or little cushion made for the purpose. "The fanga is covered from time to time with the new clothes of the dead man; they speak with the fanga and give it to eat, as if alive. But as soon as the soul is con-

[70] DeGroot, *Relig. Syst.,* II, 381. [71] Thayer, *Beethoven,* II, 111.
[72] Rohde, *Psyche,* I, 227. [73] Lippert, *Kgchte.,* II, 252, 377.
[74] Somerville, in JAI, XXVI, 403. [75] Kingsley, *Travels W. Afr.,* 517.
[76] Kropf, *Kaffir-English Dict.,* 240.

ducted into the land of souls, the cushion is torn to pieces and thrown into the fire. All relations between the dead man and his people are sundered and the widow can marry again."[77] Among the Tibetans it is believed to be impossible to quiet the soul till the fourth day after death, when a piece of paper, inscribed with prayers and requests to the soul to be quiet is burned with ceremonial by the priests. "There are other rites for the repose of the soul, with prayers that it may get a good path for its re-birth, and food is placed in conspicuous places about the house, that it may understand that its relatives are willing to support it."[78] In Samoa the unburied "occasioned great concern. No Roman was ever more grieved at the thought of his unburied friend wandering a hundred years along the banks of the Styx than were the Samoans while they thought of the spirit of one who had been drowned, or of another who had fallen in war, wandering about neglected and comfortless. They supposed the spirit haunted them everywhere, night and day, and imagined they heard it calling upon them in a most pitiful tone, and saying, 'Oh, how cold! oh, how cold!' Nor were the Samoans, like the ancient Romans, satisfied with a mere 'tumulus inanis.'" When it was impossible to get the body of a deceased person, the priest spread out before him on the ground a piece of native cloth. "Addressing some god of the family he said, 'Oh, be kind to us; let us obtain without difficulty the spirit of the young man!' The first thing that happened to light upon the sheet was supposed to be the spirit. . . . By-and-by something came; grasshopper, butterfly, ant, or whatever else it might be, it was carefully wrapped up, taken to the family, the friends assembled, and the bundle buried with all due ceremony, as if it contained the real spirit of the departed."[79]

With the Eskimo, if a taboo is violated during the three days which the soul spends near the body, "the transgression becomes attached to the soul of the deceased. The weight of the transgression causes the soul pain, and it roams about the village, endeavoring to free itself of its burden. It seeks to harm the people, who, by their disobedience to custom, are causing its suffering. It causes heavy snows to fall and brings sickness and death." Here is a typical case of religious sanction to the mores and of the solidarity in penalty for sin of the whole group, living and dead.[80] "If death results from natural causes, the spirit is supposed to dwell on the earth after having undergone a probation of four years' rest in the grave. During this time the grave may be visited and food offered and songs sung, and the offering, consisting of oil and flesh, with tobacco for smoking and chewing, is consumed by the living at the grave. Articles of clothing may also be deposited near the grave for the spirit to clothe itself after the garments have disappeared in the process of decay. It is customary to place such articles as may be deemed of immediate use for the departed soul in the grave at the time the body is interred. Ammunition, gun, kaiak [canoe] and its appurtenances, with a shirt, gloves, knife, and a cup from which to drink are usually so deposited. The spirit of the dead man appropriates the spirits of these articles as soon as they decay." It is often said of a lost article that so-and-so (mentioning a dead man's name) has

[77] Schimkjewitch, in Globus, LXXIV, 271-272.
[78] Bishop, Tibetans, 108.   [79] Turner, Samoa, 150-151.
[80] §274, below.

taken it.[81] Here is a direct reference of luck to a ghost. The Iroquois, believing that the ghost hovered near the body, lighted a fire on the grave for the spirit to cook by. If the rites were neglected, the ghosts wandered unhappily; hence the anxiety to recover dead bodies of fellow-tribesmen after a battle. A little hole was left in the grave that the soul might enter; later, holes were left in the coffin.[82] The Tarahumari dead are buried in caves and their souls remain for one year wandering on earth in the shape of animals; "the sorcerers and people who cannot pay the medicine-man always remain so."[83] The functions and power of the medicine-man or shaman should be noted throughout our cases, in anticipation of the special development of that topic.[84] The Botocudos of Brazil keep fires on the grave for some time, to repel hostile ghosts from the dead; and the neighboring Ges dig up the corpse after a year and tell it all that has happened since its death. Then the bones are painted red and buried again in the place of common burial, where later the dead are informed of events by their people.[85] It appears that the burial of the body was regarded by the Guiana Indians not as a convenient method for its final disposal but rather as a means to an end, namely, the cleaning and preservation of the bones. Exhumation was widespread in this region.[86]

The Osmanli Turks left a narrow opening in the grave "that the dead man might breathe out his soul."[87] Patroclus, in a dream, adjures Achilles to hasten his funeral so that he may pass into the spirit-world.[88] In Greece the soul of the unburied became a ghost whose wrath descended upon the land where it was detained against its will, so that hindrance of burial was even worse for the hinderers than for the hindered. It was a punishment for executed criminals to be bereft of funerary rites.[89] In White Russia, for nine days after death, the relatives put bread upon the window-sill, with salt and water, believing that the spirit is for that period on earth and will come to eat and drink every night.[90] In the fall of 1910 Viscount Terauchi, governor-general of Korea, sent to the son of Prince Ito the following telegram: "Make a report on the treaty of annexation of Korea to the spirit of the late prince, your father." Imperial messengers were sent to announce the fact at the tombs of the founders of the Japanese dynasty and of the reigning emperor's father.[91] Princes Ito and Katsura were consulted, at their graves, concerning the Russian-Japanese parley in 1923. The marriage, in 1924, of the Prince Regent was formally announced at the ancestral tombs.[92] In 1922 a pilgrimage was made to the tomb of the Sultan Osman, for consultation concerning a political project, by a parliamentary committee.[93]

The idea of the presence of the dead in the vicinity of the body has taken such hold upon mankind that it is only with the greatest

---

[81] Boas, in PSM, LVII, 629; Turner, in BAE, XI, 193.
[82] Morgan, *League of Iroq.*, 174.
[83] Lumholtz, in *Inter. Cong. Anthrop.*, Chicago, 1893, 112.
[84] §§312, 313, below.
[85] Von Martius, *Beiträge*, I, 327, 291. [86] Roth, in BAE, XXXVIII, 640.
[87] Pischon, *Islam*, 50. [88] Homer, *Iliad*, XXIII, 71 ff.
[89] Rohde, *Psyche*, I, 36, 217-218. [90] *Russian Ethnog.* (Russ.), I, 112.
[91] Assoc. Press despatch, Sept. 16, 1910; N. Y. *Times*, Aug. 5, 1923.
[92] N. Y. *Times*, Mar. 1, 1924. [93] N. Y. *Times*, Oct. 9, 1922.

difficulty shaken off. It persists, even in enlightened minds, in the form of vague fears, uneasiness, and distress; few persons, however emancipated, would care to pass a dark and stormy night in the receiving-vault of a cemetery. There exists latent in nearly all of us the fear that has remained a tradition through the successive stages of societal evolution. It cannot be explained or rationalized away; at a pinch it springs to life; for it is firmly rooted in the deepest-lying strata of the mores. The conception of the ghost, or disembodied soul, is one of the basic notions—best illustrated, perhaps, in actual mortuary practices—in the mental outfit of the race.

§219*. Disposition of the Ghost. It can be seen from the cases reviewed that peoples who believe in the ghost-theory were very anxious to bring the period of the ghost's sojourn near the body to a happy conclusion; while they wished to meet all the needs and desires of the sojourner up to the time of his departure, they did not want leave-taking to be delayed. The period was one of suspense and they speeded the parting guest. The reason for this attitude lay in their fear, for the ghost was likely to do damage, even unintentionally; and then the typical ghost was nervous, irritable, jealous of its rights, easy to offend, and swift and terrible in retribution. Some have seen in the malignancy of the ghosts evidence for the essential evilmindedness of the savage;[94] whereas it is the ills of life, rather than the disposition of men, that are responsible for the ghostly temperament. With some exceptions, presently to be noted, the ghost was intensely feared; it was only later, after the correct performance of all the mortuary and funerary rites, that it might become a beneficent and protecting daimon. Its proximity was something to be apprehensive about because of its disposition; for even though it might be well-disposed if once assured of all its "rights," no one could be certain that he had attended to or, indeed, knew all these rights. The test of duty performed was subsequent absence of ill fortune and there was always enough of the latter, in serious or petty form, to allow of inference as to the capricious and unpredictable mood of

[94] Lippert, *Kgchte.*, I, 109.

the deceased. In short, the presence of the ghost was dangerous in itself and was generally doubly so by reason of its suspicious and generally detestable disposition.

The Australian name "ulthana" is given to a spirit up to the time of a certain ceremony after which it ceases to haunt the camp and burial-ground regularly. The ulthana "is supposed to be capable, like other spirits, of hurting its enemies, and the sure sign of an attack by one of them is the presence of human teeth in the body of the victim. Medicine men will sometimes extract these."[95] "Generally it is to the ghosts of the dead that sickness is ascribed" in Melanesia, and they inflict this "not only because some offence, such as a trespass, has been committed against them, or because one familiar with them has sought their aid with sacrifice and spells, but because there is a certain malignity in the feeling of all ghosts towards the living, who offend them by being alive. All human powers which are not merely bodily are believed to be enhanced by death; the ghost therefore of an ill-conditioned powerful man is naturally thought ready to use his increased powers of mischief."[96] In Fiji there is a ridge or dyke thirty to forty feet high and fifty miles long by which the departing souls reached the jumping-off place; tradition reports that it was built to speed the departure of the ghosts who while they stayed around did mischief.[97] In the New Hebrides there is great dread of the "temes" (the term is the third person singular of the verb "to die"); such beings prowl around frightening men. They appear in dreams to their protégés and predict things.[98] In the Solomon Islands the reflection-soul is evil and the shadow-soul good; the latter goes at death to live with the good spirit, while the former "remains on earth, and lives principally in the bush, where it will fall upon anyone venturing near it, and kill him if it can. It also comes in the form of a ghost, to frighten people at night. . . . After a period of years, this 'spirit' gradually fades away and eventually dies altogether."[99] The soul has "the task of doing as much evil as possible to men, even to its own bereaved ones, unless it gets agreeable gifts to move it to omit the practice of mischief."[100] Its evil influence, exerted at night in the home-village "constitutes a perennial care in the life of the Papuan." The ghosts "play all sorts of pranks" unless carefully fed and otherwise attended to.[101]

Says Dornan[102] of certain Bushmen: "I am of the opinion that their conception of Spirit is on the whole one of a malevolent tendency." Again, on the west coast of Africa, the ghost "will, it is generally believed, do no injury to his relations, unless want of respect has been shown by not properly carrying out the funeral obsequies; hence the people like to think of the *sisa* of their deceased relatives as sitting in the house with them, and being provided for, instead of wandering to and fro outside."[103] It is likely to be the abnormal events that are accredited to souls of men recently dead. "A few hours after the death of a young man whom I knew, a furious storm broke on the town,

[95] Spencer and Gillen, *Nat. Tr. Cent. Aust.*, 515.

[96] Codrington, *Melanesians*, 194.   [97] Thomson, in PSM, XLVII, 671.

[98] Leggatt, in AAAS, 1892, 701.   [99] Somerville, in JAI, XXVI, 383.

[100] Von Pfeil, *Südsee*, 144.   [101] Krieger, *Neu-Guinea*, 182.

[102] In JAI, XLVII, 52.

[103] Frobenius, *Masken*, 162; Ellis, *Tshi*, 150.

blowing down plantain trees and working great havoc in the farms. It was stated in all seriousness by the old folk that the storm had been sent by the spirit of Mopembe—the lad's name."[104]

In Farther India, among the Palaungs, "the *kar-bu,* now a disembodied spirit, is terribly lonely; it cannot make any of its human friends hear it; it remembers everything in the past life of the body that it has just quitted; it tries to return to the house and the people that it has loved. To other spirits it appears a shadowy thing, like and yet unlike the body that it last inhabited. I remember that a Palaung girl once looked curiously at a long white glove that I had taken off, then she shuddered and said, 'I do not like it, it is like the *kar-bu* of a hand.' . . . A *kar-bu* then is a kind of ghost of the person, long, shadowy, and capable of such attenuation that it can pass through the smallest crack or hole."[105] The loneliness and the desire to attach itself to the living, together with the powers it has of slinking into the house, make the ghost, whatever its former relations to the survivors, an object of terror and one to which all manner of ill fortune is readily ascribed. Perhaps the pains taken to render a ghost propitious may suggest what is normally to be expected. Wilken[106] relates how Malay priests get hold of an orphan boy of eight to ten years of age, bury him to his neck in the ground, and stuff into his mouth a mixture of ginger, Spanish pepper, and salt. Since they give him no water, he falls into such a state that it is easy to elicit from him a promise that if they will release him at once from his torture he will serve the villagers, after his death, as a champion. When they get the promise they immediately kill him by pouring melted lead down his throat. This author makes a good deal also of the disposition of the woman who has died in childbed.[107] She becomes a sort of vampire. The lot of a woman who has died unmarried is bad enough; she has no rest but changes into an evil spirit that envies the living the enjoyment of what she has lost. Reference is made to Goethe's ballad on the Corinthian bride. Further, those who are married but have no children are in something the same situation. But the woman who has died in childbirth, who has, so to speak, been robbed of her joy just as she was about to taste it, is particularly malignant, especially to expectant and bearing mothers. She becomes a flying demon, and all sorts of practices are employed to prevent the harm she may do: glass beads are put into her mouth, a hen's egg under each arm-pit, and needles in each palm; thus she cannot open her mouth to shriek, wave her arms as wings, or open and shut her hands to assist in flight. Such ghosts are hostile to men as well as to women, and people seek to avoid disturbing them in their common resort, under the kapok-tree. If one of them gets into a pregnant woman, the latter loses her mind; hence many precautions, such as closing up the birth-room, which is a pest-house of heat and stench, conveying the pregnant woman into another house secretly, and the display of exorcising media.

Among the Sioux, "some ghosts are beneficent, but most of them are maleficent. They know all things, even the thoughts of living people."[108] The Pima "say at the grave: 'We put you here. Go to your home in the East. Do not come back.' Ghosts are uncanny things to have about and are liable to touch sleeping persons, this meaning that the one touched must accompany the visitor back to

104 Weeks, in JAI, XL, 373.

105 Milne, *Eastern Clan,* 337.

106 In VG, III, 142-143, note, 224-230.

107 §406, below.

108 Dorsey, in BAE, XI, 489.

the land of the shades."[109] "To use any clothing that belonged to a dead person would be speedy death."[110] The Navaho seem to have no ghost-doctrine, but they intensely dread all contact with corpses.[111] Naturally the revengeful soul of a slain enemy is especially to be feared; to quiet such a spirit resort is taken to all kinds of devices. "Every death that takes place within the family of the slayer during the time following the killing of the enemy is set down to the secret operation of the revengeful spirit. At a feast where I was present the slayer told me that within his family seven persons had died of mysterious diseases or through accidents during the two years which had elapsed since he had killed his enemy." The spirit of the said enemy was therefore considered to have been a particularly bad one.[112] The Fuegian word for ghost is also an adjective signifying frightful, dreadful, awful.[113]

Under advancing culture such views may suffer change. In Japan, "the belief that the dead need affection, that to neglect them is a cruelty, that their happiness depends upon duty, is a belief that has almost cast out the primitive fear of their displeasure. . . . They require nourishment; but the vapour of food contents them. They are exacting only as regards the daily fulfilment of duty. . . . To forget or neglect them, to treat them with rude indifference, is the proof of an evil heart; to cause them shame by ill-conduct, to disgrace their name by bad actions, is the supreme crime. They represent the moral experience of the race; whosoever denies that experience denies them also, and falls to the level of the beast, or below it."[114] This is a highly refined phase of ghost-belief and exhibits clearly the sanction of religion over the mores.

The cases evidently predominate in which there is revealed a lively fear of the ghost and of the ill which its presence is likely to cause. For primitives authority comes out of the other world; and submission to it is the mark of the right-minded and moral man.

§220*. Life in the Other World. The ghost is the soul that has been freed by death from the body. More exactly, it is that soul during its existence subsequent to death and prior to its departure to the spirit-world. But distinctions of this sort are misleading if one tries to carry them out logically to conclusion, for they find no lodgment in the primitive mind. The inconsistency of the savages allows of a simultaneous belief in the re-birth of every departed soul and in the fact that the spirit-world is always, and pretty densely, populated.[115] Practically, a ghost is the soul of some particular dead man; when it cannot or can no longer be

[109] Russell, in BAE, XXVI, 194.
[110] Willoughby, in *Smithson. Rep.*, 1886, pt. I, 277.
[111] Yarrow, in BAE, I, 123.
[112] Karsten, "Jibaro," in BAE, Bull. LXXIX, 41.
[113] Bridges, in *Voice for S. Amer.*, XIII, 201.
[114] Hearn, *Japan*, 52, 53, 54.   [115] Ellis, *Yoruba*, 129.

identified as such, it is a daimon. The other world is full of the souls of particular individuals who have died more or less recently. These are included under the ghost or eidolon category; they may, in fact, return as "revenants" to earth and harry the living just as do the ghosts which are not as yet "laid." Eidolism includes, therefore, theories about the nature of the other world and of life in it.

The next life is regarded in two ways: it is realistic, a replica of this life; or it is, less commonly, idealized to some degree, as happier and higher. Life in the "happy hunting-grounds" is ordinary human life minus its ill fortunes, that is, minus the aleatory element in its unpleasant aspect. The idea of heaven and hell, of reward and retribution, is conspicuously absent on the primitive stage; in general, people go on in the next life where they left off in this. Whatever the local variations in the conception of the other world, it is characteristically like this world, life in it is like life here, and it is, above all, absolutely actual. The dead are oriented, or "aimed," in the definite, proper direction. Many believers in their own heavenly destiny, for which they assert that they yearn, are in no hurry to realize it; the savage, on the contrary, will coolly lay his plans to get to the spirit-world.[116] He knows it is; he knows where it is and what it is; he knows how to get there; he wants to go; he goes. "Palaungs speak of their dead friends and kinsfolk in the same tone of voice that they used when they were alive. There is no melancholy lowering of the voice and no speaking of the dead as 'My poor husband,' or 'My poor friend.' To pity any one who has died would be an insult, a suggestion that in some way he was suffering for his sins. If a dead person has led a good life, there is no reason to deplore his death. He will be much missed by his father and mother, his wife and child, but they all believe that he will probably begin his next life under better conditions than before, so that to pity him would be wrong."[117]

---

[116] Vierkandt, *Entstehungsgrde.*, 153; on the location of the spirit-world see Spencer, *Prin. Soc.*, I, ch. XV; Tylor, *Prim. Cult.*, II, 44 ff.; Lippert, *Kgchte.*, I, 122 ff.; Wilken, in VG, III, 49 ff.; Perry, "Orientation of the Dead," in JAI, XLIV, 281 ff.

[117] Milne, *Eastern Clan*, 301.

The fact that life beyond death is conceived of in terms of life
before death is determinative of the forms of the ghost-cult or
cultus of the dead and so of its derivatives; the details of the cult
vividly reflect that conception.

The Trobriand Islanders believed that the soul "settled to his new life in
the nether world, more or less comforted concerning those left behind; having,
very likely, married again and formed ties and connections. If the man dies
young, his *baloma* is also young; but with time he will age, and finally his life
in Tuma will also come to an end. If the man was old at his death, his *baloma*
is old, and after a period his life in Tuma will also cease."[118] In the New
Hebrides, after the corpse is washed, anointed, and dressed, friends may come
and put presents of cloth on it. These are for their deceased friends to whom
he is going. All who choose may tie pig-ropes to his fingers, each of which
represents a pig to be killed whose shade will go with him.[119] A Bali chief
used to open the grave of his father to share with him the gifts of the
whites.[120] These same Bali wish to arrive in the future life whole and not
disfigured. If killed their heads will be cut off and the mouth slit for convenient carrying. They therefore leave a lock of hair on the crowns of their
shaven heads by which the trophy can be conveniently carried.[121] In Togo the
dead man is provided with a heavy knife for defense against the evil spirits
and for killing his murderer; he also gets some cowrie-shells with which "to
buy food and palm-wine on the way and to pay the passage-money."[122]

"Among the Tschwi the slaves and women killed are to form for the dead
a retinue and riches wherewith to start life in Srahmandazi where there are
markets and towns and all things as on this earth."[123] An Associated Press
despatch[124] tells how the king of Dahomi, after informing his widowed mother
of his intention to submit to the French, said he must first explain to his
father and wished her to bear the message. She was thereupon beheaded.
The coin placed in the mouth of the dead man by the southern Chinese was to
bribe the inferior officials in the realm of the dead.[125] The Santals believe
there will be nothing but hard work in the next life. "They will have but one
chance of getting a rest—that is, the men, if they can chew tobacco, can sometimes beg for a few minutes' respite under the excuse of preparing the tobacco. When the taskmaster calls them to return to their work, they say,
'Wait a moment, Sir, I have not quite finished preparing my tobacco.' Then
they make a pretence of rubbing it to a powder . . . as vigorously as possible, but as soon as the taskmaster turns his back they will again prepare
it very slowly. . . . But woe to those who cannot chew tobacco or smoke the
hukah! For this reason every Santal makes a point of learning the practice in
this world. Women who have children can also obtain a little rest under the
plea of feeding them. When told to return to work, they say—'Oh! wait a few
minutes longer, Sir, my child is very hungry,' while really the child is but
nestling in her bosom. But sad is the lot of poor women who have no fam-

[118] Malinowski, in JAI, XLVI, 402.   [119] Macdonald, in AAAS, 1892, 727.
[120] Hutter, in *Globus*, LXXVI, 307.   [121] Schmidt, *Deut. Kol.*, II, 33.
[122] Seidel, in *Globus*, LXXII, 41.   [123] Kingsley, *Travels W. Afr.*, 491.
[124] March 7, 1894.   [125] Rehatsek, in JASB, I, 306.

ily."[126] One can readily divine from such evidence the close interrelations of religion with both self-perpetuation and self-gratification.

Whether a man has been honest or dishonest in this world is of no consequence in the next; but if he has slain many people here he has many slaves to serve him there. If he has killed many wild beasts he will start well-supplied with food, for all that he lays low on earth are his in the future life. Many believe that the slain becomes the slave of the slayer in the next world, even though his death be avenged. Should the slayer himself be killed, then the first to die is the slave of the second slain, who in turn is the slave of the man who killed him.[127]

At a funeral, among certain Siberian tribes, the hope is expressed that the deceased, if unmarried, will have a happy marriage in the other world.[128] In southern India, in the case of grown-up boys and girls who die before marriage, a form of union of the dead is celebrated. The spirit of the boy takes possession of one of his relatives and suggests the marriage. The relatives seek the parents of a girl who is in a like plight. Then two clay or rice-flour figures are made and the wedding-ceremony performed as in the case of living persons.[129] The parents are then related as if their living children had married. In south China a mark is tattooed upon a young wife's face so that she may be recognized by the ancestors, after death, as belonging to their family.[130]

The tribes of the Altai Mountains say: "In the other world we shall live just as we do here; we shall sow grain, tend cattle, drink wine, and eat beef. Only there we shall live very much more richly because there we shall have not only all the cattle which we had on earth, but also those which perish."[131] "A dead person has to traverse difficult paths before reaching the other world; he has also to pass through the country of dogs, and a man who has ill-treated these animals will be severely injured by them. His dead relatives will assist him in finding the way, and he must not take with him any stolen article in case the rightful owner should meet him. In the other world the sacrificed animals form large herds belonging to the dead."[132] To be noted here is the persistence of property and its recognition beyond the grave. The foresight of the Lapps "is carried even beyond the grave, and it is no uncommon practice to bury or hide away money and other treasure for use, not only in this, but also in after life. A Mountain Lapp, once asked why he had disposed of his money in this way, instead of investing it or putting it out to interest, replied: 'To prevent it from falling into other hands after my death; for in that case what would I have to live upon in the other world?' "[133] Among the Borneans the distinction of classes remains in the life after death. He who was rich, honored, and powerful on this earth remains so, the slave is still a slave, and the poor have their subordinate position. But all in their degree enjoy superfluity of satisfactions.[134]

[126] Basu, in JASB, II, 565.

[127] Carey and Tuck, *Chin Hills,* I, 196.

[128] Michailovski, *Shamanism* (Russ.), 14.

[129] Thurston, *S. India,* 347.   [130] Andree, *Eth. Parallelen,* 79.

[131] Michailovski, *Shamanism* (Russ.), 9.

[132] Czaplicka, *Aborig. Siberia,* 148-149.

[133] Keane, in JAI, XV, 229.   [134] Schwaner, *Borneo,* I, 183.

In China, "sometimes friends and neighbors of the deceased embrace the opportunity of sending to their relatives and friends in the world of spirits boxes or trunks of clothing and money by the politeness of the individual for whose special benefit the funeral ceremonies are designed. As the living take advantage often of a neighbor or a relative who intends to travel for health, or pleasure, or business, to send to distant friends parcels of value, so the Chinese have invented the happy expedient of sending to their deceased dear ones, by the care of the dead, money and clothing. . . . It is believed that the dead man will deliver to its real owners the valuable property intrusted to his care immediately on its reaching its destination."[135]

In general, the mores of a time or place, whether life is primitive or not, appear reflected in the conception of the future life. The projectivism of the Middle Ages, for instance, was pessimistic and crushing, holding out no hope for any but nobles and ecclesiastics. Then came the Renaissance, Protestantism, adventure, the enfranchising discoveries of new lands and fresh chances, and the conception of the next life changed. It became optimistic and hopeful. Later centuries have seen it grow less material, though plenty of survivals occur. A contributor to a local newspaper[136] wants to prove that the risen Christ was not a "spiritual body," and, after citing his request for food and his eating of fish and honey, concludes triumphantly: "Tell me, do spirits eat?" The refinement of idealization no longer concerns itself with superfluity of food, or infinite leisure, or golden streets and crystal battlements, or harps and crowns. Calvinistic sermons, picturing the joys of heaven and, with still greater relish, the terrors of hell, are anachronistic; they do not elate or scare anybody. Nevertheless, whatever there is now of spirituality of conception rose by the refinement of primitive projectivism and not otherwise. As the extension of knowledge moved the spirit-world away from the immediate vicinity or the next island,[137] so has it caused men's minds to relax their preoccupation with the material in favor of the spiritual.

This belief in a future life, which is characteristic of mankind, no matter what stage of civilization is considered, is to be sharply distinguished from convictions about "immortality." The latter is a conception quite foreign to the unspeculative mind. To expect the savage to harbor it would be like counting upon a child to

135 Doolittle, *Chinese*, I, 193, quoted by Wilken, in VG, III, 121, note.
136 New Haven (Ct.) *Journal-Courier*, Dec. 7, 1916.
137 Wilken, in VG, III, 49.

understand infinity. Savages who cannot reckon above ten or twenty are not very likely to have a conception of an infinity of time.

Tylor[138] has a number of illustrations of this incapacity. Consider the Indians who call anything above twenty "much," or every higher number "plenty"; who seize a handful of hair to indicate "many cottages," or pick up a quantity of sand to signify tremendous numbers, such as fifty.[139] Of the Nyassa natives we are told that "an idea of their intellectual capacity may be formed from the fact that in a gang who worked on my plantation some four years ago the best counter owed his superiority to the size of his mouth, in which he found room to stow the ends of all his fingers one by one, counting up to ten as he did so. At this point—his fingers being all disposed of and his toes not available—he broke down. He could get as far as ten but no further, and the moment he withdrew his fingers from his mouth his mind became a blank again. However, as no other member of the gang could get as far as ten, his erudition was thought remarkable."[140] Consider the Malay chief who, being asked how old he was, answered, though he was a great-great-grandfather: "More than ten years old."[141]

It is doubtful whether anybody ever had an apprehension of life without end or anything else without end, for human beings have to think in terms of experience and that always presents matters as ending: pleasure, pain, life itself. The only way to conceive of endlessness is by imagining the opposite of all human experience—something which primitive man, at any rate, has no occasion to do. The idea of immortality has much to do with the aleatory element, in that the ills of this life are conceived to be balanced up in the next; it also reflects the conception of the relation between goodness and happiness. Such notions of balancement, reward, retribution—in fact, theorizing in general about the future life beyond mere projectivism—can find no place in the childlike mind. When it is reported that such and such a people believes in immortality, the recounter is merely deceiving himself and his readers by confusing the general belief in a future life with something else completely beyond the scope of the savage. Upon examination it will be seen that there is a "second death," even for the daimons themselves, which marks the limit of human memory. Important men are remembered awhile and may be deified and worshipped for a

138 *Prim. Cult.*, I, 240 ff.
139 Roth, in BAE, XXXVIII, 939, 940.
140 Moggridge, in JAI, XXXII, 469.
141 Skeat and Blagden, *Malay Penin.*, I, 535.

long time; the insignificant are forgotten at once. There is no "immortality" at all except in the sense of recurring reincarnation. This case is but one of a number where it is possible to arrive at totally erroneous notions by reading into the savage mind what could not under any circumstances find lodgment in it; indeed, the present instance is an aggravated one, for it is quite permissible to doubt whether the one who does the reading in has himself any realization of what immortality means. Then his misuse of the term in respect to a savage people amounts really to the misuse which he is constantly making of it in respect to himself.

The doctrine about ghosts, or eidolism, is now before us in its main outlines; out of it arises a set of expedients or an art for dealing with the ghosts which may be called the ghost-cult. The word "cult," as used in this book, means the sum of religious exercises, including, at its widest, sacrifice, prayer, praise, and ritual performances of all varieties. The cult, appearing in its simplest form in connection with the ghosts, becomes gradually more comprehensive and complicated as the ghosts develop into daimons and gods. Despite this fact, the general lines upon which the ghost-cult is laid down are not materially changed thereafter, through a long and varied series of evolutionary forms. A degree of attention is here accorded to the ghost-cult which is believed to be proportionate to its significance as a disclosing prototype. There is little in evolved religions that does not go back to animism and eidolism and to their applications in the ghost-cult; and there is much in the developed and complex faiths which cannot be understood at all without the knowledge of its simple origins in primitive beliefs and practices.

CHAPTER XXV

THE GHOST-CULT
(NEGATIVE ASPECTS)

§221. Forms of the Ghost-Cult. The common conviction that the ghost is a source of danger reflects preoccupation with the negative aspect of the aleatory element,[1] that is, with bad luck. And since the primitive mode was not speculation but action, men are found anxiously endeavoring to do concrete things by way of meeting a threatening situation.[2] They are developing a set of acts and observances of a religious nature or, in short, a cult, which is in the main a calculus of ill fortune. It is from anxiety and fear that the cult of the dead derives its reason for existence; the phenomena of the ghost-cult could hardly have resulted from the conception of beneficent superhuman powers. No other impulse than fear could have so powerfully stimulated the mind of savage man with the result of evoking such far-reaching reactions. The cult itself witnesses to concern over bad luck and hostile spirits; for its simplest forms are all negative, that is, they contemplate avoidance, expulsion, and coercion of the ghosts rather than propitiation, conciliation, and attraction; and where the latter methods do appear they are employed with the idea of avoiding ill rather than of getting good. It is only with a later and evolved theory of the nature of the higher powers that the aim of religious observances shifts somewhat away from the mere evasion of ill and they become of a more nearly positive type.

"To realise how native custom and religion are inter-related, we have only to examine the ceremonies which take place at the principal events of natives' existence, and, indeed, the fear of the wrath of the *mipashi* souls of the dead looms large even in the most minute details of the village social life."[3]

The ghost-cult represents insurance against disaster rather than investment in view of a higher return. It implies foresight; not good fortune, however, but mischance it is that has always

[1] §§194-196, above.　　　　　　　　[2] Lippert, *Kgchte.*, I, 29-30.
[3] Sheane, in JAI, XXXVI, 155.

taught and is still teaching this eminent quality—than which no other is more obviously an appanage and a measure of advancing culture.[4] The ghost-cult is a transitional form and is, in the evolutionary perspective, transitory; for the ghost becomes a spirit of a higher potency and then the ghost-cult passes into the worship of a god. The earlier form is always merging into the later; the later, in turn, is built upon the earlier and carries forward its underlying ideas and methods. Here and now we are concerned only with the ghost-cult. It is the form of religion by which the race has been characterized throughout by far the greater part of its history. Some may object to the use of the term "religion" in connection with crude views about the supernatural and practices based upon them, and may wish to dismiss the whole combination as "superstition";[5] we dissent from such views and hesitate as little to apply "religion" to eidolism and the ghost-cult as to use "trade" to cover primitive barter or "government" to include the rule of an African chief. "The two essentials of religion," says Turner,[6] are "something to be believed and something to be done."

Since the fact that life beyond death is conceived of in terms of life before death is determinative of the forms of the ghost-cult and its derivatives, the cult becomes a replica of human relations, with this one qualification that men always stand to the ghosts as the weak to the powerful. The telling analogy for the treatment of the ghosts by men is the deference accorded to chiefs and medicine-men by their lowly inferiors, especially if such dominating personages are irascible, spiteful, and malignant and let fly, without any sense of discrimination or proportion, at anyone who chances to cross them. In general, the apprehensive inferior seeks to keep out of the way of his oppressor or, where that is impossible, to placate him by catering to his appetites and whims; by fawning upon him vilely, according to our ideas; by ignoble flattery and self-abasement. This is the way men have acted and still do act before their gods; and they began to employ such methods with the ghosts. If the ghost-cult is taken to consist of negative and positive methods, the latter, covering placation, conciliation, and propitiation, are easily understandable by anyone who knows

4 §52, above.　　　　5 §199, above.　　　　6 Samoa, 77.

what bribery means. The former include avoidance in various forms and also methods of offense and defense. Man as man cannot repel or cast out the spirits; but he can avail himself of spiritual powers competent to do that. The cases will illustrate this matter. It is very important always to bear in mind that the cult is characteristically defensive in type. Preoccupation is not nearly so much with the idea of securing good fortune as with that of avoiding ill; placation is generally practised for the sake of anticipating and dodging calamity or even of simply maintaining neutrality or the existing status. Thus the predominant type of the cult is negative rather than positive. In this respect it resembles an allied manifestation, the taboo, which proscribes rather than prescribes.[7] Positive programs of achievement come much later in evolution than negative programs of limitation.

"The uncivilized man never reflects on the course of things so long as it follows its accustomed train. It requires a disturbance of the usual order to put him in the way of seeking out its cause and thus of finding means to set aside the disturbance. . . . This is the reason why we always find among the most backward people, as the rudest germs of religiosity, only disconnected phenomena of fear in the face of separate acts of some ill-disposed intervening power. Hence also the first acts of worship are solely acts of defense. We are therefore justified in regarding an unsystematized ghost-fear as the sole expression of religiosity on that stage. Such may be said to be the opinion, with scarcely an exception, of all the students of uncivilized peoples."[8]

§222*. Avoidance. The first effort is, then, toward the evasion or warding off of ill; and perhaps the simplest act of avoidance is the endeavor to prevent the soul from becoming a ghost at all. It is common enough to call upon the departing soul, adjuring it to return. "Between unconsciousness and death the native makes no distinction, so the soul will sometimes harken to his voice and the dead man return to life."[9]

"Dying, particularly in the Niger Delta, is made very unpleasant. When a person becomes insensible, violent means are resorted to. Pepper is forced up the nose and into the eyes "and other similar acts of stimulation performed; and the whole crowd of friends and relations with whom the stifling hut is tightly packed yell the dying man's name at the top of their voices, in a way that makes them hoarse for days, just as if they were calling to a person lost

---

[7] §268, below.
[8] Lippert, *Kgchte.*, I, 95-96; 110-115; 118-120.
[9] Jenness and Ballentyne, *D'Entrecasteaux*, 110.

in the bush or one struggling and being torn away from them. 'Hi, hi, don't you hear? Come back, come back. See here. This is your place.' "[10] During preparations for the Chinese funeral there are a number of occasions upon which the soul of the deceased is called back and besought to reënter the body.[11] Cases in classical literature of calling on the dead will occur to the reader.

It is, again, the regular custom in primitive religion to avoid what is "unclean," that is, charged with supernatural potency and capable of discharging it upon the unwary in the form of swift calamity. A common belief is that the corpse, as such, is unclean; that contact with it is perilous. Hence the many washings both of the corpse and of those who have handled it. Harm can indeed come from the human body in process of dissolution and from the persons of the sick as well; and uninformed people, chancing to think of that fact, have at once accredited cases of avoidance to an understanding of contagion. It may well be that avoidance-customs have shown survival-value because they have amounted to a sort of quarantine; but if so, the whole process is automatic and unconscious.[12] Death and illness are explained by the doctrines of animism, eidolism, and daimonism, not by the sciences of pathology or bacteriology.

"After the breath is out of the body it must not be brought into contact with human hands nor with the earth."[13] "The idea that the touch of the dead or dying, as well as all else that has to do with death, renders unclean, is found among the Bechuana; and if they have touched a corpse, dug a grave, or even if they are only near relatives of the dead, they subject themselves to certain ablutions, put on new clothes and cut the hair, or cleanse themselves in the smoke of a fire into which magic substances are cast. Even warriors returning from campaign wash themselves and their weapons in solemn fashion."[14] "Natives have a strong repugnance to handling dead bodies, and only near relatives prepare corpses for burial. If a stranger should undertake this kind office in case a person is found dead far from home, the reward to be paid is—according to Zulu law—a cow and a calf, together with a goat, 'for the washing of the hands.' "[15] Contact with a corpse renders the West African unclean, and he must purify himself by washing in water from head to foot; again, those who have touched the corpse and are thus unclean proceed, after the burial, in procession to the nearest well or brook, and sprinkle themselves

[10] Kingsley, *Travels W. Afr.*, 471.
[11] DeGroot, *Relig. Syst.*, I, 243 ff. A chapter is given to this practice.
[12] Keller, *Soc. Evol.*, 93-95.   [13] Smyth, *Vict.*, I, 104.
[14] Fritsch, *Eingeb. S.-Afr.*, 201.
[15] Tyler, in *Ill. Afr.* for Dec., 1895.

with water, which is the ordinary native mode of purification.[16] This use of water for ceremonial cleansing, through thorough bathing or mere sprinkling, should be noted and kept in mind; it will be met with in later connections.[17] In central Africa all fires are extinguished at a death; they are apparently polluted. Fresh fire is generated in the dead man's house and distributed. A strange case is that where friends of the family, who prepare the body for burial, may swear, use obscene language, insult people, commit adultery, or steal. They are practical jokers—funny men.[18] In Madagascar, "no one who has been at a funeral can enter the palace or approach the sovereign unless a month has elapsed, and no corpse is allowed to be buried in the capital city, or to remain in it beyond a very short time. The rough bier on which the body is carried is thrown away in the neighborhood of the grave as polluted; no one would dare to use it even for fire-wood, but it is left to decay with the weather. Besides this, after a funeral the mourners all wash their dress, or at least dip a portion of it in running water, a ceremony which is called àfana, 'freed from,' and is supposed to carry away the uncleanness contracted from contact with or proximity to a corpse."[19]

In Tibet, "no one touches the corpse but the lamas, who assemble in numbers in the case of a rich man. The senior lama offers the first prayer and lifts the lock which all Tibetans wear at the back of the head, in order to liberate the soul which is still clinging to the body."[20] The Eskimo have an intense dread of touching corpses, and clothe the dying and prepare them for burial before they are dead. For the same reason they shrink from lending assistance in case of accident lest they touch the victim after he is dead.[21] They are in such a hurry that there is some possibility of the dying being buried alive.[22] To the Maori "the remains of the dead and of all connected therewith were (and are) highly *tapu*. . . . The association of food, particularly cooked food, with anything *tapu* is most objectionable in Maori eyes. A man who handled the remains of the sacred dead became infected with a particularly powerful form of *tapu*, and could not dare to touch food with his hands until he had been freed from its malign influence." The connection of uncleanness and holiness here appears unmistakable. "Food should not be taken into a sacred house. This belief is strong to-day amongst the Maoris; an illustration of it is the custom, frequently observed, of leaving such articles as pipe and tobacco outside a church before entering. Tobacco is regarded by the Maoris as food; they speak of smoking as '*kai-paipa*,' that is 'eating-pipe.' "[23] The Jibaro warriors of Peru "never touch the manioc with their fingers, like the Jibaros generally do, but they use small wooden pins to eat with. Their hands having been polluted with the blood of their enemies, the food would become impure if they touched it, and they would expose themselves to death. . . . It is not until later, at the general ceremonial purification at home, that the warrior

---

[16] Ellis, *Ewe,* 160; Ellis, *Tshi,* 241; Thomas, in JAI, XLVII, 160 ff., and in JAI, L, 377 ff.

[17] §227, below.

[18] Stannus, in JAI, XL, 315.

[19] Sibree, *Great Afr. Isl.,* 290.

[20] Bishop, *Tibetans,* 106.

[21] Nansen, *Esk. Life,* 137; §265, below.

[22] Fries, *Grönland,* 121.

[23] Cowan, *Maoris,* 115.

himself and his weapons can be washed." During this period of his uncleanness a man must have nothing to do with a woman.[24]

In Japan the grave-diggers and coffin-carriers were outcasts, and were called "not-men."[25] Among the aborigines of the Canary Islands, cleaners of corpses lived isolated and despised. When the body had been thoroughly cleansed and dried, came the actual embalmers, a class not despised.[26] In the Crimea, those who attend to a corpse are unclean till sunset and must purify themselves by a bath.[27] The Parsees were so scrupulous about the handling of the dead that their measures have been taken to indicate a profound knowledge of hygiene and disinfection. All things that have come into contact with dead bodies are cleansed; clothes taken from bodies about to be exposed upon the "towers of silence," are never used but are thrown into a pit. The corpse-bearers may not remove the clothes with their hands, but use metallic hooks and other instruments. The corpse-tenders are provided with separate buildings to stay in; they are not allowed to enter the chief fire-temples until they purify themselves with several washings, while segregated for nine days and nights. In public feasts they cannot eat with the others.[28] In ancient Persia, "immediately after death has supervened, the evil spirit of decay, in the shape of a fly, takes possession of the body, and therewith is the corpse given over to the evil powers and makes unclean everything that touches it." The fire must be removed from the house, and can be brought back only after the interval of a month in summer or of nine days in winter. For three days after one death in the house there is danger of another. For a single individual to carry a corpse would render him unclean forever, even in the beyond. The two carriers do their work entirely unclothed and thereafter subject themselves to a special purification with urine. The author[29] thinks corpse-carriers did not adopt their profession voluntarily but were criminals forced into it. When the Greek, going out of a house of death, sprinkled himself with water from the *ardanion* at the door, it was death that he drove away from himself. "Whenever the corpse passes by, death walks with it; all along the way it has gone, from the house to its last resting-place, a spirit of death is breathing and threatening the living."[30] Even the gods left the house of the dying: Apollo withdraws from the house of Admetus when the death of Alcestis is impending.[31]

If the corpse is thought to be an agency of pollution, and the presence of the departing spirit to be perilous, the abandonment of the dying or the sick-unto-death is a logical procedure. There are also numerous cases of carrying the dying outside the house, lest they expire within. Motives here are mixed, as is often the case: there is a thrifty desire to save the house, which might other-

[24] Karsten, "Jibaro," in BAE, Bull. LXXIX, 34.

[25] Kishimoto, in PSM, XLVI, 212.   [26] Cook, in AA, II, 483.

[27] Weissenberg, in *Globus*, LXXXIV, 143.

[28] Modi, in JASB, II, 419 ff.

[29] Geiger, *Ostiran. Kultur*, 256, 258, 272-273.

[30] Müller, *Sacred Books of East*, IV (Zendavesta), pt. I, lxxxvi-lxxxviii.

[31] Euripides, *Alcestis*, 22-23.

wise have to be abandoned, and there may be some purpose of easing the soul's passing.

The Australians remove the dying and, without regard to the weather, lay him on the grass. When he is dead, the knees of the body are brought quite up to the breast, the elbows over the trunk and near the hips, and the hands raised and pressed against the chest, and in this position the corpse is made fast with cords. A pall of skins has been manipulated meanwhile so as to conceal the body, and the attendants have scrupulously avoided actual contact with the flesh.[32] Among the Zulus "burial was in earlier times only a casting-out into the wilderness and the word used for it signifies also to throw away. Among these tribes there prevails an especial fear of corpses, whose touch is held to bring ill and make unclean; therefore it happened, and still today happens . . . that the unfortunate old man who had protracted his miserable existence to an advanced age, as soon as it appeared that death had sealed him as a sure booty, was seized by the people, dragged away to the nearest ravine, and there left to his fate. They did the same thing with the sick, and it has not seldom come to pass that the supposedly dead person, in spite of his cruel treatment, has returned again to his habitation. . . . Now the custom is ameliorated through European influence but yet they always avoid letting anyone die within the hut, and carry him, before his last breath has escaped, out in front of it so that he may give up his spirit in the open air. As soon as this has taken place, the dead man's wives flee into the neighboring mountains, seeking there under rocks and in the thicket a place of refuge." They reappear only at evening "to get food, and return to their hiding-place either at once or at any rate before the dawn of the next day, until a week or so has passed; then they too [like the burial-attendants], after completion of their ablutions, put on new clothes, cut their hair off, and now may appear again, purified, in the society."[33] As a rule the Matabele "get the dying person out of his house into a small hut to die there."[34] No one whose body swells is allowed to die in the house; sometimes the dying man is carried into an inner room of a house devoted to the purpose and left to "the tender mercies of death."[35]

The Gilyak wife "never dares" to give birth at home; "she must, in spite of severity of season and stormy weather, go out of the hut for this purpose. In late autumn or in winter they build a special hut for the woman, but a very uncomfortable one, so that the mother and the child suffer the cold and feel the wind. . . . The custom of driving the woman out of the house before the delivery recalls another custom, that of carrying dying people out of the house; both practices show that the Gilyak are afraid of the dead body in the house, and a woman in confinement is in grave danger of death."[36] "In order to prevent repeated removal, which must take place at each death, they segregate the sick, when it is clear that the end is near, in a distant spot, so that they can draw their last breath there. This usage is one of the chief reasons

[32] Smyth, *Vict.*, I, 100.

[33] Fritsch, *Eingeb. S.-Afr.*, 116, 117.

[34] Decle, in "Miscellanea," in JAI, XXIII, 85.

[35] Thomas, in JAI, XLVII, 165; Binger, *Du Niger au Golfe de Guinée*, fig. 5.

[36] Czaplicka, *Aborig. Siberia*, 137, 138.

why the Alfurs of Buru, despite all the efforts of the government to unite them in regular communities, still keep on living in such scattered fashion."[37] The Veddahs expose the supposedly dying in ravines; this is from fear lest the soul take up its abode in the hut. The ravine is then figured as the dwelling-place of frightful spirits who eat the dead; but it is rather the starving village-dogs and the jackals who make a prey of the exposed sick.[38] In any case the dying Veddah must not pass away in the house; it would make the house unclean and the soul might stay about and do mischief.[39] In China "a dying person is scarcely ever allowed to remain on his bed till he has expired. Even before matters take this fatal turn, he is transported to a couch of three boards supported by a couple of trestles or benches."[40] In the Canaries, "when sickness or extreme age showed that death was near, the friends were called and the dying man said, 'I wish to die.' The request was religiously observed, and he was carried to a sepulchral cave chosen by himself, laid upon a bed of skins with his head to the north and a vase of milk beside him; then the entrance to the cave was closed and he was left to fight his last battle alone."[41]

Beside these apparently heartless procedures appear a variety of avoidance-customs whose object is the easing of the soul's exit —the speeding of the parting spirit. Though they look less barbarous, they are, in origin at least, dictated by the same self-protective considerations.

The Tibetan lama plucks a few hairs from the crown of the corpse in order to give vent to the spirit through an actual but invisibly minute perforation of the skull thus supposed to be made.[42] In Celebes "when any one lies down in the agony of death, doors and windows are thrown open, and everything in the house that is locked and bolted is unfastened, all to facilitate the departure of the soul."[43] In the Gilbert Islands a way to make smooth the path of the parting soul was to "point" him in the right direction, that is, toward the spirit-world. "The position of the body in the grave was a matter of great moment." Whatever the orientation regarded as correct, it was prescribed and others forbidden, "the belief being that they prevented the soul of the dead from reaching the land of shades, and thus turned it into a lost soul."[44] This orientation of the body in the grave is a tortuous subject, but the general principle behind divergent practice is evident enough. In China, "the most conspicuous intimation to passers-by that some one has died is a sedan-chair of bamboo splints and paper, placed outside the door for the use of the soul." The carrying-poles of the chair rest upon the shoulders of two or four human images, each of whom is regularly refreshed with a tea-cup of cooked rice and a few cakes. Also "a few threaded sheets of mock money are hung round the neck or on the arm of each, every Chinaman knowing by experience that chair-bearers are always strongly opposed to moving when no advance wages have

37 Wilken, in VG, I, 56.   38 Sarasin, *Weddas*, 496-497.
39 Schmidt, *Ceylon*, 258.   40 DeGroot, *Relig. Syst.*, I, 3.
41 Cook, in AA, II, 480.   42 Waddell, *Buddhism*, 488.
43 Van Eck, in *Indische Gids*, 1882, pt. I, 71.
44 Grimble, in JAI, LI, 47; Perry, in JAI, XLIV, 281 ff.; Rose, in JAI, LII, 127 ff.

been paid them."[45] The notion prevailed in Scotland and in many parts of England that the soul of the dying flew out of the mouth in the likeness of a bird; hence the doors must be set open when anyone was dying.[46] "The notion that an aperture is needed for the free passage of a ghost still lingers in the widespread practice among superstitious people in this country, not less than on the Continent, of opening the window of the sick chamber immediately after a death."[47] The Lithuanians make an opening in the roof over a deceased person that his soul may more quickly escape to heaven;[48] elsewhere the window is opened.[49] The Jews of South Russia think that dying on an iron bed prolongs the death-agony and so provide a wooden one. The same is true of cushions of chicken-feathers, in place of which they provide those stuffed with goose-feathers.[50] In the case of the bed, doubtless the older material was the holier.[51] In Sicily "when a person is about to die his friends and relations stand round and actually pray that the flame of life may flicker out before the hour of midnight. They have the greatest abhorrence of the time wearing on, as death in the small hours of the morning displeases the spirits and makes it more difficult for the departed one to get free and soar to heaven."[52] It is clear enough, finally, that the funerary operations, especially cremation, are calculated to free the soul: in death, "no longer do the sinews hold flesh and bone together but these the strong power of blazing fire overcomes . . . and the soul takes flight like a dream."[53]

Flight is a method of avoidance even more obvious than the preceding. Savages often vacate the house of death, leaving it to the ghost for a time or for good and all.[54] This forfeiture of comfort and capital[55] may extend to the abandonment of a village or of a whole region. The loss sustained must not be underestimated because the houses are mere huts or the land but slightly cultivated. It is felt keenly enough, and as soon as people can conceive of methods of saving their property, while avoiding ills of ghostly origin, they hasten to use them.

When an Australian dies, his hut is pulled down and the materials are often burnt. No one will inhabit a place where a death has occurred. This is not alone from fear of the ghost of the deceased; they say they believe that the wild black who has taken the kidney-fat of the deceased, or the spirit who has destroyed him, will wander about the site of the old encampment.[56] When burial has taken place, the man's or woman's camp in which death occurred is at once burnt down, all the contents destroyed—in the case of a woman noth-

[45] DeGroot, *Relig. Syst.*, I, 28, 29.   [46] Gomme, *Village Life*, 70.
[47] Discussion of Buckland, in JAI, XI, 20.
[48] *Russian Ethnog.* (Russ.), I, 176.
[49] Tetzner, in *Globus*, LXXVII, 221.
[50] Weissenberg, in *Globus*, XCI, 359-360.
[51] §324, below.   [52] Alec-Tweedie, *Sunny Sicily*, 15.
[53] Homer, *Odyssey*, XI, 218-222.   [54] §§222, 250, below.
[55] §82, above.   [56] Smyth, *Vict.*, I, xxx, 106.

ing whatever being preserved, and the whole of the local encampment is shifted to a new place. "No camp will be formed close to where a grave has been made for at least two years' time for fear of disturbing the *Ulthana*," or ghost.[57] In the New Hebrides the huts of the dead are left to rot.[58] In the Andaman Islands, even in the case of an infant's death, "all the encampment pack up the utensils most needed and go to some other camping ground, usually two or three miles distant, where they build huts to form shelter during the period of mourning, about three months."[59] The African Bushmen quit the place where anyone has died, turning it into a heap of stones.[60] At the death of a chief, the Herero tribe leaves the region, returning only after a considerable period. The chief's successor then performs sacrifices to conciliate him and the hearth and altar are erected in the old places.[61] Elsewhere in South Africa the house of the dead is burned with all it contains.[62] "The house is closed and abandoned. If the dead man was a chief the whole village is abandoned."[63] In Uganda and elsewhere the house eventually falls to pieces over the grave.[64] In one East African tribe, if an adult dies in a house it is broken down. Formerly the whole village left the region; now they remain. In another tribe, if a male child dies within three days of birth or a female within four, or if a child is still-born, it is buried in the house under the place where the water-bowls stand. With few exceptions all others are buried in the village, not far from the house in which they died. In all cases the corpse and the mourners undergo repeated washings.[65] Again, the house is burned, and also all neighboring ones, for they say: "this is a bad place here."[66] These abandoned huts are often filled with cloth, oil, and other property and sometimes with the strangled wives or slaves of the deceased.[67] Here propitiation is mingled with avoidance. After the death of a Burmese chief, "he was supposed to haunt the place as a powerful spirit, so no one has had the courage to build a house on the spot or make a garden there, as the people fear that he may be as revengeful as a spirit as he was when a Chief."[68]

The Dakotas leave their homes after a death, the dead remaining there for months, while they live in tents near by.[69] "A beneficial custom, which was probably general in former times and is still followed in many localities, is the abandonment or destruction, after the death of an adult person, of the house in which he died, and also the destruction of his clothing and other personal property. Whatever may have been the original reason for this custom, today many of the tribes recognize clearly that the burning of everything with which the deceased came in contact hinders contagion." The author instances the Utes and Navaho.[70] A Navaho would freeze rather than make a fire of the logs of a deserted hut, even though from all appearances it has

[57] Spencer and Gillen, *Nat. Tr. Cent. Aust.*, 498, 499.

[58] Leggatt, in AAAS, 1892, 700.   [59] Man, in JAI, XII, 141.

[60] Ratzel, *Vkde.*, I, 74.   [61] Fritsch, *Eingeb. S.-Afr.*, 236.

[62] Macdonald, in JAI, XIX, 276.

[63] Decle, in "New Books" in JAI, XXIII, 420.

[64] Johnston, *Uganda*, II, 715-716; Thomas, in JAI, XLVII, 179.

[65] Barrett, in JAI, XLI, 23, 34.   [66] Fabry, in *Globus*, XCI, 198.

[67] Burrows, *Pigmies*, 104, 107.   [68] Milne, *Eastern Clan*, 21-22.

[69] Beckwith, in *Smithson. Rep.*, 1886, pt. I, 253.

[70] Hrdlička, in BAE, Bull. XXXIV, 230.

been in that condition for years.[71] If one little stick of wood from such an abandoned hut "is used about a camp fire, as is sometimes done by irreverent whites, not an Indian will approach the fire; and not even under the greatest necessity would they partake of the food prepared by its aid. . . . When a person is about to die in one of the stone or log houses . . . he is carried outside and allowed to die in the open air. The house is thus preserved."[72] In Central and South America the Mayas, Paressi, Coroados, Botocudo, Lenguas of Paraguay, and others follow the same plan of abandonment of house or region.[73] Frazer[74] has collected a number of instances.

§223*. Precautions against Return. It has been seen that some peoples try to minimize the losses consequent upon wholesale abandonment by carrying the dying out of the house. There are also precautions of one kind and another, which are starkly enough self-protective, to prevent the tarrying or the return of the ghost. Among these are the "doors of the dead." It is very significant that the whole Chukchi family removes its tent "if the corpse was carried out . . . through the usual entrance."[75]

"A ghost can only find his way back to the house by the way by which he left it. Hence our ancestors carried the corpse out by a hole made in the wall, and this hole was carefully stopped up as soon as the body had passed through. The credit of this device is shared by Greenlanders, Norsemen, Hottentots, Bechuanas, Samoeids, Ojibways, Algonkins, Laosians, Hindus, Tibetans, Siamese, Chinese, Balinese, and Fijians. These 'doors of the dead,' as they are called, are still to be seen in a village near Amsterdam, and they were common in some towns of Central Italy, e.g., Perugia and Assisi."[76] The idea is simple enough, though the inconsistency involved respecting the imbecility of the ghost is apparent. A pair of concrete illustrations follow. The Hottentots take the corpse out backwards through the opening, so that the unclean thing shall not pollute the cattle-kraal; and the Bechuana try to get the body out before the last breath is drawn, and break the wall to do so.[77] Among the Ibo, a piece of wall is knocked out when a man's body is removed, while a woman's body is not carried out by the door but hoisted over the back wall. Rites are always less complex for women.[78] A rather comprehensive case of avoidance may be cited in this connection. "Among the Chukchee the whole of the funeral rites are a series of protective magical ceremonies against the evil influences of the dead. Though the latter are sometimes benevolent, the idea that they

[71] Yarrow, in BAE, I, 123.

[72] Mindeleff, in BAE, XVII, pt. II, 487.

[73] LePlongeon, in PSM, XLIV, 668; Von den Steinen, *Zent. Bras.*, 434; Spix and Martius, *Brazil*, II, 250; Wied, *Brasilien*, II, 56; Koch, in *Globus*, LXXVIII, 220.

[74] In JAI, XV, 75, note.   [75] Czaplicka, *Aborig. Siberia*, 148.

[76] Frazer, in JAI, XV, 69.

[77] Fritsch, *Eingeb. S.-Afr.*, 335; Ratzel, *Vkde.*, I, 105, 210.

[78] Thomas, in JAI, XLVII, 164, 171, 177, 184.

work harm to the living is much more prevalent. The most dangerous are the double dead, the completely dead. They are beyond being reborn into this world, and hence they become evil spirits in the other world. . . . For three days after the death no drum is beaten, and noisy domestic work by the women, such as the scraping of pans, ceases. . . . The body is usually drawn up through a hole in the roof, or in the back of the tent, and then all traces of the passage are removed to prevent the possible return of the dead. . . . On the return journey [from the burial] the people change their order of progress and perform many protective incantations, e.g., 'the fortifier' throws behind him a few small stones which shall turn into mountains. The funeral train are received on their return by the two oldest women of the place, who meet them with charms."[79] Of the removal of a corpse in Alaska it is reported: "When all was ready four men took hold of the corners of the blanket, which had been placed on the floor under the corpse, and carried all to the window, resting it on the window-sill, where it was held by four women, while the men went out through the door and again took hold outside of the window. . . . Under no circumstances will the Indians take a corpse out through the door; if there is no window, they will make a hole in the side of the house or take it out through the smoke-hole in the roof."[80] In his *Roman Questions* Plutarch says: "When a man who has been falsely reported to have died abroad, returns home alive, why is he not admitted at the door, but gets up on the tiles and so lets himself down into the house?"[81]

To these instances of the "doors of the dead" may be added here a few miscellaneous precautions of a similarly concrete character against ghostly influence. In West Africa, the bedstead in the house of mourning must be constantly occupied, even during the daytime, by some persons sitting there, lest the spirit come to take any vacant space; and the house itself must not, by day or night, be without some occupant. The near relatives, when one has occasion to go out of that house, must not go unaccompanied, lest the spirit follow them and attempt to resume earthly companionship and thus injure them."[82] This precaution against being led away by the ghost is common. A striking case of the severing of ties is shown by the Palaungs: "If a girl dies who was engaged to be married, the person she was betrothed to now breaks off the engagement. . . . Those who love each other hope to meet and become betrothed again and marry in a future existence, but they do not wish to be haunted in the present life by the ghost of the dead sweetheart. . . . If this is not done, the ghost may afterwards—it may be years afterwards—object to the lover who is yet alive paying attention to any one else."[83] "The Iroquois invariably, in former years, and still to a certain extent, perforated the soles of the baby's moccasins to prevent the ghosts from coaxing away its soul; for the child can refuse to listen to their pleadings on the ground that he has holes in the soles of his moccasins and so cannot travel the spirit trail."[84] The Lithuanians hasten to close the eyes of the dead that he may not tempt others to follow him.[85] In the Crimea, "during the agony everything eatable is removed from the deathchamber, all the cupboards in it and in neighboring

[79] Czaplicka, *Aborig. Siberia*, 146-148.
[80] Niblack, in USNM, 1888, 359.
[81] Frazer, in JAI, XV, 64.
[82] Nassau, *Fetichism*, 220.
[83] Milne, *Eastern Clan*, 293.
[84] Harrington, in AA, X, 412.
[85] *Russian Ethnog.* (Russ.), I, 176.

rooms are closed."[86] As soon as the pulse ceases to beat, the Bulgarians turn all the dishes in the house upside down in order that the soul going out from the body may not hide in them. In Wendland they carry lights into every corner, and the clock is stopped. When the coffin is carried out, they throw over the benches on which it stood and put out the lights. The straw under the coffin is thrown away; it would make the cattle sick. If the coffin is met by a man, woman, or child, soon after that someone of like age will die.[87]

By most peoples it has been thought safer to observe, in the presence of death, a more or less extended period of silence.[88] The ghost will find silent survivors less readily than noisy ones and it is believed by some also that noise irritates the departed. The time to be quiet is, in general, during the interval prior to the ghost's departure to the spirit-world,[89] and the persons upon whom chiefly silence is enjoined are the relatives of the deceased; it is part of their "mourning."[90]

An extreme case is that of the Australian women. "Until the final mourning ceremonies have been completely enacted—a period which may cover an interval of one or even two years—a strict ban of silence is laid upon those women in camp who stand to the deceased man in one or the other of the following relationships:—wife, mother, sister, daughter, or mother-in-law. . . . When once a man is dead no woman may ever again mention his name, but in the case of the men the restriction is not so absolute."[91] They converse during the silent period by signs and have developed an extensive sign-language.[92] The ban is lifted by the father of the deceased, when he bites the palm of the woman's hand.[93] "As soon as the Congo chief has breathed his last, the cloud of common mourning spreads over the whole land, which is enveloped in the deep quiet of an inviolable law of silence and fasting. . . . Nothing breaks the most undisturbed rest. The domestic animals are shut up in the yards, the negro sits in his hut unwashed and unkempt, and even the fields lie fallow, since no one may cultivate them for the next month."[94] In the East Indies deep quiet must be maintained in the house of the dead. There must be no loud speaking and no holding of markets, but fasting and silence. This lasts for a hundred days in the case of a ruling Buginese or Macassar prince; for others fifty, forty, twenty, and ten days.[95] Again, when the dead man has been buried all slink home in silence.[96]

There is, in the primitive mortuary ceremonies, plenty of opportunity for noise and the Australian case just cited is unusual

[86] Weissenberg, in *Globus,* LXXXIV, 143.
[87] Tetzner, in *Globus,* LXXVII, 221-222.
[88] Clodd, *Magic,* 99 ff. [89] Lippert, *Kgchte.,* II, 238 ff.
[90] §394, below.
[91] Spencer and Gillen, *Nat. Tr. Cent. Aust.,* 525.
[92] Davidson, in *Geog. Jr.,* XXIX, 229.
[93] Mathews, in AA, II, 500. [94] Bastian, *Afr. Reisen,* 163-164.
[95] Wilken, *Vkde.,* 314-315. [96] Lippert, *Kgchte.,* I, 115.

in its rigor; but silence has come to be the traditional attitude in
the presence of the dead. The case is illustrated with especial force
by the widespread taboo laid upon the name of the deceased.[97] The
name has been found to be intimately connected with the personality and soul,[98] and it is believed that the ghost is ready to come
at a summons by name, whether that summons is intended, as in
the custom of calling the ghosts to participate in tribal acquisitions, festivals, and other occasions, or not. To avoid the presence
of the ghost, therefore, it is necessary to refrain from mentioning
his name.[99] Further, the ghost or spirit can be thrown off the
track of a possible victim by manipulation of the latter's name or
complete suppression of it.

"It is not infrequently stated that amongst Australian tribes the name of a
dead person may never be mentioned. In some tribes this may be the case, but
amongst all of those occupying the central and northern central area of the
continent it is not so." It is upon individuals standing in certain relationships
to the deceased that the taboo always rests.[100] "There are various degrees of
silence to be observed by different persons and these are dependent upon the
mutual relationship which existed between the dead and living individual."
For instance, "the men who may lawfully marry a dead man's daughters—
whether they actually do so or not makes no difference—must not only never
mention his name, but they neither attend the actual burial, nor do they take
any part in the subsequent mourning ceremonies which are carried on at the
grave. It is their duty to cut themselves on the shoulder when the man who is
their *Ikuntera* or father-in-law dies."[101] "The deadliest insult that one southern
Papuan can offer another is to speak out the name of his dead relative; even
the slightest allusion to his death is to be avoided, otherwise 'his spirit will
come back.' "[102] The Caroline Islanders are most unwilling to repeat the name
of a dead ancestor—a typical Melanesian trait.[103] "The names of the dead are
held in great reverence, and in some islands they are never mentioned except
under the breath, or in the greatest secrecy.[104] The Bushmen "are very unwilling to speak of death, or of those who have died, and avoid the subject as much
as possible."[105] Among the Ibo silence is maintained, especially by the widow.
They use a circumlocution in referring to the death of a big man: "a stone is
broken."[106] After the death of kings, in Madagascar, "they give them a new
name, by which from that time they are always known, it being considered
as sacrilegious to speak of them by the name by which they were known while

97 Clodd, *Magic,* 121-131.   98 §212, above.
99 §243, below.
100 Spencer and Gillen, *North. Tr. Cent. Aust.,* 526, note.
101 Spencer and Gillen, *Nat. Tr. Cent. Aust.,* 498, 499, 500.
102 Krieger, *Neu-Guinea,* 322.   103 Christian, *Caroline Isl.,* 74-75.
104 Hardy and Elkington, *So. Seas,* 126.
105 Dornan, in JAI, XLVII, 52.
106 Thomas, in JAI, XLVII, 178, 188.

living."[107] A dead Samoyed "is never mentioned by name for fear his spirit might hear it and wish to return."[108]

Connected with such views about the name is the procedure of certain Siberians, who "change a name at once, if they hear that a piece of ill luck has befallen a person of the same name."[109] Among the Saoras, "were anyone to ask those carrying a body to the burning ground the name of the deceased or anything about him, they would be very angry."[110] In Celebes one gets a new name after death.[111] "The Dyaks have a great objection to uttering the name of a dead person, so if the namesake of a child dies, at once a new name is chosen. Again, if a child is liable to frequent attacks of illness, it is no uncommon thing for parents to change the name two or three times in the course of a year. The reason for this is that all sickness and death is supposed to be caused by evil spirits, who are put off the scent by this means. When they come to take the child's soul away, they do not hear his old name uttered any more, and so they conclude he no longer exists, and return without him!"[112] Sacred simplicity of the supernatural powers! Here is yet another of the glaring inconsistencies of primitive thinking.

Connected with the name-taboo is a development in language which has been called "hlonipa" from the African taboo term.[113] The general case will be taken up under another head,[114] but the custom may be illustrated here.

Among the Melanesians of New Guinea the name of a dead man is banished from the language. Thus "many words are permanently lost, or revived with modified or new meanings." It is unfriendly and even an insult to mention the names of the dead before their living relatives. When the name is not that of some common object no difficulty arises but when a person dies who is named after something that is in every day use, a new word has to be found for his name-object. To save trouble, they borrow any English word which they happen to remember. Thus a water-vessel is now called a "Finish" and a large bush-knife, in all innocence, is known as a "Go-to-hell."[115] The Sakai of Malacca believe that trees and especially animals have souls; some of them "think it is unlucky to use the proper name of an animal, when they are eating its flesh, and substitute instead another appellation which is often a periphrasis descriptive of some characteristic of it."[116] The idea here seems to be to avoid recalling the soul of the animal, which might resent what is being done to its body. Of the Angmagsalik it is reported that "by the natives themselves the name Angmagsalik is no longer used, for a man named Angmagsak died, and the heathen do not dare utter a dead man's name. . . . The inhabitants who were formerly called Angmagsalingmiut are now known as Kulusumiut." The

---

[107] Sibree, *Great Afr. Isl.*, 169; Sibree, in JAI, XXI, 229.
[108] Montefiore, in JAI, XXIV, 406.
[109] Schimkjewitch, in *Globus*, LXXIV, 270.
[110] Fawcett, in JASB, I, 248.   [111] Riedel, in *Bijd.*, XXXV, 79.
[112] Gomes, *Sea Dyaks,* 103.
[113] Lippert, *Kgchte.*, I, 115, 158, II, 160, 238; Clodd, *Magic,* 55, 112 ff., 128 ff.
[114] §§268, 315, below.   [115] Seligman, *Melanesians,* 629-630.
[116] Evans, in JAI, XLVIII, 181.

East Greenlanders avoid the name of the dead. If two men have the same name and one dies, the survivor changes his. "If the dead was named after an animal, object, or conception, the word for that animal, object, or conception is changed. Language is thereby subjected to considerable alterations, for these shifts are practised by whole communities. But it may be supposed that the old names appear again when the dead man has been wholly forgotten."[117] The taboo extends to parts of words which have the sound of the dead person's name. Thus "when Queen Pomare of Tahiti died, the word *po* (night) was dropped from the language and *viri* took its place."[118] Among the Kiowas, "the name of the dead is never spoken in the presence of the relatives, and upon the death of any member of the family all the others take new names— a custom noted by Raleigh's colonists on Roanoke Island more than three centuries ago. Moreover, all words suggesting the name of the dead person are dropped from the language for a term of years, and other words, conveying the same idea, are substituted. The same custom exists among the Comanchi and perhaps among other tribes."[119] In British Columbia "the name of the dead person must not be uttered. This is not so much out of regard to the feelings of the surviving relatives, as on account of the mystic connection which is supposed to exist between names and their owners. To utter or use the name of a dead person is to affect and disturb his ghost or spirit, and draw it back to its earthly haunts. This is inimical both to the ghost itself and to the person using the name, and thus attracting ghostly influence. It is, therefore, a thing to be avoided. Hence the taboo. Time is necessary to remove this danger. After a person has been dead a year or more his name can again be used."[120] A curious case is reported from Guiana; the Arawak use different names for certain animals according as they speak of them by day or by night. "Thus, during the working hours a jaguar is aroa, but when darkness sets in it is kabadaro (claws). Similarly, kamudu, a boa constrictor, becomes akkara (a coil); yeshi, an armadillo, is paraphrased into andajika (*anda*, close; *tejika*, ear, i.e., ears close together), and so on. I know of nothing corresponding to this, however, in the case of personal names."[121]

Much confusion for the student of language is here involved. Further taboos on speech are connected with the idea of summoning ill fortune by free use of the name. On the west coast of Africa the death of a king may never be mentioned in plain language; they refer to it in poetical circumlocutions, such as: "The great tree is falling."[122] An Egyptian denominated his death-day: "The day one does not mention."[123] Doubtless the use of the terms "unspeakable," "unutterable," "unnamable," "nameless," as well as various circumlocutions and euphemisms,[124] such as "Eumenides"

---

117 Holm, *Ethnol. Skizze.*, etc., 68-69.
118 Cited by Nansen, *Esk. Life*, 231; see citation *sub* §243, below.
119 Mooney, in BAE, XVII, pt. I, 231.
120 Hill-Tout, in JAI, XXXV, 138.   121 Roth, in BAE, XXXVIII, 676.
122 Ratzel, *Vkde.*, I, 612.   123 Meyer, *Aegypten*, II, 191.
124 Many cases in Clodd, *Magic*, 88 ff.

for "Furies," current in language at all ages, go back to the root-idea of the name-taboo.

To mislead and deceive the ghost, primitive people practise various devices which witness to a naïve confidence in the ghost's stupidity; like the usage of making doors for the dead, such precautions reveal the savage as careless of consistency. Where ordinarily the dead are so oriented as to point them to the original home of the race, undesirable ghosts are pointed the wrong way.[125] In general, the ghost here seems assimilated to the child in the matter of sagacity, though some of the precautionary measures calculated to delude have evidently become merely conventionalized and symbolic.

"Men and women are buried alike, their feet turned inland; the return from the funeral is by another road than that along which the corpse was carried, lest the ghost should follow. . . . The ghost of a *vasisgona*, a woman who has died in childbed, cannot go to Panoi if her child lives, for she cannot leave her child. They therefore deceive her ghost by making up loosely a piece of a banana trunk in leaves, and laying it on her bosom when she is buried. Then, as she departs, she thinks she has the child with her; as she goes the banana stalk slips about in the leaves and she thinks the child is moving; and this in her bewildered new condition contents her, till she gets to Panoi and finds that she has been deceived. In the meanwhile the child has been taken to another house, because they know that the mother will come back to take its soul. She seeks everywhere for the child in grief and rage without ceasing; and the ghost of a *vasisgona* therefore is particularly dreaded."[126] In the Andaman Islands, "none but infants are buried within the encampment, others being carried to some distant and secluded spot in the jungle."[127] The Chukchi of Siberia put the corpse on a sleigh and take it to a distance, on a hill; after some days, when birds have plucked out the eyes, the sleigh is brought back, for then the deceased cannot see who draws the sleigh.[128] The Votyaks, after the corpse is carried out, take the door off its hinges, and sweep off the path, that the ghost may not find the way back. Certain Tatars hang the corpse on a tree, from which they cut off all the branches, that the ghost may not let itself down again to the ground. The Tungus, departing after the burial, cover over their foot-prints with snow or branches, that the deceased may not be able to return to his former abode.[129] In south Cochin China the funeral procession wanders around to mislead the ghost as to the way back.[130]

As the Dyak corpse-carriers descend the ladder with their burden, "ashes from the fire burnt near the corpse are thrown after them by the people who are left in the house. This is done in order that the dead man may not know

[125] Rose, in JAI, LII, 131 ff.
[126] Codrington, *Melanesians*, 254, 275.
[127] Man, in JAI, XII, 144.   [128] Ratzel, *Vkde.*, II, 780.
[129] Michailovski, *Shamanism* (Russ.), 16, 17.
[130] Niemann, in *Bijd.*, 1895, 332.

his way back to the house, and may thus be unable to trouble his friends afterwards."[131] In Timorlaut the head of the dead enemy is cut off, but a coconut is put in its place to cheat and quiet the ghost. The nut is like a rude mask.[132] This practice throws light upon the reason for the corpse-mask. Among certain Brazilian Indians four young people go behind the dead, dragging a palm-leaf, in order to wipe out the foot-prints and make it harder for the deceased to find his way back.[133] In Chile they take the body out feet first, "for if the corpse is removed in another position, his errant ghost might return."[134] The Araucanians of Chile strew ashes along the way "that the spirit may not return to trouble the home."[135] The "popular objection to carrying a corpse along a private road" is attributed "to the dread lest the dead should come back by the road the corpse traveled." In England there is a custom, after a death, of unhinging the gate and placing it across the entrance, and of carrying the corpse to the grave by a roundabout way, "that there may be no return by the same path."[136]

This last case verges upon active methods of repelling the ghost, to which we shall presently come. The tenor of the foregoing examples, which can be supplemented by those of Lippert,[137] is in the direction of somehow "losing" the ghost for good and all, but by passive means.

§224*. Disguise and other Forms of "Mourning." Another method, passive in the sense that there is no assault of any kind on the ghost, is the disguise practised by survivors and especially by those standing in such relationship to the dead that he would naturally seek them out first of all. Many so-called mourning-customs, as, indeed, the name-taboo, are in origin nothing but this. However, it must be understood that motives are always mixed; and when disfigurement expresses also self-abasement the theory is that the ghosts like to see the survivors miserable—partly because this means that they have practised for the sake of the dead a self-sacrifice which witnesses to their recognition of the ghost's rights as well as to their own sense of bereavement and partly because the ghosts in general envy the living and even resent the fact that they are alive. Here is the germ of that "envy of the gods" which is roused by good luck and accounts for a lapse,

131 Gomes, *Sea Dyaks*, 135-136.   132 Andree, *Eth. Parallelen*, 133.
133 Von den Steinen, *Zent Bras.*, 510.
134 Pöppig, *Reise*, I, 393, quoted in Rohde, *Psyche*, I, 23.
135 La Fetra, in *Ill. Christian World*, Nov., 1896.
136 Gomme, *Ethnol. in Folklore*, 121, 122.
137 *Kgchte.*, I, 111 ff.

presently, into misfortune. Frazer[138] calls mourning-customs "pieces of spiritual armour, defences against ghosts or demons"; they also protect the soul of the deceased from the assaults of evil spirits that might carry it off.[139] It is no matter for marvel that the disguise is one which is, apparently, so easily penetrable. The ghosts are deceived by a "different" appearance and the practices are readily conventionalized.

Self-mutilation is a form of mourning which is reserved for another connection,[140] since in it the element of sacrifice seems predominant. The Australian women, in mourning, plaster their bodies, the men their faces, with pipe-clay.[141] "Widows and widowers cannot speak a word until the clay has worn off, no matter how long it may remain on";[142] they converse by gestures. In many tribes the men most nearly related to the deceased gash their heads, while the women burn their thighs and stomachs with fire-sticks. The heads of the women, and the beards of the men are daubed with mud, pipe-clay, or dust.[143] In Tasmania, "the ashes of the dead were collected in a kangaroo skin, and every morning, before sunrise, till they were consumed, a portion of them was smeared over the faces of the survivors, and a death song sung, with great emotion, tears clearing away lines among the ashes."[144] Papuans must not wash for a time after the death of a relative;[145] a widow's "deep mourning" is to smear herself with mud and go naked.[146] Widows "knit a net-work garment covering the whole body. They put it on when the dead husband is definitely buried, and wear it until it falls in shreds from the body, which has before been blackened with coal, and must not be washed during the entire period of mourning."[147] The chief Papuan mourner is invariably blackened all over with charcoal and it is very difficult to persuade him or her to leave the house.[148] In New Britain the hair and face, and sometimes the whole body, are blackened.[149] In the Solomon Islands, "a woman whose daughter had just died was not allowed outside her house, nor allowed even to wash herself for 150 days after the death of her daughter. The writer's visit was paid on the thirtieth day after the death, but even then there was so much dirt and filth caked upon her face and body that her features were entirely hidden."[150] Near Torres Straits, the women smeared themselves with mud and "a long fringe of frayed sago-palm leaves was tied round the neck so that it fell down in front and behind."[151] The Andamanese "smear their persons with a wash of olive-colored clay and water, shave their heads, and place a lump of this mixture

[138] In JAI, XV, 99.

[139] Wilken, in VG, III, 449 ff.

[140] §§229, 298, below.

[141] Smyth, *Vict.*, I, xxx.

[142] Howitt, in JAI, XX, 72.

[143] Curr, *Aust. Race*, I, 88.

[144] Roth, *Tasmania*, 132.

[145] Krieger, *Neu-Guinea*, 180.

[146] §394, below; Chalmers, in JAI, XXVII, 330.

[147] Semon, *Aust. Bush*, 330; Von Pfeil, *Südsee*, 317.

[148] Pratt, *New Guinea Cannibals*, 311.

[149] Danks, in JAI, XXI, 351; Jenness and Ballentyne, *D'Entrecasteaux*, 55 *et passim*.

[150] Cayley-Webster, *New Guinea*, 120.

[151] Haddon, in JAI, XIX, 416.

just above their foreheads, where it hardens and is left until the time of mourning is past. If it should fall off in the meantime, it is renewed."[152]

In West Africa, "the relations may not wash themselves or comb their hair during the funeral ceremonies, in consequence of which the rites themselves are sometimes styled *Ofo,* 'unwashed.' . . . The hair must be left unkempt as it grows, and women must cover the head with a cloth of a dark blue color. A widow remains shut up for forty days, and may not wash her cloths during that time."[153] "It is not only the widows that remain, either theoretically or practically unwashed; all the mourners do. . . . I have met peculiar forms of hair cutting—shaving the entire head, not shaving it at all, shearing half of it, etc.—when in mourning."[154] Widows go two months quite naked, smear the body with white earth, do not comb and wash, eat little, and are continent.[155] The sacrifice of hair, which goes with mutilations and other forms of exuvial sacrifice, "is one of the most widespread expressions of pain and mourning for the departed."[156] Priests mourn by rolling in filth, and the end of the funeral-celebration is a march to the sea and a bath.[157] The natives of the Lower Congo "rub themselves in the soil and wear their dirtiest garments for several days after the death of a relative, presenting a shockingly dirty figure." One has to think it strange that they cannot mourn in a more cleanly fashion, but the custom cannot be changed.[158] In Uganda the women smear themselves with white and wear a string of banana-fiber about the forehead, and a black tail fringed with white strings.[159] The Somal appears with a short growth of hair, that is, with head unshaven, only at the time of mourning.[160] The Arab women do not bathe during mourning.[161]

Tibetans formerly wore mourning for three years, not changing their clothes or washing.[162] The Ostiaks wore their scalp-locks loosened for several days after a death.[163] In the fifth century B.C., in China, it is required, in mourning, "that the face must become sharp and bony, the eyes should sink in the head, the countenance must turn black and blue, the ears and eyes ought to grow unfit for hearing and seeing distinctly, arms and legs should lose their strength and become of no use. Still further, it is ordered that high functionaries, when in mourning, should only be able to stand on their legs when supported by others, and that they should be incapable of walking without the use of a staff, and that they must remain in such a condition for three years."[164]

Among the Cheyenne Indians, "the burial took place soon after death. Because of the fear of the ghosts, dead bodies were not kept about. The dead person having become a ghost, his spirit was likely to linger near the body, and might take away with it the spirit of some person still living. This fear was felt especially as to little children. . . . Relations testified to their grief

---

152 Man, in JAI, XII, 141.
153 Ellis, *Yoruba,* 160-161; Thomas, in JAI, XLVII, 198.
154 Kingsley, *Travels W. Afr.,* 487; Thomas, in JAI, XLVII and L, *passim.*
155 Conradt, in *Globus,* LXXXI, 351.
156 Junker, *Afrika,* II, 514.   157 Frobenius, *Masken,* 112.
158 Phillips, in JAI, XVII, 219.   159 Johnston, *Uganda,* II, 793-794.
160 Paulitschke, *Nordost-Afr.,* I, 173.   161 Pommerol, *Sahariennes,* 404.
162 Rockhill, in USNM, 1893, 727.
163 Kondratowitsch, in *Globus,* LXXIV, 291.
164 DeGroot, *Relig. Syst.,* II, 671.

by cutting off the hair. The wife, the mother, and often the sisters, cut their hair short, gashed their heads, and sometimes the calves of their legs, with knives. Sometimes they cut off a finger. Male relations did not cut their legs, but they unbraided their hair and let it hang loose. Women gashed their legs in mourning only when some young male relative was wounded or killed in war. If his blood was shed, they shed theirs; but if he died from sickness, they did not cut themselves. . . . Among the Northern Cheyennes it is said that persons who at the loss of a relative did not cut off the hair or gash the person, were expected to mourn—that is, to wail—for a long time; while those who cut the hair or mutilated themselves were not obliged to wail."[165] How ritualistic the whole ceremonial is can be judged from this option.

The alteration of the Hebrew mourners' dress and the covering of the head, the "making one's self some one else," was for the sake of being unrecognizable to revenants.[166]

"During the time," generalizes Wilken,[167] "when the soul of the departed, disembodied and unreconciled, is spooking about, the surviving relations who have fallen short in their last duties to it are always exposed to its expressions of resentment. To escape these, they disguise themselves so that they are unrecognizable and give up all sorts of things which they commonly do, in order thus to mislead the ghost; in a word, they try to act so that the soul with which, while it sojourned in the body on earth, they were in daily association, can no longer recognize them. This disguise and the omission of a number of usual occupations lead to the mourning-vesture and usages." The author makes the point that the clothing worn in mourning is generally the direct opposite of the ordinary garb; gay colors are exchanged for dull ones, good clothes for rags or no covering to speak of, ornaments are left off. If it is customary to comb and wash the hair, it is left dishevelled; where the head is ordinarily covered, it is left bare; where it is little covered, veils appear. There is no question but that the main object is disguise, though not every mourning-custom is such. Particularly is the head altered or treated as a sign of mourning, for, besides being the most recognizable part of the body—the part a representation of which constitutes a "likeness"—it is widely regarded as the seat of the soul; and the hair, as a special spiritual feature of the head, comes in for much attention. Wilken's editor suggests as a parallel the covering of the head as symbolic of

[165] Grinnell, *Cheyenne*, II, 161, 162; §228, below.
[166] Maurer, *Vkde.*, I, 36.
[167] *Vkde.*, 312; and in VG, III, 420 ff.

divorce. It is worth recalling that the disguise is a ritual affair and does not need to be convincing in our sense of the term.

Certain Borneans are mentioned who appeared with crosses of charcoal on their foreheads; "they supposed that by this means they were disguised beyond all recognition by evil spirits. The belief that such a trivial alteration of appearance is sufficient disguise is probably held by most tribes; . . . a Kenyah chief when on a visit . . . discarded the leopard's teeth, which when at home he wore through the upper part of his ears, and the reason that he alleged was the same as that given" by the above-mentioned Borneo tribesmen.[168]

It is noteworthy, in the foregoing cases, how often the disguise seems to be a woman's affair; the women may be the property, and even the characteristic property, of man and are probably, as such,[169] more likely to be seized upon by the returning ghost. We turn now to a few examples of mourning-color and mourning-garb.

Red, together with the white pipe-clay, is the mourning-color with some Australians;[170] dark blue in West Africa.[171] In Thomas's[172] two articles on African burial-customs, the use of chalk appears over and over again. The Tibetans avoid color and ornaments.[173] Wilken[174] cites many instances of the use of white and black. White and blue, especially the latter, which replaces the red of non-mourning, are found in southern China.[175] Grass-shoes are often worn; but "in the northern provinces white is the only mourning color seen."[176] In the Mahabharata epic of India, red is worn, but no ornament.[177] In Borneo white is found.[178] It is stated that the Saxons used red[179] and the Frieslanders blue.[180] It has been noted that the color of the body-smearings were prevailingly black and white. Some explain this as an attempt to secure inconspicuousness; but it must also be recalled that black and white and, to some extent, red, were the tints most readily accessible to most savage peoples. Rare colors would rank as ornament, which is prevailingly tabooed in time of mourning—the ghost, it is recalled, being jealous of the survivors' pleasure. In the matter of clothing, it is less the color than the quality that counts in mourning. Thus the men in Papua wear a coarse sack around the head and the women a girdle of rattan;[181] the West African women retain signs of mourning for many months in dark, old, or scanty dress and an absence of ornament."[182] In the Congo basin pearls, cowries, false braids, and

[168] Hose and Shelford, in JAI, XXXVI, 83.

[169] §§108 ff., above.　　　[170] Howitt, *S.E. Aust.*, 469.
[171] Ellis, *Ewe*, 160.　　　[172] In JAI, XLVII and L.
[173] Rockhill, in USNM, 1893, 730.　　　[174] In VG, III, 420 ff., *passim*.
[175] Rehatsek, in JASB, I, 306.
[176] Williams, *Middle Kingdom*, II, 249.
[177] Holtzmann, *Ind. Sagen*, I, 256.　　　[178] Roth, *Sarawak*, I, 156, note.
[179] Dana, "The Color Red," in PSM, LVII, 661.
[180] Van Duyl, *Beschavingsgeschied.*, 254.
[181] Krieger, *Neu-Guinea*, 398.　　　[182] Nassau, *Fetichism*, 10.

other ornament disappear.[183] The Kayans of Borneo wear bark-cloth without ornament, the women adding a large mourning-cap;[184] the bark-cloth is the more appropriate because it is an "old" material, and therefore more sacred.[185] In Borneo music also is tabooed and all uproarious mirth; ornaments and gay clothing are laid aside.[186] In mourning the Lycians put on woman's garments; the naïve explanation of the ancient recounter is that the ridiculousness of this banishes grief.[187]

It is not necessary to illustrate further a set of practices with which we are familiar from Hebrew custom as well as from that of classical antiquity. Priam "rolled about in the filth" at the news of Hector's death and in his subsequent mourning;[188] and the Old Testament characters who wore "sackcloth and ashes" and rent their clothes have carried primitive mourning-practices over to us in such manner that, either directly or through our literature, we are familiar with them. It is interesting to hear that some modern Jews thriftily arrange to have a portion of their garments merely basted, so that they can express their grief, after a moment's orientation, both passionately and remediably.[189] Further, there is the wearing of the veil and other accessories to mourning that receives an explanation on the basis of disguise where otherwise nothing better than an accounting by way of "symbolism"[190] is available. Many and perhaps all of the traditional mourning-practices are survivals from a remote stage of societal evolution; the fact that a new content has now been put into them, whereby, for instance, mourning-clothes are interpreted as a hint to the blithesome uninformed, has nothing to do with the intellectual satisfaction or the utility of knowing the earlier stages of the evolutionary process. These remarks apply to much that follows.

§225. **Abstention.** Abstention is a winning policy; it pleases the ghosts both because if men do not take, there is the more left for them, and also because the abstaining men are in some degree of discomfort. Fasting is a typical form of abstention and may head the list. Since a ghost can be cut, burned, drowned, bruised with stones, or jammed in a door—it was a rule in parts of Ger-

183 Clozel, in PSM, XLIX, 677. 184 Nieuwenhuis, *Borneo,* I, 87-88.
185 §324, below.
186 Roth, *Sarawak,* I, 155, 156, note. 187 *Valerius Maximus, Libri,* II, 6, 13.
188 Homer, *Iliad,* XXII, 414; XXIV, 162 ff.
189 Personal communication. 190 §456, below.

many not to slam a door on Saturday, for fear of the last eventuality—it seems, Frazer[191] thinks, not unreasonable to suppose
that the ghost could be eaten, and that perhaps this supposition
furnishes a clue to the origin of fasting after a death—lest the
ghost be unwittingly taken in with the food. This may be one of
the reasons for this avoidance-practice but another seems to us
more obvious. During the time of mourning, people will eat some
things and not others; they will drink when they will not eat; so
that unless the ghost is capable of being swallowed only with certain foods and not with others or with drink, the foregoing explanation is not exhaustive. In general, there is a pronounced element
of propitiation in abstinence. Fasting, like other forms of self-
denial, is a sort of negative sacrifice—not a giving but a refraining
from taking; and again the ghosts are pleased with the discomfort
entailed. The cases, we think, support this less derived explanation, though there are certainly many instances where savages are
concerned about taking a spirit into the body—where they cover
the mouth, for instance, when yawning.[192]

In West Africa, "from the moment of death, the relatives of the deceased,
and the members of the household, abstain from food, and continue fasting as
long as their strength permits. While so fasting, they drink large quantities
of spirits, so that at funerals the greater number of the mourners are commonly in a state of intoxication."[193] In Travancore, death brings defilement,
and no one in the house can eat until after the funeral.[194] Among a potter-
tribe of the Deccan, for three days no fire may be lit nor food cooked; nutriment prepared elsewhere must be supplied to the inmates by friends.[195]
Among the Parsees, for three days after death the family abstains from every
kind of meat, taking food chiefly consisting of vegetables and fish. The nearest
and dearest friends also abstain from meat. Until recently in Bombay no food
was cooked in the house of death; the nearest relations prepare the food and
send it in.[196] The men of the Svanet tribe do not eat meat for two weeks, the
women sometimes for years, after a death. For a year at dinner and supper
they set food on the table for the deceased, and every Saturday they take to
the grave bread, arak, and cheese. At the funeral-feast, in Imeritia, only fast-
ing-food is eaten and the relatives keep this up for forty days. The members
of the family fast for a year, in which time they eat no sweet food or fruit,
and sometimes they swear off forever such dishes as the deceased especially
preferred.[197] This last case, it seems to us, is significant of the real sense of
fasting. Abstinence is plainly a case of sacrifice. In China, "as the sacrificing

191 In JAI, XV, 94.   192 Frazer, Golden Bough, I, 160 ff.
193 Ellis, Tshi, 239.   194 Painter, in JASB, II, 149.
195 Gunthorpe, in JASB, I, 414.   196 Modi, in JASB, II, 430.
197 Russian Ethnog. (Russ.), II, 272, 319.

of food to the dead in various ways anciently commenced immediately after life was extinct, fasting, being a natural result of such sacrifices, began at the same moment."[198] In Cochin China children and grandchildren of the dead renounce meat.[199] In British Columbia, "a widow or widower is forbidden to eat meat and certain vegetables for a month, and must wear quantities of spruce-bush inside the shirt, next the skin; this is done to ward off the evil spirit set free by the death of its victim, and ready to pounce upon a fresh one. It is shocking for a widow to smoke for a month after the death of her husband."[200] Main[201] has a chapter, with many apt examples, on "The Haunted Widow," showing how her deceased husband follows her up and does ill to her and to a second husband. That fasting has passed into the ritual of certain developed religions is known to all. The "Great White Fast" of the Hebrews was a "revelry of repentance . . . when they burned long candles, and whirled fowls round their heads and attired themselves in grave-clothes and saw from their seats in the synagogue the long fast-day darken slowly into dusk, while God was sealing the decrees of life and death."[202]

Abstention by way of precaution is connected with things other than food. A more or less miscellaneous list follows. It will be noted in particular that work for the winning of food was tabooed, for if the food was not appropriated the ghost could get it and the living could fast and be the more miserable. Holidays have been the cause of much economic backwardness, even in more modern times; one author[203] allows eight weeks in the year for holidays and "other disturbances" to settled life, and Colmeiro[204] calculates that at one time Spain was losing eight hundred million days' labor each year by reason of her overplus of holidays. Generally all forms of pleasure were under the ban on the primitive rest-day, for it was holy—a holy-day or holiday or Sabbath.[205]

In Dutch New Guinea men may not enter the assembly-house till their mourning is over.[206] In San Salvador, "the house remains for several days unswept in order not to irritate the ghosts with the dust."[207] On the Congo there is the same taboo on sweeping, lest the frail ghost should unwittingly be injured.[208] In Uganda, "if anyone of importance dies, the neighbours do not cultivate for three days after the death."[209] At the decease of a Malagasy king or queen numerous acts are forbidden. Almost everyone's head has to be shaved; no hat can be worn or umbrella carried; no European dress may be

[198] DeGroot, *Relig. Syst.*, II, 647.   [199] Niemann, in *Bijd.*, 1895, 332.

[200] Allison, in JAI, XXI, 313.

[201] *Relig. Chastity*, ch. II; for widow's mourning, see ch. I.

[202] Zangwill, *Ghetto*, 144.   [203] Henley, *Husbandry*, 133.

[204] *Econ. Pol. en España*, II, 53-54.

[205] See Webster, *Rest Days*, for a full treatment.

[206] Krieger, *Neu-Guinea*, 412.   [207] Bastian, *Afr. Reisen*, 227.

[208] Bastian, *Der Mensch*, II, 323.   [209] Johnston, *Uganda*, II, 794.

worn, and the native robe has to be bound under the armpits, leaving the shoulders uncovered; all singing, dancing, or playing of musical instruments is forbidden, as well as the practice of many hand-crafts, spinning, weaving, making of pottery, and gold- and silver-working. Since such occupations as tilling the soil, sowing, and planting rice, cannot be wholly abandoned, they are not called by the usual terms, but are referred to as "going into the country," or "settling down in the fields." The usual word for market is not employed during the time of mourning.[210] Thus is the spirit of the taboo evaded by hard-pressed mortals; but the holiday is not unloved for its own sake: in Surinam the bush-negroes have a great number of holidays and exhibit alacrity in their acceptance of the white man's Sunday.[211] In Borneo there is a custom for the widow or widower not to leave the house; "often the mourning spouse has to remain from three to seven months sitting idle on a mat."[212] Again, "the apartment, and the family in which a death occurs, are tabooed for seven days and nights, and if the interdict be not rigidly kept, the ghost of the departed will haunt the house."[213] All such taboos mean suspension of the occupations of ordinary life. In Sumatra, a man, after the death of wife or child, must not appear in festal garb for forty-four days, and must not engage in industry or trade except in so far as he has to for daily sustenance. He must not take part in play or go on the sea. The same period of abstinence from adorning or anointing herself rests upon the woman.[214] No cooking may be done in the house of death.[215]

"Chinese mourning for parents is supposed to consume three years, but is mercifully shortened to twenty-seven months. The observance of this mourning takes precedence of all other duties, amounting to an excision of so much of the lifetime of the sons, if they happen to be in government employ. Sometimes the son builds a hut near the grave of the parent and lives there during the whole period of mourning. The most common way, however, is to spend the night at the grave and give the day to the usual occupations. . . . The writer is acquainted with one man whose extreme devotion resulted in unsettling his mind and rendering him a burden to his family. The Chinese consider such an act commendable; the ceremonial is held to be absolute and not relative."[216]

In Greenland "those who have clothed the dead man must refrain from working iron. This precaution, it seems, must be observed for several years, lest there come upon the family some ill luck. When they begin again, a spell must first be employed."[217] Among the Central Eskimo, "on the fourth day after death the relatives may go for the first time upon the ice, but the men are not allowed to hunt; on the next day they must go sealing, but without dogs and sledge, walking to the hunting ground and dragging the seal home." This provision looks like a case of the ancient and obsolete procedure being regarded as sacred.[218] "On the sixth day they are at liberty to use their dogs again. For a whole year they must not join in any festival and are not allowed to sing certain songs. If a married woman dies, the widower is not permitted to keep any part of the first seal he catches after her death except the flesh;

210 Sibree, in JAI, XXI, 219.
211 Hostmann, *Beschaving*, I, 41.
212 Schwaner, *Borneo*, II, 77.
213 Roth, *Sarawak*, I, 154.
214 Jacobs, *Groot-Atjeh*, I, 355.
215 Kubary, in *Berl. Mus. Mittheil.*, 1885, 7.
216 Smith, *Chinese Char.*, 179, 180.
217 Holm, *Ethnol. Skizze.*, 65-66.
218 §324, below.

skin, blubber, bones, and entrails must be sunk in the sea. All the relatives must have new suits of clothes made and before the others are cast away they are not allowed to enter a hut without having asked and obtained permission."[219] Among the Bering Strait Eskimo, "during the day on which a person dies in the village no one is permitted to work, and the relatives must perform no labor during the three following days. It is especially forbidden during this period to cut with any edged instrument, such as a knife or an ax; and the use of pointed instruments, like needles or bodkins, is also forbidden. This is said to be done to avoid cutting or injuring the shade, which may be present at any time during this period, and, if accidentally injured by any of these things, it would become very angry and bring sickness or death to the people. The relatives must also be very careful at this time not to make any loud or harsh noises that may startle or anger the shade. . . . The housemates of the deceased must remain secluded for four days, and "during this time all of them must keep fur hoods drawn over their heads to prevent the influence of the shade from entering their heads and killing them."[220] Here is a mixture of motives for renouncing regular occupations. Other Eskimo must abstain from working on wood with ax or hammer, and from certain kinds of food. One woman "would not sew on clothing because there was a dead man in the village who had not yet been buried, and 'he would see her.' After consultation with her husband, she concluded that she could protect herself by drawing a circle about her on the floor with a snow knife. In this circle she did the sewing, and was careful to keep all her work inside of it."[221]

During the "great mourning" of the Hurons, "the mourners lay, face downward, upon their mats, and enveloped in their robes, speechless, or replying only by an ejaculation to those who addressed them. During this period they had no fire in the house, even in winter; they ate their food cold, and left the cabin only at night, and as secretly as possible. The 'lesser mourning' lasted a year, during which they refrained from oiling their hair, attended public festivals rarely, and only (in the case of women) when their mothers ordered, and were forbidden to marry again."[222] Certain Brazilian Indians shut themselves up for a month and live on game provided by neighbors.[223] In the funeral-meal the ghosts were present as invisible participants and were spoken of only in praise.[224] *De mortuis nil nisi bonum.* The South Russian Jews covered the face of the dead "that he need not blush for the improprieties of those round about. Since the deceased cannot participate, no eating or 'learning' must be done in the room where he lies, for it was the greatest insult for a Jew of former time not to invite him to the table and a disgrace to him to remain without a share in learning."[225] In old Holland in particular "they held the month of May to be unlucky and did not readily marry then, a notion of heathen origin, for the heathen were accustomed in that month to give offerings to the ghosts who were about at night to bring them to rest, and the churches remained closed for the month. Ovid had already said that these times were not available for marriages and that those who married then did not live long; it is a common

[219] Boas, in BAE, VI, 615.
[220] Nelson, in BAE, XVIII, pt. I, 312, 314-315.
[221] Murdoch, in BAE, IX, 424.   [222] Hale, *Iroq. Rites,* 71.
[223] Von Martius, *Beiträge,* I, 441-442.   [224] Rohde, *Psyche,* I, 231-232.
[225] Weissenberg, in *Globus,* XCI, 360.

proverb that only women of an evil life marry in May."[226] Mantegazza[227] notes that sex-abstention is a feature of mourning.

Under preceding headings there have been reviewed some of the more characteristic types of avoidance. It has been seen that through them religion enters into industry, property, government, marriage and the family, and self-gratification. Wilken[228] has made a very thorough analysis of the subject of mourning-customs and a summary of his treatment, especially concerning the re-marriage of the widow, will serve both as a summary of the chap-ter and also as a further suggestion as to the interpenetration of religion and other societal forms.

Mourning generally lasts till the feast of the dead, when those who have de-ceased within a certain period are expedited in a body to the spirit-world.[229] The intervals of sojourn on earth after death vary; in the author's cases they run from five to a hundred days and differ with age, sex, and social position. The people feel that they may not leave the village for two months and ask permission of the dead when they do. After the interval of sojourn is over the people return to regular life and get ready for the feast of the dead, which may be delayed for a year or two. Mourning goes on till that takes place. During mourning the widow must not marry; not even a levirate marriage may take place till after the feast. This re-marriage of the widow[230] is a typical case of avoidance-customs. There is a tendency against allowing a widow to re-marry at all; in some places the one who does is made to wed on Wednesday, an unlucky day, and is favored with "Katzenmusik" and a chari-vari. Hindu and Chinese prejudices in this respect are very marked; in the latter country a young girl who loses her affianced and will not marry is highly praised. In Borneo if a woman dies and then marries in the spirit-world, she yet rejoins her earthly husband when he comes. There is no idea of an absence of marrying and giving in marriage in the next life.[231] In China they have child-marriages of dead children; a paper couple is burned along with paper servants, etc. Illness may be sent by a dead unmarried son; then a betrothal is at once arranged for him. In general a wife belongs to her hus-band in the life to come, so she had better keep chaste for him. The suttee means that she goes at once to rejoin him. In view of all this, it is evident that the ghost of a dead husband can punish unfaithfulness in his relict; therefore she does not marry till he is safely off to the next world. Not only is the widow in danger; so also is the man who dares to marry her. There are all sorts of precautions when a widow re-marries; the new husband enters the house by the window, for example, and circumambulates the house three times, inside; the "Katzenmusik" is in part to drive off the evil. A finger is sometimes, on the principle of *pars pro toto*,[232] sacrificed to avert evil; it is supposed to repre-

---

[226] Schotel, *Huisgezin*, 286.
[227] *Amori*, 99; Homer, *Iliad*, XXIV, 129-130; §281, below.
[228] "Haaropfer," in VG, III, 439 ff.   [229] §230, below.
[230] §395, below.   [231] Matt., XXII, 30.
[232] §§297, 298, below.

sent the dutiful self-immolation of the spouse. Until the feast of the dead, as appears from other passages in Wilken's article, the husband's spirit is about—in fact, his body may be kept in the house till that time.

The text of the mortuary ceremonies is: "Here you have your property, leave the village in peace"; if the soul gets what it owns, there is no danger. Survivors must not show ostentation but renunciation; that makes the ghosts mild. People must fast, or eat no rice but only rough food, such as sago and maize, or renounce a certain food, as potato or fish or salt. There must be no eating in the house of death; those who attended the deceased must be fed by others, not handling food at all. The mouth must be of the natural color, not reddened by betel. Conjugal relations must be suspended. The author gives numerous instances of all these practices. He thinks Frazer's explanations of a number of them, such as not eating lest one devour the flitting ghost, or not shutting doors lest the spirit be pinched in them, are clever but somewhat artificial and forced.

Hitherto the cases have represented passive, negative methods of avoidance rather than active, positive ones calculated to resist and repel. There is no clean-cut distinction between the two classes of procedure; being evolutionary, they show transitional forms and interpenetrate somewhat. However, the ghosts are handled in an offensive as well as a defensive manner; they are resisted or even assaulted. We turn now to this aggressive aspect of the ghost-cult.

§226*. Resistance. Men do not confine themselves to a mere dodging of the ghostly peril. Ghosts may be entertained and then driven off like fleas.[233] Frazer[234] lists the various steps that are taken "to chase away the lingering ghost from his home" or to keep him from returning. They often consist in such procedure as might frighten away a small child or a half-witted person, therein again revealing the stock inconsistency of the savage in accrediting the ghosts with contradictory qualities; and they not infrequently involve rough handling of the corpse which, apparently, the soul with all its unearthly powers is unable effectually to resent. Perhaps the destruction of the body should be classified with such methods. Our cases will exhibit a variety of resistance and aggression.

The Australians tie up the remains to keep the ghost in the grave;[235] or they cut off and destroy the head. The theory of the latter procedure is "that

[233] Rohde, *Psyche,* I, 239.
[234] In JAI, XV, 66, 71; Tylor, *Prim. Cult.,* II, 181, 182.
[235] Curr, *Aust. Race,* I, 87.

the spirit rising from the grave to follow the tribe misses its head and goes groping around to find it; but being bereft of a head, it is blind and therefore, not being able to see, gets burnt in the fire. This frightens it so terribly that it retires into the grave again with all speed, and never presumes to attempt a renewal of social intercourse with the human denizens of this world."[236] In parts of Melanesia there is a sort of community-ceremony of ejection. Stones are thrown into the houses and all about and bamboos are beaten throughout the village. The people thus pass through the town till they come to the bush. "They have now driven out the ghost, who up to this time has been about the house, in which the widow has for these five days never left the dead man's bed except upon necessity; and even then she leaves a cocoa-nut to represent her till she returns." But they are not yet done with the ghost. They send word to the next village westward of the impending end of anyone badly afflicted with ulcers and sores and at his death chase him to the westward confines of his village. "The people of the next village take up the chase, and hunt the ghost westward, and so on till the sea is reached. Then they are sure he has left the island and will not strike others with his disease."[237] In the Torres Straits region they tie the thumbs and big toes of the dead together and sew or skewer him up in a mat.[238] "In many parts of Fiji the legs of the corpse are drawn up, the body is doubled together until the knees touch the chin, the elbows are drawn in to the sides with the hands uplifted, and the whole body is then securely bound in that posture. This is done to prevent the ghost of the dead man from 'walking' by night, and doing injury to the living."[239] Curious burial-postures may have been due in part to such notions. Thorn-bushes are thrown over the corpse at burial by the Zambesi tribes,[240] or a heap of stones and thorns is raised over the grave.[241] The corpse is tied heels and shoulders and pelted with stones till it is covered.[242] If the soul of the deceased is in danger, a sacrifice left at cross-paths causes the spirits that pursue him to disperse in as many directions as there are paths.[243] Again, the body is beaten into unrecognizability, or every bone is broken, especially in the case of dangerous souls. "A child dies, then another child comes to the same father and mother, and that dies, after giving the usual trouble and expense. A third arrives and if that dies, the worm—the father, I mean—turns, and if he is still desirous of more children, he just breaks one of the legs of the body before throwing it in the bush. This he thinks will act as a warning to the wanderer-soul and give it to understand that if it will persist in coming into his family, it must settle down there and give up its flighty ways. If a fourth child arrives in the family, 'it usually limps,' and if it dies, the justly irritated parent cuts its body up carefully into very small pieces, and scatters them, doing away with the soul altogether." In Togoland, the same authority[244] states that for five or six weeks "the widow remains in the hut, armed with a good stout stick, as a precaution against the ghost of her husband, so as to ward off attacks should he be ill-tempered." Near Lake Albert Edward the

[236] Urquhart, in JAI, XIV, 88.
[237] Codrington, *Melanesians,* 270-271.
[238] Haddon, in JAI, XIX, 402.   [239] Fison, in JAI, X, 145.
[240] Decle, cited in JAI, XXIII, 420.   [241] Tyler, in *Ill. Afr.,* Dec., 1895.
[242] Bent, *Ethiopians,* 78.   [243] Ellis, *Yoruba,* 155-157.
[244] Kingsley, *Travels W. Afr.,* 479, 480, 488; Nassau, *Fetichism,* 234.

dead are buried with the lower leg bent up back of the thigh.[245] Castration of the dead was practised in early Egypt.[246]

Covering the corpse with stones is common, among the Chukchi and elsewhere;[247] but this was often due solely to the desire to preserve the body from beasts. In the Naga Hills of India, "men who die violent deaths by accident are simply tied to the spot where they fell, without covering or ornament. Their death is attributed to the special disfavor of the gods."[248] The ancient Hindus bound the corpse's feet together, lest he come back and make trouble.[249] A heavy stone is laid by the Veddahs upon the breast of the corpse to hold the ghost fast to it and the cave or location is left to the deceased, at least until decay is fully accomplished.[250] The Malays have the idea that the body of the dead needs protection from spirits which seek to seize its soul; to prevent this, "two working knives are placed under the mat on which it lies, with their points projecting downwards through the floor of the house, while a spear is placed upright near the body, its butt resting on the floor and its point sticking into the sloping thatch of the roof. A fire is also lit, usually near the mat on which the body lies. If a bad thunderstorm comes on while a corpse is awaiting burial, a fire is lighted in the ground under the house."[251] Among the Sea Dyaks of Sarawak, there is a curious custom that apparently prevents the rising of a spirit which had displayed itself as reprobate in life. Beside the paths are to be seen heaps of sticks or stones, called "lying heaps." "Each heap is in remembrance of some man who has told a stupendous lie, or disgracefully failed in carrying out an engagement; and every passer-by takes a stick or a stone to add to the accumulation, saying, at the time he does it: 'For So-and-so's lying heap.' It goes on for generations, until they sometimes forget who it was that told the lie; but, notwithstanding that, they continue throwing the stone." The usage is common outside the Archipelago; it goes without the saying that the presence of these heaps is a constant reminder of what happens to the wicked. Wilken,[252] who cites the case from St. John, aligns it with European parallels in the manner of treating undesirable ghosts; thus, to prevent a person from becoming a vampire, certain Prussians entangled his corpse in a fish-net, turning his face downwards, and filled the coffin with poppy-seeds; the dead man would have to count the latter, as well as disentangle himself from the meshes of the net. Andree[253] has a number of instances: putting some earth on the body and a heavy stone on the head; nailing the corpse fast to the coffin or driving into it a strong stake. These last instances remind one of the historic custom of burying the suicide at the cross-roads, with a stake through the chest, and of the placing of a heavy stone on the chest of a dead witch.[254]

[245] Stuhlmann, *Mit Emin,* 641.

[246] Henning, in *Globus,* LXXIV, 76.   [247] Ratzel, *Vkde.,* II, 780.

[248] Woodthorpe, in JAI, XI, 203.   [249] Zimmer, *Altind. Leben,* 402.

[250] Sarasin, *Weddas,* 492; Schmidt, *Ceylon,* 278.

[251] Evans, in JAI, XLVII, 159.

[252] In VG, III, 164, 165, note, 226, note (St. John, *Life in the forests of the far East,* I, 76-77).

[253] *Eth. Parallelen,* 81 ff.

[254] Sienkiewicz, *Fire and Sword,* 618-619.

Several of the foregoing instances have illustrated directly or by implication the effectiveness, for ridding the survivors of ghostly visitations, of the destruction of the body. There is only one speedy way of totally demolishing it, namely, by cremation, though casting it into the sea means that it is disposed of, to all intents, without residue; even on the pyre, however, the bones resist the comparatively low temperatures attainable by primitive methods, and exposure to the elements or to the beasts is equally ineffective in getting rid of the bones. In view of this situation, when destruction of the body is mentioned it is disposal of the flesh that is meant; and there is usually a ceremony of collecting and treating the bones which constitutes a sort of second funeral. They are commonly cleaned, painted or otherwise decorated, and buried or stored away; this is particularly the case with the skull. The purpose in such destruction as is practised is avoidance of the continuing presence of the ghost; moreover, it must not be lost to sight that the ghost itself is eager to be "laid," to "come to rest," that is, to proceed duly to the spirit-world; thus the destruction of the body may be a service and an honor to the dead.

Lippert[255] thinks that cremation takes place where time is lacking for a slower process and that nomads, therefore, generally cremate; and he gives instances of exposure to animals as a relatively speedy method of destruction. Ridgeway[256] briefly surveys the practice of cremation over the world: "cremation is in general use amongst savage people, principally with the object of separating the inner and outer selves of the dead, of disengaging his shade from a body that has become useless and inert, and the same process logically applies to the defunct's weapons, clothing and ornaments." His weapons are "killed" by breaking them and their souls go on with that of their owner.[257] We turn to a selection of cases.

The Australians sometimes place the dead in hollow trees, which are burned; sometimes they throw corpses into the sea when they have to migrate, for fear an enemy might get them for use in magic.[258] In disposing of the dead man whose ghost is expected to possess power, there appears a belief that the ghost continues weak while the corpse continues to smell; therefore the spirit

255 *Kgchte.*, II, 253, I, 113. 256 *Early Age*, I, 481 ff.
257 Letourneau, *Prop.*, 29; Letourneau, *Soc.*, bk. III, ch. IV.
258 Ratzel, *Vkde.*, II, 76.

of the dead man who is "sunk in the sea, burnt, enclosed in a case, or rapidly denuded of flesh, is active and available at once."[259] In one district of Melanesia, the natives "are said to lay so great weight upon an ostentatious cremation that they themselves gather the wood for their pyres and keep it long in their houses, so that it will dry out and burn well."[260] Cremation is not widespread in Melanesia and the South Seas, but when it occurs, there is great ceremonial, and the ashes of big chiefs are preserved.[261] In the Solomon Islands great people are burned, while the common are buried at sea; some exposure on small islands is recorded.[262] A number of African tribes simply throw the dead into the bush.[263] In Uganda the bodies of unauthorized sorcerers are thus disposed of and those of people struck by lightning are placed on top of ant-hills and left. The Masai expose the corpse to hyænas, jackals, and vultures except in the case of a male and a chief.[264] The Chukchi cut off the clothing of the corpse exchanging for every piece a slice of reindeer-flesh until the body is entirely covered. "Then the nearest kinsman cuts the throat and opens the breast in order to lay bare a part of the heart and liver. . . . The corpse is then left to the ravages of wolves and foxes; the sooner it is consumed, the better it is thought to be for the living."[265] Another Siberian tribe exposes its ordinary dead to the wild beasts, only the priests being burned,"[266] while the Kalmuks burn the bodies of persons of distinction and bury simple people.[267] In Mongolia the dead are exposed to be eaten by wild dogs and vultures, "for as long as a rag of flesh still hangs to the skeleton, such is the local belief, the soul of the deceased may not enter the beyond"; persons of very high station are burned.[268] In Farther India, among the Palaungs, "when any one dies a mysteriously sudden death, or is killed, the body is buried as quickly as possible, in a lonely part of the jungle, at some distance from the village. The grave is generally dug beside a large tree, because the spirits of all people dying suddenly are believed to remain near their bodies, haunting the place where they are buried. Their time to die had not yet come, and the spirit could not yet go to eat the fruit of forgetfulness. Such a spirit is evil, hurtful and jealous." Again, "when a woman dies in childbirth—such a death is considered terrible—her friends hasten to bury her; so hurriedly is this done, that a woman who faints or becomes unconscious during labour runs a risk of being buried alive."[269]

The Tlinkit of the American northwest coast used to disjoint the body before burning. Ashes and burnt bones were collected and deposited in mortuary houses. Cremation was for the free; slaves were cast into the sea.[270] Cremation, says Letourneau,[271] "of all funeral customs, seems to be the most luxurious and the most coveted." If a Caddo Indian "is killed in battle, the body is never buried, but is left to be devoured by beasts or birds of prey,

[259] Codrington, *Melanesians*, 263.
[260] Von Pfeil, *Südsee*, 80.
[261] Finsch, *Ethnol. Erfahr.*, I, 143.
[262] Woodford, *Head-Hunters*, 37.
[263] Ratzel, *Vkde.*, 441, 448.
[264] Johnston, *Uganda*, II, 554-555; 589-590, 828.
[265] Bogoras, in AA, III, 95-96.
[266] Prjevalski, *Forskningsresor*, 236.
[267] *Russian Ethnog.* (Russ.), II, 469.
[268] Zichy, in *Globus*, LXXIV, 321.
[269] Milne, *Eastern Clan*, 304, 281; §406, below.
[270] Niblack, in USNM, 1888, 252, 358.
[271] *Soc.*, 233.

and the condition of such individuals in the other world is considered to be far better than that of persons dying a natural death."[272] The Urubamba Indians of South America abandon the dead to the vultures and wild animals.[273]

In Homer's time cremation was the rule, the deceased demanding it; on the other hand, to be devoured by dogs and beasts of prey was a terrible destiny. Patroclus urges Achilles in a dream to hasten his cremation; saying that the souls are withholding from him entrance to the house of Hades, and Achilles, starting up in agitation, sets about it at once. The bones are gathered from the ashes of the pyre, anointed, and stored in receptacles. It is a sad fate to miss this dignified exit from the world.[274] Beloch[275] thinks the original idea of cremation was to render return impossible by the swift destruction of the soul. Certainly in Homer the dead, once properly expedited to the spirit-world, cease to affect survivors. In later Greece burial came to be countenanced. In the Icelandic sagas, on an occasion when it was desired to get rid of a dead man's ghost, he was dug up, burnt, and the ashes cast into the sea.[276] The body was not burned except where the ghost returned and was troublesome; then they burned the body to finish him. In Scandinavian countries, Odin-worshippers burned the dead while Thor-worshippers set them in a boat and built a mound over them.[277] There was no cremation in the stone age but it appeared along with the bronze.[278] The graves opened in Slavonic territory reveal burning and burying mixed.[279] In the oldest graves in Switzerland, cremation comes later than cave-burial.[280]

In New England consumption was once regarded as a spiritual disease. As long as the heart of one dead of that disease contained blood, it was believed that the deceased was drawing blood from relations who would die of consumption one after another. The cure was to exhume and cremate the dead or his heart.[281] In December, 1923, in Jefferson, Maine, the body of a suicide was exhumed and cremated in the house in which he had killed his wife and two relatives after taking the lives of two other persons. A local attorney reports a local superstition "that if the body of a murderer is burned the ghosts of his victims will not be uneasy." One man stated that he had been out at night looking to see if the ghosts of the murdered were walking in the vicinity of the crime.[282]

Cremation of consumptives might be interpreted as an exhibition of precaution against infection. Doubtless there was in cremation, the most hygienic of all methods of disposing of the dead, an effect,

[272] Yarrow, in BAE, I, 103.
[273] Reich u. Stegelmann, in *Globus*, LXXXIII, 134.
[274] Keller, *Hom. Soc.*, 117-118, with references.
[275] *Griech. Gchte.*, I, 117-118, 116.   [276] Weinhold, *Altnord. Leben*, 499.
[277] Leo, *Island*, 544; Kålund, in *Aarbøger*, 1870, 377-378.
[278] Worsaae, *Nordens Forhist.*, 65.
[279] *Anth. Poland* (Pol.), I, 46, *et passim*.
[280] Heierli, in *Globus*, LXXII, 249.
[281] Stetson, in AA, IX, 3. Case in *New Haven* (Ct.) *Register*, June, 1854, with comment as follows: "We seem to be transported back to the darkest ages of unreasoning ignorance and blind superstition."
[282] Despatch from Damariscotta, Me., in *Nashua Telegraph*, Dec. 26, 1923.

unconsciously realized, in that direction; on the other hand, the prevalence of other highly unhygienic methods of disposition and of unhygienic practices in general, existing side by side with cremation, witnesses clearly enough against an explanation which represents the carrying back of modern knowledge into primitive life. The illustrations cited show how the mores took now this direction and now that, uniting only in the aim of destroying the body. "There is a startling contrast between the last prayer of Ajax to Zeus that he be at least buried, so that dogs and birds eat not his body, and the prayer of the devout Zoroastrian that he be *not* buried, and that dogs and birds *do* eat his remains."[283]

§227*. Expulsion. Despite the belief in the more than human power of the ghost, it is not impossible to frighten it away by plying a club or spear or by otherwise resisting it as one would resist a living being. The view appears to be widespread also that ghosts dislike or are afraid of noise. The savage funeral, or at any rate a part of it, is generally a noisy affair; the boisterous phase is usually where the ghost is being driven off and the quiet portion where the survivors are eluding its return. A good part of the uproar consists of lamentations, which must be regarded as propitiatory. There are other manifestations that are not; if they are not aimed at frightening away the recently disembodied soul, they are intended to ban the evil spirits that brought the death or that may be lying in wait for the soul of the deceased. In either case they are exorcistic.

The Papuans beat upon a big family-drum when a death has occurred;[284] then, conceiving that the ghost still lingers in the neighborhood, they try to drive it into an image which they have constructed. "Toward evening there begins, at the giving of a signal, in all houses at the same time, a hellish uproar. They beat on drums, yell, and pound, in short make as much noise as possible. This is repeated for several successive evenings, and while it is being done the sorcerer, with facial contortions and shrieks, shakes the image in his hand and suddenly falls down, an indication that the ghost has entered it."[285] In the New Hebrides one or two men watch for thirty days at the grave, blowing on conchs or bamboos.[286] The Kaffirs keep up a "perpetual clamor" and drums are beaten; other South Africans preserve a period of silence after

[283] Maine, *Early Law,* 65, note. [284] Hagen, *Papua's,* 258.
[285] Wilken, in VG, IV, 90-91. [286] Leggatt, in AAAS, 1892, 700.

the first burst of lamentation.[287] In East Central Africa "the dead are mourned for by a persistent beating of the drums by night and by day."[288] Among the Yorubas "drinking and shouting, amid the firing of muskets, the jangle of native gongs, and the dull thud of the drums, continue all night."[289] In the Chin Hills a crowd of people go to the burial-place, discharging guns and beating gongs as they go.[290] As soon as a Saora dies, a gun is fired off at the door or, if plenty of powder is to be had, several shots are fired, to frighten away the ghost. A few guns are kept for the purpose and for funeral-feasts. Guns are fired also when the body is being carried away.[291] The Dyaks of Borneo shoot off small arms at the dawn of the burial-day.[292] Elsewhere in Borneo cannons are fired over a man's grave "to arouse the spirits, who were to lead him to Kinabalu, the people shouting out, 'Turn neither to the right nor to the left, but proceed straight to Kinabalu.' "[293] Wilken[294] contrasts the great noise of the gun-firing, drum-beating, etc., with the deep silence after the ceremony. The former is exorcism, the latter avoidance. Such noise cannot be expressive of sorrow, nor yet the silence; the latter is to misguide the ghosts so that they think the settlement uninhabited. The noise-exorcism is paralleled in cases of epidemics, earthquakes, eclipses of the moon, or any other threatening situation, for the danger always comes from the ghosts; a deafening uproar is accompanied with shouts of "Depart! Go away!" Then, on the following day, the silence of death is observed; no one may be seen outside his dwelling, and all work, even cooking, is abjured. The ghosts then think they are not on their own island but on another which is uninhabited. The author adverts to the gong-beating as a sort of tolling for the dead, supposed to drive him out of the house and the village; it has its aftertype in the tolling of bells at a death. He quotes from Frazer[295] on burial customs: "In Christian times bells have been used to repel evil spirits; this, of course, was the intention of the passing bell. In Scotland funerals used to be preceded by a man ringing a bell. The idea that the sound of brass or iron has power to put spirits to flight prevailed also in classical antiquity, from which it may have been inherited by mediæval Christianity. We may perhaps see the germ of the passing bell in the kettle which the Spartan women beat up and down the streets on the death of a king. The Moquis of Arizona exorcise evil spirits by the ringing of bells; and at Port Moresby, in New Guinea, when the church bell was first used, the natives returned thanks to the missionaries for having driven away the ghosts." In Christian lands the idea prevailed that only baptized bells have the power to drive off evil spirits, "devils and tempests," while unbaptized bells are carried off by the demons. Longfellow's "Golden Legend" is quoted to illustrate.

More sophisticated peoples have preserved survivals of such noise-making. Dana[296] describes the funeral of a child, daughter of an American who had married in the place, which he witnessed in California in the 1830's. "The most singular thing of all was, that two men walked, one on each side of the coffin,

[287] Tyler, in *Ill. Afr.*, Dec., 1895.   [288] Macdonald, in JAI, XXII, 112.
[289] Ellis, *Yoruba*, 157, 158-159; Thomas, in JAI, XLVII.
[290] Carey and Tuck, *Chin Hills*, I, 192.
[291] Fawcett, in JASB, I, 248.   [292] Perelaer, *Dajaks*, 244.
[293] Roth, *Sarawak*, I, 151, 153.   [294] In VG, III, 410-413.
[295] In JAI, XV, 87-88.
[296] *Two Years before the Mast*, 142.

carrying muskets in their hands, which they continually loaded, and fired into the air. Whether this was to keep off evil spirits or not, I do not know. It was the only interpretation that I could put upon it." There are several practices, such as passing-bells,[297] musketry-discharge, "wake"-ceremonies, and the like which have descended into modern times and probably represent survivals of antique mores. They are rationalized or mythologized upon or classified conveniently as "symbolic";[298] we shall encounter many of them as we advance through the topics and cases to come.

Under the previous topic of fire in religion and later on under fetishism[299] appears evidence as to the power of this element in banning supernatural influences. Fire used in cremation provides the most efficient available agency for the destruction of the body. In the ghost-cult fire is both a bar to the return of the dead and also a protection to the dead; and the ancestral spirit, when regarded as a beneficent influence, is connected with the hearth.[300] It must always be realized that what is done in conciliation of or service to the dead is also done to "lay" the ghost and to prevent its return. "Wherever we find a so-called purification by fire or water from pollution contracted by contact with the dead, we may assume with much probability that the original intention was to place a physical barrier of fire or water between the living and the dead, and that the conceptions of pollution and purification are merely the fictions of a later age, invented to explain the purpose of a ceremony of which the original intention was forgotten."[301] Among the following cases will be found several which are propitiatory rather than exorcistic; nevertheless in such instances the exit of the ghost is eased and the underlying avoidance of its continued presence is in evidence.

Australians and others keep a fire burning at the grave for about ten days[302] and some Australians believe in an evil spirit which appears, bringing death, when the fire goes out.[303] Only the good ghost escapes the flames that rise from a cleft on the road to the spirit-world.[304] The fire on the grave is intended by the Melanesians, in certain cases to smother the ghost,[305] in others to keep the dead warm.[306] In New Guinea, "the spirits of dead warriors are allowed considerable liberty to roam about their old surroundings, and are supposed to

[297] White, Sci. and Theol., I, 343.   [298] §456, below.
[299] §§92, above, and 254, 394, below.
[300] §251, below; Lippert, Kgchte., I, 270 ff.
[301] Frazer, in JAI, XV, 80, 76.
[302] Smyth, Vict., I, 106; Urquhart, in JAI, XIV, 88.
[303] Ratzel, Vkde., II, 93.   [304] Cameron, in JAI, XIV, 365.
[305] Ratzel, Vkde., II, 339.   [306] Danks, in JAI, XXI, 349.

retain feelings of anger against old enemies, to whom they become a source of great annoyance, by making frequent visits at night and tickling their feet, so that they are unable to get any rest in sleep. To rid the village of these troublesome spirits, an occasion is set apart after every fight, when every nook and cranny of the village is switched with flaming fire-brands. . . . This procession is accompanied with the beating of drums, the blasts of the conch shell, and much noise and shouting, with a view of so frightening the spirits back to their particular spirit-land that they will never return to annoy the living again."[307] There seems to be no sense of the incongruous in the fact that dead warriors are frightened by the noises they themselves have made on many occasions in life. Again, "the native who has to traverse the woods by night often puts luminous mushrooms in his hair and on his feet. Those on his feet enable him to see his path, while the mushrooms in his hair inform other wayfarers that it is only a man they are meeting, since spirits are afraid of this light."[308] "A Bushman, after he had killed a sorceress, broke her head, buried it and then lit a large fire over the spot to prevent her shade from afterwards coming out and tormenting him."[309] Sometimes a man may struggle against spirits and even kill them but then he must be very careful to burn their bodies and to leave nothing remaining, for they will come to life again if the smallest bone is spared.[310] This case illustrates also the precaution of bodily destruction. In West Africa, the nails of a dead man and a lock of his hair are cut off and put into the interior of an ant's nest. Then all the fires in the village are extinguished and all ashes, spider-webs, and other uncleanliness removed. Fire is made by the friction-process and the ant-hill set ablaze. From it a new fire is carried to all the village-hearths, whereby the whole village is purified. "If this procedure is omitted they think that the village will no longer flourish, trade will fall off, and hunting become ever less profitable."[311] In one place in East Africa, a new chief had to stand from morning to afternoon on one foot, wrapped in the smoke of a pyre;[312] this doubtless purified him from any possible taint.

In India the dead man may have a lamp that he may not grovel in utter darkness on his way.[313] Tibetan ghosts are always malicious and their names have to be burned: "ultimately a piece of paper is thrown into the flames, on which is written the name of the deceased person—always a relative—whose ghost is to be suppressed. When this paper is burned the particular ghost has received its quietus, and never can give trouble again."[314] Among the Dyaks "a lighted torch is always carried to a funeral, and when the body is buried it is extinguished at the grave." Fires are kept burning for the use of the departed at the landing-place, "for in Hades fire is not to be procured without paying for it, and if the dead find any difficulty about obtaining fire, they can come and fetch it from the fire lit by their earthly friends. This idea does not seem consistent with the many things done to prevent the soul of the dead man finding his way back to his earthly home."[315] It is doubtless a form of

[307] Holmes, in JAI, XXXII, 428.
[308] Jenness and Ballentyne, D'Entrecasteaux, 149.
[309] Lichtenstein, Reisen, II, 102.
[310] Du Chaillu, Voy. dans. l'Afr., 228, 267, 378-380.
[311] Conradt, in Globus, LXXXI, 352.
[312] Stannus, in JAI, XL, 316.
[313] Nathubhai, in JASB, III, 431.
[314] Waddell, Buddhism, 498.
[315] Gomes, Sea Dyaks, 138, 139.

propitiation and easement of passage. In Samoa, for a great man, fires are kept burning on the line from house to grave day and night to keep away evil spirits.[316] The Indians of Virginia, as a rule, did not allow the hearth-fire to go out, as its extinction was regarded by the women as an evil sign.[317] In Alaska an old woman carried fire to the window through which the body had been removed and threw it out after the body, "as she said, to purify the house; she then took up a small dog and likewise threw it out of the window to accompany the departed."[318] In California the Yurok tribe keep a fire burning certain nights in the vicinity of the grave. They hold "that the spirits of the departed are compelled to cross an extremely attenuated greased pole, which bridges over the chasm of the 'Debatable Land,' and that they require the fire to light them on their journey. A righteous soul traverses the pole quicker than a wicked one; hence they regulate the number of nights for burning a light according to the character for goodness or the opposite which the deceased possessed in this world."[319]

It was an ancient Swedish custom to put a light in the hand of a dying person.[320] Before the Mordvins put a dead person into the coffin, one of the women moves a lighted candle three times round the inside of the coffin, wishing for the dead eternal light and warmth.[321] It is perhaps needless to recall the use of fire and lights in the funeral-ceremonies of the ancients and the moderns or the presence of a fiery river-barrier about the Greek Hades and the fire-motive as employed by Dante, Milton, Wagner, and other adapters of traditional materials. At the death of Faust, evil spirits lie in wait to snatch his soul but the angel-band pelt them with flowers, which are to them as fire, and fly away with Faust's immortal part.[322]

Last to be cited among the elements used in repelling the ghost is water. Its purificatory function has been illustrated in connection with the handling of the dead and its general function in exorcism will be considered later on;[323] here we have to do only with the ghost-cult. It is noteworthy that so many peoples conceive of a water-barrier against the return of the ghost; a commonplace of legend avers that a spirit cannot wade or swim a stream, and there is a paraphernalia of bridges and ferries which allow of crossing in one direction only.

Of the death of a Fijian hero it is related: "And while his friends were still weeping, his spirit left the body and went and stood on the banks of the 'Water of the Shades' . . . at the place called Lelele—the ferry—and cried to Ceba, the ghostly ferryman, who brought the end of his canoe which was of

[316] Ella, in AAAS, 1892, 640.   [317] Bruce, *Va.*, I, 147.
[318] Niblack, in USNM, 1888, 359.
[319] Powers, in *Contrib. N. Amer. Ethnol.*, III, 58.
[320] Stärbäck, *Guldhalsbaandet* (Danish trans.), 496.
[321] *Russian Ethnog.* (Russ.), I, 273.
[322] Goethe, *Faust*, II; Act V, 618 ff.
[323] §§222, 227, above, and 276, below; Clodd, *Magic*, 67-70.

hard vesi[-wood] if it was for a chief, but the end that was of breadfruit wood for a vulgar shade."[324] In the New Hebrides the instrument used in digging the grave is thrown into the sea and all bathe; then a taboo is laid on the shore for a mile or two, which prohibits all fishing or bathing.[325] Purification by water is common among the Bantu; one of them remarked that they had as many washings "as there were among the Jews of whom we read in the Bible. It is not a matter of dirt; it is a part of the ceremony," in this case, the ceremony of initiation. "If a person is absent from home for a year or two, he will not think of touching his friend when he returns, till water is provided, when each will take a little in the hand and sprinkle it over the other." This case is somewhat derived; still, when it is recalled that the initiation represents a death, the connection with mortuary ceremonial is evident. The detail is added that the initiates use white clay to keep from being seen by the women; it "removes the signs of boyhood."[326] The Ibo pour water on a grave and the corpse is carried under water dripping from the roof; it is said to be drinking it, a feature parallel to one occurring in birth-ceremonies.[327] East Africans sometimes sink a corpse in a lake to avoid interference from spirits. In one case, a stream was dammed and the pyre built below the dam; then, after the body was burned, the river was turned in to wash away the ashes.[328] In the Niger region, "if a person is likely to die, the soul leaves the body and goes towards the stream, which divides the next world from this. If the ghosts . . . on the other side think it time that the body died, the soul is allowed to cross the stream—by a bridge, Kagoro cannot swim—but if not they drive it back, and the sick person recovers."[329] The Fan, who regard white men as ghosts, believe that their white color is due to crossing the river of the dead and the great sea, whose waters, as every black has noted, at the end of a few days make a corpse lose its pigmentation and become a livid white.[330] Holy and purifying water is used at the West African funeral for sprinkling the corpse, the room, and the spectators. Good wishes for a speedy journey accompany the ceremony.[331] Burrows[332] once demonstrated the efficiency of water-exorcism as against the traditional methods of the Mangbattu: a native woman in hysterics was being held down and nearly smothered under grass mats, the theory being that her father's spirit had come back to call her and she must go. Burrows threw a bucket of cold water over her, to the disgust of the native theorists; but in ten minutes she was asleep and the next morning was perfectly well. We are not informed as to the effect of this demonstration upon subsequent practice. At the conclusion of the funeral the Togo negroes bathe in the sea, each bringing back a little vessel of sea-water with which the priest sprinkles the walls; "thereby return is made impossible for the dead."[333] Purification is always ceremonial rather than actual. Similar water-exorcism is found in Uganda;[334] again, the dead African chief may be buried in the bed of a diverted river, as was Alaric; and Frazer,[335] who cites such

[324] Thomson, in JAI, XXIV, 351.
[325] Macdonald, in AAAS, 1892, 727.
[326] Willoughby, in JAI, XXXIX, 235.
[327] Thomas, in JAI, XLVII, 203-204. [328] Stannus, in JAI, XL, 316.
[329] Tremearne, in JAI, XLII, 158. [330] Trilles, Fân, 4-5.
[331] Ellis, Yoruba, 153. [332] Pigmies, 103.
[333] Seidel, in Globus, LXXII, 41.
[334] Johnston, Uganda, II, 589, 693. [335] In JAI, XV, 65, 79.

cases, lists a number of instances of water-purification. The Yakut' child gets its first and often only bath when it is baptized at birth.[336] Certain Tibetans sink the body of a notable man, enclosed in a box or bag, in a stream for several weeks, to wash away the evil spirit in it.[337] That a spirit cannot cross a stream is a commonplace of western tradition, as in the legend of Sleepy Hollow and the tale of Tam o' Shanter; and the wild races of the Chittagong Hills of India hold the same view. Lewin,[338] travelling in the jungle, came upon a stream bridged by a white thread. The reason was that a man having died away from home, in a distant village, and his friends having gone thither and performed the funeral-ceremonies, it was thought that his spirit would go back with them to his former home. Spirits cannot, however, cross water without help; hence the bridging of the stream. The Borneo head-hunters believe that the soul crosses a stream into the spirit-world on the "great log."[339] Certain Indians stretch a cotton thread from the dead man's house to the interment ground, no matter how distant. "I have seen the white thread following the course of the river for many miles, crossing and re-crossing the streams several times."[340] The Chippewas believe they have to cross a stream "upon a large snake that answers the purpose of a bridge; those who die from drowning never succeed in crossing the stream." Some are prevented from crossing by the snake; these are the souls of persons in a lethargy or trance, who recover, that is, return. "They think that when a soul has crossed the stream it cannot return to its body, yet they believe in apparitions, and entertain the opinion that the spirits of the departed will frequently revisit the abodes of their friends in order to invite them to the other world, and to forewarn them of their approaching dissolution."[341]

The Chaldæans offer similar evidence as to water-beliefs; they thought that the spirit-world was separated from this one by a river.[342] "The people of the west coast of Gaul believe that their dead are carried by sailors over the sea to the foggy, dark Britain."[343] In Moldavia the corpse is carried out over a piece of cloth or carpet which represents the bridge across which the soul passes to the other world.[344] "The Wends of Geislitz make a point of passing through running water as they return from a burial; in winter, if the river is frozen, they break the ice in order to wade through the water. . . . In many parts of Germany, in modern Greece, and in Cyprus, water is poured out behind the corpse, as it is being carried from the house, in the belief that, if the ghost returns, he will not be able to cross it. Sometimes by night the Germans pour holy water before the door; the ghost is then thought to stand and whimper on the further side."[345] The case of the four rivers of the Greek Hades, one of fire and three of water, and of the ferryman Charon, as well as the conceptions of Dante and of others, derived from the classics, will again occur to the reader.

[336] Sieroshevski-Sumner, in JAI, XXXI, 80.

[337] Reid, in *Cosmopolitan Mag.*, XXVIII, 452.

[338] *S.E. India*, 209.   [339] Furness, *Head-Hunters*, 62.

[340] Wickham, quoted in JAI, XXIV, 207.

[341] Yarrow, in BAE, I, 199.   [342] Maspero, *Hist. Anc.*, I, 690.

[343] Geiger, *Ostiran. Kultur*, 276.

[344] *Russian Ethnog.* (Russ.), I, 444.   [345] Frazer, in JAI, XV, 77.

These typical methods of repelling or of "laying" the ghost may be added to by the perusal, in particular, of the works of Tylor[346] and Frazer.[347] The whole subject is treated with characteristic suggestiveness by Lippert.[348] Various substances, iron, for example, are thought to possess powerful exorcistic qualities. Frazer,[349] having noted the preference for stone implements in the cult and the tabooing of iron as of something novel and profane, finds that, as a result, iron became obnoxious to the spirits and therefore a weapon against them. Again, there may be carried along in the funeral-procession the branches of a strong-smelling tree to keep off the ghosts; salt also is much used in connection with deaths and burials;[350] and all through the ceremonies of getting a head and shrinking it, which may be many and long, the Jibaro Indians use tobacco-juice. It is given by the priest, who produces it, to the slayer and his kin to keep them safe from the spirit of the slain man. It is introduced through the nose in the case of the slayer, through the mouth in that of his wife or daughter.[351]

It is necessary here to recall the spirit-quelling powers of the dog; and with him should be associated the cock.[352] It is probably no accident that the cock in the modern and survivalistic form of the "weather-cock," still watches over house and barn. "Cock-crow" is a term associated with all sorts of traditions. Consider the behavior of the royal ghost at Elsinore: "It faded on the crowing of the cock." The passage goes on to relate that there is a time when

> The bird of dawning singeth all night long:
> And then, they say, no spirit dare stir abroad,
> The nights are wholesome; then no planets strike,
> No fairy takes, nor witch hath power to charm,
> So hallow'd and so gracious is the time.[353]

[346] *Prim. Cult.*, chs. XI ff.
[347] *Golden Bough*, III (pt. II), 142, 373-374; IX (pt. VI), 123 ff., 260 ff.; XI (pt. VIII), 59 ff. and especially Frazer, "Burial Customs," in JAI, XV.
[348] *Kgchte.*, I, 111 ff.; II, 236 ff.   [349] *Golden Bough*, I, 172 ff.
[350] Thomas, in JAI, XLVII, 165; Stannus, in JAI, XL, *passim*.
[351] Karsten, "Jibaro," in BAE, Bull. LXXIX, 30, 35, 36, 38, 61, 63, 64, 66, 68, 70, 75, *et al.*
[352] §§99, above (especially §99 of the *Case-Book*), and 256, below.
[353] Shakespeare, *Hamlet*, Act I, Sc. I, 157, 160-164.

CHAPTER XXVI

THE GHOST-CULT
(POSITIVE ASPECTS)

§228. Propitiation. The foregoing methods of avoidance and expulsion have been called the negative aspect of the ghost-cult; and propitiation would appear to be set over against them as a positive aspect. Yet propitiation in itself is really negative until it works out into a form where the supernatural being is attracted and held as a sort of familiar or guardian spirit. In reviewing propitiation, therefore, we have still to do with the unfavorable phase of the aleatory element—mischance—which so preoccupied the attention of primitive man. By far the larger number of the instances reveal propitiation as a buying-off of prospective ill rather than a winning of good, as a species of insurance wherein a regular sacrifice of wealth is acquiesced in for the sake of avoiding unreckonable ruin. Fear rather than hope underlies the ghost-cult.

It is not safe to let well enough alone. The relation to the ghosts may not be taken up or laid down at will; there is no such thing as a neutral position toward them, in the occupation of which there is nothing to hope and nothing to fear. The ghosts have rights and the survivors have duties in the nature of the case and entirely irrespective of any dealings between them. Men are duty-bound by the fact of being alive. It requires no positive act of hostility on their part to bring down ill from the ghosts; ignorance, indifference, or neglect are more than enough. There is need, in fact, of considerable attention on the part of the men if they aim at no more than the preservation of existing conditions, that is, if they are not to suffer excessively. The ghosts levy, as it were, a sort of fixed charge of propitiation to keep hands off. The struggle for existence is for them projected beyond the grave; and that struggle must be carried on for the dead by the living. To this the ghosts have a right that is as strong as their might is believed to be. The fact that they are naïvely conceived to be frightened off by noise or blows affects these rights of theirs in no permanent way; and if they are exorcised by the aid of other supernatural beings, their rights are merely transferred to those beings.

For all the phenomena which man could not explain spiritual beings were the unquestioned agency. The ghosts demanded support and punished every neglect with calamity: pain, disease, lightning, hail. Through connection with the notion of neglected duty, man's fear was ready to be awakened by any mischance; even nowadays people are terrified by their consciences in the presence of disaster. In its long history, this correlation of calamity and sin covers the whole range of notions, from that of neglected ghosts manifesting their vexation to that of a divine judgment; from punishment in this world to retribution in another; from chastisement for a time to eternal damnation; from the notion of justice consisting in the performance of ritual observances to that of a fulfillment of the most highly developed moral law.

There is no way to escape the duty fastened upon man by his helplessness in the face of the personalized luck element; hence, whatever the stage of belief, the cult includes propitiation as a form of insurance. Fire is an ill that may come despite the most scrupulous watchfulness, so that one is rightly regarded as careless, ignorant, or reckless who does not insure against it; to the savage the ills that might arise from failure to insure himself against the malicious caprice of the spirits were infinitely greater than loss of property or even life—so much greater and more fearsome that even he, in his improvidence, could not think of remaining for any period uncovered to them. Not to fulfill the duties correlative to the rights of the ghosts was sin, and the wages of sin have never been underestimated by the credulous. Hence men seek to meet the desires of the disembodied dead; and, in accordance with their conception of the ghosts, the method adopted is that which has proved itself effective in conciliating the most powerful among the living, only the effort is the more strenuous because the ghosts have transcendent power.

A number of the practices of propitiation are known as mourning-customs. There is no objection to that term if the current connotation of grief in bereavement is not carried along with it. Although pain because of the loss of loved ones is by no means wholly absent among primitive peoples, yet mourning is prevailingly ritualistic rather than what we should call genuine, as can readily be seen if one scans the evidence with the distinction in mind. Savages may be very cheerful up to the hour set for lamentation and then howl miserably for a season, shedding the while a copious flood of tears, thereafter to resume abruptly their former light-hearted mood. Professional mourners may be hired, thus relieving the family from most of the onerousness of the task. There is very little that can be referred to grief that is actual and disinterested in the sense that it is not placative, and very little also that cannot be most reasonably explained upon the basis of ghost-fear.[1]

Propitiation is generally conceived of as a positive effort to win prosperity, whereas it is based upon fear of ill luck rather than upon hope of positive good fortune. It is really another type of avoidance. It is performed because if it were omitted calamity would ensue. There is here a sort of transitional form between plain dodging, on the one hand, and a genuine effort, on the other, to serve the interests of the dead because of love and pity for them. Propitiation might be said to be a positive way of avoiding. A number of the accompanying cases will therefore present an aspect in which they look like mere avoidance; they will, at any rate, anchor the conception of propitiation in the concrete.

"According to the belief of the Papuan, the ghosts bring sickness, poor harvests, and war, as well as all other mischance. And it is not least from fear of them, and in order to get them from the outset into a good mood, that they care for the ghosts of the dead after their death."[2] In Melanesia, "the doctor called in will discover the *tindatho* who causes the complaint he has to treat, by suspending a stone or heavy ornament at the end of a string which he holds in his hand, and calling over the names of the lately deceased; when the name of him who caused the disease is called the stone swings in answer. Then it remains to ask what shall be given to appease the anger of the ghost—a mash of yams, a fish, a pig, a man. The answer is given in the same way; whatever is desired is offered on the dead man's grave, and the sickness goes."[3] The San Cristoval Islanders told Fox and Drew[4] that their fathers used to sacrifice everywhere, not alone in the shrines. "Sacrifices in the sea were made, first to the spirits of the open sea . . . and secondly to men who died and were buried in the sea. . . . For example, if one of you, Drew or Fox, were to die, and he was buried in the sea . . . next year perhaps the survivor would be thinking of his friend who died, and he would get yam and almonds and take them

---

[1] §233, below.
[2] Krieger, *Neu-Guinea*, 402.
[3] Codrington, *Melanesians*, 196.
[4] In JAI, XLV, 165-166.

to the place where the body was let down into the water, and he would throw them into the sea there with some such words as these: 'My friend (or my brother, or my uncle) this is my sacrifice to you, so that you may protect me this year when I dig my garden and look kindly on the produce of the garden.' At the rock in the sea sacred to sharks they sacrificed to sharks and to men who died and were buried there. At the shrine in the village they sacrificed to sharks, spirits of the sea and the dead, and in the village also they sacrificed to the spirits of the land, and to snakes and to those who died and were buried anywhere in the ground or in caves." Here it will be seen that the dead man took his place immediately with other spiritual powers that demanded propitiation. Infant ghosts are not feared in the Andaman Islands and infants are buried near at hand; but adults are carried to a distance and there buried or placed on a platform. The latter form is considered more complimentary, as it takes more time and labor.[5] In Africa, "if the fruitful rain fails, sacrifice is made to the dead; if some one falls ill, a discontented ghost is the cause; a pest that sweeps away the herds is brought by disgruntled dead men. If uncertainty prevails, the future appears dark and perilous, or a crime ought to be disclosed, the negroes turn to their highest court—the dead."[6] "To provide a proper burial for the dead relation is the great duty of a negro's life, its only rival in his mind is the desire to have a burial of his own. But, in a good negro, this passion will go under before the other, and he will risk his very life to do it."[7] The Mangbattu leave cooked food and oil in the forest, so that the ghost shall not return to the house for them;[8] clearly they hope from the sacrifice for nothing but to be let alone. The following cases illustrate in particular how propitiation is but one aspect of avoidance. If a certain kind of snake enters a Kikuyu hut, "it is necessary to pour some milk or fat on the floor for the reptile to drink; it may drink and leave, or it may not. If it does, well and good; if not, the owner of the village has to kill a sheep, cook some of its fat, and pour it out in the hut, saying at the same time: 'We offer you some fat to drink, we beg of you to leave us.' It is believed that an *ngoma* or spirit has come in the guise of a snake, and on no account must such a snake be killed. After the sacrifice of the sheep has been made the snake will always go, but it mysteriously disappears, no one sees it leave."[9]

When an Ainu "is about to be buried, whether man, woman, or child, the spirit is still spoken to as if it were present in the corpse, and is supposed to partake of the burial feast together with the mourners. . . . The possessions of the dead and his hut are burned. . . . To prevent the spirit of the dead from coming to disturb his relatives, prayers and sacrifices are made to him. These are the most regular ceremonies in the Ainu religion; even women, who do not join in religious ceremonies as a rule, take part in the sacrifices for dead husbands and ancestors." Their prayer is: "Watch over us and keep us from sickness. Give us a long life so that we may continue to offer such gifts."[10] "For seven days after death it is believed that the spirit, to the eyes of other spirits, appears to wear the clothes in which the dead person is buried, so the relatives try to make him look as nice as possible, so that he need not be ashamed when he meets other ghosts as he travels on the road of

[5] Man, in JAI, XII, 144.   [6] Frobenius, *Masken*, 161.
[7] Kingsley, *Travels W. Afr.*, 491.   [8] Burrows, *Pigmies*, 103.
[9] Hobley, in JAI, XLI, 408.
[10] Czaplicka, *Aborig. Siberia*, 153, 154.

the dead."[11] The Chinese have "a prevailing belief that disembodied souls continue wandering about the corpse, and enjoy the offerings that are made on the spot in their behalf."[12] "Now be off to the other world; we don't want you here any longer, now that you are dead," is the Tarahumari exhortation. "He who is above us will carry you off. What do you wish here, wandering around like a coyote? Go away from us. We don't want you. Therefore we give you provisions for the journey."[13] The Greeks attributed inexplicable misfortune to the neglect of the soul-cult and made expiation by special attention to the dead.[14] "Not out of that which we call piety, but out of fear of a 'ghost,' become mightier through its departure from the body, are to be explained such superabundant funeral gifts as are expended at the burial of Patroclus."[15] That this original fear of the dead may change into a derived emotion is not denied; but fear and avoidance are the primordial forms. Gomme[16] notes this inconsistency in Britain: "On the one hand there is a definite representation of a cult of the dead based on the fear of dead kindred and found in isolated patches of the country; on the other hand there is a definite representation of a cult of the dead based on the love of dead kindred and found generally prevalent over the country." Hearn[17] expresses very eloquently this evolved attitude of the Japanese toward their dead.

To enumerate the forms of propitiation would be to list the ways in which human beings may minister to other human beings' needs and desires. The ghosts were given what they wanted; and they wanted what men of their place and time wanted. This is a phase of projectivism.[18] In general, spirits do not call for immaterial things or states of mind in their surviving relatives but for material contributions: for meat or tobacco, for ornament, amusement, flattery, self-abasement. In short, they demand that which would have made life enjoyable to them on earth. The fact should be noted in the following groups of cases that the care and expense incurred in propitiation of ghosts is directly proportional to the importance of the deceased during life. There is no exaltation of the poor and lowly in primitive religion.

Consider the illuminating case quoted by Spencer[19] from Bishop Callaway. A Zulu has been plagued by the spirit of his brother; he has "seen" his brother. They ask what he said and the Zulu replies: "I dreamed that he was beating me, and saying, 'How is it that you do no longer know that I am?' I answered him, saying, 'When I do know you, what can I do that you may see I know you? I know that you are my brother.' He answered me as soon as I said this,

[11] Milne, *Eastern Clan*, 290.　　　[12] DeGroot, *Relig. Syst.*, I, 22.
[13] Lumholtz, in *Scribner's Mag.*, XVI, 444.
[14] Ramsay, "Relig. of Greece," in *Hastings's Dict. Bible,* extra vol., 132.
[15] Rohde, *Psyche*, I, 21.　　　[16] *Ethnol. in Folklore*, 126.
[17] *Japan*, chs. III, IV, IX.　　　[18] §206, above.
[19] *Prin. Soc.*, I, §71, from Callaway, *Relig. Amazulu*, 146-147.

and asked, 'When you sacrifice a bullock, why do you not call upon me?' I replied, 'I do call on you, and laud you by your laud-giving names. Just tell me the bullock which I have killed, without calling on you. For I killed an ox, I called on you; I killed a barren cow, I called on you.' He answered, saying, 'I wish for meat.' I refused him, saying, 'No, my brother, I have no bullock; do you see any in the cattle-pen?' He replied, 'Though there be but one, I demand it.' When I awoke, I had a pain in my side."

The spirits are jealous of their interests in the matter of food and, in general, of maintenance; they are likewise prone to insist upon their marital rights. Hobley[20] mentions a curious custom in Ukamba which throws strong light upon their spiritual beliefs. "If a young unmarried man is killed away from his village, his *muimu* or spirit will return there and speak to the people through the medium of an old woman in a dance . . . and say, 'I am so and so speaking, and I want a wife.' The youth's father will then make arrangements to buy a girl from another village and bring her to his, and she will be mentioned as the wife of the deceased, speaking of him by name. She will presently be married to a brother of the deceased, but she must continue to live in the village where the deceased had his home. If at any time the corporeal husband beats or ill-treats her, and she in consequence runs away to her father, the *muimu* of the deceased will come and pester the people of the village and they will have bad luck; it will probably ask, through the usual medium, why his wife has been ill-treated and driven away. The head of the family will then take steps to induce the girl to return for fear of the wrath of the spirit of his deceased son." Here is to be noted the fact that the girl is really married to the brother of the dead man, just as if she had been the deceased's wife during his life;[21] and also that the usual medium for receiving messages from the other world is an old woman.[22]

That the dead profit at once by the offerings made at their funerals is well known; of the king Radama, in Madagascar, "it was reported and firmly believed that his ghost was seen one night in the garden of his country-seat, dressed in one of the uniforms buried with him, *and riding on one of the horses, killed opposite his tomb.*" Such offerings are so important for well-being in the future life that a man may provide them for himself. In the East Indies, "out of fear that their heirs may forget to bring the offering, some buy, during their lifetime, a buffalo which, when they are dead, must be slaughtered. . . . The more prominent the family the more pigs are slain. Among the northern Nias islanders the number is determined according to the rank of the deceased; often it reaches eighty large and forty small ones."[23]

A further typical case of propitiation is exhibited by the Palaungs. "Ropes are passed over the coffin and under the wagon; two very long and strong ropes are fastened to the front, and two, equally long and strong, are fastened to the back. Next day the people come in great numbers, the men placing themselves before the wagon, the women behind it. As many as can do so take hold of the ropes, and then a gigantic tug-of-war takes place, the men trying to pull the wagon forward, the women trying to hold it back. There may be three hundred pulling at each end, and the ropes extend far up and down the street. . . . The idea is that if the spirit of the Chief has not yet gone to eat

---

[20] In JAI, XLI, 422. 　　　　　　　　[21] §395, below.
[22] §§58, above, and 257, below.
[23] Wilken, in VG, III, 105-106; he quotes Ellis, *Madagascar*, I, 429-430.

the fruit of forgetfulness, he will be pleased to see that the people are trying to pull his body towards them because they love him and want to keep his body near them."[24]

There is nothing spiritual, except the germs of a later development, in the primitive ghost-cult. In the impracticability of exhausting the forms of propitiation, there will be selected certain typical practices which, in addition to illustrating the ghost-cult, also offer enlightening information in themselves.

§229*. Human Sacrifice. The material wants of the ghost are met by the sacrifice of wealth in various forms; then there are other wants that can be satisfied only by human sacrifice. Cannibals naturally sacrifice human flesh to the ghosts as they do other forms of food; there are also forms of human sacrifice less obvious than this. When the soul is laid or expedited to the spirit-world, it is often accompanied by a "grave-escort" of human beings,[25] persons who have been in some way intimately connected with the earthly life of the departed: his wife; less often his children; generally some of his slaves, especially if he had been a man of position; not infrequently some of his subjects, if he had been a chief; and most often, perhaps, some of his enemies and in particular that one of them who slew him. Such procedure is strictly in accord with the idea of projectivism, for the ghost is going to pursue life as lived on earth and needs wife, slave, and subject there as here. He thirsts for vengeance upon his slayer and is pleased to have that enemy's soul accompany him as a slave. Nor does acquiescence in this practice of human sacrifice have to be forced upon its victims; they too accept the theory and even wish to accompany the dead. Wives will often commit suicide at the death of their husbands and subjects at the passing of their rulers. If the practice is inveterate in the mores, the victim thinks as little of resisting it or regarding it as cruelty or as an invasion of his rights as savage women do of protesting against man's oppression and asserting their "natural and inalienable" prerogatives.

In Melanesia "the dead man's wife and child were . . . dragged to the open grave and strangled there, and their bodies thrown in, together with his

[24] Milne, *Eastern Clan,* 311.
[25] Main, *Relig. Chastity,* ch. IV and appendix, notes III, IV, cites numerous cases.

possessions, guns, rifles, money, and valuables of all kinds."[26] In the New
Hebrides they strangle the mother, aunt, or grandmother of a beloved child
who has died, that it may have care in the next life.[27] "An excuse for the
practice of widow-strangling may be found in the fact that, according to
Fijian belief, it is a needful precautionary measure"; for at a certain place
on the road to the spirit-world lies in wait a terrible spirit which is utterly
implacable toward the ghosts of the unmarried. "Hence it is absolutely necessary for a man to have at least one of his wives, or at all events, a female
ghost of some sort following him." This need is a variant from the ordinary
ones; the case of the dead woman anticipates a following topic. "Women are
let off more easily. If the wife die before her husband, the desolate widower
cuts off his beard, and puts it under her left armpit. This serves as a certifi-
cate of marriage." She produces it when she encounters the spirit and he lets
her pass.[28] Turner[29] says that it was common in the New Hebrides, "on the
death of a chief, to strangle his wives, that they might accompany him to the
regions of the departed. The custom has been found in various parts of the
Pacific. The poor deluded woman rejoices in it, if she has any affection for
her husband, and not only shows us the strength of her attachment, but also
her firm belief in the reality of a future state. An old chief will say as he is
dying, 'Now, who will go with me?' and immediately one and another will
reply, 'I will.' "
    In South Africa, "if a boy dies before having touched a woman, a girl is
sent after him into Hades to be his wife there. Formerly, it may be, the girl
was buried with him, either alive or dead. At present the girl is sent only
ceremonially into Hades by the art of the witchdoctor."[30] It is a common
feature of the funeral in West Central Africa that human beings are sacrificed. Two hundred of each sex were slain at one king's burial. Slaves used
to be buried regularly with chiefs; now pigeons take their place. The corpse
used to lie on a number of live male slaves. If any one of these men sneezed
he was let off.[31] In the Upper Congo region, "after the coffin had been put in
the grave, men came forward, and taking a spear, called upon the spirits of
those the deceased had killed in war to attend their conqueror in the spirit
world, and every time the name was mentioned or an order given a thrust
was made with a spear. The person whose funeral I attended had killed seven
persons, and their skulls were at the base of the wild fig tree just in front of
his house. Different men called on the different spirits, and so far as I could
ascertain it was those who knew all the particulars of the slain, and the
circumstances attending their death that had to call on them to attend and
obey the deceased." This case is one of a grave-escort provided by a man
during his life-time; there are plenty of instances in which it is assembled
after a man's death by his relatives and friends. "If the family of the deceased
man were troubled with much sickness, and a witch doctor said that it was
due to the dissatisfaction of the spirit of such an one because no offering had
lately been made to him, then the family would kill a slave as a sacrifice, and
send him with a message to their troublesome relative, and a request that he

26 Codrington, *Melanesians,* 257, note.
27 Turner, *Samoa,* 326.   28 Fison, in JAI, X, 138.
29 *Samoa,* 324.   30 Gottschling, in JAI, XXXV, 381.
31 Thomas, in JAI, XLVII, 180, 184; and in JAI, L, 379; Stannus, in JAI,
XL, 315.

would not cause them any further misfortune. We induced them to give up this custom, but the timorous ones compromised the matter by burying in the grave of their deceased relative some brass rods equal to the price of a slave. The occasion was as follows: The river was rising rapidly and flooding the low lying town of Monsembe, and as the water rose higher and higher the head-men met together to decide what was to be done to cause the river to subside. I attended the conference, which lasted three hours. They suggested one reason after another for the flood, and at last they were of a unanimous opinion that the father of one of the men present was angry with his family for slighting him so long, and to show his disapprobation he had caused the river (River Congo) thus to rise, and the only way to secure its subsiding was to throw a human sacrifice into the river. I protested strongly against this murder, and pointed out to them that in order to stop the river from rising they should send their 'rain doctor' 500 miles up river to stop the rain from falling, and thus allow the waters to subside. They answered that their 'rain doctor' would have no power if he went so far, as he could stop the rain only in his own district. We had a long talk, and at last they were persuaded not to throw a person into the river. They compromised the matter, and got up a mimic canoe fight in honour of the dissatisfied spirit and scattered 600 brass rods in the river—the price of a slave—in lieu of a human sacrifice. A short time after the river began to subside and all were satisfied with the result of the conference and their compromise."[32]

In the Unyoro regions of East Africa native custom positively required the suicide of a wife on her husband's grave.[33] At the death of a certain West African king, we are told, only four men were sacrificed, but forty-two of his wives poisoned themselves in order to accompany him to the land of the dead. "At the present day [1894], amongst all the tribes, when a king or chief dies it is usual for two of his wives to commit suicide, and should no volunteers be forthcoming, two are selected and put to death."[34] In one part of the Sudan, it was customary to bury a young male and a young female slave that the dead master might have, in the spirit-world, someone to keep the flies away and to serve his food.[35]

Miss Kingsley[36] explains the murder of wives and slaves at a funeral by citing the belief that they are to be witnesses to testify to the rank of the deceased. Further, "the common-sense element in the killing of wives and slaves . . . consists in the fact that it discourages poisoning." A man's "wives and slaves, no longer restrained by the prospect of being killed at his death and sent off with him would, on very slight aggravation, put 'bush in his chop.'" Here is a quaint species of life-insurance. The negroes believe in rein-carnation and that each soul is put back into the rank and family from which it came. When a king dies, his domestics solicit the honor of being buried with him—a privilege accorded to only a few of his favorites; an observer has seen slaves of defunct chiefs appealing to be allowed to join their late master. They are let down into the vault, which is closed by a single flagstone. Each morning after the interment the stone is lifted and they are asked if they have

---

[32] Weeks, in JAI, XXXIX, 452, 454-455.
[33] Johnston, *Uganda*, II, 280.   [34] Ellis, *Yoruba*, 104, 105.
[35] Nachtigal, *Sahara*, II, 687.
[36] *W. Afr. Studies*, 146, 452; *Travels W. Afr.*, 488, 489; Oliveira Martins, *Raças*, II, 176.

found the king, until the time when, no answer being heard, it is concluded that they have. Then ensue orgies accompanied with a general relaxation of law and order; murders are committed and the bodies of the victims are brought as offerings to the departed, though at any other time murder is severely punished. This indiscriminate campaign after victims is paralleled elsewhere. In Ashanti, at the death of a king, his sons, brothers, and nephews, feigning madness, rush out and discharge their guns indiscriminately at any person they may chance to meet; similarly a Dyak who has lost a child kills the first man he meets as he leaves his house; it is to him a matter of duty.[37] On the Zanzibar Coast at the death of a chief the young men kill any stranger they encounter who is a pure black; an hereditary official must eat, unseen by anyone, the hands of the victim, and his skull is made into a cup for the new chief.[38] Servants sacrificed to the dead man have their legs cut off so that they may not run away from his service.[39] Junker[40] is astonished that female slaves follow their master voluntarily to the grave "on the hypothesis that the dead man, even in the grave, will feed and support them!"

The custom of the *suttee*, or immolation of the wife on the husband's pyre, in India is well known. In China, the burial of living beings with the dead dates doubtless "from the darkest mist of ages"; it has been traced down to the fourteenth century A.D. "Daughters, daughters-in-law and widows especially, being imbued with the doctrine that they are the property of their dead parents, parents-in-law and husbands . . . often take their own lives, in order to follow them into the next world." Such suicides increased as substitutes for immolations at burials. The Chinese came to replace real human victims with puppets that were placed near the feet of the dead, first on the water-bed and then in the coffin.[41] In old Japan, "human victims were buried up to the neck in a circle about the grave, and thus left to perish under the beaks of birds and the teeth of wild beasts." This custom was abolished over nine-teen centuries ago; but the practice of following one's master by suicide (*junshi*) was an honored usage among the samurai of the sixteenth century A.D. "Loyal retainers esteemed it a duty to kill themselves after the death of their lord, in order to wait upon him during his ghostly journey." The author[42] cites touching cases of his own time, one of which "was that of a boy fourteen years old, who killed himself in order to wait upon the spirit of a child, his master's little son." A striking modern instance is the suicide of the famous Japanese general, Nogi, who sought to follow his master, the Emperor; and it is paralleled by the suicide of Tolstoi's coachman.[43] The grave-escorts de-scribed above are typical of those reported from the Malay Archipelago,[44] North and South America,[45] and among Indo-Europeans.[46]

[37] Letourneau, *Soc.*, 242, 226.   [38] Stuhlmann, *Mit Emin*, 38.

[39] Ratzel, *Vkde.*, I, 517.   [40] *Afrika*, I, 366-367.

[41] DeGroot, *Relig. Syst.*, II, 721 ff., 735; I, 24.

[42] Hearn, *Japan*, 46, 47, 48.

[43] N. Y. *Times*, Dec. 26, 1926; Assoc. Press despatch, Nov. 28, 1910.

[44] Roth, *Sarawak*, I, 157; Veth, *Borneo's Wester-Afdeeling*, II, 280; Cayley-Webster, *New Guinea*, 160, 161.

[45] Yarrow, in BAE, I, 179, 180, 187; Nadaillac, *Preh. Amer.*, 304.

[46] Schrader, *Aryans*, 391; Ibn Fozlan, "Om Nordisk Begravelsesskikke," in *Vid. Selsk. Forh.*, XX, 9.

Wilken[47] is as satisfactory as usual on this topic. He notes that at the *tiwah*-feast, the festival of the dead, slaves and pawns are sacrificed. On the evening of the first day of the feast they are taken out of prison and their souls removed; thus their bodies, while alive, remain really soulless things, to be tortured without scruple. They are put to death the next day by being fastened to a pole and slowly executed by spear-thrusts. Perelaer,[48] from whom this is taken, saw a feast in 1863 in which in eight days forty victims were killed. Where the Dutch rule has made itself felt this custom has been suppressed, "but, in order to be faithful to tradition, one, two, or three buffaloes are bound to a stake and made way with in no less gruesome fashion with lance-stabs." Another survival is where slaves are told off to accompany the deceased, their necks stretched over a stump for beheading, and then struck lightly with the back of a sword. Some of them have lost their minds from apprehension under the ordeal. Chinese travellers have mentioned former practices of wife-sacrifice in Java; and the author quotes Valentijn as having reported that in 1691, at the death of a prince, of his four hundred wives two hundred and seventy were krissed. Each carried a turtle-dove which was allowed to escape just before the slaughter; it represented the soul of the wife. Later the usage became survivalistic; "on the death of a man the relations weep and wail, at the same time knocking their heads against the wall; while the women tie a cloth round their necks to strangle themselves, but the men interfere before any harm is done nowadays, though, in former times, the women are said to have actually strangled themselves on such occasions."

The most strenuous effort has been made by many peoples to utilize the souls of dead enemies as slaves for the departed; "in the English border custom the strength of the dead enemy is used to light the departed soul of the slayer to its rest, and the light from an enemy's strength already in ghost land would be a surer guide than any other light."[49]

The practice of head-hunting, elsewhere[50] considered, in common with most other primitive usages, is not susceptible of explanation on the basis of a single cause; certainly one of the objects aimed at is to secure an offering for the dead at the funeral, "for they believe that the souls of the slain become serviceable to the deceased in the hereafter."[51] All such views are intimately connected with the conception of the location of the soul, in this case in the head.[52]

The classic ground for head-hunting is the Malay Archipelago and environs: New Guinea and the Philippines. It is, according to Hagen,[53] "an immediate consequence of blood-vengeance." That means that the souls of the slain are propitiated by the retaliation. But even when the notion of blood-vengeance is not explicit, the idea is that the deceased shall have servants in the next

[47] In VG, III, 91-92, 97-101. Instances abound.
[48] *Dajaks,* 18, 160, 161-163, 243-246, 249.
[49] Gomme, *Ethnol. in Folklore,* 157.
[50] §292, below.
[51] Wilken, *Vkde.,* 393.
[52] §213, above.
[53] *Papua's,* 253.

life.[54] "The Dyak chief's grave is encircled with strong bamboo, upon which fresh heads are placed as the most acceptable offering to the deceased. No warrior would dare to appear before the family of the chief without at least one head as a consolatory present; these are thickly studded round the grave and occasionally renewed during the first year or two, the old ones being considered the property of the succeeding chief." It is a Bornean belief also that the persons whose heads one takes will be his slaves in the next world. Cases are found where "they will purchase a slave, guilty of any capital crime, at five-fold his value, that they may be his executioners. . . . Until a head is taken they cannot marry again, or appease the spirit of the departed, which continues to haunt the house and to make its presence known by certain ghostly rappings. They endeavor to mollify its anger by throwing a packet of rice to it under the house every day, until the spirit is laid to rest by their being able to celebrate a head feast: then the Dayaks forget their dead and the ghosts of the dead forget them."[55] "If all has been done to show befitting grief and respect—if the mourners have been on a raid and secured a nice head wherewith to decorate the grave or the household hearth,—then the spirit retires to the nether world, never again to return."[56] Wars are waged in Celebes in order to get heads, which are also trophies calculated to inspire the admiration of the women.[57]

Naturally this subject has had considerable attention from Wilken;[58] particularly in his treatment of animism, the hair-sacrifice, and skull-worship has he gathered instances of great significance; and he has applied to these his remarkable powers of interpretation. Raids for heads take place prior to a burial, the head supplying the necessary human sacrifice to lay the ghost. The person whose skull is offered to the dead man will be subject to him in the next life, just as the wife who is killed at his grave will serve him as she would have done if he had lived. Wilken's editor enlarges on the connection between head-hunting and name-giving. Before decapitating a victim he is asked his name, which is given the child. If the name is not caught clearly, they give the sound they do hear; one child bore the name "I do not know." If one gets such a name he need never fear that he will not have a slave after death; he needs only let his name be heard and the slave will appear. "Aladdin's wonder-lamp!" If a child has no such name, it is because his father is too lazy or careless to have provided a victim. There is no blood-thirst here; only a provision for the child's future life.

The Jibaro Indians of Ecuador have the custom of shrinking the human heads which they take; such an object, which is about the size of a fist, is called a *tsantsa*. There are many ceremonials connected with the preparation. Karsten,[59] who enters upon a full description of them, finds them founded upon several fundamental ideas: "(1) That in the trophy . . . the spirit or soul of the killed enemy is seated; (2) that the spirit, attached to the head, is thirsting for revenge and is trying to harm the slayer in every possible way; (3) that in case this danger is paralyzed through the different rites of the

54 Wilken, *Vkde.*, 307; Veth, *Borneo's Wester-Afdeeling*, II, 279; Bock, *Borneo*, 92.

55 Roth, *Sarawak*, I, 140, note; II, 141, 142.

56 Furness, *Head-Hunters*, 140.   57 Riedel, in *Bijd.*, XXXV, 89.

58 In VG, III, 92 ff.; IV, aanteekening IV.

59 "Jibaro," in BAE, Bull. LXXIX, 87, 89; N. Y. *Times*, April 6, 1924.

feast, the trophy is changed into a 'fetish,' a thing charged with supernatural power which the victor may make use of in different ways and in different departments of life. . . . The *tsantsa* of the Jibaro Indians, thus, is not a 'trophy' in the common sense of the word; not exclusively a mark of distinction or a visible proof that an enemy has been killed. The Jibaro warrior not only tries to take the life of his enemy, but above everything wants to secure control of his soul. Conformably to this, the so-called *einsupani* is not merely a victory feast in the sense familiar to us, but at the same time, and first of all, a kind of mystery feast." On account of the high prices now obtained for these shrunken human heads, sold mainly to tourists, the practice of head-hunting has increased and the government of Ecuador is said to be concerned over the epidemic of warfare between native tribes thus occasioned.

It is a sort of inverse idea, as compared with that of escort, when the Indian baby is buried with the dead mother lest she come back to claim it.[60]

A rather ridiculous survival of head-hunting is recounted by Hutton.[61] "In the administered village . . . war is gradually receding into the limbo of the forgotten past, except in so far as the desire to wear the warrior's pigs' tushes and cowrie gauntlets keeps the young men desirous of going as carriers on expeditions on which they hope for a chance of 'touching meat' and thus acquiring the right to put on the coveted ornaments. It is partly this desire, as well as loyalty, which at the time of writing [1921] has just taken 1,000 Semas to work in France. In their own villages they have to confine themselves to the more modest exploits of cutting off the tail of a neighbour's cow, a deed of chastened daring which is followed by the hanging up of the beast's tail and the performance of a genna [taboo] as though for the taking of a head. Incidentally, the animal . . . which is thus treated loses all its value for ceremonial purposes and becomes fit only for sale as meat, for the owner himself cannot even eat of it, much less kill it at a feast, so that the animal loses at least 50 per cent of its market value." Apparently the soul of the animal is robbed along with its tail.

Where the sacrifice of the whole body is not customary, there often occur cases of partial or exuvial sacrifice: dispensable parts of the body (*exuvies*) are cut off or blood is let; a part is offered in place of the whole. This is done at the time of the funeral and the scars witnessing to the sacrifice are for the mutilated person, when he comes to die, a sort of passport over the road to the spirit-world.

When the Australian husband dies, "the widow has to gash her scalp right down the middle line of the head, and then sear the wound thus made with a fire-stick. The husband includes, of course, any man with whom it is lawful for her to have marital relations." It is from middle age on that this rite is insisted upon and the result is that among the tribes that have the practice every elderly woman "has a more or less bare streak in the middle of the scalp marked by a hard scar."[62] In Victoria the widow cuts off her hair above her

60 Koch, in *Globus*, LXXXI, 108.   61 *Sema Nagas*, 173-174.
62 Spencer and Gillen, *North. Tr. Cent. Aust.*, 43.

forehead and in a sort of frenzy burns with fire-sticks herself and anyone who would try to interfere. At length she takes ashes and rubs them into her wounds. The only part of her not touched by the fire-sticks is her face; she scratches it, at length, "until the blood mingles with the ashes which partly hide her cruel wounds."[63] Again, members of the tribe stand or kneel over the dead in turns and are struck in turn on the head with a large boomerang until a quantity of blood flows over the body.[64] "If the deceased was highly esteemed, a second bleeding takes place."[65] In the New Hebrides the mourners gash their bodies.[66] A rather common custom is the amputation of a finger-joint the morning after the funeral. In certain districts "adults shrank from the pain this mutilation caused, so little children were made the victims, children who were often too young to know what was about to happen to them. No distinction of sex was made, but only near relatives might be made to suffer, usually the dead man's child, or younger brother or sister. . . . The thumb was always left intact, and the right-hand little finger was never mutilated in boys or men because they used it to whirl the sling. Men seldom lose more than two or three finger-joints, but it is not at all unusual for a woman to have all the fingers of one or even of both hands maimed. Only one finger was cut on each occasion, and the second knuckle-joint was never touched. The left hand suffered first."[67] Among the Jekris in the Niger region, practically all relations shave their heads, and all equally dislike doing so;[68] this is a pretty common form of partial sacrifice. In Uganda "if a man has killed an enemy in war, he propitiates his enemy's spirit by shaving his head for three days after his return.[69] "Whenever a Niam-niam has lost any very near relative, the first token of his bereavement is shown by shaving his head. His elaborate coiffure—that which had been his pride and delight, the labor of devoted conjugal hands—is all ruthlessly destroyed, the tufts, the braids, the tresses being scattered to the roads and recesses of the wilderness."[70] The Ibo put blood on the eyes of a corpse to "open his eyes."[71]

Such disfigurement may well be interpreted as disguise but better as a substitute for human sacrifice.[72] The Cherkess, mourning for his father, takes a strip of skin off his face from ear to ear.[73] Scratching the face till the blood runs, together with cutting the hair and casting it upon the dead person, is found among several tribes in Siberia.[74] Gashing and tearing the hair were common in Samoa[75] and cuttings of face or neck in New Zealand.[76] Among the Indians it is the woman who "sits by the grave to keep burning the ghost fire, brings food and water for the hungering and thirsting manes and cuts off her hair and mutilates her body if perchance she may persuade the homesick shade to depart in peace."[77] The man's tresses are of greater importance

[63] Smyth, Vict., I, 104-105.
[64] Matthews, in JAI, XXIV, 187.
[65] Bonney, in JAI, XIII, 134.
[66] Leggatt, in AAAS, 1892, 700.
[67] Jenness and Ballentyne, D'Entrecasteaux, 115, 116.
[68] Granville and Roth, in JAI, XXVIII, 108.
[69] Johnston, Uganda, II, 783.
[70] Schweinfurth, Heart of Afr., II, 34.
[71] Thomas, in JAI, XLVII, 171.
[72] §224, above; Wilken, Vkde., 317.
[73] Rubruck, Eastern Parts, 100 (Rockhill's note).
[74] Russian Ethnog. (Russ.), II, 246, 364, 388, 486.
[75] Ella, in AAAS, 1892, 640.
[76] Tregear, in JAI, XIX, 104.
[77] Mason, Woman's Share, 251.

and only a lock or two can be spared.[78] At the funeral of a Crow head-chief a chief called Long Hair "cut off a large roll of his hair; a thing he was never known to do before. The cutting and hacking of human flesh exceeded all my previous experience; fingers were dismembered as readily as twigs, and blood was poured out like water. Many of the warriors would cut two gashes nearly the entire length of their arm; then, separating the skin from the flesh at one end, would grasp it in their other hand, and rip it asunder to the shoulder. Others would carve various devices upon their breasts and shoulders, and raise the skin in the same manner to make the scars show to advantage after the wound was healed."[79] The connection here to be noted is the passage of funeral-gashing into distinguishing ornamental or tribal marks. The Botocudos had but one bond, the huge wooden plug in the lower lip, a national mark from which they were named, and a peculiar dressing of the hair.[80] Schomburgk[81] speaks of the bloody death-dance of the Arawaks. Newcomers to the funeral were switched vigorously upon the calves, holding out their legs to receive the blows. Blood flowed from the lacerations and skin and flesh hung in rags. The victims sometimes needed weeks to recover. In the case of a rich man's death the performance was repeated several times. One saw scarcely a single grown Arawak without many scars on his legs.[82]

The Jews had to be warned repeatedly not to cut hair or beard or gash themselves for the dead.[83] Achilles cut off his locks and put them into the hand of the dead Patroclus. The Greek tragedies often refer to the hair-sacrifice.[84] Roman women lacerated themselves.[85] Gladiatorial combats at funerals were largely for the entertainment of the dead but they resulted in mutilations and deaths that were really sacrificial. There was a Highland funeral-custom that the friends of the dead should fight until blood was drawn.[86]

§230*. Food-Offerings.

Human sacrifice, occurring either directly or by survival, may be no more than an offering of a contemporary or obsolete form of food. The provision of nutriment for the dead is, in general, the most fundamental of all provision, for food is the most basic of all needs whether in this life or the next. Specific and exhaustive illustration of food-sacrifice as such is impracticable; representative cases may be cited to bring out the simple directness of the primitive practices.

"The simplest and most common sacrificial act is that of throwing a small portion of food to the dead; this is probably a universal practice in Mela-

[78] Donaldson, in *Smithson. Rep.,* 1885, pt. II, 86.
[79] Yarrow, in BAE, I, 183.
[80] §445, below; von Martius, *Beiträge,* I, 315.
[81] *Brit.-Guiana,* II, 457-458.
[82] Von Martius, *Beiträge,* I, 694, 695.
[83] Levit., XIX, 27; Deut., XIV, 1 ff.; Duhm, *Geister,* 24.
[84] Homer, *Iliad,* X, 15; XXIII, 132-141; 151. Æschylus, *Choephori,* first scenes, 167 ff.; Sophocles, *Aias,* 1174-1175.
[85] Rossbach, *Röm. Ehe,* 282, note.　　[86] Gomme, *Ethnol. in Folklore,* 127.

nesia."[87] Among the Fan, "food is often set at the grave of the recently deceased, a pitcher of water, a chair for a chief, and a special Fetish emblem for a Fetish priest, so that functions similar to those of the present life may be performed beyond the tomb."[88] In the Niger region, as elsewhere over the earth, a hole is left into the grave over the head of the corpse, and palm-wine and spirits are poured in at intervals.[89] In Central Africa, if a village is moved, a pot belonging to the dead chief is set in the ground with its mouth above the surface; into this beer is poured on occasion.[90] Apparently the chief's ghost accompanies the group and continues to demand propitiation. "It is hard to say if the ghost is supposed to take the actual food offered on the grave or its essence; if the former he is evidently supposed to be easily satisfied, since he is given such a little—the Kagoro does not believe in giving him more than can be helped—but then ghosts get their own food as in life."[91] Among the Bangala, ghosts visit the towns as hippopotami; when the people are sure they are about, they put out a little food for their nightly visits; "and as the food and wine are both gone in the morning (there are plenty of dogs about)," the natives are sure that the ghosts have taken them.[92]

The Chukchi have a final meal with the corpse. A sojourner among them once shared such a meal in a room so narrow that there was scarcely space to sit about the corpse. On this account they put their dining-board on the dead man. In the board, over the mouth, they cut a hole, and on the visitor, who sat at the head, devolved the duty of feeding the dead, pouring hot tea into the hole and slipping through it morsels of tallow.[93] The Ostiaks leave on the grave a saucer and spoon for the use of the dead in eating the food which they are to bring.[94] Filling the mouth of the dead with uncooked rice was once a common custom in China; it is now obsolete, "but setting out food at the side of the corpse is still faithfully observed by all classes of society as a holy customary law allowing of no infringement whatever."[95] The Kukis fill the pipe of the dead man with tobacco and place it between his lips; they provide food and say: "You are going on a long journey; eat."[96] Other tribes put rice-paddy on the face of the corpse or dash rice into its mouth.[97] "When the owner comes to dwell in his new house, and has lighted the fire, he should carefully examine all the posts and boards of which the house is made, and wherever he finds a hole, made by some boring insect or where a knot of wood has been, he should fill it with uncooked rice."[98] Any such place affords entrance to ghosts and it is safer to propitiate. In the Philippines it is supposed that only the shadow of the food-offerings is eaten by the spirits. Food is set by the corpse and left for an hour; then the nearest relatives devour it. Ashes are strewn to discover whether the souls have come to a sacrifice, and water is left at the door for them to wash their feet.[99]

The Siouans offer food and water on the grave. "No Indian would touch

[87] Codrington, *Melanesians*, 128.   [88] Connolly, in JAI, XXVI, 149.
[89] Kingsley, *W. Afr. Studies*, 485.   [90] Stannus, in JAI, XL, 314.
[91] Tremearne, in JAI, XLII, 168.   [92] Weeks, in JAI, XL, 368, 369.
[93] Bogoras, in AA, III, 94-95.
[94] Kondratowitsch, in *Globus*, LXXIV, 291.
[95] Legge, *Li Ki*, I, 368; DeGroot, *Relig. Syst.*, I, 29; II, 383 ff.
[96] Basu, in JASB, II, 560.
[97] Thurston, *S. India*, 196; Gomes, *Sea Dyaks*, 135.
[98] Milne, *Eastern Clan*, 182.   [99] Wilken, in VG, III, 123, 124.

any article of food thus exposed; if he did, the ghost would snatch away the food and paralyze the mouth of the thief, and twist his face out of shape for the rest of his life; or else he would be pursued by the ghost, and food would lose its taste, and hunger ever after haunt the offender."[100] The Tarahumari of Mexico set beer apart for the dead who could get no rest without it.[101] In Costa Rica vessels of chocolate were set upon the graves.[102] "Clay vases full of milk and butter, dried figs or dragon-blood paste, and wooden jars of honey were put beside the dead" by the Canary Islanders.[103] Such practices were found in ancient Egypt and Persia; and the Homeric shades were eager to drink the blood of animals, even in Hades, and thus regain a sort of human existence.[104] In Cyprus food is prepared periodically after a death and is set on the grave by the priests.[105] The Russian peasants "still believe that the souls of the dead, as soon as the bodies they used to inhabit are buried, take up their quarters in the cottage behind the sacred pictures, and hence they place hot cakes upon the ledge which supports these pictures, intending them as an offering to the hungry ghosts." Crumbs also are spread there for the dead; and the Bretons leave fragments of meals on the table for them.[106]

Such offerings came, in time, to take on a survivalistic tinge. "Out of the very widespread idea that the dead do not need material nutriment but can be satisfied with merely the soul, the ghost, or the smell alone of food arose the custom of serving the food only *pro forma* and then even of dividing it among the survivors for their enjoyment or of contributing into the grave inedible imitations of food."[107]

Feeding of the ghost takes place not alone at the time of the funeral but also at intervals thereafter. The days of mourning may be largely devoted to carousing in which the ghost has his part of the "funeral baked meats" and other cheer; then there may be another feast when the bones or skull are dug up and prepared for permanent retention and exhibit—a sort of "second funeral"; and there are some peoples who have even a periodic feast of the dead, a species of All-Spirits' Day.

In New Britain the skulls of the rich are dug up after about a year and an ostentatious feast is given; there is here none of the howling characteristic of the funeral.[108] In the Trobriand Islands, "every year, after the garden crops

[100] Dorsey, in BAE, XI, 420.
[101] Lumholtz, in *Int. Cong. Anthrop.*, 1893, 108.
[102] Sapper, in *Globus*, LXXVI, 352.   [103] Cook, in AA, II, 483.
[104] Homer, *Odyssey*, XI, 147 ff.; Rohde, *Psyche*, I, 15, 54-57, 244-245.
[105] Deschamps, in *Globus*, LXXII, 349.
[106] Ralston, *Russ. People*, 136; Tylor, *Anth.*, 351.
[107] Lasch, in *Globus*, LXXXIX, 102.
[108] Finsch, *Ethnol. Erfahr.*, I, 113, 114.

have been harvested and there is a marked pause in the gardening, because the new gardens cannot be seriously tackled yet, the natives have a time of dancing, feasting, and general rejoicing called *milamila*. During the *milamila* the *baloma* [ghosts] are present in the village. They return in a body from Tuma to their own village, where preparations are made to receive them, where special platforms are erected to accommodate them, and where customary gifts are offered to them, and whence, after the full moon is over, they are ceremonially but unceremoniously driven away. . . . During my stay, the full moon, both in August and September, fell on wet, rainy and stormy days. And my informants were able to demonstrate to me by actual experience the connection between scarcity of food and a bad *milamila*, on the one hand, and the anger of the spirits and bad weather on the other. The spirits may even go further and cause drought, and thus spoil the next year's crops. This is the reason why very often several bad years follow each other, because a bad year and poor crops make it impossible for the men to arrange a good *milamila*, which again angers the *baloma*, who spoil next year's crops, and so on in a *circulus vitiosus*. . . . But the *baloma* are not entirely materialistic. They not only resent scarcity of food and poor offerings, but they also keep strict watch over the maintenance of custom, and they punish with their displeasure any infraction of the traditional customary rules which ought to be observed during the *milamila*. Thus I was told that the spirits strongly disapproved of the general laxity and slowness with which the *milamila* was at present observed. Formerly, nobody would work in the fields or do any other kind of labour during the festive period. Everybody had to be bound on pleasure, dancing and sexual licence, in order to please the *baloma*. . . . There was still another cause for their anger, connected with the ethnographer's presence in that place, and I had to hear several times reproachful allusions and remarks from the elders and from . . . the chief, himself."[109] In West Africa "the days of mourning are days of great feasting in the house of the deceased."[110]

The Kirghiz get ready during the year succeeding a death for the great celebration. The tails of the dead man's favorite horses are cut off and the beasts are pastured for the feasting and sacrifice that are to conclude the mourning; meanwhile his wives must keep their cheeks bloody the whole year. A good memorial costs thirty to forty thousand rubles and as many as fifteen thousand people come to it. The feast lasts seven days and often ruins its givers.[111] "The Japanese believe that on the sixteenth of July all the ancestors make their annual visit."[112] In the Chin Hills a costly festival takes place a year or two after a death;[113] in Travancore every year.[114] The Saoras have several such celebrations, at great cost; there is much music and dancing and gun-firing, and the ghost is so pleased as not to injure people thereafter. Finally there is a great slaughter of buffaloes: "in front of every house in which there has been a death in the previous two years, at least one buffalo, and sometimes two or three, are killed. One year there were said to be at least 1,000 buffaloes killed in Kolakotla." Every house in which there has been a death within two years is burned—for the ghosts will not return to the new

[109] Malinowski, in JAI, XLVI, 370, 379-380.
[110] Serpa Pinto, *Africa*, I, 54.
[111] *Russian Ethnog.* (Russ.), II, 194. A ruble is about half a dollar.
[112] Tamura, *Warum Heiraten Wir?* 81.
[113] Carey and Tuck, *Chin Hills*, I, 193.   [114] Painter, in JASB, II, 152.

house built on the site of the old one. "Most likely," the Saora says, "they are in the jungle or on the hill-side."[115]

In the East Indies they have an all-souls' festival for the dead at the new-year moon; in taking leave of the gathered deceased, they throw food in the direction of the spirit-world. Matter-of-fact statements are made about bringing rice to a dead child and the like. The Mohammedans opposed this practice; it was then interpreted to mean that the food was not brought to the dead but was sacrificed for their souls' rest in God. Many examples are given by the author[116] to illustrate the prevalence of the all-souls' days both within and outside the Archipelago. The Dyaks have a great "Tiwah-feast" two years after a death, accompanied with diverse carousals which Perelaer[117] does not care to rehearse. Feasting and cock-fighting are the order of the day, even in the first mourning-period.[118] The Sea Dyaks have, every year or two, a sort of festival in honor of all who have died since the last one; the dead are at this time furnished with the means of livelihood in the spirit-world and mourning is ended.[119]

The Eskimo feast of the dead "is given for the sole purpose of making offerings of food, water, and clothing to the shades of those recently deceased, and of offerings to the dead who have not yet been honored by one of the great festivals. The makers of this feast are the nearest relatives of those who have died during the preceding year, joined by all others of the village who have not given a great feast to their dead." The shades come and enter the bodies of their namesakes, thus partaking of the offerings of food and clothing—supplies necessary for their wants in the spirit-land until the time of the next festival. The essence of bits of food cast on the floor and of water poured through the cracks may be transported mysteriously to the abodes of the shades.[120] The Hurons had a festival once in twelve years, when all the bodies of those who had died during the last interval were put in one grave.[121] "Among the California tribes the Yokaia mother who has lost her babe goes every day for a year to some place where her little one has played when alive or to the spot where the body was burned and milks her breast into the air."[122] At a funeral-feast of certain Mexican Indians each drinks with the departed and exhorts him to go away now, as no one wants him any more. He has provisions and should go. They look in the ashes for animal-tracks to find out what animal-form the dead has taken.[123] In Egypt "the night of the 17th Thot was a kind of All-Saints' Day, when there was a grand illumination, and the fires were relighted before the statues of the dead and the gods. The lights were to facilitate the visits of the deceased to their former families."[124] In Rome, upon such days, thrice a year, *"mundus patet"* (the door to the spirit-world lies open); the days belonged to the dead, were unclean, and unfit for business, and the temples were closed. All sorts of means were adopted in Greece and Rome for protection against the unseen ghosts that were abroad

[115] Fawcett, in JASB, I, 250 ff.   [116] Wilken, in VG, III, 125 ff.
[117] *Dajaks*, 227, 228, 251; full description of the Tiwah, 228 ff.
[118] Roth, *Sarawak*, I, 140.   [119] Gomes, *Sea Dyaks*, 142.
[120] Nelson, in BAE, XVIII, pt. I, 363-364, 365.
[121] Thomas, in BAE, V, 112.   [122] Mason, *Woman's Share*, 253.
[123] Lumholtz, in *Scribner's Mag.*, XVI, 444.
[124] Maspero, *Hist. Anc.*, I, 322.

at the time.[125] On such an occasion in ancient Germany, the "hel" stood open; "hel" being the term for the hearth or altar,[126] corresponding to the *mundus* of the Romans.[127] In White Russia, the peasants on set days solemnly invoke the spirits of their ancestors, believing that they live and are present. The courtyard and house are cleaned and an abundant feast prepared. A libation of vodka is poured out on the table and they do not begin to eat until they have put bits of every dish of food on a special plate, which they set on the window for the spirits.[128]

§231*. Sacrifice of Property.

To catalogue the varieties of property that are sacrificed to the dead would be to list all the varieties of possession known. Property-sacrifice consists in releasing the spirit of the property, by breaking or burning, to accompany that of the dead into the next world. As in the case of food-sacrifice, so in all other cases, the notion of projectivism conjoined with the fear of the aleatory element personalized in the ghosts gives the reason for the destruction of wealth that accompanies the ghost-cult. Saving and accumulation are at a discount, for they really attract the ghosts.[129] A Saora said that if they did not burn all a man's clothes and gear, the ghost would come and ask for them and be troublesome.[130]

The present authors cannot accept the strained interpretation of Powell,[131] that the personal property of the dead is destroyed or buried with him to avoid controversy and quarrels over its disposition. If this is so, why sacrifice, later on, food and other property to the departed, not out of his stock but out of the undisputed possessions of his survivors? This theory deserves mention only because of the high position and reputation of its sponsor.

All forms of property are needed as provision for the future life. In this place there may be noticed a single aspect of property-sacrifice: the destruction of what is offered.

In Central Australia, "all the personal belongings of the dead person are broken at the grave of a man so that his spirit will not come back and use them. Women's are not broken. . . . Wood is provided so that when the dead person 'jumps up' he will have a supply of firewood handy, and the sticks and hut covering are put there in case it is cold when the dead man comes

[125] Rohde, *Psyche*, I, 237; Rossbach, *Röm. Ehe*, 270, note.
[126] §251, below.   [127] Lippert, *Kgchte.*, II, 191.
[128] *Russian Ethnog.* (Russ.), I, 110.   [129] Lippert, *Kgchte.*, I, 244 ff.
[130] Fawcett, in JASB, I, 249.
[131] In BAE, III, lvii; adopted by Jenks, in AA, IV, 202, Muñiz and McGee, in BAE, XVI, 22; McGee, in BAE, XV, 177.

back, so that he can build a shelter."[132] At a Papuan funeral the dead man's utensils, including pots, bow, and the rest, are broken and torn to pieces.[133] Elsewhere in New Guinea "some things are placed by the grave, a man's bow with string cut and some broken arrows, and his net bag containing a broken spoon, a few areca nuts, betel peppers, and broken lime calabash, and an earthen dish, broken. The dish is one last used by him. Beside a woman's grave may be seen broken cooking dishes and pots."[134] Most of the things given to the dead, in West Africa, "are deliberately damaged," but Miss Kingsley[135] does not think that "this is to prevent them from being stolen, because all are not damaged sufficiently to make them useless." "Those things which the deceased has used most are broken or thrown on the road in front of the village." Heaps of women's pots and gourds are seen there and rags, hunting-bags, and the like that have belonged to a man. On this road food is often exposed for the ghosts, a fact that shows they are there to receive whatever is thrown out.[136] All property of a barren woman is broken and buried.[137] That the crushing of breakable articles is not a provision against theft is proved, against Conradt's[138] own opinion, by the fact that the accompanying food is never touched by passers-by. "Over the grave a shelter is often built, with a rough table under it. On this table were put bottles, sauccpans, plates, mugs, etc.; under and at its side were put stools and chairs, but everything was 'killed,' i.e., broken. All the natives told me that the articles were killed to keep people from stealing them, yet they had an idea that the things thus displayed not only served as a memento of the deceased but helped him, in his present state, in some indefinable way. Undoubtedly they had forgotten the reason for 'killing' the articles. The stealing reason was not sufficient to meet the case, as no one would be found with so much hardihood as to rob a grave, they had too wholesome a fear of spirits to do that; besides detection would have been easy and dire punishment follow the theft."[139]

All the private property of the dead man is conveyed on the same sledge that carries his body; it is attached to that body. "On arrival at the appointed place, the sacrificial reindeer is killed and the sledge, which is usually specially made for the occasion, is broken up, and, with all other objects used in the ceremony, is formed into a pile on which the broken bones of the reindeer are placed.[140]

Among the Samoyeds everything deposited for the dead is somewhat damaged, even the sledge; the author hazards the surmise that it is to prevent theft.[141] The Yakuts, who break the vehicles and implements used at the funeral and formerly also the familiar tools of the deceased, said that this was done "in order that the dead might not with them hurt the living."[142] When the Gilyak ghost is ready to start on the long journey to the spirit-world, since he must travel "as the deceased was wont to do on earth, the spirits of his dogs must be 'freed.' Therefore they kill his dogs and break to pieces his

[132] Horne and Aiston, *Cent. Aust.*, 152, 153.
[133] Hagen, *Papua's*, 259. [134] Chalmers, in JAI, XXVII, 330.
[135] *Travels W. Afr.*, 493.
[136] Conrau, in *Globus*, LXXV, 250; Stannus, in JAI, XL, 314.
[137] Thomas, in JAI, XLVII, 209. [138] In *Globus*, LXXXI, 351-352.
[139] Weeks, in JAI, XXXIX, 453. [140] Czaplicka, *Aborig. Siberia*, 147.
[141] Montefiore, in JAI, XXIV, 406.
[142] Sieroshevski-Sumner, in JAI, XXXI, 99.

sleds and his weapons."[143] In some cases, doubtless, the fear of the ghost is not enough to prevent theft; graves have been rifled of offerings to the dead, among the Dyaks. "As it is almost impossible to discover the offenders, it is now the practice to break in pieces all the utensils placed in the grave, and to conceal as carefully as possible the valuable ornaments."[144] "The graves of the rich have valuable jars or gongs which are secured in their places by having a stake driven through them and thus rendered worthless."[145] When the articles deposited with the dead are broken, it is supposed that they will unite again to serve their owners in the next life. The theory that such property is destroyed to prevent stealing is unnecessary in view of the fear of the ghosts; only where aliens are in question would there be theft. The idea is to free the souls of the things.[146]

The Indians of the Columbia region break or "kill" the implements furnished to the dead man.[147] Among the Sia Indians the clothing left for the dead must never be deposited whole, as the spirit of the clothing could not leave it if the clothing were whole.[148] Sapper[149] thinks the breaking of articles left on graves in Nicaragua was to prevent theft. In Egypt the things placed in the tombs were damaged or broken to "kill" them, that their doubles might follow the double of the dead and render service.[150] Says Pietschmann[151] of the Phœnicians: "Indisputably the breaking signifies here originally what the fracture or burning of implements has signified in the burial-usages of very many people, the despatching of them to the next world." The custom was prevalent in prehistoric Scandinavia.[152] In modern Greece "vessels either especially dedicated to the deceased or else having been used in the funeral-rites are broken at the grave. . . . Today, in Greece, they cut all the clothes and wrappings of the dead, but the current reason given is that this is done to guard against depredations from the riflers of tombs, and there is no reason for going farther afield to account for it."[153] But the American ethnologist Cushing says in comment "that formerly the notion at the basis of the custom was to kill the vessel and send its spirit to dwell with the owner in the other world."[154]

Some of the explanations of this custom that accompany the cases are plainly mere surmises, caught up as the recounter went along; one of the authors quoted prefers not to go "farther afield" for an explanation than the current one of theft; another evidently has actual reported cases of grave-rifling in mind; several state plainly that the idea is to "kill" the possessions offered.

[143] Hawes, in *Globus*, LXXXVIII, 62.

[144] Roth, *Sarawak*, I, 141.   [145] Gomes, *Sea Dyaks*, 138.

[146] Wilken, in VG, III, 114, 117, 120.

[147] Bancroft, *Nat. Races*, I, 220, 247; Lewis and Clark, *Travels*, II, 396; III, 201-202.

[148] Stevenson, in BAE, XI, 145.   [149] In *Globus*, LXXVIII, 273.

[150] Maspero, *Hist. Anc.*, II, 523.   [151] *Phön.*, 211.

[152] Worsaae, *Nordens Forhist.*, 40.

[153] Politis, "Breaking of Vessels," etc., in JAI, XXIII, 29.

[154] Mason, in *Smithson. Rep.*, 1893, 624.

Doubtless there are some cases where grave-rifling was anticipated, though it is a hardy primitive who would dare to rob the
ghost; and perhaps the articles were destroyed as "unclean." It
is folly to insist upon any single explanation of such a practice.
We incline, on the evidence, and especially in view of the prevalent
belief in souls of things,[155] to accept for most cases the "killing"
theory. However, upon whatever theory, it is clear that the practice meant the destruction of wealth, which is the conclusion that
is most useful in the prosecution of our study.

§232*. Treatment of the Body. It is evident from the practice
of many peoples that the interests of the dead and, through them,
of the living are thought to be served by the preservation of the
body or of certain parts of it. The clearest case is doubtless that
of the Egyptians who, believing that the disembodied soul could
live only so long as the body was preserved, developed the practice
of mummification and hid the embalmed body deep within some
natural or artificial cave, mound, or pyramid. Many primitive
peoples take great pains to preserve the dead from the depredations of animals or men; burial under cairns of rock, disposition
of the corpse in trees or on scaffolding, in boxes, urns, sarcophagi,
or sealed caves, and the use of other protective devices, all witness
to a desire to do well by the dead. If the deceased is to arrive in
the spirit-world in the condition in which he left this one, it is
easily understandable that the proper treatment of his corpse is
one of the essential forms of propitiation.

It is not contended that the care expended in preserving the
bodies of the dead is solely propitiatory. Relics are kept as fetishes;[156] skulls may be retained as memorials or trophies; some of
the practices are plainly cases of avoidance or exorcism;[157] in
many instances the dead demand their "share of the fire" and are
propitiated by that which gets rid of or lays their ghosts. Avoidance and propitiation mingle here as elsewhere. But the cases show
a steady tendency to dispose of the dead bodies in a manner satisfactory to their former occupants, so that the latter may remain
complaisant to the survivors. Unless they thought that the trou-

---

155 §214, above; Lubbock, *Origin Civil.*, 190 ff.
156 §249, below.   157 §§222 ff., above.

ble taken would redound to their own advantage, through the evasion of ill fortune, the primitive people would scarcely have developed their often elaborate and costly ritual. Finally, it is
inconceivable that funerary practices which are actually sanitary
were devised or adopted with hygienic ends in view, though the fact
that they do realize such unplanned ends must lend them survival-
value.

"After death the chief is decapitated and the skull is cleaned and bleached,
and then, with a preparation of clay and fibre, a face representing his, as it
was while he was alive, is modelled on the bare skull; his peculiarities in
feature are emphasised to a degree bordering on caricature, but they are not
meant as caricatures, but are intended only to bring back to the beholders the
characteristic points of the chief's face."[158] Preservation of the body in the
house for a time is a mark of affection;[159] this may be followed by drying or
mummification.[160] The Papuans put chiefs' bodies in holes in coral reefs or
rocks, while the ordinary dead are thrown into the sea.[161] The Herero and
Damara of South Africa sew the dead in hides and pile stones on the graves
to keep off hyænas.[162] "The burial of a Bechuana chief takes place in his
cattle-pen, and all the cattle are driven for an hour or two around and over
the grave, so that it may be quite obliterated."[163] "Among the Wanyoro when
a king dies his body is dried, and then the lower jaw is removed and buried
by itself—the leading men of that tribe, it is said, are 'privileged to have their
heads . . . treated in the same manner.' "[164] Preservation of the corpse in the
hut is found among tribes on Lake Tanganyika;[165] and mummification of
kings and nobles is common in Uganda. Because of a belief in ghoulish witches
and wizards who eat corpses, the graves are watched for some time after
interment;[166] this ghoul-myth has a solid human origin, "since there are
depraved people all over Africa at the present day who have a mania for
eating corpse-flesh."[167]

"As a rule the burial customs depend for their character upon whether the
deceased has children or not; in a certain number of instances childless people are buried with the same ceremonies as those who have left descendants,
and this whether they are men or women; but as a rule the heirless man or
woman receives treatment little or no better than the child, who is simply
thrown into the bush. . . . Besides this there are minor variations depending
upon the rank of the deceased, such as the absence of lamentation for a poor
man." The unmarried are treated with less ceremony than the married. If a
dead child has cut its teeth both father and mother shave, for it has some
personality; for smaller children this mourning-operation is omitted. There
is much house-burial for children, except the very young, but no sacrifice. If
a corpse is not recoverable, the soul is called; then they go out and get chalk,

[158] Hardy and Elkington, *S. Seas*, 156.
[159] Codrington, *Melanesians*, 267, 268.   [160] Hunt, in JAI, XXVIII, 12.
[161] Ella, in AAAS, 1892, 642.   [162] Ratzel, *Vkde.*, I, 341.
[163] Livingstone, *Mission. Travels*, I, 104.
[164] Tyler, in *Ill. Afr.*, Dec., 1895.   [165] Stuhlmann, *Mit Emin*, 90, 186.
[166] Macdonald, in JAI, XXII, 107.   [167] Johnston, *Uganda*, II, 20.

or sticks, or cloth, pound on the ground to summon the spirit, and carry on the funeral with what they have. The chalk and the rest are the dead body. If they can bury the dead man's hair, which has been thrown on the roof as it has been cut, so much the better. A suicide's body is exposed as a sort of posthumous punishment; they may be cast into the 'bad bush' with no lamentation or sacrifice, and poor men are hired to remove their bodies."[168] Again, in East Africa, "when an ordinary person dies it is customary for the relations to throw the body out in the open, and if another relation were to die some time afterwards the same thing would be done, but if a second relation were to die very shortly after the first the second would be buried as it would be considered that the second had died as it had been unlucky to throw out the first. If a third relation were to die shortly he would also be buried, but a fourth relation dying shortly would be thrown out and they would go on ringing the changes till the deaths stopped."[169]

The Nagas of India smoke the corpse, enclose it in a coffin, and leave it in the fork of a tree. In the case of men of distinction the head is removed and deposited in an earthen pot at the foot of the tree.[170] "Ascetics, spirit mediums, elders or men of eminence are, as a rule, interred, not cremated. Such persons, if their bodies be preserved, are likely to transmit to their survivors in whose neighborhood they lie, their mystic powers, piety, and other virtues."[171] When the body is exposed the bones are collected and preserved in a receptacle of stone, mortar, or clay or even, in case of extreme poverty, in coarse cloth.[172] The Chinese erected huge grave-mounds to protect the body and possessions of the dead; ramparts and walls were constructed around such mausolea, and engines and hidden fire were utilized as defenses. The mounds "were converted into real strongholds, and, moreover, permanently garrisoned by troops and placed under the protection of a city built near the spot for this purpose."[173] Clay cylinders and stone and clay coffins were used in Japan to preserve the bodies of notables.[174] "Any Sea Dyak whom it is intended especially to honour is not buried underground, but his coffin is placed in a miniature house built for him on piles some eight or ten feet high."[175] Furness[176] thinks that scaffold-burial in Borneo is enforced by the difficulty of digging graves in the forest and the softness of the soil outside the forest. In Samoa chiefs were formerly mummified and kept in a special house or on a raised platform.[177]

In most of the observed cases the Eskimo of Point Barrow do not seem to mind the fact that dogs or other animals disturb the bodies of their dead relatives but Murdoch[178] knew of one case where childrens' remains were raised four or five feet upon a drift-wood staging to protect them. In Alaska it was customary to preserve body and head apart, the latter in an ornamented box.[179] The Kwakiutl use tree-burial and the bodies, exposed to freely circulating air, mostly mummify.[180] To strip a body of flesh, disjoint the skeleton, and pack it into a very small space, say into a jar, is a common Indian mor-

[168] Thomas, in JAI, L, 379; and in JAI, XLVII, 166, 184, 196.
[169] Hobley, A-Kamba, 67.
[170] Godden, in JAI, XXVI, 199.
[171] Crooke, in JAI, XXVIII, 246.
[172] Modi, in JASB, I, 434.
[173] DeGroot, Relig. Syst., II, 456–457.
[174] Hitchcock, in USNM, 1891, 519.
[175] Roth, Sarawak, I, 146.
[176] Head-Hunters, 143–144.
[177] Ella, in AAAS, 1892, 641.
[178] In BAE, IX, 425.
[179] Niblack, in USNM, 1888, 351.
[180] Boas, in USNM, 1895, 441.

tuary custom.[181] The Bororo of Brazil decorate the skeleton and pack it in a basket.[182] Earthenware sarcophagi have been found in Venezuela.[183] Elsewhere in South America there are to be found sham graves,[184] probably a mode of protection for the dead. "Small islands are preferred [by Fuegians] for burying-places, as there are no foxes to disturb the dead, who are but merely covered over with earth and leaves. Sometimes also the dead are buried at the foot of cliffs among the rocks, in places safe from foxes, which on account of their propensity to eat the dead are, with rats, held in the greatest detestation."[185] Mummification, especially of the rich and notables, was carried to great perfection in the Canary Islands.[186]

The foregoing illustrations will serve to show that the sedulous preservation of the bodies of the dead is a common practice upon stages of culture far below that of the Egyptians. The dead, thus preserved, are generally clothed or decorated in some manner involving sacrifice and further propitiation. This may be illustrated by the single case, among many, of bone-painting.

That the skulls of friends or enemies are profusely decorated, by carving, gilding, or otherwise, is well known and will be illustrated elsewhere;[187] but parts of the skeleton are so treated where head-hunting as such is not involved. The Maori exhumed bodies a year or two after death, under very elaborate ceremonial. "The bones were scraped, anointed, decorated, painted and set with feathers. When they had been seen or wept over by all the relatives, they were packed away in the dark ancestral burial cave, or else thrown into some inaccessible rift or deep chasm, lest some enemy might get hold of the skull, to taunt it or to use it as a baler for a canoe."[188] Presumably when there was no body to decorate with paint, the only way to cater to the ghost's vanity was to paint the bones. It was done by Indians of Ohio, Florida, and South America.[189] Some Indians of Brazil decorate the skull with feathers before depositing it in its last resting-place; the other bones are painted red.[190]

The practice of eating the dead will receive special notice under the topic of cannibalism;[191] one of its motives is the utter destruction of the soul of an enemy or a criminal, in order to get rid of a dangerous ghost. In that aspect the custom belongs with other exorcistic practices.[192] Further, even in the case of an enemy there

181 Henshaw, in AA, VII, 111.
182 Von den Steinen, Zent. Bras., 504.
183 "Precolombian Metallurgy" (Anthrop. Miscellanea), in JAI, XX, 221.
184 White, in JAI, XIII, 246.
185 Bridges, in A Voice for S. Amer., XIII, 201.
186 Cook, in AA, II, 481; Dawkins, Cave-hunting, 211.
187 §249, below.   188 Tregear, in JAI, XIX, 105.
189 Hrdlička, in AA, III, 714, 715, 718, 723.
190 Von den Steinen, Zent. Bras., 476.
191 §§290, 291, below.   192 §§226, 227, above.

is involved the idea of appropriating his strength; and the eating of the bodies of dead relatives and friends, though it may have been in origin exorcistic, has, where it has come to be conceived of as a favor to them, an unmistakably propitiatory stamp.

When the Australians were giving up cannibalism they maintained it longest in the case of their dead chiefs, that is, their powerful men. In such cases it was not needful to eat the whole body but only such parts as were conceived to contain the soul.[193] Even among the Australians the custom was declining into the survivalistic form: when the time came to eat, the mourners uttered a cannibal howl and wounded themselves with their axes but they did not eat the parts; they buried them. The prevalent native explanation was that the eating was only "a symbol of respect and regret for the dead, or to do away with the continual crying about them, which was a nuisance to those in camp."[194] However, if all this were symbolic, the question remains: Why this symbol rather than some other?[195] The strengthening power of a small piece of flesh, on mind as well as body, was regarded as supremely great.[196] The head was eaten to secure the wisdom of the deceased[197] and other parts to save what was being lost.[198] It is reported that in former days, among the Chukchi, "the flesh of the deceased was distributed and eaten by relatives; now each relative takes a small piece of fur from the clothes of the deceased and adds it to the string of such pieces which form the ancestor charms."[199] In Tibet the son eats the father's head and makes a goblet of the skull; here is the common practice of keeping the skull-fetish.[200] One people of India used to kill and eat their aged parents; it was called "eating the pumpkin."[201] Reclus[202] says that these parents beg that their corpses may find a refuge in the stomachs of their children rather than be left on the road or in the forest; hence this terrible custom is not without reasonable foundation.

Here again enters the element of apparent inconsistency; what is a service to a relative or friend may be a disservice and an insult to an enemy. The feeling which makes a savage keep the mortal remains of his ancestors in his house and regard as the severest punishment an insult to the ashes of his dead may cause him, on the other hand, to desire to inflict the extremest disgrace upon a great criminal or a detested enemy, namely, to destroy his body as completely and disgracefully as possible by eating him up. And if all ate pieces of the executed person, they had less fear of his ghost, being all alike exposed to his resentment.[203] The dust or ashes or powdered bones of the dead are sometimes imbibed by the relatives in a drink.[204] Of a South American tribe it is reported: "They are wont to burn their dead. The ashes are then pre-

[193] Lippert, *Kgchte.*, I, 233; II, 281, 284.

[194] Ratzel, *Vkde.*, II, 75; Howitt, in JAI, XX, 88; Howitt, *S.E. Aust.*, 458; Dawson, *Aust. Aborig.*, 67.

[195] §456, below.   [196] Parker, *Euahlayi*, 38.

[197] Frobenius, *Masken*, 177.

[198] Henning, in *Globus*, LXXII, 104.   [199] Czaplicka, *Aborig. Siberia*, 147.

[200] Rockhill, in USNM, 1893, 728.   [201] Basu, in JASB, II, 571.

[202] *Prim. Folk*, 249.   [203] Ratzel, *Vkde.*, II, 462.

[204] De Vaca, *Narrative*, Smith's transl., 49; Koch, in *Ztsft. f. Eth.*, XXXVI, 293-299.

served in a hollow reed and some of them eaten at every meal."[205] The practice is accomplished "that the dead may live again in them."[206] Herodotus[207] reports of the Issedones of southeastern Russia that they eat their fathers and gild and keep their skulls as sacred emblems; and Strabo[208] says of the ancient Irish: "They are more savage than the Britons, feeding on human flesh . . . and deeming it commendable to devour their deceased parents." "The eating of dead kindred is a rite practiced by savages in many parts of the world and it is founded primarily on the fear which savage man had for the spirits of the dead."[209]

§233*. Miscellaneous Forms of Propitiation. It is clear enough from the cases that the ghost takes umbrage if sufficient sorrow is not exhibited over his death and that his vanity is gratified by much and loud lamentation. That such "mourning" is largely ritualistic appears from most descriptions and especially from the prevalence of professional or hired mourners; mourning-customs include, in the main, devices for avoidance or exorcism of the ghost[210] or for its propitiation.[211] These practices are deep in the mores, so much so that most people cannot even today excuse the absence of a visible exhibition of grief at a time of bereavement. In conformity with primitive ideas, also, it is the powerful ghost which must be most ostentatiously mourned.

"As [Australian] women and children are held to be very inferior to the men whilst alive, and their spirits are but little feared after death, they are interred with but scant ceremony."[212] None but the bereaved exhibit sorrow. But with important people it is otherwise: "the females weep continuously, and, if they can, copiously. One always stands weeping in front of the corpse during the process of drying."[213] "One thing noticeable is that, however loud their moaning is, however hard they are crying, they will always stop to answer any question you like to put to them about their 'late lamented,' if you have courage enough to beard them and refuse to go away. Then, as soon as you have gained all the information you require, they will quickly resume their tears as if nothing had happened to interrupt them. But this is not unique to the savage of New Guinea. I have met with the same extraordinary species of grief amongst the women of Great Britain,—it is world-wide, this interruptable grief."[214] "Public grief is ostentatious largely because custom demands that it should be so. It would be misleading to estimate a Papuan's sorrow by the noise he makes in advertising it. All his emotions are shallow. His heart is

205 Von den Steinen, in *Globus*, LXXXIII, 137.
206 Von Martius, *Beiträge*, I, 485.   207 *Hist.*, bk. IV, §26.
208 *Geog.*, bk. IV, ch. V.
209 Gomme, *Ethnol. in Folklore*, 121.   210 §§223 ff., above.
211 Lippert, *Kgchte.*, II, 236, 238, 240, 276.
212 Curr, *Aust. Race*, I, 89.   213 Smyth, *Vict.*, I, 108, 112.
214 Hardy and Elkington, *S. Seas*, 47.

limited in feeling, as his mind is restricted in thought. He can neither hate
his enemy, nor love his friend, as civilized people can."[215]

The ritual character of mourning may appear from the following examples.
Funerals are not all sorrow among the Melanesians; "women especially love to
take part in them. A few days after one is over some old woman may meet the
dead man's brother and say to him, 'When your brother was buried the other
day I attended his funeral and wept bitterly. Now give me a little tobacco as
a reward.' It is really remarkable how easily even the youngest child can call
up a flood of crocodile tears; this professional weeping gives an air of gro-
tesqueness and unreality to every funeral. A group of women will break off
their gossip and cry as though their hearts were breaking, then a moment
afterwards cease crying just as suddenly and resume their gossip and laugh-
ter." After the mourning-time is over, "the women and girls may . . . resume
their natural tones, for throughout the mourning they make their voices thin
and piping like a little child's. At times the mourning ornaments are laid
aside, but the food restrictions are still maintained for two or three months
afterwards; the feast is then delayed to coincide with the latter occasion."[216]

Among the Yoruba, "the epithet *isokun* 'a mourner' is often applied to a
female child; a male, on the other hand, being sometimes called *iwale*, 'a digger' i.e. of a grave. A father might thus say that he had begotten two mourners and a digger, meaning two daughters and a son." Females cry longer and
better.[217] In Cameroons "the place of wailing for the dead is close to the hut
in which the body of the deceased is lying. . . . Tears . . . are forced to flow
by squeezing the eyes very tightly together, and in a short time they flow
down the cheeks making furrows on the ashes which had been smeared on the
face at the time the deceased died." Despite this artificial method, the author[218]
thinks that "there seems to be no doubt that in the majority of cases the grief
is real and not assumed." That is perfectly possible, but such an amount of
weeping is demanded by custom that nature has to be assisted to produce
enough actual tears. Thomas[219] speaks of a funeral as follows: "As they
passed my house they appeared to be talking about various things, but broke
out into wailing some fifty yards further on—one hundred yards or so from
the house; after lamenting for an hour they returned, keeping up the wailing
until they had reached a certain distance from the house; then they began
laughing and chatting. . . . After this extraordinarily barbaric scene had
gone on for twenty minutes or so, the bier was picked up and carried to the
farm, and the wailing ceased as if by magic." In West Africa "the mourning-
ceremonies over the dead are extended especially in case of the rich."[220]

Among the Ostiaks, as among many other tribes, only women ought to weep
at a burial. A widow makes an effigy of her husband which she cares for and
caresses for a year or more and then burns with weeping and lamentation.
The ghost of the deceased is supposed to see and appreciate all this. Again,
the widow is bound to weep for her husband, with expressions of despair and
self-blame.[221] In Korea, "until the funeral there is daily wailing in the dead

[215] Abel, *New Guinea*, 41.

[216] Jenness and Ballentyne, *D'Entrecasteaux*, 117, 118.

[217] Ellis, *Yoruba*, 157.   [218] Malcolm, in JAI, LIII, 400, 401.

[219] In JAI, XLVII, 180, 181.   [220] Bastian, *Deut. Exped.*, I, 164.

[221] *Russian Ethnog.* (Russ.), II, 486, 246.

man's house at meal time.[222] In DeGroot's great work[223] there are one hundred and seventy-two pages about mourning—an elaborate system connected with degrees of relationship and graded thereby; the immense detail covers also variations for many contingencies of life. Medhurst[224] gives six pages of Chinese kinship- and affinity-tables with the rules of mourning for each degree. It is interesting to note an inconsistency in this matter of mourning: first, that the loudest expressions of pain at his loss please the ghost most and then that over-vehement expressions of grief disturb the rest of the dead, so that they return.[225] A variant case is where "the Spanish custom of rejoicing rather than mourning at the death of young children is kept up by the Gauchos."[226]

A further form of propitiation of the ghost is the exaction in his behalf of the vengeance he would have taken if he could, especially upon his slayer. The classic instance of this practice is the pursuit and slaughter of Hector by Achilles, whose friend, Patroclus, Hector had slain. Achilles is represented as uneasy because he has halted his vengeance short of its utmost limit; he begs the spirit of Patroclus not to be angry because he has allowed Priam to ransom Hector's body and promises the ghost its share of the ransom.[227]

The Australian sorcerers go through an elaborate ceremony to discover the identity and whereabouts of him who has by magic encompassed any death in question. A line is finally drawn on the ground, "and to whatever point of the horizon it is directed, there must the avengers go to get the kidney-fat of the slayer of their friend. They must bring back to the tribe not only the kidney-fat, but the kidneys and a piece of the flank of the murderer, as a peace offering."[228] Among the Sea Dyaks the symbols and trophies of a head-hunting raid are placed in the middle of the public hall of the house and are then conveyed by the spirit of the winds, summoned by incantation, to the dead, "whose abode, until now full of discomfort and darkness, becomes at sight of these trophies filled with light. The spirits rejoice at the thought that their relatives have revenged upon others their own death."[229] It was incumbent on a Naga to recover or ransom the skull of a relative murdered or captured in war; to recover the skulls of their friends who had fallen in an attack made on their villages was considered a point of honor."[230] Such duties are almost always conjoined with the duty of revenge. Among the Osage Indians, every dead man, woman, and child must be avenged by the sacrifice of the scalp of an enemy over the grave by a near relative of the deceased.[231] Out of such customs arise endless blood-feuds. Vowing vengeance over the corpse of a relative or friend is common enough in history: "an ancient dame of the

222 Bishop, *Korea*, 288.
223 *Relig. Syst.*, pt. III.
224 In *China Br. Royal Asiat. Soc.*, 1853-1854, pt. IV.
225 Rohde, *Psyche,* I, 222-223.
226 Christison, in JAI, XI, 41.
227 Homer, *Iliad*, XXIV, 592-595.
228 Smyth, *Vict.*, I, 101-102.
229 Gomes, *Sea Dyaks*, 141.
230 Godden, in JAI, XXVII, 24.
231 Dorsey, in AA, IV, 404.

Buonvise house, flinging herself upon her nephew's body, vowed vengeance, after the old custom of the *Vocero,* against his murderers."[232] In such cases the primordial idea that the dead somehow profits by the accomplishment of the vow is implicit.

Besides providing for the maintenance of the ghost and often sending his wife along after him, that he may not lack the family-relations, the mourners try also to afford him a last and superlative entertainment. This is the sense of the funeral-games, gladiatorial fights, and other forms of amusement accompanying the laying of the ghost, which seemed so incongruous to many of us in our school-days. They are a part of the grand send-off accorded to people of note. Again the vanity of the ghost is taken into account, though even more is his envy avoided. It is always well not to be too hilarious but rather to dissimulate under a sad and serious mien whatever cheerfulness is felt. A few peculiar and miscellaneous cases will be presented by way of closing the topic of propitiation.

Among the Naga, "on the death of a warrior, his nearest male relation takes a spear and wounds the corpse by a blow with it on the head, so that on his arrival in the next world he may be known and received with distinctions."[233] Among the Dyaks, the mourning "includes many other restrictions beside the prohibition of ornaments and bright-coloured clothing. There must be no striking of gongs or drums or dancing or merrymaking in the house. In the old days the mourning could not end until one of the relatives managed to secure a human head."[234] Ojibway mothers who have lost a baby make a figure of feathers which they put in the cradle or carry about. The notion is that the child is too small to find its way to the spirit-world and that the mother by nursing the image affects the dead child and brings it up to an age to go on of itself.[235] Trees were planted about the grave, by the ancients, so that the soul might enjoy pleasant surroundings.[236] Ghost-huts for the deceased's protection are common;[237] in Australia the wife of the dead man remains in such a structure with him until the decay of the corpse.[238] Again the body is hung to the house-beams for seven days, "during which time the dead man's wife has to sit underneath spinning. She may not stir; and if friends do not bring her food, she must perforce starve."[239] Certain Australians have rudimentary funeral-games: at a funeral, without any provocation, two men had a contest with clubs while at the same time a few blows passed between some women and spears were thrown. It was evidently part of the ceremony.[240] In Sumatra, after digging to a convenient depth, they hollow out a lateral cavity large

[232] Symonds, *Cathol. Reaction,* I, 356-357.

[233] Godden, in JAI, XXVI, 198.   [234] Gomes, *Sea Dyaks,* 139.

[235] Andree, *Eth. Parallelen,* 92.   [236] Rohde, *Psyche,* I, 230.

[237] Frobenius, *Masken,* 255, 256.   [238] Ratzel, *Vkde.,* II, 77.

[239] Lewin, *S.E. India,* 274.   [240] Collins, *N. S. Wales,* 388.

enough to contain the body. "By this mode the earth literally lies light upon it."[241] The same practice is found among the African Bongo.[242] A certain Hindu caste sets fire to the faces of their dead.[243] The Chinese take pains to indicate to the dead the road home; they return by the same road which was followed to the grave and, to assist the ghost in finding its way, "the torches, which were extinguished on reaching the grave, are relighted and carried in the van of the tablet,"[244] which tablet the soul is thenceforth to occupy. "In the sixteenth and seventeenth centuries some people wished to be married on a grave, because they thought that this custom would afford some alleviation to the soul of the one who lay in it. . . . Thus the famous painter Marten Heemskerck set aside a certain sum of money for 'poor but honorable young people who should marry on his grave in the great chapel at Haarlem.' "[245] Modern Hebrews join with the savages and ancients in the "custom prohibiting obvious pleasures during the year of mourning."[246] Musical instruments may be removed from the house and stored for the time.

A curious and widespread funeral custom is to tell the bees, a practice which is explained "as being given to these winged messengers of the gods so that they may carry the news to spirit-land of the speedy arrival of a newcomer." In Herefordshire the yoke-horses or cattle are also told of the death of their owner.[247] If not told, they will die.[248] The tree that the dead man has planted must likewise be informed.[249]

At the memorial feast there may be presented impersonations of those who have died within the year. Chinese memorials for the dead have three purposes: "reconciliation with those left behind, reconciliation with the jurisdiction of the nether world, and reconciliation of the deceased with his fate.[250] An indispensable funerary rite of the ancient Persians is the *sag deed,* or seeing of the dog. A dog of a certain type must look upon the corpse five times a day as long as the body is in the house. Apparently this rite somehow benefits the ghost as the presence of the dog comforts the dying.[251] Many other miscellaneous cases could be cited but these may serve to suggest the endless detail of funerary rites.

§234*. Antagonism of the Dead and the Living.

Most forms of ghost-propitiation involve sacrifices on the part of the living— sacrifices not only in the technical sense of "making sacred" but also in that of giving up or renunciation. Sacrifice is, in short, loss. What the dead get the living cannot have. Yet the needs of

[241] Marsden, *Sumatra,* 287.

[242] Schweinfurth, *Heart of Afr.,* I, 303.

[243] Mitra, in JASB, III, 2.

[244] DeGroot, *Relig. Syst.,* I, 227-228.

[245] Schotel, *Huisgezin,* 288.   [246] Zangwill, *Ghetto,* 267.

[247] Gomme, *Ethnol. in Folklore,* 128; Gomme, *Village Life,* 137.

[248] Tetzner, in *Globus,* LXXVIII, 341.

[249] Carstens, in *Am Ur-Quell,* I, 10.

[250] Thilenius, in *Globus,* LXXXI, 332; Rehatsek, in JASB, I, 318.

[251] *Case-Book,* §99; Geiger, *Ostiran. Kultur,* 264-266; Modi, in JASB, II, 407.

the living are not provided for in such superfluity that the endowment for the dead can be spared with impunity. The living seem generally to need all they have. There results, therefore, an antagonism between the supposed interests of the dead and the actual interests of the living. The former are usually granted the preference without dispute and the living endure as they best can on what is left. Occasionally, as the cases will show, they try to evade the loss and save something for themselves. The reader of the following instances should note how, over and over again, the sacrificers are found trying to minimize the economic loss by various subterfuges, such as the use of paper models.[252] The antagonism is there as we, in our detachment, can readily perceive; but the primitive man senses it only in the form of discomfort and loss, to be borne along with the rest of life's irremediable ills or evaded if custom allows. He grows up into it and knows nothing different. He cannot analyze an antagonism out of the situation. We, to whom that relation is obvious, marvel at what we call "the funeral-waste,"[253] for such, to our eyes, it is. We see the destruction of human life and of property and deplore the "superstition" that apparently does nothing but hamper the race in its struggle toward self-realization. If one is an evolutionist, however, he reflects upon the virtual universality of these funerary customs and judges that they must have possessed a survival-value in their day and generation. That day, indeed, has been a long one and is not yet closed, even among civilized peoples; and the inference from both the universality and the protraction of such apparently wasteful customs cannot be other than that there exists in them a hidden expediency which dispassionate investigation will reveal.[254] For the present, however, interest lies in setting forth the antagonism in its sharpest lines, together with attempts to minimize losses; when a perspective of primitive religion is before us, it will be in order to consider the case as a whole.

Australians put into the grave all the articles owned by the dead man, tearing up such things as bags and rugs.[255] "Stone axes are excepted, as being too valuable to be thus disposed of, and are inherited by the next of kin";[256] here

[252] Examples in Main, *Relig. Chastity,* 49-52, appendix, note VI.
[253] §288, below.   [254] §§329, 330, below.
[255] Smyth, *Vict.,* I, 104.
[256] Howitt, *S.E. Aust.,* 455.

is an attempt to evade total loss. On the Murray River, the survivors never like to use a net that has belonged to a dead man.[257] Tylor[258] offers a number of well-chosen cases to illustrate how things may be taken from graves after their souls have gone on with the owners: a Fijian, for instance, took a club from a companion's grave, remarking to a missionary by way of explanation, that "the ghost of the club has gone with him." The Papuans do not wish that the dead man shall lack anything in the next life and so provide him with a stock of their simple possessions.[259] The Solomon Islanders wait for a year of good crops to bury a prominent man and sacrifice to him; "Now," they say, "we will take out Father." If a man descends to the spirit-world accompanied by pigs the ghosts will think much of him.[260] The Fijians have a "Path of the Shades," which was accidentally discovered by a surveyor. The guides were leading him along a high ridge, when "he noticed that the path was almost level and seldom more than 2 feet wide, and that the ridge joined hilltop to hilltop in an almost horizontal line." This was contrary to nature. "The surveyor had a patch of the undergrowth cleared away, and found that without doubt the embankments were artificial. Following the line of the ridge the valleys had been bridged with banks 30 or 40 feet high in the deepest part and tapering to a width of 2 feet at the top." The natives said this path extended 50 miles away. "For a people destitute of implements this was a remarkable work. Every pound of earth must have been carried up laboriously in cocoanut leaf baskets and paid for in feasts." The necessary drain on the population must have been enormous; thousands of pigs must have been slaughtered and millions of yams cultivated. With the present population the work would be impossible.[261]

On the day after the funeral, "the relatives perform the ceremony of 'visiting the dead' or 'fetching of iron,' the latter title being due to the fact that the iron implements are brought away from the pyre and wooden ones left in their stead . . . then the whole family remove their tent to another spot. Especially is this the case if the corpse was carried out, as sometimes happens, through the usual entrance."[262] Again, "after the person has been dead more than seven days, his re-birth has been settled and his ghost is not supposed to resent the stealing of the charms, or of the toll-money that has been tied to his wrists or placed on his tongue. He has by this time already paid toll with the ghostly form of the money to the guardians of the tree of the fruit of forgetfulness; so the money may be used again, as it is of no further use to the spirit."[263] In the East Indies there is a tremendous funeral-wastage; examples are given of the sacrifices of large numbers of beasts. Houses are often abandoned because they are "warm," that is, will bring ill. It is asserted that at one place there is a great treasure of gold in the ground by reason of the mortuary offerings; not seldom do they bury a value of $1200 with a corpse. There is a tendency to substitute imitations of objects; the paper house sacrificed has been inscribed "treasury" by the Chinese, to deceive the spirits. Objects are displayed on the grave, later to be reclaimed for regular use, in place of being permanently left there or broken up. The theory has been developed that the dead have the souls of the offerings and so what is left may

[257] Eyre, *Cent. Aust.*, II, 350. [258] *Prim. Cult.*, I, 482-483.
[259] Hagen, *Papua's*, 266; Krieger, *Neu-Guinea*, 397.
[260] Codrington, *Melanesians*, 262, 269. [261] Thomson, in JAI, XXIV, 350.
[262] Czaplicka, *Aborig. Siberia*, 148. [263] Milne, *Eastern Clan*, 269.

be returned to use; close upon such a view comes the notion that, since representations of a person or a thing may be his or its soul, these images are sufficient for the ghostly use. Many examples are cited. The exceeding cost of funeral-sacrifices is shown by the custom of putting off the grand feast of the dead for a good while because it takes a long time to assemble the goods to be sacrificed on that occasion; there are to be expedited in a body, to the spirit-world, all those who have died since the last big all-souls' festival, and the cost is enormous relatively to the wealth of the celebrants. This means often the retention of the body of the dead for an extended period, in his house, which demands some sort of hermetic sealing of the casket or of mummification.264 It may be recalled that a similar amelioration of practice is found in connection with human sacrifice: widows are allowed to serve the dead on earth instead of being immolated.265 Where slaves were once sacrificed, some image or substitute is used in replacement, just as counterfeits of property, such as trees, are used instead of hacking down orchards and embarking upon an indiscriminate destruction of domestic animals.

The Chinese thriftily use paper models of clothes, shoes, and other desirables, which they burn at the memorial ceremony. "For the manufacture of these things a paper industry has come into existence."266 Sheets of paper "are, according to the prevailing conviction, turned by the process of fire into real silver currency available in the world of darkness, and sent there through the smoke to the soul." The self-destitution practised of old by the Chinese on the occasion of a death was such that it literally entailed the total ruin of the family of the defunct. In the age of Confucius mourners had to throw off their own clothes so far as decency allowed when the corpse was being dressed. "It is an undisputed fact that a proper disposal of the dead was one of the main features in the social and religious life of the ancient Chinese." Of conditions in the fifth century, B.C., it is written: "A mature consideration of the matter convinces us that rich burials are identical with burying produced wealth on a large scale, and that mourning for a long time amounts to the same thing as forbidding the people to exercise their professions for that length of time." In the eleventh century, A.D., "the burning of counterfeits, after it had come into general practice, by no means did away with the older forms. Bonfires of genuine articles and valuables continued for a long time to hold a place side by side with bonfires of counterfeits."267

Among the North American Indians, the articles which the deceased had in daily use are almost invariably enclosed in his coffin; they are his intimate "property." "If there are many deaths about the same time, or an epidemic occurs, everything belonging to the dead is destroyed. The house in which a death occurs is always deserted and usually destroyed. In order to avoid this, it is not uncommon to take the sick person out of the house and put him in a tent to die."268 "With the last Indian woman who died here, a large quantity of good clothing and a nice sewing machine were buried. In old times, the ani-

264 Wilken, in VG, III, 102-122, *passim*, 102, 107, 108; his editor refers to Schurtz, H., "Die Wertvernichtung durch den Totenkult," in *Ztsft. f. Socialwiss.*, I, 41-52.

265 Main, *Relig. Chastity*, 52-58.   266 Rehatsek, in JASB, I, 321.

267 DeGroot, *Relig. Syst.*, I, 27; II, 390 ff., 474 ff., 659, 670, 718 ff., 726, 794-795.

268 Yarrow, in BAE, I, 157.

mals belonging to an Indian, his horses, cattle, etc., were killed upon the grave, but through the influence of the agents this practice is discontinued."[269] "Upon the decease of a member of a family the survivors allow their friends, relatives, and the medicine men to take away the best they have of everything."[270] The funeral-waste was avoided by certain Colorado Indians by "distributing their property among their children while they are of a very tender age, retaining to themselves only what is necessary to meet every-day requirements." Certain of the Sioux practise self-destitution to such a degree "as to leave the rest of the family not only absolutely destitute but actually naked. After continuing in this condition for a time, they gradually reach the common level again by receiving gifts from various sources."[271] "You would say that all their labor and efforts were for scarcely anything but to amass means of honoring the dead." Good robes are reserved for the dead in chests while the living are seen almost naked in mid-winter.[272] Such cases do not support Powell's theory[273] that funeral waste is the result of an effort to avoid strife over heritages; most of our examples, in fact, run counter to that notion.

The Iroquois put an end to all "the preposterous funeral usages which pervaded the lives and wasted the wealth of the other nations of this stock, by a rule in the Book of Rites. A delegation waited on the mourners and told them to be comforted; then they went on with their usual life."[274] One of the tenets of the Ghost-Dance religion was that "when your friends die, you must not cry." This "is interpreted by the prairie tribes as forbidding the killing of horses, the burning of tipis and destruction of property, the cutting off of the hair and the gashing of bodies with knives."[275] The California Indians had arrived at no such stage of reform; even for small children they strip themselves of property. "They not only burn everything that the baby had ever touched, but everything that they possess, so that they really begin life over again—naked as they were born, without an article of property left."[276] In South America only the Botocudo seem callous to the dead, not putting weapons and utensils into the grave, and seldom burning them on it.[277] The custom of most tribes is in line with preceding cases.[278] Certain Paraguay Indians always kill the dead man's favorite horse, "that nothing may be lacking to the ghost in the other world and that he may not be forced to return to earth to reclaim his property and punish the remiss."[279] Even the Fuegians so care for their dead that they often go into their graves better clad than they ever were in life.[280]

Strabo[281] tells of people of the Caucasus who surrender all to the dead, "and therefore they live on in poverty, having no inherited property." Classical literature is full of accounts of the subordination of the welfare of the living

[269] Willoughby, in *Smithson. Rep.*, 1886, pt. I, 276.
[270] Beckwith, in *Smithson. Rep.*, 1886, pt. I, 253.
[271] Yarrow, in BAE, I, 127, 159.   [272] Thomas, in BAE, V, 110.
[273] §231, above.   [274] Hale, *Iroq. Rites,* 71-73.
[275] Mooney, in BAE, XIV, 782.
[276] Powers, in *Contrib. N. Amer. Ethnol.*, III, 206.
[277] Von Martius, *Beiträge*, I, 327.
[278] Ratzel, *Vkde.*, II, 708; Von Nordenskiöld, in *Globus*, LXXXVII, 27, 28.
[279] Koch, in *Globus*, LXXXI, 45.
[280] Bridges, in *Voice for S. Amer.*, XIII, 201; Ratzel, *Vkde.*, II, 677.
[281] *Geog.*, XI, ch. IV.

to that of the dead; and the Egyptian expenditures for the dead were colossal. Even the "contemporaries of the mammoth and the cave-bear, whose energies one would have thought would have been wholly absorbed in the struggle for existence, still found time to attend to their dead, to prepare them for their future life, and to offer to them objects which they might have used for themselves, but which they preferred to bestow on the dead for their use in another life."[282] The most costly of luxuries are found in ancient Scandinavian graves,[283] though they came to be replaced by miniatures, as in antiquity.[284] The ghost was rich and honored in Valhalla in proportion to the property burned with his corpse.[285] The grave of a ruler of the Hallstatt period shows an astonishing extravagance of sacrifice, in human beings and in property.[286] In the Middle Ages, personal and movable property "was primarily a fund for the celebration of masses to deliver the soul of the owner from purgatory."[287] It is hardly necessary to cite instances of modern funerary extravagance and ostentation.

It is evident from such instances that there has existed a consistent and sharp antagonism of interest between the dead and the living. The living, while sedulously observing the rights of the dead because they conceived that to be the only safe policy, have sometimes fallen into unpremeditated ways of lessening the burden and saving something for themselves. To this several of the foregoing cases bear witness. It is only exceptionally, however, as in the case of the Iroquois, that they have deliberately abandoned the burdensome usage. It is understood that the antagonism was not recognized as such by the primitive sacrificers. They expected to get something worth while out of all their expenditure. Only unconsciously did they try to minimize the loss. The impression of this antagonism, which is proved by the cases to be actual and not theoretic, should be stored away in mind pending the development of other aspects of the cult. From this angle religion looks like a gratuitous handicap imposed upon struggling humanity; in its later evolution it shows phases even more costly and oppressive, for instance, in the priesthood with all its, to us, solemn farces and onerous exactions. But the case is nothing till it is complete; and it is not closed until the issue has been faced as to whether the duties incurred by reason of the ghost-cult represented only non-utilities in the life of society.

[282] D'Alviella, *Concep. God,* 16.
[283] Dreyer, in AA, X, 520, 525; Worsaae, *Nordens Forhist.,* 40.
[284] Müller, *Oldtid,* 375, 376, 377, 472, 491, 492.
[285] Geijer, *Svensk. Hist.,* I, 23.   [286] Ranke, *Mensch,* II, 574.
[287] Maine, *Early Law,* 79.

Looking back over the ground now traversed in the survey of the Mental Outfit, we see the ideas about the soul working out into beliefs about the ghost of the recently deceased, which issue in various forms of practice, negative and positive. In the end we apprehend the conflict of interests as between the living and the dead in which those of the latter overwhelmingly prevail. Thus upon the substratum of animistic and eidolistic conceptions there comes to be developed an art of dealing with the ghosts which is the concrete expression of an engrossing life-policy or prosperity-policy or, more accurately, of a counter-adversity-policy. This art lies, so far as we have yet followed it, in the ghost-cult. The ghost-cult, however, is no more than the vestibule to the structure of religion; in it exist the germs of more developed theories and systems dealing with the supernatural environment. These latter, in fact, may be something more than implicit. There is no difference in kind, but only in degree, to be registered as we go forward into daimonism and daimonology. The more evolved forms are there in the ghost-cult, only they are in their lower and simpler terms. It is because of this fact that the stage of eidolism is specifically marked off, in order that the essential nature of more complicated forms may be the more readily apprehended in those lower terms.

The course of the soul-idea is but begun. If animism had had no further development or sequents than eidolism, it would be a curiosity rather than the significant first stage of the evolution of a prime factor in all human life and civilization. If, in the belief of primitive men, the soul had no more than existed awhile, as an eidolon, in the neighborhood of the body and then had passed beyond the range of active interest in and power over human life, it is inconceivable that the mores and institutions which represent adjustment to the supernatural environment could have attained to any great significance. As it is in actuality, the simple beginnings of the ghost-theory and the corresponding cult of the dead represent no more than a phase of gathering momentum; they are elaborated upon, gaining power at every stage, until they sweep into the range of history as integrated systems of religion, entering as cardinal factors into the evolution of the most evolved of human societies.

CHAPTER XXVII

DAIMONISM

§235. The Extension of the Ghost-Theory. The range of phenomena classifiable under eidolism and the ghost-cult has now been surveyed. The ghost-theory, however, is far from being a temporary and sterile growth; it is susceptible of, and has attained to, wide extension and amplification. Ghost-fear has been a perennial fountain of world-philosophy. Corollary and derivative ideas and mores cluster about the central theories and practices touching the imaginary environment. An account of these is now to be given in connection with the next stage of religious development, the theory of which is Daimonism and the practice Daimonology. In eidolism and the ghost-cult appear the germ-forms of all that is to come; and these forms shade into later members of the evolutionary series in such manner as to present those constantly recurring zones of transition characteristic of all evolutionary sequences. Eidolism passes by almost imperceptible gradations into daimonism. Daimonism, in its turn, is a broadly transitional form; a number of the topics now to be treated must go back for their lower terms and simplest setting into the foregoing sections and forward for their more evolved manifestations into the range of the formal religious system—in fact, into the territory of a discipline lying beyond the scope of this book, namely, comparative religion. Thus, daimonism and daimonology become the center of our treatment.

Whereas the ghost or eidolon is the disembodied soul of a particular individual, recently dead, and the ghost-cult consists characteristically of mortuary and funerary rites, the daimon is farther along the road to godhood, being a spirit of secondary intention, generally not identifiable as the soul of any deceased person; and the cult of the daimon is a more generalized one. The term daimon covers all varieties of spirits, from the ghost, but not including it, up to and inclusive of the divinity or god.[1] Daimon-

[1] Rivers, following Codrington, makes something the same distinction, in *Melan. Soc.*, I, 15.

ism is therefore the doctrine about spirits, both good and bad; and about these as the effective agency of everything entering into human experience which is referable to luck and the imaginary environment. The term covers, however, none of the abstract and speculative conceptions of divinity. Daimonology is the science and art, corresponding to daimonism, of dealing with the superior powers which control men's welfare and destiny.

These two terms are built upon the form "daimon," which is preferable to "demon" inasmuch as it is a colorless term carrying no moral attribute of good or bad. The Greek "daimon" was simply a spirit-being or a divinity; the "demonic" connotation came with the adoption of the word by those to whom all out-group or "heathen" divinities were, as a matter of course, devils.

Eidolism and daimonism differ primarily in the fact that ghosts or eidola are the identifiable spirits of known persons while daimons are spirits whose human careers are unrevealed except through inference. The daimon, while a more evolved construction, is a replica of the ghost in all essentials of disposition and character, such likeness by itself suggesting the origin of the former in the latter. The daimons are more powerful and longer-lived ghosts, controlling the aleatory element and the unfolding of personal destiny as the recently dead cannot. They are anthropomorphic, have temperament, character, and ways of acting, and are susceptible to influences which man can cause to be exerted. They do both good and ill, the latter preponderating; "ghosts are not wholly angry, and the gentler form of ghost may and does become a god,"[2] but they are more likely to be envious and malignant toward men. Especially, therefore, are all ill-fortune and calamity to be accounted for by their agency. The life of man comes to be regarded as at the sport, from moment to moment, of these superior powers. Nothing in history is more calculated to excite pity for the human race than the existence of the set of beliefs about spirits. The immediate effect of such convictions upon human life is obviously lamentable. It requires considerable study and reflection to apprehend the remoter, impersonal, evolutionary consequences.

§236. Daimonism as a World-Philosophy. Daimonism, in-

2 Harrison, *Greek Relig.*, 257.

volving as it did all the hopes and fears of mankind, could not but become a world-philosophy. It stands forth as the salient feature of the race's mental outfit. It accounted for everything that needed accounting for. It therefore led to a complete life-policy. Some idea of its primordial quality, persistence, and scope should be acquired before entering upon an analysis of the structures which it summoned into being. First of all, it offered a sweeping explanation of two problems that are vital and ever-recurring throughout the life of the race: whence comes ill? what is the relation of goodness to happiness? The answer—that ill comes from displeasing the daimons and that goodness, consisting in pleasing them, brings happiness—naïve and childish though it may be, is the simplest solution, involving the least strain upon the mind, and it is the one to which men are always returning. Other solutions have been offered by prophets and philosophers, which have ostensibly superseded this one, but it has lasted on underneath all sophistication, in the real faith of the masses, and it is there today. Daimonism has been and now is by far the most widespread and persistent of all religious doctrines, for it has been and is present in all religions, as is revealed, if not otherwise, by a multitude of survivals, many of which will be met with in subsequent connections.

There are current among us phrases and practices, regarded sometimes as profane, which are merely survivals of daimonism: forms of swearing illustrate this point, as do euphemisms (such as "deuce [deus] take you!" or the Down-East "I swan to man," for "I swear to God") that disguise cruder forms; and the ignorant, as is fully illustrated in such stories as *Huckleberry Finn,* still expectorate, repeat formulas or execute motions, carry protective devices, "knock on wood," or otherwise endeavor to avoid or thwart daimonic influence. Such phrases and practices, when survivalistic, are not employed with serious intent, it may be, but there is no knowing how much assent one man or another may put into them or what real weight they might carry upon occasion.

Furthermore, out of the underlying strata of half-unconscious daimonism a recrudescence of supposedly discarded faith may easily emerge under pressure of calamity; people who knew better have been swept off their feet in the presence of witchcraft-manias[3] and the late war had its revival of superstition.[4] Those who think they have freed their minds of the survivals which alone deserve

[3] Sumner, "Witchcraft," in *Coll. Ess.,* I, ch. IV.
[4] Muirhead, in N. Y. *Nation,* CI, 455; Holmes, in *The Bookman,* XLIV (March, 1916).

the name of superstition[5] are in error if they judge the masses of mankind by themselves and lightly dismiss as "symbols" what are regarded by many people as firm realities.

"The belief in ghosts, and especially in ill-disposed and harmful spirits, stands at the beginning of all the religious development of the human race. It forms the deepest foundations of all the religious life of the nations. . . . Although daimonism may be superseded by higher religious conceptions, it is never rooted out or conquered. Thus, though the strong monotheistic piety of the Psalms and Prophets thrust out the lower doctrine of daimonism with un-paralleled energy, with the result that only a few traces of it are to be found in the Old Testament, nevertheless we must take it for certain that daimonism remained alive to some extent among the lower classes of the people. In the later times of Judaism, in any case, daimonism again spread with renewed energy through the upper classes, and it reveals itself with new strength in the literature. . . . In all periods of transition, the older and inferior faith breaks forth again from the depths of the national soul."[6] The despondent thinker sometimes asks himself: Do the gods rule luck, after all? Have we got the variable reduced to a constant? "Though having within me, as I hope, an understanding [of the ways of gods with men], I am at fault when I look upon the fates and works of mortals. For there is change this way and that and the life of men shifts about in endless restlessness."[7]

Daimonism is a faith shot through with emotion and calling for action; its theories demand an immediate application. If the spirits are all powerful and also prone to take offense, even where they are not regarded as spontaneously malignant; if their anger means ruin despite all mere man can do for himself; and if this ruin falls not alone upon the person immediately concerned but also upon the whole group; then the supreme prosperity-policy, which cannot be put into operation too soon, is to win the spirits to neutrality, if not to positive beneficence. If the right system can be found, prosperity must result; and, conversely, if a nation has been fortunate and prosperous, it can regard its mode of serving the gods as one truly pleasing to them.[8] Daimonism must work out into expedients to secure such ends; and the sum of these methods is daimonology.

Men have not regarded themselves as altogether helpless before

[5] §199, above; Zwemer, "The Influence of Animism on Islam, an Account of Popular Superstitions," rev. in N. Y. *Times,* July 4, 1920; Dresslar, "Suggestions on the Psychology of Superstition," report in N. Y. *Times,* June 5, 1910.
[6] Bousset, *Relig. d. Judenthums,* 331.
[7] Euripides, *Hippolytus,* 1105-1110 (chorus).
[8] Lippert, *Kgchte.,* I, 101.

the spirits. The acts, moods, and intentions of the daimons, of so
much concern to human destiny, might, it was thought, be learned
by omens, auguries, oracles, and signs offered in the incidents of
the external world to those who knew how to seize upon and interpret them; or they might be revealed by devices of divination,
soothsaying, and magic, through which men made inquiry. Or-
deals, duels, necromancy, astrology, and magic in general are more
elaborate means of discovering what the superior powers are about
to do, that is, what is going to happen. Devices against adversity
are adjusted, in general, as if the spirits enjoyed human suffering,
disappointment, and loss; men subject themselves to pain, self-
denial, and renunciation of satisfactions as if the daimons might
be induced to accept voluntary suffering instead of what they intended to inflict; and this form of buying-off, together with more
obvious forms of bribery, must be maintained all the time in order
to keep the spiritual powers well-disposed or merely neutral, or in
the effort to anticipate trouble by speedily atoning for some fault
unwittingly committed. "Redemption or salvation was necessary
because man and the world fell, at the very beginning, under the
power of the daimons. . . . Men were not to blame for ill and evil;
daimons brought sin and ill into the world."[9]

It is evident that when once the agency for incidents in human
experience had been attributed to ghosts and spirits, the interests
of man were at stake in their will and pleasure and would at last
depend for their realization upon the correct use of eidolistic and
daimonistic devices. Thus arose folkways and mores to fit the
cases and to secure the interests. Therefore the whole body of
daimonistic notions and usages belongs in the mores as an important constituent part of them. Out of the code of mores then comes
the concept of duty, as things that must be done; of truth, as the
correct world-philosophy; and of right, as the correct conduct to
satisfy interests and to win welfare. The daimonistic philosophy
opens out into a heavily sanctioned code of conduct.

In the Congo region, "the religion of the Boloki has its basis in their fear of
those numerous invisible spirits which surround them on every side, and are
constantly trying to compass their sickness, misfortune, and death; and the
Boloki's sole object in practising their religion is to cajole, or appease, cheat,

[9] Harnack, *Dogmengchte.*, I, 171.

or conquer and kill those spirits that trouble them—hence their *nganga* [medicine-men], their rites, their ceremonies and their charms. If there were no evil spirits to be circumvented there would be no need of their medicine man, and their charms."[10] Again, "hardly anything could be done without first making it known to the gods and begging a blessing, protection, or whatever the case might require. The infant, only a few seconds old, and before *anything* could be done to it, was hurried to the temple, that' its first breathing might be in the presence of the god, and his blessing invoked on the *very first* essentials of infantile life. Even the killing of a pig had to be done in the temple, and the blessing of the god asked before it could be cooked or eaten."[11]

If daimonism, along with the eidolism out of which it develops, is the most primary, universal, and persistent form of religion, it has not needed to be spread by transmission from people to people across incredible distances. It shows parallel origin in widely separated ranges; it is subject to variation, selection, and transmission, like the rest of the mores. There are in it fundamental notions and faiths which lie deep in the human mind and might seem to be ultimate components of human nature, for they belong to the first reactions of men upon experience and observation and they are the same or strangely alike for all peoples that have not risen above them. To exert their enduring influence it is not necessary that these ideas and doctrines should measure up to our standards of truth and reality. To recall a former quotation: "History shows us that the creative force exerted by an idea on the development of civilization does not depend upon its relation to reality. The power of a notion lies not in its certainty but in its vividness or in the number of people who believe in it." Because the apprehension of the spirit-environment was, among nature-peoples, vivid in the extreme and because their ideas about it were substantially the same all over the world, eidolism and daimonism could not but form the substratum upon which all subsequent religious structure has rested. The author[12] just quoted asserts that so far as experience goes, an idea which is the outcome of one man's study, or one that has been matured as the product of single culture-group, can never be so vividly apprehended, no matter what the evidence behind it, as the belief in spirits has been—a belief which, so far as the evidence for it is concerned, is extremely uncertain.

[10] Weeks, in JAI, XL, 377.   [11] Turner, *Samoa*, 290.
[12] Lippert, *Kgchte.*, I, 29; II, 45.

Simkhovitch[13] insists upon the superior potency of feeling over intellect in molding human evolution. "It may well be observed that so-called intellectual understanding does play a role only in the history of so-called ideas; that is, understanding plays a role in the history of understanding—a trite enough observation. It plays an infinitely small role in the history of mankind. Mankind and understanding are two different things. You perhaps witness from time to time great commotions in the name of ideas. . . . Do not think for a moment that it is understanding of the ideas which moves mankind; it is their faith in the ideas. This is true about the so-called masses, it is true about so-called intellectuals; when at certain times numbers of persons call themselves positivists, Kantians, Hegelians, Marxists, all you will find there is sincere and really powerful faith in the concepts of Comte or Kant or Hegel or Marx. That faith is clothed . . . in phrases and excerpts—rags of the believers' particular master. So it is with faith; and as it is, so it was, and so perhaps it will be." Malinowski[14] remarks upon the pronounced skepticism of certain primitives, to contrast it with the tenacity of belief of the great majority; "all beliefs as implied in native customs and tradition must be treated as invariably fixed items. They are believed and acted upon by all, and, as customary actions do not allow of individual varieties, this class of belief is standardized by its social embodiments. They may be called the dogmas of native belief, or the social ideas of a community, as opposed to individual ideas. . . . It seems feasible, therefore, . . . to treat elements of belief expressed by behaviour as types; that is, not to trouble about the individual variation. . . . This does not mean that they [the variations] ought to be ignored, but that, in the first approach, they may be ignored without making the information incorrect through incompleteness."

Such evidence about daimonism as is now before us, and much that is to come, but reveals in sharper relief the primordial and inveterate character of eidolism. There have been a number of cases in the foregoing citations in which it appears that while some superior spirit is recognized in a general sort of way, yet when it comes to actual life and a concrete cult it is the ghosts of the dead that hold the foreground. In a number of cases the ghost-cult has given way but slightly and partially to that of the daimons.

In the New Hebrides, "the general name for gods seemed to be *aremha;* that means a *dead man,* and hints alike at the origin and nature of their religious worship. The spirits of their departed ancestors were among their gods." Chiefs who reached an advanced age "were after death deified, addressed by name, and prayed to on various occasions. They were supposed especially to preside over the growth of the yams and the different fruit trees. The first-fruits were presented to them, and in doing this they laid a little of the fruit on some

---

13 *Understanding of Jesus,* 78.

14 In JAI, XLVI, 365-366, 423-425. See also this author's recent book: *Crime and Custom in Savage Society.*

stone, or shelving branch of the tree, or some more temporary altar of a few rough sticks."[15] This is evidently a rudimentary sort of religion and a set of gods that have scarcely parted company with the ghosts. Where there are higher spirits, worship is nevertheless accorded almost solely to the spirits of the dead.[16] In the Solomon Islands, "a difference is recognized between beings of a higher nature than human, and the spirits of dead men, but everything in the nature of a *cultus* is directed to the dead."[17] Among the Zulus, though the "Greatest Ghost," Unkulunkulu, has a high place, in daily life he does not enjoy the preference; here it is "the ensemble of the ghosts of the dead that are honored by a definite cult."[18] Among even the Phœnicians a ghost-cult was plainly antecedent to that of the gods;[19] and only with the final departure of the soul to Hades did the ancient Greek ghost-cult, later to be revived, lose its object.[20]

§237. The Art of Living. The spirits were believed to control the aleatory element;[21] they gave luck, if it came, and to them were ascribed disappointment, loss, and calamity. This good and bad luck, taken together, formed the web of life. The doctrine as to the character, ways, likes, and dislikes of the daimons and the art of avoiding, repelling, conciliating, or winning them—that is, daimonism and daimonology—were successors to eidolism and the ghost-cult as the science and art of living. Life had all the hazard of constant gambling. What one's fortune was to be was not a question of effort, industry, or talent but of the whims of daimons who, beyond the veil of the senses, were fighting or playing pranks of which the destinies of men were the resultants. The apparatus of times, words, and ritual, by which men believed that this chancy element could be controlled, admitted of no verification. The attendant practices constituted a heavy burden and made the task of living complicated and tedious; yet on account of the awful sanctions which were supposed to attend them, no one dared try the experiment of omitting them. The evolutionary process went on its automatic way. There was, along with labor and sacrifice, also care without end, and whether it did any good no one could know.

There rose no thought of rejection of the theory. Daimonology, as an art, underwent a great development of deductions and corollaries. One meets with attempts to improve the theory of it

15 Turner, *Samoa*, 318-319.
17 Codrington, in JAI, X, 298.
19 Pietschmann, *Phön.*, 191.
21 §208, above.

16 §216, above.
18 Fritsch, *Eingeb. S.-Afr.*, 139.
20 Rohde, *Psyche*, I, 21.

and new and elaborate rules for applying it, as in the case of all other folkways which have seriously affected life-interests; but attention was turned to that which, as was thought, could control the daimons and determine the aleatory element instead of toward labor and the accumulation of capital. As in all cases where the element of risk or luck is taken to be decisive, energy was lamed and rational effort debarred. There were no other departments of life in regard to which folkways were so assiduously cultivated as they were within the range of the aleatory element. The question: How shall we act in order to live well? was answered at every point by daimonism. When the answer did not verify on the test of actual experience, though the ways were altered, the principle remained unchallenged. Then the experiment went forward to the next stage.

§238. **Transition to Daimonism.** The transition from the ghost to the daimon, and so from eidolism to daimonism, was by way of a sort of competition and survival among the ghosts. Some of them were all but negligible; the bodies of the insignificant, for example of small children,[22] were disposed of in a relatively careless manner and whatever ghost-cult ensued was perfunctory. Insignificance went with lack of power, for power was what impressed the primitive mind. Physical force was the most obvious manifestation of power; and other forms included mental ability, wisdom, wealth, and control over the spirit-environment. Holders of what might be called temporal or spiritual powers were the most impressive of mankind; these were the chief and the medicine-man or priest. If the same person held both offices, as was often the case, he united in himself the several powers cited and occupied a position of supreme significance not only in life but also after death.[23] As he was sure to command an extended allegiance from his survivors, his cult, being more widely and diligently practised under a more vivid fear of his ghost, persisted beyond that of other and less prominent of the departed.

Now the chief man of a group, at a time when that group was supposed to be united by the blood-bond alone, was related to them all. Upon all, though particularly upon his nearest kin, rested the duty of seeing to his comfort in the next life, an obligation en-

22 §§218, 228, 233, above. 23 §§312, 320, below.

forced by the liveliest concern for their own well-being. Under the patriarchal family régime[24] the chief men were generally the family-heads and so the progenitors, real or fictitious, of the whole group. The deceased "father" comes readily to be singled out as the "Great Ghost" and then as the tutelary daimon, to be worshipped after the funeral and the laying of his spirit are long past.

By way of illustration of the blurred transition from eidolism to daimonism, consider the following account of the beliefs of certain Central Africans. Among them the word corresponding to *anima* is *lisoka.* "In dreams or in fainting fits the *lisoka* leaves the body but only to return to it with the awakening consciousness. At death, however, it leaves its earthly abode never to return. It is now spoken of as having gone to *mulungu."* Further, "the nature of the human *lisoka* is closely allied to that of the *masoka,* which are the inspiring agents in madness and in the ecstasy of prophecy or incantation. What the origin of these inspiring *masoka* is, or to whom they belonged when in bodily life, the Yao holds no theory. He is content to accept them as they are. . . . 'Just *masoka* and nothing more,' as he says." This word *mulungu* is taken in two broad senses. "The word *mulungu* is in the first instance applied to the human soul or *lisoka* after death when it is considered as an inhabitant of the spirit world." But the term seems also to mean the spirit-world itself. "Freed from the body it passes to *mulungu,* and there is regarded as endowed with powers which it never possessed when alive on earth. To pray to such a spirit is described as *kulomba mulungu,* to worship *mulungu,* never *lisoka* in this case. . . . Various articles of personal property were . . . placed beside the corpse, clothes, ivory, guns, axes, hoes. . . . At the head of the mound a native pot was fixed in the ground for the reception of the offering of beer which is an almost invariable accompaniment of any act of worship paid to the *mulungu* of the dead. . . . Should a long-continued drought endanger the prospects of the grain crop, the departed chief must be solicited to send the lacking rain. . . . Such shrines are to be seen in almost every Yao village where the inhabitants have been located for any length of time. They are regarded with awe—the little boys as they pass whisper to each other in a warning tone, *'masoka.'* . . . But the word *mulungu* is used by the Yao with a wider application. Etymologically the word is connected with the root *kulungwa,* which in so many of the other branches of the Bantu tongue appears as *kulu* or *kuru,* and signifies 'great' or 'old.' It is the same root which appears in the Kaffir word for God, Unkulunkulu, which may therefore be rendered as 'The old, old One,' or 'The great, great One.' A like rendering may be given of the Yao form *mulungu,* the 'Old One,' or the 'Great One.' . . . As we have already seen, the word *mulungu* is applied to the human *lisoka* when regarded as an object of worship, or as an inhabitant of the spirit world. But it is also used to denote the spirit world in general, or more properly speaking, the *aggregate of the spirits of all the dead.* . . . Among the various tribes where the word is in use . . . the missionaries have adopted it as the term for 'God.' But the untaught Yao refuses to assign to it any idea of being or personality. It is to him more a quality or faculty of the human nature whose signification

24 §419, below.

he has extended so as to embrace the whole spirit world. . . . *Mulungu* is also regarded as the agent in anything mysterious. 'It's *mulungu,*' is the Yao exclamation on being shown anything that is beyond the range of his understanding. The rainbow is always '*mulungu.*' . . . A devout native sitting down to a meal will, before beginning to eat, take out a small morsel of the food before him and throw it at the root of the nearest tree as an offering to *mulungu.* . . . Thus the Yao presents us with three stages of animistic belief:—(1) The human *lisoka* or shade, the agent in dreams, delirium, etc. (2) This *lisoka* regarded as *mulungu,* and an object of worship and reverence, the controller of the affairs of this life, the active agent in the fortunes of the human race. (3) And lastly, *mulungu* as expressing the great spirit agency, the creator of the world and all life, the source of all things animate and inanimate. And yet between these three conceptions of the spirit nature no definite boundary line can be drawn. The distinction in the native mind is ever of the haziest. No one will give you a dogmatic statement of his belief on such points."[25]

§239*. Ancestor-Worship. The ghost-cult, as the primordial expedient for dealing with the supernatural, persists either in its primitive form or in that of its lineal descendants. Of these latter, ancestor-worship appears to be the most immediate. It constitutes the stock transition leading toward daimonism, for the ancestral spirit, as the father and founder of the tribe, forms the connecting link between the ghost and the god. One would gather from Spencer[26] that it is the only such link and that ancestor-worship is a necessary stage in the evolution of religion. Still, although most peoples have traversed that stage, it cannot be regarded as the sole transitional step. Hero-worship presents another such form, if, indeed, it is not itself the inclusive one; for it is because of his position and power—his heroic qualities—that the ancestor gains his significance. The ancestor was a special sort of hero and perhaps the only sort, on the stage where the blood-tie was the sole societal bond. In any case hero-worship must be associated with ancestor-worship when considering the transition to daimonism.

In general, ancestor-worship belongs to a plane of civilization somewhat higher than that of the ghost-cult. In some cases, as in India, China, and Japan, it has remained amidst a relatively advanced civilization, although with development of culture it is more likely, as in Egypt, Greece, and Rome, to yield to a set of deities of a higher order and become no more than a popular survival. It is intensely conservative and it has acted as a fetter on

25 Hetherwick, in JAI, XXXII, 91-95.
26 *Prin. Soc.,* I, ch. XX, *et passim.*

society where it has deadened enterprise by instilling the conviction that deviation from ancestral ways is wicked and will be punished by the departed spirits. It strongly affects societal policy: if, for instance in India, a man dies leaving no son, he cannot enter the spirit-world;[27] thus marriage and all family-institutions must be molded accordingly.

When certain tribes of Australians, in fear of calamity, revert to sexual communalism, it is the ghosts of ancestors that they are trying to propitiate.[28] Hagen[29] says of the Papuans: "With a people that concerns itself in so lively a manner with the souls of its dead, it is only natural that a certain ancestor-cult has developed. . . . Dead fathers, brothers, grandfathers are the confidants in the spirit-world; they call upon them in all manner of earthly eventualities. . . . If a relative lies at the point of death, all sorts of promises are made to him by his people in order that he may, as a ghost, after his death, be always inclined to their wishes." Invocation of the ghost of a father or uncle is common on occasion of danger or illness, in the New Hebrides.[30] In Fiji offerings are made to ancestral spirits whenever their aid is invoked. These sacrifices are of articles "highly prized by the elders, and hence by the ancestors whose living representatives they are."[31] Hocart[32] contends that the Fijian *kalou* means "ancestral spirit" and not "god" in a modern sense. "The early missionaries, with their heads full of Kings and Chronicles and Greek mythology, saw nothing in Fijian religion but what they had been accustomed to expect; they mistook *kalou* for god, stripped the imagined deities of this supposed honourable title, and branded them as devils, unwitting that they were attaching infamy to departed souls, making mourning at tombs a heathenish and evil practice, and forbidding visible supports of pious remembrance to a people who think little of what they do not see and whom they already accused of a want of natural affection." Men of a higher culture have usually regarded the daimons of more primitive peoples as "demons"; here the revered souls of forebears were included under that category—another deplorable case of ignorance and prejudice.

"Another aspect of the spiritual beliefs of the A-Kamba and one which shews the intimate nature of the communion which exists in their minds between the spirits of their ancestors and the living, is demonstrated by the fact that every married woman is believed to be at the same time the wife of a living man and also the wife of some *Aiimu* or spirit of a departed ancestor. This fully explains what was not at all clear in the earlier stages of this enquiry, viz. that women are generally used as the vehicles of expression by the *Aiimu,* and the *Aiimu* who is spiritually wedded to any particular woman will often through the mouth of his corporeal wife state his name, and the old people of the village will remark on this when they hear the name, and for instance say, 'Oh, yes, that was so and so's great great grandfather.' It is firmly believed that the fertility of a wife depends to a great extent on her spiritual husband, and if a woman does not become *enceinte* during the first

27 Chowbe, in JASB, V, 227.
29 *Papua's,* 267.
31 Fison, in JAI, XIV, 26.

28 Howitt, in JAI, XIII, 189.
30 Macdonald, in AAAS, 1892, 729.
32 In JAI, XLII, 439.

six months after her marriage they consider that her particular *Aiimu* is neglecting her, and they make an offering of beer and kill a goat as a propitiatory sacrifice, and if that fails, a few months later make a bigger feast and kill a bullock."[33]

Johnston[34] says of a certain East African tribe that they "practise a vague ancestor-worship such as is universal among all Bantu Negroes." The human faces represented upon East African fetishes are those of ancestors.[35] "The religion is pure ancestor-worship. They pray for rain, good weather, and fertility to the manes of their grandparents. No important decision is reached without a sacrifice to the ancestors."[36] The development of fetishes out of the apparatus of ancestor-worship is found in Loango: "they are the objects, now become independent, in which the ancestors were thought previously to have been housed. Today each has its own power, the ability to seize in possession, that is, to throw into a state of 'possession,' to give out oracles, to animate; they are revengeful, jealous, and full of cupidity; they are, in short, genuine African, manistic godlets."[37] The Mpongwe, in times of peril or distress, collect along the brow of some commanding eminence or the skirts of a dense forest and call in most piteous and touching tones upon the spirits of their ancestors.[38] In South Africa "the system of quasi-ancestor worship enters into every relation of life, down to the remotest details. Domestic events, war, peace, agriculture, disease among cattle and goats, drought, floods, cold, heat, pestilence, etc., and almost every event of life is traced indirectly or directly to ancestor spirits, and as they are pleased or not events are propitious or otherwise."[39] Ancestor-worship is so common in Africa that an occasional exception is noteworthy.[40]

The savage peoples of Asia show the same belief and practice. Such peoples as the Votyaks and Kirghiz regularly offer prayer and sacrifice to the ancestors[41] while among certain Tibetans, twice a year the bones of the ancestors are dug up and washed with intensely solemn and sacred ceremony. "As the possession of a large 'bonery' gives to the fortunate proprietor great power in the tribe, these bones are seized upon for debt or on the inauguration of a feud" and must be redeemed.[42] "The Saora deities and ancestral spirits are said to cause all ills, and though the Saoras will not admit that the deities and ancestral spirits are the same, there is little doubt that the deities are further removed ancestral spirits"[43]—that is, the ancestral spirits, when "further removed," become deities or daimons and ancestor-worship is a stage toward daimonism.

Passing over the more civilized Asiatics for the moment, we find the Dyaks of Borneo[44] and other peoples of the Malay Archipelago and the Pacific Islands repeating the beliefs and practices already cited. "In general, the souls thus honored can be divided into two categories, namely, the souls of those

---

[33] Hobley, *A-Kamba*, 89-90.
[34] *Uganda*, II, 578; Starcke, *Prim. Fam.*, 61.
[35] Stuhlmann, *Mit Emin*, 478, 187, 554.
[36] Von Götzen, *Durch Afr.*, 83.   [37] Frobenius, *Masken*, 42, 163.
[38] Nassau, *Fetichism*, 158.   [39] Macdonald, in JAI, XIX, 276.
[40] Junker, *Afrika*, III, 313.
[41] Michailovski, *Shamanism* (Russ.), 16; *Russian Ethnog.* (Russ.), II, 188.
[42] Reid, in *Cosmopolitan Mag.*, XXVIII, 453.
[43] Fawcett, in JASB, I, 245.   [44] Gomes, *Sea Dyaks*, 142.

recently deceased and of those long dead. The former are naturally, first of all, protective spirits of the nearest kin: they are household gods, *lares privati;* the others have a wider circle of worshippers, belong no longer to any single house or kin but to several kin-groups, to families as well as to a whole village, and are thus more like *lares publici.*" Many examples are cited. Among the *lares publici* are the prominent men, founders of villages and heroes in general.[45] Certain of the Caroline Islanders would not touch a kind of big eel, "which earlier was honored as the embodied representative of the souls of ancestors. If one by chance found such a 'holy' eel dead, they buried it, carefully wrapped in mats, with the same ceremonies and honors, as if the case was that of a great chief."[46] The people of the Pacific Islands paid respect to age only because they wanted to keep in the good graces of those whose souls would soon quit their bodies and become capable of making troublesome ghost-visits.[47] The Tusayan Indians' *katcina* is the impersonation of a supernatural being of subordinate rank to the great deities; "in a general way the word Katcina may be translated 'soul' or 'deified ancestor,' and in this respect affords most valuable data to the upholders of the animistic theory."[48] The whole religion of certain Paraguay Indians "consists in an honoring of ancestors, the ghosts of the dead, which has developed out of fear of their return and vengeance."[49]

Ancestor-worship, as is well known, assumed a more highly developed form among the more highly civilized American peoples; the Sun himself was looked upon as the ancestor of the Inca rulers. But it is in China above all that the system came fully into its own, and exerted to the extreme its conservative influence upon the life of a great people. "The Chinese, prostrate bodily and mentally before the memorial tablets which contain the souls of his ancestors, little thinks that he is all the while proving to mankind how vast a power unlimited filial obedience, prohibiting change from ancestral institutions, may exert in stopping the advance of civilization."[50]

"Each Chinese house contains an ancestral shrine, in which the wooden tablets of the ancestors are placed, with the names, rank, and dates of birth and decease of various ascendants inscribed thereon. Before these incense is daily offered with prostrations, and twice a month offerings of eatables are spread, again with prostrations."[51] Upon the tablets is engraved: "To the deceased generations, first ancestors, ancestors, first grandfathers, grandfathers, and fathers."[52] "If the sacrifices are neglected the spirits will be angry. If the spirits are angry they will take revenge. It is better to worship the spirits by

45 Wilken, in VG, III, 220-221.
46 Finsch, *Ethnol. Erfahr.,* III, 200.   47 Ratzel, *Vkde.,* II, 335.
48 Fewkes, in BAE, XIX, pt. II, 1008; Fewkes, in BAE, XV, 251, 254.
49 Koch, in *Globus,* LXXXI, 45.   50 Maine, *Early Law,* 62.
51 Von Mollendorff, *Chinese,* 46-47.
52 Rehatsek, in JASB, I, 324 ff.; DeGroot, *Kongsiwezen,* 90-91.

way of insurance. This appears to be the condensed statement of the Chinese theory of all forms of worship of the dead." The system of ancestral worship, Smith[53] goes on to say, is one of the heaviest yokes which a people was ever compelled to bear. Hundreds of millions of living Chinese are under subjection to the countless thousands of millions of the dead. "The generation of today is chained to the generations of the past. . . . Ancestral worship is the best type and guarantee of that leaden conservatism" which has characterized the Chinese. The sense of the whole elaborate and expensive proceeding is to make a "good grave," out of which the deceased will cause good fortune to befall his offspring in the form of long life, health, material prosperity, luck in undertakings, rank in the state, and social prestige. Ancestor-worship may be viewed as an enterprise of the living to ensure themselves all these things. And this worship is thought to go on in the hereafter; the dead man, on rejoining his predecessors, continues his function of serving and worshipping even more assiduously than before.[54] Japanese mortuary tablets are maintained only for grandparents and parents—the recently dead. It is believed that the ancestral ghosts control nature; fire and flood, pestilence and famine, are at their disposal as means of vengeance. One act of impiety in a village may therefore bring misfortune to all. The ghost of the dead becomes a divine power to whom his children pray for the prosperity of their undertakings. "By degrees the household religion became a religion of tenderness as well as duty, and changed and softened the thoughts of men about the dead." Hearn,[55] who reports the foregoing, believes that "in all patriarchal societies with a settled civilization, there is evolved, out of the worship of ancestors, a Religion of Filial Piety."

The ancient Aryans practised a "strict ancestor-worship"; marriage, kinship, and testamentary laws are intimately bound up with this form of cult. Sons are desired because they best can make offerings to the dead. "To be a man's heir" and "to offer the dead man's meal" are convertible expressions.[56] The Pre-Mosaic Hebrews had scarcely any notion of God; they feared "the constantly threatening but always incalculable influence of demonic powers. . . . These 'demons' are partly spirits of the dead, and above all, the spirits of the nearest kin of the family."[57] Maurer[58] thinks the teraphim were ancestral figures: "it speaks for this interpretation, that the reception of the slave into the family takes place before the teraphim." The ancestors up to the latest times were supposed to watch over their offspring.[59] Homer shows no unmistakable evidence of ancestor-worship but it was well-defined in the tragedians; Æschylus makes Electra pray to her dead father quite as to a god, and in the *Alcestis* the dead heroine is to receive petitions.[60] Hesiod bears witness "that ancestor worship had come down out of gray antiquity to the time of the poet"; only the belief in the exaltation of departed souls "into powerful, con-

[53] *Chinese Char.*, 184; Harvey, *Chinese Animism.*

[54] DeGroot, *Relig. Syst.*, I, pt. I and particularly 48.

[55] *Japan*, 51, 118, 34, 49, 56.

[56] Schrader, *Aryans*, 422; Spiegel, *Eran. Alterthumskde.*, II, 98.

[57] Kautzsch, "Relig. Israel," in *Hastings's Bible Dict.*, 623.

[58] *Vkde.*, I, 129; Lippert, *Kgchte.*, II, 454.

[59] Duhm, *Geister*, 24; Jeremiah, XXXI, 15.

[60] Æschylus, *Choephori*, 124 ff.; Euripides, *Alcestis*, 995-1004; Beloch, *Griech. Gchte.*, I, 114.

sciously operating spirits" has dwindled. "For a long time the souls of the dead have fallen to Hades and his unreal realm of shades. The soul-cultus stagnates, it relates now only to those who died long ago, it does not augment the objects of its reverence." Thus the existence of ancestor-worship is a matter of inference rather than of direct evidence; of the latter little more can be presented than could be gathered to prove the same contention concerning the deity-conception of modern civilization. Zeus, for instance, like many another ranking deity, is "father of gods and men." On the other hand, "the belief in, and worship of the *dei parentes,* the *divi Manes,* the *Lares,* etc., are so ingrained in the life of the Roman that, as regards Rome, we have no reason to doubt that these ideas are primitive."[61] The Guanches of the Canaries prayed to the spirits of their ancestors,[62] and the ancient Germans, like the Hindus, Greeks, and Romans, cherished domestic deities.[63] Among the Scandinavians the older authorities "all point to the habitual and household worship of ancestors as being the main cult of the older religion."[64] The cultus of ancestors formed an important part of the religious system of the old Slavonians.[65]

Thus ancestor-worship may be considered as either a developed form of the soul-cultus or a rudimentary case of daimonology— that is, as a characteristic transitional stage. Whether one agrees or does not agree with Spencer that ancestor-worship forms an essential link in the development of religion, it undeniably appears as an important intermediary stage between the soul-cult and its sequels.

§240*. Hero-Worship. The other and allied case of transition is the deification and worship of the hero. Respect for the ghost of a great man, whether he is a member of one's own family or not, and even if he is an enemy, is a matter of observation. Tales and legends grow up about the name of the deceased man of note and presently he is the center of an extended mythology. The later interpretation of this mythology as a sort of anthropomorphic product, whether or not the hero is also an ancestor, is sometimes called euhemerism[66] after the Greek Euhemerus, who looked upon myths and hero-legends as human deeds exaggerated and inflated. Actual hero-worship, however, is due less to exaggeration of earthly deeds than to the conviction that the strong man becomes

[61] Schrader, *Aryans,* 424, 425.   [62] Cook, in AA, II, 484, note.

[63] Jolly, *Sec. Mariages,* 174.   [64] *Corp. Poet. Bor.,* I, 413.

[65] Ralston, *Russ. People,* 84.

[66] Lippert, *Kgchte.,* II, 25. Euhemerus lived about 300 B.C. For cases of the evolution from the hero and totem together to the god, see §261 of the *Case-Book.* Such cases exhibit the close relation of hero-worship and totemism.

the powerful spirit. Force is what secures recognition, after death as in life. In fact, the ancestor is worshipped less as such than as the dominating figure of a kin-group. Under the patriarchate prevailing among most peoples that have advanced far in culture, ancestor-worship as well as hero-worship concerns itself regularly with males. There is a very important sense, then, in which ancestor-worship appears as no more than a special type of hero-worship.

Among the Melanesians, "on the death of a distinguished man his ghost retains the powers that belonged to him in life, in greater activity and with stronger force; his ghost therefore is powerful and worshipful, and so long as he is remembered the aid of his powers is sought and worship is offered him." Heads are secured which are believed to add *mana*, or spiritual power, to the new spirit.[67] In Fiji "masterful and oppressive chiefs were deified because their subjects doubted whether even in death they had lost their power." Hence the Fiji gods were malevolent. "A Fijian when pressed for answer would say that kind and wise chiefs became spirits honored in the next world, but since they were inoffensive, there was no use in honoring them and so they were forgotten." Thomson[68] adds that the most important god of one section of the people was an untimely born child of a princess who had been abducted by the local chief. "Had it lived it would have been of a rank so high and sacred that it would have been deified almost while still living, but since it had never come to maturity, it called for a double measure of propitiatory sacrifice." A strange "hero," but one exhibiting the fetishistic quality inhering in the type.[69] Among the Amaxosa of South Africa, the word for the spirit "designates the ghost of a certain earlier chief, who was regarded as the greatest among them, without the people being in agreement as to exactly whom among their ancestors this honor belonged."[70] The Bahima of Uganda, who have no very clear idea of an over-ruling god or a future life for the individual man or woman, seem yet to believe in the spiritual continuance of chiefs and prominent personages, for they worship them as spirits.[71] On the Zanzibar coast, if rain fails the natives sweep off the graves of former chiefs and make sacrifice; this goes along with a strong ancestor-cult.[72] In Madagascar, "when the chiefs die, they are supposed to really become God, and to be able to bless their subjects who are still living; and the reverence in which they are held is extreme, for when their name chances to be mentioned, the utmost respect is paid to it both before and after the utterance of it." The people do not dare to clear the chief's grave of weeds without first killing oxen and offering supplication.[73]

In India one can distinctly follow the evolution into gods of the ghosts of the men whose life or death has been notorious.[74] One example—of posthumous heroism, so to speak—may stand for many. In a certain clan of northern India, many years ago, died an old lady, "not famous for anything in particular

[67] Codrington, *Melanesians,* 254, 257.
[68] In JAI, XXIV, 343.
[69] §257, below.
[70] Fritsch, *Eingeb. S.-Afr.,* 98.
[71] Johnston, *Uganda,* II, 631.
[72] Stuhlmann, *Mit Emin,* 39.
[73] Sibree, in JAI, XXI, 225.
[74] Joshi, in JASB, III, 299.

during her lifetime, but whose virtues appear to have been great after her demise, for after this the . . . clan, from being a poor one, rose gradually to considerable wealth. She, when propitiated and called on for aid, never failed her race," and the people raised to her memory a double line of well-cut stones, as to the guardian spirit of the clan.[75] Evidently her quality had not been recognized while she was alive, but was demonstrated by a sample of *post-propter* reasoning common enough among men. The case witnesses also to the connection between the aleatory element and the spirits.[76] So impressed were the Hindus with the strong and dramatic personality of Albuquerque that they still have fetishes which they call "Affonso de Albuquerques."[77] "The mythology of the Japanese is a remarkable development of ancestral worship. The Mikado traces his descent to the sun, the common ancestor of the Japanese people," and the hero is elevated to reverence and a cult. The religion "is a kind of hero-worship, but the hero may be a very wicked sinner."[78]

The Tusayan Indians, in one of their ceremonies, slaughter a huge dog and use his entrails and blood in distinguishing one of their number as the god of Death. "The Navajos say now that when one of their own number wears the mask of a god and personates a god, he is, for the time being, actually that god. A prayer to a masquerading representative of divinity is a prayer to a god." Such evidence might well be classified under the topic of the man-fetish; it shows, in any case, the ease of transition from the status of man to that of deity. "There seem to be good reasons for believing that the actor was originally considered to be identical with the being represented; in other words, that the god in his own person appeared on the stage and performed his own history in dramatic representation. On the one hand this involved priestcraft; spectators were made to suppose that the personages whom they saw, and whose disguise was assumed in secret, were none other than the veritable deities. On the other hand, the belief was not wholly deception; the priest or medicine man supposed himself, in assuming the dress, to assume also the character, to be under divine possession, to abdicate his own personality, and to present in his thoughts and actions the god whom he represented." American ethnologists have a good deal to say of the "culture-hero"—some legendary inventor or discoverer—and his worship among the Indians;[79] Hiawatha is but a type of such.

Not to prolong into historic periods illustration of a belief and cult to which readers of classical literature or of mediæval epics and tales or chronicles of the saints—or of the works of Carlyle—need only to have their attention called, we conclude the topic with several quotations from Rohde,[80] touching chiefly upon Greek hero-worship. "The 'heroes' throughout are men's souls raised to a higher power, not god-forms reduced in power. . . . The worship of heroes is not to be regarded as a strict cult of souls but rather, in a narrower definition, as ancestor-worship. . . . The gods seemed too far removed; their visible

[75] Godwin-Austen, in JAI, I, 126.   [76] §§199, 208, above.
[77] Oliveira Martins, *Hist. de Port.*, I, 267; Keller, *Colon.*, 98 ff.
[78] Hitchcock, in USNM, 1890, 483.
[79] Fewkes, in BAE, XV, 303; Matthews, in *Int. Cong. Anthrop.*, 1893, 249; Newell, in *Int. Cong. Anthrop.*, 1893, 240; Hewitt, "Mythology," in HAI, I; Boas, "Religion," in HAI, II; §§257 ff., below.
[80] *Psyche*, I, 148, note, 152-154, 191-192, 195-198 (quoted); also I, 123, 124, 150, 156-158, 172, 175, 184.

inmixture in human life seemed credible only in old legends from the past. The ghosts of the heroes hovered near the living; in good and evil fortune men detected their power." Among other services they revealed the future; consider the prophecies of Amphiaraos. "So far were the ghosts of heroes from being to the Greeks mere symbols or great names that they awaited their interference in the body at the crisis-hour. This made Greece unconquerable." The spirits formed a third class of beings, like patron saints, between men and gods. "Die Geisterwelt ist nicht verschlossen." The author follows the idea down through its later manifestations: "Charlemagne, or even Charles the Fifth, has his seat in Odenberg or in Unterberg near Salzberg, Frederick II (in a later turn of the legend, Frederick I, Barbarossa) in Kyffhäuser, Heinrich der Vogelsteller in Sudemerberg near Goslar; thus also King Artus, Holger Danske, and yet many another favorite figure in the folk-memory, lives in subterranean caves."

Alignable with the conception of the hero and hero-worship is that of the god-man, son of god, son of man, or messiah; the culture-hero is deified and his return as a ruler, under a new dispensation which he shall usher in, is expected. That a king is begotten of the god is a not uncommon belief; in any case the conception in question is that of a fetish-man, a repository of spiritual power which has been infused into him by reason of his relation to the god.[81] Prodigies surround his incarnation, such as virgin birth and other miraculous happenings.

Messianic hopes have been harbored in Mongolia and a former hero has been expected to reappear; in southern Mongolia the people look for the return of Genghis Khan who shall lead them back again to the northwestward.[82] "The doctrines of the Hindu avatar, the Hebrew Messiah, the Christian millennium, and the Hesunanin of the Indian Ghost dance are essentially the same, and have their origin in a hope and longing common to all humanity. . . . The belief in the coming of a Messiah who should restore them to their original happy condition was well nigh universal among the American tribes." He was conceived of as a white man with a flowing beard.[83] "For more than two centuries the people of Peru cherished the tradition that the last of the Incas had only retired to another kingdom beyond the mountains, from which he would return in good time to sweep their haughty oppressors from the land."[84] "Kulóskap is a god-man of truly Indian type; . . . the same culture-hero appears in the legends of the entire Algonkin family, although often under another name." He was also a sort of creator who "made the Indian (or Man; the terms are synonymous) from the ash tree."[85] There was an Indian among the California Karoks called a god-man; he fasted vicariously ten days at the annual dance of propitiation.[86]

[81] §§257, 259, 291, 310, below; Lippert, *Kgchte.*, II, 463, 479, 614.
[82] Potanin, in *Vestnik Evropi (European Messenger)*, Feb., 1888.
[83] §216, above.
[84] Mooney, in BAE, XIV, 657, 658, 660.
[85] Leland and Prince, *Kulóskap*, 33, 34, 116.
[86] Powers, in *Contrib. N. Amer. Ethnol.*, III, 28.

In India it has constantly happened that "men of high aspirations, who have laboured for the revival or reformation of religion, and received homage as inspired teachers from crowds of disciples during life, have been worshipped as actual deities at death. . . . The story has often been told of a number of Hindūs . . . who formed themselves into a sect of Nikkal Sen worshippers. The explanation of this was, that General Nicholson was a soldier of such unexampled bravery and heroism, that neither argument nor force could prevent his native admirers from worshipping him. 'This man,' they said, 'is the great power of God.' "[87] The orthodox Hindu expects reincarnations as a matter of course, and by no means doubts the Christian case. "He is only unable to admit that the nature of Christ stands alone in the history of the world, holding that his own country has seen even more than the three—Rama, Krishna, and Buddha—who were His brothers."[88]

In Babylonia the notion of a son of God and a mother of God was current. Marduk is the intercessor between men and his father, Ea; he takes their complaints to him and brings his revelations to them. "Mediators between men and God, messengers of God, who proclaim His blessings and revelations to the children of men, and conversely lay their prayers and offerings before His throne, these beings occur in every religion." The idea of a mediator between god and man is that "he stands upon the border-line between god and men." "But the idea that a god can actually become a man is an abomination to the votaries of a theocratic religion. . . . In the anthropic religions, which are wholly swayed by the conception of the theanthropos, the god-man, this, on the other hand, is precisely the favourite ideal, the goal towards which they strive with all their might. In theology this becomes the source of the boldest creations of the religious imagination. The gods to whom the devout rightly wish to draw near must themselves become men, though for a time only, and though they can never thereby wholly divest themselves of their heavenly origin or lose their divinity. Every event in their history, therefore, differs from all that happens in the case of other men. From birth to death their life is an unbroken series of miracles. Yet these sons of gods are really men so long as they dwell on earth, like Apollo and Krishna when they tend the flocks as shepherd-boys, or like Herakles and Rama when as servants or exiles they perform laborious tasks and subdue the enemies of their worshippers, or like the other avatâras of the god Vishnu, as narrated by the Indian legends."[89]

In the three centuries before Christ the word "god" was used in a manner astonishing to modern ideas. Since then the most noteworthy tendency of human ideas has been toward a discrimination between the natural and supernatural. We have learned to conceive of the natural as a field of observation and experience and of the supernatural as purely imaginary, unknown, or unknowable. The transition from one field to the other does not seem to us possible and all effect of the natural and supernatural on each other seems inconceivable. When we meet with statements from the time alluded to, made by men with the then ideas, if we try to adopt and accept what they say into our thinking, we arrive at dogmatic positions which are absurd. Passages that come under the genius of the Hebrew language, with its mode so diverse from

[87] Monier-Williams, *Brāhmanism*, 142, 269; Wilkins, *Hinduism*, 317.

[88] Nivedita, *Indian Life*, 223.

[89] Tiele, *Hist. Relig.*, I, 166-168; Hatch, *Griechentum*, 183-185; Jackson, *Zoroaster*, 52; Justi, *Persien*, 83.

ours, have produced unlimited mythology.[90] The myth about men born of gods was not rare in the Græco-Roman world and earlier. Spencer[91] has collected a number of cases of the god-man. "The idea of Christ, the son of God, as the world-redeemer, is very closely related and, as respects its origin, identical with that of an earthly king as a bringer of emancipation and a way-breaker for a new time. . . . Assurbanipal too . . . is exalted as one such, in whose reign a time of blessing began," and the Assyrian Marduk exhibits the phenomenon of resurrection.[92] Mediators between gods and men were looked upon as gods and there was a common conviction that gods appeared as men. Several messiahs emerged in Samaria in the apostolic age.[93] Historically eminent persons such as Plato, Alexander the Great, Scipio Africanus, and Augustus were said to have been begotten of the gods.[94]

The Messiah-doctrine of the Hebrews is well known. The Psalms[95] announce the coming of a personal messiah. "At certain times (especially those when Israel enjoyed outward prosperity, as happened, for instance, under the rule of the Ptolemies) or in certain circles, the expectation of a personal Messiah fell quite out of sight."[96] "The figure of the Messiah has no such secure and firm place in the hope of later Hebrewdom as is commonly assumed—the Messiah, the king of the house of David, who at the end of the ages shall establish his throne. . . . His figure appears as a quite incidental and shadowy one in the picture of the future." There develops later the conception of a non-earthly being, not the Messiah of David's house, born on earth, but the "Son of Man." "This is an angel-like being, whose dwelling is in heaven"; he is pre-existent and is the destined judge of the world. "With the title Son of Man they wished to distinguish Jesus as the heavenly, pre-existing Messiah, who will come to the tribunal as judge of the world."[97]

The various *mahdis* of the Mohammedan world are well known; the last of them to make a considerable stir in the world was the one subjugated by Lord Kitchener in southern Egypt. "At all times the Moslems have believed that toward the end of the world a man of the family of the Prophet . . . must appear to revive religion and complete the triumph of righteousness."[98]

The prodigies which precede the birth and attend the infancy of such heroes could be combined into a standing biography, impersonal and universal. "The same story of persecution is repeated everywhere in the Orient and Occident, in ancient and modern, even in most recent times, about gods and heroes." It is told of Zeus, Apollo, Horus, Cyrus, Romulus, and Remus; in Egypt of the three sons of Ra, persecuted by Cheops; in India of Krishna. The persecution by Herod has many parallels. Zoroaster

---

[90] Dan., VII, 13; Gen., VI, 2; Jubilees, II, 20.
[91] *Prim. Soc.*, I, §197.
[92] Schrader, *Keilinscriften*, 380, 388-389.
[93] Harnack, *Dogmengchte.*, I, 114, 115, 233.
[94] Gunkel, *N. Test.*, 65-66.   [95] II, LXII, CX.
[96] Kautzsch, "Relig. Israel," in *Hastings's Dict. Bible*, 727.
[97] Bousset, *Relig. Jud.*, 209, 248-250, 251-255, 348.
[98] Junker, *Afr.*, I, 57, note 3.

had to meet the temptations of Ahriman which he defeated by the law of Ormuzd and by calling upon divine spirits; there is also a tale of the temptation of Buddha. There are parallels for the ascension; there is an apotheosis of the hero whereby, having got the world in his power, he is raised to the circle of the gods and recognized. The same parallels appear in respect to the descent into hell; many gods and heroes have visited the abode of the dead: Osiris, Marduk, Tammuz, Ishtar, Eabani, Gilgamesh, Orpheus, Odysseus.[99] In particular the traditions of virgin birth elevate the hero to a plane of holiness uncontaminated by the earthiness of sex.

The Mexican god of war was said to have been a purely spiritual being, and that a woman had borne him after a miraculous conception was one of the variants of the tale.[100] "Like all the cultus heroes, Alósaka is said, in legends, to have been miraculously born of a virgin. His father was the Sun, his mother an Earth-goddess, sometimes called a maiden."[101] "Genghis Khan too was believed to be the son of a virgin and elevated above the level of human nature."[102] In Tibet there is a female savior or deliverer. "She corresponds to the goddess of mercy and queen of heaven of the Chinese, and has her literal analogy in biblical mythology and has also several analogies with 'the Virgin.' "[103] In the Mahabharata a god begets a child with a woman and promises her that she shall be a virgin afterwards.[104] Bastian[105] says that the virgin birth is amongst us a materialistic notion of a thing which, among the Hindus, is metaphysical, fantastic, symbological, and mythological. We are told that Buddha was born of a virgin.[106] The Great Mother of the Gods "was at the same time a mother and a virgin. . . . Her son, too, rose from the dead. . . . The mere title Mater Dei, then coming into frequent use, would instantly provoke a comparison with the *Mater Deum*, and the formal bestowal of the former title on the Virgin in council in 430 A.D. might well have seemed in the eyes of Pagans like despoiling their fallen goddess of even her title."[107] In Persia there was a tradition of a prophet of the tribe of Zoroaster, a savior, born of a virgin supernaturally, who would arise and help bring about the resurrection.[108] In Egypt, Apis was born of a cow impregnated by lightning and remaining virgin; and the god Ra was "not begotten, but merely born."[109] The idea of a virgin goddess and mother existed in the Phrygian religion.[110]

99 Grimm, *Sagen*, I, §§486, 489; Gunkel, *N. Test.*, 69 ff.; Müller, *Sacred Books*, IV, 206; X, 69; Ezra, IV, 13; Rev., I, 8.

100 Nadaillac, *Preh. Amer.*, 297, note.

101 Fewkes, in AA, I, 539 ff.   102 Mantegazza, *Amori*, 83.

103 Waddell, *Buddhism*, 324, 358-359.

104 Holtzmann, *Ind. Sagen*, I, 108-109.

105 *Ideale Welten*, I, 46.   106 *Hieron. adv. Jovinianum*, I, 42.

107 Showerman, *Great Mother*, 329.

108 Justi, *Persien*, 91; Bousset, *Relig. Jud.*, 477.

109 Tiele, *Gchte. Relig.*, I, 94, 111-112.   110 Farnell, *Cults*, 447, 629.

"The mystic child at Eleusis was born of a maiden; these ancients made for themselves the sacred dogma, 'A virgin shall conceive and bear a son.' It was left to Christian fathers, blending the motherhood of Demeter with the virgin mother and the parentage of Zeus, things they did not and would not understand, to make of the sacred legend a story of vile human incest."[111] The orthodox Mohammedan doctrine made of Fatima a virgin although a mother.[112] Scherr[113] speaks of "Merlin, whom the Devil, in imitation of God, begat with a pure maiden." In the year 1844 there was a centenarian who was honored in Russia as a holy virgin and mother of god.[114]

Church speculation and dogmas about virgin birth, immaculate conception, and the rest[115] will occur to the reader. "More highly endowed peoples have always had a reverential respect for virginity. They did not know how otherwise to bring about the longed-for re-birth of godhood than to have the god-become-man born of a maid. To the virgin they ascribed powers which exceeded the measure of humanity; the gift of prophecy was intrusted to her and the purity of woman was most potent to weave magic and to dissolve it."[116]

Practices reviewed under the ghost-cult and others to be considered under fetishism[117] reveal the tendency to accord an especial attention to the soul of the exceptional man, or hero. All such usages witness to the transition from eidolism to daimonism. From the succeeding treatment of daimonism and daimonology further light will be cast upon the nature of this transition. Throughout our studies we shall find the more evolved form repeating the less, not only in its broad lines but in its detail as well, and with such fidelity as to render any other theory than that of a genetic relationship incredible. Upon such evidence, if there were no other, we should be content to rest this and the other cases of transition and derivation which have been and will be encountered in this book.

§241*. Types of Daimon. Not all daimons are ghost-derived, at least in the opinion of their worshippers. Whereas some primitives, like the inhabitants of Florida in the Solomon Islands, "will

[111] Harrison, *Greek Relig.*, 553.
[112] Burton, *Arabian Nights*, VI, 397, note; Hauri, *Islam*, 111.
[113] *Deut. Kgchte.*, 132.   [114] Stern, *Russland*, 240.
[115] Lea, *Inquisition*, III, 596 ff.   [116] Weinhold, *Deut. Frauen*, I, 217.
[117] §§228, 229, 232, above, and 257, 259, below.

not allow that there are any beings of a supernatural order that have not been men,"[118] in the neighboring New Hebrides are distinguished spirits of two kinds: those of the deceased and those of unknown origin,[119] and in West Africa there appear nature-gods which are the animating principles or indwelling spirits of natural features and objects and whose cult exists side by side with that of the ghost-gods, so that "it is often difficult to decide where the one worship begins and the other ends."[120] The latter two cases indicate an origin for the daimon other than derivation from the ghost. Again, the Melanesians recognize "beings of a more or less distinctly spiritual nature, who at any rate never were men"; the author[121] quoted insists upon "the distinction which seems so important between ghosts, the disembodied spirits of men deceased, and spirits, of another order from the souls of men, which have never been connected with a human body." Thus we have a series from the daimons who were in origin always men to those who were never men. It seems certain, however, that in the development of daimonism the "trunk-line," so to speak, lies through eidolism and that the daimon "of unknown origin" turns out often, through reasonable inference, to have started in animism and to have skirted quite around the normal stage of eidolism. Consider, for example, the "nature-spirits."

Ellis[122] presents a very apt illustration of the embarrassment one might meet in seeking to connect all spirits with the ghosts of the dead; Spencer's argument, to which he refers, may well seem thin-spun in the face of actual experience.

"That the nature-gods are, as a whole, the product of manes worship," says Ellis, "is, we think, a theory not warranted by the evidence, though apparently supported by the high authority of Mr. Herbert Spencer. It often occurs that a family settles near to some river, lake, or hill, and forthwith commences a cult of the indwelling spirit, without any catastrophe having taken place to initiate it. In fact, it may be said to be the rule that whenever a Tshi group takes up its abode near any remarkable natural feature or object, it worships and seeks to propitiate its indwelling spirit, fearing that otherwise it may do some harm. Many of the nature-gods are non-terrestrial, and it is difficult to see by what process they could ever become confused with dead men. Nobody could be buried in the sky, sun, moon, rainbow, or wind,—and if these could be

[118] Codrington, in JAI, X, 303.
[119] Macdonald, in AAAS, 1892, 726.
[120] Ellis, *Yoruba*, 280.
[121] Codrington, *Melanesians*, 150, 175.
[122] *Yoruba*, 282, 291.

conceived to be animated without the intervention of the souls of the dead, why could not terrestrial objects also?"

The thick-and-thin adherent of the ghost-derivation of all spirits need not recoil utterly before this question. The origin of the nature-spirits did lie in many cases in the ghosts of the dead, and the transitional phases are now erased and forgotten. Ellis himself goes on to say:

"The origin and inception of the nature-gods, as the indwelling spirits of natural objects or phenomena, being generally lost sight of, some explanation of their existence becomes necessary, and, in consequence, we find a variety of myths dealing with the parentage and adventures of the gods."

That is to say, the negroes, in ignorance of the actuality, have proceeded in the stereotyped way to interpret in the light of their own experience and mores. They could not see, any more than or as much as we can, directly into their long past; and in their folk-lore and tradition there could scarcely be found any light upon this past, in the present case with respect to the origin of their daimons, save in the forms of survivals interpretable only in the light of science. Thus their explanations might well be wide of the mark and are generally recognized as being so. Hence there might exist in their lives and tales nothing whatever to betray to the observer a connection of their nature-deities with the dead and yet such a derivation might well have occurred, along the lines developed by Spencer.[123] In any case, nature-spirits are generally anthropomorphic and are treated as such; Xerxes even lashed the Hellespont. If they are not ghost-derived, they act and are behaved to as if they were. Primitive people get into the habit of believing as they do; though there may be no ghost in the specific case, the state of mind induced by ghost-fear underlies all their beliefs.

Science is bound to accept, at least as an alternative, a simpler explanation than Spencer's if one is available; and we think that such is the case. If all things have souls,[124] there is no especial difficulty in regarding any natural object or phenomenon, if circumstances call attention to it, as having a spirit, though the proviso needs to be made that if it merely houses a spirit, not its

123 *Prin. Soc.*, I, ch. XXIV.   124 §214, above.

own, it is really a fetish[125] and not a daimon in itself. Harried by the incalculable ills of life and in the attitude of fear, as Ellis[126] reports, the savage locates invisible agencies on all sides, as the aleatory element is conceived to exist on all sides. If pots and kettles have souls, certainly the sun and moon have; and if things are important enough their souls can come directly to the daimon-status. Even if it could be proved that the nature-spirits were all originally only human souls housed in things and the things, there-fore, were no more than fetishes, little else than a sterile, affectedly exact distinction would be established.

Ellis says in connection with the views just cited that every man worships that from which he has most to fear or most to expect and that this is com-monly something with which he is brought daily into contact. Fishermen pay much attention to the indwelling spirits of the sea and of the shoals and reefs on which their canoes might be wrecked. Here is almost a direct personifica-tion and worship of the aleatory element. In Mombasa, "there is a spring on a hill a mile from my bungalow. The year before my arrival it had ceased to flow. On consulting the medicine man the elders discovered that some person had dipped a tin vessel into its stream, and this had offended its guardian spirit. Accordingly a wooden grating was placed over it, through which only a small calabash could pass, and with the next rains the flow recommenced."[127] In this case, it may be explained, the spirit was irritated by the use of the novel, strange vessel; only the time-honored is holy or fit for the use or sight of the gods. In Siberia, the earth itself seems to be personified as a community of spirits and is honored under a designation meaning "earth-water." Sven Hedin's[128] Mongol guide explained that there were earth-spirits, sky-spirits, and lake-spirits but that there were none in the desert, and that is why men find there none of the things they most need. This community of spirits in-cludes the so-called "princes" who have their seats at the sources of streams, upon the snow-caps of the mountains.[129] In the East Indies the nature-spirits share with the souls of the dead all the real attention given to worship.[130] In West Borneo spirits occupying mountains, streams, light, and other ele-ments influence all the forces of nature; those in the sun and moon hold highest place. They govern nature for men's well-being provided that his actions do not demand punishment by illness or other calamity.[131]

The Cheyenne believe in all sorts of water-sprites and monsters; they are not by nature harmful but may become offended and work injury.[132] Among the Hopi Indians, as among the Teutons, "the nature elements are not identified with remote ancestors, nor is there evidence that their worship was derivative. . . . Animism is always and everywhere mixed up with religion; it is never

[125] §247, below.
[126] Yoruba, 277.
[127] Johnstone, in JAI, XXXII, 268.
[128] Asia, II, 1107.
[129] Radloff, Schamanenthum, 7.
[130] Wilken, in VG, III, 260.
[131] Veth, Borneo's Wester-Afdeeling, II, 305, 306.
[132] Grinnell, Cheyenne, II, 96 ff.

and nowhere the whole of religion."[133] The winged snake is seen by some Indians in the storm-clouds driven by the wind; by others in the lightning; and by still others in the wind-tossed water.[134]

The Greek world was full of daimons of an order lower than gods and connected with nature: field- and forest-spirits, "the useless race of the maleficent satyrs," the Centaurs, Daktyls, Nereids, and many others that figure in Goethe's Klassische Walpurgisnacht.[135] "The belief in these daimons goes back into the most ancient times; for the development of the Greek religion, however, they have had only a very limited significance, and only seldom has a public cultus fallen to their lot. It was left to the individual to assure himself of their favor by offering and prayer."[136] The mediæval Arabs associate a definite class of daimons with sand-whirls and apply the same term indifferently to them and to the *jinn* that accompany or cause them. "More important is the widespread belief that the stars move because they are alive, which underlies the planet and constellation worship of the Semites as of other ancient nations."[137]

Belief in nature-spirits is so abundantly preserved in legend and folklore that it is familiar to many; and Frazer's copious illustrations of the vegetation-spirit[138] form a collection to which general reference can be made. One further instance may be cited. Tree-spirits, called "vilas," occupy first place in the popular faith of the South Slavs. These are "ripened tree-souls, which chiefly appear in action outside the trees." They are in the form of beautiful winged maidens with flaxen hair and often clad in green foliage. In the regions of Adria, the Black Sea, and the Danube, the vila becomes a water-spirit. If the vila loses one hair of her head, she must die.[139] Here is a belief concerning the location of the soul already familiar to us.[140] The name "Augenblicksgötter" is given to daimons that reveal themselves suddenly to men in the manifestations of life and strength which anything offers.[141] This conception is analogous to that of *mana,* or inherent virtue, in things.[142]

§242. The Animistic Basis.

§242. The Animistic Basis. The wealth of more commonly known instances of personification in nature, barring such of them, of course, as are highly poetical and artificial, may be recalled to fortify the contention that the idea of a nature-spirit may be developed directly out of animism without traversing the stage of eidolism and attendant ancestor-worship. There is no need to assume that a dead man's spirit must have entered to possess the various venerated objects in nature, although it might be

[133] Fewkes, in BAE, XV, 254, note, 251.

[134] Preuss, in *Globus,* LXXXVI, 113.   [135] *Faust,* II, act II, 440 ff.

[136] Beloch, *Griech. Gchte.,* I, 112.   [137] Smith, *Relig. Sem.,* 134.

[138] *Golden Bough,* pt. V, vols. I and II.

[139] Krauss, in *Mem. Int. Cong. Anth.,* 1894, 367; Krauss, *Südslaven,* 69, 71, 72, 73.

[140] §213, above.

[141] Preuss, in *Arch. f. Anth.,* XXIX, 136.

[142] §§258, 303, below.

thought so to have done in almost any given case. Pending the development of the topic of fetishism, it may be said that the origin of very many of the daimons—of those of primitive peoples, at any rate—can be referred to eidolistic beliefs and all of them to an ultimate basis in animism. They could not, we think, have been derived from any other origin; and general principles forbid us to assume that they arose without antecedents.

Just as the student carries forward with him into the geometry of solids and spheres that which he has learned in plane geometry as principles settled once and for all while dealing with geometrical relations in their simpler terms, so in any advance into more evolved stages of religious belief the evolutionist will maintain connections with the simpler forms and their teachings. Certainly there have been daimons which were no more than the personification of abstractions: Tyche, Fortuna, Charity, Vice, Reason, or any other of the multitude of desirable or undesirable qualities which the poets have personified. An element of idealization also has always entered into the making of divinities, whether or not they have feet of clay; and this capacity of seeing things greater and finer than they are has led men far both toward self-realization and toward self-deception and disaster. Even in the case of supernatural beings of the vaguest character, however, these must seek their origins and prototypes where all else in the supernatural order must, namely, in the simple conceptions of primitive times, in animistic and eidolistic beliefs.

Modern thought demands such genetic connections and refuses to entertain the idea of catastrophic evolution. In many scientific fields it is not doubted by anybody that the forces now seen at work are the identical ones which have always been in operation during the ages that are gone; spontaneous generation and allied ideas have long passed away, for it is believed that everything back as far as we can yet go had its antecedents. Similarly in and throughout the field of the science of society, it is here held, the complex is a sequence or a re-combination of the simple; in particular, all daimonism comes out of animism as the branch out of the trunk. This position of rest upon a broad general principle we hope to justify in concrete connections as we go along.

The daimon reveals his origin in the fact that he is anthropomorphic or, less often, zoömorphic. Even the abstractions were, like the less shadowy daimons, formed by man in his own image.

The anthropomorphic quality of the ghosts needs no emphasis, after all the cases that have been passed in review; and those spirits which are no longer identified with men who have lived present the same character. They could not do otherwise, considering their derivation. Spirits "rove about the jungle and hunt like Dyaks themselves; and not only do *antus* hunt, but they build houses and work and farm just as the Dyaks do." And not only that: "the highest spirits are conceived of in terms of a like quality. Elders and priestesses often assert that in their dreams they have visited the mansion of Tapa and seen the Creator dwelling in a house like that of a Malay, the interior of which was adorned with guns and gongs and jars innumerable, Himself being clothed like a Dayak." Gods are altogether like men. When their altars are roofed as a house for them, they resemble a Dyak house; there is even a ladder "for facilitating the ascent of the spirit to the offerings upon the stage, which are placed there on all their festival occasions."[143] This is enough to recall the anthropomorphic character of deities; Spencer[144] has devoted considerable space to this matter. Even when it comes to spiritual abstractions, the same inherited character remains. Like all other spirits, War and Justice "were thought to be anthropomorphic. Sex, therefore, was ascribed to them: War, for instance, was regarded as a male, Justice as a female. Thus was formed the belief in the war-god Ares, or Phobos, or whatever else he was called; in the victory-goddess, Niké, in the love-god, Eros, in the destiny-goddesses, Até, Nemesis, Tyche, Moira, and innumerable other beings of a similar sort. In this way men came at length to hold a particular daimon responsible for each piece of bad luck that befel, even though it were no more than a broken pot. . . . The fourteenth Homeric Hymn gives a list of daimons which the potter has to fear."[145] This passage reveals very vividly the connection of the daimon with the aleatory element.

It is always to be understood that firm and clean-cut conceptions are not to be expected from primitive sources; language is not specific enough to admit of them, a fact which of itself indicates that they were not yet definitely formulated in the mind. A single example will illustrate the point.

It is reported of the Indians of Washington Territory:[146] "The practical part of their religion is a compound of Shamanism and Spiritism, called in Chinooks' jargon tamanous, temahnous, or tamanamus, and the word expresses their idea so completely that it has been somewhat adopted into English, for the word expresses a combination of ideas for which we have no exact English equivalent. Tamanous is a noun, and as such refers to any spiritual being, good or bad, more powerful than man and less powerful only than God or Satan. . . . It is also used to express the work of influencing any of their

---

[143] Wilken, in VG, III, 234-236, 239; he quotes St. John, *Life in the forests of the Far East,* I, 189-190 and Low, *Sarawak,* 273.

[144] *Prin. Soc.,* I, ch. XXV.   [145] Beloch, *Griech. Gchte.,* I, 111.

[146] Eels, in *Smithson. Rep.,* 1887, pt. I, 672.

spirits by incantation. The word is also an adjective, and as such is used to describe any stick, stone, or similar article in which spirits are at times supposed to dwell, and also any man, as a medicine-man, who is supposed to have more than ordinary power with these spirits; hence we often hear of tamanous sticks and tamanous men. It is likewise a verb, and to tamanous is to perform the incantations necessary to influence these spirits."

§243*. Fear of the Daimons. Though conceptions of the daimons may sometimes be indefinite, fear of them is always vivid enough. The world of spirits "is just as little organized as the primitive people themselves. All the spirits, even the highest, are but mighty magicians, mighty through their magic, sometimes beneficent according to their fancy or caprice, but always feared."[147] It is the ills of life that lead to the belief in daimons of a malevolent order; they are, again, the personification of the aleatory element.

After describing the early Israelites as a people with a certain rude joy in life, with a folk-soul resilient enough to pass lightly over the idea of evil spirits, even in times of considerable calamity, Duhm[148] goes on to rehearse the ills suffered by them in conflict with stronger peoples. These, he says, had a strong influence in the direction of confusing the people and causing them to lose their old, sound, happy folk-life. They then took refuge in strange superstitions and foreign mystery-systems. Finally, after a further visitation of calamity, "the holy place of their fathers was reduced to a heap of ruins and the whole world seemed to be laid waste"; then the Jews were filled with gloom, which "must have rendered them receptive of the beliefs in illdisposed daimons and specters."

McGee[149] dwells upon the terror of the Unknown as follows—the passage would seem to have been written with our diagram[150] illustrative of the scope of the aleatory element in mind. "The more timid tribesmen in different continents betray, in conduct and speech, a dominant intuition of a terrible Unknown opposed through self to a small but kindly Known. This intuition is not born of intertribal strife, since it is strongest in those innately amicable family groups who . . . typify lower savagery, and since it is slowly modified with the rise of self-confidence among vigorous and aggressive tribes in whose minds the good grows large with the wax of conscious power; it is merely the subjective reflection of implacable environment. . . . Over against this appalling evil there is a less completely personified good reflecting the small nucleus of confident knowledge, with its far-reaching penumbra of faith."

If the mind is concerned chiefly with the avoidance of mischance,[151] it is inevitable that the daimons which personify the ele-

---

[147] Tiele, *Sci. of Relig.*, pt. I, 79.
[149] In BAE, XIX, pt. II, 844.
[151] §196, above.

[148] *Geister*, 31, 34-35.
[150] §195, above.

ment of luck shall be for the most part malignant in general disposition or in passing mood. In any case the only safe course is to evade, exorcise, or propitiate. In some cases the belief in the powerlessness of man in the presence of the supernatural works out into pessimism and fatalism, as among the Buddhists and the later Greeks;[152] a Scandinavian hero may deride danger by proclaiming: "On one day my fate was fashioned and all my life laid down";[153] but fatalism is practically not found among primitive folk. Cases like the one of the Thracians who "mourn their newborn and bury their dead with joy as being freed and happy,"[154] are rare among nature-peoples; in childlike manner they are never discouraged for long in the search for some panacea of woes and do not settle down to resignation. Even in Homer,[155] where the idea of fate clearly appears and where occasional outbreaks of deep pessimism startle the reader of a spirited narrative, this does not seem to cripple initiative in the development of a prosperity-policy. Man may be the most miserable of all beings, "as many as breathe and creep upon the earth"; the gods may "have fated it to wretched mortals to live in woe"; but there is no sign of discouragement or letting-up in the battle of life in general or in the cult. What is to be looked for on the primitive stage, where the mind is yet unretentive of experience and unreflective, is the opposite of fatalistic resignation as a philosophy of life; rather is there in evidence a prolific development of cult-phenomena.

In their character the daimons show their derivation from the ghost;[156] even though the superior powers remain well-disposed, that is only on condition that men expend effort in keeping them in that frame of mind. If a spirit is uniformly kindly, he is likely to receive but scant attention. A status of ordinary human comfort is sometimes assumed as the natural condition, for which there is no one to thank; then it is the "fall" from this estate which must be explained so as to be avoided or made up for; and the fall

---

152 Hopkins, *Relig. Ind.*, 299 ff.; Waddell, *Buddhism*, 103, 110-111, 132-134; Burckhardt, *Gr. Kgchte.*, II, 373-416, *passim*.

153 *Corp. Poet. Bor.*, 113.

154 Herodotus, *Hist.*, bk. V, §§4, 5.

155 *Odyssey*, XVIII, 130-131; *Iliad*, XXIV, 525-526; Keller, *Hom. Soc.*, 115-116, 128.

156 §219, above.

is due to daimonic influence. The evil spirits are always menacing and they almost monopolize attention. This belief is world-wide.

To increase the misery of his existence, the Australian fills all nature with evil spirits. There is an evil divinity who tortures people at night and who is probably identical with a fire-god whose appearance brings death when the fire goes out, or a god of the South Australians who hid fire away from their ancestors.[157] In New Guinea an invisible spirit of the forest may touch a man and doom him. "After this there is nothing for you to do but go home and die; and so great is the power of suggestion, that a person who believes he has been touched by 'Wada' generally does die."[158] Pleading, protestations, and objurgation are directed toward the spirits in event of calamity, as, for example, in the case of the African father whose son was having a hemorrhage from an artery that had been closed but had broken open or the mother whose child was in convulsions. "Go away! Go away! O ye spirits! Why do you come to kill my son?"[159] A child is supposed to be under great danger from evil spirits until it has passed its seventh day.[160] Night-mare ("maere" means goblin) is an evil spirit in Africa as well as Europe;[161] in India it is always supposed to be caused by a demon, who seats himself on the chest of a sleeper and tries to suffocate him.[162] Spirits meddle in human affairs according to caprice.[163] Every disease and death is due to attack by evil spirits; the higher powers seldom come to the assistance of man in the deadly and unequal struggle and he is left to his own resources of incantation and sacrifice.[164] The traveller Gmelin saw Tatars at Tobolsk turn themselves around toward the sun every morning and say to him: "Do not kill me!"[165]

In Southern India cholera and smallpox are attributed to the spirits; when a person is stricken by the latter, the expression the people use is "The *Amman* is taking her pastime over him." Such evil spirits have a human origin, that is, are derived from ghosts. "All are powerful, malicious and interfering; and all are desirous of bloody sacrifices and frantic dances. . . . Not only the failure of rain, or a blight falling on the crops, but even the accidents and diseases which befall cattle, and trivial losses in trade, are considered instances of a devil's malevolence."[166] "Whatever the belief in a god or future state, it is certain that these people believe in an infinity of evil spirits or demons. Each disease is supposed to be in the immediate keeping of some particular demon, who goes about dealing out sickness and death at will, and to propitiate these demons is their particular care."[167]

"It is sometimes difficult to know why a spirit is offended. Without intending to be rude, an unwary person may easily make a spirit angry. For instance, a boy may jump over a small stream half a dozen times with impunity; but

[157] Ratzel, *Vkde.*, II, 93.
[158] Pratt, *New Guinea Cannibals*, 317.
[159] Nassau, *Fetichism*, 98; Kingsley, *Travels W. Afr.*, 453.
[160] Kingsley, *W. Afr. Studies*, 455.
[161] Ellis, *Yoruba*, 74-75.   [162] Caldwell, in JASB, I, 96.
[163] Shchukin, *Shamanism* (Russ.), 28, 37.
[164] Jochelson, in AA, VI, 418.   [165] Letourneau, *Soc.*, 288.
[166] Caldwell, in JASB, I, 94, 95, 96, 99.
[167] Woodthorpe, in JAI, XI, 69.

it may happen that the seventh time he may jump over a water-spirit that happens to be in a bad temper. The spirit then attacks the boy, who knows only that he does not feel well. If the spirit is not very angry, it may return to the water after the first attack, and leave the boy alone, so that his illness may only be a passing one; on the other hand, the spirit may be spiteful, and wishing to revenge itself for the slight, may follow the boy to his home and continue to attack him there until he becomes very ill. It will not do, however, for his parents, after questioning him, to jump to the conclusion that it is a water-spirit that is troubling him. The cause of his illness may not be a water-spirit; the boy, by sitting on the bank of the stream, may have closed the hole by which an earth-ogre was accustomed to issue for its airing, and it may be the earth-ogre and not the spirit of the stream that is causing the illness. Another possibility is that the boy, while idly throwing stones into the water, may have taken up one in which a spirit was living. The spirit may have chosen to make its home in the stone as it lay on a warm and sunny part of the bank, and may have been furiously angry to find itself plunged into cold water. Instead of making the boy ill, it may cause him to fall and sprain his ankle or break his leg. In serious cases the parents will go to a wise man for help in discovering which spirit has been the cause of the illness or accident."[168] This passage gives a good idea of the free and unconstrained life of the savage, to which some would wish to return, and also exhibits the strategic position of the wise man, who is generally the medicine-man, in the primitive economy.

The only safe course is one of avoidance, when dealing with supernatural forces. In Polynesia there was a prohibition of "the use for ordinary purposes of words which constituted, or formed part of, the names, not only of gods, but also of certain chiefs. . . . There was in Samoa a village god called La'ala'a, which meant 'stepping over'; and out of respect to the god the people of that village never used the word *la'ala'a* for 'stepping over,' substituting for it a new word *soposopo*, 'which is still a current synonym for *la'ala'a.'*" The author[169] cites a number of parallels: *ulu*, meaning 'breadfruit,' was called *foatau* because Ulu was the name of a great, semi-divine chief. A traveller, Krämer, whose name means 'shop-keeper' or 'grocer' in German, was honored, as a white man, with the consideration accorded to chiefs, and the people would not speak of shop-goods in his presence. "In Tahiti the sounds in the language composing the name of the king and that of his queen became taboo . . . and in consequence the original names of many of the objects with which the people were familiar used from time to time to undergo alteration." These changes were made when the king was inaugurated and any who used the old terms thereafter were put to death; after the king's death the former term could be revived. "There is a narrative of the naming of a Chilian barque, *The Pomare,* which was done in honour of queen Pomare, but was regarded by her and her people as an insult to her, and nearly caused an armed rising. . . . *Mare* was the old Tahitian word for 'cough'; but in consequence of the king Tu taking the name of Pomare . . . the word was changed to *hota.* . . . There can be little doubt that the unwillingness to use for any purpose a word which was the name of a god, and the consequent necessity for linguistic

[168] Milne, *Eastern Clan*, 243-244.

[169] Williamson, *Cent. Polyn.,* III, 93-96; on the name and its avoidance in the case of ghosts, see §§212, 223, above.

changes, was based upon fear of pronouncing the name of a deity. The avoidance of speaking of a god by his name is reported from Samoa, where we are told of the dread of a god being such that his name might not be whispered. No one in Samoa would mention the name of his tutelary animal." Many examples are cited. "The similarity as regards these matters . . . between their attitude towards the gods and towards chiefs . . . may, I think, be accepted as a further illustration of the sanctity with which the chiefs were supposed to be clothed."

"The divinities of evil among the Dakotas may be called legion. Their special delight is to make man miserable or to destroy him. Demons wander through the earth, causing sickness and death. Spirits of evil are ever ready to pounce upon and destroy the unwary. Spirits of earth, air, fire, and water surround him upon every side, and with but one great governing object in view—the misery and destruction of the human race." Among the Sioux "the ubiquitous Unktomi tortures the Indians in their hunger by bringing herds of buffaloes near the camp, which they no sooner start up to pursue than he drives away." Little devils in human form abound on the "Mountain of the Little People."[170] Sickness, destructive animals, and other harmful influences are not thought of as sent by the evil spirit but as that spirit itself in concrete guise.[171] "All the powers of nature are the influence of the good spirit so long as they do not disturb the rest and comfort of the Indian; they are the work of the evil spirits, as soon as they do."[172]

The Araucanians believed in malignant spirits, "who possessed the power of transforming themselves into any shape they wished in order to work evil. To drive them away from their dwellings the Araucanos burnt branches of . . . their sacred tree. To their influences were imputed many of their sicknesses, especially those which were not easily diagnosed. They were, in these cases, supposed to produce invisible wounds with invisible arrows. To them also were attributed all the natural phenomena, when they occurred at inopportune moments, or brought in their train any unfavourable results; as, for instance, rain in harvest-time, blight or diseases in their crops, lameness or sickness among their stock, and in general all those accidents that they could not ascribe to a direct agency."[173] No better statement of the responsibility of the spirits for the aleatory element could well be formed.

The Chaldæans peopled the world with malignant spirits who presided over all things harmful; they had a legend of the scaling of heaven and the eventual defeat of the evil powers. In Egypt ills and diseases were always due to spirits.[174] The Old Testament shows a belief in evil spirits that is much older than that in the Devil. Such a belief, it is worth repeating, is at the bottom of all the religious development of mankind. "It forms the deepest fundament of the whole religious life of peoples. Suppressed by higher forms of belief, it is never quite uprooted and conquered. . . . In all periods of transition the old, lower belief breaks forth again from the depths of the folk-soul."[175] The reality of evil spirits was not questioned in the church of the Apostolic age;

[170] Dorsey, in BAE, XI, 433, 472, 481.
[171] Spix and Martius, Bras., 1108.   [172] Martius, Beiträge, I, 646.
[173] Latcham, in JAI, XXXIX, 347.
[174] Maspero, Hist. Anc., I, 633-634; 215; Blau, Zauberwesen, 8.
[175] Bousset, Relig. d. Judentums, 331; Schrader, Keilinschriften, 459; Fairweather, "Devel. of Doctrine," in Hastings's Bible Dict., 288.

the heathen daimons were all demons.[176] "Illnesses were referred directly back to the daimons, for it was believed that the extraordinary delicacy of their bodily substance enabled them to penetrate into the human body and there evoke evil changes."[177] The doctrine of demons interested the mediæval theologian;[178] they spoiled the air and fruit and brought pestilence. The reference of tempests, sickness, and other calamities to the "judgments of God" has not yet completely disappeared.[179]

Modern backward communities still cherish the primitive ideas: the German peasantry has held to them in relatively recent times.[180] In Corsica the belief in vampires has passed but slowly; they are shapes like old women "which enter the house by night without being seen, and, fastening on the throats of little children, drink their blood. In the old days the horrible creatures were sometimes seen, but nowadays they are invisible, and the death of the little ones is the only sign of their presence."[181] The South Slavs think that a poisonous snake is the corporeal abode of a spirit hostile to man. This spirit is transferred to the human being by the bite and must then be exorcised. "Belief in the pest-women is as old as that of spirits of illness, but has received a very pronounced development as a result of the great Oriental pestilences which followed upon the big Turkish campaigns." Evil spirits are always lurking about the house of birth seeking to steal the child. They cause all trouble between spouses, to avoid which the man sacrifices a hen and the wife a cock.[182] Many fellows to Flibbertigibbet in *King Lear* are to be found in popular beliefs.

One of the specialties of daimonic malevolence lies in the attitude of evil spirits toward the departing soul. Herein the daimons reveal a strong likeness to the ghosts, for the latter are thought to lie in wait for the soul that is about to leave the body. Several of the measures of avoidance aim at the protection of the living or dying from the attacks of the recently dead.[183] Daimonistic beliefs go farther than this and afford distinct survivals of cannibalism, the daimons being often supposed to eat the souls of the dead which, unless they are fortified by all manner of ritual for the journey, may come to grief, be devoured, and robbed of the next life. The notion that the gods eat souls runs, for example, through all Polynesian mythology.[184]

A variation on this belief is found among the Haida Indians. One of their deities "has a novel way of securing his prize [a human body to eat]. He comes down on the clouds and sits watching for any stray Indian. As soon as

---

[176] Harnack, *Dogmengchte.*, I, 171.   [177] Hatch, *Griechentum*, 14.
[178] Tertullian, *Apologeticus*, XXII, XXIII.
[179] Lea, *Inquisition*, III, 417.
[180] Meyer, *Deut. Volkskunde*, 104 ff., 146.
[181] Vuillier, *Forgotten Isles*, 158.
[182] Krauss, *Südslaven*, 53, 57, 98, 155.
[183] §§222 ff., above.   [184] Ratzel, *Vkde.*, II, 126.

one comes near him he does not pounce upon his body. No! this would be too vulgar an action for a god to do. He merely seizes the spirit of the Indian, *i.e.*, he draws the spirit out of the body and takes it with him on high; and in a very short space of time the body has to go in search of his spirit, and so becomes an easy victim of this cannibal god."[185] Other cases will appear under the topic of cannibalism.[186]

In the prevalence of such beliefs and with their growth and integration, there develops the idea of a master evil spirit, the devil— a conception belonging to less primitive conditions.

§244*. The Familiar Spirit. Although the abiding danger from the daimons and even their active malevolence are thus evident and although the fear of evil underlies all of eidolism and daimonism, yet the presence of the good spirit is not ruled out. The simplest of the relatively well-disposed daimons is the guardian, or familiar, or patron, or luck spirit. The existence of such is linked with the individual rather than the group and in it lies the germ of dualism, the conception of the opposition of the good and the evil forces in the universe. Each person born into the world has his own experience of life; and this, when concentrated into a definite notion and personified, becomes the Fate or Destiny of the individual. Each is, in his degree, a Man of Destiny. As he goes through life his fortune passes into fact—into tradition or history; and if a daimon is supposed to be selected out of the host of spirits and set off to each one, to guide his destiny, this gives the general conception of the familiar spirit, tutelary genius, or luck divinity.

One who has a familiar spirit must use it as he can to evade adversity and to win prosperity; thus the shaman operates in many instances through a "familiar"—so regularly, indeed, that the term has come to be associated with magic and sorcery, for there is need, in dealing with and through the familiar, of a considerable amount of magical procedure. The topic is closely connected also with fetishism and totemism, as will soon appear.[187] Then the idea leads on to the conception of tutelary spirits and deities which are no longer protectors merely of the individual but

185 Harrison, in JAI, XXI, 16-17.   186 §290, below.
187 §§247 ff., 260, 261, below.

of a group such as a caste, gild, profession, or nation.[188] The idea
gets into mythology and poetry; the "daimon" of Socrates, the
"fortune" of Cæsar, the "star" of Napoleon (and the more dubious one which Lassalle thought he had), the "voice" of Jeanne
d'Arc. "Under him," says Macbeth of Banquo, "my Genius is
rebuked, as it is said Mark Antony's was by Cæsar."[189] "National
destiny" is still a whim of mythology.

The Australians believe that the soul of the first man whom one kills becomes his guardian spirit.[190] An individual may lose his guardian spirit if his
churinga, or sacred stone, is removed.[191] The Melanesian *mana* is the idea
which we express that one is a lucky fellow, a darling of fortune. This is
known and proved by his success, to attain which he must be gifted, endowed,
and protected by a higher power.[192] The guardian spirit is generally taken
from the outside world but may be one of the individual's own souls.[193] "Every
Fanti has his own Fetish or familiar spirit, in whose power he is considered
to some extent to be. This spirit is of a neutral character, beneficent if appeased, and mischievous if unpropitiated, but on the whole more inclined to
be of an evil disposition."[194] In Uganda, with royalty the name of the great-
grandfather is given to the eldest son; peasants do not follow this custom,
but take the name of some renowned relative. The spirit of the deceased relative enters the child and assists him through life."[195] In Nyassaland, such
spirits come in dreams and are, in fact, never seen except in dreams. A noise
seemingly without cause is often referred to them. "If you meet with trouble,
you can put white beans or flour under certain trees and ask your Azimu to
do better."[196] Among the Dyaks, each man has his special tutelary deity. "The
rich and poor are credited with rich and poor Petaras respectively, hence the
state of Dyak gods may be inferred from the varying circumstances of men
below."[197]

The Eskimo shamans (*angekoks*) have familiar spirits, which are often the
souls of the dead, especially of ancestors, and sometimes those of animals.
They may be the souls of absent Europeans. They are the helpers and avengers
of the shaman and kill his victims by showing themselves as ghosts. There is a
sort of master-familiar which, on the introduction of Christianity, suffered the
stock transformation into the devil.[198]

The connection of the familiar or tutelary spirit with Indian totemism will
be seen to be very close. "Dreams and visions are the invariable source of the
personal totem of the Salish; for even when a totem is transmitted from one
to another, as it sometimes is, the totem appears to the person or persons

[188] *Tyche Pandemos* or *Eutychia*. Krauss, *Sreća*, 60.
[189] Shakespeare, *Macbeth*, III, sc. i, 55-57.
[190] Ratzel, *Vkde.*, II, 92.
[191] Spencer and Gillen, *Nat. Tr. Cent. Aust.*, 138, note.
[192] §257, below; Codrington, *Melanesians*, 118.
[193] Kingsley, *Travels W. Afr.*, 510, 511; Ellis, *Yoruba*, 125-126.
[194] Connolly, in JAI, XXVI, 150.   [195] Roscoe, in JAI, XXXII, 32.
[196] Stigand, in JAI, XXXVII, 130.
[197] Wilken, in VG, III, 252.   [198] Nansen, *Esk. Life*, 239.

upon whom it has been bestowed in a dream or vision, acknowledging the bond and promising protection. The dream or vision is the proper and common mode of communication between the guardian spirit and its *protégé*. . . . Prolonged fasts, bathings, forced vomitings and other exhausting bodily exercises are the means adopted for inducing the mystic dreams and visions. With the body in the enervated condition which must necessarily follow such treatment, the mind becomes abnormally active and expectant; and dreams, visions and hallucinations are as natural to the novice in such a state as breathing; and we can readily understand how real to him must seem the vision of the looked-for spirit, and how firm his belief in its actual manifestation. The psychical effect of this belief upon some temperaments must be very great, for it enables them to undertake and accomplish feats of abnormal strength, agility and endurance; and gives them at times, besides a general exaltation of the senses, undoubted clairvoyant and other supernormal mental and bodily powers."[199]

In the ancient world the idea was common. In Chaldæa, each man at birth was placed under the protection of a god or goddess who was supposed to follow and guard him against evil spirits. If he is pious and faithful to this guardian his days will be prolonged to the limit of destiny; if he is not he will be tormented and cut off.[200] The thunderings against possessors of familiar spirits in the Old Testament[201] witness to the prevalence of the belief. The Phœnicians held to the current conviction.[202] The Romans believed in a *genius* or spirit that accompanied each individual from birth, the *genius domus,* and the *genius patrisfamilias;* these were often in the form of a serpent.[203] Marcus Aurelius would never allow the dedication of altars to himself but the simulacrum of his *genius,* "his spirituality or celestial counterpart," was placed among the images of past emperors.[204] In later times the idea has persisted in the North. The Valkyrs were too high for the hearts' need and so the female guardian-spirits were the *hamingjor* or luck-goddesses; when these gave a man over, "it was the end of his luck and his life."[205] The Russian *rozanitza* was a similar luck-spirit.[206]

The Dalmatian conception of *sreća*[207] is a personification of personal fortune in life as a daimon allotted at birth. It is in the form of a snake. For one to see his own protecting serpent is a very bad omen; but he never knows which one it is. Similarly one should not view the open sky at night lest he see his "star" and die; if a star falls, a man is dying; one must not spit at such a time. If the *sreća* does not discharge its function satisfactorily, it becomes *nesreća* and can be got rid of or even thrashed. One such luck-spirit excused herself for crop-failure on the ground of not understanding agriculture but only trade. These South Slav creations are akin to the Moiræ, Parcæ, and Norns. In Rumania and among the Ruthenes an attendant imp can be hatched out of a hen's egg if the latter is very hard and has black spots. It must be

[199] Hill-Tout, in JAI, XXXV, 143-144.

[200] Maspero, *Hist. Anc.,* I, 682.   [201] Levit., XIX, 31; XX, 27.

[202] Pietschmann, *Phön.,* 169-170.

[203] De Marchi, *Culto Privato di Roma Antica,* quoted in *L'Année Sociologique,* 1897, 192.

[204] Pater, *Marius,* 213.   [205] Wisen, *Qvinnan,* 7.

[206] Kostomarow, *Gt. Russians* (Russ.), 265.

[207] Krauss, *Sreća,* 62, 19, 25, 34, 60, 65, 94, 109-110.

carried for nine days under the shoulder by one who neither washes nor combs his hair during the period. The emerging devil helps the man who "broods" him but the latter's soul goes to the evil one. He cannot die, even if he wants to, till he has given the imp away.[208]

The combination of the two ideas of the inexorable malevolence of some spirits and the benevolence of others—the latter quality being generally the outcome of scrupulous attention on the part of man—has worked out in a number of primitive cases into the idea of duality. The good, familiar, or tutelary spirits may be set over against the chronically evil ones. Much of magic[209] has to do with the enlistment of spirits that have been placated into a favorable disposition. The elaboration of dualism is to be found in religions of a higher development; in this place interest centers in the fact that rudimentary dualism is to be encountered in daimonistic systems long before these have developed into historic forms.

In West Africa "the spirit of the new moon is that most commonly addressed to keep the lower spirits from molesting."[210] According to the Koryak, "Big-Raven gave light to men; he taught them to hunt sea and land animals; he also gave them reindeer, made the fire-drill, gave them the drum, left incantations for amulets, and set up shamans to struggle with the evil spirits, with whom Big-Raven himself had carried on a constant and successful warfare."[211] Siberian legends portray two antagonistic spirits, one of which helps childbirth and stands by the child while the other causes insupportable birth-pangs and pursues the child through life.[212] In Tibet, "guardians of the quarters of the sky are worshipped by the populace, who credit them with the power of conferring good luck and averting the calamities due to evil spirits."[213] In the Chittagong Hills, at the death of a priest, there is a sort of dramatization of the conflict of the good and evil spirits. "The corpse is carried to the place of cremation on a car to which ropes are attached, and the persons attending the ceremony are divided into equal bodies and set to work to pull in opposite directions. One side represents the good spirits; the other, the evil. The contest is so arranged that the former are victorious."[214] India's mythology is full of strife between the good and evil influences, in which human kings are sometimes summoned to aid.[215] The Dyaks consider the forces of nature as divided into two camps, good and evil, which are constantly at war; their belief is a "more or less perfect dualism."[216] It is reported that many Indians of North America "distinctly believe in the existence of a Great (or Good) Spirit, an Evil (or Bad) Spirit";[217] and at the

[208] Kaindl, in *Globus*, XCII, 287.
[209] §299, below.
[210] Kingsley, *Travels W. Afr.*, 452.
[211] Jochelson, in AA, VI, 417.
[212] Radloff, *Schamanenthum*, 11.
[213] Waddell, *Buddhism*, 290.
[214] Lewin, *S.E. India*, 185.
[215] Episodes in Holtzmann, *Indische Sagen*, I, 285, 292, 319; II, 198.
[216] Veth, *Borneo's Wester-Afdeeling*, II, 307-308.
[217] Donaldson, in *Smithson. Rep.*, 1885, pt. II, 351.

farther end of the double continent the Araucanians "may be classed as dual-
ists, believing in a good Spirit, who is the creator and giver of all good, and
an evil spirit, the author of all evil."[218] "Devil-worshippers," so-called, are
probably not such; they do not worship the Devil but think that as he was
once mighty he may be so again; and they keep on good terms with him.[219]

Dualism in its developed form issues not alone into complex historic religious systems but also into various categories of metaphysical speculation. These belong to the study of comparative
religion or to philosophy.

§245*. Deities. That the gods of more developed religions belong in the series with those of the ruder and cruder systems is a
natural inference for one who has followed the evolution of belief
from animism through eidolism and daimonism. The inevitable
anthropomorphic quality of the soul and ghost persists in the
gods to such an extent that the uninformed mind, impressed by the
similarities between men and their deities, can readily conclude
that the gods created man in their own image. Main[220] enlarges,
with many examples, upon the amorousness of the gods and their
unions with mortal women.

Our sets of cases enforce the essential likeness of all spiritual
beings. It was the essential likeness of organic beings which first
caught the attention of the chief proponent of organic evolution.
Such a phenomenon challenges intellectual curiosity and calls for
explanation. The case is the same in the societal range. We might
well have begun by aligning all sorts of spiritual beings with a
view to their essential similarities; but there is some advantage in
working steadily along from stage to stage, especially since virtually all of us, by reason of having passed our lives in a civilized
society, have lacked positive knowledge of the earlier forms of religion and also an objective attitude toward both those forms and
the developed types of our own time and place.

The following cases are designed to display, from various
angles, the relationship of such supernatural beings as are evidently reckoned to be deities by those who refer to them, with the

218 La Fetra, in *Ill. Christian World*, Nov., 1896.
219 Von Haxthausen, *Transkaukasia*, I, 227.
220 *Relig. Chastity*, chs. IX, X.

ghosts and daimons whose nature and characteristics we have now come to know.[221]

The Australians of certain districts recognize a sort of supreme spirit: "evidently he was not everywhere thought to be a malevolent being, but he was dreaded as one who could severely punish sins committed against those tribal ordinances and customs whose first institution is ascribed to him. . . . The knowledge of this being, and his attributes and powers, was only communicated to the youths at their initiation, and was considered something eminently secret, and not on any account to be told to women and children. It is said that the women . . . knew only that a great being lived beyond the sky"—a being referred to by them as *papang,* or father. His name is so sacred that it is spoken only in whispers; the term itself is used as little as possible, but the god is referred to as "He," "the man," "the name I told you of," the reason for this caution being "the dread of offending an unseen, powerful, and possibly present spirit." This spirit came down at the initiation-period, with a noise like thunder, that is, with the sound of the bull-roarers.[222] Beliefs about this spirit represent the nearest Australian approach to the god-idea.

Among the Fijians, "probably here and there were gods created by the priests who ministered to them, and were not the spirits of dead chiefs. For example, the god of the Bure tribe on the Ra coast (Sawakasa), who was called Tui Lagi or 'Lord of heaven.' At the approach of the missionaries, the heathen priest of this town became their staunch ally. He declared that they had come to preach the same god he had been preaching, the Tui Lagi, and that more of his mysteries had been revealed to the missionaries than to him."[223] In the New Hebrides there is a belief in Uhgen, not as a being but as a power behind all things, which is a unity and is benevolent. He gave knowledge to certain men who are the immediate agents of all things, even of the operations of nature, by means of sacred stones. "A watch, a gun-lock, a wall which a missionary will build is a thing made by a god." The caprice of these supermen controls others. The term Uhgen is applied to a mole or mark on the body, or to an indelible stain on a floor, or to a watch or gun-lock, not as superhuman but as hard to undo.[224]

Holub[225] thinks that the Bantu family before it split up into numerous tribes, had a "belief in a powerful, invisible god" who knew all things, watched the behavior of everyone narrowly and did as he pleased with each. He lived in the blue of the sky and controlled moon, stars, and men's destinies. The natives hesitate to pronounce his name, but speak of "He above" or "only He." "Mzimu is the name given to that unseen power which the natives believe in, but cannot understand. There are, in every village, small houses consecrated to the use of this spirit, and in these houses are placed grain, flour, pipes, mead, and beer, the offerings being generally accompanied by prayer or

[221] A number of writers have chapters on the deities of various peoples; for instance, Cowan, *Maoris,* ch. VII.

[222] Howitt, in JAI, XIII, 192; Howitt, *S.E. Aust.,* 533.

[223] Thomson, in JAI, XXIV, 343.   [224] Gray, in AAAS, 1892, 650, 664.

[225] *Süd-Afrika,* II, 337; Holub, *Capstadt,* II, 453; Holub, in *Illustr. Afr.,* June, 1896.

thanksgiving for some prayer granted. . . . The worship is inextricably mixed up with sorcery, sensuality and crime."[226]

Ellis[227] regards the possession of a number of general objects of worship as a step in religious evolution. The roots of the words for god signify to be afraid, harmful, or to direct, judge, or execute. From the latter are derived words for witchcraft, dream, or vision—to dream meaning literally to attain a godlike or mystic condition. "The god ranking first in the religious system of the Ewe-speaking peoples is named Mawu, a word which, besides being a proper name, has also the meanings of sky, firmament, and rain." Other gods strike with lightning, send smallpox, or excite sexual desires "without any reference or subordination to Mawu or any other god." The lightning-god is a bird-like creature hidden in the midst of the black thunder-cloud, the crash of the thunder being the flapping of his enormous wings. The god of mischief-making "can, if sufficiently bribed, be induced to take up the quarrel of a worshipper, and work evil upon the unconscious offender." A god of fire is sacrificed to when a house is first built, as a sort of insurance against a conflagration. There is a god of wisdom and earthly bliss, a benefactor of mankind who opened the eyes of the first man and woman, who were blind. "All along the western portion of the Slave Coast, the natives, like those on the Gold Coast, see in the roar and motion of the surf a multitude of gods, each of whom is worshipped in his own proper locality, so that there are two or three local sea-gods to almost every village along the shore; but at Whydah and its neighborhood this is not the case, and Wu appears to be considered the god of the sea generally, and not of some portion only." Here we have a case of the emergence of a single deity out of many. Yet the native, "while enrolling himself as a follower of a general god, likes also to have a protector whose sole business is to guard his interests; and who, though his power may be limited, is not likely to be distracted by the claims of others to his attention."

It has been noted that white men were sometimes taken to be ghosts of ancestors by tribes of color who saw them for the first time. In the Gilbert Islands, a maiden was bleached out before marriage, by being kept in seclusion. "The whole idea underlying the bleaching process is closely connected with a race-memory of certain ancestral gods who, like the famous Tangaroa of Polynesia, were fair of skin and of marvellous beauty."[228]

"The almost universal reverence of the Indians for the earth is interesting in connection with their feeling about the ownership of land. The earth is regarded as sacred, often it is called the 'mother,' and it appears to rank second among the gods. A sacrifice of food is held up first to the sky and then is deposited on the earth, perhaps rubbed into the soil. The first smoke is directed to the sky, the second to the earth, and then those to the four directions in order. Other sacrifices are commonly held up first to the sky, and then are held toward the earth. Before beginning to perform any sacred office, the priest or doctor holds his hands first toward the sky and then rubs them on the ground. 'It is by the earth,' they say, 'that we live. Without it we could not exist. It nourishes and supports us.' "[229] "The chief characters of the Huron pantheon were a female deity, Ataensic, a sort of Hecate, whom they some-

[226] Angus, in JAI, XXVII, 318.
[227] Ewe, 14, 29, 31, 33, 37, 45, 46, 56, 63; Ellis, Yoruba, 34-35.
[228] Grimble, in JAI, LI, 43.   [229] Grinnell, in AA, IX, 3.

times identified with the moon, and her grandson Juskeha, who was sometimes regarded as the sun, and as a benevolent spirit, but most commonly in their stories appears as a fantastic and capricious goblin, with no moral attributes whatever."[230] "The Ojibwa believe in a multiplicity of spirits which inhabit all space and every conspicuous object in nature. These spirits (manidos) are subservient to superior ones, either good or bad. The chief manido is termed Kitshi Manido—Great Spirit—approaching closely to the idea of God in the Christian religion; the second is Dzhe Manido, a benign being considered the guardian spirit of the Midewiwin [medicine-society], and through whose divine provision the sacred rites of the Midewiwin were given to man. The Thunder God is one of the greatest of the bad spirits, and it is from him that the Jessakkid [inferior medicine-men] are believed to obtain their powers of evil doing. There is one other who dwells in and rules the 'place of shadows,' the hereafter; he is known as Dzhibai Manido—Shadow Spirit, or the Ghost Spirit."[231] To the California Indians "God is the 'Big Man Above,' and that is the extent of their knowledge. But ask them to tell you about the creation of the world, of man, of fire, and of familiar objects, and their interest is at once aroused. Instantly God—the fabulous being—disappears and the coyote comes forward. The coyote did everything, made everything. That is what the Indian's father told him, and his father's father told *him*. If this Great Man had any existence in early days, why does he not appear sometimes in the real aboriginal legends? . . . The writer affirms unhesitatingly that there is no Indian equivalent for 'God.' There are numerous spirits, chiefly bad, some in human form, some dwelling in beasts and birds, having names which they generally refuse to reveal to mortals, and haunting chiefly the hills and forests, sometimes remaining in the Happy Western Land."[232]

It is hardly necessary to develop the essentially anthropomorphic character of the Hebrew god; in the first passages in Genesis[233] he repents that he has made man and is grieved at human wickedness. "The earliest Semites, like primitive men of other races, drew no sharp line of distinction between the nature of gods, of men, and of beasts, and had no difficulty in admitting a real kinship between (a) gods and men, (b) gods and sacred animals, (c) families of men and families of beasts."[234] It appears in Homer, as in the Mahabharata, that gods are only a higher grade of beings, in the universe along with men—not above it, out of it, merely ruling over it. "The process of evolution from spirit to god is indicated here and there, in such stories as those of Castor and Polydeuces and of Heracles. Impossible as it is to trace such processes after centuries of myth-complication and modification, still in the nature of the Greek gods were many marks of their origin from mankind. The Homeric gods were men of a larger being and power. They had human form, they had weight, could fall, could be bound with chains, could feel intense physical pain, and they could be, if not mortally, certainly very painfully wounded, even by men. They possessed this physical distinction from men, that they had no blood, but a divine fluid 'ichor' in their veins; and that, though they united with men in devouring sacrifices, still they regularly ate no flesh and grain, nor drank wine. They ate and drank immortality. Further, they possessed all the emotions and passions of men, on a grander scale; they

---

[230] Hale, *Iroq. Rites,* 74. [231] Hoffman, in BAE, VII, 163.

[232] Powers, in *Contrib. N. A. Ethnol.,* III, 413-414.

[233] VI, 6. [234] Smith, *Relig. Sem.,* 287.

feared, hated, envied, and were jealous, vain, and lustful beyond the measure of the man. There were many children born of unions of gods with men. Though in general described as 'blessed,' 'happy,' still the gods were a prey to sorrow and pain of mind, and to disappointment; they were baffled and insulted and felt the emotions natural to that state. The society of the gods was made unpleasant by mutual quarrels and bickerings; they were not omniscient or omnipotent, and their State was not stable. The entire ground-work of the Homeric system was anthropomorphic; gods were different from men chiefly in degree. The power of the gods for good or ill was, of course, far greater than that of man. Their physical force was thousands of times greater than his, and in addition, they generally possessed various attributes of spirits; quickness of movement, power of existence in various elements, etc. Besides all this, they were vested with magical powers, and were rulers over natural phenomena; in short, they were Power in the superlative."[235]

In the Greek tragedies a daughter prays to her father's spirit as to a god;[236] but the gods themselves are regarded with some resentment. This view is not exactly fatalism but is akin to it. The gods do not play fairly. They sport with men. They would punish men if the latter did what the gods do. Poor men cannot help themselves. They must make the best of it but it excites their indignation and scorn. They have standards higher than those of the gods, yet are weaker than the gods, and they are in a state of moral revolt. This is the state of mind in which men live, being brought to it by their experience of life. This is their world-philosophy. They are like slaves with base masters. They must submit and get as much joy out of life as they can on the sly, evading the notice of the gods.[237] Criticism of the gods is as ancient as Homer;[238] on one occasion Zeus is represented as exclaiming: "Ah me, how now do mortals take the gods to task! For they say that their ills are from us; while they themselves, because of their own acts of blind folly, suffer woes beyond measure." In ancient Scandinavia, Odin is at once god, hero, bard, and law-giver.[239] The anthropomorphic conception of God is well illustrated in the English mystery and miracle plays.[240]

That the beings denominated deities are of like character with those which we have called daimons is clear enough from the cases. It is as nearly impossible to determine when the daimon passes into the god or deity as to say when a folkway should be numbered among the mores, and for exactly the same reason; in the process of becoming, or of evolution, there are no clearly defined points of transition—a truth important enough to justify much iteration. Some daimons rise and others decline; a conqueror raises his tutelary deity to authority, displacing an earlier god. All changes depend upon the course of societal development and destiny.[241]

[235] Keller, *Hom. Soc.*, 107.   [236] Æschylus, *Choephori*, 124 ff.
[237] Euripides: *Ion*, 425 ff.; *Electra*, 1282-1283, 1329-1330; *Heracles*, 339-347; *Iphigenia among the Taurians*, 380 ff.
[238] *Odyssey*, I, 32-34.   [239] Geijer, *Svensk. Hist.*, 5.
[240] Spencer, *Study of Soc.*, ch. VI, 136.   [241] Lippert, *Kgchte.*, II, 247, 262.

One author[242] thinks there are three stages in what he calls "mythology." The first, to use our terminology, covers the idea of the soul and the ghost-cult; and he thinks every people on the face of the earth has traversed it. Ancestor-worship, as one of its forms, constituted the kernel of the religion of the Chinese, Egyptians, Romans, and a number of other peoples. This period, thinks the author, coincides with the stage in the history of culture in which life is supported by hunting. During the second stage the ghosts tend more and more to become spirits—of the wind, the storm, and the rain—from whom come individual spirits with mythical names. This stage of culture is the pastoral. The third period is that of agriculture and a regular form of government, and it sees spirits individualized into deities.

However risky it may be to insist upon close correlations between such things as the stage of the arts and particular religious beliefs, it is true enough that both the arts and the beliefs show a steady evolution from the crude to the more refined. Yet evolutionary forms, however advanced, retain characteristic likenesses with the earlier types out of which they have developed. It remains true of the gods as of the ghosts, that their origin lay in fear. "An eloquent French writer[243] has . . . quoted with approval, and applied to the beginnings of Semitic religion, the words of Statius, *Primus in orbe deos fecit timor.*" The deities are like the daimons and the eidola as they could not conceivably have been except by reason of a genetic relationship. In the case of the deities of advanced religions, their existing similarities with men, men's ghosts, and daimons are unmistakable to the unbiassed observer; they are surveyed very thoroughly by Spencer[244] and are likely, indeed, when once attention has been called to them sufficiently sharply to dispel conventionalization, to throng to the mind of one familiar with the Hebrew scriptures.

Among the deities, it has been noted, there is always in operation a sort of selection resulting from conquest or other form of competition between votaries whereby some gods decline and others increase in significance. Gradually a few come to surpass all their fellows; and these few are not uncommonly reduced to three.[245] It is doubtful, despite dualistic tenets, whether they are ever cut down to a smaller number until the highest reaches of understanding are attained.

[242] Meyer, *Indog. Mythen,* I, 210 ff., quoted in Schrader, *Aryans,* 409-410.
[243] Renan, *Hist. d'Israel,* I, 29, quoted by Smith, *Relig. Sem.,* 54.
[244] *Prin. Soc.,* I, ch. XXV.   [245] Paine, *Ethnic Trinities.*

Some authors[246] distinguish a type of religion which they call "henotheism" (one-god belief), where there is a single dominant deity, though there may be any number of inferior ones. Henotheism involves "the religious disposition to ascribe to each god at the moment of invocation all the attributes of supreme power," and is to be distinguished from monotheism, which recognizes one sole deity. The latter form is too abstract for the ordinary uses of mankind and the tendency, even when it is a professed creed, as in Islam, is to reverence a number of heroes and saints at whose graves miracles are wrought.[247] The typical form of religion is polytheism; if monotheism is alleged of any primitive tribe there is probably a misconstruction of the facts. "Especially through missionary influence, since 1500, ideas of dualistic and monotheistic deities, of moral government of the world, and of retribution after death for deeds done in life, have been implanted on native polytheism in various parts of the globe." There has been direct adoption from foreign teachers; observers have exaggerated genuine native deities of a lower order into gods or devils; there has been a conversion of native words denoting a whole class of minor spiritual beings, such as ghosts or daimons, into individual names alleged to be those of a supreme good deity or a rival deity.[248]

It is impossible to believe that the description of Man,[249] according to which the Andaman Islanders possess a Supreme Being, is not a reflection of previous teaching or suggestion; if not, the case is in the highest degree exceptional. Similar reports, though less detailed, speak of a "supreme creator" among the Naga of India, a "supreme being" among the Eskimo, and a god "who is in and of everything" among the Pawnees. Again, we hear that the Hindus have a trinity; "for, as we all know, this doctrine is Hindu as well as Christian and Egyptian."[250]

There is one special case which has appeared in literature, namely, that of the Great Spirit of the American Indian. Predisposed travellers have given to romantic writers a picture of the noble savage, in this respect as in others, that will not verify. Dorsey,[251] who is a reliable ethnographer, cites the assertion that the religion of the Mandans, Hidatsa, and Dakotas "consists in the belief in one Great Spirit," and comments as follows: "But such assertions are

[246] D'Alviella, *Concep. God*, 144; Lippert, *Kgchte.*, II, 249.
[247] Ratzel, *Vkde.*, III, 115.
[248] Tylor, "Savage Relig.," in JAI, XXI, 284.
[249] In JAI, XII, 157.
[250] Godden, in JAI, XXVI, 186; Boas, in BAE, VI, 583; Grinnell, *Pawnees*, xvii; Von Schkopp, in *Globus*, LXXXIII, 331; Nivedita, *Ind. Life*, 215.
[251] "Siouan Cults," in BAE, XI, 372, 423, 431, 501 (quoted).

closely followed by admissions which explain the mistake of the writer: 'Great Spirit' is synonymous with 'Great Medicine,' a name applied to everything which they do not comprehend. Among the Mandan, 'each individual selects for himself the particular object of his devotion, which is termed his medicine, and is either some visible being or more commonly some animal.' " Dorsey quotes, in order to refute them, several sentimental reports about the Indians. "The historical evidence that the Great Spirit belongs not to the untutored but to the tutored mind of the savage is preserved for us in the records of the tutors themselves, the Jesuit missionaries in Canada."[252] That great student of the Jesuit Relations, Parkman[253] asserts that "the primitive Indian yielding his untutored homage to One All-pervading and Omnipotent Spirit is a dream of poets, rhetoricians, and sentimentalists."

Herodotus[254] writes of a Thracian tribe, who believe mankind immortal, that they had only one god. Zoroaster utterly opposed demonism and the oldest form of his religion was monotheistic.[255] But the Semitic faiths which are generally regarded as such were, except for the most enlightened, at best henotheistic. "Monotheism remained an ideal of the priests and prophets."[256] The Phœnician Baals were different deities under the same name. "What is often described as the natural tendency of Semitic religion towards ethical monotheism, is in the main nothing more than a consequence of the alliance of religion with monarchy."[257] That even in the pre-prophetic period "we can speak at most of henotheism . . . but not of absolute monotheism, would be sufficiently proved by the constant inclination of the people to Baal worship." And this despite assertions that Jahweh is the true and only god. There was need of a transitional stage before monotheism could be reached; "it is impossible to get from animism to monotheism without a transition."[258] The Jewish religion had a strong influence upon Islam. "Allah was victorious over the multiplicity of gods, the community of faith over the diversity of blood, the unity of the theocratic state over the anarchy of the tribes." The Moslems came to reproach the Christians with the worship, in the Trinity, of three gods.[259] That three can be one, and one three, has been the basis of innumerable disputes, reconciliations, and interpretations.

The true monotheist is the product of long development and high enlightenment. Whether he is called religious or not, that person who stands in awe, but in the light of knowledge, before the unity of natural law is alone worthy of bearing the name of

[252] Tylor, in JAI, XXI, 284.
[253] *Jesuits,* lxxxix; Carr, in *Smithson. Rep.,* 1891, 546, note.
[254] *Hist.,* IV, 93.
[255] Tiele-Gehrich, *Gchte. Relig.,* II, 153.
[256] Maurer, *Vkde.,* 184.
[257] Pietschmann, *Phön.,* 183-184; Smith, *Relig. Sem.,* 74.
[258] Kautzsch, "Relig. Isr.," in *Hastings's Dict. Bible,* 635 (quoted), 680, 706; Deut., VI, 4; VII, 9; IV, 35, 39; I Kings, VIII, 60; Is., XXXVII, 16; II Kings, XIX, 15; D'Alviella, *Concep. God,* 200 ff.; Tiele-Gehrich, *Gchte. Relig.,* I, 295-297.
[259] Wellhausen, *Skizzen,* III, 204.

monotheist. The guess, even the inspired guess, is nothing beside
the vision that opens at length before the eye of those who have
faithfully worked through the small to the large.

The doctrine about spirits of a super-ghostly order, which is
daimonism, has now been sketched in its main outlines. When it
comes to filling in the detail, that can be done best, or perhaps
solely, by turning at once from the theory to the practice, which is
daimonology. There are, however, two related sets of beliefs which,
as immediate sequels or corollaries of daimonism, should stand
forth with some sharpness of definition before daimonology can
be treated with any degree of comprehensiveness. These are fetishism and totemism. When once these two have been considered, daimonology is to engage attention throughout the rest of our treatment of religion.

CHAPTER XXVIII

FETISHISM

§246. "Possession." With the nature and ways of the soul, the ghost, and the daimon in mind it becomes possible to follow out the further theories about them which have developed in various times and places. Prominent among these corollaries of belief is that of possession or obsession. The essence of possession is the occupation, temporary or permanent, of a person or thing by a spirit not original in him or in it. The existence of nature-spirits[1] in natural objects is not possession any more than is the presence of the soul in a man. The atmospheric movements are inexplicable to savage people and so are natural phenomena such as rain and hail; being unaccountable, they are regularly referred to spiritual agency; but the spirits indwelling in natural objects and accredited with the accomplishment of natural processes are original and permanent tenants or even personifications of these objects and processes rather than alien essences which have entered to possess them. These indwellers are always there and have always been there, as souls of things.[2] Possession is a more incidental, fortuitous matter, where a ghost or daimon, or even the soul of a living man, is conceived to have penetrated into some object or person with whom it has no original connection. The possessing spirit is imported, not innate.

There are many degrees of possession which shade into one another. Perhaps the most complete and definite is where the ghosts haunt the grave and its precincts, entering into and pervading not only the mound but also adjacent trees and other objects. Then there is the case where the daimon enters and inspires the religious votary, as Apollo seized upon the priestess of Cumæ or Dionysus instilled frenzy into the Mænads.[3] Evil spirits enter their victims to induce disease and madness, as in the story culminating in the drowning of the Gadarene swine.[4] Clean-cut cases of this

---

[1] §241, above.   [2] §214, above.
[3] Virgil, *Æneid*, VI, 45 ff., 77 ff.; Euripides, *Bacchæ*.
[4] Mark, V, 1-13; Matthew, VIII, 32.

order shade off into more ambiguous manifestations. In view of the nature of property as an adhesion to personality,[5] it is obvious that what was *proprium* to a man in life remains imbued with his spirit, and that any special mark or symbol of ownership retains similar attributes. Characteristic possessions of the dead, such as a wife, and even of the living, such as a king's throne, ring, or scepter, have in them something of the owner's personality or "virtue"; this is revealed by the taboo on the widow[6] and by the exaggerated worshipfulness accorded to the "symbol of authority." Even the "word" of the illustrious dead is regarded as "inspired" and as embodying the spirit of him who uttered it.

These various types and degrees of possession, whether clean-cut or vague, will be illustrated as fully as need be. In reviewing the cases the reader may feel that some of them are classifiable under possession only by a metaphorical extension of the term. Even so, they are being classed with their like. This is all that can be said in advance of the actual instances, except that our disposition is always to look back toward the origin of societal phenomena and to seek, under the often highly rationalized modern form, the simpler, more direct, more nearly original prototype and conception. The only alternative which we see is to meditate out an explanation on the basis of "the nature of the case," as such nature appears to a mind without perspective, which generally means an impressionistic guess.

The chief evidence of possession is abnormality. It has been seen again and again that the phenomena referred to spiritual agency are those otherwise inexplicable; those that do not accommodate themselves to the everyday routine, use, and custom so as to require no explanation; those, in a word, which are manifestations of the aleatory element. In particular also they are such phenomena as cause uneasiness and concern by rousing fear of ill, the only sort that are capable of fixing the wavering attention of the primitive mind. There are in nature and in his fellow-men a number of unusual and startling phenomena before which the savage cannot but stand aghast; and his first thought is of spiritual possession. A thing or a person that looks or acts abnormally does so, as he sees it, not of itself or himself but because of an indwelling presence. The horse of Achilles addresses his rider; that is strange enough until it is realized that a daimon is inspiring him to do so; then the master simply and naturally replies to the vocal

5 §108, above.   6 §§394, 395, below.

animal.[7] Several miscellaneous instances may serve to hold the case before us in the concrete, pending the survey of extensive evidence.

In a folk-tale of the Yorubas which reveals the local idea of spirit-possession, the mysterious disappearance of food from a locked house in which a negro father and mother were wont to leave their nine months' old baby led the father to secrete himself to watch developments. The mother laid the child upon a mat and went out, locking the door as usual. Scarcely had she gone when the baby was seen by the father to stand up and grow till he became a big boy. "Then he went to the calabashes where the food was kept, and was beginning to eat it, when the father came out from his hiding-place. Immediately the child saw his father he became a little baby again, and lay on the floor crying. He was possessed by a spirit. His mother came back, and they beat him to drive the spirit out, so that the spirit fled."[8] In India the spirits of drowned persons enter the bodies of women, generally in the effort to get some of the food which they see the women eating. The possession may have taken place months before it is known and the victim may know nothing about it. After confessing their identity, the possessing spirits are driven out by making their habitat uncomfortable.[9] The possessed are those "out of whom the god speaks and through whom he cures the sick."[10] In Samoa "men and women at times imagined they were possessed by the *ailu* and would act and speak as though under demoniacal possession." Epileptics and consumptives were influenced by the *ailu*.[11] The New Testament speaks frequently of possession by an evil spirit; in the Old there is but one instance—where Jahweh sends such a spirit to take possession of Saul and make him mad.[12] Nassau[13] comes out with the astonishing contention that "demoniac possessions in supposed lunatics are possible; they were actual and numerous in Palestine during the ministry of Christ. . . . It may be, therefore, that the missionary in his contest with heathenism has literally to fight with the devil."

These few instances will serve to open up a very wide topic into which the student must penetrate deeply if he is to understand the germ of many long-lived religious phenomena.

§247. The Fetish. Out of the doctrines about souls, ghosts, and daimons, with the added idea of possession, there arises one of the most nearly universal of human beliefs: fetishism. This is a form of eidolism or daimonism connected with a material object—the ghost or spirit acting through it or being controllable by the use of it. Fetishism, says Tylor,[14] "is the doctrine of spirits embodied in, or attached to, or conveying influence through, certain

[7] Homer, *Iliad*, XIX, 407 ff.   [8] Ellis, *Yoruba*, 120-121.
[9] Fawcett, "Obsession," in JASB, I, 534 ff.
[10] Schwaner, *Borneo*, I, 233.   [11] Ella, in AAAS, 1892, 643.
[12] Duhm, *Geister*, 15; Alexander, *Demonic Possession in the New Testament*.
[13] *Fetichism*, 136-137.   [14] *Prim. Cult.*, II, 132, 144.

material objects." A fetish is the abode, permanent or temporary, of a possessing spirit. Amulets, charms, and talismans are familiar illustrations.

Historically the word is a contribution from the Portuguese; *feitiço,* the original of *fetish, fetiche, feticcio,* and other European forms, means something fabricated (*facticium*) or *factitious.* It was applied to amulets. When the early Portuguese navigators, who were the first of Europeans to encounter blacks in their native habitat, saw them apparently worshipping more or less roughly shaped images, this term was the only one which they had available to apply to such objects.[15] Along the west-central coast of Africa the term is now used in a broader sense than the one current in scientific writings, to cover the general religious ideas and systems of the natives.[16]

When fetishes were first described and discussed, they were regarded as the product of the attribution of life to inorganic objects. This misapprehension was exposed by Spencer,[17] who saw in the fetish an indwelling spirit which was, in origin at least, the ghost of a dead man. Lippert[18] carried forward the idea of possession by the ghosts of the dead and regarded fetishism as a definite application of the ghost-theory; he cites the case of the Botocudos who along with neglect of their dead also recognize no fetishes. We do not follow Lippert in his belief that fetishes are so predominantly ghost-possessed objects but think that fetishism rises from possession by a daimon or even an anima, that is, directly out of daimonism or even animism. As eidolism is not a necessary transition from animism to daimonism,[19] though it is the regular one, so is it not the sole source of fetishism, however important a function it may be shown to discharge in this connection. In the case of many fetishes—amulets and spells, for example—it is impossible to maintain that they are always or often what they are by reason of being possessed by ghosts of dead men. The daimon as well as the ghost enters to possess things and men; and there are instances in which, as it seems, the soul of a living being extends itself beyond the body with which it is identified and lends spiritual quality to some external object.

15 Jevons, *Religion,* 166; Oliveira Martins, *Raças,* II, 93; Trilles, *Fân,* 624-625; Tiele, *Gchte. Relig.,* 7, note; D'Alviella, *Concep. God,* 39, 91, 108-110, 113; Wilken, *Vkde.,* 547.

16 Kingsley, *W. Afr. Studies,* 113.   17 *Prin. Soc.,* I, §§160 ff.

18 *Kgchte.,* II, 363-365, 367, 369, 373, 378, 380, 390, 391, 439.

19 §238, above.

"It is extremely difficult," writes Tylor,[20] "to draw a distinct line of separation between the two prevailing sets of ideas relating to spiritual action through what we call inanimate objects. Theoretically we can distinguish the notion of the object acting as it were by the will and force of its own proper soul or spirit, from the notion of some foreign spirit entering its substance or acting on it from without, and so using it as a body or instrument. But in practice these conceptions blend almost inextricably." The following extracts will enable the reader to form some conception of the difficulty referred to by Tylor; it is one that is always encountered in dealing with the products of the evolutionary process.

The Papuan concept *imunu* is discussed by Williams:[21] It cannot be said "that the real *imunu* is something immaterial, and the concrete object merely an earthly tenement for it. It would, indeed, be nearer the mark in most cases to say that the concrete object is essentially *imunu* in itself, but that it has an '*a'avaia*'—soul, spirit, shadow, or immaterial replica, however it be called— which can leave the body just as a man's *a'avaia* can leave his body in dreams." Thus the fetish-concept is regarded as very close to that of the soul of a thing. "The only fair and satisfactory way of dealing with the *imunu* concept would be to enumerate all the applications of the word"—that is, not to try to classify or explain at all; the same counsel of despair would have negatived all effort to understand the physical world around us. The author goes on to say, very aptly, that "if asked 'what is an *imunu?*' a native informant is, of course, completely nonplussed, but, pointing to this and that—and a perplexingly varied assortment of things they may be—he will say 'This is *imunu.*' . . . Such objects are queer or mysterious or secret; they are holy in the sense that they are unapproachable or untouchable; they have some kind of potency for good or evil; they are treasured with the utmost care; age seems to add to the mana [virtue] of them. . . . Anything which a native dreads for the harm it may do him, and fears because of its strangeness, and cajoles for its favours, and fondly treasures for its old associations, he will tell you is *imunu.*" Connected with this holiness-conception is the *kaiemunu,* a sort of image with a spirit in it, associated with "an individual of a certain species (usually fish, sometimes crocodile, rarely pig or snake). This fish, which is a giant among its kind—very ancient, and immortal or indestructible—is the *imunu-vii,* or 'canoe of the *imunu';* it will transport the *a'avaia* of the *kaiemunu* hither and thither. . . . This group observes a food tabu of the species to which its *imunu-vii* belongs, and professes that it would refrain from killing any member of that species. The *imunu-vii* itself would certainly be spared by a hunter or fisherman; indeed, it would be of no use to attack it. . . . Whatever may have been its origin, the *kaiemunu* is now regarded as a definitely personal being. . . . It is greatly feared and venerated; no one but certain old chiefs would dare to touch it as it stands in the *ravi-oru* [a sort of shrine]. It is continually placated with food offerings. . . . It is the very heart and the great secret of their religious life. . . . As a matter of course, the *kaiemunu* will be renewed—destroyed and re-created—when they have reached a very advanced stage of dilapidation." This fetish-figure controls success in the hunt and has to be periodically re-invigorated by ceremonies. We have here a set of ideas whose members run all the way from the soul in things to the possessed image.

---

[20] *Prim. Cult.*, II, 153.   [21] In JAI, LIII, 363, 364, 366.

The Fijian *kalou* "means nothing more or less than 'the dead'; it stands for a concept which runs unchanged through the whole of Melanesia, though many and various are the verbal forms it assumes. . . . The multitude of words for one idea requires some technical term: I suggest *manes*." This is the conception covered by our word "eidolon." The author[22] now goes on to explain how these manes come to be embodied in things. "I have never yet come across a coastal Fijian who identified the deity with the animal or spoke of it as turning into an animal; the expression is always that the *kalou* is 'embodied' . . . or 'envesseled' . . . in it or enters it; . . . both these terms are applied also to the 'priest' who is possessed by a spirit; in fact, when I have asked 'what is the "body" or "vessel" of so and so?' I have generally been told the name of the priest."

"First of all, the fetish, in itself, is nothing, whatever it is, whether statuette or any object, stone or tree, skull or some bone: it is something only if it is 'influenced,' inhabited by a spirit, depositary of some mysterious force. Consequently before its consecration, as after its execration, the fetish is nothing. The crude wooden statue which the native shapes for the European, the fetish itself which has done service but which, once sold to the white man for his museums or collections, has no further religious value, is not, correctly speaking, a fetish at all. It has been or can be. The spirit has not yet appeared in it or the mysterious influence exists no longer; in this condition it is, for the black man, an object of indifference. . . . Fetishism is then an ensemble of religious ideas and practices which includes at the same time the cult of the dead, the ghosts, the ancestors, the superior and inferior spirits of the invisible world, and, in fine, of the occult and mysterious forces of nature which do not belong to the range of these various entities but may or may not be manifestations of them."[23] This means that any of these religious ideas and practices may take form in a fetish or be put into operation in connection with one.

Wilken[24] holds that "in fetishism the spirit is wholly identified with the object in which it is housed, is not distinguished from it, so that it is really the object which is worshipped as a possessed and powerful being. . . . Many Javanese assert very succinctly and definitely that they reverence no trees, rivers, mountains, but the . . . spirit that lives in them." Others make no such fine distinctions and justify their worship by the question: "How would it be with us if there were no water, wood, and the like?"

The foregoing cases will have illustrated the complex character of fetishism and its various interrelations with other religious phenomena. What stands out from the discussion so far is that there is no warrant for confusing fetishism with animism, eidolism, or daimonism; it is, indeed, a sort of application of all three, but there is no reason for allowing theory and application to become entangled. The nature of soul, ghost, and spirit has been surveyed; either one of the three may enter to possess some object, inanimate

22 Hocart, in JAI, XLII, 448-449.
23 Trilles, *Fân*, 625-626, 627, 629-630, 633.
24 In VG, III, 132, 232.

or animate; then fetishism has to do with the phenomena and results of such possession. In the interest of lucidity there is considerable advantage in fixing attention first upon possession by the
ghost, as creative and explanatory of the fetish. The daimon being
derived from the ghost, daimon-possession is really a sort of developed ghost-possession and would be expected to show, and does
show, much the same phenomena—just as the daimon-cult echoes
the forms and ceremonies of the ghost-cult.[25] Lippert,[26] in center-
ing his treatment of fetishism about ghost-possession, has developed the topic with remarkable suggestiveness, and in what follows
we shall freely adopt and adapt from his presentation. Fetishism
as the result of ghost-possession rests upon the conception, sufficiently illustrated above,[27] of the continued presence of the eidolon
on earth. It is true that, with the easy inconsistency of the savage
the ghost may be conceived as still present, even after he has been
despatched, deliberately and with due ceremony and precaution,
to the spirit-world. It is the fact of his presence, not how he got
back, that is of interest here. If he has returned—or has never
gone at all—where is he to be looked for? Of course, in the neighborhood of his body. He returns to his own. What was his becomes
then a fetish. It is significant of the connection of fetishism with
eidolism that certain of the most unmistakable fetishes are objects
which contain or are in proximity to the dead body.

Among the objects which become fetishes through their connection with souls
of the dead the grave stands first. The grave-fetish is so obvious and remains,
as a survival, so firmly embedded in tradition that it calls for no extended
illustration. We refer, as productive of special cases of grave-fetishism, to the
foundation-sacrifice,[28] where a person is immured, dead or alive, in masonry
that his soul may watch over the structure. For instance, Polyxena is represented as having been slain at the tomb of Achilles, that her ghost might attend
upon it.[29] "Beneath the fetishes of the grave and the dead lay no mere animism. In them comparative ethnography may recognize true relics of certain
ancient forms of soul-cultus."[30]

An extension of the grave-fetish is found in the cave, mountain-top,[31] body
of water, or tree within or upon which the dead are commonly disposed. The
cave, for example, often had been the dwelling of the dead man, now conse-

25 §263, below.   26 Kgchte., II, 362 ff.
27 §§216, 217, above.   28 §294, below.
29 Euripides, Trojan Women, 622-623.   30 Krauss, Südslaven, 133.

31 Cayley-Webster, New Guinea, 186; Macdonald, in JAI, XXII, 120; Prjevalski's Forskningsresor, 242, note, 319; Roth, Sarawak, I, 185; Mitra, in
JASB, III, 254; Weston, in JAI, XXVI, 30; Smith, Relig. Sem., 457.

crated to him by his burial in it.[32] By survivalistic usage the sepulcher may still resemble a cave. Caves and holes have been the seat of a cultus and the source of oracles; for into them the ancestors have gone, in them the great ghost is supposed to dwell, and out of them the tribe in question is conceived to have issued. For peoples who inter the dead, the earth appears as a fetish, representing the abode or even the person of the oldest ghost and remotest ancestress (Chthonism): Gē-mētēr, Demeter, Tellus Mater, Mother Earth are something more than poetic personifications. Heaven-worship (Uranism) is then not so far away.[33] Accessories of the grave, such as stones, especially if shaped into images of the dead, and trees planted upon or near it become possessed by the local ghost. In general, and without further anticipation of examples—for the cases now being cited by way of preliminary illustration will be taken up in detail farther on—the grave together with its precincts forms a set of fetishes pervaded by the spirit of the dead.[34] The burial-center may even become a community-center, as in the Naga village where the whole road along which the houses stretch "was strewn with stones erected to the dead, on which their descendants sat in the evening and drank their rice-beer."[35] What looks like a parallel custom appears in the Homeric assembly, where the elders sat on the "polished stones."[36]

Further, the spirit of the dead was thought to enter and possess any being which should devour the deserted body. This is really a variety of the grave-fetish. Lippert[37] cites the vultures of Tibet which, as they soar into the sky, are supposed to be carrying the ghosts to heaven, the dogs of the Parsees, the fly among the Lapps—noting that the fly was regarded by the Christian Romans of the Middle Ages as an evil spirit. The fire-fetish has been referred to above.[38] The fetish-quality of choice animals or special types of animals[39] may have its origin, in part, in the intimacy of ownership.

It is easily possible to connect with the dead all these things and many others of their type, thus explaining the reverence and worship accorded them; but fetishism has plainly a daimonic as well as an eidolistic origin. Possession is the prerogative of higher beings, as well as of ghosts. The sacred Kaaba stone at Mecca or those of Shechem and Bethel[40] were fetishes, their indwelling spirits being full-fledged gods. Such cases do not lend themselves to an explanation on the basis of eidolism as distinguished from daimonism except under considerable strain and rather deviously. The burning bush, the sacred book, the inspired man, the infallible

[32] §250, below.

[33] Lippert, Kgchte., II, 425 ff.; Spencer, Prin. Soc., I, ch. XV.

[34] Lippert, Kgchte., II, 364, 367, 369, 373, 380, 391, 439.

[35] Godden, in JAI, XXVII, 19.

[36] Keller, Hom. Soc., 168, 169 (full references to text); Lippert, Kgchte., II, 147, 371.

[37] Kgchte., II, 390, 391.　　　[38] §92, above.

[39] §256, below; Lippert, Kgchte., II, 378, 390.

[40] §254, below; Lippert, Kgchte., II, 373.

crowd whose voice is that of God, are genuine fetishes; they are nothing in themselves, as bush, book, man, or multitude; they are taken to be possessed, genuinely enough, by an indwelling spirit that is more than a ghost. Possession is the essence of fetishism, however tenuous or unidentifiable the possessing agency. And so, whatever our idea of the nature of possession in its beginning, we are presently led far away from the simple notion of the indwelling spirits being the released souls of the dead. The idea of possession by ghost or daimon as the basic belief in fetishism represents an advance in clearness and comprehensibility over certain other conceptions. When Ratzel[41] writes that fetish-worship is probably a degenerate form of ancestor-worship, as the worship of images among civilized peoples overgrows a spiritual religion, he emits an easy generality that says little. Fetishism thus envisaged can stand in no very vital relation with the other phases of societal evolution. If, however, the ideas underlying fetishism are shown to be those of eidolism and daimonism, then we have a genetic connection and the mind that seeks for orderly sequences in evolution is at rest.

Fetishism is no "superstition" in the true sense[42] and deserves none of the contempt or ridicule often cast upon it.

It is said of one Dr. Duff "that he was once examining an Indian School, and, wishing to ridicule this idea of animal incarnation, said to the boys: 'Can any boy tell me whether it is likely that God's spirit would associate itself with a snail?' No one answered for some time; at last an intelligent lad said: 'I think He might condescend to do so, if any useful purpose were to be served thereby for the good of His creatures.' 'Then,' said Dr. Duff, 'you think as a fool.' "[43]

The domineering intolerance of the discomfited doctor is evident enough to any person of sense, yet it is more than matched by the attitude of many ostensibly enlightened people regarding certain cardinal and basic conceptions of primitive, and so of all, religion. Such tenets as those of fetishism are inevitable in their time; they are the rough blocks of crude belief about the unknown and inexplicable out of which later developed systems have evolved through the process of correction and refinement. Many of the "symbols"[44] of a more advanced stage are but survivals, somewhat adapted and

41 *Vkde.*, I, 181; Wilken, *Vkde.*, 546, 547.
42 §199, above.
43 Monier-Williams, *Brāhmanism*, 316.   44 §456, below.

rationalized, of primitive fetishism. Consider the pilgrimages to the graves of eminent and revered men, even in modern times.

§248*. Types of Fetishes. In a review of the cases there seems no point in seeking to distinguish ghost-possession from daimon-possession, though illustration will stress the former, as it is much less familiar than the latter. Evidently inanimate things are subject to possession as well as animate, and a beginning may be made with them; for the present, brief illustration is confined to objects in nature which are somehow, like the caves and mountain-tops already alluded to, repositories of ghosts and spirits.[45] Since magic is commonly worked by means of fetishes, the chapter[46] on that subject will contain many examples of the fetish.

It may be paradoxical to speak of a rock-fetish as inanimate, for possession puts life into it; but the possible paradox will mislead nobody.

In Melanesia certain spirits that are not ghosts (*Vuis*) are generally associated with stones, less commonly with snakes, owls, and sharks. "It is not that the stone is a *Vui*, or that a *Vui* is in the stone, but that there is such a connection between the *Vui* and the stone that the stone is the spirit's outward part or organ." These spirits can be readily propitiated but are jealous of neglect. The really malignant spirits are the ghosts of men; to them the natives look for spite and evil. However, there are stones near which an accident has happened, whose *Vuis* are thought to have a turn for mischief.[47] Here enters the persistent preoccupation with the aleatory element.

In North Celebes there are a number of holy stones; Wilken[48] relates a legend to account for the sacred quality of one of them. Whoever goes by it must not disturb the quiet of the place and must uncover his head; sacrifices are made to the stone on occasions of epidemics and other calamities, by some descendant of the legendary person connected with it. Stones that look like deformed animals are also holy. "It is plain that in all these cases it is the ghost of a man or an animal that is worshipped, not, however, by itself, but as identified with the stone. These stones are therefore true fetishes." The author mentions thunder-stones and bezoar-stones; the latter are found in unexpected places, such as in the insides of animals and even plants, and are regularly perfumed with incense, while the former are often old flint implements supposed to be teeth of the ox that causes the thunder. Old sacred pots are likewise fetishes; one of them brought seven hundred pounds and for another two thousand were offered in vain. Even the broken pieces of these vessels were valued at twenty-five gulden, or ten dollars. Among the inanimate fetishes are mountains and bodies of water; further, there is the heaven-fetish and that of the earth; meteorological conceptions become more definitely personalized in

[45] Cases in Spencer, *Prin. Soc.*, I, chs. XXI-XXIV.
[46] Ch. XXXVII, below.
[47] Codrington, in JAI, X, 275.   [48] In VG, III, 152 ff., 170 ff.

the monsoon-regions where irregularity means calamity. Imitative magic is employed to procure the fruitfulness of the union of heaven and earth, and there is a sacramental ceremony to the same end. Here are cases of the direct influence of physical environment on forms of religious belief.

Fire, water, precious stones, and many other natural elements may come, through possession, to be fetishes of great significance. That fire may become a fetish in a country where cremation is practised can be easily understood; then fire-worship on the Persian lines is not far off. Fire is a prominent fetish in the Bible, as in the cases of the pillar of fire, Sinai, the burning bush, and the tongues of flame.[49] Lippert[50] thinks that the sea and rivers became fetishes from the custom of throwing corpses into them: instance, not to mention the Ganges, the Scamander, Inachus, Asopus, Kephissos, and Peneus. Thus the river might ultimately become a daimon, as Father Tiber was a king and a god.

In animate nature the tree-fetish figures extensively;[51] trees in which receptacles for the dead were lodged and those planted over graves have been regarded as the abodes of ghosts. "Tree-worship is spread throughout Africa; in general it is asserted that spirits dwell in them. . . . The dead are laid away in the woods."[52] Particularly is this true of trees which have provided the ancestors with nourishment, though their fruits may no longer be used; thus the sycamore and oak became fetishes and the souls of those gone before were supposed to lodge in their branches. They might rustle in prophecy—not of themselves, it is understood, but under the control of the spirits. Thus arises the idea of a "tree of life," tabooed because of the holy character of its fruit. The "apple" (a sort of generic name for the tabooed fruit), says Gubernatis,[53] "has come to be considered in all the Oriental traditions as a symbol of seduction"; and he mentions Eve, Atalanta, and also Athena and Hera who, in the case of the Judgment of Paris, departed so widely from their matronly and virginal austerity, as its victims. The Norse sagas speak of the golden "apples which the gods must taste whensoever they grow old, and then they all become young."[54] The lotus, again, was a fetish-plant.

[49] Lippert, *Kgchte.*, II, 382, 429.
[50] *Kgchte.*, II, 423-424; Martin, in *Bijd.*, XXXV, 33, 34, 43.
[51] Lippert, *Kgchte.*, II, 380 ff.
[52] Frobenius, *Masken*, 163, 164; Chowbe, in JASB, V, 227, 228; Fawcett, "Festivals," in JASB, II, 264 ff.; Justi, *Persien*, 82; Smith, *Chinese Char.*, 290; Krauss, *Südslaven*, 36.
[53] *Usi Nuz.*, 105.   [54] Brodeur, *Prose Edda*, 39.

In New Guinea, pigs are killed slowly for the mango-tree, so that its spirit can enjoy the sacrifice the more; pigs are sacred to that tree.[55] The Africans in general attach legends and superstitions to big trees, some tribes claiming to be descended from them. The dead are buried and assemblies held beneath them. Good spirits are said to dwell in their branches.[56] In the Kilimanjaro region large trees are found in numerous groves carefully preserved from injury. These are believed to be the abodes of spirits and when a thunderstorm comes up the spirits are thought to be passing from one grove to another.[57] Among the Beduins, if one plucked a bough from a tree growing on a grave or in the vicinity of former burial-grounds, he would be caught away into the air or lose his mind. The sick are brought to sleep under such trees or undergrowth after a sacrifice has been made, the blood sprinkled on the ground, and a piece of meat fastened to a branch. During sleep a spirit, it is hoped, will come down and reveal to the sick person how to recover health.[58] Classical stories[59] of souls in trees and bushes will occur to the reader. Wilken[60] speaks of trees of gigantic size or strangely shaped, which become fetishes, mentioning one the trunk of which, where clear, was over thirty feet in diameter. The fig-tree was especially sacred, and no one would cut down a sandalwood; Sumba, with many sandalwood trees, exports hardly any wood. Stones are thrown about certain trees until they are nearly buried; everyone contributes his stone as he passes by. There is much plant-worship, which is now interpreted as worship of the soul in the plant. The ghosts of the dead live in certain trees. When cutting them down apologies and excuses are offered, such as that the foreign "preacher" ordered the cutting, which was against the will of the natives. Ill luck comes to the village if the trees suffer and they try to shift it upon the foreigner. Cowan[61] tells a story about an enchanted tree. Some Europeans split up a log from such a tree and in the course of operations a man was knocked into the water. Said an Irishman present: "Sure and the divil's in the tree!" This delighted the Maori, as a real miracle. Another daring devil split up a sacred tree and later suffered from locomotor ataxia; the Maoris knew it was a case of aggravated tapu.

There is enough evidence concerning the fetish-quality of animals[62] which eat or are supposed to eat the flesh of men to warrant the inference, without at all ignoring transmigration,[63] that connection with the ghost is at least one of the prime reasons for that quality. Since the soul is supposed to inhere in certain parts of the body,[64] it can be incorporated by another being through eating the body or some of its parts. In particular do those animals become fetishes which "bury" the dead by eating them; and it is characteristic of the fetish-animal that its flesh is tabooed as food.

[55] Haddon, in JAI, L, 248.
[56] Ratzel, *Vkde.*, I, 177, 179.
[57] Abbott, in USNM, 1891, 395.
[58] Doughty, *Arabia Deserta*, I, 449.
[59] Virgil, *Æneid*, III, 37 ff.
[60] In VG, III, 162-165, 218 ff.
[61] *Maoris*, 131, 133.
[62] §99, above.
[63] §211, above; Wilken, in VG, III, 165 ff.
[64] §213, above.

It is not meant to say, it will be recalled, that all animal or other fetishes become such through connection with the bodies of the dead; a snake, for example, by reason of its habits, may suggest the presence within it of the spirit of a dead man;[65] but it is evident that connection with the dead body and particularly the eating of the dead provide evidence for one of the simplest conclusions which the savage can draw. The taboo upon the eating of fetish-animals[66] naturally follows.

"Living sacred objects in the Solomon Islands are chiefly sharks, alligators, snakes, bonitos, and frigate birds. Snakes which haunt a sacred place are themselves sacred, as belonging to or serving as the embodiment of the ghost; there was one in Savo, to look upon which caused death. . . . Sharks are in all these islands very often thought to be the abode of ghosts, as men will before their death announce that they will appear as sharks, and afterwards any shark remarkable for size or colour which is observed to haunt a certain shore or rock is taken to be some one's ghost, and the name of the deceased is given to it. . . . A lizard seen to frequent a house after a death was taken to be the ghost returning to his old home." Among certain other Melanesians who tabooed the eel there was great reverence for one particular eel "so large that it was thought to be a *tindalo,* the abode or representative of some one dead; no one would bathe in that stream or drink from it, except one pool in its course which for convenience was not considered sacred."[67] In this quotation are to be noted the special fetish-character of the extraordinary individual; and also the fact that considerations of exigency may modify the taboo.

In West Africa the crocodile, snake, leopard, fish, shark, and a species of iguana are fetish-animals, as also are the anthropoid apes and some monkeys[68] —the latter because of their likeness to men and not because they prey upon human bodies. In Uganda, in addition to holy and tutelary snakes there are spotted hyænas which are tolerated because they are the living sepulchers of dead relations whose corpses have been placed at the outskirts of the settlements for the hyænas to devour at night.[69] "The snakes which are found, generally by pairs, in and before the Galla abodes, are not regarded as vermin; they are rather the protecting spirits of the family."[70] "None of the tribes of South East Africa catch fish. It is unclean and belongs to the category of reptiles, which are shunned and abhorred."[71] In Central Africa, "a man who loses a relation by drowning takes an oath that he will never again eat fish, and never drink water from such lake, river, etc. Here the idea is of course simply to avoid eating part of the relation."[72] Similarly, in New Zealand, "the ban of *tapu* is frequently applied to rivers, lakes, or other waters in which people have been drowned. After the wreck of the steamer 'Wairarapa' at the

[65] Lippert, *Kgchte.,* II, 403 ff.   [66] §§260, 271, below.

[67] Codrington, *Melanesians,* 178-179, 180, 177, 151.

[68] Ellis, *Ewe,* 49, 57, 58, 74; Frobenius, *Masken,* 193; Kingsley, *W. Afr. Studies,* 483, 489, 490, 515, 576.

[69] Johnston, *Uganda,* II, 19, 832.

[70] Paulitschke, *Nordost-Afr.,* I, 134, II, 24.

[71] Macdonald, in JAI, XIX, 282.   [72] Stannus, in JAI, XL, 323.

Great Barrier Island, in 1894, with the loss of a hundred and twenty-five lives, the Maoris of that island, who live in a bay a few miles from the scene of the wreck, tapu'd all fish within a certain area for a long period. During this time of interdiction no native would eat or touch any food of the salt sea."[73] The Kaffirs deduce good and bad luck in life from the souls of the dead, especially of dead chiefs. Oracles are sought at the grave, which is a fetish. And the connection of snakes with the souls of the departed is very widespread in East Africa.[74] In South Africa ghosts appear under manifold animal-forms, "but in this they choose by preference that of snakes, and if a snake shows himself in the dwelling, the Kaffir sees in this the home-seeking of a dead person, and fears by killing it to draw down on himself the vengeance of this person."[75] The people of Madagascar have, among other fabulous animals, one with seven heads, in the form of a worm, snake, or squirrel, and identified with maggots in the corpse of a noble.[76]

The topic of fetishism links on to many that have preceded but scarcely anywhere more closely than to the idea of transmigration or reincarnation.[77] Any animal into which the soul of an ancestor has been reborn is in an unmistakable sense a fetish. This allows of a universalizing of the fetish-idea not otherwise possible and affords a basis for the development of totemism, presently to be considered. It tends to the identification of fetish-species rather than fetish-individuals. Fetishes resulting from reincarnation may not be corpse-devouring species, but there are a good many instances where they have, or are accredited with displaying, that propensity.

For instance, in Tikopia Island, in Melanesia, "all the sacred beings are called atua and many of them are clearly the ghosts of ancestors. . . . The animal atua of the social divisions are clearly sacred beings. Atua are said to enter into fishes, suggesting that an animal may be only the embodiment of an atua. . . . When the people go for journeys in their canoes they throw food as an offering into the sea continually but it was said that these offerings are made to ancestral atua which enter into fish, especially the shark." There is a regular sacrifice to ancestral spirits at their graves.[78] The Masai think "that some of their more notable ancestors return to earth in the shape of snakes—either pythons or cobras." These snakes must be black because they themselves are; they live in a half-tamed state near the villages. "When a Masai marries, his wife has to be introduced to the tutelary snake of the clan and rigorously ordered to recognize it and never to harm it."[79] The "habit of worshipping a snake, alleged to be a god, whenever floods devastate China, appears to be a general one."[80] Animal-fetishes are common among Malays primarily because the souls of the dead are supposed to go into them. The tiger is a prominent

[73] Cowan, Maoris, 117.
[75] Fritsch, Eingeb. S. Afr., 106.
[77] §211, above.
[79] Johnston, Uganda, II, 832.

[74] Ratzel, Vkde., I, 174.
[76] Ratzel, Vkde., II, 521.
[78] Rivers, Melan. Soc., I, 315-316.
[80] Smith, Chinese Char., 297.

fetish and so is the crocodile. Many villages in Java have a tiger which they feed, and sacrifices are offered to crocodiles.[81] "The Eskimo believe that the souls of the dead can take up their abode in different animals, objects, mountains, and the like, from which they can issue from time to time. Hence there dwells in every natural object a being called its Inua, that is, its owner, the same word which means human being or Eskimo. Each passion or sentiment is also said to have its Inua."[82] This idea affords a connection between eidolism and the conception of a "virtue" (*mana, uhgen*)[83] in persons and things, which does not at first sight show relation with anything so concrete as eidolism but is likely to be regarded as poetical or metaphysical, indicating the "innate human perception of personality," or of the spiritual, or what not.

The snake is regarded as a fetish in India, where the annual loss of life and property due to unmolested cobras and other species is very great.[84] Injuring them would bring on leprosy, sterility, or ophthalmia and they are allowed to crawl about dwellings and drive people from their food.[85] The serpent figures in the Bible and among the Phœnicians as the agency of temptation and is raised, in effigy, to cure disease.[86] The Greek soul might go abroad in serpent-form.[87] Reverence for serpents was marked among Mayas of Yucatan[88] and among the Lithuanians and Prussians, who kept snakes under the hearth or in a corner of the smoke-house where the eating-table stood.[89] The prominent rôle played by the rattle-snake in the Moki Indians' life is well-known through popular descriptions of the Snake Dance.[90] In the picture-writing of the Sioux and Algonquins, the mystery-line (a wave-like line running down from the rattle-snake's head) is used to mark out animals, men, and even inanimate things which have the character of being inexplicable, supernatural, or holy.[91] It might be the sign for the aleatory element. The eel-fetish is encountered again in Ponapé; it is thought to enclose an ancestral spirit and the islanders flee at the sight of it.[92] Pueblo boys must not kill a rattle-snake but Pima boys may if they do not use the same arrow again; they may not kill, though they tease, the Gila monster and the horned toad.[93]

Among the ancient Persians the fly was the corpse-ghost which took possession of the unsouled body immediately after death.[94] The Parsee thought the fly the evil spirit of the northern tribes and the ancient epics represent it as assailing the dying. The vanquisher of the fly is the dog of a certain breed; by devouring the body, he saves the soul from the evil fly-spirit and thus becomes a fetish of the first order.[95] The dying Persian attained peace by seeing before

[81] Ratzel, *Vkde.*, II, 470; Perelaer, *Dajaks*, 6-7.

[82] Nansen, *Esk. Life*, 225.   [83] §258, below.

[84] Bourdeau, *Monde Animale*, 115.

[85] Thurston, *So. India*, 285, 286, 287, 288, 292; Monier-Williams, *Brāhman ism*, 320, 322; Schmidt, *Ceylon*, 290-291.

[86] Numbers, ch. XXI; Pietschmann, *Phön.*, 227-228.

[87] Rohde, *Psyche*, I, 159-163, 244-245.

[88] Le Plongeon, in PSM, XLIV, 661.

[89] Nehring, in *Globus*, LXXIII, 65-66; Stieda, in *Globus*, LXXV, 160.

[90] Account by Fewkes, in BAE, XIX, pt. II, 963 ff.; Nadaillac, *Preh. Amer.*, 126, 343.

[91] Mallery, in BAE, X, 462.   [92] Pereiro, *Ponapé*, 132-133.

[93] Russell, in BAE, XXVI, 192.   [94] Geiger, *Ostiran. Kultur*, 161.

[95] Lippert, *Kgchte.*, I, 496; II, 392.

him a dog, presumably the one which was to eat his flesh, at any rate a symbol of a desirable destiny. The case of the dog-fetish is rather complex; it has been touched upon above and will be alluded to again.[96]

§249*. The Exuvial Fetish. Thus, despite the fact that the ghost may have been expedited off to the spirit-world, enough of him remains with his corpse to make fetishes out of animals that incorporate into their own organisms even part of his discarded vesture of mortality. In considering the location of the soul[97] it has been found that that essence may reside during life in some special part or organ of the body. It may persist, further, in any fragment, after its removal or after death. In any case the portion thus disconnected is believed to have spiritual qualities and properties not of itself but by reason of its relation to the spirit of the whole organism or personality to which it has been attached.[98] Such *exuviæ*, or "strippings," are outlying, dispensable, or discarded portions of the body such as skin, hair, blood, or excreta. Their fetishistic quality is attested by their regular employment in magic[99] to produce effects of a supernatural order. If a sorcerer can get hold of a man's exuviæ he has a grip upon the spirit of the man himself. Even dust from his footprint can be used.[100]

It is clear that while a person is still alive his soul inheres in such exuviæ, whether they have been removed or not. Having some of his soul in them, they are plainly fetishes. Here is a case of fetishism derived directly from animism, for the soul does not need to be disembodied by death in order to enter the exuviæ. And not only that: virtue or personality is conceived also to exhale from a living person into things intimately connected with him but not parts of his body at all. Such objects, represented in the following examples by the "churinga" and the "medicine," are plainly not eidolistic fetishes; nor are they mere amulets, for they are more intimately, solemnly, and ceremonially tied up with the destiny of their possessors than is the typical talisman. Though it is difficult to place them exactly, they come nearer to falling under the cate-

96 *Case-Book*, §99 and §256, below.   97 §213, above.
98 Lippert, *Kgchte.*, II, 384 ff.   99 §300, below.
100 Hildburgh, in JAI, 160, 165.

gory of exuvial fetishes than under any other. We call them personal fetishes.

A chief in Togoland had a fetish-nail on his little finger: "This nail was the object of painful attention and must not be broken off, because if it were, according to the popular belief, a misfortune would occur to the owner. The finger-nail is said also to play an important rôle in the so-called fetish-drinking, because under it was often hidden the deadly poison that was to be thrown by the fetish priest, unseen, into the drinking-vessel" from which the unsuspecting victim was about to drink.[101] Allowing the nails to grow to incredible lengths is a vanity-practice but there is often something of fetishism also in the custom,[102] when it is a symbol of holiness.

The Indians of South America ascribe magical value to hair, nails, teeth, and claws, attributing their new growth, when cut, to superior power. Therefore those parts, when sound, can transfer such power to those who get them.[103] The parent gathers up a tuft of hair from the crown of the child's head, ties, and cuts it off, and lays it away in a case kept by the priest as a sacred thing.[104] In Korea the top-knot means nationality, antiquity with the sanctity derived from it, and entrance upon manhood; while marriage and ancestral worship are intimately bound up with it. The author quoted[105] goes into considerable detail concerning its significance.

In Uganda the naval-cord of a prince is dried, set with pearls, and hung up on a post. A man is set to guard it.[106] Among the Somal the navel-strand is carefully kept, sewed up in leather, "and passes for an amulet for camel-mares which then become the property of the child together with all the young which they bear."[107] In the Congo region, "the afterbirth is always buried, but the umbilical cord is hung in a plantain tree, and the fruit, when matured, is cut down and cooked with fish to make a feast for any friends and neighbours who care to partake of it. This plantain is called . . . the umbilical cord plantain . . . and the original idea underlying the feast was that the cord imparted certain properties to the plantain that made them a counteractant to sterility. There was much sterility."[108] Catlin[109] writes of a similar practice among the Indians. "In the little toy . . . which is suspended before the child's face, is carefully and superstitiously preserved the umbilicus, which is always secured at the time of its birth, and, being rolled into a little wad the size of a pea, and dried, it is inclosed in the center of this little bag and placed before the child's face, as its protector and its security for 'good luck' and 'long life.' " In Borneo, the cord is preserved in a small bamboo, together with the implements used in the puncturing of the ears and the severing of the cord. These are the beginning of a collection "which later comes to include everything of much import in the life of the Kayan, and which is hidden, after his death, under the roof and there left, under taboo, to its fate."[110] In the Pelew Islands, "the dried navel-strand is most carefully preserved by the mother."[111]

[101] Klose, *Togo*, 229.
[102] Tylor, *Anth.*, 97, 240, 241.
[103] Von Martius, *Beiträge*, 649.
[104] Fletcher, in JAI, XXVII, 441.
[105] Bishop, *Korea*, 359 ff.
[106] Stuhlmann, *Mit Emin*, 184, 588.
[107] Paulitschke, *Nordost-Afr.*, I, 192.
[108] Weeks, in JAI, XL, 419-420.
[109] *North Amer. Indians*, II, 133.
[110] Nieuwenhuis, *Borneo*, I, 64.
[111] Kubary, *Pelauer*, 55.

In Japan, the corpse was put in a jar; and just before the jar was closed, a mourning woman put into it a bit of the umbilical cord of the deceased.[112]

The following pair of cases illustrative of the personal fetish show it to be almost a repository of the owner's soul. There is a distinct shade of difference between such a conception and that of a familiar spirit or of a charm into which some outside spirit has been inducted. We wish to indicate this distinction at this juncture, though the general topic of "medicine" is to be treated under magic.[113] It seems to us quite as important to call attention to the interfusing of categories as to delimit them in the first place.

The Australian term "churinga" is applied to various objects associated with the totems, but of these "the greater number belong to that class of rounded, oval or elongated flattened stones and slabs of wood of various sizes, to the smaller ones of which the name bull-roarer is commonly applied." No woman or uninitiated man may see them. "The one point in which all the various articles agree, to which the name of Churinga is applied, is this—they are all in some way associated with individual men, women, plants, or animals of the Alcheringa [antiquity] and at the present time are strictly tabu to women. . . . The native tradition is that when a spirit-child goes inside a woman[114] the Churinga is dropped." It is, perhaps, a sort of *alter ego*. When the child is born the mother discloses the position of the tree or rock near to which she supposes the child to have entered her and a search is made for the churinga; if it is a stone, it is supposed to be marked by a device peculiar to the totem of the spirit-child and so of the newly-born. It is very likely a stone from the sacred storehouse with which the finder—most often the paternal grandfather—has provided himself. The animals associated with the location in which the churinga is found are tabooed to the child in question; the spot was the home of the spirit whose reincarnation he is. The storehouse of the churingas is often a cave, the immediate environs of which are a refuge for wild animals. Even plants in the immediate vicinity are never touched or interfered with in any way. Plainly, this churinga-idea is shot through with possession and fetishism. The churinga is supposed to endow the possessor with courage and accuracy of aim, and also to deprive his opponent of these qualities. So firm is the belief in this that, if two men were fighting and one of them knew that the other carried a churinga while he did not, he would lose heart at once and without doubt be beaten.[115]

One of the closest of personal fetishes is a man's "medicine." Medicine, as the Indians use the term, means "mystery," and is generally associated at once with magic. Each man has his mystery peculiar to himself; it is sacrificed to and is identified with his medicine-bag.[116] "The value of the medicine-bag to the Indian is beyond all price; for to sell it or give it away would subject him to such signal disgrace in his tribe that he could never rise above it; and,

112 Humbert, *Japan*, 285.   113 §300, below.
114 §§260, 334, below.
115 Spencer and Gillen, *Nat. Tr. Cent. Aust.*, 128, 130, 132, 134, 136, 156.
116 Lewis and Clark, *Travels*, I, 189, 190.

again, his superstition would stand in the way of any such disposition of it, for he considers it the gift of the Great Spirit. An Indian carries his medicine-bag into battle, and trusts to it for his protection, and if he loses it thus when fighting ever so bravely for his country, he suffers a disgrace scarcely less than that which occurs in case he sells or gives it away; his enemy carries it off— and displays it to his own people as a trophy, whilst the loser is cut short of the respect that is due to the other young men of his tribe, and forever subjected to the degrading epithet of 'a man without medicine,' or 'he who has lost his medicine,' until he can replace it again, which can only be done by rushing into battle and plundering one from an enemy whom he slays with his own hand. This done his medicine is restored, and he is reinstated again in the estimation of his tribe, and even higher than before, for such is called the best of medicine, or 'medicine honorable.'" Even though an Indian is induced to relinquish his medicine, it cannot be bought; "the Indian in such case will bury it to please a white man and save it from his sacrilegious touch, and he will linger around the spot and at regular times visit it and pay it his devotions as long as he lives." When the owner of the medicine-bag dies, it is placed in his grave and decays with his body. Such a bag may come to possess a higher degree of fetishistic potency: "When the medicine-bag is carried on a war party it is never allowed to touch the ground. Also among the Ojibwa some of the bags which are considered to have the greatest fetishistic power are not kept in the lodges, as too dangerous, but are suspended from trees."[117]

Anything that is closely associated with a person becomes imbued with his personality. The name seems to us to be rather a part of the soul than a personal fetish; yet it is a thing "to conjure with," and conjuring is done with fetishes, especially with human exuviæ.[118] The Roman word-play *nomen-numen* brings the name into conjunction with "divine essence." The king's characteristic paraphernalia, to which allusion has already been made, stand for him and possess a certain "virtue" thereby;[119] neither they nor the insignia of supreme ecclesiastical office are merely symbols, certainly not if they have, in the course of transmission across the generations, been handled by a long line of "God's anointed."

In Ashanti there is a royal stool which "is said to be about four hundred years old, and is so patched and mended with gold wire and gold plates, that the original woodwork is hardly visible. A new sovereign is not regarded as king until he has taken his seat on this stool." They speak of "The Stool," or "The Cap" as Europeans of "The Throne," meaning the royal power.[120] In East Africa, on certain occasions, the historic spears and royal ancestral

[117] Donaldson, in *Smithson. Rep.*, 1895, pt. II, 393-394; Mallery, in BAE, X, 502.

[118] §§212, above, and 299, 300, below.

[119] Lippert, *Kgchte.*, II, 385-387, 503; Keller, *Hom. Soc.*, 167, 255, 260.

[120] §120, above; Ellis, *Tshi*, 264.

stones are exhibited, being entrusted to the care of the king's mother or chief wife. No uncircumcized person may sacrifice at these stones or even touch them. "The king's mother is a most important personage—and possesses great influence over the king in his domestic affairs and in tribal matters. She exacts large contributions in money and in kind from the king . . . and is, in consequence, reported to be enormously rich. Should these contributions not be forthcoming, she threatens to make use of the power vested in her by virtue of her custody of the sacred spears; a threat that rarely fails to have the desired effect."[121] In the East Indies there are certain ancestral heritages that are reverenced as fetishes, especially the crown-ornaments. They are kept in a house-shaped chest and publicly produced once a year. The contents of the chest are perfumed with smoke from odoriferous gums and washed with water and rice-flour by the sacred man. At an exhibition of them the natives, "not even daring to look upon those miraculous relics, fell prostrate, with their foreheads pressed to the earth, exclaiming: 'Dowlet! dowlet!' . . . To this day, it is firmly credited by many of the Malays, that the elder brother of Abdul Syed was rejected from the Panghuluship solely on account of his inability to get his head through the neck of the vest, which is represented to be so small as scarcely to admit of the insertion of two fingers." Among the Macassars and Buginese, every prince has a number of such ornaments, and on their possession rests his authority. At every attempt to depose a ruler, the effort is made to lay hand on these ornaments, and if success attends, it means that he loses all power. These political fetishes consist of spears, krisses, a gun, a shield, an umbrella, a sirih-box and cuspidor, and other valuables. Of a similar nature were the European "Roland" or "Mal" columns, often decorated with the local ruler's glove or other characteristic property, and marking the community-center.[122]

It is conceded that the personal fetish, which is animistic, is less convincingly possessed than are the physical exuviæ, especially those of the dead; but they certainly fall at least upon the borders of our definition. Perhaps the most readily recognized of exuvial fetishes is the relic. This is some part of the body, often a bone, and is plainly of eidolistic origin; and if it is thought to have exhibited virtue and proved its power, it attains to unquestioned sanctity. The fact that certain bones asserted to be those of a saint have turned out to be part of the skeleton of a sheep has affected their reputation in no respect.[123] Among savages the relic is commonly a part of the skeleton, though it may be a composite collection of parts.

A piece of flesh is usually cut from the thigh or stomach of the dead persons. "The author once witnessed the burial of a very small and thin man, at which

121 Dundas, K. R., in JAI, XLIII, 30.

122 Wilken, in VG, III, 134–135, 138–139; Lippert, *Kgchte.*, II, 379; "Kl. Nachrichten," in *Globus*, XC, 227.

123 White, *Sci. and Theol.*, II, 29.

there was a discussion, as to which should be done. It was finally decided to take some hair from his head. . . . The piece of flesh from the dead body is taken to camp, and having been sun-dried, is cut into small pieces and distributed among the relatives and friends." These pieces are used as charms; from contact with them strength and courage are derived; and they may be cast into a river "to bring a flood or fish when both are wanted."[124] "A tooth, a lock of hair, a nail, or a bone is enough, in order to attach the dead to one's service."[125] The family-fetish, in one part of West Africa, "is a bundle of parts of the bodies of their dead. From time to time, as their relatives die, the first joints of their fingers and toes, especially including their nails, a small clipping from a lobe of the ear, and perhaps snippings of hair are added to it. But the chief constituents are the finger ends." They sacredly preserve "a bundle of toes, fingers, or other bones, nail clippings, eyes, brains, etc, accumulated from deceased members of successive generations."[126]

As the treatment of the skull is typical, further illustration is limited to the skull-fetish. It is often decorated, especially by painting, and is assigned a position of honor in the house or community. It is noteworthy that the skulls of persons of distinction receive honor where ordinary individuals are passed over as incapable of endowing a relic with sufficient power to make it effective. Here again, of course, we encounter the topic of head-hunting.[127]

The exhumation, drying, and preservation of skulls is common in Melanesia; in general they are those of well-to-do relations.[128] Sometimes it is the lower jaw-bone that is retained. In the Solomon Islands the bones of persons of distinction are gathered and kept—those of the chief in a coffin of shark-shape, in the tamboo- [taboo] house; here is "the devil of the natives, to whom they offer the first fruits of the season."[129]

"Like all the rest of the peoples of the earth, the Africans practise a sort of cult of relics which extends now to hair, nails, teeth, bones, and especially to the skull. People conceive that the dead expresses himself through these ruins of his body. The most important distinction between such a primitive conception and, for example, a developed Catholic conception, is that what in the former case appears natural and self-evident, in the latter is designated as supernatural and miraculous. Moreover, the conception of the nature-people is more intensive."[130] In a battle with the Ashantis, in 1826, "a head, wrapped in a silk handkerchief, and covered with a leopard-skin, the emblem of royalty, was captured. This was the head of the late king . . . and his successor had brought it with him, in the idea that he would thereby be able to obtain the support of the ghostly king against his enemies. Before the battle offerings were made to it, and the ghost was invoked to cause the heads of all the white

[124] Bonney, in JAI, XIII, 134.   [125] Frobenius, *Masken*, 162.

[126] Nassau, *Fetichism*, 159.   [127] §§229, above and 294, below.

[128] Finsch, *Ethnol. Erfahr.*, I, 114, 143; II, 18; Andree, *Eth. Parallelen*, 150.

[129] Elton, in JAI, XVII, 97.   [130] Frobenius, *Masken*, 176, 177.

men in the field to lie beside his before night."[131] In Uganda the under-jaw of a skull taken on the occasion of the former chief's death is ornamented with pearls and hung over the grave, and in important crises the king causes it to be brought to him.[132]

"The custom of using skulls as holy vessels, or even as eating bowls, is a very old one in Asia," and still persists. Out of skull-bowls was ceremonially drunk the nectar called "devil's juice" and Buddhist monks were forbidden to use them as alms-bowls because they had been the utensils of devil-worshippers.[133] The Malay Archipelago is the classic ground for head-hunting and skull-preservation; the skull serves various purposes but in general "its soul functions as a protecting spirit" over its possessors.[134] Wilken[135] is on his own heath in treating of this topic. He starts off with a description of such fetishes as old cannons, royal regalia, and amulets; then reverts to the head or skull. It provides a grave-escort, carrying its owner to the spirit-world to serve the dead man to whose spirit it is offered; then, too, it becomes a favoring spirit to the tribe that secured it from an enemy. It is treated with reverence and confers health and fecundity. The enemy's ghost is so propitiated in the skull that it will have no resentment. Thus "snatched" skulls become protective fetishes; a case is cited of a Dyak who lost all he had by fire and who mourned most bitterly over the loss of his collection of skulls. This honor of skulls as protective fetishes extends all over the Archipelago; it is paralleled by the reverence for other relics; Perelaer[136] tells how the body of a steamer-captain was cut into very small pieces and distributed among the people along the Barito River. To revert to Wilken, we learn that head-snatching was practised on the occasion of a marriage; in this case it was done in part as a test of the man, who must secure such a trophy to prove his capacity. The practice is intimately connected with ancestor-worship, for it was often the skull of a father or remoter forbear which constituted the best protection. If a skull is an amulet or talisman, a collection of them means power, as well as demonstrated courage. The author cites a number of cases where skulls were thought to have brought luck, thus bringing the custom into line as an adjustment to the aleatory element.

Furness[137] describes at length certain Bornean ceremonies connected with the loan of holy skull; and the whole picture is one of sustained and absorbed reverence. "No laugh, no jest, no light word broke the reverence of what all felt to be a holy act"—one which ended the mourning-taboo for a dead chief. Thereafter the men's locks, unshorn during the period, were trimmed, the fallen hair gathered, rolled into a ball, vigorously spat upon, and cast far from the house; and the women were sprinkled with water. The whole setting reveals the presence of a powerful fetish. The basic idea of the Dyaks is to win a spirit for the clan. The souls of those whose heads are taken become slaves in the other world; in this world the killer gets the soul of his victim as his fetish. It is the skull.[138] The head and its attachments come in for the most

[131] Ellis, *Yoruba*, 281.   [132] Stuhlmann, *Mit Emin*, 38, 186.

[133] Rockhill, in USNM, 1893, 741, 742.

[134] Wilken, *Vkde.*, 394.

[135] In VG, III, 138-150, 222; IV ("Schedelvereering"), 42 ff.; also "Haaropfer," in III.

[136] *Dajaks*, 168.

[137] *Head-Hunters*, 89, 91-93.   [138] Bock, *Borneo*, 92.

attention. A bit of the cheek-skin of a brave enemy's head is sometimes eaten as a charm to induce fearlessness and the hair is used as an ornament for sword-hilts and sheathes. As for the preserved skull, "if the jaws drop, they fasten them up, and if the real teeth fall out, or if they extract them, they fill the cavities with imitation ones of wood. They put studs in the eye sockets, but do not carve the skull, as do the Kyans. The nostrils are generally plugged with wooden stoppers. Everything is done to propitiate the head; food is put into its mouth, betel nut is prepared for it, and even a cigarette; it is implored to remain among them and to induce its friends to come that way and keep it company."[139]

It is striking to find many of these ideas paralleled in the New World. Thus, among the Jibaro Indians of Ecuador, who make much of the production of shrunken human heads (*tsantsa*), "a curious idea appears in the *tsantsa* feast, in that the victor himself on the one hand is believed to be in danger from the spirit of the killed enemy, but on the other hand, on account of his having gained possession of the enemy's head, is invested with a special mysterious power. Moreover, he is able to transfer this power by contact to other persons and to things. This explains why the victor must . . . assist, for instance, at the brewing of the manioc wine for the feast and at the preparation of the sacred drink. . . . Similarly, something of his power is transferred to his wife and daughter and may, through them, become effective in agriculture and in other departments of life."[140] The Caribs divided the cleansed and painted bones of their dead among the relatives, and if the settlement was given up, they were taken along. Decoration of the skull with parrot-feathers, each feather being dipped in pitch, indicated the respect accorded.[141] Herodotus[142] reports that the Issedones, of what is now southeastern Russia, cleaned and gilded the skulls of relatives—not enemies—and kept them as objects of annual sacrifice, whereas the Taurians thought that by having an enemy's skull they could force him to guard and to give warning.

It is scarcely necessary to refer to the prominence of relics in mediæval times. Different shrines boasted the possession of a tear of Christ, parts of his body, milk of the Holy Virgin, flesh of Paul. Many navels of God were to be encountered here and there, and the multiplied exuviæ of saints. A part of the hole in which the Cross stood was shown. Disputes, to modern taste quite unseemly, were waged over the nature and identification of relics.[143]

While upon this subject of head-hunting and the skull-fetish, we wish to emphasize the fact that practices of this sort, highly

[139] Roth, in JAI, XXII, 59; Ratzel, *Vkde.*, II, 466.

[140] Karsten, "Jibaro," in BAE, Bull. LXXIX, 89; §229, above.

[141] Schomburgk, *Brit. Guiana*, II, 431-432; Von den Steinen, *Zent. Bras.*, 508.

[142] *Hist.*, IV, 26.

[143] Bastian, *Deut. Exped.*, II, 136, 141, note; Hoensbroech, *Papstthum*, I, 254; White, *Sci. and Theol.*, index, *sub* "Relics."

repellent and even bloodthirsty and wicked as they may seem to the cultured taste, are carried through by savages in a religious mood quite comparable to the most reverential attitude of the pious adherent of any evolved faith. One should read the whole account given by Furness[144] and alluded to among the cases. Head-hunting is to the Malay an attested prosperity-policy, the regular and traditional way to attain well-being and success. His legends teach him that it was revealed to his ancestors from on high, and that after they had been taught by a benevolent deity to practise it, the boats went well, the people who were left at home ill speedily recovered health when an expedition returned with heads, and in all other respects the custom acted as an unmixed blessing to society. Faith in it is as pure as the confidence of any saintly person in similar interpositions of divine providence with which he is by tradition conversant, and is correlative with conduct no less considerate and kindly than that of a Buddhist, Mohammedan, or Christian. Candid study of codes of mores divergent from one's own issues in an enlarged tolerance for those who practise them, and even to an appreciation of the essential sincerity of uncivilized mankind in living up to the light as they see it.

§250*. The House-Fetish. The ghost being thought to haunt the region of the grave, generally for an extended period, the grave thus became a fetish. The Ainos, who give no thought to the departed, seem to dread visiting graves; on the other hand, the grave may readily become an object of pilgrimage.[145] This tenet of eidolism is now to be carried forward to several of its derived forms. First it should be noted that the custom is widespread of locating the grave within the house.[146]

The Andamanese father digs his child's grave "with an adze in the place where his hut-fire usually burns."[147] In New Britain "the grave is usually dug in the house inhabited by the deceased when alive" and "a fire is often lighted upon it or near by, which is kept burning for a considerable time."[148] The dead man is buried "near or even under his hut" in New Guinea; "a less important

144 *Head-Hunters,* 58 ff.; §294, below.
145 Hitchcock, in USNM, 1890, 466; Von Götzen, *Durch Afr.,* 83.
146 §222, above; cases in Rose, in JAI, LII, 128 ff.
147 Man, in JAI, XII, 141.   148 Danks, in JAI, XXI, 349.

man is buried in his own house. . . . The women must now go on living in the house and carry on their domestic life upon the fresh grave."[149]

In South Africa house-burial is practised, but after the ceremony the house is closed and abandoned.[150] The Kaffirs' "burial places are frequently in cattle folds. Sometimes in huts where persons have died."[151] In West Africa, "the dead are always buried in the earthen floor of the house, which, after the interment, is always smoothed down with water." Sometimes this grave is so contrived "that the head of the deceased may project beyond the line of the outer wall of the house." The exact position of the grave is obliterated.[152] In Uganda the chief is buried in his own hut only temporarily, awaiting a later and greater ceremony at the sacred burial-place, which is a grove at the top of a hill. The ordinary man is buried in the middle of his house which is not used afterward. A child is buried near the door of its mother's hut.[153] It is an honor to be buried in one's dwelling.[154] The old man is buried in the house, the young outside; a man killed by lightning is not to be buried within; a big man is buried within and the house deserted; a mother just outside or where her son will later build; a young man in his mother's house. A water-pot is thrown out and broken as a corpse is put into the house-grave.[155] In some tribes only the married are so buried and strong protest, resting upon some obscure belief, is raised against any attempt to bury the unmarried children. They are exposed.[156] The Mangbattu chief is buried in a new hut.[157]

The Chinese buried the dead of the higher classes in the house for a time, the descendants retiring into mourning-sheds.[158] Again, there may be a paper soul-house set up in the hall of the ancestors, to serve along with a tablet as a preliminary abode for the soul. Later on, house and tablet are burned and the ashes preserved for two years. Then the name of the dead, if he was prominent, is engraved on the ancestor-tablet; if not, a little portion of the ashes is placed in the censer-pot before that tablet.[159] In Micronesia the dead are generally buried in the house of a near relative.[160] In the Gilbert Islands, "the grave was generally dug in the floor of the house, though sometimes it was outside; its depth was about 18 inches, or at most, 2 feet. . . . A dear relation of the deceased would make a bed of the grave, and open it from time to time to look on the loved remains—or to appropriate a bone or two for the manufacture of the family fish-hooks, thatching tools, and other useful things. The skull was very often removed and, after being carefully cleaned in sea water, was wrapped in a mat of fine mesh and preserved in a box of pandanus wood. The widow or child of the deceased would sleep and eat beside this reliquary, carry it about in all excursions, and anoint the skull frequently with

[149] Von Pfeil, *Südsee,* 80, 317; Finsch, *Ethnol. Erfahr.,* II, 113, 336; Hagen, *Papua's,* 260, 261; Semon, *Aust. Bush,* 330.

[150] §222, above; "Review of Decle," in JAI, XXIII, 420.

[151] Tyler, in *Ill. Afr.,* Dec., 1895.

[152] Ellis, *Ewe,* 158; Ellis, *Yoruba,* 158.

[153] Johnston, *Uganda,* II, 632, 715-716, 748-749.

[154] Fabry, in *Globus,* XCI, 198.

[155] Thomas, in JAI, XLVII, 166, 169, 171, 179, 187, 189, 209; and in JAI, L, *passim.*

[156] Volkens, *Kilimandscharo,* 252-253.   [157] Burrows, *Pigmies,* 104.

[158] DeGroot, *Relig. Syst.,* II, 479.   [159] Rehatsek, in JASB, I, 328.

[160] Finsch, *Ethnol. Erfahr.,* III, 46.

coco-nut oil."[161] These practices connect the grave with the relic and show it to be a sort of altar. In the Nauru Islands, "the dead are buried in the huts, in the ground, and a near relative of the deceased sleeps upon the place."[162]

In America also house-burial is found. The Navahos bury within the hut, which is then torn down and deserted.[163] In Tennessee graves of children were found under the hard clay floors of ancient huts; this seemed to be the regular location of children's graves.[164] "In former times the Indians used to abandon a house after one died in it, because they buried the body either in the house or at the back of it, and were very much afraid of seeing the ghost of the dear departed."[165] In northern Costa Rica the most striking objects in a dwelling-place "are the graves that are found inside." These are surrounded by a frame that nobody may tread on them. The local Indians "believe that the dead man can do miracles and so pursue a sort of ancestor-cult with the grave, which is for them a holy place."[166] The Paressi of Brazil bury the dead in the house,[167] and Von Martius[168] lists a number of Brazilian and Guiana tribes who do the same, remarking in one connection that this custom, so widespread, "without doubt belongs to the numerous maladjustments which increase the mortality of the Indians." The Botocudo hut, after such burial, is, "as it were, vacated for the dead man." The custom is aligned with similar practice in Canada.[169] The Lenguas of Paraguay buried a man where he died, in his hut or elsewhere, and left the place.[170]

Rohde[171] speaks of "the memory of an earliest time when the dead man was laid away in the interior of his house, the immediate site of his cult."

These cases admit of two interpretations, neither of which will explain them all: that the dead were buried in the house because that was where they had lived; or that the house was a provision for the dead and a sacrifice to them. In any case the ghost was supposed to remain in or about the house; even the custom of abandonment shows that. The house, abandoned or not, became a fetish by reason of the presence.

§251*. Hearth- and Altar-Fetishes. House-burial not followed by abandonment leaves the ghost a frequenter of the house as he is of the grave and its environs. Ghosts thus harbored in the vicinity of men are conceived to be, as the objects of a regular propitiatory cult, reconciled and even benevolent. They are usually ancestral spirits who retain an interest in the welfare of the

[161] Grimble, in JAI, LI, 46-47.   [162] Brandeis, in *Globus*, XCI, 77.

[163] Yarrow, in BAE, I, 123.   [164] Yarrow, in BAE, I, 116.

[165] Le Plongeon, in PSM, XLIV.   [166] Sapper, in *Globus*, LXXVI, 350.

[167] Von den Steinen, *Zent. Bras.*, 434.

[168] *Beiträge*, I, 440, 621, 632, 648, 598 (quoted), 326 (quoted); Wied, *Brasilien*, II, 56.

[169] Spix and Martius, *Travels*, 250, 1238.

[170] Koch, in *Globus*, LXXVIII, 220.   [171] *Psyche*, I, 228.

family, if for no other reasons, then for their own sake. The place
of such a ghost is in the house and at its central point, the fire or
hearth, even though the body may not have been buried exactly
there; and to the hearth must be added, as a fetish-place in the
house, the door or threshold, for here too the body was sometimes
buried. A variety of customs witness to the sanctity of these spots,
particularly of the hearth. It is a true fetish and is traditionally
the habitation of the ancestral ghosts. In connection with the
hearth-fetish the various beliefs about the spiritual quality of
fire[172] should be recalled.

The kotla is the hearth-place and sacred spot of the Bechuanas as the hearth
was to the Romans; "no one may enter the kotla with his shoes on."[173] Among
the Baganda, there are two fireplaces in the hut, about which centers the most
rigid etiquette. No one but near relatives may go beyond the first one which is
near the door. It would be a great breach of good manners to sit at the second
which is near the center of the hut. Even the husbands of the owner's daughters or his son's wives are not allowed at the innermost fireplace. The sacrifice
of a goat is required to atone for transgression of these taboos; and all the
inhabitants of the house must then wear small pieces of the victim's skin.[174]
The hearth-region is sacred among the Galla also, especially the base of the
tripod, one stone of which, as the genius of the house, so to speak, is never
moved from its place. If removed by chance, the priest must proceed to a new
dedication and resetting of the stone.[175] A location in the house is set aside
for the dead, by the Alfurs; children must not play near it and care must be
taken in all ways to do it honor.[176] In Borneo, it is needful to get a head
"wherewith to decorate the grave or the household hearth," in order to lay
the ghost. At the Eskimo feast to the dead, the shades of those recently deceased come on invitation from their graves and "assemble in the fire pit,
under the floor."[177]

Among the southern Chinese "the hearth-gods or goddesses occupy an important position in every house." There is no quarreling near the hearth or
burning of paper with writing on it. These hearth-spirits report deaths in the
family to the chief spirit, and that this may be done in a way favorable to
the survivors much bribery, through burning of money, is necessary.[178] Similarly in Japan are the house-divinities lodged;[179] the spirits of the dead "hover
nightly in the glow of the shrine-lamp." The Japanese warrior may not have
fought *pro aris et focis,* like the Roman, but the ancestral spirits had their
seat in the center of his home. Among the ancient Greeks the central hearth
was the abode of the ghosts. In Homer the hearth was a sanctuary. He who as
a suppliant took his seat by the hearth, thus placing himself under the protection of the spirits there located, was safe from harm. Oaths were taken by the

[172] §§90, 92, above.   [173] Starcke, *Prim. Fam.,* 58.
[174] Johnston, *Uganda,* II, 732.
[175] Paulitschke, *Nordost-Afr.,* I, 146.   [176] Wilken, in VG, III, 211.
[177] Nelson, in BAE, XVIII, pt. I, 363-364.
[178] Rehatsek, in JASB, I, 319-320.   [179] Hearn, *Japan,* 51, 53, 59, 169.

hearth and sacrifice performed there. The threshold too was a sort of sanctuary for the suppliant.[180] The name of the goddess Hestia (Vesta) means "hearth." Among the Romans the sentiment about the hearth was very strong, as indicated by the phrase *pro aris et focis,* quoted above.

In Russia "the hearth is a holy spot and the fire divine; no one may step on the hearth." Such belief is widespread through all classes, and transgression is sin. Taboos include the prohibition of sitting down on a threshold of a door.[181] Before their removal from the ancient Scandinavian house the dead were carried three times about the hearth; and similarly did the wedding-procession appear before the seat of the spirits.[182] The old German house-spirits had a special relation to the hearth, from beneath which they often emerged and where the door of their subterranean dwelling seems to have been.[183] The Germans said: "The hel is open," where the Romans said: *Mundus patet.*[184]

Other examples of this veneration for the hearth are listed in another place.[185] The other fetish-spot in the house, the threshold, demands a word on its own account. Burial sometimes took place near the door; among the Nagas it is customary to bury in the village-street, close to the doors of the houses.[186] The custom is widespread of treating the threshold with special reverence: only the chief of highest rank may sit on the temple-threshold; no one treads on the threshold of a sacred place, persons of rank striding over it and others crossing on hands and knees. The same form is observed in passing the threshold of a chief.[187] The threshold-spirit is found among the ancient Hebrews:[188] the bride is lifted over the threshold of her new home,[189] and at the door the Hebrew slave has his ear pierced. The threshold is an important place in jural relations: on it the tenant places the rent if the lord refuses it; at it the man is summoned to the village assembly-court; he who seeks stolen goods puts three marks on it before he goes in and if he finds nothing he must pay a fine for the dishonor inflicted; at the threshold is the guest received or the stranger refused entrance. It is a symbol of home. To set foot on it is to take possession. A parishioner swears at the church-threshold, the

[180] Keller, *Hom. Soc.,* 168 (where full references to the text are cited); Lippert, *Kgchte.,* II, 191, 367.

[181] Stern, *Russland,* 96.

[182] §§371, 372, below; Lund, *Norges Hist.,* II, 25.

[183] Grimm, *Deut. Mythol.,* I, 468.   [184] Lippert, *Kgchte.,* II, 191.

[185] §§90 ff., above.

[186] Woodthorpe, in JAI, XI, 72 (discussion by Col. Godwin-Austen.).

[187] Gomme, *Village Life,* 80.

[188] Duhm, *Geister,* 7 (quoting I Sam., V, 5; Zeph., I, 9).

[189] §371, below.

church being everyone's home. He who in swearing sets foot on a house-threshold, invokes homelessness,[190] and by analogy oath-taking on the church-threshold invokes religious outlawry.

Other "spirit-places" are to be found in the house, for example, behind the head of the bed, as in Micronesia; in this case no one dares look in that direction but at the beginning of a meal throws a fragment of food over his shoulder to the spirits. If he has a pain he holds the fragment first, with his left hand, against the spot.[191] Among the Yakuts the hitching-posts are consecrated and the fate of the household is thought to be connected with them, they are invoked in imprecation and blessing; and when the family moves they are often dug up and taken along.[192] Again, the Russian ikon-shelf affords a retreat for the ancestral ghosts. When, however, all the various fetish-haunts in the house are surveyed, it is clear that the fire and hearth represent the predominant spiritual center.

As the worship of indwelling domestic spirits proceeds, the hearth becomes the altar and the house the temple. In general any meal is a sacrifice and any sacrifice involves eating,[193] the cooking-place being also the scene of the burnt offering, that is, the seat of the domestic cult. The altar is later differentiated and becomes the center of the daimon's special house or temple just as the hearth is the "focus" of domestic life; its sanctity, one might say, then infects the temple and its environs, the temple-grounds, and at length the property administered for the daimon by his priests. This is the possession of the "dead hand" or *mortmain*, in no metaphorical sense, for it is not merely given but dedicated as to the dead; it is to be devoted, under sanction of anathema, to the service of the deity.[194]

Fawcett[195] thinks that if more evidence were needed to support the Spencerian theory[196] "that the temple originated out of a sheltering structure for the dead (where it did not arise out of house-burial), it would be found in the Saora country." Hocart,[197] whose chief thesis is that the meaning of the Fijian word *kalou*, taken by many to mean the gods, is simply the dead—who thus sees as

[190] Jørgensen, in *Annaler,* 1876, 159.
[191] Finsch, *Ethnol. Erfahr.,* III, 140.
[192] Sieroshevski, *Yakuts* (Russ.), 262.   [193] §230, above.
[194] Maitland, *Domesday Book,* 242; Lippert, *Kgchte.,* II, 597.
[195] In JASB, I, 249.   [196] *Prin. Soc.,* I, ch. XIX.
[197] In JAI, XLII, 447-448.

eidolism what others have regarded as daimonism—finds much evidence in mortuary customs. "If any doubt survives as to the meaning of *kalou,* a study of temples and graves should finish it. The resemblance between a modern Fijian grave and the foundation of a house is hard to overlook. In Lau they both consist of long mounds, prevented from crumbling away by a border of rounded stones piled up or of slabs planted in the ground; chiefs' graves, like chiefs' houses, are higher. . . . It was the custom in heathen times to erect a small 'movable house' . . . consisting of a roof erected on a rectangle of four beams, so that the whole could be lifted up in order to weed the mound, and weeding was sometimes an act of propitiation." One traveller "came to an old graveyard, and noticed that the fence round it also enclosed a large native house. Here it was that the father of the present Tui Thakau was murdered and his wife strangled at the funeral. They were buried in the house, which was then abandoned and rendered *tambu* to all Fijians." "It is not proposed to derive the temple from the grave, but both from a common original, to wit, the dwelling-house, or more especially the 'hall.' . . . The men of Mbukuya regularly buried people in houses. The tribe of Yalantini . . . also buried in houses; if they selected for the purpose the foundations of an abandoned house they built up the whole again to 'cover over so and so that the rain and sun might not reach him,' and the new house was used as a dwelling. This seems decisive enough, and we can confidently affirm that in Eastern Fiji graves are degenerate houses of common people, and temples the exalted halls of chiefs."

Thus the fetish-quality of the shrine, as well as of other sacred structures and places, is derived ultimately from eidolistic beliefs.

§252*. The "Word." What has been said in life by the illustrious dead partakes of the fetish-quality characteristic of the relic; it may, indeed, be considered as in a very true and non-metaphorical sense an actual relic. Primitive people are always quoting their culture-heroes, the godlike men of old. Even with us the sayings of many a person, superior or mediocre, take on an added weight when he is dead, whether or not he has been duly canonized. The spirit of the "inspired" speaker abides in his words; they are the fetish-emissions of a fetish-man, and they must not be altered in any detail, at peril; for they are ritualized.[198] Consider the reverence accorded to the opinions of Aristotle: his statements, from the thirteenth to the eighteenth century were not tested by observation even of the most familiar objects; no one noted even the error of assigning eight legs to a fly instead of six.[199] The "authority" of Homer, Plato, Cicero, and other writers of antiquity has been the object of durable defer-

198 §§214, above, and 257, 258, 259, 279, below.
199 Weismann, *Evol. Theory,* I, 12.

ence.[200] In modern times the tendency continues; Americans are adjured from childhood to hold to the wisdom of the inspired Fathers of the Republic, even when their pronouncements are wholly out of date. The quoting of a great name will doubtless continue for many ages, while the critical faculty is further developing, to be deemed the equivalent of scientific proof.

If the reader objects that the reverence paid to the sayings of extraordinary men seems like fetishism only in case we make a sort of metaphorical extension of the term, and that such reverence simply reveals a "fetish-making tendency," we are not disposed to take serious issue with him. Such cases represent vaguer manifestations of fetishism, shading away somewhat from the literalness of definition. Even if there were here no more than a fetish-making tendency, that too belongs with fetishism. The word has had through the ages and still has, to the unsophisticated mind, a spirit within it. It has meant much in magic. Consider the repeated use of the rune in the Scandinavian sagas. All spirits bend before the word that is the name of God; it has been closely connected with deity and has even been identified as god. "In the beginning was the Word, and the Word was with God, and the Word was God."[201]

What is said by the hero, or by his familiar spirit or "genius," is inspired and is not open to discussion. It becomes a doctrine, dogma, or "eternal principle." We go counter to it when we have to, in order to adjust to changed life-conditions, but we re-interpret it as we go and refuse to admit that it is changed. "Doctrines are the most frightful tyrants to which men ever are subject, because doctrines get inside a man's own reason and betray him against himself. Civilized men have done their fiercest fighting for doctrines. The reconquest of the Holy Sepulcher, 'balance of power,' 'no universal dominion,' 'trade follows the flag,' 'he who holds the land will hold the sea,' 'the throne and the altar,' the revolution, the faith—these are the things for which men have given their lives."[202] There is fetish, or what the Indians would

200 Ridgeway, in JAI, XXXIX, 18; this author inveighs against the classical fetish.
201 §301, below; Lehmann, *Overtro*, I, 50; II, 34; Goethe, *Faust*, I, 1224-1237.
202 Sumner, *Coll. Ess.*, I, 36.

call "big medicine," in a doctrine, especially if it has been enunciated by a deceased hero.

The authority of the word is indefinitely strengthened by the apotheosis of him who has uttered it. The word then becomes the scripture and the law and a fetish of the first order. There is an assumption, says Maine,[203] that "sacred or inspired literature being once believed to exist, all knowledge is contained in it. The Hindu way of putting it was, and is, not simply that the Scripture is true, but that everything which is true is contained in the Scripture." Speaking of the rigid dogmatism formerly based upon literal readings from Jewish and Christian scripture, White[204] writes: "The most careful inductions from ascertained facts were regarded as wretchedly fallible when compared with any view of nature whatever given or even hinted at in any poem, chronicle, code, apologue, myth, legend, allegory, letter, or discourse of any sort which had happened to be preserved in the literature which had come to be held as sacred."

Plainly any such view about a body of tradition lends to it a fetish-character. To votaries there may thus be, contrary to all strictly human experience, an infallible Word as there is an infallible Man. And if this Word is literally true and perfect in whole and in every part, as it must be if it is a supernatural revelation, it becomes a sin even to harbor reservations. All sacred books are fetishes in the sense of our definition; the cruder aspects of this attitude appear when they are employed for purposes of prophecy or divination, as the ignorant would use a dream-book or other magic manual. Throwing the Bible open at random with the idea of chancing upon a verse which would lend supernatural counsel at a crisis of life or fortune is an exhibition of fetishism quite comparable to any out of primitive life; taking oath upon the book by kissing it or otherwise is, as an example of fetishism, quite the counterpart of swearing upon the relics of a martyr or upon a piece of the "True Cross." Much of this may now be survivalistic but its origin is unmistakable, like that of many another piece of ritual which is practised in ignorance of its former meaning. Religion is the more likely to reveal such survivals by reason of its essentially conservative character, for finality and complete-

203 *Early Law*, 17.   204 *Sci. and Theol.*, I, 376.

ness of original revelation do not go with adjustability to changed conditions. Religious ritual, in all places and times, has been full of the supernaturally "inspired," that is, of fetishism.

§253*. The Image. The derivation of the word "fetish"[205] indicates an artifact with a religious significance, that is, in common parlance, an idol. It was noted also that this artifact was never worshipped for itself, as a mere piece of wood or stone, but for the spirit conceived to be indwelling within it. The fetishes hitherto considered have been, one might say, of a sort of primary intention. Nobody set out to make them fetishes; they became such artlessly by reason of some association with the ghosts or the daimons. There are also images fashioned by hand into which spirits are variously and artfully inducted. These art-fetishes are numberless; we propose to treat them only sufficiently to show their position under the general head of fetishism and we think that that can be done by confining our examples mainly to those which exhibit the induction of the spirit into the image.

The very making of an image seems to exercise a compulsion upon the spirit in question to occupy or possess it. This is not so surprising when one recalls the close connection of the person with any simulacrum of him or the compulsive power of imitative magic.[206] There must often take place, however, a ceremony of invitation or induction before the image can be anything more than a material thing.

A Maori chief's signature is given by Cowan;[207] it is a full representation of his facial tattoo-pattern, very intricate, and was supposed to carry his personality. It was a sort of image of the living, a kind of projection of his soul. In Bowditch Island, "a representation of the dead person was often tattooed on the upper part of the chests of near relatives. The present king has four such figures on his chest."[208] Here is no mention of induction; the likeness is enough to secure the influence of the ghost. Among the Hindus, on the other hand, "when the image is completed it is taken to the house where it is to be worshipped, and at an auspicious moment the priest . . . goes through an interesting ceremony called the giving of life, . . . by which he invites the deity to reside in it for one, two or three days. Prior to this the image is regarded as ordinary mud . . . and any one may even touch it with impunity; but the mere repetition of certain magical words is supposed to change all this. . . . After this it would be regarded as profanation for any one except a

[205] §247, above.
[207] *Maoris*, 194.

[206] §§210, above and 302, below.
[208] Lister, in JAI, XXI, 55.

Hindu to approach the image, or for any one but a Brahman to touch it."[209]
A ruder case is where the West African, intent upon obtaining a tutelary
deity, cuts out a rude wooden effigy of a human figure, slays a fowl and otherwise prepares sacrifice, and then calls upon the spirit to enter the figure. "According to most natives he then picks certain leaves, the juice of which he
squeezes upon the object, saying, 'eat this and speak.' Then, if a spirit has
entered the object . . . a low hissing noise is heard." This fetish enables the
owner to procure the death of other people, insures against fire, accidents, and
other ills.[210] Certain African fetishes, "like many symbols used by Christians,
are not deities, but have the powers and blessings of the deities they represent,
and are able to confer boons on the possessors; through them also the deities
are approached." As for the native, "should misfortune attend him or the
jembe fail to protect him, his faith is not shattered, he attributes the failure
to stronger power working against him, or to magic which changed the normal
course of events and caused failure in a particular case, or he may have forfeited his right to help through some inadvertence or slight to the deity."[211]
There is never anything the matter with the faith; the cure for any situation is
simply more faith. Siberian "representations of gods and fetishes are made of
wood, metal, or bone. They are usually very rude in form, and now that these
people can obtain children's dolls very cheaply from Russian traders they are
ceasing to make their own fetishes."[212] Among the Koryak a small figure of
a man, called a "searching guardian" is sewed to the coats of little children, to
guard their souls. "Children particularly are subject to attacks by evil spirits,
and the children's inexperienced souls are apt to be frightened and to leave
the body. On the 'searching guardian' devolves the duty of catching the child's
soul and of restoring it to its place."[213]

In China no image is supposed to be properly an object of worship until
the spirit has been inaugurated into it by the prescribed ceremonies."[214] In the
Malay Archipelago, images are in common and constant use as mediums.
There is an image of the dead which is made directly after death and burial;
when made, the errant soul, which is round about somewhere, is driven into the
image by making "an infernal noise." If the image does not make good, it is
thrown to the ground and discarded as having no strength—as being, so to
speak, like a defective battery. Rice-kernels are scattered before the image
when it is desired to consult the dead; the sacrifice to the recently dead, whose
images are still preserved, takes place indoors, while that to those long dead,
whose images are gone, is an outdoor ceremony. Pots are used in the same
way as images and become great fetishes. Such fetishes may be conceived of
as having lost power and still remaining sacred objects by reason of the virtue
they once had. The whole body of the dead may be preserved by a sort of
mummification and relics may be retained, in the form of the skull, bones,
clothing, or other property, but the commonest fetishes are images. This parallelism between the actual exuviæ and the images clearly exhibits the quality of
the latter.[215]

[209] Wilkins, *Hinduism*, 215-216.
[210] Kingsley, *Travels W. Afr.*, 509, 510, 511.
[211] Roscoe, in JAI, XXXVII, 110.
[212] Czaplicka, *Aborig. Siberia*, 290.   [213] Jochelson, in AA, VI, 419.
[214] Williams, *Middle Kingdom*, II, 259.
[215] Wilken, in VG, III, 189 ff.

The Indians have a sort of governmental fetish. "In the process of governmental development it became expedient to have something which should symbolize the unity of the tribe and of its governing power—something which should appeal to the people, an object which they could all behold and around which they could gather to manifest their loyalty to the idea it represented." This object was a sacred cedar pole, an ancient device, "which is said to have stood as a cosmic symbol representative of supernatural authority." Its significance was twofold: it stood for authority granted and guarded by supernatural powers, and also for the men of the tribe, its defenders and providers. "Long ago, beyond the memory of the eldest, it was the custom to anoint the Pole twice a year—after the summer hunt and after the winter hunt"; recently the anointing has taken place only in the summer.[216] It is evident that whether this Sacred Pole was or was not deliberately adopted by some far-seeing primitive statesman, it could not have met the need for which it was designed if the minds of the people had not been receptive of the fetish-idea. It is probably some antique personality-symbol on the order of the mediæval "Mal" or "Roland" and, like all symbols, a survival out of remote automatic development.[217] The Finns used to make rough images called "paras" which were carried round the church nine times while the faithful muttered uninterruptedly: "Live, para." The para then began to live, that is, a spirit came to lodge within it, after which the protection of the fetish over the household became operative.[218] This procedure reminds one of the ceremonial elevation of the host that it may receive the spiritual essence.

If a spirit can be inducted into an image, it can, of course, be removed or expelled from it; the latter, having been enlivened by the former ceremony, is then dis-enlivened. What can be consecrated can be de-consecrated or disamortized or secularized as church land has sometimes been.

"On the day following the worship of the images," the above Hindu case goes on, "another interesting ceremony is performed, viz., the farewell to the deity is taken. . . . After her departure, the materials that for a time were regarded as sacred are considered so no longer. Any one may now touch them." But the image is not retained; it is rowed out to the middle of a stream and sunk.[219] In ancient India and Greece the statues of gods could be returned by ceremony to the status of ordinary metal and used for other purposes.[220] Again, if the fetish fails to function, it is thought to be empty of its spirit; where formerly, on Ruk Island, the figure of the god of the winds could not be touched or sold, after it failed to bring the west monsoon it was promptly disposed of.[221]

It is not necessary, however, that the fetish-object should be, even roughly, a likeness of the spirit inducted. It may be an amu-

[216] Fletcher and LaFlesche, in BAE, XXVII, 217, 243, 244.
[217] §248, above; Lippert, *Kgchte.*, II, 147, 167, 371.
[218] Castren, *Vorlesungen*, 166.   [219] Wilkins, *Hinduism*, 217.
[220] Lippert, *Kgchte.*, II, 439.   [221] Finsch, *Ethnol. Erfahr.*, III, 321.

let or a magical instrument, like the bull-roarer.[222] It may be a weapon; for belief in the magical powers of weapons is common among primitive peoples;[223] and the attempt is made to increase the powers of one's own weapons and to weaken that of the enemy's by coaxing away the spirits attached to the latter.

"So the Papago shaman warrior goes confidently into battle against the Apache when protected by a fetish including an Apache arrow-point taken in conflict, and feels sure of victory if his war club is made in imitation of that of the enemy and potentialized by a plume or inscription appealing to the Apache deity."[224] The earthen jars of the Dyaks provide another illustration: they are the abode of spirits, and things left in them over night are supposed to increase in quantity, like the oil in the widow's cruse. Food kept in them is thought to acquire peculiar medicinal qualities.[225]

A stone may be anointed in the induction-process and so also may the man-fetish, priest or king.[226] In form the entering spirit may be a bird, a tongue of flame, or anything else associated with the spiritual power. It may be inducted or transferred in the insignia of office or merely by the laying-on of hands. In any case the object of the induction is spiritualized, lifted to the plane of superhuman infallibility or of power and quality superior to anything which it could have by nature. In modern times this induction or transference is symbolic (survivalistic) or rationalized, as when we speak of the "influence" which flows from the "inspiring" person to those associated with him. We seldom consider the etymologies of such words as "influence" or "inspire," and it is generally a matter of surprise and interest to find that we habitually use the vocabulary of daimonism and fetishism, developed in distant days, and standing then for something very concrete and definite. If we realize that no other explanation of our expressions is plausible or even possible, we attain a better and more intelligent conception of the relation of an advanced stage of societal evolution to its antecedents.

A phase of religion of which some authors make much is the worship of the sex-organs, which is largely a cult of images—the

[222] §§163, above, and 254, below.
[223] Gröndal, in *Annaler*, 1863, 150 ff.
[224] McGee, in AA, XI, 245.   [225] Gomes, *Sea Dyaks*, 91, 92.
[226] §259, below; Lippert, *Kgchte.*, II, 375.

so-called phallic cult.[227] It is entirely probable that its importance
has been exaggerated. Much that goes under the name of phallic
does not correspond at all in the native mind to what is in the
writer's or reader's thought; many a savage figure-maker, in the
absence of skill otherwise to denote sex, has exaggerated his representation of primary sex-differences and thus given what is alleged
by some to be evidence of preoccupation with sex and sex-wor-
ship.[228] The phantasies of writers on phallicism are profitable
chiefly to those who have a taste for that sort of fiction. In general it is quite wrong to think of the savage as always preoccupied
with sex; it is much more a matter of course with him than it is
with us; systematic obscenity belongs rather to developing civilization.

However, there can be no doubt that the phallus-image has
often been a fetish, as in the Indian Archipelago,[229] affording protection against the evil eye[230] and possessing power of exorcism
over evil spirits. Only it should be noted that where the phallic
cult is ardently pursued, as at Stanley Pool, "this worship so far
as is known is conducted without any real obscene ceremonies, and
is a subject of simple reverence in the natives' eyes."[231]

The interest of the savage is absorbingly involved in the parent-
offspring relation: nothing is more unfortunate than sterility; no
magic is more feared than that which may thwart parenthood.
Where the nature of procreation is understood to be physical, the
greatest precautions against the aleatory element are taken, especially at the dangerous crisis-time of marriage. Sex and sex-relations are, in short, one of the dominating factors in the environment encountered by human society.[232] This being the case, it is
astonishing to find so little in the primitive world that deserves the
term phallic worship or phallicism. "Discoveries of phalli are rare
in America."[233] The fact that the unmentionable appeared in the
cult of India and among other more sophisticated peoples should
not be allowed to force a false interpretation of lust and obscenity

[227] Lippert, Kgchte., II, 375.
[228] Hahn, in Globus, LXXV, 285.
[229] Wilken, in VG, III, 313-322.
[230] §265, below.
[231] Johnston, in JAI, XIII, 473.
[232] §§12, above, and 334, 347, below.
[233] Nadaillac, Preh. Amer., 51.

upon the matter-of-fact adjustments of savage society to its life-conditions. The imagination that sees phallicism in every totem-post or menhir is as inflamed as was Gladstone's when he was seeking to show that his impeccable Greeks believed in a Trinity.

CHAPTER XXIX

FETISHISM: TOTEMISM

§254*. **The Extraordinary.** The object possessed by a spirit is always out of the ordinary. From this circumstance it readily eventuates that the extraordinary is accredited with fetish-quality. In a former connection it has been seen that what succeeded in arresting the vagrant attention of the primitive mind was the startling rather than the commonplace. It was not the apparent and daily progress of the sun across the sky or the nightly swinging of the stars that claimed attention and called for some explanation—not, at least, until interest was awakened by the conviction that such motion was influential over life and luck. Because the tendency is to overlook it, one must recall to mind the essentially limited field of interest of the primitive peoples and their circumscribed knowledge of things. It was the striking variation from the normal within the limited range of their interests that caught the eye and received the stock explanation along the line of animism and its derivatives. Because such a variation was inexplicable and thus belonged to the aleatory element, did it catch and hold attention; then, along with other manifestations of that element, it was doggedly ascribed to supernatural influences.

This point may be supported preliminarily by several illustrations of the attitude of the savage toward products of a higher civilization which he cannot possibly explain. Tylor[1] tells of a Polynesian, a carrier of a message written on a chip, who kept the chip as a fetish because it could talk. In New Guinea the natives feared the camera, "either as a fetish or as an implement of the white man's armoury, which might go off at any time and kill them on the spot; hence they scuttled off in all directions, and there was no little trouble in inducing the bravest of them to return and be photographed."[2] "I saw natives in the interior wearing breast ornaments of pieces of kerosene tin in the belief that the tin would endow them with strength and fearlessness, the characteristics of the white miner who had been in their district. Had those people been undisturbed for some generations, the tin and its virtues would have persisted, though the story of its origin might have disappeared."[3] "The ghosts of the dead are *mana* and work miracles; anything, therefore, that

[1] *Anth.*, 167. A similar case is portrayed by Kipling in a story called "The Tomb of His Ancestors," in *The Day's Work.*

[2] Cayley-Webster, *New Guinea*, 53.   [3] Chinnery, in JAI, XLIX, 286.

seems miraculous is *kalou,* not always metaphorically; there is no doubt that when muskets were dubbed '*kalou* bows' . . . the natives really thought they were made by spirits or were spirits themselves. A former native officer in the police told me that in the government's little war against the Highlanders, the breech-loading guns were first given out to the police; the enemy seeing their deadly effects cried out: 'yanitu, yanitu.' The white man was probably first taken for a ghost from ghost land, and later, when his humanity was proved, his wonders seemed wrought by spiritual agency. At the present day natives are firmly convinced that the circus (in which all conjuring and illusions are included) is a kind of *luveniwai,* and cannot understand why the cult is tabooed to them and allowed to the whites."[4] The Bowditch Islanders "thought a foreign ship something unearthly, and the white crew sailing gods from some region of spirits. The fire burning in their inside, and sending forth volumes of smoke (tobacco smoke) seemed superhuman, and the guns, belching out fire and smoke and 'stones,' seemed to be no work of man."[5] The case of the relics of a lost art, inexplicable save through tradition, is a striking one: pottery-making, in this instance, was no longer understood, but the old and broken pieces still to be found were held in great reverence and a legend grew up of a goddess who once broke a jar in anger.[6] The Herero of Southwest Africa are not familiar with accurate fire-arms; if one wants to sell them guns, he must not hit the mark too often while demonstrating, or they will believe the gun enchanted.[7] A central African chief is reputed to have shown with an air of deep mystery a secret treasure which he regarded as a great fetish. It was a page of an illustrated French newspaper on which was a magnificent advertisement of women's fashions.[8]

Strangeness of appearance in an object; exceptionality of the circumstances attending its advent; the suggestion of its significance through a dream or other spiritual revelation—any such condition is enough to demonstrate fetish-quality. Another and even more conclusive proof is the power revealed by an exceptional or even a familiar object to do something not in the natural order but within the range of the aleatory. Uncanny effectiveness is characteristic of a fetish; if, then, something which has not been regarded as an object of possession exhibits such potency, it is at once identified.[9] By some coincidence, let us say, an Indian is relieved of pain just after swallowing some substance which modern science has demonstrated to be quite ineffective, either for good or for ill. That substance, to the Indian mind, working as it does on the *post-propter* basis,[10] has secured the effect; it has brought about a cure by expelling the spirit of disease. That is enough.

4 Hocart, in JAI, XLII, 446-447.   5 Turner, *Samoa,* 271.
6 Hardy and Elkington, *So. Seas,* 176.   7 Büttner, *Walfischbai,* 85.
8 Brunache, *Cent. Afr.,* 97.   9 §311, below.
10 §199, above.

The remedy in question becomes forthwith a fetish to the one who took it and to all who know his story. It is not necessary to attach this incident to the Indian; the history of folk-medicine or of modern patent panaceas can be drawn upon in confirmation.

The process of reasoning involved may be tersely expressed: anything that has supernatural or magical workings is thereby proved to be a fetish. Here is the converse of the proposition illustrated by the foregoing discussion, wherein it appears that fetishes, because they have spirits in them, produce effects beyond the ordinary. Only enlightened moderns know that a converse is not always true; to assume it true is a very natural mode of reasoning. It might be said, somewhat by way of anticipation, that we believe fetishism to have come first, then magic; we cleave to this order because of the conviction that systems of magic would not have been except for fetishistic beliefs whereas, as has now become apparent, fetishism can exist without systems of magic.[11]

It is to be understood that in the explanation of fetishism not much more intelligent help is to be expected from the savage than can be elicited from a dog by an expert student of animal-behavior. One observes what the savage does; he cannot explain himself. The primitive mind is not given to analyzing, even to itself, the "how" of this union of spiritual essence and matter. That is no question for one whose attention is anxiously, exhaustively, and exhaustingly absorbed with the concrete "what" in existence. The sense of the ideas in primitive minds—in this case, what they think, or seem to think, or say they think, about fetishes—does not inhere in the indefinite, deviating, inconsistent evidence which they may excitedly or drowsily or with sly dissimulation afford, but rather in the position into which such evidence as a whole falls within the pattern of the evolution of religious belief in general. What we can be sure of is that the more burdens people have the more spiritual help will they enlist, that is, they will keep on adding fetishes and testing them out.[12] Here are variation and selection operating on the details of fetishism. The ups and downs of local creeds are reduced to regularity in the perspective-curve of general religious evolution about which they play; and it is only from the vantage-point of the perspective that beliefs which are local in time and place get their sense.

Among the objects which become fetishes because they are extraordinary are many from the inanimate world. Ordinary objects of this order are handled with indifference; others of exceptional appearance, or in connection with which circumstances arise that allow of inferences as to their being possessed, become holy and revered. If all things, whether familiar or extraordinary, were conceived to have *mana,* or "virtue" in them, we might see more in the contentions of certain writers who seem to us, as it is, both to generalize from sporadic cases and to carry back into the mind of the Melanesian and Red Indian a sophistication of which it is incapable. "*Mana,*" says Read,[13] is a generalisation, vague and mysterious; as 'cause' in popular use, is a generalisation of all the supposed 'forces' of nature. . . . It is too comprehensive a generalisation to find expression amongst savages. . . . It is unreasonable to treat it as the first source of ideas of the supernatural."

"The large rock-crystal is venerated by most blacks, and is regarded with superstitious secrecy; it is the symbol of their "Great Spirit."[14] The Melanesians make much of certain stones. "The spirits belonging to these stones are nameless; their connexion with each its own stone is not clearly defined; the stone, they say, is not the body of the spirit, nor is the spirit like the soul of the stone, for a stone certainly has no soul; they say that the spirit is at the stone, . . . or near the stone, and it is the spirit not the stone that acts."[15] Certain peculiarly shaped stones are denominated sacred and are said to contain the spirits of departed relatives." Pigs are sacrificed to the sacred stones and as each stone has to have its pig, the killing goes on till the right number has been slain.[16] In the New Hebrides, there are no idols, and stones are not worshipped as stones but for the spirits in them.[17] "Intimately associated with cultivation and fertility are ideas and practices connected with stone objects and serpents. From time to time they abandon a more or less isolated family group existence and indulge in elaborate ceremonies connected with the initiation of their young people, in some of which bullroarers and flutes are used. These, too, are definitely connected with the production of food."[18] Among the West Africans a family-deity can be obtained by securing a stone designated during a dream by a deceased ancestor; this is guarded and reverenced by the finder "as the habitation of a protecting deity for that portion of the family of which he is the head." A priest is consulted in order to be sure whether the object is one with an indwelling spirit. "Usually the priest, for his own purposes, declares that it is, and it is given a name, and receives offerings."[19] Certain sticks employed by West Africans "were abambo, or ghosts. In all native folk-lore, where spirits embody themselves, they take on absurd or singular form."[20]

[13] *Origin of Man,* 119 ff., 121 (quoted); §258, below. Read surveys the literature which theorizes over *mana* and similar conceptions.

[14] Palmer, in JAI, XIII, 297.

[15] Codrington, *Melanesians,* 182, 181, 184.

[16] Hardy and Elkington, *S. Seas,* 155-156, 161.

[17] Gray, in AAAS, 1892, 650.   [18] Chinnery, in JAI, XLIX, 280.

[19] Ellis, *Tshi,* 90-91.   [20] Nassau, *Fetichism,* 379.

The Kirghiz reverence remarkable objects in nature: a big stone or tree, a cave with a spring of pure water.[21] Among the Samoyeds, "a curiously twisted tree, a stone with an uncommon shape would receive, and in some quarters still receives, not only veneration, but actual worship."[22] Certain Siberians, like the Lapps, see spirits in characteristically shaped hills or stones; there are a number of these stones in one lake, and in this body of water only the local tribesmen might row, fish, or wash; certain regions also, having a fetish-character, were visitable only by the local tribesmen and under certain circumstances. Fire was a fetish and before eating they cast some food into it. The earth was holy and one must not stick a knife into it. Some of the author's[23] men did so and it was regarded as the cause of bad weather. The gods conceived great wrath because the earth was injured in digging up a plant—a holy one, at that—and the author's party were asked to let the sun shine again. Eight days of good weather ensued and all were friendly once more. Evans[24] reports that he found only one representation of a human figure in Borneo "that could by any possibility be called an idol. It consisted of a natural water-worn boulder of greyish stone some . . . 3 feet in height, the shape of which accidentally resembled that of a human head and bust. . . . The natural shape of the boulder would, of course, account for its being chosen as an object of veneration." In the corner of a Cambodian rice-field there often is to be found a fragment of sculptured prayer from some ancient monument, or simply an ordinary stone. They believe that a spirit dwells in this stone, give it homage, and burn fragrant sticks before it.[25] Brahmans regard a fossil ammonite as "the representative of some god, and the worship of any god may be performed before it."[26] Mexican and Zuñi Indians show similar stone-fetishes.[27] Lumholtz,[28] while among the Tarahumari of Mexico, being tired during a certain dance, went out and sat down on a stone. The dance stopped and the Indians all looked anxiously at him. Then came a medicine-man who demanded angrily that he should follow him. Upon inquiry he found that the stone he had sat on was not a stone at all but the god of the place, and now they were all afraid of his anger and vengeance.

In Egypt, wherever any remarkable rock, spring, grotto, tree, serpent, or other natural object struck the notice of a peasant, he made sacrifice to it, believing it the seat or incarnation of some superior power whose anger must be propitiated or his favor won. Individuals also had fetishes: anything odd indicated by chance or in a dream.[29] Bethel was a name given by the early Semites and retained by the Phœnicians for aërolites and other strange stones.[30] In the Bible the stone used by Jacob at Bethel, and anointed by him, was holy by reason of the vision vouchsafed him while it supported his head; the place was to him the "house of God."[31] There were the sacred stones, Urim

[21] Russian Ethnog. (Russ.), II, 181.
[22] Montefiore, in JAI, XXIV, 398.
[23] Olsen, Primitivt Folk, 141, 143.   [24] In JAI, XLII, 392.
[25] Leclère, in PSM, XLIV, 779.   [26] Thurston, S. India, 3.
[27] Cushing, in BAE, II, 35.
[28] In Scribner's Mag., XVI, 444; "Aus allen Erdteilen," in Globus, LXXII, 19.
[29] Maspero, Hist. Anc., I, 121, 122.   [30] Sayce, Anc. Empires, 200.
[31] Gen., ch. XXVIII.

and Thummim, out of whose brilliancy was drawn the will of God.[32] The stone-fetish has persisted long in isolated communities. On the island of Inniskea, in the Atlantic not far from Ireland, "a stone carefully wrapped up in flannel is brought out at certain periods to be adored by the inhabitants" who are nominally Roman Catholics.[33]

Meteoric stones have become fetishes in a number of instances. In 1880 a meteorite fell at Behor, India, and by 1882 its cult was fully established. It was worshipped as the "miraculous god."[34] Such cases recall the stone representing Cybele and also the Kaaba at Mecca.[35] Earth from the Holy Land is thought by South Russian Jews to protect the body from decay. "It is therefore one of the most ardent wishes of many a Jew to fill a head-cushion with such earth and to be mingled with it in the grave. Pilgrims to Palestine bring some earth along for this purpose, for themselves and their friends."[36] Megalithic structures, as well as stones peculiar in respects other than size, have been the objects of much veneration.[37]

The foregoing instances are almost all cases of the stone-fetish.[38] It is not difficult to see how an erupting volcano would become a fetish: Vesuvius, Ætna,[39] the mountain of Pele in the Hawaiian Islands, and many another of lesser historical note[40] were abodes of spirits. Stars as fetishes, and even the comprehensive heaven-fetish, represent possession on the grand scale;[41] practices run from the relatively simple forms of such undeveloped peoples as the Pawnees[42] to the complex Chaldæan system, to sun-worship, and at length even into the range of constituted religious systems. The origins of all in fetishism are unmistakable. The current idea that the heathen have worshipped "stocks and stones" does the heathen injustice. They know the stock and stone and their qualities and worship them, as such, as little as we do; it is when extraordinary and inexplicable peculiarities appear that the fetish-attribute is at hand. It is the volcano rather than the ordinary mountain, the comet[43] rather than the planet, the tidal wave rather than the regular ebb and flow, the "rain of blood" rather

32 Maurer, *Vkde.*, I, 137-138. On sacred stones in general, see Allen, in *Fortnightly Rev.*, XLVII, and Lang, in *Contemp. Rev.*, LVII.

33 Gomme, *Ethnol. in Folklore,* 170.

34 Hopkins, *Relig. of India,* 522-523, note.

35 Lippert, *Kgchte.*, II, 372 ff.

36 Weissenberg, in *Globus,* XCI, 361.   37 Sébillot, in AA, IV, 78 ff.

38 §313, below.   39 Vergil, *Æneid,* III, 571 ff.

40 Nutting, in *Smithson. Rep.,* 1883, 908-909; Cook, in AA, II, 492.

41 Lippert, *Kgchte.*, II, 433 ff.   42 Fletcher, in AA, IV, 733 ff.

43 On the comet, eclipse, thunderstorm, mine-gas, and other prodigies, see White, *Sci. and Theol.,* I, 173, 174-176, 182, 388, 402, *et passim.*

than the summer shower, that catch attention and seem to need, and so straightway receive, explanation upon the only basis possible under the circumstances.

§255*. **The Lucky and Unlucky.** Of old it has been thought that days, numbers, colors,[44] especially blood-color, directions, positions, and other incidents of time and space had "virtue" for good or evil in them. Extraordinary conjunctures have elevated days, for instance, into holidays; and there is food for reflection in the fact that "the records are consistent in indicating that primitive peoples used integral numbers rather as symbols of extra-natural potencies than as tokens of natural values."[45] The connection of these lucky and unlucky matters with fetishism is indirect, by way of the aleatory interest. They are evidently, as the adjectives regularly applied to them witness, involved with manifestations of the inexplicable which can be due solely to spirit-agency. Generally it is impossible to penetrate into their undisclosed past beyond the range of such a generality. We do not wish to overdo the matter of fetishism, but we are solicitous to exhibit the almost incredible penetration of spiritual influence into all aspects of society's life.

There is perhaps something a little more definite to be said about the fetish-day.[46] Under the topic of the ghost-cult the occasion for the holy day or holiday was a desire to avoid the revenant;[47] such a day is one during which spiritual influences are all about. One must not give fire or water, or work, on Friday or May Day. Days are peculiarly lucky or unlucky for certain enterprises, for example for marrying.[48] Statistics show much avoidance of Friday, especially Friday the thirteenth, which is a conjuncture of an evil day and an unlucky number as viewed by Christian tradition. The second of December was the traditional lucky day of the Napoleonic dynasty; it is improbable that Napoleon himself saw

---

[44] §440, below.

[45] §279, below; McGee, in BAE, XIX, pt. II, 842-843.

[46] See Webster, *Rest Days,* for copious illustration.

[47] §225, above; Lippert, *Kgchte.,* II, 239.

[48] *Russian Ethnog.* (Russ.), I, 103; Gomme, *Village Life,* 98; Krauss, *Sreća,* 137, note.

much that was spiritual in it, but he was too good an actor not to utilize what lay in the minds of others.

It is impossible to derive the number-fetish from any known antecedents in eidolism or daimonism, though its antecedents are probably there.[49] What we find is that certain numbers have been thought to possess a special virtue and significance. There are certain "round numbers," such as three and seven, that seem to have impressed themselves upon our cultural forebears; but they are not of universal acceptation. It must be understood that very primitive fetish-numbers are small ones, for counting does not go beyond a limited point. An offhand conclusion has been offered that the odd numbers are more likely to have fetish in them than the even; but the cases which we have collected do not support that contention.[50]

Three is sacred to the Parsees, and in India in general the odd number is the auspicious one. "The reason is that the dead bodies are always carried by an even number of corpse-bearers."[51]

Four is the sacred and ceremonial number among the Mohave Indians.[52] We are told, in fact, that "the favorite number among the aboriginal races is undoubtedly four, especially in the pueblos in which heliolatry is the fundamental basis of religion, as in Mexico and Peru. Such a predilection has generally been attributed to the knowledge possessed by these people of the equinoxes and solstices."[53] Four and five "form the basis and scaffolding of the Mexican and Maya numeral and time system."[54] "The most widespread of the mystical numbers is four; it finds expression in Cults of the Quarters in North America, South America, Asia, and Africa, and is suggested by certain customs in Australia; it is crystallized in the swastika [卍] or fylfot and other cruciform symbols on every continent; and it is established and perpetuated by association with colors, social organization, and various customs among numerous tribes. . . . The devotee of the Cult of the Quarters is unable to think or speak without habitual reference to the cardinal points; and when the quadrature is extended from space to time, as among the Papago Indians, the concept is so strong as to enthrall thought and enchain action beyond all realistic motives. . . . It is easier to represent the quatern concept graphically than verbally—indeed it has been represented graphically by unnumbered thousands of primitive thinkers on the cruciform symbols dotting the whole of human

[49] §214, above, contains an excerpt from an author who conceives that numbers and formulas have souls where we regard them as fetishes.

[50] White, *Sci. and Theol.*, I, 6, 7, 119, 154, 395-396; II, 296, 298, 299; on number-systems, see Crawley, in PSM, LI, 526; Thomas, in AA, IX, no. 12; Thomas, in BAE, XIX; Conant, in *Smithson. Rep.*, 1892.

[51] Modi, in JASB, II, 426, note; and in JASB, II, 171.

[52] Kroeber, in AA, IV, 282.   [53] Quiroga, *Cruz en Amér.*, 104.

[54] Thomas, in BAE, XIX, pt. II, 950.

history and diffused in every human province, or in the form of the equally widespread but less conspicuous quincunx."[55]

Sometimes the system of counting makes a certain number prominent. Grant mentions the case of the number seven, in South Africa. "I asked, 'Is the fine of seven head never exceeded in the case of men of rank?' The reply was, 'No, we stop at seven because the fore-finger is used to beckon with.' . . . I may say that numbers commence with the little finger, which, when elevated, indicates one; but in elevating the thumb only, the number indicated is six, and the four fingers and thumb of the other hand may be entirely out of sight. In elevating, therefore, a thumb and fore-finger only, the number meant is seven; so, as it is alleged that the fore-finger is used to beckon with, this was the reason assigned for limiting the fine to seven head of cattle."[56] Seven was the important number with the ancient Hindu and Iranian; it "is the old and original one, which both have in common with each other, and which is reproduced in both cases in the world of the gods."[57] It was prominent, as is well known, in Hebrew antiquity. "Eight frequently occurs in Shinto mythology and seems to be the most perfect and fortunate number. Japan was known as 'the land of the eight great islands.' "[58] "Nine survives as a mystical number in the muses of classical mythology, in Anglo-Saxon aphorisms emphasizing the vitality of the cat and the effeminacy of the tailor, and as a recurring tale in all of the superabundant Celtic lore such as that currently recorded by Seumas MacManus; it even survived in the schoolbooks of the early part of the century in the more curious than useful arithmetic process of 'casting out the nines'; and throughout the last decade of the nineteenth century the newspaper-writing jugglers with nines found (and diffused) much mystery-tinged amusement in almacahalic analyses of the numbers 1890-1899."[59] Nine is a rather common fetish-number.[60] Thirteen and forty-nine are in the same category: "eminently conspicuous in Europe and America is the mystical number 49 especially when expressed as 7 x 7; for, in the belief of a large element of European population, the seventh son of a seventh son needs no training to fit himself for the medical craft, while scanners of advertising columns of American newspapers may daily read anew that the seventh daughter of a seventh daughter is a predestined seeress."[61] In India, one-hundred-and-one is a sacred number; according to the Avesta the god has that many names, corresponding to the number of his virtues.[62]

Lucky and unlucky directions, positions, postures, and the rest of the multitudinous detail of the auspicious and the ill-omened, attend religious ceremonial of all kinds. It might be said that the preference of the right to the left, of one point of the compass to another, and so on, are merely ritualistic; for ritual must be car-

---

[55] McGee, in AA, I, 655-656.   [56] In JAI, XXXV, 269-270.

[57] Tiele, *Gchte. d. Relig.*, II, 66-67.

[58] Hitchcock, in USNM, 1891, 494, note.

[59] McGee, in BAE, XIX, pt. II, 849.

[60] Johnston, *Uganda*, II, 589; Lewis, in *Man*, III, 116; Keller, *Hom. Soc.*, 171-172.

[61] McGee, in BAE, XIX, pt. II, 849.   [62] Modi, in JASB, II, 426.

ried through in the "right" way in order to bring luck, and all errors of detail are sure to result in misfortune.[63] Though there is no doubt at all about ritual having spiritual virtue in it, that does not answer the question as to why the right is lucky; it is not so because it is embodied in ritual, but is embodied in ritual because it is so. The auspiciousness of ritual resides largely in its detail; vary the features of which it is composed and it is naught. The respect for the right as lucky must have long antedated the ritual in which it appears. It must be a primordial notion; certainly its origin is beyond our powers of determination, though we may guess at it; all that we can be sure of is that some circumstance, unknown, lent it at least a quasi-fetishistic quality.

The avoidance of the unlucky thing is like the avoidance of an evil spirit; it is not named. "It is a phenomenon of all languages that the utterance of ominous or ill-foreboding words is avoided. In place of such ominous words . . . euphemistic terms or expressions of pious reverence are employed. From this point of view only does it seem possible to fully understand certain words for the left in the Indo-Germanic languages."[64] The quality of right and left, up and down, may also appear in connection with what is undoubtedly a fetish, as a detail of its essence. "The usage of cutting off any corner of a manuscript, mostly the upper right-hand corner, is thought to bring luck."[65] Many such incidents speak for the regular or occasional extension of the fetish-motive.

§256*. The Animal-Fetish.

The extension of the fetish-idea to organic nature[66]—to plants, animals, and men—carries it into phases which, though more significant in religious evolution, are less generally recognized. To enter thoroughly at this point into the topic of plant-fetishism would expand our treatment unduly and would involve repetition; for fetish-plants will be found much in evidence in magic and medicine.[67] Illustration of plant-fetishism can be limited and condensed at this stage of presentation.

[63] §279, below.   [64] Schrader, *Aryans*, 255.
[65] Rohlfs, *Kufra*, 15, note.
[66] See Wilken, on the relation between human, animal, and plant life ("De Betrekking tusschen Menschen-, Dieren- en Plantenleven naar het Volksgeloof"), in VG, III, 291 ff.
[67] §§300, 301, 308, 318, below.

The Murray Islanders regarded certain objects as sacred: besides stones, also various objects from the organic world. These objects had no power in themselves; each of them merely represented some great spirit.[68] "Various kinds of trees are thought to be the abodes of spirits, especially those which have any peculiar deformations or markings . . . for instance, trees which have creepers coiled round them are supposed to be haunted. If a man has sat near one of these, and afterwards becomes unwell, he will return and cut through the creeper, as this will ensure his recovery. Owing to the same idea, it is unwise to sit down on the interlaced roots of trees."[69] The Indians spoke of the "maize mother,"[70] and many another people has woven a complex net of fetishistic beliefs about its chief food-plant. The encyclopædic work of Frazer[71] is replete with illustration of such beliefs, though his interpretation of his instances is not always convincing.

That certain plants are fetishes is often inferred from their toxic and other effects. Of the West Africans Nassau[72] writes: "What I call 'poison' is to them only another material form of a fetich power, both poison and fetich being supposed to be made efficient by the presence of an adjuvant spirit." In the toxic or stimulative action of chemicals of vegetable or other origin there was something sure to attract attention because of the life-interest involved and yet wholly aleatory and inexplicable save on the hypothesis of spiritual agency. The case of the greater and lesser poisons, narcotics, and stimulants—opium, hemp, hashish, betel, coca, tobacco—rises at once to the mind.[73] Tobacco, as we have seen,[74] is much used in connection with the Jibaro custom of shrinking human heads. Concerning the *peyote,* a plant-bud, it is reported that "at the Lake Mohonk Conferences it is anathematized as a bane to the Indian."[75]

To the savage, things which produce extraordinary effects must have a spirit in them. Are not certain alcoholic drinks still called "spirits"? This is a survival, of course, but the indwelling spirits were once real enough to be worshipped as such: witness the Soma-worship in India and the Bacchus-cult in Greece.[76] Even the laurel, once used to secure the intoxication of the Delphic Pythia,[77] became the symbol of Apollo and of poetic inspiration in general, as the "poet's plant," and provided the crowning garland for the bard "with eye in fine frenzy rolling." Of the use by the shaman of such means of inspiration we shall see more in its appointed place.[78]

Animal-fetishism is a topic that calls for present illustration, not, however, before it has been prefaced by an understanding as to the primitive attitude toward animals. One of the marked differences between primitive men and civilized lies in the divergence

[68] Hunt, in JAI, XXVIII, 7.   [69] Evans, in JAI, XLVIII, 181.
[70] Frazer, *Golden Bough,* VII (pt. V, vol. I), 172.
[71] *Golden Bough,* especially pt. I, vol. II; Lippert, *Kgchte.,* I, 577 ff.
[72] *Fetichism,* 263.
[73] Lumholtz, in *Scribner's Mag.,* XVI, 452 ff. (on the Hikori plant); on tobacco, Carr, in *Smithson. Rep.,* 1891, 539 ff.; Bruce, *Va.,* I, 160.
[74] §227, above.   [75] N. Y. *Times,* Jan. 8, 1923.
[76] Lippert, *Kgchte.,* I, 622 ff.   [77] Lucian, *Bis. Accus.,* 1.
[78] §311, below.

of their attitudes in this respect. To understand the way the savage looks at beasts, the civilized man must set aside all that sense of superiority which has been conferred upon him through the success of his cultural adjustments. He thinks he has conquered the animal kingdom and looks upon its members as "lower" and of no significance in comparison with himself. Not so the savage, who is as yet poorly equipped with cultural equipment. He does not feel himself to be the "lord of creation"; to him the animals have enviable superiorities which he cannot rival. They can outfight him, outrun him, outclimb him; they have self-preservative instincts, not to mention fighting weapons, which arouse his respect and envy. He sees no such impassable cleft between them and himself as the more sophisticated have discovered. Consider the beliefs about souls in animal-form and animal-reincarnation, recently reviewed. Animals are redoubtable competitors in the struggle for life and receive the esteem due to such.

"The relation of animals to the various rites . . . is difficult to explain for the reason that the outlook on nature and all living creatures, of the white race is so different from that of the Indian. Accustomed as we are to classify animals as domesticated or wild and to regard them as beneath man and subservient to him, it requires an effort to bring the mind to the position in which, when contemplating nature, man is viewed as no longer the master but as one of many manifestations of life, all of which are endowed with kindred powers, physical and psychical, and animated by a life force emanating from the mysterious Wakonda. . . . This view of the interrelation of men and animals, whereby in some mysterious manner, similar to the assimilation of food, man's faculties and powers can be reinforced from the animals, may assist in explaining why animals play so large a part in Omaha rites."[79] Of the Salish we read: "Their anthropomorphic conceptions of the animal and vegetable worlds coloured all their lives and thoughts. . . . Even to-day, among the most advanced and intelligent of them, there is still a strong belief in the human or man-like side of animals, plants, and other objects and forces. This universal concept of primitive man seems to be one of the most persistent of his early beliefs." The same author[80] elsewhere relates the ceremonies connected with the beginning of the salmon fishing. The first fish caught "was brought reverently and ceremoniously upon the arms of the fisherman, who never touches it with his hands, to . . . a bundle of short rods. These rods all bear the 'mystery' names and marks, and represent the elders, of the tribe." These rods are laid "on the lateral fin of the salmon on its right side, the lateral fins being regarded as the salmon's hands." The rods are formally introduced to the salmon by name and the fish is told that so-and-so wishes to welcome it and shake its hand. "When all the elders have thus been vicariously introduced, and the salmon made wel-

[79] Fletcher and LaFlesche, in BAE, XXVII, 599, 600.
[80] Hill-Tout, in JAI, XXXIV, 28; and in JAI, XXXV, 140-141.

come to the tribe, it is then ceremoniously boiled, and a small portion of its flesh given to each person present." This is a sort of communion-sacrament. "From this time onwards throughout the season, anyone is free to catch as many salmon as he likes. . . . Nothing that the Indian of this region eats is regarded by him as mere food and nothing more. Not a single plant, animal or fish, or other object upon which he feeds, is looked upon in this light, or as something he has secured for himself by his own wit and skill. He regards it rather as something which has been voluntarily and compassionately placed in his hands by the goodwill and consent of the 'spirit' of the object itself, or by the intercession and magic of his culture-heroes; to be retained and used by him only upon the fulfilment of certain conditions. These conditions include respect and reverent care in the killing or plucking of the animal or plant and proper treatment of the parts he has no use for, such as the bones, blood, and offal; and the depositing of the same in some stream or lake, so that the object may by that means renew its life and physical form." "Totemism is something more than a mere idle and meaningless whim of an ignorant people. With the natives of Alaska, it is the foundation of their entire social structure and a tangible expression of their belief. Its importance among them can scarcely be exaggerated. It expresses their belief in the kinship of men and animals, and had, doubtless, its origin in the belief of the animal ancestry of man. . . . Because of their belief that animals can understand human speech, I have been cautioned more than once, while in camp with natives, and in all seriousness, never to speak in terms of disrespect of the bear, or other animal. The natives are Darwinians to the very letter. Their belief in the origin of man from animals is expressed not only in their verbal legends, but on some of their totem poles."[81]

Wilken[82] has collected a number of instances of this feeling about animals, and even plants, some of which belong to a more modern time. He begins by citing the threat to a tree that does not bear well, that the owner will make boards of it unless things change, and the custom of telling a tree when its owner dies. So the bees are informed about marriages and deaths and urged to be diligent and do their duty. Some domestic animals have been held guilty of crimes and punished; these are the deodands alluded to above.[83] Wild animals are supposed to act according to their nature and so cannot be blamed, whereas if domesticated ones do something corresponding to a crime, they are acting against nature, and incur blame. Examples are given in generous measure all through. Punishments were sometimes preceded by regular legal process, and animals have been known to be hung as the result of a sentence, or imprisoned. When bodies of animals, such as mice, have done damage, the priestly judge has been set upon their trail and has even excommunicated them. All these are clear cases of regarding animals as men.

Probably it is only myth-making to infer that men derived specific arts and devices from the animal-world—learned to save, for instance, by noting the habits of ants and bees; and not much confidence can be lodged in guesses such as that of Starcke:[84] "Since

81 Jones, *Thlingets,* 171, 172.   82 In VG, IV, 182 ff.
83 §183, above.   84 *Prim. Fam..* 8.

man in so many ways only develops the previous achievements of animal experience, it is natural to suppose that he used the social experience of animals as the foundation of his higher advancement." It seems to us far-fetched to start the survey of various human institutions, as Letourneau does in his various books on the evolution of marriage, property, and the rest, with chapters on the forms of these institutions as exhibited by animals. There is no doubt, however, that men intensely admired the beasts, named themselves after them, gave their gods titles of honor such as "Conquering Bull," and felt a sense of affection and obligation toward the animal world before they had come to harbor any sympathy for men outside the local group.[85] And, what is of greatest importance in the present connection, they were convinced that animals like men had souls or were the repositories of men's souls and so were competent to enter into the spirit-world and to constitute part of the supernatural environment.[86]

Perhaps this topic does not need much illustration, in view of the mass of animal-stories and mythology, such as the *Jungle Book* and the *Uncle Remus* tales that have long been current in popular literature.

The horror of snakes shown on the D'Entrecasteaux Islands is hard to account for, inasmuch as large ones are rarely seen and none are particularly dangerous.[87] The Bushman does not distinguish sharply between a man and a buffalo, ascribing to the latter his own powers, even to the use of bow and arrow.[88] The Kaffirs regard the elephant with reverence; if one of them has killed an elephant after a difficult pursuit, he takes a position in front of his booty and solemnly explains to the slain animal that he has acted without intention and killed it accidentally. To take away from the elephant the power of doing harm, they cut off his trunk and bury it with ceremonies, repeating over and over that the elephant is a great lord and that the trunk is his hand.[89] Main[90] has two sections on African snake-incarnations and phallic serpents. To the West Africans, as well as other barbarians, man is not at the top of creation; that idea belongs to the revealed religions.[91] Emin Pasha's dwarf was inseparable from his dogs and apes and ate from the same plate.[92] The Arabs and Egyptians believe "that birds and beasts have a language by which

[85] Lippert, *Kgchte.*, I, 510; Spencer, *Prin. Soc.*, I, §192.

[86] Wilken, in VG, III, 289 ff.; Maine, *Early Law*, 34; Anon., "Northwestern Indians," in PSM, XLIII, 825; Thomas, in *Folklore*, XI, 227 ff.

[87] Jenness and Ballentyne, *D'Entrecasteaux*, 70.

[88] Frobenius, *Masken*, 191.   [89] Lichtenstein, *Reisen*, I, 412.

[90] *Relig. Chastity*, Appendix, notes XVI, XVII.

[91] Kingsley, *W. Afr. Studies*, 178.   [92] Stuhlmann, *Mit Emin*, 447.

they communicate their thoughts to each other, and celebrate the praises of God."[93]

Among the Soyots of Siberia the cuckoo and two varieties of swan are holy; if a man gets a certain type of swan he may ask and get the chief's daughter in marriage or, if he does not need a wife, can get a horse.[94] The Kamtschatkans hold the bear and wolf in reverence and never mention their names. Zoölatry occupies one of the most prominent places in the religious world-philosophy of the shamanists and it is even hard to decide which is more important and more characteristic for the solution of existing questions in respect to the doctrines of shamanism, the worship of animals, or the worship of ancestors.[95] Hose and McDougall[96] go to considerable length in treating of the intimate relations between men and animals in Sarawak. By the Eskimo, "nearly every attribute possessed by the shades of people is also believed to be possessed equally by the shades of animals, and the inua or shade of every animal is believed to possess semihuman form. . . . It is believed that in ancient times all animals had the power to change their forms at will. When they wished to become people they merely pushed up the muzzle or beak in front of the head and changed at once into man-like beings. The muzzle of the animal then remained like a cap on top of the head, or it might be removed altogether, and in order to become an animal again it had only to pull it down."[97]

In the Indian Archipelago, since the spirits of the dead are reverenced above all others, the animals in which these prefer to incarnate themselves are highly honored. "Various animals are found which in this manner, that is, on the ground of transmigration and the consequent conception of relationship and descent, are worshipped by the peoples of the Indian Archipelago. Among these animals the crocodile deserves to be mentioned first of all. The veneration of the crocodile appears everywhere in the Archipelago." If a man has by necessity injured one of these beasts, "his conscience pricks him more than if he had perpetrated the most dreadful murder. The native believes in the relationship between man and crocodile. . . . To be changed into a crocodile after death is the sweetest joy connected with the thought of immortality." When, in Timor, a new ruler ascended the throne, there was a sacrifice on the shore of a pig with red bristles and of a young girl decorated with flowers and anointed with sweet-smelling oil. She was fastened to a stone consecrated to the purpose, and then the crocodiles were called; the one who carried her off was supposed to have married her. The author[98] cites numbers of cases of supposed marriage between men and beasts. Special offerings are made to the crocodile if the report has spread about the neighborhood that a woman has brought forth offspring of a mating with him, a thing which takes place at the birth of twins. Further, it is believed that women bear animals from intercourse with animals. Plainly, then, animals and men may be blood-kin and animals the ancestors of human beings; this situation is close to totemism. In the Archipelago, however, there has not developed that usage of naming kin-groups after animals which goes with totemism. It might be mentioned in

[93] Lane, *Mod. Egypt.,* I, 375.   [94] Olsen, *Primitivt Folk,* 143, 144.
[95] Michailovski, *Shamanism* (Russ.), 41, 46.
[96] In JAI, XXXI, 173 ff.
[97] Nelson, in BAE, XVIII, pt. I, 423, 425.
[98] Wilken, in VG, III, 79-81, 82, 85-86, note, 88-89, note, 103-104.

passing that plants as well as animals may be reincarnations of men; hence the widespread belief that men may be derived from trees and especially from bamboo or rattan. In Sumba the apparently wild horses found in the bush are regarded as descendants of sacrificed animals and are therefore holy; no one dares to capture one of them. The horse-sacrifice is common and, in the case of the death of one chief, three hundred horses, as well as the same number of buffalo, were slaughtered—so many that there was such superfluity of meat that, even though the guests were numerous, a good part of it rotted inside and outside the village.

In Samoa, "if a man found a dead owl by the roadside, and if that happened to be the incarnation of his village god, he would sit down and weep over it, and beat his forehead with stones till the blood flowed. This was thought pleasing to the deity. Then the bird would be wrapped up and buried with care and ceremony, as if it were a human body. This, however, was not the death of the god. He was supposed to be yet alive, and incarnate in all the owls in existence. . . . A dead owl found under a tree in the settlement was the signal for all the village to assemble at the place, burn their bodies with firebrands, and beat their foreheads with stones till the blood flowed, and so they expressed their sympathy and condolence with the god over the calamity 'by an offering of blood.' "[99]

"The Jibaros still have a very vivid consciousness of their supposed relationship with the animal world, a feature which especially appears in their religion and their poetry. But they especially claim to trace the ancient human qualities in the sloth. . . . When, therefore, the Jibaros meet a sloth, they kill it with a lance, just as they kill their human enemies, and make a trophy of its head. . . . The Indian who has killed the animal has thereafter to pass through exactly the same purificatory ceremonies as one who has killed a human enemy, and even the final great victory feast is celebrated in due time with exactly the same grand preparations and with the same carefully performed ceremonies."[100]

"In an age-long contact with nature the Indian has made many observations upon the environing animal-world. His senses, sharp and active without intermission, have bound him up with it in a manner of which we, in the artificial sphere of civilization, can form no conception. . . . He knows its manner of life in all its phases, its lairs and nests, its nourishment and dainties, its season of heat, its change and wanderings. . . . Characteristic of the view of the native is it that he thinks of the life of every animal as in inborn conflict with every other one. These mutual hostilities seem to him to belong to their most essential peculiarity."[101]

"To primitive man the wild beasts were objects of reverence. With the fox, wolf, weasel, etc., that cross the path or vision of the traveller, he associates sometimes feelings of joy, but generally of gloom to such a degree that at the present time we can hardly conceive of the superstitious anxiety with which the various phenomena of nature weighed on the mind of man. . . . This holds good especially of the kingdom of birds, whose mysterious flights in the region deemed to be of the immortals seem to fit them above all other creatures to be

[99] Turner, *Samoa,* 21, 25, 26.
[100] Karsten, "Jibaro," in BAE, Bull. LXXIX, 33.
[101] Von Martius, *Beiträge,* I, 665, 666; Grinnell, *Cheyenne,* II, 97, 103 ff.

able to give mankind messages from the gods or of the future."[102] The animal-form of the soul has been mentioned[103] but an example may be added. "In the British Isles we find the following among the soul-animals—ant, butterfly, gull, moth, sparrow, goatsucker, cat, swan, and spider. In Germany we find the bat, butterfly, bee, cricket, fowl, mouse, peewit, pigeon, raven, snake, swan, toad, and weasel. In Rügen it is believed that the seal is descended from drowned human beings." Connected with such ideas is "the Icelandic idea of the aettar-fylgia: this is a guardian spirit in animal form belonging to each family, and as such attached to the dwelling of the family. . . . This leads us to the fylgia or personal guardian spirit, also conceived as an animal, which accompanies or precedes its owner on a journey in the form of a dog, raven, fly, etc. In Nor-way the fylgia is believed to take the form of the animal most appropriate to the temper of the owner."[104]

It may be said in view of these examples that the evolutionary theory, as it affects man's derivation from the animal-world, would not have encountered opposition among savages. They would have sensed no shock and might well, if they had been up to an under-standing of science, have felt such pleasure as anyone experiences at seeing a pet belief supported by scientific demonstration.

With the prevalence of such an attitude toward animals, the ascription to them of fetish-qualities is in the natural order. An animal-species may have a fetish-quality if its members are con-nected with the dead and the ghosts; then, too, both species and especially individuals may attain that quality through the fact of being extraordinary in some striking way. Thus the sacrificial ani-mal is often white, as where the Mongols slay on the holy mountain a white horse, a white cow, nine white sheep, and several white fowls.[105] They are possessed by some daimon, identifiable or not.

The insects commonly seen around corn are assimilated in name to the corn-daimon.[106] The Indians used to bury fish along with the corn-seed.[107] If this was done originally under fetish-belief, it would have proved itself an effective measure and could then await rationalization. "The bird passes as a symbol of all beings that move, apparently contrary to nature, through free space, be-cause it is believed that the phenomenon of flying is connected empirically with that of the wing-stroke. Therefore all stars, the lightning, the cloud, and the storm are fitted out with wings."[108] The mechanics of the wing-stroke were, of course, a mystery insoluble apart from the spirit-hypothesis. The thunder-bird

[102] Schrader, *Aryans*, 252.　　　　　[103] §§210, 211, above.
[104] Thomas, "Totemism," in *Folk-Lore*, XI, 235, 237-238.
[105] Prjevalski's *Forskningsresor*, 319; Main, *Relig. Chastity*, 286-287.
[106] Mannhardt, *Korndämonen*, 4.
[107] Thomas, in HAI, *sub* "agriculture."
[108] Von Negelein, in *Globus*, LXXIX, 360.

is a typically Indian construction, though the idea is found elsewhere.[109] That birds were fetish-beings in antiquity can be readily inferred from the employment of the flight of birds as omens, from the "auspices," "auguries," "inauguration," (all compounds with "avis") and other methods of divination practised in connection with them.[110] Consider the geese that saved the city. Among domestic fowl the cock is particularly noteworthy as a fetish, before whose crowing the night-prowling ghosts and spirits flee.[111] It was the crowing of the cock that killed the basilisk.[112] In Ceylon a white cock is used in religious ceremonial. People do not wish to eat charmed food; hence there is a prejudice against white cocks for eating purposes.[113] Von Negelein[114] believes that the bird is regarded as a fetish also because of the mystery of its origin from the egg. The same might be said of reptiles. "The fact that out of the unchanging body of the egg develop the most various beings led to the idea that in it was to be seen the seed of existence par excellence, and so the birds came to the front among these mythical forms." Even the nymphs were spoken of as egg-laying beings. The egg "takes a preferred place among the foods designed for the dead." But it was sometimes tabooed as food for the living; in Homer there is no case of the eating of eggs, though fowls are kept[115]—and Homer is not wont to omit mention of common foods.

The extraordinary individual may be illustrated by the goshawk from whose leg projected a supernumerary limb terminating in two toes. This peculiarity marked the dead bird as having been a fetish, and the leg was still one. The fetish was highly prized by its Indian owner, "and was believed to be a medium whereby the favor of the Great Thunderer, or Thunder God, might be invoked and his anger appeased. This deity is represented in pictography by the eagle, or frequently by one of the Falconidae; hence it is but natural that the superstitious should look with awe and reverence upon such an abnormality on one of the terrestrial representatives of this deity."[116] Grinnell[117] devotes considerable attention to the white buffalo. White or albino bison are rare; few men have seen over two or three. They were deemed mysterious, in which attitude "the Cheyennes were like other Indians." The ceremonial connected with the animal and the preparation of his hide shows it sacred; its meat must not be taken or eaten but left on the ground. Its hide was consecrated to the sun or Great Power; a religious ceremony was necessary to remove the taboo from the hide. Somewhat the same attitude was maintained toward the eagle; in eagle-catching a pipe is filled and offered to the bird and it is addressed as follows: "I did not kill you without thought," that is, without a reason. "We want to wear you." Among certain reindeer-nomads of the upper Yenesei, some reindeer, mostly white ones, over which a medicine-man has "shamanized,"

[109] Mooney, in BAE, XIV, 968, 969; Fewkes, in *Smithson. Rep.*, 1895, 584; Dellenbaugh, *North Amer.*, 167, 342, 393; Kropf, *Kaffir-English Dict.*, 324.

[110] §267, below.

[111] §227, above; Lippert, *Kgchte.*, II, 393; Modi, "Cock as Sacred Bird, etc.," in JASB, V, 346; Anon., "Das Hahnornament bei den Amurvölkern," in *Globus*, LXXVIII, 180; Harvey, *Chinese Animism.*

[112] White, *Sci. and Theol.*, I, 39.

[113] Hildburgh, in JAI, XXXVIII, 163.

[114] In *Globus*, LXXIX, 357; Lasch, in *Globus*, LXXXIX, 101.

[115] Keller, *Hom. Soc.*, 38-39. [116] Hoffman, in BAE, VII, 221.

[117] *Cheyenne*, I, 270-273, 299 ff.; II, 201 ff.

are regarded as holy and may not be used for work. In this usage the Lapps coincided. There are also horses which are flecked or reddish-yellow, as well as bears, especially yellow-flecked ones, that are holy.[118] Among the Lolos of western China, "there are three classes of evil things, which affect . . . with disease and calamity. 1st, the ghosts of those who have died unclean deaths; 2nd, demons; 3rd, *Slo-ta*. . . . *Slo-ta* are unusual appearances, unnatural phenomena, and as such, not only portend, but also cause disaster. The *Slo-ta* are, e.g., hens that crow like a cock, monstrous births, cooking vessels that make a booming noise on the fire, dogs or cows getting on the roof of a house, etc. . . . The exorcisms are long; the demons are alternately coaxed and threatened. The priest waves a thorn-branch as a whip against the evil things."[119]

"Holy mice nest under the altar of the plague-sending Apollo; golden mice are set by the Philistines beside the Ark of Jahweh to turn away the plague."[120] Here we encounter one of those cases which, in view of the fact that vermin are actually plague-carriers, look rational when viewed from the standpoint of a better-informed age. In Siam the white elephant, in India the crocodile and bull, in Egypt the peculiarly marked Apis-bull together with the crocodile and other animals that have come down to us in mummified remains, were fetish-animals. Maurer[121] speaks of the marked animal-fetishism of the Jews: the calf vied with the serpent. "Even in the temple at Jerusalem stood the effigy of the bronze serpent." The winged cherubs on the Ark were fetishes, as was the Ark itself. The demoniac swine is a haunter of Syrian houses in which there is a marriageable girl.[122] Anthropoid-fetishism is found in Borneo, suggesting a trace of totemism otherwise rare in the island. Speaking of the gibbons, a native "cast down his eyes and spoke in a voice so low we could hardly hear him, as if the very breathing of a name so sacred were profanation."[123]

Of the dog as a fetish-animal something has been said in other connections;[124] the dog-sacrifice was wide-spread in North America, among Algonquins, Iroquois, and Sioux.[125] The Cheyenne believe that the dogs are the first to become aware of the presence of ghosts and spirits.[126] Not only does the dog "bury" the dead; he can see ghosts, we recall, and by his howling or barking drive them away. Zoroaster, Homer, and Ossian agree as to this.[127] And his fetish-character is so marked that it is even possible by his actions to divine the status of the dead. "After a feast at which the Votyaks pay reverence to the ancestors, they gather up all the remnants which they give to the dogs. The more quickly these remains are consumed by the dogs, the more satisfactory to the ancestors were the sacrifices which had been offered and the better satisfied the ancestors are in the other world. The Votyaks are especially pleased when the dogs begin to fight over these remnants, for that shows that the dead are enjoying complete happiness."[128] This case verges upon divination and magic[129]—toward which all the instances of animal-fetishism point.

[118] Olsen, *Primitivt Folk*, 60, 80. [119] Henry, in JAI, XXXIII, 104.
[120] Maurer, in *Globus*, XC, 137; I Sam., VI, 11.
[121] *Vkde.*, I, 127-128. [122] Smith, *Relig. Sem.*, 291.
[123] Furness, *Head-Hunters*, 55-56. [124] *Case-Book*, §99 and §248, above.
[125] Friederici, "Indianerhund," in *Globus*, LXXVI, 364.
[126] Grinnell, *Cheyenne*, II, 101, 102. [127] Lippert, *Kgchte.*, II, 392.
[128] Michailovski, *Shamanism* (Russ.), 46.
[129] §§266, 301, 305, below.

§257*. The Man-Fetish.[130] Man too becomes a fetish by reason of possession by a spirit. Where cannibalism exists, the result, and often the purpose, of the practice is that the souls of the dead shall be merged in the living. Foregoing paragraphs on the nature of the soul and the treatment of the dead afford examples; and subsequent ones upon cannibalism and human sacrifice will reflect light upon the matter.[131] Wizards eat human flesh where others do not and become fetishes as the rest do not. Men are likewise the objects of daimonic possession, being thought to be so possessed when they exhibit extraordinary peculiarities, physical or other. The mischievous child acts "possessed." It is a survivalistic commonplace to ask, in view of some curious or inexplicable action: "What 'possessed' you to do that?" "Possessed of a devil" has been a blanket-expression to cover serious abnormality. First there are certain bodily peculiarities that have conferred the fetish-character,[132] causing now terrified avoidance and again admiring reverence. A noteworthy case is where, among the ordinarily beardless Temne of Liberia, a man who is favored with a growth on the chin is locally known as a "big daddy" and attains prestige.[133]

In the New Hebrides deformed children are well cared for; while in Samoa hunchbacks and the scrofulous are regarded as favorites of the spirits, generally, be it noted, becoming priests when grown up.[134] In Fiji, "they would make an offering of taro to 'the old, weak, and white-haired men who are *tevoro*, are nearly dead.' A similar usage was found . . . in the Solomon Islands; a very old man was asked to be propitious (*mana*) to the fishing because he was 'all the same *tomate*,' *tomate* meaning the dead. . . . A native composer once excused himself from teaching my school boys music with the flattery that he was afraid of the 'white *tevoro*,' who knew more than he did, and would pick holes in his performance. In the same way our Solomon Islanders would compare whites to *tomate* for cleverness."[135] The African Baganda, "to avert public calamity, especially war or plague . . . ascertain the facts from the . . . deity . . . and the remedy, which is usually to take a man or woman who has something peculiar about them, such as cross eye, or a light skin, etc., a white bull, and a white goat, to the border of the country from which the evil is coming; these have their legs broken to prevent them

130 The treatment of this topic by Lippert (*Kgchte.*, II, 463 ff.) is to the authors an unusually striking example of his power of presentation and suggestion. We follow him here rather closely.
131 Ch. XXIII and §§218, 227, above, and 292, 294, below.
132 §§310, 404, below.
133 Personally communicated by Mr. A. A. Ward.
134 Ella, in AAAS, 1892, 622.   135 Hocart, in JAI, XLII, 440.

escaping, and are placed in the principal roads and left to die."[136] African albinos were often kept by princes "as a fetish securing influence over the Europeans. They have everywhere the right to appropriate what pleases them, and the owner, far from raising a protest, feels himself just as highly honored by this as a pious Hindu when the ox of Siwa, at the market of Benares, empties his basket." In Loango such men are honored even more than the shamans and their hairs are sold at a high price as relics.[137] Here also was seen a hunchback, the only one in the region, who, being a prodigy, passed as a fetish. His deformity was due to the breaking of a taboo or *quixilles*.[138] The abnormality is always singled out for special precautionary treatment: women who bear twins or die in childbirth are, as far as possible, destroyed. Children "that arrive with ready cut teeth, will in a strict family be killed or thrown away in the bush to die as they please. . . . They may, if the mother chooses to be bothered with them, be reared; but the interesting point is that any property they may acquire during life has no legal heir whatsoever. It must be dissipated, thrown away. This shows clearly that such individuals are not human."[139] There is also "bodily deformity in consequence of an organic defect, on account of which even brothers are wont to abandon the victim from superstitious fear."[140] The Yakuts were terrified when a woman gave birth to a monstrosity, because they thought it a presage of calamity. In all monstrosities they see incarnation of evil spirits.[141]

Schwaner[142] found the members of one Borneo tribe afraid to look at him, a white man, "out of fear of being attacked by fever or other sicknesses by reason of the unaccustomed face. The men warned their wives and children by no means to come into my vicinity. Those who could not restrain their curiosity and acted contrary to the warnings, killed chickens by way of reconciliation with the evil spirits and smeared their bodies with the blood of the sacrifice." This case deserves alignment with conciliatory sacrifices and blood-sprinkling as developed later on.[143] Wilken[144] has a monograph on albinism in the Malay Archipelago. He notes that the nakedness of albinos seems much more noticeable to Europeans than that of dark-skinned natives. The Dyaks esteem albinos greatly; they "are fond of such monstrosities." In Nias an albino baby is an evil due to malignant spirits, and a shame to the mother; they wait to see whether the light child acquires color, and if he does not by the age of fifteen, he is killed. An albino cannot get a wife without an extra bride-price and no one wants an albino wife. The author cites Andree[145] for examples of reverence for the albino; and notes that the whiteness of the buffalo and elephant is regarded as a supernatural phenomenon. The albinos belong with the dwarfs, hunchbacks, and other abnormalities; sometimes they are court-curiosities. There are no special beliefs about partial albinism.

Occasionally, however, even so prominent an abnormality as an albino among dark-skinned races escapes especial attention. Among the Pueblo Indians, espe-

---

[136] Roscoe, in JAI, XXXII, 61.
[137] §249, above; Bastian, *Afr. Reisen*, 34.
[138] Bastian, *Deut. Exped.*, I, 58.
[139] Kingsley, *W. Afr. Studies*, 148-149.
[140] Paulitschke, *Nordost-Afr.*, I, 323.
[141] Gmelin, *Reise durch Sibirien*, II, 455-456.
[142] *Borneo*, II, 167.   [143] §§275, 298, below.
[144] In VG, IV, 272 ff.   [145] *Eth. Parallelen*, 240 ff.

cially the Zuñi and Tusayan, there are many well-marked examples of albinism; "but in no case did I learn that the individuals thus distinguished were accredited with power not ascribable to them under ordinary circumstances."[146] Perhaps the sight of many pale-faces had blunted sensibilities; yet "in certain parts of Mexico there is a tendency to congenital albinism in the native population; and before the conquest all children displaying this tendency were sacrificed to the gods before the age of puberty."[147]

"The Toba Indians kill all defective and weakly children right after birth."[148] This has been a general practice in many places and times. In ancient Iran, "corporeal defects, such as the state of being crippled, were regarded as the work of the devil."[149] Spencer[150] cites a six-fingered dynasty which reigned a century and a half and was regarded with awe because of its continuously inherited malformation. Certain bluish marks on the body, called Mongolian spots, occur in Asia, Indonesia, America, and Europe. In parts of China they are referred to the slap of a fairy or the mark of the king of the lower world, in Java to the lick of dwarf-like spirits or of a snake.[151] In India hermaphrodites are dedicated by parents. Many of them "are of unusual height and size, strong-voiced and harsh-featured, peculiarities which are made the more notable by their practice of always dressing in women's clothes. . . . They live by begging and are held in awe."[152]

Not infrequently the little black peoples or other strange aboriginal types repellent to the taste of later incomers, have been looked upon as possessed of evil spirits. It is a fact of science, according to Gomme,[153] that the hostility of races has always produced superstition; and he illustrates by the coast-tribes of New Guinea whose spirit-beliefs are derived chiefly from their fear of the aboriginal peoples.

They believe "when the natives are in the neighborhood that the whole plain is full of spirits who come with them," and to these attendants all sorts of evils are attributed. The semi-savage tribes of India are treated by their Hindu masters with contempt and loathing, and yet are objects of superstitious fear, "for they are believed to possess secret powers of magic and witchcraft and influence with the old malignant deities of the soil who can direct good or evil fortunes." The savages of Ceylon, conquered by the Hindus, are called by the chroniclers demons. Even "fairycraft has been explained as the survival of beliefs about the aborigines from Aryan sources." Such aboriginal peoples as the African Pygmies are the object of fear, not seldom because

---

[146] Bourke, in BAE, IX, 460.
[147] Brinton, in *Smithson. Rep.*, 1893, 592.
[148] Koch, in *Globus*, LXXXI, 108.
[149] Spiegel, *Erân. Alterthumskde.*, III, 682.
[150] *Prin. Soc.*, II, §478.
[151] Ten Kate, in *Globus*, LXXXVII, 53 ff.
[152] Campbell, in JASB, IV, 63.
[153] §308, below; *Ethnol. in Folklore*, 43, 46, 48, 64.

they are in reality so dangerous and yet so elusive.[154] It is a case of the extraordinary, unknown, and mysterious being referred to its stock explanation. Johnston[155] is not inclined to dismiss forthwith the theory that the lore about dwarfs and gnomes hints at the former existence of the Pygmy negro type in Europe. The dwarfs of the Congo forest live in caves and holes and disappear into them alertly, showing a "baboon-like adroitness in making themselves invisible in squatting immobility. . . . Anyone who has seen as much of the Central African Pygmies as I have, and has noted their merry, impish ways; their little songs; their little dances; their mischievous pranks; unseen, spiteful vengeance; quick gratitude; and prompt return for kindness, cannot but be struck by their singular resemblance in character to the elves and gnomes and sprites of our nursery stories." To the ancient Scandinavians the Finns and Lapps were wizards.

From instances of this order we wish to derive only the conclusion that daimonic qualities are wont to be assigned to the strange and mysterious thing, especially when it is feared, and even though it takes form in a flesh-and-blood fellow-creature.

Bodily peculiarities are likely to issue in some eminence for the abnormal person, particularly in the local religious system; the special case is that of the medicine-man or shaman, which will be considered by itself.[156] Mental peculiarities are an even greater distinction than physical;[157] they are found on both sides of the normal, the extremes being insanity and genius. That these extremes are wont to meet is a proverbial saying, and the evidence from primitive life does not disprove it; it is not always so easy to determine whether the shaman, for instance, is unsettled in mind or is simply sly and shrewd above his fellows. We may begin with insanity, which has been regarded by not a few relatively civilized peoples as evidence of possession. The very term "lunatic" indicates that the person in question is "moon-struck," and under external and supernatural influence.

In West Africa, "there is a great diversity in the treatment of the insane in different districts and different tribes. In some regions a tribe holds to the following reasoning: This person is possessed by a spirit. That spirit is occupying his body and using his voice and limbs for some reason. If we interfere with this person's doings, then we will be interfering with the spirit and may bring evil on ourselves. Therefore it is considered proper to make offerings and some degree of worship to the incarnated spirit." The author[158] is at

154 Ratzel, *Vkde.*, I, 125; Crichton-Brown, in *Nature*, XLV, 269-271.
155 *Uganda*, II, 513-514, 516-517.   156 §§309, 310, below.
157 Spencer, *Prin. Soc.*, I, chs. XVI, XVII, XVIII.
158 Nassau, *Fetichism*, 272.

pains to point out that the insane are not regarded as spiritual in themselves but by reason of this possession: "it is not true that the lunatic himself is an object of worship." Among the Arabs of Tunis, "the religious influence shows itself in the relation toward the insane. They are regarded as holy, wherefore one must endure everything from them. And so it plainly follows that the number of madmen, or of pretended madmen, is very great. People are not only happy to extend them hospitality but they can take what they will in the house." There even exists "a clear and sheer religious prostitution in favor of the insane," relations with one of them being regarded as fortunate.[159] There is here a non-eugenic practice and a case of "harmful folkways."[160]

The consideration extended by the Indians to insanity enters into the plot of one of Cooper's novels.[161] Topinard[162] goes into some detail concerning the cult-functions of two microcephalous idiots in Mexico. Burckhardt[163] gives several cases of honor accorded to idiots. A certain Christian community in Upper Egypt possessed, in 1813, an insane youth who marched about the bazaars quite naked; but the Mohammedans of the place "growing jealous, seized him one night, and converted him by circumcision into a Mohammedan saint." In Egypt, again, "an idiot or a fool is vulgarly regarded by them as a being whose mind is in heaven, while his grosser part mingles among ordinary mortals; consequently, he is considered an especial favourite of heaven. . . . Most of the reputed saints of Egypt are either lunatics, or idiots." Some of them go naked and are permitted, so highly venerated are they, to take liberties with women in a public street. Some eat straw or a mixture of that and broken glass, to attract attention.[164] Wilken[165] points out that the Sanskrit and French terms for idiot show mental defectives to be favored of heaven. It was sometimes thought that the evil spirit might be expelled by violent means or by command of a greater spirit, as in the Bible. Beating and mal-treating the insane was once a common practice; witness the term "bedlam," derived from Bethlehem, the name of a historic English insane retreat.[166] It is noteworthy that the spirit which has possessed the human victim, being allowed to take refuge in a herd of animals, at once causes them to act in a totally unnatural and insane manner.[167]

The Russians have some reputation for extending reverence to persons of weak intellect or diseased mind. When Ivan the Terrible wanted to destroy the city of Pskov, such a person, regarded as holy and a prophet, went out to meet him and shouted, addressing him by the familiar form of his name: "How long wilt thou pour out innocent Christian blood? Depart from here, or a great calamity will befall thee." Whereupon, we are told, "this mighty tyrant . . . arose and departed, in terror, as if an enemy had routed him. . . . All persons of this class are now regarded by the common people in Russia as persons in whom the divine power rules without restraint. Any village in which there is such a person thinks itself particularly fortunate, and his or her speeches are taken as oracles. The monasteries try to get possession of such

[159] Bruun, *Huleboerne*, 250. [160] Sumner, *Folkways*, §29.
[161] *The Deerslayer* (Hetty, daughter of Tom Hutter).
[162] *Anthropologie*, 726. [163] *Travels in Arabia*, II, 27-28.
[164] Lane, *Mod. Egypt.*, I, 312-313. [165] In VG, III, 330.
[166] White, *Sci. and Theol.*, II, 103, 109, 110, 112.
[167] Matthew, VIII, 32; Mark, V, 1-13.

individuals, on account of the money which can be won through them." The
author quoted[168] has a chapter on Possession by the Devil in its connection
with weakness of intellect.[169]

§258*. Ecstasy and Inspiration. Other instances of mental
aberration as a proof of possession will appear later on, in connection with shamanism. If, instead of being continuous, this aberration was sporadic, as in fits and hallucinations, then the possession was likewise occasional, though none the less significant while
it lasted. The Greeks explained such happenings as ecstasy
("standing aside") or abandonment on the part of the soul. The
ecstasy is a passing madness, as madness is a lasting ecstasy; it is
an *alienatio mentis*, a withdrawal of the mind, or a hieromania, a
holy madness, in which the soul, having deserted the body, unites
with the godhead.[170] Though we have in the Greek the origin of
the term ecstasy, we must not assume that the primitive conception knows of any speculative union with a god; its version of ecstasy means simply possession by a spirit in the absence or complete subjection of the soul. Tylor[171] speaks of how persons "who
in the natural state showed neither ability nor eloquence, would
in such convulsive delirium burst forth into earnest lofty declama-
tion, declaring the will and answers of the gods, and prophesying
future events, in well-knit harangues full of the poetic figure and
metaphor of the professional orator. But when the fit was over,
and sober reason returned, the prophet's gifts were gone." Wilken[172] expands as follows: "Insane persons and those suffering
from epilepsy, hysteria, and hypnosis are thus endowed with
prophetic gifts through the fact that a powerful spirit has entered them. . . . Hence the possession, in greater or less degree,
of the gift of prophecy by persons who get into a state wherein
their souls are thought wholly or in part to have been separated
from their bodies. This is the case, among others, with the dying.
. . . Sleepers too have to a certain degree the gift of divination;
in sleep the soul leaves the body, wanders around everywhere, and
so brings about dreams."

[168] Andree, *Eth. Parallelen*, 4-5.   [169] See Hills, in PSM, LX, 31 ff.
[170] Rohde, *Psyche*, II, 18-19; Kipling, *Kim*, last ch.
[171] *Prim. Cult.*, II, 134.   [172] In VG, III, 333.

In the Solomon Islands, possession by ghosts (*ataro*) is common. "The priest who has charge of the village shrine becomes possessed in the ordinary course of business in order that he may know the will of the ghosts. . . . But other men too become possessed. A party on the war-path will wait while one of their number becomes possessed, to learn the issue of their expedition. A possessed man sees into the future, forewarns of coming events, gives news of the absent, decides who should lead the war party, whether they should allow a school in the village, and so on. A party in a canoe wishing to know whether it is wise to go on, wait while one of them becomes possessed. The canoe rocks violently from side to side when the *ataro* comes into the man. . . . The natives remark that much deception is practised and that many cases of possession are fraudulent, but that in their opinion there is also real possession, which may be known partly by the real change of voice, and partly by the eyes, out of which a strange soul looks, not the soul of the man possessed. Possession is often brought on purposely, but is often involuntary. In the latter case the natives remark that other people of the same family are similarly affected. No doubt madness is considered to be a case of possession."[173] Among the Balinese, some person announces that he is inspired by a god or spirit; then people believe what he says is an oracle. Early in 1882 a woman of doubtful reputation asserted that she was inspired and soon had such a following that if the Dutch government had not been aware of the situation there might have been an uprising. Those who are mentally sick are inspired by a spirit, know everything, do not have to think but may answer whatever comes into their heads.[174] This is no purely savage phenomenon; it is pleasant and easy and gives one an expansive feeling of significance in the world to know it all without having to work or think; a good many writers on social topics bask in this incomparable beam of inspiration.

Inebriation, as will be seen later on,[175] forms a good example of possession; in the Congo region drunkenness "was not condemned in either men or women, but was looked upon with good-natured amusement. When a man went 'on the drink,' he pinned a leaf in his hair to show he was drinking, then if he abused anyone no notice was taken of it; and if he entered into a contract which he afterwards considered was to his disadvantage he need not ratify it, because he had a leaf in his hair—a sign of his fuddled condition."[176]

It has been frequently noted that the white man was regarded as a superior being because of his knowledge; it is not always possible to say whether he is to be viewed as a hero in process of deification or as a possessed and inspired person, for the two conceptions of hero and fetish run together.[177] The Cheyennes use the word meaning "spider," and implying superior intelligence, for white men; it is allied to the name of their high god and to the word for chief. The same is the case with the Arapaho. The spider spins a wonderful web; goes up and down on nothing; is the ablest of insects.[178] Take, again, the case of Sir James Brooke, who saved the Dyaks from their Malay masters and became rajah in Sarawak; the natives had good ground, says Wilken,[179] for according him spiritual quality and honor. "Several of their tribes have as-

[173] Fox and Drew, in JAI, XLV, 169.
[174] Wilken, in VG, I, 369.
[175] §311, below.
[176] Weeks, in JAI, XL, 416.
[177] §240, above.
[178] Grinnell, *Cheyenne*, II, 88, 89.
[179] In VG, III, 167-168; he quotes Low, *Sarawak*, 246-247, 251, 255, 259.

cribed to Mr. Brooke the attributes and powers of a superior being; and believe that he can, by his word, shed an influence over their persons or property, which will be beneficial to them. In all their prayers, he is named with the gods of their superstitions, and no feast is made at which his name is not invoked. . . . When Mr. Brooke visits their residences, instead of supplicating him, they each bring a portion of the padi-seed they intend to sow next season, and with the necklaces of the women, which are given to him for that purpose, and which, having been dipped into a mixture previously prepared, are by him shaken over the little basins which contain the seed . . . he is supposed to render them very productive. Other tribes, whom from their distance he cannot visit, send down to him for a small piece of white cloth, and a little gold or silver, which they bury in the earth of their farms, to attain the same result. On his entering a village, the women also wash and bathe his feet, first with water, and then with the milk of a young cocoa-nut, and afterwards with water again: all this water, which has touched his person, is preserved for the purpose of being distributed on their farms, being supposed to render an abundant harvest certain." Especially is he invoked at the harvest-festivals. A man who is regarded in something this manner has little trouble in ruling; native chiefs, it will be seen, are generally recipients to some degree of the reverence accorded to Brooke. It is but a step to deification; in fact, many a native ruler is deified while still living. This striking case is located here instead of under hero-worship in order to emphasize the blending of categories into one another.

In New Zealand the daimon "frequently took up his abode in the priest himself, who when thus filled with his spirit was so violently disturbed in all his limbs, so frantic in his movements, foaming at the mouth, as to appear filled with the god and no longer master of his own actions. . . . Every word he uttered while in that state was regarded as proceeding from the god and not from himself."[180] A number of instances of this order will appear in a subsequent chapter.[181] Among the American Indians, "the conception of a man under superhuman influence being obliged to believe or speak the reverse of the truth is not uncommon";[182] Grinnell[183] goes quite extensively into this notion of Contraries, or men who act by opposites. They say No for Yes; if they asked women not to bring in wood, they meant them to bring it. Many illustrations are given. These Contraries were afraid of lightning and carried magic lances that kept it off; the lances must be handled in a strange and backward manner; if anyone even touched one of them, he must be purified. Then there was the thunder-bow; "no one, not even the Contrary himself, might pass between the bow and the fire; only the pipe could pass there." No dogs were allowed in the Contrary's lodge and he might not own a dog. No one might step in the foot-prints of a Contrary or he in anyone else's, or there would result footsoreness and lameness; the Contrary's business was to step in the foot-prints of enemies. On any occasion of ceremony the Contrary must not scratch his head with his fingers; he must use a pointed stick. He could not escape his office until someone dreamed of the thunder-bow, in which case the dreamer was required to relieve the Contrary. The latter might not associate on terms of equality or familiarity with the rest of the camp; might not joke; must be alone and apart, as on some distant hill. No one became a Con-

---

[180] Taylor, *Te Ika*, 212.
[182] Mallery, in BAE, X, 466.

[181] Ch. XXXVIII, below.
[183] *Cheyenne*, II, 79 ff.

trary by choice, for the office was a great burden, but by virtue of a dream-warning from which there was no escape. There was a Contrary Society which was somewhat on the lines of the individual Contrary.

Among the Guiana Indians, "the object of the war dance was that each warrior sought to kindle in his breast the . . . Tiger (Jaguar) Spirit. Indeed, the Indian reasoned thus: 'In cold blood I am shocked and find it impossible to kill a man, let alone to split the skull of an innocent fellow. But were I to do so, then it cannot be out of my own impulse, but I must be forced into it by fury and lust of blood, which cannot be anything else but the Tiger Spirit. To arouse this spirit in me, I must dance the Jaguar dance, imitate all his movements. I growl, I hiss, I swing the club just like he does when he crushes his prey with one blow of his terrible claws. And when I have once killed my enemy, I must likewise drink his blood and taste the flesh with a view to satisfying the spirit that impels me to the deed.' Every man, animal, or living form, however kindly disposed, can rouse in himself the Tiger Spirit which compels him to perpetrate deeds over which he subsequently feels remorse."[184] Those who have followed the training of raw recruits will understand what it means to evoke the Tiger Spirit; and no one who has a memory of the late war will fail to recognize that spirit in its modern guise of Hate, followed by deeds of Frightfulness.

There should be one illustration in this place of the attainment of inspiration by the use of intoxicants; the general case, again, is taken up under shamanism. "All over the plains where the dried peyote is used, the Indians delight in peyote visions and respond to their thrill; even when the dreams are terrifying in character. The visions reported from tribe to tribe seem to imply that a certain amount of unconscious control may be exerted over the type of vision, dependent upon the picture which the Indian expects to see." Peyote is a cactus-product. The following is an affidavit from a peyote-user: "After I had taken twelve beans of peyote I saw a mountain with roads leading to the top and people dressed in white going up these roads." It may be interpolated that the modern primitive visions are not seldom colored by what has been picked up from missionaries and other white men. "I got very dizzy, and I began to see all kinds of colors, and arrows began to fly all around me. . . . I began to hear voices, just like they were all over the ceiling, and I looked around in the other room and thought I heard women singing in there; but the women were not allowed to sing in the meetings usually, and so this was kind of strange. After eating thirty-six of these peyote I got just like drunk. . . . I began to see a big bunch of snakes crawling all around in front of me, and it was a feeling like as if I was cold came over me. The treasurer of the Sacred Peyote Society was sitting near me, and I asked him if he heard young kittens. It sounded as if they were right close to me; and then I sat still for a long time and I saw a big black cat coming toward me, and I felt him just like a tiger walking up on my legs toward me; and when I felt his claws I jumped back and kind of made a sound as if I was afraid." One of the Indians "was an ordinary reservation Indian, who had had some schooling and had been in Washington and other eastern cities. On this occasion the opening reading from the Bible had been a story of the Hebrew prophet taken up to heaven in a chariot of fire. The Indian fell into a trancelike state and afterwards described his vision. He related that Jesus had come for him in an

[184] Roth, in BAE, XXXVIII, 580.

automobile and had taken him up to heaven, where he had seen God in His glory in a splendid city; and with God he had seen many of the great men of all time, more than he could remember."[185]

The idea of possession by a spirit, at the time of the departure of the soul, at the hour of death, is harbored by many peoples and found in several literatures; it is clearly marked in Homer,[186] and in the Bible,[187] where the dying prophesy. Socrates reminded his accusers, for whom he predicted chastisement: "I am now in that state in which men are most prophetic—when they are about to die."[188] As one more instance among many, may be cited the Biblical idea that insanity and prophetic ecstasy are akin, both being regarded as the work of daimons.[189]

The word "inspiration" (from *inspiro*, "to breathe in") betrays in its etymology its original significance. It may be connected with strength of mind or even with acquired dexterities as well as with mental aberrations. Thus men who are skilled in the arts are spoken of in the Bible as those that are "wise-hearted," in whom "I have put wisdom."[190] Closely allied with this idea is the conception of an inherent "virtue" or personality in a man; it is called by different names among different peoples, but is recognized widely. When present in exceptional degree it is "genius," a term which witnesses to the idea of possession.

The fact that certain writers have sought to identify such conceptions with a very primitive belief in an inherent virtue, residing in things as well as in men, leads us to develop the case in some detail in the present connection. It has been referred to above through the occasional mention of the Melanesian term *mana*. Reflection over this conception, at this point of our exposition, affords us a pretty complete example of generalized fetishism wherein men, and things as well, become repositories of a "virtue" not their own but induced or inspired in them by spiritual agencies. That the man-fetish is but a counterpart of the thing-fetish will appear quite evident, we think, as the following evidence is scanned.

"The Melanesian mind," says Codrington,[191] "is entirely possessed by the belief in a supernatural power or influence, called almost universally *mana*. This is what works to effect everything which is beyond the ordinary power of men, outside the common processes of nature; it is present in the atmosphere of life, attaches itself to persons and to things, and is manifested by results which can only be ascribed to its operation. When one has got it, he can use it and direct it, but its force may break forth at some new point; the presence

---

[185] Shonle, in AA, XXVII, 70-71; N. Y. *Times*, Jan. 8, 1923.
[186] *Iliad*, XVI, 851-854; XXII, 358-360.
[187] Gen., XLIX.
[188] Plato, *Apology*, XXX; Shakespeare, *Rich. II*, act ii.
[189] Maurer, *Vkde.*, I, 44-45.
[190] Exod., XXXI, 6; XXXV, 10, 25; XXXVI, 1.
[191] *Melanesians*, 118, 119, 120, 125.

of it is ascertained by proof. A man comes by chance upon a stone which takes his fancy; its shape is singular, it is like something; it is certainly not a common stone, there must be *mana* in it. So he argues with himself, and he puts it to the proof; he lays it at the root of a tree to the fruit of which it has a certain resemblance, or he buries it in the ground when he plants his garden; an abundant crop on the tree or in the garden shews that he is right, the stone is *mana*, has that power in it. Having that power it is a vehicle to carry *mana* to other stones. In the same way certain forms of words, generally in the form of a song, have power for certain purposes; a charm of words is called a *mana*. But this power, though itself impersonal, is always connected with some person who directs it; all spirits have it, ghosts generally, some men."

It may be interpolated here that much has been made of *mana*—and of *wakonda, orenda, oki, manitou, kutchi, agud, bu-nissi, n'ga, uhgen*, and other similar conceptions—as a sort of pre-animistic phase of belief in the supernatural. Clodd[192] who lists such terms and tries to explain many different things by *mana*, gets the following idea of it from the writers who have built upon it. "What appears to rule the life of man at his lowest, and to persist in often unsuspected form throughout his history, is the sense of a vague, impersonal, ever-acting, universally-diffused power which, borrowing the word for it common to the whole Pacific, is called *mana*." We do not share these views nor those contending for the priority of magic to other forms of religious belief and practice;[193] and call attention here to the animistic tinge of the notions recorded in the above passage from Codrington and in the following continuation of the same. *Mana*, we think, is but evidence of fetish-quality. "If a stone is found to have a supernatural power, it is because a spirit has associated itself with it; a dead man's bone has with it *mana*, because the ghost is with the bone; a man may have so close a connexion with a spirit or ghost that he has *mana* in himself also, and can so direct it as to effect what he desires; a charm is powerful because the name of a spirit or ghost expressed in the form of words brings into it the power which the ghost or spirit exercises through it." *Mana* is the superlative idea of luck as a personal attribute and gift of supernatural origin, proved by success and prosperity. In dealing with life's contingencies its possessor is truly inspired. "Thus all conspicuous success is a proof that a man has *mana;* his influences depend on the impression made on the people's mind that he has it; he becomes a chief by virtue of it. Hence a man's power, though political or social in its character, is his *mana;* the word is naturally used in accordance with the native conception of the character of all power and influence as supernatural. If a man has been successful in fighting, it has not been his natural strength of arm, quickness of eye, or readiness of resource that has won success; he has certainly got the *mana* of a spirit or of some deceased warrior to empower him, conveyed in an amulet or a stone round his neck, or a tuft of leaves in his belt, in a tooth hung upon a finger of his bow hand, or in the form of words with which he brings supernatural assistance to his side. If a man's pigs multiply, and his gardens are productive, it is not because he is industrious and looks after his property, but because of the stones full of *mana* for pigs and yams that he possesses. Of course a yam naturally grows when planted, that is well known, but it will

192 *Magic*, 2 (quoted), 3 ff.; Read, *Origin of Man*, 121, 122, 183.
193 §303, below.

not be very large unless *mana* comes into play; a canoe will not be swift unless *mana* be brought to bear upon it, a net will not catch many fish, nor an arrow inflict a mortal wound."

That *mana* is not the diffused and impersonal power which some theorists assert it to be is indicated by its unequal distribution and its persistence in the case of certain individuals. Codrington goes on, in continuation: "The ghost who is to be worshipped is the spirit of a man who in his lifetime had *mana* in him; the souls of common men are the common herd of ghosts, nobodies alike before and after death. The supernatural power abiding in the powerful living man abides in his ghost after death, with increased vigour and more ease of movement. After his death, therefore, it is expected that he should begin to work, and some one will come forward and claim particular acquaintance with the ghost; if his power should shew itself, his position is assured as one worthy to be invoked, and to receive offerings, till his cultus gives way before the rising importance of one newly dead, and the sacred place where his shrine once stood and his relics were preserved is the only memorial of him that remains; if no proof of his activity appears, he sinks into oblivion at once."

Mana in human beings seems to us, therefore, to afford evidence of possession and inspiration; and, when it occurs in things, to represent the same sort of indwelling spiritual influence. Both the persons and the objects are thereby rendered fetishistic in quality. It is quite possible, however, that the idea of *mana* may be allied to that of souls in things[194] and so go back immediately to animism, without reference to fetishism. In any case, it is our view that the primitive mind regularly works up to the abstract from the concrete and not in the opposite sense. To start, as some would wish to do, with the vague notion of inherent virtue seems to us to ignore the well-attested evidence of observation and experience. It is a species of philosophizing. The fact that the actual provenance of the spiritual influence which confers *mana* is not identifiable should not cause any more agitation of mind than the impossibility of determining the precise eidolon which has become a recognized daimon.

§259. "The Great Man" and "The People."

The genius is the "inspired" man, the "wizard"; great men of all ages, of the later as well as the earlier, have been regarded as something more than human. Their personalities and exploits have formed the evidence for this belief, their deeds ranging as they do all the way from asserted "miracles" to the exhibition in an extreme degree of com-

[194] §214, above.

monly known powers. Such men are the objects of hero-worship. Thus Napoleon evokes the wonder of all by reason of his extraordinary personality and his genius in several lines; he is the "Man of Destiny," with a "preposterous assurance" in the "star" that watched over him. And, in a totally different path of life, the lofty and intricate musical compositions of the deaf Beethoven[195] seem beyond human power. Legends gather about such extraordinary and marked men, and they are half deified; their feebler counterparts on a more primitive stage are fully apotheosized.

The typical fetish-man is the shaman or medicine-man. He is reserved for a place by himself,[196] and present interest inheres only in setting in its proper place under fetishism the general case of which he is by far the most conspicuous specific example. His nature and function demand, for their full understanding, the antecedent development of several topics not yet touched upon; further, it is out of shamanism that some of our latest phases of religion and of science almost directly spring. Though it would cripple presentation to leave the man-fetish out of a sketch of fetishism, to follow fetishism directly with shamanism would be to do the latter and indeed the whole presentation an injury. Our brief illustration at this point will confine itself chiefly to the fetish-man who is not specifically a shaman.

"In 1830 an impudent boy, who could train snakes, announced that he could work miracles." He was accepted as Vishnu's last avatar, or incarnation, hymns were sung to him, and he was worshipped as a god even after his early death from snake-bite. "A weaver came soon after to the temple, where stood the boy's now vacant shrine, and fell asleep there at night. In the morning he was perplexed to find himself a god. The people had accepted him as their snake-conquering god in a new form. The poor weaver denied his divinity, but that made no difference. In 1834 the dead boy-god was still receiving flowers and prayers."[197]

Thus do religious attachés become fetishes and gods, often quite fortuitously but oftener because of some superiority, even of assurance only, in them; and so arises a hierarchy of saints and cult-heroes. To pass over the intermediate and lesser cases, the head

195 Thayer, *Beethoven*. This author disproves and discards much rhapsodical tradition but establishes facts no less astounding.
196 Chs. XXXVIII, XXXIX, below.
197 Hopkins, *Relig. India*, 522-523, note.

of the religious system, designated by the deity as his mouth-piece, is a genuine fetish-man. Such were the founders and prophets, from Zoroaster and Moses to the Dalai Lama, Mohammed, and the Mahdi. After the Disciples had been inspired through the descent of tongues of flame, we are told that they spoke various languages and possessed certain qualities which were beyond human power of acquisition in a long life-time; they were fetish-men. One recent writer[198] contends that the modern minister should emulate their attainments. Always the race has known that "to err is human"; if, now, the head of the religious system is infallible, he is no mere man; he was not infallible just preceding his investiture with the fetish-character. It is possession by the spirit that makes the fetish-man more than human and lends him that which just before he did not have.

Pope and Emperor alike, though in different degrees, have been vessels and agents of divine power; for the ruler is another prominent type of superhuman fetish-man. It must not be forgotten that he was often both priest and king and that there was in the earlier periods of religious evolution no separation of church and state. Whenever the doctrine has prevailed that "the king can do no wrong"—and it prevails in the face of the *errare est humanum* —the king is a fetish-man, has "divine right" and all the other fetish-perquisites. When the divinity that hedges "God's anointed" ceases to protect him, the fetish-quality has passed.

"The greater part of Fiji is ruled over by chiefs who are invested with divine or ghostly attributes such as *mana*, or miraculous power. They are sometimes spoken of as gods or ghosts (*kalou*), and frequently trace their descent to an ancestor spirit (*Kalou vu*). In short, these chiefs are divine."[199] In Madagascar chiefs are considered to be far above the common herd and almost divine. If the chief curses, the people consider the words he speaks as unalterable and certain of fulfillment; those whom he curses are full of fear and distress. If he blesses, the recipients are correspondingly elated over their guaranteed good fortune. "For the chiefs are supposed to have power as regards the words they utter, not, however, merely the power which a king possesses, but power like that of God; a power which works itself on account of its inherent virtue, and not power exerted through soldiers and strong servants."[200] This "virtue" that inheres in the chief also emanates from him: in West Africa, "criminals who are doomed to death are always gagged, because if a man should speak to the king he must be pardoned. This somewhat resembles the Ashanti custom

[198] See Lewis, "The Professional Ministry," in *Atl. Mo.,* CXVI.
[199] Hocart, in JAI, XLIX, 44. [200] Sibree, in JAI, XXI, 225.

that if a criminal should succeed in swearing on the king's life he must also be pardoned, because such an oath is believed to involve danger to the king."201

Williamson202 devotes much attention to the divine or fetish-character of the chiefs of Central Polynesia, with profuse illustration. One of his summaries reads as follows: "The chief or other head of a social group, great or small, was its natural priest. This means that he was the person who, as head of the group, would *ex officio* be the medium of communication between the people and their . . . gods, the person who would, more than any of the other members of the group, be able to approach and hold intercourse with the gods, and especially . . . the tutelar god of the group, who would enter into and inspire him. This close divine association would endow the head of a group with a degree of sanctity not possessed by its other members. . . . It is therefore natural that we should find evidence of the great sanctity attributed to the chiefs, and especially to the higher chiefs or kings. . . . The first matter to which I draw attention is that of the long ancestries, some of them extending backwards to the distant mythical past, claimed by families of great chiefs or kings, and to the fact that some of these families were credited with distinguished divine descent. . . . The question is not whether these traditions were correct, it is whether they were believed to be correct, or so far accepted as to provide bases upon which the claims of the great chiefs to personal sanctity could rest and be acknowledged by their people. . . . A cult of the dead seems to have been a prominent feature in the religions of Polynesia. It is obvious that with this cult the families of the great chiefs or kings, and any other chief families whose position was such that their dead would or might be of sufficient importance to be recognized as what we may call gods, would be able to point to a whole regiment of divine ancestors, and to claim the sanctity which this ancestry involved." The fetish-quality of the priest appears in the foregoing; one case from a distant part of the world may be added. With the Jibaro Indians the priest and priestess are endowed with mysterious powers. They are much in evidence at the victory-feast succeeding the acquisition of a human head and its preparation, by shrinking, as a fetish of high potency. "As a 'priest' or conductor of the ceremonies at the feast . . . only an old warrior can officiate, who himself has killed at least one enemy and celebrated a victory feast. His insight, experience, valor and other prominent military qualities, acquired during a long life, and especially the magical power he has acquired by slaying his enemies, seems to be conceived almost as a physical reality, and his power can, like that of the victor, in a certain degree be transferred to other people. It is for this reason that he is always holding the hand of the victor at the most important ceremonies, the idea being that the action in question will thus attain more emphasis and importance. The same holds good of the priestess, through whose cooperation all actions performed by the women, and particularly by the wife and daughter of the victor, secure the tone and stress necessary."203 The emanation of virtue from the king is clearly revealed in the power of his touch to cure "the king's evil."204 The reception of Queen Victoria as Empress of India leaves little to be desired by way of illustration of the fetish-quality of the supreme ruler;

201 Ellis, *Ewe*, 224.   202 *Cent. Polyn.*, III, 61-63.

203 Karsten, "Jibaro," in BAE, Bull. LXXIX, 89.

204 White, *Sci. and Theol.*, II, 46, 49, note (attested cases); Frazer, *Golden Bough*, I (pt. I, vol. I), 368; III (pt. II), 134.

such cases have been reviewed under the topic of the kingship.[205] The "divine right" of kings and the fiction that "the king can do no wrong" were once very matter-of-fact doctrines; a ruler like Philip II of Spain plainly regarded himself as inspired of God.[206] "The King, moreover, is not only incapable of *doing* wrong, but even of *thinking* wrong: he can never mean to do an improper thing: in him is no folly or weakness."[207] The spirit that made the king a fetish was inducted into him by various ceremonies as it was into the knight with the holy mission.

In later times the fetish-quality has passed, with the extension of democracy, to "The People." *Vox populi vox dei.* The idea seems to be that individually the opinions of common men are foolish, or negligible, or even contemptible; but that when they get together to vote or otherwise to express themselves as a whole, they become inspired for the occasion and are infallible. Even if the obvious element of political diplomacy and flattery, infused into the utterances of "practical" statesmen, be discounted, there is, even at present, a widespread acceptance of this aspect of fetishism.

This belief that the people must be right does not rest upon any rational conviction: upon the consideration, for instance, that in the assembling of many judgments errors and extremes will cancel out; that on the laws of chance the truth will be revealed as it is to the actuary. There is good reason for believing that, in the long run, masses of men following their interests will work out a rejection of the less expedient in favor of the more;[208] but no such reasoned conviction supports the contention about the voice of the people being the voice of God. A vague and unintelligent inkling of the fact that the masses have always determined the mores and have stressed them in the general direction of what is taken to be expedient, that is, "right," may lurk somewhere in the background; nevertheless the actual thing that we see is a great *a priori* dogma lineally descended, through the conception of the infallibility of the directing power of a great system, religious or political, from primitive inspiration, possession, and fetishism. There is nothing rational in it except as reason has been able to disclose

[205] §§155, 156, 158, above.
[206] De Arce, in the play *El Haz de Leña,* characterizes Philip very graphically.
[207] Blackstone, *Comm.* (ed. 1850), 185.
[208] Keller, *Soc. Evol.,* 123-126.

the *rationale* of an unreasoned development;[209] for it lies, like all
the rest of such societal phenomena, in the mores. The idea of the
people-fetish is not the product of intellectual discrimination; it
has been unreflectingly received as tradition.

That God is conceived of as uttering his will, though not altogether unfail-
ingly, in an election, is shown by the case of one Thomas Withers, in 1671,
who for "surriptisiously endeavoring to prevent the Providence of God by
putting in several votes for himself as an officer at a town meeting," had to
stand two hours in the pillory at York, Maine.[210]

There has developed, finally, a sort of intellectual fetishism
which regards the "State" or even "Society" as somehow endowed
with superhuman potency. The Germans have harbored this doctrine along with that of the fetish-emperor. And the socialist, according to Pearson,[211] "finds in the moral and economic changes
in progress . . . the replacement of a worship of the unknowable
by a reverence for concrete society as embodied in the State."

§260*. Totemism: Religious Aspects. That totemism is a
topic to which it is very difficult to assign a place in any series of
religious development is brought home as closer acquaintance is
made with the manifold aspects of the subject. It may be said
preliminarily that it includes features belonging to animism, reincarnation, ancestor-worship, the familiar spirit, fetishism, the
taboo, and magic. The whole matter is complicated by a distinction which some writers very reasonably wish to draw between
"true totemism" and certain forms to which the term, they contend, has been uncritically attached. Further, totemism reveals,
along with pronounced religious aspects, also a social bearing
which cannot well be considered otherwise than in conjunction
with the religious. We shall endeavor to sketch the main lines of
the system in the text, portraying first the religious and then the
social features, and committing most of the ethnographical description to the *Case-Book*.

Though plants and even inanimate things may be totems, the
characteristic representative is the animal. That would be a reason for treating the subject in juxtaposition to animal-fetish-

209 Keller, *Soc. Evol.*, 93-95; *War to Peace*, 31-33.
210 Earle, *Curious Punishments*, 49.   211 *Free Thought*, 329.

ism. In view of the attitude of primitive man toward the animals, he does not revolt in the slightest at tracing his descent from them; and if he does that, it is natural enough that he should preserve an attitude toward the animal-ancestor not dissimilar to the one maintained toward human forefathers. Groups are found to designate themselves by animal-names, such appellation being regularly explained in some parts of the world as the name of the original ancestor. Where that is not the case, the animal-designation may be that of an ancestor's familiar spirit. In any case there is involved a special and intimate relation between a group and the living eponymic animal, meaning the one whose name the men bear, including as a typical feature a taboo at all times, or at all but brief and exceptional periods, upon eating or even upon killing the animal. Such an animal is called a totem and the views and practices involved are known as totemism. This preliminary statement is naturally the barest outline, affording the reader something to begin on; it will be much overlaid with modifying detail as he penetrates into the cases.

Totemism has left behind it many survivals, or what are interpreted to be such, in various parts of the earth; as a living system it occurs on the grand scale only in North America and Australia. The American type is the less complicated and its characteristic features may be noted first. The term "totem" is an Ojibwa Indian word rendered current by an interpreter by the name of Long.[212]

Trustworthy authority[213] on the Indian gives us to understand that "with but few exceptions, the recognized relation between the clan and gens and its patron deity is not one of descent or source, but rather that of protection, guardianship, and support." Many young Indians acquire a patron animal-spirit, sometimes called a "manitou," as the result of a revelation accorded them while under the trance-inducing discipline of initiation; then the patron thus acquired by an ancestor, especially if the latter was also a hero, descends to become the tutelary spirit of a kin-group. Thus the American totem is typically the familiar or guardian spirit[214] as

212 Dellenbaugh, *N. Amer.*, 386.
213 Hewitt, "Totem," in HAI, II, 787 ff.
214 §§163, 244, above.

derived by the individual out of personal experience. It becomes a sort of crest for a clan, though any man may have, in addition, a personal crest in the form of an individual acquisition. In general, although the Indian behaves toward his totem in much the same manner as the Australian toward his, it will become evident, upon a survey of the cases, that there clusters about the American totem no such complication of religious belief and practice as surrounds the Australian. The Australian believes and does practically all that the Indian believes and does, and a good deal more.

In Australia the totem is not a guardian spirit of the American type; it is the reincarnation of a primordial ancestor out of the Alcheringa, or "dream time." The type of reincarnation is highly original: the first ancestor is figured as a sort of combination of man, animal, and god who went about creating things, meanwhile dropping spirits like himself which took residence in rocks, trees, and other natural objects and there awaited the opportunity to enter some woman and be born. The spirit of any man, when he dies, goes back to the natural object in which it resided before birth and sooner or later is reincarnated. While discarnate as a human being, it is in animal or plant-form, and the native whose totem is a certain animal or plant regards it and himself as being "the same." These are hard sayings and passing strange; and the complication is the more astonishing in the case of so backward a people. Nevertheless the system of marriage-restrictions which rests in good part upon totemic distinctions is even more elaborate and amazing.

Australians and Indians have in common the taboo on eating or killing the totem-animal; and both display a consideration and reverence for it which go so far in the case of the Indian that he elaborately excuses himself on occasions when he must kill it. The idea in this appears to be that if the totem-animal is not irritated or alienated by rude treatment there will be plenty of game. Concern for the food-supply is never very far off from the savage mind. The Australian, here again, shows considerable elaboration in his ceremonial. It seems that each totem-group is regarded as being responsible for the proper increase of its totem-animal, which other groups can eat, as he can eat theirs—a sort of group-specialization in both production and renunciation. To secure the desirable supply of the totem-animal there is developed a ceremony that is sacramental in its nature, on the occasion of which the totem-group eats sparingly, or even by the proxy of its sorcerer, of its own ancestral daimon. It is a noteworthy fact that "the native considers that to eat none of his totem would have just as evil effects as to eat too freely. It is essential for him to partake of the totem so as to identify himself closely with it, or else he would be unable to perform the ceremony, and the supply would vanish"[215]—the supply, that is, of the totem-object which he represents. Nothing so recondite as this appears in America. One detail to be noted is the persuasion that children are produced by spiritual agencies, a conviction that has much significance in connection with the earliest ideas about the relations of the sexes.[216]

If totemism, on the religious side, is no more than a general belief in the possibility of descent from natural objects, then it is almost universal, and there is no end to the "possible survivals" of it, for instance in tree-marriage.[217] But it would hardly be worth while to distinguish it by a special name if it did not include more than that theory of descent. It has, as a matter of fact, a distinct social aspect or application, which is a sort of unplanned utilization of the religious appellations for practical purposes; and except for that aspect it is doubtful whether it would have received a distinctive name. Any conclusion as to the whole system should be held in abeyance until those social aspects have been taken into account.[218]

§261*. Totemism: Social Aspects. Totemism has been a grand parade-ground for theorists; but it would not have possessed anything like the allurement it has exerted upon speculative minds if it had not shown social as well as religious features. Extraordinary taboos and regulations have been found in vogue within and between totem-groups and they have exhibited themselves in most complicated and baffling form precisely among a people, the Australians, often rated as one of the most backward on earth. Totemism has interested the theorists most deeply, perhaps, in its

---

215 Spencer and Gillen, in JAI, XXVIII, 278.
216 §334, below.   217 Frazer, *Totemism*, 34.
218 See questionnaire on totemism in *Folk-Lore*, XII, 385 ff.

possible causal connection with the rise of exogamy.[219] It is one of the salient features of that system that no two persons of the opposite sex and of the same totem may mate; as the phrase goes, "the totem must be crossed." Since those who have the same totem are construed to be consanguine through the mythical animal-ancestor, even if not otherwise, such provision for the crossing of the totem functions as a taboo upon consanguine unions. Thus have totemism and exogamy been associated.

Nothing is to be gained by trying to simplify a difficult subject unduly; nevertheless it seems fair to infer that the totems were available labels, derived from independently developing religious beliefs, with which to designate social divisions already existing or forming, and already exogamous or strongly tending that way. If this is so, then the mystery connected with the social side of totemism is shifted over to the issue as to the origin of those divisions and of the prohibition against the mating of their members with one another. The case of the taboo on in-marriage is considered in some detail farther on;[220] regarding the origin of the social divisions not much is known. For some reason as yet not revealed a number of primitive societies have been, from remote antiquity, split up into sections variously denominated moieties, phratries, or simply divisions and sub-divisions, within and between which marriage-taboos have been in force. A number of these sections have borne animal- or plant-names and have been called totem-groups; and the rule about the crossing of the totem has been as nearly invariable as any such regulation can well be. At bottom these societal sub-divisions, whatever their origin, are of the same species as the clan and gens[221] and differ from them little except in their totem-designations—which, indeed, the clan also may have. In fact, it is contended that the only true totemism is where a clan acknowledges an animal-ancestor and from him derives its name.

Whatever the origin of the societal divisions and sub-divisions, and however they came to be designated by the totem, the adjective "totemic" has come to be applied to the sum of the interdivisional practices. There is some reason for this, apart from the

219 §§352, 353, 355, below. 220 §§349, 350, 356, below.
221 §§148, 149, above.

fact that a label of a thing not infrequently in any age comes to stand for the thing itself. If divisions were at one time forming and the mores were trending away from endogamy, existing totemic beliefs of a religious order would have appeared as if created for the explanation and justification of the rising social system. The case would not be unlike the opportuneness of the spirit environment to account for the aleatory element. As between the taboo on close in-marriage and totemism in either of its aspects, we regard the former as more ancient and original; and as between the religious and social sides of totemism, we think the former is older, for it comes down with the very ancient idea of the blood-bond. Tribal divisions and sub-divisions seem to us relatively modern, indicating tribal growth and inner differentiation or perhaps the union of original groups. It may be that this matter of priority is in itself of no more than curious interest; but if the order is as we infer, then it is certainly not the presence of societal divisions that brought about totemism. The latter is primarily a religious system capable of being used to lend plausibility to automatically developed societal structures and functions.

Totemism seems, then, to be basically a religious phenomenon, closely connected with reincarnation and ancestor-worship in Australia and with the conception of the familiar spirit in America. There are developed, subsequently or contemporaneously with it, kin-groups or other societal divisions whose unity is found in the common animal-ancestry assumed. If between such divisions exogamous relations come to exist and other social distinctions or ties are formed, these are expressed in terms of the group-designations or totems. The ensemble of societal usages thus characterized, together with the beliefs and practices connected with the religious conception of the totem, come to be referred to as totemism.

The following résumé by Rivers[222] amounts to a definition of totemism and a review of its essential features. "A general review of communities which are undoubtedly totemic shows that there are three chief features of the relation between men and the classes of animals, plants or inanimate objects which constitutes the essence of totemism. The first and most important feature is that the class of animals or other objects are definitely connected with a social division, and in the typical form of the institution this social division is exogamous. Often the division takes its name from the totem, or this may be used

222 In JAI, XXXIX, 156 ff.

as its badge or crest, but these points are less constant and essential. The second feature is the presence of a belief in kinship between the members of the social division and the totem, and in the most typical form there is belief in descent from the totem. The third feature is of a religious nature; in true totemism the members of the social division show respect to their totem, and by far the most usual method of showing this respect is the prohibition of the totem as an article of food. When these three features are present, we can be confident that we have to do with totemism. In anthropology as in other sciences, however, phenomena do not always exist in their typical form, and there are many cases to be found where totemism has departed from these typical characters and remains none the less totemism. Thus if a totemic people give up the practice of exogamy and come to regulate marriage entirely by blood-kinship, the totem will no longer be the sign of an exogamous division, but it may remain connected with some other social division, either the tribe as a whole or the people inhabiting a certain district, village or hamlet, or even a family in a sense more or less wide. If it were found that the supposed totem were connected with individuals only, or with groups of people who stood in no definite relation to other social divisions, we should have much more hesitation in accepting the connection as one indicating totemism. Again, if a relatively advanced people come to believe in their descent from heroes or gods, they may drop their belief in descent from, or even in kinship with, the animals or other objects connected with their social division and yet the transitions between their condition and that of neighbouring peoples may leave no reasonable doubt that the remaining features are those of true totemism. Once more, the value of totemic animals or plants as articles of food may lead to the disappearance of the prohibition of the totem as an article of diet, and yet some restriction on the use of such food on certain occasions, or under certain conditions, will probably survive to show the respect for the totem which once took a more complete form."

The social aspects of totemism are not exhausted until it is realized how the system pervades the whole life of a society that lives under it. Perhaps if the reader has conceived of the significance of the ghost-cult or of fetishism, he will readily appreciate how totemism, which is related to both, may form a sort of supporting dogma to all thinking and believing and also work out into practice through the various channels provided between conceptions of the world and living in it. We may conclude by offering the rather emphatic contentions of one who has had a long experience with a totemic people of backward culture.[223]

"Totemism not only controls marriages, but indicates the rank and caste of people. The higher the totem pole the greater the man who owns it. . . . Totemism governs the amount to be spent on the dead, what one shall receive at a feast, the paraphernalia he shall wear at a dance, the voice he shall have in public affairs, the size of his house, the esteem in which he is held, the nam-

[223] Jones, *Thlingets*, 173-175.

ing of children and native hospitality. It serves as a fraternal means to bind them together on the one hand, and to separate them on the other, and to mark friends from foes. . . . A woman of a superior totem, or caste, though she may live a life of shame and deepest degradation, is respected, and were she to die, would be deeply mourned and have a costly burial; her sister of an inferior totem, though she had lived an immaculate life, would receive scant recognition, and were she to die, would have few to mourn her death and a shabby burial. Totemism regulates the disposition of the dead. Those of the same totem as the deceased must not raise their hand to do a thing about the body. . . . Totemism proclaims to the world who are the occupants of a house, and denotes lineage, the children taking their mother's totem. It regulates what disposition to make of the property of the dead. It promotes hospitality and sociability, and is a spur to ambition and thrift. Many a man has laboured and saved in order to erect a costly totem pole, or to give a big feast, or to throw some glory on his family crest. Totemism binds them together for mutual help and protection. Every member of a man's totem is ready to contribute of his means and strength to help his friend in time of need. The combined crests of either grand totemic division stand ready, if necessary, to meet the liabilities of any one belonging to their side of the great Thlinget family. Totemism is recorded history, genealogy, legend, memorial, commemoration and art."

CHAPTER XXX

DAIMONOLOGY

§262. **Nature of Daimonology.** The significance of the inexplicable and unpredictable was, and still is, all but dominant in the minds of people of undeveloped culture. To account for its universal presence and effects there was need of some explanation, wide and sweeping, and also resting upon a basis of competent agency rather than of sufficient cause. The solution required was right at hand, as if created to meet the need, in the conception of an imaginary environment of ghosts and spirits. Though this construction is derived from sources which are now deemed illusory, to the primitive mind it appeared to rest four-square upon the evidence of the senses. Animism, eidolism, projectivism, daimonism, and fetishism cover the doctrine about this environment. Now that some idea of the extent and structure of the supernatural realm and of the nature of its denizens, as conceived by those who believed in it and in them, is before him, the reader is in a position better to realize the entire competence of primitive doctrine to explain the otherwise inexplicable aleatory element.

Correlative with the science and art of self-maintenance as developed in adjustment to the facts and forces resident in nature and in fellow-men are the science and art, also of self-maintenance, that secure adjustment to the supernatural environment of spiritual beings—a theory and practice comprehended under the term "daimonology." Just as the industrial and military organizations rose out of the mores as adaptations to the natural and social environments; just as the marriage-organization developed out of the same prolific soil to meet the life-condition of bi-sexuality; so did the religious organization evolve from the mores in response to the conviction that there existed round about mankind and human society a set of immaterial life-conditions not present in the course of evolution until that process had attained to its human phase.

That daimonology represents an adjustment through a set of illusions, albeit to a very real actuality, namely chance, in no way lessens its importance to the eye either of the primitive believer or of the investigating scientist. Doctrine is but embraced the closer when it is not susceptible of direct and conclusive test upon the concrete facts of life.[1] That the "-isms" (eidolism, daimonism) act as a sort of insulation that renders society less sensitive to changes in its physical and social life-conditions, and so less adaptable to them, is a fact; their net effect, nevertheless, cannot be appraised until all, not a part, of their results are before us; and however those results are adjudged, the influence of the doctrines upon society's life remains outstanding.

Not even the most practical considerations are allowed to count against religious prepossessions. Daimonology is the dominant prosperity-policy. For while self-maintenance in the face of nature and fellow-men is basic and engrossing, its eventualities do not weigh upon the primitive mind as does the necessity of adjustment to the supernatural. Fear of the unknown and the inexplicable is what lends to the mores a sanction that renders them more than humanly imperative. Men get along somehow in the struggle with nature and fellow-men and look forward with a degree of confidence to the further stages of that struggle. There is a sort of orientation in it. Men know what to expect. They are in the realm of the calculable, and so long as they can stay there they can live on with a certain assurance. But the moment they experience misfortune in a new, strange, inexplicable form, they lose this assurance and fly to daimonism as to an ultimate, all-inclusive refuge. In fact, even in the struggle with material nature and human competitors, the attitude of the daimons is determinative of any genuine and lasting success; for the aleatory element invades the range even of the commonplace. And so the accepted prosperity-policy of men who hold to daimonism lies not in their toil, forethought, and self-denial but in the success of their relations to the imaginary environment, that is, in the adequacy of their special form of daimonology. It is no wonder, then, that attention seems to be fixed upon religious exercises to the apparent exclusion of any other mode of assuring prosperity.

This accounts for the significance of the religious element in societal evolution. It enters into nearly every relation of existence

1 §198, above.

at all times and into all of them at some time; if it is not always present, the occasions of its entrance are recurrent. It permeates the rest of the societal structure in an exceptional degree. Certain forms of the industrial organization can be understood without reference to the family-organization; others that belong to the regulative system show no vital connection with forms of self-gratification; but it is a precarious business to undertake the explanation of any societal form whatever without reference to religious ideas and usages.

§263. Daimonology and the Evolutionary Series. Thus far in the study of the religious organization the matter presented has covered what people have believed rather than what, in the light of their doctrine, they have done; conceptions rather than policies have been under review. Only in connection with the ghost-cult have we, to some extent, and deliberately, anticipated the topic of practices based on beliefs. It was there found that the operations of the ghost-cult were classifiable under, first, avoid-ance and exorcism (negative methods) and, second, conciliation and propitiation (positive methods). The perspective declares it-self when the cult of the daimons is found revealing itself anew, by its exhibition of these same categories, as the lineal descendant of the ghost-cult. Though the categories in question must now be handled as covering practices less naïve, direct, and concrete, and with the modifications and reservations proper to the more ad-vanced stage of institutional evolution in which they find their setting, it should nevertheless be noted that there is no break in the course of that evolution.

To one reflecting upon its position in the evolutionary series, relatively to its antecedents, it is apparent that daimonology is farther on in the scale of societal development than is any set of doctrines and practices connected with the souls or the ghosts. It is less immediate. It is more derived. As the daimon becomes less personal and definite than the ghost of one recently departed and not yet forgotten as a personality, so do the phenomena of dai-monology become less obviously referable to obvious human quali-ties and mental reactions. They are a grade farther on and are sometimes quite inexplicable except upon the basis of unchecked imagination and sentiment unless their antecedents in the intermediate stage of the ghost-cult be kept steadily in perspective. Because these antecedents should not be lost to view at any time, they have already been covered with some completeness.

It is of the utmost importance to any scientific conception of the subject that the chain of development from animism to the developed forms of religion shall remain unbroken. The eidolon is but the anima when disembodied; the daimon is no more than the eidolon which has become disassociated from any definite origin and has attained a personality of its own. It is our idea to treat daimonology in such manner as to suggest constantly its origin in less developed forms of the cult; and yet, on the other hand, to show its forth-reachings toward those more highly evolved religious systems which, without a scientific knowledge of the course of the evolution of religion, would seem to be disconnected entirely from the complex of primitive beliefs out of which they most certainly sprang.

Since the time of Lyell and Darwin it has been the attitude of science to take for granted that the forces found in actual operation in nature and history are sufficient to account, in accordance with natural law, for any and all phenomena, however complex and seemingly far removed from explanation. This is an inference which has been repeatedly substantiated by painstaking research; it is not an *a priori* speculation. Nor is it a dogma, for it is always under test, in the argument here presented as in that of any other treatise that aims to be scientific. Science sets out to explain as much as possible of the universe and of human life without resorting to that which passes knowledge. It has successively drawn into its recognized and conceded range of explanation this and that domain within which, in former times, the supernatural alone was thought to offer a sufficient cause. Science has been modest in this procedure, whatever the antics of pseudo-scientists or heated devotees. It has not attempted to account for what is as yet outside the reach of its processes of investigation. Concerning such matters science can be nothing else than agnostic; except for its inference that natural law prevails universally, as it has been found to prevail in the several regions once assigned to the realm of the supernatural,[2] or hitherto unexplorable, it does not engage in theorizing about that concerning which no scientific evidence is available.

It follows that there is no real ground for conflict as between science and faith (though, as White[3] has shown, there has been a long and bitter feud between science and theology), for science does not aspire even to the correction of that which may be believed in the absence of scientific evidence. It does not treat of matters which are, as it is sometimes expressed, above and beyond knowledge. It does no more than maintain that the simpler and rationalistic explanation is to be accepted in place of one resting upon intuition, metaphysical speculation, dogma, or alleged miracle, where such scientific explanation, on the basis of so-called "lower" causes, is possible. In this contention science is supported by fact and record of fact; for when a set of phenomena has once become explicable by science, it has been removed immediately or eventually from the mass of phenomena, once nearly all-embracing, which traditionally called for reference to supernatural agency. The weather is no longer supposed to be determined by a god; nor earthquakes, nor geological formations, nor fossils, nor species, nor the form and structure of man, nor the institutions, laws, and destiny of nations. It is within the province of a science of society to show that human institutions are susceptible of scientific treatment and that in them too there is exhibited the reign of law and the course of an evolution. Under these institutions are to be included religious beliefs and practices in their several grades of development.

None of these evolutionary beliefs is inconsonant with belief in a God—only it must be a God of quality, a man's God and not a child's. Science is the best friend religion ever had, for it has progressively refined and elevated men's ideas concerning the Power behind the play of natural and social forces. Science has doubtless led candid and fearless men toward agnosticism, but never toward atheism. Though a scientist may well refuse to believe in an anthropomorphic god, he is the least likely of all men to fail to glimpse, and to stand in awe before, the enveloping Mystery of

[2] §195, above.
[3] *A History of the Warfare of Science with Theology in Christendom.*

life and the Power, working in accordance with inexorable law, that maintains all things. To predisposed persons, an atheist is one whose views as to God do not exactly superpose over their own; hence the agnostic has often been termed an atheist—a display of pure ignorance about on a par with the identification of socialism and anarchism.

Says White[4] of the terms "infidel" and "atheist": "They have been used against almost every man who has ever done anything new for his fellow-men. The list of those who have been denounced as 'infidel' and 'atheist' includes almost all great men of science, general scholars, inventors, and philanthropists. The purest Christian life, the noblest Christian character, have not availed to shield combatants." Examples follow. "These epithets can hardly be classed with civilized weapons. They are burning arrows; they set fire to masses of popular prejudice, always obscuring the real question, sometimes destroying the attacking party."

In pursuing the topic of daimonology beyond its most primitive phases, we shall from time to time approach near enough to doctrine and dogma to make necessary some such remarks as the above. We propose to follow our analysis as far as the facts and legitimate inference based upon them seem to warrant; but we have deemed it right to outline the scientific attitude in respect to religion before we go forward. What is beyond the bounds of scientific knowledge belongs to speculation and faith and so does not fall within the limits of science or of this book.

§264. **Ascending Complexity.** Since daimonology represents an advanced stage of religious evolution, it cannot be cramped under the simpler categories that served well enough to classify the practices of the ghost-cult. When the ghosts have evolved into daimons, the whole situation touching the aleatory element has become even more tense, complicated, and dangerous. It is no longer enough to speed the ghost to its destination and so eliminate its menacing influence once and for all. There exists now an array of supernatural potencies which, being always present, must be lived with while life lasts. They form permanent features of life's environment and to their continued presence perennial adjustment must be made. The aleatory element is now in the control of a developed and specialized set of agents, with individual and

4 *Sci. and Theol.*, I, 135.

definable predispositions, demands, tendencies to take offense, powers to punish and reward. Evidently the matter of getting on with this daimonic environment is not as simple as it was with the ghosts; in fact, it has about come to a pass where mere man, unaided, is not competent to do so.

Even in the ghost-cult it is sometimes necessary for the savage to take recourse to the aid of some element which possesses an extra-natural potency. He could abandon the dead without so doing; but when he employed fire to ban the ghosts, he was using what was to him a spiritual agency. It demanded no such accessory merely to run away or even to frighten the ghost by noise; leaving food at the grave was something anyone could do of and by himself. But the exorcism, coercion, or pacification of daimons could be done only with the aid of some special, spiritually powerful element. Such elements we have come to know as fetishes. It is typical of daimonology that the spirits of a higher potency have to be dealt with by the use of spiritual instrumentalities. In that respect they are farther from men than are the ghosts. It is safe to say that in resistance to or placation of the ghosts there are employed more practices identical with those in use for the same ends with fellow-men than is the case in the more evolved cult of the daimons. Anthropomorphism is more direct and underived in the ghost than it is in the daimon.

Ghosts were treated, in a word, more like living men, and the person who knew how to quell or to conciliate men by more or less obvious means knew also how to deal with the souls of the recently dead. But with the evolution of daimonism this condition could not persist; and so daimonology shows a characteristic difference from the ghost-cult in that most of the art of dealing with the enlarged spirits consists in the employment of spirit against spirit —in reality, a sort of undeveloped dualism, or pitting of one daimon against another. It may still be possible to avoid by simply running away; doubtless propitiation can still be accomplished by the simple giving of this or that; but exorcism and coercion demand the enlistment of spirit against spirit, or of spirit to conciliate spirit. Offensive action against the supernatural, as distinguished from defensive, cannot be without spiritual aid. In short, the typical course of daimonology is by way of fetishism and dualism. This is the mode of the cult in its evolved stages.

Despite all ascending complexity, however, the keynote of the evolving cult continues to be avoidance. The presumption is that the daimons will work ill unless they are evaded, exorcised, or bought off. They are not beneficent unless they are caused to be so.[5] Even propitiation is essentially preventive. Daimons have myriad rights and no duties; men are laden with duties and have no rights. Men are always failing in the discharge of their many and often unknown duties; and the gods are exacting. The balance is always on one side of the account and if the reckoning is squared up it does not long stay so. Ill is always to be feared and to be foreseen, evaded, and insured against, if possible. Characteristic of this preoccupation is the occasional worship of the "unknown god." Primitive peoples are credulous to all revelation, though they adhere to their own. But it was well to be sure that some vagrant daimon, unknown and so neglected, should have no cause for dissatisfaction. Even the Romans, not knowing just which god to call upon, would add to their invocations: "or the right one." Paul found the Athenians ultrareligious in that they had erected, in their prudent thoroughness, an altar to "the unknown god."[6]

This reflection of the preoccupation of men with the ill-luck aspect of the aleatory element[7] provides the cult with its characteristic key-note of avoidance. In highly evolved religious systems the gods may be conceived of as no longer malevolent; in fact, the germs of this conception can be made out even in very crude societies; but the emphasis in primitive cases is upon the evilly inclined spirits, and the good ones, or those not to be feared, are neglected and even held in some contempt. It is when the good spirits can be enlisted against the evil that the practice changes, for then avoidance is no longer the most promising prosperity-policy. That eventuality is far along the course of evolution.

Though we continue along the general lines of classification adopted under the soul-cult, distinguishing, it will be recalled, the negative and the positive methods, we shall expect to find the cases

---

5 §243, above.

6 Lippert, *Kgchte.*, I, 101; Wissowa, *Relig. Röm.*, 49; Acts, XVII, 23.

7 §§196, 197, above.

crossing these categories in an increasing degree as evolution proceeds. And it is necessary also to introduce a new element, that of coercion; for by means of practices known as coercitives it is possible to enforce the service of a daimon by a sort of irresistible propitiation. In reviewing the soul-cult there was no occasion for any such term as coercitive.

It remains, before entering upon the cases, to allude to several extensive topics that are reserved for separate treatment and are mentioned only in passing by way of indicating where and how they fit into the classification. Magic is one of these. The term is used loosely and writers not seldom refer to the cult as no more than a mass of magical practices—a slap-dash classification. Lehmann[8] remarks that a performance done by our own gods is a miracle, while that done by alien deities is magic, illustrating by the Old Testament story of the rods turning into serpents.[9] The transformation of the Egyptians' rods was black art; not so that of the rod of Moses. This is an early exhibition of the ethnocentric tendency, which still persists, to denominate primitive religion forthwith as "mere magic." Magic is an outgrowth of daimonology; it is largely exorcistic and it is also theurgic; much of it would fall readily under our categories, though it would spread over them all. The fact is that magic bears a certain stamp of its own that marks it out as a sort of species that has branched off from the cult-genus sufficiently to deserve independent consideration. It belongs, correctly understood, with sorcery and witchcraft rather than strictly with the cult. It is a derivative of daimonology rather than part and parcel of it.

Again, while the beginnings of medicine are typically exorcistic, it too has a derived evolution of its own; and the same is true of shamanism in general, though it is plainly allied to the cult. If there is recurring occasion to mention these several extensions of daimonology before they can be treated in a special manner, it is hoped that such anticipatory reference will serve to keep their connection with basic beliefs and practices before the mind, and also that the special treatment accorded them later on will recall the earlier and simpler members of the evolutionary series.

Here yet again the paramount fact is encountered that all societal institutions are enmeshed in a continuous connective tissue. They can be considered apart from one another with the purpose of understanding them better and as a device of exposition; but any classification is an artificial contrivance through which life breaks forth and escapes. Avoidance, exorcism, coercion, conciliation, propitiation run one into the other; the cult, magic, medicine, shamanism are all closely interrelated. This or any other classification can reveal no more than types, regularly intermediate between types; the individual cases straggle over from one type to

8 *Overtro*, I, 13.   9 Exod., VII, 12.

the other. In the lists of daimonological practices, certain items
will recall at once those which we have come to know in connection
with the ghost-cult;[10] others are more derived, farther removed
from the crass and obvious; and some of the latter would not be
rationally explicable at all except for the presence of transitional
forms.

§265*. Avoidance: The Evil Eye. By way of escape from the
attentions of the daimons, recourse is taken, we have seen, to various expedients that cannot be regarded as propitiatory. The simplest of these are closely parallel to the practices of avoidance as
exhibited in the ghost-cult, and need illustration rather than explanation.

Certain Papuans believe in two spirits which kill male children, not out of
malevolence, but because they wish to draw to themselves the little ones who
become their property after death. "And so the careful Papuan mother is not
willing to let her child leave the house, after the oncoming of darkness, without
an escort."[11] Among the Yoruba, when the bull-roarer, representing the voice
of a certain daimon, begins to be heard, "all women must shut themselves up
in their houses, and refrain from looking out on pain of death."[12] The Akamba
are always moving about, and for good reason: "it may be lack of water, but
more often the place has become unlucky: deaths in the family, sickness among
them or their cattle, or absence of children; any of these misfortunes will
induce the Mtumia to have recourse to the wisdom of the medicine man, and
his verdict will generally be that his village is unlucky, the haunt, perhaps,
of mischievous spirits, and then the family moves elsewhere. If they do not
move far they will often take the grass and sticks of the old huts, or may even
transport the frameworks whole, but if this is not done the entrance is closed,
the village is left standing as it is, and in perhaps six months it is a moulder-
ing heap of grass and sticks. After the next rains the bush begins to creep
over it, and in a very short time it is lost out of sight."[13]
  "Their dread of tigers is born of bitter experience, for the jungles in the
valleys are infested with them, and to the Nagas they are demons incarnate.
If a man is killed by a tiger, his house and all his belongings are burned, and
his whole family must go through elaborate purification, as if to exorcise an
evil spirit. If a man's or woman's mangled body be found in the jungle within
two or three miles of the village, his whole family divest themselves of every
thread of clothing and go to the body, and simply wrapping it in a bamboo
mat, leave it where it was found; returning to their village, they burn down
their old house and build an entirely new one; new fire is started on the hearth
by means of the fire-saw, and they wash themselves carefully, cutting their
hair and paring their nails; not a single possession of the one who has been
killed may be used again." These people seem to believe "that there is some-

10 Various cases occur under §210, above.
11 Krieger, *Neu-Guinea*, 390-391.   12 Ellis, *Yoruba,* 110.
13 Dundas, C., in JAI, XLIII, 506.

thing contagious about dying, and that association with death is liable to cause it. Merely to spread an untrue report of a man's death may cause it in itself, and the penalty for doing this serious injury is a heavy fine. . . . Possibly the fact of a man being reported dead gives malicious spirits some hold over him, just as to mention the name of an infant (or even of an adult if done often and persistently) is enough to cause death."[14] One author[15] lists the methods of protection against evil powers practised by certain Hindus as follows: "(1) *tabu,* or simple avoidance; (2) avoidance by diversion; (3) avoidance by threats or by mimetic repulsion; and (4) avoidance by actual expulsion through the help of beneficent powers. . . . The best way to safety is to keep yourself out of harm's way—to avoid contact, direct or indirect, with the harmful powers. Such an idea appears to lie at the root of the various *tabus,* or prohibitions which men of the lower culture impose on themselves—*tabus* in connection with names, birth, death, sex, food, blood, and a number of other things. In the Indian hills, when the smallpox first broke out, it was thought to be a devil. No one was allowed to go in or out of the village, and various exorcisms were employed. As these did not work, the inhabitants abandoned the village and took to the jungle."[16] Among certain Borneans one must not whistle after dark. It summons evil spirits and is sure to bring mischief into the house. Tradition has it that in the old times it was strictly against all rule ever to whistle in the house, even in the daytime.[17] With this may be compared the more modern whistling up of the wind and the taboo against whistling on Sunday. "The world of evil spirits with which his easily disturbed brain . . . peoples all fear-inspiring places in his neighborhood, prevents the Bahan from going anywhere where his needs do not drive him."[18] A child's birth is announced to the spirits, "that they may do no ill to the child." When a funeral is over, "all hasten away as fast as possible, on account of the evil spirits which are there present."[19]

In America a number of significant cases have been observed. For example, about the year 1871, Dorsey[20] was told by the Ponka "that they believed death to be caused by certain malevolent spirits, whom they feared. In order to prevent future visits of such spirits, the survivors gave away all their property, hoping that as they were in such a wretched plight the spirits would not think it worth while to make them more unhappy." Among certain tribes, it is worth repeating, "the occurrence of several years of drought in succession would be construed as a mark of disfavor of the gods, and would be followed by a movement of the people from the village. Even a series of bad dreams which might be inflicted on some prominent medicine-man by overindulgence in certain articles of food would be regarded as omens indicating a necessity for a change of location. Such instances are not unknown." Toothache is similarly ominous; "so that many a village has been abandoned simply because some prominent medicine-man was in need of the services of a dentist. Many other reasons might be stated, but these will suffice to show upon what slight and often trivial grounds great villages of stone houses, the result of much labor and the picture of permanence, are sometimes abandoned in a day."[21]

---

[14] Furness, in JAI, XXXII, 465; Hutton, *Sema Nagas,* 242-243.

[15] Roy, in JAI, XLIV, 342.   [16] Lewin, *S.E. India,* 226.

[17] Furness, *Head-Hunters,* 165-166.   [18] Nieuwenhuis, *Borneo,* II, 119.

[19] Pleyte, in *Globus,* LXXIX, 24, 27.   [20] In BAE, XI, 374.

[21] Mindeleff, in BAE, XIX, pt. II, 646.

The Guiana Indians believe that an unnamed person will be a certain victim of the first sickness or misfortune encountered by him; hence the name is a protective device and only the poorest are without names. They are bestowed by the medicine-man (piai) for a fee proportioned to the virtue of the incantations which he makes. "At the present time it would seem that the piai gives a name only if he has been called in to attend a child when sick; under such circumstances he will say that he has dreamed that the child requires a name. . . . A convalescent patient might start life afresh with a new name. . . . Among the Surinam Caribs some of the old men and women have travel names, which are used only on a journey. . . . This *nom de voyage* serves especially to trick the evil spirits . . . for which of these gentry would ever think of looking for the practically unknown real Atarwa under the pseudonym of Aliensi, a name universally known? And as far as the baptismal name is concerned anyone may know this, because the Evil One is powerless against the baptism of the whites!" Here, then, the name has its usual significance; "both on the islands and on the mainland names were exchanged in testimony of great affection and inviolable friendship."[22] One was safe if his name was held by one whom he could trust, while it was dangerous for a hostile man— much more so for a mischievous spirit—even to know that name.

In Guiana, again, "before attempting to shoot a cataract for the first time, on the first sight of any new place, every time a sculptured rock or striking mountain or stone is seen, the Indians avert the ill-will of the spirits of such places by rubbing red pepper each into his or her eyes. . . . The Indian, having prevented himself from seeing a harmful being, thinks that the latter does not see him." In particular it is the petroglyph that inspires to such practice. The author[23] just quoted tells elsewhere how, while sketching such a rock-picture, he looked up to find the Indians—men, women, and children— engaged in the pepper-rubbing. "The extreme pain of this operation when performed thoroughly by the Indians I can faintly realize from my own feelings when I have occasionally rubbed my eyes with fingers which had recently handled red-peppers; and from the fact that, though the older practitioners inflict this self-torture with the utmost stoicism, I have again and again seen that otherwise rare sight of Indians, children, and even young men, sobbing under the infliction. Yet the ceremony was never omitted. Sometimes when by a rare chance no member of the party had had the forethought to provide peppers, lime-juice was used as a substitute, and once, when neither peppers nor limes were at hand, a piece of blue indigo-dyed cloth was carefully soaked, and the dye was then rubbed into the eyes." One idea underlies all these ceremonies "and that is the attempt to avoid attracting the attention of malignant spirits."

A modern case is where Russian-American parents sold two of their children, when ill, for a nominal sum.[24] Physicians could not help them, but both later got well, which, of course, proved the theory. They had been, as it were, whisked away to a place where luck was better.

One of the most striking of the avoidance-practices is the treatment accorded to one who has obviously fallen a victim to the

[22] Roth, in BAE, XXXVIII, 677, 678.
[23] Im Thurn, *Brit-Guiana,* 368-369.   [24] N. Y. *Times,* June 26, 1925.

aleatory element through meeting with serious accident. Such a person, as one marked down by the spirits for destruction, is to be avoided, even to the extent of refusal to assist him out of his trouble.

Among the Australians, who ordinarily inter the dead, in cases of death from snake-bite, or from accident of any kind, the body is placed on a platform of sticks, in a tree. When death is caused by violence, the body is not buried, but left where it lies.[25] In some places in Melanesia, "if a sacred shark had attempted to seize a man and he had escaped, the people would be so much afraid of the shark's anger that they would throw the man back into the sea to be drowned."[26] If the daimon has sealed a victim unto himself, it is the part of discretion not to interfere but to let him have his way. Thus the Tshi negroes never attempt to rescue miners after a cave-in. The Togo tribes refuse burial to those who are struck by lightning; such people are thought to be the worst creatures under the sun and to have caused all the ill occurring in the time just preceding their death. They are assimilated, through refusal of burial, with women who die in childbirth and debtors who die without having paid.[27] In Uganda, though cases of people being struck by lightning are far from uncommon, they are occasions for a great ceremony. The victim is not moved from the spot where he met his death but nine witches or old women are sent for and a special priest, who sprinkles most of the crowd with water as a sign of purification. "Then he announces in a loud voice that the 'Bachwezi' are angry because some wrong-doing has occurred either on the part of the dead man or on the part of members of his clan. For this wrong-doing the ancestral spirits have demanded a victim." The corpse is placed on top of an ant-hill and left there unburied.[28]

Certain people in Bengal "expose in the jungle those who perish of snake-bite or other violent death, the belief being that such persons are taboo and their ghosts likely to prove malignant, in which case it is usually deemed expedient for the survivors to abandon the neighborhood, permanently or for a time."[29] Pilgrims who have fallen into the Ganges have been allowed to drown "without the slightest effort being made to save them by other Hindus near at hand, under the impression that they would be doing an injury to the drowning persons in taking them from the sacred water."[30] Perhaps this explanation is somewhat rationalized; it is generally fear for one's self that leads to abandonment of the victim of accident. In China, "at the reassembling of a class in a Christian college, the absence of a certain student was noted. It was reported that he had been drowned while on a launch trip, returning from a vacation. His small brother had been with him at the time; the boy had been pushed overboard from the crowded deck; a strong swimmer, he had been able to reach the side of the boat, but not to clamber aboard; but the pleas of the puny younger brother could not avail to move a single person to lift a helping hand, and the other passengers had looked on while the lad drowned, rather than move to save him. The teacher heard the tale in horror,

[25] Mathews, in AA, II, 500.   [26] Codrington, *Melanesians*, 179.

[27] Ellis, *Tshi*, 70; Seidel, in *Globus*, LXXII, 42.

[28] Johnston, *Uganda*, II, 589-590.

[29] Crooke, in JAI, XXVIII, 246.   [30] Wilkins, *Hinduism*, 452-453.

but the student accepted it as a matter of course, explaining that the drowning devil, who had been after the student, would certainly have taken possession of any person who attempted to rescue him. And these men, in the closing years of a Christian education, had no word of censure for people who had calmly watched a fellow drown rather than incur the wrath of a devil!"[31] Similarly the Chinese in the Malay Archipelago show themselves to be strong fatalists. "If you fall into the water they will never put out a hand to help you, as they take your fall as a sign that the god of the waters is determined to have a life, and they think if it isn't yours he gets it will be theirs. I only know of one case where a Chinaman saved a man from drowning, and that was an extraordinary exception to their rule."[32] In Sarawak the bodies of those who die from blow-pipe poison are put up on a scaffolding.[33] Certain Costa Rica Indians hold the snake to be the servant of the god, through whom he punishes men; hence the treatment accorded to one who dies of snake-bite. "He is buried outside the house, his grave is not cared for, and his wife cannot marry again, indeed is not touched again. . . . All drinking-vessels hitherto used are thrown away and new ones put in use in their place."[34]

In many Greek legends, death by lightning makes the victim holy and exalts him to the life of the gods; but snake-bite was regarded, at least in the Philoctetes legend, as a legitimate reason for desertion.[35] Among the Ossetes, "if anyone is struck by lightning, he is thought to be holy and is buried on the spot where he fell, with general jubilation; the grave becomes a place to which pilgrimages are made."[36] In such a case the interpretation of the accident has been altered, in view, probably, of a changed conception of the nature of the daimons; but, as the final instance will show, the older interpretation may long persist. Among the seamen of Orkney and Shetland it was deemed unlucky to rescue persons from drowning, since it was held as a matter of religious faith that the sea is entitled to certain victims, and if deprived would avenge itself on those who interfered.[37]

These cases represent specific attempts to avoid crossing the will of the spirits as disclosed in the play of the aleatory element. It is evident that the victim of that element is somehow accursed, and men treat him, in his hapless estate, with lack of consideration and even cold cruelty. One thinks at once of the heartless words of Kreon to the woe-smitten Œdipus.[38]

Under avoidance must be ranged likewise a set of practices consequent upon belief in the "evil eye" or "evil glance," often aligned with the "jettatura" of the Italians,[39] which is a sort of spell cast by persons supposed to be possessed of the evil eye. This belief is

[31] Hutchinson, in *Atl. Mo.,* CXXVII, 123.
[32] Cator, *Head-Hunters,* 54.   [33] Roth, *Sarawak,* I, 152, note.
[34] Sapper, in *Globus,* LXXVI, 350.
[35] Rohde, *Psyche,* I, 320; Homer, *Odyssey,* II, 721 ff.; Sophocles, *Philoctetes,* 254 ff.
[36] Stern, *Russland,* 97.   [37] Tudor, *Orkneys,* 167.
[38] Sophocles, *Œd. Tyr.,* 1515 ff.   [39] Sumner, *Folkways,* §§566 ff.

very widespread among the Old World peoples and appears everywhere to root in the same basic idea of daimonic envy of human welfare; it is best approached, perhaps, through a consideration of the attitude taken toward envy.

"As for Envy," says Bacon,[40] "that emitteth some Malign and Poisonous Spirits, which take hold of the Spirit of another, and is likewise of greatest force when the Cast of the Eye is Oblique. It hath been noted also, that it is most dangerous, where the envious Eye is cast upon Persons in Glory, and Triumph and Joy. The reason whereof is, for that at such times the Spirits come forth most into the outward parts, and so meet the percussion of the envious Eye more at hand; and therefore it hath been noted, that after great triumphs men have been ill disposed for some days following." Bacon's idea about the spirits coming forth into the outward parts is something of a rationalization. It is evident, first of all, that envy in the sense of mere human jealousy could not have produced such defensive practices as will be seen to have been evoked by fear of the evil eye. The envy of others is, rather, an agreeable titillation to vanity; the distinction of one's self or his group from others, as superior to them or more prosperous, is at the basis of many types of self-gratification.[41] If, through exhibitions of envy, those others recognize this superiority, it is the more undoubted, valid, and valued. Wherein, then, lies the "malignant and poisonous" element?

Not all human envy, despite its general pleasurableness, is free from peril. There are those whose envy is positively and practically dangerous. These are the powerful. The chief or medicineman of a savage tribe, like the despot of a more civilized state, may cast what is in truth an evil eye upon a prosperous inferior. The story of Naboth's vineyard has had many a prototype as well as aftertype. The Jews of the Middle Ages were safe only when destitute or successful in appearing so. The envy of superiors has always been perilous and to be avoided. If this is so, consider the terror with which men naturally regarded the envy of those beings which were much farther above all men than any earthly potentate over the humblest of his subjects, namely, the daimons. It was

---

[40] *Sylva Sylvarum*, 205, 206.   [41] §§444, 449, below.

their envy, the "envy of the gods," that was superlatively dangerous.

The doctrine appears almost universally among men on the earlier stages of society's evolution that human prosperity is unpleasant to the spirits and is likely to draw down adversity of a shattering order. "Good and comely things are most in danger of the evil eye, and so are also men and women in prosperity, and on festive occasions, when they put on a fine dress and wear costly ornaments."[42] Sweet are the uses of obscurity. Hence it was a device of discretion to "mortify the flesh" in various ways; and many religious forms make against happiness or, at any rate, the admission of it, and against freedom of enjoyment in good fortune. Men should never admire, congratulate, or praise—at least not very much. The friends of the fortunate man should "take him down" before the spirits become exasperated and do so. This can be accomplished, as will presently appear, by ritual abuse and vituperation. "Praise is risky; abuse and blame are safe."[43]

The connection between human envy and peril from supernatural powers lies in the fact that the former may awaken the latter by calling the attention of the spirits, who might otherwise not have noticed, to a prosperity of which they themselves straightway become envious, in their characteristic and resentful way. This is the same thing as saying that the envious eye brings bad luck to the object upon which it falls, for the aleatory element is referable to daimonic activity. Success or happiness invite calamity; the only safe policy is to divert the envious or evil glance. The expedients for accomplishing this are about to come under review.

First, however, it is necessary to explain that the eyes of some individuals are more dangerous than those of others. Any eye may be evil that is envious, for it may call daimonic attention to prosperity; nevertheless, as the quotation from Bacon indicates, a strange or abnormal eye is especially menacing. It is that not only when it expresses envy but also because it is capable of emanating evil influence of itself. Such effect is conceived to go forth from the eye and settle upon objects, which then become a menace to men. An eye of this order is, as being extraordinary and inexpli-

42 Joshi, "Evil Eye," in JASB, I, 121.
43 Campbell, in JASB, IV, 63; Clodd, *Magic,* 99.

cable, fetishistic. The possessor of the evil eye may be a fetish-man or may have, at least, some physical peculiarity, such as the oblique cast mentioned by Bacon, that is noteworthy enough to warrant the ascription of an ensuing calamity to the daimonic influence inhering in his glance. Generally there is an element of envy here, too—an envy the more ominous because of the fetish-quality behind it; but sometimes the baleful influence is independent of the volition of the person who exercises it.

"Those who are found by experience to have the evil eye seem to take a regretful pride in its possession. The horse-and-rider story told me in every village with local *dramatis personae* is typical. According to this, a villager claims to have such power; and, to convince his rather sceptical friends, expresses admiration of a stranger who happens to ride by at that particular moment; the stranger inevitably falls. Or it may be that a stranger casts doubt on the reputed skill of the villager; the latter's friends summon him to prove it at the expense of the stranger as he leaves, and the result is a triumphant vindication of the villager's claims."[44]

By such beliefs is the sum of human misery increased. Cases of this order cannot be interpreted, except by the unfettered imagination, without recourse to the ideas of fetishism as well as of daimonism. Whether there is exerted on our lives by the envy of our normal fellow-men an evil influence which calls odious daimonic attention to our prosperity, or whether a fetish-man, by reason of the activity of his indwelling daimon, may voluntarily or involuntarily cast the ominous glance upon us, the only prosperity-policy in either case is one of avoidance. We do not attempt, therefore, in our examples, to distinguish between the types of manifestation of the evil eye.

Seligmann[45] has made an exhaustive study of the evil eye; it is not often that we can refer to a work so encyclopædic upon a single topic. This author begins with the geographical distribution of the belief and goes on to catalogue the different kinds of beings who are believed to possess it. Men with rolling or fluttering eyes, or who have a cast in the eye, or double pupils, or even peculiar eyebrows, are widely suspect; also certain peoples, such as the gypsies. He lists traditional and historic persons, ranging from Medea to Leo XIII. Certain animals, birds, reptiles, and insects, not to mention fabulous beings like the basilisk, could, it is believed, exercise the malign influence. There follows a list of persons who are particularly exposed and of circum-

[44] Hardie, "Evil Eye in Macedonia," in JAI, LIII, 161.
[45] *Der Böse Blick;* also Andree, *Eth. Parallelen,* 35-45; Ploss, *Das Kind,* I, 129-143; Westropp, *Symbolism,* 58-63.

stances under which anyone is in danger. A few cases of the "good glance" are catalogued, and then the treatment advances to the diagnosis, prophylaxis, and cure of ill effects. Fetish-plants, water, and fire are found to be curative. Here we pass into medicine and therapeutics. The two volumes contain apt illustrations of a number of our foregoing and succeeding topics, as is sure to be the case when any single daimonological belief is thoroughly investigated; for all such beliefs are interwoven with one another to constitute the general fabric of daimonology.

Schweinfurth[46] reports an instructive case from equatorial Africa, where a large tree came under the malign influence of an evil glance. The negroes were "still under the influence of the astonishment and alarm that had only recently been excited. It appeared that one of the great branches, having become worm-eaten and decayed, fell to the ground, and in doing so would inevitably have utterly smashed in a contiguous hut if it had tumbled in any other direction than it did. The fall of the huge bough was attributed by the Nubians to the direct agency of an 'evil eye' which it was alleged had been directed against the tree by a soldier who had happened to be passing through the place. Just as usual the people had been collected in front of their huts under shade of the tree, when the man in question, pointing significantly to the bough, said, 'That bough up there is quite rotten; it would be a bad business if it were to come tumbling down upon your head.' The words were hardly said before there was a cracking and creaking, and down came the huge branch with a crash to the ground." This author calls the evil eye an Oriental superstition, aligned with the belief that envious looks can turn food to poison. The above case is evidently a coincidence inexplicable to anybody and as such referable to spiritual agency.

Instances from India are copious. "Many charms are used against the misfortunes which may at any time be brought about by malicious spirits, or by evil influences connected with the human eye." A tiger's claw or tooth is efficacious; so are bright ornaments which are supposed to arrest evil glances or to divert them from the person. . . . In some districts . . . I have often remarked white pots, with black marks or grotesque objects covered with streaks of white paint, placed here and there in the fields, and intended to catch the eye so as to avert envious glances of demons from the growing crops. . . . Moreover, a parent will sometimes give an infant an ugly or inauspicious name from a superstitious fear that the child's beauty may excite the envious glances or 'evil eye' of malicious persons; for it is remarkable that when a family has suffered early bereavements by death these are attributed to evil influences exerted through the instrumentality of the human eye."[47] Thurston[48] lists many devices resulting from the general belief in the evil eye; he thinks the indecent carvings on temple-cars are to avert it. Hideous, doll-like figures are suspended on houses; bogeys, often indecent, are set in the midst of gardens; conch-shells are tied to cows' horns. The crop-protectors are scare-crows as well as attractions to the envious eye. Faces of children are spotted with black dots and the eye-lids are colored with lamp-black. At weddings, vessels of turmeric-water are waved before the bridegroom's face, to ward off the evil eye; or a figure with copper coins stuck on it is waved before a sick person.

[46] *Heart of Afr.*, II, 406-407; I, 157.
[47] Monier-Williams, *Brāhmanism*, 254, 371.
[48] *S. India*, 253-258.

A sickle or other iron article is placed in front of a person suffering from sprain; here the evil-eye motive joins on with the cure of physical ill. "Some chillies, salt, human hair, nail-cuttings, and finely powdered earth from the pit of the door-post are mixed together, waved three times in front of the baby, and thrown on to the fire. Woe betide the possessor of the evil eye, if no pungent, suffocating smell arises while it is burning." Also a piece of burning camphor, or cooked rice-balls, painted red, black, and yellow, are waved before the child. "The objection which a high-caste Brahman has to being seen by a low-caste man when he is eating his food is based on a belief allied to that of the evil eye." There is some thin-spun rationalization here, for it is averred that a subtle low-caste substance passes from the eye of the low-caste man, to mix with the objects he sees. These *radii perniciosi* would defile the Brahman.

People born under certain astrological conditions have the evil eye; and "sometimes the behavior of the mother during pregnancy is also supposed to influence the child's character, and to make him evil-eyed." All witches and wizards are believed to be evil-eyed; also all beggars and people of the lowest classes. "All lingering sicknesses, pallor, want of appetite, dyspepsia, and many other like distempers are believed to be caused by the evil eye. Cows and she-buffaloes do not give milk when blighted, or, when milked, yield blood. Bullocks and horses do not eat, and become restive. Trees do not bear fruit, drop off leaves and flowers untimely, and generally wither. Stones break, pearls lose their lustre, and jewels either break or lose their brilliancy." In one Bombay caste "it is thought that the evil eye is usually attracted by one or several of the following causes: Wealth, beauty, beautiful hair, especially long eye-lashes, the drinking of milk before strangers, or the sight of a babe at its mother's breast." All these are evidences of happiness or prosperity. "Usually the lower the class and the blacker the person, the more intense is the potency of his evil eye." To avert it, iron is used; "it is not unusual to find a small knife or a nail or a scissor attached to the cradle of a child."[49]

Among the Nairs the belief in the evil eye is engrossing. "I remember being taken to task for telling a woman how healthy her boy looked, and must add that I felt as if I had been convicted of a heinous crime when four or five days later I was told that the child was ill. The entire feminine opinion of the village was convinced that the child was suffering from my evil eye, and a good many . . . magical formulae were said over it before the child was well again. With this idea of the evil eye is bound up what is known as *Kari-Nakku*, or black-tongue. When a man with *Kari-Nakku* utters anything it has effect at once. When the evil eye and *Kari-Nakku* are combined, then it has 'much orenda.' . . . If your newly built house is looked upon with an evil eye and some good expression used by such a man about it, a lightning might set fire to it and destroy it the same night. If your mango tree is full of fruit this year and a man with an evil eye and *Kari-Nakku* looks at it and says 'how fortunate,' it might happen that for years to come it would bear no more fruit. If an envious woman, aroused by the green-eyed monster of jealousy, remarks how pretty a girl is, her hair might begin to fall off, her colour might fade, her cheeks might lose their bloom. The fact to notice with regard to this is that you have to say complimentary things to effect evil. If you said how

[49] Joshi, in JASB, I, 120, 122; DeCunha, in JASB, I, 128; Modi, in JASB, II, 170 ff.

ugly a pretty girl is it would not affect her. You must say, out of your heart, how beautiful she is and then it might have effect. Everything is supposed to depend on whether it is said with or without design. If anything is said with design there would be no effect. Only when such exclamation comes out of the heart has it the power to do evil."[50] Iron is abhorred by evil spirits and disliked by lightning; miniature iron swords are worn for protection, and iron ornaments keep off the evil eye. A devil can be nailed to a tree with an iron nail. To avert the evil eye one should use a wash of water in which a smith has quenched his iron; ordinary water is good but this sort is best. Further, evil spirits hate garlic whereas good spirits like it; hence it is a good protection. Black animals are used regularly in magical ceremonies, and black glass, rings, bangles, and other ornaments are protective. White is most disliked by evil spirits and so is the best color for children's dress; yellow also is good. The star or pentacle, and also precious stones, are protective.[51]

The phallus is a protection against the evil eye; Wilken[52] connects the so-called fig-gesture with this matter; also the horn. The spread-out fingers and the number five are likewise effective. The sex-organs in general are prophylactic and curative. Wilken says that Pius IX was supposed to have the evil eye and that an Italian countess was turned out of Rome for making the sign against the evil eye while he was pronouncing a blessing. "An amusing story is also told of the late Pope, when saying prayers at the audience at the Vatican; on coming to the passage in the Lord's Prayer, 'Lead us not into temptation,' he looked over towards a very ugly old lady, upon which the lady boldly repeated aloud, 'Deliver us from the Evil Eye,' *Libera nos a malo occhio.*"

Westermarck,[53] in an article on the magic origin of Moorish designs, many of which he refers to prophylaxis against the evil eye, says that that power goes with deep-set eyes, united eye-brows, light eyes—the latter among the dark-eyed Arabs, not among the Berbers, where they are more common. The havoc wrought by the evil eye is tremendous; it "owns two-thirds of the burial ground," the people say, and is responsible for all destruction of property. The danger is greatest when eating, for a hungry looker-on is like poison in the food; if eating is going on, all must partake or go away. If someone wants to buy your gun or other possession, let him have it. A woman covers her face against the glance of a covetous man and at feasts the women eat first, lest they be hungry on-lookers. But the evil eye cannot always be avoided; hence the development of means for rendering it innocuous: gestures and formulas, such as, "May God let your look pass by!" A big pot and soot are hung in bearing trees to avert the eye. The commonest gesture is the hand of five fingers, or reproductions of them, or charms of fives, or the image of an eye or a pair of them. The hand is thrust toward the eye of a person, the gesture being known as "Five in your eye," to push back to the gazer what emanates from his eye. Thursday, the fifth day, is protective; instead of the last-quoted formula, one can say, "Today it is Thursday." It is improper to mention "five" in conversation; one should say, "Four and one." The cross is regarded as a

50 Panikkar, in JAI, XLVIII, 282-283.

51 Hildburgh, in JAI, XXXVIII, 151 ff., 175, 180.

52 In VG, III, 313 ff., 315 (quoted from Westropp, *Primitive Symbolism,* 60).

53 In JAI, XXXIV, 211 ff.; Hornell, "Survivals of the use of oculi in modern boats," in JAI, LIII; Æschylus, *Suppliants,* 716.

five (four arms and a knob in the center) which disperses the evil eye to the four winds. Now, all these figures become conventionalized, like the eye on a boat, in ornamentation; then come double fives, double crosses, and other combinations, which the author illustrates by figures, emphasizing in the end "that the student of the decorative art of a people should so far as possible make himself acquainted with their superstitions."

The belief existed among the ancient Jews: "Eat thou not the bread of him that hath an evil eye, neither desire thou his dainty meats."[54] The emphasis here seems to be upon the idea of envy and covetousness rather than on that of evil from the daimons. Eyebrows that meet were supposed, as among Greeks and Romans, to indicate the possession of the evil eye; and whole families and tribes were thought to possess it. The Jews held Babylon to be the home of the idea, and it was thought by some writers that "of a hundred men ninety-nine died of the 'eye' and only one through heaven." The seed of Joseph was thought to be immune. If anyone was afraid of the evil eye, he should put his right thumb in the hollow of his left hand and his left thumb in his right hand, and state that he is a descendant of Joseph. An obscene gesture was and still is regarded as a safeguard.[55] The heathen Arabs used to tie unclean things, such as dead men's bones, upon children to avert the *jinn* and the evil eye.[56]

Veils, amulets, and facial disfigurement were commonly used in the Orient to ward off this influence; even horses and asses were disfigured.[57] Beautiful children were kept sedulously indoors; boys were clad as girls until their beards began to grow.[58] The cloistering and veiling of women were due in good part to the same ideas.[59] Beauty attracted fatal admiration; hence it was concealed. When the usage was established for the pretty women it was sure to be adopted by all the rest. Mohammedans recited against the evil eye the one-hundred-thirteenth chapter of the Koran, which protects against all magical spells, influences of the moon, and assaults of evil spirits. Food is covered to keep it from the envious glance.[60] Fear led to the clothing of children in slovenly dress; they were unwashed and smeared with dirt, with fantastic, fluttering appendages to distract the attention.[61] "Nothing can exceed the superstition of the Turks respecting the evil eye of an enemy or infidel. Passages from the Koran are painted on the outside of the houses, globes of glass are suspended from the ceilings, and a part of the superfluous caparison of their horses is designed to attract attention and divert a similar influence."[62]

The following fragments of conversation concerning the evil eye in Sicily may conclude the cases. The speaker has said that they suffered much from the affliction in his village.

"It is a great curse," he said.
"Cannot you protect yourself from it?"

[54] Prov., XXIII, 6; Matt., XX, 15.
[55] Blau, *Zauberwesen*, 51, 152, 153, 155.
[56] Smith, *Relig. Sem.*, 448.
[57] Von Kremer, *Kgchte.*, II, 212, 253; *Jewish Encycl.*, sub "amulet."
[58] Hauri, *Islam*, 87.
[59] Snouck-Hurgronje, in *Bijd.*, XXXV, 375.
[60] Junker, *Afrika*, I, 179, note.
[61] Lane, *Thousand Nights*, I, 67, 311.   [62] Dallaway, *Constantinople*, 391.

"Yes, in a measure. I have a horseshoe over my door, and two long horns as well."

"What sort of horns?"

"Mine are only goat horns, but, of course, those of an ox are better, only they cost more money, especially when one gets long ones, and the longer they are the safer is their owner from evil. Mine are only goat horns, but they are very long, so my house is quite safe," he added complacently.

"If I see a man or a woman with evil eye," he said mysteriously, "I call out 'Corna' (horn), 'Gran corna,' 'Ritortu corna' three times. I make a sign with the index and little finger, and then I know I am all right."

"Why are you so much afraid of the evil eye?"

"Because," he replied most seriously, "a person with the evil eye has the power by legitimate or illegitimate means of bringing about every sort of evil." . . .

"The evil eye is in a thin face, with small eyes and a long nose, which is generally hooked, and the owner always has a long neck. He is unpleasant to look upon both in face and build, and is sometimes revolting in appearance. These 'evil eyes' are the safest, because we know them."

"The evil eye is called 'jettatura,' from 'to throw,' and Nature has been wise, according to the Sicilians, in showing who is a 'jettatura' so that people may avoid him."[63]

It is evident from these representative instances that the case of the evil eye witnesses yet again to the preoccupation of man with the aleatory element and in particular with ill luck. If he gets anything desirable, such as children, he cannot take open pleasure in them; he must feign always not to have his heart set upon his heart's desire lest the envious spirits thrust him down into loss and calamity. It is a wonder that the affections could have grown under this repressive influence. The idea that human happiness cannot go with piety is one that has lasted on through many successive stages of society's evolution; its survival-value probably lies in the discipline it enforced.[64]

§266*. Disparagement; Deception. Connected closely with the averting of danger involved in daimonic attention is the widespread custom of disparaging a loved object or a lucky situation. The heaping of vituperation or indignities upon one who is fortunate, in order to make him seem unfortunate and therefore no fit object of envious attention, is one of the most significant of avoidance-methods.[65] Survivals of a milder order are found in the

63 Alec-Tweedie, Sunny Sicily, 63-64.
64 §§224, 225, 234, above, and 330, below.
65 Clodd, Magic, 99.

deprecation of complimentary reference to one's self or to that which is his and, at length, in a developed restraint, modesty, and courtesy that take the place of an erstwhile swelling self-sufficiency and boastfulness.

The Nile peoples regard it as very unfortunate to give a child a good or well-sounding name. "Children are therefore called by contemptuous or even disgusting appellations ('Piece of Dung' being not an unfrequent name), or are given the names of beasts, such as dog, leopard, giraffe, and so forth."[66] To one who is aware of the significance attached by primitive peoples to the name,[67] such a practice becomes readily explicable. The Hovas of Madagascar give themselves low and ill-significant names to ward off the fate invited by grand names.[68] "I had often been surprised," writes Sibree,[69] "in considering that there were in Malagasy many offensive names, such as Rafirìnga, 'dunghill' . . . 'much dung,' etc. The first of these is an extremely common name, and is that of the present governor of Tamatave, an officer of high rank. On enquiring, however, the reason of this, I was told that it is done from a superstitious idea which some have that a pleasant-sounding name may cause envy." Among the Beduins, "the expression 'maschallah' may be translated 'God forbid evil,' and must always be added if one praises a living being. Otherwise ill or death can be averted from the man or animal in question only by giving it to the indiscreet praiser."[70]

Hindu examples are many. "Men cause their names to be cut on rocks by the wayside, or on the stones with which the path leading to the temple is paved, in the belief that good luck will result if their name is trodden on."[71] The depreciatory attitude is reflected in Kipling's *Naulahka*,[72] where the following conversation takes place between a queen-mother and another woman concerning the former's son—to whom the mother says:

"'Stay still in my arms. Oh, it is good to feel thee here again, worthless one.'

"'The Heavenborn looks as frail as dried maize,' said the woman quickly.

"'A dried monkey, rather,' returned the Queen, dropping her lips on the child's head. Both mothers spoke aloud and with emphasis, that the gods, jealous of human happiness, might hear and take for truth the disparagement that veils deepest love."

One who is familiar with the works of this author that deal with Indian subjects will recall many instances of local superstition utilized by him, not alone in respect of the present topic but generally over a wide field.

Moslems' children, horses, and asses are purposely rendered uncomely that no one may look on them with admiration. The only safeguard against admiring glances directed upon handsome children is that one shall cry, "God be gracious to you!" and spit in their faces as speedily as possible.[73] In certain backward parts of Europe, when one looks at a child, "he must say at the same time: 'How ugly!' or 'May I not bewitch you,' etc., and spit upon it three

[66] Johnston, *Uganda*, II, 779.
[67] §212, above.
[68] Ratzel, *Vkde.*, II, 511.
[69] *Great Afr. Island*, 167.
[70] R. T. K., in *Globus*, LXXV, 193.
[71] Thurston, *S. India*, 357.
[72] Ch. XIX.
[73] Pischon, *Islam*, 110.

times. . . . No one must ever admire or praise the child."[74] The South Slavs believe in a peculiar variety of evil spirits that are brought upon one by the evil glance and above all by unlucky speech. They are wandering spirits, without much courage, and are readily exorcised by powerful spells and threats. They belong to the evil glance "just as if they were its emanation." Many a good man exercises the fatal influence unawares; the way to avoid doing such harm is to cut the nails on Christmas day before sunrise and keep them. Men of exceptional beauty are exceptionally exposed to these spirits; it is enough that someone say to himself "Ah, how beautiful he is, or she!" and the damage is done. So a handsome youth is called a crazy, lame young fellow; a pretty girl is called deformed; a fine horse is called weatherbeaten. "Through this belief has come about the peculiar phenomenon in popular speech that many a word of ill significance has attained a contrary meaning." Small children are most in peril and are safeguarded by wearing a larchbark amulet.[75]

Such persuasions about envy are, it appears, not confined to primitive peoples; survivals of them, mostly unrecognized or rationalized, as in the case of so many other survivals out of the past, occur in the usages of modern and civilized nations. For example, "it is with a view to avert the influence of an evil and malicious eye from the happiness and pleasure of the newly-married couple that old shoes are thrown upon them in England."[76] Forms of disparagement, or at least a show of embarrassment and of self-depreciation in the face of expressed admiration, are exhibited as a mode of propriety.

That envy is a universal and deep-rooted human trait is evidenced by all our cases. Moreover, through them all the major strand of the aleatory element appears and reappears; no topics could form a better demonstration of its presence. Especially does it reveal itself in the case of children, so highly prized and yet so subject to influences productive of a high mortality. The search for an agency of ill, rather than for a cause, was forced upon suffering and fearful humanity.

All through the cases, also, runs the idea that it is not safe to be prosperous or happy in the sight of the daimons. The expedient policy is to appear to be miserable, especially at crises of life or at times of prosperity; for then the spirits are conceived to be near at hand and ready to pounce. This idea has persisted long after daimonism has been succeeded by more developed forms of religion. Maclaren[77] brings out strikingly, in order to refute it,

74 Temesváry, *Geburtshilfe*, 75.   75 Krauss, *Südslaven*, 41, 42, 43.
76 Modi, in JASB, II, 169.   77 *Bonnie Briar Bush*, ch. III.

the notion that God will not tolerate earthly affections, even the purest, as where a mother is devoted to her child; the child will be taken away in order that all attention may be focussed upon the jealous divinity. The canny Scot is represented as habitually understating his prosperity—though it must be admitted that it is not good fortune alone which is thus minimized, for he understates both ways. All practices calculated to present a picture of misery, including those of ascetics, may be viewed as propitiatory just as all methods of propitiation have an aspect in which they appear to aim at avoidance of ill.

Deception of the ghost is familiar to the reader of a preceding chapter;[78] and the practice of deceiving the daimons is hardly less unsophisticated. The foregoing paragraphs illustrate a sort of semi-deception; a few cases of direct misleading may be added to complete the treatment of avoidance.

When smallpox raged on the Calabar River the negroes, to cheat the disease-daimon, sprinkled the skin with chalk to make it look as if they had had the disease.[79] The negroes west of Lake Nyassa beat drums and fire guns about the dying and the dead to scare off evil spirits; but they also have a mock funeral to mislead them. "When such a decision is made, an artificial body is manufactured, and treated exactly as is done with the bodies of the dead. It is carried a considerable distance to the grave, followed by a great crowd weeping and wailing as if their hearts would break. Drums are beaten, guns fired, and all kinds of noises are made. Meantime the real corpse is quietly and stealthily interred near the dwelling, and the spirits are effectually deceived."[80] In Loango, masks are worn by physicians when visiting the sick; the disguise they afford is plainly a "means of assistance to the priests or *gangas* in their struggle against the daimons that bring illness."[81]

In Yakut families, when several children die in succession, the next child is fictitiously stolen and given to others to bring up. The stealing is accomplished with ceremonial. The mother knows it is to be done, but does not know just when. In the place of the stolen child is put a puppy or a doll. "It is required that the child should be taken out through a window, and that the story should then be set afloat that he was stolen by passing travellers."[82] Among the Nagas, the evil spirits, "in spite of all their supernatural qualities . . . are very easily deceived, and their malicious activities can be met by very simple guile, as, for instance, when the *Awou* gives out the wrong day as the date for the . . . genna [taboo] in public, though everyone knows that it is the wrong day except the spirits whose malice is feared. Again the grave is begun as soon as a man is dead, but should he prove to be merely unconscious and recover, it is essential that some substitute should be buried, and his own

[78] §§223, 224, 234, above.   [79] Andree, *Eth. Parallelen*, 111.
[80] Macdonald, in JAI, XXII, 114.   [81] Karutz, in *Globus*, LXXIX, 363.
[82] Sieroshevski-Sumner, in JAI, XXXI, 92.

stool . . . is wrapped in a cloth and put in the grave in his stead."[83] In Ceylon, a sick man may be impersonated by a dancer, who is carried to a grave like a corpse. Both the grave and the offerings are sham. Thus the evil spirit, led to believe that the sick man has died, ceases to trouble him.[84] When a certain tribe of south Cochin China goes out after aloe-wood, "during the hunt for the wood they use a sort of conventional language; many names in use in regular life are then replaced by others; so, for example, they call fire 'the red,' and a goat a 'spider.' "[85] In Polynesia skulls were set up in sepulchral inclosures to attract the notice of and so deceive predatory spirits, and keep them from seeking fresh victims.[86]

"Chinese sailors suppose that the dreaded typhoons of the China seas are caused by malignant spirits, which lie in wait to catch the junks as they navigate the dangerous waters. When the storm reaches a pitch of extreme violence, it is said that it is a habit of the mariners to have a paper junk made of the exact pattern of their own, and complete in all its details. This paper junk is then cast into the sea at the point of maximum disturbance, in order that the angry water-spirits may be deceived into thinking that this is the vessel of which they are in quest, and thus allow the real one to escape."[87] "It is no exaggeration to say that, to the average Chinese, the air is peopled with countless spirits, most of them malignant, all attempting to do him harm. . . . But there they are, millions of them. They hover around every motion and every waking hour, and they enter the sanctity of sleep. An intricate system of circumventing them, that makes the streets twist in a fashion to daze Boston's legendary cow and puts walls in front of doors to belie the hospitality within, runs throughout the social order."[88]

In London's[89] story, "Make Westing," a ship had been struggling for seven weeks against unfavorable winds trying to round Cape Horn. Now at last the wind had changed. "Mr. Turner looked happy. The end of the struggle was in sight. But Captain Cullen did not look happy. . . . Captain Cullen did not want God to know that he was pleased with that wind. He had a conception of a malicious God, and believed in his secret soul that if God knew it was a desirable wind, God would promptly efface it and send a snorter from the west. So he walked softly before God, smothering his joy down under scowls and muttered curses, and, so fooling God, for God was the only thing in the universe of which Dan Cullen was afraid." But presently the wind showed signs of changing back. "And now Captain Cullen went around brazenly before God, smoking a big cigar, smiling jubilantly, as if the failing wind delighted him, while down underneath he was raging against God for taking the life out of the blessed wind."

§267*. Anticipation and Interrogation. The chief condition of avoidance is fore-knowledge. It is not out of any intellectual curiosity that primitive people seek to know the future, but rather

[83] Hutton, Sema Nagas, 198, 242-243.
[84] Seligmann, in JAI, XXXVIII, 378. [85] Niemann, in Bijd., XLV, 335.
[86] March, in JAI, XXII, 309. [87] Smith, Chinese Char., 303.
[88] Hutchinson, in Atl. Mo., CXXVII, 121.
[89] In the volume When God Laughs.

for the sake of eluding the ills which coming days are sure to contain. Divination is not found in enlightened religion, for when the idea of arbitrary intervention on the part of spiritual agencies is not present, the only forecasting there is attaches itself to science—to the connected order of cause and effect.[90] While, however, the aleatory element was still playing the part in life for which it was cast in the absence of knowledge, the questioning of the intentions of spiritual agencies was preliminary to a proper and safe adjustment.

Actual "questioning" of the future—deliberate divination—was something of a development, and is reserved for special treatment.[91] But there is a class of traditional portents, of which all peoples have representatives; though they are not asked for, they are observed with the most scrupulous attention. These are omens. An omen, says Codrington,[92] "is a spontaneous manifestation or warning given by supernatural power, and not obtained by the arts of divination." To primitive people the dream is ominous and prophetic; so is sneezing, the flight of birds,[93] and unnumbered other phenomena to which in later stages of evolution little or no importance is attached—though practices in connection with some of them persist as survivals, often disguised by rationalization. Superstitions, as we are wont to call these survivals, attend upon special activities, for instance, hunting;[94] and stories of the sea report many deep-water omens and presages, some of which are merely traditional and not taken seriously. Such survivals, when they drop out of practice, retire, as it were, into mere language; and then we have such words as "ominous," "portentous," "ill-starred," "disaster," "sinister," which recall realities to those only who attend on etymology.

Naturally enough, since the eye is upon bad luck rather than good,[95] a large proportion of the "signs" are warnings. The homely philosophy that lies behind this fact has been cited in a former connection: "What you want to know when good luck's a-comin' for? Want to keep it off?"[96] In the present instance we

90 D'Alviella, *Concep. God*, 249.

91 Ch. XXXIX, below.

92 *Melanesians*, 220.

93 March, in JAI, XXVII, 209.

94 Andree, *Eth. Parallelen*, 42-48.

95 §196, above.

96 Clemens, *Huckleberry Finn*, end ch. VIII.

shall illustrate the spontaneous omen and portent, together with the most elementary and least specialized methods of questioning the future.

As regards the dream, its supposedly prophetic nature is a commonplace. The dead come to the living in dreams and reveal the future. Sleeping upon a grave or in a temple is a method of inviting revelation.[97] In view of the frequent reference to the dream in several other connections,[98] brief illustration will satisfy present needs.

The Dyaks lay "astonishing weight upon the advice which they get by means of dreams. . . . Those who are making ready for a head-hunting expedition often allow themselves to be scared off from it by dreams, so that their companions also give up the enterprise or go off elsewhere without them." The author[99] speaks of a Dyak who had found a large diamond in a stream; but "that night he dreamed that the stone would bring him no luck and on the next day threw it back into the water." "Houses are often deserted, and farming land on which much labour had been spent abandoned, on account of dreams. Newly-married couples often separate from the same cause."[100]

"In the Indian Archipelago . . . the belief is universal that the soul leaves the body in sleep, to have intercourse with the spirits and even to make visits to the spirit-world. Oneiromancy is therefore found among almost all tribes. Often they try to attain to prophetic dreams by incubation. Of the Sea-Dyaks of Sarawak we read that they sometimes seek communion with the dead by sleeping at their graves. . . . To *nampok* is to sleep on the tops of mountains with the hope of meeting with the good spirits of the unseen world." Examples are given. The Greeks endeavored to have such dreams by sleeping in shrines, as in that of Asklepios, or on the graves of the dead, and the same idea is implicit in the Emoy term meaning "to be-sleep a grave." The therapeutic effects of the temple-sleep will be encountered in another connection.[101]

Sneezing is a rather special case of omen. Being involuntary and uncontrollable, it was interpreted as a manifestation of a spirit which had penetrated a man. It was sometimes regarded as the departure of such a spirit or the return of one's own soul; hence the custom of blessing in connection with it.[102]

"In Florida [Melanesia] when a man sneezes they think that some one is speaking of him, is angry with him, perhaps cursing him by calling on his own *tindalo* [spirit] to eat him; the man who sneezes calls upon his *tindalo* to damage the man who is cursing him. In the same way at Saa if a man sneezes when he wakes, he cries, 'who calls me? If for good, well; if for evil, may So-and-So

97 De Goeje, in *Gids,* XXXI, pt. II, 31; Otto, *Aegypten,* I, 14; Müller, *Oldtid,* 111, 112.

98 §§163, 204, 205, 260, above, and 311, 313, below.

99 Veth, *Borneo's Wester-Afdeeling,* II, 309-310.

100 Gomes, *Sea Dyaks,* 162.

101 Wilken, in VG, III, 333-335; §317, below.

102 Lippert, *Kgchte.,* I, 109; Modi, "Superstitions," in JASB, II, 162.

[a spirit] defend me.' In the Banks' Islands also some one is supposed to be calling the name of a man when he sneezes, either for good or evil. In Motlav if a child sneezes, the mother will cry, 'Let him come back into the world! Let him remain.' In Mota they cry, 'Live, roll back to us!' The notion is that a ghost is drawing the child's soul away. It has been said that at Mota a man enquires when he sneezes by a certain divination who is cursing him; he will also stamp with his foot and cry, 'Stamp down the mischief from me! Let it be quiet! Let them say their words in vain; let them lay their plots in vain!' There is a special form of words used when one's step-father sneezes. . . . The native notions in the New Hebrides are much the same; but in Lepers' Island, if an infant sneezes, it is a sign that its soul has been away, and has just come back; the friends present cry out with good wishes. They judge in the same island by the character of the sneeze what is the motive with which the sneezer's name is being called; if it be a gentle sneeze no harm is meant, a violent paroxysm is warning of a curse."[103]

In West Africa to sneeze is a bad omen; it is an indication that something is happening to the indwelling spirit, usually that it is about to leave the body — which affords some homeless spirit a chance to slip in and cause sickness. "It is usual for persons to address wishes of long life and good health to any one who has sneezed, with the idea of thereby averting any impending ill."[104] When the king of Ashanti sneezes, "all his assistants draw two of their fingers across their forehead and across their chest; this is equivalent to asking for a benediction."[105] "The world-wide superstition of some evil influence being at work when any one sneezes is equally prevalent in Madagascar. Thus, when a child sneezes its mother or nurse always repeats the common benediction, 'God bless you,' exactly as it is done in Europe and other parts of the world."[106]

Sneezing is a bad omen to the Hindu where *crepitus ventris* is a good one.[107] Among the Parsees "if a person sneeze when another is about to leave his house for business, the latter postpones his departure for a minute or two."[108] Xenophon[109] interprets the sneeze as an immediate communication from Zeus, confirmatory of the plan he is proposing. "Sneezing appears to have been always regarded as a sign of health, even from the remotest times."[110] We have seen that this is not so; but the author is generalizing on New Zealand mores. Sneezing is reported as rare among the Indians; in South America a sneeze is regarded as a call by name, and when one sneezes a bystander will begin to ask the names of his relatives.[111] When Elisha brings the dead child to life, it sneezes seven times.[112]

The modern Hindu and Russian belief is that when a man wants to sneeze, it indicates that a lady is thinking of him.[113] Zangwill[114] has a passage where a child sneezes. "For thy Salvation do I hope, O Lord," murmured the attendant woman piously, adding triumphantly, "There! the *kind* has sneezed to the truth of it. I knew I was right." Again, "the sneeze of an innocent child silences

[103] Codrington, *Melanesians,* 226, 227.   [104] Ellis, *Ewe,* 96; Ellis, *Tshi,* 203.

[105] Letourneau, *Soc.,* 439.   [106] Sibree, *Great Afr. Isl.,* 285.

[107] Thurston, *S. India,* 248.   [108] Modi, in JASB, I, 290.

[109] *Anab.,* III, ch. II, §9.   [110] Taylor, *Te Ika,* 661.

[111] Hrdlička, in BAE, Bull. XXXIV, 155; Von den Steinen, *Zent. Bras.,* 510.

[112] II Kings, IV, 35.   [113] Gubernatis, *Usi Nuz.,* 46.

[114] *Ghetto,* 56.

everybody who is not a blasphemer." Barclay[115] has assembled an interesting collection of historical and modern cases, together with the formulas customarily uttered.

A class of portent which has always rivetted the attention of men is the prodigy—something in nature that is completely out of the ordinary, such as red rain or rain of blood.[116] White[117] refers to a number of historic prodigies that have been taken to presage local or world-wide calamity. Such portents, as has been intimated elsewhere,[118] are fetishistic in nature and are ultimately connected with the aleatory element; for they come under the category of the inexplicable. There is little or nothing prophetic about the regular course of events; it is the variation from the expected that rouses reflection, demands explanation, and is taken to be premonitory. In a general way all omens are fetishistic, and the processes of divination are not to be understood apart from a comprehension of the notions and doctrines to which the term fetishism has been applied. As representative types of omens are passed in review, this fact will receive abundant confirmation. Although among the cases there will occur many small happenings which hardly deserve the rather imposing names of "omen" or "portent," much less of "prodigy," the principle underlying them all is the same.

In New Guinea "when a particular species of firefly entered the house at night the natives immediately predicted bad luck, or impending attack and extermination by hostile tribes."[119] Natives starting on a hunt do not speak to one another and think it bad luck if they are addressed.[120] In the Solomon Islands the snakes and kingfisher are particularly ominous. "When a beginning is made of building a house or canoe, or of clearing a garden, a man will call aloud, and then if something remarkable appears it is a sign that the work will be interrupted by death or war; if nothing comes, all will be well."[121]

"It is a bad omen for a dancer to slip and fall when performing before the king of Dahomie, and, up to the reign of Gezo, any dancer who met with such an accident was put to death." Anyone who lost his footing upon a bridge across the ditch to the gates of one of the towns lost his head also.[122] In Uganda the sex of an unborn child is prefigured in the thinness or fatness of the mother. "If a man on starting for a journey strikes the big toe of his right foot twice against a stone or root, it is a bad omen." If he strikes the other foot in similar manner the greatest good luck will attend him. In all

115 "When People Sneeze," in N. Y. *Times,* July 27, 1902.
116 "Kl. Nachtr.," in *Globus,* LXXIX, 371; LXXXI, 99; LXXXIV, 181.
117 *Sci. and Theol.,* I, 171-173, 266, 323, 336, 337.
118 §254, above.   119 Pratt, *New Guinea,* 316.
120 Turner, in JAI, VII, 487.   121 Codrington, *Melanesians,* 223.
122 Ellis, *Ewe,* 95.

these omens the left side is lucky. If the first child of a pair is a girl it is very lucky, "so that very often a person starting on a journey will ask the first man he meets, 'Was your first child male or female?' If he replies, 'Male,' the traveller should return to his home, as he has started with a bad omen. . . . It is considered a very bad omen if a person shuts the door of a house after him, leaving at the time any one behind inside the hut. In such a case a goat must be sacrificed and eaten by the parties concerned to avert ill fate." If a house is struck by lightning it is abandoned, and no one is allowed to remove a single stick.[123] "At the age of about two years the child goes through the ceremony of having its legitimacy established, and is also named. . . . A vessel containing a mixture of milk, beer, and water is brought, and each mother in turn brings out the bit of the child's preserved umbilical cord and drops it into the mixture. If the cord floats the child is universally proclaimed legitimate. Should it by chance sink the child is declared illegitimate and the mother is loaded with abuse and flogged."[124] Here is another of those wholly irrational tests which have caused so much misery to unfortunate mortals. Again, if a baby's upper front teeth come through first, that is an ill omen and must be done away through dancing by the sorcerer.[125]

In Mongolia the owner of a certain house and his son became very angry when a European whistled and insisted that he should not do so in the house, as it would bring them bad luck.[126] When a mouse falls into a dish, the Cheremis consider it a divine blessing; and if there was milk in the dish, the cows will be healthy.[127] In southern India the omens for a journey are favorable if one encounters any of the following: a married woman, a virgin, a prostitute, two Brahmans, the playing of music, a person carrying a musical instrument, money, fruit or flowers, a light or a clear blazing fire, an umbrella, cooked food, milk or curds, a cow, a deer, a corpse, two fishes, a recital of the Vedas, the sound of a drum or horn, spirituous liquor, a bullock. . . . It is unlucky to encounter a widow, lightning, fuel, a smoky fire, a pot of oil, leather, or a dog barking on a house-top. A snake crossing the road is sufficient to cause the postponement of a journey. "When a student starts for the examination hall he will, if he sees a widow[128] or a Brahman, retrace his steps, and start again after the lapse of a few minutes. Meeting two Brahmans would indicate good luck, and he would press forward. . . . Among certain woodcutter classes, it is believed that, if a crane crosses from left to right, when a man is bringing home wood, he will get a third as much again for his fuel."[129]

Ancient literature is full of the belief in omens: in Assyria, in Greece and Rome, and among the Jews and Arabs, the future was thought to be revealed in dreams and in the incidents of life. The Greek and Latin classics have transmitted plentiful records of such beliefs, which have been reproduced or at least simulated, as a literary device, in classically influenced literature.[130]

[123] Johnston, *Uganda*, II, 748, 751, 752.
[124] Roscoe, in JAI, XXXII, 31-32.
[125] Ratzel, *Vkde.*, I, 469.　　[126] Rockhill, *Mongolia*, 20, note.
[127] Michailovski, *Shamanism* (Russ.), 43.
[128] §§394, 395, below.
[129] Thurston, *S. India*, 242, 243, 247, 283.
[130] Jastrow, "Relig. Babyl.," in *Hastings's Bible Dict.*, suppl. vol., 556 ff.; Blau, *Zauberwesen*, 65; Keller, *Hom. Soc.*, 141, 152 ff.; Pliny, *Hist. Nat.*, XXVIII, 4; Rossbach, *Röm. Ehe.*, 294, 296; Terence, *Phormio*, IV, 4.

Further, the ancient Teutons and mediæval Europeans were firm believers in omens,[131] and there still remains in the less developed parts of all civilized countries a lively faith in them. If the Russian peasant meets a priest first of all on setting out upon a journey, it is a bad omen; "he spits to avert the threatening ill, and acts most wisely if he gives up the journey."[132] Special writings list pages of "signs" about death.[133] "Premonitions" have been recorded by modern men of education and ability.[134] We need refer only to superstitions still harbored concerning black cats, mirrors, spilling salt, walking under a ladder, and many another.

In the preceding cases there has been no direct questioning of the future but merely action upon what were thought to be spontaneous hints. Developed divination or direct interrogation is sure to fall into the hands of specialists; it is one of the most important functions of the shaman.[135] Still there are not a few less complicated methods of deliberate interrogation that do not demand the skill of the magician or priest, to whose era most of the systematic methods and complicated processes belong. There are in divination by the non-specialist rather astonishing sets of parallelisms, as, for instance, in the widespread employment of the egg,[136] in the inspection of vital organs, and in necromancy, just as there are in mere omens, such as the flight of birds and the contrast of left and right. Attention is at this point centered upon variety of procedure rather than upon likeness.

Bolton,[137] in an interesting book on *The Counting-Out Rhymes of Children*, treats of the names of the different kinds of divination and gives many cases of lot-casting together with the formulas attending. Counting-out formulas are really magical spells and are of high antiquity.

In Borneo, where the Dyaks are deeply engrossed in natural omens, there are also methods of questioning the future in connection with all important undertakings. "Dyaks, before they dare occupy a new house, kill a pig and examine the entrails; if the reading is unfavorable, they abandon the house." A faithless native was foreordained to death by the revelation of a special fetish. "The fate foretold so clearly by the liver of the Government's albino

---

[131] Meyer, *Aberglaube*, 88, 89; Grimm, *Teut. Mythol.*, III, 1119.

[132] Stern, *Russland*, 128-129.

[133] Carstens, in *Am Urquell*, I, 7 ff., 11 ff.

[134] Marshall, *Diary*, 165 (entry for Feb. 1, 1778).

[135] §§313, 314, below.

[136] Lasch, "Verwendung der Eier," in *Globus*, LXXXIX, 102 ff.; Ellis, *Tshi*, 226.

[137] Especially 26 ff., 35 ff., 45 ff.

pig had been fulfilled. The conscience stricken soul of the faithless Aban Liah had, indeed, departed to the Fields of the Dead. From the moment that he saw that ulcerous liver, and realized its plain indication to himself he sickened, became delirious, and within forty-eight hours was dead!" An omen of ill to the rice can be tested "by killing a pig, and divining from appearances of the liver immediately after death. If the prediction of the omen be strengthened, all the rice grown on that ground must be sold; and if necessary other rice bought for their own consumption. Other people may eat it, for the omen only affects those at whom it is directly pointed."[138]

The Dyaks have a test for house-location, consisting of filling a bamboo with water and leaving it all night. "A few people remain to keep watch, and to make a great deal of noise with brass gongs and drums to frighten away the evil spirits. If in the early morning they find there is much evaporation, the place is considered unhealthy, and is abandoned." This appears, by reason of the concomitant ceremonial, to be a form of divination rather than a rational test. Some Dyaks were frightened because an omen-bird had flown through the house. "I said: 'You have fruit-trees growing thickly all round your houses, and as you leave your houses empty, I am not surprised at any bird flying through the house.' My matter-of-fact ideas were not much approved. As usual in doubtful cases, they sacrificed a pig and examined its liver." The heart and liver "are handed round to the old men present, who closely examine them, and pronounce them to augur either good or evil."[139] The cries of birds are usually listened for and not sought; but it is possible to summon them by striking a tree. If they come from the right it is lucky, from the left unlucky.[140]

The Central Eskimo have the same custom of interrogating the corpse that is practised by the Chukchi.[141] The Micmac Indians foretold the future by leaving water overnight in a shallow wooden plate and examining its appearance the next morning.[142] The Mokis had a practice closely akin to the ancient Greek crithomancy, or divination by grains of the cereals.[143] When the Peruvian Indian goes on a journey he spits a coca-ball against a rock. If he finds it, on his return, still intact, his wife has been faithful; if it has fallen, she has not.[144] This is a case of revelation of the past rather than of the future, but the general process is akin to divination.

Scrutiny of the liver was usual at Babylon; the liver of a sheep was divided by cross-lines into fifty parts and the omens were located in the checks. Hydromancy, kyklikomancy (divination by cup), and lekanomancy (divination by shell) were practised.[145] Rods and trees afforded omens to inquiring Semites.[146] The pious Jew looked to the Bible, as the Romans and mediæval Italians and French to the Æneid, for hints as to proper procedure.[147] The aborigines of the Canary Islands foretold good and ill from the direction taken

[138] Schwaner, Borneo, I, 181; Veth, Borneo's Wester-Afdeeling, II, 313-314; Roth, in JAI, XXI, 112 (quoted); Furness, Head-Hunters, 138 (quoted); Roth, Sarawak, I, 194.

[139] Gomes, Sea Dyaks, 47, 48, 158, 160.

[140] Nieuwenhuis, Borneo, I, 178.

[141] Boas, in PSM, LVII, 631.   [142] Hager, in AA, VIII, 32.

[143] Bourke, in BAE, IX, 532.   [144] Friedmann, Wahnideen, 224.

[145] Zimmern, Babyl. Relig., 84, 85; Ezek., XXI, 26.

[146] Smith, Relig. Sem., 197; Num., XVII; Isa., XVII, 10 ff.

[147] Krauss, Sreća, 155.

by the smoke of barley burned in sacrifice.[148] All the Christian orators of St. Augustine's time "denounce the popular recourse to divination unceasingly. They plainly intimate that the Christians are as bad as the pagans. Indeed, it was only the more stern priests of the Church who offered a consistent opposition to it."[149] Even in recent times, in newspapers of the lower class, there have appeared advertisements of diviners and divining apparatus.

From the above cases the conclusion emerges that divination is a process of securing from the spirits, chiefly through the use of fetishes, such glimpses into the future as enable men to foresee and avoid ill fortune. Perhaps the fetish-quality of the agencies active in divination would come out more strikingly if they could be taken one by one and followed around the earth.[150] The reader will have recalled that several of these—birds, for example—have already been treated specifically as fetishes.[151] Reappearing under magic, fetishes will be found effective to accomplish results, not by virtue of anything in themselves but through the power of their indwelling spirits; and under shamanism will be encountered the prime agency in divination, the man-fetish.

The bearing of these matters upon the topic of this chapter lies in the fact that they are daimonological procedures calculated to anticipate ill fortune by finding out the will of the spirits, so as not to run counter to it and invite destruction. They are negative and protective adjustments and belong to avoidance.

In the cases thus far cited in this chapter we have excluded as far as possible all daimonological practices other than those representing avoidance or evasion. There yet remains what is the grand case of avoidance, namely, the taboo. It deserves treatment by itself as much as do magic and shamanism.[152] Here again will occur an inevitable blurring of categories; for while the taboo is essentially a negative measure, yet it cannot be classified or treated as solely such. A taboo is essentially an evasion, and this is the place to treat of it; still it is, or becomes, broadly societal in its nature and is of a quality considerably more complex and universal than that of the several avoidance-practices hitherto considered.

---

[148] Cook, in AA, II, 493.   [149] McCabe, *St. Augustine,* 49.
[150] Lasch, in *Globus*, LXXXIX, 102 ff.; Ellis, *Tshi*, 226.
[151] §§248, 254, 256, above.   [152] §264, above.

CHAPTER XXXI

THE TABOO

§268*. Religious Nature of the Taboo. Close upon the formation of a code of mores in a society there develops a religious sanction of that code over and above the gathering conviction of its expediency for societal welfare.[1] This sanction is regularly expressed in negative form: as "Thou shalt not" rather than as "Thou shalt"; found everywhere in the world and appearing throughout history under a diversity of names,[2] it has come to be known by the Polynesian term, so that a prohibition which regularly carries a religious sanction is called a "taboo."

It is evident that the topic of taboo is nearly as wide as that of the mores themselves. A taboo is a form of avoidance or evasion of ill; in fact, all the phenomena of avoidance might, without much strain, be brought under the category of taboo. Hence, because of its indefinite extension, there is difficulty in treating this topic; it breaks through classification and ranges at large in the general field of societal phenomena, representing an interminable penetration of the religious sanction into all reaches of human activity. In a very real sense the treatment of the taboo means the examination of the interrelation of the several other institutions of society —property, marriage, and the rest—with religion. Its treatment may form, therefore, another of those horizontal surveys, like that of the energies derived from nature,[3] in which we try to indicate the cross-relations between the several institutions which have had to be traced successively and separately when under review as evolutionary series.

Some reputable writers do not recognize the religious element in the taboo: Finsch,[4] for example, assigns it, as it appears on the Gilbert Islands, to eco-

---

[1] Sumner, *Folkways*, §35.

[2] Illustrations are the West African *orunda, ibet, xina,* and *quixilles* and the Malay *pomali* or *pamali.* The Melanesian *tambu* seems to be allied with the Polynesian *tapu, tabu,* or *taboo.* Nassau, *Fetichism,* 80; Kingsley, *Travels W. Afr.,* 457; Bastian, *Deut. Exped.,* I, 183; Pechuël-Lösche, *Loango,* 4; Veth, *Borneo's Wester-Afdeeling,* II, 315-316; Codrington, *Melanesians,* 216.

[3] Chs. VIII, IX, X, above.   [4] *Ethnol. Erfahr.,* III, 29, 30.

nomic necessity. "Prohibition, that is, taboo-custom, which so often is wrongly interpreted as 'holy' . . . has chiefly utilitarian aims. Thus a palm-leaf about a coco-palm forbids the taking of nuts during a certain period, in order to spare the trees. But in times of want . . . this taboo was not kept and could not be. Under certain circumstances, too, the assembly-house was declared taboo to the women, apparently because the men wanted to carouse alone and in more undisturbed fashion. The taboo may also be extended over other things, according as the men's council finds it good; in this the belief in harmful influence on the part of spirits . . . sometimes forms a motive." It would appear from this last clause that the exclusion of daimonic elements is not so rigorous as the earlier sentences might have led one to believe. One is quite ready to concur in the opinion that it was the utilitarian character of the taboo which conferred survival-value upon it without believing that the fact that some taboos now appear to be secular proves them to have been such in origin.

Numbers of cases of the taboo are reported in which the connection with religion is not explicitly stated; yet if the context is supplied the religious element is almost always seen to be implicit. "A man being told to make a regular flight of steps to his house instead of the old notched ladder, replied 'No, that would be *pomali.'* "[5] Nothing is added concerning the reason of the taboo; it is simple adherence to the mores that appears, with nothing said about what enforces such adherence; if, however, the context is examined, in this case the Malay attitude toward *pomali,* there can be small doubt as to the daimonic sanction.

Another author,[6] referring to the Banks' Islands, thinks that there is no supernatural agency involved except as the *mana* (virtue) of the tabooing individual, one who has sufficient status to lay such a restriction, is supernatural; and he goes on to say that the transgressor of the taboo would not be sick or die in consequence but would have to give a pig or money to appease anger. "In reality the taboo generally rests upon the authority of no single person, but on that of the grade of the secret society to which the individual belongs; indeed another word and not *tapu* is used when it is a private individual in connection with no recognized and powerful body who puts up his own mark. In such a case, self assertion is likely to meet with respect, and that is all." Doubtless the political aspect of the taboo, as it shifts into a sort of ordinance, must be reckoned with here; but it is clear to the reader of foregoing chapters that most primitive secret societies are religious in their nature. Denial of the religious element in the taboo generally means that the attention of the observer is so sharply focussed upon the instance immediately before him that he does not see it in its evolutionary setting or even in its relations of parallelism with other cases of the same order.

If it is admitted that a restriction which is a mere secular ordinance should not be called a taboo, then the difficulty is shifted to the identification of the merely secular and not much is gained, for the religious and political organizations are bound to merge into one another at many points.[7] One must never leave off reminding

5 Roth, *Sarawak,* II, 6.   6 Codrington, in JAI, X, 279.
7 §§155, 161, 182, 183, above.

himself that evolution does not permit of sharp and fast distinctions, for in its range categories shade into one another by almost imperceptible gradations. It is not at all surprising, therefore, to find inferior types of taboo that are imposed by inferior and apparently purely human power alongside other grades which are sanctioned by all the gods at once. A taboo is a prohibition; but a prohibition is just as strong as the power that issues and guarantees it. "The power of the tapu," says a writer on New Zealand,[8] "mainly depended on the influence of the individual who imposed it. If it were put on by a great chief, it would not be broken, but a powerful man often broke through the tapu of an inferior." In such cases, to judge by the general context, it is not so much that the physically or politically stronger man breaks over the taboo of the weaker as it is that the greater favorite of the gods dares to ignore the daimonic sanction which the lesser thinks he has invoked; the grace of the daimons by which the one has gained and maintained his wealth or position is matched against the inferior position and claims to support possessed by the insignificant man. Taboos are in fact generally imposed by the chief or medicine-man, and both of these are fetish-men with indwelling spirits that speak and act through them. To oppose them is to challenge a daimon to his face. At the very least it is public opinion that speaks through them; but that means that the precedents are given into their hands by the gods; and the sanction of the precedents lies in the supernatural.[9]

We have met with so few of these cases where a superior feels able to defy a taboo imposed by an inferior that we cannot lay much weight upon them as disproof of the religious nature of the taboo. It is not far from the truth that no prohibition is altogether compelling which lacks the religious sanction, while all are respected scrupulously when they have it. The conclusion is that the word taboo is not employed correctly except as applied to a religiously sanctioned interdiction and that when it is used of a secular ordinance it is misapplied. Hence the taboo is a corollary of daimonism; it represents an attempt to escape a real or imagi-

[8] Taylor, *Te Ika*, 168.
[9] §§155, 156, 158, above; Keller, *Hom. Soc.*, 252.

nary peril—such mischance as can be met only by the methods of daimonology.

Taboos are expedients of insurance against the aleatory element; they are negative, with few elements of propitiation in them, and represent avoidance rather than conciliation. The savage did not accumulate much or any merit by attending to the taboos; he avoided sin and punishment by so doing. They formed for him a sort of dead-line, to stay on the right side of which indicated no higher qualities than plain discretion and caution. Merit came only with the positive cult-operations, in conciliation and propitiation. Yet the taboo was something more than mere avoidance of the spiritual presence, by abandonment of a locality, for example; it was an expedient for living on in the presence of the daimons. Men recognized that there was no way to exorcise or force the spirits so that they would cease to sanction their taboos; hence there was no recourse left except to submit to the drawing of the dead-line, keep its location ever in mind, and devote all attention to getting on the safe side of it and staying there.

The taboo, by its nature, does not admit of experimental verification. The native does not dare, by ignoring it, to make the test; or if by chance, involuntarily, he does, still he is more likely to support the theory by promptly dying of fright than to live to note the non-appearance of the consequences.[10]

The taboo is extended generally to prohibit what would bring bad luck; it proscribes words and names, days and seasons, attitudes and actions.[11] The cases to be cited in illustration are unusually numerous because of the range covered by the topic. What might offend the spirits or might attract them when not wanted is the object of strenuous taboo. Notions of ritual uncleanness lead to a ban of segregation, silence, and secrecy. Certain places, as a church or king's court, are tabooed for profane purposes such as fighting. Religious apparatus, for instance the Ark, is tabooed from the gaze of the people; there was a taboo on Mount Sinai and on the Tree of Life. In short, sanctity, consecration, and holiness represent taboo. In the light of these generalities the cases may seem less confused.[12]

10 Jevons, *Relig.*, 90.   11 §§223, 255, above.
12 For an encyclopædic collection of taboos, see Frazer, *Golden Bough*, I, 170 ff.; II, 86 ff.; 117-118; 225 ff.; *et passim*.

The Melanesian "tambu" never, like the Polynesian "tapu," signifies "any inherent holiness or awfulness, but always a sacred and unapproachable character which is imposed." In the Solomon Islands everything connected with a ghost is itself tambu. "In cases where the English word taboo can be employed there is always in Melanesia human sanction and prohibition. Some thing, action, or place· is made *tambu* or *tapu* by one who has the power to do it, any one whose standing among the people gives him confidence to lay this character upon it. The power at the back of the *tapu* or *tambu* is that of the ghost or spirit in whose name, or in reliance upon whom, it is pronounced; for the *tapu* is a prohibition with a curse expressed or implied." When a chief lays a *tambu* whose violation must be atoned for by payment to him, "it seems to the European a proof of the power of the chief; but to the native the power of the chief, in this and in everything else, rests on the persuasion that the chief has his *tindalo* [spirit] at his back."[13] A Papuan taboo may forbid certain foods, actions, the wearing of ornaments, sleeping in a house, or uttering certain words or names. "Noteworthy is the striking parallelism between the last-named usage and the Zulu custom called 'Hlonipa.' "[14] Again, in New Georgia, at the launching of a new war-canoe, one of two virgins is publicly sacrificed and the other kept in seclusion from four to five years. Should she break the taboo, she is put to death.[15] Seligmann[16] distinguishes two kinds of taboo in southeastern New Guinea: "those of a magical kind, an infringement of which is believed to be followed automatically by the physical penalty of illness, and those having no magical force so that their neglect involves no certain penalty and the force causing them to be obeyed is merely the weight of public opinion and long established custom. The former class of taboo can only be imposed by certain individuals, who are recognized as being able by their magic to render the breaking of the taboo physically painful or dangerous. The second class includes two very different forms or species of taboo. The first of these embraces all those cases in which objects are protected by signs which imply that the taboo is imposed as an expression of the wishes of the owner by the old men of the hamlet or hamlet-group, or as an expression of public opinion after the matter has been discussed. The other form of taboo includes all those cases of abstinence from naming or doing things at special times, prohibitions which have the binding force of old established habit, and to which every native submits as a matter of course under the appropriate circumstances, and which for the sake of brevity may be called taboos of custom. . . . In the case of certain foods not protected by 'medicine,' the imposition of the taboo is notified by taboo signs, which are, generally speaking, the same as those used for objects protected by taboos with magical content." Examples follow. We are unable to see any very great difference between the two types named; if the taboo is one of custom, it has the ghosts behind it, ready to guarantee it.

From his African experience, Trilles[17] finds the ordinary sense of the word taboo to be "sacred," in the signification of "appropriated to things and to beings considered as sacred." He finds it "essentially religious," issuing from chiefs, priests, and sorcerers. Everything is taboo on occasion: the chief, the

---

[13] Codrington, *Melanesians*, 215.
[14] §223, above; Von Pfeil, *Südsee*, 163-164.
[15] Hardy and Elkington, *S. Seas*, 136-137.
[16] *Melanesians*, 574-575.   [17] *Fán*, 601.

place, the fire, the word. "The taboo therefore extends to all domains, as well to the political as to the religious, to the moral as to the human. In fact, it becomes for the chiefs a potent means of domination by adding to the civil power all the force of the religious power." In East Africa they have an affliction called *makwa* or *thabu,* which is characterized by eruptions, sores, and wasting away. It is supposed to be the consequence of violating the taboo. A person gets *makwa* if he fails to observe purification-rules after a death; if he lies on his mother's bed or takes an article from it; if a son cohabits with his father's wife, after the father's death, without the elders having performed certain ceremonies (the brother of the deceased has to cohabit with the woman first, to take the curse off). If a woman's breasts are not ceremonially purified by an elder she will have future children with *makwa;* if a man cohabits with a woman where cattle are grazing they will get the disease; if a woman with children is forced by a man, her children will suffer; if a hyæna defecates in a village during the night, *makwa* will fall on the village. There are many other contingencies that may produce this trouble; in all of them the curse can be taken off by ceremonies including sacrifice.[18] "The ten commandments, as apprehended by the white man in their ethical splendor, are not so apprehended by the black man when God 'ties him with ten tyings' in the 'early morning' of his Christian day. They are not then to him the expressions of ideals; they are facts, definite laws of abstainings, of omission and commission. They are the Eldorado of taboo. They replace with a great calm the agitations of the experimental efforts of the past, when everything was at stake and nothing was sure; when man was exhausted in his effort to fill his side of the contract, but might never count upon the party of the second part. In this they are emancipating; they are the way of escape from a man-made yoke. Given a Father-God, there is no greater benefit that He could have conferred upon our pragmatic Bulu than ten explicit tyings. The practice of the law promises at first to be an exact science—the perfect taboo for which our Bulu has blindly searched and which is here given him with the marks of divine authority."[19]

In West Africa, *ekis* cover certain diseases and mark off certain ranks and social conditions. A food-eki may be remitted in time of famine by means of certain ritual ceremonies.[20] Togo temples are taboo to Europeans; it is believed that all the people would die overnight if clothed foreigners should enter one of them. Certain animals may be tabooed in the region of the temple; "the fetish suddenly announces that . . . he cannot any longer endure dogs, horses, goats, or swine, and therefore desires their death if they appear at the places where he is worshipped, or otherwise in his presence."[21] Fowls and dogs are *fadi* in southern Madagascar, and dreams often cause the taboo to be laid.[22]

Taboo among the Nairs "is essentially an arrangement to keep the ghosts and spirits pacified; for it is clear to them from the tested experience of past ages that to break any of these rules is to challenge those who have power to do them great harm."[23] "After I had been working among the Todas for about

[18] Hobley, in JAI, XLI, 411-413.
[19] Mackenzie, in *Atl. Mo.,* CXVIII, 794.
[20] Martrou, "Les 'eki' des Fang," in *Anthropos,* I, 745-761.
[21] Seidel, "Fetischverbote," in *Globus,* LXXIII, 342, 355.
[22] Ratzel, *Vkde.,* II, 455.   [23] Panikkar, in JAI, XLVIII, 284.

four months," says Rivers,[24] "various misfortunes befell some of those who had been my chief guides to Toda lore. One man who had pointed out to me certain sacred places fell ill and made up his mind that he was going to die. Another man lost his wife a few days after he had shown me the method of performing one of the most sacred of Toda ceremonies. A third man who had revealed to me the details of the ceremonial of the most sacred Toda dairy, suffered the loss of his own village dairy by fire. The Todas consulted their diviners, who ascribed these events to the anger of the gods because their secrets had been revealed to the stranger. In consequence my sources of information ran dry to a large extent, and the difficulties in the way of the investigation of the more sacred topics were greatly increased. . . . Among the many aspects of social life and religion, I soon found that there were some about which there was no reticence, and these could be discussed in public with men, women, or children standing by and perhaps taking part. There were others of a more sacred nature, and, if they were approached in public, it was immediately obvious that the people were ill at ease and their answers became hesitating and unsatisfactory." Rivers got around this situation by interviewing one or two at a time and by having his guide signal to him if he approached a dangerous topic. "One of the difficulties of anthropological inquiry is that the good and trustworthy narrators are often the most reticent. They are trustworthy because they are honest and pious members of their community, and are therefore naturally reluctant to offend against the sanctity of their religious customs by talking of them to a stranger."

The word for taboo in Assam is "genna." "If a man falls from a tree and is killed, the headman of the clan declares that particular tree to be genna to the members of the clan. . . . It is clear that the fiat of the headman could have no validity unless it were in accord with the mental level of the clan that they should recognise that that tree had some special danger for it, and that this danger could be avoided by placing the tree under ban. . . . There is no genna which is limited to one individual only. The tie which binds the members of a household together is the tie of blood, and although the consanguinity of the members of a household is more apparent than the relationship of the several subdivisions, the tie is yet the same. . . . I have referred to the atmosphere of exaltation, which gennas produce, and I need hardly mention that, though the means differ, this state of excitement and anticipation is a notable feature of the 'mysteries' of the classical past, and of primitive peoples of to-day. So, too, the association of the mysteries with certain prohibitions which are of a practical nature as those which . . . give a close-time to the game, or which surround the headman with sacred attributes, finds its parallel in the lessons which are taught to the young initiate as he is gradually made perfect in tribal lore. . . . In so far as the genna is intended to mitigate the displeasure of the spirits, I should regard it as religious, but, since the general belief is that the performance of the rite prevents the spirits from doing further damage, the genna is magical. . . . Those connected with sickness are magical, for the theory of sickness is that all illness is due to possession by some spirit. Even the cases where the genna is preliminary to a sacrifice are instances of magic where the sacrifice is not intended to propitiate the spirit, but to lure him from the body of the patient. I am quite prepared to admit that these cases are on the border line between religion and magic, because the control of the operat-

24 *Todas*, 2-3, 12-13.

ing priest or magician is to be regarded as rather less complete than in the cases where the spirit is held to have no option but to obey. Individual gennas such as those at birth, name giving, marriage, are certainly magical and intended to afford protection against harm from spirits who at those moments are specially active." This citation has been made, not with the idea of reproducing the author's[25] distinction between religion and magic, which is rather trifling, but to bring out the essentially religious nature of the taboo—taking the term in the broad sense, as is done in this book. To resume the quotation: "It will have been observed that the negative aspect of the genna is prominent. Most, if not all of them, prohibit some act which may at other times or by other persons be performed with immunity from bad results. Positive gennas which enjoin the performance of acts, under penalty, are rare, but, as some at least of the gennas are in effect legislative, the form they assume is worthy of note." This comment is exceedingly apt; the negative quality of the taboo is a constant character. "I see in these genna customs the foundation of all communal life, for the primary lesson they teach, whether directly or indirectly, is that harm to one is harm to all, and that the strength of all is greater than the strength of one. They give force to social and industrial legislation and, by creating an artificial atmosphere of exaltation, they stimulate the feelings of mystery and awe which are at the bottom of a good deal of what is popularly called religion. . . . When events indicate that 'the electric current is on the rails,' none dare move across or into the danger zone unless duly insulated by a genna. When a man inherits or arrogates to himself the high privileges attaching to the headship of one of these clans, he is placed on an eminence of danger. On him will fall the first discharge of supernatural activity. Therefore he protects himself by all this ritual of genna."

The connection of the taboo with the dead appears in India, where "one very common method of guarding against the evil influences of persons in a state of taboo is to bury the dead face downwards; to fill the grave with thorns, to pile a heavy cairn over the remains." These are, as we know, funerary practices calculated to lay the ghost.[26] Among the Parsees, at funerals and in other sacred ceremonies the taboo-line is represented by a shallow trench called "pavi," a word derived from "pav," meaning sacred. To make a thing "pav" is to wash it properly in pure water. In fire-temples the sacred fire burns within such an enclosed space.[27]

In Borneo, when anyone is ill and the exorciser is called in, the room is put under taboo; only members of the family may enter, and even they under certain restrictions. "They seem to regard this custom with such reverence that we availed ourselves of its privileges whenever we wished for privacy, and although the natives laughed at our adoption of their customs, they left us nevertheless strictly alone when we tied a basket or a bunch of leaves in front of our little apartment in the veranda."[28] Besides the *pamali* for the dead, there is one for the sick and one for the field. The sickness-taboo "often takes in a whole village when a dangerous sickness is prevalent; there is held a sacrificial feast to conciliate the angry god and during, at the maximum, eight days all occupations of the village stand idle and the inhabitants shut themselves up in their houses. Sometimes also the dwellers in a particular

25 Hodson, in JAI, XXXVI, 100, 102, 103.
26 §223, above; Crooke, in JAI, XXVIII, 247.
27 Modi, in JASB, II, 425, note.   28 Furness, *Head-Hunters,* 12.

house subject themselves to this *pamali,* hoping that by laying this sort of penance upon themselves, they may move the gods to avert a danger that threatens a sick person among their beloved relations." The field-taboo lasts for four days subsequent to the completion of the sowing; nobody belonging to the tribe dares step upon the fields during that time. Here, as in the death-taboo, a feast with the sacrifice of a pig is demanded for the lifting of the *pamali.*[29]

The closeness of connection between the taboo and daimonism is unmistakable. "From the cradle to the grave they live under these bonds, since the priests play a great rôle in every period of life, and then too the religious service comes in with its restrictions."[30] The taboo of the Mentawei Islands "forms an integral part of the cult, for the *punan* enters almost everywhere": when a new boat or house is done, at a marriage, in case of births, deaths, and illness. Sacrifice is performed by the priests, who are called in.[31]

In Polynesia the laws of taboo constituted a network of restrictions around the entirety of life, comparable only with the caste-system of India. All things on earth, except men, were divided into holy and common; the former were regarded as the property of gods or nobles while the latter were allowed to all men, unless touched by someone conveying taboo. In all cases there is a religious kernel to the taboo; it probably began in religion and was extended to politics. It was useful to discipline wild men accustomed to little check. It secured property; and Europeans have been able to get it extended over their possessions. By it short crops have been preserved against improvident consumption; and winter supplies of fish, have thus been rendered secure. An intoxicating drink has been held, by the taboo, in reserve for the nobles. It has thus been made use of for private and selfish purposes; thus, Kamehameha the First tabooed a mountain near Honolulu because he thought the quartz-crystals found there were diamonds. In 1840, the Hawaiian government tabooed cattle for five years, because they were being exterminated. Violation of the taboo accounts for the cases where Europeans have been suddenly massacred by natives who had just before seemed most friendly. Even animals were punished for breach of taboo. It was necessary, of course, to have persons who were free from restriction to feed those upon whom it rested, since the latter might touch no food; slaves were used to this end, for they were out of the ban of their own deities and had not been received into that of others, and so were held incompetent to violate taboo. And there had to be ceremonies to raise taboos, since otherwise they would smother a whole people.[32]

"The system of *tapu,* so widely spread throughout the islands of the Pacific, was carried to its highest pitch of development as a social law in the land of the Maori. Its operation was arbitrary, and often ridiculous to European ideas, but it has its uses. It was really the only law save that of the spear and the *patu* that the Maori possessed, and the fear of *tapu* and the unseen tempered the too free exercise of brute force in a community where war was the chief end of man. *Tapu* was the *'noli me tangere'* of Maori land. Literally the word may be briefly translated as 'sacred' or 'holy' or 'forbidden,' but its variations and peculiar applications are innumerable." A number of illustrations are given. A great chief was exceedingly *tapu,* his head especially so. No one

[29] Veth, *Borneo's Wester-Afdeeling,* II, 315-316.
[30] Nieuwenhuis, *Borneo,* I, 139-140.   [31] Pleyte, in *Globus,* LXXIX, 31.
[32] Ratzel, *Vkde.,* II, 211 ff.

would dare to touch any remains of food of which he had partaken, to use his drinking-vessel, or to lay a finger on his sleeping-mat. "His *mana-tapu* —an expression which it is very difficult to translate into English that will convey its true sense, but which may be baldly rendered as personal sacred power and essential psychic force—was something of which the ordinary man stood much in awe."[33] "In a speech made to his pupils . . . years ago . . . one of the last teachers of the *tapu* lore of the Maori, explained why such lore should not be divulged to Europeans, and how it was that missionaries were not allowed to become acquainted with it." Such knowledge was withheld "for reasons obvious to those who know the native mind, and the attitude of the average missionary towards such matters. . . . All of this goes to show that, when you wish to gain an insight into the occult lore of the Maori, it is not desirable to go to him as a missionary; also that you should treat his beliefs with respect; nor try to force your own upon him; and that it is a wise thing to imitate his dignity and politeness, and treat him as you would one of your own folk whose knowledge exceeds your own, and whom you look upon as a master."[34]

In Deuteronomy[35] are mentioned twelve curses or taboos. The Jahweh-taboo covered everything belonging to the god or his service, for instance the Ark; for whoever touched it must die, and when it was stolen, it caused severe illness in the land of the Philistines and had to be brought back. For it was Jahweh's seat.[36] Similarly Sinai was surrounded by a barrier and no one might tread on it. Into the sanctuary at Shiloh and later at Jerusalem, only priests might enter, and into the Holy of Holies only the high priest, once a year; also, before doing so, "he must fill the whole place with incense that he might not die." "The presence of the god makes the sacrifice and meal taboo. The participators wash themselves and put on other clothes, in order that the taboo may not go over upon the ordinary clothes." The common taboos upon death, sex-relations, women, and illness appear among the Hebrews; "the idea of the taboo extends over wide ranges, but is only in part still demonstrable in the Old Testament."[37]

It is significant of the religious nature of the taboo to find it intimately connected with the idea of "holiness." The taboo-day is, we have seen, also the holiday. The tabooed thing is likely to be "unclean" or "holy" or both at once, for the two terms run together. Smith[38] goes rather fully into this idea of holiness, connecting it with the taboo but reserving the latter term for the idea of holiness on the primitive stage as distinguished from the conception in advanced religions. He says:

"The most general terms to express the relation of natural things to the gods which our language affords is the word 'holy'; thus when we speak of holy places, holy things, holy persons, holy times, we imply that the places,

[33] Cowan, *Maoris*, 114–115.   [34] Best, in JAI, XLIV, 129.
[35] XXVII, 15 ff.   [36] I Sam., VI, 7.
[37] Maurer, *Vkdliches*, 76; Maurer, in *Globus*, XC, 136–138.
[38] *Relig. Sem.*, 91, 150, 152, 158, 163, 167–168, 451.

things, persons, and times stand in some special relation to the godhead or to its manifestation. But the word 'holy' has had a long and complicated history, and has various shades of meaning according to the connection in which it is used." Holiness "is essentially a restriction on the license of man in the free use of natural things." Rules of holiness in this matter of restriction, "enforced by the dread of supernatural penalties, are found among all primitive peoples. It is convenient to have a distinct name for this primitive institution, to mark it off from the later developments of the idea of holiness in advanced religions, and for this purpose the Polynesian term *taboo* has been selected. . . . In the oldest type of society impious acts or breaches of taboo were the only offences treated as crimes;[39] e.g., there is no such crime as theft, but a man can save his property from invasion by placing it under a taboo, when it becomes an act of impiety to touch it. . . . I believe that in early society (and not merely in the very earliest) we may safely affirm that every offence to which death or outlawry is attached was primarily viewed as a breach of holiness; e.g., murder within the kin, and incest, are breaches of the holiness of tribal blood, which would be supernaturally avenged if men overlooked them." And the very land might be holy; "thus in Canaan where the whole land was holy, the hunter was allowed to kill game if he returned the life to the god by pouring it on the ground"—the blood being the life. Thus holiness makes a close connection with fetishism, the more clearly so in the case of ritual holiness attributed to certain pools, notably the Zamzam well at Mecca. Holiness attached to the clothing of anyone who made the sacred circuit of the Kaaba stone at Mecca; such clothing could not be worn again or sold, but must be left at the gate of the sanctuary.

"Even a person by unauthorized touching of what is itself holy may 'become holy,' i.e. fall forfeit to the sanctuary, enter into a special relation to God; so, for instance, by touching the altar or the sacred paraphernalia.[40] In such an event, special offerings and atonements are needed in order to remove the condition of 'being holy,' which presses upon the individual as a danger. The danger lies in the fact that, while he is in this condition, every species of defilement, whether due to his own fault or no, may readily prove fatal to him."[41]

The essential likeness between the tabooed and the holy comes out automatically in translations of the Bible into native tongues. In West Africa the word corresponding to taboo is *orunda*, meaning originally *prohibited from* human use—as *ibet* means a command, law, abstinence, and *xina* or *quixilles* an injunction of abstinence. This word *orunda* "grew under missionary hands into its related meaning of *sacred to* spiritual use. It is the word by which the Mpongwe Scriptures translate our word 'holy.' "[42]

§269. Societal Function. It is the religious sanction of the taboo that confers upon it that surpassing disciplinary function

[39] §182, above.   [40] Exod., XXIX, 37, XXX, 26 ff.
[41] Kautzsch, "Relig. Israel," in *Hastings's Bible Dict.*, 682.
[42] Nassau, *Fetichism*, 80.

which makes it a factor almost without peer in the formation of societal structure. Ghost-fear supports it at every turn and actual penalties due to terror attend breaches of its provisions.[43]

"Tapu is an awful weapon. I have seen a strong young man die the same day he was tapued; the victims die under it as though their strength ran out as water."[44] How effective the taboo is, and how it may demonstrate the validity of its supporting sanction is illustrated by the case of the "strong and healthy black boy" employed by an Australian settler. One day he was found to be ill. He explained that he had 'stolen some female opossum' before he was permitted to eat it, and that the old men had discovered it and he should never grow up to be a man. In fact, he lay down under the belief, so to speak, and died within three weeks."[45] Clearly he died of fright. If a man took anything with a *sabi* or taboo, indicated by a piece of wood, bunch of grass, or the like tied to it, he would die.[46] "An Australian black-fellow, who discovered that his wife had lain on his blanket at her menstrual period, killed her and died of terror himself within a fortnight."[47] The accidental eating of the meat of a female animal brought a Malekula native to his end.[48] "Blacks die off very quickly, once they have lost heart."[49] "A Maori woman, having eaten of some fruit and being afterward told that the fruit had been taken from a tabooed place, exclaimed that the spirit of the chief whose sanctity had been thus profaned would kill her. This was in the afternoon and next day by 12 o'clock she was dead."[50] To the savage there is evidently no lack of verification of the theory he is going by. In cases like these, no indication is to be found of any discrimination against the taboo set by an inferior; the implication always is that a taboo is a taboo—each proscription has infinite spiritual power behind it. Once again, "it is evident that a tambu approaches to a curse, when it is a prohibition resting on the invocation of an unseen power."[51]

Hardy and Elkington[52] give a rather complete picture of the taboo or "hope" of the South Seas. The Solomon Islanders use a "hope" to keep a place free from trespassers. "It is a strange custom and difficult to fathom, but the belief in it is so strong that the most daring native would not dream of testing its powers. There are various kinds of 'hopes,' some will result in the death of any one trespassing on them, whilst others will only bring sickness upon him. A death 'hope' will have a skull on it, or a piece of shell, or part of an ants' nest, and on seeing these signs the intruder knows what to expect—that he will die as the man has died whose skull is there, or die as surely as the fish which once lived in the shell has died, or as the ants which inhabited the nest." This prefiguring of the fate of the trespasser is distinctly magical.[53]

---

[43] §306, below; cases in Frazer, *Golden Bough*, I, 168 ff.

[44] Tregear, in JAI, XIX, 100.　　　[45] Howitt, in JAI, XVI, 42, note.

[46] Haddon, in JAI, XIX, 405.

[47] Anon., "Aust. Aborig.," in JAI, IX, 459.

[48] Somerville, in JAI, XXIII, 381.

[49] Glave, in *Century Mag.*, XXX, 927.

[50] Brown, *New Zealand*, 76, quoted in Frazer, *Golden Bough*, I, 168.

[51] Codrington, *Melanesians*, 216.

[52] *S. Seas*, 134-137.　　　[53] §302, below.

Chiefs' houses are "hope"; so are crocodiles, which may not be killed; "but in one of the rivers where crocodiles abound a youth was killed by them, and the chief took the 'hope' off until the boy's father had slain a sufficient number to satisfy his anger, and then back went the 'hope.'"

One voyager had with him two natives who did not like to land on an islet that had been "hoped" by their chief. They finally did land but one of them went under the taboo-barricade, picked the central shoot of a fern, nibbled it a bit, and passed it to the other native. "They assured me that now the 'hope' would have no effect as long as they did not steal any nuts. There seem to be various methods of overcoming 'hope,' the chief being by a payment to the owner of it. He will extort what he considers a sufficiently large sum of money to take away the ill effects which would otherwise have followed if the 'hope' had been scouted. . . . In spite of the fact that white men scorn these 'hopes' and do not suffer any bad results, it has in no way brought discredit on them; the belief is quite as strong now as it ever was, but the natives think that the white man is guarded by a special providence and so cling to their belief." Thus no verification is possible, first because no native dares to put his fortune to the test and, second, because when he sees someone else dare and escape scatheless, he has an explanation right at hand which strengthens rather than weakens his theory.

These illustrations bear witness, preliminary to the body of our cases, to the disciplinary fear that lies back of the taboo. There was nothing else in primitive life, not even the terror of a ruthless despot, that could come anywhere near the taboo in effectiveness—that could actually scare healthy people to death. Thus the taboo was an unconsciously evolved warning and restraint in societies which had no other means of combating things harmful to themselves. Taboo was the primordial form of societal regulation; it reduced society to order for expedient ends and thus gave it shape and consistency. It had a competence not of this world and strength sufficient to control action. In the earliest stages of civilization, though conservative to a degree shown by no other regulative force, it gradually expanded to cover an increasing body of notions concerning what must not be done in order to live successfully. As it lay in the mores, both mores and morals came to be built around it. It is thus, at last analysis, a development by which fear of the supernatural comes into play to prevent actions which are believed to be harmful to health, industry, war, sex, family, religion, or any other social interest. What violates taboo is profane and irreligious. It works over into a proscription of "bad form."

A single instance will recall many an illustration of this last point. Among the Pelew Islanders, "the word *mugul* and its opposite, *tokoi* constitute every third word in conversation. The latter means 'good usage,' the former 'bad form.' . . . When, as a joke, I took off my hat and set it on the head of one of them—she seemed to me on account of her icy, silent dignity to be the most distinguished—she threw it off with great agitation and, springing up in anger, read me a sermon of rebuke that I, already so long in the country, did not yet know even that it was in the highest degree *mugul* for a native to cover the head."[54]

In the long run the taboo makes for society's well-being. Occasionally this is strikingly evident. McGee[55] tells of how the Seri taboo the smaller rodents, so that these have increased to incredible numbers. Their burrows honeycomb the country and make it nearly impassable, even for pedestrians; and they thus have rewarded their benefactors "by protecting their territory for centuries." Of course the ancestors of these Indians planned no such thing. The services of the taboo to society have been in the main quite unforeseen; their rationality is discoverable long after the act and only subsequently to long eras of automatic selection.[56]

A single additional quotation will serve to set the general topic of the societal services of taboo before us. "The possession of Tambu has a very important influence on the lives of the New Britain people." Thus: first, it minimizes the evil and fatality of war, by enforcing compensation for every life taken and every wound inflicted. It also establishes personal right to property and the right to alienate it. It makes the people frugal and industrious. Nothing is wasted and the rare spendthrift is held in contempt. It makes the people commercial, because it allows of intermediaries who carry transactions to places their principals have never visited. But even so, it is added, tambu has not been an unmixed blessing, for to it "may be attributed in no small degree their intense selfishness and their glaring ingratitude."[57]

Within the society the taboo is the great institution-builder, for, as we have seen,[58] it cuts away at the amorphous mass of folkways, eliminating this and that, until what is left shows a shape and consistency that is more permanent and institutional. This the taboo is able to do in its function as an instrument of selection. It is clear enough from the cases cited that such selection is not often rational; a course of action may be banned merely because of a dream; yet a great many of the taboos, whatever the circumstances of their origin, show a rationality in retrospect that is analogous to the rationality of nature-processes. And the ta-

54 Semper, *Palau-Ins.*, 66, note, 97.   55 In BAE, XVII, pt. I, 203*.
56 Keller, *Soc. Evol.*, 93 ff.   57 Danks, in JAI, XVII, 314.
58 §46, above.

boos are themselves, like original folkways, subject to automatic selection whereby in general, though with noteworthy exceptions, those that make for societal welfare are retained at the expense of many that do not survive the test of competition. Taboos are, in a sense, negative mores and as such are subject to the same evolutionary process that acts upon the mores.

The taboo, coming into societal life with its daimonic sanction, profoundly affects all human conduct. It defines the code and in so doing establishes norms; it upholds standards of decency and propriety by proscribing the indecent and improper. It secures privacy to natural functions. In general it governs that aspect of societal life called by Spencer "ceremonial." It is impossible to pursue the taboo in detail; what we propose to do is to exhibit representative instances of its entrance into the several major phases of societal life: into self-maintenance in its several forms, into self-perpetuation, and into the various unclassifiable types of self-gratification. It checks and disciplines into definite courses the forces—hunger, love, vanity, and ghost-fear—that lie behind all these manifestations. Its effectiveness could not be except for its daimonic nature, for it enlists ghost-fear, the most compelling sanction known to undisciplined man.

§270*. The Industrial Taboo. When a taboo within the field of primary self-maintenance sanctions a vitally inexpedient variation in policy, it cannot long withstand selection unless the society which exhibits it is isolated from competition. Taboos of such stripe are to be found persisting under such conditions; and sometimes where the society is not pressing heavily upon its means of subsistence but is living in easy circumstances, a moderately inexpedient practice guaranteed by taboo may not cause sufficient ill or discomfort to lead to selection. If, for example, the taboo against anyone walking about over the head of another[59] results in the limitation of house-building to one story, not much is lost, especially on the stage of primitive architecture. In distinction from such cases, others are to be found where the prohibition debars an inexpedient policy and soundly guarantees the continuance of an expedient one against tampering or even criticism.

[59] Examples in Frazer, *Golden Bough*, I, 188 ff.

Whatever is of economic value to primitive societies, such as property and women, is subject to taboo.[60] The nearer such regulation comes to covering direct reactions of a given society upon its natural environment the surer is it of justification on the ground of rationality. Not that the presence of such a taboo is at all a proof, we reiterate, of rational choice; it merely indicates that the automatic process has resulted in an expedient adjustment, which can then be shown to be rational.

As we go forward to examples from the more derived parts of society's maintenance-organization, such as property, we shall find this rational aspect of the taboo much less clearly in evidence, for there the test of the mores is much less concrete and conclusive —inexpediency or expediency much less demonstrable—than it is in the simpler departments of the industrial organization, such as the food-quest or direct food-production.

In British New Guinea a series of solemn taboos surrounds the chase of the dugong, or sea-cow. The weaver of the net must not leave the house in which he is working till he is done. He cuts his hair close and paints his body black; may have no relations with any woman; has his food brought by men, who sedulously remove all fragments; must not touch the food with his fingers; must eat as little as possible; and must not speak aloud. When the net is done a stern "helega" is extended over all the villagers; all noise is forbidden; the women and children must not speak aloud and must stay outside the village, coming in only at evening to sleep. The silence-taboo is particularly severe upon such a talkative race. Restrictions upon the hunters are still more strict, especially for the leader, who may not bathe, sleep, or speak, but gives orders by signs. The hunters' canoe may not touch any other, and if another craft crosses its bow, all hope of success is dashed. An unfortunate hunt is, in view of these various conditions, easily accounted for. All restrictions lapse at once when the prey is caught.[61] The rational element, in this case, is very slight.

Some Solomon Islanders, out walking with Woodford,[62] took a long circle around a yam-patch, while he struck across the middle of it. "On their rejoining me I inquired whether I had done wrong, as I was always most particular not to do any damage knowingly. They replied, 'No,' but that if a native walked across a patch of growing yams, a devil, I suppose a kind of 'genius loci,' would assuredly make him sick." Evidently such a belief protected the growing crops and guaranteed property in them.

In Togo there was a taboo on white men, their dress, ways, money, and tools. In a certain village where no white man had yet been, no one might enter in European clothes, no shade be spread or hammock seen there. But German coins at length displaced cowries. Then a man was struck by light-

60 De Greef, *Soc.*, 141; Letourneau, *Soc.*, 466-467.
61 Finsch, *Ethnol. Erfahr.*, III, 403, 404.
62 *Head-Hunters*, 170.

ning, and the shamans announced that the gods were angry at the change of money; that the shell-money was for the blacks, the metal for the whites. There was in this same region a local god who could forbid planting, getting water at the watering-places, or even cooking.[63] In the Loango region the burning off of the bush was forbidden by a "quixilles."[64] Such provisions rendered possible a serious interference with economic life. Cotton cloth is tabooed in Liberia, in favor of nakedness or bast-clothing, for initiates into their clubs;[65] this is doubtless an interdiction of the new material in favor of the time-hallowed old vesture or an absence of clothing. Rohlfs[66] was angrily warned, while botanizing, that it was forbidden by religion to go through a sowed field otherwise than barefoot and that he must instantly take off his shoes. He later learned that the scruple about treading down with shod feet a grain that served as food for man existed also in the Egyptian and Nubian sections of the Nile valley, where it was forbidden also to spit upon the crop.

In Assam, India, "a woman whom I knew had come from a cloth-weaving village, was settled with her husband in an outlying village where I saw her. I asked her if she had woven any cloths recently, and she told me her husband's village people forbade her weaving because it was genna to them. I was well aware that by discouraging the marriage of their girls outside the group of cloth-weaving villages, they were fast making themselves a close corporation in enjoyment of a valuable monopoly. . . . Race, religion, political power, have been and still are factors in the growth of caste. We know that caste is partly occupational in its origin, but this incident illustrates how the sanctity of an industrial monopoly comes to be recognised by others. I asked a headman why they forbade the woman to weave cloths, and he told me that all feared something terrible would happen to them if they allowed her to make cloths. There is also the fear of the magic of the craftsmen being directed against them, for in these tribes the villages which have a special industry are regarded as possessing remarkable powers which they claim, and which others believe to have been taught them by some divine being."[67] Such an arrangement defeats the transfer of culture much as do the rules of a mediæval gild or the high tariff of a modern state, neutralizing, in particular, one of the chief services of exogamy.[68]

Alongside rational measures the most irrational prevail. "Since the Kayans think that the rice has a soul which is sensitive to the same impressions as we are, a variety of things are forbidden in the first period after sowing. . . . People may kill no animals, for fear the blood may scare off the rice-soul. For the same reason it is not allowed at that time to marry or have one's self tattooed."[69]

The taboo often works out naturally into a "game-law," which may or may not be rational in its effects but is generally irrational in theory. Among the East Greenlanders, if the first seal is taken in the spring while the taker is still living in his snow-house, it must not be eaten for three days, even if the people are suffering from hunger. Again, if the tent has not been provided with new skin-coverings in the spring, seal or whale must not be taken into it until several days have intervened. "Early in the spring a man got a share in

[63] Seidel, in *Globus*, LXXIII, 342, 343, 358.

[64] Bastian, *Deut. Exped.*, I, 64.

[66] *Drei Monate*, 274-275.

[68] §356, below.

[65] Frobenius, *Masken*, 118, 121.

[67] Hodson, in JAI, XXXVI, 94-95.

[69] Nieuwenhuis, *Borneo*, I, 180.

a seal and took it into his tent to cut it up and get the sinews out. The tent-covering was right good but had been used the previous autumn. Upon the seals later becoming very scarce, that man was looked upon with evil eye by the rest because by his conduct he had brought it about that the seals had become angry and left the coast. . . . . The natives did not dare sell us a whole seal without the catchers holding on to something of it, preferably a fragment of the snout. A number of times we had at length to promise to throw the heads of purchased seals, when we had eaten them, into the sea."[70]

Although certain Zuñis lived only two days' walk from the lake of salt where they got their supply, it was a dire sacrilege to get it except at a certain time of the year.[71] Shingu native boatmen followed every winding of the river and never would cross them.[72]

These cases illustrate restrictions upon various forms of maintenance-activity, some well-advised from the standpoint of better knowledge, others distinctly adverse to success in living. The presence of general false premises, derived from the conception of the imaginary environment, is unmistakable. In connection too with the maintenance-activities there is also a time-taboo or holiday whose effect is to slow up the pace of work, so much so that it is difficult not to regard this form of prohibition, however salutary in moderation, as readily productive of maladjustment; in Webster's *Rest Days* occur many examples of the protracted cessation of economic activity, sometimes to the distinct impoverishment of the society in question.

"It may be forbidden to the negro by his 'quixilles' to travel on certain days; on these days he must rest"; for instance, on Sona-day, their Sunday or rest-day, beyond visiting the market no other business may be done, at peril of illness sent by the fetish.[73] The Yoruba *ako-ojo*, or "first day," is a Sabbath or day of general rest. "It is considered unlucky, and no business of importance is ever undertaken on it." It exists alongside special days of rest for worshippers of particular divinities. Monthly moon-sabbaths are observed by peoples who do not reckon by weeks; and it is plausibly maintained that the sabbath goes back in origin to moon-worship. For a follower of a god to violate the day sacred to the god is as serious an offense as to break the Sabbath was among the Jews; "and, as with the Jews, is punished with death, the notion being that if the honour of the god is not vindicated by his followers, they will suffer for the neglect. The Sabbath-breaker is, in fact, killed by the other worshippers of the god from motives of self-protection."[74]

Among the Central Eskimo, "in winter a long spell of bad weather occasions privation, since the hunters are then prevented from leaving their huts. If by chance some one should happen to die during this time, famine is inevi-

70 Holm, *Ethnol. Skizze*, 34, 35.   71 Cushing, in BAE, XIII, 352.
72 Von den Steinen, *Zent. Bras.*, 102.
73 Bastian, *Deut. Exped.*, I, 185; II, 79.
74 Ellis, *Yoruba*, 145, 146, 149.

table, for a strict law prevents the performance of any kind of work during the days of mourning."[75] Again, the Caribs think that the clay of which their pottery is to be made must be obtained from the deposit at a particular place and only on the first night of the full moon. Pots made of clay obtained at other times will not only break, but will cause diseases in those who eat out of them.[76] Every day except the one is therefore a "sabbath" so far as getting clay is concerned.

The Jewish sabbath and jubilee are well known. The Levitical prescriptions[77] could not be carried out in full, demanding as they did cessation of field-labors every seventh year, and other arbitrary restrictions; for living up to them, "so far as this was possible at all, would have led to a total want of certainty as to all matters of property and a consequent paralyzing of economic relations."[78] Here is a case where societal selection suppresses the traditional mores when they and their sanction constitute an impossible or painful maladjustment to life-conditions. The jubilee year "was regarded by the Jews themselves as merely an utopia and was so handled."[79] The Assyrians furnished a model for the Jews in their weekly day, the seventh, fourteenth, twenty-first, and twenty-eighth of the months, on which there was a general prohibition of work.[80] Ellis[81] believes the Jewish sabbath to be connected primarily with moon-worship, and thinks it was at first monthly but became weekly after the adoption of the seven-day week from the Babylonians. "In all the later works, written after contact with the Babylonians, we find frequent mention of Sabbaths, but nearly always in connection with new moons."

The Cheremis do not labor at all during the blossoming of the corn. To do work during this time—about three weeks—is sin; only the uprooting of weeds is allowable. "After the three weeks they betake themselves—among the Christian Cheremis too—into the woods to the ancient places of sacrifice, and there kill cows, sheep, and domestic fowl in honor of the gods."[82] "As in the German folk-tales, so in those of the southern Slavs, the man in the moon is a profaner of the holy Sunday rest. Sometimes the story is that the man was a woodcutter, sometimes a smith."[83]

The taboo, reacting upon the industrial organization, now lends strong sanction to the obviously expedient and again supports equally powerfully some course of action that cannot be for the welfare of society. In its latter phase it may, if the society is protected from competition, continue for a long time to preserve an outworn habitude; but such restrictions drop progressively away where the group-struggle is intense enough to test out the mores

[75] Boas, in BAE, VI, 427.   [76] Schomburgk, Brit.-Guiana, I, 261.
[77] Levit., XXV, 1-7, 18-22; Neh., X, 32; I Macc., VI, 49, 53; II Chron., XXXVI, 21; Buhl, Israeliten, 63, 64.
[78] Kautzsch, "Relig. Israel," in Hastings's Bible Dict., 718.
[79] Buhl, Israeliten, 110.
[80] Wellhausen, Hist. Israel, 112, note; 116-119.
[81] Yoruba, 147-148.   [82] Stern, Russland, 99.
[83] Krauss, Südslaven, 12.

conclusively, laying ever severer penalties upon the maladapted. A later age may, however, approve of any one of the persisting taboos, for instance the one calling for rest-days, upon rational grounds; and it may then last on for a long time, ostensibly under its obsolete form or under some reinterpretation of its origins, now long lost to memory. To many persons Sunday is an economic holiday, profitable to national life upon demonstrated grounds, namely, the need of periodic rest, recreation, and change. Its religious aspects may even seem to them incidental whereas, had there been no religion, the rest-day might have been very late of development. It is the rest-idea that is incidental.

§271*. Food-Taboo. Taboos upon activities in the maintenance-organization often amount to food-taboos, for they prevent the getting of any food at all or of particular varieties. There are numerous special forms of the food-prohibition.[84] Certain of them amount to a closed season on different kinds of game; sometimes they represent a policy as to the use of a food supposed to be very strengthening but limited in amount or harmful at some crisis in the individual's or society's life. Many of them appear to root in selfishness and in what we should regard as abuse of power, as in the prohibition of certain foods to women and children or to the lower classes; but the great majority seem to be laid as self-denial to conciliate the spirits,[85] especially when some offense has been committed. They thus represent a sort of negative or passive sacrifice—a refraining from getting so that the spirits may get—plus an averting of possible ill through self-discipline. Such a taboo for a time is a fast.[86]

These taboos, like the time-taboo, entirely arbitrary so far as is revealed, are sometimes rationalized upon and their origins reinterpreted; they are thus justified in an age where the mores have changed. For instance, the fruit of one tree in Eden was tabooed; it was a sin to eat of it; and, as usual in the primitive relation of taboo and its transgression, the wage of sin was death. The later notion that it was the tree of the knowledge of good and evil ex-

[84] Lippert, *Kgchte.*, I, 118, 119, 121, 248.
[85] §280, below.
[86] §225, above; Lippert, *Kgchte.*, I, 119.

plained the prohibition to a more sophisticated age by rationalizing upon it—else it would have remained entirely unintelligible and arbitrary and therefore unjustifiable.

Of Tasmanian taboos there were three forms: that on the names of deceased or absent relatives and friends, upon their burial-places, and upon certain kinds of food, such as the wallaby and scaled fish. "Of shell fish there were few or none, and no other fish would any native of Tasmania even touch . . .; they would rather starve than eat it."[87] This case reminds us that fish were often fetishes by reason of their real or supposed "burial" of the dead;[88] the fish-taboo will appear several times in what follows.

There is a long list of Australian foods forbidden on the basis of age, sex, and time.[89] Much of the Australian restriction "is associated with the idea, firstly, of reserving the best things for the older people, secondly, of reserving certain things for the men as opposed to the women, while, thirdly, there are restrictions which deal with the food of individuals at particular times."[90] Women and boys are not allowed to eat the wallaby or bandicoot lest the women have fewer children and the boys grow beards of a faded color.[91] "The old men are privileged to eat every kind of food that it is lawful for any of their tribe to eat, but there are kinds of food which a tribe will eat in one district and which tribes in another part of the continent will not touch. The women may not eat of the flesh of certain animals; certain kinds of meat are prohibited to children and young persons; young married women are interdicted from partaking of dainties that delight the palates of older women; and men may not touch the flesh of some animals until a mystic ceremony has been duly celebrated. . . . In looking over the list of animals prohibited to young men, to women, and to children, one fails to see, however, any good reasons for the selection—unless we regard nearly the whole of the prohibitions as having their source in superstitious beliefs."[92] There is sometimes a progressive emancipation for men; at the end of specified periods the taboo is removed. After the third of these periods, for instance, a man could eat fish, after a fourth, honey, after a fifth, whatever he liked. Then he was taught the meanings of the tribal message-sticks.[93] Evidently the release from the taboo accompanies the stages of initiation.

Arbitrary rules are that fish is forbidden to women during menstruation; that widows may eat the females of any animals or that they may not for about two years eat animals that run on the ground but only those that climb trees.[94] "There are some kinds of food, however, which seem to be universally abhorred—as, for instance, the fat of swine. As a rule, the natives will not eat pork, or any kind of fat the nature and origin of which are not known to them."[95] This abstention may be connected with the notion that the seat of the soul is in the fat.[96]

[87] Roth, *Tasmania*, 74, 101.   [88] §§247, 248, 256, above.
[89] Eyre, *Cent. Aust.*, II, 293-295.
[90] Spencer and Gillen, *Nat. Tr. Cent. Aust.*, 470.
[91] Ratzel, *Vkde.*, II, 53.   [92] Smyth, *Vict.*, I, 234.
[93] Parker, *Euahlayi*, 81.
[94] Gason, in JAI, XXIV, 171; Palmer, in JAI, XIII, 298, 299.
[95] Smyth, *Vict.*, I, 237.   [96] §213, above.

The Australian food-taboos furnish about as complete a series as can be found. Parallels occur throughout Melanesia: thus, so long as a Papuan boy is not circumcized, "he may eat neither swine-flesh nor dog-flesh, which are tabooed to women also, but only fish, crayfish, and varieties of shellfish that are allowed to men; for certain varieties of crayfish and shellfish are allowed to women only. It is to be said parenthetically that the menu of the Papuans is so arranged that the good things, the dainties, are reserved exclusively for the men."[97] In New Britain the dog, iguana, and a certain kind of pudding are reserved for women; the last especially for mothers-in-law. Chiefs and men under vows in connection with a society eat no pork or fish of certain kinds, including sharks. In the New Hebrides women and children eat sow's flesh, men never. Again the streams are full of eels, but they are tabooed; for there are ghosts in them, especially the big ones.[98]

In the Andaman Islands there is a taboo which amounts to a reservation of food supposed to be strengthening to warriors;[99] according to their lights the Andamanese are acting with the same rationality that civilized nations exhibit when the population "behind the lines" deny themselves for those at the front.

Trilles[100] tells a story of a man who went to the village of his parents-in-law, probably to take an instalment of the bride-price for his wife; he stayed quite a while and returned to find, to his joy, that his wife was pregnant. She had a fine boy who, unfortunately, died before any ceremony could be carried out. The parents-in-law came at once, sought the cause of the death, and found it promptly. During his absence the husband had killed an antelope and eaten of it. This was interdicted to an *enceinte* woman and to her husband, during the period of gestation and lactation. The father had therefore, in ignorance, broken a taboo. In expiation, since the child was a first-born, the wife returned to her parents, there was a divorce, and the husband lost all right to a return of the bride-price. If the child had lived the father would have paid amends to the parents of his wife and the boy would have been "vowed" to the antelope.

In general, African food-taboos rest upon irrational daimonistic notions and there is more than an indication that they are imposed chiefly upon the flesh of fetish-animals. Since almost every tribe has its special tribal animal, there is probably a considerable admixture of totemism in the restrictive measures.[101] The food-taboos of the black races are typical; those found elsewhere are confirmatory or serve to fill in the picture.

In Samoa, "a man would not eat a fish which was supposed to be under the protection and care of his household god; but he would eat, without scruple, fish sacred to the gods of other families. The dog, and some kinds of fish and birds, were sacred to the greater deities . . . and, of course, all the peo-

---

[97] Hagen, *Papua's*, 234.
[98] Danks, in AAAS, 1892, 618; Leggatt, in AAAS, 1892, 699; Codrington, *Melanesians*, 177.
[99] Man, in JAI, XII, 354.   [100] *Fân*, 166.
[101] Ratzel, *Vkde.*, I, 176.

ple rigidly abstained from these things. . . . The same idea seems to have been a check on cannibalism, as there was a fear lest the god of the deceased would be avenged on those who might cook and eat the body."[102] There is, in a number of these cases, a connection with the totemic taboo[103] which the reader will have noted. In one of the Hervey Islands, there were officers known as "rulers of food." During the reign of one of these there was extreme scarcity; and not only was the responsibility for the famine attributed to him, but his failure was in matters supernatural. He did not control cultivation and consumption aright by proclaiming the correct taboos. In the Marquesas Islands, "the chiefs could interdict the use of a food or drink by their subjects completely, and for an unlimited time, and no one would dream of raising the slightest complaint, or violating the taboo. The taboo was divided into several classes, some of which, being measures of precaution, might be called economic, and these are the taboos with which we are now concerned. The object of these economic taboos . . . was to prevent the too rapid destruction of an edible commodity, or one useful for any other purpose. If the quantity of . . . breadfruit was diminishing in a district, the chief had the right to lay a taboo on all or part of the fruit-trees for twenty months, in order to give the trees time to regain strength. In the same way, if fish was beginning to fail, the taboo was laid on one part of the bay in order to allow the fish to spawn without being disturbed and so replenish the sea in the neighbourhood of the inhabited places." During these taboo-periods the people ate fermented breadfruit and fished in the open sea or another part of their fishing-grounds.[104]

Among the Salish Indians, "the heart, liver, kidneys and spinal-cord of deer were especially tabooed. It was not easy to learn much on these points, or to gather the origin or significance of these restrictions. The usual reply to all inquiries of the kind is that it was the 'custom.' That in the native mind is an all-sufficient reason for the practice, and old François, whom I interrogated on the matter, had probably never before in his life had his attention directed to the question of 'why' or 'wherefore' he practised this or that custom. That it was dangerous to disregard these things he knew, for had he not himself suffered by so doing?"[105]

Several illustrations from Semitic practice will reveal the persistence of food-taboos into stages of civilization more familiar to most readers. The injunction to the Israelites was: "Every moving thing that liveth shall be food for you; as the green herb have I given you all. But flesh with the life thereof, which is the blood thereof, shall ye not eat."[106] If a man kill a beast or fowl, "he shall pour out the blood thereof, and cover it with dust. For as to the life of all flesh, the blood thereof is all one with the life thereof; therefore I said unto the children of Israel, Ye shall eat the blood of no manner of flesh: for the life of all flesh is the blood thereof: whosoever eateth it shall be cut off."[107] The *nervus ischiadicus* of the hip was not eaten;[108] it was the ancient custom in taking oath with a person to lay the hand on his hip. Maurer[109] gives a list of the chief animals that might be, or must not be, eaten by the Hebrews. The

[102] Turner, *Samoa*, 112-113.   [103] §§260, 261, above.

[104] Williamson, *Cent. Polyn.*, III, 329-330, 331-332.

[105] Hill-Tout, in JAI, XXXIV, 323.   [106] Gen., IX, 3, 4.

[107] Levit., XVII, 13, 14.   [108] Gen., XXXII, 32.

[109] In *Globus*, XC, 136, 137; Maurer, *Vkde.*, I, 18.

allowed animals were those that chewed the cud and had cleft hooves.[110] The fruit of new trees was eaten only in the fifth year; in the fourth it was consecrated to Jahweh, "but the produce of the first three years was 'uncircumcized,' i.e., taboo, and might not be eaten at all."[111] "Fish were eaten by the Israelites, but not sacrificed; among their heathen neighbors, on the contrary, fish—or certain kinds of fish—were forbidden food, and were sacrificed only in exceptional cases." Among the Syrians pork was taboo, "but it was an open question whether this was because the animal was holy or because it was unclean." Mohammed avoided the eating of lizards because he thought them the offspring of a metamorphosed clan of Israelites.[112]

Evidently all these food-taboos are guaranteed by such power that they tend to endure, resisting almost anything short of the annihilation or utter subjugation of the group in question at the hand of some other group widely differing in code, or short of the automatic process of more gradual readjustment, operating over longer periods. Even in the case of subjugation, since the codes of primitive peoples are so much alike, selection may be delayed for a long time where only primitive peoples come into contact with one another.

Further extensions of the taboo laid upon plants and animals have appeared under the topic of totemism.[113] The detail might be added that special luxuries come frequently under the ban and that, chiefly among more advanced societies, intoxicants of various sorts have occasionally been forbidden. In such cases the taboo operates in the field of self-gratification.[114]

The Brahmans consider the drinking of spirituous liquors one of the five great sins, and Mohammed forbade wine. So did Manu in India, the penalty for drinking spirits being "to commit suicide by drinking them when in a boiling state." Intoxicants are, here as in other more familiar cases, permitted only at special religious ceremonials. Wine was proscribed among the ancient Semites when the vine stood in relation with an alien cult.[115] Coffee and tea are sometimes allowed to men only. Certain negroes may smoke only in their huts and not in the presence of strangers; others *vice versa*. Again, every year five men must abstain a hundred days from betel-chewing, along with sex-relations, and may eat only fish and field-products.[116]

[110] Levit., XI; Deut., XIV.   [111] Levit., XIX, 23 ff.
[112] Smith, *Relig. Sem.*, 153, 159, 219, 88.
[113] §260, above.   [114] §§437, 438, below.
[115] Tylor, *Anth.*, 269; Monier-Williams, *Brāhmanism*, 194-195, 369; Maurer, *Vkde.*, I, 91.
[116] Duveyrier, *Touâreg*, 430; Bastian, *Deut. Exped.*, I, 185; Senfft, in *Globus*, XCI, 174.

It is not alone the food upon which restriction descends; the manner of eating also comes in for attention. The taboo, here again, has had a great deal to do with the development of standards of propriety and decency, of good manners, and of what is sometimes called "finer feeling." It is quite wrong to assume that the more intimate and private functions of the body are concealed because of any innate "instinct" or "sense" of shame, propriety, or the like. All such so-called senses, like the "moral sense," are in the mores, are learned and not transmitted by heredity, are acquired and not inborn. No young child has them. The fact is that they are largely, if not wholly, the by-product of religious fear. The section on magic[117] will reveal a universality of belief in the perils surrounding the publicity of private functions; the evil eye of envy is always menacing; and the taboo is the prime means of avoidance. The following cases will illustrate the manner in which the taboo hovers about the process of eating. Such restrictions are the beginning not only of decency, but even of etiquette and nicety of behavior; when their original daimonistic sense has long been lost, such forms as covering the mouth in yawning or repressing a sneeze are reinterpreted on the basis of delicacy of manners and concern for the comfort of one's fellows.

The oldest reports represent the king of Loango as never to be seen eating and drinking, and still he draws his garment over his face when he is to drink in the presence of others.[118] An observer[119] remarks: "The negro is really more consistent or of finer feeling than the European civilized man; even the taking of food at meals he generally hides from the glances of others, at least of strangers." In the Egyptian Sudan neither bread nor other food was eaten on the streets, for "the people fear the evil eye which a passer-by might let fall on it. Sickness—yes, even death—would then, according to the superstitious persuasion of all Sudanese, be the sure consequence."[120] "Everywhere in northern Abyssinia, people, when they eat, are hidden from public gaze by having sheets hung over them." At a wedding-feast the guests eat in little groups of four or six, each group being covered with a sheet. "This custom is universal, whether the meal is partaken of by the roadside or in their huts." Some rationalize the custom, not understanding it, as due to a fear of having to give to beggars if seen eating.[121] India exhibits the same custom.[122] "I never once saw a single Hindu, except of the lower caste, either preparing or eating cooked food of any kind. . . . The merest glance of a man of inferior caste makes the

---

117 Ch. XXXVII, below; Sumner, *Folkways,* ch. XI.
118 Bastian, *Deut. Exped.,* I, 262-263; Kingsley, *W. Afr. Studies,* 455-456.
119 Hutter, in *Globus,* LXXVI, 307.   120 Junker, *Africa,* I, 156.
121 Bent, *Ethiopians,* 32.   122 Joshi, in JASB, I, 126.

greatest delicacies uneatable, and if such a glance happens to fall on the family supplies during the cooking operations, when the ceremonial purity of the water used is a matter of life and death to every member of the household, the whole repast has to be thrown away as if poisoned. The family is for that day dinnerless. Food thus contaminated would, if eaten, communicate a taint to the souls as well as the bodies of the eaters—a taint which could only be removed by long and painful expiation."[123] In Borneo, "they seem to regard their family meals as strictly private, and would always announce to us that they were going to eat,—possibly to give us warning not to visit them at that time, and they were also quite as punctilious to leave us at the moment that our food was served." Says another traveller: "While I ate they went modestly one side."[124]

Concealment of eating is not the whole content of the taboo; there are strange rules about the touching of the food which one may be eating publicly. "A singular custom which prevailed through the entire extent of Polynesia consisted in making any person, place, or thing sacred for a longer or shorter period; if it were a person, during the time of the Tapu, he could not be touched by any one, or even put his own hand to his head; but he was either fed by another who was appointed for the purpose, or took up his food with his mouth from a small stage, with his hands behind him, or by a fern stalk, and thus conveyed it to his mouth; in drinking, the water was poured in a very expert manner from a calabash into his mouth, or on his hands, when he needed it for washing, so that he should not touch the vessel, which otherwise could not have been used again for ordinary purposes."[125] In Samoa, anyone who touched a corpse became taboo; he might not touch food, even to feed himself. He was fed by others or took up the food with his mouth.[126] The Maori, when on a war-party, "are very particular that food is not passed by one in front of another, or put near a weapon, or touched by the right hand. It must be carried and eaten with the left." Generally the women eat together, but the sexes are separated at meals, and usually each man eats apart. Eating is always done in the open air, for food would taboo a house and then anyone entering it.[127] Certain South American tribes were ashamed to eat in the presence of another or to see anybody eat. One who eats in the presence of others is, however, no more than derided. Von den Steinen[128] thinks the origin of the custom is to be found in lack of food; he was himself so hungry while among these peoples that he often cast covetous glances on food that was being consumed by others.

In Greece the poorest people ate behind closed doors; but the Egyptians felt no repugnance to eating and drinking in the open air, for, said they, ugly and low things should be done in secret but honest ones in public.[129] On the other hand, a Roman prefect ordered all respectable men to eat in private.[130]

There are occasional abstentions connected with drinking. Of the Tasmanians it is said: "Their meal had continued a long time and we were much surprised that not one of them had yet drank; but this they deferred till they were fully

[123] Monier-Williams, *Brāhmanism*, 128.
[124] Furness, *Head-Hunters*, 12; Schwaner, *Borneo*, II, 168.
[125] Taylor, *Te Ika*, 163.   [126] Ella, in AAAS, 1892, 640.
[127] Tregear, in JAI, XIX, 107, 111.   [128] *Zent. Bras.*, 66.
[129] Maspero, *Hist. Anc.*, III, 796; Herodotus, *Hist.*, II, 35.
[130] Valerius Maximus, *Libri*, XXVIII, 4.

satisfied with eating."[131] Bourke[132] reports drinking-tubes and regulations forbidding direct modes of drinking.

One author[133] explains the shame of eating before others thus: when famine was frequent people were ashamed or feared to eat when others were hungry; and women were more sensitive to the feelings of onlookers. Here is a fair sample of psychologizing upon the mores of others from the standpoint of a more developed code. Eating was one of the operations during which there might be introduced into the body some spirit-element which would then "possess" it, with resulting ill; or it might be an occasion for rousing envy and covetousness and thus attracting the evil eye; magic too could be carried on, by the use of fragments and remnants, to the detriment of the public as well as of the careless eater. Most of these taboos make for careful and private eating, that is, for etiquette and manners, but altruistic sentiments concerning the feeling of onlookers and non-sharers are present only in the imagination. The discipline is through religious awe and fear.

§272*. The Property and Civic Taboos. The very essence of property, as elsewhere demonstrated,[134] lies in adverse possession; and the title to property resides in force of some sort. No other power was so competent to guarantee this adverse possession or monopoly as was ghost-fear; and so its sanction has always, both in ruder times and even among more developed peoples, constituted the strongest support of property. Perhaps this was most directly and obviously the case in the matter of the grave; but even the property-mark was a taboo, with a strong religious aspect to it.[135] This taboo amounted in the Saxon land-books, the Domesday Book, and elsewhere, to an anathema upon the transgressor. "The origin of property was a rite in the shape of a taboo consecrating it to individual use, and temple lands in the village system even now prove this fact."[136] Though the representative cases to be cited show that the real driving power of the religious sanction to property is sometimes lost sight of, one who would understand the institution must keep that sanction ever in mind and note its im-

---

[131] Roth, *Tasmania*, 102.
[132] In BAE, IX, 494.
[133] Ellis, in *Psychol. Rev.*, VI, 138.
[134] §§108, 110, above.
[135] §§116, 121, above and 382, 395, below.
[136] Da Cunha, in JASB, II, 547.

plied presence where it is not explicitly brought out or where, even, it is explicitly minimized or denied.

Finsch,[137] repeating his assertion that "the taboo has nothing to do with religion but serves practical ends," cites the interdict on coco-palms in New Britain as "a very useful arrangement to increase the yield of the palms by a closed season. The mission too derived advantage from this custom and placed the churches, as inviolable, under the native taboo." In the Mortlock Islands a taboo is laid upon the landed property of the departed and remains till lifted by the chief. On the death of a chief an isolation-taboo covers the whole of an island so that no canoe from any other island of the lagoon may touch its shore. Generally in Melanesia the taboo reserves owner's rights in fruits or prohibits the common use of a path or part of the seashore for a time.[138] In the Solomon Islands trespass and robbery are prevented by the "hope," which warns that the place is forbidden and also carries mysterious punishment if the warning is disregarded.[139] A traveller in these islands got a chief, Gorei, to accept the responsibility of his protection. "That afternoon," he reports, "all my possessions were landed and stowed away in an empty house upon which was placed Gorei's special taboo, the consequences of the violation of which would have been, in the native's eyes, fearful to contemplate."[140]

In West Africa, crops are tabooed by being left under the protection of amulets, and thus guarded are quite safe from pillage. Articles left for sale by the side of the frequented paths are under amulet-protection; "and no native would dare to take anything without depositing its stipulated value, for fear of the unknown evil the god to whom the amulet belonged might bring upon him."[141] In some localities "you often see on fields, houses, and tools bundles of grass or banana-leaves hung up, or even gourd-bottles. These are called 'ju-ju' and have the purpose of securing the objects in question against theft. They think that the man who touches these marked objects will be seized by the *elung* and die a painful death."[142] The *elung* is the local secret association. These African taboo-methods were carried across the Atlantic by the slaves. Among the bush-negroes of Surinam, "not seldom does one see standing before the separate dwellings a *kifunga* or wooden doll; and if the owner leaves it for some time, he provides the generally unlocked door with still another protection, an *obia*, which, again, consists of the most insignificant things: a wisp of straw, an object out of the animal kingdom, or the like. But in spite of the insignificance, the protection exerts an unfailing magic in which everyone believes, and thus secures the property. We were glad to make use of this recourse, in that we represented our instruments as *obia*, and they then protected themselves and all our other possessions from unwelcome contact."[143]

In Borneo a whole river may be tabooed. "That the river was pre-empted was manifest; across its mouth had been stretched a rope of rattan, and from it dangled wooden models of parongs, billiongs [axes], and spears. These models indicated that the river was claimed by the camphor collectors; to disregard this warning exposed the offender to the malignity of all evil Spirits. The only way whereby such a taboo may be counteracted is to build a fire, and

137 *Ethnol. Erfahr.*, I, 115, III, 319.
139 Woodford, *Head-Hunters*, 18.
141 §77, above; Ellis, *Ewe*, 92.
143 Martin, in *Bijd.*, XXXV, 30.

138 Codrington, in JAI, X, 279.
140 Somerville, in JAI, XXVI, 387.
142 Frobenius, *Masken*, 79.

erect over it an arch of twigs and sticks cut at the ends and down the sides into curled shavings; when the fire burns up briskly, he who would break the taboo must carefully explain to the fire that he is a near friend to the claimants of the river, and entreat the flame and smoke to convey his message of good-will both to them and to the Spirits of the jungle. After this ceremony he may, in perfect safety, pass under the rattan and ascend the river."[144]

In Rotuma a discarded food-plant, called *ranji*, "was, for some reason now apparently forgotten, strictly *ha*, or taboo, for any man to dig and cook it by himself. It was only dug by a whole district at a time, and then all took part." The reason for this practice is "that the ranji was the food of the *atua* [spirits], and could only be eaten when their priests gave leave."[145] The taboo in Samoa is chiefly to protect fruit-plantations from robbery; each man can taboo his own, marking it with some symbol, and his own imprecation avails to curse the robber.[146] By a sort of imitative magic the symbol indicated what might be expected by the transgressor: that a sea-pike might run into his body, a white shark seize him, disease run right across his body (indicated by a stick suspended horizontally), ulcers break out all over him, lightning strike him, or death in some unspecified form overtake him.[147]

The central idea of these instances is the protection of property-rights. We need only to call attention once again to the closeness of relation between the taboo and various religious practices, such as imprecation, magic, fetishism, and avoidance in general.

Under civic taboos we aim to throw together representative instances exhibiting the influence of such interdictions in the regulative organization. A beginning may be made with the taboo upon the chief executive. Frazer[148] assembles many of these restrictions. That the king or chief, along with the shaman, is a typical fetish-man has been elsewhere[149] indicated.

In many African regions the chief is surrounded by circles of peculiar restrictions. He must not leave his house; all who enter it, except one old woman, must come in crouching and backwards; he must not look upon the sea; must wear only stuffs of native manufacture, live in a straw-hut, and go barefoot; must see no white people; must not touch the ground; must not eat certain foods. In one African case, he must pass his life with fettered limbs and in semi-darkness. It is no wonder that certain African princes have to be forced to receive the crown.[150] Of course he has privileges, such as that of being borne in a hammock; but he must not sleep on an island. The husband of a princess is preceded upon his promenades by a bell so that he may not be viewed by other women. The higher the rank, the heavier the *quixilles;* the king of Loango would die if he saw the water of a river or of the sea. "If one of the women from the capitol of the king of Angoy is condemned to death

144 Furness, *Head-Hunters,* 115; Bartels, *Medicin,* 98.
145 Gardiner, in JAI, XXVII, 423.   146 Ella, in AAAS, 1892, 638.
147 Turner, *Samoa,* 185-187.   148 *Golden Bough,* I, 233 ff., 297 ff.
149 §§156, 257, 259, above.   150 Frobenius, *Masken,* 228, 229.

for her misdemeanors, she is customarily executed by crushing her ribs to-gether, for she may be touched by no man—as the Siamese stamp princes to death in a sack." The kings of Angoy, besides being forbidden the sight of white men, must go about clothed in palm-bast garments.[151] The unapproach-able character of the king extends even to his cattle, which must be guarded against the evil eye of his subjects. At Kubla Khan's hunting-castle a herd of ten thousand snow-white horses were kept whose milk was reserved for the descendants of Genghis Khan and another favored class.[152] The lives of great chieftains were, by ancient custom, inviolable in war; "this usage is sealed, from time to time, by sprinkling cow's milk on the path where the enemy is coming."[153] The king's war-trumpet is reserved to him alone.[154] A Shan ruler "must avoid passing a house in which there is a dead person, and no marriage or funeral processions may pass by the palace enclosure."[155]

In Polynesia and Micronesia the king, as the bearer of taboo, has a majesty which is dangerous to himself. Originally he could touch no land or house, because it would thereby become his; hence he was carried over the land from one of his own houses to another. As soon as the crown prince was born the taboo was transferred to him.[156] An old Maori chief threw over a precipice a very good mat because it was too heavy to carry, and was asked by Taylor[157] why he did not hang it on a tree so that someone else could find and take it. The chief gravely said that it was the fear of its being taken by another that caused him to throw it where he did, for if worn his tapu would kill the person. Another chief's lost tinder-box killed several who were unfortunate enough to find it and light their pipes from it, without knowing that it belonged to so sacred an owner; they actually died of fright. If a chief's blood flows on any-thing, it is tabooed or consecrated to him, and becomes his property. Taylor recites a number of other Maori instances, one or two of which have been alluded to under the topic of property.[158] A great chief got into a fine, large, new canoe in which a party had come to visit him, to go a short distance, and in so doing stuck a splinter in his foot, and the blood flowed from the wound into the canoe, which at once tapued it to him; the owner immediately jumped out, and dragged it on shore, opposite the chief's house, and there left it; a gentleman entering the author's house, knocked his head against a beam, which made the blood flow, and the natives present said that in former times the house would have belonged to that individual. A chief's house was tapu, no person could eat therein, or even light his pipe from the fire; and until a certain service had been gone through, even a woman could not enter; the chief being sacred, had his food to himself, generally in his veranda or apart from the rest. No chief could carry food lest it should occasion his death by destroying his tapu, or lest a slave should eat of it and so cause him to die. A chief would not pass under a wata, or food store. The head of the chief was the most sacred part of the body; if he only touched it with his fingers, he was obliged immediately to apply them to his nose, snuff up the sanctity which they had acquired by the touch, and thus restore it to the part from whence it was taken; for the same reason a chief could not blow the fire with his mouth, for

151 Bastian, *Deut. Exped.*, I, 197, 198, note, 200, 216.
152 Ritter, *Asien*, I, 144. ·
153 Junker, *Afrika*, III, 583, 593.
154 Ratzel, *Vkde.*, II, 501.
155 Woodthorpe, in JAI, XXVI, 23.
156 Ratzel, *Vkde.*, II, 201.
157 *Te Ika*, 164-165, 168.
158 §108, above.

his breath, being sacred, would communicate sanctity to it; then a brand might be taken by a slave or a man of another tribe, or the fire might be used for other purposes, such as cooking, and so cause his death. "The males could not eat with their wives, nor their wives with the male children, lest their tapu or sanctity should kill them." In Bagdad one might not spit in the presence of the chalif or blow the nose, yawn, cough, or sneeze.[159]

Evidently the taboo played a strong rôle in sustaining and guaranteeing power: that of men over women and, in particular, that of the civil head, which means the authority of society and law.[160] It is patent also from what has been said about war that the taboo was the guarantee of peace as well as of war-customs. Inside the group the first guarantees of peace and order were by taboo: the king's peace, the temple-peace, the peace of God. Acts, words, days, persons, and places came under it and it proscribed indecency, impropriety, and immorality. Relations of persons, for example in marriage, were defined by taboo, and the whole intricate network of rights and duties in society was held in form by the same agency. Between groups it availed for safe-conduct, embassies, trade, and other relations. It is manifestly impossible either to list or to illustrate these wider functions of the taboo exhaustively; the following cases are cited by way of suggestion rather than of demonstration.

In Australia, "when a young man for the first time takes blood from another man, the latter becomes for the first time tabu to him until he chooses to release him from the *intherta,* or ban of silence, by singing over his mouth."[161] This performance brings home the new status of the young man, both to himself and to others. Similarly the bull-roarer is tabooed to males until initiation, and to women always.[162] Again, the taboo guarantees social policy: "a bit of rag, a few sticks, a stone, or a little mud, are the only visible signs, but the results where these are found, are: water is kept uncontaminated; trees laden with fruit are not touched, except by the owner; the entrances of villages and special bush-paths are kept clean; fish is preserved when necessary, and a man's property is absolutely safe."[163] If a Papuan breaks a *sabi,* he must pay; if he does not pay he is not allowed to enter the council-house and is held in contempt.[164] The taboo is of the utmost utility where, as in the New Hebrides, there are no courts of justice. The rule is to steal what you can without being caught; but the taboo is more effective than any police.[165] The penalties are diseases, which only the maker of the taboo-symbol can cure. If anyone is ill he tries one taboo-maker after another; and if none of them suc-

[159] Von Kremer, *Kgchte.,* II, 247.   [160] §§155, 156, above.

[161] Spencer and Gillen, *Nat. Tr. Cent. Aust.,* 462.

[162] Chalmers, in JAI, XXVII, 329.   [163] Cator, *Head-Hunters,* 192.

[164] Krieger, *Neu-Guinea,* 314.   [165] Ch. XIX, above.

ceed in curing him, the disease is of foreign origin and no one knows the cure.[166] The taboo on foreigners has been alluded to; in Togo it lies against Europeans or against European dress, tools, ships, money, usages, churches and schools, medicines, and cemeteries.[167] In the Loango region spirituous drinks are tabooed, since intoxication may lead to murder or other crimes.[168]

In Borneo a chief has the right to lay a *pamali* which prevents ingress into a district; this may last for several years, and is imposed in consequence of the death of some eminent member of the family. It often prohibits trade and communication in a very inexpedient manner or entails great loss and increase of expense to merchants.[169] Ratzel[170] gives a full account of Polynesian taboos; he thinks they were originally religious but were carried over into the political organization by rulers who saw their advantage in so doing.

Among the ancient Canary Islanders, the taboo made a man's house his castle and secured privacy. "When a person went to the house of another, he seated himself on the stone before the door and whistled or sang until invited to enter. To go in unbidden was a punishable offence."[171]

When the Israelites first entered Canaan, they "placed a number of the chief heads of public morality under the protection of a solemn taboo by a great act of public cursing."[172] A light ban was laid on marriages with heathen women, covering a thirty-day exclusion from the cult-community; and there was a heavy one, always accompanied by a curse and involving perpetual exclusion. In cases of leprosy there was a strict taboo; the afflicted must show himself to the priest who decided as to the length of the exclusion and performed the reception into the cult-association after recovery. The irrational element in this taboo appears in the provision that linen, woollen, and leather stuffs shall be shown to the priest if they show greenish or reddish spots. If greenish or reddish depressions appear on the walls of a house, the priest must likewise interfere. For the house is afflicted with leprosy. In the case of the leprosy of fabrics and homes, the commentators think of stains produced by mold or the results of chemical action. The author quoted[173] goes on to say that "the Jahweh-taboo carries at times the character of punishment for subjugated peoples. . . . All that falls into the hands of the Jahweh-warriors is sacrificed to Jahweh or consecrated to his use. This latter signifies a great advance in civilization: the original ferocity in war is subordinated to a humanitarianism motived in religion. Everything that is conquered belongs to the victorious gods and comes into their country and territory. Canaan is therefore the land of Jahweh and Israel the people consecrated to him. . . . Whoever wants to belong to it must wear Jahweh's mark, that is, must be circumcized."

Much is made in the Bible and elsewhere of sanctuary: the neighborhood of the altar is such, and so are certain cities. Certainly as late as the fourteenth century, even in England, the right of sanctuary existed and had become a nuisance; for "any criminal escaping from royal justice for felony or murder had only to reach the nearest church and he was perfectly safe." Also the

166 Gray, in AAAS, 1892, 651.
167 Seidel, in *Globus*, LXXIII, 340, 341.
168 Bastian, *Deut. Exped.*, I, 187.
169 Schwaner, *Borneo*, II, 148-149; Roth, *Sarawak*, II, ccv.
170 §268, above; *Vkde.*, II, 211-214.   171 Cook, in AA, II, 487.
172 Deut., XXVII; Josh., VIII, 30 ff.; Smith, *Relig. Sem.*, 164.
173 Maurer, *Vkde.*, I, 107-108; Maurer, in *Globus*, XC, 137, 138.

church protected fraudulent debtors who would escape with their gains to sacred ground and there live till they could tire out their creditors' patience or escape. "The precincts of the Abbey," says Dean Stanley, "were a vast cave of Adullam, for all the distressed and discontented in the Metropolis, who desired, according to the phrase of the time, to 'take Westminster.'" In 1540 sanctuary was abolished for murder, rape, and highway robbery with violence, and in 1623 for all crimes; but it was traditionally tolerated for many years.[174]

In the last case we have the passing of a taboo which once debarred hasty punishment because, in its phase of maladjustment, it exempted from all punishment.

There are also taboos that represent what might be called sanitary regulation, for they proscribe defilement of rivers, of the ground beneath shade-trees in a country with few trees, and similar social assets.[175] "There is little doubt that the common practice of retiring into the sea or a river has its origin in the belief that water is a bar to the use of excrement in charms. It is remarkable that at Mota, where clefts in rocks are used . . . the word used is *tas*, which means sea."[176] Clearly enough, the reason for such retirement is often far from rational, going back as it does in this last example to ideas about water as a purifying element and to magical beliefs about exuviæ;[177] however, in whatever sort of variation it originated, such a taboo stands upon its own actual serviceability to society; and out of it come standards of cleanliness and decency.

§273. Miscellaneous Taboos. The thoroughgoing differences between the sexes have been referred to several times in preceding connections; and it has been seen that they have had as an inevitable consequence the development of diverse sex-mores and codes.[178] These differences have been felt and recognized by the veriest savages and restrictions have been laid, both within and without the institutions of marriage and the family, upon the relations of the sexes. Reference need be made only to the interdictions imposed upon the woman by reason of the conviction that

[174] Trevelyan, *Eng. in Age of Wycliffe*, 91 ff.
[175] Brunache, *Cent. Afr.*, 276.
[176] Codrington, *Melanesians*, 203, note.
[177] §§227, 249, above, and 300, below.
[178] §§58-60, above, and 331, 333, below.

she is at all times, though at certain times more than at others, perilous to man.[179] These sex-differences are recognized by taboos strengthening or declining in intensity with woman's approach to or recession from sex-maturity, and enforcing a sex-separation even between spouses and within the family.

Women are under taboo in Australia as in Polynesia and are not allowed to eat with the men.[180] Eating food tabooed to women is actually visited with death from fright.[181] In the New Hebrides women must not see the newly initiated till they have washed. "Not long ago a girl from *Uta,* inland, saw by accident this washing. She fled to Tanoriki, where the Mission school is, for refuge, but they could not protect her. The Uta people sent for her and she went, knowing that she could not fail to die, and they buried her, unresisting, alive." After the boy goes to the club-house, there "begins his strange and strict reserve of intercourse with his sisters and his mother. This begins in full force towards his sisters; he must not use as a common noun the word which is the name or makes part of the name of any of them, and they avoid his name as carefully. He may go to his father's house to ask for food, but if his sister is within he has to go away before he eats; if no sister is there he can sit down near the door and eat. If by chance brother and sister meet in the path she runs away or hides. If a boy on the sands knows that certain footsteps are his sister's he will not follow them, nor will she his. This mutual avoidance begins when the boy is clothed or the girl tattooed. The partition between boys and girls without which a school cannot be carried on is not there to divide the sexes generally, but to separate brothers and sisters. This avoidance continues through life. The reserve between son and mother increases as the boy grows up, and is much more on her side than his. He goes to the house and asks for food; his mother brings it out but does not give it him, she puts it down for him to take; if she calls him to come, she speaks to him in the plural, in a more distant manner; 'Come ye,' she says . . . not 'Come thou.' If they talk together she sits at a little distance and turns away, for she is shy of her grown-up son. The meaning of all this is obvious. At Santa Cruz and the neighboring islands the separation of the sexes in daily life is carried far, but has not this character. At Santa Cruz the men and women never work together promiscuously or assemble in one group; men with their wives and children only, and men with their mothers, work in the gardens; when a crowd assembles the women collect aloof. In Nufilole, one of the Swallow group, the separation is complete; men and women are never out together; in the morning the men go out first and come back, after that the women go and fetch water, when they return the men go out again."[182] The meaning of the above seems to us less obvious than this author thinks; however, the fact of separation stands out.

The cook of the king of Angoy, in Loango, must remain chaste; in Angola the presence of a woman would spoil the iron-manufacture, elsewhere the copper-mining. In French West Africa the men and women must be separated at the dances; it would be death to a woman to dance beyond the set boundary,

179 §§388, 407 ff., below.   180 Ratzel, *Vkde.,* II, 67.
181 §269, above.
182 Codrington, *Melanesians,* 87, 232, 233; §425, below.

as an evil spirit would seize her. Women must not see men eating; must not see the ancestral images; and must not be seen while making oil.[183] In the Congo region, the taboos "touch every kind of food, every place, and every action. There is not a single article of food that is not tabu to some one, there is not a place that has not been tabued at some time or other, and there is not a possible action that has not been or is not affected by tabu. The tabus are many and various, but most of them will fall under the following heads: 1. The totem tabu. . . . A woman brought her totem with her when she married, and observed her own totem and that of her husband. A child born to them took the totems of both parents until there was a council of both families, the paternal and maternal branches, and then it was generally arranged that the child should take its father's totem. . . . 2. *Ngili* or permanent tabu. This is a tabu that is put on any kind of food, as, 'You must not eat goat's flesh'; or an interdiction not to go to a certain place, as, 'You must not go across the river to a particular island'; or a prohibition not to perform a certain action, as, 'You must not drink native wine except through a reed, and never straight out of a vessel of any kind.' . . . There was, whether through tabu or not, a very strong aversion to milk and raw eggs. To drink milk or eat a raw egg rendered the person unclean for several days, and he was not allowed to eat with his family until the uncleanness . . . had passed away. They could and did eat well-cooked eggs no matter how savoury through age they might be at the time. Very frequently this *ngili* becomes an inherited tabu. A man has, say, elephantiasis, and the medicine-man says he is not to eat either elephant or hippopotamus meat, and he will pass this *ngili* on to his sons, who will carefully observe it lest their legs become swollen like an elephant's. 3. *Mungilu* or temporary tabu. . . . Men engaged in making fishing and hunting traps were under a tabu not to have sexual intercourse until they had been successful in catching something and eating it. . . . Sometimes a man in a rage will put himself under a tabu. A wife by her conduct has irritated him beyond endurance, and at last he strikes on the ground with a stick . . . and says: 'May I be cursed if ever I eat food cooked by you.' He is now under *mungilu* not to eat food from that woman's hands. This as a rule brings the woman to her senses, and after a time she prevails on her husband to remove the tabu."[184]

In Assam, "warriors, both before and after a raid, are subject to gennas of an interesting nature. They may not cohabit with their wives, and may not eat food cooked by a woman. Indeed, so strong is the genna against any intercourse with women, that on one occasion a woman, the wife of the headman, who was quite ignorant of the fact that her husband was returning with a party of warriors to lay the heads before the war stone, spoke to him. He was under the same genna disability as the warriors, and I was told that, when she learnt the awful thing she had done, she sickened and died."[185] "The sexual act is a mysterious power, and is consequently tabued during and immediately before such auspicious occasions as a religious festival, the first sowing of one's rice-field, and a hunting expedition."[186] Williamson[187] thinks that water was a "conductor of taboo, a medium through which the taboo of what we should in some cases call sanctity, and should in others designate as

---

[183] Bastian, *Deut. Exped.*, I, 216; Serpa Pinto, *África*, I, 109; Lenz, *Westafr.*, 207; Grabowsky, in *Globus*, LXXIX, 164; Frobenius, *Masken*, 225.

[184] Weeks, in JAI, XL, 365-367.   [185] Hodson, in JAI, XXXVI, 100.
[186] Roy, in JAI, XLIV, 343, 344.   [187] *Cent. Polyn.*, III, 215-218.

uncleanness, could pass into a person, or by means of which he could lose or get rid of it." He thinks this is the sense of anointing kings; Samoan chiefs might be sprinkled with coconut-water to make them sacred or to take away their titles. In one island a chief was installed by seating him on a special stone and anointing him.

The taboos of the Polynesians make a gulf between the two sexes, so that man and wife can never eat at the same table or play at the same fireside with their own children, nor may the woman cook at the same fire with her husband. Among the heaviest curses are: "May you become a bottle to hold salt water for your mother!" "May you be roasted as food for your mother!" "Pull out your eye and give it to your mother to eat!"[188] Besides never being allowed to enter the men's house, the women are restricted for ten months out of twelve from going outside the reefs in canoes.[189] They must keep away from the men's range. In Alaska, "on one occasion we saw a man who was blocked in a seat by three women get up and climb over the backs of several seats in order to get out; and that in the presence of a large congregation. This he did rather than ask the women to let him pass. To speak to the women would, in his estimation be a great breach of propriety, but climbing over the seats was nothing out of the way."[190]

These taboos are as if directed against a different and alien creature, so that the female, in so far as they reach, is in but not of the community and is systematically separated from the male members who have demonstrated themselves to be of real account.

Marriage is itself a case of taboo, securing adverse possession and monopoly much as does a property-interdiction. Endogamy and exogamy, the provisions about incest—in fact, all cases of forbidden unions—are instances of the taboo. It is the restriction that makes the institution. This is to be brought out in such detail later on[191] that special evidence need not be cited here. A single quotation may serve as illustration.

"As all important happenings in the life of the Kayans give occasion for the laying of special prohibitions, so do these exist also for the first period of marriage up to the next following new year. In order to shorten them as much as possible, they thus marry preferably shortly before that festival."[192]

Thus men are always trying to escape or shift the burden of the taboo, remaining the while unshakenly convinced of the necessity of restriction. The evolution of marriage and the family consists largely of the development of interdictions upon freedom of sex-union and upon other relations consequent to it; if the idea of the

188 Ratzel, *Vkde.*, II, 183.

190 Jones, *Thlingets,* 209.

192 Nieuwenhuis, *Borneo*, I, 77.

189 Kubary, *Núkuóro*, 21.

191 Ch. XLIV, below.

taboo is grasped, it will receive recurrent illustration in the section on societal self-perpetuation. The preliminaries to marriage, the wedding-ceremony, the marriage-mark, the treatment of adultery, the lot of the widow, the practices surrounding pregnancy and child-birth—all these are encircled and permeated by the taboo, that is, by religious limitation. So too are the relations within the family, for the taboo defines rights between its members; it also ranges widely over relationships by marriage and those of the general kin-group, clan, and tribe.[193] It would be possible to follow religious restriction through these various topics in great detail; probably, however, enough cases of taboo in the industrial, familial, and civil organization have been presented to bring out the essential nature of the usage.

Beside the industrial organization, property, the regulative organization, marriage and the family, there are two other departments of societal life in which the action of the taboo is displayed, namely, in self-gratification and in religion itself. Inhibition descends heavily upon forms of pleasure-seeking. It is safer to seem unhappy and unlucky; especially in proximity of the ghosts and spirits, for example at mourning-time, must ornament, ostentation, play, and pastime in general be renounced. There is in the matter of self-assertion and display a subtle balance to be preserved: while it is desirable to impress fellow-men with one's magnificence it is at the same time most indiscreet to make parade before the spirits. Self-gratification covers a great complexity of practices that are difficult of classification;[194] and the taboo has ranged over the entire field, prohibiting this and that, reserving certain luxuries and enjoyments for the old, the noble, the rich, for men over women and children, for the shaman over the ordinary man. It has forbidden delicate food to warriors, special dances and play-acting to women. The interdiction of self-gratification has been a time-taboo rather than a thing-taboo: it is not so much that fine clothes, ornament, music, or play is tabooed to everybody, or to anybody, for all time; it is rather that everybody, or certain specially involved persons, must refrain for a period. Partly for this reason the taboo has never shaped up real

193 §§366, 368, 372, 373, 382, 384, 394, 407, 408, below.
194 §434, below.

institutions of self-gratification; and so its constructive action in this range is far less imposing in results than where it has been formative of property or law or a peace-group.

That the taboo, finally, religious as it is in nature, has wrought mightily upon the religious system of which it is a part is evident, implicitly if not explicitly, in every paragraph which will have been devoted to the evolution of that system. After all is said and done, the object of evolving religion is insurance against the aleatory element, and the methods pursued have been consistently and characteristically those of avoidance. But the taboo is the very formulation of the avoidance-policy: Thou shalt not. The theories of animism, eidolism, and daimonism set conditions amidst which men think they must live in their relations with the supernatural; and there follows immediately upon this theory the practice of the ghost-cult and daimonology. Taboos then call for abandonment, silence, disguise, abstention, and the rest. Fetishism abounds in taboos which cover the grave, the hearth, the altar, the word, the day, the image. The fetish-man is set apart and is inviolable; the fetish-people must not be criticized or derided. In daimonology avoidance still persists;[195] the evil eye is tabooed, and disparagement is a virtual extension of the inhibition upon self-praise. Thus the religious system, so far as we have yet followed it, is shot through with prohibitions effectively formative of the institution; and however far we may go in tracing its evolution we shall still find the taboo-factor saliently in evidence.

Thus the taboo is seen to permeate the whole societal structure, bringing everywhere to bear the unrivalled disciplinary and selective powers with which it is endowed. It is virtually co-extensive with the mores; nevertheless it cannot be fully appreciated nor its power assessed without a comprehension of the doctrines held wellnigh universally, about souls, ghosts, and daimons. The taboo is a negative method of control rooted in the acceptation of such doctrines, and that is why it has been considered at this point.

195 §264, above.

CHAPTER XXXII

SIN, EXORCISM, COERCION

§274*. **Sin.** All cases of avoidance represent resignation to a situation where there is nothing else to be done; a pertinent instance is that of the people who tried exorcism awhile without relief, and then fled the region. The taboo is typically immutable. The alternatives presented are obedience or calamity; and penalties are believed to be inflicted with inexorable severity. The transgressor is exposed, in the resentment of the daimons, to the full sweep of the aleatory element; for he has whistled up that blast by neglect of scrupulous respect for the limitations set on conduct. The man who has broken a taboo has sinned, and the wages of sin must be apportioned to him. One tree in Eden was put under taboo; man must renounce its fruit, for on the day on which he ate of it he would surely die.[1] Breaking the taboo is a sin of commission. Then there is the sin of omission, which belongs under the positive or propitiatory aspect of the cult and consists in failure to recognize the rights of the ghosts and daimons to food, flattery, and other perquisites.[2] In the former case, one has done the things that he ought not to have done; in the latter he has left undone the things he ought to have done; in either case there is presently no health in him. The sin of commission is evidently a conception following immediately upon that of the taboo, and as such receives the bulk of attention at this point. The variety of possible sins of this type corresponds with the multiplicity of forms taken by the taboo. Despite the fact that the daimons are inflexible sponsors of the taboos, as well as ever jealous of their prerogatives, there is yet something that can be done, even after one has sinned. There is a sort of belated avoidance, an evasion of the consequences, which passes into forms of exorcism of the evil influences. The review of the notions about what sin may be, and of what can be done about it, forms a useful transition to the topic of exorcism. We shall begin with representative illustrations of the endless

[1] Lippert, *Kgchte.*, I, 105, 121, 123, 98.
[2] §289, below.

varieties of sin. It should be noted at the outset that sin is ritual, not rational; and that it is a matter of act, not of thought, intent, or state of mind. Primitive people do not get entangled in the purpose-consequence relation because they consider results only. They have no problem as to the relative importance of faith and works. It is all works with them; faith has nothing to do with the matter. Their attitude here is entirely consistent with the one they maintain toward secular crime and punishment.[3]

There is a New Guinea legend that once tattooing gave no pain, "but that this exemption came to an end one day long ago when a girl who was being tattooed irreverently laughed." It is no laughing matter now; and everyone remains reverently silent while it is being done.[4] Generally any disaster, especially to hunting and fishing expeditions, is referred by the Papuan "to the breach of one or other of these things, having been with wife or other woman or having eaten of forbidden food."[5] That the Andamanese "are not entirely devoid of moral consciousness, may, I think, in some measure, be demonstrated by the fact of their possessing a word . . . signifying sin or wrong doing, which is used in connection with falsehood, theft, grave assault, murder, adultery, and—burning wax(!), which deeds are believed to anger . . . the Creator." The latter visits with storms "the burning of beeswax, the smell of which is said to be particularly obnoxious to him. Owing to this belief, it is a common practice, when one person has a grudge against another, to burn wax when such an one is engaged in hunting, fishing, etc., the object being to cause as much discomfort as possible. Hence it is a common saying, when a storm arises, that someone must be burning wax." Again, this great spirit "is so disturbed at seeing a pig badly quartered and carved that he points out the offender to a class of evil spirits, one of whom at once dispatches the sinner." Roasting pig's flesh causes an odor disagreeable to the spirits and to the Creator, "who often assists in discovering the offender. The same risk does not attend boiling pork."[6]

A West African sin is to spit on the earth,[7] and an East African to eat eggs and chickens. Some Italian prisoners got hold of a thin fowl and some eggs but were not permitted to enjoy them; when their sacrilege became known through the neighborhood, they were held in such aversion that the women, passing by, held their noses so as not to smell the evil odor of fowl. Not only that, but when the foreigners wanted to drink, they had to use the palms of their hands, for the natives believed they would call down the wrath of heaven and contaminate themselves if they let their drinking-vessels approach the polluted lips.[8] It is to be noted in passing that it is easy to become a partner in a neighbor's sin.

On the Amur it was a great sin to rock an empty cradle; only the ghost might do this while a child was being buried.[9] To the Yakuts it is a sin not to

3 §182, above.   4 Barton, in JAI, XLVIII, 26.
5 Chalmers, in JAI, XXVII, 333.
6 Man, in JAI, XII, 112, 154, 158, 159.   7 Bastian, *Afr. Reisen,* 261.
8 Vannutelli e Citerni, *L'Omo,* 436, 437.
9 Schimkjewitsch, in *Globus,* LXXIV, 270.

pull a man out if he falls into the water, provided he is a ninth generation relation or nearer; if he is beyond that degree, it is not.[10] "The Mongolians who filled Asia with pyramids of skulls, in order to carry out the will of heaven, feared its wrath if they should not expel at once from human society the death-deserving sinner who had laid a knife in the fire or had leaned on a whip."[11] The various Mongol taboos connected with fire are mentioned elsewhere;[12] to violate any one of them was a grave transgression. In the same region it is a great sin to name one's own father or mother; and certain lamas reckon it a sin to kill their parasites. One cloister has the environs "overrun with antelopes, which live a peaceful life, inasmuch as the lamas regard it as a sin to kill an animal in the neighborhood of the holy temple."[13] An unclean person should not wear, and so pollute, anything good and valuable—such things as the gods like.[14]

The sins of the ancient Hebrews were mainly ritual ones. Zangwill[15] speaks of the "heinousness of frying steaks in butter," a tradition that reaches far back to the time when Jahweh, like the Greek gods and the African fetishes, delighted in the odor of burning grease. To eat of this sacred grease or of blood is for the Jew a capital crime. There are many Old Testament taboos in addition to those in the decalogue—for example, that beasts should not be killed except in sacrifice—the transgression of which is sin; and these run on through the Bible and are imposed upon converts from heathendom.[16] A certain puritanical Mohammedan sect of the eighteenth century asserted that the greatest sin was to give divine honors to a creature. The second was using tobacco. There was no other. As to murder, adultery, and false witness, "God is merciful."[17]

Among the aborigines of the Canaries a candidate for nobility must be cleared of the suspicion that he has entered a slaughter-house to take or kill goats, has prepared his meal with his own hands, has committed rapine in time of peace, or has shown disloyalty in word or action, especially toward women.[18] In Scandinavia, "the almost superstitious piety which is, in the North, directed to the seed and to bread meets us at every turn. To throw away even the smallest bread-crust ranked and ranks among the people as a great sin; likewise the treading down of a corn-ear."[19] In Great Russia, several centuries ago, the Church forbade the use of wall-mirrors and pious people avoided them as a foreign sin. Small hand-mirrors were imported in great numbers and used for the women's toilet.[20] Mantegazza[21] reports the story of a brigand captain who had murdered a whole family and who saw one of his men licking butter with his tongue. He gave him a blow on the head, exclaiming: "Pagan! Thou dost not fear God! Dost thou not know that it is Friday!"

[10] Sieroshevski, *Yakuts* (Russ.), 434, 435.

[11] Bastian, *Afr. Reisen,* 206, note.

[12] §§88, 89, 92, above; Shchukin, *Shamanism* (Russ.), 31.

[13] Prjevalski's *Forskningsresor,* 302; Prjevalski, *Erste Reise,* 27, 68.

[14] Hildburgh, in JAI, XXXVIII, 151.

[15] *Ghetto,* 320.

[16] Levit., VII, 25; XVII, 3; Deut., XII, 16; Acts, XV; Maurer, *Vkde.,* I, 184.

[17] Palgrave, *Arabia,* 282.   [18] Cook, in AA, II, 487.

[19] Wadenstjerna, in *Globus,* LXXII, 373.

[20] Kostamarov, *Gt. Russ.* (Russ.), 73.   [21] *Rio de la Plata,* 429.

The belief is always present, by implication at least, that there was once a sinless time, when all were happy; this was the Golden Age. There were once perfect people, like Homer's[22] "blameless Ethiopians, some at the rising sun, some at the setting." Fancies of this sort rest upon tricky "logical" constructions, and have filled the minds of men to the exclusion of useful knowledge. Eve and Pandora are racial phantasms.

A single example may be cited. The Hausa believe "that the people of old were formed just as we of to-day are, but were giants. Everything in the world was in proportion, the ears of barleycorn being as large as ostrich eggs. But gradually men and plants degenerated until they became no larger than they are at present. We are becoming smaller, for not so very long ago the Hausa hunters could overcome elephants in a fair fight, and carry them home on their shoulders; now they have to use magic—also the poisoned arrow."[23]

Generally such beliefs in the good old times are accompanied by explanations of their disappearance wherein it appears that man was responsible, by reason of his injudicious and sinful behavior, for the existence of death and woes of every description.

The drawing of a distinction between sin, crime, and vice may help to clarify all three conceptions. Vice is individual and is the original and real thing. Religion makes it a sin; law a crime.[24] Among primitive people, since law is so largely a matter of religious taboo, sin and crime are pretty much the same thing.

It is characteristic of sin, as viewed by the primitive mind, that it cannot be solely an individual matter; there is a societal interest in it. For anyone who violates a taboo brings down the consequences not upon himself alone but upon the whole community as well. This is yet another indication of how primitive men think in terms of the group rather than of the individual, a tendency that has lasted on at least down to the persecution of heretics in avoidance of the wrath of God. It is as if the sinner were a sort of selected mark for thunderbolts which might not be rifle-sure of hitting only the devoted target but might spread their charge over both the target and its vicinity; or as if he were a contagion-bearer capable of involving all his neighbors. This conception leads to a group-responsibility for the actions of all members and thereby to the regulation of individual liberty. It is a principle

22 *Odyssey*, I, 22; *Iliad*, I, 423-424; Keller, *Hom. Soc.*, 2.
23 Tremearne, in JAI, XLV, 24.   24 §182, above.

of wide generality[25] which deserves special illustration in its application to sin.

The people of a certain East Indian tribe "are of opinion that an unmarried girl proving with child must be offensive to the superior powers, who, instead of always chastising the individual, punish the tribe by misfortunes happening to its members. They, therefore, on the discovery of the pregnancy, fine the lovers and sacrifice a pig to propitiate offended Heaven, and to avert that sickness or those misfortunes that might otherwise follow; and they inflict heavy mulcts for every one who may have suffered from any severe accident, or who may have been drowned within a month before the religious atonement was made." Among the Land and Sea Dyaks a man "may not marry his first cousin, except he perform a special act . . . to avert evil consequences to the land." This ceremony includes sacrifice of personal ornaments and other property, the sacrifice of a pig, the bathing of the pair in the river into which the foregoing have been cast, and the sprinkling upon the ground and in the villages round about of pig's blood. The parties are then free to marry. They must ask pardon. "I once tried to make out of whom they asked pardon, and I was told, as I always am 'sighi adat komi—only our custom.' They said it was to no evil spirit, but to the whole country, in order that their paddy might not be blasted."[26]

This case is a pretty full one. Among the most primitive peoples there is, as many examples throughout this book show, a general avoidance and abhorrence of the sinner that witness very clearly to fear of something happening to the rest because of his transgression; but there is generally no such elaborate precautionary system as the one just cited until a higher level of culture is reached. In Japan, "the ghosts of the ancestors controlled nature;—fire and flood, pestilence and famine were at their disposal as means of vengeance. One act of impiety in a village might, therefore, bring about misfortune to all." In 1911 it was reported that, owing to certain anarchistic movements subversive of loyalty, Japan was inspired to start a sort of religious revival—a "return to the gods."[27] Thus too among the Greeks of Homer[28] the man who failed in the cult brought woe upon all his fellows; "the sin of one man, especially of an important man, might descend upon a whole community and make it unclean, in which case reparation was made by the community." A king of Persia feared the presence of his Christian subjects. "I look on you," he told them, "as scattered sheep wandering in the desert, and I fear that the gods, in anger on account of you, will inflict punishment on us."[29]

"A bold man might venture to violate a taboo and take his risk of supernatural danger; but if his comrades were not equally bold they would immediately shun him lest the danger should spread to them." Thus Achan's breach of the taboo involved the whole host. "On this principle most ancient societies attached the penalty of outlawry or death to impious offences, such as the violation of holy things, without waiting for the god to vindicate his own

25 §176, above. 26 Roth, *Sarawak*, I, 116, 123.

27 Hearn, *Japan*, 118; N. Y. *Times*, May 11, 1911.

28 *Iliad*, I, 9 ff.; *Odyssey*, IV, 351 ff.; Keller, *Hom. Soc.*, 126. In the *Eumenides* of Æschylus (475, 443-453), Orestes is no menace to his city, as a mere murderer, for he has performed the proper purificatory rites.

29 Justi, *Persien*, 199.

cause." If the people of the land do not slay the impious person, Jehovah will destroy him and all his clan, for he is a plague-center, menacing everybody; he is like a leper. Thus the penalty of sin may seem to be a civil one. "In the Pentateuch it is sometimes difficult to decide whether the penalty invoked on impious offences is civil or supernatural."[30]

The idea of community-solidarity and responsibility comes out sharply in the treatment of Moriscos, Jews, and heretics in Spain, and not seldom in later times. The Spanish ecclesiastics urged the expulsion of the Moors in order to make Spain pleasing to God, so as to win his favor and get prosperity. In 1664 there was a petition urging the suppression of the sinful and scandalous bacchanalian Shrovetide festivities in New Amsterdam; the petitioners fear that if the revellers still indulge, "they will more and more provoke God to bring his wrath on the settlement" (which had already been destroyed by savages during the previous year). Governor Stuyvesant issued an order forbidding the festivities.[31] The 1679 synod of the churches in Massachusetts Colony set itself to ferret out the sinners by proposing two questions for investigation: "1st. What are the reasons that have provoked the Lord to bring his judgments upon New England? 2nd. What is to be done, so that those evils may be removed?"[32] Judge Sewall was convicted of his wrong-doing in his judicial capacity during the Salem witchcraft frenzy, "not by any human power, or any knowledge derived from without, but by the direct visitations of Divine Providence, as he regards them." He asks for the prayers of his brethren that God may "not visit the sin of him, or of any other, upon himself or any of his, nor upon the land." Early New England records are full of similar cases.[33]

Of course if there were no sin, but piety and obedience, then happiness, alloyed with profit, would result. Jeremiah[34] threatens woes from Jehovah against those who worship the "queen of heaven"; but they answer that they have had prosperity while serving her, and since they have ceased they have had adversity. The *post-propter* conclusion is that they had not sinned in challenging the prophet's taboo. Hull, a merchant and treasurer of Massachusetts, enjoined his captains "to see to the worship of God every day in the vessel, & to the sanctification of the Lord's day & suppression of all prophainess that the Lord may delight to be with you & his blessing upon you which is the hearty prayer of youre frend & ownr."[35]

Calamity to the community is proof positive of the presence of sin. Hence sin is abjured at such a time. Whenever the aleatory element oppresses men beyond measure, they fly to religion and seek to rectify delinquencies. They "reform" and pledge themselves not to repeat transgression. Then very often they become more

30 Smith, *Relig. Sem.*, 162; Josh., VI, 18, VII, 1, 11 ff.; Levit., XVII, 4, XIX, 8, XX, 4, 5.
31 Assoc. Press Rep. for Dec. 4, 1900 (N. Y. *Times*).
32 Hutchinson, *Hist. Mass. Bay*, I, 324.
33 Weeden, *New Eng.*, I, 421; Hubbard, *New Eng.*, 376, 377.
34 Ch. XXXIV.   35 Weeden, *New Eng.*, I, 250.

prosperous, lose their fright, forget, and "backslide." This is a general and obvious phenomenon.

Because business was bad, the barbers of Bombay decided, in 1890, to stop shaving the heads of widows; if any barber did this he would be excommunicated.[36] In view of a long drought the Chinese Mohammedans forbade the slaughter of animals, thus conforming to Buddhism. After all, they seemed to think, the Buddhists might be right. But after rain came the markets were full of beasts again.[37] Inspection of a list of earthquakes, famines, and pestilences from the time of Augustus[38] reveals contemporary reactions toward repentance and religion. "The oracles, which had long ceased, were partially restored under the Antonines; the calamities and visible decline of the Empire withdrew the minds of men from that proud patriotic worship of Roman greatness, which was long a substitute for religious feeling; and the frightful pestilence that swept over the land in the reigns of Marcus Aurelius and his successor was followed by a blind, feverish, and spasmodic superstition."[39]

During the World War frequent notices appeared signalizing the increase of religious observance and the decline of frivolity and sin. Religious retreats, according to the Bishop of Winchester, replaced cricket, golf, and the theater. Dreams were dreamed and visions vouchsafed. The end of the world was seen to be imminent. The ignorant harked back to discarded beliefs and practices. It has not been proved that the world is more religious now, several years after the war, than it was before; we learn, however, that a "wave of mysticism sways Russia" and that the peasants of many communities have endowed the holy icons with supernatural powers of healing and their religious fervor has alarmed the government.[40]

Stopping a sinful practice when frightened is a case of avoidance; so is the suppression of the sinner by the community. Both practices, however, might be interpreted as exorcistic: the sin is due to an evil influence which by abjuration is ejected; the sinner is possessed of an evil spirit which, with the execution or banishment of his human domicile, is cast out of the community. Such border-line cases, interpretable in either direction, are common enough in evolutionary zones of transition.

Most of the instances cited have had to do with the detection of the presence of sin through the descent of calamity. The converse of this preoccupation with bad luck is the inference from the experience of prosperity to a condition of sinlessness. The Old Testament doctrine assimilated prosperity with righteousness. "I considered in my heart that I was full of righteousness because I

---

[36] "Meeting of Bombay Barbers," in JASB, II, 172.
[37] Mitra, in JASB, III, 32. [38] Zumpt, *Bevölkerung*, 84.
[39] Lecky, *Europ. Morals*, 319-320.
[40] N. Y. *Times*, Oct. 8, 1916, and May 17, 1925.

was prosperous and had become plenteous in children." The wealthy appear like the righteous.[41] This attitude, however, is much less marked than the one to which the bulk of attention has been here assigned; for no one dared talk much about good luck; it was, indeed, something to fear and to dissimulate.[42] That calamity was due to sin was sure; that prosperity witnessed to a sinless state was debatable, for it might be only a prelude to the deeper damnation.

Men have exercised themselves in all ages concerning the relation of goodness and happiness.[43] Theoretically they ought to go together; but there were instances enough where the wicked flourished like the green bay tree. The pious have always clung desperately to the theory and have interpreted the facts as consonant, after all, with it. If not in this life, then in that which is to come, the theory must verify. Let Dives preen himself as he will; it is for the unlucky righteous that Abraham's bosom is prepared.

"I was envious at the arrogant when I saw the prosperity of the wicked. . . . They are not in trouble like other men. . . . They have more than heart could wish . . . and they say, How doth God know? . . . Behold they are the wicked and being always at ease they increase in riches. Surely in vain have I cleansed my heart and washed my hands in innocency for all day long have I been plagued and chastened every morning." However, the Psalmist sees that the wicked are at last cast down and destroyed. He himself was brutish and ignorant not to have seen the solution. He will cleave unto God.[44]

In later times, when people have become less certain about the recompenses to be looked for in a future existence, if not in this, they are more inclined to demand equalization here and now. This is one of the generally unrecognized elements in communistic agitation.

§275*. Remission. Before coming to sharply marked exorcism, and while still on the topic of sin, it remains for us to consider remission of sin through confession, purification, and other expedients. It is plain enough that people do not want to sin; if they know what to avoid and can keep an endless and complicated set

41 Ryle and James, *Psalms Solomon*, I, 3, xxxviii; Charles, *Enoch*, 96, 4, note.
42 §§265-267, above.   43 §327, below.
44 Psalms, LXXIII.

of taboos before their minds, they will not bid defiance to the daimons. Ajax had to be "greatly infatuated" before he would do so.[45]
The desire not to sin is evidenced by the various means of solicit-
ously questioning the future and also by many magical practices which will be reviewed later on. It is worth reiterating also
that sin is a matter of act and of objective fact rather than of
intention. Primitive people do not consider the state of mind of the
actor but what he does. This comes out in the punishment of
secular crime, if that may be distinguished from sin; and what was
done in the matter of relations between men finds its counterpart
in the anthropomorphism of cult-relations. To begin with, sin was
factual; the inclusion of the element of motive was a much later
development in the relations of man and daimon, as it was in
those of man and man.

The taboo has been spoken of as something immutable, inexorable, and implacable. That is its general character. Thus it appears to the primitive savage and even to the not altogether unsophisticated human being who is living under it; and from that
conception the best start can be made for the understanding of its
evolution. Nevertheless, viewed over an extended period, as science
alone is able to scan it, no societal form is immutable; in the long
run the taboo is found subject to variation and selection like the
rest of the mores and institutions. Selection over the ages has
established certain taboos as measures of permanent societal expediency; for instance, most of the interdictions of the Decalogue
are accepted by all societies that have attained any organization
worthy of the name. The recognition and enforcement of these
essential taboos, whether they remain within religion or work out
into the range of the secular, is the condition under which the
maintenance of societal existence is alone possible. This is a matter of experience, of trial and failure, of automatic selection, and,
at length and in part, of rational policy. Other taboos of less
permanent and general expediency disappear unnoticed or, in a
minority of cases, are even subjected to rational criticism and are
deliberately abrogated. If the primitive taboos have been presented as immutable, that is in consequence of an attempt to take

45 Homer, *Odyssey*, IV, 502 ff.

the viewpoint of the peoples of short memory and undeveloped
critical sense, to whom they are really changeless.

For the same reason sin has thus far been represented as an
error of avoidance, irrevocable and inexpiable. Yet "atonement for
sin" is a current phrase, and the reader knows that there have been
conceptions of purification, expiation, purgation, ransom, and
redemption.[46] As the cult kept on developing from form to form
and as the taboos underwent alteration, so did the conception of
sin change and also the method of dealing with the fact of sin. It
came to be believed that even if a taboo had been broken, something could be done about it. The main strand of evolution here is
that of the general theory and art of daimonology; and as these
outgrew their simplest form of mere avoidance of the presence and
resentment of the daimons, the alterations in the subordinate and
derived religious ideas and practices involved in or attached to
them are seen to have taken place as a natural accompaniment—
as a corollary might be conceived to change with its supporting
proposition. As development of the theory and practice of daimonism and daimonology advanced, men no longer laid them down and
died forthwith in helpless terror because they had sinned but set
about betimes to clear themselves of transgression so as to escape
its consequences. One of the prime methods of self-clearance is
confession.

Confession is a sort of exorcism by ritual. When a man has
sinned, though he may not realize the fact until he begins to experience the consequences, there are things he can do to cleanse himself of the taint. It is as if the sin, or the spirit causing it, were
residing in him and could be got rid of by the proper performance
of ritual. For there is a fetish-quality in ritual; and fetishes are
the prime instrumentality in overcoming noxious spiritual influences. Further, a man must clear himself of sin not only in his own
interest but in that of the community as well. Though later ideas
demand admission of sin as the first preliminary to remission, the
original object of insisting upon confession seems to have been the
same as that for requiring a notification of the presence of disease,
like the "Unclean! unclean!" of the leper.[47]

46 §§286, 295, below.   47 Levit., XIII, 45.

Among the Eskimo "it has come to be an act required by custom and morals to confess any and every transgression of the taboo, in order to protect the community from the evil influence of contact with the evil-doer." The author quoted[48] holds that this importance of the confession of transgressions, with a view to warning others to keep at a distance from the transgressor, has gradually led to the idea that a sin can be atoned by a confession. Acknowledgment of delinquencies in the face of a life-crisis is thought of as a measure of protection against ill luck. Ostiak husband and wife confess prior to the confinement of the latter. "If the married pair have concealed no sins in their confessions, an easy, painless birth is expected; if they have, a painful labor is looked for, in which the concealed sins shall be expiated."[49]

"A partial remission of sin by means of confession to the priest is found in Brahmanic literature." A repentant pilgrim was once heard seeking remission, both after and before the act, as follows: "I confess here that many a time have I killed traveling strangers; oft have I committed robberies; the wives of other people have I appropriated; quarrels and incidental thrashings of others have I indulged in time out of number; and hosts of other grave crimes and dark sins am I guilty of. . . . Clearly and unmistakably have I made this confession, and I believe I am now absolved of my transgressions. And (now while I am at it) I confess here also to the homicides, robberies, the appropriations of other men's wives, beating of others, etc., that I may perpetrate in the future."[50]

Aside from confession there are other expedients for clearing one's self from sin; it can sometimes be cast off by calling down upon one's head abuse or vituperation.[51]

One can be rendered sinful, in one district of India, by looking at the moon on a certain day; and "he is absolved from all sin if he gets abused by anybody. In order to insure getting abused, the person rendered sinful takes care to throw brick-bats into the house of a neighbor who abuses him for pelting in this way. This abuse absolves him from all sin caused by looking at the moon. Similarly, in Bengal, the sinful man robs a neighbor's orchard of fruits, or cuts down his plants for which he is abused by the latter and thus rendered clean of all sin caused by looking at the 'moon of ill omen.'" The author[52] quoted thinks that "the principle of vicarious sacrifice underlies the act of abusing the proprietor . . . of a village. By getting abused these men are supposed to be offered as sacrifices to appease the wrath of the rain-god."

In Togo the men march out of town to a certain tree where they all rub down the body. This clears them, they think, of all guilt.[53] Personal ablution is enjoined in Tibet but the purification is merely ceremonial, seldom extending to more than finger-dipping, and often not even that, for these people do not love water and soap.[54] In Sumatra people who have been killed by some

[48] Boas, in PSM, LVII, 627.

[49] Kondratowitsch, in *Globus*, LXXIV, 290.

[50] Hopkins, *Relig. Ind.*, 329; Kawaguchi, in *Century Mag.*, XLV, 390.

[51] §266, above.

[52] Mitra, in JASB, IV, 393-394, 391; §295, below.

[53] Klose, *Togo*, 302.   [54] Waddell, *Buddhism*, 423.

mischance, as by a fall, attack of a wild beast, deluge, earthquake, or lightning, are supposed to have a quarter of their sins forgiven. But they must also, if possible, undergo ritual purification. Then they can, "when they knock at the gates of heaven, show a check which gives them a claim to a twenty-five per-cent reduction of their account." Women who die in childbirth are similarly regarded, and are equally in need of the purification.[55] Application of earth and bathing cleanse impurities, according to Manu; and the Japanese sprinkle salt to purify.[56]

The Eskimo use switching and wiping motions over the body, followed by stamping and slapping the thighs, to cast off uncleanness; also a peculiar form of ablution.[57] The Chinook and other neighboring Indian tribes believe that spirits kill the unclean man, who cleanses himself by fasting and bathing.[58]

In South Germany, self-clearance from sin takes somewhat the form of an ordeal; strength and conscience are both tested in connection with the manipu-lation of certain iron figures. "The young fellow who can lift them upon his shoulders and then cast them over back into the sand, protects himself thereby against sickness in the year to come, and at the same time proves that he is not burdened with a deadly sin."[59]

§276*. Exorcism. In the ghost-cult has been displayed a set of practices calculated to banish or exorcise the souls of the recently dead,[60] some of which have been recalled in the cases just cited. They are in the main simply an extension upon offensive opera-tions as directed against human enemies; the ghosts were still so like men that they could be treated in much the same manner. Since, however, the daimons were the ghosts raised to a higher power and to a quality somewhat more complex and derived, the methods of forcing or exorcising a daimon could not remain as simple as those of the ghost-cult. Such forms as baptism could still be used;[61] but in general, man as man could not compel the dai-mons; to coerce a spirit there was need of some accessory in the shape of a coöperative spiritual agency. Hence the offensive opera-tions directed against the daimons must include an element of dualism, though they do not deserve the name as ordinarily em-ployed. For the simplest exorcism that makes use of spiritual aid —as has indeed appeared in connection with the ghost-cult—does not consist of setting one great spirit to combating another: Ormuzd against Ahriman, angel against demon, God against the

55 Jacobs, *Groot-Atjeh*, I, 439.
56 Bühler, *Manu*, V, 135; Kishimoto, in PSM, XLVI, 213.
57 Nelson, in BAE, XVIII, pt. I, 371; Fulcomer, in AA, XI, 58.
58 Boas, in USNM, 1895, 393.
59 Sartori, in *Globus*, LXXXVII, 93.   60 §§226, 227, above.
61 Clodd, *Magic*, 67-70; White, *Sci. and Theol.*, II, 117.

Devil. That is further along on the course of evolution. The commonest agency for repelling or compelling a spirit is the fetish, which is identified with a daimon only so far as it is the abode of such; it is, very often, something that embodies spiritual power of unknown, undefined, unidentified origin.[62]

With the aid of the fetish-object or material or practice the supernatural influences can be repelled or controlled. The sum of such operations might perhaps be called magic; in any case, a selection of typical methods of exorcism that would not ordinarily be thought of as magical may be cited by way of preliminary. It is to be noted that methods of exorcism are not seldom the sort of operations that drive off wild animals.[63]

Among certain Papuans, when sickness is about, they blow conch-shells, beat drums, throw fire-sticks, and keep up a continuous yelling for some time.[64] In Creek Town, West Africa, certain images were taken periodically from the houses, amidst a terrible din of screaming and tomtoming, and thrown into the river; then the town was cleared of spirits. "The rationale of the affair is this. The wandering spirits are attracted by the images, and take shelter among their rags, like earwigs or something of that kind. The *charivari* is to drive any of the spirits who might be away from their shelters back to them. The shouting of the mob is to keep the spirits from venturing out again while they are being carried to the river. The throwing of the images, rags and all, into the river, is to destroy the spirits or at least send them elsewhere." Then fresh images are set up pending the next exorcism.[65] West African witches are supposed to meet at midnight at a sort of Brocken and plot sickness; while their corporeal bodies lie asleep in their huts, their spirit-bodies, unimpeded by walls or other physical objects, pass with instant rapidity through the air, over the tree-tops, to the place of assembly. Here they have visible, audible, and tangible communication with evil spirits and feast on some human's "heart-life," the loss of which involves his illness and death unless it be restored. "The early cock-crowing is a warning for them to disperse; the advent of the morning star they fear, as it compels them to hasten back to their bodies. Should the sun rise upon them before they reach their corporeal 'home,' their plans would fail, and themselves would sicken. They dread cayenne pepper. Should its bruised leaves or pods have been rubbed over their body-home by anyone during their absence, they would be unable to re-enter it, and would die or miserably waste away."[66]

Exorcisms at weddings, after puberty and initiations, and at other crises are common. Meal is sprinkled on all paths leading into camp, to keep off evil spirits—a case of protection verging upon propitiation. Whistling while going home at night keeps off evil spirits; though sometimes silence is better.[67] A

[62] §247, above.   [63] Pietschmann, *Phön.*, 174.

[64] Chalmers, in JAI, XXXIII, 124.

[65] Kingsley, *Travels W. Afr.*, 495.   [66] Nassau, *Fetichism,* 123.

[67] §223, above; Kolben, *Beschreibung,* 127, 148, 150; Stuhlmann, *Mit Emin,* 89; Brunache, *Cent. Afr.,* 133.

naïve case of setting the daimon aside is related of the West African negro: "It happens not so very seldom that he simply buries his fetish-idol, which in this case is an uncomfortable conscience, that it may not be a witness to his misdeed. And in so doing the depth to which he hides his god may stand in a direct relation to the shamefulness of the intended undertaking."[68] There is no doubt about the efficacy of iron in exorcising spirits; they seem to have a sort of aversion to it. "It is a very common belief among natives that iron is antagonistic to rain; in Ukamba the women for long refused to use iron hoes for this reason. . . . Probably the same idea underlies the objection to the railway. I talked once to an old man on the subject, but got very little out of him, excepting a look, which plainly said that if I did not know that to lay an iron band all across the country was enough to drive all rain away, what did I know. Unfortunately, there have been a series of dry years for about the last ten years or more."[69] The way in which coincidence supports primitive theory is no less than uncanny.

Among the Nagas, the spirits "are a timid crew and may be frightened from molesting men on the march by singing and shouting, a notion which may have something to do with the incessant 'ho, ho'-ing kept up by a Sema working or carrying a load. They are also easily kept at a distance by a sprig of wormwood and are generally very sensitive to strong or unpleasant odours." This, despite the fact that they "generally have the dispositions of the more unpleasant of humans."[70] "The aid of the *mantram*, or word of power is invoked not only to forestall but also to exorcise evil powers." These utterances "may be described as a curious combination of suggestion, abjuration, coaxing, and threat."[71]

Such precautions, some of which suggest the simplicity of the traditional ostrich, with head in the sand, are not confined to primitive peoples. China is a vast hunting-ground for expedients in exorcism. Chinese gunpowder was developed as a spirit-repeller; "strings of crackling fireworks are burned at the door-posts, before the outgoing and incoming of the year, designed to expel and deter evil spirits from the house." The portrait of a tiger keeps them away from the coffin; a pair of trousers of a child's father, hung on the bedstead, will gather all unfavorable influences that might affect the child; in both ancient and modern China, "ghost-papers" have been widely used as prophylactic expedients.[72] The body of a deceased infant is crushed into pulp to prevent the devil in it from vexing the family. "Taoism has degenerated into a system of incantations against evil spirits," for Confucianism was too refined and high to satisfy the common man.[73] "In China, the streets along which a funeral is to pass are first sprinkled with holy water, and even the houses and warehouses, lest some demon should be lurking ready to pounce on the dead man as he passed. During the passage of the funeral, in addition to the noise of gongs and crackers, bank-notes are scattered along the road to the grave, and while the demons are supposed to be pursuing these deceitful riches—for the notes are bad ones—the soul of the man goes tranquilly behind the coffin

[68] Lenz, *Westafr.*, 193.
[69] Dundas, C., in JAI, LI, 238, note; and in JAI, XLIII, 525.
[70] Hutton, *Sema Nagas*, 199.   [71] Roy, in JAI, XLIV, 348.
[72] Williams, *Middle Kingdom*, I, 813; De Groot, *Relig. Syst.*, I, 181; Gomme, *Village Life*, 181-182; N. Y. *Times*, Dec. 16, 1894; Letourneau, *Soc.*, 289.
[73] Smith, *Chinese Char.*, 206, 293.

to the grave."[74] Here we see, along with the exorcistic efforts, also the attempt to buy off and at the same time to deceive and overreach the threatening influences.

In ancient Chaldæa, man in his war against the evil spirits needed every help he could get. Fire was his most efficacious ally, the greatest enemy of evil spirits. It put them to flight and dissipated their power. The Chaldæan never moved a step except in fear of them, especially at night, and then even in his house. In the ninth century B.C. there were sixty-five thousand great gods of heaven and earth; how many secondary ones there were is not divulged. Sacred images were brought into the chambers of the sick to exorcise the spirits that were plaguing them; texts from sacred books were placed on the walls and bound around the patient's brow. His sins and the evil spirits must loose their hold on him when he held a holy object in a white cloth in his right hand and had a black cloth wrapped about his left.[75]

According to ancient Hebrew belief, since evil spirits attacked men at night, "therefore one should not, in the early morning, touch the eye with the hand before it has been washed; for otherwise one might become blind. Therefore the body is unclean early in the day and must be bathed every morning. Any one who sets himself on his way before cock-crow, runs the risk of his life, while from any one who reads the Schema on his couch the spirits remain afar off." If anyone is married, let him read the Schema.[76] There were formulas for banning: "The gods that have not made the heavens and the earth, these shall perish from the earth, and from under the heaven."[77] The daimons did, it seems, come to inhabit mainly the deserted cities and ruins. Mid-day was, as with the Greeks and Romans, one of the times of the daimons; but when they came at night, the light from the seven-branched candlestick drove them off.[78] In Homer there is little or no definite exorcism, but there are unnamed evil daimons and practices witnessing to a desire to be rid of some interfering supernatural agency.[79]

The five-pointed star, or pentagram, was an effective defense against evil spirits. Röck[80] says that the Christian cultus took over this holy astral symbol from a heathen source, and little silver medallions were sold with the local mother-of-God on one side and the pentagram in red on the other. This sign protected from the snares of the devil and hell, and promised luck; the circumscription read: "May this be your lucky star!" The author remarks upon the presence of the pentagram, cross, and swastika in pre-Columbian America. It was really a magical or fetish-sign. Its employment in Goethe's *Faust*[81] is well known; the fact that the dog that became Mephistopheles could not get out over the pentagram on the threshold, though he had been able to slip in because the outward-directed point of the star had not been completed, illustrates the rigidity of the ritual connected with such protective devices. The Middle Ages were full of doctrine about spirits and their exorcism, and the Church Fathers exercised themselves very earnestly concerning such matters. Devil-atoms could be swallowed unless the sign of the cross were made over the mouth. Relics of saints about the neck, the Evangel of John on the heart, a sanctified host—

74 Frazer, in JAI, XV, 86.
75 Maspero, *Hist. Anc.*, I, 635-636 (quoted); *Records of the Past*, III, 139.
76 Blau, *Zauberwesen*, 146, 162-163.   77 Jer., X, 11.
78 Maurer, *Vkde.*, I, 29, 66, 133.   79 Keller, *Hom. Soc.*, 110.
80 "Pentagramm," in *Globus*, XCV, 8.   81 Pt. I, ll. 1039-1048.

"these were infallible protection against devilish temptation and persecution, which everyone could get from the caretaker of his soul."[82] The "book, bell, and candle" as exorcistic fetishes have taken a stock place in literature. Even in the seventeenth and eighteenth centuries, peasants relied upon exorcism and excommunication against worms, insects, and other destructive agencies. A full description of an exorcism in a castle at Darmstadt, in 1717-1718, brings out many curious details.[83]

In Ireland "when anyone gets a fall, he springs up, and turning about three times to the right, digs a hole in the ground with his knife or sword, and cuts out a turf, for they imagine there is a spirit in the earth."[84] Masks are traced down from devices for avoidance and exorcism to their survivals employed on holidays to frighten people.[85] In Great Russia the bread and salt ceremony, besides indicating good-will, was thought to expel evil spirits and malign influences. Bread and salt were laid on the ground under the floor-beams of a new house in Bukowina, and twigs consecrated on Palm Sunday were set in the wall as protection against all evils such as lightning. "Whenever unclean spirits make themselves evident in a house, they buy six new earthen pots and wait until the spirits begin again to make confusion. Then a man puts the six pots beside him, and taking one of them at a time, always with the left hand, throws it behind him. After each throw he must say: 'If you are good, remain; but if you are evil, disappear!' "[86]

Anything less than an encyclopædic treatment of exorcism would fail to bring out the infinite variety of means adopted for banning evil spirits. Throughout this variety, however, resemblances appear which are highly significant; for peoples so widely separated from one another that acculturation seems out of the question exhibit closely similar practices. It is well to consider the variety of exorcistic devices; but one should not lose sight of the similarities. With a view to emphasizing the latter we shall consider three very widely encountered methods, beginning with baptism.

The use of fire and water for removing "uncleanness" and in banning the ghost is a familiar detail of the ghost-cult.[87] In particular is baptism a rite of wide prevalence over the earth. "In Africa 'baptism' is just as anciently indigenous as in Oceania."[88] "With few exceptions . . . bathing of the new-born infant takes

[82] Lea, *Inquisition*, III, 381; Heyer, *Priesterherrschaft*, 23, 24; Sumner, in *Coll. Ess.*, I, ch. IV.

[83] D'Avenel, *Hist. Écon.*, I, 298; Hermann, in *Hess. Bl. Vkde.*, IV, 167-176.

[84] Gomme, *Village Life*, 130.

[85] Rütimeyer, in *Globus*, XCI, 203, 213-214; Andree, *Eth. Parallelen*, 109.

[86] Kostomarov, *Gt. Russ.* (Russ.), 252; Kaindl, in *Globus*, XCII, 284.

[87] §§88, 92, 222, 227, above.   [88] Frobenius, *Masken*, 78.

place among most peoples; a purification of the mother always."[89]
The aim is not physical cleanliness, for sanitary conditions are a
matter of concern to but few of the peoples in question. It would
be difficult indeed to account for the prevalence of baptism on
other than religious grounds.[90]

Several West African tribes carry out a ceremony combining fire-purifica-
tion with that by water. The mother and child must pass through a sort of
rain formed by the dripping from the eaves of sacred water thrown upon the
roof. When the child is named, his head is bathed in a special water of purification. After the ceremony, the fire is put out and a fresh one lighted.[91] In
ancient India, eight days after birth there was a solemn ablution of the new-
born child.[92] The tribes at the head-waters of the Yangtse-Kiang wash the
year-old boy in some sacred pool.[93] In central Borneo the Kayan children
receive a name with the new year and are sprinkled with water by the head
of the household.[94] In New Zealand baptism the eight-day old infant was taken
to a running stream. A branch was stuck upright in the water, to which the
navel-strand of the child, being cut off with a shell, was fastened. The water
that flowed about the branch was sprinkled over the child, who now received
a name. Sometimes there was immersion in the stream.[95]

Wilken[96] goes into this banning function of water as he does into so many
other of the funeral-ceremonies. It is employed not only at death, but at betrothal or the occupation of a new dwelling. Regular bathing has a religious
aspect; there are formulas for bathing and the water is to be struck in a
certain way while uttering them. Epidemics are followed by a flight to the
vicinity of water. Child-baptism is but another illustration of the subject; the
infant is let down into the stream and an invocation made: "May the sicknesses
go forth with the water." Baptism means literally "to bathe the child." Both
sprinkling and immersion are practised and name-giving follows upon the
bath. When a new name is attained, there is another baptism. The ceremony is thought by the Indians to keep off ill and the Filipinos use it against
the spirit of a woman who has died in childbirth. European baptism safeguarded the child against the devil; an unbaptized child could not rest nor
get into Paradise. Hence a rule that midwives might baptize, lest there might
not be time to get a priest. Even things can be baptized, for example, bells.[97]
There was a baptism of bells in France under Napoleon III, on which occasion all those condemned to death were pardoned.

In Greenland "baptism is looked upon as being the infallible means of protection" against evil spirits;[98] perhaps early contact with Christianity is responsible in this case. Among the Oregon Indians, after a month, "the child
was taken to the river and waved five times over the water as a sort of 'baptismal' rite."[99] Other Indians baptize after three days; "they believe that with-

---

[89] Mucke, *Horde,* 84; §§408, 409, below.
[90] Lippert, *Kgchte.,* II, 344 ff.   [91] Ellis, *Yoruba,* 153.
[92] Zimmer, *Altind. Leben,* 320.
[93] Reid, in *Cosmopolitan Mag.,* XXVIII, 443.
[94] Nieuwenhuis, *Borneo,* I, 174.   [95] Taylor, *Te Ika,* 185.
[96] In VG, III, 428 ff.   [97] §227, above.
[98] Fries, *Grönland,* 149.   [99] Sapir, in AA, IX, 275.

out this rite the child can not live," and they add sacrifices and burnt offerings.[100] Under Nagualism, in Mexico, there was a kind of baptismal sacrament
with water; and in Peru baptism took place a few days after birth.[101] Fuegian
children are immersed in the sea immediately after birth.[102]

The invulnerability of Achilles and other mythical heroes—never complete,
of course—was secured by baptism. There are a number of cases in Norse mythology. The Norse sagas represent Haakon the Good as being baptized at
birth; then, though a heathen, he was baptized in Christian fashion in England,
and he baptized his own son.[103] A Russian sect, called the "Underground People," re-baptize a man just before death, so that the devils, when they look
for "Peter" or "John," to punish him for the sins of this life, may not find him
under his alias. *Non est.*[104]

Baptism may be by immersion or by sprinkling; "it is only since the twelfth
and thirteenth centuries that the method of sprinkling has become general, the
western churches demanding immersion, of the head at least."[105]

Another special case of exorcism is by the use of a bodily secre-
tion. The numerous instances of this order need not be detailed;
the employment of spittle may serve as a type. To spit on a person
is to drive off evil spirits from him. In one sense, the saliva is
fetishistic, just as the rest of the exuviæ are;[106] and its use is in so
far magical, for magic is carried out through the agency of fetishes. But the use of saliva, like that of water, is perhaps more
generally religious than specifically magical. In any case, it constitutes a form transitional toward magic.

In central Africa, "a man on experiencing a disagreeable odour spits."[107]
The Masai attached much importance to the act of spitting. To spit at a
person is, with them, a great compliment. "The earlier travellers in Masailand
were astonished, when making friendship with old Masai chiefs and head-men,
to be constantly spat at. When I entered the Uganda Protectorate and met
the Masai of the Rift Valley for the first time, every man, before extending
his hand to me, would spit on the palm. When they came into my temporary
house . . . they would spit to the north, east, south, and west before entering
the house. Every unknown object which they regard with reverence, such as a
passing train, is spat at. Newly born children are spat on by everyone who
sees them."[108] Nassau[109] has a rather far-fetched explanation of the African
mode of honoring a guest by spitting on his hand. He thinks that the sudden
and violent expulsion of the breath is apt to bring away some moisture, but
that "the kernel of the custom lies in the prayer of blessing accompanying the

[100] Russell, in BAE, XXVI, 188.
[101] Brinton, *Nagualism,* 60; Müller, *Amer. Urrelig.,* 389.
[102] Ratzel, *Vkde.,* II, 677.
[103] Laing, *Sturlason's Sagas,* I, 391, 394, II, 15.
[104] "St. Petersburg Correspondence," in *Lit. Digest,* Apr. 21, 1894.
[105] Bastian, *Deut. Exped.,* II, 142, note.
[106] §249, above.   [107] Stannus, in JAI, XL, 286.
[108] Johnston, *Uganda,* II, 833.   [109] *Fetichism,* 99.

act." This veteran missionary is strong on facts of experience, but subject to bias in interpretation. In central Africa a curse is removed through the elders spitting on the victim. "The spitting of an old man confers a blessing. It is customary for an elder meeting anyone whom he wishes well, to spit on his chest or hand."[110] It is reported of some East Africans that "in pointing out a direction they use their tongues; and the Scotch and Irish habit of spitting upon a gift for good luck is carried to a vast extent. They even offer their faces to be spat upon as an evidence of good feeling."[111]

The Persian Yezidis "are shocked if one spits upon the earth, because they interpret this as an insult to the devil," that is, as exorcistic. Some authorities interpret this abhorrence as one of defilement of the earth.[112] Here appears the more modern and rational idea of expectoration. New Testament examples will occur to the reader.[113] In parts of Europe spitting is "a general favorite amongst magical devices. In Erdely the midwife spits in every bath of the child. The mother too always spits where she lays the child down—until it is confirmed"[114] and so relieved once for all from peril of evil influences. Spitting on the bait is a traditional practice among fishermen; and spitting upon the hands or upon implements is not altogether free of ritual. There are, or were, a good many expectoration-practices among boys' devices to win good luck or better, perhaps, to exclude bad luck. And there still persist persuasions as to the curative effect of saliva and urine.

It is doubtless true that the saliva has an antiseptic quality; animals persistently lick their open wounds, and dentists say that lacerations of the mouth are far less subject to infection than those of the external parts. On the other hand the secretions in the mouth regularly transport disease-germs. It cannot be conceived, of course, that such considerations, one way or the other, weighed in the minds of savages. If they have developed practices that prove to be rational, the rationality is the product of the winnowing action of societal selection over long periods during which men have been aware but vaguely, if at all, that alteration is taking place, much less that it is in this direction or that, and subject to control.

The last of the special cases here to be considered is the one that is doubtless the most generally familiar: that of the amulet,[115] talisman, or charm. It is commonly a fetish, so that it would be fair to say that its effect is magical; and yet there are talismans enough employed even today whose wearers or sponsors would

110 Dundas, C., in JAI, XLV, 258.
111 French-Sheldon, in JAI, XXI, 383.
112 Jackson, in *Jr. Amer. Orient Soc.*, XXV, pt. I, 179-180.
113 Mark, VIII, 23; John, IX, 6; Mark, VII, 33.
114 Temesváry, *Geburtshilfe*, 75.
115 Etymology extensively considered by Wünsch, in *Glotta*, II, 219 ff.

strenuously repel the suggestion that they are that. Such amulets, it would be explained, are religious, not magical—a distinction, in many cases, without a difference except in angle of vision.[116] There is no object to be gained, however, by forcing things into categories in violence to ordinary usage; and in many respects, indeed, the amulet deserves to be considered by itself and apart from other magical or semi-magical apparatus.

In all probability the amulet was also the first ornament, and so of an unreckonable antiquity; it is entirely likely, too, that it was one of the first pieces of personal property.[117] In those instances where the quality which makes it ornamental is likewise the attribute that lends it protective power, it is, perhaps, least fetish-like; even so, however, its rarity or peculiarity is what sets it apart from other objects of less or no talismanic potency. One of the essential properties of this type of amulet is that it glitters, flutters, swings, or jingles, with the result, through attracting the evil eye, of averting it from the wearer.[118] "The constantly menacing and greatest danger is the evil glance, that of envy as well as of admiration; it has as a consequence sickness and death. Especially to avert this danger are amulets worn. Every ornament that draws this glance to itself turns it off from the wearer. The conceptions 'ornament' and 'amulet' pass over into one another and are scarcely to be distinguished; everything that springs into the eye serves for an ornament as well as for an amulet."[119]

Consider the precious stones and the beliefs that have centered about them. In some parts of Europe, in the Middle Ages, the diamond was classed with the animals; the amethyst, as its etymology indicates, was deemed by the Greeks an antidote for intoxication; the topaz cured lunacy and other affections of mind and body; amber defended against witchcraft and sorcery; the agate was "almost a universal remedy"; jade warded off kidney-disease; and many other specific qualities became identified with other stones.[120]

These are objects that are extraordinary in themselves and so

[116] §303, below; Lehmann, *Overtro*, I, 9 ff.; Schulze (*Fetischismus*, 174, quoted by Krauss, *Sreća*, 156) draws a rather formal distinction between a fetish and an amulet.

[117] §§112, above, and 447, below.　　　[118] §265, above.

[119] Wellhausen, *Skizzen*, III, 143-144.

[120] Curtin, in *Bull. Amer. Acad. Med.*, 1907, VII, rep., 51 ff.; Kunz, *Curious Lore of Precious Stones*, and *The Magic of Jewels and Charms*.

become fetishes;[121] a number of the amulets have, however, a much closer and more definite connection with the spirit-world and are of far less pronounced ornamental quality. Illustrations of both types, and of intermediate ones, are now to be listed. It must be noted that it is impracticable to classify amulets into those purely defensive against ill and those exercising positive effects in securing good luck. Because the positive and negative functions are thus inseparable, even in the same amulet, the general treatment of the topic forms a natural transition to the following sections on coercion, conciliation, and propitiation.

The Namaqua of South Africa have an amulet consisting of two sticks called "white-forgetting" which causes the white man to forget injuries done them by the wearer; also another set of sticks called "girl-love," which secure favor with the women. To the Zulu the tuft of an ox-tail prevents childlessness. It was near the Cape that the first South African diamond was discovered, in a leather bag hung about the neck of a sorcerer.[122] West Africa is a land of amulets: iron arm-rings; fringes of dried palm-leaves, which insure against injury in war, being killed if taken prisoner, and witchcraft; the tail of a horse, cow, or goat, which, waved to and fro in front of the body, causes the foe's missiles to deviate to the right and left; a sentence or verse of the Koran, written on paper and sewed up in leather.[123] Says Miss Kingsley:[124] "The two chiefs saw us courteously out of the town, as far as where the river crosses the outgoing path again, and the blue-hatted one gave me some charms 'to keep my foot in path.' . . . Charms are made for every occupation and desire in life—loving, hating, buying, selling, fishing, travelling, hunting, etc." Even human eye-balls, particularly of white men, are powerful charms. Water from around a floating corpse is a good death-charm. On the Loango coast the tongue is rubbed, for protection's sake, with a mixture of powder and rum. The common soldiers have war-amulets while the leader is safeguarded by spitting the juice of a certain plant on the ground before him, to ward off bullets.[125]

Of three Pygmies who came into camp each carried a talisman which he held out against the white men for self-defense. Amulets on the abdomen protect the pregnant. Camphor has the reputation, in a large part of the Mohammedan world, of infallibly repelling devilish influences. A tale is told of an Algerian Arab who offered for sale, for twenty-five francs, a book wrapped up in rags, which turned out to be a text-book on trigonometry; "the leaves of the book—doubtless on account of the highly mystical figures—were regarded, over a wide area as very efficacious amulets against all sorts of illnesses and spirits, and were worn, enclosed in little cases, around the neck.

121 §254, above.
122 Fritsch, Eingeb. S.-Afr., 360-361; Middlebrook, in Globus, LXXV, 271; Ratzel, Vkde., I, 36.
123 Ellis, Ewe, 38, 69, 94.
124 Travels W. Afr., 288, 448, 449, 478.
125 Bastian, Deut. Exped., I, 203.

. . . Some parts of the book had been sold, even in the Sudan, at very high prices."126

The Koryak use crude representations of animals or men, or parts of animals (hair, beak, nose, portion of ear), or inanimate objects, as amulets. In Tibet "prayer-flags are used by Lamas as luck-commanding talismans." Reading holy writ also operates to relieve the sinner; but the "result of the wholesale reading of the scriptures is that, in order to get through the prescribed reading of the several bulky scriptures within a reasonable time, a dozen or so Lamas are usually called in, each of whom reads aloud, all at the same time, a different book or chapter for the benefit of the sinner."127

The close connection between the extraordinary object, which readily becomes a fetish, and the luck-piece, amulet, or charm, is revealed in Furness's[128] account of a trouble-maker in Borneo. This man was always stirring up strife between the Kenyahs and the Sarawak Government, "until Dr. Hose one day obtained possession of an invaluable charm of his, consisting of a small misshapen hen's egg, whereon he based all his good luck. Only by the ever-present threat that his egg would be broken by Dr. Hose at the least sign of treason on his part, can he be controlled and kept peaceable, even, I believe, to this hour."

In antiquity the cords tied on mummies' necks, arms, and legs were intended, like all mystic knots, "to ward off evil influences. Gum of acacia had value as an amulet by reason of the idea that it was a clot of blood, the tree being a woman. So much are amulets in demand in Cairo that the vendors have shops at street-corners or at the entrances to mosques.129 Among the Hebrews, "amulets were used to protect in a prophylactic way man and his possessions, as house, cattle, etc., against the evil workings of magic, demons, and other circumstances, or to turn away ill, sickness, and damage of the most diverse sort that was already present. . . . The amulet was like a weapon held out before. As a father gives such a staff to his son, so that he may thereby be protected against magic and the evil eye, thus God gave Israel the Thora to protect it." Knots and bells on clothing were a protection; they were not merely ornaments and could be worn even on the Sabbath. The heathen, too, wore tintinnabula.130 In two places in the Bible a magical element called "mandrake . . . is mentioned as bringing blessing, protecting against dangers and sicknesses, easing birth-pangs, and making the unfruitful fruitful."131

126 Schweinfurth, Heart of Afr., 439; Lessner, in Globus, LXXXVI, 338; Nachtigal, Sahara, II, 527; Hammer, in Umschau, IV, 936-937 (quoted).

127 Jochelson, in AA, VI, 418; Waddell, Buddhism, 410, 411, 412, 464.

128 Head-Hunters, 104.

129 Maspero, Hist. Anc., II, 526; Smith, Relig. Sem., 133; Pischon, Islam, 110.

130 Blau, Zauberwesen, 86, 91, 164; Duhm, Geister, 26; Exod., XI, 2 ff.; XII, 35 ff.; Jewish Encyclop., sub "Amulet."

131 Gen., XXX, 14; Song of Songs, VII, 13; Maurer, Vkde., I, 139.

Roman children wore a charm (fascinus) to ward off witchcraft; and there was a sign for it.[132] A runic sign was scratched on the cradle to protect the child against all ill; later the pentagram was painted on it, against witches. The holly was a guard against evil fairies and the mistletoe was hung as part of the Druid-ceremony. In East Prussia, when the milk was bewitched, the cows were milked through the hole in a stone axe and in the eighteenth century, in Hesse, if they did not give milk, their udders were rubbed with a stone axe. In the Rhine district this superstition long persisted and in almost every house there was one of these implements. "The preventive magic power of the horse, of which animal the shoe must be taken to form part, is bound up, in the shoe, with the protective and preventive power of steel and iron." To the horse-shoe, nailed up or burned in, great protective power has been ascribed.[133]

"Books and letters fallen from heaven belong to the inventory of the mediæ-val Christian folk-beliefs of Germans and Slavs"; the samples of such alleged revelations reveal their fetishistic and talismanic quality.[134] The Puritans were described as embroidering texts and proverbs on underclothing.[135] In all parts of Scotland the ancient spindle-whorls and other tools and weapons are sup-posed to have increased the birth of children, to increase the milk of cows, cure diseases of the eye, protect houses from lightning, etc." But they may be regarded, on the contrary, as dangerous. In the west of Ireland the celts and stone implements are supposed to be fairy arrows. "The finder of one should put it in a hole in a wall or ditch. It should not be brought into a house or given to anyone."[136] "A luck-fetish well known and highly esteemed in all Europe is the luck-caul. It is obtained 'when the membranes which enclose the fœtus do not tear, as commonly happens, before the passage of the child's head but rather cover the head when born, like a cap.' "[137]

When one considers the endless variety of amulets in almost universal use through the earlier stages of society's evolution, and not unrepresented in the later, the reflection rises as to what sort of a world it was where such means were unshakenly accepted as constituting the normal and indispensable apparatus for living. It looks as if personal responsibility and initiative could have been but feebly developed where accountability was so habitually shifted over to the supernatural. The major premise of the imaginary environment was so strong that verification was not even imag-ined; if experience did not check up with theory, so much the worse for the former. If alteration of practice was imperatively called for, whatever substitution was made must be justified as a better interpretation and realization of the enduring doctrine. Only after

[132] Andrews, *Latin Dict.*, *sub* "fascinus," "lunulae," and references.

[133] Weinhold, *Deut. Frauen,* I, 102; Nassau, *Fetichism,* 101; Andree, *Eth. Parallelen,* 32; Schell, in *Globus,* XCI, 364.

[134] Bitterfield, in *Am Ur-Quell,* I, 66, 67.

[135] Mayne, *City Match,* Act II, scene 2.

[136] Gomme, *Village Life,* 161.   [137] Krauss, *Sreća,* 158.

ages could the dogma be questioned; and it is not seriously criticized by mankind as a whole today. Almost any doctrine can be made to cover almost any practice if the interpretation is subtle enough. And the fact always remains that the amulet gave confidence and faith to its wearer. Although there is not much that is rational in the practices just reviewed, they were relatively harmless, as some of the religious mores were not, and they all made for organization and discipline. The validity of the amulet may be challenged; that it had value admits of no doubt; its case goes in as a corollary of the justification of primitive religion as a whole, an issue which we are not yet ready to consider.[138]

§277*. Coercitives. The amulet is prevailingly a defensive and offensive weapon against the supernatural, though it works over on occasion nearly into the character of a propitiatory device. The next set of practices to be reviewed has a positive cast. These are not propitiatory, though they verge still farther than preceding expedients in that direction; they seem, rather, to exert over the spirit at which they are directed a sort of compulsion to do this or that. There seems to be fetish in them; for, since man of himself could not force the daimons, it is to be supposed that some spiritual power inheres in the practices and ritual effectively employed in coercion. If correctly performed they can be as little resisted as was the rubbing of Aladdin's lamp or the pronouncing of "Open, Sesame!" To such compulsive measures the name coercitives is given. Coercitives represent yet another device for controlling the aleatory element.

Primitive people are found now and then treating their gods in a most cavalier manner, beating their images, dragging them in the mud, or casting them into the water.[139] This is when the idols seem to have lost virtue, that is, when their spiritual possession is doubtful or weak.

Images of Hindu divinities are sometimes treated as the people of a Portuguese village once treated their patron, Saint Anthony; they knocked his head off and substituted for it the head of St. Francis because, contrary to agree-

138 §§329, 330, below.
139 D'Alviella, *Concep. God,* 113; Spencer, *Study Soc.,* 301.

ment, he allowed the Spaniards to plunder the town. The author[140] quoted saw nothing of this sort in connection with village-goddesses.

An alien god is subject to indignities. He is presumably hostile anyway, and there is nothing to expect in the way of conciliating him. However, threats directed at one's own divinities are not uncommon.

When Burton spoke to certain East Africans about God, they asked eagerly where this god was, so they could go and kill him. "Who but he," they said, "lays waste our homes, and kills our wives and cattle?"[141] Again, the foreign god may be imprisoned. The Aztecs constructed a large cage to receive the images of foreign gods, "so that they might not be able to use their liberty for succoring their worshippers."[142] Spencer[143] quotes a vigorous denunciation of the patron saint of a boat sailing from Goa, because the weather was squally, ending with a threat of heaving the said saint overboard the next time he failed. The customary offering to him was omitted because of his demonstrated incompetence. The Albans, after being subjugated by the Romans, deserted their cult in wrath.[144] Augustus punished Neptune in effigy because he had behaved badly. The ancient Arcadians used to beat their god Pan if they came back from the chase empty-handed. On the day of the death of Germanicus, all the altars in Rome were cast to the earth.[145] Frazer[146] devotes considerable space to the coercion of the gods to give rain.

Instances of this kind are rather exceptional and it is to be conjectured that a spirit treated in such manner cannot be conceived of as very powerful. Regularly the daimons are so potent and so resentful of anything that can be construed as even a piece of negligence—whether wilful or not does not matter—that the general case must be conceived of about as follows: the only way to coerce a spirit is by the enlistment of a more powerful one, either in his own person or in some fetish-object which he affects or in some ritual that is fetishistic in quality.

The fact that the coercitive does not run precisely with this general case, for it does not enlist one spirit against another, is the reason for setting coercion somewhat apart from magic. Coercion represents a sort of irresistible propitiation. Chastity and the ordeal are examples.[147] Men act in a certain way and the daimons cannot but meet their wishes; men revert, for instance, to a cruder code of mores and thus move the spirits to favor them: they fall

[140] Fawcett, in JASB, II, 281.   [141] Lubbock, *Origin Civil.*, 131.

[142] Nadaillac, *Preh. Amer.*, 360.   [143] *Study Soc.*, 160.

[144] Livy, *Hist.*, I, ch. 31.   [145] Suetonius, *Caligula*, V.

[146] *Golden Bough*, I, 18 ff.

[147] §§183, above, 281, 283, below; Maine, *Relig. Chastity*, ch. XV.

back on promiscuity,[148] they revive cannibalism, they return to older or discarded forms of worship. This is analogous to the abjuration of sin in calamity. In view of the fact that what is archaic is holy and what is new is profane, it would appear that the daimons in their inveterate conservatism cherish that which is old, even when it is obsolete; and are so pleased by a return to the ancient forms as to be coerced by so doing. These were the mores they themselves, when they lived on earth, were used to and approved and they have still their erstwhile likes and dislikes. Reversion in worship is to them a sort of vindication. Furthermore, they get offerings on all such occasions.

Hearing of a pest at the Murray River, the old men of a neighboring tribe proposed an exchange of wives to avert it.[149] In making peace, the ordinary Australian sex-taboo was raised to lend solemnity to the occasion.[150] The Italian Lokri of antiquity sacrificed the chastity of daughters to move the gods to favor. "Why? They sought to conciliate the gods and make them propitious by returning from the new customs, thought to be unpleasant to them, to the usages of the very ancient past—the primitive time, which was regarded as golden and divinely favored."[151]
The spirits "need much propitiation, and are very apt to be annoyed by the abandonment of ancient customs, which is not perhaps entirely unnatural, as by the abandonment of a custom they usually lose offerings of some sort. Thus when the harvest has been bad a 'Morung' [club-house] is sometimes built . . . to fulfil no other purpose than obedience to a custom the lapse of which has conceivably angered the spirits. Again a village which has for years lived under the protection of the *Pax Britannica* continues to make an occasional pretence at erecting defences and the accompanying ceremony, as this is believed to propitiate the spirits, who certainly receive some sort of offering on that occasion."[152]

The daimons seem always to have delighted in survivals, and religion is still full of them; there is, for instance, something hardly reverent in an English prayer that does not use "thou" in its several cases. In a general way survivals are still, if not coercive, at least propitiatory. Among the coercitives one that exhibits a more than ordinary generality is nudity, though there are instances where it seems propitiatory or exorcistic. In any case it is frequently an adjunct to worship and to sorcery.

148 §344, below.   149 Cunow, *Australneger,* 69.
150 Spencer and Gillen, *Nat. Tr. Cent. Aust.,* 97, 98.
151 Justinus, *Hist.,* XXI, 3; Athenæus, *Deipnosophists,* XIII, ch. 573, 574; §343, below.
152 Hutton, *Sema Nagas,* 198-199.

One African tribe has a great fear of the sorceress of another. Hence, on a night-journey to another village they generally go naked, thinking they will thus remain unseen. In Senegambia the ritual element comes out more clearly; where an accused person is put to the ordeal of drinking poisoned water, he must be naked. In Ashanti, when the men are thought to be in battle, the women run about with sticks, representing guns, and naked. Their whole idea seems to be to invoke the gods in behalf of their men. In Cameroons, after a man accused of witchcraft was sacrificed, the whole community, males and females, went naked into the sea to wash away the magic. In Madagascar, witches are supposed to go about naked.[153] In these cases there is always some idea of moving the spirits, and nudity is part of the process. Penance preceding head-hunting expeditions in Borneo includes confession, fasting, omen-taking, and nudity.[154] A report on Formosa says "that for certain rites the priestess has to strip naked; if true, this would be analogous to the same custom in religious dances . . . in eastern Africa, and to the modern incantations used by a girl seeking to learn of her future husband in Bavaria."[155] It is sometimes plainly stated that nudity is repellent. Ghosts abominate nudity; hence the procedure of the man whose wife is being confined, in mounting the roof naked to scare off the evil influences. If the Tagal gets off the road, he ascribes it to the ghost of a woman, who has died in childbirth, and strips to frighten her off.[156]

"The female worshippers of Dionysus attending in a nude state . . . formed a counterpart of the naked female votaries who attended at the Indian festival of Potraj. Both women and girls in Britain took part in sacred rites with naked, woad-stained bodies. Hail, whirlwind, and lightning are dispelled by female nudity under certain conditions, and a storm at sea yields to it. In Italy a priest and a naked girl go into a field, early in the morning, to drive out caterpillars. When a woman walked naked around a field, caterpillars and all loathesome insects fell dead before her. In Umbria, on the evening of Epiphany, girls go naked to pick a green olive twig, to learn whether they will find husbands. In Russia, at one time, at the baptism of proselytes men and women had to strip naked and before the gathering be totally submerged in a tub or in a ditch. This custom, which was demanded by the church as something immutable, is certainly not adapted to ennobling the in any case lax sense of shame of the Russian men and women."[157]

Krauss[158] describes at length a Slavic ceremony where nudity is coercive. Twelve young men and twelve young women of spotless reputation strip and drag a plow seven times around the village, until the furrow becomes a little ditch; then "the enclosed area is formally consecrated and freed from the pest-woman." The author makes it clear that the ceremony is a solemn and devout one, entirely free from sexual license or incitement.

[153] Conradt, in *Globus*, LXXXI, 351; Frobenius, *Masken*, 135; Ellis, *Tshi*, 226; Ratzel, *Hist. of Mankind*, II, 352; Sibree, *Great Afr. Isl.*, 292.

[154] Bock, *Borneo*, 93. [155] Wirth, in AA, X, 367.

[156] Wilken, in VG, III, 320; §408, below.

[157] Gomme, *Ethnol. in Folklore*, 28, 39; Pliny, *Hist. Nat.*, XXII, ch. 1; XXVIII, ch. 23; Ellis, *Man and Woman*, 262; Lecky, *Europ. Morals*, II, 300; De Gubernatis, *Usi Nuz.*, 29; Stern, *Russland*, 115.

[158] *Südslaven*, 66, 67.

Although these cases are variant and even contradictory, they unite in ascribing to nudity an occult power with respect to the daimons. There are a number of highly sensual religious rites,[159] whose origin is not known, that may at one time have been reversions; the Walpurgisnacht will occur to the reader of mediæval writers or of Goethe.[160] Such rites in their most objectionable form are practices peculiar to sects and, whatever their origin, are of no significance to the present topic. To be noted in connection with any ritual is the fact that, when performed correctly, it seems to exercise a coercion upon the daimons comparable with that of a magical formula and especially, perhaps, of imitative magic. It is related also to the vow.[161]

One other form of coercitive remains to be considered. If cursing and imprecation are not coercitive upon the spiritual powers, they are hard to classify. There is no propitiation about cursing, though antecedent attentions to the daimons may be necessary in order to give the maledictions effect; Apollo, being reminded of the services of Chryses, heeds at once his call for vengeance.[162] Nor is cursing always an appeal to the gods as guarantors of the mores. Nevertheless it regularly inspires lively fear and anticipation on the part of its object, sentiments which go to show that the daimons are likely to bring it to pass. It is as if they were obliged to do so.[163]

"I recollect one amusing incident in which a policeman was sent to hear what certain persons affirmed before a *kithito* [fetish] of particular merit; one wily Mkamba taking the oath added, 'If the policeman does not tell the European truly what we have said let him die,' and the result was that the unfortunate policeman was afraid to tell anything lest by the slightest error he should fall a victim to the oath." In East Africa, "the functions of the elders being both religious and judicial, they exercised powers spiritual and temporal over the people. Of the former order the most commonly known was the cursing of a disobedient person by the elders. This was a very potent curse, but it could be removed again on submission and petition for forgiveness. . . . The elders assembled and a large fire was made, beside which was laid a palm leaf; an elder stood up and proclaimed, 'As this leaf shall wither and the fire burn, so let him wither and die.' . . . The curse was removed through the elders spitting on the victim."[164] Again, a curse, called a *thahu*, affected the hut and the latter had to be demolished unless the imprecation was removed.

159 Mason, *Woman's Share*, 258.   160 *Faust*, pt. I, ll. 3478 ff.
161 §§279, 283, 302, below.   162 Homer, *Iliad*, I, 43 ff.
163 §281, below.
164 Dundas, C., in JAI, XLV, 253, 257-258.

This actually accounts in part for the low type of domestic architecture, for there was small incentive to build well if a *thahu* might fall upon the hut and the owner be obliged to tear it down at any moment.[165]

The jungle Dyak is remarkably honest; during long absences of families things are seldom stolen. "I have not been able to discover any enactment of traditional law which fixes the punishment for theft. It has not been necessary to deal with the subject at all." This is the setting; now what is done if thieving actually occurs? "I have known of only two instances of theft among the Dyaks. One was a theft of rice. The woman who lost the rice most solemnly and publicly cursed the thief, whoever it might be. The next night the rice was secretly left at her door. The other was a theft of money. In this case, too, the thief was cursed. The greater part of the money was afterwards found returned to the box from which it had been abstracted. Both these instances show the great dread the Dyak has of a curse. Even an undeserved curse is considered a terrible thing, and, according to Dyak law, to curse a person for no reason at all is a fineable offence. A Dyak curse is a terrible thing to listen to." The author[166] describes the performance of a woman whose coffee had been stolen. "She began in a calm voice, but worked herself up into a frenzy. We all listened horror-struck, and no one interrupted her. She began by saying what had happened, and how these thefts had gone on for some time. She had said nothing before, hoping that the thief would mend his ways; but the matter had gone on long enough, and she was going to curse the thief, as nothing, she felt sure, would make him give up his evil ways. She called on all the spirits of the waters and the hills and the air to listen to her words and to aid her. She said something of this kind:—

" 'If the thief be a man, may he be unfortunate in all he undertakes! May he suffer from a disease that does not kill him, but makes him helpless— always in pain—and a burden to others. May his wife be unfaithful to him, and his children become as lazy and dishonest as he is himself. If he go out on the war-path, may he be killed and his head smoked over the enemy's fire. If he be out fishing, may an alligator kill him suddenly, and may his relatives never find his body. If he be cutting down a tree in the jungle, may the tree fall on him and crush him to death. May the gods curse his farm so that he may have no crops, and have nothing to eat, and when he begs for food, may he be refused, and die of starvation.' " It will be noted that this curse invokes all the things most terrible to a primitive person, especially in respect to the manner of death; for the forms of dissolution called down upon him mean that he is execrated for the future life as well as for this one. The following curse for the woman-thief, cited by the same author, is equally acute, blasting as it does her hopes for that one supreme dignity of woman, motherhood.

" 'If the thief be a woman, may she be childless, or if she happen to be with child let her be disappointed, and let her child be stillborn, or, better still, let her die in childbirth. May her husband be untrue to her, and despise her and ill-treat her. May her children all desert her if she live to grow old. May she suffer from such diseases as are peculiar to women, and may her eyesight grow dim as the years go on, and may there be no one to help her or lead her about when she is blind.' "

In the case of liars, "the persons deceived start a *tugong bula*—'the liar's

[165] Hobley, in JAI, XLI, 406.
[166] Gomes, *Sea Dyaks*, 63, 64, 65, 66, 67.

mount'—by heaping up a large number of branches in some conspicuous spot by the side of the path from one village to another. Every passerby contributes to it, and at the same time curses the man in memory of whom it is. The Dyaks consider the adding to any *tugong bula* they may pass a sacred duty, the omission of which will meet with supernatural punishment, and so, however pressed for time a Dyak may be, he stops to throw on the pile some branches or twigs." The curse thus becomes a vigorous factor in societal regulation. "It has often been remarked by Dyaks that any other punishment would, if the man had his choice, be much preferred to having a *tugong bula* put up in his memory. Other punishments are soon forgotten, but this remains as a testimony to a man's untruthfulness for succeeding generations to witness, and is a standing disgrace to his children's children. Believing, as the Dyaks do, in the efficacy of curses, it is easy to understand how a Dyak would dread the accumulation of curses which would necessarily accompany the formation of a *tugong bula*. . . . A deep fear of curses, especially from parents, appears in the myths and also in the way of thinking of the historic time. Once spoken, they are an objective force."

Literature is full of this persuasion about curses, and fiction has witnessed to the popular belief by making curses come true.[167] In another set of cases, the curse is pronounced, contingently, against one's self; it calls the daimons to witness that the oath-taker will or will not do this or that; it is often a taboo laid voluntarily upon one's self, and the consequences of dereliction are vividly symbolized. There is here a degree of kinship with the ordeal.[168]

"It is difficult to find an oath that the average Sema, or at any rate many Semas, will not take recklessly and indiscriminately, except oaths of such weight that guilty and innocent alike hesitate to take them. Such an oath is the oath on the water of the Tapu (Dayang) river. No man who took a false oath on that water could ever cross the river or even enter it again, for it would certainly drown him, nor could he eat fish from the river during his whole life or he would die of it for sure. But then a man whose cause is really just will usually shy at taking this oath, for it is not a thing to be lightly undertaken, and the writer has known men content to lose their cause rather than take oath to its truth, even when there could have been little or no doubt but that they had the right on their side. The oath, too, on a village spring is another serious matter. . . . Oaths regarding ownership of land are taken on the earth in dispute, which is bitten and swallowed. So also is the earth from a grave, while the oath on one's own flesh, though sometimes merely entailing biting one's finger, sometimes also, if great emphasis is desired, entails the swallowing of one's own flesh. The writer has seen a man accused of murder (and undoubtedly guilty) chop off the end of his forefinger and swallow it to add force to his asseverations of innocence. Oaths are also taken on a tiger's tooth. And this form of oath is very popular with perjurers, as tigers are

167 Kipling, *Courting of Dinah Shadd*, 30-33.
168 §183, above.

becoming so scarce that no one is afraid of being carried off if he bites the tooth on a false oath. . . . A rare but serious form of oath is that by cutting iron, which if a man do falsely, members of his clan die off without apparent cause, such is the power of the metal when treated disrespectfully. The writer has known a man come into court with a . . . bit of umbrella wire prepared to take this oath." . . . A certain man is mentioned who had to desert his house and site and build a fresh one in another place because in a fit of temper he had cut a bit of iron in his house.[169]

In the Indian Archipelago, the commonest way of taking oath is by the drinking of a little water in which certain articles are placed. All of these have a symbolic significance; salt, a piece of wax, a bullet, a knife or other cutting tool. The idea is that as the salt melts in the water, the wax in the fire, so the perjurer will waste away; that he will not die a natural death but lose his life by a bullet or weapon. In the Moluccas they do not speak of swearing an oath but of drinking an oath. Swearing is also called "salt-drinking."[170] In Sumatra swearing is done upon certain implements and articles that are thought to have a supernatural power. "They consist of an old rusty kris, a broken gun-barrel, or any ancient trumpery, to which chance or caprice has annexed an idea of extraordinary virtue. This they generally dip in water, which the person who swears drinks off." This author,[171] as well as the preceding one, offers a number of cases. "The taking of oaths with the peoples of the Indian Archipelago consists chiefly in this: that the persons who take the oath utter a curse upon themselves and symbolize it by some action." Thus the Bataks cut up a frog, the Nias Islanders a pig, and the Dyaks decapitate a hen, as symbolical of the lot which they, in case of perjury, call down on themselves. Sometimes fern-leaves are stripped off while taking oath.[172]

The case is rather fully worked out in Homer.[173] Taking oath is called "cutting sacred oaths"; to take an oath was to "give the gods" to each other, for they were the best guardians of agreements. The form of oath was a calling of the gods to witness; and a penalty was usually attached to perjury in the form of a curse, pronounced upon himself by the one taking oath. A man might swear by his own head, his son, or his scepter. This is the general form of oath between man and man; the deities ordinarily called upon were those of the spirit-world who punished oath-breakers. The gods, in their own swearing, also called upon the older gods, especially upon the Titans, and upon the river Styx, the latter being the greatest oath possible to immortals. As the Styx was symbolic of death, and the Titans of power that had passed away, probably this oath was one which staked both power and immortality. A guest might swear by his host's hearth and hospitality, and oaths were sometimes accompanied with libation.

The most important social agreement calling for oaths was the conclusion of a quarrel or war: a reconciliation or a truce. Ceremonies in connection with such oaths had some features peculiar to themselves. When Agamemnon and Achilles were reconciled, and the former swore that Briseis had not been violated while in his possession, the ceremony was thought important enough to be worthy of a special victim, a boar. Hairs were cut from the animal, and

---

[169] Hutton, *Sema Nagas*, 164-166.   [170] Wilken, in VG, II, 498-499.
[171] Marsden, *Sumatra*, 242.   [172] Wilken, *Vkde.*, 469 ff.
[173] The following is adapted somewhat from Keller, *Hom. Soc.*, 175 ff., where full references to the Homeric text are given.

prayers was made to Zeus by the son of Atreus; the rest "kept silence fit-
tingly, listening to the king." First, he called Zeus, Earth, Sun, and the Erinyes
to witness that what he had said was true, and then cursed himself if it were
not so. The throat of the victim was cut, but the flesh was not burned; it was
hurled into the sea "as food for the fish." No fire is mentioned; evidently the
boar symbolized in some degree the quarrel whose ill-feeling was now to be
cast away and annihilated.

Oath-ceremonies sometimes took on a still greater social import. The "sacred
oaths" of truce were of this variety. In the oath-ceremonies preceding the
great truce of the *Iliad,* the victims were to be three in number; from the
Trojan side, two lambs, one light-coloured male for the Sun, and one dark
female for the Earth. The Greeks were to furnish one for Zeus. The truce was
to be concluded by Priam, as the most illustrious of the Trojans in age and
honor; an old man was needed, in so solemn an affair, who could perform
or oversee the ceremony correctly, for "the minds of the youth are unstable,
but the old man from his wide experience plans the best." All gathered about
the kings while the heralds led in the victims and mixed wine. Water was
poured over the hands of the princes, and Agamemnon, with his sacrificial
knife, cut hairs from the heads of the victims, which were distributed to all
the noblest of the Greeks and Trojans. Agamemnon then prayed, lifting up his
hands, to Sun, Earth, and Rivers, and to the gods of the spirit-world who were
wont to punish oath-breakers, invoking them to guard the truce of which they
were witnesses, and to fulfil the conditions of the ordeal-trial about to take
place. The throats of the lambs were then cut with the copper knife carried
always by the king, wine was drawn and distributed, and, as they poured it
out upon the earth, the members of both armies cursed the truce-breaker and
all his family: "May their brains run out upon the ground as does this wine."
The victims, or at least two of them, were then carried back to Ilion, probably
to be buried there after the manner of the foundation-sacrifice.

Although an oath-ceremony, as the last example shows, may
approach the sacrificial form, most oaths are unaccompanied by
anything interpretable as propitiation. It would seem that it was
coercive on the spirits, in event of perjury or non-fulfilment, to
bring to pass the consequences invoked by the oath-taker; the daimons, when called to witness, must uphold agreements of this sort
in their capacity as guarantors of the mores or the precedents.
Without the security that oaths would be kept no society could
persist, and if it did not, its gods would disappear along with it;
it is thus to the maintenance-interest of the daimons, as it were, to
punish at the call of the curse. In the case of an anti-social practice, then, such act becomes a sin which the gods, having their
attention called to it by a curse, have no choice but to punish. It
must be recalled, however, that this covers only part of the case;
for curses are far too indiscriminate to be assembled under any

one category. They are not uttered solely against practices inexpedient for societal welfare.

Many of the phenomena of daimonology exhibit coercitive elements or a coercitive tinge: self-immolation, self-mutilation, asceticism, abstinence, continence, cleanliness or uncleanliness, and a number of others.[174] This set of ideas runs out at last into all ritual and magical theories of rites, sacrifices, fasting, prayer, vows, and sacraments. Coercion is plainly one of the major phases of daimonology, along with the avoidance, exorcism, and propitiation to which it is related. The grand case of coercion is magic. It is, however, a sort of extra-cult phenomenon, better understood after the cult has been reviewed in all its aspects. It is sufficiently developed and complicated to require a chapter for itself; along with shamanism, which also is reserved for separate treatment, it amounts to a sort of synopsis of the whole subject of religion. For these several reasons we have chosen, before considering magic, to complete the study of the cult by moving at once to a consideration of its positive or propitiatory aspects.

[174] §§279, 282, above.

CHAPTER XXXIII

PROPITIATION

§278. Nature of Propitiation. The type of daimonology farthest removed from the avoidance of the spirits is the winning of the higher powers to man's side through conciliation or propitiation. The sense of propitiation rests squarely upon the original and inevitable conception of the nature of the daimons, namely, that they are anthropomorphic; having the origin they do, it could not be otherwise than that they should be made in man's image. The abundant evidence as to their anthropomorphic quality renders their derivation through animism about as conclusive as any theory concerning institutional development can be. It follows that to conciliate and propitiate them the procedure must be like that employed to win over fellow-men, in particular the important and powerful. This is the broadest consideration behind the positive developments of the cult; if it is kept steadily in mind, much that would otherwise remain confused falls into order and perspective.

The case of the propitiatory cult is simplified somewhat by the fact that the consistently good spirits generally do not come into it. It is only the evil spirits, or the good ones in evil mood, that demand propitiation; for they will cause calamity unless bought off in some way. Considerable development is called for before people arrive at the idea of a consistently benevolent god. The connection of this conviction with the attitude taken toward the aleatory element[1] is unmistakable: while men hope for good luck, they are truly preoccupied with the question of how to avoid ill luck. Misfortune will come of itself unless something is done to prevent it, whereas fortune will not arrive unless something is done to bring it. Propitiation, in fact, is rather a mode of dodging great ill fortune through acquiescing in an endurable, recurring present loss than it is a deliberate policy of getting good luck. It is insurance rather than investment. Thus viewed, all cult-activities are seen, once more, to be fundamentally negative in character—all of them

---

[1] §196, above.

basically avoidance-policies. Nowhere does this come out more clearly than in the fact that it is the power for ill which has to be conciliated and propitiated, that is, bought off or bribed.

It is to be noted in the cases that the line between coercion and conciliation is not hard and fast; in fact, avoidance, exorcism, coercion, and propitiation merge into one another. Consider a typical case of transition.

Certain of the Bantu "regard their god as the creator of man, plants, animals, and the earth, and they hold that having made them, he takes no further interest in the affair. But not so the crowd of spirits with which the universe is peopled, they take only too much interest and the Bantu wishes they would not and is perpetually saying so in his prayers, a large percentage whereof amounts to 'Go away, we don't want you.' 'Come not unto this house, this village, or its plantations.' He knows from experience that the spirits pay little heed to these objurgations, and as they are the people who must be attended to, he develops a cult whereby they may be managed, used, and understood."[2]

This case might be considered as transitional from exorcism to coercion. Nudity, again, though it seems to be generally coercitive, is often interpretable as propitiatory, for the daimons get satisfaction out of the sight of human misery, humiliation, and self-discipline. Borderline cases are always in evidence between the types that can be distinguished.

Among certain backward savages it is believed "that the Supreme Spirit is the embodiment of good, and yet in the same breath they will tell you that He becomes angry and needs that His anger should be appeased either by incantations or the sacrifice of human beings." Again there is a "confused notion of good and evil spirits," with a sort of general propitiation prior to any undertaking.[3] In South Africa there is a strong belief in the power of spirits to injure or aid; and a conviction that they must be kept in a good humor.[4] Evil spirits, sometimes of ancestors or kings, are propitiated; the good ones are so good that they do not need attention.[5] Miniature huts are built for the former, so they will not enter the huts of the people.[6] Again, good deeds—adherence to the mores—mark the "just" man, and if they do not win anything they insure against loss. A venerable African chief stood in the open street, addressing the spirits of the air "and begged them, 'Come ye not into my town'; he then recounted his good deeds, praising himself as good, just, honest, kind to his neighbors, etc. This man had not been in touch with Europeans, so that his ideal of goodness was a native one, which can be found everywhere among the

[2] Kingsley, *Travels W. Afr.*, 442.
[3] Hardy and Elkington, *S. Seas*, 126; Williams, in J AI, XXVII, 345.
[4] Fritsch, *Eingeb. S.-Afr.*, 57.
[5] Schmidt, *Deut. Kol.*, II, 166, 242, 244.
[6] Junker, *Afrika*, II, 124-125; Burns, in *Wide World Mag.*, I, 478.

most remote West Coast natives. He urged these things as a reason why no evil should befall him and closed with an impassioned appeal to the spirits to stay away."[7]

"In the case of smallpox, the universal scourge of Korean childhood, the daemon is treated with the utmost respect." The priest is called in "to honor the arrival of the spirit with a feast and fitting ceremonial. Little or no work is done, and if there are neighbors whose children have not had the malady, they rest likewise, lest, displeased with their lack of respect, he should deal hardly with them."[8]

In the Indian hills there are spirits of the village, of the family or clan, residing in trees, of the household, of the fields, and of specific spots in the air, streams, jungles, and hills. Of these, "none can bestow blessings, but all are prone to do damage and inflict loss and suffering: therefore they must be propitiated by sacrifices."[9] The perils of the climbers of the palmyra-palm are great and there are many fatal accidents from falls; they have, therefore, a religious ceremonial at the beginning of the sugar-producing season. "Bishop Caldwell adopted the custom, and a solemn service in church was held, when one set of all the implements used in the occupation of palmyra-climbing was brought to the church, and presented at the altar. . . . A religious service of the kind was particularly acceptable and peculiarly appropriate to our people."[10] Here was effected a skilful adjustment of the missionary religion to local mores.

"The Dyak's feeling toward prominent members of the snake tribe is more than reverential. . . . The python and cobra are the snakes generally selected by the spirits for their habitation"; but not all the snakes are thus regarded as fetishes—"only individuals which have become known as spirit-possessed through dreams, or inference from other signs. . . . In a certain case a python came at night and astonished the community by swallowing one of their pigs. This bold attack was thought to mean that they had been guilty of neglect of duty to his spiritship; so with all haste an offering was prepared, and laid out on the floor of the house, the snake, gorged with the pig, being still underneath; some words of entreaty and submission were said, and lo! the beast vomited up the pig, thereby affording indubitable proof that their view of the case was right! They then managed to secure it in a bambu cage. . . . A company afterwards took it into the jungle, where they offered it another sacrifice, and then freed it."[11] This case is full of details recalling fetishistic and other tenets; the inference as to the peril of neglect or sin is a regular one. The Sea Dyaks, for another instance, strive to get themselves into a sort of "state of grace" by staging a general confession before a kidnapping or head-hunting foray; infringement of the recognized marriage-system is thus detected and punished.[12]

The Eskimo's thoughts are always bent upon treating the sea-mammals in such a way that they may allow themselves to be caught; they form one of the main subjects of his religious beliefs and customs. "The mother of the sea-mammals may be considered the principal deity of the Central Eskimo. She has supreme sway over the destinies of mankind, and almost all the observances of these tribes are for the purpose of retaining her good-will or of

[7] Kingsley, *Travels W. Afr.*, 452.　　[8] Bishop, *Korea*, 413.
[9] Carey and Tuck, *Chin Hills*, I, 195.　　[10] Thurston, *S. India*, 359-360.
[11] Roth, *Sarawak*, I, 187.　　[12] Bock, *Borneo*, 218.

propitiating her if she has been offended."[13] The sense of danger has not only developed the social structure of the Omaha tribe and given the warrior a position of vital importance, "but it seems to have been equally potent in stimulating the growth of religious observances. A feeling of insecurity and of dependence lay beneath them all."[14]

The need of keeping up an unremitting propitiation is evidenced in the matter of sins of omission.[15] The faults hitherto considered have been almost wholly those of commission: something wrong has been done; some taboo broken. But even if a man were guiltless of sins of commission, he would not be safe; to keep the daimons well-disposed it is not enough merely to refrain, by staying within the taboo, from doing what they prohibit. It is also necessary to perform positive cult-obligations and to incur no guilt by reason of omissions; for the daimons have might-supported rights that root ultimately in the supposed needs of the ghosts. Neglect of these obligations—omission to do something positive—is as much sin as is the transgression of the taboo.

The notion of sin has undergone an enormous change of sense, says Lippert,[16] in the course of time. A start is made with the belief that the dead torment the living; then the latter seek by rites of various sorts to evade or repel the annoyance, or to conciliate the ill-disposed ghost. According to the early notion of worship the living owe these rites to the dead and it is sin and guilt to fail in them. The idea that sin entails death is the abstract and sublimated expression of the crude, original notion that the unconciliated dead will kill the living who have failed in their duties. In the Bible the original sin is expressly presented as a violation of the oldest sacrifice of renunciation.

Whatever the nature of the sin, whether of commission or of omission, there was but one recourse for the sinner if he were to evade or lessen the penalty: conciliation or propitiation.

The Homeric case is typical. "In connection with regular offerings come reparation-sacrifices, in consequence of sin. Sin was the violation of any one of the multitudinous rights of the gods; failure in sacrifice and the like, or transgression against any of the norms of life which had received the sanction of the superior powers. The oncoming of a sudden and great calamity enabled one to deduce at once the fact of sin; all evil was due to sin. One who had transgressed was no longer justified with the gods, and was exposed to endless

---

13 Boas, in PSM, LVII, 624, 626.   14 Fletcher, in JAI, XXVII, 437.
15 §274, above.   16 *Kgchte.*, I, 105.

misfortune; the only course to pursue was to find out at once which god was angry, and then to make all efforts to appease that wrath and to justify one's self." Sin was a matter entirely of form; no repentent frame of mind was required. "The gods were not inexorable, and rich reparation and praise procured instant justification. The sin of one man, especially of an important man, might descend upon a whole community and make it unclean, in which case reparation was made by the community."[17] For some reason unknown, "either because he was careless or forgetful," Oineus made the grave error of omitting Artemis when he was sacrificing to all the gods; and she despatched a wild boar that devastated his rich orchards and vineyards. Further, "in the hunt for this boar a cumulation of woe arose from the anger of the offended goddess, which led to a destructive war."[18]

A few representative cases of sin followed by reparation and propitiation, taken from accounts of more primitive societies, will serve to fill out the conception.

It is an offense against the totem, resented as the members of a secret society resent the disregard of their esoteric symbol, if an Australian woman sees blood drawn in a quarrel. And so the man whose blood is first shed usually performs a ceremony by way of reconciliation.[19] Among the Dyaks, "rice is strewn on the dead man's chest. This is a propitiation to the gods for any wrong he may have done when alive. According to Dyak ideas, death is the punishment for some sin, and for that sin some sacrifice must be made, or the living may also suffer for it. By sin is meant either the doing of any of the thousand and one things which a Dyak considers forbidden by the gods, or the disregarding of the warnings of birds or dreams." "In cases where propitiation for sin is the esoteric basis of the institution, e.g., in the slaying of sacrifice after an act of adultery, the thoughts of the Dyak are not directed to the cleansing of the offenders, but to the appeasing of the anger of the gods, in order to preserve their land and crops from blight and ravage. . . . If it rain continually day after day, and week after week, and there is no promise of continued fine weather, the Sea Dyaks are apt to imagine that some impurity has defiled the tribe and that the face of the Great Spirit is hid from them. So the elders go to work to find it out, and adjudicate on all cases of incest and bigamy, and purify the earth with the blood of pigs. Prayers are offered . . . from one end of the country to the other; for the space of three days the villages are tabued and all labor discontinued; the inhabitants remain at home and strangers are not admitted." Again certain Dyaks found the reason for daimonic displeasure in the acts of an unmarried man and woman who were living together. A party went under the house with gongs to drive away the spirits, and the man and woman were put on a raft, with a pig, and set afloat on the river. They jumped off and swam ashore, but the pig disappeared down the rapids.[20] Here we have the sanction of the mores by the spirits, and also

[17] Keller, *Hom. Soc.*, 125-126 (where all references are cited).

[18] *Iliad*, IX, 536 ff.; Keller, *Hom. Soc.*, 135.

[19] Spencer and Gillen, *Nat. Tr. Cent. Aust.*, 463; Codrington, *Melanesians*, 216.

[20] Gomes, *Sea Dyaks*, 134; Roth, *Sarawak*, I, 191, 401; Nieuwenhuis, *Borneo*, II, 136.

a combination of exorcism and propitiation. "Almost the sole object of the religious ceremonies of the Eskimo is to appease the wrath of Sedna [the mother of the sea-mammals, alluded to above], of the souls of animals, or the souls of the dead, that have been offended by the transgressions of taboos."[21]

§279*. **Ritual.** When there appears at the end of a list of sins, "the non-performance of religious rites,"[22] that amounts to a sort of unspecified residue or miscellany, including many and important items. Incorrect performance, furthermore, is a delinquency scarcely less serious than omission itself. Whatever the nature of a religious exercise, whether propitiatory or other, it must be done aright. The rites must be right. To secure the hearing and favor of the daimons is something like the opening of a combination-lock: it is not sufficient to make approximately the right number of turns to left or right—it is necessary to make exactly the right number, or the whole procedure is futile. Similarly with religious ritual: the results are not attainable unless the traditional forms are scrupulously followed. In fact, the daimons are so wedded to those forms that they are as disquieted and angered by error as any imperious earthly sovereign by a blunder in court-etiquette; and the daimons, when irritated, are wont to lash out without measure, visiting the same severity of punishment upon the unwitting peccadillo as upon a deliberate, heinous sin. It is true, too, that if the ritual is correct it seems to exert a coercitive influence upon the daimons; it becomes fetishistic like a magical formula.[23] Vinogradoff,[24] referring to the swearing of oaths, states that "the swearer was to pronounce a formula which was supposed to call forth the action of divine Power, so that truth might be made known and untruth detected. . . . These formulae were occasionally very intricate, and a slip of the tongue was taken as a sign of divine interference to disclose the falsehood of an assertion." Hence the absolute need of exactitude in ritual; hence also the need of a trained and leisure class that can make a business of its correct performance. If ritual is simple, as in Homer, the need of intermediaries is not felt;[25] if it is so long and complicated that,

21 Boas, in PSM, LVII, 630.   22 Phillips, *Vedas*, 154.
23 §301, below.   24 *Hist. Jurispr.*, I, 349.
25 Keller, *Hom. Soc.*, 145 ff.

in his engrossment with toil and his ensuing weariness, the common man cannot be sure of mastering it, the priest is indispensable.

We are treating of ritual under the general topic of propitiation, because we conceive of most cases of ritual as propitiatory; however, the necessity of performing rites in the correct manner applies generally. Our list of cases will contain examples of exorcistic and coercitive ritual as well as propitiatory; and in some of the instances the types will be mixed or uncertain. There is one essential element which all forms of ritual must exhibit. It comes out in drawing the distinction between liturgy, mere ceremonial, and true ritual. A liturgy is only an established form of procedure. The order of exercises of a legislative body is liturgical; there are rubrics to prescribe what shall be done and formulas to be recited at various stages. Ceremonial is a looser form of procedure. What the man and woman say and do in the wedding-ceremony is convention and is important only for that reason, not for its rational content. If a woman is not willing to promise to obey, that makes no difference; it is only a formula and what is being done is understandable enough without it. The effect would be the same if the established custom were that when a man and a woman joined hands and said together, "Abracadabra," that should be a wedding. Ritual, however, means set actions and words[26] which have "virtue" and are effective to produce results. If the priest says, "By virtue of what you have done, I declare that you are man and wife," that is liturgical. If he says, "By virtue of my sacerdotal character and authority I join you in marriage," that is ritual. An English coronation is liturgical; a Russian coronation was ritualistic because, when the ecclesiastic had poured oil upon the prospective Tzar's head, the latter was made a different man from what he had been, namely, a fetish-man. That did not mean a functionary, but a man different from all other men as well as from his former self. All orthodox Russians would now obey him as a religious duty because he was now the "Little Father," authorized by God to command. If they obeyed him before he was anointed, that was a concession, not on account of his divine authority. Of course the pouring of oil on a man's head has no

---

26 §252, above.

effect upon his character or ability and so does not give him rational authority.

There is always an irrational, fetishistic element in ritual. It implies an operation which has an irrational, occult effect; there is no true causal relation between the act and its supposed consequence. The priest or ritual-specialist is a fetish-man discharging functions proper to his status. The origin of all ritual is in ghost-fear; rites are such performances as persuade or coerce the superior powers to avert their harmful interposition. As ritual is the only means of creating or changing jural relations when written records are not yet in easy and current use, it appears in law as much as in religion. To strike the scales with a coin, to hand over a sod with a sprig set up in it, to raise the hand in oath, to hold or kiss the Bible, are usually described as symbolic acts. They are really ritual. Such doings are definitive and irrevocable; they are actually performed and witnessed; they are acts, not negotiation. Other symbols used in ceremony very often have the same effect, as would be readily seen had not the modern use of oral statements and written records done away with symbolism and ritual to such an extent that the sense of them is lost to us. When they are understood, they always have a great effect upon the reason and conscience through the senses.[27]

Of ritual as connected with the attainment of possession Bartels[28] says: "We have to conceive of it as a religious act of purgation, as a solemn preparation of the human body for the reception of the immortal godhood, quite similar to the way in which one prepares himself by strict fasting when he wishes to come into a nearer relation to the gods."

This book is full of cases of ritual; it occurs in connection with property, marriage, sacrifice and other cult-operations, shamanism, law, and government. Cases here cited are designed to bring out the scrupulous care taken to have the rites correct and invariable. It must be borne in mind, of course, that complicated ritual belongs rather to evolved than to primitive forms of the cult.

There is a certain place in which the king of Angoy, in Angola, has to stay just previous to being crowned. "But if there, by chance, a fly settles upon his body, he will die very soon, and in any case the value of all the preceding ceremonies is null and worthless, and he must begin them all over again, to-

27 Sumner, "Mod. Marriage," in *Yale Rev.*, XIII, 249 ff.
28 *Medicin*, 122.

gether with all the accompanying costs—if, after the disappointment of half a lifetime, he holds firmly to the purpose of attaining the crown. Generally the candidates come to grief even earlier, since the severe prohibitions whose transgression would nullify all that went before, increase from step to step, as do likewise the costs."[29]

India is a country full of interminable ceremonial. People are preoccupied with the terrors of bad luck, the evil eye, and daimonic influence in general, and are always practising protective rites. Rites are conceived as alone maintaining life and making and sustaining society. Formulas are reiterated endlessly. Alms-giving is a rite, not to relieve poverty but to store up rite-credits.[30] "The gods live by sacrifice: 'the sun would not rise if the priest did not make sacrifice.' . . . Even the order of things would change if the order of ceremonial were varied: night would be eternal if the priests did so and so; the months would not pass, one following the other, if the priests walked out or entered together. . . . As dependent as is man on what is given by the gods, so dependent are the gods on what is offered to them by men. . . . Even the gods are now not native to heaven. They win heaven by sacrifice, by metres. . . . What, then, is sacrifice? A means to enter into the godhead of the gods, and even to control the gods; a ceremony where every word was pregnant with consequences; every movement momentous. . . . It is sufficient to understand that according to the house-ritual and the law-ritual, for every change in life there was an appropriate ceremony and a religious observance." Of the sacraments alone, such as investiture with the sacred cord, there were forty. "The pious householder who had once set up his own fire, that is, got married, must have spent most of his time, if he followed directions, in attending to some religious ceremony. He had several little rites to attend to even before he might say his prayers in the morning; and since even to-day most of these personal regulations are dutifully observed, one may assume that in the full power of Brahmanhood they were very strictly enforced."[31]

"Brahmans have assured me, and I have no reason for doubting their truthfulness in this matter, that if they perform their daily religious rites properly, at least two hours in the morning and the same time in the evening would be fully occupied with them; and an hour or so in the middle of the day should also be devoted to similar work." "Each man finds himself cribbed and confined in all his movements, bound and fettered in all he does by minute traditional regulations. He sleeps and wakes, dresses and undresses, sits down and stands up, goes out and comes in, eats and drinks, speaks and is silent, acts and refrains from acting, according to ancient rule."[32]

In Ceylon, "should a charmer make even a slight mistake during the performance of a 'serious' charming ceremony (i.e., a ceremony for which he has summoned the 'sight' of powerful and malignant devils), he renders himself liable to an immediate attack by the devils he has called upon, resulting in serious injury and perhaps in death. It is for this reason that the mantras for such ceremonies must be learned by heart, and not read from a book during the performance, since in reading a mistake may easily be made. A charmer prefers to learn from an old book rather than from a new one, because there

[29] Bastian, *Deut. Exped.*, I, 220-221.
[30] Lippert, *Kgchte.*, II, 271, 447, 449.
[31] Hopkins, *Relig. India*, 187, 188, 245, 246.
[32] Wilkins, *Hinduism*, 195; Monier-Williams, *Brāhmanism*, 352, 393.

is a smaller chance of errors, due to copying, in the former."[33] This is a case of magic, but whatever is said about magical ritual is applicable to that which is distinguished as genuinely religious. In Samoa, "all listened carefully to the enunciation of this prayer by the priest, for if he was observed to *stutter* in a single word it was a bad omen."[34] In New Zealand, "a dour, tattooed, white moustached old warrior died suddenly . . . in 1900, shortly after performing the ceremony of . . . removing the *tapu* from a newly-built carved house. His death was by some of his people attributed to his having inadvertently committed what is known as a *whati*, that is an omission or mistake in repeating some of the incantations, and also to . . . the exercise of the 'black art,' by a rival *tohunga*."[35] Thus the Polynesian ritual must be performed correctly or it is worse than of no account; and the American Indian ceremonies call for the same exactitude.[36]

The extreme complexity of ritual is to be found among more developed peoples; the Chinese have ritualized ceremonial, religious and other, to an extraordinary degree, and even have a textbook dating from about 200 A.D. in which their regulations are assembled.[37] In China, ritual grows up in the soil of ghost-fear and issues in self-gratification. It interlocks with self-maintenance; for instance, no one collects a debt without accepting a formal cup of tea from the debtor. If he should refuse the tea the debtor would decline to pay the debt.[38] An Assyrian text prays that the enemy's ritual may go wrong and fail. "May the lips of the priest's son hurry and stumble over a word." Farnell[39] comments: "The idea seems to be that a single slip in the ritual-formulae destroyed their whole value." In the Egyptian sacrificial meal, the first requirement was absolute cleanliness. The ceremony was regulated to its utmost details, and accompanied by formulas which must be recited with absolute exactitude of tone and movement, or else the sacrifice was null. The god was bound by a kind of contract that if all this was done correctly he would be propitious. If it was not properly performed the sacrifice passed to the temple, but secured nothing. Hence the immense responsibility of the priest to the worshippers; for, as the prince could not maintain the necessary dexterity, the priests must make a profession of it, cultivating the necessary cleanliness of person, skill of voice, etc., in a great hierarchy.[40]

Tullus, in trouble, tried to pacify Jove, but the rite he used was not correctly begun or carried out; as a consequence he and his house were struck by lightning and burned to ashes, for Jove was exasperated at being approached with improper ceremonial.[41] By due rites there could be secured, out of a world full of spirits, one which could be evoked for any service. The Romans set one over each function; hence the *indigetes*, or spirits with vocations. But the all-essential matter was the rites.[42] In the Church the host was not consecrated if "Hoc est corpus meum" was not correctly pronounced.[43]

[33] Hildburgh, in JAI, XXXVIII, 156.

[34] Turner, *Samoa*, 28.   [35] Cowan, *Maoris*, 118.

[36] Moerenhout, *Voyages*, I, 502 ff.; Boas, in USNM, 1895, 443 ff.; Fewkes, in BAE, XIX, 1006.

[37] Legge, *Li Ki*.

[38] Personally communicated by Dr. Harvey.

[39] *Greece and Babylon*, 297; Maspero, *Hist. Anc.*, III, 208-209.

[40] Maspero, *Hist. Anc.*, I, 122.   [41] Livy, I, ch. XXXI.

[42] Lippert, *Kgchte.*, II, 270, 271; Rossbach, *Röm. Ehe*, 126-127.

[43] Clodd, *Magic*, 139; this author cites several cases.

The Turks wash themselves from the fingers up to the elbow and from the toes to the ankles; the Persians contrariwise. The Turks wash first the right and then the left arm in ritual; also the right and then the left foot. The nose may not be blown using the right hand. In Islam every movement was executed with military precision.[44]

The preceding paragraph refers to the ritualistic bearing of right and left. There is fetish in these terms and they figure largely in omens and divination.[45] "This venerable division is still retained when we speak of a *sinister* portent, or a *right* judgment."[46]

In the Himalayan region there are piles of stone on the mountain-passes which are invariably kept on the right by travellers in token of respect. "This is an old-world custom which still survives in the West, where it is considered the 'lucky-way.' Thus it is practiced in stirring the Christmas puddings, etc., in passing the wine at table, from right to left; in cattle treading the corn in this direction; and among the Scotch Highlanders, in walking thrice in this way around those to whom they wish well, 'to make the deazel,' as it is called."[47] There was also a Hindu funeral-rite of circumambulation with the left shoulder toward the revered object.[48] The fire should be kept to the right in circumambulation; also a mound, a cow, a Brahman, clarified butter, honey, a crossway, a well-known tree. "The sun, the moon, and the stars show their reverence for the holy mountain by moving about it to the right."[49] Dextral and sinistral circuits were made by the Osages, always with scrupulous ceremonial.[50] "This distinction between left and right was of the utmost importance among the Chaldæans, and among the Greeks it is further witnessed in several ceremonies of serving, drinking, etc., where the custom of passing the cup toward the right was scrupulously maintained."[51] Roman circumambulation, in weddings as in funerals, was always from left to right.[52] It was the fashion in the sixteenth and seventeenth century, as in modern military usage, to keep the superior on the right.[53]

A sacrament may be taken to mean a solemn ritual, effective for a religious upbuilding toward a religious ideal. The term has been applied, although in a somewhat strained and figurative sense, to many forms of marriage; the Council of Trent anathematized

[44] Thevenot, *Voyages*, I, 148, 150, in Stoll, *Geschlechtsleben*, 279, 280; Hauri, *Islam*, 255.

[45] §§255, 267, above, and 313, below. [46] Brinton, *Relig. Sent.*, 184.

[47] Waddell, *Himalayas*, 115; Waddell, *Buddhism*, 287, 420; Francke, in *Globus*, LXXVIII, 223-224.

[48] Monier-Williams, *Brāhmanism*, 303.

[49] Bühler, *Manu*, II, 48; Holtzmann, *Ind. Sagen*, II, 42, 94, 102, 198, 268, 269, 319.

[50] Dorsey, in AA, IV, 405, 408. [51] Keller, *Hom. Soc.*, 156.

[52] Rossbach, *Röm. Ehe*, 109, 315, 316. [53] Denecke, *Anstandsgefühl*, xxv.

anyone who should deny that marriage was one of the seven sacraments established by Jesus in the Gospels.[54] Here was a strain to make marriage holy. Cannibalism or its survivals may be sacramental; for such ceremony is conceived to make sacred and to save from the degradation of sin, nature, evil, baseness, into some ideal of a superior condition.[55] The Australian totem-sacrament meant such union with the ancestral spirits that direct control was won over the food-supply.[56] Foot-washing may be sacramental, as in the case of the Dunkards, though the example in Scripture seems not to have occasioned a church-sacrament. A vow may be taken sacramentally; initiation-ceremonies are often typically sacramental, and primitive secret societies make use of this sort of ritual.[57]

Sixteen Hindu sacraments are cited: conception, male-bearing, pregnancy, birth-ceremony, naming-ceremony, taking the child out of doors, feeding with rice, shaving, thread-girdling, cutting of the hair, studying the four Vedas (each forming a separate sacrament), returning from the preceptor's house, and marriage.[58] The marriage-ceremony is the Vedic sacrament for woman just as the initiation with sacred texts is for man.[59] The bride is, in one district, "not allowed to enter her new home until she and her husband eat rice boiled in milk; and to illustrate the sacramental conception of this meal, we find that the Dhobi youth does not eat boiled rice until he tastes it for the first time at his own wedding feast, and the Sansya and Majhwar bride after her home-coming has to cook for the kinsfolk of her husband, while among the Masahars new fire is solemnly made for the cooking sacrament."[60]

The Navaho have a ceremony like the sacrament for the sick; the god-masks and other paraphernalia are watched through the fourth night of a nine days' ceremony.[61] Savages have often developed the sacramental eating of dough images in human form, so that the Catholic fathers have been scandalized to find wafers and cakes utilized in a manner so nearly parallel to their own usages that they have concluded that "the devil mimics the Catholic Church."[62] A gruesome Greek ceremony involved the eating by unwitting participants of the vitals of a murdered man and the drinking of his blood in wine; this magically united them with the dead man.[63]

54 Holtzmann, in *Arch. f. Religw.*, VII, 58 ff.

55 §§300, 301, and ch. XXXVII, below.

56 §260, above.

57 §163, above; on sacraments in general, see Frazer, *Golden Bough*, II, 318 ff.

58 Nathubhai, in JASB, III, 394; Risley, *Eth. Ind.*, I, 112.

59 Bühler, *Manu*, II, 27, 28, 67.   60 Crooke, in JAI, XXVIII, 241.

61 Mathews, in AA, IX, 50.

62 Jevons, *Relig.*, 214 ff.; Frazer, *Golden Bough*, II, 318 ff.; Lippert, *Kgchte.*, II, 275 ff.; Loeb, *Human Sacr.*

63 Burckhardt, *Griech. Kgchte.*, I, 213.

Ritual develops easily into drama. There can be no doubt that the great bulk of primitive stage-performances was religious in nature;[64] the fact that the plays represent the acting out of myths is in no wise inconsistent with the contention. Myth and ritual are closely related, though the former is often erroneously assumed to be the cause of the latter. "While many cases can be shown in which a myth has been invented to explain a rite, it would be hard to point to a single case in which a myth has given rise to a rite. Ritual may be the parent of myth, but can never be its child."[65]

§280*. Renunciation. The cult includes several practices which, though they are thought to please the daimons and make them propitious, yet call for the offer of no actual gifts or bribes. These are fasting, continence, self-discipline, and ascetic practices in general; and they constitute the sacrifice of renunciation. We have referred so often to the pleasure the spirits are conceived to take in human lack and misery that we scarcely need to do so again; even very primitive people seem to have felt what, in a more developed form, the Greeks called the envy of the gods.

If the aleatory element is in the hands of the daimons, then men are only the sport of malevolent powers. Often enough life has looked like that, and it still bears such aspect on occasion; for a series of strokes of bad luck may be so grotesquely ruinous that men can believe with difficulty that they merely "happened"; it seems as if some very superior intelligence were needed to secure such perfection of mischief-making. Particularly is one subject to change of fortune when he is happy; to have been lucky for a long period is to be in great peril of a reversal. From the day of legend down, men have become uneasy when favored by fortune. Even the child seems to feel that to appear miserable is somehow propitiatory. A slight shift in this conception and there emerges the widespread conviction that the gods delight in human pain and misfortune. If they do, then one of the ways to propitiate them is through renunciation, actual or ostensible, of life's goods and pleasures; and another is positive self-torture or "mortification of the flesh." This is particularly needful at some crisis in life, some

---

[64] §442, below. [65] Frazer, *Golden Bough,* II, 246.

occasion of rejoicing or of high vital activity such as marriage, which affords the spirits a special and welcome opportunity to vex men and must be safeguarded not only by defensive practices but also by renunciations.[66] The so-called Puritan sabbath, on which pleasure and levity of all kinds are renounced in favor of sober and holy discomfort, is a survival of this primitive attitude.

Renunciation is sacrifice, though it might be termed negative as compared with the offering of actual goods. Take the case of fasting, which may be interpreted as either avoidance or propitiation according to the point of view occupied: people may fast because they wish to avoid any possible competition with the spirits in food-getting by vacating the field for them and letting them take it all; or there may be, in fasting, less of fear than of a desire actually to give what is thereby saved. In either case the sacrifice is one of renunciation. Fasting is found in the ghost-cult and persists in that of the daimons; so does the renunciation of operations in self-maintenance, that is, of labor,[67] which really, inasmuch as most primitive labor goes into the food-quest, amounts to about the same thing as renunciation of food. Then there is the renunciation of sex-relations and social ties in general, and at length the system of asceticism appears. Brief reflection will show that a good number of the taboos represent renunciation for the sake of propitiation. The taboo, coercitives, asceticism, penance, and the "state of grace" are all interconnected; the tangle which they form gets firmly intrenched in the mores and persists in spite of acculturative influences.[68]

The Murray Islanders fasted when going to war or on a long journey.[69] In Fanti-land, "one may often meet women, known to be well off, or of good families, poorly clad, half-naked, with black daubs on the face and chest, who will answer the question as to what is the matter by saying, 'I am doing my Fetish.' This consists of the observance of a fast for a few days in the year, abstinence from sexual intercourse, or indeed from work, frequent invocation of the Fetish or familiar spirit, and a great bath at the end, putting on of clean or new garments, and a hearty meal."[70] The Six Nations bewailed their decline and misfortunes, attributing them to neglect of their retreats and fasts.[71] John Smith tells how medicine-men carried out ceremonies lasting

66 §§373, 374, below.   67 §§225, 228, above.
68 Sapper, in *Globus*, LXXXVII, 130.
69 Hunt, in JAI, XXVIII, 13.   70 Connolly, in JAI, XXVI, 152.
71 Lafitau, *Mœurs*, I, 340 (Dutch edition).

twelve hours, fasting, to find out whether he had evil designs against the tribe.[72] To some of the South American tribes abstention from food in many exigencies of life has seemingly become a sort of second nature. As soon as pregnancy declares itself, for example, both spouses impose on themselves a strict fast, eating only ants, mushrooms, and other less esteemed foods.[73] It would appear that they thus revert to an older, inferior, but holier food, thus presenting a picture of reduced and unfortunate circumstances.

As the list of food-taboos given in another connection[74] demonstrates, abstention may be partial and special, covering certain varieties of food, especially luxuries.

In the Andaman Islands both sexes, beginning between the eleventh and thirteenth year, abstain for from one to five years from turtle, honey, pork, fish, and several other favorite foods. As the one who is fasting "makes up for the restrictions by eating more of other kinds of food, the physical welfare does not suffer. The chief is the one who decides the time when the period of fasting may be stopped, according to the individual's powers of endurance and self-denial."[75] Among the Sea Dyaks "are youths who appear at birth to have had certain marks, signs of misfortune, on them, and who, in order to get the marks to disappear and to prevent the evil which their presence forebodes, must atone, or go through penitential performances, such as depriving themselves during a certain portion of their lives of salt or fish, or of every kind of clothing."[76] "The chief and, under certain circumstances, every older Botocudo is wont to claim nothing or only a very small portion of the game killed by them. At the basis of this custom lies the notion that the eating of the flesh will be harmful to the killer."[77]

In Japan, Shinto communities appointed a member to pray and to abstain vicariously for them, from women, wine, and amusements, for a year. If any public misfortune occurred, there was a suspicion that he had broken his vows and of old he would have been put to death.[78] The ancient Arabs abstained from wine while under some obligation or vow; the abstinence was to stimulate them to fulfilment. Others made the abstention from wine, and also anything else connected with the wine, the real content of the vow. Priests must abstain from wine while they were discharging temple-functions.[79] "In Egypt the doctrine that the highest degree of holiness can only be attained by abstinence from all animal food, was the result of the political fusion of a number of local cults in one national religion, with a national priesthood that represented imperial ideas. Nothing of this sort took place in Greece or in most of the Semitic lands, and in these accordingly we find no developed doctrine of priestly asceticism in the matter of food."[80]

Into the fasting and other renunciations of pilgrims and holy men we need

[72] Bruce, *Va.*, I, 160 (quoting Smith's *Works*, 399).

[73] Spix and Martius, *Brasilien*, 1318-1319.

[74] §271, above.   [75] Man, in JAI, XII, 130.

[76] Bock, *Borneo*, 218; Roth, *Sarawak*, II, 104, note.

[77] Von Martius, *Beiträge*, I, 325.   [78] Hearn, *Japan*, 166.

[79] Buhl, *Israeliten*, 10, 11, note.   [80] Smith, *Relig. Sem.*, 302-303.

not go very far. The beggar-pilgrim of the Hindu epic took a vow to be always alone and chaste and without house or property. He bathed in holy water, visited all the holy places, mortified the flesh, and fasted strictly, "so that he became day by day more shrunken."[81] Thereby he was storing up merit with the daimons, just as if he had sacrificed liberally to them. Pictures of this kind are familiar enough to readers of books on India or mediæval Europe.

Fasting was doubtless often a good thing for the savage, though he went through periods of involuntary abstention too, when the food-quest failed. It was at any rate disciplinary. And perhaps something can be said for the renunciation of labor during the rest-days, although this latter abstention was not felt to be so much of a sacrifice and was easily overdone. Renunciation of social intercourse was more of a deprivation. We add a pair of examples to those already cited in another connection.[82]

In Borneo, "when the rice is all harvested, the household is lali [taboo] to strangers, and for eight days no one can go off on an expedition nor return to the house from an expedition. No sooner does this lali end, than another begins, while the rice is being stored in the granaries." Again, a *pamali* "is undertaken by individuals when any member of the family is sick; thus, parents often put themselves under its regulations, fondly hoping that by denying themselves for a time the pleasures of intercourse with their fellow creatures, they will prevail upon the malignant spirit, which is supposed to have shed its withering influence over their offspring, to restore it to its wonted health and strength." The *pamali* is also undertaken "by a whole village during any sickness which prevails generally amongst the members of the tribe; it is marked by a pig slain and a feast being made in order to propitiate the divinity who has sent the malady among them; in its severest form it is of eight days' continence, and during this period everything in the village is at a standstill, inhabitants shutting themselves up from all intercourse with strangers."[83]

Among the Central Eskimo, "a religious custom compels the women to leave off working when the hunters return, and they cannot resume their sewing and the preparation of skins until the seal is cut up. This custom is founded on the tradition that all kinds of sea-animals have risen from the fingers of their supreme goddess, who must be propitiated after being offended by the murder of her offspring."[84]

Renunciation really taught a great life-policy, though no one was aware of it. It is the method, in its refined form, of increasing life's fraction by lowering the denominator of demands instead of striving always to increase the numerator of satisfactions. It comes to be one of the great life-philosophies.[85]

[81] Holtzmann, *Ind. Sagen*, II, 157.   [82] §§225, 255, above.
[83] Furness, *Head-Hunters*, 164; Roth, *Sarawak*, I, 261, note.
[84] Boas, in BAE, VI, 562.
[85] "Entbehren sollst du, sollst entbehren." Goethe, *Faust*, I, 1549.

§281*. Continence. There is a long series of renunciations connected with sex, some of which are noted in treating of the taboo and of the various aspects of marriage and the family.[86] Continence is a propitiatory if not a coercitive practice and is employed on occasions of crisis in individual or societal life. Fear enters into the list of motives to continence, especially fear of woman's "uncleanness."[87] Since avoidance and propitiation are often in mind at one and the same time, their several effects cannot be disentangled. Main[88] regards continence as a coercitive, effective in mourning, getting game, crop-planting, and weather-making; it is demanded at sacred times, such as that of prayer, religious festivals, and initiation. "Among his other ungracious views of conjugal intimacy Paul held that it was incompatible with prayer."[89] In its strictest form it is a duty imposed upon priests and especially priestesses, with the consequence that the old, who are beyond temptation, or the very young are selected as intermediaries with the gods. Especially do virgins possess magic power; "suppression of the sexual, undoubtedly stimulates the religious impulse." The case is cited of a Pima Indian woman, unmarried, "who *because of her spinsterhood* is believed to be possessed of supernatural power";[90] the fact that celibacy is so rare among primitive peoples[91] doubtless points the contrast with a sharpness foreign to the civilized. Main quotes as follows from Plutarch:[92] "Some are of the opinion that these vestals had no other business than the preservation of this fire; but others hold that they were keepers of other divine secrets, hidden from all but themselves." The classical authority goes on to tell what the Vestals did, exhibiting them as really holy, in good part by reason of their virginity. With this general introduction to the subject, we may pass on to the ethnographic cases.

Among the Melanesians, "when the yam vines are being trained the men sleep near the gardens, and never approach their wives; should they do so and tread the garden it would be spoilt." Men "setting out on a hunting, fish-

86 §§273, above, and 347, 349, 368, 374, 408, below.
87 §378, below.
88 *Relig. Chastity*, chs. XV, XVI, XVII, XVIII; 176, 201, 212, 259 ff., 276.
89 I Cor., VII, 5.   90 Russell, in BAE, XXVI, 184.
91 §342, below.
92 *Numa*, IX, X; these facts are brought out in a novel by White, called *The Unwilling Vestal*.

ing, or war expedition, must have nothing to do with women, only eat certain foods and sparingly." The old men who remain behind to look after the men's house are under like restriction, "lest the expedition should fail." The owner of a big tree, which is about to be cut down to make a trading-canoe, eats only sago and keeps away from all women. Similarly with the owner of land that is about to be cleared; such a man must talk but little.[93] In working up copper and copper rings, nobody may be present who has not been continent, or the operations will fail.[94] The militaristic Zulus renounce marriage altogether till their period of service is over, and the chief is supposed not to marry at all. The business of life is war, and celibacy, if not continence, is in order.[95]

Abstinence from women while on the war-path is practiced by Hindu Koosh tribes; and in one district in India, during the ceremonies over the skulls of slain enemies, the warriors may eat no food cooked by women or in their accustomed pots nor have for five days any communication with their wives.[96] One might well believe that there was something rational in such sex-taboos prior to strenuous exertion; but they are combined with fasting or special food-taboos, last over beyond the period of campaign, and, as several of the cases show, are imposed when no such strenuosity is in prospect. The fact that those also that remain behind are subject to the same limitations reveals the essentially formal and ritual nature of the abstention. When going out after aloe-wood all must be continent and not eat a certain kind of fish and during their absence their families must avoid the use of offensive words or quarrels. Village-approaches are closed to strangers.[97]

When the Maori went to war, "they were separated from their wives, and did not again approach them until peace was proclaimed; hence, during a period of long-continued fighting, they remarked that their wives were widows."[98] For four days before the Caroline Islanders go on a fishing expedition, they remain continent. When the distribution of the fish commences, if women or children come near and break the taboo by helping themselves, they will get swelled ankles or elephantiasis as a visible token of daimonic resentment. The rule of continence applies throughout the South Seas; in the Pelew Islands, fishing is religious and the leader's skill not only technical but magical. He knows the rites, and one of them that contributes indispensably to success is the ritual continence.[99]

During the Eskimo bladder-festival the men and large boys sleep apart and the men keep rigidly away from the women. They avoid going into their own or any other house for fear of becoming unclean; and bathe twice a day. No females who have reached puberty are permitted near or under the bladders while they hang in the men's house. They say that if they fail in continence the shades will be offended.[100] The Indian spirit that "dwells among the Indians during the dancing season, dislikes people who are unclean or such as have

[93] Codrington, *Melanesians*, 134; Chalmers, in JAI, XXVII, 332, 333.

[94] Bastian, *Deut. Exped.*, I, 158; note in *Globus*, LXXII, 164; Mantegazza, *Amori*, 98, 99.

[95] Ratzel, *Hist. of Mankind*, II, 434.

[96] Mitra, in JASB, VI, 120; Godden, in JAI, XXVII, 39.

[97] Niemann, in *Bijd.*, XIV, 335.   [98] Taylor, *Te Ika*, 189.

[99] Christian, *Caroline Isl.*, 249; Kubary, *Karolinen-arch.*, 127.

[100] Nelson, in BAE, XVIII, pt. I, 393, 440.

had intercourse with women."[101] Continence is enjoined before a hunt, and for four days before a ceremonial succeeding the planting of grain. An emetic is taken as purification from conjugal relations, and on the fourth day married men bathe and have their heads washed with yucca suds, to the same end. "The exempting of those who have not been married and those who have lost a spouse seems a strange and unreasonable edict in a community where there is an indiscriminate living together of the people."[102] It is a matter of ritual, not of reason.

Though the trend of these last cases is all toward avoidance, the idea of pleasing through renunciation is always present. In the healing ceremony of the Navaho the impersonators of the gods must be continent till all the paint is removed from their bodies. In the worship of a holy plant by the Tarahumari shamans, there must be continence for three days before and after the ceremony; for the laity the period is one day. Again, where the Indians go annually to get a kind of cactus, spending twenty-three days going and coming, they must observe continence, eat no salt, and not bathe for the four months previous. Thus sex-renunciation is not set off by itself but goes with other forms of propitiatory renunciation. Every Aztec man must marry when he comes to the age of twenty, except certain priests who took a vow of chastity in honor of the gods they served.[103]

When Jahweh revealed himself to Israel at Sinai, the men were ordered to abstain from women for a time, and Moses forever. Those who hoped for a divine revelation must be continent. The bread of the priest was hallowed, "if the young men have kept themselves at least from women."[104] Frankincense was the gum of a holy tree, collected with religious precautions; only certain holy families could see the trees, and when collecting there must be no relations with women or participation in funerals. In old Arabia, one in a blood-feud must renounce women, wine, and unguents. The sex-act, being regarded as impure, was followed by Babylonians and Arabs with ablution and fumigation, as is still the practice in the Sudan.[105] Many Greek priests must be chaste for life or during priestly activity and the abstention extended to certain foods, even for all who entered the temples. Roman women remained continent in connection with certain festivals, and the flamens were forbidden to marry more than once.[106] Among the Armenians certain groups hold continence-days. Bulgar men abstain at the time of one of their festivals, "that the child, if there is one, shall not be sickly. Continence at plowing-time is a precaution against rusty grain.[107]

Here is a number of rather primitive cases showing some mixture of motive, but one and all exhibiting the idea either that continence is pleasing to the daimons or that incontinence is ab-

[101] Boas, in USNM, 1895, 501.
[102] Bourke, in BAE, IX, 460; Stevenson, in BAE, XI, 75.
[103] Stevenson, in BAE, VIII, 248; Lumholtz, in *Int. Cong. Anthrop.*, 1893, 111; note in *Globus*, LXXIII, 330; Nadaillac, *Preh. Amer.*, 311.
[104] Exod., XIX, 15; *Jew. Encycl.*, V, 226; I Sam., XXI, 4.
[105] Pliny, *Hist. Nat.*, XII, 54; Smith, *Relig. Sem.*, 427, 454, 482.
[106] Stengel, *Gr. Kultusalt.*, 35; Rossbach, *Röm. Ehe.*, 262, 130-131.
[107] Seidlitz, in *Globus*, LXXVIII, 244; Strauss, *Bulgaren*, 290; Temesváry, *Geburtshilfe*, 16.

horrent. It is not proposed to enter exhaustively into the ascetic continence-practices of a more developed religious system. Enough instances have been cited to indicate the origin of such ideas and habitudes. The nature of the Christian structure erected upon this primitive practice may be dismissed briefly.

"Monkish asceticism," remarks Lippert,[108] "saw woman only in the distorting mirror of desire suppressed by torture." The sex-function came to be thought base and shameful; there was no purity except in complete renunciation—in trying to annul one of nature's most compelling laws. Anything else was, to morbid reasoners from a grotesque premise, mere concession and compromise. Christianity involved itself in a sort of hopeless inner war; "the flesh lusteth against the spirit and the spirit against the flesh."[109] It is true that there is always some such contest in us, though it does not follow that wherever there is a war there is virtue or vice. In any case, the notion developed that there was positive merit in renunciation of sex: the "fanciful purity of celibacy."[110] It was better not to marry; the blessed are they "who were not defiled with women, for they are virgins."[111] Scriptural denunciations of ascetics[112] and cases of married ecclesiastics were overlooked in the development of the doctrine. Continent marriages were the holy ones. At the end of the eleventh century, "throughout Germany, husbands and wives separated from each other in vast numbers, and devoted themselves to the service of the church, without taking vows or assuming ecclesiastical garments; while those who were unmarried renounced the pleasures of the world, and placing themselves under the direction of spiritual guides, abandoned themselves entirely to religious duties."[113] When minds were saturated with these ideas of sex-renunciation, and also in a condition of pruriency from morbid meditations, it is not strange to find actual tests of the power of renunciation, to demonstrate exceeding sanctity.[114] Though asceticism was supposed to free men from sensuality, ritual celibacy, as Lea demonstrates, is consistent with unstinted sensual indulgence. The sophistry necessary to reconcile the two was easily supplied.

A special word should be added concerning the exaltation of virginity; it is an ideal not at all peculiar to any one time or religion. It is propitiative and is a way to daimonic favor.

In West Africa is a god who was once an earthly king, chiefly remembered because he murdered his father-in-law. He is the object of human sacrifice. "Young girls who are dedicated to his service are obliged to remain virgins;

[108] Kgchte., II, 520; cases in Sumner, Folkways, ch. XVIII.

[109] Gal., V, 17; Rom., VII, 18, 25.   [110] Lea, Sacerd. Celib., 32.

[111] I Cor., VII; Rev., XIV, 4.   [112] I Tim., IV, 3; III, 2; Titus, I, 6.

[113] Lea, Sacerd. Celib., 254. Cases of alleged continent marriages in Eicken, Weltanschauung, 456; Payne, Eng. Med., 22-23; Lea, Sacerd. Celib., 181-182; Lecky, Europ. Morals, II, 314, 315, 336, et passim.

[114] Lea, Inquisition, II, 357; III, 109; Lea, Sacerd. Celib., 167; Todd, St. Patrick, 91; Main, Relig. Chastity, Appendix, note XXXIII.

they have charge of the temple and make the daily offerings."[115] Among the Blackfeet Indians, "in time of scarcity of food, seven vestals of the sun dance along in a circle, invoking the starry heaven for food."[116] Virgins dedicated to the sun appear also in prehistoric Mexico; "homes of the selected," containing several hundred virgins, some of them consecrated for sacrifice, were maintained by the Inca.[117] On the island of Grand Canary there were sacred women who left their houses or caves only in case of famine or on fixed days to bathe in the sea. If by chance a man met them, he lost his life. After the age of thirty they might marry, "but any failure in virtue before that time was punished by imprisonment and starving to death in a stone cell."[118] In the regular line of ascent from European celibacy are the temple-girls of Hammurabi's time, 2250 B.C.; those consecrated to the Mithra cult with an imposition of perpetual chastity; the virgin goddesses and others of classical times; and the Roman Vestal Virgins.[119] Some female Druids were perpetually celibate.[120] The dogma of virginity in the Christian Church placed the virgin far above marriage; the body of that soul which aspired to be the bride of Christ must be virgin.[121]

A strange aberration, one might say, viewing without its antecedents the astounding development of these nature-challenging theories and dogmas. In many cases, as Lea shows in his *History of Sacerdotal Celibacy in the Christian Church*, nature threw back the challenge and swept through man's films of fancy like a cannon-ball through a spider's web. But, however inexplicable by itself, this system is seen to be merely the exaggeration of a primitive form embodying purposes of avoidance and evasion but predominantly those of propitiation.

§282*. Self-Discipline. Continence, though a special form of self-discipline, is not perhaps so classified in most people's minds; in its connection with sex it has other bearings; in any case, however, it has deserved a place by itself. Self-discipline means to the majority of readers something like self-torture. The extreme is self-immolation before the altar as a coercitive upon the deity to accede to demands.[122] Where the practice is not so rigorous it always implies the endurance of some selected pain or discomfort in order to stand well, or especially well, with the daimons. The

[115] Ellis, *Ewe*, 89.   [116] L'Heureux, in JAI, XV, 302.
[117] Nadaillac, *Preh. Amer.*, 409; Prescott, *Peru*, I, 109 ff.
[118] Cook, in AA, II, 491.
[119] Winckler, Hammurabi, *Absatz* 23; *Umschau*, VII, 91; Maspero, *Hist. Anc.*, III, 763; Euripides, *Hippolytus*, 1301-1302, 1440 ff.; Euripides, *Trojan Women*, 41-42, 980.
[120] Von Pflugk-Harttung, in *Trans. Roy. Hist. Soc.*, VII, 73.
[121] Harnack, *Dogmengchte.*, II, 747.   [122] Joshi, in JASB, III, 289.

idea seems to be that while the latter must be able to gloat over a certain amount of human suffering, rather indiscriminately imposed, yet they may be satisfied with samples of it which men can choose to endure. The aleatory element, striking indiscriminately and capriciously, is thus reduced from an unmanageable variable of unpredictable pain and loss to a constant that can be dealt with.[123]

Self-discipline, as developed in widely separated places and times, is multiform; we have met with it already in ceremonies of self-torture connected with the ghost-cult.[124] It is not possible to say just where self-discipline ends and an actual sacrifice of part of the body, the blood, for instance, begins. A man who has had bad luck in hunting cuts his body that his pain may get attention and his luck change. The results of such practice are skin-markings, which may come, as in the case of tribal marks or tattooing, to be motived quite otherwise than in the original intention. Most societal practices and institutions have such a multiple origin, as, for example, the potlatch,[125] which may have in it an element of propitiation by self-destitution. Most of the following cases, chiefly from the Indians of the two hemispheres, are less complicated with accessory motives, though the stock interplay between avoidance and propitiation is usually in evidence.

Whether holy uncleanliness is to be considered as self-discipline or as priestly license, in any case it is often the holy people who do not wash where the rest do.[126] Abstention from washing is certainly regarded as propitiatory in some parts of the world. As the crop last year, runs a report, "was a complete failure, so it happens that the women abstain from washing themselves for a whole year, a time-honored method of averting the wrath of Heaven." Mongols and Tibetans hardly ever dare to wash their clothes.[127] Rubruck[128] is quoted in this connection as follows: "They never wash their clothes, because they say that God then becomes angry, and because thunder comes if they are hung up to dry. In fact they lash the washers and snatch away from them the garments they are washing. The Mongolians even go so far as to assert that Heaven "is not gracious to him who has no vermin."[129] The priests of Dodona slept on the ground and did not wash the feet.[130] "Bathing was regarded by mediæval people as a necessity of life, and so renunciation of the bath also was imposed as a church penance."[131] The Anglo-Saxons, who were fond of hot baths, used cold ones as a penance.[132]

[123] §197, above.
[124] §§228, 229, above.
[125] §113, above.
[126] Schultz, Höf. Leben, I, 173.
[127] Rockhill, Mongolia and Tibet, 154.
[128] Eastern Parts, 234.
[129] Prjevalski's Forskningsresor, 225.
[130] Homer, Iliad, XVI, 235.
[131] Weinhold, Deut. Frauen, II, 114.
[132] Garnier, Brit. Peasantry, I, 100.

Coming now to the more serious forms of self-discipline and "mortification of the flesh," we meet first the so-called swinging festival, of India. Two iron tenter-hooks are passed through the skin of the votary's back and he is lifted high in the air by a lever whose fulcrum is a post twenty feet high; then he is turned about. He goes through the motions of fighting, often with sword and shield in his hands, and must appear cheerful, whatever his pain, for if tears escape him he is driven from his caste. A person might swing by proxy. A case is reported of an old woman who vowed to swing if her daughter's coming child was a boy and did so with great resolution. Sometimes the whole apparatus was upon a car, which was dragged slowly around the temple, doubtless in order that the god should get a good look. Children had wires put through pinched-up flesh on their sides, and were led round and round the temple as with leading-strings. The so-called lifting ceremony becomes milder and at length a substitute—a sheep, together with the victim's clothes—appears or the swinger is suspended by a cloth passing under the arms.[133] Many other forms of self-discipline appear in India, from living on alms, through affectation of extreme penance, to incredible extremes of bodily torture. The "Up-arms" hold up their arms till they cannot lower them again; "Sky-faces" look at the sky until their muscles stiffen in that position. The nails are permitted to grow through the clenched fists until work can no longer be done. Passions are subdued, literally, with lock and key.[134] Lying on beds of spikes makes the victim acceptable to the gods and therefore holy. Members of one sect break all the taboos relating to caste, food, and drink, use foul and indecorous language, and wander about begging alms. "They believe that by leading such lives God would be pleased and save them."[135] Flagellating themselves while dancing for miles along the road, for days together, is another device. Some of these self-torturing groups are declining in numbers.[136] "Female ascetics were probably in ancient India as common as they are now, and were considered equally disruptable."[137]

A case is reported where a man started from a valley to ascend a mountain, perfectly nude. His vow was never to remain even for an instant on his feet until he reached a shrine over ten thousand feet from the base of the mountain. A further condition was that he would crawl back two body-lengths for every three forward—and all this over sharp rocks and ledges. The feat took five years; and when he had arrived, received absolution and given up all his property, he could not stand erect. He remained for several weeks, nude in the cold mountain air, tied to a pillar in the temple.[138]

The belief that the spirits were pleased with personal suffering was common among the American Indians; a somewhat extended description of their forms of self-discipline appears in the *Case-Book*. The Cheyennes promised suffering in case of success on the war-path just as other peoples have promised material sacrifices. They starved to conciliate the spirits, skewered their bodies, faced the sun, and otherwise mortified the flesh, as a later stage of civilization denominated it, till they attained to dreams and visions. "The strongly religious character of the Indian, and his simplicity, tend to keep alive in him these

[133] Thurston, *S. India*, 488, 489, 490, 493, 495-497, 499, 501.
[134] Hopkins, *Relig. Ind.*, 486.   [135] Basu, in JASB, I, 497.
[136] Fawcett, in JASB, II, 278; Monier-Williams, *Brāhmanism*, 87.
[137] Bühler, *Manu*, 363, note.
[138] Lecture by Boeck, rep. in N. Y. *Times*, Feb. 28, 1898.

notions which in others we call primitive, but which we regard as wholly natural if they are found in the sacred books in which we believe." The author[139] has just remarked that the parallel between Indian practices and those of the Old Testament is close and that "analogous offerings are made by Christians at the present day." Several details in this author's excellent treatment deserve to be singled out. In the finger-amputation and the cutting off of pieces of skin and flesh, a regular knife must not be used; formerly a flint was employed and of late a bit of sharpened tin. The flint was holy because it was old; the tin, perhaps, because it was regarded as fetishistic. After a description of the skewering, pole-swinging, skull-dragging, etc., all of which are instanced in the *Case-Book,* the author calls attention to the fact that sacrificial blood is regarded as something precious all over the world. Here is where the parallels to more modern religions come in; the modern practices and dogmas are rationalized somewhat and also are so conventionalized that their origin is not apprehended. But then too the Indians have modified their ceremonies in the direction of mitigation; in some cases, instead of skewering the self-torturers, they are merely painted; the practices are mainly obsolete and are represented by occasional reversions and by such survivals. Of the Sun Dance we read that "refusal of the red men to discontinue part of the barbaric rites led to an absolute ban of the dance four years ago. The revival was agreed to when the Indians promised to abandon the practice of slashing their chests with knives and suspending themselves from poles by means of deer sinews passed under the chest muscles."

Nakedness, besides being a coercitive, may be taken as a form of renunciation. Saul, seized by the spirit of prophecy, stripped himself naked and "prophesied before Samuel." David danced before the Ark "with all his might" and was sneered at for uncovering himself before the handmaids "as one of the vain fellows shamelessly uncovereth himself." But David gloried in his own debasement before the Lord. "And I will be yet more vile than thus, and will be base in mine own sight." That he was acting properly in the sight of Heaven is to be inferred from the fact that the woman who sneered at his self-abasement "had no child unto the day of her death." When Bathsheba's child was sick, David fasted and lay on the ground six days, hoping thus to win divine pity.[140]

When the priests of Baal could not secure the presence of their god, they seized knives and awls and cut their bodies so that the blood ran.[141] This is construed as a return to exuvial sacrifice. "In such cases it was simply a crafty way out of it, to use the lust of the god for the life-element, for blood and especially for human blood, in order to coerce him despite his resistance, to give ear to the requests directed to him." The same procedure appears in Syria and among several peoples of Asia Minor. Scourging, too, is found. "In the last periods of heathendom it certainly has been forgotten that originally the spilled blood was intended to be offered to the god himself, in order by it to coerce his presence; and then this practice came to be regarded as a form of penitential chastisement, which likewise had the purpose of securing the presence of the deity."[142] Islam gradually lost its original ascetic tendency; but

[139] Grinnell, *Cheyenne,* I, 79-83, II, 196, 211 ff., especially 212, 214; N. Y. *Times,* July 18, 1926.

[140] I Sam., XIX, 24; II Sam., VI, 14 ff.; XII, 16 ff.

[141] I Kings, XVIII, 28.   [142] Pietschmann, *Phön.,* 164-165.

before Mohammed vigils were frequent and there were even regular night-watches, with prayer.[143]

Isolated fanatics have in recent times returned to self-discipline to secure salvation, as where a Russian lay brother had himself buried up to the armpits in a cave because he was anxious to be saved by mortifying the flesh. After a week he hoped to have found salvation. He was discovered dead.[144]

What is known in European history as asceticism was an organized system of struggle to escape from the body and sense, so as to become "pure" or live a detached soul-life; that its origins were primitive has now been seen. The adherents and philosophers of a developed religion took up the idea and the practices of renunciation and self-discipline and refined upon them, interpreting them in the light of a more sophisticated age. Neo-Platonists adopted such devices in order to lead a morally clean life and to insure themselves against daimonic assaults. Then came exaggerations: Simeon Stylites is reported to have remained thirty years upon a pillar forty cubits high.[145]

In the second century A.D. asceticism began to be organized. The neophyte must endure hardships, subject himself to flogging, and otherwise systematically mortify the flesh. "This not seldom degenerated into ostentation over the capacity to bear pain. . . . It was in the fourth century, under Christianity, that people first came to regard an ascetic life as something existing for itself. . . . What identified the cynics also characterized the Christian ascetics: rough clothes and unshorn hair."[146] Here was the basis for the erection of a whole system, and one completely at odds with the obvious conditions of human life on earth. "There is, perhaps, no phase in the moral history of mankind of a deeper or more painful interest than this ascetic epidemic. A hideous, sordid, and emaciated maniac, without knowledge, without patriotism, without natural affection, passing his life in a long routine of useless and atrocious self-torture, and quailing before the ghastly phantoms of his delirious brain, had become the ideal of the nations. . . . For about two centuries, the hideous maceration of the body was regarded as the highest proof of excellence."[147]

Because this system was a variation in the mores that could not have permanent survival-value, its elimination awaited merely the deliberate arrival, in its own good time, of societal selection. Advances, through a process of correction and substitution, in the understanding of natural law and of societal life, swept away this set of practices as they did witchcraft. By 1500 asceticism was gone, overwhelmed by the advance of commerce, wealth, and pro-

---

[143] Wellhausen, *Skizzen*, III, 210.   [144] N. Y. *Times*, Sept. 26, 1897.
[145] Lehmann, *Overtro*, I, 93; Stoll, *Suggestion*, 255; Tennyson, *Stylites*.
[146] Hatch, *Griechentum*, 108, 109; Lea, *Sacerd. Celib.*, 29, 41.
[147] Lecky, *Europ. Morals*, II, 107.

ductive power; and then came the contrasting pagan ways of the Renaissance. The prescriptions of asceticism which controverted most harshly the social relations under which men are bound to live were never enforceable in fact, except for a group of fanatics. Asceticism shut out from the heights of religion all but those who could practise it; and most people could not. The ascetic was a deserter. In renouncing the world to attain heaven, he turned his back on all the duties that lay upon him as a member of society. He lived for the future life, not for this one. The system was anti-social and society could endure it but for a time. What Lea shows as to the impracticability of ever enforcing sacerdotal celibacy applies to any and all prescriptions and practices that become obvious and distressing maladjustments to actual life-conditions.

Other renunciatory and debasing practices may be passed rapidly in review. Though they are not all strictly propitiatory, they have the element in them and fall most readily into classification at this point.

Drunkenness is taken by some peoples to be propitiatory. American Indian chiefs of the pre-Spanish period thus incapacitated themselves at certain festivals, appointing substitutes to carry on the needful functions of government. The kings of Persia renounced their habitual sobriety on the day of the Mithra festival. Drunkenness at the Dionysus celebrations was in the order of events. The connection of shamanism with the use of drugs and poisons will appear farther on.[148]

Eating and drinking loathsome things forms part of the religious exercises of certain sects. Such fakirs make themselves "all that is terrible and hideous, filthy and formidable," using human bones as wands and the upper half of a human skull as a drinking-vessel. Cannibalism is sometimes practised. One such sect claims that its "monstrous doctrines are those of equality and humanity. All castes are equal with them, and they make no distinction between good and bad." The eating of filth means the subjugation of natural tastes.[149] It is believed by Bourke[150] that these disgusting usages are in many cases the result of an aim to do what one abominates in a superlative degree for the greater merit; they are the greater sacrifice or self-abnegation.

The erotic and the religious seem often to be closely allied one to the other. Religion runs out into sensuality and obscenity beyond description. It is not necessary to go beyond the mention of this matter: there is unlimited license and debauch; all taboos, even that proscribing incest, are suspended; the carnal runs out into unimagined variety and inventiveness. Some of these practices are difficult to discover and punish, for they are kept secret in associa-

---

148 Sapper, in *Globus,* LXXXVII, 130; Maspero, *Hist. Anc.,* III, 744; Euripides, *Bacchæ;* §§313, 317, 318, below.

149 Balfour, in JAI, XXVI, 341, 342; Barrow, in JASB, III, 201.

150 *Scatalogic Rites,* 40; Ezek., IV, 12, 15.

tions and sects.[151] One curious phase of sexual practice in religion is the practice of men posing and living as women, and *vice versa*.[152] It is sometimes the result of a vow, in the hope of restoring health or virile power.[153] The few cases which we have gathered of this obscure practice may be listed here. In Siberia, a number of tribes exhibit it, and it is connected in the main with the shaman. Such men do their hair like woman's, imitate her dress, habits, and pronunciation, and do some of woman's work. Rarely, "the 'soft man' begins to feel himself a woman; he seeks for a lover, and sometimes marries." Public opinion is against such creatures but they are regarded as very dangerous. Few cases occur of transformation of women into men. There are some genuine perversions here, but "it does not follow that every pathological individual is the subject of magical worship." The authoress[154] quoted has an explanation of this change of sex, in the practice of degrading the cowardly, infirm, and conquered to the position of women. "Keep him with the women, put their clothes on him, and he is no longer dangerous, if hostile, and may be made useful in occupations suitable to females." In short, this is believed to be a case of feminizing captives. This does not seem to us to explain all the cases, at best. Shakespear[155] speaks of a man who "dressed himself up as a woman, smoked a woman's pipe, wore a woman's petticoat and cloth, carried a small basket, span a cotton spindle, wore ivory earrings, let his hair down and wrapped a mottled cloth, which was said to be of an ancient pattern, round his head as a turban. . . . The idea of the performer disguising himself as a woman is that the spirit of the dead tiger may be humbled, thinking that it has been shot by a woman." "There was in Tahiti a strange class of society . . . spoken of by writers as *mawhoo*. . . . They were men who adopted the rôle of women. According to the missionaries, these people adopted the *mawhoo* life when young; they dressed like women, followed their employments, including cloth making, and lived with and waited on women, and an example is given of one of them seen in Pomare's train who mimicked the voice and every peculiarity of the sex. They sought the courtship of men, just as women did so, were even more jealous than were women of the men who cohabited with them, and always refused to sleep with women. . . . They were kept only by the principal chiefs. They were treated as women, and not as men, in the application of all the rules of the taboo. They were under the prohibitions to which women were subject as regards food, not being allowed to eat with men, or to eat their food, and having separate plantations for their own use; but they might gather and dress the women's food. They might not kindle fire from a fire made by other men, but women might kindle it from fire made by them. They were excluded from all religious assemblies, might not tread

[151] Preuss, in *Globus*, LXXXVI, 358; Hahn, in *Globus*, LXXV, 286; McGee, in BAE, XV, 201; McGee, in AA, IX, 371; Hopkins, *Relig. Ind.*, 448, 455, 450, 491; Wilkins, *Hinduism*, ch. III, 235; Monier-Williams, *Brāhmanism*, 185; Dubois, *Mœurs*, 434; Basu, in JASB, I, 478 ff.; Boshart, *Afr. Lebens*, 201.

[152] Cases in Main, *Relig. Chastity*, ch. XIV, and Appendix, notes XXV, XXVI.

[153] Fawcett, in JASB, II, 331, 343; Dymock, in JASB, II, 345; Basu, in JASB, I, 502.

[154] Czaplicka, *Aborig. Siberia*, 250-255.

[155] In JAI, XXXIX, 380-381 (on the Kuki-Lushai of India).

the sacred ground of the *marae* [public enclosure], or eat of food which had been there, or had been touched by those who officiated at the altar."[156]

It is evident that there is a religious element in all these cases; others occur in connection with the shaman.[157] They are oddities that seem to us to belong with the rest of the religious sexual perversions. The aspects of this general topic of religious sex-license that bears more directly upon marriage and the family are treated elsewhere.[158]

By renunciatory and other propitiatory practices it is thought possible not only to avoid present or immediately impending evil but to store up insurance against the more distant future. Pious works not alone pile up credits for the individual; a surplus of them is also available for all in the cult-union, including both the living and the dead.[159] Hence the pious man is a social asset and receives reverence due both to admiration and to personal interest in the store of daimonic good-will which he is accumulating and in which his fellows may hope to share. This sentiment is the opposite of the one harbored in respect to the sinner and heretic.[160]

"It is a most common and widespread notion that a man by doing any extraordinary deed (supererogation), such as the setting up of an image in his house, visiting the shrine of any deity, bathing, pilgrimage, incurring bodily suffering, can have a certain number of good deeds written down to his credit, which will be an equivalent for a certain amount of sins, caused by neglect of duty or by the committal of actual offences. A balance will be struck when he leaves the world, and his future condition depend upon the preponderance of good or evil. If good outweighs the evil, his next birth will be higher; if the evil preponderate, he will sink in the scale of creation. A low-caste man may, by his meritorious acts, become a Brahman in a succeeding birth; and, in like manner, a Brahman through sin may sink into a lower caste. Hence the religious are ever trying to lay up a stock of punya [merit], which will stand on the credit side of their account in the days of judgment."[161] In ancient Persia, "under certain circumstances it seems to have been allowable that a specially pious soul should, out of its superfluity of merits, assist another who was deficient in them; this would be, in any case, a noteworthy analogy to the belief about the saints of the Catholic folk of many regions."[162]

The foregoing introduces us bluntly to the idea that the cult-activities in propitiation are to be regarded as resting upon a sort of ledger account kept by some supernatural recording agency. The bargain-element is marked. Men dicker with one another for benefits and they atone by gifts and fines for transgressions of

156 Williamson, *Cent. Polyn.*, II, 393.
157 §310, below.
158 §§343, 365, 366, below.
159 Lippert, *Kgchte.*, II, 450.
160 §274, above.
161 Wilkins, *Hinduism*, 312-313.
162 Geiger, *Ostiran. Kult.*, 280.

rights; it is but natural that the same methods should be employed between human beings and anthropomorphic spirits.

§283. **Vows.** The vow is a sort of contract with the spirits; and it may promise either renunciation or positive sacrifice. A vow of renunciation is a voluntary taboo laid on one's self, thus differing from the socially prescribed interdiction. It may determine the whole mode of life; or it may affect merely such details as those of dress. By its very nature it is self-disciplinary, for it does not prescribe what one would do anyway, or want to do; nor does it debar the doing of what one does not want to do. Its disciplinary function lies in the control it exercises over voluntary behavior. The vow is also related to the prayer and the curse[163] and often is no more than a malediction on one's self in event of his not carrying out the terms of the vow. It is the sort of thing vowed, which is chiefly self-discipline, rather than the form of the vow that interests us here; a number of cases have appeared incidentally under the taboo.[164]

The personal *quixilles* of West Africa is paralleled among Australians, Americans, and other peoples: men "swear off" from fowl, fish, or fruits, often for life. A negro will vow that he will not eat such and such animals, birds, fish, herbs or fruits, or, if he does, he will devour the whole beast without anyone's help, and bury the bones. . . . Others are prevented from crossing any water, however thin the stream.[165] The Gold Coast negro takes vows of renunciation at marriage, probably in the effort to win vigor so that he can give life to a child.[166]

India is a land of extreme vows, as has already appeared. "A curious and perhaps not very well known form of vow which Hindus make to deities is that of the mouth-lock, an instrument fashioned like a large safety-pin, usually made of silver, and worn with the pin stuck through both cheeks between the teeth so as to keep the mouth open. . . . It is supposed to be one of abstinence [from food] and silence, but seems to have almost lost this significance, and become a mild form of self-mutilation and temporary inconvenience." The vow is generally on condition of being cured of ailments of the head or neck. These mouth-locks are afterwards sold at auction for their intrinsic value for the benefit of the temple.[167] The fakir may be under a vow not to sit down or rest himself during his whole life. The only rest he allows himself night or day, year in and year out, is to lean slightly with his elbows on a suspended stick of wood. "There can be no manner of doubt that these men do undergo most ghastly sufferings, and yet, somehow, they live to a fairly old age, and never seem to come to much harm. Furthermore, as every Anglo-Indian knows, they

163 §277, above.
165 Bastian, *Afr. Reisen*, 253.
167 Fawcett, in JASB, II, 97 ff.

164 §§268, 270, 271, 273, above.
166 Frobenius, *Masken*, 218.

possess, or seem to possess, certain apparently supernatural powers in the way of divination, prophecy, and miracle working. All these are no doubt tricks, but they are tricks of a particularly obscure kind."[168] Among some of the aborigines of India, "the only form of worship is sacrifice, but oaths are taken on rice, beasts, ants, water, earth, etc."[169] Lippert[170] thinks these vows of self-torture in India were the substitute for positive sacrifice of which poverty did not permit.

The so-called "Crazy Dance" of an Arapaho organization was performed only for a vow concerning the recovery of a sick child. Recovery, or some other blessing, was expected.[171]

Among the early Arabs a man "swore not to wash his head till his revenge was complete; to remain apart from women; to renounce wine; and not to anoint himself."[172] Achilles vowed not to eat or drink until Patroclus was avenged; and when vengeance was accomplished, not to bathe until the funeral was completed and Patroclus provided with what he needed in the other world. Similarly Priam did not sleep after Hector's death, but lay in the courtyard, nor would he eat till the corpse was ransomed and cared for.[173] A vow of chastity is mentioned by Euripides.[174]

The vow of renunciation is paralleled by that of positive sacrifice. The latter is more like a prayer, except for its element of malediction—an element rather essential to any vow.

The Zanzibar negro vows to give certain things if his wish is fulfilled; these things are hung on trees before or after the fulfilment, as in the temples of more developed cults.[175] In India, "vows are made with regard to the depredations of wild beasts, that if they cease, an image of the troublesome animal shall be made and placed in the shrine."[176] The Phœnicians of Cyprus had a custom of consecrating to certain divinities, as the outcome of a vow, statues of themselves instead of votive stones. Thus they expressed the fulfilment of personal religious obligation. The blessing which such a gift was thought to bring was so highly esteemed that at length in late Greek and Roman times associations caused to be erected in the temples, at their expense, statues of persons who had won the good-will of the associations.[177] If the Greek gods took oath, it was by the elder gods, or by the Styx, or otherwise in such manner as to put at stake their immortality.[178]

Involving a self-curse as it did, the oath or vow was conceived to have unparalleled power over destiny. In the unshaken and unshakable belief that such a curse would come true, the vow-taker had little temptation to prove false. A vow was more than a mere

[168] Burns, in Wide World Mag., I, 475.

[169] Hopkins, Relig. Ind., 534.   [170] Kgchte., II, 294, 314.

[171] Mooney, in BAE, XIV, 1033.   [172] Procksch, Blutrache, 5.

[173] Homer, Iliad, XIX, 208-210, 304-308, 346-348; XXIII, 50; XXIV, 161-166, 553.

[174] Electra, 256.   [175] Stuhlmann, Mit Emin, 24.

[176] Painter, in JASB, II, 153.   [177] Pietschmann, Phön., 211.

[178] Keller, Hom. Soc., 176.

promise, for the supernatural powers were called to witness. A statement "under oath" is still regarded as peculiarly trustworthy and falsity under oath is not only a lie but perjury. Oaths and oath-making embrace a large group of usages which testify to the high importance of societal coöperation. Concordant understandings, promises, and elementary contracts are essential to that. Fidelity, confidence, and mutual responsibility are indispensable to societal well-being. There must be sanctions to insure all this. Eidolism and daimonism furnish the philosophy and suggest the devices; then comes an application of daimonistic doctrine which develops that philosophy and also builds up mentality and character.

CHAPTER XXXIV

SACRIFICE

§284*. **Nature of Sacrifice.** A gift or a bribe may be "given" to a human being; when it is presented to a daimon, however, the proper term is to "dedicate" or "make sacred" or "sacrifice." From renunciatory forms of propitiation the series now passes to the positive giving or sacrifice of property, and even of life itself, in order to avoid misfortune or to secure good luck. Sacrifice appears as an insurance in advance or as an atonement afterwards; it is accompanied by a lurking fear lest it be not satisfactory. Positive methods of propitiation include, in addition, whatever else would please and predispose human beings, such as praise, glorification, flattery, and entertainment in general. Main[1] has a chapter on the sacrifice of virgins to the gods, pandering to their lust. No actual sacrifice of property is involved, it is true, in most of these latter forms of "worship"; nevertheless worship, accompanied or not by sacrifice, is something considerably more positive in nature than the avoiding, exorcistic, coercitive, and renunciatory practices hitherto considered, however regularly it may be associated with them.[2]

The whole medley of forms taken by sacrifice and worship becomes ritualized just as do the negative forms of the cult; and—what is more significant—the elements of reverence, awe, dread, devotion, and adoration inherent in the former are merely extensions and refinements of original ghost-fear. Reverence, in its etymology, signifies fear; and the cases, corroborating the etymology, leave no manner of doubt that the element of dread is always present. So long as the aleatory element lies behind religious constructions, it could scarcely be otherwise. The most obvious and visible demonstration of the evolutionary nature of these religious phenomena is the close connection of sacrifice and worship with the ghost-cult.[3]

[1] *Relig. Chastity*, ch. IX.   [2] Lippert, *Kgchte.*, II, 331.
[3] Ch. XXVI, above.

But, before coming to the cases, there are a number of considerations touching upon the nature of sacrifice which can be brought out by reviewing an article by Wilken[4] on "The Origin of Sacrifice" in which he takes issue with a theory propounded by Robertson Smith, in his *Religion of the Semites*. Smith makes much of the reverence and trust felt toward the gods on account of the common consanguineal bonds existing between them and their worshippers. Even the victim, an animal, was within the sacred circle of kin; and the sacrificial meal was therefore a sort of communion between blood-kin. There was therefore no fear but a feeling of oneness between gods and men; Smith rejects the famous saying: *Primus in orbe deos fecit timor*. Wilken retorts that there is little if any evidence for this view; there is no such relationship to the gods; their "fatherhood" is not to be taken in the emotional sense. What is demonstrable is the soul-cult and the fear of ghosts; the cult is "no worship of piety but of self-interest and fear." The theory of the sacrifice is *Do ut des*. The gods are not friends but jealous enemies. Illustration is copious, here as in Wilken's other publications. "Need and fear are the factors through which the relation between men and gods is regulated and the character of the worship is determined." Men serve the ghosts the better the more frightened they are. Hence a sacrifice is no spontaneous gift to the gods but a means to get on with them. The two ideas are contradictory. The eating of the sacrifice is simply the utilization of a residue; the spirits have had its substance, its soul, which is released by breaking or killing, as men are rendered inanimate. The gods feast on the "smell" or savor, which is the quintessence of the offering. Whatever idea there is of communion is secondary, not primary. We have not gone into the detail of this refutation, having contented ourselves with the general outlines, which the detail seems to us to support.

We turn now to the cases illustrative of the nature of sacrifice. "The sacrifices of the Solomon Islands may well be traced to the desire of making the deceased still sharers of the common meal; what is offered and burnt is common food. The further step of begging the offended ghost to take all and spare the sick is taken in several localities." This is the ghost-cult. Codrington,[5] who writes the above, has reservations about the derivation of the daimon from the ghost and consequently runs into puzzles when he comes to daimonology. "To connect the offering of money," he goes on, "to a spirit who is never the ghost of a man, nor at all the animating spirit of a natural object, with the sharing of the common meal with the deceased, is much more difficult." It seems to Codrington, apparently, more than a little strange that the daimons are so human: "to offer money is apparently to give what man most values, and what the spirit also loves."

"The fear of damaging their material well-being, their property, is for the Koi-koin the chief incentive for respecting supernatural influences, and to the beings they fear is oftener accorded consideration than to the good ones who bring blessings. The sacrifices . . . are therefore . . . means for rendering the supernatural powers favorable to those who offer them."[6] The fact is that the daimons love just what anthropomorphic creations might be supposed to love, and are not even above sharing a meal. The ghost-cult and the more evolved forms of sacrifice and worship are always merging into one another: the Chukchi shamans, at feasts, make sacrifices and recite incantations, but "at the same

---

4 In VG, IV, 161 ff.   5 *Melanesians*, 144, note.
6 Fritsch, *Eingeb. S.-Afr.*, 339.

time they do not forget to send gifts to the deceased relatives of the host, by means of burning."[7] Skeat and Blagden[8] have seen among certain Malays, "on the occasion of their rice-harvest feast, a small quantity of boiled rice deposited on the top of a low tree-stump, and offered by way of compliment to all the enemies of the rice, as represented by noxious insects and the wild beasts of the jungle. Here we see the idea of sacrifice in one of its most rudimentary stages, that of a mere complimentary present intended to establish a truce with avowed and acknowledged foes."

In the East Indies the evil spirits are appeased more than the good, the lower rather than the higher, the present more than the absent. The fortune, good or ill, that comes from the spirits is given, not according to any deeds of men but according to the gifts which they offer to the higher powers. Some sacrifices are simple, others full of ceremonial; the common daily offering is done by each man for himself. In the great offerings the shamans play an important rôle; from being merely seers they come to be priests. The sacrifice is mostly food and drink, though clothing is included; the best gifts are pigs and dogs. The formula used is: "Here is your share, from the first fruits. Give us luck." The spirits cannot eat material things; they eat the souls of the offering and the sacrificer eats the flesh. This is the conception with all the people of the Indian Archipelago. During sacrifice no work may be done and silence must be preserved; the sacrifice is a great prohibition and there is hardly any occurrence in public or private life that does not demand it. The *adat* (code) regulates all this to the least detail. Sacrifices can be made at all times and places; though the Archipelago knows almost no native temples, the offerings, are made most often in localities where the spirits are supposed to love to be. In some regions a little house is built to lay the offering in, such structures being later torn down. An exceptional temple, covered with pictures, generally obscene, was used by all the tribe and was probably erected in honor of ancestors.[9]

Dogma is as difficult to confute in its primitive as in its developed form; take the case of the spirit eating the food sacrificed. Roth[10] "once remonstrated on the futility of the custom, on the ground that the food was clearly not eaten by any invisible being, but by fowls or pigs, or perhaps by reckless boys. Their answer was ready. The *antu*, whatever form it may take in showing itself to human eyes, is, as a spirit, invisible, a thing of soul, not of matter: now, they said, the soul spirit comes and eats the soul of the food: what is left on the altar is only its husk, its accidents, not its true essence." Thus dogma is unassailable; there is no verification on facts of observation but merely progressively deeper dives into mystery. The cure for faith that does not verify is merely more faith. You always get back to an original premise,

[7] Elenitzki, *The Strangers of Siberia* (Russ.), 67.

[8] *Malay Penin.*, II, 199-200.   [9] Wilken, *Vkde.*, 573-577.

[10] *Sarawak*, I, 189.

capable of a chameleon-interpretation; and the stark primitiveness of that premise is always there for the eye that is open.

Sacrifice is so regularly connected with eating that the two operations are not readily separable. "That the Babylonians originally regarded the sacrifice as food for the gods comes out clearly from numerous passages of the cuneiform inscriptions."[11] The ghosts had their share of the family or tribal meal, and so did the more evolved spirits. In Homer, "meals were generally sacrifices, and sacrifices meals; drinking was likewise inseparable from libation."[12] "In old Israel all slaughter was sacrifice, and a man could never eat beef or mutton except as a religious act." The sacrificial feast goes back to the public meal of clansmen; "the Passover became a sort of household sacrifice after the exile, but was not so originally."[13] Not food alone, but clothing, ornament, and other desirables found their way to the altar; in general, anything was material for sacrifice to anthropomorphic spirits that was of value to men. This statement, however, though broadly true, needs a little qualification, for there were articles of sacrifice which men might not eat because of their sacred character. They were fetishes, and came, as such, under the food-taboo.

The Hebrews might not eat the seat of life[14]—the blood or viscera of victims, especially the kidneys or liver or the omental fat; in case of sacrifice these were burned on the altar. "The importance attached by various nations to these vital parts of the body is very ancient, and extends to regions where sacrifice by fire is unknown. The point of view from which we are to regard the reluctance to eat of them is that, being more vital, they are more holy than other parts, and therefore at once more potent and more dangerous. All sacrificial flesh is charged with an awful virtue, and all *sacra* are dangerous to the unclean or to those who are not duly prepared; but these are so holy and so awful that they are not eaten at all, but dealt with in special ways, and in particular are used as powerful charms." Similarly the flesh of the totem-animal was eaten only by exception: "it is akin to the men who acknowledge its sanctity, and if there is a god it is akin to the god. And, finally, the totem is sometimes sacrificed at an annual feast, with special and solemn ritual. In such cases the flesh may be buried or cast into a river, as the horses of the sun were cast into the sea, but at other times it is eaten as a mystic sacrament."[15]

It is worth while to notice especially the function of blood in sacrifice. We have seen that the soul was connected with the vital fluid and shall find that blood comes to represent the bond between individuals and groups.[16] All sorts of notions of a derived nature surround the blood.[17] It is widely used as food. Perhaps "it is unnecessary to quote examples of the world-wide rite of offering the

11 Schrader, *Keilinschriften,* 594-595.
12 Lippert, *Kgchte.,* II, 140; Keller, *Hom. Soc.,* 126-127; 134-135.
13 Smith, *Relig. Sem.,* 142, 270-280.   14 §213, above.
15 Smith, *Relig. Sem.,* 379, 381, 295; §260, above.
16 §§146, 147, above, and 411, 412, below.
17 Strack, *Blutaberglaube.*

blood, the vehicle of life to the primitive mind, to the god, while the material flesh is eaten by the worshippers";[18] but we shall cite a few cases.

In West Africa, "the blood of the living sacrifice is regarded as the portion of the offering which specially belongs to or is particularly acceptable to the god, because the natives suppose it to be the vital principle." When the British invaded Benin, "the natives had hoped by a great blood-bath again to reconcile the spirits of the . . . fetishes, and to be able to win for themselves the fortune of arms."[19] "Peculiar is the conception of the strengthening, even healing quality of animal-blood as of the most precious fluid of the animal-body. The Galla not only anoint their faces with it, in the desire to remain strong and well; not only sprinkle house and servants; not only wet their hands with blood when taking oath; not only taste of the blood of the big animals, for instance the elephant, which they have killed—but they also drench with blood the roots of consecrated trees, to protect them from withering; . . . offer it to the gods in sacrifice, in order to get riches in return; anoint with it the chin of the chief, to make him more powerful and unconquerable; wet with blood the face of the corpse reposing in the grave as a sign that its rest is to be a profound one and that nobody may disturb it. The princely bridegroom anoints forehead, nose, and cheek-bones with blood before the marriage, to make the union lucky." By blood-ceremonial is made "a marriage that is absolutely irrevocable. Bride and groom dip their fingers in the blood and color each other in turn . . . in order to get strength and blessing for the progeny to come. Relatives of the bride anoint her whole body with blood, to give her strength in the period of pregnancy, and the husband pours blood into the hollow of the wife's neck, in the hope thus never to let her love grow cold. Everything indicates that they ascribe to blood a magic power which then comes to belong quite especially to the individual who has imbibed it."[20]

At a Sea Dyak funeral, "a fowl is killed, and the blood is collected in a cup and mixed with a little water. Each person present is touched with the blood, to propitiate the gods of the infernal world and to secure immunity from any evil consequences to the persons engaged in the funeral rites."[21] Among the Eskimo, "the tail of a living dog is often cut from its body in order that the fresh blood may be cast upon the ground to be seen by the spirit who has caused the alarm, and thus he may be appeased."[22]

In the "Nekuia" of the *Odyssey*,[23] the ghosts drink eagerly of the sacrificial blood, by which their memories are restored for the time and they regain a semblance of being. To the Semites, "this ritual of blood is the essence of the offering; no part of the flesh falls as a rule to the god, but the whole is distributed among the men who assist at the sacrifice. . . . The law of Deuteronomy allows men to slay and eat domestic animals everywhere, provided only that the blood—the ancient share of the god—is poured out on the ground. . . . The fat of the intestines was also from ancient times reserved for the deity, and therefore it also was forbidden food. The prohibition did not extend

[18] Smith, *Relig. Sem.*, 234; Godden, in JAI, XXVI, 189 (quoted).
[19] Ellis, *Ewe*, 79; Seidel, in *Globus*, LXXIV, 6.
[20] Paulitschke, *Nordost-Afr.*, I, 152.   [21] Gomes, *Sea Dyaks*, 136.
[22] Turner, in BAE, XI, 196.   [23] Bk. XI; Keller, *Hom. Soc.*, 105.

to the fat distributed through other parts of the body."[24] Lippert[25] notes that tribes that loathed blood drank it to come into communion with the spirits and learn the future; and that some modern Jews mix blood drawn from their fingers at marriage.

It appears that in certain varieties of sacrifice the victims were not eaten, because they would appear to be somehow tainted by sin or to be otherwise undesirable. Such cases have been utilized in other connections.[26]

In Homeric Greece, as in Borneo,[27] the sacrifices accompanying oaths of truce or reconciliation were not even burned, much less eaten; the Borneo pig was left in its gore while the Greek boar thus sacrificed was hurled into the sea, "as food for the fish"; and lambs, after their throats had been cut, were merely carried away again.

In both cases, hairs had been cut from the heads of the victims and distributed to all participators in the vows; in fact the taking of oaths was called "cutting sacred oaths" and the verb "cut" is even used by itself to designate the ceremony.[28] Certain plants and animals are sacrificed which men no longer eat. Their identity is always significant. Conversely, "the sacrifices of animals not ordinarily eaten, are not the invention of later times, but have preserved with great accuracy the features of a sacrificial ritual of extreme antiquity."[29] This consideration qualifies further the generalization that the materials of sacrifice are those of human use. The old is holy and the new profane; and the former, not only in the matter of foods but also of dress, language, actions, and mores in general, is adhered to in the cult long after it has been superseded in common life. Unleavened bread and bitter herbs are cult-foods centuries after leaven and modern condiments have become known. To a special consideration of this fact and of the broad results of it we shall later come; its bearing upon the materials of sacrifice is obvious when attention is once lent to the matter. A number of articles are offered which, though men once ate or otherwise used them, are employed no longer. Once desirable to the living, and so also to the dead, while mortals have since discarded

---

[24] Smith, *Relig. Sem.*, 201, 235, 238, note; he refers to Deut., XII, 15, 16; Levit., III, 17; XVII, 10 ff.; I Sam., II, 16; Exod., XXIV, 8.

[25] *Kgchte.*, II, 336, 337.   [26] §§142, 277, above.

[27] Furness, *Head-Hunters*, 128; §295, below.

[28] Homer, *Iliad*, XIX, 250-267; III, 260-313; II, 124; III, 297.

[29] Smith, *Relig. Sem.*, 295.

them, the daimons still retain a preference for what they used to desire. Hence it is that the sacrifice is seldom the modern novelty but rather the "old" food which men either do not eat at all or eat only ceremonially, that is, merely taste.[30]

That the superior powers can be drawn this way and that by propitiation—that every god, so to speak, has his price—appears in most accounts and especially in such practices as concealment of the favoring or tutelary divinity's name, lest he be lured away. While the Roman priests called upon the tutelary divinity of a besieged town, promising a new and better worship at Rome, they kept the name of their own god secret lest the same thing should be done to them.[31] In the *Iliad*,[32] before the ordeal-trial, Ajax advises the Achæans to pray "in silence, to yourselves, lest the Trojans hear," though he corrects himself, in a burst of confidence, on the ground that there is in any event nothing to be afraid of.

It is worth noting that propitiation, being a method of securing tangible and verifiable results—for example, of making crops grow by fasting in the spring or sprinkling the ground with blood —forms a practice subject to correction. The soil may be seen to respond to chance fertilization and then irrational methods may be succeeded by rational. Although it cannot be contended that much science emerged out of such emendation, there was, at any rate, a development in what might be called the artistic side of the propitiatory cult, comprising music, art, and dramatic representation. These, fostered by religion, were eventually to have careers of their own when freed from cult-connections. Their emancipation has been broadly parallel to that of the evolving sciences.

§285*. Bargain-Sacrifice; Prayer. Perhaps the most outstanding feature of the sacrifice as a process of dealing with the daimons is the fact that it is a bargain. It is a piece of the business of living; a premium paid on an insurance policy against the aleatory element; a purchase of good luck. It is not at all intended to be a free gift, something for nothing, given purely out of love for the spirits or a disinterested desire to see them pleased. The defi-

30 Lippert, *Kgchte.*, II, 286; Keller, *Hom. Soc.*, 134; §324, below.
31 Pliny, *Hist. Nat.*, XXVIII, ch. IV.
32 VII, 193-196; Keller, *Hom. Soc.*, 113-114.

nite practical interest of men in what the daimons do, or do not do, is a constant factor that must be regularly reckoned with throughout the evolution of society. Thanksgiving for favors accorded without the asking is rare enough in ethnography to be virtually non-existent; the whole relation between men and daimons is a sort of debit and credit account where satisfaction, if given at all by the latter, is strictly for value received.

Certain tribes in the Philippines believe in *anitos* that are ever ready to do one evil; and ceremonies for their placation form an uninterrupted series. It is a strange sort of thanksgiving where they "give thanks to the *anitos* for not having destroyed their possessions."[33]

An extreme case of bargaining with a divinity, where the latter acts as a debt-collecting agency, receiving commissions, is afforded by a "quaint custom" of southern India. "The goddess Kulanthat-Amman has established for herself a useful reputation as a settler of debts. When a creditor cannot recover a debt, he writes down his claim on a scroll of palmyra leaves, and offers the goddess a part of the debt, if it is paid. The palmyra scroll is hung up on an iron spear in the compound of the temple before the shrine. If the claim is just, and the debtor does not pay, it is believed that he will be afflicted with sickness and bad dreams. In his dreams he will be told to pay the debt at once, if he wishes to be freed from his misfortune. If, however, the debtor disputes the claim, he draws up a counter-statement, and hangs it on the same spear. Then the deity decides which claim is true, and afflicts with sickness and bad dreams the man whose claim is false. When a claim is acknowledged, the debtor brings the money, and gives it to the pujari, who places it before the image of Kulanthat-Amman, and sends word to the creditor. The whole amount is then handed over to the creditor, who pays the sum vowed to the goddess into the temple coffers. . . . So great is the reputation of the goddess, that Hindus come from about ten miles round to seek her aid in recovering their debts. The goddess may sometimes make mistakes, but, at any rate, it is cheaper than an appeal to an ordinary court of law, and probably almost as effective as a means of securing justice. In former times no written statements were presented: people simply came and represented their claims by word of mouth to the deity, promising to give her a share." Since the written claim has come into use probably more debts have been collected and more money gathered into the treasury.[34]

Not much reflection is needed to realize that the priests of this divinity have a good business here, and one capable of considerable development. It is perfectly possible that they have built up an excellent system of self-maintenance without deliberate rascality, for the shaman is generally self-deceived while he is mystifying the rest.[35] The fact that everyone, including the priests, believes that it is the goddess who is the effective agency, need not prevent

[33] Scheidnagel, *Isl. Filip.*, 63.   [34] Thurston, *S. India*, 358-359.
[35] §309, below.

her servants from informing themselves as to the local economic and financial situation and developing considerable shrewdness in settling claims. A sound human judgment is not weakened by the preface: Thus saith the Lord.

The contractual aspect of sacrifice is a general one which will appear throughout the cases. There is small need of special illustration when attention has once fastened upon it. It is plainly developed in prayer; as prayers and vows belong to the same species of performance,[36] the bargain-element is not new to the reader. The verbal dealings of men with the dead in the ghost-cult[37] have shown, in their measure, the same contractual character. The prayer, though it frequently partakes somewhat of the nature of incantation and of imitative magic[38] and, in so far as it does that, reveals a coercitive aspect, is really the oral part of the sacrificial ceremonial, wherein attention is called to the offering and the *quid pro quo* is stated; it is the contract itself, the rest being the performance.

In the New Hebrides, if one man is oppressing another, the latter goes with an offering to the grave of a chief and begs him to punish the offender. Then the latter is killed in some disaster.[39] In Uganda, in times of adversity, there is a tribal prayer. "The people meet together, bringing a sheep, some flour, and some milk and honey. Three holes are dug in the ground, one for the oldest man of the tribe, one for the oldest woman, and one for a child. The food is cooked and mixed together, and portions are given to the man, woman, and child, who bury it in the holes allotted to them. The remainder of the sacrifice is then eaten by the old men of the tribe, and while this is proceeding, the rest of the people pray very solemnly. . . . It is thought that by burying this food in the ground the spirits of departed chiefs, together with, perhaps, the omnipotent Deity, may eat the buried food and accept the sacrifice of the tribe." The selection of the old and young symbolizes the whole tribe, from the oldest to the youngest.[40] The feature of eating with the spirits in a communal meal should be noted.[41]

The essence of primitive prayer, and of much that is offered by more developed peoples, comes out clearly in the Homeric type of invocation. "Prayers and vows were much the same thing; as the word for prayer indicates, prayers were mostly vows. These vows were then followed by a request, and thus belong really to the machinery of the bargain-sacrifice. Promises of sacrifice were held binding by the gods, who might conceive great anger if they were not performed. The prayer was often preceded by ceremonial hand-washings or by a bath and putting on of clean clothes. It was generally pronounced aloud, with hands reached out to the god; indeed, the expression 'lift up the

---

36 §283, above.
37 §228, above.
38 §§301, 302, below.
39 Macdonald, in AAAS, 1892, 729.
40 Johnston, *Uganda*, II, 883-884.
41 §§230, 260, above, and 297, below.

hands' is equivalent to 'pray.' Yet prayer might be uttered 'in the heart,' and before the enemy it was the part of caution to pray in silence. Prayer was offered in need to the god likely to be nearest at hand. It was a good time to pray when the god's attention was attracted to one's vicinity, that is, when an omen occurred. . . . Prayer was, with few exceptions, egoistic, and there are in Homer no prayers of thanksgiving which may not be more simply interpreted as promises."[42]

Where prayer does not include the element of promise of sacrifice, or a reminder of its performance, that element resides in the common assumption that only the prayers of the "just" stand much chance of being answered. But the just, or the "justified" are those whose cult-obligations have been scrupulously discharged. Their debt, guilt, failure in covenant, or sin is thus expunged. Their accounts are squared up with the spirits. This is now a lost idea, but it was very vivid once. It is better, if one is in doubt about his own status, to have some just person offer his petition for him. The man just above all others is of course the priest, who spends all his time attending to the god; then too there are laymen of notable piety whom the daimons do not readily fail. It does not matter much what a man's private life is, so long as he is justified: consider Jacob and David. The idea of the justified man is presented in typical clearness by Homer.[43]

From the words of the gods themselves, it was only with regret that they failed a "just" man. Of mortals who are in Ilion "he was the dearest to the gods," says Zeus of Hector: "dearest to me also, since he never failed in acceptable gifts. For never did my altar lack a proper feast, neither libation nor savor." And of Odysseus in the same tenor: "How then could I be unmindful of the godlike Odysseus, who exceeds men in wisdom, and who surpasses in the sacrifices which he offers to the immortals?"

Louis XIV, when disaster overtook his armies, thought that God must have forgotten what the king had done for him. Sometimes God is thought to be showing off. When President Garfield was shot, one clergyman said that God sometimes wanted to remind men of his awfulness. These are fine examples of anthropomorphism, and the latter of how a man can understand a god or be in his confidence.

Primitive prayers, as the reader of them observes at once, do not ask for spiritual things; much less are they an expression of "attitude of soul." They have to do with temporal happenings which represent the impact of the aleatory element upon actual

42 Keller, *Hom. Soc.*, 141-144 (where references to text are given).
43 *Iliad*, XXIII, 862-879; XXIV, 66-70; *Odyssey*, I, 65-67 and ff.; Keller, *Hom. Soc.*, 127.

living. It is entirely typical of prayer that the requests are, above all, for the life, health, and wealth of the individual and his immediate circle and for offspring. They ask for success in self-maintenance and in self-perpetuation, to live and to procreate—the common interests of all living things. Practically all prayers of primitive man are variations, details, or derivations of these main interests. Only in more sophisticated times are the less tangible and more tenuous things besought; and even then the bulk of the people who pray still cling to requests for temporal blessings.

A typical African case is where the formulas run: "God give you to pasture and to bind!" that is, give you riches in cattle, the engrossing local form of wealth; and "God waken you with the anointing butter!" The latter phrase needs the comment that a woman happily recovered from child-bearing carries a lump of butter on her head when she goes out the first time, as a sign of the blessing she has received. "Thus should God accord to the receiver of the wish a surprising blessing of children, for every Wachaga wants a rich progeny in spite of all the need and cares which, even upon him, children may impose."[44] The prime care, in India, is "how to avert, control, or conciliate . . . evil powers, not for any spiritual benefit to himself—in the sense in which the man of higher culture understands spiritual benefit—but for securing the only treasures he cares for—his crops and his cattle and his own health and that of his own wife and children—from every possible harm."[45]

Homer gives several stock forms of prayer which are not materially different one from the other or from the forms common throughout the world. The following is typical: (a) invocation of the deity; (b) review of reasons establishing a claim for answer; (c) object of the request.[46] The second and third portions of the formula are simply an exposure of the nature of the prayer as an oral contract preceding or fixing the terms of the bargain and are readily understandable. The invocation of the daimon is worth considering by itself, for it is no mere call to attention but a distinct form of propitiation. It is usually highly flattering and subservient, rehearsing, as it does, the honorable titles of the god, just as the several titles of a Tatar prince had to be duly recited, unless he dispensed for some reason with the ceremonial, before embarking upon a request or even a message.[47] Herein is the anthropomorphic quality of the daimon again betrayed; for his attention

[44] Gutmann, in *Globus*, XCIII, 299.   [45] Roy, in JAI, XLIV, 350.

[46] Naegelsbach, *Hom. Theol.*, §13 (where a number of prayers are cited); Keller, *Hom. Soc.*, 142.

[47] Sienkiewicz, *Fire and Sword*, 673.

is drawn to the man of just ideas whose sentiments concerning his deity fit in so well with those which the latter holds about himself.

This phase of prayer belongs to active worship and will recur. Thus far it is clear, that out of such ideas comes the notion that men will be heard for their "much shouting," that prayer by itself is propitiatory, and that it turns readily into ritual—into such mechanical ritual, indeed, that it can be performed, as it were, by machinery. Witness the Tibetan device. A recent traveller encountered monasteries "containing enormous prayer-wheels in which they said there were one million prayers. Each time the wheel is turned a bell rings, and one million prayers have ascended to Heaven." Water-power and wind-power are used in a number of localities.[48] There are even wooden idols in Japan that are covered with spit-balls shot at them by pilgrims, the petition, written on the paper, in this way reaching the god.[49]

§286*. Atonement. It has been noted that sacrifice often represents a sort of neutrality-toll levied by the gods. There are a number of ancestral spirits that are supposed to be always good; and yet even they are the recipients of gifts and sacrifices, on the theory, it would seem, that it is safer that way. Faith in the goodness of the spirits, unless they are insignificant ones, seldom goes to the limit of permitting negligence; men are too unsure of themselves and of their own adroitness in not becoming irritating to the daimons. In fact, there lies behind the aforesaid neutrality-toll the widespread notion that man is by his actions, wittingly or unwittingly, always in sin—even that he has come into the world already sinful and under peril. "Original sin" may belong, as a dogma, to a more developed stage of civilization, but the conviction that anyone may at any time sin, and so be a candidate for punishment, is entirely correlative with the common experience of all mankind; for there is always the chance of running foul of the aleatory element and falling into unforeseeable disaster. It was thought possible for one to become, in various ways and not by his own knowledge or intent, "unclean"; and then he has stood in a

[48] Howard-Bury, in *Jr. Roy. Geog. Soc.*, LIX, 85-86.
[49] Humbert, *Japan*, 118.

relation to the daimons that was gravely perilous both to himself and to his neighbors.

"The Hausa is pursued all through his life by the fear of the bori, and various measures are taken to avoid the attentions of these demons. . . . The rite of initiation into the sect is supposed to render the dancers themselves immune from the attacks of the particular demons which they profess to follow, while the periodical ceremonies seem to inoculate them afresh on behalf of the whole community. These ceremonies are akin to the early sacrifices, in which a selected human being (not an animal) suffered to save others."[50] This appears to be a periodic removal of uncleanness. The pursuit of blood-vengeance has a like aim in view for the Albanian. "After living some eight months among blood-hunters, I perceived what *ghak* meant to them. It is not so much a punishment which they inflict, as an act performed for self-purification, and as such a solemn and necessary act. For there are certain offences that blacken, not merely the honour of the man against whom they have been committed, but blacken also the honour of his whole house and even of his tribe. Only blood can cleanse the stain. And the man whose honour is blackened is obsessed with the idea of his own impurity. It gives him no rest. Blood he must have. . . . In such cases an absolutely innocent man who is ignorant of the cause of offence may be sacrificed; and his blood cleanses the other's honour, who, triumphant, announces his deed. He is now in turn liable to be shot, and should he have slain a man of his own tribe, by tribe law his house will be burnt, his corn burnt, and in some districts his trees felled and his cattle slaughtered too. But all this is of but small moment. His honour is clean, and if he must die he dies happy. A man of the Christian tribe of Nikaj who was seeking blood was exhorted by the Franciscan to desist, and threatened with the torments of hell. 'I would rather clean my honour and go to hell,' he replied, and went out to slay. He slew, but was himself mortally wounded. The Franciscan hastened to the spot, and begged him to confess and repent while yet there was time. The dying man said, 'I do not want your absolution or your heaven, for I have cleaned my honour.' And he died."[51] "It is highly significant that young pigeons and turtle-doves were sacrificed to Jahveh, under the Levitical law, as an atonement for the impurity of child-birth, while similar offerings were brought by the Virgin to the Temple at Jerusalem after the birth of Christ."[52]

Sins of omission were easy to fall into; where it was comparatively a simple matter to avoid definitely tabooed actions, it was impossible to meet positive requirements that were not known, much less formulated. An "unknown god" might, at any time, resent lack of propitiation. The only safe course, under these circumstances, was to atone regularly and punctiliously for what sins one must have committed or must be committing that he could not know about. It was a sort of blanket insurance-device, cover-

50 Tremearne, in JAI, XLV, 20, 23.   51 Durham, in JAI, XL, 465.
52 March, in JAI, XXVII, 227; §388, below.

ing visitations of the aleatory element not otherwise provided against.

A method of atonement that is not far short of sacrifice is that connected with the scape-goat. The idea is familiar to those acquainted with the Hebrew scriptures[53] and has been exhaustively illustrated by Frazer.[54]

The idea of the scape-goat is not uncommon in India; "during a severe outbreak of smallpox, the people of Jeypur made some 'puja' to a goat and marched it into the Ghats and let it loose on the plains."[55] In Korea, on New Year's Day, rude straw dolls stuffed with a little money were thrown into the street. Such an effigy "is believed to take away troubles and foist them on whoever picks it up. To prevent such a calamity more than one mother on that evening pounced upon a child who had picked up the doll, and threw it far from him." Another such Korean custom "causes people to paint images on paper, and to write against them their troubles of body or mind, afterwards giving the paper to a boy who burns it."[56]

This idea and practice of putting off sin may be extended to apply to a human victim; thus emerges vicarious atonement, wherein the one suffers in expiation of the sins of the rest, and other more refined and developed conceptions. Such a human scape-goat of a crude order is the "sin-eater."[57]

"Not long ago, in upper Bavaria, when a man died and had been laid out, a cake was made of ordinary flour. The corpse was placed before the fire, and this cake, called the corpse cake, was put upon his breast to rise. The dough, in rising, was believed to absorb all the virtues of the deceased, and the cake was afterward eaten by his nearest relatives." This is a species of cannibalism. "In the Balkan Peninsula an edible image of the dead was carried in the funeral procession. When the body was buried the mourners ate this image above the grave, saying 'God rest him!'" These cases introduce us to the veritable "sin-eater," whose function, in Wales, "has only ceased within the memory of men still living. It was the custom for the nearest relative, usually a woman, to hand across the bier, or place upon the breast of the corpse, bread, cheese, and beer, which were eaten by the sin-eater, who pronounced everlasting rest to the departed. It was believed that the sin-eater thus appropriated to himself all the sins which the deceased had committed."[58] "In the county of Hereford was an old custome at funeralls to have poor people who were to take upon them all the sinnes of the party deceased!"[59] The last author remarks that the object of sin-eating was to keep the ghost from returning; it is clear that this custom is, in any case, one whereby sins are assumed, with

53 §§275, above, and 295, below; Levit., XVI, 8, 10, 21 ff.; Duhm, *Geister,* 55.
54 *Golden Bough,* II, 182 ff.   55 Fawcett, in JASB, I, 213, note.
56 Bishop, *Korea,* 265 ff.
57 Hartland, "Sin-eater," in *Folk-Lore,* III, 145-157.
58 Anon., in PSM, XLVIII, 411, note.
59 Gomme, *Ethnol. in Folklore,* 117, 120.

the result that consequent suffering or risk or requirement of expiation is incurred.

Thus the idea of atonement for something in the way of a delinquency is prominent in sacrifice, even though there may be no formulated doctrine of natural and original sin. The latter conception is not, however, without representation on the earlier stages, as will appear under the topic of redemption.[60]

§287*. Insurance and Investment. Most sacrifices, bargains as they are, fall into one of two categories: insurance or investment. In the former, there is, as in the case of the Melanesians, a combination of fear and distrust with crass materialism; the idea of the sacrifice is "to move ill-disposed spirits to omit the evil they plan."[61] Here is evasion through bribery. It has been repeatedly noted that insurance against bad luck is the dominant principle of the cult; men had long been working on this negative or avoidance side before they arrived at the idea of attaining anything positive through sacrificial operations—of actually setting out to buy good luck; of investing with the hope of a positive return. Several representative cases will set these and other general aspects of sacrifice before us, after which we can go on to more special types.

In the South Seas men's ills and successes have a good deal to do with the sea, and sailing is intimately connected with spirit-influences; "during the voyage certain foods are cast out of the canoe to induce the spirits not to stir up the sea by winds." Melanesian sacrifice is connected with magic at almost every turn: "if a man goes to sacrifice for success in fighting, he takes great care that nothing sharp should prick or scratch him, or a stone bruise him; in the one case he would be shot, in the other he would be clubbed." The familiar spirit is in evidence also. "Money in this same way of sacrifice, if so it can be called, is scattered in a deep hole in a stream, or in a pool among the rocks upon the beach. . . . The number of men who in old times had a sacred place with a familiar spirit of their own was large, probably most of the grown-up men had one." Also "offerings are made at sea near certain dangerous rocks; a tuft of pig's hair or a fowl's feather from the cargo, or a bit of food, is thrown into the sea for Tagaro, that he may give a safe passage to the canoe." The Solomon Islanders picture the ghosts that haunt the sea as having suffered a "sea change"; they are composed of fishes, their spears and arrows being long-bodied garfish and flying fish. "If a man on returning from a canoe voyage or from fishing on the rocks falls ill, it is because one of these sea ghosts has shot him. These ghosts are therefore propitiated in any danger

[60] §295, below.　　　　　　　　　　[61] Von Pfeil, *Südsee,* 164.

at sea with areca-nuts and fragments of food cast to them among the waves, and their anger is deprecated in prayers."[62] Despite their powers, such spirits "are evidently easily taken in." In the New Hebrides the distinction between good and bad people is that between liberal and stingy givers of food at feasts in honor of the spirits;[63] thus the moral element enters into the cult in a form characteristic of the local mores.

It is the object, in this place, to list a number of forms of sacrifice which will disclose the varying practice, together with the unvarying theory, of spirit-worship. Some of the practices are strangely divergent; a number are intertwined with magic; but all are mainly defensive.

Thus the Hottentots have various usages in sorcery called "making different"; they consist in sacrificing animals and giving the meat away. In Fanti-land there are to be seen, in fields and at boundaries, empty bottles from which rum and gin have been poured into the soil; also small wicker structures enclosing a few bananas, eggs, and a flask of gin to propitiate the fetish of the region.[64]

The reverential feeling of the Mongols toward fire is such that they will drink no wine or tea without first pouring out a few drops on the fire.[65] The Gilyaks have a "bear-feast," in connection with which the bear is to serve as a messenger to the "Great Master of the Mountains," as a witness to the value of the sacrifice.[66] The sacrifice of a cock takes place among certain classes in Bombay "to influence the incidence and progress of an epidemic of cholera."[67] In a field in which a house is to be built there is sometimes rudely drawn a human figure, together with magic symbols. Flowers and boiled rice are laid upon leaves about the figure, which represents the earth-spirit dwelling in the ground. If this ceremony should be omitted there would be no luck in the house.[68] In 1809, a wounded English officer died in an Indian desert; thereafter the natives paid sacrifices of ardent liquors and cigars to his spirit, feeling that it could not rest since he had died in so sad a way.[69] Among the Saoras there is a spirit that is very malevolent, always going about from one village to another to cause illness and death, and even devouring men. He is much feared; and before the new mangoes are eaten cooked—they may be eaten raw—a sacrifice of goats is made to him.[70]

There is in India a form of cult called demonolatry. Besides the gods of household, village, and locality, a number of devils are worshipped. "But, as a rule the worship of these devils is strictly confined to the lower classes and the aboriginal tribes."[71] Similarly in Tibet the devout burn every morning, "in

[62] Von Pfeil, *Südsee*, 143; Codrington, *Melanesians*, 141, 142, 143, 144, 258, 259.

[63] Cator, *Head-Hunters*, 187; Lawrie, in AAAS, 1892, 712.

[64] Ratzel, *Vkde.*, I, 104; Connolly, in JAI, XXVI, 149.

[65] Shchukin, *Shamanism* (Russ.), 31.

[66] Hawes, in *Globus*, LXXXVIII, 61.

[67] Weir, in JASB, I, 35.   [68] Thurston, *S. India*, 327, 328.

[69] Caldwell, in JASB, I, 104; Kipling, *Tomb of His Ancestors*, 136.

[70] Fawcett, in JASB, I, 242, 243.   [71] Joshi, in JASB, II, 202.

honor of the devil, sweet-smelling wood, little twigs of cypress or pine."[72] This classification well illustrates the ethnocentric tendency to degrade the daimons of another age, class, or people to the status of devil or demon; the word is used loosely, and many cases of so-called demonolatry are simply regular or special forms of the cult, where the evil spirits rather than the good are propitiated. Demonolatry is well developed in South India, in order through sacrifice to secure the removal of calamities already inflicted or threatening. The victim, generally a goat, must be a male and perfectly black. It is tested by dashing it with water; if it shakes itself, it is acceptable. Then the head must be struck off by a single blow, after which the body is held up so that all the blood may flow out upon the altar. It is then cut up and made into curry, which, with boiled rice and fruit, forms a sacred meal of which each participator in the sacrifice receives a share. "Sacrifices are *never* offered because of the sins of the worshippers and the devil's anger is not supposed to be excited by any moral offence." Sickness is the commonest reason for sacrifice. The demon is offered life for life—blood for blood. "The demon thirsts for the life of his votary or for that of his child; and by a little ceremony and coaxing he may be prevailed upon to be satisfied with the life of the goat instead."[73] Here is more than a suggestion of ransom or redemption.[74]

It is to be noted, in connection with what is called demonolatry, that primitive people seldom even approximate to a recognition of what we mean by "demon" or "devil"—a spirit antithetical to and in a constant duel with a great and good spirit. All the supernatural powers that need attention in order that men may live well are classed together without invidious distinction; all demand sacrifice and worship because all have rights that can be neglected only at peril. And, however careful one may be, he is sure sooner or later to violate some of these rights—if in no other way, then through ignorance of spiritual claims newly risen. Primitive "demons" or "devils" are simply evil spirits. "Demonolatry" is no more than the cult of the daimons; the Indian and the Chinese cases are not to be set apart from those which precede and follow because of the terminology employed by those who report them.

In China, "all the lofty maxims of Confucianism have been wholly ineffective in guarding the Confucianists from fear of the goblins and devils which figure so largely in Taoism. It has often been remarked, and with every appearance of truth, that there is no other civilized nation in existence which is under such bondage to superstition and credulity as the Chinese. Wealthy merchants and learned scholars are not ashamed to be seen, on the two days of the month set apart for that purpose, worshipping the fox, the weasel, the hedgehog, the snake, and the rat, all of which in printed placards are styled 'Their Excel-

[72] Rockhill, in USNM, 1893, 706.
[73] Caldwell, "Demonolatry," in JASB, I, 103 ff.
[74] §295, below.

lencies,' and are thought to have an important effect on human destiny."[75] Again, the function of the "paper-scatterer" is "to strew round or octangular sheets of tinned paper . . . along the road, and also in the water when the [funeral-]train has to cross a creek or stream by a bridge or in boats. . . . This paper money is destined for the malevolent spirits who, according to the popular conception, prowl about everywhere and infest streets and thoroughfares, mountains and forests, rivers and creeks, causing all sorts of mishap to befall men." Trumpets also are used to keep away from the funeral train those on whom the distribution of money has had no effect; and to the noise of the trumpets that of fire-crackers may be added.[76]

In Borneo one of the duties of survivors is to see to it that evil spirits do not take possession of the corpses; "and so beads are fastened in all the openings, on arms and legs, to pacify them." Offerings "to attract the good spirits and to propitiate the evil" are things which men themselves like.[77] A cobra is kept in the Dyak house as a tutelary spirit; "and everywhere among them these spirit-possessed reptiles are regarded as friendly visitors sent by some higher power for good, and the sacrifice becomes an acknowledgment of some obligation, and a gift to keep them in good humor, according to the maxim— 'Presents win the gods as well as men.'" Before starting to build a boat, plates were loaded with rice and other food and with betel for the spirits to enjoy.[78]

When an operation on the body is contemplated, "as an indispensable preliminary, before the skin is touched, several beads must be given to the operator, who may not keep them all, but must hand over some to the 'Toh,'—the demons who are always lurking about to see that the rules of the house are obeyed. It is lali [taboo] to draw human blood in a house unless the Toh be previously informed that it is for a lawful purpose. Some of the beads are, therefore, flung broadcast out of doors, for the Toh to gather up at their leisure."[79]

Pietschmann[80] enters somewhat into the theory of the Semitic sacrifice: "Animation does not rise exclusively from the life-force belonging to the object animated; there are mysterious powers who, as they please, can allow or hinder propagation and survival. . . . To them, therefore, and not to man, belongs in the fullest sense everything which they animate. If man uses for purposes of nourishment that which derives from their sphere of activity, he must not do this without assuring them a portion of it in the form of sacrifice, or without letting them join in the enjoyment of it. Their right precedes; therefore first fruits are especially appropriate to them—the first fruits of the cattle, the first fruits of the products of the field." The idea of first fruits is, to most people, wholly Biblical; but parallels occur widely over the earth.[81] "Among the Hebrews, as among many other agricultural peoples, the offering of first-fruits was connected with the idea that it is not lawful or safe to eat of the new fruit until the god has received his due." Cereal food had no such sacred association, however, as did flesh; "as soon as God had received His due of first-fruits, the whole domestic store was common." The Levitical distinction between the sacrifice of cereals and of animals "rests upon an ancient principle; that the idea of communion with the deity in a sacrificial meal of

75 Smith, *Chinese Char.*, 296.
77 Nieuwenhuis, *Borneo*, I, 85, 146.
79 Furness, *Head-Hunters*, 151.
81 Frazer, *Golden Bough*, II, 373 ff.

76 DeGroot, *Relig. Syst.*, I, 154 ff.
78 Roth, *Sarawak*, I, 188; II, 246.
80 *Phön.*, 165.

holy food was primarily confined to the . . . animal victim, and that the proper significance of the cereal offering is that of a tribute paid by the worshipper from the produce of the soil."[82] Here we verge upon the mysteries of the communion-ceremonies.[83]

The Greek mysteries "were probably the survivals of the oldest religion of the Greek tribes and of the people who had gone before them. They were not in honor of the heaven-gods, Zeus, Apollo, and Athene but of the gods of the earth and the under-world, those of the productive nature-forces and of death."[84] These elder gods are generally evil and demand a special and antiquated sort of propitiation. It is to be noted that Ægisthus, after killing Agamemnon and marrying his wife, made a rich sacrifice because he had accomplished a "great work" which he had never hoped to effect. "These offerings, however, as he had been warned by the gods not to pursue the above-mentioned crimes, are to be taken rather as a buying-off of punishment for disobedience. In this case it was entirely ineffective."[85] It appears that there might have been some hope of atoning for moral wrong-doing had there been no definite warning.

Among the Jews of South Russia, when a person is very ill, often "the field is measured." A piece of cloth in length corresponding to the circumference of the "field," that is, the cemetery, "is bought and given to the poor or to a hospital. . . . This probably happens with the idea of buying-off the sick person from death."[86]

It is impossible to exhaust the endless types of sacrifice. Many details are stored in the works of writers like Frazer.[87] The outstanding intention in the foregoing cases is the avoidance of ill luck through propitiation. It is desirable, however, to realize that the other aspect of sacrifice—the intention of getting good luck, of investing rather than insuring—is not altogether unrepresented. The two aspects merge one into the other; and they have in common a very practical aim. Religion has no sense except to ward off ill or to get good. The worship of the Christian god seems to savages to lack rational ground. If they worship they want a return, either from the god or from his representatives. "No more blanket, no more hallelujah!"[88] A few cases that are more in the modern mode of seeking positive good may be cited.

A young Melanesian "wishes to get on in the Loli Society, to become rich, to live to be old, the main object being to be a great man in the Loli. Such a person makes his offering of a pig or mats to the man who is acquainted with the spirit, . . . for they say . . . that the offering is not made to the spirit,

[82] Smith, *Relig. Sem.*, 142, 241, 244; Levit., XXIII, 14.
[83] §§230, 260, above, and 297, 325, below.
[84] Hatch, *Griechentum*, 210; §279 of the *Case-Book.*
[85] Keller, *Hom. Soc.*, 130, 141, 176; 136 (quoted).
[86] Weissenberg, in *Globus*, XCI, 359.
[87] Andree, in *Globus*, XCIII, 257.   [88] Von Martius, *Beiträge*, I, 463.

but to the man who knows him. This go-between keeps the pig for himself. He goes to the sacred place taking the supplicant with him; then he mutters to Tagaro, the spirit, 'This man has given us two a pig, let him be great, let him be a full-grown man.' After this introduction and recommendation the suppliant can go and make his requests in the sacred place by himself."[89] On Chatham Island, "they make a little canoe which they fill with wooden figures, hooks, and paddles, and with good wind send out upon the sea as sacrifice to Rongomoona that he may send plenty of fish."[90] The Koryaks are willing to discharge their part of the sacrifice-bargain in the hope that the spirits will carry out theirs. Such trustfulness is relatively rare; primitive people generally go on the theory of "no cure no pay." These natives are Christians in name, but sacrifice dogs and reindeer from time to time, although they do not know to whom. They say, in making an offering: "There is something for you. Do you give something to us."[91]

Among the Indian Khonds, "the priest goes from house to house, performing the ceremony of the cow-shed. . . . The ropes of the cattle (buffalo) which are grazing, are tied to the central point in the cow-shed, and the other ends are laid along the ground across the shed. These ropes are the visible objects to which sacrifice is made. The head of a chicken is buried near the ends tied to the post, a little to the left being ranged the leaves on which are placed rice, flesh of the pig, and a bit of its ear. A little in front of these is buried a rotten egg. The chicken whose head is buried is then and there boiled and eaten by children who have not yet donned a cloth. The priest goes thus around the village. The ceremony is performed for favors to come."[92] When the Malays go to get guttapercha, their wives set coconut-shells, filled with oil and lighted, afloat on the river to bring them luck.[93]

Alaskan masks are used "to propitiate and do honor to the animals or beings represented by them, and thus to bring about plenty of game during the coming year and to ward off evil influences.[94] In their war-sacrifices the Iroquois use "the leg of a deer or bear, or some other wild beast, rub it with fat, and then throw it on the fire, praying the sun to accept the offering, to light their paths, to lead them and give them the victory over their enemies, to make the corn of their fields to grow, to give them a successful hunt or fish."[95]

The wild-rice feast in Minnesota is stated to be "a sort of thanksgiving."[96] If it is really that, it is exceptional. The reader of ethnography seldom meets with a case where the spirits have spontaneously blessed men and the men have sacrificed in gratitude; primitive gratitude is predominantly of the type identified by Talleyrand as a lively sense of benefits to come. "It does not lie in the character of the natives to give thanks for benefits received."[97] There are no thank-offerings in Homer.[98] What has been received is merely history. In antiquity the sacrifice of the investment-type was common enough. Offerings were made to Hecate as mistress of the spirits to keep the house clear of evil phantoms. In the time of Augustus the knights threw pieces of money

[89] Codrington, *Melanesians,* 143.   [90] Weiss, *Chatham Ins.,* 19.
[91] Elenitski, *The Strangers of Siberia* (Russ.), 73.
[92] Fawcett, in JASB, II, 250.   [93] Bock, *Borneo,* 29.
[94] Nelson, in BAE, XVIII, pt. I, 358, 359.
[95] Carr, in *Smithson. Rep.,* 1891, 551.
[96] Jenks, in BAE, XIX, pt. II, 1091.
[97] Fritsch, *Eingeb. S.-Afr.,* 339.   [98] Keller, *Hom. Soc.,* 136.

into a lake for the preservation of the Emperor's life and health.[99] Dualism
enters largely into the more developed forms: the good or white spirit is enlisted to overcome the evil or black.

How far sacrifice and worship have come in their evolution to
be directed toward avoidance of ill and how far toward securing
good is a question that is considerably obscured by the development of dogmas and theories. There has been much rationalization
and the æsthetic element has entered largely into religious ritual;
nevertheless the primordial elements are still there and play their
part.

§288. The Burden of Sacrifice. "Sacrifice" has come to mean
self-denial, surrender, and loss; that is what the word generally
signifies to those who now use it, for the term is no longer connected, in current usage, with making something sacred or even
with the religion out of which it originated. When parents are said
to make sacrifices for their children, there is nothing religious
implied; it means that they go without that the children may have.
Similarly one may sacrifice present comfort in prospect of future
satisfaction; an architect may even sacrifice strength and utility
to beauty of construction. Sacrifice in its primordial sense has
gone out of fashion and is historical; the significance of the word
has shifted because that which has lingered in the mind respecting
sacrifice has been, it seems, the painful results of the practice as
felt by its performers rather than the practice itself and the beliefs
upon which it was once based.

The burdens entailed upon humanity by this detail of the cult
have been amply sufficient to stamp a lasting impression; they
represent a weighty factor when it comes to a final summing up
of the case of religion as an adjustment in the mores.[100] In this
place we should acquire some realization of the nature and weight
of the burden, in so far as it inheres in sacrifice, and add that impression to the one already derived from study of the ghost-cult,
of the antagonism of the living and the dead.[101] The existence and
pressure of this burden is implicitly if not explicitly suggested in
most of our cases of sacrifice, foregoing and to come; and we have

[99] Farnell, *Cults*, 511; Suetonius, *Augustus*, §57.
[100] §§329, 330, below.   [101] §234, above.

seen some, and shall see more, of the thrifty reactions of men in their effort to discharge their duties to the spirits and yet evade some of the loss attendant upon so doing. The fact that the work-animal is not sacrificed is significant.[102]

In Mombasa, "the daughter of one of my elders had been possessed of an evil spirit, and her father consulted the medicine man as to her condition. The seer sent her into a trance, and while she was lying unconscious, the spirit spoke through her mouth, saying he would leave her, were a dance given in his honour. The father was at the time too poor to hold the dance, which entailed expenses in palm toddy and rewards to the performers, but he undertook that it should take place in three months after the harvest of his maize. The spirit then, on his side, promised to desist from tormenting the woman."[103]

The killing of dogs cripples the domestic economy of the maritime Koryak: "At one time I came to a settlement of twelve houses, and found there more than forty slaughtered dogs hanging on posts."[104] The Indians depleted their stock in similar manner; "and in making these sacrifices, and all gifts to the Great Spirit, there is one thing yet to be told—that, whatever gift is made, whether a horse, a dog, or other article, it is sure to be the best of its kind that the giver possesses, otherwise he subjects himself to disgrace in his tribe, and to the ill will of the power he is endeavoring to conciliate. . . . Lewis and Clark, in their tour across the Rocky Mountains, have given an account of a Mandan chief who had sacrificed seventeen horses to his medicine-bag, to conciliate the good will of the Great Spirit; and I have met many instances where, while boasting to me of their exploits and their liberality, they have claimed to have given several of their horses to the Great Spirit." The speaker is the artist, Catlin.[105]

In Borneo, "the belief in an innumerable crowd of supermundane beings, populating the air, the water, and the woods, endowed with powers by which they rule all possible actions of mankind, causing now profit, now loss, exercises a great influence on the mode of life of the natives, hinders them in the development of their intellectual and moral qualities, and prejudices their material welfare. Offerings and prayers to the gods, consultations with them on the issue of enterprises, and thanksgivings by means of feasts on account of the fulfillment of wishes, occupy a great part of their time."[106]

Among the nomad Arabs the flesh of domestic animals—"the only class of victims admitted among the Semites as ordinary and regular sacrifices"—was not a common article of diet. "The everyday food of the nomad consisted of milk, of game, when he could get it, and to a limited extent of dates and meal—the latter for the most part being attainable only by purchase or robbery. Flesh of domestic animals was eaten only as a luxury or in times of famine."[107] Thus have valuable foods been systematically renounced, as has been noticed above,[108] in favor of the gods.

[102] Lippert, *Kgchte.*, I, 494, 510.
[103] Johnstone, in JAI, XXXII, 265-266.
[104] Jochelson, in AA, VI, 419.
[105] Quoted by Donaldson, in *Smithson. Rep.,* 1885, pt. II, 398.
[106] Schwaner, *Borneo,* 180-181 (trans. by Roth, *Sarawak,* II, clxxii).
[107] Smith, *Relig. Sem.,* 222, 223.   [108] §271, above.

Erman[109] thinks the boastful records of a Rameses III worthy of credence. In a reign of thirty-three years, he had given to the various temples 113,433 slaves, 493,386 head of cattle, 88 barks and galleys, and 2,756 golden images. Further contributions were 331,702 jars of incense, honey, and oil; 228,380 jars of wine and drink; 680,714 geese; 6,744,428 loaves of bread; and 5,740,352 sacks of coin. To get this wealth the king taxed his subjects; he did not create it himself. The burden rested squarely and heavily upon the population. Such extravagance seems less incredible to a generation which has been edified by glowing accounts of the contents of recently discovered royal tombs.

In Homer a case is mentioned of an offering of eighty-one oxen at a time; sacrifices succeeded each other closely; sometimes all the gods had to be propitiated in order. The term "hecatomb" (hundred oxen), though used no longer by Homer in its original signification, either of number or kind of animals, points to great prodigality.[110] Furthermore, the victims, here as among the Indians and elsewhere, are "unblemished," "fat," "young," and otherwise select. It would not do to sacrifice anything short of the best.

If one were to add to the list of sacrifices, as he might justifiably do, the materials and labor involved in erecting tombs, alignments, pyramids, and temples and in providing the endless and costly ecclesiastical paraphernalia of all places and times, he would arrive at stupendous totals of self-denial and cost. The loss involved could generally be but ill afforded; that men felt it and tried to evade or lessen the burden is evident enough.

"The Chukchi, who bears his lot with patience and is commonly lacking in all energy, believes in spirits in the earth, the sea, rivers and mountains, the sun and moon. Without doubt, on the basis of his general character we must conclude that the strongest side of his religion is fear. By sacrifice he seeks to win the good will of the superhuman beings but, just as he enjoys deceiving strangers, so is he niggardly with his sacrifices. To get good fishing the Chukchi . . . regarded it as necessary to sacrifice to the sea-spirit, but of the crust which he got for such purpose he thought the spirit did not require more than a few crumbs."[111] Instead of real animals, Tibetans now sacrifice dough-images; so in Rome models of wax or dough were substituted; and the same thing occurred at Athens.[112] Chinese thrift in the sacrifice of gilt-paper images, parchment-figures, and worthless money will be recalled from several preceding examples.[113] In the case of a compact in Borneo, a "wee pig was sacrificed on the beach and there left in its gore. Such a sacrifice, when made in ratification of a compact, renders the flesh inedible to all participants in the ceremony; hence the diminutive size of the pig."[114] Thrift was evidently at work among the Homeric Greeks who cut out the thigh-bones of victims, covering them with fat, and then making them deceptively attractive by laying

---

[109] *Aegypten*, II, 406-408.
[110] Keller, *Hom. Soc.*, 138-139 (where full references to text are given).
[111] Nordenskiöld, *Studier*, 313, 314.
[112] Waddell, *Buddhism*, 498-499; Smith, *Relig. Sem.*, 240.
[113] Yule, *Marco Polo*, I, 207, 208.
[114] Furness, *Head-Hunters*, 128; §284, above.

pieces of meat on the top. The rest of the animal was eaten by the participants, except that the vitals were merely tasted, that is, ceremonially eaten.[115]

The fact that the victim was devoured in good part by the sacrificers, while the god was there to eat his part, makes of the sacrifice a sort of communion-meal, with a large significance of its own.[116] Even though the sacrifice was not utterly removed from human use, still there was a considerable waste in the recurrent gorgings of what might otherwise have been saved for distribution over lean seasons. It is necessary to look squarely at the actual loss and waste of sacrifice, for they were actual. No evolutionist can believe, however, that there were no compensating advantages capable of conferring survival-value upon the practice. Sacrifice, by destroying capital and other advantages in living, entailed increased effort and exercised a "discipline through fear."[117] The reality of the loss is undeniable; it cannot be argued away; the only question is as to the value of the compensating advantages which were conferred by the system.

[115] Keller, *Hom. Soc.*, 133-134; Letourneau, *Prop.*, 87, 320.
[116] §§230, 260, above, and 297, 325, below.
[117] Lippert, *Kgchte.*, I, 127.

CHAPTER XXXV

ANTECEDENTS OF HUMAN SACRIFICE

§289. The Food-Interest. Just as fetishism reaches certain of its most significant aspects in the spirit-possessed man, so does propitiation attain what is perhaps its most unique and important phase in human sacrifice. That usage rests upon no theory that is as yet unrevealed to the reader; it is no more than a special development of daimonology, here reserved for separate treatment because of its consequences rather than of its antecedents, for it leads directly into the evolved religious ideas and practices to be reviewed in what follows.

It is useful at this point to recall the general aspects of sacrifice as these have emerged from evidence hitherto cited. Given the aleatory element and the spirit-environment conceived of in terms of projectivism and anthropomorphism, the theory and practice of sacrifice are seen to be inevitable in the setting of their time. Men dealt with the daimons as with human beings raised to a higher power, thinking to coerce or conciliate them by recourse to means proved effective, in experience, to force or win over fellow-beings. With the higher development of spiritual conceptions, methods of conciliation and propitiation worked toward the front, replacing, at least in outward form, the negative recourse of avoidance and exorcism. Gifts and service became the acceptable and successful way of getting results.

Of all gifts to the spirits a large fraction have consisted of food; it was the vital interest, the thing most generally and steadily in demand. The first need, for spirit as for man, was to be nourished, as any unselected collection of instances, no matter how exhaustive, reveals. It could not be otherwise upon the undeveloped stages; only with the accumulation of capital and the growth of economic security does mankind get the opportunity to fix an eye upon needs other than immediate and material. That the food-interest may be an original factor where it does not appear obviously as such is illustrated in the case of domestication.[1] In

[1] §95, above.

conformity with regular usage, the food offered to the anthropomorphic daimons was that which was, or had been in former time,
the food of men. The spirits could not be put off with any inferior
article—not, at least, until men had developed subtlety in subterfuge; they were given what they liked, not what they did not like.
They received good food that men knew to be such by their own
experience; to sacrifice poor or blemished stuff would have been
not only fruitless in result but perilous in the extreme. In short,
the daimons got what men regarded as the best there was.

It immediately follows that if human flesh was sacrificed upon
the altar that was because it was desirable, and not for any other
purpose than eating; the instances, in any case, fail to reveal any
other utility. The sacrifice of human flesh cannot be disassociated
from the eating of it any more than can the offering of the substance of plant or animal. The conclusion is, then, that the performance of human sacrifice means that the daimons are anthro-
pophagous; then a short inference allows of the conviction that
people who immolate their fellow-men either are now cannibals or
have been at some previous time. The cult, in its conservatory of
survivals, contains much material for reconstructing the past;[2]
cult-cannibalism indicates the preëxistence of the practice among
men just as the vestigial dentition of the baleen whale betrays its
toothed ancestry.

Though there were other motives for human sacrifice, such as
the provision of a grave-escort,[3] cannibalism is the primordial one
from which to make a start. The approach to the topic of human
sacrifice will be, therefore, by way of a survey of cannibalism.
This will involve a certain degree of digression from the direct
course of cult-evolution, for it is necessary to consider the practice in its several phases by way of gathering up all the strands.
The topic of cannibalism will form, in some measure, another of
those cross-surveys[4] which assist in keeping before the mind the
truth that all societal forms and institutions are interrelated and
interpenetrating; treated separately for the sake of convenience,
they must all be put back into their natural contacts and inter-
lacings if one would see society as a whole.

2 §324, below.   3 §229, above.
4 Chs. VIII-X, XXXI, above, are of a similar type.

§290*. **Cannibalism.** If it were not for the long-standing taboo against the eating of human flesh, the contention that cannibalism was widespread and perhaps universal amongst mankind[5] would rouse little opposition. There would be no talk about an "instinctive revulsion" against the eating of the human body—a revulsion parallel to the asserted instinctive horror of incest, elsewhere[6] shown to be non-existent. It is the regular tendency of prepossessed minds, as was sufficiently exhibited in the opposition to geological and biological science, to assert upon *a priori* grounds the impossibility of whatever they do not wish to believe, and in default of evidence to hunt up some "instinct" that "must" have been present to render impossible the practices now regarded as revolting. There are many ways of persuading one's self that unacceptable conclusions are untenable; plenty of "axioms" can be thought up to support any position already taken; major premises yielding agreeable conclusions lie all about us; reason can be found for anything. Nothing can ever prevail against such easy recourse to the axiomatic, followed by a dialectical development of the same, except masses of facts under whose brute weight the axioms and major premises collapse.

There are enough facts at disposal to dispel the fancy of an instinctive revulsion against human flesh. Even without them, it would be a hardy partisan who would maintain that a man, civilized or savage, would instinctively recognize and revolt at human flesh if he did not know it to be such. There are several sorts of animal-flesh, considered revolting, which one could not bear to swallow if he knew their identity; even physical sickness might ensue upon eating them—if one knew what he had eaten. No instinct would reveal and no revulsion occur unless he were undeceived. And if anyone takes refuge in the position that instinct, now weakened by civilization, would have warned the unspoiled nature-man, let him reflect upon the cases where the savage eats tabooed food which he does not recognize to be such and then, upon realizing what he has done, manifests the signs of revulsion and fear appropriate to the situation.[7] The fact is that all these taboos are in the mores and are therefore societal and traditional,

---

[5] Schaaffhausen, in *Arch. f. Anth.*, IV, 245.

[6] §§348, 349, below.   [7] §§268, 271, above.

not innate or natural. Like the so-called natural rights, again, they are societal acquisitions of such long standing that their origins cannot be readily apprehended; and so they are referred to "nature."[8]

In fixing upon some point of departure, here as in the case of marriage,[9] the evidence from the ways of animals carries but slight weight. Animal-ways present no series, no significant and steady tendency, which would force us to any conclusion as to the original state of man. Some of the animals are cannibals; some are not. It depends upon circumstances of various sorts. All that we could conclude from the facts about animals is that some men were cannibals and some were not, which we know already. Always we are driven back to the evidence which we can make available about *Homo* himself, if we are to arrive at any reliable results. Facts about the animals' organic makeup are quite germane to any discussion of man's organic structure, for all such matters come under a single type of evolution; but facts from the range of organic evolution have no direct value in determining relations upon the plane of societal and institutional development. Further, we are not disturbed in our use of ethnography by the objection, on the part of those who revolt at facing truths unpalatable to their taste, that all cases of cannibalism represent mere degeneration. Some of them do;[10] but there is nothing behind the general challenge to ethnographic evidence except sentimentality.[11]

We wish always to start, not with a conjecture, but with a body of facts about the most primitive condition accessible to study; these can then be followed up through periods and stages where information is relatively plentiful. Our inferences as to stages earlier than those for which we possess actual evidence are intended to be reasonable and modest. The conclusion seems inevitable, on the basis of the cases which will be cited here as well as of those listed in special and more exhaustive monographs,[12] that the differentiation of human flesh from other meat by taboo was a product of societal evolution; that is to say, it was as likely to be used as food as was any other nutritious article[13] prior to the imposition of a restriction that did not exist in nature. It is not asserted that

8 §§171, 172, above; Keller, *Soc. Evol.*, 55.
9 §343, below.
10 Andree, *Eth. Parallelen*, 43; Lippert, *Kgchte.*, II, 291.
11 §455, below.
12 Steinmetz, *Endokann.* (this author gives in tabular form cases of known cannibalism, with the causes or motives, p. 25); Andree, *Eth. Parallelen;* Nadaillac, in *Rev. Deux Mondes*, LXVI; Koch, in *Intern. Archiv. Anth.*, XII, 78; Loeb, *Hum. Sacr.* See indexes to Pinkerton's *Voyages* (70) and to other collections of the same order. Sumner, *Folkways*, ch. VIII.
13 Vierkandt, *Entstehungsgr.*, 149.

cannibalism was universal—we cannot know whether it was or not —but that there was no general factor in the situation to prevent it from being universal, though special factors may well have excluded it in any given case.

Peschel[14] says that the Papuans and Polynesians are the only races pervaded by cannibalism; that it occurs only in isolated cases in Africa and America, while in Asia it is almost wholly absent and in Europe belongs only to an uncertain antiquity; and that it cannot be proved that all societies went through a stage where they practised it. Peschel is one of those who, though candid, are rather reluctant to admit the extension of a revolting custom; his statement is conservative.

The New York *Times*[15] remarks that "it is a curious and interesting fact that though many students and observers of our Indians in days not at all remote came across traces of cannibalism among them, there has been a sort of 'conspiracy of silence' on the subject. . . . The North American Indians have been spared an accusation warranted by the facts because, apparently, the white folks for once had a regard for the red man's reputation."

The geographical distribution of man-eating is, in itself, of no great importance unless it throws light upon the evolution of the practice, and we cannot see that it does. It has been held that the distribution of fauna and fish, entailing for some a lack of meat-food, is responsible for the presence or persistence of cannibalism; but there appears to be no true correlation of this sort.

What we find is, first, that in a "pervaded" region such as Melanesia there occur side by side tribes wholly given over to anthropophagy and tribes that regard it with horror; that cannibalism by no means goes with degradation of physique or character; that it is not correlative with destitution or with lack of meat-food; that human flesh is used merely as food rather rarely, chiefly by the black races of Australasia and Africa; that it is eaten much more generally for religious reasons; and that traces of its former employment are very widespread, indicating a condition in the remote past verging upon the universality of the practice among all races. Taking these findings up in order in the text and the *Case-Book*, and without attempting to plot out the geographical distribution of cannibalism, we hope to present the several stages

[14] *Races*, 164.   [15] June 26, 1925.

through which the evolution of the usage has gone. First, then, with regard to the pervasiveness of the habit in its very foci, some evidence may be cited as to conditions in Melanesia.

In formerly German Melanesia, "the sole genuine delicacy in the eyes of the Kanakas is meat, especially human flesh; and so the men reserve the enjoyment of it to themselves, and the women may for the most part only prepare it." The tendency to cannibalism is strong enough, joined with the resultant intertribal hostility, to affect social life profoundly. This author[16] would like to know "what limits the natives themselves set for cannibalism and at what grade of relationship or of tribal membership man ceases to be appraised according to his lesser or greater degree of toothsomeness." These tribes might well be described as pervaded with anthropophagy; but Codrington's[17] general survey of Melanesia rather upsets the impression. In the Banks' Islands and Santa Cruz "there has been no cannibalism, though the natives were not ignorant of the practice of it by others." The horror and rage felt toward a party of Tongans who had eaten those whom they had killed in battle led to an immediate attack upon another party that returned the year after. On the other hand cannibalism became more extensive in recent times on the Solomon Islands. "It is asserted by the elder natives of Florida that man's flesh was never eaten except in sacrifice, and that the sacrificing of men is an introduction of late times from further west." Coast peoples accuse inlanders of being cannibals. "A few years ago one Nunn, an inland chief, was believed to say that pig's flesh was bad and man's flesh sweet to him; a man who had mounted to his place and found himself in a sweat would sit down to cool before he showed himself; Nunn took the sweat as a sign of fatness and would desire to eat him." Elsewhere it is thought that the ghosts do not like the eating of men; again, the older men will have nothing to do with it, though the younger have learned it. "The natives of San Cristoval not only eat the bodies of those who are slain in battle, but sell the flesh." In the northern New Hebrides, "after a bitter fight they would take a slain enemy and eat him, as a sign of rage and indignation; they would cook him in an oven, and each would eat a bit of him, women and children too. When there was a less bitter feeling, the flesh of a dead enemy was taken away by the conquerors to be cooked and given to their friends." In Lepers' Island, "it was a murderer or particularly detested enemy who was eaten, in anger, and to treat him ill; such a one was cooked like a pig, and men, elder women and boys ate him. The boys were afraid, but were made to do it. It is the feeling there that to eat human flesh is a dreadful thing, a man-eater is one afraid of nothing; on this ground men will buy flesh when some one has been killed, that they may get the name of valiant men by eating it. A certain man in Lepers' Island mourned many days for his son and could not eat till he bought a piece of human flesh for himself and his remaining boy; it was a horrid thing to do, appropriate to his gloomy grief." Other writers confirm and extend the conflicting cases in Codrington's report.

Some African cases illustrate the fact that rejection of cannibalism does not signify tribal quality nor its practice the reverse. It is noteworthy that the Pygmies scorn cannibalism. They do not file their incisors to points, which

16 Von Pfeil, *Südsee*, 41, 288.
17 *Melanesians*, 343-344; Codrington, in JAI, X, 285.

is thought by some to be a sign of cannibalistic propensities, and are said to be too low of culture to be cannibals. With this may be put the fact that cannibalism was absent in Tasmania.[18] "In the Congo basin it is the more gifted, the most handsome and energetic races that follow this gruesome, fastidious, evil habitude."[19] Other authors comment upon the correlation between good qualities and cannibalism. The cannibalism of the Monbuttoo is unsurpassed by any nation in the world. But with it all, the Monbuttoo are a noble race; they display a national pride and are endowed with an intellect and judgment such as few natives of the African wilderness can boast; if asked a reasonable question, they will return a reasonable answer. The Nubians can never say enough in praise of their faithfulness in friendly intercourse and of the order and stability of their national life.[20] A similar report is at hand regarding the Bangwa: they are physically symmetrical, upright as a dart, bright and intelligent in appearance; they do not grovel before one's face and then stick a spear into his back but are straightforward and brave. Yet they are advanced cannibals and, unlike many others, do not mind being known as such.[21] "Why it is precisely the more gifted nature-peoples—those that stand upon a higher grade of culture—that are given over to anthropophagy certainly remains an unsolved riddle; but it is a fact not to be contravened. The inhabitants of the equatorial Congo region are more or less addicted to cannibalism and yet, in respect to their capacity, they occupy a superior position among the river-peoples. Similar considerations forced themselves upon me in the comparison of the most diverse peoples in the many districts over which I have travelled."[22] A supporting instance from the Indian Archipelago is the comparison of the backward, non-anthropophagous Kubus with the Bataks, among whom cannibalism has prevailed "from time immemorial."[23] Such cases dispose of the contention that cannibalism always goes with a degraded physique, vitality, or culture.

These cases, besides illustrating the points at issue, also reveal some of the general aspects of cannibalism. Some of those who have described and undertaken to explain this practice assume that men would not have followed it unless they had been forced to do so, a view illustrative of the tendency to project evolved notions into the unevolved mind. There is nothing to show that man had to be compelled to eat anything possessing nutritive value; the evidence lies the other way: that he had to be forced if he were to renounce anything that would satisfy hunger. The

[18] Quatrefages, *Hommes Sauvages*, 340.

[19] Stuhlmann, *Mit Emin*, 457; Burrows, in JAI, XXVIII, 39; Davids, in *Globus*, LXXXV, 229.

[20] Schweinfurth, *Heart of Afr.*, II, 92, 94, 95; Ratzel, *Vkde.*, I, 536.

[21] Lloyd, *Cannibal Country*, 345, 346, 347.

[22] Junker, *Afrika*, II, 297.

[23] Shufeldt, in PSM, L, 40; Volz, in *Globus*, XCV, 3; Anon., "Kubus," in *Globus*, XXVI, 45.

proper question is not: Why does cannibalism exist? but rather: Why does it persist or not persist?

Though cannibalism must have been tried out, as a variation, almost everywhere, it has been, in historic times, very unevenly represented over the earth. It is now practised by no peoples who have succeeded in the struggle for existence and for an elevated standard of living. It is a desperate reversion, accompanying the breakdown of all the safeguards of civilization, when it appears in the modern world, as we are told that it did in starving Russia.[24] It must, then, have come to constitute a maladjustment and to have been eliminated by the action of societal selection, persisting only in isolation, like slavery or polyandry. Indications of its course, from the stage where it was practised as a regular and recognized part of the mores down to those survivals and derivatives which are all that is left of it among developed human societies, occur in sufficient number to provide a perspective of its evolution. The particular one of its derivatives in which we are most interested and toward which we are working is human sacrifice. The next phase of the matter is the use of the human body as mere food.

§291. Corporeal Cannibalism. The explanation of cannibalism as due to lack of meat-food, or of food in general, though supported by some little evidence, is controverted by the great preponderance of cases. The more irregular and inadequate the food-supply, it is thought, especially if it is intermitted by absolute want, the more ravenous is the appetite for flesh and blood. Particularly in time of famine do savages, even though they have begun to refrain, fall back upon the nearest and always available nutrition. It is deficient nourishment, we are told, that creates an insatiable desire for salts, acids, condiments, and stimulants; and there is also the reaction against a monotonous unseasoned diet which, as in the Middle Ages, led to the high valuation put upon pepper and other spices.[25] Something such, it is held, stressed toward cannibalism.

24 N. Y. *Times,* Feb. 28, 1922; Sept. 8, 1922.
25 Lippert, *Kgchte.,* I, 60; 479-480; II, 281; Keller, *Colon.,* 12, 111, 176, 342, 388.

Instances of cannibalism due to utter destitution, as where the Eskimo are cannibals only in time of famine,[26] are not marvellous or even significant; stories of shipwrecks in relatively recent times show the breakdown of any food-taboo under stress. There is no evidence here as to the origin of cannibalism that is not general evidence as to the satisfaction of hunger. On the other hand, there are plenty of cases of the eating of human flesh under no compulsion or provocation whatever but merely because it is desirable as a food or even as a luxury; it is tabooed, as luxuries often are, from the women and children. There is nothing to show that primitive people were always driven to cannibalism against their will, or against their preference, or as a last resort, or in the teeth of an innate instinct, or by a perverted preference, or by anything else exceptional or abnormal. It seems to have taken no driving to develop cannibalism; the need of coercion, we repeat, came in when people were caused to refrain. The elemental force of automatic selection among the mores was what brought about the elimination of the custom when it had become inexpedient for societal welfare; then only came into play the taboos and the loathings that seem to us now, because they are so incalculably old, to be instinctive and "in nature."

The alleged correlation of cannibalism with scarcity of meat-food is supported by such evidence as the following.

In some parts of Australia a man who has a fat wife is afraid to let her go anywhere alone, while in other districts cannibalism is abominated. It is suggested that the practice remains in Central Australia and Queensland because there is no game; and the appetite for meat-food, after eating the local starchy substances, is said to amount almost to a passion.[27] "It is certain that cannibalism has been much more general and common in the northern than in the southern portion of the continent. This may be accounted for partly on the ground that meat was more plentiful in the south."[28] "It cannot be denied that cannibalism prevailed at one time throughout the whole of Australia. The natives killed and ate little children, and the bodies of warriors slain in battle were eaten. They did not feast on human flesh, however, like the natives of Fiji. They appear to have eaten portions of the bodies of the slain in obedience to customs arising out of their superstitions, and very rarely to have sacrificed a human life merely that they might cook and eat the flesh. This, however, was done under some circumstances. When tribes assembled to eat the fruit of the Bunyabunya, they were not permitted to take any game, and at length the

26 Letourneau, *Soc.*, 201; Fairclough, "Basuto," in *Jr. Afr. Soc.*, London, IV, 194 ff.

27 Ratzel, *Vkde.*, II, 55.   28 Curr, *Aust. Race*, I, 77.

craving for flesh was so intense that they were impelled to kill one of their own number in order that their appetites might be satisfied."[29] The New Caledonians carried on war only to get meat-food, since the only mammal native to their country is a bat which is not eatable; and when the desired object had been attained—as soon as a few men had been killed—the struggle was over. Similarly in New Zealand, since the dog was the only mammal of account, a supply of meat-food was absent.[30]

Such cases, though striking, are few in comparison with the instances where cannibalism persists along with an abundance of available animal-food. It appears that by the time a people has advanced to herding it has also passed beyond the eating of human flesh; doubtless the owners of flocks and herds felt much less temptation to reversion; there are, however, a number of tribes whose range is rich in game and who yet continue to be cannibals. The fact is that there are relatively very few parts of the earth where meat or fish cannot be had; even in the cases just cited, barring northern Australia, fish are available; and if it is asserted that fish do not fill the place of meat, there are still a number of sea-mammals such as the whale or seal that are warm-blooded and yield animal-meat.

The East Greenlanders "say that human flesh tastes just as good as bear-meat but that they can always tell by people's exterior whether they have eaten it; and those who have been obliged to eat it are ashamed to tell it."[31]

The African Monbuttoo have been mentioned as inveterate cannibals; yet there is plenty of meat to be secured from the abundant wild life of their region. There are not so many elephants, buffaloes, and other larger animals as elsewhere; "yet the yield of the chase would be adequate for their own wants, because the abundance of their supply at certain seasons is very great, and they have the art of preserving it so that it remains fit for food for a very considerable time. With this fact capable of being substantiated, it is altogether a fallacy to pretend to represent that the Monbuttoo are driven to cannibalism through the lack of ordinary meat."[32] In New Zealand war was carried on to get human victims; no secret was made of the object of such a raid, nor was there any self-consciousness or embarrassment about participating in the ensuing cannibal meal; "human flesh is regarded as an especial delicacy, and is preferred to pork. The lack of animal-food is in no manner the cause for this, for in actuality, while all South Sea tribes live on plant-food only, there are wide ranges where cannibalism is unknown. Moreover, where it does prevail, human flesh forms no part of the nourishment of the crowd, but only a supplement to the feast of which each participant gets only

[29] Smyth, *Vict.*, I, xxxvii-xxxviii.
[30] Letourneau, *Soc.*, 193; Andree, *Eth. Parallelen*, 57.
[31] Holm, *Eth. Skizze*, 123.
[32] Ratzel, *Vkde.*, I, 538; Schweinfurth, *Heart of Afr.*, II, 89.

just so much."[33] In Tanna and Fiji the passion for human flesh co-existed with an abundance of vegetable food, but there were also pigs and fowls; on the other hand, in Tahiti where were chiefly fruits and fish, cannibalism was little more than traditional.[34]

Wilken[35] comes out flatly against the theory that the custom goes with lack of meat-food. It is not so with the Bataks or Dyaks, and even the South Sea Islanders have a superfluity of pigs and dogs. Finsch[36] thinks cannibalism was very rare in Micronesia and only sporadic in Polynesia; and that when present it was always in places particularly rich in resources. The Maori of New Zealand, mentioned above as having but one mammal, were not driven to their man-eating by lack of meat-food, as they had plenty.[37]

Our cases show that human flesh is for the anthropophagist a desirable food, irrespective of the other constituents of the supply; or that it is a special or holy food. The religious bearings of cannibalism indicated in the latter alternative are of great significance and will come to the fore a little later on; for the present it should be noted that human flesh has been treated, in its time, like any other food-commodity; it has been exposed for sale in public; it has become an object of pure gluttony.[38]

In one Melanesian district anyone who can make a feast of human flesh becomes at one step a big man. The body is carved with as great care as is displayed by expert carvers of fowls in Europe. Women may not share in the feast, but may lick the leaves in which the flesh is wrapped for cooking.[39] In one district of the Solomon Islands victims, mostly women, were purchased in a neighboring island, fattened for the feast, and "killed and eaten as pigs would have been."[40] In the Congo basin "cannibalism, originating apparently from stress of adverse circumstances, has become an acquired taste, the indulgence of which has created a peculiar form of mental disorder; with lack of feeling, love of fighting, cruelty and general human degeneracy as prominent attributes. . . . An organized traffic in human flesh still exists in many parts of the Upper Congo; men, women, and children being continually purchased and sold expressly for cannibal purposes."[41] Some of the comments in the above may be rejected as fanciful; but there is little doubt that, in the Congo region, much of the eating of human flesh is simply out of voracity; it is a case of a delicacy. The local cannibalism is not bound up at all with religious beliefs; an old chief said that human flesh was eaten because it was "extraordinarily savory, much sweeter than goat's flesh or mutton."[42] "Although human

---

[33] Finsch, *Ethnol. Erfahr.*, I, 125.

[34] Letourneau, *Soc.*, 192, 199 (quoting Cook, *Second and Third Voy.*).

[35] *Vkde.*, 27.   [36] *Ethnol. Erfahr.*, III, 5.

[37] Quatrefages, *Hommes Sauvages*, 442-443.

[38] Andree, *Eth. Parallelen*, 32; Letourneau, *Soc.*, 194; cases in Loeb, *Human Sacrifice*.

[39] Von Pfeil, *Südsee*, 131.   [40] Elton, in JAI, XVII, 99.

[41] Ward, in JAI, XXIV, 298.

[42] "Kl. Nachrichten," in *Globus*, XC, 228, 355.

flesh is forbidden to women, nevertheless, on the evidence of an old Mo-Mbala woman, there are many who partake of it in secret. 'When the sun shines we say:—"Eat *Misuni?* Bah! Never!" and we spit on the ground; but when night comes we steal to the grave and take our share as well as the men.' "[43]

Similarly in Brazil: "I inquired of the chief about the causes of anthropophagy in his tribe, and his answers showed that he and his had remained utter strangers to the sentiment which makes the eating of human flesh abominable to more civilized peoples. 'You whites,' he said, 'do not want to eat either crocodiles or apes, though they taste good. If you had had fewer turtles and hogs, you would certainly have fallen into this [i.e., cannibalism], for hunger hurts. All this is merely custom. When I have slain an enemy, it is surely better to eat him rather than let him waste. . . . The worst is not being eaten, but death; if I am killed it is all the same whether my . . . tribal enemy eats me or not. But I could not think of any game that would taste better than he would. You whites, really, are too dainty.' "[44] "In connection with cannibalism a distinction should be understood between the actual ingestion of human flesh, a practice to which the term is specially applied, and the drinking of fluid in which human ashes, powdered bones, etc., have been mixed. . . . The former habit would appear to have been associated with their slain enemies, the latter with their deceased chiefs, friends and relatives, but not strictly so. . . . There is evidence of its practice as a matter of ceremony, for taste, hunger, or vindictiveness, while records of its existence are obtainable throughout the length and breadth of the Guianas, including the islands. Indeed, so prevalent was the custom that it is not surprising to learn, on the authority of Bishop las Casas, that the conquerors actually made special provision for this weakness of their Indian allies." Of the Spaniards it is said that "these inhuman creatures were wont, when they declared war against any city or province, to bring with them as many of the conquered Indians as they could to make them fight against their countrymen. . . . But because they were not able to furnish them with all necessary provisions, they allowed them to eat those other Indians whom they took in war, so that in their camp they had shambles stored with human flesh. Infants were killed in their sight and then broiled and eaten. Men were slaughtered like beasts and their legs and arms dressed for food, for the Indians like the taste of these parts better than others. . . . The Holy Roman Church, through its ecclesiastical subordinates, also regarded cannibalism, under certain circumstances, in no sinister light. So fully were the missionaries persuaded that the only way to bring the savages within the pale of the church was to give them the tastes and habits of civilized life that it became a matter of dispute whether they ought to be permitted to eat human flesh. And what adds to the singularity of the question is that it was decided in the affirmative."[45]

Such matter-of-fact notions on this subject show how automatic the whole development has been. When slaves are eaten as being cheaper than buffalo,[46] there is evinced the same artless thrift that is shown by the housewife who orders a pot-roast in-

[43] Torday and Joyce, in JAI, XXXV, 403 (East Cent. Africa).
[44] Spix u. Martius, *Bras.*, 1249-1250, note.
[45] Roth, in BAE, XXXVIII, 590-591.　　[46] Ratzel, *Vkde.*, II, 451.

stead of a choice cut. Sometimes cannibalism seems even to be a sort of groping population-policy, "to keep the tribe from increasing beyond the carrying capacity of the territory."[47] Though the custom was to become idealized in ceremonial, both judicial and sacramental, it began in simple reactions upon life-conditions; and the beginnings have no marks indicative of the presence of reversion or degeneration.

An example of genuine reversion may clarify by contrast. In the year 1200 A.D. the Nile failed and famine ensued. Children were eaten by their parents. The civil authorities burned such cannibals alive and all was astonishment and horror over this outbreak of savagery. But the people got used to the practice and acquired a taste for human flesh. "Men were seen to make ordinary meals of it, to use it as a dainty, to lay up provision of it." Different methods of preparing it were invented, and the usage having been introduced, spread to all the provinces. The art caused no surprise. The horror of it which was felt at first passed away. People talked of it as of an ordinary and indifferent thing.[48]

The primitive cases are not at all of this complexion but represent simple adjustments in self-maintenance and self-gratification. No religious ideas are present in any definite form. All is matter-of-course and matter-of-fact. Original cannibalism must have been based upon some such direct reaction of society to its environment and the theories connected with it must have been simple and underived.

§292*. Animistic Cannibalism. It is rather surprising to one who realizes the penetration of religious ideas into the body of societal practices and institutions to find that cannibalism can be treated, even to the extent represented by the foregoing paragraphs, with almost no reference to animistic beliefs and their outreachings and derivatives. However, the subject cannot be pursued beyond these simplest and most elementary aspects without hitting upon its connections with animism, eidolism,[49] and daimonism. To these connections, as strands of great significance in the development of the cult and of religion, we now give attention, returning at this point from a necessary digression back toward the main

[47] §§402 ff., below; Whitmarsh, *World's Rough Hand*, 178; Oliveira Martins, *Raças*, II, 62.

[48] Abd-Allatif, *Rélation de l'Égypte*, 360, 361; Sumner, *Folkways*, §348.

[49] §229, above.

topic of religious evolution; when we arrive, presently, at human sacrifice, we shall have reached the trunk-line of thought again.

If the phenomena of cannibalism are viewed as a whole, it is clear that man-eating is a matter of ceremonial and ritual rather than of mere alimentation. Among the West African tribes, for instance, sacrificial and ceremonial cannibalism in fetish-affairs is almost universal.[50] It is well to set out from food and eating, nevertheless; for to him who so starts much is explicable that is not, except by way of metaphysical abstraction, religious dogma, or pure guess-work, for one who begins with his feet less firmly on the ground.

How inseparably, according to primitive belief, the soul clings to the body has been demonstrated in preceding connections. In view of these serenely unshaken animistic convictions, it is not to be expected that the bodies of some human beings can be devoured by others without attendant notions and theories as to supernatural influence. Such notions abound. In the cases already cited there appear hints of the persuasion that the body includes something more than the flesh; and in those to come it will seem that cannibalism may have nothing, or next to nothing, to do with alimentation but is directed toward the realization of religious relations and purposes that have almost completely overlain the material ones. It is not the whole body that is eaten; it is the few and selected parts, those supposed to contain the vital principle. Thus cannibalism passes out of the range of material self-maintenance into that of ceremonial and ritual, later to dwindle away into a set of survivalistic practices and formulas which betray their origin only to the unprepossessed student of their evolution.

Though long ages ago the eating of fellow-men became for advancing peoples a societal maladjustment destined to be selected away in the conflict of human groups and persisting only where that conflict and competition were not rigorous, yet, closely connected as it was with religion, that fossil-bearing institution above all others, it has left many noteworthy survivals down to our time. Relics of a custom we abhor lie unrecognized about us and are interpreted as "symbols," when the simple question: Why this symbol rather than some other? is enough to expose any explana-

50 Kingsley, *Travels W. Afr.*, 287; Serpa Pinto, *Africa*, 148.

tion except the one that rests upon the derivation of form out of form back to the primitive prototype. It is to the further development of the evolutionary series which began with the idea of the soul that this entering element of cannibalism is to contribute. Hence it is treated less for itself than as an accessory factor.

Animistic cannibalism means, first of all, the appropriation of the soul of the person devoured. There seems to have been an idea among primitive races that by eating the flesh or some portion of the body recognized as the seat of power, or by drinking the blood of a human being, the person so doing absorbs the nature or life of the one sacrificed.[51] Such appropriation secures strength for the eater. It is to be noted in passing that many cannibals will devour only their fellow-tribesmen; there is a so-called "endo-cannibalism,"[52] by which is preserved in the tribe the whole body of soul-strength belonging to it. In such case the eating of the deceased is an honor to them.[53] Here is a sort of exclusive spiritual in-breeding, of interest chiefly in its accentuation of familial and tribal solidarity.[54]

Within the family the strength of bearing women is thought to be restored by the eating of their deceased children. Sometimes too the child of a woman regarded as too young to rear it is killed and eaten. In general, the first-born incurs the greatest risk of infanticide; and it is asserted that, since the first-born of a young mother is less vigorous, its demise amounts to a sort of selection.[55] A common practice also is to eat the body of an enemy, with a view to the appropriation of his valor and strength, just as the heart of the lion is devoured to increase one's own heart-quality or "courage." Other seats of the soul[56] are singled out for appropriation and there appears, further, the notion that some extra punishment is thus inflicted upon the dead foe; that his soul is destroyed or damaged in some way. For the present these various motives need only be noted, for the object here is simply to bring out the general relation of cannibalism with religion as it develops into ritual and ceremonial.

[51] Gomme, *Ethnol. in Folklore,* 152.
[52] Steinmetz, *Endokann.;* instances in Jevons, *Relig.,* 202 ff.
[53] Lippert, *Kgchte.,* I, 233-235; §§226, 232, above.
[54] §§151, 176, 274, above.   [55] Lippert, *Kgchte.,* II, 289.
[56] §213, above.

In Queensland women kill and eat their children in order to recover their strength. Fathers do not eat their children nor sons their parents. If a child dies the other children eat part of it, in order to grow faster.[57] "Children are eaten when they die, but the crime of infanticide is not very common, unless in the case of a first child."[58] Among the Dieri, while the fathers do not eat of their offspring, the mothers and female relatives must, in order to have the dead in their livers, their seats of feeling.[59] "Cannibalism is practised occasionally, but only by old men and women who eat a baby, thereby thinking they will get the youngster's strength."[60]

The custom of cannibalism for hatred or vengeance is found throughout Polynesia.[61] In Tahiti, "the sacrifice of prisoners was followed by cannibal feasts; the honor of eating the eyes of the victims being reserved to the king. The first name of Queen Pomare (*Aimata, I eat the eye*) is a last souvenir of the royal privilege."[62] After a battle the Maori, collecting the corpses, cut off the scalps and right ears for the gods. The chief began the feast by eating the uncooked brain and eyes of one victim. They packed in baskets what was left and sent it to their neighbors who, by consuming it, showed themselves friends of the victors and enemies of the defeated. In the Marquesas Islands, before a cannibal feast the hair of the victims was cut off and made into magical rings; thus the use of human hair for ornament, or of human bones for implements— for instance, of the skull as a drinking-cup—has cannibalistic significance.[63] The bearing of such ceremonial survivals should never be overlooked.

The Bella-Coola Indians have cannibalism and human sacrifice as a sacrament, the victims, who were formerly captives or slaves, being children of the poor, bought from their parents. Where the English government set out to stop these human sacrifices, the priests dug up corpses and ate them, several being thus poisoned.[64] The Tlinkits ate enemies to get courage. At a certain feast men offered their bare arms to the chief, who bit out pieces and ate them. This meant glory for both parties. Nutka chiefs ate human flesh before entering battle; and their sorcerers fasted, lived in solitude, and ate the dead. A sacrificial victim was regarded as the son of the one who offered him. Mexican sacrifices were of a cannibalistic tinge: the king ate some of the victims, who were captives and children; and human blood was mixed with sacrificial wafers. There were prolonged cannibal feasts among the Nahuas and Mayas; and the Nicaraguans held a dozen or so of them each year, in which everyone had a share.[65] In Guatemala, seeresses were fed certain parts of war-captives.[66] "The practice of eating prisoners has been and perhaps is still common among South Americans. Humboldt saw traces of it along the Orinoco."[67] Several Brazilian tribes cook up and pulverize their dead, using the powder in a drink which is supposed to carry over to them the virtues of their fathers.[68] Tribes

[57] Ratzel, *Vkde.*, II, 55; Lippert, *Kgchte.*, I, 209.

[58] Palmer, in JAI, XIII, 283.   [59] Gason, in JAI, XVII, 186.

[60] Crauford, in JAI, XXIV, 182; Foelsche, quoted in JAI, XXIV, 196.

[61] Radiguet, *Sauvages,* 170; Johnson, *Cannibal Land,* 189-191.

[62] Nadaillac, *Preh. Amer.,* 63.   [63] Ratzel, *Vkde.*, II, 124, 126.

[64] Goeken, in *Mittheil. aus d. Königl. Museen zu Berlin,* I, 184, 185.

[65] Bancroft, *Nat. Races,* I, 106, 170, 189; II, 176, 305, 357, 395, 430, 689, 708; III, 150, 152, 413, 415; Preuss, in *Globus,* LXXXVI, 109.

[66] Coto, *Dicc., sub* "sacrificar."   [67] Nadaillac, *Preh. Amer.,* 63.

[68] Von Martius, *Beiträge,* I, 599.

in Uruguay eat their children in order to get back their souls into their own souls. This applies especially to young mothers who are regarded as having too soon given up part of their souls to their children.[69]

Herodotus[70] tells of the Massagetæ who sacrificed and ate the old; those dying of disease were buried, which was less fortunate. Others put the sick to death and ate them. In the Norse sagas much is heard of eating the heart of Fafnir. Siegfried roasts the heart and, having eaten a bit of it, understands the birds. He gives Gudrun a morsel of it and "she was ever afterwards crueller and wiser than before."[71] The ancient Irish thought it honorable to eat dead parents, and by so doing prevented the ghosts from returning. Various survivals occurred among them in the treatment of enemies' bodies, largely with the idea of increasing courage.[72] So the Turks ate the heart of Vishnevitsky, a brave Polish soldier whom they executed in 1564.[73]

In West Prussia, in 1865, a burglar, after killing a maid-servant, "cut a large piece of flesh out of the body of the murdered girl in order to make candles for his protection on further occasions of this sort. The talismanic light, which he kept in a tin tube, did not prevent him from being caught in the act of committing another burglary about six weeks later. During the trial . . . he confessed that he had eaten some of the maid-servant's flesh in order to appease his conscience." The "thieves' candle" is interpreted as a survival of primitive cannibalism, and appears also in a Russian folk-song: "I bake a cake out of the hands and feet, out of the silly head I form a goblet, out of the eyes I cast drinking glasses, out of the blood I brew an intoxicating beer, and out of the fat I mold a candle." The writer quoted[74] goes on to mention the persistence of the eating of the heart—in this case that of an unborn male child—in order to acquire supernatural powers. "The modern European cannibal believes that by eating nine hearts, or parts of them, he can make himself invisible and even fly through the air. He can thus commit crime without detection, and defy all efforts to arrest or imprison him, releasing himself with ease from fetters and passing through stone walls."

The vengeance-motive for cannibalism is expressed or implied in several of the foregoing examples. Apart from what the eater of an enemy's soul may gain for himself is the damage he can inflict upon the dead. The usage is widespread and deserves special illustration.

In the Solomon Islands, cannibalism is not referable to lack of food. It seems due originally to the desire to humiliate the enemy—both the slain individual and his tribe. But "appetite comes with the eating," and human flesh comes to be a much desired dainty.[75] In the New Hebrides, eating an enemy is the greatest indignity that can be put upon him—worse than giving him over to dogs and swine, or mutilating him. Likewise strength is to be gained by such cannibal-

[69] Lippert, I, 209. [70] *Hist.*, I, 216; III, 99.
[71] *Corp. Poet. Bor.*, 38, 157, 393; Lippert, *Kgchte.*, I, 482.
[72] Gomme, *Ethnol. in Folklore*, 121, 148, 149, 152.
[73] Evarnitzky, *Cossacks* (Russ.), I, 209.
[74] Evans, in PSM, LIV, 217, 218. [75] Parkinson, *Südsee*, 486.

ism.[76] In Fiji, not only were war-captives eaten but certain tribes were compelled, probably as punishment, to give every year one member for a cannibal feast.[77] African tribes who do not hunt men for food yet eat those they have slain in battle.[78] One Central African chief said that it was a very fine thing to enjoy the flesh of a man whom one hates and whom he has killed in a battle or duel. Cannibalism is not for lack of food; they never kill a slave to eat him unless by some accident he is rendered incapable of work. It is war and vengeance that keep up the widespread cannibalism of Central Africa.[79]

Wilken[80] agrees that cannibalism develops and the taste arises out of the vengeance-motive; it cannot be due, in the regions he covers, to lack of meat-food, as they have plenty of pigs. The heart of an enemy is roasted and divided. Prisoners are often eaten alive, piecemeal. "The most acceptable explanation is that men, driven by a far-reaching desire for revenge, ate the war-prisoners or the slain, to the end of annihilating them utterly and in the most shameful manner." But this motive may exist side by side with others. In some places, if prisoners and slaves fail, children are eaten, where there are over two in the family; and the old are devoured as the "ripe fruit falling from the tree." In New Zealand, "cannibalism was due to a desire for revenge, cooking and eating being the greatest of insults. They seemed to have some idea that the courage of the person eaten would come to them, but this was not true of the majority. Possibly scarcity of food during siege-time helped the practice—there was ordinarily plenty of food."[81]

In Brazil there are a number of tribes among whom war-captives are, as such, sacrifices to the blood-vengeance of their captors: they are forthwith eaten. "These Indians do not eat their enemies from hunger but apparently from a misguided national feeling, from a crude over-valuation of bravery and a false thirst for honor. The victor has the right to the life of his prisoner. He may, when the latter is led, in festal dress, with a cord about his body, into the circle of dancers, smash his head in with a war-club; may, as he wills, choose a part of the body as food; and trace on his own body, by an addition of tattoo or paint, the living memorial of his heroic deed." Regarding the Miranhas, "it is neither gnawing hunger nor national hatred that makes these savages cannibals, but rather the reckoning upon a rare, appetizing meal, that satisfies their rude pride and, in certain cases, probably also blood-revenge and superstition."[82]

Achilles wishes he could summon the resolution to cut off and eat Hector's flesh raw, for what he had done to Patroclus; and Hector's mother would like to take similar vengeance on Achilles: "Might I have the center of his liver, fastening upon it, to eat! Then would works of revenge come about for my son!"[83] There is no reason for the form of such expressions unless they are survivalistic.

[76] Gray, in AAAS, 1892, 649, 663. [77] Ratzel, *Vkde.*, II, 288.
[78] Burrows, *Pigmies,* 58, 61; Burrows, in JAI, XXVIII, 44.
[79] Brunache, *Cent. Afr.,* 108.
[80] *Vkde.*, 21-24, 27 (where a number of references are given).
[81] Tregear, in JAI, XIX, 108.
[82] Von Martius, *Beiträge,* I, 129-130, 201-202, 538-539.
[83] Homer, *Iliad,* XXII, 346-347; XXIV, 212-216 (quoted), IV, 35; Keller, *Hom. Soc.,* 129-130.

Thus cannibalism was a sort of war-measure and a means of infusing terror. Especially when the custom was passing away did men feel fear as well as repulsion toward those who still practised it; one who ate human flesh, even the local shaman, was accredited with an appetite that made him dangerous, and he was shunned.[84] Cannibalism might then be retained by an individual or group as a measure of "frightfulness";[85] cases of modern "outbreaks of savagery" are familiar. It remains to explain why they take the particular forms that they do; and there is no other explanation than that the wild passion of revenge tears away the taboos that have long overlain deep-seated and primitive impulses, loosing them once more upon society. All such acts are reversions; they are not newly invented but, on the contrary, have their source in the crude primitive habits and notions which we have been reviewing. It is not enough to account for them as mere acts of fury or unbridled passion; the question remains: Why just these acts rather than others? The root-idea is to do some irreparable damage to the hated person.

From the idea of cannibalism for vengeance, finally, it is but a step to judicial cannibalism.[86] The idea of taking vengeance upon an alien foe has its counterpart in the punishment of the enemy within; condign measures are employed against the flagrant transgressor of the mores.[87] After its general disappearance, cannibalism may persist in the form of punishment, the underlying motive being utterly to destroy the soul of the criminal or to inflict damage and penalty, even after death, upon the element that alone survives death. In some cases, however, the criminal's blood, like that of the enemy, is supposed to confer strength.

Perhaps also there may be in the communal eating of the criminal the idea of collective responsibility for putting to death a tribal comrade. The blood-guilt, if any, must be incurred by all. The ritual of execution is like that of sacrifice; it ceases to be a crime only when done by all. There is in this a truth of social philosophy; many fallacies in our discussions of punishment and

84 Andree, *Anthropophagie*, 91.
85 Gomme, *Ethnol. in Folklore*, 149; Dozy, *Musulmans*, I, 47; II, 226.
86 Good cases in Wilken, VG, II, 482 ff.
87 §226, above.

of war are due to the fact that we have lost the drift of something which uncivilized man saw.

In South Australia the condemned man being killed, the weapons used in the execution are washed in a small wooden vessel and the bloody mixture apportioned among the tribesmen. In this case the idea is to get redoubled courage, strength, and nerve for the future.[88] In parts of Africa, no death is regarded as a natural one, but the agent must always be found. He is then eaten, together with meal-porridge.[89] A man found in the harem of an African chief "was quartered and given to the people to eat, raw and warm."[90]

"Far and away the most remarkable example of cannibalism in the Indian Archipelago is found among the Bataks. Cannibalism exists here under a regulated form, solely as a punishment for certain misdeeds. Adulterers are killed and afterward eaten. Also upon the commission of incest rests the penalty, as it appears, of being killed and eaten." Anyone who has had relations with the widow of his younger brother, which is considered as incest, meets this fate. "Traitors and spies are executed with the same purpose; and also prisoners taken with weapon in hand. . . . All captives are eaten alive, that is, pieces of flesh are cut off their bodies while yet alive, so that they are already partly devoured before they give up the ghost."[91] "For crimes for which we have but light penalties, or a few years in jail, the Battaks cut up their perpetrators alive, and I dare say eat them afterward; indeed, cases are on record where a Battak has been convicted of adultery, and his discoverers, members of his own tribe, have cut him up alive and then feasted upon his remains."[92] "They do not eat human flesh as the means of satisfying the cravings of nature, for there can be no want of sustenance to the inhabitants of such a country and climate, who reject no animal food of any kind; nor is it sought after as a gluttonous delicacy. The *Battas* eat it as a species of ceremony; as a mode of showing their detestation of certain crimes by an ignominious punishment; and as a savage display of revenge and insult to their unfortunate enemies. The objects of this barbarous repast are prisoners taken in war, especially if badly wounded, the bodies of the slain, and offenders condemned for certain capital crimes, especially for adultery."[93] There are five crimes for which the criminals are eaten, dead or alive: adultery, theft at night, being captured in war, marrying a wife from the same tribe, and attacking a man or a village when there has been no declaration of war.[94] In other islands, enemies, compatriots fallen in battle, the violently killed, and thieves and assassins are eaten; and on Easter Island children, captives, and condemned persons.[95]

The Chinese, according to Marco Polo, formerly ate all who were executed by authority. Modern cases of cannibalism are reported, especially in famine-times. Pith-balls stained with the blood of decapitated criminals have been used as medicine for consumption. The Tartars are said to have devoured traitors and culprits.[96]

[88] Gason, in JAI, XXIV, 172.   [89] Junker, *Afrika*, II, 316-317.
[90] Oliveira Martins, *Raças*, II, 67.   [91] Wilken, *Vkde.*, 23, 24.
[92] Shufeldt, in PSM, L, 41.   [93] Marsden, *Sumatra*, 391.
[94] Von Hellwald, "Battak," in *Jäger's Handwörterbuch d. Zoologie*, I, 372.
[95] Letourneau, *Morale*, 96; Thomson, in USNM, 1889, 472.
[96] Yule, *Marco Polo*, I, 266, 275, note.

§293. **Survivals and Legends.** Cannibalism becomes narrowed down in practice, becoming a prerogative only of men, of chiefs, of shamans, and it takes on the quality of the antique and traditional, the holy, solemn, ritual, and judicial. This is its mode of passing away. Perhaps it forms one of the sources of slavery and merges imperceptibly into that, as the captive kept for later eating is retained as a worker.[97] It passes into practices that recall it more or less distinctly, such as the concoction of various medicines from parts of the human body[98] and the animal-substitutions connected with human sacrifice, which is itself the chief survival of cannibalism.

A case of limitation is where only certain experienced men could eat a piece of the victim, no others being allowed even to see this done.[99] Again, as illustrating the dwindling of the custom: "their disposition was to demand a life for a life, that they might stay and eat, although curiously enough, they would not have committed cannibalism in the presence of a white man or a native woman!"[100] "According to their own account, the Florida [Island] people till lately did not eat human flesh, and now only eat it in sacrifice." It is chiefly the inland people in all the islands who are cannibals, and the great object is to get *mana* (virtue) by it. This author[101] seems to assert that some people who had not the custom are learning it; that it is, however, generally characteristic of isolation. "Formerly it was customary among the Jibaros for the victor, before he took on the trophy, to swallow a small piece of skin which the medicine man had cut off from the neck of the trophy, 'in order to manifest that he was eating his enemy.' This custom is now seldom followed, and the piece of skin is generally simply thrown away."[102]

In some cases, though cannibalism seems to be passing away, a closer knowledge of the local situation reveals its persistence or, it may be, the lack of promise in an apparent reformation.

"In one part of New Georgia the chief, some years ago, gave orders that no more human flesh was to be eaten, which to many might look as if his cannibalistic views were changing, but the cause of it was not a moral, but a physical one: the last feast of man they had indulged in caused an epidemic of sickness to run through the tribe, and the chief did not wish such a thing to occur again. . . . In other parts certain chiefs boast that they do not eat human flesh, and hope is again raised that these savages are reforming, but a little closer scrutiny shows that the particular chief deals in human flesh, trading it to other natives, and, like the man who makes the sausage, he does not eat it." Cannibalism is likely to recur at short notice: "You may live on the most friendly terms with a tribe for months, and go away with the idea

---

[97] Letourneau, *Morale,* 182.
[98] §318, below.
[99] Parker, *Euahlayi,* 73.
[100] Pratt, *New Guinea Cannibals,* 224. [101] Codrington, in JAI, X, 305.
[102] Karsten, "Jibaro," in BAE, Bull. LXXIX, 84 (Ecuador).

that cannibalism is dead, and laugh at those who have tried to make you believe otherwise, but had you remained one day longer, or the chief's son died one day sooner, that laugh would never have come off, but instead your head would have, and your comely carcase would have been frizzling in the kai-kai dish; and the very men who had made so much of you a little before, would with equal glee have made less of you."[103]

A pronounced exception is a certain West African people which "have a horror of cannibalism, and apparently never practice it, even for fetish affairs, which is a rare thing in a West African tribe where sacrificial and ceremonial cannibalism is nearly universal."[104] Of some tribes it is possible to say that "they are not positively cannibals, but eat from time to time a morsel of cooked man." Such a special occasion demanded one man (a deer-hunter) and four women, as follows: one pot-maker, one just delivered of a first child, one who has goitre, and one basket-maker.[105] Such specifications represent obvious ritual features. A curious survival is where certain Mongols "kill the mother of the bride in performing their marriage ceremony when they do not find any wild men, and eat her flesh."[106] In a Ladak cloister a trumpet is used which is made out of a human thigh-bone; "and since the maker of such an instrument is obliged, under ancient custom, to eat a part of the periosteum of the thigh, the English investigator Waddell thinks he sees in this usage the last relic of a cannibalism formerly prevalent in Tibet."[107]

There is a theory, interesting rather than demonstrable, according to which dog-eating is to be regarded as a survival of cannibalism. It seems to have started the other way round, in a wild guess offered by a sentimentalist.

St. Pierre,[108] in his *Études de la Nature,* emitted the fancy that dog-eating was the first step toward cannibalism. The strange result was that a pair of excellent scientists thought there might be something in the correlation. Cases of dog-eaters who have apparently never known cannibalism are readily found.[109] The dog was undoubtedly the earliest and most widespread domestic animal and so, very likely, the first to act as a substitute for a human victim, as he is now a substitute in the New Hebrides;[110] but substitution is a step away from rather than toward cannibalism. The fetish-character of the dog[111] probably indicates that he was closely connected with the cult and sacrifice; and perhaps the spirits that are specially propitiated by dog-flesh are those that are not so far from being pleased by a human sacrifice. In the absence of evidence as to the closeness of correlation nothing better than a guess can be offered. The instance is cited partly to illustrate how shaky theories get

[103] Hardy and Elkington, *S. Seas,* 95, 96, 97.

[104] Kingsley, *Travels W. Afr.,* 287; Nassau, *Fetichism,* 11.

[105] Serpa Pinto, *África,* I, 148.

[106] Rockhill, *Mongolia,* 144; Rockhill, in *Smithson. Rep.,* 1892, 770, note.

[107] Francke, in *Globus,* LXXIII, 4.

[108] Schweinfurth, *Heart of Afr.,* I, 191; Peschel, *Races,* 163; Bourke, *Scatalogic Rites,* 63.

[109] Allison, in JAI, XXI, 313; Clozel, in PSM, XLIX, 675.

[110] Macdonald, in AAAS, 1892, 727; Lippert, *Kgchte.,* I, 493-494.

[111] *Case-Book,* §99.

ANTECEDENTS OF HUMAN SACRIFICE 1245

afloat; the tracing of a notion back to a St. Pierre ought to be enough to dispose of it.

There are a number of cases where cannibalism, though not at all a common usage, is practised now and then or periodically, on solemn occasions, and often with a sort of exaltation or timorous bravado. Such instances, some of which have already appeared above, are typically animistic and sacrificial, like the totem-eating of the Australians.[112] Strictly belonging under human sacrifice, they should be mentioned here as plainly survivalistic of cannibalism and as indicative of the passing of the custom; they are regularly sacramental in nature, involving religious union between the god and the sacrificers and also between the sacrificers themselves.[113]

Before arriving at human sacrifice, that most significant derivative of cannibalism, toward which, in fact, this whole discussion is working, and in default of which as an objective so extended a digression would be out of order, we turn briefly to the appearance of anthropophagy in legend. Myth, tradition, and folklore are full of it; for ages it has adorned the nursery tale, so that each new generation learns about it early. An abiding reminiscence of cannibalism seems to be of the race's patrimony.

A tribe of Indians explains how it drove another tribe away toward the south because it was learned that the latter's members were addicted to cannibalism.[114] In the ancient epic of India the ogre is made to say: "I smell the flesh of men. It is long since I have eaten of men, who are to me the food best loved."[115] "The legends of Atreus and Lycaon show us plainly that the ancient custom had not long fallen into disuse."[116] To Homer cannibalism is a work of abominable barbarism. "The custom is found in actual and common existence only in the ruder tribes mentioned by Homer; among the Greeks themselves it was only in isolated cases of extreme anger toward an enemy that a savage desire to devour his flesh might arise. . . . The practice was held in great abhorrence, and direst need did not reduce them to so shameful an act. The whole force of the cult was thrown against it, and it is thus relegated to a somewhat remote past."[117]

The reader can supply other instances from well-known folklore. In these days the old indulgent attitude toward legend and

112 §260, above.
113 Cases in Frazer, *Golden Bough,* II, 318 ff.
114 Grinnell, *Folk Tales,* 220.
115 Holtzmann, *Ind. Sagen,* I, 130-131.
116 Letourneau, *Soc.,* 202.   117 Keller, *Hom. Soc.,* 129-130.

folk-tale, as toward that which can have interest only to a child-intelligence, is out of date; and so is the strained interpretation of them as pure phantasy and imagination. Enough legendary material has withstood verification to give pause to the candid student.[118] Handled with due regard to their qualities, myth and tradition are informative concerning periods where other evidence is lacking. In the present case, the appearance of cannibalism in the legends of so many peoples argues for its widespread prevalence in the remoter past.

Many peoples who once practised anthropophagy have dropped it and now, as is the normal consequence, view it with aversion; and in a number of places native tribes have been persuaded or forced by outsiders to give it up. Cannibalism is one of those practices, like polyandry or communal property, which seem inconsonant with advancing civilization and persist only in a protected station. That it has been automatically selected away because it became a maladjustment no evolutionist can doubt. Still it is not enough to say that a usage disappears because it is broadly inexpedient. It ought to be possible to show why it must needs die out; how it came to be tabooed as, for instance, endogamy was;[119] but the explanation is not ready at hand. There is nothing poisonous about human flesh and no instinct against eating it has been developed under natural selection; as in the case of endogamy the issue must be settled, if at all, upon the plane of general societal evolution.

It is possible to compare the qualities and services of endogamy, to its distinct disadvantage, with those of exogamy; the former system had not the survival-value of the latter. Where, now, slavery replaced cannibalism the case is parallel; the more expedient supplanted the less; only there are too many peoples who have given up man-eating without having developed slavery to render this correlation of much value. Again, if cannibalism were due to destitution in general and lack of meat-food in particular, it could be inferred that the practice declined as power in self-maintenance increased; even so, however, there is no reason why any particular

118 Tylor, *Anth.*, ch. XV; §455, below.
119 §356, below.

kind of food, unless there is something specific against it, should be renounced just because there is an abundance of other kinds. If, again, it is held that cannibalism, with its constant raiding for human victims, makes against peace and acculturation and is therefore detrimental to society, then the same charge lies patent against whatever leads to violence, such as raiding for women or property, and not against cannibalism in particular; further, there is thus furnished no explanation of the decline of endocannibalism, where the victims often consider themselves beneficiaries, which involves no war, and which is really an expression of group-solidarity. And if, once more, it is contended that the eating of tribal members, especially infants, means numerical weakening, the same cannot be said of the eating of those who have died without violence, of slain or captured enemies, or of children who were marked in any case for infanticide. Some truth inheres in each of these considerations; but almost any general explanation of the taboo upon human flesh is found to be untenable in the face of all the facts.

As accounting for the decline of cannibalism, a line of thought which seems to cover a maximum of the facts and to incur a minimum of the objections is as follows.[120] Human flesh is, first, a preferred food; where cannibalism exists, it is tabooed against women and children in favor of men, against inferior men in favor of men of position. There is no doubt that the procurement of enemies' bodies for cannibalistic purposes is a notable feat, entitling the successful both to the glory attendant and also to the lion's share in whatever pleasure or spiritual upbuilding may accrue from the appropriation of the victim's body or soul. The greatest and the strongest come to be characterized by the frequency of their cannibalistic privileges. Human flesh is their food as it is not of the inferior. How, then, of the spirits? They exceed all men in position and power. Shall they not be characterized by their participation in the preferred food? It will be clear enough as we go on with human sacrifice that human flesh is a food much prized by the daimons, if not for itself then for the soul-essence that is in it.

If, then, human flesh is tabooed in favor of superiors, it is in

120 See also Loeb, *Human Sacrifice.*

the natural order that it shall come to be set apart for the daimons. Such is the case, for it comes to be a holy food, reserved for them; it is "unclean," as holy things are wont to be, and man may not eat of it except on special religious occasions. Later, even after a revulsion to it has developed, as is the way with tabooed foods, he must needs eat or taste of it on such occasions. It is to be recalled that many of the taboos on certain foods, that is, the eating of specified animals and even plants, represented avoidance of the eating of a relative; and yet that, on occasion, that plant or animal was solemnly devoured as a sort of sacrament.[121] The case is quite parallel to that of the eating of swine or other unclean animals or of "old foods" in general;[122] only the taboo on human flesh is much more widespread and attended by a much deeper loathing—is much older, therefore, as can be inferred—than that upon any other sort of food. There has been plenty of time for this revulsion to have become firmly established in the mores and for sentiments to develop about the whole matter which have entered as independent factors into human relations.

Returning now to the fact that cannibalism, like slavery, while well enough in its time, when human relations were rudimentary, has long been a maladjustment in the evolution of society, we can see that the variation in the mores represented by the taboo of human flesh in favor of the gods was seized upon by selection and elevated into something well-nigh universal among all peoples who had passed the vestibule of civilization. The disgust that had come to be felt for the food readily extended to include those who ate it and ethnocentrism rose to a pitch where cannibals were thought fit only for annihilation.[123] That it has persisted among relatively advanced populations, as in Africa, while it is not represented among relatively backward ones should cause no misgiving; societal adjustments do not move with an unbroken front.

Though the renunciation of human flesh may be physiologically unjustifiable; though it may constitute an economic waste; yet there is no doubt that a return to cannibalism would run counter to and probably bring about the collapse of the societal codes by which we live. There is economic wastage to which we have to be

---

121 §§256, 260, 271, above.   122 §324, below.
123 Keller, Soc. Evol., 58 ff., 64 ff.

resigned. It is a waste to take care of the aged, the crippled, the insane, and other members of society who are useless in themselves; still no one advocates the adoption of the methods of natural selection. The essential sense of humanitarianism, for it has sense, is cloaked over by sentimental phrases about rights to life, liberty, and other things, about duties to our "common humanity," and the like, whereas the essence of the matter is that society is an organization that gets on better if all its members stick together, even though they pay a price for so doing. They cannot be eating each other. So long as the price is no higher than it has to be, it is better to pay it than not to pay it. We can readily shoulder the waste of not having cannibalism, just as we can that involved in a reasonable policy of humanitarianism.

Civilized men might think that cannibalism was a usage of low savagery, far removed from our interest and serving only to show how low human beings can sink. Evidently that is a gross misconception of it. It was a leading feature of society at a certain stage, around which a great cluster of mores centered; ideas of interest were cultivated by it which became directive and regulative as to what ought to be done; it intertwined with kin-notions, filial piety, civil discipline, societal coöperation, war-policy, vicarious sacrifice, communion, and sacrament. Sympathy and piety toward children and parents once dictated it; they came to proscribe it; but sympathy and sentiment do not necessarily run upon rational lines. They might well get started on a reverse current and run with equal strength. That is what has happened to later ages. The eidolistic notion that cannibalism might offend the ghosts replaced the eidolistic notion that it would please them. The history of the folkways and of the speculative opinions connected with them is full of such reversals.

Our horror of cannibalism is due to a long tradition, broken only by hearsay of some far distant and extremely savage people who practise it; therefore we think it, in itself, and "naturally," revolting to everybody and possible only to degraded races. Some of the best scholars, in writing about it, intersperse their text with adjectives conveying horror and repugnance. It is evident that when the matter is treated in such fashion the reader is blinded to the reality and significance of the custom. A usage which has existed so widely and so long and in so many forms is a component of civilization. Though now obsolete, it has contributed, like infanticide, slavery, and polygamy, to the structure which later generations have inherited. We should not read of these things as boys batten on horror-stories; we study them because they give knowledge and insight into human nature and into the conditions of human life, and because, as phenomena of group-existence, they set forth better than the commonplace things the competition of life and the organized effort by which men have tried to win mastery over circumstances. If for any society the struggle for existence was so hard that it cost the full strength of all, the support of non-workers would imperil the whole. In migration or flight before the enemy, to wait for the weak would mean death to all. Where everybody believed that cannibalism was the only expedient possible under certain circumstances, beneficent alike for the eater and the eaten, or necessary for the preservation of the strength of the former alone, group-interest called for the practice. "Group-interest" is not a vague phrase or a name for the selfish action of a majority. It is a positive fact. To pass casual judgment upon peoples on other stages of culture, without a careful and candid effort to realize their circumstances, is as risky as it admittedly is to dispense praise or blame to one's fellows on the basis of the superficial appearance of things.

The steps by which cannibalism passed away will appear as we go on. This chapter demonstrates, at least, that man-eating was once no isolated phenomenon, still less a morbid and pathological usage. It has been practised very widely over the earth and in a manner that does not set it hopelessly apart from the eating of any other sort of animal-flesh. With such considerations in mind one can perceive the position of the otherwise inexplicable usage of human sacrifice in the evolutionary perspective.

CHAPTER XXXVI

HUMAN SACRIFICE

§294*. Nature of the Offering. The immolation of human beings, like any of the other forms of sacrifice, is part of the cult. Though it does not derive solely from cannibalism, there is much connected with it, as will appear from the cases, that cannot be understood without reference to the facts and conclusions with which the last chapter was mainly concerned. The question as to why human beings are sacrificed can be fully answered only by having already in mind the utility—the full, sordid, or even abhorrent utility—of man to man. For the daimons remain anthropomorphic, to be served as men are served, and it is not until a long course of development has been left behind that this manlikeness of the spirits can be transcendentalized, etherealized, interpreted as symbolism, or otherwise shorn of its obvious and direct meaning and results. As a general rule, human sacrifice attends cannibalism just as the sharing of any other sort of food with the spirits accompanies the eating of it; but cannibalism does not necessarily attend human sacrifice any more than the eating of a particular food accompanies its presence on the altar. There has already come before us a type of human sacrifice that is neither directly nor indirectly connected with man-eating: the provision of an escort for the dead to the spirit-world.[1] All such offerings conform, however, to the general idea of sacrifice as propitiation of anthropomorphic spirits living a life like that of men.

It is astonishing to one who holds the current notions about human sacrifice to read that "there is not a people that has not practised this custom at some period or other of its history. Hindus, Egyptians, Greeks, Romans, even Israelites, differ, in this matter, from the negroes of our own times in nothing save the object they assign to this kind of sacrifice."[2] The longer the matter is studied, the less is one inclined to balk at this universal. Particularly convincing is the body of survivals of human sacri-

[1] §229, above.
[2] D'Alviella, *Concep. God,* 86; Lippert, *Kgchte.,* II, 275.

fice, appearing and reappearing in various connections throughout
societal evolution, which cannot be explained in any convincing
or consistent manner apart from the hypothesis that the practice
was once exceedingly widespread over the earth.

"That human sacrifice is still practiced in some parts of the Old World was
shown recently when six members of a local tribe were sentenced to death for
burning alive a young man named Manduza in order to appease the rain goddess. Rhodesia had been suffering from a severe drought, and some of the
native tribes ascribed it to the wrath of the goddess, who, they believed, had
been violated. The chief of the tribes conducted inquiries, which led them to
believe that his son Manduza was guilty of assailing the virtue of the goddess,
and he thereupon ordered him to be burned. The rain goddess, incarnated in
a young and handsome girl, was produced in court, but did not give evidence.
Counsel for the defense commented on the high motives which led the chief
tribesman to sacrifice his own son for rain in order to save his people from
drought, and referred to parallel cases in Biblical history. It is noteworthy that
the natives are firmly convinced of the efficacy of human sacrifice, especially
as rain fell soon after Manduza was burned alive."[3]

Any explanation of human sacrifice that assumes reflection and
reasoning among savages—that sees its purpose, for instance, in
the effort to counteract over-population—is ruled out upon general considerations.[4] The spirits are believed to want what men
want. If men want human flesh, the spirits also want it. Then when
men change, the gods do not, and the rite keeps up a custom that
incites abhorrence and loathing unless it is somehow interpreted or
made mystical. Whatever loathing is felt is part of the sacrifice.
Later the rite may be whittled down, pass into symbolism, lose all
meaning, and finally be selected away, to persist only in shadowy,
survivalistic form.[5] It is in simple motives, obviously derived from
eidolism and daimonism, that the springs of action must be sought.
The sense of the custom of sending a man's wives and servants into
the other world with him lay in the wish to assure him a retinue
of friendly or subject spirits; instances of the husband being
sacrificed at the wife's death, unless the wife is of much higher
station, are virtually non-existent. In the case of children, a care-
taker was often sent along: mother, grandmother, or aunt was
strangled; or if there was no one left to nourish the child, in case
of the mother's death in child-birth, the infant was expedited along

[3] N. Y. Times, June 6, 1923.
[4] §§36, 42, above, and 402, below; Goldstein, in Globus, LXXXIX, 37, 40.
[5] Lippert, Kgchte., II, 292, 309.

with its natural care-taker.[6] Other equally uncomplicated motives will appear in the cases to be cited.

In New Georgia slaves are kept chiefly for their heads, and are put to death when the owner dies.[7] Certain secret societies of the South Sea islanders "offer human sacrifices from time to time, in obedience to some awful superstition which gives good luck to whole districts as long as they contain medicine made of the entrails of human beings. . . . All those who are proved to have had anything to do with these sacrifices are hanged, and the Commissioners do everything they can to track down the culprits; but constantly nothing can be found out."[8] "Travellers, scientists, and traders still visit the interior and some come out all right, but to everyone that survives a dozen succumb, simply because cannibalism is to a certain extent a religious ceremony to these natives. They do not kill and eat human beings for the sake of their taste, or because they are hungry. . . . In nearly every case where human beings are killed and eaten, it is on occasions when such a sacrifice is necessary, according to the natives' religious beliefs. Like the prophets and priests of old they believe in sacrifices; they honestly consider that they are doing the correct thing when they kill, cook, and eat a man or woman, and it will take many years and many missionaries to persuade them to the contrary."[9] "A slight earthquake occurred one day, and when we asked old Yanavolewa about it he said, 'It is the spirits that cause them, spirits that live underground. . . . Many years ago there were two earthquakes, one on the land and the other on the sea. The people fled to the hills, but the sea followed after them. Finally some one suggested that they should throw an albino into the water, and when this was done the sea retired."[10]

In New Calabar, "the shark is the chief animal deity, to which they were in the habit of sacrificing a light-colored child every seven years." It is interesting to note the three types of fetishes in this quotation: the shark, the abnormal human type, and the sacred number. The authoress[11] says elsewhere: "You can always read human sacrifice for goats and fowls when you are considering a district inhabited by true negroes, and the occasion is an important one, because in West Africa a human sacrifice is the most persuasive one to the fetishes. It is just with them as with a chief—if you want to get some favor from him, you must give him a present. A fowl or a goat or a basket of vegetables, or anything like that is quite enough for most favors, but if you want a big thing, and want it badly, you had better give him a slave, because the slave is alike more intrinsically valuable and also more useful. So far as I know, all human beings sacrificed pass into the service of the fetish they are sacrificed to. They are not merely killed that he may enjoy their blood, but that he may have their assistance. Fetishes have much to do, and an extra pair of hands is to them always acceptable." There is even a device for stretching the neck of the human victim preparatory to his beheading.[12] In Uganda, during dances to celebrate the new moon, "a white cock is thrown up alive

[6] Ratzel, *Vkde.*, II, 335; Letourneau, *Soc.*, 220; §405, below.
[7] Somerville, in JAI, XXVI, 400.   [8] Cator, *Head-Hunters*, 168, 170.
[9] Hardy and Elkington, *S. Seas*, 94, 95.
[10] Jenness and Ballentyne, *D'Entrecasteaux*, 150.
[11] Kingsley, *W. Afr. Studies*, 501; 176.
[12] Burrows, *Pigmies*, 144.

into the air, having its wings clipped, and as it falls it is caught and plucked by the eunuchs. It is said that originally this was a human sacrifice, a young boy or girl being thrown into the air and torn to pieces as he or she fell, but of late years, as slaves grew scarce and manners better, the white cock has been substituted."[13]

The Chukchi are devoted to shamanism. In 1814, on the appearance of a contagion affecting men and reindeer, the shamans called for a human sacrifice as the only recourse, naming one of the most respected and beloved elderly men of the tribe. The people would not kill him but, as the disease did not abate, the old man devoted himself for his people. Nobody would execute him until finally his own son, at his command, put the knife into his breast.[14] The Buryats used formerly to sacrifice a man to the evil spirits in order that a sick person might get well.[15] Here we have an adumbration to the vicarious or ransom sacrifice. In 1892 a begging rustic was killed by the Votyaks; the head was lacking to the body, and heart and lungs had been removed to be offered by the Votyaks to their heathen god. This was in consequence of the famine and typhus experiences of 1891 and 1892, which "evoked among the superstitious Votyaks the desire to beseech the evil heathen gods for sympathy —a sacrifice had to be offered to them."[16] This case illustrates the tendency to revert, under some extraordinary visitation of the aleatory element, to the more primitive means of propitiation. Among the Shans certain spirits are appeased only by human sacrifices. The guardian spirit of ferries claims a victim every year—preferably a Chinaman—and saves trouble by capsizing a boat and taking him. The ferry is then safe for the rest of the year. "Shans still believe in the efficacy of human sacrifice to procure a good harvest. . . . The manner nowadays is to poison someone at the state festival."[17]

Certain Dyaks, "when they lay off their mourning and erect their memorial poles for the dead, always sacrifice a slave, who is slowly killed by spear-thrusts, and whose corpse comes to lie under the pole on which they stick his head. At their harvest-festivals too custom calls for the sacrifice of a slave."[18] At the death of a big chief, a victim was obtained and caged. When the feast was over, "and a bloodthirsty instinct had been stimulated to a high pitch by arrack, each one in turn thrust a spear into the slave. No one was allowed to give a fatal thrust until everyone to the last man had felt the delight of drawing blood from living, human flesh." The victim often survived several hundred wounds. "Frequently, some of the guests worked themselves into such a bloodthirsty frenzy that they bit pieces from the body, and were vehemently applauded when they swallowed the raw morsel at a gulp."[19] Running amuck is a sort of human sacrifice of both one's victim and himself. "The Moros believe that one who takes the life of a Christian thereby increases his chance of a good time in the world to come; the more Christians killed, the brighter the prospect of the future, and if one is only fortunate enough to be himself killed while slaughtering the enemies of the faithful, he is at once transported to the seventh heaven." Before setting out on his enterprise, the candidate for all this

13 Johnston, in JAI, XIII, 473.
14 Russ. Ethnog. (Russ.), II, 578.
15 Melnikow, in Globus, LXXV, 132, 133.
16 Iwanowski, in Globus, LXXIV, 101.
17 Woodthorpe, in JAI, XXVI, 24.
18 Nieuwenhuis, Borneo, II, 143.   19 Furness, Head-Hunters, 140.

takes a bath in a sacred spring, shaves off his eye-brows, takes a solemn oath, dresses in white, and hides his *kris* or *barong* in his clothes. He will fight to the last breath, seizing the rifle-barrel when bayonetted to draw in the bayonet and reach the soldier. There is more here than mere hemp-intoxication. That it is a service to a god to sacrifice his enemies to him is a frequent obsession of religious warriors.[20]

Mexico of the Aztecs stands out as a classic region for human sacrifice. Readers of Prescott,[21] and even of fiction based upon various historical accounts, retain an impression of blood-thirstiness that is the more vivid and persistent if it has been received in early years. The victims were for the most part captives taken in war, and war was often made solely with a view to obtaining them. A large proportion, however, consisted of condemned criminals, or slaves, or even of children, bought or presented for the purpose. The greater part of the victims died under the knife but some were drowned, others were shut up in caves and starved to death, while still others fell in gladiatorial sacrifice. But the most cruel sacrifice of all, and yet the most common, was performed by tearing out the heart of a living human creature at the sacrificial stone. There is no doubt that many thousands were slaughtered each year for this purpose. According to some authorities, in the capital alone, the annual sacrifice amounted to no less than twenty thousand.[22] But "recent researches justify us in believing that the number of the victims has been greatly exaggerated by the Spanish historians. Conceding this exaggeration, it is probable that only in the interior of Africa could such wholesale slaughter as really occurred in Mexico be paralleled."[23] The Inca religion set aside cannibalism but human sacrifice went on.[24]

The cases of the intended sacrifice of Isaac and that of Jephtha's daughter will occur to the reader of the Old Testament; and the fact that child-sacrifice is forbidden witnesses to its existence. This sacrifice was not for fear of poverty, even in much later Semitic history.[25] Smith[26] refers copiously to the practice: he thinks "that human sacrifice is not more ancient than the sacrifice of sacred animals, and that the prevalent belief of ancient heathenism, that animal victims are an imperfect substitute for a human life, arose by a false inference from traditional forms of ritual that had ceased to be understood." In old Arabia "little girls were often buried alive by their fathers, apparently as sacrifices to the goddess. . . . At Hieropolis the sacrificed children are called oxen"—doubtless an effort to reconcile ancient ritual with a newly rising code of mores. The captive in war is simply the choicest part of the booty and is as such reserved for the god: "Saul undoubtedly spares Agag in order that he may be sacrificed, and Samuel actually accomplishes this offering by slaying him

[20] Worcester, *Philippine Isl.*, 175-176; Sienkiewicz, *Deluge*, I, 561; II, 182, 598, 626.

[21] *Conquest of Mexico;* Haggard, *Montezuma's Daughter;* Wallace, *Fair God.*

[22] Bancroft, *Nat. Races*, II, 304-306; Biart, *Aztèques*, 118.

[23] Nadaillac, *Preh. Amer.*, 297, note, 295, 277, 266, 268.

[24] Von Martius, *Beiträge*, I, 464.

[25] Gen., XXII; Judges, XI; Levit., XVIII, 21; XX, 2; Sale, *Koran*, 112, 113, 114, 218, 230, 481.

[26] *Relig. Sem.*, 67, 362, 365, 370, 375, 491-492; Smith, *Kinship*, 281.

'before the Lord' in Gilgal."[27] Archæological discoveries in Syria witness to the sacrifice of the first-born and of twins, the children having been suffocated with dry earth and ashes filled into jars.[28]

Among the northern peoples there is evidence of human sacrifice until late in the Christian era.[29] The sagas and legends of northern Europe contain many references to the practice. About 900 A.D., the Norsemen were in the Orkneys, and their leader, catching a defeated enemy "made them carve an eagle on his back with a sword and cut the ribs all from the back-bone and draw the lungs out, and gave him to Odin for the victory he had won."[30] Odin's victims were swung up in the air, being marked on the breast with Odin's mark, that of a spear-point. Men sacrificed to Thor had their backs broken on a stone. Those who were executed for public crimes, the only capital offenses, were devoted to the gods. This is what execution meant; it was *ipso facto* a sacrifice. The Vikings made human sacrifices at the launching of their ships.[31] King Haakon of Norway sacrificed his son to get victory.[32] The Swedes prepared for sea-roving raids by human sacrifice, and every nine years there was a sacrifice of thralls, in the heroic age, at Upsala—they were thrown from cliffs, or tortured, or hung up, or their spines broken.[33] "The already converted Franks, at the crossing of the Po, made a great sacrifice of Gothic women and children as the first-fruits of the war."[34] Of the Druid rites much has been written.[35] Of the Saxon it is said: "The gods of his bloody creed called for the slaughter and torture of his captives; when he was about to turn his sails from the main land to his own home, he deemed it a sacred duty to pick out one man out of every ten to perish by a cruel death as the thank-offering of their captor's piety."[36]

The Lithuanians have maintained heathen customs down to our time. Human sacrifices were kept up, and the sick and maimed gave themselves as victims. Esthonian tradition speaks of sacrifice, sometimes of little children.[37] In Dragomanov's *Slavonic Folk-Tales about the Sacrifice of One's Own Children*,[38] there is, among other selections, a ballad called "The Merciful Woman"; wherein the faithful are adjured to throw themselves in the fire, to throw in sinless babes, "and all suffer for the name of Christ."

A special variety of human sacrifice, represented incidentally in foregoing examples, is one which occurs in connection with the beginning of some important undertaking. As it is often found attendant upon the laying of a foundation, it has been called

[27] I Sam., XV, 33.
[28] *Daily Consular Reports*, no. 2010, for July 22, 1904.
[29] Schrader, *Aryans*, 422; Grimm, *Deut. Myth*, 38.
[30] Vigfússon and Dasent, *Icelandic Sagas*, III, 8.
[31] *Corp. Poet. Bor.*, I, 408-410, II, 50.
[32] Vigfusson and Powell, in *Corp. Poet. Bor.*, II, 306.
[33] Geijer, *Svensk. Hist.*, I, 123; Estrup, *Skrifter*, I, 261; Freytag, in *Am Ur-Quell*, I, 180.
[34] Weinhold, *Deut. Frauen*, I, 218.
[35] Joyce, *Anc. Ireland*, I, 221 ff.; Borlase, *Antiq.*, 63 ff.
[36] Freeman, *W. Eur.*, 40-41.
[37] *Russ. Ethnog.* (Russ.), I, 170; Gomme, *Ethnol. in Folklore*, 73.
[38] Quoted in JAI, XXI, 458.

"foundation-sacrifice." The original purpose was to secure a ghost to watch over, to defend, or to give notice of any peril to some valued structure. This idea was extended to cover cases where the ghost was needed to protect important enterprises, agreements, or arrangements; later on it was modified so that no human victim was needed; for it was conceived that, since the world was full of spirits, one of them could be evoked for a special need by employing the proper coercitive or propitiatory rite. The Romans set such a spirit over each function; hence the *indigetes*, or ghosts with vocations.[39] Faint survivals of foundation-sacrifice appear in the dedication of a modern structure, where the articles deposited in the hollow of the foundation-stone are far from including anything as impressive as an immured victim.

Haddon[40] lists a number of cases of sacrifice at the erection of Papuan men's houses and at the making of a war-canoe; later dog's and pig's blood was put into the post-holes of the houses instead of a human victim or human blood. The King of Siam instructed three persons, who were to be sacrificed and immured in a foundation, to guard the gate well after death and to give notice of coming harm.[41] The Chinese and Tatars, in building a city-wall, interred within it the bodies of workmen who died. "In this manner, it is estimated, that one million human beings found their last resting places in the walls surrounding Peking."[42] It is reported that the Chinese used to throw a young girl into melted bell-metal, to better the tone of the bell.[43]

In one district of Borneo, "at the erection of the largest house, a deep hole was dug to receive the first post, which was then suspended over it; a slave girl was placed in the excavation, and at a signal the lashings were cut, and the enormous timber descended, crushing the girl to death. It was a sacrifice to the spirits." The passage of human sacrifice into a substitute form is indicated where "every family must kill a fowl or a pig before the post holes for a new house can be dug, and the blood must be smeared on the feet and sprinkled on the posts to pacify . . . the tutelary deity of the earth."[44] Again, they put an egg in every hole, "a sacrifice which is found in one form or another all over Borneo."[45]

Wilken[46] considers the foundation-sacrifice at some length, especially in the matter of survivals of the practice. A skull is put under a new building as a living child may be; this is a substitute for a real human sacrifice. The Dyaks must get a fresh head in founding a new edifice. Animal-substitutes are common, though all the victims at a foundation-ceremony are not such. Even the skulls or bones of animals may be used. It is not always clear whether

[39] Lippert, *Kgchte.*, II, 270.   [40] In JAI, L, 239, 240, 260, 272.
[41] Lippert, *Kgchte.*, II, 323.
[42] Anon., "China," in *Scientif. Amer.*, LXXXIII, 37-38.
[43] Letourneau, *Morale*, 23.
[44] Roth, *Sarawak*, II, 15, 215; Gomme, *Village Life*, 25.
[45] Nieuwenhuis, *Borneo*, II, 180.   [46] Wilken, in VG, IV, 57 ff., 70 ff.

the foundation-sacrifice is connected with skull-worship or is a mere sacrifice; sometimes there is a prayer to the earth to support the structure, that is, a mere sacrifice to the earth, with no idea of the victim's soul watching over the house. Of course there is no substitute possible where man or beast is sacrificed to make of the soul of the victim a protecting spirit. Sometimes the skull of the protecting victim is not put under the posts but hung up within; the custom of hanging up carabao-skulls in profusion is as common as the Indian use of bison-skulls. Then the animal-skull becomes a decoration in the form of an imitative carving, and finally a mere crescent moon, symbolical of the horns. The use of the horse-shoe, while it involves also the fetishistic quality of iron, probably points back to the horse as a foundation-sacrifice. The horse-shoe is an Arabic sign for the waxing moon. In Polynesia, where human sacrifices, with cannibalism, and the grave-escort were common, men, or parts of men, especially the eye, were buried under the foundations of temples. Human sacrifices, the best means to secure the favor of the gods, were offered when war-ships were built.[47] "In New Zealand, the bottom of the columns which support the house are carved to represent prostrate figures of slaves; a survival of the old custom of foundation sacrifice."[48]

In America, the Tlinkits buried a living slave under the corner post of a new house.[49] "Formerly the custom obtained of killing several slaves when a person of consequence built a house, the victims being selected sometime before the ceremony. The bodies of those slain were accorded the right of burial, and in this much were deemed very fortunate. . . . If an intended victim managed to escape or to conceal himself he was allowed to live, and might return after the conclusion of the festivities at the house of his master without incurring punishment. It frequently occurred that powerful chiefs assisted favorite slaves on such occasions to make their escape."[50] The Iowas developed a parallel foundation-sacrifice of tobacco: "whenever they halt upon a ground for the establishment of their village, the doctor, or mystery man, regularly, and in due form, walks on to the ground, and having designated the spot for each wigwam, invokes the favor and protection of the Great Spirit by throwing tobacco on to the ground designated for each wigwam."[51] Human foundation-sacrifice is an extreme of this sort of offering.

"More or less authentic traditions pretend to state that preliminary to the opening of the canals a young girl of noble family, decorated as for her wedding, was thrown into the Nile."[52] According to one interpretation of an Old Testament passage,[53] Jericho was built upon a foundation-sacrifice of the founder's oldest and youngest sons. The foundation-sacrifice both of human beings and more especially of animals is in evidence among the Canaanites. The Rabbinical tradition also knew it. "Pharaoh had the Israelites and their children immured in place of the lacking bricks." Oriental proverbs read: "No start on building without spilling of blood"; "Every house must have its dead, whether man, woman, child, or beast."[54] "The custom of the building-sacrifice is said still to exist secretly in Palestine. They told me that it was practiced especially in connection with the building of Turkish baths, soap-

[47] Ratzel, *Vkde.*, II, 124.
[48] Gomme, *Village Life*, 27.
[49] Ratzel, *Vkde.*, II, 698.
[50] Niblack, in USNM, 1888, 375.
[51] Donaldson, in *Smithson. Rep.*, 1885, pt. II, 149.
[52] Maspero, *Hist. Anc.*, III, 75, 76, note 5; Saad, in *Globus*, XCV, 173.
[53] I Kings, XVI, 34.
[54] Maurer, *Vkde.*, I, 69-72.

boiling plants, and here and there even in the case of private dwellings. When the four chief pillars of the bath, which carry the arch, are to be set, the chief builder sends the workmen off to their noon-hour, and a youth (whom they think to be an orphan or one that will not be searched for much) is put into the hole, of two meters or so in depth, prepared for the rectangular pillar, and as if by accident earth and sand are poured on him till he is smothered."[55]

In Iceland, victims were bound to the rollers by which boats were launched, and so made into sacrifices. This was most common when a new boat was launched or a great expedition undertaken.[56]

The Southern Slavs wall in the shadow of a passer-by; and the immuring of a girl or woman in the foundation of a new house is referred to in Bosnian and Herzogovinian songs.[57] "In Germany it is often an empty coffin that is built into the foundations; whilst the Bulgarians confine themselves to the pantomime of throwing in the shadow of some passer-by."[58]

If anyone is disposed to question the evidence from legend and folklore, he should ask himself whence the legends come and why they repeat with such unanimity a motif whose multiple invention out of pure imagination is all but incredible. Men do not fabricate the grotesque and bizarre from whole cloth: least of all does it get into primitive legend. The fidelity with which folk-tales reflect existing notions and practices, or those obsolete ones whose prevalence in the past is well authenticated, is enough to guarantee that they are founded upon actualities.[59]

A form of human sacrifice, common in certain parts of the earth, centers upon the dedication of the head. In order to secure this supremely important offering there has been developed the practice of head-hunting. Heads are fit funerary gifts, as has been seen under the ghost-cult;[60] and the fact that they are sacrificed to the daimons reveals once more the lineal connection between the ghost-cult and daimonology. The most obvious motive for head-hunting is doubtless the acquisition of a trophy of skill and daring; it is a pursuit of glory;[61] it is evident, however, to one who scans a number of cases of the practice, that this is not the only motive nor yet, in all likelihood, an underived one. The idea of propitiation is present in the sacrifice or dedication of the soul that resides in the head. "The extension of the principle of

---

[55] Saad, in *Globus,* XCV, 173.

[56] Vigfusson and Powell, in *Corp. Poet. Bor.,* I, 410.

[57] Krauss, *Südslaven,* 161 (detail in his "Bauopfer bei d. Südslaven," in *Mitth. d. Gesellsft. Wien,* 16-23); Letourneau, *Morale,* 23.

[58] D'Alviella, *Concep. God,* 32.   [59] §455, below.

[60] §229, above.   [61] §§444, 449, below.

head hunting and skulls hung up as trophies to the heads of animals confirms the fact of some primitive belief lying behind an apparently merely barbarous trophy."[62] The contention is offered that where head-hunting prevails, cannibalism does not, although the two usages are not antagonistic to one another;[63] if this is so, the inference would be that head-hunting, as a development of human sacrifice, arose after the latter had ceased to reflect cannibalism as a contemporary usage. However that may be, the connection of head-hunting with human sacrifice cannot fail to appear in any collection of representative examples.

On the island of Florida the chief must have a head as a foundation-sacrifice for a new canoe; that the possession of many heads is a sign of greatness and power is understandable enough if each trophy means that a sacrifice has been made. "The practice . . . of taking heads and preserving them as signs of power and success belongs to the Solomon Islands generally."[64] "Tribe after tribe has been completely wiped out by certain powerful chiefs through a continued series of head-hunting expeditions."[65] Captives are "on a perfect footing of equality and familiarity with their captors. But any day a head may be wanted to celebrate the completion of a new canoe or other work, and one of the luckless slaves is unexpectedly called upon to furnish it."[66] The dead enemies "are hung up for several days in the neighborhood of the taboo-house. Then they take down the bodies, remove and clean the head, and keep the skull in the taboo-house."[67]

Furness[68] has a very graphic, though perhaps somewhat impressionistic report of a conversation with a native blood-brother concerning the merits and demerits of head-hunting. The latter asserts that the custom is not horrible at all. "It is an ancient custom, a good, beneficent custom, bequeathed to us by our fathers and our fathers' fathers; it brings us blessings, plentiful harvests, and keeps off sickness, and pains. Those who were once our enemies, hereby become our guardians, our friends, our benefactors." He goes on to tell the tradition concerning the development of the custom. When it had been adopted, miracles began to appear: boats were all ready and launched, and moved off of themselves when occupied; the current of streams turned and ran up hill, "as it does at flood-tide at the mouth of a river." Crops were found almost ready for harvesting only fifteen days after planting. The ill got well, the lame walked, and the blind saw. The firm belief is that, even if one loses his own head, his second self goes to a happy place if he has been brave and taken heads. "When I die my friends will beat the gongs loud and shout out my name, so that those who are already in Bulun Matai, will know that I am coming, and meet me when I cross over the stream on Bintong Sikòpa"—

[62] Godden, in JAI, XXVII, 16.   [63] Ratzel, Vkde., II, 448.
[64] Codrington, Melanesians, 297, note, 345.
[65] Hardy and Elkington, S. Seas, 97.   [66] Woodford, Head-Hunters, 155.
[67] Parkinson, in Dresden. K. Zoöl. u. Anth.-Ethnog. Mus. Abhandl., VII, pt. VI, 13.
[68] Head-Hunters, 59-63, 64-65.

the great log. This chief says that he could not, as a boy, bear the thought of hurting people, but his father set him and his brother to spearing to death an old nurse of his, and he quickly got all over it. "That's the way to become a Man; a baby is afraid of blood, Tuan. My father was right. No man can be brave who doesn't love to see his spear draw blood."

The heads are fetishes and only the very aged may touch them. "Sickness, possibly death, follows a disregard of this rule; but the aged, who are at any rate on the brink of the grave, may fearlessly handle them." They are fed with rice and arrack at the festivals.

Head-hunting extended to Formosa and the Philippines and out into Micronesia and Polynesia; one traveller saw eighty-five Chinese skulls hanging in one of the Formosan men's houses.[69] The stealing of heads in Micronesia, where the prince has to defray all state-expenses, and the people pay no taxes, provides a method of raising revenue. The principal chief travels about with a head which his warriors have taken, through the districts with which he is at peace. He conducts the war-dance and receives money for it. When one district has done this with one head, the turn comes to another, in order that the money may be made to circulate.[70] In America, too, though there was no such organized head-hunting, the head was a trophy.[71]

Relics of head-hunting appear in classical accounts. Herodotus[72] tells of the Taurians of the Crimea that they cut off enemies' heads and fixed them on long poles above the smoke-holes in their roofs, in the belief that they would watch over the dwelling. "The special sanctity of the head of the sacrificed victim, so apparent in the Indian festival, appears in European paganism and folklore."[73]

It is evident from several of these examples that the idea of sacrifice does not cover all cases of head-hunting. Among the Malays it is as if they set out to get and bind to themselves, by a species of coercion, the ghosts of those whose heads they secure; to procure fetishes of high potentiality both for protection and for the attainment of well-being. Allusion to this aspect of the custom occurs under the topic of fetishism.[74] It is the connection of the practice with the ghost-cult and the evident sacrificial nature of most of the cases that lead us to align the treatment accorded to the head with human sacrifice and related ceremonies.

There is another type or modification of human sacrifice which is approached from another angle elsewhere in this book:[75] infanticide and the exposure of children. Exposure was often a dedication

[69] Yamasaki, in *Mitth. Anth. Gesell. Wien*, XXXI, 27; *Globus*, LXXII, 323.

[70] Ratzel, *Vkde.*, II, 206.

[71] Friederici, *Skalpieren*, 77-90; Spix und Martius, *Brasilien*, 1314; Koch, in *Globus*, LXXXI, 70.

[72] *Hist.*, IV, 103.   [73] Gomme, *Ethnol. in Folklore*, 84.

[74] §§248, 249, above.

[75] §§404, 405, below; Sumner, *Folkways*, ch. XVI.

to the gods just as was infanticide; only there was, in the former case, an amelioration and a hope that the child might be preserved. This hope is reflected in the outcome of a number of legendary tales.

"The exposed and later famous men, like Sargon, Cyrus, Moses, Romulus and Remus, play a great rôle. Exposure presents an effort at commutation of the child-sacrifice. Without sacrificing the child, it is offered to the god who expresses his satisfaction by preserving the child. The god has spoken and has accepted the commutation."[76] In mourning for Germanicus, Roman women exposed their children.[77]

Another modified form of human sacrifice is the Roman *ver sacrum*, or "sacred springtime." Though all the first-born of a year were vowed to Mars, that is, to death, they might save their lives, if they could, outside the tribe. This amounted to mass-exposure and led to colonization.[78] There was an official formula for the vow of *ver sacrum*, communicated to the people by a magistrate,[79] and the exposed were veiled, supposably as a sign of dedication. Ihering's[80] account of the practice sets it before us in sufficient detail:

"According to the account of Festus, accepted by modern scholars, the *ver sacrum* took the following shape: In times of severe distress the Government dedicated to the gods, for the purpose of moving them to compassion for the people, the entire offspring of both man and beast during the forth-coming spring. The children were allowed to live until they had grown up; then the marriageable youth of both sexes had to leave the town and seek their fortunes abroad, and make a new home for themselves elsewhere. The nation severed all further connection with them, wherein lay the difference between the *ver sacrum* and colonization. The people did not concern themselves as to the fate of the wanderers, who were given over absolutely into the hands of the deity, who might do with them as he would. Hence the name of *ver sacrum*, and for those who took part in it of *sacrani*. . . . It is not true that the entire birth of the following spring was dedicated to the gods. The dedication would in that case have been unqualified, whereas each *votum* was given in true Roman fashion, on condition that the deity would first grant that which had been prayed for. . . . The Romans never mention over-crowding as one of the grounds of the *ver sacrum*, but refer to other calamities, such as pestilence and war, which are not in the slightest degree remedied by migration; and the fact that in the *ver sacrum* the execution of the vow is separated from the vow itself by an interval of twenty or twenty-one years does not harmonize with the idea of alleviating an existing over-population." It was the non-

76 Maurer, *Vkde.*, I, 239-240.   77 Suetonius, *Caligula*, V.
78 Lippert, *Kgchte.*, II, 309; Keller, *Colon.*, ch. II.
79 In Livy, *Hist.*, XXII, 10; Harrison, *Greek Relig.*, 522-523.
80 *Evol. of Aryan*, 249, 250-251, 257-258, 261, 262-263, 280-281.

propertied class that formed the chief contingent in the migration and the exiles were young. "With the Greeks it assumed the form of the tithes offered to the gods. With the Scandinavians it was decided by lot who had to emigrate: with them, it is said, in times of great famine a third, on another occasion half, of the population emigrated."

Throughout the foregoing illustrations, and especially in the case of exposure and the *ver sacrum*, there will have been recurrently observed a tendency to ameliorate the practice of slaying human beings. Substitutes have been employed; the victims have been accorded a chance for their lives; or the whole ceremony has been diluted down into survivalistic and symbolic forms. The cannibalistic element has been modified away. The general trend of evolution in these matters has been toward a less harsh and savage code.

§295*. Redemption and Covenant. The germs, at least, of ransom and redemption are explicitly revealed under foregoing topics, in particular that of atonement.[81] One of the widest phases of religious sentiment represents all men as under debt to the spirits. This may be merely because the latter have held off and not inflicted damage when they might have done so. In any case there must be a buying-off or "redemption"—it is salutary to reflect upon the etymology of the latter term. The thing to be bought off or ransomed is not infrequently life itself; the "ransomed soul" is a more developed conception. It is as if life comes into the world under forfeit, by reason of some original obligation or "original sin." The idea is that one can keep his life, demanded though it is by the god of death or the evil spirits, by rendering another life in its stead.[82]

This topic is closely allied to that of the scape-goat.[83] Among the Bahima, "if at any time disease breaks out amongst the cattle, a priest is called in and has the symptoms of the disease described to him; after hearing how the disease first began and all about it, he resorts to divination to discover the cause of the sickness. When the cause has been decided, he collects herbs and other remedies to attract the disease from the cattle. An animal is chosen from the herd in the evening, which is to be the scapegoat for the herd; the herbs, etc., are tied round its neck, with certain fetiches to ensure the illness leaving the other animals; the cow is driven round the outside of the kraal several times, and afterwards placed inside with the herd for the night. Early the

[81] §§275, 286, 287, above. [82] Wilken, in VG, III, 471.
[83] §286, above.

following morning the animal is taken out and again driven round the kraal; the priest then kills it in the gateway, and some of the blood is sprinkled over the people belonging to the kraal, and also over the herd. The people next file out, each one jumping over the carcase of the cow, and all the animals are driven over it in the same way. The disease is thus transferred to the scapegoat and the herd is saved. All the fetiches and herbs, which were upon the scapegoat, are fastened upon the doorposts and lintel of the kraal to prevent the disease from entering again."[84]

Wilken[85] connects skull- and hair-sacrifice with redemption. Head-hunting, besides being a result of skull-worship, also provides a substitute for one's own life. He recalls the Admetus story. Vicarious sacrifice also is a sequel of the procuring of a head, as is shown in the puberty-ceremonies and in marriage. Citing the case of the Inca who, in illness, would offer to the deity one of his sons, imploring him to take this victim in his stead; that of the Gauls, who tried to escape death from illness by human sacrifice; and that of the Norse king who sacrificed to Odin in succession nine of his sons, in order to attain longevity, this author collates with them a number of cases from the Indian Archipelago. For example, in the island of Bali, "for weeks the village had been wasted by an epidemic. In their resourceless condition the people had turned to the priest who revealed to them, after the appropriate prayers, that the plague would not wane before the community had offered one of its members to the gods as a reconciliation-sacrifice." Said a native to the recounter: "And look you, sir! that is happening. To N. N., who lies there, has fallen the high honor of being allowed to die for his fellow-citizens. The gods ought, however, to be content with our good will and give him back to us living straightway. Then N. N. is to be brought to the river, in order to dedicate himself, and thereafter returns to the village-temple where for three days he must segregate himself in prayer and the doing of penance." This is evidently an amelioration of an ancient bloodier custom; in remote districts a real human sacrifice of a vicarious order, though not always of a village-member, is practised. The Arab, on slaying a victim, should say: "O God, verily this . . . is a ransom for my son such a one; its blood for his blood, and its flesh for his flesh, and its bone for his bone, and its skin for his skin, and its hair for his hair. O God, make it a ransom for my son from hell fire." "The sacrifice is meant, as the prophet, himself says, *to avert evil from the child by shedding blood on his behalf.*" Later blood was merely smeared on the child's head, and finally saffron took its place. The hair-offering for children is a common phenomenon, here and there even in Europe. Polynesian mothers are wont to shave their children's heads or cut the hair as close as possible. Here the offering is really exuvial sacrifice.[86] Main[87] has a chapter on "Vowed Offspring" which has a good deal to say about ransom, though children were also vowed, in case they should have them, by the childless. The Jewish doctrine of the first-fruits is elaborated.

[84] Roscoe, in JAI, XXXVII, 111.

[85] Wilken, in VG, IV, 63 ff.; III, 498-500. This author presents many cases and quotes Tylor, *Prim. Cult.*, II, 403; Cæsar, *Bell. Gall.*, VI, 16; Grimm, *Deut. Mythol.*, 40; Frazer, *Golden Bough*, pt. III, chs. II, IV, V, VI; Smith, *Kinship*, 153; Ploss, *Kind*, I, 289-295; Ellis, *Polyn. Researches*, I, 261.

[86] §298, below.

[87] *Relig. Chastity*, ch. XIII; Judges, XIII, 3, 5; I Sam., I, 11, 28; II, 18, 19; Luke, I, 15, 16; and the Apocrypha.

Illustration may include citations from two writers of fiction who have taken up into their stories much of an ethnographical nature.

An Englishman in India is figured as having had a son by a native woman, and as, at the instance of an old gate-keeper, performing the customary sacrifice by beheading two goats. While so doing he mutters the prayer: "Almighty! In place of this my son I offer life for life, blood for blood, head for head, bone for bone, hair for hair, skin for skin."[88] Previous to this the father had stepped upon a naked dagger that had been laid upon the threshold to avert ill luck; and when it broke at the hilt under his tread, the native mother had murmured: "God is great! Thou hast taken his misfortunes on thy head." To this assumption of another's guilt we shall presently come. Again, in Zangwill's[89] story of modern Jewish life in the London Ghetto, the father of a son is represented as handing him to the cohen, a priestly functionary, and speaking as follows: "This is my first-born son, is the first-born of his mother, and the Holy One, blessed be He, hath given command to redeem him, as it is said, and those that are to be redeemed of them from a month old, shalt thou redeem according to thine estimation for the money of five shekels after the shekel of the sanctuary, the shekel being twenty gerabs; and it is said, 'Sanctify unto me all the first-born, whatsoever openeth the womb among the children of Israel, both of man and of beast; it is mine.'" The father then places fifteen shillings of silver before the cohen who next inquires in Chaldaic: "Which wouldst thou rather—give me thy first-born son, the first-born of his mother, or redeem him for five selaim, which thou art bound to give according to the Law?" The father answers and the cohen takes the money, holds it over the head of the infant, and says: "This instead of that, this in exchange for that, this in remission of that. May this child enter into life, into the Law, into the fear of Heaven." Orthodox Jews still have a custom which requires the ransoming of the first-born son from the church.

Something in exchange for or in remission of something—this is the kernel of procedure in all cases. The child's life is redeemed by a substitute value and the impending punishment is remitted. Here are conceptions, commonly dismissed as symbolic, which are survivalistic and capable of explanation only in the light of the evolution of religion. Ransom and redemption go back to the body of primitive ideas and practices which we have been reviewing, and especially and most directly to human sacrifice as a means of reconciliation and propitiation, and to the conception of original sin and guilt and of the rights of the gods; they can be derived from no other antecedents and so cannot otherwise be included under the scientifically accountable. If one desires rather to consult his fancy or intuition in matters of this sort, though he may

[88] Kipling, "Without Benefit of Clergy," in *Life's Handicap*, 219, 216.
[89] *Ghetto*, 52.

satisfy prejudices and yearnings, he must be content to fail of a genuine explanation.

The dread of higher powers long cast a chill over all enjoyment that men had a chance to attain. Many encountered ill luck, perishing by accident, disease, sorcery, or other calamity. Anyone was liable to be the next victim. How could the danger be set aside? Obviously by providing a substitute or vicarious sacrifice. One's child, especially his first-born, was the most obvious life to give for his own; then a slave or a prisoner. Here was furnished a strong motive for war. In the case of the Phœnicians child-sacrifice developed, on such lines of logic, into an important societal institution.[90] The Romans could not stamp it out.[91]

The two incidents quoted from fiction are typical of a modified redemption; the crude instance is where there is not merely "life for life," but human life for human life; where, for example, the first-born's death redeems the life of the father or that of brothers and sisters yet to come, just as the first-fruits of the field insure the later-maturing crops. It can be seen from some of the following examples that redemption is intimately related to the common custom of buying one's self off from ill-fortune or from the consequences of sin;[92] the only added conception in the developed form of redemption is that of an indefinite accountability incurred merely by being alive and belonging to a race that has forfeited the right to live or, at any rate, has no such right except as its members are ransomed. This developed theory belongs, naturally, to a stage of greater sophistication.

In Australia, the body of the dead must not touch the earth. It is dropped heavily on bark and the sorcerer cries: "Blood for blood" or "Life for life,"[93] meaning, apparently, that now the debt of life which the deceased has long owed, is discharged. In one New Guinea district there are two spirits which kill male children, not out of malevolence, but because they wish to draw to themselves beings who become their property after death. And so "the corpses of their little children are not buried in the earth, but laid in the highest branches of trees" in the hope that these two spirits will take them and spare the other children.[94] In another Melanesian case, when a man becomes ill and a certain malignant spirit is believed to have seized his soul and bound it to a banyan-tree, some person who has access to the spirit is employed to intercede;

[90] Not, as Lippert (Kgchte., I, 441) infers, for merely selfish reasons, in order to evade the care and expense attendant.

[91] Tiele-Gehrich, Relig., I, 242.   [92] §§275, 286, above.

[93] Smyth, Vict., I, 104.   [94] Krieger, Neu-Guinea, 390-391.

"he takes a pig or fish to the sacred place and offers it, saying, 'This is for you to eat in place of that man; eat this, don't kill him'; and he is then able to loose and take back the sick man's soul so that he may recover."[95]

In Korea, "the arranging for the sale of children to daemons is a function of the *mu-tang* [sorceress] and is carried on to a great extent. The Korean father desires prosperity and long life for his boy (the girl being of little account), and the sale of his child to a spirit he believes is the best way of attaining the object." But the child is not passed over, life and all; the *mu-tang* "takes in its stead one of its rice bowls and a spoon, and these, together with a piece of cotton cloth on which the facts concerning the sale of the child are written, are laid up in her own house in the room devoted to her daemon."[96] In India, ransom is by a head or image, in metal or cake; even animals were ransomed by images, to save capital. Elsewhere it took heroes to free men from human tribute to supernatural beings.[97] In an Indian epic episode a king refused to give up to a hawk a dove which had sought shelter in his bosom. At last the hawk demanded as ransom a weight of the king's flesh equal to that of the dove. He cut off the flesh and put it in the scales, but could not equal the dove's weight. Then he gave his whole body. The hawk was Indra and the king had withstood a test.[98] The idea underlying certain Hindu sacrifices is that "evil comes to man out of the displeasure of the gods, who will allow an afflicted person to substitute an animal in lieu of himself, and that the offering of the same may be made with a view to mitigate their wrath."[99]

In Sumatra a father is in duty bound to make a substitute sacrifice on the day when his child's hair is first cut, that is, when he becomes a member of the great household and is dedicated to Allah. "In proportion to his social position the father offers at the birth of his child a she-goat, sheep, cow, or carabao. . . . Hardly any Mohammedan will fail to do this for his sons; but for his daughters he often neglects it."[100] The members of the Polynesian Arreoi society slew and ate their first-born; it was a sacrifice in the sense of being a meal to which the gods came.[101] The Indians of Florida are represented as sacrificing their first-born to the sun.[102] A man's captive was sacrificed for him. He could not eat the flesh himself, since the victim was, in a sense, his son.[103]

Lippert[104] collects several examples of redemption: the South American father ransomed his child with his own blood; the North American child was redeemed with its own blood, drawn, in Mexico, from the tongue, from behind the ear, or elsewhere. Flogging the Spartan youth at the altar of Artemis was a method of blood-letting, resulting in a covenant with the goddess. In Rome, boy-sacrifice was occasionally demanded; after the overthrow of the custom, heads of poppies and onions were offered vicariously, being hung at the door. Children were saved by the substitution of a kid, whose heart and entrails stood for theirs—this revealing in full the vicarious quality of the sacrifice.

The most familiar case of ransom is the Semitic one, which has

[95] Codrington, *Melanesians,* 138, 139.   [96] Bishop, *Korea,* 412.
[97] Lippert, *Kgchte.,* II, 320.   [98] Holtzmann, *Ind. Sagen,* I, 277.
[99] Deshmukh, in JASB, I, 113.
[100] Jacobs, *Groot-Atjeh,* I, 180, 181.   [101] Lippert, *Kgchte.,* II, 306.
[102] Carr, in *Smithson. Rep.,* 1891, 538, note.
[103] Bancroft, *Nat. Races,* II, 309.   [104] *Kgchte.,* II, 317, 312, 322, 323.

entered into the Christian system. Were it not for this development, it would perhaps have seemed unnecessary to single out the
special topic of redemption and covenant from the mass of similar
usages. Ransom and redemption are closely allied with covenant—
are, in fact, the expression and visible sign of it; the ransomed
and redeemed are under covenant with the god and are his chosen
people. The Old Testament is permeated with the idea and its
attendant ritual.

"Even the first-born child, in the same fashion as the animals, had at first
been sacrificed to a bloody Jehovah. Later on it was still in theory dedicated
to the Lord but its ransom was compulsory. Five shekels of silver paid to the
Levites redeemed it." Each grown man was to pay a half-shekel as "a ransom
for his soul to the Lord." The Baalim demand human sacrifice; the first-born
is theirs unless redeemed by money or circumcision. In distress it is asked what
God demands: "Shall I give my first-born for my sin; the fruit of my body
for my transgression?" The first-born is to be given, like the first-fruits.
Earlier, no one devoted to God is to be ransomed; he must be killed according
to the original intent. The burning of sons in the fire, though denounced, is
witness to the pre-ransom stage.[105]
These redemption-rites indicate antecedent human sacrifice; no amount of
interpretation can alter that. The prophet[106] knows it but cannot, in his enlightenment, regard it as one of the laws of God "by which man lives." He
explains it by the "awfulness" of God and as a punishment for apostasy in
the wilderness. "Moreover also I gave them statutes that were not good, and
judgments wherein they should not live; and I polluted them in their own
gifts in that they caused to pass through the fire all that openeth the womb
that I might make them desolate, to the end that they might know that I am
the Lord." Here the god seems to warrant what has come to be considered
immoral, provided it conduces to his power. In the story of Abraham, his will-
ingness to comply with the divine demand for the sacrifice of his son is construed as a merit to be richly rewarded.[107]
"A sheikh east of the Sea of Galilee declared: 'Every place, every land, yes,
every spot on the earth has its inhabitants. Now, in order that no one of the
family in this land may die, since evidently it does not belong to him, the
whole family is redeemed by a fedu [redemption-sacrifice].'" "The numerous
redemption-myths show how man sought gradually to escape the noose which
the inevitable course of his own thought had wound around his neck." The
author quoted[108] cites different redemption-customs which are remote survivals
of human sacrifice. "Exposure," he continues, "represents an attempt at redemption of the child-sacrifice. Without slaying the child it is offered to the
god, who expresses his pleasure by preserving it. The god has spoken and approved the redemption. This form of ransom is encountered on Israelite soil in

[105] Levit., XXVII; Maspero, *Hist. Anc.*, II, 160; Num., XVIII, 15, 16;
Micah, VI, 7; Exod., IV, 24; XXII, 29; XXX, 12-16; XXXIV, 20; Deut.,
XII, 31; II Kings, III, 27; Ezek., XX, 26.
[106] Ezek., XX, 25, 26.   [107] Gen., XXII, 1 ff.
[108] Maurer, *Vkde.*, I, 72, 240, 241, 242; Maurer, in *Globus*, XCI, 111, 112.

the life-history of Moses."[109] Redemption by animal-substitution occurs several times in the cuneiform inscriptions.[110]

Redemption by animal-sacrifice lies also at the base of the Passover-myth. Among the Mexicans the divine primordial mother, Centeotl, at her festivals, goes about through the land and abodes of men. To protect life, they pierced their ears, noses, tongues, arms, thighs, collected the blood and hung it in ancient vessels on the door-posts of the houses. The same thought comes to expression in the Passover-myth. At the festal time comes the angel of Jahweh and kills the first-born of the Egyptians. The Israelites, however, had protected themselves by sacrificing a lamb and sprinkling their door-posts with blood. The place of the first-born of the Israelites was taken by those of the Egyptians." It is to be noted that the Passover-lamb was roasted whole, with bitter herbs—the primitive meal; and that the ceremony implied a covenant.[111] The latest Israelite form of redemption resulted in the hierodule, or sacred slave—the first-born, who took up duties in the temple.[112]

Smith[113] makes the evolution of the redemption-idea somewhat more complicated, though his interpretation amounts, in the end, to the same explanation of it. "I apprehend that all the prerogatives of the first born among the Semitic peoples are originally prerogatives of sanctity; the sacred blood of the kin flows purest and strongest in him.[114] Neither in the case of children, nor in that of cattle, did the congenital holiness of the first-born originally imply that they must be sacrificed or given to the deity on the altar, but only that if sacrifice was to be made they were the best and fittest, because the holiest, victims." This theory seems to us less inevitable than the one amply illustrated above, of the gods' claim to being served first. That is what made firstfruits "holy." The author goes on, involving himself, we think, by trying to see the primordial as the derived: "But when the old ideas of holiness became unintelligible, and holy beasts came to mean beasts set aside for sacrifice, an obvious extension of this new view of holiness demanded that the human firstborn should be redeemed, by the substitution of an animal victim;[115] and from this usage, again, the Moloch sacrifices were easily developed in the seventh century, when ordinary means seemed too weak to conjure the divine anger." Then, "for many centuries the official theology of the Church was content to interpret the death of Christ as a ransom for mankind paid to the devil, or as a satisfaction to the divine honour, rather than as a recognition of the sovereignty of the moral law of justice." As another writer[116] puts it, "theology made of Jesus an expiatory victim immolated by his celestial father."

The Thargelia were ancient sanguinary festivals celebrated in Greece in honor of Apollo and Artemis. Two men or a man and a woman were immolated in Attica to expiate the sins of the people. "The circular dances of the Greeks around the victims, or later around the altar, can be compared only with the songs and furious dances of the Iroquois and Brazilians around their prisoners."[117]

"There is a story that in 1588, Hector Monro, Baron of Fowlis, being taken ill, sent for a notorious witch, who informed the Baron that he could not

[109] Exod., II.
[110] Schrader, *Keilinschriften,* 596-597.
[112] Num., III, 39-46.
[114] Gen., XLIX, 3; Deut., XXI, 17.
[116] Oliveira Martins, *Raças,* II, 49.
[111] Lippert, *Kgchte.,* II, 314 ff.
[113] *Relig. Sem.,* 465, 424.
[115] Gen., XXII.
[117] Magnin, *Théâtre,* 30.

recover unless 'the principal man of his bluid should die for him.' The Baron's half brother was selected. In 1590, the Baron was tried for 'sorcery, incantation, witchcraft, and slaughter.' "[118]

Survivalistic practices, presently to receive mention, will reflect light not only upon human sacrifice but also upon redemption and allied topics. Man is always at fault. "How now do mortals take the gods to task!" says Zeus, "for they say that their evils are from us, while they themselves, because of their acts of blind folly, suffer woes beyond measure."[119] In the *Roman de la Rose*[120] it is noted that in an unfortunate marriage man says God made it; but God is good and the evil is due to man. Man's duty, and his neglected duty, are always there; and he is ever under a censure from which he must buy himself off.

The establishment of what was thought to be a successful adjustment for conciliation and propitiation leads to the conception of a covenant, that is, of a contract or alliance between the men who owe to the god their blood and that of their children and the divinity that takes the ransom. All who are in the covenant form a society not necessarily resting on kinship but having a common debt and duty to the daimon—an original obligation to pay to him which they admit and which he, by reason of that admission, will perhaps not so jealously enforce. Between god and chosen people there is mutual service and good will, and the men are marked for the covenant, generally by some scar resulting from exuvial sacrifice.[121] The covenant has a double aspect: that of the worshippers to their divinity and that of the cult-members to one another. Those who participate in the sacrificial eating of the victim, or in the drinking of his blood, are brought into sacred relations. The use of blood to lend sanctity to acts, even between groups or between members of different groups, is common enough; brotherhoods are thus formed and agreements are sanctioned by dipping weapons in the blood of sacrifice;[122] "the blood of the everlasting covenant"[123] is a familiar expression. The covenant-factor comes out strongly in the rite of mutilation or other initiation, either at birth—to ransom the child—or at puberty—

118 Gomme, *Ethnol. in Folklore,* 142.   119 Homer, *Odyssey,* I, 32-34.
120 18,580 ff.   121 §298, below.
122 §§108, 141, 297, above; Xenophon, *Anab.,* II, 2.
123 Heb., X, 29; XIII, 20; Exod., XXIV, 8; Zech., IX, 11.

to introduce him into his father's organization. Naturally the place for making the covenant is the location occupied by the daimon, the fetish-spot; hence, among other forms, the threshold-covenant.[124]

The idea of sacrament enters into the sacrifice; that is, all who participate in a thing which, occurring in religion, is rare, terrible, mysterious, of powerful effect upon the imagination, yet effective for salvation from danger and from evil—which, outside of religion, may be shocking and abominable—all such come into close communion with one another. Each one who desires to share in the good to be gained must participate in the ceremony and the offering. All must do it that no one may blame another. The amount of cannibal food is reduced to a small crumb or to a drop of blood, mixed with other edibles or drinks. The usage becomes ritual and ceremonial. Later the original food is merely represented—for instance, by cakes in human form. Such cases appear under the survivals of human sacrifice.[125]

By the sacred relations into which the covenanted worshippers are inducted, bonds of mutual obligation are created which the parties dare not break; hence guarantees are established. Contracts thus coming into existence are good within the cult-bond, which becomes a social tie of the first order.[126] The composite idea of ransom, redemption, and covenant has been developed, interpreted, rationalized, and refined from its original, to become one of the profoundest and most transcendental of religious mysteries; and at the same time it has exercised a powerful socializing influence upon ever wider groups of fellow-worshippers. The ethnocentric sentiments harbored by a chosen people[127] for aliens produce arrogant patriotism, national pride and delusion, isolation, endogamy, and holy war for propaganda and plunder, at one and the same time. When such a notion as that of being a peculiar and chosen people has once found lodgment, it has far greater effect on the mores than any theological dogma.

---

[124] Lippert, *Kgchte.*, II, 306, 311, 316, 336, 339, 397.

[125] §§293, above, and 297, below.   [126] §151, above.

[127] Case of the Jews: Deut., IV, 20, 37; VII, 6; X, 15; XIV, 2; Ps., XXXIII, 12; XLVII, 5; CXXXV, 4; Is., XL, 66. Case of Arabs: Koran, sura II, 137; III, 106.

§296*. Sacral or Sacrificial "Prostitution." This practice, termed also temple-harlotry, has its relation to human sacrifice, obligation, and ransom. In most of its aspects it is not described by the designation "prostitution." The underlying idea is not unlike what was in the minds of the people concerned when a woman who met a party of head-hunters was allowed to surrender herself sexually to save her life.[128] A girl might be dedicated, in such a relation, to the god instead of being slain in sacrifice; then she might be bought off with the earnings of her sojourn in the temple. The mores can legitimize anything; they can relieve a course of action of all odium; thus the dignity and value of the women who had lived in the temple were in no way impaired. Though sacrificial prostitution is found more commonly in connection with rather highly developed religion, suggestions of it appear upon the less evolved stages. Among the instances of premarital license[129] will be found a number of cases approaching it.

This subject is treated extensively and with many examples by Main.[130] He cites cases of virginity, as of the vestals, and of consecration to perpetual virginity of infant daughters as a recognition of divine aid in winning a victory. He makes much also of temple-attendance by widows as a substitute for their immolation. The conclusion, however, is that "man's relations to his gods are always modelled on his relations to man, and except under the monogamous wage-earning systems of modern civilization it is but very rarely that female service does not imply sexual intercourse." Perhaps this exception is not universally valid.

There were women in the Guinea region who were married to the fetish. "The chief business of the female *kosi* is prostitution, and in every town there is at least one institution in which the best-looking girls, between 10 and 12, are received. Here they remain for three years, learning the chants and dances peculiar to the worship of the gods, and prostituting themselves to the priests and inmates of the male seminaries; and at the end of their novitiate they become public prostitutes. This condition, however, is not regarded as one for reproach; they are considered to be married to the god, and their excesses are supposed to be caused and directed by him. . . . Children who are born from such unions belong to the god." The practice "is essentially religious in its origin, and intimately connected with phallic worship."[131] Among the Dyaks of Borneo there is a class of priestesses whose loose mode of life does not make marriage impossible for them but rather the contrary.[132] Mexican courtesans often immolated themselves; they were not disgraced by unchastity.[133]

128 Riedel, *Rassen*, 118 (quoted in Stoll, *Geschlechtsl.*, 483).
129 §§343, 344, below.
130 *Relig. Chastity*, 163-164, 191, 52-58; ch. VI, appendix, note XXII, 78.
131 Ellis, *Ewe*, 38, 141; Bastian, *Deut. Exped.*, I, 172.
132 Ratzel, *Vkde.*, II, 431.   133 Bancroft, *Nat. Races*, II, 336.

Sacral prostitution was known in Egypt and Assyria,[134] and to the ancient Semites; it spread westward with the Babylonian and Phœnician religions and "flourished in Israel down into the later era of kings."[135] Passages[136] are cited to substantiate this statement, some of them by reason of their repeated denunciation affording proof of the fact that the custom was firmly rooted; it "appears ethnologically less an outflow of the originally universal priestly right than a form of ransom of the human sacrifice." The Israelites dedicated both males and females as hierodules; it is cast up to the people that the service of the temple is being discharged by heathen.[137] Temple-prostitution is distinguished from this and is found in all Semitic nature-religions. To the ancient Israelites association with prostitutes was not a matter of shame. Temple-prostitutes were commoner in the north, owing to connections with the Phœnicians; but even in the time of Josiah they had their own quarters in the temple at Jerusalem. Especially, however, did the practice flourish in Babylon where "fathers rich in daughters were all the more happy to use this opportunity for providing for a daughter because it was enveloped in a religious nimbus. . . . This custom, thus widely extended, is pretty good proof that the practice in question goes back to primitive Semitic times."[138] The harlots were "holy" on account of their connection with the temple; but Herodotus[139] says that they retired with their partners outside the edifice.

One writer,[140] in some irritation, refuses to believe at all in sacral harlotry on account of "woman's nature" and "man's jealousy." Plainly we have here a subject concerning which much legitimate difference of interpretation may be recorded—a topic of such nature also that a predisposed person may wave aside any number of relevant considerations if his prepossessions are impenetrable to evidence and reason. Here are our cases.[141] There runs through them that strong strain of dedication and consecration which goes with sacrifice, justifying the alternative adjective used in the topic title.

§297*. Survivals of Human Sacrifice. Perhaps redemption and sacral prostitution might be called modifications or mitigations rather than survivals of the sacrifice of human beings; and

---

[134] Maspero, *Hist. Anc.,* II, 50, 51, 126, 577, note; II, 536; Winckler, *Hammurabi,* 19.

[135] Maurer, *Vkde.,* I, 52, 93-95; Farnell, "Relig. of Greece," in *Hastings's Dict. Bible,* suppl. vol., 130.

[136] Gen., XXXVIII, 21-22; Amos, II, 7; Hos., IV, 14, IX, 10; I Kings, XIV, 24, XV, 12, XXII, 46; II Kings, XXIII, 7; Levit., XIX, 29; Deut., XXIII, 18.

[137] Jos., IX, 27; Ezek., XLIV, 8.

[138] Barton, *Semitic Origins,* 43-44; 251, 253, 258.

[139] *Hist.,* I, 199; Smith, *Relig. Sem.,* 141.   [140] Warner, *Jewish Spectre,* 207.

[141] See also Sumner, *Folkways,* ch. XVI.

the same might be thought of several usages about to be mentioned. It is a question chiefly of terminology and of deciding when a practice has been so modified away that only a survival is left. Whatever these dwindling relics may be called, it is strong evidence for the generality of human sacrifice that they have been found so copiously among so many peoples. Modifications have been instanced over and over in what precedes; in fact, lists of our examples—those, say, of substitute-sacrifice—might be taken to be illustrative of obvious mitigations rather than of the practice itself. In the present connection, therefore, we are gathering up strands rather than spinning new ones.

The attempt is often made to interpret away evidence for the former existence of a practice now regarded as unsavory; and there may well be divergencies of interpretation of special cases between disputants who are both competent and unprejudiced; but the available collections of facts, such as those of Frazer,[142] represent a weight of testimony heavy with significance. Main[143] finds the vowing of offspring by the childless to be a substitute for human sacrifice. The following representative instances should recall others cited here and there in what precedes.

In New Guinea once a young man must kill and deliver a man for the chief to eat; now a wild pig is the substitute.[144] In Uganda, at the cessation of a dance, a little girl "was laid out at the base of the tree as though she was to be sacrificed, and every detail of the sacrifice was gone through in mock fashion. A slight incision was made in the child's neck, but not such as to seriously hurt her. She was then caught up and thrown into the water of the lake close at hand. Here a man was standing ready to save her from being drowned. The girl on whom this ceremony was performed, was, my informant learnt, dedicated by native custom to a life of perpetual virginity."[145] In India, "from Coorg to Mysore we have examples of village festivals in which substitution of animals for human beings is traceable." We are told that at first a man was given as a victim. "When he was offered up the essential essence went out of him. It entered into the horse—and so on to the ox, sheep, goat, wheat, barley."[146] Again, "the bridegroom, as part of the wedding ceremony, cuts off the head of a human figure of dough with a knife supplied by the bride's family. This shows that human sacrifice was once part of a Hindu marriage."[147]

In Samoa, "if any visitor caught a cuttle-fish and cooked it, or if any member of that family had been where a cuttle-fish was eaten, the family would

[142] *Golden Bough*, especially II, 247 ff.
[143] *Relig. Chastity*, ch. XIII, 191. [144] Haddon, in JAI, L, 270.
[145] Johnston, *Uganda*, II, 720. [146] Fawcett, in JASB, II, 281 ff.
[147] Athalye, in JASB, I, 76.

meet over the case, and a man or woman would be selected to go and lie down in a *cold* oven, and be covered over with leaves, as in the process of baking, and all this as a would-be or mock burnt-offering to avert the wrath of the god. While this was being done the family united in praying: 'O bald-headed Fe'e! forgive what has been done—it was all the work of a *stranger*.' Failing such signs of respect and humility, it was supposed the god would come to the family, and cause a cuttle-fish to grow internally, and be the death of some of them." Again, there was a deity incarnate in the sea-eel, and some boys had eaten one. "As soon as the people heard that these lads had 'eaten the god,' they mustered, gave them a beating, and dragged them off to a cooking house. They laid them down in the oven pit, and covered them with leaves *as if* they had been killed, and were now to be cooked as a peace-offering to avert the wrath of the deity. . . . If, through a stranger or by any member of the family, an incarnation had been cooked in the family oven, it could not be used again until some one had been laid there as a mock burnt-offering, and gone through the 'make-believe' process of cooking. It was death to the family if the oven was used without this ceremony."[148]

MacLeod[149] finds no mortuary immolation of widows on the aboriginal North American northwest coast; there is, however, a practice which has been explained as a "mitigated survival" of widow-burning. The body is put on a pyre; "during the process of burning . . . the bystanders appear to be in a high state of merriment. If a stranger happen to be present they invariably plunder him; but if that pleasure be denied them they never separate without quarreling among themselves. . . . If the doctor who attended him has escaped uninjured, he is obliged to be present at the ceremony, and for the last time tries his skill in restoring the defunct to life." If he fails in this the medicine-man throws a "present" on the burning body, "which in some measure appeases the resentment of the relatives, and preserves the unfortunate quack from being maltreated." The same resentment seems to be harbored toward the widow; "while the doctor is performing his last operation she must lie on the pile, and after the fire is applied she cannot stir until the doctor orders her to be removed, which is, however, never done until her body is completely covered with blisters. . . . If, during her husband's lifetime she has been known to have committed any act of infidelity, or omitted administering to him savory food, or neglected his clothing, . . . she is now made to suffer severely for such lapses of duty by his relations, who frequently fling her into the funeral pile, from which she is dragged by her friends, and thus, between alternate scorching and cooling, she is dragged backwards and forwards until she falls into a state of insensibility. . . . The wretched widows, to avoid this complicated cruelty, frequently commit suicide. . . . The men are condemned to a similar ordeal, but they do not bear it with equal fortitude, and numbers fly to different quarters to avoid the brutal treatment which custom has established as a kind of religious rite." The author sees here "a tendency towards the mortuary burning of both widower and widow. . . . The fact that certain post-cremation duties await the survivor may be considered as tending to prevent actual immolation. The fact that the widower is accorded the same

148 Turner, *Samoa,* 31-32, 58, 59.
149 "The Incipient Suttee," in AA, XXVII, 122-126 (author's italics are removed).

treatment makes it very unlikely that we have a case of 'mitigated survival,'" as Tylor has thought, of mere widow-immolation.

Cutting off the head of a figure or mutilating it in the presence of the gods is common, not alone in India but in America and elsewhere. Bourke[150] gives a number of cases where ancient kinds of meal derived from grasses—"old foods"[151]—were used to make dough-images of men which were eaten sacrificially. The blood of a human sacrifice was often mixed in. Here are human sacrifice and cannibalism reduced to a ceremonial meal. The Pawnees have a folk-tale about "The Boy who was Sacrificed."[152] A father offered up his son and cast his body into a river. The animals discovered the body and restored it to life. The boy was made a doctor and was taught the art of restoring people to life. It was never known that the father had sacrificed his boy. The boy knew he could never have done these wonderful things unless his father had sacrificed him. Here is evidence from legend paralleling and supporting that from survivals. Among the Karoks of California, as has been noted elsewhere,[153] appears the god-man who propitiates vicariously by suffering for all. "In the summer when there is no rain, and not much to eat, the Tarahumaris are very religious and sacrifice animals to their god. After many have been given up and no rain comes, the Indian argues with his god that he must not be so greedy, but his mouth is shut with the query: 'What would you say if I asked for a Tarahumari to be killed for me?'"[154] It is significant that, among the Chibchas, parrots which had been taught to speak took the place of human beings as sacrifices.[155]

In Japan, "human sacrifice appears to have been practiced, and, if we may judge by the numerous legends handed down, was not entirely suppressed until long after the period when clay images were produced as a substitute." Legend ascribes the substitute images to about the beginning of the Christian era.[156] Human sacrifice is said to have been abolished through the compassion of the Emperor, when he heard the weeping and crying of victims who had been buried alive. The edict reads: "Let there be complete cessation of all such ancient practices as strangling oneself to follow the dead, or strangling others to make them follow the dead, or of killing the dead man's horse, or burying treasures in the tomb for the dead man's sake, or cutting the hair, or stabbing the thigh, or wailing for the dead man's sake." Figures of clay were introduced as substitutes for horses as well as men.[157]

The legend which tells us why the Egyptians did not have human sacrifice proves that they once had it. There is evidence that they had the custom of killing slaves to serve the deceased in the other world; also the chief prisoners of war were sacrificed to the gods. In places, human sacrifice continued until the Roman period but was very rare. Men were replaced by cakes of a certain form, or by animals.[158] In the Greek rites there was, together with a disguised amelioration, also a curious case of pretending that human beings about to be sacrificed were animals—instead of substituting the latter for the former. "We have before us Greek rites where the victim is disguised as a man; but con-

---

[150] In BAE, IX, 526.

[151] §324, below.

[152] Grinnell, *Folk Tales*, 161 ff.

[153] §291, above.

[154] Lumholtz, in *Int. Cong. Anthrop.*, 1893, 110.

[155] Bastian, *Culturländer*, II, 178.

[156] Pfoundes, in JAI, XII, 222.

[157] Hitchcock, in USNM, 1891, 523.

[158] Maspero, *Hist. Anc.*, I, 168, note.

versely human sacrifices are often dressed up as animals, or said to represent animals . . . fathers sacrificing their children say that they are not children but beeves."[159] This latter looks like a disguised reversion, as the opposite case is a disguised modification. In Roman times, "for a long period the ancient human sacrifice was recalled by rush dolls called . . . 'Greeks,' that is, enemies in general, which they threw into the Tiber, and woollen dolls, called 'oscilla,' which they suspended on house-doors and at cross-ways against the blood-thirsty manes, that they might spare the living members of the family."[160]

"Our knowledge of heathen antiquities will gain," says Grimm,[161] "by the study . . . of the shapes given to *baked meats,* which either retained the actual forms of ancient idols, or were accompanied by sacrificial observances. A history of German cakes and bread-rolls might contain some unexpected disclosures. . . . Even the shape of cakes is a reminiscence of the sacrifices of heathenism." The traditions of the Welsh and Irish contain many traces of the custom of human sacrifice; a belief still lurks among the Irish peasantry that every seven years the fairies have to offer a child to the evil one and that they try to decoy a fair earth-child.[162] The charges of human sacrifice bandied about between religious sects in the Middle Ages amount to the recognition of a discarded habitude. A saint of the fourth century says of the Gnostics "that some of their sects were accustomed to kill, to dress with spices, and to eat the children born of their promiscuous intercourse."[163]

That certain savage customs connected with human sacrifice, vicarious and other, have prefigured the ceremonial of more advanced religious systems can admit of no doubt. Such usages are plainly sacramental, for they feature the union between deity and men and that between men adhering to the same deity. They do not aim at religious edification for itself but at a closer understanding and conciliation that will result in a more secure prosperity. The parallelism between the savage and the civilized systems has been too close not to have forced itself upon even the unwilling attention of observers. Spanish ecclesiastics in the New World inferred that Satan had visited the field in advance of them and had scoffingly taught the natives the sign of the cross[164] and a parody on the sacraments. Frazer[165] and others have made collections of such savage rites. That the sacrament of communion

---

[159] Smith, *Relig. Sem.,* 366, note.

[160] §265, above; Grupp, *Kgchte.,* I, 19.

[161] *Teut. Myth.,* I, 63.

[162] Gomme, *Ethnol. in Folklore,* 61; Von Pflugk-Harttung, in *Trans. Roy. Hist. Soc.,* N. S. VII, 62.

[163] Lecky, *Europ. Morals,* I, 417.

[164] Quiroga, *Cruz in Amér.;* §244, of *Case-Book;* index of this book, *sub* "cross."

[165] *Golden Bough,* II, 318 ff.

was viewed in the Middle Ages as something far less spiritual than it has become is attested by the fact that the popular imagination conjured up operations upon the host alleged to have been performed by Jews and sorcerers, which would be applicable only to a human body. Further, a great variety of usages in connection with blood and of superstitions about it appear to be survivals of human sacrifice or deductions from it.[166]

In Mexico, Central America, and British Columbia there was an extravagant development of cannibalism is connection with religious festivals and human sacrifice; the latter was sacramental and vicarious, as the attendant rites show. The combination of sorcery, religion, and cannibalism exhibited deserves close attention; shamans ate the flesh of the dead in connection with fasting and solitude as means to their professional stimulation.[167] Torquemada tells of how the Mexicans made images of their god of war out of grains and seeds kneaded with the blood of boys sacrificed for the purpose. The image was broken into crumbs and distributed among the males who ate it after the manner of communion: "este era su manera de comunión." Similarly "the Peruvians made use of sacrificial cakes kneaded with the blood of human victims."[168] Fainter and European survivals are the forms taken by the "baked meats," to which allusion has been made, and the baking of loaves into the shape of a human figure representing the spirit of the corn, which are broken up and distributed for eating among the villagers.[169]

Latent and lurking beliefs of this sort provide, to some degree, for the reception by savages of similar beliefs developed elsewhere and endowed by more developed peoples with a refined interpretation; those who have participated in the attempt to uplift backward races have had the ground somewhat prepared for them, though primitive peoples can see in the developed system only that to which their own minds are attuned.

§298*. Exuvial Sacrifice. All religious and magical practices show cross-strands connecting them, more or less loosely, with all the rest. Vituperation of another or cursing him[170] might be about equivalent to the sacrifice of him. However, that which has been taken to be most directly and indisputably survivalistic of human sacrifice is the actual offering of parts of the body. The sacrifice

[166] §298, immediately following.
[167] Bancroft, *Nat. Races,* I, 170; II, 176, 395, 689, 708; III, 150, 413; Preuss, in *Globus,* LXXXVI, 109, 112, 152.
[168] Bourke, in BAE, IX, 523 ff.
[169] "Cannibalism," in PSM, XLVIII, 411, note.
[170] §283, above.

of such parts as can be spared without danger to life—the outlying parts, or *exuviæ*—is a well-developed daimonological practice. It is evidence of the lineal descent of the more developed cult of the daimons out of the simpler cult of the dead that exuvial sacrifice, as well as that of the body as a whole, is common to both. There is the same cutting of hair, amputation of finger-joints, and drawing of blood in the one cult-form as in the other —practices which will need less illustration here for having been treated in former connections.[171]

Exuvial sacrifice is interpreted as a survival of the sacrifice of the whole body[172] and without doubt, in many instances, is such; yet it is impossible to refute the contention that it may have risen independently.[173] It may have been a substitute for or an insurance against the loss or death of the whole. The order may have been: fear of death, exuvial sacrifice as insurance, sacrifice of the whole body. There is no way of determining the general case. The offering of exuvial parts seems to exist in the ghost-cult in as primordial a form as does the larger dedication of the whole body and is found among peoples who are described as never having been accustomed to cannibalism. We are so confident, however, that cannibalism, out of which exuvial sacrifice could scarcely have come directly, lies at the basis of much of human sacrifice that we have preferred to align exuvial sacrifice among the modifications or survivals of human sacrifice—always meaning by that term the offering of the body as a whole. Although it pleased the daimons to see the pain inflicted in mutilation and blood-letting, there was, even in exuvial sacrifice, for instance in circumcision, an element of redemption and covenant that points back to the comprehensive offering. This will be clearer a little farther on, when the nature and significance of the tribal marks left by exuvial sacrifice are considered. In any case, exuvial sacrifice, as partial human sacrifice, is not far out of place at this point.

It is permitted to doubt, concerning the report that the first canine teeth and the uvula of certain Saharan children are sacrificed "on hygienic grounds,"[174] that the grounds are correctly represented; nevertheless the fact

171 §229, above.
172 Lippert, *Kgchte.*, II, 295 ff.; Wilken, in VG, III, 1 ff., 399 ff.; IV, 1 ff., repeatedly refers to it as a *pars pro toto* offering.
173 Loeb, *Human Sacrifice.*   174 Nachtigal, *Sahara*, II, 178.

of sacrifice is there. An Indian case is where "a woman cut off a piece of her tongue and offered it to the insatiable goddess, who would not let any child of hers live."[175] Again, the Chinese think there are cases of obstinate illness of parents, curable only by sacrificing a portion of the flesh of a son or daughter, which must be cooked and unwittingly eaten by the parent. Favorable results, though not certain, are very probable. The *Peking Gazette* frequently contains references to cases of this kind. "The writer is personally acquainted with a young man who cut off a slice of his leg to cure his mother, and who exhibited the scar with the pardonable pride of an old soldier."[176]

Ideas concerning the fetish-quality of hair and nails and their use in magic[177] lend them especial importance as exuvial sacrifices. Though offered chiefly in the ghost-cult, they appear also as sacrifices to the daimons.

Wilken[178] copiously illustrates hair-sacrifice, and Tylor[179] devotes briefer attention to it. There follows a brief extract from the former author's treatment. Numerous instances are given to show how persons in danger make an offering of the hair to save themselves; this explains the sacrifice at births or at entrance into manhood. The hair-sacrifice often accompanies that of an animal; the hair of an infant is cut in preparation for his sacrifice, and then an animal is killed instead. The animal is the redemption-sacrifice in place of the head that is owed to the spirits; the blood of the animal frees the child from all danger. Then there is the hair-sacrifice at marriage; this is often the puberty-sacrifice pushed on a little. Only part of the hair, say that in front of the forehead, may be shorn. These forms are abundantly illustrated from the ethnography of the Indian Archipelago. An instance from the mainland of Farther India may be interpolated: "if a child breaks the tabu with regard to teasing domestic animals, and a storm comes up soon afterwards, its mother cuts some hair from its head, wraps it in a piece of thatch, goes out of the house and places it on the ground, where she strikes it with a working-knife or a billet of wood. Up-country Sakai are also said to cut a piece of hair from a friend's head, place it on the ground, and strike it with a working-knife, whenever a thunder-storm overtakes them in the jungle."[180] To resume with Wilken: cutting of the hair is often a religious ceremony and has so remained; oaths are taken by the hair or beard, as seats of strength or soul. If slaves are allowed to live, their hair is cut as a partial sacrifice; the coiffure is a mark, therefore, of social position and it is a shame for a free person to be shorn. No one needs to be informed of the cruelties perpetrated by the ancient Hebrews in the name of their god;[181] captives were dedicated to him for destruction and he received human sacrifices. Here the hair-sacrifice meant redemption, on the principle of *pars pro toto;* hence the hair of those who were spared was shorn, especially that of women kept for sexual uses. The

175 Fawcett, in JASB, I, 466.   176 Smith, *Chinese Char.,* 178.
177 §§213, 283, above, and 300, below.
178 "Haar-opfer," in VG, III, 399-550.
179 *Prim. Cult.,* II, 364.   180 Evans, in JAI, XLVIII, 189.
181 Josh., VI, 21; VIII, 22-26; X, 28-40; XI, 8; also Deut., XX, 16-18; XXI, 10-12; Levit., XIV, 8; XXVII, 29; Num., XXI, 1-3; VI, 1-21; VIII, 7.

trophy-motive in acquiring the hair is later and derived. Head-hunting is alignable with the foregoing; scalping and head-hunting go together in the Archipelago. The possession of the skull or scalp makes an enemy the slave of the dead. The cutting of prisoners' hair was later extended to that of any-one in slavery; then the hair was cut as a symbol of subjection. Later on, the handing of a few hairs to a master was an acceptation of inferior status and came to be used in greeting; pulling the moustache or forelock appears to be a survival of this. The cutting of a woman's hair at marriage was symbolic of her subjection, for her soul went into someone else's keeping. Hence brides are represented with flowing hair where wives are shorn; then the locks were cut or, later on, bound up and covered with a cloth or cap. This was a Jewish custom and still prevails. Long hair, then, is symbolical of chastity and vir-ginity, as any reader of Major's novel, *When Knighthood Was in Flower,* will recall. Fallen girls had their hair shorn; it was cut with violence if a girl was suspected by her lover. Then shearing came to be an insult, a punish-ment by a sort of scalping; General Arolas thus punished the Moros with effect, after trying other penalties.[182] The Javanese partially shave an unfaith-ful wife's head, thus imposing deep degradation. The author refers to a hu-morous handling of the topic in Ovid's *Fasti:*[183] Jupiter wanted a head and they were going to bring him an onion; he demanded a human head. "You mean a hair from the pate?" was the query. "No, I mean the life."[184]

The Omaha belief is that the hair cut from the crown of a child's head really goes to the thunder god who dwells "far above, on high" and is addressed as "grandfather," the term of highest respect in the language. A Pawnee chief, telling how he had sacrificed a scalp, said: "It was a greater sacrifice than the sacrifice of the buffalo meat. Not many men have made it."[185] At the first name-giving of a child it was immersed in water; at the second, its hair and nails were solemnly cut and either preserved or offered to the sun or to the protecting spirits.[186] In ancient Persia hair and nails should never be allowed to fall to the earth when being sacrificed; otherwise the evil spirits "gather as harmful animals and vermin which devour the grain and clothes."[187] "Arab women laid their hair on the tomb of the dead; young men and maidens in Syria cut off their flowing tresses and deposited them in caskets of gold and silver in the temples. . . . Quite distinct from the hair offering are the cases in which the hair is shaved off (but not consecrated) as a means of purification after pollution. . . . In such cases the hair is cut off because defilement is specially likely to cling to it."[188] The modern Semite is represented as sharing similar notions of sacrifice about exuviæ; instance the old Jew in Zangwill's[189] story who "cut a chip of mahogany out of her best round table. He had finished cutting his nails and wanted a morsel of wood to burn with them

[182] Worcester, *Philippine Isl.,* 170, 190.

[183] III, 339-344.

[184] The foregoing is from Wilken, in VG, III, 495-497, 506-508, 512-531. He cites Turner, *Samoa,* 122; Weinhold, *Deut. Frauen,* 183; I Cor., XI, 3-15 (on Paul's dictum concerning women's hair); Bancroft, *Nat. Races,* II, 251-252, 469, 461, 675.

[185] Fletcher, in JAI, XXVII, 443; Grinnell, *Folk Tales,* 349.

[186] Müller, *Amer. Urrelig.,* 389.   [187] Müller, *Sacred Bks.,* IV, 185 ff.

[188] Smith, *Relig. Sem.,* 325, 333-334; 321; Levit., XIV, 9; Deut., XXI, 12.

[189] *Ghetto,* 41.

in witness of his fulfilment of the pious custom." Though Achilles sacrificed his hair to the dead Patroclus, he had vowed it to a river-god if he should return home; this is interpreted as a substitution for the older human sacrifice.[190]

One of the most consistent of exuvial sacrifices is that of the blood. In the ghost-cult blood is often necessary to bring the spirit to rest; hence blood-revenge, running amuck, mutilation in blood-letting, and other funerary customs.[191] The blood-sacrifice gets into the cult and becomes stereotyped in a number of forms; religious formulas and hymns are full of it. Of course the original sense of the practice has been interpreted away and it has been elevated into the realm of mystery; its incongruity with modern ideas is thus remedied by adjustment and no one thinks of the original notion any more than he reflects upon the etymology of a word like "halcyon" (sea-dog) or "cynosure" (dog-tail), unless his attention is especially directed to the matter. That which is holy, whether thing, act, or word, is viewed in a marvellous detachment from its original sense. It is conventionalized to the utter non-perception of its obvious meaning, much as if black should be called white and thereafter, under a sort of hypnotism, be seen as such. The African dance is sometimes accompanied with obscene gestures, but their meaning is so overlaid with sanctity that they are nothing to the natives if not solemn and reverent.

Many cases of blood-letting have appeared in foregoing connections. Some Papuans pierce the ears and noses of children; "any child not being pierced would be a scandal, and could not, under any circumstances, marry when grown up."[192] The following examples are out of the life of relatively advanced peoples. A Tarahumari of Mexico "never kills another, except when drunk, for the blood is God's, he says."[193] This is like the Israelitish view. It is a widespread custom in America to sprinkle blood upon maize, which is then eaten with great solemnity; such blood-letting and that from the ear being a substitute for human sacrifice.[194] Acosta[195] speaks of the transubstantiation of the maize-cake wet with infants' blood. There is found in "this blood-letting from the tongue, ears, and softer parts of the body a cult-operation that had developed to a monstrous degree."[196] Among the Peruvians too, a ceremony for the expulsion of evils required that a paste be made of maize

190 Homer, *Iliad*, XXIII, 20; Rohde, *Psyche*, I, 15, 17.
191 Lippert, *Kgchte.*, II, 325; §229, above.
192 Chalmers, in JAI, XXXIII, 121.
193 Lumholtz, in *Int. Cong. Anthrop.*, 1893, 109.
194 Andree, *Eth. Parallelen*, 202.
195 *Hist. Indias*, X, cap. XXIV (quoted in Letourneau, *Morale*, 248).
196 Preuss, in *Globus*, LXXXVI, 118; Prescott, *Mexico*, I, 59, 63, 64.

mixed with the blood of children between five and ten years old. This blood was taken from between the eyebrows. Each family assembled at the home of the eldest brother. The head, face, and most of the body of each was rubbed with this paste and then the threshold was anointed with the mixture, in order that it might be seen that the members of the household had performed their devotions.[197]

"In the ritual of the Semites and other nations, both ancient and modern, we find many cases in which the worshipper sheds his own blood at the altar, as a means of recommending himself and his prayers to the deity. A classical instance is that of the priests of Baal at the contest between the god of Tyre and the God of Israel.[198] . . '. The blood-offering in particular frequently takes a form which makes it a severe test of the neophyte's courage—as in the cruel flagellations of Spartan ephebi at the altar of Artemis Orthia, in the frightful ordeal which takes the place of simple circumcision in some of the wilder mountain tribes of Arabia." This blood-offering "continued to be practiced among the civilized Semites, by certain priesthoods and societies of devotees; but in the habitual worship of laymen it either fell out of use or was retained in a very attenuated form, in the custom of tattooing the flesh with punctures in honour of the deity. The hair-offering, on the other hand, which involved nothing offensive to civilized feelings, continued to play an important part in religion to the close of paganism, and even entered into Christian ritual in the tonsure of priests and nuns."[199] The blood-letting persisted a long time: in 1492 a sorcerer is said to have promised to heal Innocent VIII with the blood of three boys; that, however, both the children and the Pope died and the doctor took to flight.[200]

Blood-letting and ransom are related. The Jews, like other nations, were ransomed by the blood-letting of circumcision and by a vicarious beast. Their peculiarity was that they sacrificed all the blood of all things slain, the notion being, it will be recalled, that the soul or life was in the blood. This made the Jews a peculiar people. After the Flood the covenant was that God would not destroy all life again if the blood was sacrificed. The dogmatic ground was not to eat blood because the life that resided in it was given for men to ransom their souls with, for blood ransoms life.[201]

Mutilations are another form of the exuvial sacrifice. Like the scars from blood-letting, they afford evidence of the discharge of cult-obligations belonging to the type of human sacrifice. Thus mutilations, along with blood-letting, appear at life-crises: at the death of relatives, for instance, at the puberty-celebration, or in preparation for marriage.[202] Spencer's[203] chapter on mutilations supplies instances and interpretation; scars and other disfigure-

---

[197] Gomme, *Ethnol. in Folklore*, 166.   [198] I Kings, XVIII, 28.

[199] Smith, *Relig. Sem.*, 321, 328, 334-335.

[200] Reumont, *Gchte. d. Stadt Rom*, III, 198.

[201] Lippert, *Kgchte.*, II, 318; Levit., XVII, 11.

[202] Letourneau, *Soc.*, 210-212; Spencer and Gillen, *North. Tr. Cent. Aust.*, 134-135.

[203] *Prin. Soc.*, II, ch. 3; Lippert, *Kgchte.*, I, 393-394.

ment come to identify a people ransomed, reconciled with their god, and chosen and marked for him.

Take, for example, the sacrifice of finger-joints, noting the persistence of the practice in survivalistic form. In one Indian district, one hundred years ago, every woman, "previous to piercing the ears of her eldest daughter, preparatory to her being betrothed in marriage, must undergo the amputation of the first joints of the third and fourth fingers of her right hand." The operation is performed with a chisel by the village smith. "If the girl to be betrothed is motherless, and the mother of the boy has not before been subjected to the amputation, it is incumbent on her to suffer the operation." But the mores have become milder. "Instead of the two fingers being amputated, they are now merely bound together and thus rendered unfit for use."[204] It is interesting to speculate upon the interpretations that a sentimentalist might put upon this finger-binding—the "symbolism" that he might discover—if its origin were unknown. The severed finger-ends were put into a snake's hole as an offering to a certain spirit. Some say the women wish to be allowed to revive the amputation, as they are not held in as high esteem as formerly. At present, some take gold and silver pieces, stick them to the finger ends with flour paste, and either cut or pull them off; others simply substitute an offering of small pieces of gold or silver for the amputation. Flowers have been tied to the fingers that used to be cut, and then followed the pantomime of cutting by putting the chisel on the joint and then taking it away. All the rest of the ceremony is as it used to be.[205] To be noted, as a case of blood-letting, is the ear-piercing to which this mutilation of the mother is attendant.

In Polynesia, "after the death of a chief the people used to shave their hair, lacerate their faces and bodies; they used to torture themselves by burning their skins, by driving sharp points into their thighs, sides, and cheeks; they broke the bones of their little fingers and also those of the ring-finger, as was the custom in Australia and other places."[206] Here is a case where mutilation verges upon propitiatory self-discipline.[207]

In a portrait of an Arapaho chief, "a number of scars appear on chest and arms. There are seventy of them, arranged in various patterns of lines, circles, crosses, etc., with a long figure of the sacred pipe on one arm. His own statement is that they were made in obedience to a dream as a sacrifice to save the lives of his children. Several of his children had died in rapid succession, and in accordance with Indian custom he undertook a fast of four days as an expiation to the overruling spirit. During this time, while lying on his bed, he heard a voice, resembling the cry of an owl or the subdued bark of a dog. This voice told him that if he wished to save his other children he must cut out seventy pieces of skin and offer them to the sun. He did as directed, cutting out the pieces of skin in the various patterns indicated offering each in turn to the sun with a prayer for the health of his family, and then burying them. Since then there has been no death in his family."[208] One tribe of northern California "are inveterate gamblers, either with the game of 'guessing the sticks' or with cards; and they have a curious way of punishing or mortifying

204 Thurston, S. India, 391.
205 Fawcett, in JASB, I, 450, 454, 457, 466.
206 Letourneau, Soc., 216-217 (where original sources are given).
207 §291, above.   208 Mooney, in BAE, XIV, 898.

themselves for failure therein. When one has been unsuccessful in gaming, he frequently scarifies himself with flints or glass on the outside of the leg from the knee down to the ankle, scratching the limb all up criss-cross until it bleeds freely. He does this 'for luck,' believing that it will appease some bad spirit who is against him."[209] A clearer case of the connection of religion with the aleatory element would be hard to find.

Of the various exuvial sacrifices effected by mutilation, with consequent blood-letting and identifying scars, the one performed in circumcision is perhaps the most historic. This is a practice found in all parts of the world[210] and under conditions precluding origination elsewhere than in daimonism. That it comes, in later ages, to be a hygienic device disconnected with any faith, has led some to believe that it was originally a rational procedure; they should realize that many unpremeditated primitive practices reveal the rationality of that which has survived the automatic processes of selection.[211] With circumcision are to be classified other mutilations of males that can have no hygienic value, and corresponding operations upon females.[212] The scar of circumcision is the mark of selection by the god; "uncircumcized" comes to mean unregenerate, heathen, barbarian, irreligious. Circumcision is regularly part of the puberty-ceremony.[213]

An interesting story is told by Grant[214] of the introduction of the custom among the Mavenda of South Africa. The chief Magato's commander-in-chief made up his mind that, in order to secure the adherence of some smaller tribes that practised circumcision, the rite ought to be introduced. He succeeded in his purpose. Magato was the first chief of the tribe to adopt the mutilation. "Now an uncircumcised person is looked upon by Magato and his indunas [sub-chiefs]—all of whom are circumcised—as unclean." How little this custom has to do with ideals of cleanliness in the material sense may be made out from another passage: "A Zulu hut can only be entered on the hands and knees, an attitude which brings the visitor into a much closer contact with mother earth than is desirable."

In West Africa, "circumcision among the Yorubas, as among the Ewes, is connected with the worship of Elegba, and appears to be a sacrifice of a portion of the organ which the god inspires, to ensure the well-being of the remainder." It is called "the cutting that saves." "No woman would have connection with an uncircumcised man. A similar operation is performed on

209 Powers, in *Contrib. N. Amer. Ethnol.*, III, 90-91.
210 Lippert, *Kgchte.*, I, 390-392.
211 Keller, *Soc. Evol.*, 94. For a fanciful theory see Westermarck, *Marriage*, I, 561-564.
212 Roth, *N. W. Cent. Queensland*, 180.
213 §163, above; Webster, *Prim. Secret Soc., passim.*
214 In JAI, XXXV, 267-268, 269.

girls."[215] In Mysore, India, among certain hunters, the rite is performed on boys of ten or twelve; while simultaneously other rites, including the burning of the tongue, are practised prior to their reception into communion. There is a mock circumcision of men, wherein a betel-leaf is snipped off, on conversion to Mohammedanism.[216] Rose[217] notes that in the Punjab, among the Mohammedans, "the keynote to the observances connected with the operation lie in the fact that it is regarded as a wedding—indeed, in the south-west of Bahâwalpur it is actually termed *shâdi*. In accordance with this idea the boy is treated like a bridegroom." This statement is not so surprising when one reflects that circumcision goes with initiation and that initiation is the vestibule to marriage; nevertheless the making of the correlation is almost unique to this writer.

Circumcision or incision is performed by all the tribes of the East Indian Archipelago, on both boys and girls. Wilken[218] gives copious illustration. The part removed is preserved and used to drive off evil influences, if the young fellow falls ill. This author has a queer theory about circumcision which seems to stand out from his other ideas as quite forced and artificial; he connects it with fecundity in a strange way. Yet he says that, although there is no connection between circumcision and religion, "this, however, does not prevent it from having a religious character among many peoples." Among the cases cited is an extraordinary one where a tribe gave up circumcision because of the death of several members owing to the fact that the knives used in the operation had accidentally been placed in a vessel containing arrow-poison; the tribesmen say that this happened two or three hundred years ago. "Undeniably we have in the segregation of the boys in the temple, after their circumcision, one proof more . . . that circumcision among the several peoples must be conceived of as a sacrifice. . . . Among many, assuredly, the significance is lost, but among the aborigines circumcision could have had no other object than that of a sacrifice of a part of the life-making organ to the life-making god (the sun), a *pars pro toto*. And from the moment when the sacrifice was made, the young men remained devoted to the god, until the time came when they too were called to coöperate in the task that is laid on every living individual—the preservation of the species."[219]

In the minds of those who have encountered it only casually, circumcision is connected with a single race and religion. It is worth while to dispel that misconception. The Jewish custom but follows the general type, with some specialties and an added intensity going with a higher development. To the Jews circumcision was the covenant; later this covenant was the Passover; but the former was the condition of a share in the latter.[220] To be uncircumcized was to be unredeemed and in danger; witness the story of the son of Moses.[221] The later tradition reported that some of the patriarchs were born circumcized and that the angels were so created.[222] Circumcision was sanctification. It became later a question whether converts from heathendom must be circum-

[215] Ellis, *Yoruba*, 66-67.

[216] Thurston, *S. India*, 388, 389, 390.   [217] In JAI, XXXVII, 254.

[218] *Vkde.*, 225-232; "Besnijdenis," in VG, IV.

[219] Jacobs, *Groot-Atjeh*, I, 198, 199, 201.

[220] Lippert, *Kgchte.*, II, 317.

[221] Exod., IV, 24; Maurer, in *Globus*, XCI, 111.

[222] *Jubilees*, XV, 27 and note.

cized, that is, introduced to the rite-religion of the Jews.[223] In the matter of redemption, "the oldest form might well be the sacrifice of a part for the whole life and blood." Hence the wide-spread practice of circumcision. "Circumcision becomes a mark of bond with Jahweh which is to be borne by each male Israelite. For it is prescribed expressly: 'Sanctify unto me all the first-born, whatsoever openeth the womb among the children of Israel, both of man and of beast, it is mine.'" Circumcision meant community in sacred things; it was connected with puberty, for Abraham circumcized the fourteen-year-old Ishmael; it was a tribal mark, for all the fighting men were circumcized at Gilgal; it stood in relation to inheritance and the ancestral cult; and it may be regarded as a form of redemption from human sacrifice. It was connected with marriage, for the same root-word means bridegroom and to circumcize; the young man was thereby declared fit for the performance of cult, defense, and marriage. Thus the practice is entangled with many of the major strands of social life. "The use of stone knives indicates the antiquity of the usage and refers it to the stone age."[224]

The mutilation of the sex-organs extended even to castration, a practice of the priests of certain cults, preserved in classical legend, and prolonged into the eunuch-making of relatively recent times.[225]

The scars left by mutilations of various sorts become, as has been intimated, identifying marks set upon those who belong or are in bond to the god of the group; and so they readily come to be tribal marks, then crests or mere ornamentation, and their original religious significance may be utterly lost and irrecoverable. Says Oliveira Martins:[226] "The human body is the first text of histories and codes: on it man inscribed the tribe to which he belonged and the acts that rendered his life illustrious. A dawn of reflection, a herald of knowledge, appears when social forms attain a certain grade of cohesion and when ideas proclaim the solidarity of generations under the formula of animistic conceptions." This passage is perhaps a little impressionistic, but there is more than a grain of sense in it; the tribal marks and the tattooed records were labels of identification not at all incomparable to the heraldic devices upon clothing which succeeded them.

In Queensland, "a boy of the White Cliff tribe was marked with five vertical scars down the centre of the chest, and he pointed out to me that he differed from those of Bundaberg in so far that they had three horizontally round the front of the body." Again, in one of the coastal regions, each woman had two joints of one little finger removed, which distinguished her from the women of

223 Acts, XV.
224 Maurer, *Vkde.*, I, 240-241; Exod., XIII, 2; Reinach, excerpt in *Globus*, XCIV, 323.
225 Tiele-Gehrich, *Gchte. Relig.*, I, 247; Catullus, *Attis*.
226 *Raças*, II, 86.

other groups. "It is not done to give them any power of catching fish." The custom extends far along the coast and is said always to indicate a coast-woman. It also indicates, in places where it is not universal to the women, one who is appointed to the office of fisherwoman to the family. The custom not seldom exists where no reason for it can be ascertained.[227] In British New Guinea, "when the boy is six years old, his nose-cartilage is bored and the indispensable nose-ornament attached. According to the belief of the natives, one has to be provided with that in order, after death, to enter a land where superfluity of food and luxuries reigns. . . . If a child dies whose nose-bone has not yet been perforated, they do not neglect to make it up by an operation on the small corpse, out of fear that . . . entrance after death into the 'good land' might be closed to it."[228] In the island of Florida the ghosts are finally taken, after a sojourn at the western point of the island, in a canoe across the sea. "They land on a rock near the shore, and there for the first time they become aware that they are dead. They then meet with a *Tindalo,* who carries a rod, which he thrusts through the cartilage of their noses to prove whether they are pierced; if so, there is a good path which they can follow. . . . If the nose is not pierced, the ghost is not allowed to follow the path, but has to make his way with difficulty and pain."[229] In the New Hebrides there is a belief that people are met in the spirit world by a daimon that cuts off their noses with a tomahawk unless they can show certain tattoo-marks, mostly of lizards.[230] Again there is a great snake over which each soul must pass. When the ghost approaches, the snake asks for the tattoo-marks, which the soul takes off and gives to the snake. "Appeased by this ransom, the snake makes itself flat and broad, so that the soul can get to the spirit-world as over a bridge. Since the snake lets powerful people by unchallenged, chiefs need no tattooing; the lower people do not count at all, since their souls without further ado pass over into fish. But if the soul of a noble woman comes to the snake without the tattoo then it stretches itself so that its body is narrow and serrated. Now the soul must slip off; it falls into the sea and can never reach Vatum. In the end such souls enter into fish, and they think that fish with no fat, and dry, are their dwellings."[231] Certain Christians of Malabar branded the cross on their children's foreheads.[232] The tattoo is of high totemic importance; there is no Fan who does not wear it. Only those who from their infancy have lived in contact with Europeans, on the coast, for instance, have lost it. The first tattoo is a "remedy" and is applied after birth; the second is the "beauty tattoo"; the third the totemic marking, the most important of all.[233] In the Gilbert Islands the natives believe that a fearsome hag guards Bouru, the land of the dead. "Fast she clutched the soul and searched it for the marks of the tattooing-needle; these she scraped away with her long nails and swallowed, saying, 'Pass from Maura, land of the living, to Bouru, land of the dead.' Then she touched the soul's eyes with her hand, bestowing upon them the vision of spirits, so that the way seemed no more dark, but clear and easy. But if she found no tattoo-marks, since food she must have, she plucked out the pupils of the soul's eyes and devoured them."[234] This last detail is

[227] Howitt, *S. E. Aust.,* 746-747.   [228] Krieger, *Neu-Guinea,* 295.

[229] Codrington, in JAI, X, 304; Codrington, *Melanesians,* 256.

[230] Leggatt, in AAAS, 1892, 700.

[231] Thilenius, in *Globus,* LXXXI, 47.   [232] Reclus, *Prim. Folk,* 152.

[233] Trilles, *Fân,* 617.   [234] Grimble, in JAI, LI, 50.

highly significant of the soul's location.[235] Cowan[236] treats quite fully of the Maori tattooing and patterns, reproducing, as has been noted elsewhere, the signature of a great chief, which was the intricate tattoo-pattern on his face. To march safely over the ghost-road to the "Many Lodges," the Indian must bear the tattoo-mark.[237] Jacob, going to war, made a covenant with Jahweh and obliged all his men to renounce other gods and all their marks. Ear-rings are mentioned, which were doubtless, besides being ornaments, also calculated to throw into relief the scars of blood-letting through piercing. All such things were buried.[238]

The absence of any of these evidences would betray the fact that the mutilation necessary for reconciliation with the spirit had not been performed. It is not necessary to multiply examples. As foregoing cases indicate, many of these marks, originally religious, became ornamental as well as political; and rude scarring developed into artistic tattooing with intricate ornamental patterns. Then, when the body came to be covered, the designs shifted from the skin to the clothing.

There are multitudes of common formulas, usages, observances, ornaments, designs, and other everyday phenomena which, like bodily deformations and their refined modifications, are the survivals of a very remote antiquity. Their sense has been so altered by time and readjustments that we have no thought of connecting them with anything anterior and primitive until some series is set before us in which they manifestly take their rightful place.

[235] §213, above. [236] *Maoris,* ch. XIV, 194.
[237] Dorsey, in BAE, XI, 486.
[238] Gen., XXXV, 4; Lippert, *Kgchte.,* II, 346.

In absence of any of these evidences would betray the fact that the mutilation necessary for reconciliation with the spirit had not been performed. It is not necessary to multiply examples. As foregoing cases indicate, many of these bark hats, originally rude gods, became ornamented as well as political and rude-serving developed into artistic tattooing with intricate, ornamented patterns. Thus, when the body came to be covered, the designs shifted from the skin to the clothing.

There are multitudes of common formulas, usages, observances, ornaments, designs, and other everyday phenomena which, like slightly deformations and their refined modifications, are the survivals of a very remote antiquity. Their sense has been so altered by time and readjustments that we have no thought of connecting them with anything anterior and primitive until some series is set before us in which they unobtrusively take their rightful place.

CHAPTER XXXVII

MAGIC

§299. Methods of Magic. Magic is the production of effects by inexplicable means; it thus involves an appeal to supernatural agencies and belongs under daimonology, the science and art of dealing with such agencies. The unaided efforts of mere human beings cannot bring it to pass. Since there are so many tales and traditions illustrative of the magic art that nearly everyone must have in his mind a working idea of what magic is, we might come almost at once to the actual cases; there are, however, a few preliminary connections to be made with what precedes and what follows. The methods and processes of magic represent, in the main, an effort to coerce spirits to accomplish things desired, through the agency of other spirits and in particular by means of fetishes. It is not asserted that all so-called magical operations are coercive nor yet that all are performed by the use of fetishes, such as the "medicine," the wand, or the incantation, but that it is typical of the magician to operate in such manner. Part of the evidence is already before us; in the chapters on fetishism occur a number of cases where the fetish is shown to have magical potency of a coercive order; and in the section on shamanism there will be reviewed a number of instances where fetishes are employed not only to exorcise spirits but also to coerce them to positive action.

The connection of magic with coercion is illustrated by the fact that nakedness is often regarded as an essential to the production of magical effects. In a West African story, women perform magic in night orgies, naked, as in the revels of the Walpurgisnacht. Among the Hebrews, "in performing magic they aimed, as far as possible, to have few clothes on the body, for clothes break the magic"; while among the southern Slavs "the sorcerers and sorceresses are accustomed to be entirely unclad, 'naked as their mothers bore them,' when they undertake their major magical operations."[1] Again, the connection of magic with taboo and sin

[1] §277, above; Nassau, *Fetichism*, 279; Blau, *Zauberwesen*, 151-152; Krauss, *Südslaven*, 55.

is illustrated by the Maori belief that "one way to bewitch a man is to get him to break the *tapu;* another one to bury a *tapued* image or stone in his courtyard at night."[2] Further, part of the method of magic is the self-discipline which, as a form of propitiation, made so strongly for favor with the spirits: "Especially extensive are the examples of abstention from sex-intercourse before war and other great enterprises; particularly also for the successful accomplishment of all magical ceremonies and holy procedures."[3]

The following instance illustrates several lines of connection with the cult, together with the greater susceptibility of women to possession and the costliness of magic as well as of religion in the stricter sense. "An offence to a god can easily be rectified if one does some elementary sacrifices, but the performance of counter-magic is neither so inexpensive nor so easy. First of all one has to get rid of the evil already done. For that elaborate ceremonies may be necessary. Secondly, ceremonies to keep one immune from future attacks are essential. If it is any woman who is possessed of the devil, and it is women who generally suffer from these things, an expensive and elaborate devil dance . . . has to be performed. For this the village has to be informed, and each family in the village is supposed to contribute something in kind to the expenses and take its share in the work."[4]

Thus magic is aligned with a number of cult-procedures. This is inevitable, for in magic too it is the aleatory element and the spirit-environment that must be encountered; nevertheless magic is generally conceived to be outside the regular cult, based upon an old and submerged or a foreign religion, and its forms often represent a parody upon those of the regular and accepted faith. The focus of magical operations is the employment of objects and ritual that have a fetish-quality. These several points, and others like them, will come out as we review, in order, the magical use of exuviæ, inorganic and organic substances, ritual, the rehearsal of hoped-for issues, and the employment of effigies and images. Thereafter, in the light of the cases, we may gather together a series of generalizations concerning the nature of magic.

§300*. Exuvial Magic. That the exuviæ are fetishistic, as containing part of the soul inhabiting the body from which they

[2] Tregear, in JAI, XIX, 116.
[3] §§281, 282, above; Preuss, in *Globus,* LXXXVII, 399.
[4] Panikkar, in JAI, XLVIII, 280.

come, is evident. One of the stock resources of magical practice is some exuvial part of the victim. Such objects, including not alone physical fragments such as hair but also remnants of food, clothing, property, and likewise the name—things assimilated to personality—are part of their owner in the sense of containing some fraction of his soul.[5] With such samples of a person, it is thought, much damage can be done, for by the induction of spiritual influence into them, supernatural power may be exerted over the whole of which they are or have been parts. What is done to them is done to their erstwhile owners; it should be recalled that the nails, clothing, or property of a deceased person can be used for his funeral when there is no corpse.[6] A common practice in sorcery is to steal food which an enemy has begun to eat, and thus to "appropriate," and hide it in a tomb; then the dead, by finishing it, come into communication with the victim and are able to consume him.[7] In a case of illness and death, the vengeance of survivors can be carried out through the use of exuviæ.[8] Perhaps such ideas were at the bottom of the belief, as among the Hebrews, that magic was more effective when accomplished with vessels that had been stolen.[9] Ideas of this sort enforce, where they do not originate, the taboos against public eating or against carelessness in the disposition of what has once been of or within the body. It is fear of the magic that can be worked by the use of exuviæ, for instance saliva,[10] which has made a good part of men's manners, as well as their so-called hygienic and sanitary practice. Thus magic has not been altogether inexpedient.

Australia affords full illustration of this topic. The strongest medicine, that is, magical means, that the Australians know is some part of the human body or human food. If a man can get the bone from which another has eaten the meat, he gets an instrument of magic against the eater which extends to life and death; hence each man carefully buries his own bones. But the bone itself is not the medicine; they know a mere bone when they see one. To make medicine out of it, they first bury it awhile, then stick on it a lump of red ocher, fish oil, a fish's eye, and flesh from a corpse; and the whole is laid for a time on the breast of a dead man.[11] In Victoria, if any object belonging to one of a hostile tribe is found, it is carefully preserved until somebody wants to do harm to a member of that tribe. Then it is smeared with fat mixed with red

---

5 §§213, 249, 257, above.
7 Reclus, *Prim. Folk*, 82.
9 Blau, *Zauberwesen*, 52.
10 Instances in Clodd, *Magic*, 17-23.

6 §218, above.
8 Friedmann, *Wahnideen*, 225.
11 Ratzel, *Vkde.*, II, 95.

clay, and tied on a throwstick set in the ground by the fire. The natives sit in a circle around it, at such distance that their shadows are sure not to fall on it, and chant incantations until the stick falls over in the direction of the tribe to a member of which the object belonged. Then they throw hot ashes in that direction, whistling and cursing and invoking disease and all kinds of misfortune on the enemy.[12] Here is a case of group-solidarity, for it is dangerous to a whole tribe if one member furnishes the enemy with a means of magic.

The shaman may make a charm out of the hair of a dead man mixed with his fat and that of a lizard, rolled into a ball and affixed to a stick. It is concealed carefully until the shaman is ready for action, and then unwrapped and laid by the fire, pointing in the direction of the intended victim. "It is believed that the spirit of the dead man whose fat has been used will help the charm to act." A girdle made of a dead man's hair descends to his eldest son or, failing him, to a younger brother or to the eldest son of an elder brother, in order of inheritance, and then on down in the family. "It is supposed to be endowed with magic power and to add to its possessor all the war-like attributes of the dead man from whose hair it was made. It ensures accuracy of aim and at the same time destroys that of an adversary."[13] Giving a lock of hair as a token of affection is a mark of the greatest confidence; for thus one puts himself in the power of another. "The blacks are very superstitious about such matters; they will always take care to destroy the hair they cut off. It would frighten a black very much if he or she knew that another black had some of his or her hair"; but the young woman forgets these fears when she feels safe in the hands of her lover.[14]

Another charm is made out of the fibula of a dead friend, wrapped in the sun-dried flesh of another friend and tied with hair of a third. It is placed in the hot ashes of a sleeping enemy's fire, where it is warmed and then pointed at the person to be killed. It is then taken away and in about five weeks laid underground with a slow fire lit over it. "The person at whom it has been aimed sickens after it is burnt a little, and dies unless the doctor sucks out the bone which is supposed to have entered the sick person's body." A similar charm is built up upon a rough piece of white quartz and similarly used. "The possession of one of these charms aids a man in composing and devising a new corroboree," or dance; it evidently inspires him to artistic effort. Such valuable charms are kept hidden from view.[15]

"The death-bone, or bone-apparatus, and its property of producing sickness and death, which, in the absence of sufficiently demonstrable causes cannot otherwise be accounted for, is one of the most dreaded, as it is universal, of the aboriginal superstitions" over a good part of Australia. One that is found is destroyed; a woman would immediately fall sick were she to touch or even look at it. "It is most important to remember that in all cases while the death-bone is being 'pointed,' the blood of the victim passes invisibly across the intervening space to the 'pointer,' and so along the connecting-string, into the receptacle, where it is collected: at the same time one of the doctor's gew-gaws, or stock-in-trade, bone, pebble, etc., passes invisibly from the 'pointer'

---

12 Dawson, *Aust. Aborig.*, 54.

13 Howitt, *S.E. Aust.*, 361; Spencer and Gillen, *Nat. Tr. Cent. Aust.*, 538, 539.

14 Smyth, *Vict.*, I, 83.   15 Bonney, in JAI, XIII, 130.

to be inserted into the body of the victim, who thus contracts his sickness." Men threaten their wives with the bone to keep them in order. "So strongly are men, women, and children convinced of the power of the bone, that no reasoning can shake their belief."[16] The fat-taking operations of Australian wizards by which they are supposed to sneak up on a sleeping victim, overcome him by means partly magical, cut open his right side, and remove the omental fat—without leaving a scar, thus making him ill and at length killing him—are carried out with the idea of making out of the fat charms of high potency.[17]

There are many cases where an impression of the body seems to be regarded as exuvial; thus in Papua "the people seem to regard it as hopeless to pursue a fugitive enemy after he has got a start, and the only thing they do is to shoot off their arrows in his foot-prints or perform some other act which is thought to hurt him from a distance."[18] Similarly in Ceylon: the attempt is made to get dust from an enemy's footprint and drop it into a receptacle with a picture representing the victim; this they do in connection with images made from the wild yam. Further, they try to catch a thief by using dust from his footprint.[19]

It follows that one has to be very careful about his exuviæ. Certain Africans keep their nails short to prevent them from splitting, and bury the cuttings on the spot where they were cut. If they spit, they cover it with earth. If the spittle accidentally falls upon another, it is a sign that the two are friendly disposed.[20]

The bearing of magical beliefs upon hygiene and sanitation is evident from such passages as the following. "It is worthy of remark that nothing offensive is ever to be seen near the habitations of the aborigines, or in the neighborhood of their camps; and although their sanitary laws are apparently attributable to superstition and prejudice, the principles of these laws must have been suggested by experience of the dangers attendant on uncleanness in a warm climate, and more deeply impressed on their minds by faith in supernatural action and sorcery. It is believed that if enemies get possession of anything that has belonged to a person, they can by its means make him ill; hence every uncleanness belonging to adults and half-grown children is buried at a distance from their dwellings. . . . Children under four or five years of age, not having strength to comply with this wholesome practice, are not required to do so; and their excreta are deposited in one spot and covered with a sheet of bark, and when dry they are burned."[21] No one can believe that the "principles of these laws must have been suggested by experience of the dangers" involved, if that means that there was deliberate reflection over the matter; doubtless the sanitary practices rose automatically in the mores and then were, in the usual fashion, sanctioned by religion.

[16] Roth, *N.W. Cent. Queensland,* 152, 156; Howitt, *S.E. Aust.,* 360; Howitt, in JAI, XX, 90; Smyth, *Vict.,* I, 102. Pictures of this instrument and of a man using it, in Spencer and Gillen, *North. Tr. Cent. Aust.,* 456, 457.

[17] Howitt, in JAI, XVI, 31, 33.

[18] Landtmann, in JAI, XLVI, 330.

[19] Hildburgh, in JAI, XXXVIII, 160, 165.

[20] Barrett, in JAI, XLI, 36.   [21] Dawson, *Aust. Aborig.,* 12.

§301*. Other Instrumentalities. Beside the exuviæ there is a great variety of objects, substances, mixtures, and preparations used in making magic. Perhaps the best inclusive name for these is the Indian one, "medicine," which meant to the Indian what he took out of the English or French words,[22] that is, "mystery." We do not wish at this point to consider medicaments used in case of illness—what is ordinarily meant by "medicine"—having reserved all such cases for a later connection.[23] For the occasion the Indian meaning of the word stands, in accordance with which anything inexplicable is a mystery, or "medicine." What Mr. Worcester did to entertain the mountaineers of the Philippines would have been "big medicine" to an Indian, and evidently was all of that, whatever their local term may have been, to his audience. He astonished them by causing water to run up hill, through a syphon, and by the display of a magnet.

"One night," he writes,[24] "I over-did it, first hypnotizing a rooster, and then working the time-honoured trick of 'chewing together' the cut ends of a bit of cord. I scared my audience nearly to death. They hardly dared move, much less speak, during the remainder of the evening, and left the next morning without waiting to eat." The author had a man come to him who wished to exhibit the power of his charm to ward off bullets, and wanted to be shot at with a powerful rifle. It was an awkward situation, but Worcester offered to shoot at the charm when hung against a tree. He demolished it; and finally destroyed or got possession of almost all the charms in the tribe. "When the supply was exhausted, I was the possessor of a large collection of curious articles, and of a reputation which was worth more to us than two regiments of soldiers would have been." The collection included a betel-nut and an old lead bullet tied together; a small joint of bamboo, closed with a dirty rag, and containing a stone from the stomach of a crocodile; but the charms were mostly small books "in which had been written a good deal of extraordinarily bad Latin, some Tagalog, and a lot of mummery made up of letters of the alphabet and cabalistic marks. A facsimile is given."

This quotation gives the conception of "medicine." It is some fetish-article or substance, an amulet in so far as it will protect but more than an amulet in that with it effects can be produced upon others' destinies.

22 It is said that the French word *médecin* (physician) was responsible, at least in part, for the Indian term. On Indian medicine and medicine-men, see Hrdlička, in HAI, I, 836-839.

23 §318, below.

24 Worcester, *Philippine Isl.*, 267-268, 429, 433.

The Fans "believe that fetish priests, witches, and sorcerers have the power of inflicting bodily harm on their enemies or on others for lucre, by burying objects in the ground to be trodden on or hanging them over the pathway, making at the same time an invocation." In West Africa, "there is everywhere a belief that it is possible to put medicine on a path for your enemy which, when he steps over it, will cause him to fall sick and die. Other people can walk uninjured over the spot, but the moment the man for whom the medicine is laid reaches the place, he succumbs, often dying within an hour or two."[25]

The effectiveness of such "medicine" seems to us to reside in its coercitive power, inherent in it as a fetish, over spiritual beings. It would be impossible, if it were worth while, to enumerate the articles and substances, apart from exuviæ, by the use of which as "medicine" magical results are supposed to be attained; our foregoing lists of fetishes[26] will furnish enough examples. Certain plants are held to possess magic qualities; the familiar "apple" figures here: Eve, Atalanta, Hera, and Athena, not to mention Aphrodite, were irresistibly charmed by its use.[27] Most of these vegetable fetishes are to be considered under therapeutics,[28] where the magical qualities of certain animal-derived medicines also will be noticed. The cases about to be cited are miscellaneous and designed to illustrate the topic from many angles; they are chiefly those which are left over after reserving for the topic of the shaman as a healer of disease all that might reasonably go under medicine.

In the New Hebrides the love-charm is a piece of a banana-leaf and a lizard, burned to charcoal and kept in a section of bamboo.[29] In the French Congo, "a great love charm is made of the water the lover has washed in, and this, mingled with the drink of the loved one, is held to soften the hardest heart." Friendship-compelling charms are made, on the Ivory Coast, of chalk saturated with the blood of some one "you know really cared for you."[30] Elephant-medicine, which makes the killing of elephants easy, is rubbed, in the form of a blackish powder, into incisions on the arms and thighs.[31] Hair from the tail-brush of cattle, signifying a state of right, property, or ownership in them, is fastened around the neck or arm of young people, especially girls, when they have some heart-sickness and nobody knows what is the matter with them or what can help them. This is a case of administering a dose of property to cheer them up; likewise the belief is entertained that the wearing of these hairs wards off calamity.[32] Among the Hausa, "charms may be made

[25] Connolly, in JAI, XXVI, 151; Nassau, *Fetichism*, 264-265.
[26] §§248, 249, 252, 254, above.
[27] §248, above; Gubernatis, *Usi Nuz.*, 105.
[28] §316, below.   [29] Lawrie, in AAAS, 1892, 711.
[30] Kingsley, *Travels W. Afr.*, 488.   [31] Holub, *Süd-Afrika*, II, 405.
[32] Kropf, *Kaffir-Engl. Dict.*, 212.

from moon's juice. . . . The woman takes a large calabash of water, places it so as to reflect the moon's beams, and stirs it round and round 'so as to mix the moon up with the water.' The worst of this method is that the moon will never go back until the woman has promised it the life of a member of her own family, or that of some child. No one else knows that the moon has come, for all seem to see it still in the sky, but on the day upon which it really returns the person who has been named will die. The woman can practically work any evil she likes with the water."[33]

The Singhalese make medicine for some ills from the milk of a pure black cow, which animal, like the black cat so much in evidence here as elsewhere, is a fetish. This medicine is intended to secure fecundity. With a certain discretion, it is applicable only to cases of people within ages commonly suitable for the production of children; for those beyond these ages it is valueless.[34] In ancient India the magic potion doubled the power of the drinker and reddened his eyes.[35] In China, under the name of "corpse oil," "the luminiferous liquid of the lamp plays an important part in the black art. Women generally ascribe to it the power of creating discord between married people; hence many a principal wife, if jealous of a concubine who enjoys more of their common lord's love than herself, does not shrink from smearing the dangerous stuff on the garments of her rival, feeling sure she shall in this way put a stop to the good understanding which excites her jealousy."[36] In Persia magic qualities are ascribed to saffron, which is called "peasant's magic"; pregnant women wear a ball of it to ensure against calamities attendant upon their condition.[37] A certain Dyak is reported never to have had a child till he killed a pig and made part of it into a lotion with water, the rest being eaten at a feast.[38]

To the Indian, hairs shed by bison were strong medicine; and otter-skin was the proper material for the medicine-bag.[39] Among the Ojibwa, "love powder is held in high esteem, and its composition is held a profound secret, to be transmitted only when a great fee is paid." It consists of the following ingredients: vermilion, powdered snake-root, a drop of blood from a woman in a special condition, and a piece of ginseng cut from the bifurcation of a root and powdered. These are mixed and put into a small buckskin bag.[40] Bourke[41] treats at some length of the Indian "hoddentin" and "kunque." The former is a yellow-colored flour or powder, resembling corn-meal, derived from a variety of the cat-tail rush. No Apache would go on the war-path without a bag of it, if it could possibly be got, attached generally to his ammunition-belt; "whenever one was wounded, hurt, or taken sick while on a scout, the medicine-man of the party would walk in front of the horse or mule ridden by the patient and scatter at intervals little pinches of hoddentin, that his path might be made easier." If hoddentin is a prehistoric food, its fetishistic quality is readily understood.[42] It "found its place as part of the necessary ritual at weddings or connected with the earliest hours of a child's life, just

33 Tremearne, in JAI, XLV, 56-57.   34 Hildburgh, in JAI, 184, 185, 164.
35 Holtzmann, *Ind. Sagen*, I, 125.   36 DeGroot, *Relig. Syst.*, I, 23.
37 Dymock, in JASB, II, 443.   38 Cator, *Head-Hunters*, 68.
39 Mooney, in BAE, XIV, 1033; Hoffman, *Writing*, 171.
40 Hoffman, in BAE, VII, 258; Dorsey, in BAE, XI, 416.
41 In BAE, IX, 500, 507, 509, 510, 521, 527.
42 §324, below; Lippert, *Kgchte.*, I, 578 ff.

as rice has been freely used in other parts of the world." Illustrations of ritual use are given. Similarly with "kunque," another sort of sacred meal; almost universally through the pueblos the families keep a vessel of it, "of which the good housewife is careful to throw a pinch to the sun at early dawn and to the twilight at eventide." Every Zuñi carries a bag of it. "Kunque" contains meal of blue and yellow corn, a small quantity of pulverized sea-shell, some sand, and, wherever possible, a fragment of a peculiar blue stone. "In grinding the meal on the metates the squaws are stimulated by the medicine-men who keep up a constant singing and drumming." The Peruvian "kunque" is very like that of the Zuñi. The author finds a number of ethnographical parallels to the use of a vegetable magic powder, some of them among peoples no longer primitive, for instance, the "carnestolendas" in Spain, "in which, on Shrove Tuesday, the women and girls cover all the men they meet with flour. The men are not at all backward in returning the compliment, and the streets are at times filled with the farinaceous dust."

The fetish-quality of the magical substances employed is explicit in many of the cases cited; it seems to us implicit in the others; and the fact is confirmative that the stock modes of ghost- and spirit-exorcism are taken recourse to against magic. "Of the means used in magic, most are protective, serving to ward off or break the sorcery. In the first rank must be mentioned water, which dissolves every sorcery."[43] Magic of the foregoing orders is still practised in civilized countries and is even openly advertised in newspapers of the baser sort.

An Associated Press despatch of November 1, 1925, reports the use of mercury in bread to find the body of a drowned person—a method familiar to readers of *Huckleberry Finn*. "Following superstition, thirty loaves of bread and mercury were cast upon the waters today in the hope that at least one of the loaves with its lodestone would come to rest above the spot where the body is believed to be resting on the bottom of the lake."[44]

The simplest instrument which is perhaps most commonly associated with magic is the staff or wand. Most modern "magicians" carry the latter during their ministrations. The wand may be a whip or a stick otherwise modified. It is a little like the "pointing-bone" of the Australians; in fact, pointed sticks occasionally take the place of the bone, one being used in "sickening" or killing men and a smaller one for women.[45] The wand is peculiar to no time or place: a Homeric god or magician wielded one;[46] so does the Afri-

43 Blau, *Zauberwesen*, 158.   44 N. Y. *Times*, November 2, 1925.
45 Parker, *Euahlayi*, 31; Spencer and Gillen, *Nat. Tr. Cent. Aust.*, 333.
46 Keller, *Hom. Soc.*, 172, 173.

can sorcerer; and, along with the drum, it distinguishes the medicine-man in Indian picture-writing.

The drum—a powerful instrument of magic—and the magical compound
are set in operation, in West Africa, by blows from the fetish-stick. In the
case of the compound, composed of dead man's bone, smoked herbs, ant-hill
earth, and charcoal, it has a small live animal or insect tied to it and is fixed
with wooden forks by a path. The victim "is allowed to pass just by, and then
his enemy breaks a dry bamboo stick; the noise causes the victim to turn and
look in the direction of the noise—i.e. on to the charm—and then the murderer
hits the live animal on it, calling his victim's name, and the charm is on him."
The type of affliction is determined by the part of the animal's body that is
struck by the fetish-stick. "The interesting point, however, is the necessity of
establishing the personal connection between the victim and the charm by
means of making him look on the charm and calling his name. Without his
looking it is no good."[47] Again, there is an apparatus consisting of two sticks
jointed so as to contract or extend, which is used in adjudging guilt.[48] Among
the Kalmuks the wand is a whip; it is said that when they first came to
the Volga and saw the fish, they tried to catch them by striking at them with
their whips.[49] In Korea, "a bottle with a wide mouth is put on the floor, and
alongside it a piece of paper inscribed with the name of the unclean daemon,
which has been obtained by divination and parley. The paper being touched
with the magic wand jumps into the bottle, which is hastily corked and buried
on the hillside or at the crossroads."[50] Among the South Slavs the tree at the
grave is a fetish of the dead. "Whoever breaks a twig from it gives pain to the
dead, but also can do much mischievous magic with the stick, because the soul
living in the wood becomes subservient to him."[51] Here is a clear case of
fetishism.

Besides the wand and the drum, the magician may use a variety
of implements, like the bell, or the knot,[52] most of which have,
aside from magic, a fetishistic quality. The local forms of fetish-
implement are too numerous and various to be listed or classified.

Thus the Australian uses a small wooden *Churinga* or sacred emblem, which
is whirled about and struck on the ground, to the accompaniment of amorous
song, to charm a woman. Or he may use a head-band to which virtue has been
imparted by singing over it and which he wears about the camp for the woman
to see. A certain shell-ornament or a horn will infallibly effect the same ends.
Australian women use magic less than men but they can charm a necklet or
food.[53] Quartz is supposed to be a substance which wizards can project against
their victims; the doctors always carry crystals about with them, carefully

[47] Kingsley, *W. Afr. Studies,* 164, 165, 166.
[48] Junker, *Afrika,* II, 471.
[49] *Russian Ethnog.* (Russ.), II, 453.
[50] Bishop, *Korea,* 406.   [51] Krauss, *Südslaven,* 36.
[52] §265, above; *Records of the Past,* III, 141.
[53] Spencer and Gillen, *Nat. Tr. Cent. Aust.,* 541-548.

concealing them, especially from women.[54] In Mota Island, "the more beneficent forms of magic are the appanage of certain men who have usually inherited their powers from the maternal uncle and only exceptionally from the
father even now when, so far as other property is concerned, inheritance from
the father is becoming frequent. The efficacy here is inherent in certain objects
and it would seem that this efficacy or *mana* belongs to the object, such as a
stone, rather than to the possessor of the stone. In this island a person who
steals a stone with *mana* may acquire the power of carrying out the rite effectively, and I was told that it was not uncommon for stones to be stolen for
this purpose." The author[55] cites instances. Weeks[56] mentions a charm to
prevent the owner from being wounded in a fight; the name for it, *mpete*, "is
given to the brass ornaments on a state officer's uniform as the natives thought
they were worn for that purpose, and not as a sign of rank." In South Africa
a lion's claw worn on forehead or neck made enemies sluggish and the wearer
nimble and even invulnerable to bullets; and a shell-whorl was a love-charm.[57]
A quill taken from an enemy was great medicine to an Indian.[58] An Omaha,
by fasting and prayer, sought to fall into a trance, "in which he should see
some object, that forever after would be his particular medium of help from
the supernatural"; it might be a feather, a tuft of hair from some animal,
"the small black stone emblematic of thunder, or the pebble representative
of water."[59]

Ancient objects are likely to be regarded as fetishes and to be available for
magic. Thus the Australians use the stone ax for bewitching men and women;
they touch the former with the sharp edge, the latter with the blunt one.[60]
"Each Hopi clan possesses one or more ancient objects, called wimi, which
it has inherited from the past and regards with special reverence." They are
generally supposed to be endowed with occult powers, like the Australian
"churinga," and it is believed that the priests can get certain results from
their manipulation.[61]

The use of grave-earth is almost exuvial. It is employed by the southern
Slavs for magic affecting love, marriage, and children. "The ghost of the buried
person becomes the intermediary. If a widow wants to marry again, she takes
earth from the grave of her first husband and casts it, when he does not know
it, over the man she wants for a second husband. Barren women who want to
be fruitful betake themselves to the grave of a woman who died in childbed,
call the dead woman by name, bite off with the teeth the grass growing on the
grave, at the same time repeatedly calling upon the woman who is resting in
the grave, and conjure her to send them pregnancy. Finally they take along
some of the grave-earth and always carry it about with them in a girdle. . . .
In the Croatian mountain-region they believe . . . that if anybody picks up,
in a cemetery, any earth thrust up there by a mole, and throws it between a
bridal couple when they are entering the church for the wedding, these people
will live in discord all their lives." An especial power resides in coffin-nails
and grave-crosses. With the former a husband's unfaithfulness can be pre-

54 Howitt, in JAI, XVI, 26.   55 Rivers, *Melan. Soc.*, I, 156-157.
56 In JAI, XL, 392-393.
57 Holub, *Süd-Afrika*, I, 416; Bent, *Mashonaland*, 272.
58 Donaldson, in *Smithson. Rep.*, 1885, pt. II, 404.
59 Fletcher, in JAI, XXVII, 437.
60 Ratzel, *Vkde.*, II, 95.   61 Fewkes, in AA, III, 211.

vented, and "the grave-cross nail in the gun makes the hunter a sure marksman. . . . If anyone wants to work evil magic on another, he takes, on a Tuesday or Friday at the new moon, a broom with which a house has been swept after the removal of a dead person, burns the broom and sprinkles with the ashes the person it is desired to bewitch. This instrumentality works all the better if it can be given to the victim baked in a cake, to eat, or in a liquid, to drink."[62]

Another set of instrumentalities of magic, to the savage mind, are the inexplicable products and processes of civilization. Writing, for example, is to one unacquainted with it pure magic; and the written or printed signs that convey meaning without a voice have powerful "medicine" in them. Recall the leaves of the trigonometry text-book, mentioned above, or the "small books" treasured by the Filipinos;[63] or consider the small piece of paper in which there were many beatings that was left in the top of a tree where it could do no further harm.[64] The camera, the siphon, the gun (called fire-tube by the Eskimo), fire-water, and other white man's instruments are as inexplicable to ignorance as are certain ciliary motions of parts of a dissected body;[65] they are normally and naturally regarded as magical and their manipulators as magicians.

The Hovas of Madagascar believe that paper, written upon, has evil powers, but that such magical instruments may also ward off ills.[66] "When I made inquiries of several people," says Lenz,[67] "and then noted down the words, the negroes ran away with a cry and asserted that I was making fetish and wanted to kill them. The whole village ran together, and the chief interpellated me seriously about my undertaking." Only after much talk could the excited parties be quieted; "but they always cherished a powerful respect for my book." A young Borneo woman "was exceedingly worried by the appearance of my camera and assumed, so she declared, that with it I could see her through and through and know her very thoughts." The camera was called a "box-with-an-eye." The author's[68] description of the perils of making likenesses, as felt by the natives, is quite full and complete. If a man were to be photographed, he must have all his best charms upon him, in order to offset his exposure and, in one case, the author's likeness was demanded so that if evil were to be worked by the foreigner the native would have means of retaliation. As is so often the case, the coincidence of a death following the taking of a likeness served to substantiate the native beliefs. Sioux chiefs,

62 Krauss, *Südslaven,* 135, 136, 137, 138.
63 §161, above; Tylor, *Anth.,* 167.
64 Kipling, "Tomb of his Ancestors," in *The Day's Work,* 145.
65 Nassau, *Fetichism,* 242.   66 Ratzel, *Vkde.,* II, 520.
67 *Westafr.,* 279.
68 Furness, *Head-Hunters,* 62 (description of plate; quoted), 100, 174, 179 ff.

some time ago, much resented the presence of a young man with a tripod camera at a council; one of them kicked it over and made gestures significant enough to discourage further enterprise.[69] "Even today tickets and ticket-clipping are dark oppression to Indian rustics. They do not understand why, when they have paid for a magic piece of paper, strangers should punch great pieces out of the charm. So, many and furious are the debates between travellers and Eurasian ticket-collectors."[70]

There is a story of some Indians who had captured, and intended to torture at the stake, a white man with a wooden leg well concealed by clothing, and with false teeth and a glass eye. Pending his torture, the prisoner was fed; and, being experienced in the savage attitude toward mysteries, at the conclusion of his meal he casually stuck his knife through his trousers into his leg, took out and washed his teeth, and removed and polished his eye. The circle of his captors widened at each stage of his self-revelation, as they moved toward their horses, and at the end he found himself alone in a vast solitude. This story, read long ago and, to the best of the reader's recollection, in an old book of travels through Texas and the West, deserves to be true in its portrayal of native terror before the inexplicable white man's magic.

A final type of magical instrumentality is ritual, whether of word or of action. Fetishism is not, as we have seen, confined to material objects; the "word" was a fetish, even when it was no more than the name;[71] combinations of words constituted formulas and prayers;[72] and when actions—which may likewise be fetishistic—were added, there appeared a ritual of greater or less complexity, in which, if carried out with exactitude, there was conceived to reside power capable of securing otherwise inexplicable results. For the moment we are interested chiefly in the spoken spell or incantation. In it barbaric and obsolete words were thought to be especially powerful, the more so the harder it was to give them sense. Thus was the element of mystery enhanced.

The Australians repeat incantations while on the hunt, believing that they will weaken the beasts.[73] Preuss[74] reproduces a Hottentot magical song wherein a mother names the various parts of a child's body, kissing them. Stigand,[75] the African hunter, found that a proverb, especially if in archaic language, had a magical force: "I have found that the quoting of a proverb often proves a point completely to the native satisfaction. . . . Often old Swahili words, which have completely gone out of use in the modern language, are retained in these proverbs. The very fact that they are unintelligible to him would make them even more convincing. They bear for him the magic of an unknown incantation." This attitude is not unlike that of modern strivers who are so deeply impressed with the unintelligible book, picture, or musical

[69] Personally communicated by the would-be photographer.
[70] Kipling, Kim, 313.   [71] §§212, 252, above.
[72] §285, above.   [73] Ratzel, Vkde., II, 53.
[74] In Globus, LXXXVII, 397.   [75] Elephant, 281.

composition as straightway to revere it. "Making juju" for a town is a yearly ceremony in the Niger region—"to preserve its health, to prevent death and war, to maintain friendly relations with the neighboring villages, to keep on good terms with the consuls, to bring good generally to the inhabitants." The natives dance, scream, play, drink gin—sprinkling some of it on the walk— and sometimes paint themselves quite white, leaving the paint on till it wears off.[76]

Incantations flourish in Siberia, and the shamans use much ritual in their practice.[77] In Tibet, from the local translation of the Buddhist scriptures "are culled out the Indian mystic formulas, mostly unintelligible gibberish, which are deemed most potent as charms. These formulas are not used in the worship of the Buddhas and superior gods, but only as priestly incantations in the treatment of disease and ill-fortune. As these spells enter into the worship of which the laity have most experience, small pocket editions of one or other of these mystic *Sutras* are to be found in the possession of all literate laymen, as the mere act of reading these charms suffices to ward off the demon-bred disease and misfortune."[78] The syllable "om" is one that no one is worthy to pronounce save under ritual prescriptions; rites and sacrifices pass away, but the "om" is imperishable.[79] "It is well known that the Hindu ascetics lay great importance upon the frequent repetition of the holy formula: *Om manî padmî hum.*" This is paralleled by the repetition "for hours at a stretch, in chorus or even alone, [of] the name *Allâh* or the formula: *lâ ilâha illâ-llâh.*"[80]

Formulas are potent in themselves; they do not have to be connected with sacrifice. "Mysterious *mantras,* used alike by priest and warrior, serve every end of magic." Extraordinary power resides in the mere repetition of holy texts. "These are applied on all occasions without the slightest reference to the subject."[81]

The East Greenlanders use spells against all manner of peril. "They are most effective the first time they are used and thereafter lose their power; wherefore one must not use them unless he is in danger or when they are transmitted to a second person. . . . Spell-formulas are uttered slowly and in a suppressed, mystic tone but the significance of the words is not known."[82]

There are Indian magic songs that "entice all birds and animals," "which all the Whales obey," which "are heard to any distance away over forests and mountains."[83] The snake-ceremonies of the Hopi Indians, where the snakes are intercessors with the rain-gods, are permeated with magic. "If the proper ceremonies with them are performed in prescribed sequence and in traditional ways," there is "a compulsion of the rain and growth supernaturals to perform their functions, which is brought about by the use of proper charms."[84] "The Choctas, Chickasaws, and allied tribes of Indian Territory frequently perform acts of conjuring in the ball field to invoke the assistance of their

[76] Granville and Roth, in JAI, XXVIII, 111.
[77] Full account in Radloff, *Schamanenthum.*
[78] Waddell, *Buddhism,* 163.   [79] Bühler, *Manu,* II, 75, 77, 83, 84.
[80] Von Kremer, *Kgchte.,* II, 40, 41.
[81] Hopkins, *Relig. Ind.,* 351-352, 374.
[82] Holm, *Ethnol. Skizze,* 77, 78.
[83] Leland and Prince, *Kulóskap,* 118, 166, 196.
[84] Fewkes, in BAE, XIX, pt. II, 1008.

tutelary daimons." By sorcery too they expect to find out the plans of the enemy.[85]

Antiquity is full of magic by words and formulas. The Assyrians had charms and counter-charms in profusion.[86] Among the Hebrews the angels had names and could be conjured; they had to come, after the proper rites, at the proper time and place, had been performed.[87] There is but one spell in Homer,[88] which is sung over a wound, to stop the flow of blood. Latin literature teems with references to magic.[89] Homer and the Norse sagas, says Lehmann,[90] show no demons; and in the North operative magic is mainly by words or by runes. He cites four means of magic: the runes, which were engraved magic signs ascribed to Odin, good for all events, but seldom used alone; the *galder,* songs or spoken magic formulas; magical drinks and foods; and the *sejden,* strongest of all, which were magic songs combined probably with quite unknown secret operations. In *Egil's Saga* the runes in a charm were carved wrongly so that it caused sickness instead of health; in the *Njala,* a wife leaves a husband because she is spell-bound—for a former mistress has uttered a spell on him against his wife.[91]

It might be contended, with no small show of plausibility, that the printed word is a fetish capable of exercising magic influence. Certainly there are many people ranked as civilized, or even as cultured, who have no critical sense as respects what they see in type. The printed page, especially if it exhibits a certain pretentiousness of form, seems to exert a benumbing influence over common sense, and the attitude evoked has a family-likeness to that assumed worshipfully, aforetime, before "authority." It is an echo of the stock imputation of wizardry to which ignorance takes recourse in the presence of that which is vaguely, if at all, understood. One of the ways sometimes adopted for disconcerting even an intelligent adversary is to overwhelm him with mathematical formulas, graphs, and other esoteric devices which he cannot withstand because he cannot understand them. They are similar to the secret, fetishistic jargon of the medicine-man. In a similar manner, floods of wild and whirling words impose upon the less criti-

[85] Hoffman, "Menomini," in BAE, XIV, pt. I, 129; Leland and Prince, *Kulóskap,* 187.

[86] *Records of the Past,* I, 131-135; III, 147.

[87] Blau, "Angelology," in *Jew. Encycl.,* I, 588; Blau, *Zauberwesen,* 92.

[88] *Odyssey,* XIX, 457-458.

[89] Tavenner, *Studies in Magic from Latin Literature,* is a laborious collection of materials scattered through the writings of eighty or more Latin writers.

[90] *Overtro,* I, 100, 110-112.

[91] *Corp. Poet. Bor.,* 373; Dasent, *Burnt Njal,* 19, 25.

cal, often exerting effects that deserve the name "magical" in a sense not wholly metaphorical.

Says the New York *Times*,[92] editorially: "Some sociologists hold that national conventions, so far as their exterior forms and observances are concerned, are essentially a survival of primitive magic. Others have been impressed by the strong infantile element in them, and have classed much of their ritual and proceedings with nursery rhymes, children's games, college cheers. These, too, may be regarded, in part, as the detritus of 'words of power,' 'relics of mythology and shamanism.' Whatever anthropologists say, the layman knows by observation that politicians are most superstitious."

The connection between incantation and prayer has been developed, with illustrations;[93] it is true enough that prayer, though it is primarily part of the propitiation-ritual, sometimes exercises coercitive power.

§302*. Imitative Magic. There remains a form of magic of which much is made, especially in Frazer's *Golden Bough*, and which he calls "sympathetic." It forms one of the grand cases of the *post-propter* fallacy.[94] A typical form is the rehearsal of some desirable event, with the idea of making it come off; the "buffalo-dance," wherein the chase and taking of the bison are enacted, with certain Indians made up as the quarry, is perhaps as characteristic an example of this sort of magic as could be found. It is evident that there is ritual[95] in such performances, together with a strong presumption that they will attain their ends; in some cases and aspects they are plainly coercitive, though the propitiatory element also is likely to be present. It is possible to regard them as acted prayers. In the poverty of undeveloped speech, the conveyance of meaning by signs was of the highest utility in attaining precision; even now gesticulation is still much in vogue to clarify and emphasize meaning. It is not at all fanciful to regard much of what goes under the name of sympathetic magic as simply the sort of prayer which the spirits will be sure to apprehend, appealing as it does to the eye rather than to, or in addition to, the ear. And perhaps gesture, being older, is more holy than speech.

Whatever the ritual, its mimetic character is what secures

92 June 5, 1924.   93 Marett, in *Folklore*, XV, 132 ff.
94 §199, above.   95 §279, above.

magical results; in it resides a power that is spiritual in nature and compelling in effect. It is a force beyond that of a mere action performed by a mere man. It has fetish in it. And so, though a number of the alleged cases of sympathetic magic are not really magic at all, yet there are in most of them such characteristics as have led us to classify them here, under the general caption of magical coercitives. If they can be so regarded there is no trouble at all in explaining why they have their power, whereas if they are vaguely referred to some subtle "sympathy" between things and things, or actions and things, or performances and results, there is little but assumption to explain why the rehearsal of a situation can be thought an effective means of bringing it about. To say that it is charactcristic of savages so to believe is merely to re-state the question in other and often more pretentious "psychological" terms. But if solemn ritual is taken to be fetishistic— and it will have been seen often enough throughout this book to be that—then this form of ritual falls in readily with a large category of cases that allow of a simple and direct interpretation on the basis of a universal primitive belief and practice.

We do not like the term "sympathetic," which seems to us to involve subtleties that are not to be found among primitive men; "imitative," on the other hand, implies fetishistic practice. If you have an imitation of a man's features, you can play havoc with his destiny; if you know his name, you have a hold over him.

"The word is no magic proceeding forth from man alone but is an independently effective thing, a representation of the object which it designates. We can recognize this best in the names of persons which, as is well known, are unwillingly told, because of fear lest magic may through them be practised upon the person himself. And so it is just about the same with the name as it is with the picture of a man who, for example, can be killed by means of the likeness." Musical instruments, when they are magic-exerting objects, are often viewed as images of a god; and it is believed that a daimon has crept into the instrument or that a god manipulates it. "So, for example, the sound of the bull-roarers, used in ceremonies in Australia, is often the voice of a particular daimon, that is, the bull-roarer itself is the image of him."[96]

Now it seems to us but a step farther on to hold that if you can imitate the actions of a man, or of an animal, or of rain, you have a similar control over each one of these, by way of the fetish-

---

[96] Preuss, in *Globus,* LXXXVII, 395.

quality of your mimetic ritual. But let us work up to that point through a simpler stage.

It will be recalled that the soul, ghost, and daimon enter to "possess" counterfeit presentments of themselves. Such simulacra are often, as shown by Spencer,[97] composed in part of actual exuviæ. These then become fetishes. In magic the use of such images, especially *envoûtement*, or wax-figure sorcery, long antedated the "Sorceresses" of Theocritus[98] and has persisted down to the present.

A Loango fetish is described which "carried a saber at its side, whose face was represented by a lump of clay, whose eyes and ears had been painted on," and into which, "for magical purposes nails were driven."[99] Evidently something unpleasant was being done to or by the agency of some saber-bearing person by way of his image. In one part of Africa, "a woman who loses a child carries a wooden doll representing it until she bears another." Of certain tribes of India it is said that "this process of sympathetic magic, in its two branches of imitative or homeopathic magic and contagious magic, will be found to lie at the root of most of the quasi-religious, social, domestic, and other ritual of the aborigines."[100] In Ceylon, the mouth of a person may be paralyzed by charming the palms and then clapping them together suddenly. Images of boiled rice are made to cure children's illnesses; the sickness goes into them. In cases of barrenness, an image of a child is made and then rocked by a man with padded breasts; it is given to the sufferer, kissed like a real child, and kept in a cradle till she conceives.[101] In some parts of the South Seas the method "is similar in many respects to the usual custom, that of making an image of the man or woman whose death is required, and then doing to it what it is wished shall happen to the original. In the island of Tanna the method differs slightly, for here, instead of an image being made, part of the person's property is stolen and taken to the sacred man who works destruction to its late owner, but he must have this property in his possession, or his maledictions will fail." It is noticeable here, both that a man's property is so much a part of him that what is done to it is done to him,[102] and that the magic done is by cursing, that is, invoking spiritual powers, not merely relying upon "sympathy." These sacred men, called Narak-burners, hold their position through the ownership of certain Narak-stones, and their procedure is the cremation of locks of hair or bits of food of their victims over a sacred fire lit over or near the place where the Narak-stones lie hidden. As usual, the victim sickens and dies as the exuviæ or food is consumed. "If a man hears that his effigy is being thus dealt with, or fancies it is because he feels sick, he will hurry off to the 'burner' and offer him a bigger price for his freedom than his enemy has paid for his death. The result of this may be guessed, and

[97] *Prin. Soc.*, I, ch. XXI.

[98] "Pharmaceutriæ," *Idyll* II; Ovid, *Amores*, III, 7, 29; Horace, *Epod.*, XVII, 6; Lenormant, *Chald. Magic*, 5-40.

[99] Bastian, *Deut. Exped.*, I, 42. [100] Roy, in JAI, XLIV, 329.

[101] Hildburgh, in JAI, XXXVIII, 160, 181, 182, 184.

[102] §108, above.

a keen bidding often results; if he be rich he is allowed to live, but a poor man has no chance." Of course this belief leads to a careful burial of clipped hair and the throwing of half-finished food and refuse into a stream, for water removes the Narak-burner's power.[103]

In Mexico, "the sorcerers make little images of rags or of clay, then stick into them the thorn of the maguey and place them in some secret place; you can be sure that the person against whom the conjuration is practiced will feel pain in the part where the thorn is inserted."[104] Not so different from such an image is the "vengeance-puppet" in its Japanese and Scotch forms.[105] After a theft, the Japanese woman puts up a rude figure drawn on paper, heels up and head down, with the feet transfixed by a needle. "The thief, on account of the pierced feet, was not to run any further and could thus be more easily caught"; until he was, the likeness remained hanging. The Scotch puppet was of clayey silt left after an overflow, and was to be set in the house-door of the person against whom ill-will was to be expressed. Images of witches were burned by the ancients, while images of good spirits afforded protection, especially if supported by a formula. "He who makes images corresponding to my whole person has bewitched my whole person."[106]

Thus imitative representations have, to practitioners of magic, a power over the object or person imitated. They are assimilated to the original somewhat as exuviæ are to the body from which they have been detached; and working upon or through them is operation upon the object or person itself. In view of such facts, then, it seems to us no long stride from the magical imitation of things to that of acts, especially characteristic ones, as a means of exercising power to secure the performance of those acts thus rehearsed. "It is a common idea amongst savages that to prefigure an event assures its occurrence; hence the veritable pantomimes in which the Redskins represent the capture of game or the defeat of the enemy before starting on the chase or the war-path."[107] Before going farther than to suggest this point of view, we let some typical cases of imitative magic speak for themselves.[108]

The Australians of the northwest make magic by rhythmic labor-movements without actual labor-performance. They carry out the ceremony in connection

[103] Hardy and Elkington, *S. Seas,* 163, 164, 165.

[104] Brinton, *Nagualism,* 10.

[105] Ten Kate, in *Globus,* LXXIX, 109; Karutz, in *Globus,* LXXIX, 110.

[106] Schrader, *Keilinschriften,* 605; Blau, *Zauberwesen,* 47, 48; Bartels, *Medicin,* 34.

[107] D'Alviella, *Concep. God,* 94, note.

[108] For collections of cases, see Havemeyer, *Drama,* chs. II, III; Andree, *Eth. Parallelen,* 8 ff.; see bibliog. by Eberman in *Ztsft. d. Vereins f. Vkde.,* XXIII, Heft 1, 14.

with great heaps of stones when there is lack of animal and plant food. In the case of the lack of edible seeds, grass-seeds are swung in wooden bowls and hand-mills play a big rôle. The women go through the procedure of swinging and grinding while singing and dancing go on. The mere movements were effective, just as the feigned sleep of men represented "a simple analogy to the condition" they would like the spirits to be in.[109]

In Melanesia, if an arrow-head that has inflicted a wound can be recovered as a whole or in part, "it is kept in a damp place or cool leaves; the inflammation is little, or subsides. Shells are kept rattling over the house where the wounded man lies to keep off the hostile ghost. In the same way the enemy who has inflicted the wound has by no means done all that he can do. He and his friends will drink hot and burning juices, and chew irritating leaves; pungent and bitter herbs will be burnt to make an irritating smoke, and will be tied upon the bow that sent the arrow; the arrow-head, if recovered, will be put into the fire. The bow will be kept near the fire, its string kept taut, and occasionally pulled, to bring on tension of the nerves and the spasms of tetanus."[110]

The Zulu, buying cattle, chews a bit of wood to soften the hard heart of the seller. On the Gold Coast, when the men go to war, the women at home dance the fetish-dance to help them.[111] In southern India, childless persons perform on carved wooden figurines the ear-boring ceremony, in the belief that they will soon be doing the same thing to genuine children born to them. "Or, if there are grown-up boys and girls in a family who remain unmarried, the parents celebrate the marriage ceremony between a pair of dolls, in the hope that the marriage of their children will speedily follow. . . . Some there are who have spent as much money on a doll's wedding as on a wedding in real life." Again, on the way to a certain hill-temple there may be seen small stones heaped up in the form of hearths and knots tied in the leaves of young date-palms. "These are the work of virgins who accompany the parties of pilgrims. The knots are tied to ensure the tying of the tāli string on their necks, and the heaping up of stones is done with a view of ensuring the birth of children to them. If the girls revisit the hill after marriage and the birth of offspring, they untie the knot on the leaf, and disarrange one of the hearths."[112]

In the East Indies the natives of some districts, believing that rice has a soul and sex-passion, seek to rouse the latter to get a good harvest.[113] An analogous "renewing" of nature by the magic of cohabitation is found in Mexico and Peru. The explanation of the use of the whirr-stick in the Tusayan snake-dances is that its sound, being like that of wind-blown rain, is rain-compelling.[114] The Ojibwa medicine-man, in producing hunter's medicine, "draws with a sharp-pointed bone or nail upon a piece of birch-bark the outline of the animal desired. He indicates the place of the animal's heart by a puncture upon which a little vermilion is carefully rubbed, as this color is thought to be very efficacious toward effecting the capture of the animal and

[109] Clement, in *Int. Archiv. f. Ethnog.*, XVI, 6-7; Preuss, in *Globus,* LXXXVII, 335, 347, 350.

[110] Codrington, in JAI, XIX, 217.   [111] Tylor, *Anth.*, 296, 298, 340.

[112] Thurston, *S. India,* 347, 357.

[113] Wilken, *Vkde.*, 550; Preuss, in *Globus,* LXXXVII.

[114] Bourke, in BAE, IX, 476.

the punctured heart is thought to insure its death."[115] Among certain California Indians, when a wife is childless, "her sympathizing friends sometimes make a rude image of a baby out of grass, and tie it in a miniature baby-basket, according to the Indian custom. . . . She takes it up, holds it to her breast, pretends to nurse it, and sings it lullaby-songs. This is done as a sort of conjuration, which it is hoped will have the effect of causing the barren woman to become fertile."[116] Such ceremonies recall part of the wedding-ceremony, where symbols portray the hoped-for fecundity of the union, and also the customs surrounding pregnancy and child-birth, such as the couvade.[117]

There is plenty of imitative magic in the oath or ordeal.[118] The parties act out the invoked consequences of perjury or guilt in a very realistic manner. "May their brains run out upon the ground as does this wine!"[119] In view of the numerous illustrations of these topics we shall cite but one case by way of recalling them.

"If the persons buying and selling cannot read, they burn the agreement (after it has been read to them) on a large flat stone, then carefully taking the charred pieces of paper they beat them into powder and sprinkle them on water in a bowl. The water is then stirred with a spear or a sword, or with the barrel of a gun, and the persons say, 'May I die by spear (or sword, or gun) if I do not keep this agreement!' Then they each drink half of the water. A few drops may be poured out on the ground, so that the earth also is a witness to the transaction."[120] This citation contains the further fetishistic belief in the written word.

One of the characteristic developments of imitative magic lies in the dance, especially as it passes into dramatic representation. It possesses coercive power. Perhaps the most typical of magical dances are those which precede the chase and war. In the former, alluded to above, there are men in appropriate disguises, to represent the prey, which is finally brought down and "killed" with much realistic display; in the latter there is a similar rehearsal of hoped-for accomplishment.[121] It should be noted in scanning detailed descriptions[122] that the magical dance always presents, in some of its aspects and generally as a whole, the features of a dramatic prayer. It is with the steady development of the regular

[115] Hoffman, in BAE, VII, 221.
[116] Powers, in *Contrib. N. A. Ethnol.*, III, 318.
[117] §§371, 407, 408, below.   [118] §§183, 277, above.
[119] Homer, *Iliad*, III, 298-301; Keller, *Hom. Soc.*, 175 ff.
[120] Milne, *Eastern Clan*, 216.
[121] §140, above; for full description of buffalo-dance, see Donaldson, in *Smithson. Rep.*, 1885, II, 358 ff.
[122] Several are collected in Havemeyer, *Drama*, chs. II, VI.

cult that "prayer and sacrifice assume the leading place in religious ritual; and magic, which once ranked with them as a legitimate equal, is gradually relegated to the background and sinks to the level of a black art." Then inexplicable and prodigious performances are referred to the regular gods as "miracles" worked by them, which "are not considered as breaches of natural laws. Not conceiving the existence of natural law, primitive man cannot conceive a breach of it."[123]

§303. Nature of Magic. It is now possible, with representative cases in mind, to enter more fully into the nature of magic. Magic, it will be recalled, is thought to exist alongside the cult or outside of it or, very often, in a sort of opposition and antithesis to it. It is generally quite outside "our" cult. What our own gods do is miraculous; what is done by supernatural powers other than our own deities is magic, sorcery, or witchcraft. The Biblical instance is worth repetition as wholly typical: when the rod of Aaron turned into a serpent, that was a miracle; when those of the Egyptian priests did the same thing, on the same occasion, that was magic or "black art."[124] Peoples far more primitive than the Hebrews seem to draw something the same distinction, and it persists on into the "league with Satan," a feature of the witch-processes of later times.[125] A plague among the Indians prior to the arrival of the Plymouth colony "was attributed in a notable work of that period to the Divine purpose of clearing New England for the heralds of the gospel; on the other hand, the plagues which destroyed the *white* population were attributed by the same authority to devils and witches."[126]

Though this distinction between magic and miracle is traditional, it is not, after all, a real one, so far as daimonology in general is concerned; both magic and the cult belong under that category. The power involved is more than human. Also there are plenty of likenesses between magic and the cult, for magic itself implies or actually exhibits a condemned, despised, and feared form of worship. "The subject of magic," says Sir Charles

---

[123] Preuss, in *Globus*, LXXXVII, 347; Frazer, *Golden Bough*, I, 31, 33; Rivers, *Medicine, Magic, and Religion, passim*.
[124] Lehmann, *Overtro*, I, 13.   [125] Sumner, in *Coll. Ess.*, I, ch. IV.
[126] White, *Sci. and Theol.*, II, 85.

Dundas,[127] "has led me to think that between this and the knowledge of how to please or ward off the spirits there is very little
difference, if any at all, and that there is therefore no special art
which can be called magic: it is simply the cult of the spirits.
The contrary of the making of charms to ward off evil is the construction of spells or curses for the purpose of bringing evil upon
others. The art is closely allied to that of witchcraft." There are
in magic some elements of avoidance, propitiation, and conciliation, as will appear, and its effect is typically exorcistic; its
operation, however, is essentially coercitive upon the spirit-world
whose powers cannot but yield to the stress exercised by the magical operations. Even the Earth-Spirit is obliged to appear before
Faust, though he speedily vanishes in contempt of his summoner.

> Thou hast drawn me with power,
> Hast long tugged at my sphere. . . .
> Thou resemblest the spirit thou comprehendest,
> Not me.[128]

The daimon is not bribed to appear or serve; but if the magic is
right he always must do so. If there is here a coercitive influence,
exerted to secure results that only some superhuman power,
whether identifiable or not, can compass, then the subject of magic
belongs with the other slighter forms of coercion[129] as the ranking
member of the category. In fact, magic is set apart with a name
of its own chiefly by virtue of the fact that the powers it controls
are generally, whether identifiable or not, outside the regular cult
and that they are coerced rather than avoided or propitiated.
Magic is, in short, a specific kind of coercitive.

Less purely magical is the production of results through the
agency of a familiar spirit,[130] somehow bound and coercible by the
human master, as were those of Aladdin and Prospero. Into this
form there often enters some form of propitiation, in that the
spirit is bound by interest, gratitude, oath, or otherwise to repay
a service rendered. Thus was Ariel bound. In typical magic this
coercion is secured by the use of the fetish: some substance or
article, some ritual act, word, or formula, is the repository of

---

[127] In JAI, XLIII, 528.
[128] Goethe, *Faust,* pt. I, act I, 130-131; 159-160.
[129] §277, above.   [130] §244, above.

spiritual power. Commonly there is simply the compelling fetish, like Aladdin's lamp or his "Open, Sesame!" where there can be no question of prior relations of spirit and man because there was between them no antecedent knowledge or acquaintance at all.

Most broadly, next to its coercive quality, magic is a case of dualism, that is, of the enlistment of spirit against spirit. The most familiar instance of dualism is the eternal opposition of the White and the Black, the Good and the Evil, God and Satan; only, on the less sophisticated stage, the moral quality of the spirit invoked as resident in the fetish is not a matter of much attention. In fact, it is generally supposed that magic deals with the control of evil influences rather than good. There is such a thing as "white magic," but the words "sorcery," "witchcraft," "black art," have a suggestion of evil about them. Sometimes the gods themselves are controllable by appeal to the dark and menacing powers of a more ancient dynasty of divinities.

The magic power of Greek witches "was gained by *compelling* the gods; in other words, by appealing to a higher and supreme power to which the gods must bow. Magical art, then, was associated with an older pre-Hellenic religion and the divine power of a more ancient system, and was always related to the Chthonian religion and the gods of the world of death."[131]

Lehmann[132] distinguishes between official and private magic. The latter is employed by the individual, usually a witch or wizard, without the sanction of the group, for his own benefit and generally to the injury of others. The former is the type which enjoys the sanction of the society—in later development, that of the state; it is for the benefit of the group at large and for any individual who wishes to take advantage of it, but involves no danger to others of the in-group. This is "white art" where the private type is "black art"; it is manipulated by the official representative, shaman or priest, and is not far from being the group-religion itself.

There are some writers[133] who seem to believe that magic is antecedent even to animism and go on to show how out of a basic belief in "orenda," "mana," or "virtue," which we are inclined to

[131] Ramsay, "Relig. Greece," in *Hastings's Dict. Bible,* 154.
[132] *Overtro,* I, 32-33, 50 ff.
[133] Vierkandt, in *Globus,* XCII, 21-25; 40-45; 61-65; Preuss, in *Globus,* LXXXVII, 381 ff.; Lévy-Bruhl, *Fonctions Mentales.*

regard as an animistic or fetishistic quality,[134] might come the notion of the soul and ghost. Their contentions, we have said, seem to us highly psychological and tenuous and without a spacious basis in ethnography; but they may be briefly reviewed, in their present connection with magic, from a résumé.[135]

The case is based upon the Iroquoian "orenda," the Siouan "wakanda," the Melanesian "mana," and a few other similar conceptions. "Orenda" is a hypothetical or "subsumed" potence or potentiality to do or effect results mystically. Much is made of "the confusion of subjectivity and objectivity in both the practical and the theoretical field"; the primitive man gets his own personality mixed up with the external world.

A shaman's orenda is great and powerful; a fine hunter's is superior, and when he is successful, it has baffled or thwarted the orenda of the quarry. The winning of a game of chance or skill is due to a superior orenda; and when there are inter-tribal games, shamans are hired by both parties to exercise their orenda to win victory. The brewing of a storm is the storm-maker preparing its orenda. Similarly with animal or human anger, with shyness, cleverness, and other qualities: they are all states of orenda. "Anything whose orenda is reputed or believed to have been instrumental in obtaining some good or in accomplishing some purpose is said 'to possess orenda.'" The rabbit, "by barking the underbrush at a suitable height, indicates the depth to which the snow must fall. Thus his orenda controlled the snow."

These beliefs now pass into experience, and man begins to personalize them more sharply. "In the stress of life, coming into contact or more or less close relation with certain bodies of his environment more frequently and in a more decided manner than with the other environing bodies, and learning from these constraining relations to feel that these bodies, through the exercise of their orenda, controlled the conditions of his welfare and in like manner shaped his ill-fare, he came gradually to regard these bodies as the masters, the arbiters, the gods, of his environment, whose aid, good will, and even existence were absolutely necessary to his well-being and his preservation of life itself. And these relations and the manner of obtaining the favor and gifts of these bodies gradually grew into tradition and vigorous custom, and in the flux of time developed into rite, ceremony, and a more or less elaborate ritual." Orenda is "the executive power of men and devils, angels and gods; it can destroy the living and can as well bring back to life the dead; in fact, it is omnipresent, omniscient, and omnipotent; enchantment, exorcism, the evil eye, relics, holy springs, ordeal, bedevilment, and all the arts of soothsaying, are one and all activities arising from the faith and trust in the efficacy of this subsumed magic potence or orenda." The Iroquois names for life, soul, ghost, mind, and brain are cited by this author, to show that orenda is not one of them.

Against such a view may be set evidence such as the following: "*Mena* is probably a form of the widespread *mana,* and also occurs in another form in San Cristoval as *manawa,* the breath or to breathe; *mana* or *mena* perhaps means originally the breath, and power is a secondary meaning, owing to the fact that it is the breathing upon an object which imparts power."[136]

---

[134] §210, 254, 258, above.   [135] By Hewitt, in AA, IV, 37 ff.
[136] Fox and Drew, in JAI, XLV, 153; §210 of *Case-Book.*

Differences of opinion as to origins, in their place proper enough for discussion and, if possible, settlement, do not concern us here. The present interest is magic, and the only reason for recurring to the above views, is that adherents of them allege that they afford a much more profound explanation of religion and magic than otherwise attainable, and indicate that magic antedates animism. Let the reader strive to align with this *orenda*-theory the cases which are to follow and make his own choice between it and the animistic theory of Tylor to which, in its essentials, we adhere. In our opinion the *orenda*-potency is nearly enough a part of the soul while this is still in the living body to be considered along with it; and when it comes to inanimate objects, we think that potency is probably an evidence of possession by some unidentified ghost or spirit. We think, in short, that magic is a form of daimonology and is hardly understandable if regarded as so far antecedent to it as we are urged to believe. In our inferences as to primitive matters we always take it for granted that the simple and unspeculative precedes the complex and abstruse, just as a knowledge of simple elements must precede that of compounds, like bronze. Certain vague conceptions of "virtue" are doubtless rather widespread; but we do not believe that a theory inspired by such, though it may be an interesting toy for the speculative schematizer, can be universalized to any useful purpose.

§304. **Sway of Magic.** The object of magic is stated by one writer[137] to be twofold: to secure insight; to exert effect on environment. It might be noted at once that these are the objects of science also; men's aims must needs be the same, however diverse the means employed for their attainment. If, our author goes on, these objects are secured by recourse to higher, intelligent beings, it is spiritism; if by recourse to unknown nature-forces, it is occultism. But "every acceptation based upon certain experiences vanishes if experience no longer supports it." These remarks align magic perfectly with the rest of the practices for dealing with the aleatory element and show its procedure subject

137 Lehmann, *Overtro,* IV, 3-5.

to correction through advancing knowledge—as a vague notion of "subsumed mystic potency" is not.

There is always about life an eternal encircling mystery. Daimonology, with its antecedents, animism and eidolism, was the first world-philosophy. Science is the last. All the religions and philosophies which have ever existed are strung along a line which leads from the former of these to the latter. Magic and sorcery rest on theories of the past that have not been corrected, the deductions from which have been drawn not by reason but by phantasy. In the absence of any knowledge of natural law, "primitive man's experience must have consisted of a stream of events as disjointed and disconnected as the successive incidents in a dream."[138] Existing in a high civilization, magic is a superstition and a survival.[139] A species of occultism persisting today, which is also truly superstitious, is the notion that the longings of men are any proof that there must be—somehow, somewhere—a satisfaction for them; that immortality must be, because generations of men have so ardently desired it. This is the fanciful vagary concerning the objective truth of ideas. It includes the conviction that the presence of personal discontent is proof that something which is ought not to be or that something which is not ought to be; that some change in conditions, instead of adjustment to them, is called for.

No profit comes out of dabbling about in dialectics over mysteries. Much enlightenment, however, can be gained by noting how, entirely automatically, the race has stumbled upon a working hypothesis, has carried it to the facts of life, has corrected it gradually and painfully (by experience, not by meditation), and has finally emerged with highly effective sciences which provide both insight and also power over environment—the original objects at which magic aimed. All the sciences, we shall see over and over again, rose out of what is now called superstition; indeed, they could not have risen had it not been for the spur to observation, collection, and comparison of facts that a lively interest and fear never ceased to ply. Our interest lies in the evolution out of unverifiable fancies of the tested expedients by which we all live, and not at all in dialectics over the fancies.

[138] Jevons, *Relig.*, 16.   [139] §199, above.

Nothing has perhaps appeared so inexplicable to a later age as the obsession of magic, sorcery, and witchcraft.[140] The same might be said in general of daimonism and its derivative forms and recurrences. Here we need yet again to recall the comment of Lippert[141] about how the creative force exerted by a notion in the development of civilization depends, not upon how true it is, but on its vividness and the numbers who believe in it; about how greater vividness more than offsets higher certainty, especially since the more vivid notions are produced by the more elementary thinking, so that a man feels that he has found them out for himself. "Never will the established doctrines of Newton and Copernicus furnish anything like such motives for conduct as the childish notions about ghost-fear. The reason for this inheres not in the quality of the ideas but in the way in which they come to be. . . . The farther a notion reaches back into primitive times the more universal must be its extent, and its power in history is rooted in this universality."

The belief in magic is wholly natural to the savage; given his premises, it is also rational and logical. Says a writer[142] on New Guinea: "While I have spoken of this native belief as belief in 'magic,' we must remember that it really is not magic from the native point of view. From his point of view it is just as natural for a person to be killed by treating his hair after it has been cut off, as it is to kill him by giving him a grain or two of strychnine." Where modern civilized man is not checked up by the verification now possible owing to the labors of science, he is about as likely to believe in magic as was his cultural progenitor of long ages ago; the less exact the science the more does he run to this racial tendency.[143] Political and social magicians, if they can display qualities enough like those of the medicine-man, never lack a following.

The belief in magic has been sufficiently vivid and also universal upon earth. If occasionally it is reported that a people puts no faith in witchcraft,[144] that is most exceptional. Belief in magic is profoundly deep-rooted, is seldom extirpated altogether, and is

140 Sumner, "Witchcraft," in *Coll. Ess.*, I, ch. IV.
141 *Kgchte.*, I, 29; II, 45.
142 Strong, in JAI, XLIX, 294.   143 Keller, *Soc. Evol.*, 1 ff.
144 Schweinfurth, *Heart of Afr.*, I, 307.

generally ready to break out, especially under stress. If European influence, through missionaries or otherwise, is exerted to eradicate such belief, the latter is dissembled or perhaps defended on some grounds thought to be plausible and acceptable to the critic, while the practice is merely intermitted or perhaps carried on clandestinely.

"The distinction," writes a veteran missionary to West Africa,[145] "sought to be made by the half-civilized Negro between a white art and a black art, as a justification of his practice of fetich enchantments, lies in the object to be obtained by their use. He vainly tries to find a parallel to them in Christian use of fire-arms,—proper for defence, improper for unprovoked assault. The black art he admits is wrong, its object being to kill or injure some one else; the white he thinks allowable, because with it he acts simply on the defensive."

As for the belief in witchcraft, "it is latent and may burst forth anew at any moment. . . . At the present day it is in politics. . . . Anarchists who are fanatical enough to throw bombs into theaters and restaurants, or to murder kings and presidents, just because they are such, are capable of anything which witch-judges or inquisitors have done, if they should think that party success called for it. If bad times should come again upon the civilized world, through overpopulation and an unfavorable economic conjuncture, popular education would decline and classes would be more widely separated. It must then be expected that the old demonism would burst forth again and would reproduce the old phenomena."[146] And now, in confirmation of this forecast, comes the following concerning popular credulity in England: "At the opposite pole from this reinvigorated atheism there has taken place a most extraordinary recrudescence of the belief in magic, miracle, and the direct intervention of the supernatural."[147] This was under the stress and misery of war.

§305*. Applications of Magic. Magic, like the rest of the daimonological system, plays about the aleatory element. A great many of its applications center about death. As has been shown in another connection, "primitive man is unable to conceive the idea of natural death—every death is attributed to sorcery or to

---

[145] Nassau, *Fetichism*, 116.   [146] Sumner, *Coll. Ess.*, I, 125, 126.
[147] Muirhead, in N. Y. *Nation*, CI, 455.

some malicious act."[148] This being the theory, the practice is to ferret out by magic the perpetrators of death-dealing operations, a custom so common that it is made use of as the most obvious means to attain political ends through the accusation of troublesome persons or of those whose goods, if they are condemned, can be confiscated by persons in power—chiefs or priests.[149] Around a case of death, therefore, there center investigations, which are largely magical, of acts which are almost always magical.[150] Murder by magic is plainly "black art," and "sorcery" and "witchcraft" are other names for it. The so-called detective function of "smelling-out" the murderer connects up with the topic of omen-taking;[151] but the atmosphere of magic in it is unmistakable.

In Australia, a relative of the dead lies with his head on the corpse that he may have a dream fixing the identity of the sorcerer. Some tribes watch the movements of an insect, some the direction taken by a lizard, some question the corpse, some watch the drying of damp clay over the grave to detect in the line of the principal fissures an indication of the locality of the murderer. Sometimes, when the dead man has many relatives, a council is held and some-one accused and condemned; or young men are selected who shall proceed upon a path indicated by an insect and kill, as the guilty party, the first native they meet. "When a man falls ill, some one is at once suspected of having cast a spell over him. If he dies, the person thus suspected is killed, especially if the man had been a person of importance."[152]

In New Guinea the epidermis is stripped from the corpse, after certain portions of the body are allotted to certain relatives. "Should it fail to come off on some part of the body, the relative to whom that part has been allotted has been the cause of the death." For "in their belief no one dies a natural death"; some sorcerer has accomplished it.[153] In New Britain, a man lies down at right angles and head on to the corpse, with a pearl shell in hand. An old man then calls out, one by one, the names of all the men in the village—all the villagers being assembled—and then, if nothing happens, the names of men in other villages, until a rapping is heard in the shell. This is done by a spirit to which they are appealing for information. "The individual at the utterance of whose name the rapping is heard is at once accused of causing the death of the deceased, and if possible, immediate compensation is sought or vengeance taken. Nothing that may be said or done will convince the people that the man indicated is innocent of the charge. I have known persons thus accused to be seized at night and literally hacked to pieces."[154]

"Belief in witchcraft is the cause of more African deaths than anything else.

[148] §203, above; Basu, in JASB, II, 557.
[149] §§155, 158, 179, 184, above, and 313, 320, below.
[150] Crawley, in JAI, XXIV, 221.   [151] §§267, above, and 313, below.
[152] Ratzel, Vkde., II, 73; Smyth, Vict., I, xxviii, 103, 110; Howitt, in JAI, XX, 90.
[153] Guise, in JAI, XXVIII, 211, 216.   [154] Danks, in JAI, XXI, 350.

It has killed and still kills more men and women than the slave trade. Its only rival perhaps is the smallpox, the Grand Kraw-Kraw, as the Krumen graphically call it." The widows of a dead man are subjected to ordeal, their guilt being established by the failure of a fowl to cluck at the sight of fire. The authoress[155] says that the abolition of the custom of killing wives and slaves at the death of a man leaves a temptation to poison him which did not exist when they were killed on his grave. Wife-sacrifice was a sort of insurance to a man. As it is, however, ten or more die for one death, "and thus, over immense tracts of country, the death rate exceeds the birth rate." This startling expression from a firstrate authority is backed up by Nassau,[156] himself long a missionary in West Africa, who says that "for every natural death at least one, and often ten or more, have been executed under witchcraft accusation." He tells of a man lacerated by an elephant who lived long enough to accuse twelve of his women and other slaves of having bewitched his gun so that it wounded but did not kill the elephant. On that charge four of the accused were put to death. It is generally the aged, the defenseless, and slaves who are the victims; but "no one is secure." If the foreign authorities were to withdraw from Sierra Leone, Congo-Français, and other districts, "the witchcraft ordeal and murder would be at once resumed." Evidently the missionaries have made no permanent impression, to judge by this admission of one of the most ardent of them. The "smelling-out" goes on right along; the chiefs, through their tools, the shamans, get rid of suspects of disloyalty by having, for instance, a whole army smelt over—"in this way hundreds of people were killed every year during the big dance." But Nassau knows of certain exceptional cases where death was considered natural; "for it is not unqualifiedly true that all tribes of Africa regard all deaths as caused by black art. There are some deaths that are admitted to be by the call of God, and for these there is no witchcraft investigation." Similar suspicion of wives, ordeal-potions, priestly investigations, property-confiscations, and the rest are common throughout Africa.[157] They are sufficiently illustrative of the application of magic to cases of death.

Among the Indians of the northwest coast of North America are to be found the same startling confessions of impossible guilt that were made by victims of the mediæval witch-processes.[158] Indian villages were bombarded and destroyed in the effort to compel the natives to abandon the punishment of victims accused of witchcraft; "but the chief stumbling block has been the surprising admission of guilt which nearly all the accused Indians make when charged with charming away life, and this, too, in the face of the death penalty. Such is their credulity that when accused they believe they must be guilty." The ferreting process in America is not dissimilar to that encountered in Africa. In case of sickness and death three men are selected who first pulverize a dried frog, mix it with salt water, and drink the mixture, thus securing the purification through vomiting and purging that renders them able to judge of the case submitted. A wood-mouse is caught and caged. "They then commence naming over suspected persons, and presently the little mouse nods its head."[159] In British Guiana, finally, the detection-process is by cutting off all the digits of the dead person's hands and toes and boiling them in a pot,

[155] Kingsley, *Travels W. Afr.*, 462, 463, 466, 467, 488.
[156] *Fetichism*, 86, 124, 118, 170, 239, 241-242.
[157] Stuhlmann, *Mit Emin*, 394; Nachtigal, *Sahara*, II, 686.
[158] Sumner, in *Coll. Ess.*, I, ch. IV.   [159] Niblack, in USNM, 1888, 348.

while singing a gruesome mourning-song. On the side where the first member is cast over the pot's rim they expect to find the hostile unknown.[160]

These cases exhibit the vividness of the persuasion that death is due to magic and that the death-dealing agency can be identified by magic. Many other exhibitions of the aleatory element are similarly referred to witchcraft and sorcery. An assortment of cases will serve to illustrate the manifold applications of magic to the various vicissitudes of life.

In terms implying somewhat too great sophistication in the savage mind, the primitive attitude is thus summarized: "The need of causality, the strain to discover the cause for everything, which is as much alive in the Papuan as in us, for him puts a soul into each separate object in nature; and by means of magic, the sole higher 'science' of the nature-man, he rules his world. Soul-faith and magic are inseparable. Because everything is be-souled, everything also can be bewitched." In corroboration it is elsewhere reported of the Papuan that, while his idea of a higher being has next to no influence on him, his belief in magic and witchcraft governs his doings in the highest degree; this assertion is reiterated, and supplemented by the opinion that every effort to draw him away from this belief and practice would be a vain one.[161]

"There is in these [Australians], as in other savage tribes, an undercurrent of anxious feeling which, though it may be stilled and forgotten for a time, is yet always present. In his natural state the native is often thinking that some enemy is attempting to harm him by means of evil magic, and, on the other hand, he never knows when a medicine man in some distant group may not point him out as guilty of killing some one else by magic."[162] It may be added that if he is so pointed out he can convince nobody, not even himself, that he is guiltless. "In connection with manners and customs of our Aboriginal race a great motor power is the belief in sorcery or witchcraft. In the everyday life of the Black, a pressure originating in this source may be said to be always at work." In Australia, self-deception naturally flourishes along with inconsistency. "One black fellow will often tell you that he can and does do something magical whilst all the time he is perfectly well aware that he cannot, and yet firmly believes that some other man can really do it. In order that his fellows may not be considered in this respect as superior to himself he is obliged to resort to what is really a fraud, but in the course of time he may even come to lose sight of the fact that it is a fraud which he is practising upon himself and his fellows."[163]

It might be added that if one grows up into the acceptation of any doctrine as a natural feature in the landscape of societal life, he is not in a position to criticize it or to become self-undeceived. These generalities on the Papuans and Australians are so suscep-

160 Schomburgk, *Brit.-Guiana*, I, 325.
161 Hagen, *Papua's*, 275; Krieger, *Neu-Guinea*, 184.
162 Spencer and Gillen, *Nat. Tr. Cent. Aust.*, 53, 54.
163 Curr, *Aust. Race*, I, 45; Spencer and Gillen, *Nat. Tr. Cent. Aust.*, 130.

tible of general application to primitive peoples that they are singled out for attention. We turn now to several more specific cases.

One of the four main Australian ways of getting a wife is by charming through magic. "Throughout all the tribes there are certain well-recognized methods of obtaining a wife by magic, and they vary very little from tribe to tribe. In all cases the woman so obtained is supposed to belong to the proper class into which the man may lawfully marry." Any irregularity in this respect is likely to be punished by death. "The obtaining of a woman by magic is one of the most fruitful sources of quarrels amongst all of the tribes." The method is by nocturnal singing and swinging of the bull-roarer, which is supposed to entice the woman irresistibly. Or the admirer wears a magical head-band, shell-ornament, or tassel.[164] Magic also plays a rôle in connection with the food-taboos: "the old Australians may therefore eat many animals which are forbidden to the younger classes, plainly because the former are in a position to meet the evil influences of the dead animals . . . that is, to withstand the magical effect that goes with the eating."[165] "All ill luck and calamity which befalls a Jabim he refers to the magic of a man ill-disposed to him, and if he thinks he knows him he tries to take vengeance."[166] Here is a prolific cause of disorder.

"My men," writes Livingstone,[167] "having never had fire-arms in their hands before, found it so difficult to hold the musket steady at the flash of fire in the pan, that they naturally expected me to furnish them with 'gun medicine,' without which, it is almost universally believed, no one can shoot straight." In South Africa we encounter again the "smelling-out" process, in this case for the detection of the bewitchment of men or cattle. It rarely strikes the poor man, being a sort of tax on large possessions. "Sometimes the sentence is merely a fine of cattle, but generally it is 'eating up,' which may mean anything—from stripping him of all that is worth taking, to destroying him and all that belong to him." The posse sent by the chief to do this is called an "impi," and its attacks generally take place at night. If a Kaffir be asked why there are so many dogs around his kraal at night, he will say that they are for safety and often adds that "if from the mode in which the dogs bark, he suspects an 'impi' is coming, he would creep out and hide in the nearest thicket; for if the 'impi' returns to head-quarters, and reports that they were unable to find the accused, and inflict the sentence on him, it appears to be generally held that the accused is free, and may, and indeed ought to go to the chief who sent the 'impi' and claim immunity from further punishment for that offence." "The property of a detected wizard, whether he escapes or is executed, is divided between the chief of the clan and the magician, and it is curious to find that no poor man is ever found guilty of practicing this art."[168]

The early Greeks seem singularly free from the terror of black art as felt by many other peoples upon a similar or more advanced stage of civilization.[169]

[164] Spencer and Gillen, *North. Tr. Cent. Aust.*, 472.

[165] Spencer and Gillen, *Nat. Tr. Cent. Aust.*, 554; Preuss, in *Globus*, LXXXVII, 399.

[166] Von Pfeil, *Südsee*, 318.   [167] *Mission. Travels*, I, 279.

[168] Frere, in JAI, XII, 263; Macdonald, in JAI, XIX, 274.

[169] Keller, *Hom. Soc.*, 174.

The Roman Laws of the Twelve Tables provided against enchanting harvests and employing incantations; even Cæsar, otherwise a derider of the other world, valued omens and magic. Almost nobody doubted the potency of sorcery and the Code of Justinian provided for the expulsion from cities of sects that might by means of it upset the elements. There was a popular belief that grain could be bewitched over from someone else's field to one's own. Once the people lodged such a charge against a freedman. The latter appeared for trial accompanied by his slaves, carts, and well-kept oxen. "Look upon my magical implements," he said; "there is yet lacking only my unceasing labor, which I cannot show you."[170]

Here is exemplified the tendency to call magical, or to ascribe to extra-human power, that which can be attained by sustained and well-directed effort along lines admitted by everyone to be within the scope of powers no more than human. The prevalence of belief in magic undoubtedly fathers the conviction that it is the unpredictable whims of the supernatural that determine human destiny, thereby both reducing confidence in labor and economy and furnishing subterfuges to those who shun them. Further, ignorance and sloth are always ready, having ascribed the results of knowledge and energy to wizardry, then to confiscate them. The story illustrates also the shifting boundary that exists between the realm of the known and the range of the aleatory element; what is to be referred to human power or to divine power is a relative matter and depends upon point of view.

"The church had already in the first four or five Christian centuries not only condemned all the old heathen magic as black art, as devilish art, but itself had adopted a great part of it and turned it into Christian forms." Passages of Scripture replaced former exorcisms; amulets and relics abounded. Prophecy was made by chance opening of the Bible. Then, later, the reformers, while repudiating all the holy apparatus of the church against magic, agreed with the notions of the time about magic. And, in ignorance of the Greek language, the term "black art" was erratically derived out of "necromancy," the first part of the compound being taken to be the Latin "niger."[171]

We shall not attempt to present, even by sample, the rank development of magic in the Middle Ages.[172] There was at that time a consistent exhibition of the stock attitude of ignorance in the presence of knowledge: the ascription

[170] Pliny, *Hist. Nat.*, XXVIII, ch. iv; Grupp, *Kgchte.*, I, 24, 26-27; Vergil, *Ecl.*, VIII, 99; Seneca, *Quaest., nat.* IV, 7; *Cod. Just.*, I, tit. 5, §5; IX, tit. 18; Lehmann, *Overtro,* I, 80-84.

[171] Lehmann, *Overtro,* I, 94-97, 157, 32, note.

[172] Conspectus in White's remarkable *History of the Warfare of Science with Theology in Christendom.* Thorndike, *History of Magic and Experimental Science during the First Thirteen Centuries of our Era* is a very thorough study, without much perspective, of the chief treatises bearing upon the subject.

of sorcery. It was not safe to know anything, as many a learned Jew or Arab found out. Astrology and alchemy flourished, and the extension of the witch-mania was unparalleled outside of Africa.[173] In northern Europe the magic operations, like those of the Greeks, were directed "not against spirits but against the nature itself of things," and "distinctions between black and white art seem scarcely to exist. . . . The result, not the means, made the act dishonorable." Storms were produced by enchantment. In Britain courts were held in the open air where magic had less control. Henry VIII alleged seduction by witchcraft in his marriage to Anne, "and this was evident because God did not permit them to have male issue." Illness came from being "overlooked" by some old woman. A royal marriage-bed was sprinkled with holy water and formulas of exorcism pronounced over it.[174] Among the South Slavs there is a widespread magic having to do with the milk-supply and among the Bulgars impotence and childlessness are looked upon as the results of sorcery worked by an enemy.[175]

The preceding paragraphs will have got before the mind the prevalence and main features of the belief in magic and will have lent still more point to the idea, to which we often return, about the power of a notion being proportional, not to the truth in it but to its vividness. That the race has been long and thoroughly steeped in magic is indicated by the number of terms to be found in modern languages—terms whose origin lies in very real conceptions of enchantment, bewitchment, charming, and other magical conceptions and operations. Words such as "spell-bound," recalling magic; "saturnine," "mercurial," "ill-starred," or "disaster," recalling astrological beliefs; "possession" or "inspiration," recalling fetishism; "night-mare," to "spirit away," "ingenuity," "entrancing," "ecstasy," "inauspicious," "abominable," "thunder-struck," "astonished," and a host of other terms that recall animistic and daimonistic doctrines[176]—all are embedded fossils or survivals that witness to preceding stages of evolution just as clearly as silent letters in words, like "phthisis," betray linguistic genealogy or as vestigial organs, such as the appendix in man, indicate animal-ancestry.

Belief in magic in the stricter sense, to say nothing of that wider sense which makes it virtually synonymous with all religious exercises of a primitive order, has been nearly if not quite univer-

[173] Sumner, in *Coll. Ess.*, I, ch. IV.

[174] Lehmann, *Overtro*, I, 117-118; *Laxdaela Saga*, 112; Gomme, *Ethnol. in Folklore*, 68; Creighton, *Hist. Ess.*, 352; Garnier, *Brit. Peasantry*, 385; Æneas Sylvius, *Fried. III*, II, 96; Clemens, *Prince and Pauper*, 188 ff., 408.

[175] Krauss, *Südslaven*, 55; Strauss, *Bulgaren*, 290.

[176] Tylor, *Anth.*, 345.

sal among all peoples. And if anyone thinks that belief to be defunct in civilized states, he is unacquainted with the mode of thought of the ignorant, as well as with various weaknesses and vagaries of those who ought to know better.[177] Consider a "cure" for obesity which consists in dwelling only upon one-dimensional figures and resolutely banishing all thought of circles, spheres, and other rotundities. It is mere imitative or sympathetic magic.

§306. Effectiveness of Magic.

The power of magic over those who believe in it is attested by trustworthy observers. The fatalities attending the breaking of a taboo should be recalled, to point the moral that "there is nothing either good or bad but thinking makes it so."[178] Let us get before us a few examples of the fatal power of magic.[179]

"There is no doubt whatever that a native will die after the infliction of even the most superficial wound if only he believes the weapon which inflicted the wound had been sung over and thus endowed with *Arungquiltha* [magical poisonous properties]. He simply lies down, refuses food, and pines away. Not long ago a man . . . received a slight wound in the groin. Though there was apparently nothing serious the matter with him, still he persisted in saying that the spear had been charmed and that he must die, which he did in a few days."[180] A Papuan who gets a notion that a daimon is meddling with his affairs will lie down and die. "It will no doubt surprise you to be told that a strong healthy man can walk away into the bush, and because another man has told him to die, he lies down and dies. . . . The man dies because the Papuan's brain is so weak that he cannot resist the enchantment under which the sorcerer has placed him. He believes he must die, and uses no effort of will to oppose the authoritative will of the magician."[181] This statement is unfair to the Papuan's brain; it is the content of his mind rather than its quality that is the trouble. He grows up into his belief in magic and is no more weak-minded than is a modern man who inherits his politics.

"The extraordinary part of the magic in savage lands is that it always works, and if men or women are properly cursed and their death prophesied by the magician, they die, and in the way their death has been foretold. . . . I once was at the death-bed of an old [Maori] chief, who was supposed to be dying of typhoid, but the real cause of his death was fear. In some way he had offended another chief, and that man had cursed him by a Tohunga or priest. I was unable to ascertain exactly what he had done, but the result of it was that an image made of clay, which was supposed to represent him, was placed in a creek, and as the water washed away the figure, so the chief gradu-

---

[177] Cases in N. Y. *Times*, November 29 and December 4, 1925.
[178] Shakspeare, *Hamlet*, Act II, Sc. II, 256.
[179] §268, above; numbers of cases in Frazer, *Golden Bough*, I, 168 ff.
[180] Spencer and Gillen, *Nat. Tr. Cent. Aust.*, 537.
[181] Abel, *New Guinea*, 110, 111.

ally sank; and, when the last particle was softened by the slowly trickling water and vanished down the stream, so that moment the soul of the old chief passed over the border. So strong is the superstition regarding these things that a man who is cursed never dreams of attempting to overcome the disaster foretold him, he simply goes home and dies, and it is in this way that this particular superstition, and others like it, live."[182] These observations deserve attention, and we shall recur to them; the case illustrates the effectiveness of cursing[183] as well as of magic.

If you nag an African, he gets sulky and will die to spite you;[184] but if this is true, how much more likely is he to die if he knows he is doomed. Processes of "praying to death," called "anaana," were practised in the Hawaiian Islands: "Any native *whose goods were desired,* or who might otherwise have given cause of offense, summoned by anaana instantly suspended his avocation and, hastening to the kahuna [shaman], crouched in abject submission to his will, until death took place, usually in a few hours, and apparently from exhaustion."[185]

The reader should note in these examples, aside from their bearing upon magic, the utilization of native religious beliefs for secular and especially sacerdotal ends. This could not be were it not for the absolute enthralment of the victim to his faith. Here, as in many another connection there are revealed the personal prestige of the shaman and also, more generally, the disciplinary power of primitive, literally accepted, uninterpreted religious doctrine.[186]

The chief interest here is in the effectiveness of magic. It is almost a truism that that thing is effective which "works"; and the extraordinary thing about magic in savage lands is that it always works, for if it seems to fail in any particular case, that is due simply to neutralization by an opposing magic that is still more powerful. If the performance does not come off, there is always an excuse which is plausible enough to a believer. The cure for magic is more magic.

"In the same certain way that death is brought about by a mental process—cursing—so miraculous cures are effected. . . . Should the god fail and the sick one die, the natives do not lose faith in their god, but decide that the patient was either too good to live, or so bad he had to die."[187]

Methods that are utter hocus-pocus get results—arrive at predetermined aims. In authentic cases of the effectiveness of fear

[182] Hardy and Elkington, *S. Seas,* 44, 45.
[183] §277, above.   [184] Kingsley, *Travels W. Afr.,* 655.
[185] Nichols, in *Pop. Sci. News,* XXVII, 77 ff.
[186] §§312, 330, below.
[187] §268, above; Hardy and Elkington, *S. Seas,* 46.

consequent upon taboo-breaking, being cursed, or being bewitched, there is no doubt whatever that the mental state affects the physical processes. Certainly the history of the witch-manias in mediæval and later times confirms the power of faith and suggestion to secure results that were concrete, unmistakable, and undeniable. Consideration of this point is more in place perhaps under the treatment of disease.[188] For now reflection is suggested upon the fact that, apart from any rational establishment of a cause-and-effect relation between magical operations and their actual working, there seems over and over again to exist a chronological relation of coincidence. To the savage mind, which has not of course succeeded in distinguishing chronological from causal sequence, such coincidence is the best of proof, as it still is to uncritical intelligence. This is an illustration of the *post hoc ergo propter hoc* fallacy.[189]

No one who has lived and observed at all reflectively can fail to be astonished at the number of coincidences which he has encountered. He may not be able to list a large number of them at will; but when he strikes a new and inexplicable one, there rises in his mind the feeling that he ought not to be immeasurably astonished, after all, for this situation has been duplicated many times before; he can recall several striking cases, perhaps, and has the sense of familiarity with others that have slipped below the horizon of memory. Some coincidences turn out, of course, not to be "mere coincidences"; a hidden cause-and-effect relation is discoverable. *Propter hoc, ergo post hoc* is all right enough and many *posts* are also *propters*. However, even where all allowance is made for the possible resolution of the coincidence into a sequence or correlation, there still remain many cases that cannot thinkably be so resolved. It is an unlucky coincidence to sneeze just as one is making an important shot in a game or, to cite the classic instance, to have inflammatory rheumatism and St. Vitus's dance at the same time; still, though each of the two happenings so linked together has its own antecedents and is inevitable at the moment, the fact that the times have synchronized is incidental, or coincidental, only.

188 §§315, 316, below.   189 §199, above.

There are, on the one hand, many such coincidences between operations, magical and other, which enlist the supernatural, and on the other what are taken to be the results of those operations. In view of certain truly damnable coincidences, it would almost seem, even to one who knows better, that some higher power has been pleased to trifle with men by thus leading them astray. Take the case of the tree-limb that fell at the glance, of course the evil glance, of the soldier; take the birth of a son to the late Czarina of Russia when, after all suggestions of science had failed, the images at Moscow had been displayed in solemn procession. There are a good many cases cited in various connections throughout this book that reveal similar coincidences. The coincidences seem particularly significant because they are forced upon attention and remembered, whereas there is nothing in the ordinary course of events, casually viewed, to enlist astonishment.

In any case the coincidences men encountered—belonging as they did to the aleatory element—strongly enforced convictions about sorcery. If real effects, together with coincidences interpreted as effects, appeared with some regularity, there can be no wonder that belief in magic was strong as well as widespread.

§307. **Correction into Science.** Out of the magic that branched off from the stem of religion sprang an important line of evolutionary development which, passing through pseudo-science, culminates in the sciences of today. Folk-magic, says Lehmann,[190] is a pile of stones which the "secret sciences," fitting the blocks neatly, have worked up into a wall. The first is an automatic growth among the people, the latter a construction by the best drilled, reflective minds of the time. The Jewish Kabbala was constructed on the basis of numbers and of the peculiarities of the Hebrew alphabet; "cabalistic" occultism is found elsewhere also.[191] Most of this sort of development started with the Chaldæans; and "witchcraft played a very great part in the whole of ancient Egyptian life."[192] The Arabs and to a less extent the

190 *Overtro,* II, 4, 8 ff.   191 Rehatsek, in JASB, I, 415.

192 Lehmann, *Overtro,* II, 37 ff.; Gessmann, *Geheimsymbole,* 3 ff.; Steindorff, *Relig. Anc. Egypt.,* 106; Meyer, *Aberglaube,* 1 ff.

Jews and classical peoples transmitted magic, now systematized into a branching pseudo-science, on down to later ages.[193]

Some of the cases previously cited bear evidence that the belief in magic is by no means obsolete in civilized countries; it may be added that the lower class of news-sheets carry advertisements of practitioners of the occult arts in their grosser forms and the higher type record punishments inflicted upon these specialists. Astrological predictions occasionally appear among the letters to editors; in a communication to the New York *Times*,[194] a certain gentleman is at some pains to explain that his prediction of the Democratic candidate's election in 1924 was based upon defective information, namely, that Mr. Davis was born on April 13, whereas the right date was April 12, this making "a marked difference in the horoscope." As for Mr. Coolidge, "his natal and progressed charts, his nomination at a favorable Jupiter hour, together with the fact that we find the benefic Venus in the ascendant Nov. 4, is favorable to him. He will have the love and esteem of the people."

It is not within the plan of this book to trace the history of magic or witchcraft through the systematic development of the former into the sciences or of the latter into the witch-processes of relatively modern times.[195] However, from the further evolution of the secret or pseudo-sciences there emerges a principle of wide significance in society's evolution. Taken by themselves, the early stages in the evolution of a human institution are of no importance except as curiosities; it is their genetic connection with the later members of the series that lends them real scientific significance. The establishment of this connection generally leads to the disengagement of some element of insight into the process through which society is automatically adjusting itself to its life-conditions; in these sweeps of societal evolution rather than in its detailed episodes is illumination attained. If the history of any one of the modern sciences is investigated, it is found rooting at last in what is to us superstition.[196] Astronomy and chemistry reach back through astrology and alchemy into fetishism and animism. Medicine comes out of exorcism and magic. They all go

---

[193] Blau, *Zauberwesen*, 21, 36, 37, 38, 43, 48, 49; Kautzsch, "Relig. Israel," in *Hastings's Dict. Bible*, 651, *et passim;* Maurer, *Vkde.*, I, 5, 136-137; Debschütz, *Christian Life*, 100-101; Pliny, *Hist. Nat.*, XXX, 2, 5, *et passim;* Charles, *Enoch*, LXV, 6, 7, 8.

[194] August 10, 1925.

[195] Tylor, *Anth.*, ch. XIII; White, *Sci. and Theol.*, II, chs. XI, XII; Sumner, in *Coll. Ess.*, I, ch. IV.

[196] White's chapters are headed: "From Magic to Chemistry and Physics"; "From Miracles to Medicine," etc.; *Sci. and Theol.*, I, chs. III, IV, XII; II, ch. XIII; Thorndike, *Magic;* Libby, *Hist. Medicine*.

back to the primitive mental outfit for their origin; and that outfit was for a long time not only very meager but, small as it was,
also full of error. Deriving as they did from this source, the sciences found parentage likewise in the illusory major premise of
it, namely, that which assumes, on the basis of what looks like
actual evidence, the imaginary environment of ghosts and spirits.
All of them go back ultimately to the aleatory element and are
the evolved forms of the originally blundering attempts to adjust
to that life-condition and deal with it.

The aleatory element, at least, was real; hence it may be said
that both the pseudo-sciences and the real sciences rest, in their
course of evolution, eventually upon reality. It is none the less
true, though, that this basic reality was seen in such form as to
render the reactions to it largely mistaken in the light of knowledge. A real thing at the bottom; the adjustments to it erratic.
Yet the irrational and erratic is subject to correction—indeed,
correction upon the basis of experience and under societal selection is enforced upon all viable societies.

There was no doubt in the primitive mind about the correctness
and expediency of its existing forms of reaction and adjustment,
that is, of its code of mores. Action was always taken under the
conviction, which no one dared to challenge even if it had come
into his head to do so, of the indisputable and final responsibility
of the spirits for the vicissitudes, and especially for the horizon-
filling ill chances, of human life. Hence the eagerness of men to
avail themselves of the only sure way—in fact, the only known
way—of avoiding calamity and attaining to well-being. Suppose
that men now believed that the stars ruled all life; would not
attention to the stars take precedence over all other human occupations? Suppose that men still believed that some philosopher's
stone could be found which would readily and cheaply transmute
baser substances into precious ones; would not the study of substances be pursued at a fever heat? Suppose that men still believed
in a fountain of perpetual youth; and then reflect upon the expeditions that would be fitted out, financed by rich men whose shadows
had begun to fall toward the east, and eagerly joined by everyone
who had caught sight of *sæva senectus* and was only theoretically
and in exalted moments persuaded that "the best is yet to be."

Suppose, on the other hand, that the ideas of star-rule had never existed; would such efforts have been devoted to the charting of the constellations and the observation of celestial movements? Would men have studied the metals and elements so assiduously and piled up accumulations of observations for science to build upon, if there had been nothing in it beyond the satisfaction of intellectual curiosity?

The chase after the philosopher's stone must have been exciting and engrossing, granted that men were convinced beyond peradventure that there was one and labored under no limitations of scepticism or criticism. You might get something big at any moment. It was a grand gamble with luck; and the race has always been fascinated by playing with chance. Even now, under accepted limits of what one can expect to get, the study of natural science is exciting. Fancy, then, how engrossing the pseudo-sciences must have been to the initiates. There was an element of enthusiasm about the study of them that drove minds to work.

It was the conviction that lay in what we now call superstition that put the emotional motive behind these studies, labors, and renunciations. Without the fear and the hope, but especially without the fear, the activity would not have been there; for it is emotion that is dynamic. And the emotion would not have been present save for the to us illusory major premise of the imaginary environment. It was "superstition" that made the sciences possible. Animism, daimonism, and fetishism were really not superstition,[197] however; they were the normal modes of thought at the time and place; they were the best that men could do under the circumstances to account for the chances of life. The ablest minds of the time could find no better. They were not, therefore, superstition in the derogatory sense but were the religion of their time. If it is pleasing or easier to call an undeveloped religion superstition, there should be no contempt in the term. In any case it had in it, right or wrong, the dynamic power, capable of inspiring mankind to effort and to action, which has brought us where we now are.

The only difference between superstition and science is that the latter consists of processes by which associations and se-

197 §199, above.

quences are critically examined over and over again until the
nexus is verified—not explained—and brought under generalizations which have been ratified by long experience and the consensus of highly trained men. All of human knowledge has come in
this way: first man has seized upon an aspect of a thing suggested
to him by the immediate effect of a phenomenon on his feelings,
for instance in dreams. The first desire was to be; the first struggle was for existence; the first exertion was by necessity. To die
was to fail. Then he began to correct his first apprehension. By
constant further correction he backed, as it were, into all he
knows; and he is doing it still. All that men have learned has been
won, so to speak, backwards. It began in error; then error was
corrected a bit at a time, for in the place of the old mistake there
was generally put a new error which was only a little better. It is
only since modern science came into general authority that the
race has been able to face forwards and to undertake free and
original investigation into truth. One thing we have learned, or
should have learned, is that all we hold to be true is infected by
error.

It is not always realized that primitive man had to experiment
or perish, even though the danger of experimentation was always
great; indeed it is even yet not infrequently at the risk of his life
that man discovers the laws of nature.[198] Further, though his so-
called superstition was based upon a misunderstanding of the
causes of natural phenomena that proved to be gross, it is impossible to contend that mere meditation along the lines of his
beliefs ever lessened that superstition by revealing the truth concerning those causes. Nothing but experience has been competent
to do that. Speculation has always been a brittle reed to lean upon
and the meditators and contemplators have had to depend, for
very life, as well as for the continued opportunity to spin out
their imaginings, upon the solid common sense of men of action
which, when organized and systematized, became science.

Any mental adjustment is subject to correction on the criterion
of experience. The essential is to have something positive there to
correct. It was the theory that men held, even though wrongly,
that forced them to observe, record, and experiment; to approach

[198] Jevons, *Relig.*, 17.

the facts at all, and then to study them. Correction of maladjustments of theory to fact was sure to come when the theory proved to be irreconcilable with the actual, concrete, economic conditions of living. Direct contact with these conditions molds the mores and the mores determine the philosophy of the age. Thus comes about a correction which is for the most part automatic and unconscious; yet the way is opened for rational correction or selection where tests show an unmistakable verdict.[199] And presently the old theory becomes a maladjustment, whether or not it is seen to be obsolete, and it fades away. The cocoon, though indispensable in its time, is no longer needed. Men now study the stars, even though there is nothing crucial to gain or lose by so doing. The imagination, availing itself of the poetic and dramatic means of expression, breaks new ground for the intellect, and phantasms hold the field until concepts are ready. Here is a parallel to the function of play in advance of new arts or on their flanks. Here are societal structures, again, that seem very different in character and tendency from the forms out of which they sprang and upon whose reason for existence or validity the nature of their origin has no bearing at all.

[199] Keller, *Soc. Evol.*, chs. III, IV, V.

CHAPTER XXXVIII

SHAMANISM

§308*. **The Black Art.** To attain a proper conception of shamanism it is necessary to start with some sort of distinction between "black art" and "white art" and the practitioners of each. Terminology here is very loose and confused; the literature shows an interchangeable use of priest, medicine-man, sorcerer, magician, wizard or witch, enchanter, necromancer, conjurer, soothsayer. Which of these belong to religion and which do not? The very confusion of terminology is evidence of the fact that no sharp lines of distinction have been drawn in popular usage between religion and allied beliefs and practices; and the absence of such discrimination suggests strongly that the differences have not been striking enough to evoke a sense of contrast. Perhaps if an effort were made to arrange the above list of terms in a series, "priest" would stand at one end, as being most evidently associated with religion, and "sorcerer" at the other. Over against religion might stand sorcery or witchcraft; or, to employ the other terminology, "white art" might be contrasted with "black art." In any case, it is necessary to fix upon some distinction of types and hold to it, for if that is once done, intermediate forms may be allowed to intermingle and overlap without producing a confusion in the general perspective.

Most of the entanglement of terminology is due to variation in viewpoint. Observers of primitive peoples, for example, who are unenlightened and therefore unsympathetic, indiscriminatingly apply the term sorcerer to functionaries upon whom the savages look with all the respect and reverence accorded by the observer to his priest. The only way to get at the truth is to strive to occupy the point of view of the peoples under observation; to do that is to clear up much of the confusion otherwise inevitable.

The two extreme types here distinguished are witchcraft and shamancraft, and we shall try to make the distinction between them and between their exponents by first setting witchcraft before us, as one extreme, and then devoting the rest of our space to shamanism. The attempt to draw fine distinctions where there is not much difference has no place in a general survey.

The difference between witchcraft and shamancraft is parallel to the distinction between magic and miracle; the former is performed by the aid of evil or unrecognized spirits, the latter by that of our own daimons. Quite often the former category of supernatural beings represents a set of older, superseded, or evicted gods—daimons which have become demons.[1] The wizard or witch came in Europe to be associated with the devil, as possessed by him or under compact with him and exercising, through his support, a private "black art" that lay outside the legitimate official activity of the recognized priest or shaman.[2] To have genuine witchcraft there must be an accepted religion and ritual or at least a recognized set of spirits, as a background for the irregular practice and the outlaw powers associated with wizardry and magic.

It follows from these facts that primitive peoples can display no such sharp distinction between witchcraft and religion as appeared, to take the extreme example, in the witch-persecutions of the Middle Ages. Primitive religions are too much alike and also too hospitable to each other's deities and practice to allow of a thoroughgoing intolerance. Yet there is, especially in Africa, a considerable amount of attention paid to extra-cult dealings with the supernatural. Cases have already appeared under the topic of magic. In the present connection we wish to treat less of the activities of witch and wizard than of their personality and characteristics and the way in which they are regarded by the communities in which they dwell.

Seligmann[3] speaks of certain Melanesians who, "as is only natural . . . make the strongest distinction between (1) the magic that produces disease and death, which may be called sorcery, (2) the specialized and the beneficent magic of departmental experts and (3) minor magic, a class of magical practices known to many of the laity, and consequently used by them in their daily life without special ceremony. It must be remembered that the practices included in the third category do not imply to the native mind that element of strangeness or disorder in the usual course of events, which Europeans invariably associate with the term magic." Miss Kingsley[4] says that in one way

[1] Lippert, *Kgchte.*, I, 124.   [2] §§303, above, and 309, below.
[3] *Melanesians*, 281.
[4] *W. Afr. Studies*, 157-158; *Travels W. Afr.*, 442-443, 445.

of looking at it, "there was no witchcraft whatever in West Africa, nothing having 'a true distinction' in the native mind from religion." Elsewhere, speaking of the crowding spirits, she writes regarding the native: "As they are the people who must be attended to, he develops a cult whereby they may be managed, used, and understood. This cult is what we call witchcraft." All these spirits can be "influenced, and made subservient to human wishes by proper incantations." Evidently that which has been called witchcraft in West Africa is as much the religion of the peoples there as any system to which we accord the term is to those who profess it.

African witch-meetings take place secretly, in the forest or distant from a village, and near midnight. Their signal-call is the hoot of an owl, their sacred bird. They profess to leave their bodies lying asleep in their huts, the spirit being that which, unhindered by walls or other physical obstacles, hastens to the meeting-place. They can pass with instant rapidity over the tree-tops. At the meetings they see, hear, and communicate with evil spirits and they eat the "heart-life" of some human being at their feasts. They must disperse at cock-crow and they fear the advent of the morning star which compels them to hurry back to their bodies; the light from the rising sun would thwart their plans and they would sicken.[5] If the Loango people suspect one of their number of witchcraft, they fall upon him, cut him up, and devour him. This fear of witches and the consequent persecution of them is a world-wide phenomenon "which is found among all the native tribes in Polynesia and especially in the remote islands of Melanesia, as well as among the Patagonians or northerly Indian tribes, and then throughout Africa." Revelation of the witch may come through a dream.[6]

"Witches in India are supposed to be able to remove all the bones out of a man's body, or to deposit a fish, ball of hair, or rags in his stomach. The town of Jeypore was said to be haunted by a ghost. It was described as a woman, who paraded the town at midnight in a state of nudity, and from her mouth proceeded flames of fire. She sucked the blood of any loose cattle she found about, and, in the same way, revenged herself on any man who had insulted her." Here we have the close relation between the witch and the ghost; witches are often, indeed, those who are possessed by some evil ghost. Again, a girl suffering from mental disease, and believed to be possessed of a devil, accused a man of having bewitched her. Her friends and relatives waylaid the man, held him down, and extracted his two front teeth with a hammer and pincers. In another case the front teeth were knocked loose with a big stone and a total of nine teeth extracted. Various expedients in the nature of divination are practised in order to ascertain the person guilty of witchcraft.[7] The Hindu widow is looked upon as possessing supernatural powers.[8] The same idea of blood-sucking sorcerers who prey on children and whom it is meritorious to kill, prevailed in native America.[9]

Egyptian magicians sometimes threatened to overturn the pillars that supported the sky if the gods did not obey their orders; they used the stock methods of magic by means of images of the victim, remnants of his food, or

5 Nassau, *Fetichism*, 123.

6 Bastian, *Deut. Exped.*, I, 62, note; II, 155, 165.

7 Thurston, *S. India*, 324, 325, 425-426.

8 Zachariae, in *Ztsft. Verein f. Vkde.*, XVIII, 177 ff.

9 Russell, in BAE, XXVI, 198; Brinton, *Nagualism*, 5.

things which had touched him. This magic was offset by other magic, but it could not defeat destiny.[10] The Bible[11] is full of references to witchcraft as an abhorrent practice, and Judaism was very severe against it.[12] "Turn ye not unto them that have familiar spirits nor unto the wizards; seek them not out, to be defiled by them."[13] To the teachers of the Talmud, who knew him only from popular accounts, Jesus was a magician.[14] From the New Testament point of view he was the opposite, for he cast out unclean spirits, and when the disciples were sent out the only commission mentioned is that of "authority over the unclean spirits." What they did was miracle, not magic or witchcraft.[15] Evidently, however, magic was the life-policy of the age. In the Arabian stories there are many more witches than wizards; the water-ordeal was used to test alleged witches.[16] Lehmann[17] undertakes to trace the witchcraft practices from the Chaldæans down to the Middle Ages—something that is beyond our province. The mediæval witch-processes represent a set of phenomena almost unbelievable in their exhibition of mental perversion and of terror-inspired cruelty.[18] People would believe any story against any man—the more monstrous the more easily—with consequences frightful to contemplate; and the accused would even admit the most ridiculous accusations, though he well knew that such admission meant present ruin and death. These mediæval beliefs have been taken up by Marlowe and Goethe in connection with the story of Faust.

The case of Jeanne d'Arc illustrates once again the relation between magic and miracle. "It was a matter of absolute necessity to the English to have her, not only to prevent her ransom by the French, but to neutralize her sorceries by condemning and executing her under the jurisdiction of the Church." There was much doubt about whether she was a woman or a phantasm. A later age sees much of autosuggestion in her mental states. To her defenders "the main difficulty was her wearing male attire and cutting her hair short—an offence which in the end proved to be the most tangible one to justify her condemnation."[19] It was the confusion or association of sorcery with heresy that produced the mediæval type of witchcraft—a type impossible under looser primitive conditions. That there were love-affairs between evil spirits and men became a cardinal belief, and with the entrance of the amorous element the way is opened for all sorts of obscenity of imagination.

Several other modern instances may serve to represent many. There are Scottish cases at the end of the sixteenth century where it is asserted that

[10] Maspero, *Hist. Anc.*, II, 17, 212.

[11] Exod., XXII, 18; Deut., XVIII, 10; I Sam., XV, 23; XXVIII, 7; II Kings, IX, 22; II Chron., XXXIII, 6; Micah, V, 12; Nahum, III, 4; Enoch, VII, 1; VIII, 1; IX, 7; XVI, 3; Tobit, VI, 4-8; VIII, 2; XI, 11; Gal., V, 20.

[12] Blau, *Zauberwesen*, 23, 24, 29; *Jew. Encyclop.*, XI, 358 *sub* "Simeon ben Shetah"; Lea, *Inquisition*, III, 396.

[13] Levit., XIX, 31.   [14] Blau, *Zauberwesen*, 29.

[15] Acts, X, 38; Mark, I, 27; III, 11; VI, 7, 17; Acts, V, 16; VIII, 7; XVI, 18; XIX, 15, 16.

[16] Lane, *Thousand Nights*, I, 70 (edit. 1841); Smith, *Relig. Sem.*, 179; Wellhausen, *Skizzen*, III, 143.

[17] *Overtro*, I, 77 ff.; Burr, *Lit. of Witchcraft*.

[18] See Sumner, "Witchcraft," in *Coll. Ess.*, I, ch. IV.

[19] Lea, *Inquisition*, III, 352, 357; Zürcher, *Jeanne d'Arc*.

women went to sea in a sieve; and where victims have their finger-nails torn off, their legs crushed in the "boot," and suffer other tortures on suspicion.[20] Capital punishment for witchcraft was abolished in England only in 1736; the *De Coverley Papers* portray the popular beliefs in Queen Anne's reign.[21] Under Ivan the Terrible Russia experienced a veritable orgy of witch-persecution.[22] The South Slavs think that in every witch "there lives a hellish spirit which leaves her at night and transforms itself into a fly, a butterfly (nightmoth), a hen, a turkey-cock, or a crow (daw)—preferably, however, into a toad. If the spirit has left the witch, her body lies as if wholly lifeless, and if one changes the position of the body so that the head comes to lie where the feet were, the witch remains forever dead; for the spirit, returning later, could no longer find the entrance into the body. . . . In Serbia and Bulgaria, however, there is not even any legend of witch-burning, which is a proof that the Turks did not allow any such usage to come into existence."[23] The Rumanians of the Bukowina are much concerned over the possible bewitchment of their cows. Twigs are placed so as to prevent witches from entering the yards. If a cow is really bewitched she can be restored, particularly by milking her through a stone with a natural perforation (which is supposed to be the result of a lightning stroke), or over a sickle, letting the milk strike the edge. There is a strong belief that people may be summoned and transported through the air by witchcraft—the witch blowing into the stove at midnight, and muttering a certain formula.[24]

More or less well authenticated cases of witchcraft-beliefs appear from time to time in the contemporary press.[25] The faith is by no means defunct. Its sudden reappearance at Salem is a commonplace of American history.

It is to be noted that the foreigner, especially if he belongs to a despised, aboriginal race, and is of a consequence more or less a creature of mystery, is likely to be feared as a sorcerer.[26] Two distinct tribes inhabited the villages in Port Moresby, New Guinea. "The Koitapus were undoubtedly the original inhabitants, and in colour are somewhat darker . . . and have narrower heads . . . but in their manners, customs, and language there is a marked difference. The Motu tribe consider themselves the superior of the two, though they live in great fear of the mysterious powers the Koitapus are said to possess, and were it not for this superstition the Motus would soon overrule and probably vanquish the other tribe. So strong is their superstitious belief in the powers of the Koitapus, that directly one of them falls ill, presents are immediately dispatched to a Koitapu man or woman with instructions to remove the evil influence that has brought the sickness or calamity. The weather also is supposed to be in the hands of the Koitapus," and the Motus have to pay if they want it changed.[27] Of the Finns, Lehmann[28] writes: "This folk stood in the whole

---

[20] Sharpe, *Witchcraft in Scotland,* 64, 70, 86.

[21] Ashton, *Queen Anne,* 93.   [22] Stern, *Russland,* 82-83, 97.

[23] Krauss, *Südslaven,* 112, 123.

[24] Kaindl, in *Globus,* XCII, 284, 285.

[25] Murray, *Witch-cult;* Sumner, "Witchcraft," in *Coll. Ess.,* I; Assoc. Press Repts. for March 31, 1895; April 7, 1895; July 11, 1897; Oct. 17, 1898; March 24, 1909; May 7, 1909; Jan. 20, 1922; Feb. 28, 1923; March 11, 1923.

[26] §257, above.

[27] Hardy and Elkington, *S. Seas,* 22, 23.

[28] *Overtro,* I, 99-100; Laing, *Heimskringla Saga,* I, 85.

North in great repute as magicians, and the most powerful and most feared
magicians and witches that appear in the sagas are almost always Finns."
Many of the Finns are red-headed.[29] In Norway the Lapps were believed to
know sorcery; there was a Blocksberg near Tromsø.[30]

In general, though the witch or wizard is the exponent of extra-
cult relations with the supernatural; though she or he performs
magic or black art, not miracles; yet the qualities that characterize the misprized witch are of the same category, at least in primitive times, as those demanded of the revered exponent of the
orthodox cult. In fact, not a few of the black-artists were orthodox enough so long as their religion stood firm; only when it was
superseded did their gods become devils and the priests of their
gods turn into mere magicians, sorcerers, wizards. Whatever is
learned, therefore, about the persons who attend upon the out-
cast gods or upon evil spirits is always in point when one comes
to study the shaman; and whatever is understood about magical
performances has a direct bearing upon the study of the sacerdotal function. Only ignorance can hold that all savage religion is
"mere magic" or superstitious sorcery, as if there could be no connection between phases of the same thing. The distinction between
religion and magic or between the priest and the sorcerer whereby
"our" beliefs are religion and "our" religious functionaries are
priests, whereas "their" beliefs are superstitions and magic and
"their" functionaries are black-artists, represents no more than
a case of ethnocentrism.

§309. The Shaman.[31] Man as a fetish has been considered
under the general topic of fetishism.[32] We come now to the ranking fetish-man: the medicine-man or shaman. Here is a functionary of such significance, of qualities so complex and of an activity
so varied, that he could not well be treated prior to the development of the chief aspects of daimonology. For he is the daimon-

[29] Topinard, *Anthropologie,* 340.   [30] Lund, *Norges Hist.,* I, 126.

[31] The best general sketch of the shaman is that of Maddox, *The Medicine
Man.* Other less comprehensive studies are: Bartels, *Medicin;* Wilken, "Sha-
manisme," in VG, III; Shchukin, *Shamanism* (Russ.); Radloff, *Schamanenthum;* Michailovski, *Shamanism* (Russ.); Bourke, "Med.-Men," in BAE, IX;
Krauss, "Schamanenthum der Jakuten," in *Mitth. Anthr. Gesell. Wien,* 1887-
1888; Hoffman, "Midē'wiwin," in BAE, VII.

[32] §§257 ff., above.

ologist in chief; and since daimonology is the great prosperity-policy of any primitive society, the shaman is the prime agency for prosperity. His arts penetrate into all the details of life where results are wanted and means are deficient or unknown. His importance can scarcely be exaggerated; and, because in his person and his function he collects together most of the strands of evolving religion which then, when he has worked them into new combinations, radiate forth into unforeseen possibilities, the review of his person and his function amounts to a sort of epitome of religion and also affords one of those cross-sectional summaries which we aim to include from time to time in our treatment of societal evolution.

The word "medicine-man" means "mystery-man."[33] It has no necessary relation to acquaintance with medicaments and drugs, except as the latter are means of dealing with the mystery of disease or other spiritual phenomena. The word "shaman," meaning "excited," "smitten," "inspired," was derived by the Russians from the Tungus form. The significance of its meaning is already apparent to one who is familiar with the idea of "possession."[34] Partially because it lends itself readily to the formation of adjectival and other variants, "shaman" has come into common usage. The essence of the matter is that the functionary in question is the mystery-man, the man who deals in the mysterious, inexplicable, occult, in that which can be accounted for only by eidolism and daimonism. In short, the shaman is the expert as respects the aleatory element and the imaginary environment.

Such being his capacity, it is evident that he outranks all merely earthly functionaries. The war-chief is something and so is the great hunter or artisan or counsellor or ruler; yet all these, since they have to do with the physical or social environment only, are less than the medicine-man, just as the calculable natural environment is less in the minds of men than is the incalculable environment of ghosts and spirits before which man, unaided, is so helpless. As the aleatory element enters into all phases of life,

---

33 §300, above.

34 Shchukin, *Shamanism* (Russ.), 25; §§246, 257, 258, above. By some the term is traced back to a Pali word meaning mendicant-monk, but this is uncertain. Wilken, in VG, III, 339, 358; Wilken, *Vkde.*, 564; Mallery, in BAE, IV, 190; Laufer, in AA, XIX, 362.

so does the function of the shaman; hence he is enabled to interfere in the business of any mere lay functionary while he suffers
little or no control within his own range. In practice there is no
such distinction between secular and sacerdotal as might be inferred from this contrast; the temporal power is likely to be
lodged in the same hands that hold the spiritual; the state and
church, if such high-sounding terms may be used of primitive
arrangements, are not separated but form a composite; generally,
indeed, the former is subjected to the latter. This fact witnesses
strongly to the pervasion by religion of the whole societal structure.

The word "sacerdotal" has been used in the foregoing paragraph; for the shaman is also the priest in the more special sense
of that word. The specific priestly function is correlative with
complicated ritual, not appearing in any pronounced form where
the ritual is simple.[35] It will be recalled that the rites must be
rightly performed or they have no effect except to irritate the
spirits. When, now, they are lengthy and complicated it is only
the specialist who can be sure of carrying them through without
error. It is the priest alone who knows the exact combination of
the lock which must be opened in order to secure well-being. There
is a terror of a spirit-horde "swarming around men with mysterious threats and reaching towards them out of the dark with thousands of terrible hands; hence the demand for intermediaries to
purify and absolve and to give protection against frightful
fancies."[36] Hence the added function of the fetish-man, the intermediary between the imaginary environment and man, the ranking agent of prosperity. Some writers attempt to distinguish between shaman and priest while others make no distinction. The
two functions run one into the other.

Among the Melanesians, "there is no priestly order, and no persons who can
properly be called priests. Any man can have access to some object of worship, and most men in fact do have it, either by discovery of their own or by
knowledge imparted to them by those who have before employed it. If the
object of worship, as in some sacrifices, is one common to the members of a
community, the man who knows how to approach that object is in a way their
priest and sacrifices for them all; but it is in respect of that particular function only that he has a sacred character; and it is very much by virtue of that
function that a man is a chief, and not at all because he is chief that he per-

35 §279, above; Rohde, *Psyche,* I, 44.   36 Rohde, *Psyche,* II, 79.

forms the sacrifice. . . . In close connexion with religious observances come the various practices of magic and witchcraft, of doctoring and weather-doctoring; for all is done by the aid of ghosts and spirits."[37] The shaman is the real specialist and is recognized as such, as compared with casual performers. "The opinions of the specialists have a traditional basis: they are clearly and categorically formulated and, in the eyes of the native, they represent the orthodox version of the belief."[38] Among the Shilluk of Africa there is a class of priests who form a sort of ecclesiastical caste. They have a share in all booty.[39]

Says Wilken[40] of the East Indian shamans: "They are consulted, in the moments when they are inspired, over all sorts of affairs; they are in the first instance magic-doctors but no real priests. Yet they are the leaders of ceremonies in several big sacrificial occasions and in so far they may be in a sense compared with priests, although their most notable function is to loan their bodies to the spirits so that the latter can reveal themselves to man and speak to him." "Priesthood in the proper sense of the term does not exist among the Sea Dyaks, for the Manang or medicine man does not fulfill the necessary conditions. Any man who is a chief, or who has been fortunate in life, or who is well up in ancient lore, and who knows the form of address to the deities, may perform the sacrificial function."[41] "It is generally believed that among the Indians of North America, the priests and the shamans, 'medicine men,' or doctors, are the same. This is not the case with the Pawnees." Among them the priest is entirely distinct from the doctor. "A priest might be a doctor as well, but not because he was a priest."[42]

It takes a pretty highly integrated religion to develop a real priesthood, such as that of the Jews after the exile.[43] In Greece those who served at the shrine at Delphi were merely the noblest Delphians, selected by lot;[44] here were military and subsequently political societies, in which religion was always subservient. Private shrines were served by their owners, the heads of families.[45] It was the Oriental religions that possessed the numerous and highly organized priesthood, even in Rome; and the Romans ridiculed the priestly tonsure and other distinguishing marks.[46] "The Eastern Slavonians seem to have built no regular temples, and—in striking contrast with the Lithuanians, not to speak of some of the Western Slavonians—they appear not to have acknowledged any regular class of priests. Their sacrifices were offered up under a tree—generally an oak—or beside running water, and the sacred rites were performed by the Elders, or heads of family communities."[47]

Strictly speaking, the priest was the intermediary between men and gods, who attended to the ritual of the cult. In the less developed religions, as there was no settled cult, the functions of the holy man were not much differentiated.

[37] Codrington, *Melanesians*, 127.
[38] Malinowski, in JAI, XLVI, 427.
[39] Ratzel, *Vkde.*, I, 520.
[40] *Vkde.*, 564.
[41] Roth, *Sarawak*, I, 190.
[42] Grinnell, *Folk Tales*, 350, 374.
[43] Lippert, *Kgchte.*, II, 319.
[44] Euripides, *Ion*, 420 ff.
[45] Otto, *Aegypten*, I, 133, 169.
[46] Dill, *Nero*, 580-583.
[47] Ralston, *Russ. People*, 83.

§310*. The Fetish-Man. The shaman has been referred to as the fetish-man. To be recognized as such, it will be recalled, he must exhibit certain qualities indicative of possession by a spirit. He is always an exceptional person. Evidences of possession may be physical, mental, or other;[48] and they may be natural or induced. In any case the fetish-man must be different from the ordinary; he must be abnormal and as such inexplicable except by reference to spirit-influence. Bodily deformation, albinism or peculiar skin-markings, polydactyly, dwarfism or gigantism, and other physical peculiarities have at various times and places led savages to single out those who exhibit them as possessed of a spirit. Abnormalities of the nervous system above all others rivet this sort of attention. Insanity at one end of the scale and genius at the other have been commonly interpreted as evidence of spirit-possession; and there are all grades of distinctive peculiarity between these two. Epilepsy, catalepsy (both meaning "seizure"—by a spirit), hysteria (from "hystera," womb), ecstasy ("putting out" of place), apoplexy (a crippling "stroke"), paroxysms, somnambulism, fainting-fits—all these mental abnormalities are taken to be significant of possession.[49] Mental quickness, cleverness, or cunning is likewise referred by those who cannot vie with it or understand its superiorities to inspiration or an indwelling genius.

Lehmann,[50] who goes very thoroughly into what he calls the psychology of magic, describes in some detail, and with pictorial illustration, the phenomena of hysteria major. Prior to the attack the person is melancholy and irritable. There follow darkness before the eyes, noises in the ears, stiffness of the body except for some incessantly moving limb, then collapse and relaxation of the muscles. The second period, called the "clown-phase," shows the assumption of strange positions, for instance the bending of the body backwards almost into a circle. Postures are taken that seem contrary to nature's laws; there is much movement, including struggles with imagined enemies, and hallucinations of all kinds appear. The third period, called the "expressive," continues the hallucinations and there are shouts and postures indicative of what the victim thinks he sees. He is generally terrified, loses all self-control, seems to be shaken by some immense power and flung exhausted; in an unnatural and unearthly voice and with supplicating gestures he begs to be spared; he is

48 §§257, 258, above.
49 Spencer, *Prin. Soc.*, I, ch. XI; consider the epileptic lama in Kipling's *Kim*.
50 *Overtro*, IV, 339 ff. This is a book of great suggestiveness and significance. It is translated into German, under the title *Aberglaube und Zauberei*.

often under the delusion of not being himself but another. He is attempting to escape from a Something that has a demon voice. Such hysterical subjects, "under delusion or diseased imagination, so lose their sense of being themselves as to talk with what they take to be the voice of the demon within them, answering in its name." In short, the attack is accompanied by unearthly, inexplicable phenomena sufficient to awe even the sophisticated mind—something the same phenomena as are shown in an attack of delirium tremens.

Dr. Bälz,[51] who had many years of experience as a physician in the Orient, has written a brief article upon possession and related conditions which deserves a synopsis. He has himself observed in East Asia cases of possession which are fully identical with those described in the Bible. The conviction that illnesses in general, but in particular those which are signalized by the apparent appearance of a new personality, are due to the influence of evil spirits, "is as old as mankind itself. It is found at all times, among all peoples, in all races, with savages and civilized." At the core of the phenomenon is suggestion, which is responsible for mystic religious ecstasy and for so-called stigmatism, whereby the wounds of Christ were visible upon the bodies of certain women. Predisposed individuals fall into a hypnotic or hysterical state "with limitation or exclusion of certain ranges of nerve and soul life and abnormal acuteness of others." The author has seen hysterical phenomena in Methodist revivals, as well as at the grave of a Buddhist saint. The witch-processes of the Middle Ages, with all their horrors, rested upon pathological suggestion, and masses were infected by it. Catholic and Protestant clergy have utilized the Chinese belief in a fox-demon in order to demonstrate the ability to exorcise it with the name of Christ. The native Christians in China publicly declare that they see in this devil-exorcism a means of propaganda for their faith. And a highly educated Christian missionary in China has written a thick book in which he demonstrates, or claims to demonstrate, that Satan and the fox-demon are identical; the proof of this he sees in the efficacy of the name of Christ upon the demon which, thus threatened, leaves the man. "I have had opportunity to study in Tokio cases of such possession and no doubt remains to me that it is always a matter of auto-suggestion." He has noticed also the intelligence and eloquence of the demon "which seem to stand far and away above those of the possessed subject." This he explains as follows: "With illnesses, especially those of the mind, abnormal amounts of energy flow into single areas, by a sort of short circuit abnormal unions between various courses of association are set up, and so are evoked the phenomena of force which we call convulsions, deliria, illusions, mania, etc. The most successful treatment is based, like the origin, on suggestion, which may be of a religious or other variety."

It is little wonder that simple savages should attribute abnormal mental states to possession by a spirit. The person sustaining an attack or, better, recurrent attacks of hysteria readily acquires the fetish-character and becomes eligible to the office of intermediary between men and the spirits. D'Alviella[52] says that "the still undistinguished functions of the diviner, sorcerer and

[51] "Besessenheit und verwandte Zustände," in *Pol.-Anth. Rev.*, X, 790-791.
[52] *Concep. God*, 95.

doctor, were assigned to individuals singled out for their performance by the command of more or less real information, or by
a predisposition to hysteria, which is easily taken for inspiration." Medical experience witnesses to nocturnal and waking hallucinations, especially by older persons and particularly by old
women[53]—visions of which only the enlightened are critical. Para-
noia, with illusions of grandeur or of persecution, is a phenomenon calculated to impose upon the ignorant; many of the prophets and founders of sects have shown it. When a person is once
set apart from the rest in some such manner, he becomes a fetish-
man and is no longer to be judged by ordinary standards; for
instance, if the common man's sneeze is interpreted as evidence of
perilous possession, that of the shaman indicates inspiration.[54]

We shall first illustrate the natural qualifications for the shamanistic function and then those which are induced, noting, however, that it is not always possible to distinguish just where the
natural ends and the artificial begins.

Spencer and Gillen[55] say that medicine-men and allied functionaries "are
characteristically the reverse of nervous or excitable in temperament"; but
they are disposed to lay stress upon the imaginative quality. "So far as we
could ascertain,—though of course the natives concerned do not admit, probably indeed they do not realize, that such is the case,—the simple fact is that
there are some individuals who are more highly gifted with imagination than
others. Possibly the performances which they originate may be due in the
first instance to dreams. What a savage experiences during a dream is just
as real to him as what he sees when he is awake." It seems that inequality
between men, whether unrecognized by primitive peoples or disavowed by
civilized nations, is perennially effective as constituting the element of variation indispensable to societal adjustment. The Australian shaman sucks stones,
nails, or wire out of his patients. "But the *koonki's* actual belief that he produced the articles by sucking is hard to understand. What one cannot grasp
is such an example as is given by . . . Howitt,[56] of a man who possessed these
powers and lost them. He then believed that he could no longer suck stones
out of another, and so he surrendered . . . a position which brought him
credit and went back to mediocrity."[57]

In certain of the islands, a magician is called a "runner-about while
asleep."[58] In New Guinea "all is still united in one hand, in that of the wiser,
more intelligent, more mentally superior; the conceptions of physician, priest,
philosopher, sorcerer, chief have not yet been differentiated and monopolized.

[53] Friedmann, *Wahnideen*, 249.   [54] Lippert, *Kgchte.*, II, 415.
[55] *Nat. Tr. Cent. Aust.*, 278, note; and *North. Tr. Cent. Aust.*, 450.
[56] *S.E. Aust.*, 409.
[57] Horne and Aiston, *Cent. Aust.*, 122.
[58] Jenness and Ballentyne, *D'Entrecasteaux*, 77.

Any adult who has the luck or understanding for it may be one of these or all of them at once."[59] Piebald people, who are in some regions looked upon with awe, are not a class apart but share village life in every respect.[60] There is, however, a strong belief in "second-sight." Some old woman, seats herself at the foot of a grave, at sundown on the day of burial, and "peers into the darkening shadows beneath the cocoa-nut palms. She remains perfectly still in this position, all the relatives of the deceased regarding her with deepest anxiety. Presently her looks become more intense, and lowering her head, but still gazing into the depths of the forest, she says in low and solemn tones, 'I see coming hither the spirit of Kalo Kava's (dead man's name) *tupuku* (grandfather). He says he is glad to welcome his grandson to his abode. I see now his father and his own little son also, who died in infancy.' She gradually becomes more excited, swaying her body from side to side, and waving her arms. 'Now they come,' she says, 'I can see all our forefathers in a fast-gathering crowd; they are coming closer and yet closer. Make room, make room for the spirits of our departed ancestors.' By this time she has worked herself into a frenzy; she throws herself on the ground, beating her head with her closed fist. The foam flies from her lips, her eyes become fixed, and she rolls over insensible."[61]

Again, "if it occurs to anyone that he wants to be a priest, he has only to announce that he frequently hears the voices of the ghosts and to resort often to the forest, ostensibly with the purpose of meeting them."[62] "The knowledge of future events is believed to be conveyed to the people by a spirit or a ghost speaking with the voice of a man, one of the wizards, who is himself unconscious while he speaks. In Florida [Island] the men of a village would be sitting in their . . . canoe-house, and discussing some undertaking, an expedition probably to attack some unsuspecting village. One among them, known to have his own *tindalo* ghost of prophecy, would sneeze and begin to shake, a sign that the *tindalo* had entered into him; his eyes would glare, his limbs twist, his whole body be convulsed, foam would burst from his lips; then a voice, not his own, would be heard in his throat, allowing or disapproving of what was proposed. Such a man used no means of bringing on the ghost; it came upon him, as he believed himself, at its own will, its *mana* overpowered him, and when it departed it left him quite exhausted. Still a man to whom this happened, when he had a reputation as a prophet, would be employed to assist in the council, and make that a branch of his profession as a wizard."[63] Such a person has no control over his own potency; "the wizard must be careful not to swallow any of his own spittle while muttering his charm, or he himself will be bewitched."[64]

In West Africa, "in old days an albino had only to name anywhere a person Aynfwa [the local god] wished for, and that person was forthwith killed."[65] "I asked such a man once many questions to which some of his answers were true, and found that like European fortune tellers his oracular replies were either vaguely framed or they showed that he was possessed of a very shrewd mind which from obvious circumstances could deduce facts which the ordinary individual could not surmise."[66] In South Africa, ventriloquism plays a good

[59] Hagen, *Papua's*, 276.
[61] Guise, in JAI, XXVIII, 210, 211.
[63] Codrington, *Melanesians*, 209.
[65] Kingsley, *Travels W. Afr.*, 513.

[60] Pratt, *New Guinea*, 172.
[62] Von Pfeil, *Südsee*, 138.
[64] Danks, in JAI, XXI, 350, note.
[66] Dundas, C., in JAI, XLIII, 530.

part in the shaman's business and those who have such powers enjoy increased reputation. "Their influence is strengthened by their keen powers of observation and a most retentive memory, especially for trifles. . . . They work themselves up into a state of great excitement before giving their revelation."[67] Of conditions in India it is said: "It is a little difficult to enter into the religious beliefs of other people, especially if they are in a different stage of civilization from our own, but the general idea of our riverain folk seems to be that the Deity is a busy person, and that his hall of audience is of limited capacity. Only a certain proportion of mankind can hope to attain to the presence of God; but when certain individuals have got there, they may have opportunities of representing the wishes and desires of other members of the human race. Thus, all human beings require an intervener between them and God."[68]

It is difficult to condense the remarkable treatment of shamanism given by Wilken[69] and, of course, impossible to reproduce his copious and apt illustration. He begins by citing the various beliefs about possession; the insane, for example, are favorites of the gods; he says that the Sanskrit term for idiot literally means that, and aligns with it the French *benêt,* "qui veut dire benit," and the saying that children and fools speak the truth. This attitude is marked in the East Indies; hysteria, epilepsy, catalepsy, lethargy, somnambulism, hypnotism, are all due to possession. The author mentions a man who had so much *embonpoint* that it suffocated him and he often fell into a cataleptic sleep; thus he attained the divinatory faculty and gave oracles. The shamans of Siberia take as neophytes children who are excitable and have a tendency to paroxysms, and women, "for not less natural reasons," are chosen for this function among a number of peoples. In Borneo there are those who fall into the so-called magnetic sleep where they develop anæsthesia; "their revelations they give in words and in writing, but in both cases commonly so unintelligibly that another person has to be present to clarify." Further reference to Wilken will appear as we go on.

In Paumotu, "one of the missionaries dug a well, the people laughing at him and saying he would never find water, or that if he did so it would be only sea water. When water was found and proved to be fresh they were much impressed and they afterwards called the missionary 'the man who gives water.' We are not told to what the people attributed this mysterious success, but there can be little doubt that they would credit the missionary with some supernatural power."[70]

Says Hill-Tout[71] of the medicine-man of British Columbia: "No one, I believe, is less a conscious humbug than the average Indian 'Doctor,' though it has been common to regard him as such. His belief in the efficacy of his own practices and in the power of his nagual [personal spirit] to effect the cures he undertakes, is as sincere as the belief of his more sophisticated brother in his trained professional skill and in his powerful drugs." The author cites the case of an ex-shaman: "touching this and other abnormal powers he formerly possessed, he said the reason that he no longer possessed them was partly because he had given up 'exercising' himself since his conversion to

[67] Garbutt, in JAI, XXXIX, 534, 535, 537.
[68] O'Brien, in JAI, XLI, 511.
[69] In VG, III, 337, 338; see also Kruijt, *Animisme in den Indischen Archipel.*
[70] Williamson, *Cent. Polyn.,* III, 333.   [71] In JAI, XXXV, 144–145.

Christianity, but more particularly because his present wife, who had been the widow of another man, had been careless about carrying out the purificatory ceremonies after the decease of her former husband, who had been a white man. She had also married him within a few months of her first husband's death. This, which is contrary to the mortuary regulations, and her 'bad medicine' consequent upon her non-purification from the death defilement, robbed him of his mystery powers. . . . Though 'Captain Paul' has outwardly long given up the practices of his forefathers, and is one of the chief catechists of his Church, his belief in *snam* powers is at bottom as firm and real as ever it was. A little incident he related to me regarding the source or origin of the name of one of his grandchildren makes this very clear." The girl was given a name in accord with ancient Indian custom, "in spite of the fact that she possessed already a baptismal name; though few, if any, outside the immediate family circle, besides myself, know of it or its origin and significance." The author seems to believe that this man was an exceptional person in the matter of "the abnormal sight powers he claimed to have formerly possessed. I do not, for my part, doubt his possession of them for a moment; the known phenomena of hypnotism make them quite possible, and fully justify one in holding such a belief. That some of the old Indians had power to exalt their senses and faculties by invocation of their *snam* is quite clear, I think, from the feats they frequently attempted and accomplished." In all these cases we verge somewhat upon the next topic, of induced possession; still there appears to be in the nature of the shaman a basis to start with; and it is that which we are trying to illustrate in the present instance.

Among the Omahas it is believed that certain persons understand the talk of children: "if a little child cries unceasingly, as if it were in pain, one of these people is sent to the child to find out what ails him."[72] It is also not an uncommon notion among the Indians that a man under superhuman influences believes and speaks the reverse of the truth.[73] Indian myth conceives of a young magician so gifted, though blind, that his mother could not determine whether he saw all things by clairvoyance or natural vision.[74] Among the Maricopa the medicine-men become such through the influence of dreams, which begin in their childhood to forecast their destiny. A medicine-man is believed to be endowed with his powers from birth, having lived in another world before this and there attained his qualifications as healer.[75] Many try to see visions but by no means all succeed; those who do become shamans.[76] The test of the medicine-man, where he appears, is supernatural endowment.[77] In one Brazilian tribe the person who can hold out the longest in their palm-wine drinking-bouts becomes a medicine-man.[78] The members of the medicine-societies in South America are not frauds; "they are, like so many deceivers, deceived by their own superstitions and fancy themselves in the immediate power of dark powers, hostile to them themselves." In one case, where a peculiar skin-disease was not uncommon, "the magician and his wife were on many parts of their bodies black as Moors, on others lighter than I."[79]

---

[72] Fletcher, in *Globus*, LXXIII, 254. [73] Mallery, in BAE, X, 466.
[74] Leland and Prince, *Kulóskap*, 307.
[75] Hrdlička, in BAE, XXXIV, 228; Russell, in BAE, XXVI, 253-254.
[76] Dixon, in AA, X, 216. [77] Wickham, quoted in JAI, XXIV, 207.
[78] Von den Steinen, *Zent. Bras.*, 491.
[79] Von Martius, *Beiträge*, I, 77, 419; Koch-Grünberg, in *Globus*, XC, 122.

To enforce the fact that special abilities confer the fetish-quality, there should be recalled the special case of the smith;[80] for he was not alone one of the very earliest specialists in the industrial organization but also one of the first of mystery-men.

Hobley[81] has collected a number of Bantu cases where this artisan, according to the local belief, possesses magical powers. Even "a medicine man has no power over a smith's magic." It is noteworthy that "iron has always played a great part in ancient magic, and continues to do so in many parts of the world," while the processes of smithery have been invested with an atmosphere of mystery. These African smiths have formed a gild which is a sort of medicine-society. "The smiths of Agades are very skilful; they mix in all political situations, rank as physicians and magicians, and are the strongest pillars of Islam."[82] In West Africa, "when the embers are red and the metal is red, it is then tabu for a blacksmith to open his mouth." He greets people then by two little blows on his anvil. As for cleverness, "there is not a man of the forest tribes who will compete with a blacksmith for that distinction; it is agreed that they are as clever as they claim to be, and there is an understood element of divinity in their skill."[83] Blacksmiths attend the black shamans of the Buryats; "the smith makes out of iron a model of a man, then smashes it with his hammer—and the man whom the model represented dies shortly thereafter."[84] In Borneo those who stand under the special protection of spirits are smiths and artists in the carving of hartshorn.[85] Dwarfs, we are told, "are as good physicians as smiths"; this was in ancient Scandinavia, where the smith enjoyed consistent repute as a magician.[86]

The shamans are marked out from the common herd not only by personal peculiarities but also by special practices and taboos which surround them with an atmosphere of aloofness and mystery. Tibetan lamas, for instance, may take tobacco only in the form of snuff;[87] Indian shamans in Guiana may not eat the flesh of the larger animals and must confine themselves to those original to Guiana, refraining carefully from the novel importations of Europeans.[88] The old is holy and the holy man must cleave to it. The taboos that surrounded the Flamen Dialis, or priest of Jupiter, at Rome, and his wife as well, were incredibly arbitrary and oppressive.[89] And to such renunciations were added, for the sake of aloof holiness, the self-disciplinary and ascetic practices

80 §72, above; Lippert, *Kgchte.*, II, 215, 216, 217, 221, 410.
81 *Bantu Beliefs*, 167 ff.   82 Goldstein, in *Globus*, XCII, 187.
83 Mackenzie, in *Atl. Mo.*, CXXXI, 489.
84 Melnikow, in *Globus*, LXXV, 133.   85 Nieuwenhuis, *Borneo*, II, 229.
86 Gröndal, in *Annaler*, 1863, 31.   87 Rockhill, *Tibet*, 709.
88 Schomburgk, *Brit.-Guiana*, I, 173.
89 Frazer, *Golden Bough*, I, 117-118.

which have been treated by themselves elsewhere in this book.[90] Priests are often not allowed to marry, though the opposite is more common; cases where marriage is a precondition are very rare.[91] The fetish-man is not seldom a woman; in fact, the sex-qualities of woman[92] are thought by some to make her more susceptible than man to spiritual influences.

Lehmann[93] remarks that "women have in general a lighter sleep than men and they also dream much more. Clearness of dreams is greatest with women" and "the oftener one dreams the more easily are dreams remembered." He finds normal spontaneous hallucinations much more frequent in women; they have convulsions in hysteria four times as frequently as do men. They are the best mediums and crystal-gazers. We still speak of a person being "nervous as a witch." Crawley,[94] commenting upon the fact that "Patagonian sorcerers who are chosen from children who have St. Vitus dance, go in women's clothes," writes: "Doubtless the idea is to assume the emotional peculiarities of women so essential to the priest. To the savage mind, the donning of another's dress is more than a token of the new position: it completes identity by communicating the qualities of the original owner."

However this may be, there is no doubt that the medicine-woman or shamaness exists, though not in such numbers as her male counterpart. The immediately following cases are about all which we have encountered as compared with almost innumerable instances of the male functionary. It may be said that women are more likely to be witches where men are wizards than they are to vie with men in the regular shamanship. This may be due in part to their "uncleanness."[95] Further, they are more likely to be used, in a subsidiary capacity, as mediums, than to direct shamanistic operations.

A shamaness is reported in South Africa who practised the usual hocus-pocus over the sick.[96] In West Africa the priestesses do not marry or in any way become the property of a man, but they are licentious to a degree.[97] On the Gold Coast maidens are necessary assistants to the priests and have a priestly character.[98] In East Central Africa priestesses, in consequence of revelations, can impose impossible tasks on men or order human sacrifices, and no one will dare oppose. Prophetesses have dreams and visions revealing the will of ancestral spirits. Their oracles are generally delivered in a sort of hysterical frenzy. A prophetess "throws herself on the ground and remains in a state of catalepsy for some time, while the awe-stricken villagers gather

[90] §§280-282, above.
[91] Niemann, in *Bijd.*, XLV, 331.
[92] §58, above.
[93] *Overtro*, IV, 139, 325 ff.
[94] §282, above; in JAI, XXIV, 223, note.
[95] §388, below.
[96] Decle, in JAI, XXIII, 421.
[97] Ellis, *Tshi*, 121.
[98] Ratzel, *Vkde.*, I, 609.

around her, waiting for revelations. At last she speaks and her words are accepted unquestioned as the oracles of God, for she has seen the ancestors face to face."[99] One of the tribes of Uganda had no professional medicine-men but only woman-doctors.[100] In Northeast Africa old women who claim to be versed in magic are addressed as men and are designated by the masculine article.[101] A female marabout's grave was pointed out in South Tunis.[102] Amongst the Tungus beyond Lake Baikal, either men or women, married or single, may be shamans. Old women exercised shamanistic functions in Kamchatka, but among the Buryats no women dared touch the sacred robe in which a shaman was buried.[103] In Korea the whole class of shamans was spoken of as female; they wore woman's clothing, so strongly did the female idea prevail.[104] In Persia there was a sort of ascetic order of women corresponding to the *fakirs* among the men.[105] Among the Kurds, all the medical knowledge was in the hands of female hereditary *hakims*.[106]

In the East Indies shamans are of both sexes but more commonly female. The shamanesses are mostly public women and are highly honored, an injury to one of them being visited with double penalty.[107] Male shamans often live and dress as women; where the office is not open to women, some of the shamans "pretend to be women, or rather dress as such and like to be treated as females," and are called "pseudo-women." They are often impotent, miserable creatures, with dull eyes and harsh voice, pale and thin. They talk in the usual Delphic and disconnected manner. It is to be noted that change of clothing between the sexes is one of the forms of disguise in mourning.[108] Especially do the Dyaks of Borneo affect the shamaness, who are sometimes supposed to be sex-associates of the spirits. They thus attain to possession and can effect cures; and also stir the imagination of the men and urge them to wars and commercial undertakings which have important consequences. It never occurs to anyone to reproach them for the licentious lives they lead. Certain men dress like these shamanesses and lead an even less respectable life; they may be married to a "husband." "The femininity of the deities of these *manangs* is worth considering in regard to a question much discussed, namely, whether the original *manangs* were all women."[109] In Celebes old women read the omens from cries of birds and the condition of pigs' livers, and give orders. Women who heal disease may not marry.[110]

Among the Aleuts a graceful boy may be dressed as a girl and brought up among girls, later to become an *angakok* (shaman). Then the finest girls are given him to be educated and initiated and if they are clever they become

[99] Macdonald, in JAI, XXII, 105.   [100] Johnston, *Uganda*, II, 750.
[101] Paulitschke, *Nordost-Afr.*, II, 95.   [102] Bruun, *Huleboerne*, 65.
[103] Michailovski, *Shamanism*, 57, 89, 93.
[104] Bishop, *Korea*, 409.
[105] Jackson, *Persia*, I, 22 (in *Amer. Orient. Soc., Section for Hist. Study of Relig.*, VII).
[106] Bartels, *Medicin*, 52, 53; Ellis, *Man and Woman*, 6, note.
[107] Wilken, *Vkde.*, 563 ff.; Wilken, in VG, III, 353 ff.; 375, note 151.
[108] §224, of *Case-Book*.
[109] Ratzel, *Vkde.*, II, 486; Perelaer, *Dajaks*, 32, 35; Schwaner, *Borneo*, I, 186; Roth, *Sarawak*, II, clxxv; Bock, *Borneo*, 104; Gomes, *Sea Dyaks*, 180; Morris, in *Amer. Orient. Soc., Section for Hist. Study of Relig.*, VII, 40-41.
[110] Riedel, in *Bijd.*, XXXV, 83.

prophetesses and shamanesses.[111] A shamaness of the Apache, called Pretty-mouth, "seems to have no better claim to her position than that she escaped from a lightning stroke and from the bites of a mountain lion, which seized her one night but did not kill her."[112] Among the Bella-Coola Indians women are sometimes shamans.[113] Among some California tribes the shamaness is consecrated through a rigorous ordeal, involving nine days of fasting. "During the daytime the dance is intermitted, but the woman is straitly guarded throughout the whole period of consecration, lest the flesh should prevail over the spirit, and her ravenous hunger should cause her to profane the ceremony and invoke the wrath of the spirits by secretly eating."[114] Female shamans are found, exceptionally, in Brazil.[115]

In Egypt women more than men enjoy the powers of magic, having more acute senses and greater power in the art of calling or driving away the invisible ones. They held high priestly positions in the Hellenistic period.[116] Homer[117] shows but a single priestess among few priests. Prophecy and divination, among the ancient Germans, were always practised by women, who were supposed to possess a certain inherent prophetic power. In the North the prophetesses seem to have been largely of Lappish or Finnish nationality; and the Norns embody the same tradition of female powers. Woman's place was to stay at home, warn of doom, wait for return, and weep over the slain. They had oracle-dreams, could read and write runes and work magic by drink from a cup on which runes were written.[118] In hydromancy, girls, boys, and pregnant women were the ones who looked into the moved waters, especially if the experimenter himself could see nothing.[119] The pagan cult of the Slavs was supervised by old women of dignity.[120]

The foregoing cases illustrate various inexplicable peculiarities of person and sex which set off the possessed or inspired person from the rest and confer on him or her the fetish-quality. Where the quality is hereditary, we encounter a fetish-stock; in Palermo there were families whose members, as such, were believed to be able to cure this or that disease.[121]

§311*. Induced Possession. Already some of the cases have verged toward the category of what might be called artificial possession. Possession is evidently an asset if it elevates one into the

[111] Reclus, *Prim. Folk*, 68.   [112] Bourke, in BAE, IX, 456.
[113] Von Goeken, in *Mitth. Berl. Mus.*, 1885, 185.
[114] Powers, in *Contrib. N. Amer. Ethnol.*, III, 67, 68.
[115] Von Martius, *Beiträge*, I, 78, 79.
[116] Maspero, *Hist. Anc.*, II, 271-272; Otto, *Aegypten*, I, 93.
[117] *Iliad*, VI, 269 ff.
[118] Chadwick, in *Folk-Lore*, XI, 273-274; 298-299; Grimm, *Teut. Myth.*, III, 1038-1039; IV, 1396; Tacitus, *Germ.*, ch. VIII; Cæsar, *Bell. Gall.*, I, 50; Strabo, *Geog.*, VII, 294; Uhland, *Dichtung und Sage*, 314.
[119] Lehmann, *Overtro*, II, 144.   [120] Krauss, *Südslaven*, 111.
[121] Pitre, in *Am Ur-Quell*, I, 90, 91.

status of intermediary between the spirit-environment and human life; and the aspirant to spiritual powers does not have to wait for accidental proofs of his quality, for it is possible by artificial means to attain to the peculiarities of appearance, and especially to the mental states, characteristic of possession. The adventitious aids to a striking individuality, in the shape of grotesque and imposing dress, masks, and other paraphernalia, not to mention professional manner, which still clings to both priest and doctor, may be dismissed with a single graphic illustration; their variety has been limited only by the bounds of a rich inventiveness.

"The medicine man of the Black Feet Indian tribes, when exercising this art upon a sick person, arrayed himself in the most absurd costume which the mind of man ever conceived. For a coat he wore the skin of a yellow bear. The skin of the head was formed into a mask, which entirely hid the features of the enchanter. On his person in addition to the skin of the yellow bear—an article exceedingly rare and, therefore, in itself a powerful medicine—were the skins of various wild animals which were also anomalies or deformities and hence, in the savage estimation, medicine. There were also skins of snakes, frogs, field mice, snails, the beaks and tails of birds, hoofs of deer, goats, and antelopes, in a word, the odds and ends, the fag ends and tips, of everything that swims, flies, or runs. In one hand he held a magic wand, in the other a fearful rattle which contained the arcana of his order. On coming into the lodge where a sick man lay, he shook the rattle and brandished the magic wand, to the clatter, din, and discord of which he added wild startling jumps and Indian yells, and the horrid and appalling grunts, growls and snarls of the grizzly bear, calling on the bad daimon to leave the patient. It was necessary to see the dress of that medicine man before a person could form a just conception of his frightful appearance."[122]

Such external and crude accessories and other deliberately adopted singularities, however, or even the tricks with which the uninitiated were imposed upon, counted for relatively little in establishing the repute of a shaman compared with manifest relations with the spirit-world. Despite the fact that the durability of his fame depended, in the long run, upon the success of his performances in curing disease, in rain-making, in prophecy, and in other daimonological functions, he could never even get a start in the profession unless he could demonstrate clear evidence of possession; nor was it possible for many aspirants to exhibit recurrently, or even a single time, the phenomena of physical or mental

[122] Catlin, *N.A. Ind.*, I, 39-40 (Donaldson, "Catlin Gallery," in *Smithson. Rep.*, 1885, pt. II, 419), condensed in Maddox, *Med. Man*, 101-102. The portrait in question is reproduced by both Catlin and Donaldson.

peculiarity which were taken to be proof positive of the indwelling of a spirit. It was chiefly the power to operate upon one's own mental states, and those of others, by which the fetish-quality was confirmed.

The shaman had learned means of inducing the phenomena characteristic of possession. He kept them secret from the common herd, but saw to it that they were not lost to the elect. By gyrations he produced in himself a vertigo and frenzy far enough from normal to impose awe and fear; the "whirling dervish" has had many an ethnographical counterpart. And there were discovered by a series of shamans a variety of poisons, ranging from alcohol and nicotine to hashish and the juice of the deadly fly-mushroom (*amanita muscaria*), which, taken in proper quantities, induced intoxication or mental states indistinguishable to simple minds from mania, hysteria, catalepsy, and the other evidences of possession listed above. Further, there can be no doubt that the shaman long ago practised hypnotism and autohypnotism and that both the hypnotizer and the hypnotized were regarded as possessed. If a trance did not come naturally it could be produced. The technique included, besides point-gazing, crystal-gazing, "meditation," and other stupefying or intensifying practices,[123] also the use of drugs, rhythmic and monotonous motions, strokings, and sounds, and the "mortification of the flesh" by fasting, flagellation, and other forms of self-torture. By such means the nervous system was stimulated, undernourished, jangled, or otherwise thrown out of normal; and there resulted visions and other illusory mental phenomena and exhibitions of unhinged reason, awe-inspiring and incomprehensible, which could not fail to be ascribed, because they were both extraordinary and inexplicable, to spiritual possession. The pathological aspects of such exhibitions have been set forth by Lehmann;[124] we cannot undertake to rehearse them here. However, since the candidate had to go through a severe strain, to which he must at length give way physically in order to prove himself inspired, it is not so

[123] An Associated Press report states that a British aviator, becoming hypnotized by the revolving propeller of an airplane, walked slowly into it and was killed. N. Y. *Times,* April 5, 1923.

[124] *Overtro,* IV, 226 ff., 308 ff.; Lippert, *Kgchte.,* II, 410 ff.; Preuss, in *Globus,* LXXXVII, 398.

strange that successful novices were often those of weak or abnormal constitution. An author,[125] who is also a physician, writes as follows: "In view of the fact that candidates for the position of shaman have to undergo fasting and hyper-excitement of the nervous system in order to arrive at hysteria or states bordering on the hypnotic, it is evident that a person with an irritable nervous system is peculiarly fitted to be a shaman. Neurotic, melancholic, and epileptic subjects are the best candidates."

It is essential to realize that the shaman, in cases of this order, is as little able to explain his own actions and states as is anyone else. He is convinced of his own fetishistic quality in precisely the same way in which others are convinced; if they are dupes, so is he. His view of his own performances is the same as theirs, namely, that he is possessed by a spirit which has entered into and assumed control of him so that what he does is not of himself and by his own will but involuntary and spiritually directed. If, as a piece of foolery, one person accidentally, by making the traditional passes and droning the characteristic formulas, manages to hypnotize another, how is he to explain his performance? Such things have happened; and when the successful but frightened "mesmerist" has had to call in expert aid in order to get his subject restored to normal, he has sworn off further experimentation altogether. Not so the shaman, for he feels that his powers clearly indicate possession. He is "inspired" and can look forward to an honored and prosperous future. Many self-styled mouth-pieces of revelation, in more sophisticated times, have been equally honest in their persuasions concerning their own qualities. While it is true that the shaman sometimes becomes a mere trickster and deliberately imposes upon the ignorant, yet one who conceives charlatanry to be the rule has altogether missed the truth and failed to apprehend the essential candor of primitive peoples in dealing not only with the environment of things and of men but with themselves.

In reviewing the methods employed in order to attain possession or inspiration, it should be noted that though they aim at the production of a state of illusion—at the unstabilizing of the central nervous system through the introduction of toxic sub-

[125] Bartels, *Medicin*, 79.

stances into the body, through bodily undernourishment and torture, or otherwise—yet that no one regards the states thus produced as unfitting the mind for the discharge of its functions. Quite the reverse; for it is precisely while in such a condition that the intellect is conceived to transcend its ordinary powers because it is under spiritual control. The shamans have learned what substances or actions will throw their own minds or those of others into such states; but they do not know why. The whole matter is inexplicable and aleatory. No explanation is possible except that the various means of inducing possession have fetish in them. The spirit-hypothesis is everywhere in evidence and of rational criticism there is a vanishing minimum.

An Australian boy who can see the ghost of his mother sitting by her grave is taken in hand by the medicine-man and trained into the profession. He is a susceptible, suggestible subject. Sleeping on a grave is important for the would-be shaman, for his sensitive soul thereby attains to strange pains and thrills. "During that awful sleep the spirit of the deceased would visit him, seize him by the throat, and opening him, take out his bowels, which he replaced, and the wound closed up."[126] In the Torres Strait Islands, "a kind of exhilarated madness or frenzy was undoubtedly induced in the sorcery men by partaking of the decomposing flesh and oil of human corpses."[127] Stoll[128] finds autosuggestion at the bottom of possession by the shaman and the mediæval nuns.

The "smellers-out" of the Zulus "study a year or two in the school of African prophets, clothe themselves with the skins of serpents and wild beasts, attach to their heads bladders of birds and small animals, tie about their neck dried roots, lions' and panthers' claws, crocodiles' teeth, etc., also fasten a leopard's skin about the loins, frequenting desert places, talking to the moon until they become semilunatics."[129] Liberian shamans are supposed to have extraordinary powers, so that they can, for example, uproot trees. This state is often arrived at by hypnotism or by the use of certain plants. A ghost, the soul of a relative or ancestor, is said to inhabit and control such a person.[130] In Uganda there are "sorcerers who use their knowledge of poisons, their unconscious mesmeric powers, and their charlatanry for bad purposes; and the real medicine men or women who apply a knowledge of drugs and therapeutics to the healing of diseases." There is a lingering suspicion that the sorcerer is a corpse-eater, either from a morbid taste or the desire to invest himself with magical powers. Again, the shaman "has some power of self-hypnotism, and undoubtedly exercises a mesmeric influence over weak-minded people."[131] "Sakai and Jakun medicine-men . . . practise abstinence in order to acquire the power of seeing visions."[132]

[126] Howitt, *S.E. Aust.*, 404, 415. [127] Haddon, in JAI, XIX, 312.
[128] *Suggestion*, 105. [129] Tyler, in *Illust. Afr.*, Dec., 1895.
[130] Frobenius, *Masken*, 126. [131] Johnston, *Uganda*, II, 578, 676.
[132] Skeat and Blagden, *Malay Penin.*, II, 200.

Wilken[133] says that the medium between spirit and mortal must be in a condition to receive the former into his body. This is done by much magical music and the singing of magical songs, by burning incense, and by intoxicating drinks, whereby the shaman's soul leaves his body and makes room for the possessing spirit. The entrance of the latter is announced by loss of sense or ecstasy, paroxysms, hysteria, the hypnotic state, or other phenomena of that order. It seems to be necessary that the shaman's soul shall leave his body. He stares at an object or point, he listens to monotonous rhythm, he snuffs incense or smoke, he dances or repeats monotonous movements—that is, all the senses are operated upon to acquire the proper state. Then the soul takes flight and the daimon possesses the body, or the soul goes off to mingle with the denizens of the spirit-world in order to get revelations as to the cause of illness, the complexion of the future, or other desirable information. The Delphic Pythia, to use an "energetic metaphor," was supposed to be pregnant of the god. The word for shaman may mean "word," since he is supposed to speak the word of the spirits, or "he in whom the spirit comes," "he against whom the spirit leans." Formerly East Indian chiefs had to show possession of some sort, which reveals the close connection between the priesthood and the chieftainship. To get possession speedily, often the head is covered, with incense burning beneath the covering, and the answers of the possessed are in a peculiar speech, called the tongue of the descending spirit, full of circumlocution and personification of objects by their qualities. Wilken gives many pages of illustration of the peculiar behavior of the possessed: the strong twitching of the body, the turning of the head on the shoulders in an abnormal manner, so that it looks as if it must come off; the voice, now high, now low, now whinnying like a horse. The possessed person commonly knows or claims to know nothing of what has happened.

The preparations for possession include many details: the body is covered with oil which the spirits like; rice-grains are strewn upon it; the spirits are addressed in a soft tone in a tongue not understood; the medium is incessantly fanned by a helper, who speaks to her in a singing tone when recalling her from her madness. In one case Malay words were spoken with the intonation of the Sakai aborigines, and Sakai words and phrases unintelligible to the Malays were uttered. The mediums are largely women, and if they are men, they live and dress like women. The operations are accompanied by "deafening noises, sufficient to kill a person in ordinary health," and this at the side of the bed of illness; and the operator grimaces fearfully and jumps about so violently as to shake the house.

It is to be noted that the novice must be able to get into a state of possession and break involuntarily into violent dancing or he is rejected, and that the excesses practised lead to poor health and an early death. Some of the successful candidates have been sickly persons of a neuropathic character, "women whose menses are accompanied with lethargic sleep for several days."

Wilken's summary of his extended treatment lays stress on intoxication and sense-derangement. He notes that it is commoner to have the spirit enter the shaman than that his own spirit should merely free itself and seek revelation in the spirit-world. There is no gild of medicine-men, with three tribal exceptions in which there are colleges and hierarchies. The shamans are natural and spontaneous, or trained and artificial. They treat illness by spitting on the

[133] In VG, III, 326, 332, 336 ff., 341 ff.; summary begins on 374.

location of pain, kneading and pinching, removing objects such as fish-bones by sucking, throwing their own spirits into the patient, driving out the illness into some house or vehicle. In some cases they are real priests or religious officials. The dance is regarded less as a means of inducing ecstasy than as an expression of ecstasy, the presence of the spirit. The female shamans are often professional dancers; in their profession there is no ecstasy; they tend to become prostitutes and the men who imitate them practise sex-vices.

In conclusion the question is raised as to how far the shaman is a charlatan, and the answer is that there is little conscious deception practised. The lapse of memory is normal in such states as the shaman attains by his fasting and intoxication; in the seventeenth century hysterico-epileptics and somnambulists regarded themselves as possessed because they lost all sense of individuality. The hallucinations under ecstasy are spontaneous; suggestion in such states can make people actually seem to see spirits. The shaman is serious enough about himself and his powers. Further, in such states the senses and powers actually become super-normal and there is undoubted anæsthesia, with cessation of the blood-flow from the anæsthetized parts. Anæsthesia is a characteristic of hystero-epilepsy; and there is a similar phenomenon in ecstasy and somnambulism. There is very little, if any, pretended ecstasy. If the mediums are weak and neurotic women, there is every likelihood that they can be upset by the performances they go through. Some tribes believe the shaman's gifts are hereditary, and are probably correct, so far as the susceptible disposition and the unbalanced nervous system go. The conclusion is, therefore, that possession is real and not simulated. Wilken's editor adds that shamans and mediums are now of the same old sort, but that there is a tendency to lend a scientific tinge to their performances. He lists a rather full bibliography of shamanism. This treatment of Wilken's is located here because so many of its cases, not elsewhere duplicated, are derived from the Indian Archipelago; he cites many recondite Dutch authorities besides calling upon his own extended store of personal experience.

To enter upon this subject as it is exhibited in China would carry us into a maze of examples illustrative of the various aspects brought out in our text and cases.[134]

Dixon[135] considers the American medicine-man from several angles. Women are widely permitted to discharge the office. The indications of such destiny are dreams, visions, and extraordinary experiences, and the sources of power are spirits of various kinds. Control of this power is gained by fasting and solitude, bathing, purgation, offerings, and sacrifice; the use of drugs is rather rare. The shaman may be self-developed or taught by an older shaman. Charms, tricks, and legerdemain are employed and there is a special jargon spoken by the medicine-men.[136] According to Mooney[137] the most important features of the Ghost Dance and the secret of the trances is hypnotism. "It has been hastily assumed that hypnotic knowledge and ability belong only to overripe civilization, such as that of India and ancient Egypt, or to the most modern period of scientific observation. The fact is, however, that practical knowledge, if not understanding, of such things belongs to people who live

---

[134] Harvey, *Chinese Animism*, ch. IV, presents a selection from this wealth of material.

[135] In *Jr. Amer. Folklore*, XXI, 1-12.

[136] Dellenbaugh, *North Amer.*, 28-29. [137] In BAE, XIV, 922.

near to nature, and many of the stories told by reliable travelers of the strange performances of savage shamans can be explained only on this theory. Numerous references in the works of the early Jesuit missionaries, of the Puritan writers of New England and of English explorers farther to the south, would indicate that hypnotic ability no less than sleight-of-hand dexterity formed part of the medicine-man's equipment from the St. Lawrence to the Gulf."

The Sioux practise self-torture. Catlin has a picture of a man "with splints or skewers run through the flesh of both breasts, leaning back and hanging with the weight of his body to the top of a pole which was fastened in the ground, and to the upper end of which he was fastened by a cord which was tied to the splints. . . . His feet were still upon the ground, supporting a small part of his weight. . . . In this condition, with the blood trickling down over his body, which was covered with white and yellow clay, and amidst a great crowd who were looking on, sympathizing with and encouraging him, he was hanging, and looking at the sun, without paying the least attention to anyone about him. In the group that was reclining about him were several *mystery-men*, beating their drums and shaking their rattles, and singing as loud as they could yell, to encourage him and strengthen his heart to stand and look at the sun from its rising in the morning till its setting at night; at which time, if his heart and strength have not failed him, he is cut down, receives the liberal donation of presents (which have been thrown into a pile before him during the day), and also the name and the style of a doctor or *medicine-man*, which lasts him and insures him respect through life."[138] "Wizards sometimes chew the seeds of the jimson-weed . . . to induce delirium, which their dupes regard as the touch of an unseen power, and their crazy ravings as divinely-inspired oracles."[139] They are supposed to have the power to sink into hard ground; this is a trick of stooping or is done "possibly by means of hypnotic influence." The Indian wizard is supposed sometimes to be a cannibal.[140]

In antiquity there were fetish-drinks that brought on divine efflatus, inspiration, and enthusiasm; such were the soma and the wine of the Mænads. Hashish has incited to religious visions and the phenomena of possession. The laurel was the plant of the inspired poet; it was used by the Delphic priestesses, to drive out consciousness so that the god could take possession. Music and the dance in their way exhibited intoxicating qualities comparable with those of opium and other drugs. Antiquity is full of the fasting and self-discipline of prophets, who frequently retired into the desert, to meditate in solitude, for a time prior to the practice of their profession.[141] Meditation, with the eyes fixed upon some

[138] Donaldson, in *Smithson. Rep.*, 1885, pt. II, 320.
[139] Powers, in *Contrib. N. Amer. Ethnol.*, III, 380.
[140] Leland and Prince, *Kulóskap*, 36, 257.
[141] §254, above; Lippert, *Kgchte.*, I, 625; II, 46, 435; Rohde, *Psyche*, II, 16, 17, 20, 21; Euripides, *Bacchæ, passim;* Maurer, *Vkde.*, I, 89, 105.

object or point—as the monks of Mount Athos stared at their navels[142]—is yet another method of autohypnosis. As all microscopists know, the eye cannot be used for long periods, especially when the observer is weary or weakened, and still remain trustworthy. After a time one comes to see what he wants to see.

The early Greeks had also a form of concentration analogous to crystal-gazing, namely, finger-nail-gazing, or onychomancy. This was employed in mediæval Europe by smearing the nail of an uncorrupted boy with a mixture of soot and oil, or of wax and oil, or with suet. Certain magical charms were then muttered by the magician, who made the boy hold his finger against the sun-light and look fixedly at his nail. In a short while the boy is said to have seen various images appear upon it.[143]

It is hardly necessary, in view of the foregoing, to advert to the vision-securing procedure of mediæval times. Let one example stand for many. It is said of a certain saint that "he habitually never broke his fast before sunset, and that he passed most of the night in prayer, restricting his sleep to the least that was compatible with life." If this is so, "his career became easily intelligible. Deficiency of nourishment, replaced by unceasing and unnatural nervous exaltation, must have rendered him virtually an irresponsible being."[144] One of the latest cases of inspiration is that of Joseph Smith, Jr., who alleged that he had recovered the gems Urim and Thummim and by their agency had been able to translate from gold plates the Book of Mormon. "The paper bears marks of being written under the influence of veritable crystal gazing. . . . Joseph's condition, under the influence of his 'Urim and Thummim,' was semi-hypnotic."[145]

The foregoing cases make it evident that primitive men had got hold of a working knowledge of mental aberration and how to produce it. They stumbled upon this as they did upon many another piece of information. It is not difficult, even now, to get into a mood of awe before such impressive and inexplicable phenomena; how much more of concern must the savage have felt in encountering what he took to be the undebatable evidences of the immediate presence and working of fearful supernatural potency!

The practices of self-discipline as a part of the cult have been considered elsewhere.[146] Whether or not they were entered upon with knowledge of their effects upon mental states, they were sure to result in forms of hallucination and worse. Even the robust

[142] Lehmann, *Overtro,* IV, 316.   [143] Meyer, *Aberglaube,* 283-284.
[144] Lea, *Inquisition,* II, 214.
[145] Riley, *Founder of Mormonism,* 81, 84, 86; Exod., XXVIII, 30; Levit., VIII, 8; Num., XXVII, 21; Deut., XXX, 8; I Sam., XXVIII, 6; Ezra, II, 63; Neh., VII, 65.
[146] §§281, 282, above.

Luther was brought into a precarious state of bodily and mental health by his self-discipline and brooding. Much of the fanaticism of mediæval monks was certainly due to such unsettlement of mind; Lehmann[147] cites striking examples of anæsthesia and visions under torture and before death, as well as under self-discipline in its several forms, and analyzes the phenomena of auto-hypnosis involved.

Ghost-fear itself has always been paralyzing enough to the race; such adjuncts as induced insanity, with the secrets of its production lodged in the shaman, sharpened that fear and gave it definite embodiment. The states into which the medicine-men learned to throw themselves could be explained only by way of eidolism and daimonism and confirmed those doctrines at every point, not alone to the minds of the laity but to those of the professionals themselves; for originally the latter must have hit unwittingly upon the means and processes of inducing states of possession. All these things entered into the range of experience and were reacted upon conformably to the mental outfit of the time. Then they, and the way they were interpreted and adjustment was made to them, entered in turn into the mental outfit and constituted the basis of action for the next period.

§312*. Reputed Powers of the Shaman. Even where the performances of the shaman are mere trickery, they are subjected to no critical examination by those to whom they are inexplicable. Scepticism is a product of evolution on a higher grade. Let it be recalled that the regular attitude of ignorance toward knowledge is the ascription of wizardry. Some of the demonstrations of the shaman are clumsy enough to our eyes; but it is not our eyes that are doing the observing. Of the much-vaunted Hindu tricks, such as growing trees, or throwing ropes into the air and climbing up,[148] White[149] says: "Count de Gubernatis, the eminent professor and oriental scholar at Florence, informed the present writer that

---

[147] *Overtro*, I, 137 ff.; IV, 301, 312 ff., 330 ff.

[148] Ibn Batuta's account, in Yule, *Cathay*, 500; Hoffman, in BAE, VII, 157; Grinnell, *Folk Tales*, 377 ff. On "The Fire Walkers of Fiji," see Burke, in *Frank Leslie's Monthly* for April, 1903 ("with photographs by the author, an eye witness"), 588 ff.; Langley, in *Smithson. Rep.*, 1901, 539.

[149] *Sci. and Theol.*, II, 166-167. On a hoax concerning "crowd-hypnotism," see Lehmann, *Overtro*, III, 157-159.

he had recently seen and studied these exhibitions, and that so far from being wonderful, they were much inferior to the jugglery so well known in all our western capitals." Despite this weighty evidence, there are many of the performances of the primitive shaman that defy explanation as successfully as do the feats of the modern wizard. We are not especially interested in the legerdemain, optical illusions, ventriloquism, and other dexterities of the shaman—or of the modern spiritualist—except to note that so long as they are not understood they constitute, both to the observer and to the artist himself, evidences of fetishistic quality; for, however attained, that quality is the indispensable attribute of its possessor and out of it comes his power. After he has somehow shown himself to be possessed and to constitute a mouthpiece of spiritual revelation,[150] both he and others harbor various theories as to the sort of spirit that dwells in him, as to the powers which such possession confers upon him, and as to the way in which his supernatural endowment may be kept up.

It must be understood, however, that it is dangerous for the shaman to fail. In that case, he may not only be demoted from his position but runs considerable risk of losing his life. Part of his equipment is his adroitness, through plausible excuses and counter-accusations, in shifting the blame and keeping his failures from counting.[151]

Australian shamans allege that they must eat human flesh to keep up their supernatural powers; each has a special animal, for instance, a huge, supernatural water-snake with a mane-like head of hair, by virtue of which he does his work.[152] "The wizards were everywhere credited with the power of conveying themselves through the air, or of being conveyed by the ghosts from place to place, or from earth to sky."[153] "The belief in magic in its various forms—in dreams, omens, and warnings—is so universal, and mingles so intimately with the daily life of the aborigines, that no one, not even those who practise deceit themselves, doubts the power of other medicine-men, or that if men fail to effect their magical purposes the failure is due to error in the practice, or to the superior skill or power of some adverse practitioner."[154]

In New Guinea a girl who is supposed to be the medium of the power is told off to communicate with the spirit, Fi-fi, and "from that moment, by a peculiar confusion in their minds between the spirit and the medium, she becomes Fi-fi to all intents and purposes. She retires to some corner near at hand, where she is not seen, and from there she whistles in different keys. The

150 Lippert, *Kgchte.*, I, 100.   151 Maddox, *Med. Man,* 151 ff.
152 Ratzel, *Vkde.*, II, 56, 96; Roth, *N.W. Cent. Queensland,* 153.
153 Howitt, in JAI, XVI, 25.   154 Howitt, *S.E. Aust.,* 356.

sound is made entirely at the medium's discretion, but the moment it is heard the people exclaim that Fi-fi has come, and they judge by the whistling whether the omens are favourable or not."[155] In the New Hebrides the shaman's power is gained by devotion to the spirits; he can make thunder and lightning, bring fish, cause crops to grow, and prepare sacred earth for young men to lure young women with.[156] "The sacred men . . . will tell you that they periodically visit the first stopping-place of the departed souls, and they say it is a long way under the ground. In this place all the important affairs of the world are discussed and arranged, and it is from here that the spirits work and punish those who do not follow the dictates of the sacred men. These priests or sacred men in this way have gained a tremendous control over their fellow-men, for superstition is strong and no native dare disobey a sacred man."[157] If a Papuan shaman tells a man to go off and die, he does it[158]—not because his brain is weak but by reason of the strength of the mores. The boy who used to fear to go in swimming on Sunday had the same sort of feeling, only far less in degree.

Kaffir sorcerers are supposed to possess supernatural powers derived from lions, leopards, elephants, boa-constrictors, alligators, or Hottentot women in the region above, enabling them to supply charms and to "smell out" counter-charms.[159] "In 1857 an impostor . . . predicted that if the confederate tribes killed all their cattle, destroyed all their corn, and left the ground untilled in the spring, at a given time their ancestors would rise and drive the English into the sea. He also said that he had visions of cattle belonging to the ancestors coming in huge droves over the hills and that after the English had been driven out every man could have as many as he had folds for. The corn-pits also were to be filled from the same source. A number of tribes believed this and destroyed all their chances of food for the season."[160]

The East Greenlanders "believe in spirits that everywhere surround them but are not visible and are seen by only a few consecrated people, namely the *angakoks*. "By the help of these the spirits come to harm or to bless men. . . . When we asked the *angakoks* how they performed their arts, they asked us first whether we believed in them. If we answered that we did not know what we should believe as to that, they told a mass of lies and untruths. If on the contrary we answered that we did not believe in them, they were quite willing themselves to reveal to us all their secrets and tricks and declared that they were good for nothing as *angakoks;* for all that they did was a game. But at the same time they expressed their belief that other *angakoks* could stand in relationship to the spirit-world." If a person studying to be an *angakok* fell ill he lost the ability to work as a shaman in the future. An inferior order of shaman, who worked in secret where the *angakok* operated in the open, could make a *tupilek* out of an animal which would kill the man it was sent against; it should contain a piece of the catch which its victim had made. The *tupilek* is made alive by singing a spell over it and grows by reason of its maker sucking through a bone.[161] An *angakok* can send his soul to interrogate

[155] Pratt, *New Guinea*, 315.   [156] Lawrie, in AAAS, 1892, 711.
[157] Hardy and Elkington, *S. Seas*, 155.
[158] Abel, *New Guinea*, 111.   [159] Kropf, *Kaffir-Eng. Dict.*, 9.
[160] Macdonald, in JAI, XIX, 280, 281.
[161] Holm, *Ethnol. Skizze*, 72, 85, 90, 93, 94.

the good spirits or the bad. He struggles to bring his familiar, who answers questions as an oracle.[162]

Among the Minnesota Ojibwa there are four classes of mystery men: the *Midē* or medicine-man, who exorcises, performs incantations, and administers shamanic or magic remedies; the Jessakkid, who professes prophecy and antagonizes the evil charms of rivals; the Wabeno, who purveys hunting-charms and love-powders; and an herbalist, who professes a knowledge of plants and administers "medicine-broths," or decoctions and infusions.[163] The Wabeno and Jessakkid deserve, perhaps, special mention. "When a hunter has been successful, as he thinks, through the aid of a Wabeno, he supplies the latter with part of his game, when, in giving a feast to his tutelary daimon, the Wabeno will invite friends, though all wishing to come are welcome. The feast is given at night; there is boisterous singing and dancing, and the Wabeno entertains his visitors with a further exhibition of his skill. By the use of plants he is supposed to be able to handle red-hot stones and burning brands, and it is said that he can easily bathe his hands in boiling water or maple sirup." An inferior shaman is the Jessakkid, who is a seer and prophet; he is commonly called a juggler, but the Indians define him as a "revealer of hidden truth." The gift is given by the thunder-god at long intervals to a chosen few, being received in youth when the individual fasts and sees visions. He is thought to be able to deprive his victim of reason and even of life; but he cannot injure the real shaman (Midē) or expel evil spirits in a patient. Tales are told of how the Jessakkid can instantly disengage himself from the most complicated rope-fetters.[164]

"It is no easy matter to secure osteological material from the Tlingits, for until within a very few years the dead were cremated. This rule, however, did not apply to the shamans, for it was believed that their bodies would not burn, and consequently they were placed in little house graves usually erected upon some lonely rock or picturesque promontory."[165]

It seems that a magician might lose for a time his powers of magic, "as all magicians are often all exhausted." It is bad to be a wizard, and use black art for evil purposes; but the real medicine-man is a good magician and can break the wizard's spell. The Mayas "are very careful to make this distinction between magician and sorcerer."[166] The Nicaraguan shaman catches the soul, in which process he works himself up through drink and autosuggestion into a sort of ecstasy, and returns it into the breast of its ailing owner.[167] The Guiana shaman is "priest, physician, and magician at the same time, a powerful and feared being, in whose hand it lies either to give free rein to the persecutions of the spirits that serve him or to lend protection against their influences."[168] A great meteor which fell was held to be the soul of a medicine-man, which had come to tell the Bororo that he wanted the flesh of a hunter, and would send the dysentery to one of them.[169] "The magic-doctors are more feared than honored by certain South American peoples. Frequently the rage

[162] Fries, *Grönland*, 144.   [163] Hoffman, in BAE, XIV, 66.
[164] Hoffman, in BAE, VII, 157.   [165] Dorsey, in PSM, LIII, 171.
[166] Leland and Prince, *Kulóskap*, 196, 233; Le Plongeon, in PSM, XLIV, 670.
[167] Sapper, in *Globus*, LXXVIII, 273-274.
[168] Schomburgk, *Brit.-Guiana*, I, 170; Southey, *Brazil*, I, 237.
[169] Von den Steinen, *Zent. Bras.*, 513.

of the whole tribe is directed against them when drought, inundation, or epidemics are ascribed to their ill-will."[170] Such shamans can handle all kinds of snakes with impunity.[171] Fuegian "doctors are supposed to have the power of killing persons in their dreams, and the expression is very common of eating persons, referring to this power."[172]

These examples of what the Germans might call the "indomitable will to believe" are prototypes for the many historical examples of uncritical submission to the superficially or fundamentally mysterious. The savage, as a rule, could not possibly know better, while more civilized peoples have looked down on his childlike beliefs with the supreme contempt of devotees of genuine and self-confident superstition.

What the shaman is supposed to be is reflected to a considerable extent in his initiation into office, just as the status of wedlock is to some extent rehearsed in the wedding-ceremony.[173] It is not necessary to illustrate the initiation very copiously, as the general topic occurs elsewhere;[174] but several representative cases may be summarized.

An Australian, feeling that he is capable of becoming a medicine-man, resorts quite alone to the mouth of a cave inhabited by spirits, and, with much trepidation, lies down there to sleep. He does not venture within lest he be spirited away forever instead of acquiring magic powers. A spirit, finding him, throws an invisible lance which pierces his neck from behind, passing through the tongue, and coming out through the mouth. "The tongue remains throughout life perforated in the centre with a hole large enough to admit the little finger." A second lance pierces the head from ear to ear, the victim falls dead and is carried into the depths of the cave. There all his internal organs are removed and a new set substituted, after which the victim comes to life again, but in an insane condition. Upon recovery from this he is led by the spirits back to his people. He presently decorates his nose with a broad band of charcoal and fat. He may now practise for a year, but if in that time the hole in his tongue closes up, his virtues have departed, and he will cease to practise. "He dwells upon his experiences, doubtless persuading himself that he has actually passed through those which are recognized as accompanying the making of a medicine man . . . and at the same time he cultivates the acquaintance of other medicine men, and learns from them the secrets of the craft, which consist principally in the ability to hide about his person and to produce at will small quartz pebbles or bits of stick; and, of hardly less importance than this sleight of hand, the power of looking preternaturally solemn, as if he were the possessor of knowledge quite hidden from ordinary men." Women may go through exactly the same process of initiation into the profession. A

[170] Koch, in *Globus,* LXXXI, 108.
[171] Koch, in *Globus,* LXXXIII, 121.
[172] Bridges, in *Voice f. S. Amer.,* XIII, 201.
[173] §§369, 371, below.　　　　　　　　　[174] §163, above.

lesser shaman is made by other shamans and not directly by the spirits. Old medicine-men press quartz crystals slowly and firmly up the legs of the candidate and then up the body as high as the breast-bone. This is repeated three times, with much scarification. "By this means the magic crystals are supposed to be forced into the body of the man." An incision half an inch long is then made in the tongue, and the body of the candidate is greased and painted with special designs. After recovery he must, for about a month, talk very little and be in every way abstemious, sleeping always with the fire between him and his wife.[175]

The same theme is played upon elsewhere in Australia, and the crystals are in evidence, for every medicine-man is supposed to be able to produce them at will from his body through which they are conceived to be distributed. The possession of these fetishes is what gives his virtue to the shaman. Again, the candidate, on returning to his people, is supposed to be a new man who has forgotten all about who he was and all about his past life. He has to be told who is his wife. If a candidate carried the situation off aright, "his coming back in this way and his strange behaviour at once showed the other natives that he had been made into a medicine man."[176]

In the Torres Straits tribes the novice has to swallow filthy messes with fortitude.[177] Among the Yakuts the old shaman puts the candidate through a set of vows to renounce God and consecrate his life to the demon who is to execute his demands, and teaches him to call up spirits.[178] In Borneo, at initiation into the order, the candidate's "body is supposed to undergo a complete change, he assumes a new name, and among other things his fingers are furnished with fish-hooks to enable him to clutch the human soul about to fly away, and reintroduce it into the body, thereby prolonging life."[179] Among the Dyaks, "manangs are generally called to their profession by a revelation made to them in dreams by some spirit. Each manang, therefore, claims to have a familiar spirit, whom he can call to his aid when necessary. When a person receives a call from the spirit, he bids adieu for a while to his relatives, abandons his former occupations, and attaches himself to some other experienced manang, who, for a consideration, will take him in hand and instruct him in the incantations, a knowledge of which is necessary for his calling. . . . The aspirant to the office of manang must first commit to memory a certain amount of Dyak traditional lore, to enable him to take part in the incantations in company with other witch-doctors. But in addition to this, before he can accomplish the more important parts, such as pretending to catch the soul of a sick man, he must be publicly initiated." The author[180] cites the three types of initiation, the last of which attains to the highest grade but demands a considerable outlay possible only to rich people. In New Zealand there was a kind of school for priests, and they were at length initiated into the secrets of the caste with elaborate ceremonies. The doctrines taught to the novices were the secret explanations of religion and they were given

[175] Spencer and Gillen, *Nat. Tr. Cent. Aust.*, 523 ff.
[176] Spencer and Gillen, *North. Tr. Cent. Aust.*, 480-481; Howitt, *S.E. Aust.*, 407-408.
[177] Haddon, in JAI, XIX, 398.
[178] Michailovski, *Shamanism* (Russ.), 73.
[179] Roth, in JAI, XXI, 115.
[180] Gomes, *Sea Dyaks*, 164, 177, 178, 179.

with great care, since a single false word in invocations not only made them vain but might kill the priest.[181]

An Eskimo *angakok* requires an apprenticeship up to ten years long, with protracted periods of solitary retirement. He must evoke a spirit by stone-rubbing, die of fright, and later come to life again. Thus he gradually gets the mastery over his familiar. To reach the top of his profession he must be dragged to the seashore by a bear and eaten up by a walrus; then his bones set off homewards and meet the shreds of flesh on the way. All grows together and he is whole again. His art of healing is of no avail unless he is well paid; but the gifts are supposed to go to his familiar.[182] The *piai* of Guinea inherits his profession and is secretly inducted into its mysteries by his father. When the latter feels too weak to combat the spirits further, he passes his function ceremonially over to the son. To the tests of the latter belongs the swallowing of great quantities of tobacco-juice, which must be done without betraying his feelings.[183] The drinking of abominable mixtures of herb-solutions is the test elsewhere in South America.[184]

There are occasional cases which reveal disbelief or a critical attitude toward the alleged powers of the shaman. These are of a different class from the sentiments which drive a people to kill or demote an unsuccessful performer, for there is no revelation of a critical spirit in such action except as some given individual is found wanting; the doctrine is not touched—it is even strengthened by the punishment of one who has shown himself unfit to be a mouthpiece for it.

To Europeans a certain Melanesian shaman "strenuously denies that he is a sorcerer at all, and when at one time he was under arrest on a charge of sorcery he put the case to Captain Barton in this way: 'If a man falls sick, his family come to me and ask me to make him well. If I don't do something for them they say "Tata Ko the sorcerer desires to kill our brother," and they are angry and will perhaps try to kill me. If I do give them something they insist on paying me well for it; should I refuse to take their presents they would not understand it, and they would think I was trying to kill their friend, but when I do take what they give me, you arrest me on a charge of sorcery or blackmail.' "[185] Here is a case of a man who was forced to be a medicine-man in spite of himself; he was a spirit critical enough to understand the situation as respects himself, in any case, and to plot correctly the reactions to be expected from the populace. In the next case it appears that savages are not insusceptible to a visual demonstration. Says Weeks:[186] "One day I heard Mayeya boasting outside my house of the seven days he had spent under the water in company with the water spirits; so going up to him, I said: 'Mayeya, I hear you have lived under the river for seven days.' 'Yes,' he said, 'I have.' 'Well,' I replied, 'I will give you 5,000 brass rods'—the currency of that dis-

181 Ratzel, *Vkde.*, II, 325.   182 Nansen, *Esk. Life*, 281.
183 Schomburgk, *Brit.-Guiana*, I, 172.
184 Hassler, in *Cong. Anth. Chicago*, 1893, 356.
185 Seligmann, *Melanesians*, 280.   186 In JAI, XL, 381-382.

trict—'if you will stay under the water here in front of my house while I count them.' He replied: 'I cannot do it just now, but I will return on another day and do it.' Whenever I saw Mayeya after that I always reminded him of my offer. The people at last used to urge him to accept my challenge and offer of 5,000 brass rods. They argued with him saying: 'You have remained under the water for seven days, surely you can stay under it while the white man counts 5,000, for you know he counts very quickly. Go and get your 5,000 rods and then you will be able to buy two more wives.' He, however, put them off with first one excuse and then another, until at last they chaffed him about it, laughed at him, doubted whether he had stayed under the water half a day, much less seven whole days and nights. As he still made excuses the natives lost faith in him, his practice fell off, and the last I saw of Mayeya was his coming to borrow of me 100 brass rods, for he was in difficulties. I said: 'No! you have imposed on many people, and done to death many a person by your false charges of witchcraft; I will not lend you a brass rod, but there are 5,000 waiting for you if you will only stay under the water while I count them.' "

In another place[187] there is related the device by which an African chief unmasked a wizard. Garbutt[188] relates a companion-piece. He dilates on the "smelling-out" process of the South African shaman which he says is full of deceit, lying, and devilry, one of the blackest blots of heathenism. "It is an historical fact that the great Zulu king, Tshaka, put the *izanusi* to a practical test. He secretly smeared the ground in front of the royal hut . . . with blood —an act of treason if committed by any member of the tribe. Naturally the next morning there was a great outcry. All the witchdoctors were summoned in order to discover the perpetrators of this outrage. Numerous persons were pointed out by them as the guilty party." One of the doctors, however, exclaimed that a greater power had done it, "which pleased Tshaka, and which he interpreted to mean him. The doctor in question was the only one spared, all the others were slain by their would-be victims on Tshaka's orders. It is stated that ever after, he would not order a man's execution because of having been 'smelled out.' Umziligazi, to prove the nonsense of witchcraft, once put a stone in his mouth to represent a swollen cheek. He then called all his witchdoctors to 'smell out' the person who had done it. After several of them had smelt out their victim he spat out the stone."

The doctrines of shamanism and the qualities of the shaman should come out with especial vividness in a survey of shamanistic practice. The fact is that most of the salient points in the evolution of primitive religion are epitomized in that practice, for as animism is taken up and carried on in eidolism, and eidolism in daimonism, so too is the ghost-cult taken up, with all its underlying doctrines and practices, into daimonology. Daimonology is the most evolved stage of religion thus far encountered in this book and the understanding of its processes involves the retention of all that has gone before, back to the first consideration of the

[187] §155, above. [188] In JAI, XXXIX, 536.

aleatory element and the spirit-environment. Now the supreme daimonologist is the shaman. In his hands is reposed the system as we have seen it developed out of simpler forms. In his practice we may hope to see exemplified and summarized the whole subject of religious evolution as heretofore considered. By focussing attention upon him for a time we may hope, then, to draw together virtually all of the strands which we have been pursuing and attain to a general perspective of the road traversed up to this point in the study of adjustment to the supernatural environment.

CHAPTER XXXIX

FUNCTIONS OF THE SHAMAN

§313*. **Shamanistic Practice.** It is evident from what has gone before that the field of operations of the shaman is coterminous with the range of the aleatory element; for he is the functionary who, through his special relations with the spirit-world, is enabled to control or at least to predict, those hazards of life which are a closed book to the mere human mind. The common conception of the medicine-man is that of a healer of disease. This is in fact one of his chief functions; but there are shamans who do not heal, and those who attend the sick discharge also other offices of scarcely less importance. If the shaman is conceived of as an indispensable middle-man or intercessor between the aleatory element in all its forms and man, we have the covering truth of the matter. He comes in where the layman can do no more for himself or where the event touches the whole tribe so that the efficacy of the human individual is ruled out. "Since the number of the good and evil spirits is so great and since a piece of conjuring that is incorrectly performed will bring evil, the individual man cannot think of accomplishing the magic operations."[1]

Uncivilized people who live under the immediate influence of the forces of nature and of blind chance are interested above all in the means of escaping evil fortune and in propitiating the forces of evil. They want protection from drought, lightning, storm, disease, death, and enemies. Not all can attain the means of winning good and averting ill. Some persons are endowed with the requisite knowledge and are thus fitted to be intercessors between their fellow-men and the unknown powers. These are the shamans and their art is shamanism. The more developed the people, the better defined is the position of the shamans and the more systematic is the organization of shamanism. Although the system thus covers a wide range of civilization, yet the philosophy of life included in it has broad, common features.[2]

Viewed from a slightly different angle, the shaman is the person to whom revelation is vouchsafed. The notion of revelation is not confined to religions founded by great law-givers. Even the lower varieties of a priesthood have for their chief business the obtain-

[1] Lehmann, *Overtro*, I, 21; 43 (quoted).
[2] Michailovski, *Shamanism* (Russ.), 5.

ing of divine disclosures. The shaman keeps up the rites of the particular familiar spirit from whom he derives his information; the spirit helps him and he, in his turn, elevates the spirit to honor. In this way a cult develops. A god is a spirit which gets a continuous worship and, while an inferior spirit may be evoked and then dismissed when the occasion passes, if he is called up oftener and oftener, he becomes a god.[3]

The miscellaneous cases of shamanistic practice immediately following will illustrate the range of the shaman's activity in control of the aleatory element, as he applies the revelations accorded him by his indwelling spirit. Several of his most general and important functions, however, and above all his profession of healer, have been set aside for special and detailed treatment. His miscellaneous practice may be passed over more superficially in the prospect of such an intensive examination of his more consistent and typical offices.

The Australians have innumerable rules and processes for warding off the evil spirit whom their imagination has invented and the priests or sorcerers have for their chief business the affording of help in this respect. The natives have the strongest faith in their shamans who are for the most part old men having some knowledge of medicine, of the traditions for finding the cause of death or identifying the persons who cause death, and of the proper measures for funeral-ceremonies, initiations, and incantations.[4] In nearly every New Guinea village "is a man who puts on the mien of an exorcist and in all difficult cases, such as sickness, the apprehension of an evil-doer, or the like, they take recourse to him."[5] "Charms were worn for protection, and the aid of the diviner was often called in to prophesy as to the prospect of success in war."[6]

In Togo, as elsewhere recounted, German coins displaced the cowrie-shells. Now the temple-riches were in cowries, and the shamans took advantage of the death of a man by lightning to announce that the gods were angry at the change; that blacks must keep to the cowries, since the coins were for whites.[7] In East Central Africa "the magicians are useful in every detail of life." Especially is the prophetess in demand as a detective of witches and wizards. In detection, she first shouts and rants frantically, shaking the rattles with which she is covered from head to foot, and then goes about quietly touching each person's hand. When she touches that of the victim, she starts back and yells: "This is he, the murderer, blood is in his hand." The accused may be allowed to demand the poison-ordeal but the verdict of the prophetess is likely to be absolute and final and the condemned man is put to death. His guilt is proved by the priestess who, after wandering all night, listening to spirit-voices,[8] "smells out" the "horns" which he used.

[3] Lippert, *Kgchte.*, I, 100; II, 250.   [4] Ratzel, *Vkde.*, II, 93, 94.
[5] Von Pfeil, *Südsee*, 318.   [6] Hunt, in JAI, XXVIII, 12.
[7] Seidel, in *Globus*, LXXIII, 343.
[8] Macdonald, in JAI, XXII, 104, 106.

"The great medicine-man has a sort of international status, for to him the chiefs in particular turn to get him to predict, from the position of the entrails of a butchered animal, the future, the outcome of a prospective war, the course of an illness, or the like. The little medicine-men devote themselves chiefly to the healing of man and beast within their districts, but also make the weather, bind and loose the rain, and by magic regain stolen property."[9] In the case of a much-feared chief, who was held to be a powerful magician, the negroes gave him gifts freely that he might not close off the water in the river.[10]

Sir Charles Dundas[11] assigns great importance to the mental impression made by the shaman upon his patients. "The native is a marvellously impressionable creature, as is often proved. Supposing a man has an enemy and he lays medicine outside his hut designed to make him mad, the owner of the hut will see it, or, if not, one may be sure that he will be told about it, and thenceforth even the most sceptical native's life is full of fears. For generations the evil power of the medicine has been known, and the fear preys on his mind until it is too much, and the medicine has done its work. This I have seen more than once, and the truth of it has often made me ask myself whether, if the medicine man's art can bring about this, it can also bring about the opposite effect. The Mkamba knows well how easily life is lost, and on the slightest sickness he will think himself dying, but on the other hand he knows that if he can be helped it will be through the medicine man, and therefore all his hopes rest in him. His hopes in the latter will therefore be as strong as his fear of death, and lightened with this hope his mind is in the best state to assist his cure; thus I think many a cure may at any rate be facilitated by the influence of the medicine man. There is only one person who cannot be either cured or aided by his charms, and that is the medicine man himself. Curiously enough, most medicine men evince a shyness and nervousness very often which may be so pronounced at times that one would think them mentally deficient. As a matter of fact, such is often, I think, the case, and the natives regard them as nothing but imbeciles in ordinary matters. They are said to be extraordinarily absent-minded and thriftless, which accounts for the fact that they are generally poor, and the more proficient they are in their art the less sane they are held to be. I believe that in an account of the Congo people it is stated that a foolish person is supposed to be particularly favoured by God, wherefore such persons are much respected. Possibly something of the same sort underlies the opinion as to the medicine man's insanity, for, as one man said to me, 'he has a spirit in his head like a madman.'" Cummins,[12] in speaking of the production by the Dinka shaman of some foreign body alleged to have been removed from a patient's body, asserts that "the mental relief afforded to credulous patients by the sight of what they believe to be the cause of their sufferings, thus removed, must often be beneficial. Certainly the magician in question enjoyed a great reputation. He was suspected, however, of being a dangerous man because, to quote the criticism I once heard passed on him, 'as he knew the way out, he must also know the way in.'" In the case of the abstraction of a bone or pebble from the body "the instant relief afforded

9 Volkens, *Kilimandscharo*, 254.
10 Passarge, in *Globus*, LXXXVII, 229.
11 In JAI, XLIII, 533-534.   12 In JAI, XXXIV, 159.

by this treatment is wonderful."[13] Dr. Puckett[14] has collected a mass of instances from the American negro's folk-beliefs which bear very cogently upon the survival of shamanism in this country; voodooism, positive and negative sign-controls, prophetic omens, ecstasy, and conjuring in general are shown to be widespread in the South. The preacher particularly, a man with a great flow of words, intoxicates himself with his own eloquence; and if, on any occasion, he seems to be running dry, the audience is adjured to "Mourn him up, chillun!" "Words," says Kipling,[15] "are the most powerful drug used by mankind. Not only do words infect, egotize, narcotize and paralyze, but they enter into and color the minutest cells of the brain."

The name of the Prophet, brother of Tecumseh, was "Open Door," meaning the "way or door which had opened for the deliverance of the red people." "There is a distinction between the 'doctors' of the Apache, Mohave and other tribes; some doctors are the bringers of rain, some have special power over snakes, some profess to consult the spirits only, and do not treat the sick unless no other practitioner is near. Among the Mohave the relatives of a dead man will consult a spirit-doctor and have him interview the ghosts who respond to his call, and learn from them whether the patient died from ignorance or neglect on the part of the doctor in charge. If the spirits assert that such was the case, the culprit doctor must either flee for his life or throw the crime upon some witch."[16] The Tarahumari medicine-man carries a new-born child thrice to and fro, east, west, north, and south, through the smoke of a corncob fire to make him strong and a good farmer. He is needed also to rub runners with a smooth stone that they may win foot-races.[17]

The ancient Hebrews had seers alongside the priests, who imparted information in return for gifts. The hand of Jahweh was upon the prophets.[18] The seer knew even the language of trees.[19] In Greece the interpreter of omens wielded great influence, especially since the people, as a rule, accepted his word without further ceremony. Though Homer[20] speaks of the best omen being to fight for the fatherland, the heyday of divination was yet to come.[21]

The foregoing quotations will serve to introduce the shaman in a general way. It is next to impossible to isolate his various activities in the cases, for they merge into one another and are interdependent in any given situation. It will be understood that the examples, as they are to be presented, are roughly classified by type. The first set will envisage the prophetic function of the

[13] Seligmann, in JAI, XXXII, 300.
[14] Folk-Beliefs of the Southern Negro.
[15] "Speech to the Royal College of Surgeons," reported in N. Y. Times, March 22, 1925.
[16] Donaldson, in Smithson. Rep., 1885, pt. II, 202; Bourke, in BAE, IX, 454.
[17] Lumholtz, in Scribner's Mag., XVI, 298, 305.
[18] Is., VIII, 11; Ezek., I, 3; III, 14, 22; VIII, 1; XXXIII, 22; XXXVII, 1; XL, 1; Jer., XV, 17.
[19] Maurer, Vkde., I, 89; Blau, Zauberwesen, 47.
[20] Iliad, XII, 254-255.
[21] Beloch, Griech. Gchte., I, 128-129.

shaman; the second, his rain-making activities, and the third, which will be developed at much greater length, his system of dealing with disease. The first of these is an advanced divination; the second, a matter largely of coercion and magic; the third, exorcism by a specialist. All the functions of this specialist are plainly derived out of the more general practices of the ghost-cult and daimonology; they are focussed more sharply and their details developed as they could not have been except for the rise of a class of men who had both the leisure and also the incentive to specialization.

It is evident that the divination practised by the shaman was not in general on the order of mere omen-interpreting.[22] The way he learned the future was not so much from happenings in the world of nature as from direct consultation with the ghosts and spirits. He had his apparatus for divination—some animal, plant, or inanimate thing, which is always, of course, a fetish.

The New Hebrides shaman pens a snake or lizard in a little enclosure, where it presently is supposed to turn to stone, somewhat as did the ominous serpent in Homer. He operates by the use of this stone, in which dwells a spirit of the dead or of unknown origin.[23] The African shaman uses a cup and bees-wax as an oracle; or practises water-gazing, earth-knocking, tobacco-shaking, pebble-counting; or uses sand and small shells, throwing the sand and divining through the figures it seems to form.[24] In Western Siberia, the shaman divines the future by means of a little stick which he throws; if it falls with the mark upon it down that means bad luck; in the contrary case, success.[25] Amongst the Buryats and quite widely in Central Asia, every shamanistic undertaking begins by divination on the shoulder-blade of a sheep or goat. The bone is roasted and the cracks produced are studied.[26] Again, the Kirghiz sorcerers try to drive a wild black horse over a man whom they have stupefied with hashish.[27] Masks are in use in many shamanistic ceremonies.[28] In Borneo divination is by cabalistic figures picked out by trained birds;[29] in the Carolines, the shaman uses figures drawn on the sand to support his magic, and also ferns and leaves.[30] Augury was practised in Mexico and Peru by "those who work with smoke," and in the former region by the elaborate counting of

[22] §267, above. [23] Macdonald, in AAAS, 1892, 726.
[24] Angus, in JAI, XXVII, 319; Gutmann, in Globus, XCII, 166-167; Paulitschke, Nordost-Afr., II, 60; Junker, Afrika, III, 582.
[25] Michailovski, Shamanism (Russ.), 56.
[26] Michailovski, Shamanism (Russ.), 85; Rubruck, Eastern Parts, 187; Prjevalski's Forskningsresor, 282; Shchukin, Shamanism (Russ.), pt. II, 24; Pinkerton's Voy., III, 314; VII, 65, 99; IX, 390.
[27] Karasin, In the Rushes (Russ.), 243 ff.
[28] Andree, Eth. Parallelen, 115. [29] DeGroot, Kongsiwezen, 6.
[30] Kubary, Núkuóro, 26; Kubary, Karolinen-Archip., 100.

beans. There were various specialties in divination, including prophecy by "the shapes of grains of maize taken at random."[31]

Sacred trees, as, for example, the Armenian poplars, were questioned by priests, who interpreted from the rustling of their leaves.[32] David got omens from sounds in the tops of trees; Joseph divined with a cup; and lot-casting was common in Israel.[33] Urim and Thummim were gems for divination.[34] In the Roman law a mathematician is a soothsayer who uses numbers and figures.[35] The Druids divined by smoke, by the chirpings of the wren, by throwing stones, and by eating.[36]

We need not rehearse such methods as the above, as they appear in later times; but certain of them have remained in the mores, under conditions where their significance is not widely recognized. Shamanistic divination survives in survivalistic form, for instance, in counting-out rhymes, which "have a twofold aspect; the end in view is to determine an unknown factor by casting lots, the use of rhymes and doggerels is merely the outward and visible means to this end. . . . Tylor, in his *Primitive Culture*,[37] holds that things which occupy an important place in the life-history of grown men in a savage state, become the playthings of children in a period of civilization; thus the sling and the bow and arrow, which formed the weapons of mankind in an early stage of its existence, and are still the reliance of savage tribes, have become toys in the hands of all civilised children of the present day. Many games current in Europe and America are known to be sportive imitations of customs which formerly had a significant and serious aspect. Adopting this theory, we hold that games of chance are in part survivals of the practices of the sorcerer, using this word in its restricted and etymological meaning [Latin *sors*, a lot]; we maintain further that the spoken and written charms originally used to enforce priestly power, have become adjuncts to these juvenile games, and the basis of the counting-out doggerels under consideration. The idea that European and American children engaged in 'counting-out' for games are repeating in innocent ignorance the practices and language of a sorcerer of a dark age, is perhaps startling, but can be shown to have a high degree of probability. The leader in counting-out performs an incantation, but the children grouped around him are free from that awe and superstitious reverence which characterised the procedure in its earlier state."[38] Where once the person counted out was designated to die, he is now merely the "it" in a game. And the counter realizes as little the original import of his formula as do most persons who use, for instance, the word "hocus-pocus" (*hoc est corpus*).

The prophetic function of the shaman deserves to be singled out from among his miscellaneous activities. In no respect does he

---

[31] Brinton, *Nagualism*, 10, note, 15; Bourke, in BAE, IX, 532.

[32] Justi, *Persien*, 82; §§254-256, above.

[33] II Sam., V, 24; Gen., XLIV, 5; I Sam., X, 10; XIV, 41; Josh., XIV, 2; Deut., XVIII, 10, 11; Num., XXIV, 1; Ezek., XXI; *Jewish Encycl.*, XII, 544.

[34] Exod., XXVIII, 30; Levit., VIII, 8; I Sam., XXVIII, 6; XXX, 7; Lippert, *Kgchte.*, II, 458.

[35] *Codex*, IX, t. 18; *Pandects*, V, t. 21; §255, above.

[36] Von Pflugk-Harttung, in *Trans. Roy. Hist. Soc. N. S.*, VII, 66.

[37] I, 75 ff.

[38] Bolton, *Counting-Out Rhymes*, 26, 35, 41, 45 ff.

appear more obviously as the intermediary between the aleatory element and man. All peoples have exhibited a strong desire to know the future, in order to avoid ill fortune by anticipating the conditions to be encountered and adjusting to them. It is always easier to receive a revelation uncritically than to study the facts and painfully think a situation out. It is impossible in any case, especially for the savage, to analyze everything that comes before the mind. Attention flags, the intellect tires, and action slips into the customary grooves as the easiest way. Furthermore, there is usually some striking coincidence to support any revelation, however fantastic, whether in law, politics, or religion. It is no wonder that the unsophisticated nature-man pinned his faith on amulets or medicine-men.

The situation might be put in this way: the spirits rule all life; sin is action contrary to their will; their will must be known as a precondition to avoidance of calamity; prevision of that will is veiled to merely human intelligence; hence the imperative need of the seer, the inspired person who can reveal that will, not by reason of any human attribute possessed by him but by the revelation vouchsafed through him by his indwelling spirit. It is the spirit that prophesies; hence the need of a peculiar state in the fetish-man, indicative of the presence of the spirit and a guarantee of the validity of the prophecy. The shaman may dream or suffer from induced illusions and then rise to interpret the former; he may utter, while under the influence of drugs or autohypnotism, prophecies just wild, ambiguous, and oracular enough not to be refutable, verifiable, or even understandable save under credulous conjecture.

A contradiction, curious enough to strictly logical thinking, appears where a people has arrived at a conception of fate and yet clings still to exploration of the future. What is to be, must be; and yet, if conditions can only be known beforehand, it need not be. It is fated; and yet it may perhaps be avoided.

Among the Homeric Greeks, fate was the "portion" assigned to man; for example, men were "long ago fated to die."[39] Fate was both superior and inferior to the gods. "If we ask . . . how Zeus himself is bound by Fate, we come only upon a rough form of the general problem of free-will and deter-

[39] Homer, *Iliad*, XVI, 441.

minism, such as certainly would have been unintelligible in an age which had not yet thought out even the relation of cause and effect."[40]

One should not be much disturbed by the inconsistency of undeveloped peoples—no more than he would be by that of children.[41] The fact remains that human interests drove men to interrogate the aleatory element as it existed in the unrevealed future and to seek revelation that would permit of adjustment in advance, thus rendering possible the avoidance of sin and calamity. To this natural longing the shaman alone could secure satisfaction through his confidential relations with the makers of the future, the spirits. How he is believed to accomplish this function has come out in many preceding connections; he is usually ready for a consideration to avert the evil that he believes or pretends that he foresees.

The prophetic function of the shaman is enhanced, upon a somewhat advanced stage of development, by his reputed astrological powers. The casting of horoscopes has been alluded to again and again in preceding connections; in China, India, and mediæval Europe, for example, astrology became a veritable obsession.[42]

"It is well known that nothing of importance is done by a true Hindu without consulting the stars." "In Hindu homes, the parents, as a rule, maintain the horoscopes of their children as the most important records from which the destinies of their children can be ascertained. With regard to males, the one that is written at their birth holds good forever, but for females two horoscopes are mentioned; one which is written at their birth, and the other which is written when they attain puberty; of these two the latter one is of the utmost importance."[43] Horoscopes at marriage are regarded in Tibet as of the weightiest significance; and this persuasion is quite general where astrology is practised. The astrologer-lamas "have always a constant stream of persons coming to them for prescriptions as to what deities and demons require appeasing and the remedies necessary to neutralize these portending evils."[44] Mexican shamans were able to read and interpret the books of fate and to tell from the calendar of lucky and unlucky days what a man's future was to be.[45] In the Middle Ages, "there were few who could take the common-sense view of Petrarch, that astrologers might be useful if they confined themselves to predicting eclipses and storms, and heat and cold, but that when they talked

40 Leaf, *Companion to Iliad,* 162; Keller, *Hom. Soc.,* 128, 187.
41 §§199, 215, above.   42 §307, above.
43 Monier-Williams, *Brāhmanism,* 372; Naidoo, in JASB, II, 382.
44 Rockhill, in USNM, 1893, 725; Waddell, *Buddhism,* 451; §372, below.
45 Preuss, in *Globus,* LXXIX, 261.

about the fate of men, known only to God, they simply proved themselves to be liars."[46]

Any layman can forecast the future to some degree, through traditional signs and omens traditionally interpreted.[47] The medicine-man is, for all that, the inspired professional observer and interpreter; and in the course of time, by reason of the fact that religious traditions and methods of all kinds are preserved and elaborated within the ranks of the shamans—who, in addition, are likely to be the ablest and most imaginative members of the society—the function of prophecy comes to be assigned, in all important instances, to the shaman. Where the laity do not hesitate to interpret ordinary dreams and portents, they yet hasten to the prophet when the extraordinary experience occurs. Everybody knew what it meant when the serpent and the eagle were wounding each other over the Greek and Trojan camps; but when the serpent at Aulis concluded his startling performances by turning to stone—a "great sign"—the rest were dumbfounded and only the seer could elucidate. Dream-interpreting was rather small business, though "even the dream is from Zeus."[48]

It seems from the chorus in the Agamemnon of Æschylus[49] that the prophet was wont to stick to the presaging of ill luck:

I would not boast to be a topping critic
Of oracles: but to some sort of evil
I liken these. From oracles, what good speech
To mortals, beside, is sent?
It comes of their evils: these arts word-abounding that sing the event
Bring the fear 't is their office to teach.

The more derived and complicated the theories and practices connected with prophecy the more secure became the monopoly of the fetish-man as prophet; questioning of the future is one of his major functions and is involved in all phases of his practice.

§314*. Rain-Making. The shaman is not infrequently referred to as the "weather-doctor." Despite the advances of the science of meteorology, the weather is even yet an incalculable matter,

---

[46] Lea, *Inquisition*, III, 444.   [47] §267, above.
[48] *Iliad*, XII, 199-208, 218 ff.; II, 300 ff.; I, 62-63; Keller, *Hom. Soc.*, 152 ff. (where full references to text are given).
[49] 1130 ff. (Browning's translation); Homer, *Iliad*, I, 106 ff.

especially over protracted periods. To the undeveloped races, in any case, it belongs within the range of the aleatory element and is something upon which anxious attention centers. The weather, and more especially the matter of rainfall, is to the uncivilized, and especially to those of them who depend upon tillage, of an importance hardly to be appreciated by the civilized man. Whereas the latter may lose a crop and suffer financially as a result, among the primitive tillers, as is illustrated by the famines in India that result from the irregularity of the monsoons, the absence of rainfall means widespread desolation and death. Particularly in parts of the world where the rainfall is slight in any case and where what there is must come at a certain season in order to render a harvest possible, is preoccupation with the weather a most engrossing affair. Why the rain comes, and in particular why it does not, are matters veiled to savages and, as such, are universally referred to the aleatory element in the form of the spirits. Here again the medicine-man, who is often also the chief,[50] is present to explain, to prophesy, and to arrange all such vital conditions through the fetishistic quality with which he is endowed. In arid regions his function as rain-doctor periodically dwarfs his other powers.

It is proposed to cite ceremonies of rain-making both as practised by the shaman and also as attempted by the layman; the dominance of the former will appear the more strikingly by reason of the collocation. In these ceremonies there is a pronounced element of imitative magic.[51]

In Central Australia, rather exceptionally, "the performers and the tribes generally do not seem to have much faith in their ability to make rain, but they boast a good deal when they have the luck to fluke it. Somebody always gets the credit for having done the trick every time it rains, but still the rain-makers get to work every time it looks cloudy. One old *kurdaitcha* man that I asked about not making rain, one dry time, answered me: 'No good make 'em rain this time. Too much dry fella. By and by cloud come up, me make 'em rain.' . . . The making of rain is of supreme importance to the aborigines, but its actual occurrence is so rare that the blacks' faith must often be severely tried, and many excuses are necessary to account for the failure. Either an opposition man's magic is too strong, or, as they explained the continued dry weather after trying three months ago, "Too much not chuck 'em white fella clothes,' or . . . 'No good try make 'em rain, no clouds.' . . . Twelve rainy days a year is the average fall in Mungeranie district, so rain-

50 §§155, 156, above.   51 §302, above.

making on any particular day must depend largely on luck." The rainfall is a little over five and a half inches a year.[52] It is no wonder that they are both dubious and discreet in the matter.

In New Guinea the professional shaman is not seldom exposed to dangers and unpleasantness. Thus he is often called upon for damages where he has not performed according to desire. For instance, if he is applied to concerning rain and the rain which then falls in streams will not stop, he must bear the damage which the crops have suffered from the excessive down-pour. Rain is sometimes very bad, especially for the tobacco-plants, and if it comes in excess it is thought to have been made by neighboring tribes with hostile intent.[53] "In times of severe drought the sorcerer is appealed to, who, if well paid, will make rain; he also can stop it. He also causes heavy seas so that canoes are not able to get out, but, if paid, will give calm by speaking to the spirit in his bone calabash and squirting his saliva all about."[54]

"Rain-making is almost as universal as feeding, and every race has its rain-maker, who, for a consideration, will tap the cloudless sky and bring torrents of water down to quench the thirst of the dry earth. In the New Hebrides the rain-maker goes into the forest and there collects the branches of a certain tree, which he cuts into lengths and lays a dozen or so of them parallel to each other. He then takes another dozen and threads them through the parallel ones, forming a kind of flat basket-work hurdle. Over this contrivance he mutters prayers, and then buries it in a dried-up creek. . . . More incantations follow this proceeding, and then heavy stones and rocks are placed over the rain producer, and the inhabitants all wait for the rain, which, strange to say, generally comes. . . . There is no lack of faith in these natives, and when once they have applied to the rain-maker they set to work to make preparation for the rain." The authors quoted[55] are reminded of the anecdote of the American child who went back for an umbrella as the family was starting to church on a cloudless Sunday that had been appointed as a day of prayer for rain; when derided, the child replied, "Aren't we going to pray for rain?" "The natives of the New Hebrides are very much like this little girl, and perhaps their faith brings about the results they desire. Who knows? Sometimes, however, they get more than they desire." In 1890 the natives of one of the small islands of the New Hebrides besought rain of the shaman. "The wise man consented, and after the machine, described above, was duly placed in the water-hole, the rain came down in torrents and did not cease for forty-eight hours. It was so severe that the entire surface of the harbour was fresh to the depth of three or four inches; and the water-hole, where the machine had been placed, had ten feet of water in it; whilst the yams in the plantation were being literally washed out of the ground. So great was the consternation of the natives that they were beside themselves with fear, and rushing to the rain-maker implored him to stop the rain. This, however, was no easy task, as the old man explained, because his machine was buried under ten feet of rushing water. Being unable to dive he could not get it out, and until it was fished out the rain would continue. The scene can be better pictured than described. At last in desperation the aid of the shore natives, who are good divers and swimmers, was sought,

[52] Horne and Aiston, *Cent. Aust.*, 116, 118.
[53] Krieger, *Neu-Guinea*, 185; Schleiermacher, in *Globus*, LXXVIII, 6.
[54] Chalmers, in JAI, XXVII, 333.
[55] Hardy and Elkington, *S. Seas*, 168, 169, 170, 171.

and soon the machine was brought out of the creek, and the rain stopped immediately afterward. The most remarkable thing about these and like superstitions is that more often than not they come off as the sages predict they will; and when once one does there is no longer any room for doubt, in the minds of those who wish to believe. That incident of rain-making in 1890 will be talked about for years, and the name of the rain-maker will be handed down to future generations."

The South African shaman attempts to stop a hail-storm which he sees coming by spitting against the storm, swinging his arms and calling for aid against it.[56] In equatorial Africa the wet season is the rain-making time; at other seasons the natives are incredulous. Previous to British occupation, unsuccessful rain-makers were killed or severely punished.[57] Again, "the wind-maker has become an important person since the negroes have become accustomed to the use of European manufactures and so are often exposed to lack through the delay of trading-vessels. Since they do not themselves frequent the sea, the shaman can find no sale for . . . Æolus-bags and instead generates the favorable breezes in his hut, which smokes and shakes from the violence of the process." From the east coast to the west most negro tribes have their rain-makers; in one case the subsidized functionary buries a pot with magical herbs and roots in the earth, "whereupon rain must certainly come."[58] Where the houses, built of salty earth, would melt in the rain the people pray to keep it off.[59] Emin Pasha once did a little medicine-business, on complaint that the local wizard was keeping back the rain. Emin said he could make rain. He had noted the barometer. The negroes hastened to bring goats, and rain fell soon after.[60] In Uganda the people buy rain-medicine; it is a root which, if kept dry in a house, produces no rain, "but if after a drought the root is thrown into a river, or kept soaked within a large pot of water, rain is sure to fall soon afterwards."[61] Again, "a personage of great authority in the land is the Father of Rain. . . . When they want rain, he is loaded with gifts of every description and receives the greatest honors. But his life cannot be very tranquil; if the water does not come to satisfy the desires of the country the fault becomes his, and at times . . . he may even be killed. The title and the faculty then pass to another of his family who cannot withdraw from the advantages and perils inherent in the office."[62]

The Yakuts put a stone found in the viscera of an animal into a bag on the end of a willow wand and dip it in the blood of birds. It is waved after sundown, with invocations, and laid on a tree. This causes rain, hail, wind, and cold at the will of the conjurer.[63] In Mongolia, on one occasion, "the Jalang had to burn up all his little snakes and bears and talk pretty rough to the gods, but he at last got them under control, for no snow and very little hail fell during the night. The medicine man was consequently very proud, and insisted that but for him they would have been snowbound for at least a week."[64]

[56] Macdonald, in JAI, XIX, 295.
[57] Spire, in Jr. Afric. Soc. London, V, 15 ff.
[58] Junker, Afrika, I, 404.
[59] Rohlfs, "N.-Afr.," in Mitth. Perthes' Geog. Anst., Ergänzheft., 25, 5.
[60] Stuhlmann, Mit Emin, 588.   [61] Johnston, Uganda, II, 881-882.
[62] Vannutelli e Citerni, L'Omo, 196-197.
[63] Shchukin, Shamanism (Russ.), 39.   [64] Rockhill, Mongolia, 202.

"Strange as it may seem to us, almost all primitive peoples believe that rain-making is an art to which men can attain, and some of them expect their kings to exercise it."[65] Elisha made rain or at least drew down a supply of water.[66] In Arabia Petræa when rain fails the women go in procession to the house of the village-chief with songs which are really prayers, carrying a cross with a woman's under-garment hung upon it.[67]

It can be seen from the foregoing cases that though ceremonies looking to rain-making may occur with or without the participation of the shaman, yet in a large proportion of the instances where need is pressing, that functionary is thought to be indispensable. Where the ceremonies are protracted and complicated he is the more likely to appear. It is fair to say that rain-making is one of his typical functions.

§315*. Theory of Disease. Among all the woes that flesh is heir to, sickness and death have always held a dominant position. While prayers have been offered by generations of fearful and hopeful men for offspring and wealth, the most fervent petitions have generally besought the higher powers for health and long life. Insurance-policies are the rational means adopted by developed peoples in the face of the aleatory element as it reveals itself in death, illness, and accident, in "acts of Providence" which no one can predict or foresee. The savage anxiously plies his best cult-measures against such eventualities. Then when, despite all prophylactic measures, sickness comes, whereas the civilized man sends for the scientifically trained physician or surgeon or at length, in weariness and disappointment, falls back upon any recourse that offers hope to his weakened and uncritical mind, the savage, whose original theory is daimonistic, loses no time in summoning the professional daimonologist. Unlike civilized man, there is nothing for him to revert to; he himself stands near the beginnings of things. Nor is he exhorted to embrace old superstitions under new and pretentious names that affront both religion and science. He knows exactly what to do; there is nothing else; and he does it and sticks to it.

It is not wholly correct to say that the undeveloped peoples

[65] Smith, *Relig. Sem.*, 83, 231; Frazer, *Golden Bough*, I, 13 ff.; Wellhausen, *Skizzen*, III, 157.

[66] II Kings, III, 17.   [67] Goldziher, in *Globus*, XCIII, 285.

always have recourse to the spirit-hypothesis in case of bodily damage. They recognize a plain wound, for instance, when they see it; they know how it was made and are likely to treat it in what we should call a rational way. Not always, however; for the most skilful treatment will not avert mortification if the spirits are adverse. Several cases will appear below illustrating the use of magic in dealing with hurts whose cause seems to us simple and obvious. The theory of disease is, in any case, almost purely daimonistic, for here there is no concrete, material inflicting agency, such as a hatchet, which has laid a man's flesh open as naturally as it cuts into a tree. Here, as elsewhere, ghost-fear is the constant fountain to which men return for a new supply of world-philosophy. Here, too, the daimonistic and the rational element play into one another's hands; for while a rational method may come to be practised under what is later seen to be a wholly spurious theory, yet, provided only that method works, it persists and confers benefits irrespective of the unsoundness of the premises upon the basis of which it is launched.

Sickness, like other inexplicable calamities, is referred to the agency of spirits, generally set in operation by sorcery. Hence the avoidance and neglect of the sick, through fear of the spirits possessing them or interested in their destruction, referred to above.[68] It was really a long step in evolution when rites developed by which the sick could receive care, even though those rites are in retrospect only sorcery and magic, often in a highly repulsive form.[69] Where the cause of illness is less obvious and especially where the patient is delirious and makes involuntary movements, as in hysteria or epilepsy, there appears a case of possession to be cured only by exorcistic processes. Such processes work or do not work, and in the course of time are subjected to selection and correction; thus, though leechcraft must be addressed to the spirits and is largely magical, yet a true science and art grow out of the daimonistic theory and the daimonological practice. Various phases of this theory and practice will come out in the following representative cases.

[68] §222, above.
[69] Lippert, *Kgchte.*, I, 110, II, 329, 415; Rivers, *Medicine, Magic, and Religion.*

Bartels[70] summarizes as follows. The disease is a daimon or several of them. It may be the ghost of a dead man or an animal; or be due to the sucking and gnawing of a daimonic human being. It is an animated something that can wander about and reply to questionings. It is an alien body, visible or not, in the victim; or a poison; or the displacement of some bodily part, which has left the body or taken a wrong position in it; or "the supernatural loss of some bodily constituent; or a bewitchment, a curse, a punishment, the will or gift of the gods. . . . Among the animals which force their way into the human body as an illness the worm stands far ahead in the matter of geographical distribution."

In Australia rheumatic afflictions are often attributed to the placing of sharp fragments of quartz, glass, bone, or charcoal in a person's footprints or in the impression of his body where he has lain down. "Once, seeing a . . . man very lame, I asked him what was the matter. He replied, 'Some fellow put bottle into my foot.' I found out that he had acute rheumatism, and he believed that some enemy had found his footprint, and buried in it a fragment of a broken bottle, the magic of which had entered into his foot."[71] A person becoming unaccountably sick believes himself to have been "pointed at" with a "pointing-bone."[72] He first finds out the doctor and the enemy who have made him ill, then employs another doctor to retaliate upon his would-be destroyer; and when he is sure that his adversary is equally in his power, the mutual fear tends to break the spell, with the result of restoration of health and harmony.[73] There is no natural cause for disease; it is always produced magically by an enemy and the doctors are called in at once to beat out the spirit sent to do damage. This is done by belaboring the ground in and about the camp with the stuffed tail of a kangaroo, after which all faithfully believe the evil spirit has been chased out.[74] That illness is of spirit-origin is clearly seen in the measures adopted by the father of a sick child, who dances before the child, stark naked, a solemn dance accompanied with a song.[75] Of the Melanesian it is said that "in sickness a feeling of apathy and indifference comes over him from which he is with difficulty aroused. Since the usual cause of sickness is to their minds evil magic, its only remedy must be magical too, and the man himself is merely a fighting-ground for two contesting forces over neither of which has he much control."[76] "New, rare, or obscure complaints, especially if they should prove fatal, are put down to the machinations of a sorcerer . . . generally belonging to a distant tribe. An ill-defined supernatural agency . . . was also held responsible for unexpected deaths." In cases of death by natural causes the evil spirit has fixed the time beforehand for the victim to meet the accident, for instance, to be bitten by a snake.[77]

In East Africa, "natives do not believe that a man's life ceases from any natural cause other than sickness, but sickness may be due to many things. Therefore, when a man dies his relatives will review the whole of his life, and enquire if at any time he was struck or injured, and if such was the case they very naturally try to prove that this was the cause of his death. In some

[70] Medicin, 10.   [71] Howitt, S.E. Aust., 366.
[72] §301, above.
[73] Roth, N.W. Cent. Queensland, 154.
[74] Gason, cited in JAI, XXIV, 170.   [75] Ratzel, Vkde., II, 96.
[76] Jenness and Ballentyne, D'Entrecasteaux, 109.
[77] Seligmann, in JAI, XXXII, 300.

cases the proof will be that, ever since the deceased was damaged in such and such a way, he had been known to be ailing. If there is no such proof, or the injury was of recent date, or showed external symptoms, elders are summoned and the corpse is dissected. They do this with considerable skill, and undoubtedly by long practice they are often able to detect an injury to some organ. On the other hand, ignorance results often in the most absurd diagnosis. If none of this appears likely, the death is invariably put down to witchcraft. The medicine men from far and near are consulted, and such and such a one is fixed upon as the culprit. Although, however, innumerable deaths, diseases, lunacy, and injuries to people and stock, are all attributed to witchcraft, and the evidence of medicine men supported by suspicions of others is accepted as conclusive proof, there is in none of these tribes any legal compensation due, or admission of litigations in respect to witchcraft. It seems that a man must resign himself to regarding such as part and parcel of the everyday risks of life, and the work of supernatural powers no less than of the wizard. On the other hand, a wizard ran great risk of suffering death by the speedy method of public execution. The justice of this appears to us, of course, extremely doubtful, but the native spares no means to obtain proof, which to him is conclusive, and it is certain that many cases of so-called sorcery are real instances of poisoning."[78]

The Yakut regards even childbirth as a sickness caused by evil spirits; "no consideration is shown either mother or child; for women possessed of evil spirits are regarded by the Yakut as no less perilous to society than those infected with epidemic germs. This accounts for the entire absence of compassion, and for the cruelty manifested by the Yakut towards women suffering the pains of labour."[79]

In Borneo there is exorcism plus the recovery of the sick person's vagrant soul; but there is also some appreciation of rational measures, such as abstinence from certain foods, from bathing, and from heavy work.[80] "The peculiar attribute of the *manang* is the possession of mysterious powers over the spirits, rather than any special knowledge of medicines." Maladies come from the touch of spirits; "the Dyak description of most diseases is . . . 'something passed him.'" It is the *manang's* duty to hurry to the other world and recover the wandering soul. While he does so, in a sort of trance, the people wait the result. He seems to awake from sleep and raises his right hand as if clenching something. "That hand contains the soul, and he proceeds to the patient and solemnly returns it to the body of the sick man through the crown of his head, muttering at the same time more words of incantation." Finally, a live fowl must be waved over the patient, with a further invocation, and then killed as an offering to the spirits. It is eaten by the *manangs*.[81] However much of a free-thinker the Sumatran may be, he still sticks to the spirit-theory of disease.[82] Similar beliefs prevail in Formosa.[83] Up to about 1830 the goddess Pele of the great volcano of Hawaii had her priestesses whom she used to come up out of the crater to possess or inspire; they were then gifted with the power to cure illnesses.[84] "Sickness and death were viewed by the Samoans

[78] Dundas, C., in JAI, XLV, 277-278.
[79] Czaplicka, *Aborig. Siberia,* 141.
[80] Nieuwenhuis, *Borneo,* I, 114.
[81] Gomes, *Sea Dyaks,* 163, 164, 168.
[82] Jacobs, *Groot-Atjeh,* I, 179.
[83] Pickering, *Formosa,* 73.
[84] Letourneau, *Soc.,* 282.

as proceeding from the anger of their tutelary deities, or produced by an evil spirit, or by the spirit of a dead relative entering the body of the victim."[85]

Holm[86] was requested, on one occasion, by a sick *angakok*, to send back a lock of hair which he had permitted Holm to cut off; "for he was apprehensive lest otherwise he should die." The Eskimo believe every part of the body has a soul of its own, and falls ill if it loses it; it takes the *angakok* to recover and restore the soul.[87] Turner[88] "heard of a son who took his mother to wife, and when the sentiment of the community compelled him to discard her he took two other women, who were so persecuted by the mother that they believed themselves to be wholly under her influence. She even caused them to believe that they were ill, and when they actually did become so they both died." Here is a case of powerful suggestion, quite inexplicable save under the spirit-hypothesis. The Aleuts believe that all diseases and bodily calamities are due to the will of someone, living or dead. The shaman is the defender against them; he exorcises by sprinkling the sick person with urine.[89]

The Dakotas and Ojibwa mixed the delicate spines of the cactus with grease and anointed their arrow-shafts and depressions bored in lead bullets. The spines caused extreme pain and were believed to travel forward in pursuit of life; but the medicine-man, if very powerful, might succeed in calling back the life of a victim, provided the attendant gifts are valuable enough to secure the necessary aid of the spirits.[90] An epidemic caused the execution, on one occasion, of two medicine-men who were suspected of bringing the visitation upon the tribe[91]—by recourse to their spiritual powers, naturally. The belief that a spirit comes from the spirit-world to carry off a living person's soul to that place is prevalent among Indians of Washington. "There are those who profess to discover when this is done, and if by any of their incantations they can compel that spirit to return, the person will not die, but if they are not able, then the person will become dead at heart and in time die, though it may not be for six months or even twelve."[92] In 1917 died Chief No Shirt of the Walla Walla Indians of Oregon. He steadfastly refused to be treated by a white physician, for his guardian fox-spirit was in the clutches of his enemy's eagle-spirit. It might have escaped but for the fact that the latter was under the control of a powerful medicine-man. "The white doctor he knew would be unavailing, for how could a white man cope with the malevolence of a superior weyekin [spirit] when he did not even believe in the existence of such things? And so the old chief laid himself down stoically to die."[93] "Stitches in the side and rheumatic pains, which are frequent among them [the Creeks], are often regarded as the effect of magic wounds. They believe firmly that their enemies among the Indians have the power to shoot them when they lie in sleep, from a distance of five hundred miles."[94]

The Tarahumari think that "all sicknesses have their origin either from the wind or witchcraft. If of the first kind, nobody dies from it."[95] Certain Colombia Indians object to taking medicine, regarding all sickness as a punishment

[85] Ella, in AAAS, 1892, 639.
[86] *Ethnol. Skizze,* 77.
[87] MacCurdy, in AA, X, 652.
[88] In BAE, XI, 180.
[89] Reclus, *Prim. Folk,* 83.
[90] Hoffman, in BAE, XIV, 285.
[91] Russell, in BAE, XXVI, 59.
[92] Yarrow, in BAE, I, 176; Eels, in *Smithson. Rep.,* 1887, pt. I, 677.
[93] N. Y. *Times,* March 26, 1917.
[94] Bartels, *Medicin,* 25.
[95] Lumholtz, in *Int. Cong. Anthrop.,* 1893, 107.

for sin. The sick man sends for the shaman (*mama*) to make a full confession. The latter makes a series of passes over the patient and receives the confession. He then decides whether the sins are mortal or whether they may be forgiven and health recovered. "This requires some judgment; the mama must decide from the condition of the patient, because he can become equally famous by telling a patient that he must die for his sins (which on being so informed he usually does without much further delay), as he can by predicting renewed health and prescribing the formula for recovery."[96] A Miranha chief advised relations with a woman to resist fever; men got all their ills from women, and woman might cure them on the principle of *venenum veneno*[97]—poison counteracting poison. "The Jibaros make a distinction between evil caused by witchcraft . . . and disease. . . . The illness of a patient is generally attributed to witchcraft when it consists of violent pains in some part of the body, especially when the pain is accompanied by swelling of that part. Thus, for instance, headache, rheumatic pains, and colic are ascribed to witchcraft. On the other hand, to the category 'disease' . . . the Jibaros set down especially such illnesses as have originally been brought to them by the whites and which are not particularly accompanied by pains, like dysentery, smallpox, and most other fever diseases."[98]

This daimonistic theory of disease, consistent throughout the world despite the multitude of details which it must cover, was the principle upon which the shaman did his work. It is as impracticable to catalogue all his methods as it is to list all the ramifying outgrowths and expressions of the theory itself; but they are all of a kind, just as are the applications of the theory, and their type may be clearly indicated by representative illustrations. Before coming to actual diagnosis and treatment, however, a word should be given to prophylaxis, especially since the methods employed so well reveal the daimonistic theory of disease. Prophylaxis, we are often told, is now coming belatedly into its heritage of appreciation, and we are adjured not to wait till disease appears but to anticipate and avoid its onslaughts. Scientific prophylaxis is novel enough, it is true; nevertheless the primitive peoples were eager to anticipate illnesses and did all the avoiding they knew how to do. They fled from unwholesome places on the ground that they were the abodes of evil spirits. The Australians' camps were surprisingly clean; if they got too bad, the group simply moved on.[99] That the whole cult is, in a sense, one great organization for avoidance and insurance—a huge prophylactic

96 Nicholas, in AA, III, 639-640.
97 Spix u. Martius, *Brasilien,* 1251, note.
98 Karsten, "Jibaro," in BAE, Bull. LXXIX, 9.
99 Horne and Aiston, *Cent. Aust.,* 18.

affair—has appeared again and again in the foregoing; since one of the chief dangers from the aleatory element was ill-health, there was no lack of ritual calculated to anticipate and fend it off. The taboo operated strongly in the same direction. Actual prophylaxis, however irrational its motive, began in the ghost-cult, as a few instances will recall.

The coldest-blooded exhibition of anticipation and avoidance is the abandonment of the sick.[100] Thus the Lopliks of central Asia fear smallpox so intensely that when anyone is supposed to be ill with it, they put food beside him and then flee to a new village, abandoning their reed houses, and even their scanty furniture.[101] In Nicaragua if a sick man is likely to die, they give up their efforts and go away, leaving no food or drink, but rather the implements needed in the next world.[102] The Macusi are indifferent and unsympathetic with the sick; and so are the Arawaks, who seem to be frightened off by their misfortune.[103]

In such cases it cannot be inferred that the natives have any conception of contagion; if they really secure what amounts to quarantine of the sick, it is from fear of the ghost or of the disease-daimon, and the good result, if there is one, is, like fasting at a time of plague, unforeseen and unplanned on rational grounds. If it seems rational after the act and in retrospect, that is another matter altogether.[104] If the Scandinavians had had any rational idea of prophylaxis, the churches would not have been pest-houses from the dead buried in them.[105]

Most of the following instances illustrate the taboo or the propitiatory cult or other foregoing topics as well as prophylaxis against disease. Their citation here should serve to draw those topics together into a focus upon daimonological practice.

In the Torres Straits Islands, many kinds of fish are forbidden to women because it is thought they cause one of the diseases of women. A kind of turtle and its eggs are tabooed to nursing mothers and no woman until beyond childbearing age may eat pigeons.[106] The Coast negroes take great care of their teeth; they are frequently seen working at them with a chewed piece of wood and the result is that the teeth are "dazzling white."[107] The women of some aboriginal tribes of the Malakka Peninsula wear combs with figures in parallel lines which represent disease and flowers; the latter are prophylactic. If wind bearing disease approaches a head in the hair of which the correct preventive

[100] §222, above.
[101] Huntington, *Pulse of Asia*, 247.
[102] Sapper, in *Globus*, LXXVIII, 273.
[103] Schomburgk, *Brit.-Guiana*, I, 227, 419.
[104] Keller, *Soc. Evol.*, 93 ff.
[105] Lund, *Norges Hist.*, II, 89.
[106] Haddon, in JAI, XIX, 309.
[107] Fabry, in *Globus*, XCI, 199.

flowers are represented, the ill is warded off.[108] In Togo, a dog beaten to death and hung by the heels to a scaffold in the market-place is held to prevent disease.[109] How far the Congo negroes are from scientific prophylaxis may be judged from the following. "The women were so fond of attending the sick, i.e., sitting in the house and giving advice, that they neglected their work and various duties to do so. Hence a sick person would often have a house full of visitors, attendants, and advisers, and if the complaint was infectious it was thus quickly spread through the town. I have gone to see a smallpox patient, and found the house literally packed with folk. Isolation was derided, and precautions were foolish, for none of them would take the complaint unless they were bewitched."[110] To be aligned with the above is the following, from the island of Cebu, during the prevalence of smallpox: "The clothes of the dead were turned over' to the living without being washed, while the victims bathed in a cold stream at the very crisis of the disease."[111] In Borku Arabs have adopted the negro and half-breed custom of clipping the uvula with scissors as protection against a number of maladies.[112]

The Samoyed shamans hold a solemn magical performance every year, at the approach of winter, when diseases begin to appear among them. An old seer drinks blood and performs sorcery in the presence of the other shamans and of the old people.[113] Certain Finns of northeast Russia regard bathing, which they practise in the bitterest weather, as their most important method of escaping disease.[114] Cow's urine is used as a disinfectant by Persians and also by peasants in several parts of Europe.[115] Gourd-shell charms are common in China. "The shell of this vegetable is sometimes hung up near the place where the children who have not yet had the small-pox sleep during the last night of the year. This custom is explained by the Chinese by saying that a certain god of the small-pox and measles will 'empty' the small-pox into the gourd-shell, and not into the children, if he should observe one ready. Afterward, when they break out with the small-pox, they will have it slightly." A lantern bound on the neck of a child during the last night of the year will have the same effect; and paper masks are worn during that evening to make the children appear ugly so that the smallpox spirit will pass them by.[116] Here is one of the stock attempts to turn aside bad luck by appearing to be already ill-favored and unfortunate. In Japan, the moxa, a sort of cautery, is applied to possible seats of pain. It is difficult to find natives who have not the marks upon calves or back; in the former location they protect from a disease called kak-ke, in the latter against leprosy and brain-troubles. The soles of the feet are treated against cramps, the elbows against rheumatism of the shoulders. The cauterized place is supposed to derive fresh life-force from the application and so to be more resistant to disease; the immediate effect is said not to be exorcistic or repellent of spirits.[117]

"When the natives of Borneo are selecting the site for a new village, a piece

[108] Preuss, in Globus, LXXV, 345.

[109] Ellis, Ewe, 93; Seidel, in Globus, LXXII, 23.

[110] Weeks, in JAI, XXXIX, 450.

[111] Worcester, Philippine Isl., 313.　　[112] Nachtigal, Sahara, II, 93.

[113] Michailovski, Shamanism (Russ.), 78.

[114] Russian Ethnog. (Russ.), I, 316.　　[115] Modi, in JASB, II, 419, note.

[116] Doolittle, Soc. Life of Chinese, 315-316.

[117] Bartels, Medicin, 223.

of bamboo is stuck in the ground, filled with water, and the aperture covered with leaves. A spear and a shield are placed beside it, and the whole is surrounded by a rail. The latter is to protect the bamboo from being upset by wild animals and the weapons are to warn strangers not to touch it. If there is much evaporation by the morning, the place is considered hot and unhealthy, and is abandoned."[118] In Samoa, if it was thought that a person died of a disease which might be hereditary, his body was cut open, and any inflamed or otherwise abnormal organ was removed and burned. That stopped descent.[119] In the Nauru Islands, "every morning young and old wash their teeth with salt water; dark spots are rubbed with fine sand. Old teeth are drawn with a string, molars with two little pieces of wood tied together. The teeth of the Nauru people are very white and regular but fracture quite easily."[120]

The Pima Indians throw away the broth of boiled meat lest it cause consumption.[121] The Mohave have ceremonies to insure good health, called saltsinging or crow-singing.[122] All the medicine-men of the Yuma meet occasionally and with considerable ceremony to "make medicine"; this was done, in the summer of 1874, "for the purpose of averting diseases with which the Indians were afflicted the summer previous."[123] The Seminole Indians have a "Black Drink," with a nauseating smell and taste, which acts as an emetic and cathartic; and the Indians believe that unless one drinks it, he will be sick at some time during the year and cannot eat of the green corn during the feast. They think they can commence on the green corn with an empty and keen stomach if they purge themselves beforehand.[124] Certain of the South American Indians induce daily vomiting with the idea of freeing the stomach of any superfluous materials, so as to be healthy and energetic. Bartels[125] recalls the weekly or at least monthly purge to which German children have been subjected within recent decades.

An Egyptian prophylactic measure was to write passages from the Koran on the inner surface of a dish, soak the script off, and take the water.[126] In the prophylaxis of the Jews of southern Russia amulets play a strong rôle; the sickness-bringing spirits are frightened off either by strong-smelling stuffs, by fear-inspiring objects, or by prayer. Children wear, during an epidemic of scarlet-fever or diphtheria, little bags filled with garlic, pepper, cloves, etc. Other prophylactics are wolf-teeth and needles in a package, which are believed somehow to stand in relation with the disease-process. A little bundle of strong-smelling grasses is good protection against nausea and stomachtroubles. Mouse-eyes are a common constituent of many amulets; a little package of dirt wards off fever; weakly or long-desired boys are provided with ear-rings.[127]

It seems that inoculation against smallpox was practised of old in China, and the African Unyamwesi say it is a very ancient custom with them.[128] The Masai adopted it, after suffering terribly from the time of the scourge of 1850

[118] Roth, in JAI, XXII, 31.   [119] Ella, in AAAS, 1892, 639.
[120] Brandeis, in *Globus*, XCI, 60.   [121] Russell, in BAE, XXVI, 69.
[122] Kroeber, in AA, IV, 281-282.   [123] Mallery, in BAE, X, 505.
[124] MacCauley, in BAE, V, 522; Donaldson, in *Smithson. Rep.*, 1885, pt. II, 316.
[125] *Medicin*, 121.   [126] Hauri, *Islam*, 87-88.
[127] Weissenberg, in *Globus*, XCI, 358.
[128] Bartels, *Medicin*, 128, 129; Stuhlmann, *Mit Emin*, 85.

(before which it seems to have been unknown) till about 1892; "I verily believe that but for the advent of the European the pastoral Masai would in a few years have become absolutely extinct between smallpox and the cattle plague which induced famine."[129] Bordier[130] cites several peoples who had blundered upon a species of inoculation. As is well known, vaccination, after its introduction, was repeatedly forbidden in eighteenth-century Europe, and still has its bitter opponents amongst the ignorant or fanatical.

To have presented the theory of disease and to have touched, however lightly, upon prophylaxis, is to have foreshadowed the topics of diagnosis and treatment. In a similar manner has the ghost-cult prefigured daimonology, and daimonology the more evolved forms of later elaborated religious systems. Interest now turns not only to the actual working out of the theory of disease but also to the incipient revamping of that theory in the light of knowledge unpremeditatedly acquired in its application. In the light of that theory many an otherwise grotesque and irrational-seeming practice will take its place in an understandable series, and will actually figure as the germ-form of later and accepted practice.

§316*. Diagnosis and Treatment.[131] The treatment of disease was generally preceded by a sort of diagnosis which was, conformably with the current theory, entirely daimonistic, being confined to the identification of the spirit causing the malady or of the action on the part of the patient which might have brought down daimonic wrath. Diagnosis amounts, in fact, merely to divination;[132] and it extends to the determination of the outcome of the illness. Doubtless the shaman becomes in time quite expert in judging whether a patient is or is not likely to die, and can prophesy accordingly. This merely illustrates anew the gradual and inevitable infiltration of real observation and inference into the daimonological process.

The sick Melanesian wants to know what spirit is "eating" him, and summons the shaman. The latter slaps with one hand the end of a bamboo stick, "calling one after another the names of men not very long deceased; when he

129 Johnston, Uganda, II, 828-829.
130 Géog. Méd., 555 ff.; Van Duyl, Beschavingsgeschied., 310-311.
131 The cases under this section and the two that follow of necessity run together in a manner to defy strict classification.
132 §267, above; ch. VII of Seligmann, Der Böse Blick, covers diagnosis of the evil eye.

names the one who is afflicting the sick man the stick of itself becomes violently agitated."[133] The Saora shaman attains the same end by using a saucer, with oil and a lighted wick in it. The patient holds this and the shaman, with his left hand on the patient's wrist, drops grains upon the flame, calling out as he drops them the names of deities and ghosts. Whichever spirit is being named as a grain catches fire is responsible for the illness.[134] In South Africa, the doctor "smells out" the agent which has produced illness by witchcraft, and tells how the person who has bewitched the deceased will now die from sunstroke, snake-bite, lightning, or otherwise. "Needless to say, the next person who dies of a curious malady or by accident is considered to be the one who bewitched the person whose grave was struck by the doctor. . . . The natives call the doctor 'he who performs a difficult work.'" This sort of diagnosis comes nearer criminal detection, perhaps, than medical practice, but it is well to collate it with the other instances of diagnosis, for it is after all a determination of the agency for disease. The ordeal is applied to the same end, as we have seen it in operation under the administration of justice.[135] The shaman concocts a noxious mixture of the castor-oil bean, and excrement of hyæna "forms a portion of the mixture in all cases." The accused drinks till he vomits or purges, that is, till he is proved, respectively, innocent or guilty. In some cases there is an insistence upon proving guilt; "as many as twenty plates full were given," in one case, twenty-four—the accused vomited repeatedly and finally, at the twenty-fourth, purged, and was adjudged guilty.[136] It is a common belief that evil spirits, when they want to torture a man, insert foreign articles into his body, whereby he becomes sick and dies; in the East Indies these are little stones, to make the body cumbersome; bones and coral, to dry up the body and make it thin; chalk, to induce coughing and wasting away; fish-bones, to produce shooting pains; and hair, to cause the hair of the head to fall.[137]

When an Eskimo is ill, so long as there is hope, he receives careful nursing. To find out whether he is to live, a matron places under his pillow a stone, which is weighed every morning with incantation. If it gets heavier the case is desperate. Then they build a snow-house at some distance and fit it out somewhat, take the patient there, and bid him farewell. They do not stay, for if he should die all present must strip off and throw away the clothes they are wearing.[138] The chief function of the *angakok* is "to find out the reason of sickness and death or of any other misfortune visiting the natives." Coming to the house of the sick, he lowers the lamps, pulls his hood over his head, sits in the back of the hut facing the wall, claps his mittened hands, "and, shaking his whole body, utters sounds which one would hardly recognize as human." He invokes his familiar spirit and then questions the sick person: "Did you work when it was forbidden?" or "Did you eat when you were not allowed to eat?" If the poor fellow remembers any transgression, he cries: "Yes, I have worked," or "Yes, I have eaten"; and the *angakok* rejoins: "I thought so" and issues his orders about the atonement. Forms of atonement are manifold, including exchange of wives, taboo on bathing or scraping ice from the

[133] Codrington, *Melanesians*, 210.
[134] Fawcett, in JASB, I, 261.   [135] §183, above.
[136] Garbutt, in JAI, XXXIX, 551, 555.
[137] Wilken, in VG, III, 383.   [138] Reclus, *Prim. Folk*, 39.

windows, throwing away of clothing, abstention from the eating of venison, working of deerskins, or filing of iron.[139]

The California Karoks have two classes of shamans, the root-doctor and the barking doctor. The business of the latter, who is generally a woman, is diagnosis, which she does "by squatting down like a dog on his haunches before the patient, and barking at him dog-fashion for hours."[140] In ancient Mexico, staring into water was much used to discover whether a sick child's soul had got lost. If the child's face looked dark in the water, the worst fears were justified; if bright, the sickness was of no consequence. Then there was diagnosis with a knotted cord; if the knots were readily loosed the sick man would get well, if they tightened he would get worse or die. "There is of course no doubt but that in both cases the skilled medicine-man had the outcome of the divination in a certain manner in his own hands, and that, according to his estimate of the severity of the case, he could arrange the questioning." Divination was practised also by the fall of grains of maize.[141] Bourke[142] reports "the last trial for witchcraft and its punishment within United States territory," in 1876, at Rio Grande City. A sick young Mexican had been given up by the local medical talent, and one of the "numerous old hags," called *curanderas,* was called in. These functionaries are described by Bourke "as possessing in equal portions a knowledge of kitchen botany, the black art, humbuggery pure and simple, and a familiarity with just enough prayers and litanies to give a specious varnish to the more objectionable features of their profession." One old woman declared that cats had jumped down the patient's throat; another asserted that it was frogs. The wise women, having been fined, asked for remission as "they were poor, humble women." The judge replied: "That's nothing. You can all get through keyholes, and you all know where to find buried money to pay your fines. That's all there is about it."

Great faith is reposed in the diagnosis; in fact, it is the faith that verifies the divination. Among the Bororo of Brazil when a child was sick, the medicine-man predicted its death at a certain time, at which time the father strangled it. The medicine-men foretell the death of a sick person correctly; for he is put to death at the time indicated.[143] Jewish priests had rules for the identification of leprosy and ritual dealings with it.[144]

Such methods of diagnosis, though a modern would regard most of them as wholly irrational, are capable of being modified by experience until they come to have real sense in them. Just as from much observing the rain-makers get to know about the weather-probabilities or the astrologers about the regular movements of the heavenly bodies, so does the shaman arrive at a certain objectiveness and correctness in his judgment about the status of the sick. The truth or falsity of the theory upon which he starts has

139 Boas, in BAE, VI, 592.
140 Powers, in *Contrib. N. Amer. Ethnol.,* III, 26.
141 Seler, in *Globus,* LXXVIII, 89.
142 Reported in N. Y. *Times* for March 17, 1895.
143 Von den Steinen, *Zent. Bras.,* 461, 511.
144 Levit., XIII.

nothing to do with the quality of the results ultimately attained; the theory gives him a foothold, a method, and especially a zeal that are indispensable. Had he been bereft of his "superstition" he could have acquired no one of these.

There is no question as to the importance in therapeutics of the degree of confidence and faith that can be inspired in the patient; other things being equal, the sick man who believes in his doctor has an added chance of recovery. Just because of the religious element in primitive medicine is the trust reposed in the shaman well-nigh implicit; for he handles and administers not mere chemical substances but fetish-materials; and it is not his own fallible human mind that directs him but the all-knowing spirit that has taken up its abode in him. The shaman is a fetish, that is, and his whole procedure is fetishistic. If he brings the patient, the lookers-on, and himself all into an ecstatic state, he enhances the "faith-cure" element in his therapeutics.[145] If fear because of the transgression of a taboo or by reason of the knowledge that one has been bewitched or cursed can bring speedy death to a healthy person, then utter confidence in the enlistment of spiritual favor and aid through the shaman should be capable of much in the restoration of health. One of the best examples of the faith-cure is the temple-sleep or "incubation"; and the theory of it is in nowise affected by the fact that in Greek times the temples of the healing god stood in fresh air, were sunny, and in the neighborhood of springs which might have had mineral elements, and that the priests possessed actual medical knowledge.[146] "We see that it is the imagination or, as one would say today, autosuggestion, which causes all kinds of illnesses among the nature-peoples; and it is through the skilfully applied suggestion of their medicine-men that they are cured."[147] The shaman has been known to effect cures where the efforts of the white physician had been expended in vain.

The great bulk of the medicine-man's procedure, on the prevailing theory of disease, could scarcely be other than exorcistic. Consider the long list of prophylactic and therapeutic measures

145 Lehmann, *Overtro,* I, 21 ff.

146 Meyer, *Aberglaube,* 93, 94, 95, 96; Lehmann, *Overtro,* I, 73-74; IV, 294-296; Stoll, *Suggestion,* 329; §317, below.

147 Bartels, *Medicin,* 50.

against the evil eye,[148] no one of which could be rational in the sense of aiming to neutralize or to combat an authentic cause. The astonishing fact about primitive therapeutics is that by the process of experimentation, still under the spiritual hypothesis, remedies were discovered which have vindicated themselves in practice and the effectiveness of which has at length been demonstrated at the hand of modern science.

A description of the procedure of the shaman amounts to an extension into a special field of the methods of exorcism in general;[149] the salient feature of any such survey may well be the indication of what might be called the permanent product of primitive therapeutics. Special books on the subject[150] emphasize this aspect of the matter and should be consulted for exhaustive illustration. We shall begin with what might be called the irrational methods of healing, that is, the methods whose efficacy, except in so far as they inspire confidence and work "faith-cures," could not withstand scientific examination and appraisal. There is one method which deserves special mention, namely, what might be called "passing the buck" in the matter of disease; this is illustrated by the device of rubbing some article on warts and thus luring them into it, and then throwing it away somewhere in order that a stranger may pick it up and take the warts with it. This method is quite common among primitive peoples. Further, it must be noted that, whatever the mode of treatment, it is hardly complete unless some spell is uttered to strengthen it. Again, it is common to use the stock fetishes in exorcism, for example, iron.[151]

A good many of the cures are attempted without specific activity on the part of a shaman; this is really "folk-medicine"; but the need of the specialist in serious cases is the more conclusively exhibited.

Australian therapeutics[152] have to do very largely with blood-letting, which will be touched upon below. In New Guinea "nursing, according to our ideas,

148 §§265, 266, above; Seligmann, Der Böse Blick, I, ch. VIII, and nearly all of Vol. II.

149 §§226, 227, 276, 313, above.

150 Maddox, Med. Man; Bartels, Medicin; Pinkerton, Voy., XVII, index, sub "cure"; Adams, "Domestic and Quack Remedies in the Levant," in Bull. Amer. Acad. Med., X, 659 ff.

151 Cases in Hildburgh, in JAI, XXXVIII, 176 ff., 186, 187, 192, 194.

152 Dawson, Aust. Aborig., 56 ff. (long passage on diseases and remedies).

was of course impossible, for you cannot induce a savage to keep himself covered up."[153] In New Britain the Duk-Duk ceremony is performed when any of the chief's family is ill. The natives say that when a sick man sees a Duk-Duk he either gets well or soon dies. It is a case of kill or cure. The dance takes place in a tabooed enclosure where women and children may not go on pain of death. The chief performer is supposed to be a deity and, having first taken a canoe to another island, generally makes his first appearance coming out of the water. He is masked; and if the mask should come off, he would be killed.[154] In West Africa, "when the patient is a rich man, several sheep are sacrificed, and he is fetished until the last moment arrives amidst the howls of a number of old Fetish Women, who continue to besmear with eggs and other medicine the walls and doorposts of his house and everything that is around him until he has ceased to breathe."[155] In eastern Angola there are three shamanistic functionaries: the first cures with roots and herbs empirically but uses absurd decoctions made under incantation; the second divines only and is the diagnostician who identifies the illness as being due to ghosts or witchcraft; the third is the exorciser who operates in the stock manner.[156] "Medicine among most Africans easily tails off into witchcraft," which is of two kinds in Uganda: a kind of white magic, involving the use of hypnotism and powers of divination for innocent purposes and a black art which is "little else than poisoning or scaring people into fits by uncanny practices. . . . Their therapeutics are very simple. They can make salves for wounds out of the leaves of certain plants, but apart from that they attempt to cure most illnesses by putting pebbles in a gourd and rattling them over the head of the sick person until he is nearly deafened. If that fails to cure him, they cut off the head of a fowl or of a quail, and hang it to a string round his neck, to be worn until the cure is effected."[157]

The shaman sometimes tells a sick Buryat that the ruler of the lower world demands another soul if he gives up that of the sick man; and he asks who is the near friend of the latter. If he is told, he catches the soul of the friend during sleep and gives it to the ruler of the lower world.[158] A Chukchi who has been sick seven days has a rope tied round his neck and is dragged at a run around the house. If he falls, they go on, and he dies or recovers. If he lingers, he is stoned or speared.[159] The Siberian shaman's performances have been described above;[160] it is evident that the sick-room is not a place of quiet and low voices. "Obviously sleep is highly dangerous to the sick, for if in sleep the soul departs, how can we be sure that it will come back? Hence to ensure recovery one of the first requisites is to keep a man from sleeping. With this in mind, the Circassians dance, sing, play, and tell stories to the sick by the hour. Fifteen or twenty young fellows with strong lungs are selected to sit by a sick man and make all possible and horrible noises to keep sleep away; but if by any chance it should come they immediately dash water over his face. This is a last effort to stop the soul about to take flight."[161]

[153] Pratt, *New Guinea*, 214.   [154] Dall, in BAE, III, 100.

[155] Kingsley, *W. Afr. Studies*, 173; Nassau, *Fetichism*, ch. XII.

[156] Serpa Pinto, *África*, I, 112.   [157] Johnston, *Uganda*, II, 750, 751.

[158] Michailovski, *Shamanism* (Russ.), 59.

[159] Reclus, *Prim. Folk*, 41.

[160] §311; Assoc. Press. Desp., in N. H. *Register* for Nov. 28, 1895.

[161] Frazer, in JAI, XV, 82.

Catlin[162] describes the operations of an Indian medicine-man over an Indian who had been shot, two bullets having passed through the center of his body. "He was lying on the ground in the agonies of death and no one could indulge the slightest hope of his recovery, yet the medicine-man must needs be called . . . and hocus pocus applied to the dying man as the dernier resort when all drugs and all specifics were useless and after all possibility of recovery was extinct." Catlin presents a drawing of this shaman, in full regalia. He made a frightful din and discord, adding "the wild and startling jumps and yelps of the Indian and the horrid and appalling grunts, and snarls, and growls of the grizzly bear, . . . ejaculatory and guttural incantations to the Good and Bad Spirits, in behalf of his patient, who was rolling and groaning in the agonies of death while he was dancing around him, jumping over him, and pawing him about, and rolling him in every direction. In this wise this strange operation proceeded for half an hour, to the surprise of a numerous and death-like silent audience, until the man died, and the medicine-man danced off to his quarters, and packed up and tied and secured from the sight of the world his mystery dress and equipments."

Of the Sia of New Mexico we learn that "it is only upon acquaintance with the secret cult societies that one may glean something of the Indians' conception of disease, its cause and cure. It is supposed to be produced almost wholly through one or two agencies—the occult powers of wizards and witches, and the anger of certain animals, often insects. Therefore, though some plant medicines are known to these Indians, their materia medica may be said to be purely fetichistic; for when anything of a medicinal character is used by the theurgist it must be supplemented with fetich medicine and magical craft."[163] A Spanish historian reports the existence among the lower classes in Mexico, of "medicine men, who treat the sick by means of strange contortions, call upon the spirits, pronounce magical incantations, blow upon the part where the pain is, and draw forth from the patient thorns, worms, or pieces of stone."[164] "Stronger than any herb, are the words which are spoken over it before it is used. These are not prayers, but accounts of a previous cure. The repetition of the words has power again to cure."[165]

The shaman of British Guiana begins his exorcism right after sunset, after putting out every spark of fire in the house and sending away the inmates. He swings his clapper to the accompaniment of a monotonous song. He now commands the disease-spirit, now beseeches him to release the patient. Meanwhile he blows tobacco-smoke from a consecrated cigar at intervals into the latter's face. If during the ceremony it begins to rain the operations are put off until the next evening. At length the spirit is forced to appear and the medicine-man enters into negotiations with him. Two different voices are always heard at this juncture, but the sick man cannot understand what is being said. When the strange voice ceases, the medicine-man is ready to inform the patient as to the cause of the spirits' wrath and the nature of the malady; "this explanation is at the beginning of the trouble commonly very unclear and ambiguous, like the profoundest oracles of the Pythia. If the illness increases the exorcism is continued every evening until a favorable crisis ensues. By that time the shaman has forced the spirit to tell him everything

162 Quoted by Donaldson, in *Smithson. Rep.*, 1885, pt. II, 418, 419.
163 Stevenson, in BAE, XI, 73.   164 Brinton, *Nagualism*, 11.
165 Preuss, in *Globus*, LXXXVII, 396.

and he knows the actual seat of the illness. He lays his mouth upon the most painful part of the body and sucks until after a time he brings out of his mouth a mass of fish-bones, thorns, or the like, which the spirit has introduced into the body. "The imagination of the patient now takes over the completion of the cure." A few medicaments, chiefly plant-juices, are used, their value being in the main to hasten the confession of the spirit. If the conjurings have no result and no means, drink or magic formula, can move the spirit, and the patient dies, naturally several ways lie open for the shaman to save his reputation and explain his lack of success. If the sick man or one of his relatives has injured another shaman, the latter sets up his art against that of the attending doctor and neutralizes his efforts.[166] In Brazil, shamans break out the teeth of venomous serpents and use the snakes in their magic arts, and especially in curing snake-bites.[167]

Among American medical biographies[168] occurs that of a physician who was born in Maryland and lived there till his death in 1858. He listened to his patients' whims and utilized them on occasion. "A hypochondriac labored under the insane delusion that he had swallowed a spider which was consuming his vitals; all efforts to dispel the crazy notion were in vain when old Dorsey was summoned. He humored the notion and declared the case was a bad one, and laid his strategy to oust the noxious tenant. After much pomp and parade of preparation, and ejecting the inquisitive from the darkened room and bandaging the patient's eyes, the mouth was pried open and a captive bluebottle fly, held by a thread to his leg, was sent buzzing across the yawning cavity, while the doctor peered anxiously in. From time to time Dr. Dorsey was heard to ejaculate: 'I see him! He is coming,' and the like. At last the sick man tore off the bandage and sprang to his feet, and there stood the doctor triumphant with the spider captured in his hand. The cure was perfect and lasting. No wonder the more ignorant neighbors marvelled that such wisdom and skill were vouchsafed to mere mortals." In this case the physician had merely adopted the characteristic method of the shaman.

These cases have exhibited what might be called the irrational methods of healing. Except for their effect upon the mind of the patient, few of them lead anywhere. They were impressive in their day and that is what lent them their effectiveness. Wherever the spiritual theory of disease has persisted, they have maintained themselves, either in the hands of the shaman or in the body of folk-medicine; but with the advance of knowledge, though they are periodically resurrected in the shape of systems wholly discreditable to an age that knows science, they have lost their force and have become grotesque and ridiculous, even—in fact, chiefly— in the eyes of those who are now involved in revived supersti-

[166] Schomburgk, *Brit.-Guiana*, 171-172.
[167] Spix u. Martius, *Bras.*, 1210.
[168] Kelly and Burrage, *Amer. Med. Biog.*, sub "Frederick Dorsey"; Foote, "Medicine Fakes and Fakers," in *Nat. Geog. Mag.*, XXXV, 67 ff.

tions.[169] The superstitions about health and disease prevalent at the present day are as gross as those of primitive savages and, in addition, have no excuse for existing.[170] To judge by the tenets of some sects there might as well have been no development of science at all, for all the effect it seems to have had upon primordial fetishism. It is truly incongruous that those who scorn science should have their existence, as well as their antics, made possible by the services of science.

Certain variations in primitive therapeutics have, however, been preserved and extended by science itself because of the actual, though accidentally discovered, efficacy which they have revealed. A few of the foregoing cases have shown something of this character; we turn now to a survey of some shamanistic methods which have survived in modern practice.

§317*. Therapeutics. It will be seen that what we should call a rational method of dealing with bodily ills emerges only unconsciously and slowly out of the mass of daimonistic theory and daimonological practice now before us. What we find is that the shaman tries in various ways to expel the disease-spirit from the suffering body. To a number of his methods modern knowledge can assign no efficacy whatever; they were simply ineffective variations. Others have been taken over and are used in the healing art of today. Something has been seen of the former type in preceding paragraphs. We now come to some of the shaman's real discoveries upon which he blundered while proceeding on an untenable hypothesis. He kneads, squeezes, and pounds the seat of pain, and in so doing is executing a rude massage. He sucks at the sore spot and thus performs a sort of cupping operation; perhaps "kissing the pain away" is remotely alignable with this. He applies heat, for fire is a sovereign exorcistic element, and thus increases the flow of blood to the part treated. He uses water, another spirit-banishing element, and secures a certain larger

---

[169] Geare, "Healing by Magic and Mummery," in *Amer. Med.*, XXII, 644-650.

[170] Consider the situation which makes advisable and appropriate such a broadcast address by a state health-officer as that upon "Superstitions about Health" delivered by Dr. W. L. Munson, and reported in the N. Y. *Times* for June 24, 1925.

degree of cleanliness and perhaps a "water-cure." He scarifies and draws blood; then ensues whatever relief bleeding confers. He develops "incubation" or the "temple-sleep," thus securing quiet in what is often the most wholesome location in the settlement, and also employing powerful suggestion.[171] As all these processes are fathered by the daimonistic theory, it is to be expected that the cases will show throughout a mixture of the relevant and irrelevant, the rational and the irrational. It is only gradually that experience leads to a selection of the remedies which, since they actually meet the situation in a positive and objective manner, are fitted to persist under the régime of science. For the most part our cases illustrate the period of variation and unconscious experimentation; promising and unpromising procedure occur together.[172] However, if one keeps his eye upon essentials, he can make out the gradual and unplanned emergence, despite many backslidings and much attendant spuriousness, of methods approved by modern science. There are grains of wheat in the bushels of chaff that are capable of growth and eventual reproduction as the chaff is not.

Massage is known to the Papuans as well as everywhere in the eastern tropics and is much employed, especially after strenuous marches.[173] The Kaffirs treat a sick member of the body by smearing cow-dung upon it and kneading it in order to extract the cause of sickness.[174] "The kneading of the body which is practised by the Somali . . . consists in treading upon the back with the bare feet. To this end the person to be massaged lies stretched out or squatting with the abdomen downwards and a person treads upon his back with unshod feet, not softly but heavily—trampling, as we should put it. This exercise is of excellent hygienic effect."[175] In South Africa an incision is made into the patient's back and sucked, the result being the production, from the doctor's mouth, of a caterpillar or other small object. "Horrible stews" are given and massage applied, the patient's hands being beaten with red coals.[176] The Borneans practise bleeding, tattooing, and massage.[177] A stock Polynesian remedy, especially for rheumatism, was kneading.[178] "The practice of relieving pain by manipulation of the body was the effective movement cure resorted to by the [Easter] islanders years before the Swedish or massage treatment assumed its present importance. . . . I may testify to the physical regeneration of this titillant manipulation. On more than one occasion I have thrown

[171] §316, above.
[172] For more exhaustive illustration, see Maddox, *Med. Man,* and Bartels, *Medicin;* Geare, in *Amer. Medicine,* XXII, 644-650.
[173] Hagen, *Papua's,* 258.   [174] Kropf, *Kaffir-Eng. Dict.,* 308.
[175] Paulitschke, *Nordost-Afr.,* I, 174.   [176] Garbutt, in JAI, XXXIX, 551.
[177] Nieuwenhuis, *Borneo,* I, 118.   [178] Ratzel, *Vkde.,* II, 132.

myself upon the ground, completely exhausted by over-exertion, and yielded
to the dexterous kneadings and frictions and palmings and pinchings of those
skilled in the treatment. The hard-fistcd native is by no means gentle in the
operation, but with palms and knuckles vigorously tests every muscle and
tendon, as well as every joint of the vertebræ, until the exhausted patient
sinks into a state of oblivious somnolence."[179] The Guiana shamans have no
deep knowledge of medicine; "their whole activity consists in wild and at the
same time rude exorcisms, with expectoration, stroking, pressing, and smoking
of the ailing part, in the ejaculation of unintelligible words, in the ability to
get themselves into a sort of wild ecstasy by the use of a narcotic powder,
but particularly in the art of ventriloquy."[180] The Shingu shaman blows clouds
of tobacco-smoke over the body of the sick and kneads the patient with all his
might, while he and not the patient groans. Then he sucks the affected part
and at last pretends to spit out the cause of the pain.[181] One must recall here
the fetishistic quality of tobacco.[182]

The Papuans treat fever by binding the temples and back of the head with
a string, or by placing the sufferer near a hot fire to drive off the fever. Also
they seek to smoke out the fever.[183] They hold a glowing coal as close as possible to a wound, which is quite rational and also painful, and for fevers they use
exposure to the glowing sun as well as to the fire.[184] The Yakuts are very much
afraid of smallpox, calling it and measles "old women," and "say that they are
two Russian sisters dressed in Russian fashion, who go to visit in person those
houses where they have marked their victims. All diseases come from evil
spirits who have taken possession of men. . . . The simplest method of cure
is by fire. A boy whose wounded finger became inflamed, came to the conclusion, which the bystanders shared, that a *yor* had established itself in the
finger. Desiring to drive it out, he took a burning coal and began to apply
it around the place while blowing upon it. When the burned flesh began to
blister and then burst with a little crackle, the curious group which had
crowded around him flew back with a cry of terror and the wounded boy, with
a smile of self-satisfaction, said:—'You saw how he jumped out.' A man who
had the rheumatism had his body marked all over with deep burnings. As soon
as he had any pain, he applied fire to the seat of it."[185]

The water-cure is widespread over the earth. Among the Australians the
sorcerers employ the steam-bath against rheumatism.[186] The Papuans use
certain vegetable juices but resort also to hot and cold washes; the sick person
is bathed daily in the sea.[187] In Togo a very sick woman was treated by having mouthfuls of water, mixed with sand and holy ashes, twice squirted into
her eyes.[188] In West Africa baths accompanied by massage are much esteemed.
Sometimes the bath is prepared by digging a hole and putting in a quantity
of herbs, then pouring boiling water plentifully over them. The patient is
covered over with the parboiled green stuff and a coating of clay is placed

[179] Thomson, in USNM, 1889, 471.
[180] Schomburgk, *Brit.-Guiana,* I, 423.
[181] Von den Steinen, *Zent. Bras.,* 345.   [182] §256, above.
[183] Krieger, *Neu-Guinea,* 177; Chalmers, in JAI, XXXIII, 121.
[184] Hagen, *Papua's,* 258.
[185] Sieroshevski-Sumner, in JAI, XXXI, 105.
[186] Ratzel, *Vkde.,* II, 96.   [187] Hagen, *Papua's,* 257.
[188] Seidel, in *Globus,* LXXII, 41.

over all, leaving just the head sticking out. The patient stays in the bath from a few hours up to a day and a half, and when removed is well rubbed and kneaded. Such a bath is undoubtedly good for many diseases, notably rheumatism, which afflicts both black and white. The authoress[189] has seen in few herbal remedies any trace of a really valuable drug.

In the therapeutics of the American Indians different kinds of baths play a leading part. Among the Tlinkit there is no house without a hut for the steam-bath. Other tribes have a common bath-house in the middle of the village, and still others bathe much in the open air. In northwestern America a cold bath in the morning is customary, though dwellings and dress are dirty. Remedial measures include bleeding, kneading, and sucking the sore place. The Arawaks and Botocudo when they have overloaded their stomachs, tread each other's abdomens with their feet. Other South Americans induce vomiting every morning by tickling the palate with a feather, thinking that whatever remains in the stomach overnight is injurious.[190] In British Columbia, "the sweat-bath is the cure-all; this is nothing more than a hole dug in the ground and covered by a conical roof of green branches and earth, a small opening being left for the bather to crawl into. A fire is built outside and a number of stones are heated. When these are sufficiently hot, they are placed in the sweat-house; the bather crawls in, taking with him a small kettle of water; he closes the opening and drops the water gradually on the hot stones, until the house is filled with steam and heat; he endures this as long as possible, and then rushes out and plunges into the cold river; the performance is repeated three or four times. When the doctor cured, he was paid in blankets, horses, or cattle, according to agreement; when he did not cure, he often forfeited his life."[191] If the Guiana Indian fails to profit by rest and the heat of a fire under his hammock, he sends for the shaman who does magic and then proceeds to the steam-bath and the cold plunge in the river. Whatever the nature of the disease, the bath is the indicated cure. In the heat of fever the patient is steamed or dashed with cold water.[192] It is easily seen why the American Indians should have died in such great numbers, when they subjected those who had taken measles, smallpox, and other eruptive diseases from the whites to such unsuitable treatment.

Scarification and real bleeding or phlebotomy may be taken together. All medical practice was at first a cult-performance to appease the gods to whom illness was due;[193] and, as we have seen elsewhere, blood-letting was one of the stock means of propitiation.[194] Further, scarification is thought to let out the evil spirit. In Australia, "in cases of rheumatism, tight bandages are applied to the affected part; headache is often treated by making a number of small incisions on the temples; snake-bites are sucked in some cases at least; and fractures are bound up with splints." Incantations and rude vapor-baths are other measures. "It has been noticed that the treatment of disease, according to European rules, instead of resulting in cures, or temporary alleviation, generally hastens the end of the Blacks, and yet drugs seem to act on them in

[189] Kingsley, *Travels W. Afr.*, 469.

[190] Ratzel, *Vkde.*, II, 561; Donaldson, in *Smithson. Rep.*, 1885, pt. II, 455.

[191] Allison, in JAI, XXI, 311.

[192] Schomburgk, *Brit.-Guiana*, II, 333-334.

[193] Lippert, *Kgchte.*, II, 329.   [194] §§224, 228, 229, 291, 306, above.

the same manner as on us."[195] In Papua, as a remedy for headache, the sufferer sits opposite to the person applying the treatment. The latter takes a little bow and arrow and puts the arrow to the other's forehead, drawing it slowly and discharging it again and again till blood flows. They bleed for nearly every ache, using a shell to scarify; later they employed splinters of glass if they could get bottles. Fever is treated by blood-letting from forehead or back.[196] In case of inflammation and ulcers that have not yet broken they often make hundreds of little cuts, with a piece of glass, over the seat of the difficulty. Malaria, persisting beyond childhood, is treated by tattooing; a couple of lines are made over the enlarged spleen. Rheumatism is common and is treated by an elaborate tattoo. It is not possible to ascertain the origin and meaning of the marks.[197] In the Torres Straits region "scarification of the affected part is a common mode of treating local inflammatory complaints."[198] Blood-letting and tattooing are applied in Borneo to painful, swollen spots.[199] On the island of Ponapé, "in certain ailments, such as the formation of abscesses, in rheumatic and certain paralytic cases, and especially in all those whose cause and treatment they do not know and which thus appear to them strange, they undertake to extract the bad blood, as they think, by practising bleeding, which sometimes they repeat with such frequency that they end up by becoming completely debilitated."[200]

It is clear that we have in these cases the beginnings of several processes which have been approved by the practice of more evolved peoples and times. When it comes to primitive surgery, we find some very cold-blooded performances. The use of splints has been alluded to as practised by the Australians. Some very astonishing cases of surgery, calculated to strain credulity, are cited by Bartels.[201] External operations are sometimes performed in a skilful way and the wound sterilized; the patient is even deliberately narcotized with opium or hemp.[202] Nevertheless there is very little that deserves the name of surgery among the primitive peoples; the body was mutilated in various ways,[203] but of actual curative operations there are but few to be cited.

Bandelier[204] states that trephining of the skull is practised still, at the time he writes (1904), by Bolivian medicine-men. He cites cases of patients who lived through the operation and for years afterwards. The trephining was done, in one case of a fractured skull, "with simple, well-sharpened pocket-knives." "Indians, like other mortals, suffer from pain in the head; when the pain becomes persistent, suspicion of evil powers dwelling within the cranium, or of some evil substance smuggled inside it through sorcery, naturally follows. In such cases, after all other charms have proved ineffectual, the final resort is to perforate the skull and let the evil out. This is a religious act, and

195 Curr, *Aust. Race,* I, 98, 209.

196 Pratt, in *Nat. Geog. Mag.,* XVIII, 572; Krieger, *Neu-Guinea,* 177.

197 Hagen, *Papua's,* 257, 258; Seligmann, in JAI, XXXII, 297, 298.

198 Haddon, in JAI, XIX, 306.   199 Nieuwenhuis, *Borneo,* I, 118.

200 Pereiro, *Ponapé,* 134, 135.   201 *Medicin,* chs. XIV, XV.

202 Thurston, *S. India,* 397. For a report on anæsthesia by deep breathing, cited in *American Medicine,* see N. Y. *Times* for Feb. 4, 1923.

203 §§229, 307, above, and 445, below.

204 In AA, VI, 441, 442, 443, 444 (quoted). Full discussion, with plates, of Peruvian trephining, in Muñiz and McGee, in BAE, XVI.

trephining in such cases is accompanied by ceremonies, which are as yet unknown to us."[205]

Trepanation was done in neolithic times in Europe.[206] Horsley[207] finds that the openings are generally over that region of the brain which "is the seat of origin of that special form of convulsions which is known as Jacksonian epilepsy, and which so frequently follows injuries to the skull and brain." He suggests that the scar might first have been excised as the source of pain, then the bone removed to secure further relief; after which that particular portion of the skull might have been removed in case of convulsions, where there had been no fracture, "among savages to whom pain is of slight consequence." Such a speculation is perhaps as good as any other in a case where, though the facts are present, their interpretation can only be guessed at.

Primitive obstetrics are a combination of magic, rude manipulation, and rational procedure. In Australia the woman is sprinkled with water and later is well steamed. This is probably purificatory rather than therapeutic, as "she is not allowed to return to the general camp for about three months after the birth of her child." The Australian child is tempted into the world by a woman who descants upon the beauty of nature; charms are added in case of the child's reluctance.[208] In New Guinea the woman is belabored on breast and back and water is poured over her head.[209] The woman may hold a rope suspended from the ceiling, and in difficult cases magic is the resort.[210] No medicines are used in New Britain, and in the New Hebrides the women have to attend to themselves throughout.[211] Bechuana women also are almost unattended, since they are believed to be unclean while child-bearing.[212] The Jekris use massage to facilitate the process.[213] Pygmy women generally give birth in the forest; the placenta is buried.[214] Bartels[215] cites a case in Uganda of the Cæsarian section, where the patient has been half intoxicated with banana-wine. Again, the woman is kneaded and her mouth covered to prevent her crying; in difficult cases the wizard gives her a root-decoction.[216] Among the Veddahs the woman when delivered goes forward, if on the march, or attends to her usual duties.[217]

Among the Sia, "though the woman is considered an invalid and exempt from all household duties until the tenth morning after childbirth, she passes in and out of the house after the fourth morning and occupies herself sewing, not more than half of her time being spent in a reclining position."[218] Of one California tribe it is reported that "their practice in midwifery is sometimes terribly severe, though effectual," including kneading and even treading.[219]

[205] D'Alviella, Concep. God, 25-27.
[206] Topinard, in Rev. d'anthrop., III; Jónsson, in Aarbøger, 1889, 176 ff.; MacCurdy, Human Origins, II, 160 ff.
[207] In JAI, XVII, 101, 102.　　　[208] Parker, Euahlayi, 39, 40.
[209] Krieger, Neu-Guinea, 389.　　　[210] Guise, in JAI, XXVIII, 206.
[211] Danks, in JAI, XVIII, 292; Gray, in JAI, XXVIII, 129.
[212] Fritsch, Süd-Afr., 204.
[213] Granville and Roth, in JAI, XXVIII, 106.
[214] Johnston, Uganda, II, 539.　　　[215] Medicin, 125.
[216] Stuhlmann, Mit Emin, 82.
[217] Rütimeyer, in Globus, LXXXIII, 203.
[218] Stevenson, in BAE, XI, 143.
[219] Powers, in Contrib. N. Amer. Ethnol., III, 239.

Light massage and a bath immediately after delivery are practised by the Tupis, and the woman is fully recovered in three or four days.[220]

In backward parts of Europe the methods are not much better than among savages. In a number of places, to hurry the delivery, the woman cudgels her husband; if she omits this, birth will be slow. Various magical processes are employed, especially in difficult cases.[221] In a number of cases much attention is paid to the placenta, which appears to be regarded as a fetish-object.[222]

§318*. Medicines. To be distinguished from other healing processes, though not in theory, is the administration of medicaments—not in theory, we say, for here too the notions remain daimonistic and the practice exorcistic. In general that is given which is thought effective to cast out the disease-spirit. It is easy to see why the emetic or the cathartic would be regarded as competent to secure such expulsion, particularly if the patient, as is so often the case in many forms of illness, needed relief of that sort. It is thought that certain decoctions of ill appearance, smell, and taste render the body a repulsive habitation for the disease-spirit; and again that the medicine is itself a spirit or a spirit-possessed fetish so that, by administering it, one spirit is set to drive out another. It is not very profitable to try to distinguish between these two details of theory; the fact is that in either case the medicine is regarded as fetishistic. Healing, like magic, relies largely upon the use of fetishes.[223] They may be such, as will be observed in the cases, because, like relics, they contain a virtue referable to the soul still possessing them; or they may be extraordinary in themselves or, more particularly, in their effects, like ardent "spirits." To make an exhaustive list of medicines would be impossible here and unprofitable; it is for more special works[224] to aim at more detailed treatment of this topic. The reader will note, however, the regular tendency toward automatic selection and retention of such drugs and other remedies as are capable, whatever the theory, of proving themselves therapeutic in fact.

220 Ambrosetti, in *Globus,* LXXIV, 245; Hassler, in *Anthrop. Cong. Chicago,* 1893, 354.

221 Temesváry, *Geburtshilfe,* 16, 44, 45, 48, 49, 122; Kaumanns, in *Hess. Bl. f. Vkde.,* V, 133 ff., review in AA, IX, 411.

222 Stuhlmann, *Mit Emin,* 653; Hiekisch, *Tungusen,* 84–85; Wilken, *Vkde.,* 205; Riedel, in *Bijd.,* XXXV, 92; Hassler, in *Anthrop. Cong. Chicago,* 1893, 355.

223 §§299-301, above.

224 Maddox, *Med. Man,* especially chs. VI and VII.

The Australians are prone to use blood as a medicine, a wife drawing it from her own body to administer to a sick husband. It is also rubbed over the body; and where there is a similar anointment with red ocher there can be little doubt that it is a substitute for blood—for ceremonial objects are sometimes rubbed with that substance instead of the usual blood. In fact, deposits of ocher are attributed to blood which has flowed from women.[225] Earth-eating is supposed in New Guinea to alleviate distress, particularly after overeating on fish; this is another thing from geophagy to satisfy hunger.[226] Cator[227] cites a case of a woman "with a dreadful disease in her face," for whom the European doctors could do nothing. She was brought up into the interior to be cured "country fashion" by a shaman and was getting better every day, having become free of pain after intense suffering. "For fevers, too, some of these native doctors have splendid medicines; but, on the other hand, many of them are awful humbugs, and ascribe every kind of magical power to some absolutely rubbishy concoction and charge accordingly."

The Hottentots have a medicine called "burmeester," a mineral, of which they always carry samples with them to rub into a snake-bite or scorpion-sting. Experimentation caused German doctors to believe it "a rational means against snake-bite" and one of them identified it as an ammoniac-salt.[228] Stigand[229] speaks of certain native remedies as "real medicines, which are often wonderfully efficacious."

"The ground principle of all West African physic is that everything works by spirit on spirit. Therefore the spirit of the medicine works on the spirit of the disease. Certain diseases are combatable by certain spirits in certain herbs. Other diseases are caused by spirits not amenable to herb-dwelling spirits; they must be tackled by spirits of a more powerful grade. . . . Before passing on to the great witch doctor, the physician, we must have an account of the neglected-by-traveller-because-less-showy African village apothecary, a really worthy person who exists in every known West African district. . . . These apothecaries are learned in the properties of herbs, and they are the surgeons in so far as surgery is ventured on. A witch doctor would not dream of performing an operation. Amongst these apothecaries there are lady doctors, who, though a bit dangerous in pharmacy, yet, as they do not venture on surgery, are, on the whole, safer than their confrères, for African surgery is heroic. The Dualla practitioner is truly great on poultices for extracting foreign substances from wounds, such as bits of old iron cooking pot, a very frequent foreign substance for a man to get into him in West Africa, owing to pots being broken up and used as bullets. . . . Dr. Nassau says that the efficacy of drugs is held to depend on their benevolent spirits, which, on being put into the body, drive away the malevolent disease-causing spirits."[230] The African expects an instant cure from medicine. Why not, if it is to expel the evil spirit? He takes drugs in big doses, for logic tells him that the greater the quantity taken the more effective the cure. The Basuto reasoned from the

[225] Smyth, *Vict.*, I, 263; Spencer and Gillen, *Nat. Tr. Cent. Aust.*, 464; Ellis, in PSM, LVII, 523-524.

[226] Meigen, in *Ztsft. d. deut. geolog. Gesell.*, Jahrgang 57, 1905 (résumé in *Globus*, XC, 259).

[227] *Head-Hunters*, 189.   [228] Gentz, in *Globus*, LXXXV, 82.
[229] In JAI, XXXVII, 127.
[230] Kingsley, *W. Afr. Studies*, 180, 181, 182, 490.

small fee charged by government doctors that the remedy was worth nothing —was merely water. What could they afford to give for a mere trifle except water? They believe that those who go to the hospital get their clothes taken away, never to be seen again, are stinted in food, and their bodies cut up if they die. Especially do they distrust the length of time required for a cure. What is the intention of the doctor who detains them thus? What is he going to practise on them?[231]

In Ceylon, for snake-bite a black stone is applied which, it is believed, adheres to the wound till it sucks out the poison; then it drops off.[232] This treatment reminds one of the "mad-stone" that was used in his boyhood to suck the poison out of the bite of a rabid dog. In Tibet "the eating of a paper on which a charm has been written is an ordinary way of curing disease. A still more mystical way of applying remedies is by the washings of the reflec- tion of the writing in a mirror." The author[233] cites a parallel from Gambia where extracts from the Koran are written on a wooden tablet, which is then washed; and the dirty infusion is drunk by the sick person. "The Chinese give a very high price for tigers' bones as a medicine, considering them a specific for strength and courage."[234] The Chinese idea is that nourishment is an animistic process; though the corporeal constituents of food leave the body, its incorporeal essence remains and elevates the soul-qualities of the eater. Bodily strength and health are therefore strength and health of the soul and various substances can restore them. Medicines are derived from certain ani- mals and "the list of medicaments which include parts of the human body is extraordinarily long. The ground for this is the idea that man is more strongly souled than animal or plant, and that therefore parts of his body exercise a correspondingly higher effect upon the soul of the eater." These parts are of unequal significance to medicine. The liver ranks first, being often identified with the soul; and the heart is scarcely inferior. The gall is the seat of courage and soldiers on the battle-field drink the gall of their enemies mixed with spirits. The blood of decapitated criminals is especially effective: "an eye-wit- ness tells of an execution which took place in 1862, in Tientsin, where the executioner's assistants dipped balls of plant-pith in the blood of the criminal and sold them as curatives. . . . Human secretions and excretions take up a very wide space in Chinese medicine." Sweat, saliva, and other secretions heal specific diseases. Preparations of charred skull are often used; and "still to be mentioned is the eating of earth taken from a burial-place."[235] This variety of "cannibalism," as the author[236] quoted calls it, is paralleled elsewhere.

Honey enters largely into Dyak medical practice, and to it are ascribed peculiar healing qualities; it will be recalled that honey plays a considerable part in mortuary ceremonies.[237] The so-called Bezoar stones obtained by the natives "are held in great repute by the Chinese, who buy them readily at a high price, for use as medicine in all kinds of ailments. They are reported to

[231] Marcosson, *Afr. Adv.*, 183; Lévy-Bruhl, *Ment. Prim.*, 484-485, 492.

[232] Hildburgh, in JAI, XXXVIII, 182.

[233] Waddell, *Tibet*, 401.   [234] Bishop, *Korea*, 73.

[235] Behrens, in *Globus*, LXXXI, 96, 97; Grube, in *Berl. Mus.*, VII, 3; Bourke, *Skatalog. Rites, passim.*

[236] Kern, "Menschenfleisch als Arznei," in *Int. Archiv. f. Ethnog.*, IX, suppl., 37-40.

[237] §§228, 230, 284, 285, above, and 437, below; Roth, *Sarawak*, I, 290.

be found both in the intestines and gall bladder of the monkey." Some of them are thought to be coagulated blood. In the Middle Ages they were brought to Europe as a sovereign remedy against poison.[238] In Sumatra plant-medicines, gathered during an eclipse of sun or moon, are in much repute but they must not be picked by hand and are gathered preferably by women, who use their mouths. The plants are chewed and the sufferer bespewed with them.[239] The Kubus use various decoctions made of different kinds of leaves. Their stock is very limited; it does not appear that they have many poisons but know best the plants possessing aphrodisiac qualities or those that produce abortion.[240] The gathering, preparation, and application of such medicines is done only on certain days and to the accompaniment of prayer by the shamans.[241] Worcester[242] treated neuralgia of the face with gum camphor saturated with ninety-six per cent alcohol, shampooing the sufferer and "taking especial pains to get it into his eyes, nose, and mouth, in order that he might not fail to note that we were using *strong medicine*." After application of the above for two hours some laudanum was given. An abscess burst and the cure was effected. Then flocks of natives came with all sorts of ailments, mostly stomach-ache and chills-and-fever. Jamaica ginger and quinine were dealt out liberally. The white men got a great reputation and had everything they wanted. By one tribe "crocodiles' teeth, filed to dust, are believed to be potent in checking some diseases, and the gall of pythons is also highly esteemed." Tongan doctors use some herbs, often successfully; they also employ massage and anoint with oil.[243]

Reclus,[244] speaking of the liberal use of urine by the Eskimo, cites many parallel cases from history. "Among the Indians of North America, and indeed as far as Alaska, the drug does not work in and for itself, but through the medicine-man's magic power only is curative quality imparted to it. All nature-products which he proposes to make serviceable for his medical use must be boiled, stirred, shaken, and filtered in a secret manner, and rattling with the magic rattle, humming, murmuring, and singing of incantations must accompany all these processes. Only thus do they attain the right and curative effectiveness."[245] Yet it was the American medicine-man who "first discovered the virtues of coca, sarsaparilla, jalap, cinchona, and guiacum."[246] It is truly "marvelous that in spite of the false reasoning by which they reached the results, in spite of their illusory major premises, and, one might almost say, in spite of themselves," so many of the medicaments applied by those primitive doctors had real medical properties.[247]

Saliva as a remedy was common among the Jews. Eye-troubles were cured by spitting into the eye. Most powerful was the saliva of a man who had not yet eaten.[248] In Arabia, as in Germany and Italy, woman's blood was a medi-

[238] Roth, *Sarawak*, I, 446; Bock, *Borneo*, 88. The oldest work on them is stated to be that of Wittich, *Von den wunderbaren Bezoarischen Steinen*, Leipzig, 1592. An article on the reputed medical qualities of precious stones, by Ponder, appears in the *Pharmaceutical Jr.* of London (abridged in N. Y. *Times*, June 3, 1926).

[239] Jacobs, *Groot-Atjeh*, I, 395. [240] Forbes, in JAI, XIV, 125.
[241] Bartels, *Medicin*, 108. [242] *Philippine Isl.*, 368-370, 494-495.
[243] Ella, in AAAS, 1892, 639.
[244] *Prim. Folk*, 36, 60, 61; Murdoch, in BAE, IX, 421.
[245] Bartels, *Medicin*, 109. [246] Bourke, in BAE, IX, 471.
[247] Maddox, *Med. Man*, 278-279. [248] Blau, *Zauberwesen*, 162-163.

cine.[249] Pliny[250] cites many remedies derived from the human body in his long lists of diseases and cures. White's[251] chapter on the evolution of medicine out of magic is highly enlightening in respect to mediæval conditions. From a very ancient period people have broken fragments from tombs and statues to pulverize and use as specifics for several diseases. Water that remained in the depressions of such fetish-stones[252] was effective in illness.[253] Healers among the southern Slavs asserted that they owed their knowledge of the curative qualities of plants to the tree-souls, and no peasant would dare question the assertion, from fear both of those souls and of the healers.[254] In Styria, in 1911, a law-suit for libel is reported to have revealed the popular belief that apothecaries and doctors had the right to kill at least one man and one woman every year in order to make medicines out of their bodies.[255] East Prussian remedies follow the stock primitive lines.[256] Irish peasants used urine much as the Eskimo did,[257] while "in Lincolnshire a small portion of the human skull was taken from the graveyard and grated, to be used in a mixture and eaten for the cure of fits. For the cure of epilepsy, near Kirkwall, a similar practice was resorted to, while in Caithness and the western isles the patient was made to drink from a suicide's skull."[258] The medical effects of the touch of the body of an executed criminal are widely recognized.[259]

The reports of healing and of the discovery of the herbs and other medicaments with which it was done go back into the time of the myths, just as in the case of other magical medicines effective for hunting and fishing, for play, for the crossing of a swollen river, for the success of magic dances, for good fortune in childbearing, for the protection of the child, for success in love, and all the rest.[260] The point of interest is less in the probable or possible origin of this or that medicament than in the process of trial and failure or of trial and success—in the groping empiric effort through which alone the beginnings could have been made. A comparison between the Cherokee pharmacopœia and the United States Dispensatory reveals that about one-third of twenty remedies investigated were correctly used.[261] It is true that, while many

[249] Durkheim, in *Année Soc.*, I, 56.
[250] *Nat. Hist.*, chs. XXVIII, XXIX, XXX.
[251] *Sci. and Theol.*, II, ch. XIII.   [252] §254, above.
[253] Sébillot, in AA, IV, 93, 94-96, 98-99, 101.
[254] Krauss, *Südslaven*, 97.
[255] New Haven *Jour.-Cour.*, for Sept. 16, 1911 (from London *Standard*).
[256] Sembrzycki, in *Am Ur-Quell*, I, 136.
[257] Preuss, in *Globus*, LXXXVI, 326.
[258] Gomme, *Ethnol. in Folklore*, 116.
[259] Peacock, in *Folk-Lore*, VII, 268 ff.
[260] Preuss, in *Globus*, LXXXVII, 396.
[261] Mooney, in BAE, VII, 323; Maddox, *Med. Man*, ch. VII, cites the most important medicines discovered by the shaman.

medicines possessing no medical properties have been retained even down to the present day, still among primitive peoples themselves there has been some selection upon the basis of observation and experience; and further along the line there have developed deliberate experimentation and scientific assessment of remedies both old and new. Without the daimonistic theory at the outset, nevertheless, it is hard to see how there would have been anything to give up or to retain or any basis in experience—in short, any development at all.

§319. Science and "Superstition." It should be clear from the preceding survey, not only of the medicines but also of the methods of the shaman, that we are again in the presence of the evolutionary process under which astronomy developed out of astrology and chemistry out of alchemy—under which, in a word, science developed out of what is generally called superstition. There is no science without laws; but there are no laws without records of phenomena—no records without observation—no observation without interest—and, we might almost add, in respect to the matters here under review, no interest without ghost-fear. Mental curiosity was lacking; to make a beginning it was needful that the emotions should be stirred; and in the case of medicine, at least, ghost-fear did that. It was the daimonistic theory of disease that set the process going and gave a chance for the development, in the fullness of time, of a quite different theory. This came to pass when it was observed that the phenomena recorded in memory, tradition, or otherwise, could be better explained by a modification of the original hypothesis into virtually its opposite. The old theory did duty as a point of departure, as a supporting framework, until the structure was set up; then it had served its purpose and might fall away, leaving, however, a solid edifice where there might have been none without it. Though the supports and braces are now rejected and forgotten, it is enlightening to know that they were once there and carried all the weight.

The most satisfying outcome of any scientific study is the conviction that truth has prevailed, and so, presumably, will prevail. And in no other range of observation is this conviction more enheartening than in the field of societal phenomena. The beginnings of what we now most prize have been childish, laughable, grotesque, revolting, or downright horrible. But this was not because men were wrong-headed and perverse; it was simply because they did not know, as the child does not. They were doing the best they could, under the circumstances. They had wrong premises from which they deduced, logically enough, conclusions that were wrong. With no external or adventitious aids, they sized up the problem of living as it appeared to them and evolved a life-policy which they put unflinchingly into practice.

In this practice the adequacy of the theory was always challenged by and tested on the actual conditions of living. However strongly supported by tradition and by what advanced peoples call superstition, the theory could not indefinitely stand if it involved maladjustment to these conditions; and even if adjustment had been for the moment secured, it presently turned, with the inevitable change of the life-conditions, into maladjustment. Of a consequence it was provided that life-theories should be subject to correction just as it is provided that bodies fall toward the earth's center.

If, however, the correction of error is provided for, then it matters little what you start with, if there is time enough—and there is no lack of that when it comes to cosmic processes. You are sure to work out toward the truth. Whenever you take hold of the societal fabric, you find its strands, however orderly and symmetrical their present arrangement, running back into a snarl of the fantastic and irrational. Out of this unpromising and often ludicrous beginning has come all that we now value; and without those beliefs which we wonder at as we reject them, but which spurred our forebears to an activity in whose absence there would have been no observation and verification, society and civilization could not have been what they now are. It is no small service to the race to demonstrate that truth comes out of the automatic correction of natural error, and not otherwise; for it gives a true perspective of human life and a clearer understanding of what men are doing and can do to live better in the future. It is also possible, in the light of such knowledge, to believe that the process will never end while men live on earth. Societal evolution teaches that the race began in destitution and error and has, by the exercise of its own powers and not by outside aid, worked itself up, for the most part unconsciously, to what is now prized as culture or civilization. There is no more reason to believe that this process will ever stop than there is to believe that arbitrary intervention at any time interrupted its course in the past.

This is the broadest generalization to be derived from detailed studies such as that of the medicine-man's character, functions, and methods; and it represents their widest human interest. Any such study makes substantial contribution to our enlightenment concerning the evolution and life of human society.[262]

§320*. Social Position of the Shaman. There will be no better time or place than the present to sketch briefly the position taken in society by the professional daimonologist. It is evident, first of all, that the healer of disease, to say nothing of the priest, is in a position readily to increase his own possessions. A few examples are representative of many.[263]

Kipling,[264] who portrays so vividly the life of India, makes a Jat say, with bitterness, of the priests: "They are all most holy and—most greedy"; and, again, concerning a sick child: "Now I am a poor man—many priests have dealt with me,—but my son is my son." In Tibet, "when, despite the execution of all this costly worship, sickness still happens, it necessitates the further employment of Lamas, and the recourse by the more wealthy to a devil-dancer or to a special additional horoscope by the Lama. So that [to] one family alone is prescribed a sufficient number of sacerdotal tasks to engage a couple of Lamas fairly fully for several months of every year."[265] In Borneo, "whether the patient live or die, the *manang* is rewarded for his trouble. He makes sure of this before he undertakes a case, as he is put to considerable inconvenience by being fetched away from his own home and his own work. He takes up his abode with the patient, and has his meals with the family, and in other ways makes himself at home. If a cure be effected, he receives a present in addition to his regular fee." The author[266] gives a list of "different kinds of ceremonies, according to the advice of the *manang* or the fee the patient is prepared to pay. . . . If a patient fail to recover after one kind of ceremony, the *manangs* often recommend another and more expensive one."

The Cherokee shamans disclaim that the consideration, often cloth, which the doctor receives for his services is "pay, in our sense of the word, but assert that it is one of the agencies in the removal and banishment of the disease spirit. Their explanation is somewhat obscure; the cloth seems to be intended

[262] The foregoing three paragraphs are adapted from Keller, in Foreword to Maddox, *Med. Man*, ix-x.

[263] Maddox, *Med. Man*, ch. V.   [264] *Kim*, 296.

[265] Waddell, *Buddhism*, 464.

[266] Gomes, *Sea Dyaks*, 165, 168, 169.

either as an offering to the disease spirit, as a ransom to procure the release of his intended victim, or as a covering to protect the hand of a shaman while engaged in pulling the disease from the body of the patient. The first theory, which includes also the idea of vicarious atonement, is common to many primitive peoples."[267]

It was hardly possible for the shaman, unless he was an utter lunatic, to remain poor; and his wealth meant, among primitive peoples, position and power. If the holy man, whether shaman or priest, represented the intermediary between the supernatural and man, the latter being as concerned as we have seen him to be about his relations with the supernatural, then the mediating agent stood for prosperity and was sure to hold a preferred position in society. He must be well-dressed, for instance, if he was to represent the people to the gods. Through his power of denunciation of rivals whom he, as the official and ranking exponent of the public cult, might at any time accuse of witchcraft, the shaman was firmly established—provided, of course, that he could continue to demonstrate his abilities and gloze over his failures.[268] A list of his exemptions and privileges would be very extensive; Main[269] makes a good deal of his sexual prerogatives, whereby he is likely to have a plurality of wives or to be able to commandeer women who are dedicated to the daimon. A few representative illustrations follow.[270]

Australian medicine-men and medicine-women are not subject to special tribal restrictions while actually practising their profession; for instance, that one which prohibits any intercourse whatever between men and their tribal mothers-in-law.[271] The prime offender in an affair involving interference with another man's wife was not touched, being a shaman, while the woman concerned, and the others who were connected with the matter, "came in for very severe handling."[272] Occasionally, however, "the doctor had to undergo the ordeal of spears when a member of the tribe lost his life, who should have been protected by his incantations."[273] In Melanesia, as has been noted before, a man becomes chief because he performs the sacrifices, not *vice versa*.[274] "Medicine men here, as in most other places, hold unique positions, and many a smart villain prospers owing to the belief that he has power over the unseen —to kill or cure at will. Their houses are taboo or 'hope,' the same as the

[267] Mooney, in BAE, VII, 337.
[268] Lehmann, *Overtro*, I, 21-22, 27-33; Lippert, *Kgchte.*, I, 32.
[269] *Relig. Chastity*, Appendix, notes XIII, XIV, XXXII.
[270] Maddox, *Med. Man*, chs. IV and V.
[271] Spencer and Gillen, *Nat. Tr. Cent. Aust.*, 530, note.
[272] Spencer and Gillen, *North. Tr. Cent. Aust*, 486.
[273] Curr, *Aust. Race*, I, 47.   [274] Codrington, *Melanesians*, 127.

chief's, and in many villages they are held in far greater awe than the chief himself."[275] "It is a striking fact that, when division of social function first appears, it is often in connexion with religion or the closely allied leechcraft. Thus, in Eddystone Island in the Solomons, where most arts are practised by all, there is a high degree of specialization of function in relation to disease and its treatment. In that island it is believed that each recognized disease arises through the infraction of a taboo. . . . There are nearly a hundred such taboos, each with its special ritual and confined to a small group of practitioners, sometimes to one only. Since the disease dependent upon infraction of each taboo can only be cured by a man who knows the appropriate rites, there has arisen a state of affairs in which each disease has its own specialists, leading to a degree of specialism in leechcraft exceeding that of modern medicine."[276] The Andamanese curry favor with the shaman with all sorts of bribes. "Sometimes these gifts are so numerous that they would, if given at once, inconvenience the seer; hence he requests that they be set aside for his future use." Many persons possess such "bespoken" property.[277]

In Africa, if a holy woman who serves the fetish marries, her mastery is acknowledged by her husband. If she thinks she is injured, she simulates madness; then the husband, or anyone else who has angered her, must sacrifice in expiation. Such an offering is generally spirits, of which she and her sister-priestesses drink the greater part.[278] The controllers of the Ju-Ju, in West Africa, sell their victims into slavery "in as far distant a country as possible; but occasionally one of these men has drifted down to the coast again, but does not return to his own country as no one would believe he was anything but a spirit."[279] In northeast Africa the shamans are greedy and even murderous; yet "each chief has a number of them by him and even the poorest man of the people is a client of one of these persons." They sell means to prevent sterility and to produce abortion and often do not hesitate to make common cause with robbers. Seamen beg for their blessing upon voyages; warriors, sick people, and lovers turn trustingly to them. They "go about elegantly clad and live high."[280]

Evidence from the Society Islands "points to the relationship of head priests to the higher chiefs, and to the appointment by chiefs of persons who were to act as official priests, and to the tendency of the office thus created to become hereditary." In one island there was "a king, attended by a priest, who was one of the two highest of the chiefs of the king's people, and who acted as the king's mouthpiece at council meetings . . . and therefore performed both sacred and secular duties. . . . In the Marquesas nothing could be done in the political or religious sphere without the consent of the high priests, the gravest questions of state always having to be submitted to them. . . . The priesthood should be divided broadly into two classes, of which one, the real priests, belonged to noble families . . . whilst the other, the more numerous class, were really inspired persons." These latter were the general priests. In another island there was, in 1845, no king. "In olden days they had kings; but as they were high priests also, and were supposed to cause the food to grow, the people became angry with them in times of scarcity and killed them. One

[275] Hardy and Elkington, *S. Seas,* 139.
[276] Rivers, *Soc. Org.,* 148.
[277] Man, in JAI, XII, 96.
[278] Frobenius, *Masken,* 102, 103.
[279] Kingsley, *W. Afr. Studies,* 498.
[280] Paulitschke, *Nordost-Afr.,* II, 61.

after another of them was killed; therefore no one wished to be king, so afterwards affairs were managed by councils of heads of families."[281]

In America the shaman is the educator and the preserver of myth and tradition and of the arts of writing and of divination. His power is often greatest in time of peace. The organization of the priesthood is slight where there is little specialization and highest in Mexico, Central America, and Peru.[282] Much more care and expense were undergone in burying the medicine-man than in the case of anyone else.[283] "Instances are not rare where medicine men or shamans on the northwest coast of America have been head chiefs of villages."[284] Among certain Alaskan Indians the shamans were influential, rich, respected, and feared. "The social standing of a medicine-man is, on the whole, a desirable one; but it has also its drawbacks and its dark side. The medicine-man is decidedly influential among his fellow savages. He is consulted and listened to, on account of the superior knowledge imparted to him by the spirits. He is feared, on account of his power to do evil, viz., to cause the death of a person, to ruin his undertakings, to render him unsuccessful in the hunt by driving away the game from his path, to cause the loss of his property, of his strength, of his health, of his faculties. . . . The medicine-man is rich, because his services, when summoned, or even when accepted though uncalled for, are generously remunerated. He is respected on account of his continual intercourse with the supernatural world. His words, when said in a peculiar low tone, with a momentary glow in the eyes, which he seems able to control at will, or when uttered during his sleep (real or feigned), are taken as oracles, as the very words of the spirit. In short, for these tribes who have no chiefs, no religion, no medical knowledge, he is the nearest approach to a chief, a priest, and a physician: to the chief, because he practically forms and models the public opinion, the only rule among Ten'a, to a priest, because he acts as the intermediary between the visible and invisible world, to a physician, because his power enables him to cast away devils by which diseases are caused. One ought to add that all diseases, according to Ten'a medicine, originate in a spirit locating himself in a person's body. The medicine-man, having a devil at his service, may, by means of it, expel the intruding spirit, provided, of course, that his own demon be more powerful than the intruder. If the reverse happens, he fails in his attempts to cure the sick person, and incurs no odium by the fact. It is not his fault, if his spirit is not stronger than the opposing one, and he is not made responsible for it." This is a keen statement and exact except for the "devil" and "demon" terminology which is natural enough to the priest who writes.[285] In Mexico the medicine-men had control of education, in songs and prayers, national legends, religious dogmas, medicine, conjurations, music and dance, painting, drawing ideographic signs and phonetic hieroglyphics. Supposed communication with the spirits raised them in the eyes of the people but all elements of science lay smothered in this spirit-service. Where religion is the whole of immaterial life, it means that all intellectual life is frozen fast.[286] Contemporary with the Zapotec chief lived a chief priest, who "took an important part in the government of the country." He

[281] Williamson, *Cent. Polyn.*, III, 51-52, 333-335.
[282] Dixon, "Amer. Shaman," in *Jr. Amer. Folklore,* XXI, 1 ff.
[283] Dorsey, in PSM, LIII, 169.   [284] Niblack, in USNM, 1888, 251.
[285] Jetté, in JAI, XXXVII, 157 ff., 163-164.
[286] Ratzel, *Vkde.,* III, 14.

could not marry and was bound to continence "but on a certain day of the year he had a right to become intoxicated, and when he was in that state, a young and beautiful virgin was brought to him; and it was the eldest of the children born of this union of a single day who inherited the sacerdotal dignity."[287] People who cannot pay the medicine-man must always remain in the shape of animals.[288]

The immunity from blame instanced in foregoing connections is, however, not at all universal. "Since supposed sorcery is nearly always the nearest cause of murders within the tribe, it is clear that the professional sorcerers or medicine men are those members of Jibaro society which are most frequently exposed to the revengeful attacks of their enemies. As a matter of fact, in large Indian societies sorcerers are almost continually assassinated, or at least threatened with death, by their enemies. When a medicine man has undertaken to cure a sick person and the latter dies in spite of the treatment, the 'doctor' is also generally made responsible for the death, the relatives of the dead reasoning that the medicine man, instead of curing the patient, on the contrary used his art to kill him. The unsuccessful curer is therefore murdered unless he escapes by flight."[289] It is evident that, whatever the treatment accorded the unsuccessful medicine-man, it is because of firm belief in shamanism and its powers rather than of doubt of either.

In ancient Persia and Egypt, as in India, the priestly class was above all others.[290] Rich Egyptians gave property and land to the patron god to secure prayers and sacrifices for themselves. In the course of time these formed great estates, and masses of gold and silver were collected in the temple. All this was managed by the priests. If the nobles and kings had not laid hand on the revenues of the temples, the whole territory of Egypt would have become sacerdotal. The priests were a great privileged body, secure in their existence and free from all civil burdens. The author quoted[291] gives an estimate of the ecclesiastical property at the accession of Rameses IV. The priests formed colleges or schools and engaged in studying the holy texts and in theological speculation. Greek tragedy has some hard things to say of the seer: that the desire for money is the prophet's plague;[292] that the whole ambitious tribe of seers is a curse and good for nothing. What is a seer? One who by luck sometimes gets it right, but often wrong; when his luck fails him that is the end of him.[293] But the so-called Oath of Hippocrates presents the ideal of a sober, self-respecting, humane, and reticent public functionary out of whose character, along with priestly pretensions, have departed all the arrogance and other objectionable qualities of the primitive shaman.[294]

Chadwick, in his "Ancient Teutonic Priesthood,"[295] makes the points "(1)

[287] Nadaillac, *Preh. Amer.*, 363.

[288] Lumholtz, in *Int. Cong. Anthrop.*, 1893, 112.

[289] Karsten, "Jibaro," in BAE, Bull. LXXIX, 9.

[290] Geiger, *Ostiran. Kultur*, 463, 464; Letourneau, *Prop.*, 145.

[291] Maspero, *Hist. Anc.*, II, 126, 303, 305, 558; Tiele-Gehrich, *Gchte. Relig.*, I, 54, 99-100.

[292] Sophocles, *Antigone*, 1055.

[293] Euripides, *Iphigenia in Aulis*, 520, 956-958.

[294] *Hippocratis Opera Omnia*, I, 1-2; translation of oath in *Works of Hippocrates* (Adams), II, 779-780.

[295] In *Folk-Lore*, XI, 285-286 (quoted); Geijer, *Svensk. Hist.*, I, 24.

that the priest of the ancient Germans was not a person endowed with secret knowledge but a tribal official; (2) that in the North priestly duties were always combined with temporal power." We have met this connection before, under the topic of kingship.296 The Druids ruled over all the Celtic peoples. In Cæsar's time many Gauls went to Britain to study Druidism; and in Gaul this priesthood occupied a social rank like that of Brahmans. "They formed a powerful order, influenced and decided the choice of magistrates; performed divine service; brought offerings and explained oracles; were doctors and teachers, and acted as arbitrators in the absence of state jurisdiction, enforcing their decision by a kind of civil outlawry. They possessed privileges and revenues, were rich and despotic, and held the people in subjection." The Druids of Ireland never attained such power, though the chief Druid lived at a king's court and his power was pretty much the same as the king's. The Druids' knowledge was remarkable for their time. Their teaching consisted of a public part and a secret part; to the latter belonged hymns, rules for prophecy, formulas for charms, and knowledge of ancient hieroglyphics. The Irish even asserted that the Druids had created heaven, earth, sea, sun, moon, and stars. In Gaul they kept schools for the sons of the nobility, some features of which seem to have been handed down to the Irish monasteries. The Roman writers charge them with rudeness, stupidity, vanity, pride, and hardness of heart; and Rome broke their social position and ended their judicial powers.297

Maddox[298] well accounts for the social position of the medicine-man by reference to the fear he inspires through his aloofness and by reason of the popular belief in his influence with and power over the spirits. "The conviction of his supernatural origin, the effect of his adventitious aids, his superior mental and moral qualities, in addition to the exhibition of truly wonderful powers, cause in the savage mind a feeling of veneration and awe which does not fail to assist in extending the temporal and spiritual sway of the shaman over all classes throughout the land. . . . He must be treated with reverence and his wishes consulted, lest in anger he consume the recalcitrants. . . . It is to the advantage, therefore, of every tribal member to ingratiate himself with the medicine man. If there be a person who can so influence the spirits that they will do his behest, it is obvious that everybody will want to make friends with him. Even if he has no mystical power, if by

296 §155, above.

297 Von Pflugk-Harttung, in *Trans. Roy. Hist. Soc.*, VII, 55 ff.; Cæsar, *Bell. Gall.*, VI, 13. Hilton Gregory (the *nom de plume* of a Methodist clergyman), in "A Note on Priestcraft" (*Amer. Mercury*, VIII, 148 ff.), treats rather bitterly of the modern clergyman as a sort of medicine-man and self-styled friend of God. He says that some clerics resist modernism because it would pull them down from their pedestals and lower their perquisites. The most ignoble of modern priests are here closely aligned with their primitive prototypes.

298 *Med. Man,* 114 ff.

using his detective function he can throw the blame of evil fortune on the insubordinate, every person in the group will dread him to the extent of showing him respect, reverence, and even worship. . . . The medicine man is naturally keen in turning to advantage the unusual esteem and privileges which come to him by virtue of his office. . . . He is the most influential man of primitive times. . . . In view of his social prominence, it is not surprising that this personage makes use of his power to elevate himself to the highest position in the land—that of chief. . . . The medicine man in some cases exercises not only kingly power, but pretends divinity. . . . The shaman 'goes from strength to strength.' "

§321. Shamanism as a Recapitulation. The shaman is a sort of culminating and epitomizing functionary, so far as religion is concerned, and shamanism may be said to recapitulate the views and practices of the race with respect to the supernatural. It touches the aleatory element at every turn, for it has to do with the inexplicable, and in practice it concerns itself almost altogether with the spirit-environment. Animistic doctrines are illustrated in the theories about disease: that it is due to absence of the soul and to experiences undergone by that errant "double." The shamans are all-powerful against the ghosts of the dead, though they may receive their endowments from them; and they themselves become powerful ghosts; the ghost-cult is recalled over and over again in the operations of the medicine-man. Daimonism, or the theory about spirits, is similarly exemplified in the personality and performances of the shaman; and he is not seldom the hero who rises to the status of godhood. Of fetishism the shaman is an even stricter epitome; for he himself is a fetish-man and he works constantly with fetish-instrumentalities. Daimonology is exhaustively illustrated in his professional activities and the taboo both rests upon him and is by him extended over others. In his capacity as priestly intermediary between men and gods he deals with sins and penalties and with the means of clearance from spiritual resentment and censure. He knows the ritual, practises and imposes renunciation and self-discipline, attends to the sacrifices, prescribes atonement and ransom, and secures redemption. As a hero he may become a veritable messiah.[299]

[299] §240, above.

In short, the shaman-priest is the great exponent of religion. Out of a study of his nature and doings a complete panorama of primitive beliefs could be deduced. He stands or falls, therefore, as an adjustment by society to the supernatural environment, along with the religion which he represents and recapitulates—except, indeed, as he escapes, with the development of science out of "superstition," into the scientific professions and thus detaches his interests and destiny from the narrowly spiritual. When we come to the final assessment of religion as an adjustment it will be necessary to refer repeatedly to the results attained by shamanism and its exponents. Until that time are reserved any further generalities concerning the shamanistic function and functionary.

A final truth, and a weighty, to be drawn from the study of the shaman is the respect of primitive mankind for what they took to be, and what was in many respects, superior knowledge. For those who knew, for those who saw (the seers), there was high honor. We, to be sure, realize that the shaman did not know or see, as alleged; we accord him no respect by reason of his association with spirits in whose existence we do not believe. That, however, has no bearing upon the fact that what stood for knowledge among savages was highly prized; that the primitive man was no fool, but knew it was better to know. If ignorance has always ascribed superior knowledge to wizardry, if it has stood in awe before the empty occult, it has yet reverenced the best there was available, the germ out of which real knowledge was to evolve. The savages were too near to the raw struggle for existence to hold in light esteem that which they thought contributed strongly to their insurance against ill; it has been reserved for civilized man, secure behind the bulwarks of which the savage laid the foundations, to play the wanton fool, as no nature-man could or would, with fanciful and perverse floutings of the knowledge—of the science—he ought to reverence. Only civilized man is secure enough, by virtue of the work and thought and suffering of those who gained knowledge for mankind, and for him, to affect contempt and condescension for their indispensable labors.

CHAPTER XL

RELIGION IN GENERAL

§322*. Alleged Absence of Religion. In scanning ethnographical literature a reader comes rather frequently upon the statement that such and such a people has no religion. Although certain of these assertions are isolated and therefore not subject to critical examination, most of them are embedded in a context which reveals the angle of view of the writer. This is the chief point of interest in them all—not that one is much concerned as to what any particular author defines, implicitly or explicitly, as religion or no-religion, but rather because, taken all together and even in their conflicts, they contribute powerfully to the conclusion, familiar enough to the evolutionist in any field, that hard and fast lines of demarcation do not exist in any evolutionary series. In connection with most of the alleged cases of the absence of religion there are yet indications of belief in a supernatural environment and in a life beyond death. From the evolutionary point of view, peoples who hold such convictions have a religion; we think it as unjustifiable to deny such title to their beliefs as to withhold the application of the term culture from the germs of what is now called civilization or to refuse to call a child a human being. Religion is to us a series of adjustments to that salient set of life-conditions represented by the aleatory element as personalized in the spirit-environment.

A review of the cases[1] in which religion is alleged to be absent or to exist in a rudimentary phase not conceived to deserve the name will make for an understanding of the essential nature of religion. Unqualified denials of its presence are not only few but dubious, for the most sweeping assertions of its utter absence are often contradicted by their context.

---

[1] Lippert (*Kgchte.*, I, 103) quotes the testimony of a number of travellers that certain peoples have no religion but ghost-fear and Spencer (*Prin. Soc.*, I, §146) lists several cases of the alleged absence of religion, referring also to kindred instances cited by Lubbock and Tylor (*Preh. Times,* 564 ff., and *Prim. Cult.,* I, 377 ff., respectively); §216, above.

A beginning may be made with the African Pygmies who are in many respects the most backward of peoples. Of them it is reported that no religion, so far as could be discovered, had ever been in use; they do not know the totem and have no fetish-rites whatsoever. Where one of their number dies he is buried, and there is an end to him and his memory. They neither wear mourning nor erect memorials over the graves of their dead. "Some of the tribes have neither religion nor superstition, nor do they practice any occult or fetish rites. Others have a vivid belief in the unseen world, in a god, and in the spirits of the departed, and so are higher in the scale of civilization than their more agnostic neighbors."[2] Among the Wambutti dwarfs there were no fetishes; "I have looked about in the two dozen Wambutti settlements and never noticed a fetish-hut, otherwise so tremendously numerous in the villages of the primeval Ituri forests. And I have not yet encountered any graves. . . . I came later to the view that they possess no trace of religion, of veneration, or of metaphysical ideas in general, yet feel themselves constantly opposed and thwarted by the hostile powers of nature."[3] The dwarfs of Cameroons "know only evil supramundane powers, for the conciliation of which they do nothing, since they feel themselves powerless against them."[4] Without exception inquiries elicited a disbelief in a higher being.[5] "Their whole faith seems to me to reach its peak in fear of magic, which is artificially instilled in them by the sorcerers. Though as a means to their ends idols and fetishes are of service, otherwise they are by no means prayed to or honored by the people." It is to be noted that great difficulty is encountered in getting information about the religion of these peoples; "among all heathen negroes who really hold their gods in honor there is found a reluctance, to be overcome only by protracted association, to tell anything at all about them."[6] Lloyd[7] thinks the Pygmies have their religion. It has been said that they have none, but in passing through the forest he has often found signs of Pygmy worship. At the foot of some of the huge trees he has several times picked up little bundles of food neatly tied up in rough bark cloth; he has also seen little pots of honey placed at the foot of these trees. This indicated veneration for the spirits of the great trees among which they made their homes. He found also some little shrines, very neatly made, that must have belonged to the Pygmies. Upon their arms and around their necks, some of them, especially the women, wore charms to ward off leopards and also disease, especially smallpox.

"There is no lack of people who assert that the Kaffirs possessed no religion and, in fact, in a special sense, the observation can be justified. On the other hand, if certain muddled conceptions of super-earthly things and the superstition connected therewith be held sufficient to indicate the presence of religion, the said tribes all have religion as well as religious usages and the fundamental notions of the different tribes do indeed agree in essentials. They have unclear ideas about persistence beyond death and the ghosts of dead ancestors become, among most of them, the object of a certain cultus." The author[8] quotes a missionary as follows: "If by religion we mean reverence for God, or the

[2] Burrows, in JAI, XXVIII, 37; Burrows, *Pygmies,* 100, 182, 197.

[3] David, in *Globus,* LXXXV, 118; LXXXVI, 196-197.

[4] Von Schkopp, in *Globus,* LXXXIII, 285.

[5] Lessner, in *Globus,* LXXXVI, 395.

[6] Zöller, *Kamerun,* 73.   [7] *Dwarf Land,* 324.

[8] Fritsch, *Eingeb. S.-Afr.,* 57, 98, note, 233.

external action by which that reverence is expressed, I never could perceive that they had any religion nor any idea of the existence of God." With the Herero too, "the religious ideas are never consistently thought out but external superstitious usages form the real heart of their so-called religion."

The Nature-Veddahs have no idea, or a very uncertain one, of the further life of the soul of the dead at the place of death and do not sacrifice to the ghosts; and the Culture-Veddahs have advanced little farther, for when questioned they reply that they do not know whether the soul lives on after death or that they have never thought about it. Of the former type of Veddah it is stated that "he has no conception of a soul, a highest being, or a future life. He says he sees the sun rise each morning and the darkness come at evening, and that is all he knows . . . and he thinks there is no existence after the body is once dead. He does not know who made the world but now believes that One must have made it." Formerly he did not bury corpses, letting them lie where they fell; he had at most a misgiving as to a future life. If he is found practising funerary usages, the cult of the dead, and memorial festivals, it is in imitation of more cultured neighbors.[9] There is no distinct belief in a god, no ancestor-worship, no cult of the stars, no daimon-fear. "At the question as to whether they admitted that there were gods, or a god, the answer was: 'We do not know'; likewise, concerning what idea they had of sun and moon: 'We do not know.' Plainly they have never thought about it. At the query as to whether they were afraid, anywhere at night in the forest, of evil ghosts and spirits, the answer was definitely, 'No.' At the question as to the persistence of soul-life after death, the answer was again similarly guarded: 'We do not know.' "[10] "They have no knowledge of a Supreme Being. 'Is he on a rock? On a white ant-hill? On a tree? I never saw a God!' was the only reply to repeated questions." They have no idols, offer no sacrifices, and pour no libations; nor can they be said to have any temples, for the few sticks sometimes erected, with a branch thrown over them, are, the author[11] quoted thinks, simply to protect their votive offerings.

Of certain Dyaks it is reported: "The people are like babes, they have no religion of their own, no gods to worship. They pay attention to the cries of birds of good or ill omen, observe strictly the traditions of their forefathers, and have a very strict code of moral laws, which they administer with as fair justice as any one could get in England." This author[12] quotes as follows: "Were I asked what is the religion of the Land Dyaks, I should say none worthy of the name, but their *religious observances* may be classed as follows"—a list including killing and eating fowls and pigs, with a portion set aside for the deity; propitiation of demons and ghosts; the taboo; obedience to and belief in priestesses; dancing; the use of omens from the notes of birds.

The Kubus of Sumatra seemed to have no idea of a state after death; "when we are dead, we're dead."[13] From southern Celebes is reported the following dialogue: "Who made the earth and the heaven?" "I do not know." "When anyone dies, where does his soul go?" "I do not know." "Do you know who Mohammed is?" "I do not know." "Do you sacrifice to the daimons?" "Yes, sirih, rice, and the like, to beg for rain." "How do you conceive of them?" "We

---

[9] Sarasin, *Weddas*, 495, 498-499.
[10] Rütimeyer, in *Globus*, LXXXIII, 207, 264.
[11] Bailey, in *Trans. Ethnol. Soc. London*, II, 302-303.
[12] Roth, *Sarawak*, I, 76, 165. [13] Forbes, in JAI, XIV, 125.

know nothing of them, but we take a man along who knows something about them." They have no religion, unless traces of tree-worship be so considered.[14] Wallace[15] saw no traces of any religion in the Aru Islands. In the Poggi Islands there was no religion but demonism, no idols or idol-worship, but some practice of auguries.[16] In the Moluccan Archipelago, the Arafuras knew of no future life. "No Arafura has ever returned to us after death, therefore we know nothing of a future state." They contended that when you are dead there is an end of you; yet they tried to scare off evil spirits by snake-symbols.[17]

The Marshall Islanders are said to have no religion and no priests, yet there exists a rather rude fetishism, and there are diviners. Certain Caroline Islanders "have never possessed a religion."[18] The Ponapé people "in their relatively rich language lack the word to express the idea of God; only the lightning, not very common there, did they apprehend to be a supernatural thing which they fear but do not worship."[19] Of the natives of Rotuma Gardiner[20] writes: "Faith they had not; their own religion was founded merely on fear of the *atua*, who had to be propitiated; their good spirit was entirely neglected."

Among the Eskimo, "there is no knowledge and no idea of a Supreme Being or of a future state, so far as I could discover. One whom I questioned said: 'Husky die. No more Husky.'"[21] The great majority of the Indians did not rise to any idea of a single god. As with the Hottentots and Malays, the missionaries in America have had the greatest difficulty to find in the Indian glossary a word for our term "God." The abstract notions reach no farther than soul or ghost, or perhaps shadow, or their words mean only "wonderful." They designate no personal unity. The word "manitu" of the Algonquins does not mean at all "Great Spirit," but only that which is mysterious and incomprehensible. The notion becomes concrete only in connection with creation. The only question is whether the creator in the Indian myth is the ultimate force of existence, or only an assistant god who executes creation, or only the first created, who then carries out the rest of the process. The Indians had a belief that the men of light would come one day to make good their right to the land which the god of light had created and possessed before he returned to heaven. This belief greatly helped the white conquerors of the sixteenth century.[22] That "fear created the gods" seems to be substantiated by the observations of Von Martius[23] upon the Brazilian tribes. Most of the tribes had no word for god until the missionaries introduced one. The Botocudos had no religion but ghost-fear,[24] and "the Mundrucus do not believe in immortality."[25] The Tupis did not get beyond an "innate terror," for example of the lightning.[26] The commandant of a Spanish post in Peru, a good Catholic, attempted to instil in several natives some idea of God. "They listened apparently in vague wonder, and when asked if their people had no such belief, replied in the negative. The

[14] Sarasin, in *Globus*, LXXXIII, 279-280.
[15] *Malay Arch.*, 481.
[16] Severijn, in *Tijds. T. L. Vkde.*, III, 329.
[17] Spencer, *Prin. Soc.*, II, §575, note.
[18] Finsch, *Ethnol. Erfahr.*, III, 139, 200.
[19] Pereiro, *Ponapé*, 132.   [20] In JAI, XXVII, 409.
[21] Hanbury, *Canada*, 67.   [22] Ratzel, *Vkde.*, II, 679.
[23] *Beiträge*, I, 463, 464.
[24] Ehrenreich, in *Ztsft. f. Ethnol.*, XIX, 34.
[25] Markham, in JAI, XXIV, 268.   [26] Varnhagen, *Brazil*, I, 123.

idea of a future life after death, so far as we could learn, was not familiar to them."[27] The Caïngua of Paraguay retain a little of what their ancestors learned from the Jesuits two hundred years ago, "but aside from these rudimentary notions, their religion is null and destitute of every kind of outer worship." The author[28] goes on to say, however, that "notwithstanding their entire want of religion, the Caïngua have a vague idea of a future life; for after the interment of a deceased relative they deposit on the new grave the arms of the departed and provisions for the journey which they evidently suppose to be possible."

The Reverend Dr. La Fetra[29] speaks rather disconsolately of the Araucanians. "Nowhere at any time, in all these centuries of contact with them, has any religious worship been found among the Araucanians. They have no priests, make no public prayers, have no religious ceremonies, and no domestic idols nor charms. They are simple children of nature, rising to the sublimity of belief in a Creator, the giver of all good, and yet they are able to form no very definite ideas of the attributes of this Good Spirit. The efforts of the Jesuits and other Roman Catholic missionaries among them for more than three hundred years have been almost unavailing. Here and there a cross in their burying ground indicates that the inmate of that grave had been baptized in the Christian faith, but that simple ceremony was probably all the difference between him and his people." Among the Fuegians there is "no word for deity or a future existence."[30]

To take one case of a highly developed belief, we are told that Buddhism is "a system which knows no God in the Western sense; which denies a soul to man; which counts the belief in immortality a blunder, and the hope of it a sin; which refuses any efficacy to prayer and sacrifice; and which bids men look to nothing but their own efforts for salvation."[31] By many such a system would not be accorded the name of religion, though it is one of the few great faiths.

Whether animism, eidolism, daimonism, or fetishism is denied the name of religion, or is not, is a matter of small consequence; interest lies only in showing that, whatever they may be called, they represent the necessary antecedent members of a connected series of adjustments to the supernatural environment, of which later religions are the lineal consequents. Religion is not absent, even if represented only by its germ. Nearly all of these alleged cases of lack of religion—barring the few in which, the context offering no contradiction, there is a categorical denial of the presence of even animistic phenomena—fit readily into the evolutionary series of religious forms as it has been developed in foregoing chapters. They could have been classified here and there in that

[27] Bailey, in *Nat. Geog. Mag.*, XVII, 448.
[28] Machon, in PSM, LII, 400, 405.
[29] "Araucanians," in *Illust. Christian World* for December, 1896.
[30] Spears, in *Scribner's Mag.*, XVII, 224.
[31] Huxley, in PSM, XLIV, 35.

series and really belong for the most part in its earliest categories; they were saved out for citation at this point, after the
series should have been spread before us, in order to enforce the
contention that all types of adjustment to that salient life-condition represented by the aleatory element, however poor and naïve
or rich and sophisticated they may be, and whatever name may be
given them, belong genetically together. In particular, the foregoing instances furnish a minimum or base-line from which to
reckon the degree of development attained by human adjustment
to the unseen environment. The distinctions present in this series
are those of degree and not of kind, just as in the other series of
adjustments in societal self-maintenance and self-perpetuation.

§323. Nature of Religion. The grounds explicitly or implicitly
taken in reports such as the foregoing, either for denying religion
to the primitive peoples or for rebutting such denial by others,
amount to a series of judgments as to the nature of religion. It
is evident on the face of the reports that most of them, when
adverse to the existence of religion among savages, have been
made by using as a measuring-stick the faith to which the observer
was committed. All that such judgments say is that "their religion is not ours and ours is the only one that deserves the name."
That is what a Buddhist might say to a Christian; it is what
many a Christian sect has said of another. Assertions of this tenor
merely afford illustrations of ethnocentrism. In general, the
grounds on which the possession of a religion has been denied to
the savage have had to do with only partially relevant details,
such as faith in "immortality"[32] or recognition of a "Supreme
Being"; they have not included the distinguishing features of the
institution, namely, a belief in the supernatural and a method of
dealing with it. If we ask, What is religion? What does the term
mean? we are thrown back, of course, upon current usage. Anyone can call a horse a frog if he wants to, and if he can get enough
persons to follow his lead the horse will come to be known as a
frog. Terminology-fixing is a case of evolution, with the term
following the successful variation. In any case, the review of the
alleged instances of no religion, together with those that reject

32 §220, above.

that allegation, opens the way for a consideration of the essential nature of the institution. There may be some profit in citing a few actual definitions as formulated by men conversant with the evolution of societal institutions.

D'Alviella[33] begins by listing the elements which he regards as "common to all organized religions," as follows: "(1) The belief in the existence of superhuman beings who intervene in a mysterious manner in the destinies of man and the course of nature. (2) Attempts to draw near to these beings or to escape them, to forecast the object of their intervention and the form it will take, or to modify their action by conciliation or compulsion. (3) Recourse to the mediation of certain individuals supposed to have special qualifications for success in such attempts. (4) The placing of certain customs under the sanction of the superhuman powers." This author then works up to a definition in the following terms: "The conception man forms of his relations with the superhuman and mysterious powers on which he believes himself to depend." Later on it is added that religion as defined implies "something exalted and mysterious in the character of the being adored." Brinton[34] finds the prevailing sentiment in fetishism, animism, and all the polytheisms to be fear of the unknown; and elsewhere remarks: "What I think is the essence . . . in all religions is their supposed control over the destiny of the individual." Mason[35] comes through with the simple definition that, "in a general sense, religion is the sum of what is thought or believed about a spirit world and what is done in consequence of such thinking." He very naturally wants the "verbal elements" of such a definition as Caird's[36] explained—the latter's formula running to the effect that religion is "man's ultimate attitude toward the universe." Ratzel[37] declares with pompous Teutonic vagueness that religion is an "affirmative relation of human consciousness to something objectively perceived, which determines things in the highest instance and to which man stands in personal relation." A culture-historian writes: "All that is religion which unites man, as such, with something which he has recognized or regards as above himself, on which he feels himself dependent, and to which he therefore pays reverence."[38] Gumplowicz[39] regards religion as "the conception of those ideas which rise in the human spirit concerning all those things which it is not in a position to apprehend through its senses but to know which it is driven by an unconquerable need of its nature. . . . Religion is therefore no artificial product of human imagination but a *naturally-necessary function* of his [man's] finite and limited spirit, which is ever coerced by a longing that is not to be quieted—coerced to pass the boundaries set by nature. . . . All religion is merely a spirit-reflex," called into being by the unknowable. Lippert[40] warns us that religion and mythology are not the same thing. "Any fabulation whatever about heavenly or other natural phenomena may be made perfectly

[33] *Concep. God*, 4, 47, 63.

[34] *Races*, 68; Brinton, *Relig. Sent.*, 155 *et passim;* Brinton, *Amer. Hero-Myths*, 19.

[35] *Woman's Share*, 241; Mason, in *Smithson. Rep.*, 1893, 623.

[36] *Evol. of Relig.*, I, ch. III, 53, 250.   [37] *Vkde.*, I, 41.

[38] Henne am Rhyn, *Kgchtl. Skizzen*, 197.

[39] *Rassenkampf*, 139.   [40] *Kgchte.*, I, 98.

manifest as a fact; but if it cannot be demonstrated that it serves in some form or other as a support of the cult, we have no right to designate it as the expression of *religious* ideas, unless we want to dilute and delete the concept 'religion.' "

Several competent writers define from the standpoint of a special and engrossing interest. "Religion, albeit a most highly developed expression of human activity, may be defined as any system of words, acts, or devices, or combinations of these, employed to obtain welfare or to avert ill-fare through the use, exercise, or favor of the orenda of another body or bodies."[41] Robertson Smith[42] tries to distinguish religion from magic or sorcery, as follows: "From the earliest times, religion, as distinct from magic or sorcery, addresses itself to kindred and friendly beings, who may indeed be angry with their people for a time, but are always placable except to the enemies of their worshippers or to renegade members of the community. It is not with a vague fear of unknown powers, but with a loving reverence for known gods who are knit to their worshippers by strong bonds of kinship, that religion in the only true sense of the word begins. Religion in this sense is not the child of terror; and the difference between it and the savage's dread of unseen foes is as absolute and fundamental in the earliest as in the latest stages of development. . . . Religion is not an arbitrary relation of the individual man to a supernatural power, it is a relation of all the members of a community to a power that has the good of the community at heart, and protects its law and moral order. This distinction seems to have escaped some modern theorists, but it was plain enough to the common sense of antiquity, in which private and magical superstitions were habitually regarded as offences against morals and the state." If this distinction, which is parallel to that drawn by Lehmann between white and black art,[43] is accepted, then plainly many peoples can have no religion. DeGroot[44] writes: "From what has heretofore been written on the subject in Europe and America, it is tolerably manifest that Religion in China is but little more than a great art, or combination of arts, for promoting welfare in this present life and future salvation, by following certain lines of conduct and by propitiating or rendering harmless certain classes of invisible beings and agencies." This conception of the art-aspect of religion is confirmed for the Romans: "their religion was essentially an art—the art of discovering the designs of the gods and of acting upon them by various rites."[45]

Any such set of definitions of a human institution by scientists who are not also narrow specialists or mere speculative thinkers serves to bring out salient aspects of the institution in question. The formulation of an inclusive definition is another matter. It is impossible to make a definition of religion which shall cover all forms of it from the lowest to the highest and will yet describe to the satisfaction of devotees the characteristics of the most evolved forms. No more could a definition of a machine be formulated which would take in the primitive loom at one end and the modern

41 Hewitt, in AA, IV, 42.   42 *Relig. Sem.*, 54, 55.
43 §303, above.   44 *Relig. Syst.*, I, vii.
45 Lecky, *Europ. Morals*, I, 398.

type at the other and yet do justice to the special features and refinements of the latter. That is no reason, however, for denying the name of machine to the former. It is futile to say that if religion is characterized as reverence for higher powers and belief in a future life, that formulation excludes nothing and so defines nothing; and it is equally absurd to assert that civilized religion is degraded by such a definition. The fact is that if we adopt a formula that covers the basic essentials of the modern loom, or of a modern religion, we cannot draw a hard and fast line between that and the primitive form. If the ethnographers mention instances in which the religious element seems small, the reflection is in point that a minimum is not a negative. They often also contradict themselves by other statements which show that they have not settled in their own minds what definitions they want to use for various terms current in this connection. Unless one is bold enough to arrogate to his own faith a term which unquestionably covers a series, he must be content with a considerable latitude in definition.

As an illustration of what should not be included under the name religion, though it is not by any means regularly ruled out, is the so-called "scientific religion." Galton,[46] for instance, wanted eugenics to be introduced "into the national conscience like a new religion"; but no religion was ever sired by a statistical table. The first form of religion is ritual and the second is belief in a dogmatic creed. In the first, religious duty consists in performing the appointed rites with fidelity. In the second, it inheres in orthodoxy; it is duty to believe faithfully in the specified articles. The second does not entirely supersede the first but unites with it and gives the rites a new character; with it, mysticism and transcendentalism are developed. A proposed third type of religion is rationalistic. This is the one which is ruled out. In all religion there are and must be effects assumed for which there are no causes that are real within the sphere of human experience or subject to experiment or other proper verification. Although tradition supported by ritual and sentiment enables men to hold inconsistent opinions and ideas through life and to swear loyally to two or three standards of truth at the same time, yet the sceptical and rationalistic habit will force ever new attempts to resolve these inconsistencies, for if its tests are accepted as conclusive no religious notions can satisfy them. A scientific religion is an absolute contradiction in terms. It is a philosophy which contains two different and irreconcilable conceptions of causation. Only by keeping each to its own range can religion and science exist peaceably side by side and jointly account for all things.

Reverting to the religion-series as a whole, and including all members of it, we find that just as all forms of the industrial

[46] *Eugenics,* 38.

organization, property, war, and government represent adjustment to the natural and social environment, and as all forms of marriage represent adjustment to the life-condition of bi-sexuality, so do all forms of religion represent adjustment to the supernatural environment. In the presence of the aleatory element and of the conception of a spirit-environment society could not do otherwise than develop a set of mores, involving both theory and practice, for getting along under these life-conditions. Religion is, in a word, society's adjustment to that which is, in any age, beyond knowledge—to the aleatory element, as personalized, through the long ages of human evolution, in the spirit-environment. As an institution, it is a framework of customs, rites, symbols, phrases, scriptures, apparatus, altars, temples, costumes, and various other details. The institution holds the ideas together and perpetuates them.

§324*. Conservatism of Religion. "Experience shows," says Robertson Smith,[47] "that primitive religious beliefs are practically indestructible, except by the destruction of the race in which they are ingrained." "The last thing to perish in a nation is its faith. The whole history of the world proves that no anomalies are so glaring, no inconsistencies so paradoxical, as to sap the credit of a religious system which has once been firmly rooted in the habits, instincts, and traditions of a race: and what remains longest is often the least rational portion. Religions from the first are not the product of logical reflection or experiment, but of sentiment and aspiration. They come into being as pure intuitions, and afterwards invade the province of the reason and assimilate the thought of centuries in their own synthesis."[48] "As soon as a religion no longer possesses the power to present its dogmas . . . as indisputable truth, as soon as it is not in a position to choke every doubt, it is all up with its vital force."[49] Expressions like these represent the mood of writers who have been impressed with the toughness of religious belief. There is another side to the matter, for religion is alterable over long periods of time; nevertheless it is characteristically and essentially conservative and, in

---

[47] *Relig. Sem.*, 355-356.   [48] Symonds, *Renaissance*, I, 403.
[49] Von Kremer, *Kgchte.*, II, 42.

comparison with other human institutions, it gives the impression of a "resisting inertia."

"What to a western mind seems but a natural process, the evolution of a custom or a principle beginning in religious motives and divesting them in its progress, assuming a purely secular character, is almost, if not absolutely, unknown in India. . . . Religion has never been and can never be anything but religion with the Hindus, and it engrosses all their mind to the exclusion of all secular motives to an extent that, as has been remarked by some one cynically, 'the Hindus even sin religiously.' "[50] Cicero[51] defines all religious beliefs or practices that go beyond the prescription of ancestral usage as superstition. "Those sides of the popular Catholicism where it harmonizes with the ancient, heathen invocation, donation, and conciliation of the gods have rooted themselves most stubbornly in the knowledge of the people. . . . Perhaps it is only apparently paradoxical to say that popular belief had been quite especially firmly grounded in Italy in so far as it was heathenish."[52]

It would seem, at first thought, unnecessary to equip this paragraph with copious illustration, inasmuch as any reasonably informed person can summon many instances to mind. Since, however, the whole of religion is so insulated from candid assessment by reason of conventionalization, the most obvious of rationalistic contentions need full support in concrete fact.

One of the chief tenets of religion is that the familiar and especially the archaic are holy, while the novel and strange are profane. This comes out of the function of religion as a sanction of the mores.[53] In the modern as well as the ancient world, as the observer of the present and the reader of history well knows, religion has clung resolutely to ancient and therefore holy forms of language, dress, architecture, furniture, music, and instruments and ceremonial in general. Spencer[54] speaks of the "pertinacity with which the oldest part of the regulative organization maintains its original traits in the teeth of influences that modify things around it." He cites the persistence of cutting instruments of stone for sacrificial purposes "when implements of bronze, or even of iron are used for all other purposes." The Hebrews are commanded to build altars of stone without using iron tools which would dese-

[50] Nathubhai, in JASB, V, 35.

[51] De Nat. Deorum, I, 17, 42, §117; II, 28, §70; De Div., II, 72 (quoted in Dill, Nero, 443).

[52] Burckhardt, Renaissance, 483, 484.

[53] §20, above.

[54] Study Soc., 107; I Kings, VI, 7; Exod., XX, 25; Kautzsch, in Hastings's Dict. Bible, 661; case of iron in Frazer, Golden Bough, I, 172 ff.

crate them; nor might the altar be ascended by means of steps. "Both these regulations are plainly intended by way of protest against innovations that had crept in, and in favour of the ancient simple ritual usages, which were as yet quite uninfluenced by art and higher culture." The high priest of Jupiter at Rome was shaved with a bronze knife. "Further the primitive method of obtaining fire by the friction of two pieces of wood, survives in religious ceremonies ages after its abandonment in the household; and even now, among the Hindus, the flame for the altar is kindled by the 'fire drill.' " Tylor[55] too cites a number of cases of such conservatism: where the ascetic Brahman, going into the forest to end his days, or the Bornean while in mourning, reverts to the ancient bark-clothing; where the "leaf-wearers" of India drop back upon the garb of Adam and Eve after the Fall; where the extinguished fire of Vesta, the fire that is to cure sick cattle, and the "new fire" must be kindled by friction—the last instance of this practice having occurred in Scotland in 1826. Hieroglyphics were "kept up for sacred purposes."

So much for the classical writers, by way of preliminary. It is readily enough appreciated that the employment of any novelty in connection with religion may easily be regarded as sacrilegious. Consider the use of a modern breakfast-food, with its perhaps grotesque name, in a church-ceremony. Rather does religion go back and select a food so antique as no longer to be in common use, as, for example, the lotus, unleavened bread, bitter herbs.[56] The retention of the old is not wholly confined to religion; all solemn ceremonial is full of survivals.[57] The court of justice, the wedding, or the academic procession illustrates the same conservatism. It is probable that a great deal of the survivalistic practice to be observed in other parts of the societal field originated in religion or at any rate in the religious sanction connected with the major activities of life. If there are any ceremonies which have been performed at the important crises of human and social life

[55] *Anth.*, 244, 245, 262, 174; Ratzel, *Vkde.*, I, 65; Rivers, quoted in §261, above.

[56] Lippert, *Kgchte.*, I, 453, 545-549, 579-581, 588; Ratzel, *Vkde.*, I, 371; Exod., XII, 8, 15; XIII, 6, 7; XXIII, 18; Levit., II, 4; VII, 12; VIII, 26; XXIII, 6; Num., VI, 19; IX, 11; Deut., XVI, 3, 4; I Cor., V, 8.

[57] See index to this book, *sub* "old" foods, "the old as holy," "survivals," "symbols."

that are not tinctured by religion, they are yet to be discovered. Men did not dare to ignore the aleatory element at such junctures. Let one try to invent a solemn ceremonial without religious elements and he becomes aware from another angle of the situation before us.

It is to be noted also that the new and strange, as being inexplicable, are commonly referred to the spirits and so may constitute fetishes which, like the white man's camera, inspire immediate suspicion or terror;[58] but such are seldom sacred in the sense in which the archaic and time-honored appurtenances of the cult are holy.

The cases may begin with a reference to the Australian reversion to ancient custom in time of calamity, wherein the natives proposed to exchange wives to ward off a pestilence.[59] "Even in savage tribes, such as those of Central Australia, we meet with evidence of the remarkable way in which ancient customs are preserved in connection with 'sacred' rites. The retention of the fire-stick at circumcision, after the use of stone implements was evidently known, finds its parallel in the retention of stone implements for the same operation after the use of iron was well known." When a man has his hair cut he always squats facing the ancient ancestral camp of his mother, or some great calamity will befall him.[60] In Melanesia a stone adze, never iron, is used in the initiation-ceremonies, and circumcision is performed with obsidian flakes.[61] In South African songs and proverbs, "many old words occur, and the present generation seem able to give one no more than a tentative explanation of them."[62] The Hovas of Madagascar never cleared away the long strings of black soot that hung from inside the lofty high-pitched roofs of old-fashioned houses; "for they were considered as a proof of an old and long-established family having inhabited that house, a kind of patent of respectability; and thus the word has become equivalent to what is ancient and venerable from age."[63]

Iron is the correct thing in Singhalese ceremonial where steel is rejected.[64] In one district in India the people provide by general subscription a small black ram for their goddess which is offered for them by a special person. "Standing before the goddess he holds the ram in his arms, and seizing the animal by the throat with his teeth, bites it till he kills it. He tears the ram's bleeding flesh *with his teeth* and holds it in his mouth to the goddess."[65] Here, apparently, the use of any sacrificial implement whatever is held to be less holy. "Those who have seen a genuine crowd of shrine-farers, in some place remote from a stream, cannot wonder at the shock which the pious imagina-

---

58 §254, above.
59 §§275, 277, above, and 344, below; Cunow, *Australneger*, 69.
60 Spencer and Gillen, *Nat. Tr. Cent. Aust.*, 401, note, 466.
61 Haddon, in JAI, L, 266, 272.
62 Willoughby, in JAI, XXXIX, 237, 238.
63 Sibree, *Great Afr. Isl.*, 159.
64 Hildburgh, in JAI, XXXVIII, 186, 187, 192, 194.
65 Fawcett, in JASB, II, 266.

tion suffers at the sight of a locomotive."[66] At the funeral of a Borneo rajah,
men and women dance in old-fashioned clothes. In this country once a pen-
sioned European soldier set up a water-mill to grind rice. The Malays would
have nothing to do with it because Satan was in it. The capital was a total
loss.[67] The dress of the corpse, in central Borneo, is of a style no longer worn
except by tribes who because of isolation have clung longer to the old ways.[68]
In Malacca, when a more permanent settlement is made, the first fire must be
kindled by a "clean" unmarried girl with the aid of a fire-drill, for "good
luck."[69] "In Tahiti . . . the dialect of the church often differed from the common dialect, and thus religion was veiled in mysteries, especially where there
were priests. . . . The language used in prayer seemed to be more formal and
sententious and almost totally different from that used in common life." The
author[70] quoted gives examples; there was in the Society Islands a special
language used by priests and chiefs. Sometimes such an esoteric speech is
specially devised, but it is far more likely to be of ancient derivation. Some
Japanese, if they want to eat meat, go out of doors to do it; they may not eat
meat in the presence of the ancestral tablets.[71]

The East Greenland Eskimo will not let iron come into contact with their
hair. They cut it with the jaw-bone of a shark, if at all.[72] When an Alaskan
Eskimo does work with iron, he must first put the fetish which the shaman
carves for every child at its birth in a sack and take it outside the hut. Otherwise the child will be ill.[73] Harrington[74] shows how at festivals the older forms
of corn-preparation supplant those in common secular use. Parched corn "was
in former days a very important article of Iroquois diet; but at the present
time it is used mainly at certain ceremonial functions . . . and but rarely at
other times." There is also a special wedding-bread. In the sacred dog-feasts
of the Indians, the dog is roasted whole, in a pit filled with heated stones. This
is a method for the sacred feasts, not the ordinary one.[75] "The reversion of the
Apache to the food of his ancestors—the hoddentin—as a religious offering
has its analogue in the unleavened bread and other obsolete farinaceous products which the ceremonial of more enlightened races has preserved from oblivion."[76] There is a belief among the Plains Indians "that the ancient stone
arrow heads were peculiarly deadly, and possessed this property, that even a
slight touch with them made a wound which was likely to be fatal"; after
arrowheads "ceased to be used for general purposes, they took on a sacred
character and were employed to slay the sacrifices."[77] The subterranean *estu-
fas* of the pueblos, being sacred, have retained the pristine, circular form
long after the adoption of the rectangular type of structure for ordinary or
secular purposes, "according to the well known law of survival in ceremonial
appurtenances."[78] Among the mourning-customs of the Pima widows, along

[66] Nivedita, *Ind. Life*, 265.   [67] Bock, *Borneo*, 99, 126.
[68] Nieuwenhuis, *Borneo*, I, 85.
[69] Stevens, in *Ztsft. f. Ethnol.*, XXVIII, 168.
[70] Williamson, *Cent. Polyn.*, III, 91-92.
[71] Kishimoto, in PSM, XLVI, 208.
[72] Nansen, *Esk. Life*, 174.   [73] Ranke, *Mensch*, II, 511.
[74] Seneca, "Corn-Foods," in AA, IX, 586-588.
[75] Gomme, *Village Life*, 171; *Case-Book*, §99.
[76] §301, above; Bourke, in BAE, IX, 519.
[77] Grinnell, *Folk Tales*, 250, 253.   [78] Cushing, in BAE, IV, 476.

with staying at home, not washing their hair, and crying the name of the deceased at daybreak, was a taboo upon bringing their blankets over their shoulders, even in the coldest weather. "When the chemise was adopted, as the blankets went out of use, it was customary to revert to the blankets during the period of mourning."[79] "Leaning against the drying-frame we see a notched log. This is an old-fashioned ladder, such as these Indians used almost exclusively thirty years ago. In the meantime many of the young men have been taught carpentry in the industrial schools of the East and the government has supplied them with plenty of tools for woodwork; yet the Indians cling to the rude ladder of their savage days."[80] The Diggers dare not use stone mortars which they dig up, holding them in superstitious dread.[81] In the Pacific region the stone implements laid aside after intercourse with the white man become holy. The Yurok will not cut open the first salmon with an iron knife, saying that it makes the flesh poisonous.[82]

"Since the fall of the second Temple," writes Zangwill,[83] "we have dropped out of our worship all musical instruments connected with the old Temple worship, especially such as have become associated with Christianity. But the ram's horn on the New Year is an institution older than the Temple, and specially enjoined by the Bible." "The Moslem worshipper must, while repeating his formulas, be covered, if a man or a female slave, from navel to knees, if a woman from head to foot except for face and hands—but for the Mecca pilgrimage the covering of more than the private parts is forbidden."[84]

Urns as tombstones may recall the Greek period when they were real receptacles for ashes. In a sacrifice preceding the battle of the Horatii, the victim's throat was cut with a stone knife;[85] so, before mummifying the dead, the Egyptians made an incision, in order to remove the entrails, with a stone knife.[86] In the sale of house or land, at Rome, it remained the custom to pass one of the ancient ingots of copper, to confirm the transaction. This sale *per aes et libram* was solemn and irrevocable.[87] In Scotland a live coal is thrown into the water in which a newborn babe is washed, a symbolic survival of heating water by a hot stone, which was thought to make the children stronger.[88] Until 1878 the bulls of the Pope were written in a special Old Gothic script.[89]

Christianity retained enough similarity to the old Egyptian religion—in its life after death, its judgment, its conception of life as a pilgrimage to death, its eternal gods, who procreate themselves, and its trinity of deities, to allow of easy acceptance by the Egyptians. It was "only an advance along the old way. The Serapis-cult had a fully organized system of monks and cloisters."[90] Whether or not there was an early acculturation here, the old elements persisted. Similarly with the Roman Catholic and Buddhistic systems. "Many of the details in the Roman Catholic worship may have been derived from Buddhism; from this source comes the rosary. . . . By an extraordinary coinci-

[79] Russell, in BAE, XXVI, 195.   [80] Matthews, in AA, IV, 3.

[81] Skertchly, in JAI, XVII, 335.   [82] Ratzel, *Vkde.*, II, 587.

[83] *Ghetto,* 97.

[84] Snouck-Hurgronje, "Twee Populaire Dwalingen," in *Bijd.,* XXXV, 366, 367.

[85] Livy, *Hist.,* I, 24.   [86] Herodotus, *Hist.,* II, 86.

[87] Gaius, *Commentaries,* I, 119, 122; III, 174.

[88] Gomme, *Village Life,* 167.   [89] Pierer, *Konv. Lex., sub* "Bulle."

[90] Junker, *Afr.,* I, 40.

dence, each of these churches is conspicuous for its use of holy water, choirs, sacred pictures, tonsure, vestments, the bell in religious service, the orders of nuns, monks, and the vows of the monastic system. . . . Buddha has found a niche as a saint in the row of canonized Catholic worthies, and has his saint-day in the calendar of the Greek and Roman churches. But it is not his mother who is the Virgin of Lamaism, which has made of Buddha the Supreme God. . . . In Lamaism there is also the tiara-crowned pope, and the transubstantiation theory; the reverence to Virgin and Child, confessions, fasts, purgatory, abbots, cardinals, etc."[91] And Platonism brought over a mass of daimonism into Christian philosophy.[92]

Throughout this book[93] occur cases of survivals illustrative of the conservative character of religion. So pronounced is this trait that the study of the cult is not unlike the exploration of fossil-bearing strata. Further, as in the case of zoölogical fossils, so here, is it possible to reconstruct from the findings a picture of an epoch that is past and gone. We know the story of the persistence in religion of old forms of language, music, and the rest; we ourselves do not have to infer from its preservation in religion that Latin was once a secular spoken language, for we know from recorded history that that is a fact. Our historical knowledge simply confirms the validity of similar inferences where knowledge is deficient. If a visiting Martian were equipped with the conception of cult-conservatism, it would not be difficult for him, scrutinizing contemporary cult-forms or cult-derived ceremonial, to infer, in complete ignorance of past history, that Latin was once a secular tongue. By such processes of inference from religious phenomena not a few facts of culture-historical value may be surmised. Survivals constitute one of the forms of evidence as to the past, whether or not they are visibly connected with the cult;[94] it is by reason of the surpassingly conservative character of religious forms and ceremony that they occur in far greater profusion in them than elsewhere. Selection does not operate as sharply in the rest of the societal system as it does in the region of the maintenance-mores;[95] and by the very nature of the case, and in the almost utter absence of the possibility of test and verification, it is conspicuously ineffective, except automatically and over long periods, in the realm of religion—so much so, indeed, that the

91 Hopkins, *Relig. Ind.*, 557.   92 Lippert, *Kgchte.*, II, 459.

93 See index *sub* "survival," "symbol"; Lippert, *Kgchte.*, I, 126.

94 Tylor, *Anth.*, 15.   95 Keller, *Soc. Evol.*, ch. V.

reputable authors quoted above express themselves to the effect that religion is virtually unmodifiable.

A quotation from a speech of a negro chief in Dahomi runs as follows: "Have you not seen, when I not long ago gave a feast in honor of the third king of Dahomi . . . that on the occasion there hung on my shoulders a quiver of arrows? That was the symbol of the times when the stouthearted forefathers fought their neighbors with such weapons."[96] Bourke[97] develops the already cited evidence for "hoddentin" as an ancient food. "The peculiar manner in which the medicine-men of the Apache use the hoddentin (that is, by putting a pinch upon their own tongues); the fact that men and women make use of it in the same way, as a restorative when exhausted; its appearance in myth in connection with Assanutlije, the goddess who supplied the Apache and Navajo with so many material benefits, all combine to awaken the suspicion that in hoddentin we have stumbled upon a prehistoric food now reserved for sacrificial purposes only." An examination of the Spanish writers who most carefully transmitted their observations upon the religious ceremonies of the Aztecs and other Mexican and South American nations brings out two most interesting features. First, that there were commemorative feasts of prehistoric foods and, second, that one or more of these foods has played an important part in the religion of tribes farther north. "The first of these foods is the 'tzoalli,' which was the same as 'bledos,' which latter would seem beyond question to have been hoddentin or yiauhtli." The author interjects the remark that "in our own country all military reunions make it a point to revert to the 'hard tack' issued during the campaigns in Virginia and Tennessee." The shaman sprinkled the sick man with "powder of the artemisia" which was "supposed to be the food of the ghosts," that is, it was the food of the tribal ancestors. "An accurate examination of the subject of hoddentin must include the curious analogue of 'down' throwing and sprinkling which seemingly obtains with tribes which at some period have been compelled to rely upon birds as a main component of their diet. Examples of this are to be found on both sides of the Pacific and in Australia, and doubtless they could be met with in other very unexpected quarters. The down used by the Tchuktchi on occasions of ceremony had a suggestion of religion about it. 'On leaving the shore, they sung and danced. One who stood at the head of the boat was employed in plucking out the feathers of a bird's skin and blowing them in the air.' " Fewkes[98] finds in the persistence of the rites of each of several uniting clans an indication of the original forms of worship; so that here too the cult affords a clue to local history.

Concerning barley in Homer's day, "probably since it was recognized as the oldest of the grains, it was used chiefly in sacrifice, only partially bruised or ground." Acorns, honey, and perhaps the smaller quadrupeds appear to be ancient foods, and milk, only infrequently a food of the living, was offered to the dead in Hades. Fish were eaten only at necessity and were called

[96] Hostmann, *Beschaving*, II, 168.

[97] In BAE, IX, 518, 523, 525, 527, 533; "Cannibalism," in PSM, XLVIII, 411, note.

[98] In BAE, XIX, pt. II, 1006.

"sacred."[99] We know from Homer[100] that salt was not universally in use in his day and learn from later writers that "the use of salt for seasoning was a comparatively late discovery and therefore excluded from certain sacrifices to the gods . . . 'Because at first they knew no use for salt. And even when they knew and loved its savour They kept their fathers' sacred written precepts.' Plutarch in his *Roman Questions* says that 'when the women poured libations of wine to Bona Dea, they called it by the name of milk,' and Macrobius adds that 'wine could not be brought in under its own name, but the wine was called milk and the vessel containing it a honey-jar.' . . . These forms of primitive sacrifice—the *pelanos,* the barley grains, the *nephalia,* the fireless rites . . . remain broadly speaking and in their simplest forms characteristic of the lower stratum and of the worship of underworld spirits. . . . Between the chthonic gods and the whole class of dead men, heroes and daemons, the only distinction observed is . . . that certain chthonic gods from sheer conservatism reject the service of wine, whereas it is apparently acceptable to dead men, to heroes and to daemons not fully divinized."[101] At marriages a child with a crown of acanthus and acorns carried around a basket of bread and said as he offered it: "I have fled the bad. I have found the better," meaning that acorns have been given up and better food substituted.[102] Wissowa[103] remarks on the great stability in all religion and religious affairs. In later sacrificial customs are relics of old usages: sacrificed animals are killed with a stone (*silex*); bronze, not iron, is used in the cult; pottery for the cult is not made with the potter's wheel; fire is renewed with the fire-drill; grain for the sacrifice is pounded, not ground.

The foregoing cases have to do, in the main, with survivals of a material order from which can be reconstructed a picture of antecedent material culture. In many small details of ceremonial, religion and magic tend to cling to the obsolete forms which lend them dignity and mystery. This must have become apparent in the discussion and cases of previous chapters and is easily verifiable from observation at the present day. We add several examples in which the survivalistic quality is not evident upon casual inspection. From another angle survivalism appears in the life attributed to the daimons; what they have and do, or do not have and do not do, gives a strong hint as to the mores of the past. If they are cannibalistic where their worshippers are not, or if their cult warrants plain inferences as to human sacrifice, the only conclusion to be drawn is that these practices once existed. Many of the bloody usages in conciliation and coercion, if traced down to the present time, have shifted over into poetry or been conventional-

[99] Seymour, *Hom. Age,* 327; Keller, *Hom. Soc.,* 47, 48, 132, 140, 171.
[100] *Odyssey,* XVII, 455-457; *Iliad,* IX, 214.
[101] Harrison, *Greek Relig.,* 87, 91, 95, 351.
[102] Foucart, *Assoc. Relig.,* 74.   [103] *Relig. Römer,* 30.

ized so as to lose their original significance. If the gods of a slave-keeping people have few slaves or none at all, the inference is that slavery is recent. It is significant that magical property is inheritable through the female line whereas other property follows the male. "The more beneficent forms of magic are the appanage of certain men who have usually inherited their powers from the maternal uncle and only exceptionally from the father even now when, so far as other property is concerned, inheritance from the father is becoming frequent."[104] Suppose, however, that the gods exhibit conduct which men no longer countenance—what then is the inference? If there appears a goddess of what is to us impure love, that fact is unreflectingly referred to some base aberration or abuse of religion. It is easy to evade the truth by such assertions or by interpretation on the basis of an insubstantial symbolism. The reason for the cruder morals of the gods is the same as for the obsolete character of their food: they were the morals of an antecedent state before the rise of mores of restriction. They are a picture of the past.

Among the Tuareg, in certain of their ceremonies, the participants simulate drunkenness. "This circumstance deserves to be noted among a people who have not the usage of drinking fermented beverages and whose sobriety is proverbial; nevertheless it has been confirmed to me by a number of reliable natives and admits of no doubt."[105] In India "when a man wishes to indulge in bhang, or any other intoxicant, he has simply to engage in the worship of Siva, who, when incarnate, was particularly addicted to the use of intoxicants." In the mythologies, stories, drama, and mysteries the cruder usages are preserved. "It has passed into a proverb, that whilst the teaching the gods have given is good and worthy to be followed, the example they have set is bad and unfit to be copied. In the present day there are philosophizing men who try to explain away a good deal of the worst teaching . . . and to give a poetical interpretation to the stories of the varied immoralities of the gods; but the mass of the people believe these accounts in their most literal form, and merely say that acts permitted to the gods are forbidden to men."[106] In the *Ion* of Euripides,[107] Ion says that if Zeus and Poseidon paid the penalties for all their adulteries as men do they would empty their temples and treasuries. They act unjustly when they pursue pleasure without due restraint. It is not fair to call men wicked when they imitate the gods; rather blame the examples. Perhaps the most striking case is the practice of incest among the gods where men revolt at it with the utmost horror. In Homer the Œdipus union is abominable while Zeus and Hera and the sons and daughters of Æolus present prosperous pictures of fraternal incest.[108] It cannot be said that the god of the Old Testa-

[104] Rivers, *Melan. Soc.*, I, 156.   [105] Zeltner, in JAI, XLIV, 357.
[106] Wilkins, *Hinduism*, 169, 317.   [107] 442 ff.
[108] Keller, *Hom. Soc.*, 204-205; 232-233.

ment affords a model for human behavior in all respects, even to wild tribes like those of the ancient Hebrews or the fanatical Boers of South Africa who adhered most worshipfully to the old dispensation.

In moral as well as material things religion is prepared to divulge a revelation of the remote past. Consider the license as regards property and marriage that is often a feature of the initiation.[109] It hardly need be said that the record thus rendered available is defective in the same way as are the geological and embryological records utilized so enlighteningly by the organic evolutionist; and that inference must be as cautiously and conscientiously made in the one case as in the other.

The *Kulturgeschichte* of Lippert, who has developed this matter of cult-evidence in an original and brilliant manner, contains many examples of significant survivals, together with interpretation along the lines indicated. He says that the cult results from the conception of the inmixture of the spirit-world into the life of man; that its forms rise exclusively from conceptions as to the anthropomorphic nature of the ghosts. "Nothing remains alien to it which can be the object of human desire," but everything first appears in forms corresponding to the stage of cultural development contemporaneous with its rise. When this stage passes and new cultural forms appear, the once-developed cult-forms do not, however, at once fall away. They persist alongside the new economic and other structures and become inconsistent with the latter. "And so a later time gradually learns to know cult-forms which, disengaged as they are from each and every other life-custom, seem to have been invented solely for the cult. On the other hand, precisely in consequence of this relation, the several cult-forms reveal to us, as in a changing picture, the life-forms of long past times." The cult presents a "picture of the past." This contention is elaborated as occasion is found, and with compelling persuasiveness, throughout Lippert's two volumes.[110]

Religion does not, like science, look to its own correction and readjustment. In science man can advance in a straight line indefinitely, while in religion he has had to revolve around certain fixed points from which he could not depart far.[111] It is next to impossible with the weapon of reason to attack and carry a position held by religion; for religion can at any juncture fall back upon its characteristic "doctrine of mystery." Science may present what it regards as unanswerable contentions; to any rational being operating upon the basis of reason they could not be otherwise regarded; but then theology extricates itself from the ration-

109 §163, above.
110 *Kgchte.*, I, 116-117 (quoted), 117 ff., 348, 480, 532; II, 139.
111 Ratzel, *Vkde.*, III, 15.

ally untenable situation by declaring that its dogmas "are not contrary to reason but are above reason."[112] In a very true sense, religion is within its rights when it states that its range is that of mystery—in which it originated—outside and beyond the reach of science. But the range of theology is not thus exempt from criticism and attack; as White[113] asserts, there is no clash between religion and science but only between science and dogmatic theology.

§325*. **Religion is Evolutionary.** If the statements of the writers quoted at the outset of the last caption were strictly true, then religion could show no adjustment. There could be no variation in this range and no selection except by the utter destruction of the adherents of some ill-starred faith; there could be nothing except unvaried transmission. Such a view would be absurd on the face of it; otherwise a special revelation must needs be assumed to have taken place in the case of every minute peculiarity of every religion. If, instead of attempting to play the treacherous and futile logical game, the candid searcher goes to the facts, he finds that religion, like every other societal product, is in and of the mores and, like them, shows adjustment to life-conditions in the usual way. Its conservative quality renders its adjustments slower and more painful than those in, say, the industrial organization; but the time-element is not important in cosmic processes where there are no anxious, short-lived observers and actors to become impatient and dismayed.

"It sounds paradoxical to say that all civilization had its cradle in daimonism, yet that daimonism and civilization are inversely proportional"; that development dissolves the cult, though the cult resists development; that the world-philosophy that corrodes daimonism is rooted in daimonism.[114] "The religion of rude tribes is at the same time their philosophy, containing such explanation of themselves and the world they live in as their uneducated minds are able to receive";[115] that primitive beliefs strike us as foolish and repulsive has nothing to do with their survival-value in their day nor yet any bearing upon the expediency or acceptabil-

---

[112] Lippert, *Kgchte.*, I, 116.
[113] *Sci. and Theol.*, I, viii, xii, 113, 168, 169, *et passim*.
[114] Lippert, *Kgchte.*, II, 411.   [115] Tylor, *Anth.*, 342.

ity of the more refined forms that grew out of them. "The impossibility of inventing a new religion is generally acknowledged. One might as well try to build a tree."[116] "No lasting change takes place in the religious belief and usage of a people which is not rooted in the previous faith and custom."[117] Any new religion has to take up the features of the old and assume its place in the unbroken series. So too the old does not pass away but merges into the later.[118] The ideas of incarnation, inspiration, revelation, propitiation, contrition, repentance, atonement, intercession, vicarious sacrifice, expiation, prayer, confession, worship, another life, ritual sacrifice, sacrament, ransom, salvation, redemption, covenant, superior existences, uncleanness, purification, prophecy, men's duties, sin, original sin, and all the rest go back to the limit of our knowledge of man on earth. They were all implicit in the primordial ghost-fear and have all been evolved so gradually and steadily that beginnings cannot be found for them. Further, religions borrow and lend; in the savage particularly there is no feeling that his own religion is the only one for all men.

"It is not at all incredulity that makes the labors of the missionary among the 'savages' hard. Most readily do they believe everything that he tells them out of his revelation; only it does not take hold on them and does not influence their lives in the desired way. They distinguish it—in this very many accounts agree—always as the revelation of a stranger-god to a stranger-man; it is not *their* revelation. It may be excellent, they often say in support of their declination, but for the stranger-men, not for *them*."[119] Zoroastrianism took up the ancient fetishism, Buddhism could include ancestor-worship, Mohammedanism made much of the Kaaba, Christianity adopted asceticism and also pagan rites in connection with the cultus of the dead to which it had at first been averse.[120] The religious system of Moses is the adoption and perpetuation of an existing customary system.[121] John the Baptist and his disciples were ascetic in their practice and used baptism; Jesus, who had been circumcized in the orthodox manner, prepared for his work by entering John's association and by asceticism. He received inspiration in the descent of a fetish-bird, was anointed, and cast out devils in the usual manner. Later he repudiated certain fixed forms, such as the fast and the sabbath. The process was one of elimination from within rather than new invention or a wholesale clearing of the board. In the New Testament many figurative phrases are current which are derived from the antecedent cult: the bread of life; the tree, fruit, water,

[116] Inge, "Cath. Ch.," in *Atl. Mo.*, CXXXI, 445.
[117] Hatch, *Griechentum*, 3.   [118] Justi, *Persien*, 73, 93.
[119] Lippert, *Kgchte.*, I, 101.
[120] Hearn, *Japan*, ch. X; De Marchi, *Cult. Priv.*, in *Année Soc.*, I, 208.
[121] Kautzsch, in *Hastings's Dict. Bible*, extra vol., 633; Barton, *Sem. Orig.*, 291 ff.; Paine, *Ethnic Trinities*.

fountain, river, way, word, and book of life. Gradually ethics took the place of the formal cult. Fear of hell superseded that of the ghosts and spirits, rose to a veritable terror, and has eventually all but disappeared. Concern about atonement and redemption has followed a like course. Insistence upon the correct belief, resulting in dogmas, succeeded the enforcement of ritual acts. The priesthood, originally but feebly represented, once rose into a world-system and hierarchy and has since declined. Independent thinkers, like Paul, threw off cult-ideas and burdens while introducing new religious attitudes, for instance in regard to marriage. The Germans developed the notion of compounding for breaches of the cult-association. In the Middle Ages the idea of purgatory, indulgences, and compositions ran rife; and the religion of the time reverted to a ruder stage and blocked the way of learning. The idea of the "needs" of the ghosts and gods, upon which ancient cults depend, was metamorphosed for the first time during the Reformation into a doctrine of free grace and forgiveness, and the latter ideas became prominent in speculation. The Protestants elevated the Scriptures to high authority, yet abandoned and ignored the plain doctrines of the New Testament about virginity, assuming rationalistic ground. The ideal of Protestantism was not celibacy but the family. It was and is middle-class and its ideals are domestic and conjugal. It fostered conjugal love, a typically modern novelty.[122]

Concerning the doctrinal controversy that has arisen within recent years the faculty of the Cambridge Episcopal Theological School, pleading for a "permissive" creed, expressed itself as follows: "This is not the first time the Church has been confronted with changes in its belief, nor the first time it has allowed freedom of interpretation, nor the first time violence seems to have been done to its formularies. The Reformation brought changes in the doctrine of the Lord's Supper, a doctrine which had been established for centuries and which men claimed was found in the Scriptures. The last fifty years have brought changes in the views of the Bible, a book which has been regarded as the inerrant Word of God from the first centuries until modern times. In any society, civil or religious, when the formularies in their original intention have ceased to represent the mind of the society or of a large section of it, the alternatives to literal adherence or withdrawal are interpretation and restatement. In the case of the creeds interpretation is not an attempt to explain away plain historical meanings, but a discovery, in the only language now authorized by the Church, of the underlying religious meaning. We believe that a large proportion of the Church now finds itself forced to this expedient in the use of various parts of our formularies."[123] Creeds are frameworks to hold ideas as these take form in an age, and with the modification of the ideas to accord with changed conditions the frameworks must be repaired, revamped, or altogether superseded.[124] In its spread among the less developed races, Christianity constantly adjusted itself to a greater or less degree, by necessity, accommodating its terminology to the notions of these races or at least allowing them to see in its creeds and forms what they, on their stage of eidolism or daimonism, could understand.[125]

[122] Sumner, "Mod. Marr.," in *Yale Rev.,* XIII, 263.
[123] N. Y. *Times,* January 6, 1924.   [124] Keller, *Soc. Evol.,* 318 ff.
[125] Lippert, *Kgchte.,* II, 611, 613 ff., 624 ff.

Here is a casual selection of facts, mainly out of the history of the religion we know most about, illustrative of alterations that take place through time in any religion. Such changes represent a development of form out of form, in a connected series, with survival of some forms over others, in adjustment to life-conditions. This is the evolutionary formula. Religion must, like other societal forms, conform to life-conditions at a time and place, for it is only a world-philosophy, a view of the order and system of all things. "Religion changes with culture. As the Hebrews after their settlement carried over to Jahweh the cult of the Canaanitish god of the land, so did the Arabs act under similar circumstances."[126] Temporarily, fantastic religious ideas of the world are disturbing to societal order, though they may serve individual or sub-group interests.[127] It should be clear enough that any people's religion is of a type with the rest of its institutions, in that they must all be consistent one with another as representing, in their ensemble, the adjustment of the society in question to its life-conditions. The native Zulu religion is no more adequate to the needs of the United States than is the Zulu government by despotic chiefs; nor can the highly refined religious system of a cultured people be transferred unmodified to savages, and meet their needs, any more than can a highly organized and specialized system of government and law.

If the preceding chapters have not exhibited religion as an evolving institution, then there is no object in trying to labor the point here. We have noted the strain toward consistency[128] between the religious mores and the rest of the societal code; we turn now to cases of the adjustment of religion to the general type of that code.

Nassau[129] enforces a truth to which we have often adverted when he says that in West Africa "religion is intimately mixed with every one of these . . . sociological aspects of family, rights of property, authority, tribal organization, judicial trials, punishments, intertribal relations, and commerce." Says Sir Charles Dundas:[130] "If we now look back into any of the previous chapters it will be seen that almost every subject either directly brings us to the question of religion or hints at the influence and presence of the spirits. The tilling of the fields, the building of a house, are practically acts of religion, the law is

---

126 Wellhausen, *Skizzen*, III, 47.
127 Ratzenhofer, *Soc. Erkennt.*, 224. 128 Sumner, *Folkways*, §5.
129 *Fetichism*, 25. 130 In JAI, XLIII, 538.

in the hands of those who more particularly are dedicated to the service of the spirits, and its provisions frequently are ultimately religious observances; in fact, compensation seems to be as much a religious observance as a legal requirement. The whole of the medicine art seems to be derived from, to merge into the religious sphere and to be largely dependent on the spirits. . . . So also the spirits are everywhere, in the hut of a dead wife, in the village and field, in trees, rocks and hills, and in all these places they may manifest themselves or have sacrifices made to them." "This influence of the spirits, or the belief in this influence, which is in effect the same thing, is the real key to a close understanding of the native mind; the natives' life is so permeated with these beliefs, and they have consequently such a profound effect on their actions, that until we thoroughly understand this question we are bound to be perpetually brought face to face with what appear to be absolute enigmas. Progressive Europeans in East Africa are apt to pooh-pooh these beliefs, and to feel very impatient with them, as they undoubtedly, in general effect, tend to conservatism, and to check development according to our standards. This is probably the case, but the fact must, however, not be lost sight of that on the whole they act as moral restraints, and perform the functions which a religion fulfils among people of a higher culture, and even if Government formally abolished them by legislation it would not affect the belief one iota, and before these beliefs are officially discountenanced we must be quite certain that we have something better and something equally adapted to the native mind to put in their place, or blank materialism will result, and the effect of this negation of faith and the freedom from all moral restraint upon a savage is appalling to contemplate. . . . As far as can be seen we have nothing to hand at present which is quite suited to people at this stage of culture, and it would therefore appear that the best policy will be carefully to study their present beliefs and encourage them, at the same time with the help of that knowledge, and influence based on that knowledge, to induce the people gradually to give up any repugnant features of their ritual and retain the better elements. It is of great interest to note how the more intelligent elders respond to enquiry into their beliefs once they are convinced that such enquiry is undertaken in the proper spirit, and nothing convinces them so much of the *bona fides* of our intentions as a sympathetic study of their own customs and a demonstration of one's knowledge of them."[131] The opposite policy has been too often followed. The missionaries, bringing one set of mores to face another, experience opposition that they often fail to understand. Where the mother-family exists, the tie of the children is closer to the mother than to the father. The innovators try to change this and meet the opposition of the women. The blacks conceive that man and wife have each his or her own goods in marriage, whereas the whites insist that they all belong to the man, who "endows" the wife with his property, the result amounting to community of possessions. But the man does not like to confer this endowment and be saddled with the children. "White culture expects him to think more of his wife and children than he does of his mother and sisters, which to the uncultured African is absurd."[132]

This instance, which is referred to in another connection, may stand for hundreds of others in missionary experience where ignorance has encountered disillusion and pain. It is only an illustration of the assertion of Renan:[133]

[131] Hobley, in JAI, XLI, 407.
[132] Kingsley, *W. Afr. Studies,* 377.   [133] *Averroès,* 162.

"Religion being the most profound expression of the conscience of humanity at a given epoch, to understand well the religious system of an age, it would be necessary to live its life with a thoroughness of which the most penetrating historian would be scarcely capable." Says Oliveira Martins[134] of Mohammedanism: "Out of that religion which unites with great refinements of intelligence a singular moral obscurity and a materialism without charity, the Berber or Tuareg, the negroid, and the negro comprehend and so take over only the second part, which is compatible with their respective capacities. . . . Whatever may be the moral value of a religion, the people that accepts it will derive from it that which is compatible with its genius and with the evolutionary stage of its civilization." The bulk of the Egyptians never understood the priestly system but clung to animal-worship, the cult of the dead, and magic. Over the Arabs "the public religion of the cult has little practical influence; superstition is the private working religion of life." The desert Arab, except in a few districts, is only externally a Moslem.[135] Says a competent observer[136] concerning the acceptation of Christianity by the Chinese: "Always, when I have tried to sound the spiritual depths of Christianity in China, I feel as if walking on ether. I never have talked about religion with a Chinese Christian without a sensation that somewhere in the back of his mind Christianity is given a twist which, if it was accurately translated to us, would not be orthodox." The "Christian General," Feng, perpetrated an act of gross treachery in deserting Wu Pei-fu, which was justified by a prominent missionary on the ground that he had sought guidance in prayer and was doing what he did for the good of China, as revealed.

"In its peaceful ethics, and in its exaltation of the feminine, the influence of the agricultural organization has permeated all the Dyak religion, endowing even the virile war-gods . . . with influential wives. Agriculture claims as its exclusive province a group of deities."[137] In New Zealand, in 1862, there rose the Hau Hau religion, the name of it being derived from "Jehovah." It was a mixture of Christian, Mosaic, and Buddhist elements. Highly grotesque ceremonies were developed which in many respects recalled Druid rites. The priests spread the tidings that they received direct commands from Jehovah through the Angel Gabriel and that the Maoris had been marked out to be a chosen people. The priesthood had its secret signs and several grades, like a secret society. Adultery was allowed by the religion and concubinage was reckoned a virtue. Those who had belonged to the Christian church went over by preference to Hauism.[138]

It is believed by specialists that the aridity of the climate of northwestern Arizona has had a profound effect on the religious beliefs and practices of the Hopi.[139] The type of religion universal to America "has found among the Incas, in culture-myths, star-worship, polytheism, and in the hierarchic arrangements attendant upon them a refined peak. On the other hand we meet here in the Amazon-country some few usages, sporadic and limited to a weak horde, in the midst of the levelling barbarism of the generality of this popula-

[134] Civ. Iber., 73.

[135] Bousset, Relig., 458-459; Wellhausen, Skizzen, III, 193; Müller, Islam, I, 50.

[136] Millard, in N. Y. Times, Sept. 8, 1925.

[137] Morris, "Borneo," in Am. Or. Soc., Sec. for Hist. Stud. Relig., VII, 42.

[138] Weiss, Chatham Isl., 67.   [139] Hough, in AA, X, 33.

tion, which are explicable only as the echo of a neighboring higher culture."[140] Upon most of these savages, evidently, the Inca-religion could make no impression.

"I wish," writes Müller,[141] "we could explore together . . . the ancient religions of mankind, for I feel convinced that the more we know of them the more we shall see that there is not one which is entirely false; nay, that in one sense every religion was a true religion, being the only religion which was possible at the time, which was compatible with the language, the thoughts and the sentiments of each generation, which was appropriate to the age of the world."

"It is a law which may be regarded as practically universal, that the religious conceptions of a people are expressed in forms which are modelled, in large degree, on those political and social institutions which the economical conditions of their situation have produced. Thus, a god could not be conceived as a father where marriage was so unstable that fatherhood was no recognized feature of the social structure, nor as a king among a people into whose experience the institution of kingship had never entered. An illustration of this principle may be found in the fact that republican institutions are, by their influence, gradually banishing the kingly idea of God from theological discussions, and are leading to an emphasis of the fatherhood, and even brotherhood of God. We should therefore, on general principles, be led to suppose that the prominence of the mother and the institutions of maternal kinship among the primitive Semitic clans, as well as their tendency to unregulated intercourse and the important functions of the date palm, all left a deep impress on their religious ideas and practices. Indeed, we may be sure that this is the case, especially as a large mass of evidence has survived which is only intelligible when interpreted in the light of these general laws." The author[142] follows this statement with several pages of rather technical detail. Judaism adopted many fantastic and superstitious ideas during the Babylonian captivity, incorporating them, and passing them on to orthodox Christianity. The Old Testament is full of battles between the prophets and the religion popular in the mores. A modern device to bridge over inconsistency between religion and the economic mores is cited by Zangwill:[143] "Time was when the Passover dietary was restricted to fruit and meat and vegetables, but year by year the circle is expanding, and it should not be beyond the reach of ingenuity to make bread itself Passoverian. It is now that the pious shopkeeper whose store is tainted with leaven sells his business to a friendly Christian, buying it back at the conclusion of the festival."

Among the Phœnicians the change to sedentary life brought a development of sacrificial and other ritual and a greater attention to holy places.[144] "The cult rises and grows with the people and the state but both are subject too, as homogeneous creations, to the same laws of growth and decay."[145] Frazer[146] finds the history of the Egyptian religion to have been largely a struggle between the localization and the amalgamation of cults. "On the one side there was the conservative tendency to preserve the local cults with all their distinctive features, fresh, sharp and crisp, as they had been handed down from an

[140] Von Martius, *Beiträge,* I, 462.
[141] *Sci. Relig.,* 115.
[142] Barton, *Sem. Orig.,* 82.
[143] *Ghetto,* 266.
[144] Pietschmann, *Phön.,* 221.
[145] Von Kremer, *Kgchte.,* II, 1.
[146] *Golden Bough,* I, 313-314.

immemorial past. On the other side there was the progressive tendency, favoured by the gradual fusion of the people under a powerful central government, first to dull the edge of these provincial distinctions, and finally to break them down completely and merge them in a single national religion." The bulk of the people was conservative; the kings were the champions of unity; and the unity was attained in part by discovering points of similarity.

We hear of a "religious particularism that can appear only among an agricultural people, and only then, too, when this people has a cult-center and is jealous of its nationality." Again, "every religious reform of a people still roots in its past, provided the new doctrine is not of foreign origin as, later on, Islam was in Persia, Christianity with the Germans, Buddhism in China. Then it forms an opposition to the national religion, fights it, seeks to crush it out, and must only, in order to get a firm foothold, respect certain ineradicable folk-notions, traditions, and usages, and seek to bring them, as far as possible, into harmony with its own."[147]

"Christianity floated into the Roman Empire on the wave of credulity that brought with it this long train of Oriental superstitions and legends. In its moral aspect it was broadly distinguished from the systems around it, but its miracles were accepted by both friend and foe as the ordinary accompaniments of religious teaching. The Jews, in the eyes of the Pagans, had long been proverbial for their credulity, and the Christians inherited a double measure of their reputation. Nor is it possible to deny that in the matter of the miraculous the reputation was deserved. . . . Without a single exception the Fathers maintained the reality of the Pagan miracles as fully as their own. The oracles, as we have seen, had been ridiculed and rejected by numbers of the philosophers, but the Christians unanimously admitted their reality. . . . To suppose that men who held these opinions were capable, in the second or third centuries, of ascertaining with any degree of just confidence whether miracles had taken place in Judea in the first century," is highly venturesome. "Epictetus, whose austere creed rises to the purest monotheism, teaches as a fundamental religious maxim that every man in his devotions should 'conform to the customs of his country.' The Jews and Christians, who alone refused to do so, were the representatives of a moral principle that was unknown to the Pagan world."[148] All the great advances in culture, such as the utilization of fire, or agriculture, have their myths and their divine cults. Christian saints follow heathen gods, and the church has simply glorified many primitive ideas.[149] Seeck[150] generalizes as follows: "We all follow the teachings of our religion precisely as far as they correspond to our moral impulses, that is, we are led by these impulses, not by religion. . . . Morality is not determined by religion but on the contrary religions have been modelled over and over again according to the changing conceptions of morals." "Religions," writes Symonds,[151] having in mind the use of assassination by the Church in the sixteenth century, "except in the first fervor of their growth and forward progress, recognize the moral conventions of the society which they pretend to regulate. . . . It is well-nigh impossible for the men of one century to sympathize with the ethics of a past and different epoch." The Christian practice in regard to marriage shows religious re-

---

[147] Tiele-Gehrich, *Gchte. Rel.*, I, 271; II, 81.
[148] Lecky, *Europ. Morals*, I, 373, 375, 405.
[149] Usener, "Mythol.," in *Arch. f. Religw.*, VII, 6 ff.
[150] *Antik. Welt*, II, 340, 342.   [151] *Cath. Reaction*, I, 337.

form coming from the mores and impressing itself on religion. The Reformation abjured asceticism, reduced sacrament, and opposed celibacy. Most of the matters that were offensive to the reformers had either not been in the New Testament at all or had been developed in extreme form. In the end, sacramental monogamy came out of the mores.[152]

In no community does religion stand still. The Anglican Church has had a half-dozen phases. Congregationalism in New England is far from being what it once was. Not seldom has theology warranted Frazer's[153] characterization: "The history of religion is a long attempt to reconcile old custom with new reason; to find a sound theory for an absurd practice."

§326. Religion and the Mores. This last citation implies that religion is not readily adjustable. This is the fact. It is by nature less adjustable than any other institution of society, for it is farthest from conclusive test and selection.

"Man," says Bagehot,[154] "may be described as a custom-making animal. . . . In whatever way a man has done anything once, he has a tendency to do it again: if he has done it several times he has a great tendency so to do it, and what is more, he has a great tendency to make others do it also. He transmits his formed customs to his children by example and by teaching. This is true now of human nature, and will always be true, no doubt. . . . What is peculiar in early societies is, that over most of these customs there grows sooner or later a semi-supernatural sanction. The whole community is possessed with the idea, that if the primal usages of the tribe be broken, harm unspeakable will happen in ways you cannot think of, and from sources you cannot imagine."

Yet religion does adjust, tardily and almost grudgingly, in the course of time. Its very substructure alters its shape and so its supporting power as the ages go by: for from the aleatory element much has been subtracted and transferred to the non-spiritual range; and the spirit-environment, by reason of its very anthropomorphic character, must keep some pace with the altering complexion of human life as it is being lived on earth. Ultimately religion must reflect the mores in their alteration, as the next life and the spirit-world, on the principle of projectivism, repeat this life and this world.

One of the authors[155] of this book has worked out the relation of religion and the mores and concludes as follows.

[152] Sumner, "Mod. Marr.," in *Yale Rev.,* XIII, 249 ff.
[153] *Golden Bough,* II, 62.   [154] *Physics and Politics,* 141-142.
[155] Sumner, in *Coll. Ess.,* I, ch. V (129-131 quoted).

Mohammedanism, Romanism, and Protestanism contain systems of world-philosophy which have been deduced from religious dogmas. The world-philosophy is in each case removed by several steps of deduction from the religious postulates. In each case customs have grown up from the unavoidable compromise between metaphysical dogmas and interests, and these customs, so far as they inhere in essential traits of human nature or in fundamental conditions of human life, or as far as they have taken on the sanctity of wide and ancient authority, so that they seem to be above discussion, are the mores. Does a Roman Catholic, or a Mohammedan, or a Protestant child begin by learning the dogmas of his religion and then build a life-code on them? Not at all. He begins by living in and according to the mores of his family and societal environment. The vast mass of men in each case never do anything else but thus imbibe a character from the environment. If they learn the religious dogmas at all, it is superficially, negligently, erroneously. They are trained in the ritual, habituated to the usages, imbued with the notions of the societal environment. They hear and repeat the proverbs, sayings, and maxims which are current in it. They perceive what is admired, ridiculed, abominated, desired by the people about them. They learn the code of conduct—what is considered stupid, smart, stylish, clever, or foolish, and they form themselves on these ideas. They get their standards from the standards of their environment. Behind this, but far behind it for all but the scholars, are the history and logic by which the mores are connected with the religious facts or dogmas, and when the scholars investigate the history and logic they find that the supposed history is a tissue of myths and legends and that the logic is like a thread broken at a hundred points, twisted into myriad windings, and snarled into innumerable knots.

But now it follows that the mores are affected all the time by changes in environmental conditions and societal growth and by changes in the arts, and they follow these influences without regard to religious institutions or doctrines; or at most, compromises are continually made between inherited institutions and notions on one side and interests on the other. The religion has to follow the mores. In its nature, no religion ever changes, for every religion is absolute and eternal truth. It never contains any provision for its own amendment or "evolution." It would stultify itself if it should say: I am temporarily or contingently true, and I shall give way to something truer. I am a working hypothesis only. I am a constitution which may be amended whenever you please. "The faith once delivered to the saints" must claim to be perfect, and the formula itself means that the faith is changeless. A scientific or developing religion is an absurdity. But then again nothing is absolutely and eternally true. Everything must change, and religion is no exception. Therefore every religion is a resisting inertia which is being overcome by moving forces. Interests are the forces, because they respond, in men, to hunger, love, vanity, and fear, and the actual mores of a time are the resultant of the force of interests and the inertia of religion. The leaders of a period enlist on the side either of the interests or the resistance, and the mass of men float on the resultant current of the mores.

The essay quoted cites a number of cases, including that of our own country during the last fifty or sixty years, and concludes: I have maintained that the religion comes out of the mores and is controlled by them. The religion, however, sums up the most general and philosophic elements in the mores and inculcates them as religious dogmas. It also forms precepts on them. For an example we may note how the humanitarianism of modern mores has colored and warped Christianity. Humanitarianism grew out of economic power developed by commerce, inventions, steam, and electricity. Humanitarianism led to opposition to slavery, and to the emancipation of women. These are not doctrines of the Bible or of Middle-Age Christianity. They were imposed on modern religion by the mores. Then they came from the religion to the modern world as religious ideas and duties, with religious and ecclesiastical sanctions. This is the usual interplay of the mores and religion.

The relation of religion to the rest of the mores is that of a sanction upon them. This has been seen in the section dealing with the mode of origin of the mores.[156] When in the Pentateuch the reason given for a command is: "I am the Lord thy God," what it means is that such are the mores. By the very nature of this sanction religion must retain, support, and render holy the old rather than the new and must thereby in some degree oppose the variations by which alone further adjustment is possible. Strictly speaking, therefore, it is in the nature of religion to oppose adjustment. So candid and thoughtful a writer as Galton[157] has asserted that "the religious instructor, in every creed, is one who makes it his profession to saturate his pupils with prejudice." "Few things in the past," says White,[158] "are to the sentimental mind more pathetic, to the philosophical mind more natural, and to the progressive mind more ludicrous, than addresses at high festivals of theological schools. The audience has generally consisted mainly of estimable elderly gentlemen, who received their theology in their youth, and who in their old age have watched over it with jealous care to keep it well protected from every fresh breeze of thought. Naturally, a theological professor inaugurated under such auspices endeavours to propitiate his audience." It is as difficult to find any type of religion which has welcomed free inquiry as it is easy to cite eminent inquirers who have been executed or persecuted by religious authorities. Despite such opposition, however, free inquiry has always won; it has been inevitable, because the necessity of adjustment is perennial and imperative and the prime method of adjustment has been that of free inquiry. Despite the loves and hatreds of individuals and sects, society could not allow the suppression of that activity by which its life is sustained.

156 §§18, 19, above.   157 *Human Fac.*, 210.
158 *Sci. and Theol.*, II, 185.

Even primitive life is not without its variations of belief or at least its out-reachings toward examination of accredited faith. Says Malinowski[159] of the Trobriand Islanders—and the observation has been made by other ethnographers, as some of our citations have indicated: "If you examine the 'broad masses' of the community, the women and children included (a proceeding which is easy enough when you speak the language well and have lived for months in the same village, but which otherwise is impossible), you will find that, whenever they grasp your questions, their answers will not vary: they will never venture into private speculations. . . . As to the danger of their views being modified by missionary teaching, well, I can only say that I was amazed at the absolute impermeability of the native mind to those things. The very small amount of our creed and ideas they acquire remains in a watertight compartment in their mind. Thus the general tribal opinion in which practically no variety is to be found can be ascertained even from the humblest informants." This is fine evidence as to the residence of the mores in the masses.[160] The author goes on: "When dealing with intelligent grown-up informants, things are quite different. And as they are a class with whom an ethnographer has to do most of his work, the variety of their opinion comes very much to the fore, unless the inquirer is satisfied in taking one version of each subject and sticking to it through thick and thin. Such opinions of intelligent, mentally enterprising informants, as far as I can see, cannot be reduced or simplified according to any principles: they are important documents, illustrating the mental faculties of a community. Further on, they very often represent certain typical ways of conceiving a belief, or of solving a difficulty. But it must be clearly borne in mind that such opinions are sociologically quite different from what we called above dogmas or social ideas. They are also different from generally accepted or popular ideas. They form a class of interpretation of belief, which closely corresponds to our free speculation on belief. They are characterized by their variety, by not being expressed in customary or traditional formulae, by being neither the orthodox expert opinion, nor the popular view."

One should not be surprised that variations of this sort refuse to submit to reduction or simplification; they play about on the surface of the main current of conviction held by the unthinking masses, and are, like all other variations, the initial factor in the further evolution of religion and other institutions. That such variations seem irrational or even imbecile to a sophisticated mind is quite irrelevant. All through the evolution of religion variations have sprung up that seem totally irrational, such as making a fetish out of an albino; but the only question of any importance connected with them is whether or not they worked, in the sense of contributing survival-value to the system in which they were embodied. This they could do only by showing expediency for

[159] In JAI, XLVI, 428; see his recent volume, *Crime and Custom in Savage Society.*
[160] Sumner, *Folkways,* §§47 ff.

tribal life and welfare, by meeting societal interests. The same touchstone is the only one by which whole religious systems can be assessed.[161]

The history of the warfare between science and theology has been written by a competent hand and often quoted in this book. It might well have been called the history of the conflict between new societal adjustments and the sanction of old mores that have become maladjustments. Science appears as a protagonist in this duel because science is the surest and speediest instrument of adjustment ever developed by human society. It has, within its range, superseded the old groping process or that by rule of thumb. In all cases it informs us what it is that we must adjust to, so that we can make our adaptations with more intelligence and success. Though what we have to adjust to is something we cannot alter, nevertheless if we know just what to expect, or even approximately what to expect, we are immeasurably more likely to succeed in our adaptation than if we go at it blindly and hit-or-miss. Aided by science, one does not have to stumble about in peril like a person in a dark room full of live wires. He knows, at least, now that the light of science has been let in, where some of the wires are; and he has learned to avoid them or even how to put to his own use the fearful powers which they carry.[162] Such procedure is now in the mores; but it is futile to proclaim the conclusion of the war between science and theology while the sounding brass of the anti-evolution stump-orator and the tinkling cymbal of the sanctimonious heresy-hunter agitate every breeze.

Anything that gets in the way of science—of "trained and organized commonsense"—an instrument of such effectiveness that even those who scoff at it are living by its grace and are even circulating their foolish libels by its aid—is sure to emerge from the shock badly crippled. That has happened over and over again to theology. It was an advance in the mores, accompanied by an increase in knowledge, that made the Greeks of the fifth century denounce their own gods. Commonly so-called religion has begun by violently assaulting the new and by killing or driving out of its jurisdiction all persons having intellect enough to think independently; then, as the new has persisted and gained strength,

161 §330, below.   162 Keller, *Starting-Points*, ch. XII.

the tactics have been changed, and there has been made that attempt to "confiscate science to the uses of theology which we so constantly find whenever the triumph of science in any field has become inevitable." White,[163] from whom we quote, speaks of a high ecclesiastical dignitary as having displayed "one of the best examples of a method which has been used with considerable effect during the latest stages of nearly all the controversies between theology and science. It consists in stating, with much fairness, the conclusions of the scientific authorities, and then in persuading one's self and trying to persuade others that the Church has always accepted them and accepts them now as 'additional proofs of the truth of Scripture.' A little juggling with words, a little amalgamation of texts, a little judicious suppression, a little imaginative deduction, a little unctuous phrasing, and the thing is done." At the close of such a controversy, "we only have efforts to save theological appearances, and these only by men whose zeal outran their discretion."

Despite all bluster and subterfuge, the mores have always succeeded eventually in dictating the interpretation of the sacred screeds; for science has moved irresistibly forward, to the advantage even of those who were bent upon thwarting it. "In all modern history, interference with science in the supposed interest of religion, no matter how conscientious such interference may have been, has resulted in the direst evils both to religion and to science, and invariably; and, on the other hand, all untrammelled scientific investigation, no matter how dangerous to religion some of its stages may have seemed for the time to be, has invariably resulted in the highest good both of religion and of science."[164]

Recently the press has reported that the Episcopal bishops are "softening" the burial-service by cutting out references to worms, and are even going to allow it to be read over suicides and unbaptized adults.[165] When Princess Mary of England was married, certain phrases that have become utterly offensive to a refined taste were omitted from the service. They would have gone long ago had it not been for a mysterious sort of insulation that sur-

163 *Sci. and Theol.*, I, 186-187; II, 201-202; Lippert, *Kgchte.*, II, 628.
164 White, *Sci. and Theol.*, I, viii (italics omitted).
165 N. Y. *Times*, August 6, Sept. 3 and 15, 1922; *Literary Digest*, July 25, 1925 (quoting Bishop Slattery).

rounds the traditionally holy, whereby even the obscene may be handled by the clean-minded without a shock—without revulsion because without realization. This phenomenon is undoubtedly an exhibition of fetishism, and by reason of such insulation religion is less speedily checked up by the considerations of decency and propriety that have evolved in the mores. It is a privileged subject.[166]

This insulation is really conventionalization. Conventionalized pictures and statues are not improper. Conventionalization occurs in medical books. Reverence is convention: certain things are, for reverence sake, to be ignored and not heard, or seen, or realized. When an old usage becomes vulgar and is abandoned as such, it may nevertheless pass into worship or myth and be preserved there.

Among the East Greenlanders "in the long winter evenings time is killed by telling old tales the content of which is often of an obscene nature. But no attention is paid to that. They are recounted in the presence of children and young girls and all are diverted by them."[167]

Language which we think coarse in common life is used in church, and good taste demands that the Bible be expurgated for children. The stories of their mythology have been conventionalized even by the Hindus.[168] All this is in the mores. Respectability itself is convention; though it be sneered at, it is a safeguard, for free and easy behavior may degenerate into rowdyism and blackguardism. The sanction of religion lends a peculiar power to the common phenomenon of conventionalization, while rationalization undoes conventionalism and ritualism.

In still another way is religion following the mores, in that the original sense of its formulas has lost its drive and become only partially intelligible. Only upon special scrutiny does the empty survival reveal its maladjustment and meet its elimination.

The contention that religion does not make the mores but is no more than a sanction upon them does not involve the assertion that it has no influence upon them, that it may not make changes in them, or at any rate seem to do so, if circumstances are favorable. It certainly conserves them, to the extent of enforcing an

[166] Lippert, *Kgchte.*, II, 512; Sumner, *Folkways*, §74.
[167] Holm, *Ethnol. Skizze*, 112.   [168] Wilkins, *Hinduism*, 317.

obsolete code upon men long after it has ceased to do them any good whatsoever. Though the sanction of anything is evidently subsequent and secondary to what it sanctions, that it enters powerfully into the making of the destiny of that which it guarantees is self-evident. The general effect of a sanction is naturally conservative rather than progressive. Its operation can better be illustrated than described.

People are to be heard passing judgment on the Bible on account of the things in it which are contrary to our own mores, such as adulteries, incestuous marriages, acts of violence, falsehoods, polygamy, concubinage, slavery, and witchcraft. If the Bible is offered as a single, complete, universal, and eternal norm of truth and right, such criticisms are in order and are necessary to the preservation of our own mores and to the elasticity of our moral judgment. If we know that there never can be a universal and eternal norm of truth and right, then the mores of the Bible are those of successive periods of history covered in the book. They are thus material for the student of society, like the mores of the Phœnicians or Egyptians. Then it is idle to expend adjectives on them; but then also they have no authority. Nansen tells how the Eskimo applied their naïve and childish minds to the stories in the Bible; their logic tempts a smile but it is uncontrovertible. Children often express similarly keen comments. Missionaries are often confronted by them. When we hear them we learn to what an extent our attitude toward the Bible is conventional and different from that toward any other book to a degree which begs the question, if we ever dare raise it, as to what the Bible is. This attitude toward the Scriptures is a part of the mores of Protestant societies. It reveals a point in which we fail to be true to the code of life which ordains that always and in all things we shall strive to get at the truth and shall face it as we find it, the only code which an educated and honest man can today profess. The fact is that the Bible has had a tremendous influence upon our mores. Its phraseology enters into our vernacular. Yet let anyone read, for instance, the twenty-second to the twenty-sixth chapters of Deuteronomy and see how independently our mores have formed themselves in regard to the matters there treated. Some of the positions taken we agree with; some we reject; others seem to us too trivial to deserve an opinion. That the mores have taken their own course, in spite of the high authority and specific injunctions of the book, is obvious.

Take a few historic cases, out of the sixteenth century. In Scandinavia it was almost sinful to observe hygienic habits. The dead were buried beneath the churches and the air in them was foul and pestilential. When it was proposed to discontinue the custom the reply was that what the Church taught as right could not be abolished from considerations of bodily health.[169] Here is a fine example of the secondary or tertiary logical deduction turned into an arbitrary dogma of right conduct, over-ruling reason and expediency.

In the Bible, again, the existence of spirits is generally assumed in such a natural way that it is impossible to understand that any question is left open. Any simple, pious reader of the Bible is led to believe in them; to disbelieve is to meet a necessity for a special interpretation over and over again. The

[169] Lund, *Norges Hist.*, 36, 73, 83, 86, 89.

Protestants of the sixteenth and seventeenth centuries were led by their doctrine about the Scriptures to believe in demons and witches. Since the belief in ghosts, spirits, demons, and witches has been abandoned the doctrine of Scripture has been modified, although no adjustment has yet been reached. It is quite impossible to hold the traditional doctrine of the Bible and reject all such constructions. If ghosts do not exist, then the doctrine of the soul suffers mortally and with it the tenets about immortality and retribution. In few cases has the argument that a thing must be true, on account of the dogmatic disasters which would result from denying it, been so strong as in the case of witches. We have been taught to think of religions as coming into society through some law-giver and reforming its mores. We shall get better intellectual satisfaction if we look first to the mores as antecedents and then to the religions as consequents. Changes in a society bring it about that old religious ideas no longer fit the new mores. A new construction is needed and is eventually provided. It must be accordant with the interests and the arrangements which the interests have brought about; also with the general ideas or doctrines by which those arrangements are adjusted to traditions which already hold place in public opinion. The religion therefore follows the mores and out of any new religion offered to a people they select what suits their mores and fits their interests as they see them. Such a selection is the process of syncretism. For an understanding of the real process of change in religion and the mores too much attention has been paid to the expressions of great men who never won more than a few adherents and never, therefore, greatly affected the course of things. The secret is in those popular mores which so generally elude all our means of investigation.

For all men in the sixteenth century who saw that the then current law of correlation between goodness and prosperity did not verify in this world, scepticism had found lodgment in the citadel of world-philosophy. When they were bold enough to disbelieve in ghosts, the whole fabric of projectivism began to fall to pieces. With the loss of belief in ghosts and demons the notion of sorcery and magic also was lost and this was the real death-blow to witchcraft. The men who had to learn that there was no sky and that the earth floated in space found courage to give up purgatory altogether. Then the correlation between goodness and prosperity in the other world was broken and the notion of hell faded away too. The disappearance of purgatory as a positive concept and the disbelief in ghosts, demons, magic, and witchcraft was what produced the real issue between ritualistic-sacramentarian religion and rationalistic-realistic world-philosophy. The former survived only as an exercise which produced emotional sensation. The revolution was in the mores; the children had rejected the traditions of the fathers as to what the earth is, what man is, what goodness is, and then they revolted against the dogmas and sanctions of religion. It is instructive to notice the scorn of Protestants and Catholics of the sixteenth century for each others' mores of marriage and the family. The former dwell on the immorality of priests and monks, the latter on divorce. The revolution in the mores is marked by the difference in the standards of the two parties as to what was important and what unimportant. The history of the last four hundred years shows how slowly any great transformation in the mores is brought about. The institutions and ritual last on while the mores are changing. The mores of Protestantism have infected the Roman nations and are spreading now. This is a controlling fact of the present and future. Protestantism was a readjustment of the religion to the new mores; it was a metaphysical system built partly on the old theology and partly on the Bible interpreted without adequate criticism or knowledge. Therefore it produced sects which imposed, as conducive to welfare, dogmas of duty and right which would not verify in experience. They were rooted in metaphysical deduction, not in the mores. They aimed to control the latter. Every year we see the dogmas fade out as the mores prevail. It is by them that we live, even if we let the dogmas pass unchallenged. This indifference is the fatal sign.

Catholicity was in the Middle Ages a great and moving notion. In a political chaos it had great meaning. When great states arose, since it meant the world-dominion of the Church, it came into antagonism with the States. The Crusades are another instance of a great moving idea which enthused Europe for centuries and then proved to have been a folly. The modern thirst for social equality is a similar passion for an unverified notion. Such ideas color the mores of an age; they become guiding principles of action which men obey although they cost heavy sacrifices.

Such philosophical deductions as were made in the period which we have been examining have been in the taste of the last three centuries. They culminated in the eighteenth, when it became the fashion to regard logical deductions as revelations of actual sequences and relations in the world of perception. When men are willing directly to face the question whether the experience of life verifies the doctrines which their seniors have taught them, that is rationalism.

Thus deductions from religion may temporarily become independent rules of action. The cult-observances, rooting in projectivism, are what ought to be done—what a good man will do. But no such norms have in them anything of the original and permanent.

Religious persons, with visions or revelations, may start variations in the mores as have the Mormons and the Christian Scientists; then, whether these variations persist in the long run depends upon whether they constitute better adjustments of society to its life-conditions. If they do not, no amount of supernatural sanction can save the variations. The tendency of partisans, in the religious as in the political field, is to claim everything for their favorite belief, ignoring the underlying, constant, inevitable, though less dramatic multiple factor represented by environment, physical and social, and the fact of automatic adjustment to it. Both religious and political claims to the origination of all that is desirable are abating under the searching scrutiny of science.

§327. Religion and Morals. Morals are the part of the mores which have become positive in dogma and rule on account of their importance, real or assumed. "The morality of a group at a time is the sum of the taboos and prescriptions in the folkways by which right conduct is defined. Therefore morals can never be intuitive. They are historical, institutional, and empirical."[170] Then the relation of religion to morals must be the same as to the mores, that is, it acts as a sanction to a settled code.[171] "Morals," writes Oliveira Martins,[172] "in establishing societies, impose their stamp on religion which, reacting, gives a transcendent sanction to a socialized will." The "touchstone of all religions," says Lippert,[173] is "the unconquerable awe before the transgression of the moral code." The code came out of the business of living and religion lent the sanction of ghost-fear, without which men on the lower stages could not have been disciplined into morality. It is true that religion followed with its sanction all the correct and incorrect variations of self-maintenance and often imposed restraint on improvement; but one thing always persisted: the disinclination to violate the moral law, whatever it was. Several ethnographers contend for the entire disassociation of religion and morals, while others find various degrees of connection.[174]

"The Central Australian natives . . . have no idea whatever of the existence of any supreme being who is pleased if they follow a certain line of what we call moral conduct and displeased if they do not do so. They have not the vaguest idea of a personal individual other than an actual living member of the tribe who approves or disapproves of their conduct, so far as anything like what we call morality is concerned. Any such idea as that of a future life of happiness or the reverse, as a reward for meritorious or as a punishment for blameworthy conduct is quite foreign to them. . . . It must not, however, be imagined that the Central Australian native has nothing in the nature of a moral code. As a matter of fact he has a very strict one, and during the initiation ceremonies the youth is told that there are certain things which he must do and certain others which he must not do, but he quite understands that any punishment for the infringement of these rules of conduct, which are thus laid down for him, will come from the older men." He is told that the "spirit" he has heard of is only an invention to impose on women and children.[175]

"Religion, at the stage of growth in which we find it, among these three groups of [West-African] tribes, has no connection with morals, or the relations of men to one another. It consists solely of ceremonial worship and the gods are only offended when some rite or ceremony has been neglected or

---

170 Sumner, *Folkways*, §31.
171 Starcke, *Samvittighedslivet*, 43 ff.; Gumplowicz, *Soc.*, 179 ff., 183.
172 *Raças*, II, 153.   173 *Kgchte.*, I, 28, 93.
174 For a collection of cases, see Letourneau, *Morale*.
175 Spencer and Gillen, *North. Tr. Cent. Aust.*, 490; §163, above.

omitted. If the omission be quite unintentional the result is just the same, as the gods, like uncivilised man, judge by acts and not by motives. In all ages man makes God the moral counterpart of himself, and in savage life he only revenges that which affects himself. With the wrongs of others he has nothing to do."[176] Miss Kingsley[177] develops the West African system in further detail. "We have in Fetish a religion in which its believers do not hold that devotion to religion constitutes Virtue. The ordinary citizen is held to be most virtuous who is least mixed up in religious affairs. He can attain Virtue, the love and honor of his fellow-men, by being a good husband and father, an honest man in trade, a just man in the palaver-house, and he must, for the protection of his interests, that is to say, not only his individual well-being, but the well-being of those dependent on him, go in to a certain extent for religious practices. He must associate with spirits because spirits are in all things and everywhere and over everything; and the good citizen deals with the other spirits as he deals with that class of spirits we call human beings; he does not cheat the big ones of their dues; he spills a portion of his rum to them; he gives them their white calicoes; he treats his slave spirits honorably, and he uses his slave spirits for no bad purpose, and if any great grief falls on him he calls on the great over-lord of gods, mentioning these things. But men are not all private citizens; there are men whose destiny puts them in high places —men who are not only house fathers but who are tribe fathers. They, to protect and further the interests of those under them, must venture greatly and further, and deal with more powerful spirits, as it were, their social equals in spiritdom. These good chiefs in their higher grade dealings preserve the same cleanhanded conduct. And besides these there are those men, the Fetish men, who devote their lives to combating evil actions through witches and miscellaneous spirits who prey on mankind. These men have to make themselves important to important spirits. It is risky for them, for spirits are a risky set to deal with."

In Siberia there is evidently no canon of morality unless it is to get on well with the spirits and the shamans. "There is in the world of shamanism, however, no eternal justice. The gods of light, as well as the gods of darkness, do not act simply on ethical principles but let themselves be won over by sweet sacrificial foods and gladly shut their eyes when they are richly endowed; they are envious of men's wealth and above all want their gifts. Therefore it is a duty always to come into union with the spirits of light and of darkness through men specially gifted to this end. This task of mediation is undertaken by the shamans."[178] Among the Osetins each family secretly from every other family treats some particular object with a kind of worship, under a complete conviction of its unconquerable strength; one is afraid to enrage this fetish-object, for instance by a false oath in its presence.[179] In Japan the ethical sentiment "was exactly adapted to social requirements"[180] but the same thing cannot be said of the religion.

"It is true that the whole life of the Hindu is religious. His Scriptures teach him how he must dress, eat, work, and conduct himself in all his various relationships. According to the belief of a Hindu, he is as guilty, in many respects more guilty, in the sight of God, when he violates some apparently trivial

176 Ellis, *Yoruba*, 293.   177 *W. Afr. Studies*, 178, 179.
178 Radloff, *Schamanenthum*, 13.
179 *Russian Ethnog.* (Russ.), II, 354.   180 Hearn, *Japan*, 177.

caste regulation, as when he is guilty of falsehood, dishonesty, or immorality. . . . As there are so many deities, and so great a variety of character in these deities, and such various kinds of work are pleasing to them, it is a fact that almost any habit can be indulged in, almost any vice committed, under the impression that it is pleasing to some deity or other. Is a man inclined to drink spirits, bhang, or use opium? He can do this as an act pleasing to Siva. Does he wish to eat flesh? This can be done as part of the worship of Kali. Is he lustful? He has an example in Krishna. . . . A man who strictly observes the rules of his particular caste, and repeats the mantras of his guru [spiritual adviser], and is liberal in his offerings to the temples or gurus, is accounted a good Hindu, whatever his moral character may be."[181] Since 600 A.D., of the Hindu religion, the "gist, in a word, is this: 'If you feel able to endure it, the best thing to do is to study the plan of the universe, and then conform to it. By severe mental discipline you can attain to this knowledge, and for reward you will be immortally united with God.' To this the sectarian adds: 'Or believe in my god and the result will be the same.' But both philosopher and sectarian continue: 'If, however, you do not want to be united with the Supreme Spirit so soon as this, then be virtuous and devout, or simply be brave if you are a warrior; do whatever the rules of morality and caste-custom bid you do, and you will go to heaven for thousands of ages; at the end of which time you will be re-born in a fine family on earth, and may again decide to repeat the process of gaining heaven or to join God and become absorbed into the World-Spirit at once.' "[182]

The Brahmans "did not pretend to be teachers of ethics. The standard books they used when Buddhism arose . . . are the most unmoral literature imaginable. They only claimed to be able to perform accurately certain sacrificial rites which would ensure to the sacrificer desirable results—cattle, sons, wealth, or victory. Neither did their lives tend to show that there was the slightest necessary connection between the cult of the gods and purity of life. . . . Even among the Jews it was to the prophets, rather than to the priests, that any forward steps in ethical theory or practice were due."[183] The Dyaks conceive of a spirit that questions the ghost of the deceased about his misdeeds; the former falls lifeless if the latter details a list of them but strikes dead for seven days any ghost which reports a blameless life.[184] Even when sacrifice is made after adultery, the Dyak does not think of the cleansing of the offenders but of the appeasing of divine anger in order to preserve the land and crops from blight and ravage.[185] Thus adultery has the aspect of a crime against the community.

Parallel to the Hindu case is that of the ancient Hebrews. "The correctness of the view which emphasizes the non-ethical aspect of the Decalogue is specially evident in connexion with the prohibition of adultery. The object is not to keep the youth or the married man from immorality in general, as our catechisms are wont to explain the matter, but to ward off attack from one of the most important of a neighbour's rights of property. It is only in this sense that the notion of adultery is known to the ancient Hebrew mind; while, on the other hand, no limits are placed upon a married man's sexual intercourse with female slaves. In like manner, the seduction or violation of a

[181] Wilkins, *Hinduism*, 193, 309, 321.   [182] Hopkins, *Relig. Ind.*, 418.
[183] Rhys-Davids, in *Intern. Quart.*, VII, 10, 11.
[184] Perelaer, *Dajaks*, 220.   [185] Roth, *Sarawak*, I, 191.

virgin was plainly regarded in the earliest times more as a damage to one's rights (notably, for instance, in the way of lowering the selling price of a daughter) than as a moral transgression."[186] "Though the earliest nature-religion was fully identified with the earliest morality, it was not fitted to raise morality towards higher ideals; and instead of leading the way in social and ethical progress, it was often content to follow or even to lag behind. . . . Among the Semites, as among other races, religion often came to work against a higher morality, not because it was in its essence a power for evil (or good), but because it clung to the obsolete ethical standard of a bygone stage of society. . . . The evils that slowly sap society, the vices that at first sight seem too private to be matters of national concern, the disorders that accompany the increase and unequal distribution of wealth, the relaxation of moral fibre produced by luxury and sensuality, were things that religion hardly touched at all, and that the easy, indulgent god could hardly be thought to take note of."[187] The Moslem does not understand the difference between religiosity and morality. He would never admit that it is more meritorious before God to be an honorable man than to fulfil ritual prayers and washings.[188]

The Assyrian gods appear "as protectors of truth and right, as the regents of a natural and moral world-order, even if it is as yet so inadequately conceived."[189] "The purity which was required of the Zoroastrian was of two kinds, moral and legal. Moral purity comprised all that Christianity includes under it—truth, justice, chastity, and general sinlessness. It was coextensive with the whole sphere of human activity, embracing not only words and acts, but even the secret thoughts of the heart. Legal purity was to be obtained only by the observance of a multitude of trifling ceremonies and the abstinence from ten thousand acts in their nature wholly indifferent. Especially, everything was to be avoided which could be thought to pollute the four elements—all of them sacred to the Zoroastrian of Sassanian times,—fire, water, earth, and air."[190] The duties of men to the gods of Homer's time were ritualistic rather than ethical.[191] Beloch[192] refers the moral code of Greece to the poets and the seven wise men; their injunctions were then inscribed upon the walls of the Delphic temple. "The pure morality of the Mithraist creed might seem to have little in common with the orgies of the devotees of Attis and the Great Mother. But religious sentiment has a miraculous power both to reject and to transmute. The costume and Phrygian cap of Attis appear on all the monuments of Mithra to the end."[193]

"The chief objects of Pagan religions were to foretell the future, to explain the universe, to avert calamity, to obtain the assistance of the gods. . . . To make men virtuous was no more the function of the priest than of the physician. On the other hand, the philosophic expositions of duty were wholly unconnected with the religious ceremonies of the temple. . . . The love of truth in many forms was exhibited among the Pagan philosophers to a degree which has never been surpassed; but there was one form in which it was absolutely unknown. The belief that it is wrong for a man in religious matters to act a lie, to sanction by his presence and by his example what he regards as baseless

[186] Kautzsch, "Relig. Israel," in *Hastings's Dict. Bible,* 634.
[187] Smith, *Relig. Sem.,* 53, 65.   [188] Müller, *Islam,* I, 207.
[189] Tiele-Gehrich, *Gchte. Relig.,* I, 58, 215.
[190] Rawlinson, *Or. Mon.,* 635.   [191] Seymour, *Hom. Age,* 445, 446.
[192] *Griech. Gchte.,* I, 233-234.   [193] Dill, *Nero,* 588-589.

superstitions, had no place in the ethics of antiquity."[194] In the Middle Ages the fear of hell and other punishments affected men, not to make them good but only to cause them to attend on ritual.

Throughout this book religion is shown to have sanctioned a great variety of conduct.[195] It is perhaps worth while to recall some instances. It has supported the use of the old, in the matter of foods, instruments, processes, and products; has favored both war and peace, wealth and poverty, diligence and idleness, virginity and prostitution, humility and ostentation, indulgence and austerity. It has prescribed game-laws, cannibalism, human sacrifice, the killing of the old, suicide, incest, polyandry, polygyny, slavery, and the levirate; has guaranteed all forms of property-holding, of inheritance, and of government; has both favored and proscribed commerce and the taking of interest; it has been forced to bend to new vices.[196] It has therefore offered no absolute standard of morality, for there is none, but has sanctioned what lay in the mores of the time and place—or, often, what lay in the mores of the place at some previous time. For morals push on faster than religion. Long after private morals as to sex-relations have advanced beyond prostitution, it is practised under the ægis of the cult. The morals of the gods are generally those of a former and cruder generation; they persisted in incest long after it had become abhorrent in human relations. The fact that men can accept in the case of the gods that which society outlaws is an illustration of conventionalization. Where a fluent liar, like Odysseus, was an object of admiration there was a liar-god and the thieves were not without a patron-deity; according to Ellis[197] there is still a certain religious character to crime. Saintliness has often been no more than technical goodness; such was that of the Pharisees.

All this is to be expected if one has grasped the idea of the mores and their evolution. The mores will both tighten up after a period of laxity and relax after a period of stringency, and the sanction of the mores will follow after, perhaps afar off, and sometimes so tardily that it will be ready to guarantee stringency or the reverse when the mores are about to desert that alternative

[194] Lecky, *Europ. Morals*, II, 2; I, 404.
[195] *Hastings's Encyclopædia of Religion and Ethics*, in over ten volumes, covers thousands of correlations between the two.
[196] Lecky, *Europ. Morals*, II, 294.   [197] *The Criminal*, 156, 161.

in their swing toward its opposite. In general, the system of morality was formed by the societal economy in the mores; "but religion lent it that strong and meaning sanction of penalty without which the education of man, on the lower and middle stages, to morality . . . would never have taken place."[198] It should never be lost to sight that whatever early religion did toward the development of morality was strictly confined to the in-group. To steal a group-comrade's wife was bad, and the local deity, who belonged to the kin-group as a ghost or ancestor, would not fail to exact a penalty; on the other hand, it was good to steal the wife of a member of the out-group, and the home-deity would rejoice over the exploit as much as any mortal could. Relics of this way of looking at morality still exist; a deity may be more than paternally indulgent to the questionable deeds of his votaries.

Religion in history, from the earliest to very recent days, has not been a matter of morality at all but of rites, ritual, observance, and ceremony; it has expressed political traditions and ties or sustained political power or nourished sanitary and hygienic practices believed from experience to conduce to societal welfare. Even this last rationalistic element has always tended to become stereotyped and traditional, that is, irrational, and so to degenerate into further cases of rites and ceremonies. It is the practice of prescribed rites and usages in all the great religions which gives a man something to do; then he learns to revere a person who has performed them long and faithfully. The latter becomes the type, ideal, and model. Prayers, pilgrimages, fasts, alms, washings, and prescriptions are before the eye, external and physical; by repetition they become a part of life. It is the habit of doing things, as when the Moslem prays five times a day, which holds a man for life, which drills him in acts that become his life.

Religion has been shown to have been a sanction to mores and morals. That function is, however, incidental to the nature of religion and not at all its original or essential characteristic. It is a fallacy and is disastrous to religion to suppose that "the essential elements in all religious beliefs must be the ultrarational sanction which they provide for social conduct."[199] The whole religious and moral structure would collapse together if that were true, for it

---

[198] Lippert, *Kgchte.*, I, 28, 93.   [199] Kidd, *Soc. Evol.*, ch. III.

would have no natural cohesion. If social codes have any rational guarantee, it is one independent of religion; it is one discernible to the eye of the evolutionist only and resides in the expediency of those codes as societal adjustments to life-conditions. If the codes had no such guarantee, and a religion were maintained in order to sanction them, that religion would be no support but a dead weight. The remark that if the French people had had no God, one would have had to be invented for the purpose in hand was a piece of whimsical wit with more facets to it than appear at first sight. A religion is a matter of ancient faith, not of reason or casual invention; and men will give it their trust in proportion as it offers a solution of the problem of life satisfactory to them on their stage of culture.

§328. The Power of Religion.

For countless generations, says Lippert,[200] religion was nothing else than a struggle for existence projected beyond the grave, for the domain beyond death was introduced, as it were, into the range of the struggle in this world. In a sense, men here had to carry on the conflict not only for themselves but for those who had gone before and whose needs in the beyond must be met by men here. Religion for the primitive man was not speculation but worship; and worship was nothing but the extension of the self-maintenance struggle into a spirit-world of which all primitive men, with remarkable unanimity, cherish the same childish conception. Whether this conception corresponds to reality or not has no effect upon its influence. One of Lippert's significant passages may be quoted yet again:

"History shows us that the creative force exerted by a notion on the development of civilization does not depend upon its relation to reality. The power of an idea lies, not in its certainty but in its vividness and in the number of people who believe in it. Our faith in the power of 'the truth' rests on the principle that in the conflict of ideas those which are the more certain will become also the more widely accepted. Often, however, greater vividness more than offsets greater certainty; and the notions which are more vivid are also produced by the more elementary thinking, so that men believe they have found them out for themselves. Such were the ideas which produced the rites of religion." Elsewhere the author recurs to the power of the ghost-belief: "So far as experience allows us to make a comparison, a notion, when it is the product of the study of a single man, and when it has been matured by a single culture-

[200] *Kgchte.*, I, 29; II, 45; I, 30; II, 462, 511, in order of quotation.

group only, can never win such currency, and can never be so vividly apprehended, no matter what the evidence for it may be, as, for instance, the belief
in ghosts, which is as respects evidence extremely uncertain. Never will the
established doctrines of Newton and Copernicus furnish anything like such
motives of conduct as the childish notions of ghost-fear. The reason for this
is not in the quality of the notions but in the way in which they come to be.
. . . The farther a notion reaches back into primitive times for its origin, the
more universal must be its extent, and its power in history is rooted in this
universality." The influence of religion on history has never been fully realized.
"Inasmuch as it is a mark of man that he puts his own ideas, as if they were
natural forces, into the mechanism of his social progress, and inasmuch as,
historically, no other motive has ever had anything like the same strength as
religious notions, there is much ground for the attempt to separate man from
all other creatures by the characteristic of religiosity. The overwhelming influence of religion, not only on the history of civilization but also on what we call
political history, has hardly yet been justly appreciated. . . . Just as man is
distinguished from all other living beings by having developed a cult, so the
historical development of social organization, upon which all further evolution
of self-maintenance and so all civilization depends, has been such that it never
could have taken place as it has but for the influence of the cult." The fact
is, however, that societal gain is never a motive; for if it is at the expense of
the individual, or even though it benefits him, no one sees it otherwise than
from the restricted point of view of his own narrow interest. It takes other
and more impersonal factors to attend to the welfare of society as a whole;
and among them is the impulse that comes from religion, to which men ascribe
whatever is by experience advantageous but the causal relation of which they
cannot perceive.

No one who has read ethnography and history reflectively can
be in any doubt as to the power residing in religion. It is a potence
capable of dealing, to the satisfied conviction of men, with the
aleatory element; and concern with that element has occupied the
minds of all mankind. It is also the sole means of adjustment to
the dark mystery which, in all ages surrounding the slight circle
of human knowledge, has been figured in the form of a supernatural, spiritual world. All races have known that man lives not by
bread alone and that the anxious spirit may rest, in the end, only
in harmony and reconciliation with the supernatural and altogether irresistible Power. Not having felt so helpless before the
other exigencies of life, men have dared to adopt positive methods
of dealing with them. Most religions, however, have been developed
on the principle of avoidance and escape, as if in the presence of
insufferable power against which it was hopeless to strive. And
there has even been conceived, beyond the gods and controlling
them too, a Fate, utterly inescapable, and in the presence of which

the only possible attitude is that of resignation.[201] Only that which is necessary happens, said the Stoics; hence if a man desires no more than that, his wishes will be fulfilled.

The power of "the faith," which did not exist on the earlier stages of religious evolution, has been illustrated throughout history. It has inspired men to superhuman effort and also to subhuman atrocities. All the mediæval sectarians took the risk of the stake, and knew they were doing so.[202] No one would go to the stake for the doctrine of the conservation of energy or natural selection with such fervor as men have exhibited in self-immolation for some absurdity of creed.

§329. Disservices of Religion. No intellect, however emancipated, can get away from the conception of the enveloping mystery of the unknown and the unknowable; in fact, it is precisely the mind which is best stocked and most scientifically trained that senses the mystery most poignantly. Various degrees of perception equip themselves with their own grades of anthropomorphic or more highly refined theory; and each and every type of theory is explicable in the setting of its time and in the state of knowledge of its votaries. There is therefore no moral judgment to be passed upon primitive beliefs, such as we are accustomed to deliver when we call them superstitions. Things went that way, and that is all there is to it. To say that the course of religious evolution was senseless or faulty or unworthy of the human race, and that it might have been better otherwise, is to betray the type of one's intelligence. It is like asserting that it would have been better if objects fell up instead of down or if water had been composed of different constituent elements.

It is possible, however, for anyone who is immersing himself for the first time in the details of primitive religion to revolt at the picture and to ask himself whether the race would not have been better off if it had not developed religion at all or, at any rate, if men had not been subject to illusions in dreams and otherwise and had developed their adjustments to the aleatory element along

[201] Vierkandt, *Naturvölker,* 146, 147; Starcke, *Samvittighedslivet,* 85-86.
[202] Lippert, *Kgchte.,* II, 619; Lecky, *Europ. Morals,* II, 251; Friedmann, *Wahnideen,* 219.

lines other than those which they followed. Such impressions are so strong and compelling that it is worth while to balance the services of religion in society's evolution against the disservices which it seems to reveal throughout the various stages of its development.

It is possible to make out a strong *prima facie* case against religion, since its apparent disservices are concrete and evident, while to appreciate its services to society one must have done enough reflection to realize that methods of indirection may be quite as effective as those which are direct and obvious. Short-sighted preoccupation with the obvious has convinced not a few emotional people that religion must be uprooted, along with private property, the monogamic family, and government. It is needless to say that such persons are not intelligent evolutionists, accustomed to discounting incidentals in favor of a long perspective. The case against religion, if it may be so designated for the sake of brevity, consists of a set of detailed complaints concerning the weight of its incidence upon human prosperity and happiness. There is plenty of truth in them—enough, in the absence of countervailing considerations, to arraign the institution once and for all. It is in point to note that about the same could be said of most societal institutions, though perhaps without so high a grade of intensity.

In the case against religion appear such considerations as the following— there is no object in attempting an exhaustive survey or of citing matter that is inferential; most of the facts are already in the hands of the reader of our previous chapters. Religion has hampered the industrial organization[203] by cult-exactions in food and materials in general, in labor, time, and thought. It has prevented the accumulation of capital, by disallowing and diverting inheritance, and otherwise. Much of what it has exacted has been wasted, in an economic sense, in funeral-ceremonies, sacrifices, and tomb-building. It has tampered with family-organization to the detriment of the latter, and in group-relations it has caused wars, prevented the spread of peace, and otherwise kept peoples apart. It has been the enemy of advancing knowledge and has retarded education. It is our purpose here to illustrate this typical set of charges, without attempting to enforce, refute, or systematize them to any extent. First, then, concerning the relations between religion and economic life. In both Egyptian and mediæval history, says Lippert,[204] who treats the evolution of religion with such acumen, we see what an immense influence was

203 Diamond, "Cult and Econ. Org.," in *Sci. Mo.*, XVIII, 66 ff. (a portion of a dissertation on the relation of religion and capital) ; §265, above.

204 Lippert, *Kgchte.*, I, 30; II, 604, 605, 273, 622, 626; §§234, 237, 270, above.

exerted upon the economic life by the conception of a struggle for self-maintenance beyond death. The cathedrals and the monasteries, with treasures, lands, and serfs, by the side of the huts of the poor, like the grand temples and pyramids by the side of the mud hovels, show how the struggle was diverted from this world to the next, and how "Life has played the miser for the enrichment of Death." Each man's desire to preserve his own soul created for survivors a duty which took precedence of all others and from whose weight there was no relief. It was enforced on conscience by fear. The man's own notion weighed upon him more heavily than any external power. Religion drew a veil over nature and fact and led technical effort in self-maintenance astray; the only cause for ill was the unappeased ghost, the unpaid atonement. Men have done what religion has ordered, not what self-maintenance required and prompted. Rites replaced industry and the accumulation of capital; preoccupation with the aleatory element crippled labor and thrift. The cult-cure for ills caused misery, inequality of unproductive accumulations, and poverty. When it failed there was no rejection of it but rather new rites, new outlay, more loss, more misery. Religion, by turning all attention to the future life, has discouraged initiative in this one. The cult has absorbed human attention and, where great importance has been assigned to it, has been the greatest clog on progress. Economic mischief was done by elevating poverty and beggary to honor and saintliness and by plans somehow to buy heaven. The priesthood absorbed the property, even of the poorest classes, and provided examples of insatiable greed coupled with offensive parasitism.

Entering somewhat more into the concrete, we find, even among quite primitive tribes, religious considerations operating against success in winning a livelihood. Consider the spirit-theory of fishing, which lays stress on silence alone,[205] or that of agriculture, which insists upon an application of fowl's blood—upon ritual instead of upon industry.[206] It takes sophistication to be able to say: "No idler, though he has the names of the gods upon his lips, can win a livelihood without hard work."[207] The Eskimo have killed animals recklessly, undermining their livelihood, because they believed the souls of the beasts could not be destroyed by any amount of slaughter but would simply reanimate new prey.[208] Religion laid its stress upon the accessory or wholly irrelevant. In religion the human notion enters the parallelogram of forces as a motive, so that men cannot rely upon a solely physical analysis, and confusion ensues.

Of the fetishes in Madagascar we read: "Many were the curious antipathies they were supposed to entertain; one of the most foolish of these was the dislike to houses with walls made of non-combustible materials, so that until about nine or ten years ago no stone, brick, or earthen building could be erected in the capital city or the other principal towns of the central province."[209]

In Tibet, "you see, on the one hand, numerous and rich monasteries, large stone temples, paved courts, gilded roofs, wide groves—within the temples; statues, life-size, of gilded brass, pictured walls, orchestras and dancers composed of clergy, in expensive silk costumes and various kinds of masks. There also, in tiny cells on winter evenings, by the light of tallow or wax candles, goes on the copying of clerical books, the study of medicine, the carving of images of

[205] Krieger, *Neu-Guinea*, 186.
[206] Roth, *Sarawak*, I, 190.
[207] Euripides, *Electra*, 80-81.
[208] Turner, in BAE, XI, 200.
[209] Sibree, *Great Afr. Isl.* (1880), 301.

the gods. And by the side of these monasteries lives a whole nation of barbarians in garments of undressed fur put on the naked body, satisfied with a most meager stock of household utensils, and living in the same dwellings with their cattle."[210] "Not long ago, a teacher in the city of Foochow began to investigate the relation of idolatry to the industries of that city. Foochow contains approximately 700,000 inhabitants. Such a survey as has been possible, using student investigators, has shown that at least 80 per cent of the population is, to some degree, dependent for its livelihood upon the popularity of idol-worship. Thirty per cent of the people were found to be entirely dependent upon it. Some day the manifold ramifications of idolatry through Chinese society will be adequately discussed. Here it can only be said that it has its economic stakes set where even many of the missionaries never suspect them to be. Mohammedanism and Christianity combined have scarcely begun to affect idolatry."[211]

The extremest inferences are drawn in India from the doctrine of sparing life; there prevails "a rejection of meat and drink which still limits the food supply of an over-populated country, and contributes to its periodical famines."[212] "Whatever differences exist between the sects of Hinduism, there are two characters common to all . . . a pessimistic view of life and salvation by works."[213]

Prolific food-supplies have been tabooed to peoples that were starving, noxious animals protected in their forays on human life, and men have had to stand by and see the fruits of their industry destroyed by holy beasts. So difficult was the situation that men tried to save something from the wreck by deceiving their gods. The people were oppressed by ecclesiastical tithes and the best land was drawn under the mortmain. Egypt was "wholly exhausted" by the extravagance of her cult-outlays.[214] Consider the time, effort, and wealth expended upon the Pyramids; Cheops is said to have had 300,000 subjects working on his tomb in shifts of 100,000, for many years.[215] Even more striking, in their time, are the megalithic structures of neolithic ages, which required the systematic coöperation of a large number of men whose duty it was to honor the dead.[216]

At some periods, "poverty and beggary are raised to a cult; enterprise, technique, knowledge, and art are not even recognized."[217] Again, the latter are fostered and turned to religious uses. Adams[218] writes of the devotion shown to the Virgin in the Middle Ages. "The measure of this devotion, which proves to any religious American mind, beyond possible cavil, its serious and practical reality, is the money it cost. According to statistics, in the single century between 1170 and 1270, the French built eighty cathedrals and nearly five hundred churches of the cathedral class, which would have cost,

[210] Potanin, in *Vestnik Evropi (European Messenger)*, Feb., 1888.
[211] Hutchinson, in *Atl. Mo.*, CXXVII, 123.
[212] Deshmukh, in JASB, I, 85; Maine, *Early Law*, 48.
[213] Monier-Williams, *Brāhmanism*, 71.
[214] Tiele-Gehrich, *Gchte. Relig.*, I, 99-100.
[215] Maspero, *Hist. Anc.*, II, 378.
[216] Ranke, *Mensch*, II, 499; Nadaillac, *Preh. Amer.*, 83, note; Thomson, "Easter Isl.," in USNM, 1889.
[217] Kurnig, *Pessimismus*, 3.
[218] *Mont-Saint-Michel*, 94, 95, 98, 99.

according to an estimate made in 1840, more than five thousand millions to replace. Five thousand million francs is a thousand million dollars, and this covered only the great churches of a single century. The same scale of expenditure had been going on since the year 1000 and almost every parish in France had rebuilt its church in stone. . . . The share of this capital which was—if one may use a commercial figure—invested in the Virgin cannot be fixed, any more than the total sum given to religious objects between 1000 and 1300; but in a spiritual and artistic sense, it was almost the whole, and expressed an intensity of conviction never again reached by any passion, whether of religion, of loyalty, of patriotism, or of wealth; perhaps never even paralleled by any single economic effort, except in war." Later the bourgeois, after 1300, became doubtful about this investment, feeling "that neither the road to Heaven nor Heaven itself had been made surer or brought nearer by an investment of capital which amounted to the best part of the wealth of France. Economically speaking, he became satisfied that his enormous money-investment had proved to be an almost total loss, and the reaction on his mind was as violent as the emotion. For three hundred years it prostrated France. The efforts of the bourgeoisie and the peasantry to recover their property, so far as it was recoverable, have lasted to the present day and we had best take care not to get mixed in those passions."

It can be seen that the whole theory under which men lived tended to a sort of paralysis of economic activity. A fatalistic mood sometimes appeared. Ancestor-worship in China has been frequently cited as a prime cause of the unprogressive quality of a once leading civilization.[219] In the Middle Ages too each man's desire to save his own soul created for survivors a duty which took precedence over all others and from the weight of which there was no relief. It was enforced on conscience by fear. Thus man's own notions bore more heavily upon him than any external power. When religion is fatalistic, it dampens initiative. All forms of daimonism and daimonology go on the assumption that the ills of life are due to sin and can be atoned for; that the future can be molded by devices. This fosters optimism and the belief in a free will. When that does not verify, there comes reaction, resignation, and despair, such as that of Job. It is all of no avail; "necessity" and fate rule all; what is the use? " 'It is written on my forehead,' is a sufficient reason for the greatest calamities and troubles in after life. This superstitious belief largely accounts for the stoical endurance of physical pain, disappointment, and loss, that is so noticeable in the Hindu. What Vidhātā (Fate) has written must come to pass; it is useless, therefore, to attempt to oppose the inevitable. . . . The common phrase the people use is that creation is the play or sport of God. He was tired of being alone, and for His own amusement formed the world from Himself; all the pains and miseries and vexations of life come from the influence of Māyā (illusion), from the individual imagining himself to be something distinct from God. There are several ways by which this illusion can be overcome. . . . The best way of all is by meditating on the identity of the soul with God, until the mind becomes conscious of nothing else. In other words, as it seems to an outsider, supreme bliss consists in having no knowledge and no desires; indifference to heat and cold, hunger and thirst, day and night, self and the world. A life of inaction is the noblest man can live; and a life without thought is better than an active, self-denying one. . . . No doc-

[219] Harvey, *Chinese Animism*.

trine is more commonly and implicitly believed than this, that all man's life is arranged by the deity, and that it is useless for him to attempt to go against the Divine decrees; all that man can do is to submit. . . . There is only one way, so far as I know, of gaining an alteration of this destiny, viz., by bathing in a tank at Benares, where it is promised to the bathers that they can obtain a successful issue for their plans, although the opposite has been written by the gods."[220] "The deep-rooted fatalism that is common to Buddhists and Mohammedans plays a great rôle in all Ladakh cultivation. As a consequence of it, valleys whose water-supply is of itself sufficient for tillage are wholly deserted because once the terraces were destroyed by a great spring flood. The Ladakh native, conceiving that a higher being does not favor settlement of the place in question, does not make the least effort to cultivate it again."[221]

It is stated that religion interferes with the matter of self-perpetuation through its prescriptions of celibacy, infanticide, and other perversions of what is thought to be natural and expedient, not to mention its emphasis upon the uncleanness and general undesirability of one sex. Many texts can be cited from the Bible which decry the family-relations as bonds upon the religious man, and the Christian Fathers had much to find fault with in women. "What does it matter whether it be in the person of wife or mother, since we have to beware of Eve in every woman?"[222]

Religion is charged with the paternity of not a few wars. These include the primitive head-hunting expeditions, for example, as well as the real religious wars, so-called, characteristic of more developed peoples. The religion of Odin which in some cases made for peace, in others called for blood-vengeance as the holiest duty and thereby caused constant war between families; this was but little softened by the fixed money-payments whereby the laws opened the way to reconciliation.[223] A people which regards itself as "chosen"[224] is likely to develop ethnocentrism to an offensive degree and to encroach upon the rights of others or, stubborn in its defeat, to suffer through centuries. A French statesman of the sixteenth century asserted that it was folly to hope for peace between persons of different religions; that a Frenchman and an Englishman, "who are of the same religion have more affection for one another than citizens of the same city, or vassals of the same lord, who hold to different creeds."[225] It can be seen, then, that religion has hindered the development of the state by keeping up traditional or religious distinctions. Protestantism was in no way responsible for the modern state, with its constitution and freedom, its bureaucracy and military establishment, its modern stratification into economic and other classes, its science and art; these rose before and without it.[226] The church and the state have fought it out from the time when they ceased to be united in the priest-chief until they were separated as utterly incom-

[220] Wilkins, *Hinduism*, 11, 318, 319, 320.

[221] Francke, in *Globus*, LXXVIII, 225.

[222] Exod., XXXII, 29; Deut., XIII, 6-10; Zech., XIII, 3; Matt., X, 37; Luke, XIV, 26; McCabe, *St. Augustine*, 213; Sumner, "Status of Woman," in *Coll. Ess.*, I, chs. II, III.

[223] Geijer, *Svensk. Hist.*, I, 115.

[224] Kautzsch, "Relig. Israel," in *Hastings's Dict. Bible*, 684.

[225] §295, above; Johnson, *Europe*, 399, 400.

[226] Troeltsch, in *Hist. Ztsft.*, Folge 3, Bd. 1, Hft. 1.

patible.[227] Consider the efficiency in interference with the course of things lodged in a Pope who could partition the world between two favored nations.

Today, in the face of all the tendencies of civilization to bring the whole human race into one coöperative organization, religion produces deep and radical divisions and fosters prejudices resting on ignorance, hate, and false pride. Each division is either actively or passively hostile to the rest. In the best case they ignore each other, forming groups that are estranged and suspicious, so that coöperation is difficult or out of the question, while the welfare of mankind depends upon harmonious coöperation more than upon anything else.

Perhaps the most consistent charge against religion is that it has always opposed the advance of knowledge. Such a usage as refusal to speak ill of the dead fosters untruthfulness and leads to distorted traditional valuations, for example in the case of historic national figures. In the Laws of Manu[228] it is set down that "unless one be asked one must not explain anything to anybody nor must one answer a person who asks improperly; let a wise man, though he knows the answer, behave amongst men as if he were an idiot." This is an extreme case; the charge is generally not that religious experts have not been ready to answer questions but that they have been too eager in their officious ignorance to answer and to insist upon that answer; that they have wished to rule conduct, and not only that but also thought; and that they have balked at no means for securing their desires. The story of the Inquisition, of the Index, and of enforced recantations under torture or threat of it, need not be rehearsed, nor yet the later conflict between theology and science. It is contended that religion has inculcated contempt for reason by treating all unpleasant evidence as non-existent. Sects and parties have claimed divine protection and favor. Which one of them, when it met calamity, ever accepted that as a proof that it was in error? When the Spanish Armada was destroyed, did any Churchman infer that they had been mistaken in supposing that the expedition had been in God's service and under his favoring providence? Yet did they not seize upon every iota of evidence favorable or capable of being interpreted as favorable to their dogmas? There were those at the time of the Crusades who argued that the Mohammedans must be right and the Christians wrong on account of the misfortunes and failures of the Crusaders. The Templars were charged with this deduction. It was branded as a heresy. To draw such an inference was not permitted. Not the candid reasoner but the equivocal interpreter was called for at such a juncture. Powerful support was afforded to the normal and disastrous human tendency to resist learning the lessons of history. It is also charged that religion foisted metaphysics on the world, by substituting pallid entities for crude divinities. Among other things it developed an idealism which "allows everyone, with his little outfit of notions, to help build the world-temple; hence its attractiveness." It is even stated that socialism, now become "a religion, a faith and a hope that have nothing to do with nature-science" but are loaded with metaphysics, is one of the results of the metaphysical state which Comte derives from the religious. We are bidden to note how religion hampered art as well as science, fixing it within inalterable categories, and that it has been unfriendly to education.[229] As late as 1515,

---

[227] Caine, *Christian,* 525-526.   [228] Bühler, *Manu,* II, 110.
[229] De Greef, *Soc.,* II, 163, 194, 218; Topinard, *Anth.,* 33 ff.; Letourneau,

Leonardo da Vinci suffered because he practised dissection while the Church "taught the sacredness of the human corpse, and was ready to punish as a sacrilege the use of the anatomist's scalpel."[230]

The low state of many tribes is accounted for, according to Ratzel,[231] by the making of all mental acquisitions the possession of a priestly class and locking them up in superstition. Religion is so far from having its origin in causation that daimonism is antagonistic to causation. A daimon-agent is always assumed. Sacred books, with priests or sages to interpret them, have become the authority for rules of right, deductions being made and imposed independently of their social effects. Such a thing must be or must be done because the scriptures say so, or are understood to say so, or say so by inference. Such inferences have caused great wrong and woe: torture, ordeal, duel, witchcraft and witch-processes, the beggary of children disinherited by parents in order that the latter might escape purgatory. All the sects claim to have the truth; therefore it is wrong for anyone to persecute us but right for us to persecute anybody. Heretics were criminals who deserved all they got. It took a long time to carry people over to doubt and then to criticism. Things which no one could know were always being stated as facts and acted upon. Sacred books hold a world-philosophy and may carry it over to a subsequent period, in which it is survivalistic, with an authority that negatives adjustment.

A church, sect, party, or association has a program. It is formed to do something. Such a union does not exist in order to find out the truth. It assumes some dogma to be true; and "there is no dogma so absurd that it has not been admitted by men endowed as to everything else with a great *finesse* of spirit."[232] That dogma is made the postulate of its action and the purpose of the union is to bring those together who have a common conviction and to organize them for action which will propagate their faith or realize its application to life. Hence "toleration" never can be rational *inside* any such union. It would be absurd. In science, on the other hand, toleration and discussion are absolutely essential. No one knows what is "eternally true." The question is always open.

There can be no object in prolonging the foregoing. There is enough in it to indicate the grounds of assault. It is unnecessary to say that, though there are two sides to a number of the issues raised, we are not interested in rebutting details.

§330. The Survival-Value of Religion. The case for religion rests, scientifically speaking, upon a few broad and related considerations. If they are accepted, the value of religion in societal evolution is removed from the range of doubt and the debatable details need not be labored over. If not, then we, at least, see no way of assessing the sets of pros and cons that can be presented

Morale, 369 ff.; Lippert, *Kgchte.*, II, 459; Spencer, *Soc. Stat.*, 167; Anon., "Naturwissenschaft u. Religion," in *Pol. Anth. Rev.*, III, 279.

[230] McCurdy, *Da Vinci's Note-books*, 6.

[231] *Vkde.*, III, 14.   [232] Renan, *Averroès*, 163.

concerning the value of religion. In what follows, further, it is not the validity of any particular faith but the survival-value of religion as an institution that is in question.

As has been heretofore noted, it is no charge against any human institution that it began in crudity, brutality, or illusion. The doctrine of natural rights and liberty never had any historical foundation; it is a pure example of *a priori* dogma. Does this render invalid a single institution that professes to rest upon it now? Shall we return into serfdom because it is proved that our ancestors were emancipated under a delusion or a superstition?[233]

An evolutionist, viewing the universal existence of religion throughout the races of mankind, cannot but believe that it has possessed survival-value, for there must once have been races without it and it must on a time have risen as a variation that has withstood selection and has persisted. If one considers, further, that it is precisely the most advanced races that have suffered most and longest under the cult-burdens and other alleged disadvantages accruing from religion, he comes unavoidably to the conclusion that religion constitutes for a society an adjustment with high survival-value. Along with the family, property, and government, religion has taken its place as one of the major institutional adjustments in the evolution of society.

There is always reason behind the success of a persisting adjustment, whether in the organic or the societal realm; in fact, our very idea of reason is derived from observation of the constitution and operation of things that "work." Adjustments do not survive selection and last on when they are wrong-headed and contrary to reason or despite the fact that they are whimsical, capricious, and unamenable to law. If one looks dispassionately into the charges against religion and admits all of them, either wholly or in some degree, and then surveys and acknowledges the costs in capital, effort, and pain that religious systems have imposed cold-bloodedly and offensively upon mankind, he is yet, in the end, constrained to believe that the article was worth the cost. Exceedingly expensive, it has also been incomparably effective. The costs were paid by some and the rewards were enjoyed by others, which is highly unfair viewed from a selected position from which one

233 Sumner, *Coll. Ess.,* II, 112 ff.; §171, above.

can see only the individual or the present generation and always in the light of his own mores. In appraising human institutions as evolutionary products, all local situations, codes, and biases must drop out of account and the arbiter must view the landscape from a high and detached place, from horizon to horizon. In no other way can the nature and service of a great institution of society be visualized. Only the evolutionist can "justify" religion.

It has been the failure to realize "the inconscient processes that make manners, faith, patriotism" which has rendered the labors of great souls like Robert G. Ingersoll ephemeral. "Error to him was always definite and personal, the offence of a given bigot, priest, or council. He never saw or admitted the inevitableness of much that outrages isolated common sense. . . . It is strange that so sympathetic and humorous a man should not have understood how cleverly life saves itself from the literal cruelty of creeds. . . . He was too intolerant of those bonds which human nature gladly, and on the whole wisely, forges for its own better control."[234]

Religion caused labor to be performed—as slavery did—which would otherwise not have been done. This is not the "make-work fallacy," for the alternative was generally idleness, not productive labor. It destroyed much capital, but also caused its accumulation.[235] That this hoard was in the hands of the priesthood who robbed the people and lived parasitically upon them has no bearing, detestable as it is to our mores, upon the result. The priests could hold the treasure from dissipation as no other class could; no one cared to steal from the temple, which was on its way to become a safe-deposit and bank.[236] That the advantage of his labor shall not accrue to the slave or the priest-ridden devotee was better than that the spur of a special necessity should not be applied. The very fact that accumulation of capital by inheritance was negatived by the priesthood has its favorable aspect. It is edifying to think of the new generation climbing up from the shoulders of the old but the question always is as to whether it will climb or only sit; and there is little doubt that the primitive

234 Anon., "The Old Skepticism," in N. Y. *Nation*, XCIII, 313-315.
235 Lippert, *Kgchte.*, I, 30 ff., 126.
236 Otto, *Priester*, I, 318-320; Letourneau, *Prop.*, 212.

heir was likely to content himself with "possession," or "being seated," in the original sense of the word.

Their ill-gotten gains made of the priesthood a leisure class. The capital they appropriated was not destroyed but transmuted; and it was returned to a later age in the form of culture. This was an alchemy of which no other class was capable. It is not to be understood that the priest planned any such endowment. He lived along with the interests of himself and his gild filling his whole horizon; those of the people he was bleeding, or of the far-off generations which he was ultimately to bless, had no place in his mind or heart. He was an unconscious factor in a great automatic process, as most human beings are all of the time and as all of them are most of the time. He experimented to find medicines, he worked up devices and tricks, which sometimes became arts, like that of writing, all to further his special purposes.[237] He had the leisure to do this sort of thing, which involved at least the rudiments of intellectual exercise, and, later, to found libraries and undertake literary labors,[238] just because he was supported by others. Without this "injustice" to them, he could not have laid the foundations of a higher culture; what to them was a loss was for the race a gain. The great processes of nature and society take no account of our little ideas of "justice." Inequality was permitted to work out what, under a general levelling process, could not have been. In the long view, then, even the shamans, whether tricksters or self-deceived, were worth to society what they cost.

"What an emancipating advance must it have meant to that time to discover cult-means through which the sick could be, if not cured, at least brought into the range of human care! Yet this is a discovery which we still condemn as vile, black sorcery, for whose practice we carp at poor savages, and on suspicion of which a more enlightened age kindled the fagot-pile!"[239] We must not forget that sorcery and magic provided that basis of observation and experimentation upon which, by correction, science was erected.[240] The development of most of the learned professions is referable, at least in high degree, to the priesthood. The temples

---

[237] §161, above.
[238] Otto, *Priester*, I, 339.
[239] Lippert, *Kgchte.*, I, 111.
[240] §307, above.

discharged a distinct social function; they "served the purpose of public parks and public halls and the treasures of the gods, accumulated within them, were a kind of state treasure, preserved by religious sanctions against peculation and individual encroachment but available for public objects in time of need. The Canaanites of Shechem took money from their temple to provide means for Abimelech's enterprise, when they resolved to make him their king; and the sacred treasure of Jerusalem, originally derived from the fruits of David's campaigns, was used by his successors as a reserve fund available in great emergencies. On the whole, then, it is evident that the difference between holy things and common things does not originally turn on ownership, as if common things belonged to men and holy things to the gods. Indeed there are many holy things which are also private property, images, for example, and the other appurtenances of domestic sanctuaries."[241] Hall[242] waxes eloquent over the function of the Church in the Middle Ages: "We shall have recognized in the church the professional peacemaker between states and factions, as between man and man; the equitable mediator between rulers and their subjects; the consistent champion of constitutional liberty; the alleviator of the inequalities of birth; the uninterested and industrious disseminator of letters; the refiner of habits and manners; the well-meaning guardian of the national wealth, health, and intellect, and the fearless censor of public and private morality."

If anyone recalls that the sanction of religion tends to preserve the old and to oppose the new, let it be said, first, that tradition is as important in societal evolution as the corresponding factor, heredity, is in the organic process. If all were variation, life would be an unrelated chaos, just as, if all were tradition, it would take on the immobility of death. This is no apology for the discreditable view that has been harbored by not a few of the orthodox as to their function in the world, which they have interpreted to be that of brakemen, but merely the suggestion that religion has a distinct function and one useful to society in connection with the upholding of tradition. Such conservatism cannot continue to be indiscriminate nor can important services to society any longer be

---

[241] Smith, *Relig. Sem.*, 147.   [242] *Eliz. Age*, 103.

discharged by an agency that is not adjustable to the spirit of its age.

Not to prolong a discussion of relatively minor matters, much less to try to combat the detailed complaints about religion and the priesthood, let us consider what is, after all, the first and last service of religion to society, namely, the discipline it exercises. Not without justice has it been written that fear is the beginning of knowledge.[243] It is certainly the beginning of that discipline through which alone wisdom arrives. Discipline was precisely what men needed in the childhood of the race and have continued to require ever since. Men must learn to control themselves. Though the regulative organization exercised considerable discipline, its agents were merely human; the chief had to sleep occasionally, could not be everywhere at once, and might be deceived and evaded. Not so the ghosts and spirits. The all-seeing daimonic eye was sleepless; no time or place was immune from its surveillance. Detection was sure. Further, the penalty inflicted was awesome. Granted that the chief might beat or maim or fine or kill, there were yet limits to what he could do. The spirits, on the other hand, could inflict strange agonies and frightful malformations and transformations. Their powers extended even beyond the grave and their resources for harm outran the liveliest imaginings. In short, they inspired, not a daylight-fear but a grisly, gruesome terror—ghost-fear. Consider the threat of the taboo, and its effectiveness.[244] It is beneath this unearthly whip of scorpions that humanity has cringed for long ages and there is no doubt that its disciplinary value has superseded all other compulsions to which mankind has ever been subject.

Here appears again the supernatural sanction of the mores; this book contains many instances of its effectiveness. Consider again the Hindu village proprietor who, "while deprecating the action of Government in withholding support from the higher education in the country, was on his own part doing everything in his power to thwart the spread of primary education among the peasantry of his village. On being asked why he delighted in keeping the peasantry in ignorance, he observed that it was a great blessing to him and other respectable members of the village that the peasantry were left uneducated and engrossed in superstition. 'At present,' he says, 'I am not obliged to undergo the expense of keeping men to watch my fields and my mango

[243] Prov., I, 7; Lippert, *Kgchte.*, I, 125; Oliveira Martins, *Raças*, II, 154.
[244] §§268, 269, above.

trees, because the village god does the duty for me either without any remuneration or at the cost of a fowl or a cocoanut. But once the peasants are educated and made to believe that the great Gramadev, of whom they are so much now in awe, is nothing more than a block of stone capable of doing neither good nor evil, thefts and impudence will increase in the village, and there will be no end to my troubles.' "[245] Here was a plain preference for the ghostly discipline over any other. Turner[246] dilates upon the function of religious fear in maintaining order, and cites in illustration oath-taking and curses against thieves. Consider the force invoked to sanction the various "commandments" of the Egyptians, Hebrews, or Mohammedans—injunctions making for the welfare of society and having behind them not only the public opinion of men, as befits the folkways, but the sanction of a religious fear presently to be stamped upon men in the form of conscience.[247] The Jew wanted to be different from others; and while we may marvel at the apparently foolish means he adopted, we must respect the product he attained, which has proved itself by the existence of the Jewish religious society through thousands of years.

"Cursed be he who dishonors father or mother"; this imprecatory nature of the commandment is what inspires the unearthly fear and compels an unreflecting and uncritical obedience beside which that accorded to military authority is a pale and shadowy counterpart. Religion "developed the spirit of subordination, prevented the scattering of the tribe, and formed a link between successive generations; and . . . it favored the sacrifice of a direct and immediate satisfaction to a greater but more distant and indirect good."[248] It is perhaps superfluous to recall its effectiveness in the protection of property and other major institutions of society.

The value of discipline is a topic that deserves extended treatment for its own sake;[249] if its surpassing importance is realized, and especially its indispensability upon early stages of civilization, then the services of religion as an unrivalled dispenser of discipline are readily appreciated. Religion is both doctrine and institution, the latter growing out of the former; for to preserve its doctrine it must be an institution. The institution is a framework of disciplinary habit, education, symbol, and usage—the most powerful educators that mankind has ever known. Its power of discipline alone, wielded so strongly albeit sternly, might well be enough to assure religion of survival-value as an effective agency of adjustment to life-conditions. The existence of religion among all races means that they all were disciplined; the presence of its heavy hand, in particular wherever civilization has devel-

[245] Joshi, in JASB, II, 206.   [246] Samoa, 183 ff.
[247] Maurer, Vkde., 179 ff.; Deut., XXVII, 15-26; Koran, Sura, VI; Joshi, in JASB, III, 275.
[248] D'Alviella, Concep. God., 179.
[249] §§143, 144, above; Sumner, "Discipline," in Coll. Ess., IV, 423 ff.

oped, means that it was those who were becoming most cultured who were being disciplined most severely. "The man who is not flayed is not educated."[250] It is thus as a stern sanction of the mores that religion reaches its acme of value.

It is a striking fact that through the ages of evolution there has occurred a progressive de-personalization of the supernatural. The ghost was wholly, and the spirit characteristically, anthropomorphic. Men must needs be driven to anthropomorphism when they wish to portray a spiritual being; even Goethe's Earth-Spirit itself was envisaged by him as a "great gray face in the clouds." But the tendency has long been away from the personal god and toward the First Cause. The members of the series between the primordial ghost-fear of the Unknown as conceived in human terms and the awe of the scientist who has insight[251] enough to realize the presence of impersonal Law and Order, under Power, throughout the universe, form a long array; yet the series is unbroken. Awe grows, says Spencer,[252] from "something special and occasional to something universal and unceasing." It has developed as a result of constant refinement of crude conceptions in the light of advancing knowledge. No other agency has purged religious conceptions of their gross elements as has science. It has been the prime instrument in securing society's adjustments to its material life-conditions; the mores have followed upon its trail; and religion has fallen in behind the mores. If the conferring of refinement is a friendly function, even though it involves faithful wounds, then science is the best friend religion has ever had.

[250] Epigraph to Goethe's *Dichtung und Wahrheit;* from Menander. Liddell and Scott, *Gk.-Eng. Lex., sub* "dero."
[251] §464, below.
[252] *Stud. Soc.,* 310.

END OF VOL. II.